MW01053107

HANDBOOK OF
POLICE PSYCHOLOGY

Gregory Bedny and David Meister
The Russian Theory of Activity: Current Applications to Design and Learning

Winston Bennett, David Woehr, and Charles Lance
Performance Measurement: Current Perspectives and Future Challenges

Michael T. Brannick, Eduardo Salas, and Carolyn Prince
Team Performance Assessment and Measurement: Theory, Research, and Applications

Jeanette N. Cleveland, Margaret Stockdale, and Kevin R. Murphy
Women and Men in Organizations: Sex and Gender Issues at Work

Aaron Cohen
Multiple Commitments in the Workplace: An Integrative Approach

Russell Cropanzano
Justice in the Workplace: Approaching Fairness in Human Resource Management, Volume 1

Russell Cropanzano
Justice in the Workplace: From Theory to Practice, Volume 2

David V. Day, Stephen Zaccaro, Stanley M. Halpin
Leader Development for Transforming Organizations: Growing Leaders for Tomorrow's Teams and Organizations

James E. Driskell and Eduardo Salas
Stress and Human Performance

Sidney A. Fine and Steven F. Cronshaw
Functional Job Analysis: A Foundation for Human Resources Management

Sidney A. Fine and Maury Getkate
Benchmark Tasks for Job Analysis: A Guide for Functional Job Analysis (FJA) Scales

J. Kevin Ford, Steve W. J. Kozlowski, Kurt Kraiger, Eduardo Salas, and Mark S. Teachout
Improving Training Effectiveness in Work Organizations

Jerald Greenberg
Organizational Behavior: The State of the Science, Second Edition

Jerald Greenberg
Insidious Workplace Behavior

Edwin Hollander
Inclusive Leadership: The Essential Leader-Follower Relationship

Jack Kitaeff
Handbook of Police Psychology

Uwe E. Kleinbeck, Hans-Henning Quast, Henk Thierry, and Hartmut Häcker
Work Motivation

Laura L. Koppes
Historical Perspectives in Industrial and Organizational Psychology

Ellen Kossek and Susan Lambert
Work and Life Integration: Organizational, Cultural and Individual Perspectives

Martin I. Kurke and Ellen M. Scrivner
Police Psychology into the 21st Century

Joel Lefkowitz
Ethics and Values in Industrial and Organizational Psychology

Manuel London
Job Feedback: Giving, Seeking, and Using Feedback for Performance Improvement, Second Edition

Manuel London
How People Evaluate Others in Organizations

Manuel London
Leadership Development: Paths to Self-Insight and Professional Growth

Robert F. Morrison and Jerome Adams
Contemporary Career Development Issues

Michael D. Mumford, Garnett Stokes, and William A. Owens
Patterns of Life History: The Ecology of Human Individuality

Michael D. Mumford
Pathways to Outstanding Leadership: A Comparative Analysis of Charismatic, Ideological, and Pragmatic Leaders

Kevin R. Murphy
Validity Generalization: A Critical Review

Kevin R. Murphy and Frank E. Saal
Psychology in Organizations: Integrating Science and Practice

Kevin Murphy
A Critique of Emotional Intelligence: What Are the Problems and How Can They Be Fixed?

Susan E. Murphy and Ronald E. Riggio
The Future of Leadership Development

Margaret A. Neal and Leslie Brett Hammer
Working Couples Caring for Children and Aging Parents: Effects on Work and Well-Being

HANDBOOK OF POLICE PSYCHOLOGY

Edited by

Jack Kitaeff

Private Practice of Police Psychology
Arlington, Virginia

Routledge
Taylor & Francis Group
New York   London

Routledge
Taylor & Francis Group
711 Third Avenue
New York, NY 10017

Routledge
Taylor & Francis Group
2 Park Square
Milton Park, Abingdon
Oxon OX14 4RN

© 2011 by Taylor and Francis Group, LLC
Routledge is an imprint of Taylor & Francis Group, an Informa business

International Standard Book Number: 978-0-415-87766-4 (Hardback)

Visit the Taylor & Francis Web site at
http://www.taylorandfrancis.com

and the Psychology Press Web site at
http://www.psypress.com

To my wife Tress, my mother Gertrude, my sister Ellen, my children Isaiah, Moriah, Mordechai, Hayleigh, and Myles. And to June and Stella, two good friends, gone, but never forgotten.

Contents

PART III   Training and Evaluation

PART IV   Police Procedure

PART V Clinical Practice

PART VI Treatment and Dysfunction

Series Foreword

There is a compelling need for innovative approaches to the solution of many pressing problems involving human relationships in today's society. Such approaches are more likely to be successful when they are based on sound research and applications. Our *Series in Applied Psychology* offers publications that emphasize state-of-the-art research and its application to important issues of human behavior in a variety of social settings. The objective is to bridge both academic and applied interests.

We are very pleased to have the book *Handbook of Police Psychology* in our *Series in Applied Psychology*. Dr. Jack Kitaeff has provided us with outstanding examples of how recent scientific and applied developments from various fields of psychological research can, and are, currently being applied to the solution of many of the problems faced by individuals involved with the many different aspects of police administration and allied fields. He has brought together an outstanding group of experts involved in the relevant research and its applications to a wide variety of law enforcement, forensics, ethical, legal, and policing issues.

Dr. Kitaeff is particularly well qualified to undertake this effort. He is a licensed clinical psychologist in Virginia specializing in forensic and police psychology. He graduated from the City University of New York, has a master's degree in experimental psychology from the State University of New York, and received his PhD from the University of Mississippi. He completed his internship in clinical psychology at Walter Reed Army Medical Center in Washington, D.C.

He received his legal education from George Mason University, where he was awarded his JD degree, and he served his legal clerkship with the U.S. Attorney's Office. His private practice has involved consulting with police and sheriff departments, conducting pre-employment screening of law enforcement candidates, and carrying out fitness-for-duty evaluations. He has held teaching positions and has produced several books, including the recently published *Forensic Psychology*. He has appeared on several television and radio programs.

In his preface to this book, Dr. Kitaeff acknowledges that an earlier book in our series, *Police Psychology Into the 21st Century* (1995, edited by Martin Kurke and Ellen Scrivner), was a successful groundbreaking work that attempted to examine some of the connections between psychological research with needs in different areas of practice in law enforcement. It is interesting to note that these chapter authors in the 1995 book were mainly individuals looking at the available research from their standpoints as law enforcement area job incumbents. There is a great deal of discussion about what needs to be done, and the chapters provided some directions to be pursued. The editors had projected the needs and some of the ways of getting there in the future. The current book provides a remarkable display of progress in achieving many of the objectives set out by Kurke and Scrivner's volume. The earlier volume is still available and would serve as a nice companion to the present new Kiteaff book.

The present volume is an ambitious and comprehensive view of a growing field. Chapter 1 presents a very comprehensive historical review of the long history of the relationships between psychological research and different areas of police psychology. Examples of chapters that follow include ones on legal and ethical issues related to public safety, methods for hiring and promotion of police officers, and issues between police and probation officers. The next section deals with many issues in the screening, selection, and evaluation of police officers. Subsequent sections deal with training, counseling, stress reduction, and evaluation issues. Next, several chapters deal with police procedures, such as hostage negotiations, domestic violence, use of force, and still other issues with international perspectives in law enforcement. The next chapters are concerned with aspects of clinical practice in situations involving grief, public safety, and even suicide in law enforcement. A final section deals with the treatment of certain dysfunctions, such as helping officers under investigation or prosecution, the use of critical incidents to provide early interventions, developing peer support programs, and improving healthy habits for coping with stress.

Readers will find an extensive list of approximately 150 helpful references for those interested in pursuing some of the sources and issues in more detail. Another feature is the specification of 27 key court cases that proved relevant to some of the issues discussed.

This *Handbook of Police Psychology* makes available needed information that will be of use to the growing community of individuals working in or with law enforcement agencies. The chapter authors have been specifically chosen for their expertise and reputation in working at the local, state, and federal levels of law enforcement. They include psychologists who are or were officers, federal agents, and civilian employees of law enforcement agencies, and other psychologists who provide consulting psychological services to law enforcement agencies. They have broken new ground and contributed to the establishment of environments that have enabled psychologists and police personnel to respect each other and to contribute to the bodies of knowledge of each other's profession.

Edwin A. Fleishman
George Mason University

Jeanette N. Cleveland
Pennsylvania State University

Series Editors

Preface

In 1995, when Martin I. Kurke and Ellen M. Scrivner wrote the preface to their groundbreaking work, *Police Psychology Into the 21st Century* (the precursor to the present book), their title alone bore witness of things to come. More specifically, the title of their book was more than insightful alone; it revealed an understanding of what had been taking place at the dawn of the new century in police psychology. The title of the book was not *Police Psychology "in" the 21st Century*, which would be a static description of the way things were, but rather *Police Psychology "Into" the 21st Century*, which was a dynamic description—bordering on prophetic—of what was happening and transpiring even as these words were written.

In 1995, the authors described police psychology as "an evolving area in which psychological science is applied in the law enforcement managerial and operational environments." Police psychology (as known in 1995) was regarded as a "relatively new phenomenon" in the history of psychology. The book *Police Psychology Into the 21st Century* was presented as a "core technology consisting of psychological evaluations, counseling, and training."

In the original book, the careers of the 21 authors contributing to the book were seen as testimony to the growth and adaptation of the field. Each author was regarded by the editors as "experienced police psychologist[s]…some [as] civilian members of a federal, state, or local enforcement agencies…[and] others [as] consultant-contractors to the law enforcement community [at large]." Most authors were presented as having been trained as mental health experts, whereas other authors were described as having backgrounds in industrial and organizational psychology and other nonmental health disciplines.

The editors of the original book viewed it as one "in which experts in different aspects of psychological support to law enforcement agencies would write on police psychology from their own idiosyncratic perspectives." Authors were seen as practicing psychologists within "working public safety environments [which resulted] in a variety of approaches to the subject and of presentation styles." Kurke and Scrivner believed that police psychology "must continue to grow in pace, scope, and direction, and that such growth [was] dependent on the development and inclusion of new methods and technologies in support of police officers and their families, police management, and police operations." The editors saw their book as being a "snapshot of police psychology," as it turned into the 21st century. They added prophetically, "We can hardly wait to watch and participate in its future." Well, the future is here.

This book is divided into six parts: General Practice, Pre-Employment Psychological Screening, Training and Evaluation, Police Procedure, Clinical Practice, and Treatment and Dysfunction. Each category presents chapters that are relevant to the general practice and procedures of police psychology as they stand 10 years into the 21st century.

The first section is preceded by the chapter "The Introduction and History of Police Psychology" (Kitaeff), which presents an overall picture of where we are as a profession, the definitions of the profession, and how we got here.

The section General Practice covers police psychological consultation to public safety as a whole (Davis), legal issues involved in the hiring and promotion of police officers (Gutman), ethical issues in police psychology (McCutcheon), and police versus probation and surveillance differences (Herrmann & Broderick).

The section Pre-Employment Psychological Screening contains chapters on psychological evaluations of an actuarial and clinical nature (Weiss & Weiss, and Cutler), appraising and managing police officer performance (Jacobs, Thoroughgood, & Sawyer), the selection and promotion of police officers (Jacobs, Cushenbery, & Grabarek), the integration of psychological reports (Johnson), and a challenge to the deselection process of police applicants based on interview aspects (Arcaya).

The Training and Evaluation section includes chapters on couples' counseling and assessment (Inwald, Willman, & Inwald), fitness-for-duty-evaluations (Corey), and biological indicators of stress during police tactical training (Fenici, Brisinda, & Sorbo).

The section Police Procedure includes chapters on police use of force (Gallo), hostage negotiations (Mullins & McMains), domestic violence (Straus & Brooke), police interviews with suspects (Roberts & Herrington), and applying restorative justice principles in law enforcement (Myers).

The Clinical Practice section contains chapters on the police personality (Gerber & Ward), complex trauma and grief (Rudofossi), and suicide in law enforcement (Abrams, Liang, Stevens, & Frechette).

Finally, the section Treatment and Dysfunction contains chapters on psychological strategies for helping officers in trouble (Miller), critical incident reactions (Best, Artwohl, & Kirschman), peer support programs in law enforcement (Roland), and a brief intervention model for improving healthy habits and coping skills (Anshel).

Some of the chapters in this book would be barely unrecognizable when *Police Psychology Into the 21st Century* was published in 1995. But the chapters, recognizable or not, are of equal importance in the current field and state of practice of police psychology. As will be repeated several times throughout this book, the professions of police and police psychology have continued to grow geometrically, yet there is a familiar thread that runs through every decade and every topic. It is the thread of professionalism that continues to bind our young profession.

Although Hugo Münsterberg advocated for psychology's involvement in the detection of crime and the presence of psychologists in the criminal process, he could barely imagine the extent to which this now takes place on a daily basis. Although in 1917 Lewis Terman advocated for testing using the Stanford-Binet in the hiring of police officers, he could hardly imagine the breadth of present-day pre-employment applicant-screening programs. Nor could L. L. Thurstone in 1922 have imagined the same thing. Certainly, in 1954, when Martin Reiser became this nation's first full-time police department psychologist, could he ever had foreseen the extent of the influence that present-day psychologists would have in the selection, hiring, and management of present-day police officers at all levels and how *police psychology* itself would come to be recognized as a legitimate psychological specialty by the American Psychological Association.

Although Kurke and Scrivner saw *Police Psychology Into the 21st Century* as a snapshot of police psychology as it existed in 1995, the present *Handbook of Police Psychology* represents a panoramic digital image of how police psychology appears in 2010 and how it stands poised to change even further over the coming decades.

Jack Kitaeff

About the Editor

Jack Kitaeff, PhD, JD, is a licensed clinical psychologist in the Commonwealth of Virginia specializing in police and forensic psychology. He received his undergraduate education at Brooklyn College, and his graduate psychology education at the State University of New York at Cortland and the University of Mississippi. He received his law degree from the George Mason University School of Law, and completed a legal clerkship with the U.S. Attorney's Office, Eastern District of Virginia.

Dr. Kitaeff completed a clinical psychology internship at Walter Reed Army Medical Center, and served as a psychologist and Major in the U.S. Army Medical Service Corps. He became the first police psychologist for the Arlington County Police Department, where he established a pre-employment psychological screening program for police applicants. From 1984 to the present, he has been the consulting police psychologist for numerous law enforcement agencies in the northern Virginia area, including the Arlington County Sheriff's Office, among others. Dr. Kitaeff is an adjunct professor of psychology with the University of Maryland, University College. He is also a faculty member in the School of Psychology at Walden University. He is a Diplomate in Police Psychology from the Society of Police and Criminal Psychology, and a member of the American Psychological Association.

Dr. Kitaeff is the editor of *Malingering, Lies, and Junk Science in the Courtroom* (Cambria Press, 2007), and the author of *Jews in Blue* (Cambria Press, 2006) and *Forensic Psychology* (Prentice-Hall, 2010).

About the Contributors

Alan A. Abrams
California Department of Corrections,
    California Facility
Vacaville, California

Mark H. Anshel
Middle Tennessee State University
Murfreesboro, Tennessee

Jose M. Arcaya
John Jay College of Criminal Justice
New York, New York

Alexis Artwohl
Private Behavioral Sciences Consultant
    to Law Enforcement
Tucson, Arizona

Suzanne Best
Lewis and Clark Graduate School of Education
    and Counseling
Portland, Oregon

Donatella Brisinda
Clinical Physiology-Biomagnetism Center
Catholic University of Sacred Heart
Rome, Italy

Barbara Broderick
Maricopa County Adult Probation Department
Phoenix, Arizona

Stephanie L. Brooke
Capella University
Lakeville, New York

David M. Corey
Consulting and Forensic Psychology
Lake Oswego, Oregon

Lily Cushenbery
Pennsylvania State University
State College, Pennsylvania

Michael J. Cuttler
Law Enforcement Services, Inc.
Greensboro, North Carolina

Joseph A. Davis
California Department of Justice
Institute of Criminal Investigations
San Diego, California

Riccardo Fenici
Catholic University of Sacred Heart
Rome, Italy

Brenda Frechette
California Department of Corrections,
    California Facility
Vacaville, California

Frank J. Gallo
Western New England College
Springfield, Massachusetts

Gwendolyn L. Gerber
John Jay College of Criminal Justice
City University of New York
New York, New York

Patricia Grabarek
Pennsylvania State University
State College, Pennsylvania

Arthur Gutman
Florida Institute of Technology
Melbourne, Florida

Victoria Herrington
Australian Graduate School of Policing
Charles Sturt University
New South Wales, Australia

D. Scott Herrmann
Superior Court of Arizona
Phoenix, Arizona

Robin Inwald
Inwald Research, Inc.
Cleverdale, New York

Stephanie Inwald
Inwald Research, Inc.
Cleverdale, New York

Rick Jacobs
Pennsylvania State University
State College, Pennsylvania

Ronn Johnson
University of San Diego
San Diego, California

Ellen Kirschman
Private Practice
Redwood City, California

Jack Kitaeff
Private Practice of Police Psychology
Arlington, Virginia

Alice Liang
California Department of Mental Health,
    Napa State Hospital
Napa, California

Jeni L. McCutcheon
Independent Public Safety and Clinical
    Psychology Practice
Phoenix, Arizona

Michael J. McMains
Retired, San Antonio Police Department
San Antonio, Texas

Laurence Miller
Clinical and Forensic Psychologist and Law
    Enforcement Educator
Boca Raton, Florida

Wayman C. Mullins
Texas State University
San Marcos, Texas

Roslyn Myers
John Jay College of Criminal Justice
New York, New York

Karl A. Roberts
Australian Graduate School of Policing,
Charles Sturt University
New South Wales, Australia

Jocelyn E. Roland
Independent Practitioner
Modesto, California

Daniel Rudofossi
New York University
Retired NYPD Uniform Psychologist/Police
    Sergeant
New York, New York

Katina Sawyer
Pennsylvania State University
State College, Pennsylvania

Anna Rita Sorbo
Clinical Physiology-Biomagnetism Center
Catholic University of Sacred Heart
Rome, Italy

Kyleeann Stevens
St. Elizabeth's Hospital
Washington, District of Columbia

Trisha K. Straus
Attorney-at-Law
Granger, Georgia

Christian Thoroughgood
Pennsylvania State University
State College, Pennsylvania

Kyle C. Ward
John Jay College of Criminal Justice
City University of New York
New York, New York

Peter A. Weiss
University of Hartford
West Hartford, Connecticut

William U. Weiss
Portland State University
Portland, Oregon

Elizabeth Willman
Inwald Research, Inc.
Cleverdale, New York

1 History of Police Psychology

Jack Kitaeff

The professions of policing, psychology, and police psychology have grown geometrically in the United States during the last 100 years. When American colonist Asser Levy and his brothers-in-arms served on the Burgher Guard in New Amsterdam (New York City) in 1657, they in essence became this country's first policemen. Levy and his brethren could never imagine the current levels of technology and professionalism of modern police work and of the modern application of psychological principles to police work and law enforcement.

Today, psychology applied to policing, or *police psychology,* can broadly be defined as the application of psychological principles and methods to law enforcement. This broad and growing area includes topics such as screening and hiring police officers, conducting screenings for specials quads (e.g., SWAT), fitness-for-duty evaluations, investigations, hostage negotiations, training and consultation, and stress counseling, among others (Kitaeff, 2010).

POLICE PSYCHOLOGY: THE BEGINNINGS

Hugo Munsterberg is often called the first *forensic* psychologist. Yet in many ways he was also the first *police* psychologist because he wrote, at the beginning of the 20th century, how the law, the criminal investigator, the mechanisms of the courtroom, and the detection of criminals all came together under the watchful eye of the experimental psychologist. In his book *On the Witness Stand* (1908), Munsterberg talked about many topics such as illusions, the memory of witnesses, the effects of emotions, untrue confessions, the suggestibility of witnesses, hypnosis, and crime prevention. But it was perhaps his work on the detection of crime (and hence the use of primitive "criminal profiling" and "hypnosis") that stands out as the forerunners of the modern tools of the same names that have been used by police psychologists during the last 100 years. Munsterberg said:

> The psychologist who seeks to discover the secret connections of ideas may thus, by his association method, not only protect the innocent and unmask the guilty, but bring health and strength to the nervous wreck.
>
> Yet our chief interest belongs to the legal aspect of this method [free association and hypnosis]. Carried out with the skill which only long laboratory training can give, it has become, indeed, a magnifying-glass for the most subtle mental mechanism, and by it the secrets of the criminal mind may be unveiled. All this has, of course, no legal standing to-day, and there is probably no one who desires to increase the number of "experts" in our criminal courts. But justice demands that truth and lies be disentangled. The time will come when the methods of experimental psychology cannot longer be excluded from the court of law. It is well known that the use of stenographers in trials once met with vehement opposition, while now the shorthand record of the court procedure seems a matter of course.
>
> The help of the psychologist will become not less indispensable. The vulgar ordeals of the "third degree" in every form belong to the Middle Ages, and much of the wrangling of attorneys about technicalities in admitting the "evidence" appears to not a few somewhat out of date, too: the methods of experimental psychology are working in the spirit of the twentieth century. The "third degree" may brutalize the mind and force either correct or falsified secrets to light; the time-measurement of association is swifter and cleaner, more scientific, more humane, and more reliable in bringing out the truth which justice demands.
>
> Of course, we are only at the beginning of its development; the new method is still in many ways imperfect, and if clumsily applied it may be misleading; moreover, there exists no hard and fast rule

which fits every case mechanically. But all this indicates only that, just as the bodily facts have to be examined by the chemist or the physiologist, the mental facts must be examined also, not by the layman, but by the scientific psychologist, with the training of a psychological laboratory. (1908, pp. 109–110)

POLICE PSYCHOLOGY: THE EARLY YEARS

Other early psychologists who influenced the fledgling field of police psychology included William Stern, Alfred Binet, and Lewis Terman. William Stern (1912) decided that "personalistic psychology" or "individuality" was destined to be the main psychological problems of the 20th century. He attempted to classify people according to types, norms, and aberrations. To Stern, it was in the process of investigating individuality that the real essence of personality and intelligence could be discovered. Stern was influenced by the work of Alfred Binet and his studies of intelligence in children. As a result, Stern reviewed the principle findings in the field and developed the idea of expressing intelligence test results in the form of a single number, the *intelligence quotient.*

While Terman's (1916) study was the first to suggest that testing using the Stanford-Binet was useful for pre-employment evaluations, his results lacked information about the actual criterion-related validity of the Stanford-Binet for the specific purpose of police officer selection. However, Terman did feel that testing would one day be valuable as a selection tool for certain types of occupations and stressed the importance of establishing correlations between test scores and future performance, and in establishing norms of performance for different occupational groups. While Terman's study was speculative and did not involve the kinds of personality tests used in law enforcement selection today, he was a forerunner for using these evaluations as a means of obtaining the needed research data to make such evaluations viable (Inwald, 1990, 1992).

In the early 1920s, a few experimental investigations of psychological testing on police attitude and performance were conducted. For example, in 1922, L. L. Thurstone gave the Army Alpha Intelligence test to a group of officers serving in the Detroit Police Department. He found that, in general, patrolmen scored higher than the lieutenants who commanded them. Thurstone concluded that this may have been due to the fact that the most intelligent law enforcement officers often moved out of police work altogether to other, higher-paying occupations rather than waiting for promotions that took too long to come or never came at all. Kates (1950) administered the Rorschach inkblot test (Klopfer scoring system) to a group of New York City police officers and found that some Rorschach variables could be used to predict job satisfaction and motivation for promotion.

In the 1950s, psychology became increasingly utilized in many areas beyond testing and classification in the military, and this included increased involvement in police work of various sorts and to various degrees. During World War II and the Korean War, psychologists were employed by the military service to assist Selective Service Boards in identifying individuals who were psychologically unfit for military service. In addition, they became involved in conducting evaluations for purposes of selecting spies, saboteurs, and intelligence operatives (Janik, 1990). Most notable in this area was the work of Henry Murray and colleagues, who used personality assessment instruments to perform personnel selection evaluations for the Office of Strategic Services (OSS), the precursor to the CIA. Success in these areas quickly expanded to postwar civilian life.

In 1954, Martin Reiser became the nation's first full-time police psychologist, when he began screening all applicants to the Los Angeles Police Department using the Minnesota Multiphasic Personality Inventory (MMPI), a group Rorschach, a tree drawing, and a brief psychiatric interview (Blau & Super, 1997). A date that further stands out in importance for police psychology is 1972, when Martin Reiser presented a paper titled *The Police Department Psychologist* at the Western Psychological Association Convention. Reese (1987a, 1987b), a historian on psychological services to police and law enforcement, has estimated that only six police agencies in the United States had full-time psychologists prior to 1977. The same had not been true in Europe, however, where police departments in Germany were using psychologists in a variety of capacities as early as 1919. In 1966, the Munich police were employing a full-time police psychologist to train officers to deal with various patrol situations, such as crowd control.

In 1958, Harvey Schlossberg (shield number 16844) became a patrolman with the New York City Police Department. As he was in college at the time and contemplating attending graduate school, he felt that this might be a job in which he could earn money while he attended to his studies. He didn't know a lot about what the police job entailed but heard they were recruiting, so he figured he would give it a try. He learned that he would have to attend an academy where he would learn how to shoot a pistol. Most of all, he knew that he would get paid a salary during this time. He could never have imagined back then that he would remain with the police department for 20 years (Kitaeff, 2006a).

In his book *Psychologist With a Gun,* Schlossberg (1974) recounts the first time he wore his police uniform home. His mother didn't even recognize him. He didn't even recognize himself when he looked in the mirror. He knew one thing: With that uniform, his badge, and his gun, he felt different. "The first day I wore the uniform of a cop I felt taller than usual" (p. 29). After earning his bachelor's degree from Brooklyn College, Schlossberg went on for his master's degree at C.W. Post College and his doctorate at Yeshiva University. In 1971, Harvey Schlossberg became the first known police officer in the United States to earn a doctorate in psychology while still a full-time police officer in uniform.

In 1972, when Police Commissioner Patrick Murphy heard that one of his officers (a detective by now) had earned a doctorate in psychology, he asked Harvey Schlossberg to design a police psychological service unit. In many ways, Schlossberg can be considered the father of modern police psychology in the United States.

In *Psychologist With a Gun*, Schlossberg (1974) outlined his thoughts for establishing a psychological services unit within the police department (the second in the country after Martin Reiser established his with the Los Angeles Police Department). But Reiser was a psychologist, not a police officer. Schlossberg was both—a very important distinction. He listed the services this new psychological services unit would provide. They included:

1. The conducting of psychological evaluations, consisting of psychological testing.
2. Psychiatric interviews, diagnosis and prognosis, all in an attempt to discover if certain policemen sent to [him] by their superiors or coming to [his] office voluntarily were too emotionally upset to be allowed to carry a gun. If they were found to be, then either short-term or long-term therapy would be recommended and an attempt made to find psychiatrists to treat them.
3. Marriage counseling, where marital problems impaired a policeman's work.
4. Guidance and counseling to police who had minor problems.
5. Referral of families, wives, or children for treatment if they needed it.
6. Psychological testing and evaluation of candidates for promotion.
7. Psychological testing and evaluation of all recruits.
8. Research and operational consultations to other units within the department for personnel selection and research into function.
9. Instructional services to promotion classes on recognition of psychiatric problems commonly encountered by supervisors.
10. Continued administration of a pilot program for certain officers who needed therapy, which would include referral, payment, and supervision of the therapeutic process.
11. Maintaining of liaison with the honorary psychiatrists who served the Medical Division as consultants.
12. Acting as consultant to the district surgeons on psychological matters concerning members of the force.

13. Conducting of special lectures on psychological problems related to special police functions.
14. Representing the department on psychological matters in lectures before lay and professional organizations.
15. Consultant on behavioral patterns in crime situations.
16. Teaching of specialized courses for department units.
17. Acting as liaison with civilian psychiatrists and psychologists and as advisor to them on special problems relating to the demands of police work. (p. 93)

In the psychological screening of police recruits, Schlossberg instituted an assessment battery that included a structured clinical interview along with the administration of certain psychological tests. These tests included the *Thorndike Dimensions of Temperament Scale*, the *Cornell Medical Index* (CMI), the *Edwards Personal Preference Schedule* (EPPS), the *Minnesota Multiphasic Personality Inventory* (MMPI), and the *House-Tree-Person Test* (H-T-P) (Kitaeff, 2006b).

The *Thorndike Dimensions of Temperament Scale* was originally published in 1966 and was a self-report inventory through which the individual describes himself with respect to 10 dimensions of temperament: Sociable, Ascendant, Cheerful, Placid, Accepting, Tough-Minded, Reflective, Impulsive, Active, and Responsible.

The *Cornell Medical Index* (CMI) was created in 1949 and was a self-administered health questionnaire developed to obtain details of the person's medical history as an adjunct to the medical interview. It consisted of 195 questions divided into 18 sections; the first 12 sections dealt with somatic complaints, and the last 6 with mood and feeling patterns.

The *Edwards Personal Preference Schedule* (EPPS) was developed in 1959 based on the "manifest need system" theory of H. S. Murray and his associates at the Harvard Psychological Clinic. Beginning with 15 needs drawn from Murray's list of manifest needs, Edwards prepared sets of items whose content appeared to fit each need. Examples included the *need for achievement* (to do one's best and accomplish something difficult), *deference* (to conform to what is expected), *exhibition* (to be the center of attention), *intraception* (to analyze the motives and feelings of oneself and others), *dominance* (to influence others and to be regarded as a leader), and *nurturance* (to help others in trouble).

The original *Minnesota Multiphasic Personality Inventory* (MMPI) was developed in the late 1930s by a psychologist and a psychiatrist at the University of Minnesota. The test had 10 clinical scales and three validity scales plus various supplementary scales. The clinical scales were intended to distinguish groups of people with psychiatric disorders that have somewhat exotic-sounding names such as *hysteria*, *psychopathic deviate*, and *psychesthenia*. The names of these primary clinical scales have remained the same for the last 75 years even through a restandardization process took place in 1989.

The *House-Tree-Person Test* (H-T-P) is a projective technique developed by John Buck, and was originally an outgrowth of the "Goodenough" scale that was used to assess intellectual functioning. In administering the H-T-P, the subject is asked to draw alternately a house, a tree, and a person. Buck felt artistic creativity represented a stream of personality characteristics that flowed onto graphic art. He believed that through drawings, subjects objectified unconscious difficulties by sketching the inner image of primary process. Because it was assumed that the content and quality of the H-T-P were not attributable to the stimulus itself, he believed they had to be rooted in the individual's basic personality.

This screening process was designed to ensure that only the psychologically fit and "normal" person became a police officer. But there was (and is) much to suggest that even the most emotionally stable individual "changes" when he becomes a police officer. Accordingly, Schlossberg knew that it was not enough to psychologically screen police recruits; it would be necessary to provide psychological counseling for them as well. Accordingly, the psychological services unit of the police department offered a full array of individual and group psychotherapy.

Schlossberg knew that for almost all police officers, the credibility of anyone offering therapy for officers would be a major issue. Police officers are traditionally very distrustful and wary of outsiders who they perceive as not understanding what the world of a police officer is like.

For Schlossberg, this was not an issue because, in addition to being a psychologist, he was also a cop. "I ran after bad guys on the same rooftops as they did," he would say (Kitaeff, 2006a). Peer counseling, or having cops counsel other cops, was a technique brought to the forefront by Schlossberg. He trained police officers to help other officers in trouble and to be "group leaders" of police group counseling sessions. Interestingly, he found, for example, that these lay therapist-cops who were leading these groups were often more accurate than Schlossberg in spotting the violent-prone officers in the groups. Schlossberg felt strongly that it was best to catch problems before they developed into nightmares. He instituted what he called an "early warning system" in which certain markers or signals in a policeman's performance would set off a "psychological alarm" that therapeutic intervention was needed. Schlossberg also recommended to the police brass that officers have regular therapy sessions as a means of warding off problems before they grew into bigger ones. A major advantage of such an approach would be to remove the stigma of seeing the "shrink," which so often occurs in police work. By making such visits mandatory, the officer's macho self-image could be maintained. Unfortunately, police department higher-ups shot down this idea as taking up too many man-hours.

The 1960s witnessed significant legal and cultural changes that led to the expansion of psychologists' roles and applications in the law enforcement field. In 1963, James Shaw of Washington State was appointed by the King County Sheriff's Department as the first "in-house" police psychologist working half-time, conducting research, and providing consultations and pre-employment evaluations for sheriff's deputies.

In 1967, the release of the Presidential Commission on Law Enforcement and the Administration of Justice (1967) report on law enforcement slowly set in motion a trend that would eventually result in the psychological screening of *all* law enforcement candidates (Janik, 1993; Ostrov, 1990). The report emphasized the importance of assessing emotional stability in officer candidates. Specifically, The National Advisory Commission on Annual Justice Standards and Goals (1967) recommended that, by 1975, every law enforcement agency employ a trained professional who could administer psychological tests for purposes of evaluating applicants for characteristics that would be detrimental to police work.

As a result of these and other developments, the concept of *pre-employment selection evaluations* for police candidates became more acceptable to police administrators than in the past. Still, during the late 1960s and 1970s, most chiefs continued to believe that the pre-employment interviews they conducted completely by themselves, along with the medical and physical examination requirements, were sufficient for selecting the best candidates for the job. Some psychologists in the late 1960s conducted research as external consultants to law enforcement agencies, and agencies began to have more direct contact with psychologists and the services they could provide through grant projects. For example, in 1969, Joseph Fabricatore of California began working as a graduate student research associate for the Los Angeles Sheriff's Department on a Law Enforcement Assistance Administration (LEAA) study focused on predicting patrol officer behavior from psychological variables (Inwald, 1998, 2006, 2008).

It has also been expressed that the beginning of the profession of police psychology officially began at the National Symposium on Police Psychological Services (NSPPS), held at the FBI Academy in 1984 (Bartol, 1991; McKenzie, 1986). What is clear, however, is that since the 1960s, the application of psychological services and research to law enforcement settings has gone from just about nil to almost omnipresent. What is further known for sure is that by 1985, 11 states had passed statutes requiring police departments to psychologically screen their applicants, and by 1990, 64 percent of state police departments and 73 percent of municipal police departments required psychological screening. Today, most large and many medium-sized police departments have a full-time police psychologist on staff or utilize part-time police psychologist consultants.

In September 1984, James T. Reese (from the FBI) and Harvey Goldstein organized and conducted a 5-day National Symposium on Police Psychological Services at the FBI Academy in Quantico, Virginia. At this conference, approximately 150 police psychologists and other professionals working in the field from around the United States began to develop a strong national network. During and after the presentations, many active discussions took place about various testing programs and selection techniques. In 1984, Jack Kitaeff became the first police psychologist for the Arlington County Police Department. In this role, he developed a set of local norms using standardized psychological tests, including the *Wechsler Adult Intelligence Scale* (WAIS), MMPI, and the *Sixteen Personality Factor* (16PF) test, which he used as a guide in his applicant selection process. He also spent hundreds of hours riding in police cars in an attempt to gain a true awareness of the nature of the job of being a police officer, a knowledge that helped him tremendously in both the assessment and the counseling of officers.

In 1987, Daniel Rudofossi joined the New York City Police Department at the rank of patrolman. He served as a street officer for 9 years, but in 1996 received his doctorate in clinical psychology and subsequently became a uniformed member (sergeant) of the Membership Assistance Program (MAP), which was the first joint Police Department–Police Union employee assistance program created by the Office of the Mayor. Rudofossi was also appointed as the official Medical Division Uniform Psychologist by the agreement of the police union presidents (PBA, SBA, LBA, and CBA) and by order of the Chief of Police Personnel. In this new role, Rudofossi made the clinical decisions regarding all sick, restricted duty, modified duty, restoration of firearms, removal of firearms, and ambulatory assessments and interventions for all affected officers in the city. His work required services to be provided throughout the city on a "24/7" basis for 4 years.

Rudofossi—now a published author, poet, lecturer, and professor—forged a new direction in police psychology, having written his first book on his work with traumatized police officers in the New York City Police Department. "Dr. Dan" as he was known, has had a unique method for the treatment of trauma and grief. Part of this involves making sense of the chaotic experimental traumatic neurosis alive in scientific terms, in the "eco-ethological niches" of police work.

Rudofossi's multi-axial diagnosis and multiple therapeutic approaches are anchored in real clinical illustrations leading to conceptually fleshed-out public safety personality styles. He did research involving 2% of NYPD's 40,000 officers and applied those findings into his knowledge gained from his therapy experiences with police and other emergency responders. "Working With Traumatized Police Officer-Patients: A Clinician's Guide to Complex PTSD" is a unique and holistic approach about the understanding and treatment of police and public safety personnel. The genesis of this work may have been in the urban intensity of the NYPD, yet it is relevant to emergency responders and public safety personnel anywhere. Rudofossi's supervisors included Dr. Albert Ellis, founder of Rational Emotive Behavior Therapy (REBT); the famed psychoanalyst Dr. Charles Brenner; and Dr. Bob Barnes, who was a supervisee of the famed Dr. Viktor Frankl, founder of Logotherapy.

Rudofossi eventually became the Chief Psychologist for the Detective Crime Clinic of New York and New Jersey, a consultant to the Saybrook University Police Clinical Psychology doctoral program, and a professor at New York University, where he received two master's degrees and another doctoral degree while still an active duty police officer. Rudofossi is currently the Administrative Psychologist and Training and Curriculum Director for the Drug Enforcement Administration's (DEA) Employee Assistance Program. He sees his learned predecessors as Dr. (Detective) Harvey Schlossberg of the NYPD, San Francisco Police Department Captain Dr. Al Benner, and Dr. James Reese of the FBI's Behavioral Science Unit, who assisted Rudofossi in developing an initial proposal and content validity analysis when designing his assessment instrument, which would allow him to gain a foothold on police trauma and the public safety officers' experiences.

In 1989, Michael Roberts and Michael Johnson of Johnson Roberts & Associates published their automated Johnson, Roberts Personal History Questionnaire (PHQ), a 300-item questionnaire for evaluating public safety officer applicants.

In 1993, Ones and associates published a monograph in the *Journal of Applied Psychology* that included Inwald Personality Inventory (IPI) validity data previously mentioned in the APA Task Force report. The generalizability and test validities of "integrity" tests were established, which essentially stopped any movement to ban these instruments (Ones et al., 1993). And in 1995, Robin Inwald's Hilson Safety/Security Risk Inventory (HSRI) was published for use in preconditional offers (see ADA material later in this chapter) for police screening (Inwald, 1995). The HSRI, with its scales focusing on attitudes and behaviors related to safety issues, as well as self-control in other areas, was developed for use in the police/public safety field after police administrators continued to complain about the recurring problem of vehicular accidents in their departments. Inwald's instruments saw an increased role of police psychologists in the 1990s as evaluators sought to use personality instruments that tapped job-related behavioral characteristics in pre-employment, fitness-for-duty evaluations (FFDE), and the growing special duty assignment evaluations for hostage negotiators, SWAT team members, and so forth.

In 1996, Hilson Research published Inwald's Hilson Management Survey (HMS) for promotional screening. This instrument was used for public safety officer promotions and public safety administrator screening, including some assessments conducted by police psychologists for police chief and assistant police chief positions (Inwald et al., 1996).

New instruments for public safety assessment purposes were also developed during the first decade of the 21st century. In 2000, Law Enforcement Services, Inc. (LESI), published Michael Cuttler's "online PHQ" for evaluating public safety officer applicants. This new instrument grew from research conducted on the validity of individual life history items that was also published in the *Journal of Applied Psychology* in 1998 (Sarchione et al., 1998).

In 2002, Hilson Research published Robin Inwald's Hilson Trauma Recovery Inventory (HTRI) as a result of discussions at the 1998 FBI Conference on Domestic Violence by Police Officers and the recent influx of officers returning from overseas military duty in the Middle East (Inwald, 2002, 2006).

Additional independent IPI validation research was completed during these years (Chibnall & Detrick, 2003; Detrick & Chibnall, 2002), including comparisons of IPI scores with those of newly developed research scales for the MMPI-2 (Ben-Porath, 2006).

In 2005, IntegriQuest, LLC, published Andrew Ryan's RPIQ, an automated biodata collection instrument for public safety officer candidates.

In 2007, Inwald Research, Inc., published the Inwald Couples Compatibility Questionnaire (ICCQ), Inwald Partners Personality Inventory (IPPI), Inwald Personality Survey (IPS), and Inwald Attitude Survey (IPS) for use with police couples (Inwald, 2007, 2008). In 2008, Multi Health Systems, Inc. (MHS), published Robert Davis and Cary Rostow's "M-PULSE," a personality test developed for public safety officer screening (Davis & Rostow, 2008).

In 2008, Peter Weiss, William Weiss, and Carl Gacono reviewed the use of the Rorschach inkblot method (Exner, 2003) for police psychological assessments (Weiss, 2002; Weiss, Weiss, & Gacono, 2008; Zacker, 1997). This review was completed for several reasons. One was the wealth of personality-related information that can be gleaned from the Rorschach Comprehensive System, and another was the impression management limitations of self-report measures such as the MMPI and other instruments. In 2008, Pearson Assessments, Inc., published the MMPI-2 Restructured Form (MMPI-2RF), a revised form of the MMPI-2 that included a set of law enforcement norms in its technical manual (Tellegen & Ben-Porath, 2008).

THE NATURE OF POLICING: WHAT MAKES A GOOD POLICE OFFICER?

Who are the police, and how are they expected to behave? For one thing, the police are expected to be conscientious, agreeable, emotionally stable, self-controlled, honest, and morally upright (Berry, Ones, & Sackett, 2007; Kitaeff, 2006b).

Controlled experiments have been designed and conducted to identify the personality traits, or degrees of traits, that are correlated with or significantly predict discrete aspects of future successful police performance. As psychologists trained in research, empiricism, and the scientific method, we appreciate the importance of these studies and try to incorporate their findings into our daily work in the selection of police recruits, the evaluation of present officers, and our consultation with police administration. As any practicing clinician will also disclose, however, years of experience and observation "on the firing line" have allowed us to also develop certain working hypotheses that are perfectly appropriate to be used as one part of our clinical armamentarium. The present author is no different. Some of the personality attributes the author has found important in police work—assessed primarily from the 16PF—include emotional warmth, dominance, conscientiousness, social boldness, self-reliance, organization, and high energy level (Kitaeff, 2010).

Of course, complete reliance on these factors without the use of empirically derived personality traits and standardized psychological inventories and tests would be inappropriate. What makes a *good* police officer? Hogan (1971) reported that supervisors described their best *officers* as functionally intelligent, sociable, and self-assured. A decade later, using the Inwald Personality Inventory and the MMPI, Inwald and Shusman (1984) found that patrol officers who exhibited heightened awareness and discernment tended to receive better supervisory ratings. Having conventional attitudes and being free of "neurosis" (excessive anxiety, worry, self-doubt, and phobias) have also been shown to predict fewer serious job problems among *police officers* (Hiatt & Hargrave, 1988). The pre-DSM-IV-TR term neurosis refers to generalized anxiety, phobias, self-doubts, and feelings of helplessness and hopelessness. Yet some degree of guardedness and circumspection appears to be a desirable personality characteristic for effective policing (Detrick & Chibnall, 2002).

The police in the United States are the major representatives of the government and the legal system in their transactions with citizens. They are responsible for enforcing the criminal laws, keeping the peace, and responding to calls for service. They are also required to exercise discretion in determining whether or not a violation of the law has taken place and whether someone should be arrested and charged with a particular criminal offense. They are put in the position of mediating disputes between people from all walks of life and making immediate decisions on who might be in the wrong or the right. Indeed, for better or worse, police officers are possessors of inordinate amounts of power. Furthermore, the average officer is continuously exposed to temptation and opportunities for corruption with only limited likelihood of getting caught (Kitaeff, 2010).

PRE-EMPLOYMENT PSYCHOLOGICAL SELECTION: COGNITIVE ASSESSMENT

THE WONDERLIC PERSONNEL TEST

The *Wonderlic Personnel Test* (WPT) is one of the most frequently used cognitive testing devices in private industry as well as law enforcement. The publishers describe the test as a short-form test of general cognitive ability (Aamodt, 2004). Such cognitive ability is often referred to as general intelligence or "g" and is a measure of the level at which an individual learns, understands instructions, and solves problems. It provides a measurable and quantitative look into how easily individuals can be trained, how well they can adjust and adapt to changing situations and demands, how easily they can solve problems on the job, and how satisfied they are likely to be with the demands of their chosen career. The publishers claim that higher scoring individuals will not only gain more from individualized training but also be more likely to learn effectively from on-the-job experience. Modest scoring individuals will need more detailed supervision, greater hands-on practice, more time and repetition, and closer supervision (Wonderlic, 1999).

The WPT consists of 50 questions, including word comparisons, disarranged sentences, sentence parallelism, the need to follow directions, number comparisons, number series, analysis of geometric figures, and story problems requiring either mathematical or logical solutions. Questions are arranged in order of difficulty and allow the test taker 12 minutes to complete the test before being stopped by the proctor. Computerized, large-print, and 11 alternate language versions of the test are available.

The WPT correlates highly with the Wechsler Adult Intelligence Scale (WAIS) (r = .92), which suggests that the Wonderlic taps various intellectual functions and may be a test of global intelligence (Dodrill, 1980, 1981, 1983; Dodrill & Warner, 1988). Research also suggests that scores on the Wonderlic have a test–retest reliability, ranging from .82 to .94 (Dodrill, 1983). Alternate form reliabilities range from .73 to .95, and correlation of odd items on the test to even items on the test ranges from .88 to .94 (McKelvie, 1989). The average score of police applicants taking the Wonderlic as part of pre-employment job screening is 20.91 with a standard deviation of 6.14. Super (1995) has found correlations of .19 between Wonderlic scores and patrol performance. Hankey (1968) has found correlations of .06 with patrol performance and .28 with academy performance.

THE WECHSLER ADULT INTELLIGENCE SCALE

The *Wechsler Adult Intelligence Scale* (WAIS) is one of the most common and "global" tests of intelligence in use today. It has been an integral part of clinical and educational psychology practice and research since 1939, starting with the introduction of the original Wechsler-Bellevue Intelligence Scale (Wechsler, 1939). Since the original version, the Wechsler Scale has been restandardized three times: once in 1955 as the WAIS, again in 1981 as the WAIS-R, and most recently in 2000 as the WAIS-3. The tests cannot be proctored for group administration (as the Wonderlic can) but must be individually administered by a qualified and appropriately trained psychologist, and it consists of various verbal and performance measures.

The tests are useful in assessing general intelligence as well as more specific components of intelligence such as judgment and common sense, general knowledge and information vocabulary, speed of eye–hand coordination, concentration and attentiveness, and social awareness. Results from these tests can indicate various forms of psychopathology as well as neuropathology and associated problems. The reason for this is that brain damage, psychotic deterioration, and emotional difficulties seem to affect some intellectual functions more than others. And a pattern analysis of WAIS scores may reveal certain disorders. Indeed, the WAIS is recognized as a valid and reliable test of intelligence but has not been researched to any great extent regarding its ability to predict law enforcement performance.

From the limited research available, a correlation of .61 was found between WAIS scores with academy grades, and a correlation of .38 between WAIS scores and performance ratings of police officers after one year on the job was also found (Aamodt, 2004). One of the major drawbacks of the WAIS (in any of its various incarnations) is the time it takes to properly administer the test. The test is designed to be individually administered. The WAIS-R, for example, requires one and one-half hours to properly administer. This does not include the time needed for proper scoring and interpretation.

NELSON-DENNY READING TEST

The *Nelson-Denny Reading Test* is a 118-item test designed to measure reading comprehension and vocabulary. The test takes about 45 minutes to complete and has a test–retest reliability of .77, internal reliability of .96, and alternate form reliability of .90. Some research suggests that Nelson-Denny scores correlate between (r = .38) and (r = .59) with police academy grades (Rose, 1995; Surrette, Aamodt, & Serafino, 1990).

SHIPLEY INSTITUTE OF LIVING SCALE

The *Shipley Institute of Living Scale* consists of 60 items, and measures vocabulary and abstract thinking. The test can be administered to a group of individuals and takes about 20 minutes to complete. Most of the uses of the Shipley scale have been in clinical and neuropsychological settings and not for the pre-employment selection of police personnel. Gardner (1994) found a correlation of .16 between Shipley scores and police probationary performance. Other research has found correlations of .39 and .50 (Mullins & McMains, 1996; Scogin, Schumacher, Gardner, & Chapin, 1995). Davis and Rostow (2003) found a significant negative correlation (r = -.09) between Shipley scores and being terminated for cause.

PERSONALITY ASSESSMENT INSTRUMENTS

THE MINNESOTA MULTIPHASIC PERSONALITY INVENTORY

The Minnesota Multiphasic Personality Inventory (MMPI) was first published in 1937 and consists of 566 forced-choice true or false questions related to various forms of clinical psychopathology. It is an empirical criterion-keyed test that pretests items used on the various clinical scales. The validity scales consist of scales L (Lie), F (Frequency), and K (Defensiveness). The 10 clinical scales are scales 1 (Hypochondriasis), 2 (Depression), 3 (Hysteria), 4 (Psychopathic Deviate), 5 (Masculinity–Femininity), 6 (Paranoia), 7 (Psychesthenia), 8 (Schizophrenia), 9 (Hypomania), and 0 (Social Affiliation). In response to concerns that the original MMPI contained dated, objectionable items (e.g., items that were religious, sexual, and intrusive), it was republished in 1989 to address these issues and increase its face validity as well (Daniels & King, 2002).

The new version of the MMPI was a vast improvement over the older one as it satisfied the criticisms leveled against it but maintained its usefulness. The MMPI, and later the MMPI-2, has been and remains the most commonly used psychological test in the assessment of police officer applicants. As Blau (1994) observed, it has been the workhorse of paper-and-pencil personality assessment for more than half a century.

Police officers as a group tend to fall in the "normal" MMPI (or MMPI-2) range on clinical scales and generally present an emotionally healthy image (Mills & Stratton, 1982). Studies have found that police officers tend somewhat to score higher than non–police officers on scales K (Defensiveness), 3 (Hysteria), 4 (Psychopathic Deviate), and 9 (Hypomania) (Bernstein, Schoenfeld, & Costello, 1982; Raza & Carpenter, 1987).

A study performed by Hargrave (1987) found that the L scale and the F scale tended to distinguish between satisfactory and unsatisfactory officer criterion groups. Herndon (1998) found that elevations on the L scale of the MMPI-2 appeared related to subsequent poor behavior of police officers after being hired. Boes, Chandler, and Timm (1997) found that corrupt officers were likely to obtain high scores on the L scale. Scores on the L scale also have been found to correlate generally with future problematic police performance.

Overall, research has found that elevated L scores are correlated with poor police performance. Weiss, Davis, Rostow, and Kinsman (2003) suggest that the L scale is a valuable predictor of problematic police officer behavior. This is not surprising considering the descriptors of high L scores given by Graham (2000). He describes these individuals as trying to create a favorable impression of themselves by not being honest in their responses to the MMPI-2 test items. These individuals are described as defensive, denying, and repressing. They tend to claim virtues to a greater extent than most people. They manifest little or no insight into their own motivations. They show little awareness of consequences to other people of their own behavior. They overevaluate their own worth. They have poor tolerance for stress and pressure. They are unoriginal in thinking and inflexible in problem solving.

It should be noted that the types of police applicants who would obtain high L scores on the MMPI-2, without an actual MMPI-2 administration, may very easily be misidentified as good candidates for police work because they appear so "normal." The L scale measures a cluster of personality attributes and attitudes that can most certainly negatively impact police performance but are not obvious; rather, they are subtle. These applicants tend to be rigid, moralistic, conventional, and socially conforming. Police department background investigations often fail to discover any criminal behavior or behavioral aberrations with these individuals. However, the very inadequate stress tolerance of these applicants, along with their defensiveness and inflated sense of self-worth, makes them particularly susceptible to impulsive, aggressive, or abusive behavior in their roles as police officers.

Scale 4 (Psychopathic Deviate) of the MMPI is generally thought to have particular relevance in the selection of police officers because the scale was developed to assist in identifying persons with psychopathic personality disorders (Weiss, Bueher, & Yates, 1996). A psychopathic personality pattern involves a repeated and flagrant disregard for social customs and mores, an inability to profit from experience, emotional shallowness, and the strongly held belief (whether conscious or not) that "the world is my oyster." Males who score high on scale 4 are further described as hostile and aggressive in their interpersonal relationships, sarcastic and cynical, ostentatious, exhibitionistic, moody, thrill-seeking, and resentful. Women are described as aggressive, emotionally changeable, and high-strung. Shusman, Inwald, and Knatz (1987) found scale 4 to be important in separating good and poor performance groups of police officers; Weiss, Buehler, and Yates (1995) found that scale 4 correlated with dissatisfaction as a police officer when the "Subtle-Obvious" distinction on scale 4 is more closely examined. Other researchers have found that scale 4 subtle items were associated with termination of probationary officers (Weiss, Serafino, Serafino, Wilson, & Knoll, 1998).

Overall, various studies have suggested that officers rated as unsatisfactory by their supervisors tend to score significantly higher on scale 4 (Psychopathic Deviate), scale 6 (Paranoia), and scale 9 (Hypomania) than satisfactory officers (Hargrave, 1987; Hargrave, Hiatt, & Gaffney, 1988). Building on this idea, Bartol (1991) followed 600 police officers from 34 small-town police departments over 13 years to determine which officers were eventually terminated. He concluded that an "immaturity index" consisted of a combination of scales 4 and 9 plus the L scale and was a strong predictor of termination. Other researchers such as Hargrave et al. (1988) have used a composite of MMPI scores (F, 4, 9, and CYN) to identify highly aggressive law enforcement officers and applicants. And Weiss et al. (1998) found that scale 4 has predictive power for both job retention and supervisory ratings in police officer candidates.

Although the research indicates modest success using the validity and clinical scales of the MMPI and MMPI-2 in predicting future police officer functioning, very few studies have addressed the various content scales of tests. The content scales were designed to provide relevant data on certain traits and behaviors not available from the standard MMPI-2 scales (Clark, 1994). Content scales include, but are not limited to, Anxiety (ANX), Obsessiveness (OBS), Health Concerns (HEA), Bizarre Mentation (BIZ), Cynicism (CYN), Family Problems (FAM), and Work Interference (WRK). Daniels and King (2003) examined the predictive ability of the MMPI-2 content scales in differentiating successful and unsuccessful small-town police officers and found that although the scores of police officers differed somewhat from the MMPI-2 normative sample, the content scales were not able to predict police officer performance.

THE CALIFORNIA PSYCHOLOGICAL INVENTORY

The *California Psychological Inventory* (CPI), one of the oldest and most respected of the personality inventories, is similar in format to the MMPI, but its subscales include such personal traits as dominance, sociability, and flexibility. These subscales stand in contrast to the diagnostic categories of the MMPI (e.g., Psychopathic Deviate and Depression). Answers to the 434 items yield scores on 20 dimensions in four primary areas:

1. Measures of Poise—dominance, capacity for status, sociability, social presence, self-acceptance, independence, and empathy
2. Measures of Normative Orientation and Values—responsibility, socialization, self-control, good impression, communality, well-being, and tolerance

3. Measures of Cognitive and Intellectual Functioning—achievement via conformance, achievement via independence, and intellectual efficiency
4. Measures of Role and Interpersonal Style—psychological mindedness, flexibility, and femininity

The CPI also yields scores on several special scales such as managerial potential (Mp), work orientation (Wo), creative temperament (Ct), leadership potential (Lp), amicability (Ami), law enforcement orientation (Leo), anxiety (ANX), narcissism (NAR), and tough-mindedness (Tm).

Scale scores on the CPI have been found to be related to police trainees' academy performance and to supervisors' ratings (Bartol, 1991). Hargrave and Hiatt (1989) tested 575 police recruits with the CPI and found that CPI profiles distinguished between those suitable and unsuitable for training. The authors concluded that CPI profiles have a more consistent relationship with future job performance than police academy variables. The higher rated officers generally scored higher on the CPI primary areas assessing socialization, responsibility, interpersonal values, and character.

THE INWALD PERSONALITY INVENTORY

The *Inwald Personality Inventory* (IPI) was developed with the express purpose of directly questioning public safety/law enforcement candidates and documenting their admitted behaviors, rather than inferring those behaviors from statistically derived personality indicators specifically for the pre-employment personality screening of police applicants (Inwald, 1992).

The test is a 310-item, true–false questionnaire that usually requires about 45 minutes to complete. It consists of 25 scales and one validity scale (Guardedness). The 25 constructs measured by the IPI are:

- Acting Out Behavior: Alcohol use (AL), Drug use (DG), Driving violation (DV), Job difficulties (JD), Trouble with society and the law (TL0), and Absence Abuse (AA)
- Acting Out Attitudes: Substance abuse (SA), Antisocial attitudes (AS), Hyperactivity (HP), Rigid style (RT), and Type A (TA)
- Internalized Conflict: Illness concerns (IC), Treatment programs (TP), Anxiety (AN), Phobic personality (PH), Obsessive personality (OB), Depression (DE), Loner type (LO), and Unusual experiences and thoughts (EU)
- Interpersonal Conflict: Lack of assertiveness (LA), Interpersonal difficulties (ID), Undue suspiciousness (US), Family conflicts (FC), Sexual concerns (SC), and Spouse/mate conflicts (SP)

Some studies have found the IPI predicting criterion measures such as retention or termination, absences, lateness, and disciplinary measures more often than the MMPI (Inwald & Shusman, 1984; Shusman & Inwald, 1991). In a cross-validation study, Shusman, Inwald, and Knatz (1987) found the IPI to be superior to the MMPI in predicting police academy success. Several studies have found that a combination of the IPI and MMPI is the most successful approach for predicting maladaptive behavior in police and corrections officers (Inwald, 1992; Scogin, Schumacher, Gardner, & Chapin, 1995).

THE SIXTEEN PERSONALITY FACTOR QUESTIONNAIRE

The *Sixteen Personality Factor Questionnaire* (16PF) is a 187-item personality inventory that usually requires about one hour to complete. The original test—published in 1949 by R.B. Cattell—yielded 16 scores in such traits as reserved vs. outgoing, humble vs. assertive, shy vs. venturesome, and trusting vs. suspicious (Cattell, Eber, & Tatsuoka, 1970). Since 1949, the 16PF has been revised six times, with the most recent revisions (1993 and 1998) used by many law enforcement agencies today.

The 16 primary factors of the 16PF consist of "A" (Interpersonal warmth), "B" (Abstract reasoning), "C" (Emotional stability), "E" (Dominance), "F" (Enthusiasm), "G" (Conscientiousness), "H" (Social boldness), "I" (Sensitivity), "L" (Vigilance), "M" (Imagination), "N" (Forthrightness), "O" (Apprehensiveness), "Q1" (Openness), "Q2" (Self-reliance), "Q3" (Perfectionism), and "Q4" (Tension). Results of one meta-analysis suggest that of the 16 scales, only two—Dominance and Conscientiousness—were significantly related to police performance (Aamodt, 2004). As indicated earlier, the test is used frequently in pre-employment psychological assessment in law enforcement, and individuals scoring high on certain scales are described alternatively as assertive and competitive, and conscientious and responsible, depending on the scales examined.

THE EDWARDS PERSONAL PREFERENCE SCHEDULE

The *Edwards Personal Preference Schedule* (EPPS) was developed in 1959 based on the manifest need system theory of H. S. Murray and his associates at the Harvard Psychological Clinic (Anastasi, 1976). Beginning with 15 needs drawn from Murray's list of manifest needs, Edwards prepared sets of items whose content appeared to fit each need (Murray, 1938). Examples included the *Need for Achievement* (to do one's best and accomplish something difficult), *Deference* (to conform to what is expected), *Exhibition* (to be the center of attention), *Intraception* (to analyze the motives and feelings of oneself and others), *Dominance* (to influence others and to be regarded as a leader), and *Nurturance* (to help others in trouble).

In its present form, the EPPS consists of 225 pairs of psychological needs, and yields a test consistency score and scores on 15 dimensions of manifest needs. These are Achievement, Deference, Order, Exhibition, Autonomy, Affiliation, Intraception, Succorance, Dominance, Abasement, Nurturance, Change, Endurance, Heterosexuality, and Aggression. Law enforcement research using the EPPS has been rather limited (Aamodt, 2004). But Balch (1977) found that higher scores on Need for Achievement (r = .37) and consistency in completing the test (r = .22) were associated with completing a police academy, and Shaffer (1996) found that higher scores on the Dominance scale were related to increased traffic accidents.

PERSONALITY ASSESSMENT INVENTORY

The *Personality Assessment Inventory* (PAI) is an objective inventory of adult personality designed to assess various psychopathological syndromes. This test, introduced in 2004, consists of 344 items and requires about one hour to complete (Weiss, Rostow, Davis, & DeCoster-Martin, 2004).

The PAI contains the following scales:

- Validity scales: inconsistency, infrequency, negative impression (NIM), and positive impression
- Clinical scales: somatic complaints (SOM), anxiety (ANX), anxiety related disorders (ARD), depression (DEP), mania (MAN), paranoia (PAR), schizophrenia (SCZ), borderline personality (BOR), antisocial personality (ANTA), antisocial-stimulus seeking (ANTS), antisocial-egocentricity (ANTE), aggression (AGG), and substance abuse (DRG)
- Treatment consideration scales: aggression (AGG), suicidal ideation (SUI), stress (STR), nonsupport (NON), and treatment rejection (RXR)
- Interpersonal scales: dominance (DOM) and warmth (WRM) (Aamodt, 2004)

In a study by Weiss, Zehner, Davis, and Rostow (2005), PAI results of 800 male and female police officer candidates were examined as possible predictors of the criterion variables insubordination, excessive citizen complaints, and neglect of duty. The results indicated highly significant coefficients for antisocial-egocentricity (ANTE) as a predictor of insubordination and excessive citizen complaints. Significant coefficients were also obtained for antisocial-stimulus seeking (ANTS) and negative impression (NIM) as predictors of neglect of duty.

Rorschach Inkblot Test

The *Rorschach Inkblot Test* has been one of the most popular techniques for personality assessment for the last 90 years. Developed by the Swiss psychiatrist Hermann Rorschach, the Rorschach technique utilizes 10 stimulus cards. Five of the stimulus cards are in shades of gray and black only, two contain additional touches of bright red, and the remaining three combine several pastel shades. As the examinee is shown each inkblot, he or she is asked to tell the examiner what the blot could be. Besides keeping a verbatim record of the responses to each card, the examiner notes times of responses, position or positions in which cards are held, spontaneous remarks, emotional expressions, and other incidental behavior of the examinee during the test session. Following the presentation of all 10 cards, the examiner questions the individual systematically regarding the parts and aspects of each blot to which the associations were given. During this inquiry, the respondents also have the opportunity to clarify and elaborate their earlier responses.

The Rorschach test has been subjected to several major scoring and interpretive systems through the years. But the most ambitious effort at developing a psychometrically sound system was undertaken by Exner (1974, 1978, 1993), who presented a standardized system for the administration, scoring, and interpretation of Rorschach responses. He used ratios, indices, and combinations of variables in his comprehensive system (Exner, 1978).

Some researchers and clinicians believe that, considering the Rorschach's utility as a diagnostic and assessment devise in other areas, it could be employed effectively in hitherto unused areas that could include law enforcement selection (Meyer, 2004; Meyer, Mihura, & Smith, 2005). Indeed, the Board of Trustees of the Society for Personality Assessment concluded that "the Rorschach possesses documented reliability and validity similar to other generally accepted test instruments used in the assessment of personality and psychopathology and that its responsible use in personality assessment is appropriate and justified" (2005, p. 221).

While no data for the successful use of the Rorschach in selecting police officers currently exist, the test has been used successfully in other settings, including employment-related screenings in other fields (Exner & Weiner, 1994). The Rorschach has also been used for fitness-for-duty evaluations for employees, including airline pilots (Ganellen, 1996). But in order for the Rorschach to be considered acceptable as an assessment tool for the screening of police applicants, considerable research must be undertaken to determine its appropriateness and effectiveness.

VOCATIONAL INTEREST INVENTORIES

Kuder Occupational Interest Inventory

The *Kuder Preference Record* was developed in 1948 and then replaced in 1971 by the *Kuder Occupational Interest Inventory* (Aamodt, 2004). The Kuder is a 100-item interest inventory developed through criterion keying procedures for the purpose of measuring vocational interests (Kuder, 1985). The inventory takes about 45 minutes to complete and yields scores on 119 occupational groups (including police) and 10 occupational areas (outdoor, mechanical, computational, scientific, persuasive, artistic, literary, musical, clerical, and social service).

There have been recommendations that an interest inventory be included as part of any testing battery to assess police applicants (Spielberger, 1979). Azen, Snibbe, and Montgomery (1973) found a correlation of .24 between the Mechanical Interest scale and supervisor ratings of performance.

The same authors used the Kuder to select police officer candidates in the city of Los Angeles and found that the Kuder Mechanic Scale was also a predictor of success in police work.

STRONG INTEREST INVENTORY

The *Strong Interest Inventory* (SII) was originally formulated in 1920 by E. K. Strong Jr. and has been revised many times since then. The inventory was based on the work of John Holland, who defined six basic occupational themes (called *Holland codes*) that can be used to categorize occupations as well as individuals (Anastasi, 1976): Realistic (machines, tools, outdoors), Investigative (science, theories, ideas, data), Artistic (self-expression, art appreciation), Social (people, team work, human welfare, community services), Enterprising (business, politics, leadership, influence), and Conventional (organization, data, finance). The most recent version produces 30 Basic Interest Scales, 244 Occupational Scales, and more than 120 specific jobs. The research supporting the Strong as a predictor of police suitability or performance is meager.

SITUATIONAL TESTS

As will be discussed in greater depth later in this volume, besides the administration of paper-and-pencil tests, psychologists may administer computerized situational tests designed to measure what applicants might say or what they might do in response to interactive videos that depict police work–related events. For example, a psychologist can present an applicant a video that shows a potential interaction with someone. The applicant must quickly make an appraisal (judgment) as to how dangerous the person's behavior is (e.g., using a scale ranging from *not at all dangerous* to *very dangerous*). Then the applicant is required to make a decision as to how forcefully he or she would respond (e.g., using a scale ranging from an *escapable action* to a *lethal action*). The psychologist can evaluate the applicant's judgments and decisions, which may reveal aggressive inclinations.

Results from situational tests can greatly add to the applicant's pre-employment screening and evaluation. However, when performing such evaluations, psychologists should not expect police applicants to have the same fund of knowledge as someone who has been a police officer for an appreciable amount of time. What psychologists should assess is the personal experiences and judgment inclinations applicants bring to the job assessment and to the job itself. But it should be noted that situational tests using the computer are very expensive and are not backed up by empirical psychological literature, which would be needed to validate them.

In 1989, a major revision of the MMPI was published (Butcher et al., 2001), resulting in the MMPI-2, which in turn caused police psychologists to attempt further validation studies with the new test. While welcoming obsolete item revisions, police psychologists, who were accustomed to interpreting MMPI profiles using the original clinical norms, expressed concern that the new updated norms showed far fewer elevations for the more "normal" and defensive police/public safety officer candidates. This led many psychologists involved in pre-employment assessment to add additional tests (sometimes nonpsychological in nature) to their standard batteries in order to either augment or to replace the MMPI-2.

Also, when the Polygraph Act of 1988 banned the use of the pre-employment polygraph for nonfederal police agencies, newly unemployed polygraph examiners became interested in promoting the use of paper-and-pencil honesty tests and "integrity tests." But integrity tests have not been studied much. In his 1994 book, Theodore Blau indicated that of the 40 integrity tests available at the time, few studies of these tests had been published in peer-reviewed journals. Today, mostly the National Security Agency and the Central Intelligence Agency make significant use of the polygraph for personnel security and pre-employment screening. But it seems to slowly be making a comeback as an adjunct to pre-employment psychological screening for police applicants.

THE POLYGRAPH MACHINE IN HISTORICAL CONTEXT: EARLY PIONEERS

The modern polygraph has been used in one form or another for nearly a century, and much cruder versions of its components existed as far back as 300 B.C.E. The Bedouins of Arabia, for example, required the authors of conflicting statements to lick a hot iron. The one whose tongue was not burned was considered truthful. The common principle underlying this primitive test as well as others (e.g., spitting drier rice powder that had been placed in one's mouth, or being less able to swallow a "trial slice" of bread, as practiced centuries ago in England) is that the tense, nervous person (the one who is lying) has less saliva (dry mouth and tongue) and thus is more likely to have their tongue burned, spit dry rice, or have difficulty swallowing a piece of bread (Smith, 1967). As indicated previously, in modern times, the admissibility of voice identification evidence into court is usually evaluated using the Daubert standard, which allows such evidence into testimony if the judge assesses that such evidence will assist the jury in better understanding the case as a whole.

In 1878, Italian physiologist Angelo Mosso used an instrument called a *plethysmograph* (an instrument for measuring changes in volume within an organ or whole body, usually resulting from fluctuations in the amount of blood or air it contains) in his research on emotion and fear in subjects undergoing questioning. He studied, in particular, the effects of emotions such as fear on subjects' cardiovascular and respiratory activity. He also studied blood circulation and breathing patterns and how these changed under specified conditions. The use of the plethysmograph revealed periodic waves in a subject's blood pressure caused by changes in the respiratory cycle in response to certain stimuli (Kitaeff, 2010). Mosso was the first scientist to report on experiments in which he observed that a person's breathing pattern changed under certain stimuli, and that this change, in turn, caused variations in their blood pressure and pulse rate. Although not for the purpose of detecting deception, Sir James Mackenzie constructed the first *clinical polygraph* in 1892, an instrument to be used for medical examinations with the capability to simultaneously record undulated line tracings of the vascular pulses (radial, venous, and arterial) by way of a stylus onto a revolving drum of smoked paper. Until the end of the 19th century, no measuring device for the detection of deception had ever been used. The first use of a scientific instrument designed to measure physiological responses for this purpose came in 1895 when Italian physician, psychiatrist, and pioneer criminologist Cesare Lombroso modified an existing instrument called a *hydrosphygmograph* and used this modified device in his experiments to measure the physiological changes that occurred in a crime suspect's blood pressure and pulse rate during a police interrogation.

In 1914, Italian psychologist Vittorio Benussi invented a method to calculate the quotient of the inhalation to exhalation time as a means of verifying the truth and detecting deception in a subject. Using a *pneumograph*—a device that recorded a subject's breathing patterns—Benussi conducted experiments regarding the respiratory symptoms of lying. He concluded that lying caused an emotional change within a subject that resulted in detectable respiratory changes that were indicative of deception.

William Moulton Marston, a U.S. attorney and psychologist, is credited with inventing an early form of the *lie detector* when, in 1915, he developed the discontinuous systolic blood pressure test that would later become one component of the modern polygraph. Marston's technique used a standard blood pressure cuff and a stethoscope to take intermittent systolic blood pressure readings of a suspect during questioning for the purpose of detecting deception (Lykken, 1988).

The idea of "lie detection" caught on rapidly in the United States during the 1920s and 1930s after John Larson was asked by the chief of police in Berkeley, California, to develop a lie detector to solve a case under investigation (Larson, 1969). This instrument, to many, became the first true polygraph used for lie detection purposes (Bartol & Bartol, 2004). In the 1930s, the increasing demand for polygraph examiners resulted in at least 30 polygraph schools opening across the United States (Barland & Raskin, 1976; Lykken, 1988).

A modern polygraph machine is an instrument that simultaneously records changes in physiological processes such as heartbeat, blood pressure, respiration, and electrical resistance (galvanic skin response or GSR). The underlying theory of the polygraph is that when people lie, they also get measurably nervous about lying. The heartbeat increases, blood pressure goes up, breathing rhythms change, perspiration increases, and so on. A baseline for these physiological characteristics is established by asking the subject questions whose answers the investigator knows. Deviations from the baseline for truthfulness are usually taken as signs of lying (Kitaeff, 2010).

APPROACHES TO THE POLYGRAPH TEST

There are three basic approaches to the polygraph test: (1) the Control Question Test (CQT) (also referred to as the relevant–irrelevant technique), (2) the Directed Lie Test (DLT), and (3) the Guilty Knowledge Test (GKT). The details of each of these tests is beyond the scope of this chapter, but suffice it to say, they are all used with varying degrees of success to help ascertain if an individual is telling the truth (Allen, 2002; Allen & Iacono, 2001; Kitaeff, 2010).

From a theoretical standpoint, truthful responses are accompanied by relatively flat reaction lines, whereas untruthful responses are hypothesized to cause significant fluctuations in physiological measures such as heart rate, perspiration, and respiration. In addition, some evidence suggests that the accuracy of polygraphs can even be increased through intensive training of the examiner and by using computerized systems. But the majority of the scientific evidence indicates that whatever accuracy the polygraph examination does provide seems to come from the conclusions made by individual examiners of such factors such as the subject's general demeanor rather than his or her actual chart responses. Most experienced examiners would even concur that the key ingredient for a competently administered polygraph is the examiner—regardless of whether a computerized scoring procedure is used (Iacono, 2008).

Currently, the research conducted under laboratory or controlled conditions indicates that the correct classification of truthful and deceptive examinees ranges between 70% and 80% at best (Kitaeff, 2010).

CRITICISMS OF THE POLYGRAPH TEST

One of the problems with the polygraph is its susceptibility to countermeasures used by examinees to fool the machine and the examiner (Bartol & Bartol, 2004). Countermeasures can be physical or psychological. The most common countermeasures used are either pain or muscle tension. For example, in an effort to deceive the polygrapher, "biting one's lip or tongue or subtly jabbing oneself with a pin may induce enough pain to promote a physiological response that masks the subject's response to questions from the polygrapher" (Bartol & Bartol, 2004, p. 86). Mental countermeasures include deliberate attempts at distortion using techniques such as counting backward from 100 or thinking of a peaceful or arousing scene. In this way, the examinee tries to either minimize or maximize the emotional impact of questions. Although physical countermeasures can often be detected by experienced polygraphers, mental countermeasures are far more difficult to detect (Ben-Shakhar & Dolev, 1996).

Overall, it is generally recognized that no physiological response is uniquely associated with lying. Moreover, the brain mechanisms involved in lying are unknown, rendering it difficult to develop techniques that can distinguish liars from truth tellers. Indeed, a person's physiological reactions in response to lying are likely similar in nature to those resulting from the passionate denial that occurs when false charges are leveled against him. The fear of detection is indistinguishable from the fear of false detection, and the physiological reactions recorded by the polygraph under these two circumstances cannot be discriminated from each other. Scientists with no direct involvement in the polygraph profession have repeatedly reviewed the scientific literature and concluded that the accuracy claims of the polygraph profession are exaggerated and indefensible. Carroll (1988) summarized the results of a series of laboratory experiments on the polygraph using mock crimes and blind scoring (where examiners had no knowledge of guilt or innocence).

The results suggested a "staggering high rate of false positives and a dearth of contribution to the process of establishing innocence" (p. 27). These opinions are reflected in reviews spanning several decades (Lykken, 1988; Saxe, Dougherty, & Cross, 1985) as well as in more recent evaluations of the literature carried out for texts in polygraphy and forensic psychology (Ben-Shakar, 2008; Iacono & Patrick, 1999; Oksol & O'Donohue, 2003).

In a 1997 survey of 195 psychologists from the Society for Psychophysiological Research, most respondents answered that polygraphic lie detection is not theoretically sound, that the test can be beaten by easily learned countermeasures, and that test results should not be admitted in courts of law (Lacono & Lykken, 1997). The issue was settled in 1998 with the U.S. Supreme Court case of *U.S. v. Scheffer,* where in an 8-to-1 decision the Court emphasized the poor reliability of polygraph evidence as a whole. Justice Thomas, writing for the majority, stressed that a fundamental premise of the criminal justice system is that jurors are the ultimate and most reliable evaluators of credibility and truthfulness (*U.S. v. Scheffer* at 313). Since 1998, almost all courts reject polygraph results or only allow them if their admissibility is stipulated by both parties prior to the polygraph examination taking place. Only a few courts leave their admissibility up to the judge (Kitaeff, 2010).

PRE-EMPLOYMENT, PSYCHOLOGICAL SCREENING, AND THE LAW

In general, psychologists have designed pre-employment psychological screening programs by attempting to "screen out" those applicants found to be psychologically inappropriate for police work and to "screen in" those with positive characteristics, attitudes, and traits known to be associated with highly functioning officers. The screening-out method is based on the hypothesis that an officer who is "psychologically unstable" is more likely to violate the civil rights of citizens and contribute to community unrest than a "stable" officer. Most psychologists who work with law enforcement agencies employ a screening battery composed of an interview, a cognitive test, and two or more personality tests.

There are legal and liability-related reasons why the pre-employment screening of police applicants is necessary. Suing the police is very popular in the United States. It can also be very profitable, as the average jury award is over $2 million. This does not take into account the hundreds of cases settled out of court likely amounting to hundreds of millions of dollars. Lawsuits against the police may be filed in state court as a tort law claim. This is the preferred method because a tort (a "wrong" in the legal sense) can usually only be settled by monetary awards for damages done to the plaintiff. In addition, courts may impose punitive damages against the police department as punishment if the wrong done to the plaintiff was particularly severe in the eyes of the court. Under the law, the failure of a police department to properly select police officers can easily be considered a severe form of neglect. A department may be liable for a charge of negligence by employing an individual who possesses personality attributes or prior conduct that would create an undue risk of harming others in carrying out his or her official responsibilities. Furthermore, the standard of proof in these civil cases is "by a preponderance of the evidence," which is much easier to meet than the criminal standard of "beyond a reasonable doubt."

Tort liability associated with lawsuits against police departments may also include wrongful death, assault and battery, false arrest, and false imprisonment. Gross negligence may be assumed by a department's failure to conduct full background investigations of applicants. Police departments can also be charged with negligent retention (keeping employees on the job when they clearly should have been disciplined, demoted, or dismissed) and negligent entrustment (inadequately preparing officers prior to entrusting them with police responsibilities).

The risk to municipal government (and to the public) is considerable when a potential employee is a police officer. This increased risk stems from the privileges granted to commissioned police officers to take "life and liberty" under special circumstances. In U.S. society, this privilege to exert lawful, sometimes deadly force and restraint is why the hiring of police applicants known to possess destructive characteristics can make a department so legally liable. *Deliberate indifference* may be said to apply when a police department should have had the ability to foresee a risk to the public, but for any reason did not take possible steps to minimize that danger. In instances such as these, a lawsuit may be filed in federal court as a violation of Title 42 of the U.S. Code. This is a legal claim that alleges that there has been a violation of someone's civil rights under the U.S. Constitution.

Although individual states cannot be sued in federal court under a civil rights claim, municipalities (and their employees), police departments (and their employees), and sheriffs' departments (and their employees) can be sued if it is shown that they were acting "under color of law," and violated a specific amendment of the Constitution. The standards used in federal courts in this regard are *custom or policy* and *deliberate indifference*, both of which are loosely defined concepts but similar to *totality of the circumstances*. Although such suits can result in monetary awards, the amounts are usually not great because the purpose of civil rights suits filed under 42 U.S.C. 1983 is essentially injunctive (i.e., to force the municipality or department to change its procedures or behaviors).

A lawsuit against a police department by a present employee or police applicant may also be filed in federal court stemming from a complaint filed with the U.S. Equal Employment Opportunity Commissions (EEOC). Such complaints could be based on race, age, or sex discrimination in hiring, retention, or promotions.

During the late 1970s, the personality tests most commonly used with public safety office candidates included the MMPI, the CPI, the 16PF, the EPPS, and various projective tests. Because the MMPI was the most widely used nonprojective personality assessment instrument available to clinical psychologists at the time, it was a natural choice to be used by psychologists who began working in the police and public safety officer selection field (Murphy, 1972). It was first used in police research in an attempt to predict police academy grades (King, Norrell, & Erlandson, 1959). Articles suggesting the usefulness of the MMPI in police settings, particularly for pre-employment screening, began to appear in the 1970s (Azen, 1974; Azen, Snibbe, & Montgomery, 1973; Saccuzo, Higgins, & Lewandowski, 1974; Saxe & Reiser, 1976). However, the MMPI originally had been developed and normed for use with inpatients in psychiatric hospitals and not with more highly functioning and symptom-denying job applicants for law enforcement officer positions. It was noticed by practitioners that the norms for the MMPI often showed "normal" ranges for individual candidates, whereas the job histories and antisocial behavior patterns discovered in background investigations and psychological interviews for these same individuals suggested potential difficulties for high-risk positions (Inwald, 1982). There was growing concern about the inadequacy of available instruments, or of evidence to support the MMPI as a predictor of police performance (Mills & Stratton, 1982).

The 1980s represented another decade of change for police psychology. With much growing interest and development in police/public safety personality testing, a larger number of research articles and instrument publications began to appear as more psychologists became involved in conducting pre-employment evaluations for police departments and the need to firmly establish the validity of the instruments used for this application was recognized.

In 1981, police psychologists became aware of an important lawsuit in New York City. On December 20, 1976, NYC police officer Blase A. Bonsignore used his off-duty revolver to shoot his wife and then to commit suicide. His wife suffered brain damage and serious motor dysfunction as a result. In the lawsuit that followed, the jury awarded his wife $425,000 in damages on her negligence claim. (*Bonsignore v. the City of N.Y.*, 1982). This was a very important case in the development of police psychological-screening programs in that its outcome persuaded many reluctant chiefs that they could have serious difficulties defending hiring decisions if they failed to provide adequate psychological screening at the outset.

Meanwhile, the shorter, 310-item IPI soon gained considerable popularity with police psychologists, especially as its validity for pre-employment screening became established during the 1980s. Several IPI research publications and independent studies were completed, including the first longitudinal cross-validation studies and the first publications that directly compared law enforcement candidate test results by gender and ethnicity (Inwald, 1988; Inwald & Shusman, 1984; Scogin & Beutler, 1986). Also at this time, there was some early recognition of the emerging area of police–public safety assessment by professional psychology organizations. For example, in 1982, the New York State Psychological Association's "Meritorious Research Award" was presented to Inwald for "contribution to test construction in an important new area."

After the IPI computerized report was published in 1982, specifying how test results could be interpreted using public safety officer applicant norms, National Computer Systems (NCS) introduced an MMPI computer-generated narrative report, the "Minnesota Report: Personnel Selection System," in 1984. The original MMPI clinical norms still were used in the MMPI profile graphs, and no cutoff scores were suggested for law enforcement officer candidates or for other job applicants.

In 1985, police psychologists began to expand their practices to include "fitness-for-duty" testing. When some psychologists who were using the IPI for pre-employment screening began to readminister this test as an aid for determining fitness-for-duty of already hired officers (Rice, 1985), it was clear there was a need for more specialized assessment instruments. In 1986, the first comprehensive personality inventory developed for "fitness-for-duty" evaluations of public safety officers, the Hilson Career Satisfaction Index (HCSI), was developed and validated by Robin Inwald (Inwald & Kaufman, 1989).

In 1988, at the IACP annual convention, Inwald introduced the Hilson Personnel Profile/Success Quotient (HPP/SQ), the first comprehensive personality inventory measuring "emotional intelligence" (Inwald, 2004; Inwald & Brobst, 1988; Inwald & Brockwell, 1988). Validated for police personnel hiring and promotion, and based on Inwald's "Success Quotient Theory," this measure focused on a combination of characteristics such as initiative, "winner's image," work ethic, popularity/charisma, and social sensitivity. Norms were collected for police chiefs at the 1988 IACP convention and, after validation data were analyzed for law enforcement officer applicants throughout the United States, the HPP/SQ became a standard addition to many police psychologists' pre-employment and promotional test batteries.

In 1988, Inwald also added discriminant-function-derived prediction equations for termination, absence, lateness, and disciplinary actions to the IPI's computerized report. These equations were based on the first 5-year longitudinal prediction study, including cross-validation, for public safety officers. The results were published in the *Journal of Applied Psychology* (Inwald, 1988).

Because of complaints about "honesty/integrity" tests received by members of Congress, its Office of Technology Assessment (OTA) launched an investigation into the validity of these tests now flooding the market (though mostly in the retail area). With similar concerns, the American Psychological Association (APA) also organized a special task force to review available research. At this time, practicing police psychologists expressed growing concerns about claims of validity for tests not previously used to screen law enforcement applicants. Because these tests, with little or no published research connected with police performance, were marketed directly to police chiefs and others for use without the input of a psychologist, several articles and research reviews were published on the subject (Inwald, 1984b, 1988, 1992; Sackett & Harris, 1984; Sackett et al., 1989). When the final reports from OTA (1990) and APA (1991) were published, they showed conflicting results. The OTA report concluded that "existing research is insufficient as a basis for supporting the assertion that (honesty tests) can reliably predict dishonest behavior in the workplace." In any case, the Polygraph Act and subsequent "honesty test debate" of the late 1980s certainly encouraged increased scholarship and validation research in the area of public safety/police assessment.

A complaint may also be based on alleged violation of the Americans with Disabilities Act (ADA). The provisions of the ADA state that individuals who believe they have been discriminated against on the basis of their disability can file a charge with the Commission at any of its offices located throughout the United States. The Commission will investigate and initially attempt to resolve the charge through conciliation following the same procedures used to handle charges of discrimination filed under Title VII of the Civil Rights Act of 1964. A charging party may file a lawsuit within 90 days after receiving a notice of a "right to sue" from the EEOC. The ADA also incorporates the remedies contained in Title VII. These remedies can include rehiring, promotion, reinstatement, back pay, and attorney's fees.

REASONABLE ACCOMMODATIONS

Reasonable accommodation (making changes in the nature of the employee's job) is also available as a remedy under the ADA. Under most EEOC-enforced laws, compensatory and punitive damages also may be available where intentional discrimination is found. Damages may be available to compensate for actual monetary losses, future monetary losses, and mental anguish and inconvenience. Punitive damages (used to punish an agency for wrongdoings) also may be available if an employer acted with malice or reckless indifference; however, such damages are not available against the federal, state, or local governments.

Certainly there are numerous reasons from legal, psychological, safety, and commonsense standpoints why police departments and other law enforcement agencies should perform some form of pre-employment psychological screening. Perhaps an Indiana appellate court said it best when it opined that a "policeman frequently works alone, wields great authority, carries lethal weapons" and, "It is not an occupation for … a person with questionable emotional stability" (*City of Greenwood v. Dowler*, 1986 at 1081).

FITNESS-FOR-DUTY EVALUATIONS

Police employers have a legal duty to ensure that police officers under their command are mentally and emotionally fit to perform their duties, and failure to do so can result in significant civil liability (*Bonsignore v. City of New York*, 1982) and serious consequences to citizens, the examinee, other officers, an employing agency's reputation, and the trust of the community. Various courts have interpreted this duty to include the authority to mandate psychological fitness-for-duty (FFD) evaluations of police officers reasonably believed to be impaired in their ability to perform their job functions because of a known or suspected psychological condition (*Colon v. City of Newark*, 2006; *Conte v. Horcher*, 1977; *Deen v. Darosa*, 2005; *Kraft v. Police Commissioner of Boston*, 1994; *McKnight v. Monroe Co. Sheriff's Dept.*, 2002; *Tingler v. City of Tampa*, 1981; *Watson v. City of Miami Beach*, 1999).

In Chapter 13 of this volume, Cory expresses that the circumstances giving rise to fitness-for-duty evaluations (FFDEs)—they are many and varied. They may involve suspicion of job relevant psychopathology associated with on-duty performance (e.g., excessive force, repeated problems of judgment), off-duty conduct (e.g., domestic violence, driving while intoxicated), a suicide attempt, psychiatric hospitalization, or a disability claim. Stone (2000) reported that 26% of the cases from his own practice in the southern region of the United States resulted from suspected psychopathology (i.e., diagnosable mental condition), 19% from excessive force issues, 15% from substance abuse, 13% from behavior implicating poor judgment, and 9% from domestic violence.

Dawkins, Griffin, and Dawkins (2006) utilized an alternative classification scheme for their analysis of the FFD referrals in their own Midwestern practice. Similar to Stone, they found that 16.5% of the more than 200 referrals they analyzed involved alcohol use, but they reported more than twice as many referrals involving domestic violence (20.5%). They reported that 16.3% involved other behavioral concerns, 36.9% pertained to psychopathology or emotional distress, and 4.7% were for officers being considered for rehire following an employment separation.

The right of a police employer to intrude on the medical and personal privacy of its officers derives from two special features of police work: the power of the position and the fact that police officers are public employees. Police officers are members of quasi-military organizations, "called upon for duty at all times, armed at almost all times, and exercising the most awesome and dangerous power that a democratic state possesses with respect to its residents—the power to use lawful force to arrest and detain them" (*Policemen's Benevolent Association of New Jersey v. Township of*

Washington, 1988, at 141). As citizens, police officers retain their constitutional rights (e.g., *Garrity v. New Jersey*, 1967), but as public employees, they "subordinate their right to privacy as a private citizen to the superior right of the public to have an efficient and credible police department" (*Richardson v. City of Pasadena*, 1973/1974, at headnote 1). In the words of the U.S. Supreme Court, "the public should not bear the risk that employees who may suffer from impaired perception and judgment will be [in] positions where they may need to employ deadly force" (*National Treasury Employees Union v. Von Raab*, 1989, at 671).

The employer's duty to ensure a psychologically fit workforce does not, however, extend an unfettered right to require such evaluations of any police officer in any instance (*Denhof v. City of Grand Rapids*, 2005; *Holst v. Veterans Affairs*, 2007; *Jackson v. Lake County*, 2003; *McGreal v. Ostrov*, 2004). Instead, the employer's duty is balanced by public interests and the employee's constitutional, civil, and property rights and interests. But how do we determine truth telling on the part of an officer-employee?

Cory (see Chapter 13 in this volume) points out two primary means for assessing the response style of an officer: third-party information and psychological assessment instruments, or tests, with built-in measures of response style. It is important to gather third-party information. Its utility is tied not only to the improved depth and breadth of information obtained through collateral sources but also to its potential for detecting malingering, defensiveness, dishonesty, and uncooperativeness. Melton et al. (1997) observed that "obtaining information contradicting the client's version of events is probably the most accurate means of detecting fabrication and may be the only viable one with clients who sabotage interview and testing efforts" (pp. 57–58). This is not to say that any given collateral source should be considered to be more reliable than the examinee, but rather that consistencies and discrepancies across and within data sources are important means of weighing validity.

Standardized assessment instruments with validity scales or indices, such as the MMPI-2, MMPI-2-RF, PAI, CPI, MCMI-III, and 16PF, also can serve useful roles in evaluating response style, especially when used in conjunction with third-party information. Consideration should always be given, however, to the base rates of these scales in a particular norm group, such that examinees in an FFDE are not judged to be defensive or dissimulating on the basis of validity scales alone when the scale norms were derived from respondents from a decidedly different context (i.e., police applicants in a pre-employment evaluation may not be comparable on validity scales to incumbent employees in an FFD examination) (Heilbrun, 2001). Evidence of frank lying, dissimulation, falsification, or overt concealment should always be reported to the referring party along with any reservations or limitations in the reliability of the examiner's opinions as a result of the employee's response style. In general, however, when the examinee's response style, based on evidence from third-party sources and psychological testing, suggests that his or her responses are unreliable, they should be regarded as less probative than information obtained from other sources with higher reliability.

TREATMENT

If causation is a compelling topic for clinicians, it pales in comparison to the attraction to treatment. Clinicians generally wish to be helpful, and this is especially true when faced with an examinee who is psychologically injured, suffering, or otherwise distressed. Indeed, when an evaluator concludes that an employee is psychologically unfit for duty, the referring party often requests that the examiner address how fitness might be restored. When this is the case, evaluators should still be careful to limit their treatment recommendations, including modalities and duration, to those for which there is adequate evidence of effectiveness.

Most importantly, examiners should be careful not to *condition* a determination of fitness on an employee's participation in counseling or other therapy. When such a condition is stipulated, it typically is rationalized in one of two ways: either because the examiner believes the employee's current fitness is unlikely to be sustained without additional or ongoing treatment, or because the employee's current unfitness results from a minor impairment expected to respond quickly to treatment.

In cases where the employee is judged to be currently unfit for duty because of a remediable condition, it is usually more prudent to acknowledge the current unfit status and not address recommendations designed to restore fitness unless requested by the referring party. When an employer requires treatment as an employment condition, some jurisdictions have held that the employer is responsible for the cost of treatment and compensation to the employee for any on-duty time used to engage in treatment (*Sehie v. City of Aurora*, 2005; see also *Todd v. Lexington Fayette Urban County Government*, 2009, where the court reached a different conclusion when the mandated conditions are for the benefit of the employee and not the employer). Furthermore, employees required to engage in treatment can easily come to believe (erroneously) that treatment compliance will or should shield them from consequences for persistent problematic behavior. Unless the referring party has specifically requested the examiner to opine on treatment or restoration of fitness, the report should be silent on this question. When the employer does request treatment recommendations from the examiner, it may be useful to reference the practical guidance of the EEOC:

> Regardless of whether employers believe they are trying to help employees who have medical conditions, employers should focus instead on addressing unacceptable workplace conduct. Employer comments about the disability and its treatment could lead to potential ADA claims (e.g., the employer "regarded" the employee as having a disability or the employer engaged in disparate treatment). (EEOC, 2008, p. 12)

ACCOMMODATION

Under the ADA, an employer "must provide a reasonable accommodation to the known physical or mental limitations of a qualified individual with a disability unless it can show that the accommodation would impose an undue hardship" (EEOC, 1997, p. 12). A *reasonable accommodation* is defined as "any change in the work environment or in the way things are customarily done that enables an individual with a disability to enjoy equal employment opportunities" (29 C.F.R. §1630.9). This may include job restructuring, part-time or modified work schedules, reassignment to a vacant position, and providing additional unpaid leave for necessary treatment.

Employers are only responsible, however, for providing a reasonable accommodation to a *known* limitation of a qualified individual with a disability. Even when an employee has a psychological condition that renders him or her unfit for duty, it is not *per se* legally equivalent to a disability under the terms of the ADA. Indeed, some conditions that may not meet the ADA's definition of a disability may nevertheless render an employee unfit for duty. Moreover, except in cases of obvious disabilities, it is generally the case that the employer's obligation to explore accommodation arises only when the employee tells the employer he is disabled (*Hammon v. DHL*, 1997). The employee need not use the word *disabled* or *disability* to formally initiate the accommodation exploration process (*Cannice v. Norwest Bank Iowa N.A.*, 1999); on the other hand, where the employee openly denies having a disabling condition, even an FFD examiner's finding to the contrary may not be sufficient to require accommodation efforts on the part of the employer (*Larson v. Koch Refining Co.*, 1996).

Once an employee specifically requests an accommodation for a work-impairing condition, the employer has an affirmative duty to engage in the "interactive process" to obtain relevant information about the employee's condition and the basis for requesting an accommodation (*Barnett v. U.S. Air., Inc.*, 2000). Thus, employers may prefer—and usually are best advised—to separate questions of reasonable accommodation from the FFD question. However, when in the interests of expediency and/or compassion an employer asks the examiner to make recommendations regarding accommodation, the examiner should become knowledgeable about the types of accommodation regarded by the courts as reasonable (e.g., an employer is not required to restructure or reallocate the essential functions of a job as a reasonable accommodation, and the essential functions may include the start and stop time of an employee's work schedule; see *Guice-Mills v. Derwinski*, 1992). Unless the examiner is familiar with the statutes, regulations, and case law pertinent to reasonable accommodation, it is best to inform the referring party; police department) that questions about accommodations be deferred to a separate stage of the evaluation. Under any circumstances, reasonable accommodations are always *an employer's decision, not an examiner's.*

As noted elsewhere, in 1990, the Americans with Disabilities Act was passed by Congress. This law prohibited "pre-conditional offer psychological/medical" testing and became effective in 1992. Passed with the American Psychological Association's written support, and before APA executives had notified Division 18 police psychologists of ADA's ramifications for their assessment work, this new law had a major, mostly negative, impact on police assessment. Police psychologists, prior to 1992, were saving departments large sums of money and resources by inquiring about alcohol/drug use during the early stages of applicant investigations and screening. Robin Inwald and Michael Roberts, who between them at that time had the largest collection of pre-employment test data in the country, pooled these data from various testing instruments and databases. They collaborated on an article about the job-relatedness of such questions (Inwald, Kaufman, & Roberts, 1991) in an attempt to influence the writers of the government's upcoming ADA Guidance report (guidelines for the new law). Despite the admittedly clear evidence that patterns of alcohol and/or past drug use on written personality/psychological instruments did, in fact, predict poor police officer performance across many test scales and performance variables, Inwald and Roberts's campaign for an ADA exclusion of public safety organizations on behalf of practicing police psychologists failed. The published ADA guidelines required that police agencies adhere to the requirement that such questions only be asked after an actual "conditional offer of employment" had been made near the end of the screening process. Whereas some psychologists continued to conduct "psychological/medical" screenings using the MMPI or IPI prior to conditional job offers in their departments, most police psychologists changed their pre-employment assessment practices after the passage of the ADA in order to avoid lawsuits and to clearly be within the law.

But the choice between administering the MMPI and associated tests, along with inquiring into psychological/mental health issues after the job offer or not at all, was not actually dichotomous. In other words, there was another option available to police psychologists who desired to retain the information of all the hitherto (i.e., pre-ADA) administered psychological tests interview questions yet at the same time not running afoul of the ADA. One of these solutions was developed by this author and consisted of conducting pre-employment psychological screening in two phases. More specifically, a general interview devoid of a mental status examination or questions that could reveal a disability was coupled with a "general personality test" such as the 16PF that only indicated degrees of "normal" personality traits such as interpersonal warmth, dominance, seriousness, conformity vs. nonconformity, being solution oriented, self-assuredness, being open to change, and self-discipline would be administered as part of the "Phase 1" psychological screening. Any other factors that could possibly hint at a disability were not used. If the applicant passed "Phase 1" of the screening, he or she was invited back for "Phase 2," which consisted of the MMPI-2, the Wonderlic Personnel Test, and a clinical interview combined with a mental status evaluation. This technique for working within the requirements of the ADA was utilized by the author with various police and sheriff's departments in the northern Virginia area. The downside of this process was the additional time burden on the applicant, the department, and the psychologist, for scheduling two interviews and for the additional work needed by the psychologist in writing two reports, one based on Phase 1 and the other based on Phase 2. Accordingly, this author, together with the various law enforcements served, decided to administer the entire psychological at the end of the applicant screening process. In this manner, it would be the last appointment for any given applicant. Under such an arrangement, if an applicant had been successful up until the psychological and was then rejected, the reason would be clear, and the need for the cryptic and misleading "other more qualified applicants" letter would be unnecessary. This is not to say, however, that rejected applicants still did not receive this generic form of rejection letter.

A second law passed subsequent to the ADA was the Civil Rights Act of 1991, which also had a strong impact on assessment practices and instrument development in the police/public safety field. With concerns that police assessment validity would be decreased should it become illegal to use separate gender norms, APA's Diane Brown organized a meeting with EEOC representatives and two researchers in the field. Paul Sackett and Robin Inwald presented research data supporting the value of using separate group norms to best predict police and other employee's performance. Despite their efforts to preserve the best predictions possible for employee selection, the Civil Right Act of 1991 resulted in responsible selection test publishers having to change available separate norms by gender and ethnicity and merge groups into one overall norm. It became (for all intents and purposes) illegal to consider ethnicity or gender during employee selection, thus making the most accurate prediction equations also illegal.

In 1991, the IACP's Psychological Services Section formally adopted Inwald's revised "Fitness-for-Duty Evaluation Guidelines" at its Annual Section Meeting. In a conference program titled "Fitness for Duty: Standards and Practices for the '90's," which included presentations by Catherine Flanagan (New York), Stephen Curran (Maryland), and James Janik (Illinois), Robin Inwald formally presented these guidelines to the IACP membership during the 98th Annual IACP Conference in Minneapolis, Minnesota.

Rather than alter items and scales of the IPI so that it could continue to be used as a "pre-conditional offer" test under the new ADA guidelines, Inwald wrote a series of new personality assessment instruments that were normed and validated on public safety officer applicants and did not contain items that would reveal psychopathology or past substance abuse (included in the ADA definition of "medical" diagnoses). In 1992, the Inwald Survey 5 (IS5), which included scales measuring areas of integrity and anger management, among others, was published by Hilson Research (Inwald & Gebbia, 1992). Inwald developed the IS5 in an effort to give police psychologists' critical behavioral information at the "pre-conditional offer" phase of screening because the administration of the IPI or MMPI now was illegal under ADA until the end of the screening process. Police agencies began to use this test as part of their "pre-conditional-offer" screening programs and many police psychologists also added it to their "post-conditional-offer" and "fitness-for-duty" batteries.

In 1993, the FBI sponsored a conference titled "Law Enforcement Families: Issues & Answers" at the FBI Academy in Quantico, Virginia. Robin Inwald conducted a research study for this conference and developed the Hilson Spouse/Mate Inventory, the first assessment instrument for evaluating relationship issues specific to police personnel and their spouses or partners (Inwald, 1993).

In 1995, the FBI sponsored a conference titled "Organizational Issues in Law Enforcement" at the FBI Academy in Quantico. At this conference, Inwald presented summary research on those police/public safety officers who had been tested during the 1970s or 1980s and later became involved in inappropriate violent behavior as officers (Inwald, 1995). As a direct result of discussions at this FBI conference, the Inwald Survey 2 (IS2) was published by Hilson Research the following year (Inwald et al., 1996). This 110-item inventory, along with its shorter version, the Inwald Survey 8 (IS8), was the first personality inventory developed for public safety officers and applicants that focused specifically on the identification of characteristics associated with violent behavior.

Because many police psychologists and public safety administrators, who conducted or organized pre-employment screening programs, often complained about the length of the personality inventories being administered, Inwald developed the "Hilson Life Adjustment Profile ("HLAP")," a 110-item inventory for identifying psychopathology as well as assessing a police candidate or officer's actual functioning in personal, social, and family life. Also published in 1996, this inventory was offered as a possible replacement for the much lengthier MMPI, and correlations between these two instruments were included in the HLAP Technical Manual (Inwald et al., 1996).

In 1997, Psychological Assessment Resources, Inc. published the "PAI Law Enforcement, Corrections, and Public Safety Selection Report" to be used with Morey's 1991 Personality Assessment Inventory. Like the IPI and the other Hilson Research test reports, this report relied on law enforcement norms for evaluating public safety applicants.

The first comprehensive psychological job analysis, focusing on personality variables found in published psychological tests and documenting their relative importance to subject matter experts such as police chiefs and administrators, was conducted by Michael Cuttler and Robin Inwald in the mid-1990s. In this study, more than 1,500 police administrators, representing every public safety agency in the state of North Carolina, identified the personality variables they believed most important for police officer performance on the Hilson Job Analysis Questionnaire (HJAQ). Using this and other studies, the HJAQ was published in 1998 and was the first computerized job analysis assessment tool used by administrators to evaluate the relative importance of different personality variables in their agencies (Inwald, 1998).

In the fall of 1998, as the result of increasing concerns about domestic violence in police families, the FBI sponsored a "Domestic Violence by Police Officers" conference at Quantico. After the week long presentations and discussions on this topic concluded, Robin Inwald developed a scale for identifying those individuals most likely to become involved in domestic violence. This scale was added to the updated and renormed Inwald Survey 5-Revised (IS5R) in 1999.

Additional IPI studies from independent researchers also were published in the 1990s (Mufson et al. 1994), including one linking the IPI and MMPI with the "Big Five" Personality Factors (Cortina et al., 1992). During this time, several researchers continued to examine the validity of the revised MMPI-2. Examples from this period include articles by Brewster (1996); Hargrave, Hiatt, and Gaffney (1986); and Kornfeld (1995).

However, research efforts in the field soon were hampered by the fact that police departments, unlike in earlier years, began to take their psychologist's ratings very seriously. During the 1980s, police administrators continued to hire many officers despite their questionable suitability based on psychological tests. This allowed for validation studies to be conducted where there were a larger number of "failures." This situation changed during the 1990s, when police psychologists had gained respect in their departments and when the testing came at the end of the screening process (because of the new requirements of the ADA). Now agencies rarely hired officers with "questionable" psychological results. Although beneficial for society, the rejection of nearly all poorly rated candidates restricted the range of officers who could be followed in predictive research studies, limiting a researcher's ability to directly compare the validities of different tests.

In 1999, Deniz Ones began a project for the California Police Officer Selection and Training (POST) organization in its efforts to update psychological screening guidelines. Over 19,000 validity coefficients from all personality-based tests available at the time were presented at numerous professional conferences. This firmly established the validity of personality tests, such as the MMPI, CPI, and IPI, among others (Ones, 2009).

NEGLIGENT HIRING AND "TORT" LIABILITY

Tort liability associated with lawsuits against police departments also include wrongful death, assault and battery, false arrest, and false imprisonment (Kitaeff, 2006b). Gross negligence may be assumed by a department's failure to conduct a full background investigation on a prospective police applicant. Police departments can also be charged with negligent retention (keeping employees on the job when there is significant evidence that they should have been disciplined, demoted, or even dismissed) and negligent entrustment (inadequately preparing officers prior to entrusting them with law enforcement powers and responsibilities) (Kitaeff, 2006b).

NEGLIGENT HIRING AND RETENTION, AND DUTY TO ADEQUATELY TRAIN AND SUPERVISE

In *Hild v. Bruner*, a federal district court in New Jersey upheld a jury finding of municipal liability for excessive force during an arrest (1980). Although the city required its officers to carry guns both on and off duty, the city had no consistent psychological testing in place to help ensure the officers' fitness to carry weapons. Based on the city's failure to implement an effective psychological testing program to identify officers unfit to carry guns, the court held the city liable for the injuries its officer inflicted. In *Hardy v. Town of Hayneville,* a city was held responsible for the negligent hiring of an officer deemed unfit by later review of his background (1999). In a similar case, *Geidel v. City of Bradenton Beach*, the court held that the city could be liable for any intentional tort by their police officer if it could be shown that the municipality had been negligent in its duty to select, train, and supervise the officer (1999). In *Bonsignore v. City of New York*, the failure to adopt a meaningful psychological testing procedure resulted in the award of $300,000 in compensation and $125,000 in punitive damages when an off-duty officer, known generally to have emotional problems, wounded his wife and killed himself (1982). In another case, the court concluded that periodic psychological screening is constitutional, provided that management provides for the privacy of officers' files and records and respects their right of due process (1998).

In *Miller v. City of Springfield* (1998), a New Jersey court upheld periodic psychological testing of all police officers. Two officers and the union challenged a 12-year-old policy requiring officers of all ranks to be tested every 3 years. One of the officers was later directed to participate in counseling for anger management. The lawsuit, filed in state court, claimed:

1. Officers were forced to reveal personal and private information which was unrelated to the work performance and their fitness for duty as police officers.
2. The process violates officers' rights of due process.
3. The screening causes "humiliation, embarrassment, emotional distress, anguish and harm to [officers'] personal reputations."

The judge dismissed the suit.

While personality assessment in law enforcement settings came of age in the 1970s and 1980s, reflecting changes in both society and the professional role of psychology, the 1990s were a decade of continued expansion. In 1990, a survey of 72 major law enforcement agencies was conducted in order to determine the tests used for applicant selection. Results of this survey revealed that 51% did not use any psychological tests, and the three most widely used tests were the MMPI, CPI, and IPI (Blau, 1994; Strawbridge & Strawbridge, 1990). But then again, the MMPI was (and is) the most commonly used psychological test in the world.

POLICE STRESS, PSYCHOLOGICAL DYSFUNCTION, AND POSTTRAUMATIC STRESS DISORDER

Police officers regularly deal with the most violent, impulsive, and predatory members of society. They put their lives on the line and confront miseries and horrors the rest of us can't even imagine. In addition, officers are always in the spotlight and open to complaints and criticism from citizens, the media, and the judiciary. This may skew the officer's opinions on the character of the average human being and create a cynicism, isolation, and difficulty trusting people in general. Although the stress of viewing many horrific events, violence, and trauma can be substantial in police work, it is exacerbated by its intermittent nature interspersed with periods of boredom and calm. Officers cannot usually control entrance into most traumatic and dangerous situations that they face; they have to "react" to problems and typically do so without sufficient warning or preparation.

Officers are also required to always be in emotional control and must show extreme restraint even under highly emotionally charged circumstances. They must wear a social mask that they put on with the uniform. A former president of the International Association of Chiefs of Police has said:

> What our society expects from police officers is a perfect blend of robot and person. In any confrontation, no matter the potential for violence, we're not supposed to display emotion or the human characteristics that result from adrenalin…. People realize officers are human, but they don't understand that we can't train them to a point where we override every human emotion. (Miller, 1998)

One of the most poignant descriptions of the ways police officers are different from the rest of us has been provided by police psychologists Daniel A. Goldfarb and Gary S. Aumiller in their groundbreaking work *The Heavy Badge*. In it, they express:

> Law enforcement officers are seen as authority figures. People deal with them differently and treat them differently, even when they are not working.... [They are] are isolated. The wearing of a badge, uniform and gun makes a law officer separate from society.
>
> Law enforcement officers work in a quasi-military, structured institution. These are [often associated with mental health concerns such as sacrificing] the individual for the good of society. The "rotating shift" schedule is very taxing on an officer's life. [Their] bodies are adjusted on what is called "circadian schedules" which is a repetitive daily cycle.... An officer doing shift work never gets a chance to stay on a schedule. This upsets his physical and mental balance in life.
>
> ...Officers have a different kind of stress in their jobs, called "burst stress." Burst stress means there is not always a steady stressor, but at times, there is an immediate "burst" from low stress to a high stress state. In other words, officers go from complete calm, to high activity and pressure in one "burst." The normal stress situation for most of the rest of the work force consists of a stress building process that can be either reduced or adapted to before it gets "out of control." This is not the case for the officer, because "out of control" can happen in seconds....
>
> [Officers] need to be in constant emotional control. [They] have a job that requires extreme restraint under highly emotional circumstances. They are told when they are extremely excited, they have to act calm. They are told when they are nervous, they have to be in charge. They are taught to be stoic when emotional. They are to interact with the world in a role. The emotional constraint of the role takes tremendous mental energy, much more energy than expressing true emotions. When the energy drain is very strong, it may make the officer more prone to exhaustion outside of work, such as not wanting to participate in social or family life. This energy drain can also create a sense of job and social burnout.
>
> The "at work" world of the officer is very negative. He sees the bad part of society—the criminal, the abuser of the rules. This may skew the officer's opinions on the character of the average human being. It creates a cynicism, a critical view of the world. It is hard to adjust to trusting a fellow human being when so much of the day is spent with people who are not trustworthy. It is hard to believe in positive intentions of people, when the day is spent with people who are intending to hurt each other. This lack of trust can show up in the way the officer deals with people on a personal level, with neighbors, with a spouse. It can even show up in the way children are raised, as police parents may tend to be stricter in discipline and more careful with privilege.

According to Goldfarb and Aumiller, these "differences" between police officers and other members of the public can lead to increased alcohol use, attitudinal problems, behavioral problems, intimacy and relationship problems, overall increased stress, and even suicide.

What is stress? In a very broad sense, *stress* is a reaction to both internal and external stimuli. Often the external stimuli causing stress are referred to as *stressor* and include events such as pressure from superiors, excessive traffic, and gunfights. In general terms, stress is the nonspecific "response of the body to any demand" (Selye, 1979b, p. 3). Stress can assume other meanings. For instance, stress can be a perceived imbalance between what is required of the officer and what he is capable of giving, under conditions where failure may have dire consequences.

Implicit in these definitions is the notion that stress is a fundamental part of being alive. That is, any demand placed on an individual to change can produce a physical response to some degree or another, with or without the individual's knowledge or consent. Thus, just being alive creates a demand on the body. When an individual perceives danger, there is an outpouring of hormones that create alterations in bodily processes and can produce, among other things, an increased heart rate, sweating, trembling, and fatigue (Monat & Lazarus, 1977). In addition, the mere perception of fear can produce fearful consequences in the body. Especially among police officers, finding ways of coping with stress is in both their individual best interest and in the interest of public safety as well.

Job stress for police officers or regular civilians can be defined as the harmful physical and emotional responses that occur when the requirements of the job do not match the capabilities, resources, needs, or expectations of the worker (Stevens, 1999c). For police officers, in addition to the daily grind, officers are frequently the target of criticism and complaints by citizens, the media, the judicial system, opportunistic politicians, hostile attorneys, "do-gooder" clinicians and social service personnel, and their own administrators and law enforcement agencies (Blau, 1994).

Dr. Larry Miller, in his comprehensive and poignant book *Shocks to the System*, describes stress specifically as it relates to the police officer when he states, "Police officers regularly deal with the most violent, impulsive, and predatory members of society, put their lives on the line, and confront miseries and horrors that the rest of us view from the sanitized distance of our newspapers and TV screens" (1998, p. 216).

Miller stresses:

Police officers generally carry out their duties and responsibilities with dedication and valor, but that some stresses are too much to bear, and every officer has his breaking point. For some, it may come in the form of a particular dramatic event, such as a gruesome accident or homicide, the killing or wounding of a partner, the mistaken shooting of an innocent civilian, or an especially grisly accident or crime scene.... For other officers, there may be no single major trauma, but the identified mental breakdown occurs under the cumulative weight of a number of more moderate stresses over the course of the officer's career. In either case, all too often the officer feels that the department doesn't support him and that there is nowhere else to vent his distress. So he bottles up his feelings, acts snappish with coworkers, superiors, civilians, and family members, and becomes hypersensitive to small annoyances on and off the job. (p. 217)

The result of prolonged stress may be posttraumatic stress disorder (PTSD). The DSM-IV-TR (American Psychiatric Association, 2000) defines PTSD as follows:

The essential feature of Posttraumatic Stress Disorder is the development of characteristic symptoms following exposure to an extreme traumatic stressor involving direct personal experience of an event that involves actual or threatened death or serious injury, or other threat to one's phsical integrity; or witnessing an event that involves death, injury or a threat to the physical integrity of another person; or learning about unexpected or violent death, serious harm, or threat of death or injury experienced by a family member or other close associate.... The person's response to the event must involve intense fear, helplessness, or horror.... The characteristic symptoms include persistent reexperiencing...persistent avoidance of stimuli associated with the trauma...persistent symptoms of increased arousal...the disturbance must cause clinically significant distress or impairment in social, occupational, or other important areas of functioning. (pp. 463–464)

Miller (1998) points out that if no treatment is provided for PTSD, symptoms may persist for many months or even longer, and anger, hostility, irritability, problems with authority, fatigue, inability to concentrate, loss of self-confidence, and increased use of food or mood-altering substances may also be the result. Many of these long-term effects can interfere with a police officer's job functioning for months, if not years. In some cases, delayed or prolonged stress reactions manifest themselves in the form of psychosomatic physical complaints, or in a tendency to "snap" at minor provocations, irritations, or events that would have not hitherto caused any such reactions in the officer. All this underscores the importance for police officers to receive treatment as soon as possible after traumatic events occur, and certainly as soon as possible after the appearance of symptoms of PTSD.

PSYCHOLOGICAL DEBRIEFING

Police work is stressful and unpredictable. Officers must have the emotional resources to perform multiple tasks without losing control in the face of physical threats. They need to exhibit dominance and assertiveness, and at the same time restraint and empathy. They must be able to complete their tasks despite provocation, ambiguity, and the ever-present threat of psychological or physical injury (Shusman, Inwald, & Knatz, 1987).

Although most people do not seek crises in their lives, police officers respond to and immerse themselves daily into the chaos and confusion of other people's lives, and by doing so they put themselves at risk of becoming victims of traumatic incidents. Yet, they do so willingly and without hesitation. One only needs to stand back and watch officers responding to a call of a "man with a gun" to appreciate their coping abilities. Because officers comfort trauma victims and operate in the wake of traumatic events, it should be expected that they will be exposed to the problematic and undesired effects of stress.

The National Organization for Victim Assistance (NOVA) identifies nine categories of trauma workers. Law enforcement personnel and firefighters are listed as immediate responders and trauma workers (NOVA, 1991, as cited in Harris, 1995).

In law enforcement, stressful or traumatic incidents are often referred to as *critical incidents*. A critical incident is any situation faced by an officer that causes him to experience unusually strong emotional or physical reactions. These reactions may have the potential to interfere with the officer's abilities to function either at the scene or later in life. The reactions are a normal person's response to an abnormal event, although because of officers' training, belief, and experience, they may believe the opposite to be true.

A critical incident can also be a time when an officer's expectations about his ability to handle stressful situations are called into question (Mitchell, 1990b; Ryan & Brewster, 1994). The officer's reaction to this event may also interfere with his family life (Hartsough, 1995; Sheehan, 1995). It is important to keep the definition of a critical incident flexible because of the varying effects an incident has on different officers (FBI Bulletin, 1996).

The following events are typical of those that may cause unusual distress for emergency personnel (Mitchell & Bray, 1990):

- Death of a fellow officer
- Serious injury to a fellow officer
- Serious multiple-casualty incident/accident
- Suicide of a fellow officer
- Traumatic deaths involving children
- Events that attract "excessive" media interest and public scrutiny
- An event involving victims known to the officer
- Exposure to infectious diseases
- Being the subject of a lawsuit
- Any event that has an unusually powerful impact on the officer

How a person reacts to these events, the meaning he or she attributes to his performance, and the circumstances surrounding the incident can cause a psychological crisis. It is important to remember that a critical incident should not be defined in terms of the event but rather in terms of the impact it has on the individual. An event that is less-than-critical (subcritical) can still have an impact on an officer's performance and functioning. Psychotraumatologist Pierre Janet wrote that it is how a person thinks about and reacts to a traumatic event that ultimately determines how quickly the person recovers from the experience (Everly, 1995a).

Psychological crises violate or contradict the beliefs a person has about the world. A crisis may shatter a person's assumptions regarding the world as a safe and orderly place. It may also challenge how a person evaluates his competency and gives rise to self-doubt (Everly, 1995a). When a person is victimized, three basic assumptions or beliefs about the self and the world are challenged: the belief in personal invulnerability, the view of oneself in a positive light, and the belief in a meaningful and orderly world. When a person faces a loss, as in the loss of the feeling of invulnerability, there must be some adjustment in order to go on living. The interval between the recognition of the loss and the subsequent adjustment can be difficult with symptoms such as intrusive ideas and numbing of emotions (Horowitz & Kaltreider, 1995).

Frankl (1959) felt that the failure to find meaning and a sense of responsibility in one's life lies at the root of psychopathology. Trauma challenges previously held assumptions, beliefs, and understandings about the world and oneself in the world (Everly, 1995b).

In a critical incident, how an officer responds in one moment might serve to define the entire event (FBI Bulletin, 1996). That meaning comes from the socially, and sometimes personally, constructed belief an officer has about the "correct" way to respond. It is the meaning that an officer attributes to an event that determines his or her behavior and reactions after the event. George Everly (1994a) provided another perspective when he stated, "Practically speaking, there is simply no such thing as reality without considering the human perspective" (p. 178).

The term *critical incident* has been defined in a number of ways since it was first used in the early 1990s (Best, Artwohl, & Kirschman, Chapter 24, this volume). As will be seen later in this volume, rather than insisting on a universally agreed upon meaning, law enforcement experts have actually stressed the importance of maintaining a flexible definition because of the wide variation in officer responses to duty-related events (Bohl, 1995; FBI Bulletin, 1996). Therefore, although definitions vary, it is generally understood that line-of-duty events, which for officers are "outside the range of normal activity" (Patton & Violanti, 1996, p. 183) or involve serious threat or loss (Gentz, 1990), are considered critical incidents . Some experts maintain that it is the individual officer's reactions that make an incident *critical*. This mirrors the American Psychiatric Association's criteria of an event eliciting an intense emotional reaction in the exposed individual in order for it to be considered "traumatic" in the *Diagnostic and Statistical Manual* (DSM-IV-TR, 2000).

Police departments are well advised to educate their personnel when a stressful, high-profile event has occurred involving its officers. As Best et al. in this volume point out, lack of knowledge about the details of the event can fuel rumors and does nothing to allay the anxiety of the personnel who were not directly impacted but may still have concerns. Rumors that begin to circulate may also be harmful to the involved personnel when inaccuracies and speculations about their performance come to their attention (Artwohl & Christensen, 1977). Neither agency nor tactical/operational debriefings in first responder settings should take the form of a psychological intervention. Rather, such debriefings are forums in which information is shared in order to assist agency personnel in developing a more coherent narrative of the incident from which they can learn and better support affected officers.

WHEN PROVIDERS BECOME PATIENTS

Police officers, as will be seen later in this volume, may be in need of critical incident stress debriefing, yet they also serve as *providers* of such debriefing for others in their role as first responders. There are a variety of models and strategies that can be used to provide mental health support and services to officers. Substantial research supports the indication of two primary targets for on-scene interventions: physiological arousal and emotional distress (Ozer et al., 2003).

Miller (1998) describes how in order to accomplish dealing with physiological arousal and emotional distress, many agencies have organizationally formalized *critical incident stress debriefing* (CISD) teams to deal with the therapeutic work for traumatized officers (Miller, 1998). Such teams have been implemented throughout the United States, Britain, and other parts of the world as well. "Such teams have often been organizationally subsumed under the broader category of *critical incident stress management* (CISM), which includes a range of crisis intervention strategies in addition to CISD" (Miller, 1998, p. 228).

FORMAL MODELS OF POLICE POSTTRAUMATIC STRESS DISORDER

Miller (1998) describe CISD intervention as designed to promote the emotional processing of traumatic events through the ventilation and normalization of reactions as well as preparations for possible future experiences. Although CISD is designed for use in groups, other debriefing-type models have been used with individuals, couples, and families.

Most CISD takes place 2–3 days after a suspected trauma-inducing event and is structured as a single group meeting lasting approximately 2 hours. A CISD is run by a psychologist or other trained mental health professional and a member of a peer support team (Mitchell & Everly, 1996).

There are a variety of CISD formats (Benner & Quinn, 1993; Blak, 1990; Bohl, 1995; Mitchell & Everly, 1995b). In general, these formats involve taking an officer through a number of stages designed to alleviate symptoms of stress and educate the officer about normal reactions to abnormal events. A detailed discussion of various forms of psychological debriefings is provided below.

The San Jose Police Department, for example, reported that between 1972 and 1987, 52 officers were involved in shootings and 17 of those officers subsequently left the department. SJPD did not have a CISD team in place during this time period. Since the inception of their CISD team, 122 officers have been involved in shootings, and none of the involved officers have left the department (Benner, 1994).

Officers are by nature suspicious of psychology professionals, who are often seen by them as "the enemy" (Benner, 1982). These professionals are first encountered by officers when they apply for a law enforcement job. Subsequent contacts are at the request of the police department for a "fitness for duty" evaluation. Officers are concerned that mental health professionals who work for a police department will align themselves with the administrators who provide them with a job (Benner, 1982). Further, because the psychologists work for the police department, the holder of privilege is the department administration and not the officers. When officers are sent to a department psychologist, they do not know what can be discussed in confidence. The issue of confidentiality is murky at best and varies from agency to agency (Super & Blau, 1997). Relationships between an officer and a psychologist are also strained when a psychologist is not familiar with police culture (Benner, 1982).

Peer counseling can be described as a process whereby officers can talk about their feelings to another officer. The idea behind peer counseling is that an officer who has experienced a line-of-duty traumatic event can empathize with and validate another officer's reaction as being normal. Officers tend to trust other officers who have experienced a similar incident.

One of the most common types of CISD models in use today consists of several phases (Miller, 1998; Mitchell & Everly, 1996). In the *Introduction*, the team leader—either a mental health professional or peer debriefer—introduces the CISD process and encourages all members to participate. In the *Fact Phase*, each member is asked to describe his or her role during the incident; it is basically a process of "What did you do?" The *Thought Phase* is where the leader asks the group members to discuss what went through their minds as the incident unfolded. This is followed by the *Reaction Phase*, during which members move from providing cognitive descriptions to relaying their emotional reactions during the event and sharing in so many words, "What was the worst part of the incident for you?" It is during this phase that group leaders (especially if they are trained mental health professionals) look for adverse emotional reactions on the part of participants. In the *Symptom Phase*, participants are asked to describe cognitive, physical, emotional, and behavioral signs and symptoms of distress that appeared at the scene and at various points after the scene. In essence, members are asked, "What have you been experiencing since the incident?" The *Education Phase* provides participants with factual information about stress and adverse emotional reactions. This serves to normalize the stress and coping responses and provides a basis for questions and answers. The final stage is the *Reentry Phase,* which provides a wrapup of sorts during which participants can ask any final questions, and general group bonding is reinforced. In essence, members are asked, "Is there anything positive that can come out of this experience that can help you grow personally or professionally?" Or "How can you help one another in the future?"

It should be noted that to encourage participation and reduce fear of stigmatization, the administrators of any given police department or law enforcement agency should make clear that these kinds of debriefings are 100% confidential. The only exception to this general rule is where there is a clear and present danger to self or others that is revealed during the process.

To reduce the stigmatization of individual members, it is sometimes beneficial to have a policy in place that makes postdebriefing participation automatically followed by referral to a mental health professional (Everly & Mitchell, 1997; Horn & Dunning, 1990; McMains, 1990).

One of the most extensive and comprehensive adaptations of the CISD process for police officers has been developed by Bohl (1995), who explicitly compares and contrasts the steps or phases in her program with the phases of the Mitchell CISD program. In the Bohl model, there is little distinction between the cognitive and emotional phases of the debriefing. Officers are free to express emotional reactions during the cognitive phase, and the other way around.

What is important in the Bohl model is not the mere act of venting, but rather the opportunity to validate feelings. Under the Bohl model, the leader does not ask whether anything positive has arisen from the incident. Expecting officers to find a "growth experience" after seeing their partner shot and killed, for example, is seen as ridiculous. Last, under the Bohl model of CISD, is the final *round robin* in which participants are invited to say anything on their minds, whatever it may be. Remarks can be addressed to anyone, but others cannot respond directly; this is to provide a feeling of safety to participants (Miller, 1998).

Although peer counseling services and CISDs in general have been shown to be a very effective way to help officers, getting officers to accept the help has been difficult. Police officers have traditionally avoided seeking therapy or help. Officers tend to believe that other people can't really understand their problems and that "real officers" shouldn't have any problems (Linden & Klein, 1988). The issue of requiring an officer or making it optional for an officer to attend a CISD varies from department to department (Super & Blau, 1997). A formalized departmental understanding of the nature of stress and a departmental order requiring officers to attend a debriefing are preferred to waiting until the officer is calling for help (McMains, 1990).

Fay (2000) reports a study by Beijen (1995a), who attempted to determine to whom a veteran police officer is most likely to turn for help. His results showed that 80% of the responding officers would seek help from a friend and fellow officer, but only 35% would seek help from a peer counselor. The majority of officers would, if necessary, seek out a friend for an informal debriefing. Informal discussions of traumatic events among emergency personnel have been going on for many years (Kaufmann & Beehr, 1989). Friends listening to, supporting, and encouraging each other are an important part of reducing stress for officers (Mitchell, 1996). However, the police culture doesn't easily accept the open expression of feelings and emotions. Further complicating the situation is the internal, organizationally generated stress from the semimilitaristic environment in police departments. Policies, rules, and political alignments within an organization make it important for an officer to choose his confidants wisely (Beijen, 1995b).

Finally, unfortunately, despite the best efforts of many dedicated police officers and police psychologists, police officers continue to commit suicide at a rate twice that of the general population (Beijen, 1995b; Gibbs, 1994; McCafferty et al., 1992). Psychological services have been developed to try to meet the specific needs of police officers, but officers are still wary of utilizing professional psychological services. Police job-related stress and trauma continue to impact officers, their families, and taxpayers. It is clear that officers need to talk about job stress and trauma, and the people they prefer to talk with are their self-chosen colleagues and friends (Beijen, 1995a). For this reason, further ways of addressing the impact of job stress need to be developed.

POLICE OFFICERS AS FIRST RESPONDERS

As mentioned previously, the history of police psychology reveals that police officers are not only the recipients of critical incident stress debriefing but also the providers of such debriefing. Certain traumas do much more than injure us physically and even psychologically. They violate our very sense of safety, and stability, and what theorists refer to as *ontological security*. Ontological security is a stable mental state derived from a sense of continuity in regard to the events in one's life (Giddens, 1991). It is a sense of order and an absence of chaos and anxiety that give meaning to a person's life. Even being the victim of a violent crime is not consistent with the meaning of an individual's life, as this tends to threaten that individual's sense of ontological security.

More than traumas such as hurricanes, train accidents, and plane crashes, violence intentionally caused by other people and aimed directly at us robs us of our sense that the world can ever be a safe place again. Victim services are helpful in this regard, are available in all 50 states, and are particularly useful for sexual assault victims, domestic violence victims, and children. One such victim service entity is the National Organization for Victim Assistance (NOVA), which has developed a generic model of victim services that contains three major components: (1) emergency response at the time of the crisis, (2) victim stabilization in the days following the trauma, and (3) resource mobilization in the aftermath of the crime (Young, 1991).

Miller (1998) and Clark and Friedman (1992) also offer some very commonsense suggestions for first responders who must deal with the victims of crime. The responder's first concern is to see that serious injuries get treated. It is vitally important that a first responder (police officer, fire fighter, crisis worker, medic, or mental health professional) introduce him- or herself to the victim as well as bystanders. Regardless of any uniform that the first responder may be wearing, it may be necessary to repeat the introduction several times. The victim should be heard by the first responder in an understanding, sympathetic, and nonjudgmental fashion. There is no need to press for details regarding the crime as there will sufficient time for this later by local or federal authorities. Instilling a sense of safety, comfort, and trust is much more important at this point.

The importance of trauma counseling and psychological intervention cannot be overstated. Kilpatrick et al. (1985) reported that 19% of rape victims attempt suicide, 44% report suicide ideation, and 16% say that they had "a nervous breakdown" following the rape. But the degree of susceptibility to developing actual stress-related disorders such as PTSD varies from person to person and seems to depend on psychological, social, demographic, and environmental factors. Demographic factors include ethnic background, religious beliefs, socioeconomic status, gender, age, and, most importantly, the presence of supportive relationships. Psychological factors include coping mechanisms, self-confidence and self-esteem, emotional stability, and resiliency. Environmental factors include the degree of violence involved in the incident and the location of the crime or attack. For example, victims who are attacked in an environment they had formerly perceived as being "safe" tend to experience more negative reactions than those attacked in" unsafe" locations (Markesteyn, 1992).

The psychological reactions to violent crime can include minor sleep disturbances, irritability and worry, depression, anxiety disorders, alcohol and drug abuse, suicidal thoughts (and attempts), and PTSD. PTSD symptoms include intense fear, feeling of helplessness, or horror, agitation, persistent reexperiencing of the traumatic event in the form of flashbacks, increased arousal, avoidance of stimuli associated with the trauma, emotional numbing, and clinically significant distress or impairment in social, occupational, or other important areas of functioning (American Psychiatric Association, 2000). Most of the research on PTSD indicates that treatment is most effective when begun soon after the traumatic event, and should consist of some combination of pharmacotherapy and cognitive behavioral therapy. But it is important for PTSD survivors to know that recovery is still possible even if treatment is not received immediately (Shalev, 2007).

Only in the last 20 years has terrorism become a significant fact of life for Americans. Accordingly, the body of clinical psychological literature on terrorism has lagged behind that of other types of traumatic events. Unfortunately, these events have been increasing in frequency, and many experts maintain that the worst is yet to come.

Terrorist attacks, such as those on Oklahoma City and the World Trade Center, combine features of a criminal assault, a disaster, and an act of war (Hills, 2002). Accordingly, many of the treatment approaches combine what we know from treating victims of criminal assault, grief, natural and manmade disasters, riots, war, workplace violence, and school shootings (Miller, 2001a, 2001b, 2002c).

A study cited in Miller (2002a) of the devastating 2001 World Trade Center attack found that 11% of all New Yorkers showed symptoms of PTSD 2 months following the incident, which is almost three times the national average. An additional finding was that the degree of PTSD distress was most strongly related to the amount of television coverage watched. This suggests that potentially vulnerable victims may have attempted to use information gathering via television as a coping mechanism but instead ended up retraumatizing themselves.

Following a terror attack, many survivors experience a type of "pan phobia" accompanied by a heightened sense of vulnerability and an avoidance of anything related to the trauma. Survivors may have frequent nightmares of the imagined horrifying death of victim they have known, or wish-fulfillment fantasies of rescuing the victim. Their grief may be compounded by guilt if they feel they should have foreseen the attack or done more to keep their loved ones safe (Sprang & McNeil, 1995).

The first responder on the scene of a terrorist attack may be a police officer, emergency medical technician, firefighter, or mental health crisis counselor. Miller (2002b) recommends that such people should obtain as much information as possible from the victim about the terrorist crime itself, and begin a plan for aiding other potential victims. Collaborative work with other first responders is essential to ensure that investigators obtain valuable data while victims receive optimal care. First responders should avoid empty statements such as "Everything will be all right," and instead offer more concrete and realistic information such as "We're going to take you to a safe hospital." A victim's wishes should be accommodated as much as reasonably possible, if, for example, the victim wants a family member or friend to remain during treatment or questioning. Victims should be allowed to talk and express their emotions even if they may seem somewhat digressive or rambling. First responders should provide basic, understandable education about the onset and course of possible posttraumatic symptoms and attempt to normalize the traumatic stress experience while discouraging a sense of severe stress-related disability to come.

Outreach programs in the community should be identified around which psychological care can be organized. Identifying high-risk groups is one of the most important aspects of any disaster consultation (Ursano, Fullerton, & Norwood, 2003). If possible, help to identify the remains of loved ones. Although this may shatter any hope that the person may still be alive, the actual sight of the deceased often provides a strange sort of reassuring confirmation that the victim's death agonies may have fallen short of the survivor's imagined horrors, and even if not, that the physical presence of the body at least means that the victim's suffering is finally over . Outcome studies of mourners of a death from natural causes report shorter periods of denial and higher total recall of the deceased in those who were able to view the body prior to burial (Sprang & McNeil, 1995). When no definitive remains are found, symbolic remains may serve as a surrogate. For example, an urn of ashes from Ground Zero was offered by the City of New York to each family of a missing person.

INDIVIDUAL PSYCHOTHERAPY

Although it may not always be a comfortable experience, psychotherapy for PTSD often involves facing the memories and images of trauma head on. There is a time in the treatment of the PTSD patient, for example, where the psychologist must take the patient back to the original traumatic event and have him or her discuss it in step-by-step detail. The goal, according to Miller, is to "counteract maladaptive avoidance tendencies and to diminish the chance that they will congeal into longstanding patterns of behavior" (p. 33). Miller cautions, however, that sometimes it is necessary to work through the patient's other "peripheral issues" before the traumatic event can be adequately explored (Everstine & Everstine, 1993).

Therapy should increase adaptive defense mechanisms and allow a patient to reenter normal life and reassume normal social roles with the understanding that problems along the way are not signs of regression but merely necessary bumps in the road to recovery (Miller, 1998).

For victims of violent crimes who decide to press charges and testify in court, the recovery process from PTSD can seem even longer than with noncriminal traumatic events. This is because of the time it takes for the criminal justice system to run its course, cross-examinations by defense counsel, and so on.

Studies have shown, for example, that the prevalence of PTSD is higher among victims who wade through the criminal justice system than among crime victims in general (Freedy et al., 1994). But if the decision has been made to proceed through the criminal justice system, it may be somewhat therapeutic for victims of violent crimes to file a request for restitution as part of the sentence as well as a victim impact statement. The assistance of a mental health professional during these times to help prevent a replay of the original traumatizing effects is highly recommended.

Sprang and McNeil (1995) have presented a phased treatment model originally designed for survivors of murder victims that can productively be applied to the treatment of survivors of terrorist homicide.

An initial evaluation and debriefing phase occurs immediately following the traumatic event and focuses on crisis intervention and stabilization of the individual's emotional, social, and physical environment. At this stage, the individual's defenses should not be challenged. Instead, the intervention should include empathic support, validation, and normalization of the patient's reaction to the traumatic loss. Survivors should be prepared for the emotional, financial, practical, and social losses that follow the terrorist killing of a family member. Therapists should encourage a graded and dosed ventilation of emotion and provide necessary support.

Then, therapists should gradually begin to educate family members as to what they can expect and try to dispel unrealistic expectations. Other aspects of this educative process include providing concrete information about such victim resources as the Red Cross, National Organization for Victim Assistance, Crime Victims Compensation Fund, employee assistance programs, and so on. At each step, the therapist should monitor patients' reactions to avoid overwhelming them with too much information too quickly (Sprang & McNeil, 1995). When trust and therapeutic rapport have developed, relaxation training, biofeedback, desensitization, and cognitive behavioral techniques can be applied to symptom management. Opportunities should be provided, arranged, or planned for patients to take back some control of their lives, for example by helping and educating others or running support groups.

The patient should be helped to reduce self-blame through the use of cognitive or existential therapeutic approaches. Psychological mastery over the traumatic bereavement can be encouraged by asking patients to describe the future: "If you were not struggling with your grief anymore, what would you be doing?" A related process involves helping the patient say a psychological goodbye to the slain loved one, realizing that there will always be painful memories but that the survivors have a right to continue their own lives (Sprang & McNeil, 1995).

A far more productive therapeutic approach involves validating the survivors' pain while supporting their strengths and helping them to live as normal a life as possible, albeit a life that will be radically different from the one they led before (Spungen, 1998). For such patients, Spungen (1998) recommends they keep a daily diary or journal and write down their thoughts and feelings about the murder and about their deceased loved one. This notebook should be portable enough to carry around so patients can jot down their thoughts as they occur. Another suggestion is to tape-record thoughts into a portable recorder; these can later be transcribed, if desired. Even if the survivor never reads the diary again, the act of writing itself can be therapeutic; clinicians will recognize this as the technique of *journaling* or *narrative therapy*. Spungen has found that some covictims may create several volumes of such notes before they realize they have made progress. The only caveat is that this exercise should not become a prolonged obsessive preoccupation to the exclusion of other therapeutic strategies and participation in life generally.

By simply asking what the victim saw, heard, felt, touched, or tasted, the clinician opens additional channels of information and facilitates additional narrative working-through. Hanscom (2001) described a *treatment* model that emerged from her work with survivors of torture and that may be applied to victims of terrorism, especially incidents involving abduction, hostage taking, and abuse. In this model, an essential condition of healing of torture and trauma survivors is the reestablishment of the experience of trust, safety, and the ability to have an effect on the world. This relearning relies less on particular therapeutic techniques and procedures than on the compassionate human interaction and therapeutic alliance between the survivor and a counselor who is willing and able to listen effectively.

A HEARTS model to deal with the aftermath of terror has been suggested by Miller (2002c), Hanscom (2001), and others. HEARTS is an acronym for:

> *H = Listening to the **history**.* This includes providing a gentle environment, listening with body language, attending the flow of speech, hearing the voice and tone of the speaker, observing the speaker's movements and reactions, looking at facial expressions, remaining quietly patient, and listening compassionately. Clinicians will recognize this as a basic description of *active listening.*
>
> *E = Focusing on **emotions** and reactions.* This involves using reflective listening, asking gentle questions, and naming the emotions.
>
> *A = **Asking** about symptoms.* This involves using one's personal and therapeutic style to investigate current physical symptoms, current psychological symptoms, and suicidal tendencies.
>
> *R = Explaining the **reason** for symptoms.* This includes showing how the symptoms fit together, describing how the body reacts to stress and trauma, explaining the interaction between the body and mind, and emphasizing that these are normal symptoms that normal people have to a very abnormal event.
>
> *T = **Teaching** relaxation and coping skills.* This involves instructing the patient in relaxation skills, such as abdominal breathing, meditation, prayer, imagery, visualization, and others; and discussing coping strategies (e.g., recognizing how they have coped in the past, reinforcing old and healthy strategies, and teaching new coping skills).
>
> *S = Helping with **self-change**.* This involves discussing the person's worldview—the original view and any changes, adaptations, or similarities—and recognizing the positive changes in the self.

FAMILY THERAPY

Whether it is a single family member who is hurt or killed in a terrorist attack, or a mass terrorist casualty incident where hundreds of families are killed, injured, or displaced, family members can act as both exacerbating and mitigating factors to one another in their efforts to cope with trauma. Accordingly, a key therapeutic task often involves turning vicious cycles of recrimination and despair into positive cycles of support and hope.

Family therapists have long recognized that the effects of successive traumas are often cumulative (Alarcon, 1999; Catherall, 1995). Accordingly, therapy for terrorist bereavement may have to deal with unresolved traumatic material from the past, which will almost certainly be re-evoked by the more recent trauma of the murder. In addition, other aspects of life cannot automatically be put on hold when the death occurs, so therapy must address coexisting issues such as school and job problems, marital conflict, substance abuse, or other preexisting family stresses.

Therapists should inquire about individual family members' private perceptions of death. Nihilism and despair are common early responses, and helping patients and families to recover or develop sustaining spiritual or philosophical beliefs or actions can buffer the destabilizing and disintegratory effects of the murder. Therapeutic measures may involve exploring the family members' concepts of life and death, as well as encouraging both private meditative and socially committed activities, such as support groups or political or religious antiterrorism activities (Rynearson, 1996). Many Oklahoma City and World Trade Center survivors started or joined various charitable or social service foundations as a way of memorializing their slain loved ones.

Pictures and other mementos of the deceased family member can serve as comforting images for survivors. In looking at family picture albums together, therapists and survivors can bring up positive imagery that may counterbalance the grotesque recollections of the terror attack. Similar memorializing activities include writing about the deceased or creating a scrapbook, but these activities should never be part of an unhealthy obsessive preoccupation (Spungen, 1998).

COMMUNITY RESPONSES

By definition, mass-casualty terrorist disasters are community events, and there is much that community leaders can do to offer support and increase therapeutic and social morale. Commendations and awards to professional first responders, volunteer rescue workers, service providers, and others who have distinguished themselves are important components of the community recovery process. Memorials to the victims of the terrorist disaster are part of the healing process and should be encouraged. Leaders are powerful symbols. Local and regional leaders should be encouraged to set an example of expressing their own grief in a healthy and mature way, to lead the community in recognizing the appropriateness of constructive mourning (Ursano, Fullerton, & Norwood, 1995).

EMERGENCY RESPONSE UNIT AND HOSTAGE NEGOTIATIONS: MUNICH

One of the most notable and far-reaching initiatives taken by Harvey Schlossberg was his part in developing the nation's first true Hostage Negotiation Team in 1972.

An eye-opening hostage event took place in the summer of 1972. Simon Eisdorfer, Assistant Chief Inspector at the New York Police Department, watched as a hostage drama unfolded on television. What became known as the "Munich massacre" occurred at the 1972 Summer Olympics in Munich, Germany, when members of the Israeli Olympic team were taken hostage by the Palestinian terrorist organization Black September—a group within Yasser Arafat's Fatah organization. The attack, miserable and failed attempts at negotiations, and a botched rescue attempt eventually led to the deaths of 11 Israeli athletes and one German police officer.

According to news sources, the Israeli athletes had enjoyed a night out on September 4, 1972, watching a performance of *Fiddler on the Roof* before returning to the Olympic Village. At 4:30 a.m. on September 5, as the athletes slept, eight terrorists clad in tracksuits and carrying guns and grenades in duffel bags scaled a chain-link fence with the help of unsuspecting U.S. athletes who, too, were sneaking into the Olympic Village compound. The Palestinians then used stolen keys to enter two apartments used by the Israeli team.

Israeli wrestling referee Yossef Gutfreund heard a faint scratching noise at the door of the first apartment. When he investigated, he saw the door begin to open and masked men with guns on the other side. He shouted, "Hevretistalku!" (Guys, get out of here!) and threw his nearly 300-pound weight against the door to try to stop the Palestinians from forcing their way in. The wrestling coach Moshe Weinberg, age 33, attacked the kidnappers as the hostages were being moved from one apartment to another, allowing one of his wrestlers, Gad Tsobari, to escape. The burly Weinberg knocked one of the intruders unconscious and stabbed another with a fruit knife before being shot to death. Weightlifter Yossef Romano, 31 and the father of three, also attacked and wounded one of the intruders before being killed.

The kidnappers were left with nine living hostages: wrestling referee Yossef Gutfreund, age 40; American-born weightlifter David Berger, 28; wrestler Mark Slavin, 18; weightlifting judge Yacov Springer, 51; weightlifter Ze'ev Friedman, 28; track coach Amitzur Shapira, 40; wrestler Eliezer Halfin, 24; shooting coach Kehat Shorr, 53; and fencing coach Andre Spitzer, 27.

The terrorists demanded the release and safe passage to Egypt of 234 Palestinians and non-Arabs jailed in Israel. The German authorities, under the leadership of Chancellor Willy Brandt and Minister for the Interior Hans-Dietrich Genscher, rejected Israel's offer to send an Israeli special forces unit to Germany. Instead, a small squad of German police was dispatched to the Olympic Village. Dressed in Olympic sweatsuits and carrying machine guns, these were members of the

German border police, untrained in any sort of counterterrorist response, and without specific tactics in place for the rescue. The police took up positions and awaited orders that never came.

In the meantime, camera crews filmed the police actions from German apartments and broadcast the images live on television. With televisions on, the terrorists were able to watch the police as they prepared to attack. Footage shows the terrorists leaning over to look at the police who were in hiding on the roof. In the end, the police simply left.

At one point during the crisis, the negotiators demanded direct contact with the hostages in order to satisfy themselves that the Israelis were still alive. Fencing coach Andre Spitzer, who spoke fluent German, and shooting coach Kehat Shorr, the senior member of the Israeli delegation, had a brief conversation with Schreiber and Genscher while standing at the second-floor window of the besieged building, with two kidnappers holding guns on them. When the kidnappers became impatient with Spitzer's prolonged answers to the negotiators' questions, the coach was pistol-whipped in full view of international television cameras and pulled away from the window.

The kidnappers demanded transportation to Cairo. The German authorities feigned agreement and at 10:10 p.m., two helicopters transported both the kidnappers and their hostages to nearby Fürstenfeldbruck airbase, where a Boeing 727 aircraft was waiting. The kidnappers believed they were on their way to Riem, the international airport near Munich, but the authorities planned an assault on the kidnappers at the airport.

Five German snipers, none of whom had any special training, were chosen to shoot the kidnappers. All had been chosen simply because they "shot competitively on weekends" (Kitaeff, 2006a, p. 87). No tanks or armored personnel carriers were at the scene. A Boeing 727 jet was positioned on the tarmac with five or six armed German police inside, who volunteered to do the job, dressed as the flight crew. The plan was for them to overpower the terrorists with the pretense of inspecting the plane, and give the German snipers a chance to kill the terrorists remaining at the helicopters. But they were ordinary police officers who had not been trained for such a mission. At the last minute, as the helicopters were arriving on the tarmac, the German police aboard the airplane voted on and then abandoned their mission, without contact to or from any central command.

The helicopters landed just after 10:30 p.m., and the four pilots and six of the kidnappers emerged. While four of the Black September members held the pilots at gunpoint, Issa and Tony walked over to inspect the jet, only to find it empty. Knowing they had been duped, they jogged hastily back toward the helicopters, and at approximately 11:00 p.m., the German authorities gave the order to the police snipers positioned nearby to open fire.

There was instant chaos. The four German members of the chopper crews began sprinting for safety in all directions. In the ensuing frenzy, two kidnappers standing near the pilots were killed, and a third was mortally wounded as he fled the scene. The three remaining exposed kidnappers scrambled to safety, and began to return fire and shoot out as many airport lights as they could from behind the helicopters, out of the snipers' line of sight. A German policeman in the control tower, Anton Fliegerbauer, was killed by the gunfire. The helicopter pilots fled, but the hostages, who were tied up inside the craft, could not. A stalemate developed. During the gun battle, wrote Groussard, the hostages secretly worked on loosening their bonds. Teeth marks, evidence of the hostages' determination, were found on some of the ropes after the gunfire had ended.

The five German snipers did not have radio contact with each other and were unable to coordinate their fire. None of the snipers were equipped with steel helmets or bulletproof vests, proving an egregious lack of preparation. None of the rifles were equipped with telescopic sights or night vision scopes. Later, it was discovered that one of the snipers never fired a shot because he was positioned directly in the line of friendly fire, without any protective gear. Later in the battle, when kidnapper Khalid Jawad attempted to escape on foot, this sniper shot and killed the fleeing kidnapper, and was in turn wounded by one of his fellow policemen, who was unaware that he was shooting at one of his own men.

At 4 minutes past midnight, by now into September 6, one of the kidnappers jumped out of one of the helicopters. He turned and sprayed the helicopter and hostages with gunfire, killing Springer, Halfin, and Friedman, and wounding Berger in the leg. The kidnapper then pulled the pin on a grenade and tossed it back into the cockpit, where it detonated. While the first helicopter was burning, writes Cooley, the surviving kidnappers kept fire trucks at bay by shooting at them.

What happened to the remaining hostages is still a matter of dispute. However, it is likely that a third kidnapper stood at the door of the helicopter and riddled the remaining five hostages—Gutfreund, Shorr, Slavin, Spitzer, and Shapira—with fatal gunfire. Jim McKay, who was covering the Olympics that year for ABC, had taken on the job of reporting the events as Roone Arledge fed them into his earpiece. After the botched rescue attempt, he came on the air with this statement: "Our worst fears have been realized tonight. They've now said that there were 11 hostages; 2 were killed in their rooms yesterday morning, 9 were killed at the airport tonight. They're all gone" (Kitaeff, 2006a, p. 89). But almost beyond comprehension, the massacre of 11 Israeli athletes was not considered sufficiently serious to merit canceling or postponing the Olympics.

A little over a month later, on October 29, a Lufthansa jet was hijacked by terrorists demanding that the Munich killers be released. The Germans capitulated and the terrorists were let go, but an Israeli assassination squad tracked down the terrorists along with those responsible for planning the massacre. Eight of the 11 men targeted for death were killed. Of the remaining three, one died of natural causes and the other two were assassinated, but it is not known for sure if they were killed by Israeli agents.

THE AFTEREFFECTS OF MUNICH: THE BIRTH OF THE ESU

Many counterterrorism experts have theorized that the Munich massacre was one of the most significant terror attacks of recent times, one that set the tone for decades of conflict in the Middle East and launched a new era of international terrorism.

As the commanding officer of the NYPD's Special Operations division, Eisdorfer realized that such an event could actually happen in New York City. He also knew that the police department was not prepared to deal with it. Accordingly, he developed the operational plans for the nation's first Hostage Negotiation Team. The team became reality in the spring of 1973, months after a high-profile standoff in January in which armed robbers seized a dozen hostages at a Brooklyn sporting goods store and one police officer was killed.

Eisdorfer knew that by putting fresh cops into a hostage situation, he could wear down hostage takers. He realized that negotiators could subtly turn a siege into a waiting game that played out in their favor. Police officers could change shifts but the suspects could not, and the latter would become tired and hungry and more likely to surrender. His emphasis was saving lives, not ending things quickly as had unfortunately, and tragically, been done in the past.

As both a psychologist and a police detective, Harvey Schlossberg provided most of the psychological consultation needed in all aspects of the new team. What resulted was a 48-hour siege involving 11 hostages and 4 armed men. "In a way," Schlossberg recalled, "the Brooklyn siege was like a final exam for our hostage negotiations training" (H. Schlossberg, personal communication, February 1, 2006).

The gunmen had barricaded themselves with the hostages inside the store, where they were pinned down by police fire. One of the first things Schlossberg did when arriving on the scene was to calm things down. He ordered the cops to stop shooting and wait it out. "I didn't want to storm the place; I wanted to talk to them," he recalls (H. Schlossberg, personal communication, February 1, 2006). The gunmen had recently sent out a note stating that one of their comrades was injured. They requested medical aid and food. This made Schlossberg believe that these men were more concerned with staying alive than with suicide. He sent in a police radio and initiated a dialog.

In the end, the hostages escaped by a clever trick: They had persuaded their captors to let them go to the rear of the store in anticipation of a shootout. Instead, they broke a plasterboard wall and exited to the roof through a hidden stairway. In his book, *Psychologist With a Gun,* Schlossberg expressed that by basically "doing nothing" and waiting out the situation, the gunmen's alertness relaxed and they fell for the hostages' ruse.

Eisdorfer and Schlossberg's techniques worked and would be studied and emulated by police departments all over the world (Kitaeff, 2006). A special hostage negotiation team is now a permanent fixture of the police department and is incorporated within the Emergency Service Unit (ESU).

The ESU is considered very elite. It is said that when someone needs help they call the police, when the police need help they call the ESU. The unit provides specialized equipment, expertise, and support to the various units within the NYPD. From auto accidents to building collapses to hostage situations, the ESU is called in when the situation requires advanced equipment and expertise.

Also included within the ESU is what is commonly referred to in other agencies as the Special Weapons and Tactics team (SWAT). For possible hostage situation, on-scene psychologists and trained police negotiators profile hostage takers; determine their motivation, vulnerabilities, and dangerousness; suggest dialogue strategies or psychological tactics that would defuse the situation; and spend equal time analyzing which hostages might engage in behaviors that diminish or enhance their chances for survival. A trained hostage negotiator will be able to advise police on whether a hostage taker might be mentally ill (about 50% of them are) and what the extent of their life crisis might be. This is particularly important because some hostage takers may be out of touch with reality or even attempting to commit "suicide by cop."

In contrast to Eisdorfer's time, crisis/hostage teams now usually consist of at least five people. These include the primary negotiator (who does most of the active negotiations), a secondary negotiator (who monitors negotiations and makes suggestions), an intelligence officer (who seeks and organizes incoming information), a psychologist (who serves as a consultant or advisor), and a tactical liaison (who maintains communications with command)

The first 15 to 45 minutes of a hostage situation are the most dangerous. This is because the hostage takers are still going through a panic reaction. This is when most hostages get injured or killed, either because they tried to be a hero, made some remark or suggestion, stood out in some symbolic way, or were just picked at random to make a point. Unless the hostage takers are under the influence of some chemical stimulant, they are likely to calm down after a while, appear to be exhausted, and tell everyone to get some rest. Hostages may be traded for food, drink, and/or toilet facilities, and these released hostages will be interviewed for what they observed (i.e., numbers of hostage takers, weapons present, routine, and chain of command). Sleep may occur, and this is not uncommon, especially when there are a small number of perpetrators or a solo suspect who has handled all the details alone. Authorities use surveillance devices to tell when everyone falls asleep, and have at times surprised everyone by ending a hostage situation during this time (Kitaeff, 2006b).

THE INTERNATIONAL ASSOCIATION OF CHIEFS OF POLICE, PSYCHOLOGICAL SERVICES SECTION RELEVANT POLICE ORGANIZATIONS

The International Association of Chiefs of Police (IACP) Psychological Services Section has progressed from 1984 to the present time. (see Fischler, 2001, 2010; IACP, 2006, 2009).

During August 1984, a gathering of police psychologists attending a conference at the FBI Academy discussed how police psychologists could serve IACP membership and agreed to work toward forming an IACP police psychological services committee. This group met again at the October 1984 IACP Annual Conference in Salt Lake City as an ad hoc committee. The ad hoc committee developed an outline of interests and responsibilities and made a formal presentation to IACP Executive Board members, who voted to establish the Police Psychological Services Committee on October 25, 1984.

Initial objectives of the committee were to:

1. Provide an immediate and knowledgeable information source on police psychology and related mental health fields to law enforcement in general, and to the IACP in particular.
2. Advance police psychological services in general.
3. Identify police psychology resources, including the development of a directory of law enforcement mental health professionals.
4. Make training available to IACP membership concerning police psychology and related fields.
5. Provide information and training to mental health professionals so they might develop and upgrade skills in the law enforcement mental health area.

The new Police Psychological Services Committee first met on October 13, 1985, at the IACP Annual Conference in Houston, Texas, to further develop initial goals. It immediately began to plan how to advance these goals through presentations at IACP annual conferences and publications in *Police Chief* magazine. The committee consented that its primary role was to serve IACP member needs. Committee members met again on December 17, 1985, at the FBI Academy to finalize workshops for the 1986 Annual Conference. The committee was elevated to full section status in 1986 at the Annual Conference in Nashville. Since that time, the Psychological Services Section has grown to over 80 police psychologists. The section continues to adhere to the original objectives of the Psychological Services Committee by contributing to *Police Chief* magazine, presenting training programs at the annual conferences, and scheduling in-service training for police psychologists at each annual conference. The section has also been instrumental in the development of standards relating to police psychology and has developed standards for pre-employment, duty-related shootings and other traumatic incidents, fitness for duty, and use of peer support.

Membership in the section is open to licensed psychologists who are members of IACP and who work as psychologists with public law enforcement agencies. The Psychological Services Section has developed, among other things, guidelines for issues relating to:

1. Peer support
2. Officer-involved shootings
3. Pre-employment psychological evaluations
4. Fitness-for-duty evaluations

SOCIETY OF POLICE AND CRIMINAL PSYCHOLOGY

The Society for Police and Criminal Psychology (SPCP) is an eclectic professional organization that encourages the scientific study of police and criminal psychology and the application of scientific knowledge to problems in criminal justice. It focuses on law enforcement, judicial, and corrections systems. Members of the SPCP study the full range of human behaviors, motivations, and actions within the framework of the criminal justice system. Consequently, the SPCP encourages input from psychologists, social workers, psychiatrists, lawyers, police officers, corrections personnel, and other professionals concerned with the criminal justice system (SPCP, 2010).

The SPCP sponsors an annual conference held during the fall at varying locations. The conference focuses on the interface between criminal justice and the behavioral sciences. It includes presentations on international perspectives in policing, specialized police procedures and techniques, personnel decision-making issues in criminal justice agencies, the law and criminal justice, litigation issues, inmate populations, issues in probation and parole, and other issues affecting those in the criminal justice system. The SPCP invites individuals from all over the world, with expertise from every relevant discipline, to present their work on police and criminal psychology, including topics relating to mental health and the criminal justice system. Proposals are welcomed regarding research, theory, and applications that may be of interest to the members, who are encouraged to share their expertise by making a presentation or conducting a workshop at the conference. The SPCP welcomes presentations from psychologists, psychiatrists, lawyers, police officers, corrections personnel, social workers, and professionals involved in the study of the criminal justice system.

The SPCP also publishes the *Journal of Police and Criminal Psychology* through Springer Publications. The journal is published twice per year and focuses on issues relevant to practitioners and academicians in the field of criminal justice. The journal has a worldwide subscription base, and a subscription is included with membership in the SPCP.

The "Diplomate" designator is designed to recognize the special expertise and contributions made by psychologists who work with law enforcement, as either clinicians or academics. The diploma awarded by the SPCP is the premier board certification in this specialty area of applied psychology. Only psychologists are eligible for the Diplomate certification in police psychology. Police psychology encompasses many specialized services provided to law enforcement agencies by psychologists, such as pre-employment psychological testing, specialty assignment and fitness-for-duty evaluations, organization development, training, hostage negotiation team consultation, and critical incident stress debriefing.

In order to assess these areas of knowledge, written and oral examinations in person are required of all candidates for the Diplomate. These examinations are designed and administered by currently active Diplomates in police psychology. Attainment of this high and rare distinction signifies that the holder has demonstrated to a board of peers his or her expertise in the history, theory, principles, practices, techniques, and ethics of police psychology. Those who qualify are recognized by their peers as capable and accomplished in police psychology. Diplomate status is a level above graduate training and state licensure requirements. As a minimum, police psychologists hold a doctoral degree in professional psychology and have appropriate credentials to practice psychology within the jurisdictions of their respective states, typically requiring years of supervised experience and postgraduate training. SPCP provides an advanced venue in which police psychologists continue their postgraduate educational experiences. In its more than 30 years as a professional association, SPCP has awarded the Diplomate to only 60 people (the author of this chapter [and editor of this book] is one of these individuals) (SPCP, 2010).

DIVISION 18 OF THE AMERICAN PSYCHOLOGICAL ASSOCIATION: PSYCHOLOGISTS IN PUBLIC SERVICE

According to APA, the Division of Psychologists in Public Service (Division 18) was established in 1946 as a founding division of APA. It was created in response to the needs of the public in such areas as psychological practice, research, training, program development, and outcome evaluation. Among its goals, Division 18 works to protect and advance the profession, foster ethical practice, advocate for persons with mental illness, and promote quality care.

Public service psychologists are practitioners, researchers, university professors, legislators, program developers, clinical coordinators, managers, administrators, and more. Their clients include consumers of mental health services, managers, administrators, policy makers, elected officials, and the public. They work in a variety of settings, including state hospitals, community mental health systems, VA medical centers, criminal justice systems, police and public safety settings, state legislatures, and academic institutions. In general, the services they provide are as varied as the persons they serve and the places they work.

Members of Division 18 help train more than half the clinical and counseling psychologists in the United States by providing the internship sites and administering the internship programs. Its members develop and implement mental health treatment programs for millions of persons in inpatient and outpatient settings, as well as community support systems. Through the work of its members, Division 18 has the potential to directly or indirectly touch the lives of most people living in the United States.

POLICE AND PUBLIC SAFETY SECTION OF DIVISION 18

Members of this section work with law enforcement, fire departments, nuclear regulatory agencies, emergency medical services, and other public safety entities. They are involved in the selection of employees, fitness-for-duty evaluations, mental health programs, criminal investigative analysis (profiling), and hostage negotiations. They participate in the development of training, research, and implementation of effective mental health programs, including critical incident stress debriefing.

CRIMINAL JUSTICE SECTION OF DIVISION 18

Members of this section work primarily with incarcerated people and with administrators who operate state or federal correctional facilities and detention centers. They provide professional support to one another through an exchange of information concerning the administration, assessment, treatment, and ethical and training issues involved in this challenging line of work.

DIVISION 41 OF THE AMERICAN PSYCHOLOGICAL ASSOCIATION
(THE AMERICAN PSYCHOLOGY-LAW ASSOCIATION)

According to the APA, Division 41—the American Psychology-Law Society—promotes the contributions of psychology to the understanding of law and legal institutions, the education of psychologists in legal matters and law personnel in psychological matters, and the application of psychology in the legal system. The Division holds a biennial two-and-one-half-day spring meeting that includes paper and plenary sessions. Members receive the bimonthly journal *Law and Human Behavior* and the *American Psychology-Law Society Newsletter* three times per year.

THE AMERICAN SOCIETY OF CRIMINOLOGY

The American Society of Criminology (ASC) is an international organization whose members pursue scholarly, scientific, and professional knowledge concerning the measurement, etiology, consequences, prevention, control, and treatment of crime and delinquency. The ASC's objectives are to encourage the exchange, in a multidisciplinary setting, of those engaged in research, teaching, and practice so as to foster criminological scholarship, and to serve as a forum for the dissemination of criminological knowledge. Members include students, practitioners, and academicians from the many fields of criminal justice and criminology.

The ASC conducts an annual meeting devoted to discussions of topics of general interest. The ASC also sponsors an employment exchange at the annual meetings and maintains an active professional employment and position-listing service on the Web. Members receive the journals *Criminology* and *Criminology & Public Policy*, and a newsletter, *The Criminologist*. The ASC has specialized divisions such as Corrections and Sentencing, Critical Criminology, Women and Crime, International Criminology, and People of Color and Crime, which also distribute newsletters, journals, and announcements on a regular basis.

CERTIFICATION

Now aware of recent court cases and the growing potential for publicity and lawsuits in this area, practicing police psychologists have worried about either *negligent hiring* cases (when officers were hired who initially had "passed" the psychological evaluations and then did something wrong) or charges of *discrimination* (when candidates were not hired and believed the psychological assessments were unfair). Police psychologists searched for a credential beyond the PhD and state license to practice psychology that would add credibility in the courtroom for those who conducted police evaluations. Some police psychologists were, granted Diplomate status in forensic psychology by the American Board of Forensic Psychology (ABFP) or in clinical psychology by the American Board of Professional Psychology (ABPP). But unfortunately ABPP was still not the post-PhD credentialing body that police psychologists so desperately need. Most police psychologists don't even bother pursuing Diplomate status within ABPP as there was simply not a "home" for them there. But all this may be changing. On September 8, 2010, the Council of Organizations in Police Psychology, Inc. submitted an initial application for ABPP affiliation in "Police and Public Safety Psychology" to the American Board of Professional Psychology. The Council of Organizations in Police Psychology is comprised of the Police & Public Safety Section of Division 18 of the American Psychological Association, the Police Psychological Services Section of the International Association of Chiefs of Police, and the Society for Police & Criminal Psychology (see Initial Application for ABPP Affiliation of Police & Public Safety Psychology as a Specialty Board, 2010).

Fortunately, as indicated earlier in this chapter, the Society of Police and Criminal Psychology (SPCC) already offers a Diplomate in Police Psychology for police psychologists who complete an academic review, a rigorous examination, and an oral interview.

OFFICIAL RECOGNITION OF POLICE PSYCHOLOGY AS A SPECIALTY

On August 10, 2008, at its annual convention in Boston, APA officially acknowledged "police psychology" as a true psychological specialty.

THE CURRENT STATUS OF THE PROFESSION OF POLICE PSYCHOLOGY

The IACP Police Psychological Services Section, in conjunction with members of the Society for Police and Criminal Psychology and the American Psychological Association (Division 18, Police and Public Safety Section), recently carried out a comprehensive survey of the field of police psychology. The Joint Committee on Police Psychology Competencies identified 57 separate competencies clustered or organized into four distinct domains of practice: assessment-related activities, intervention services, operational support, and organizational/management consultation (Aumiller & Corey, 2007). These core domains of practices include proficiencies such as job analyses; pre-employment psychological evaluations of police candidates; psychological fitness-for-duty evaluations; threat assessments; promotional assessments; psychological autopsies; test development; employee assistance counseling, individual therapy and counseling; group, couple, and family therapy; critical incident intervention; critical incident counseling; substance abuse treatment; wellness programs; and intervention-related consultation (Aumiller & Corey, 2007).

These practice domains represent the past in police psychology, the present, and the future. But what is most important is that the American Psychological Association has now recognized police psychology (inclusive of all the listed 57 competencies) as a true psychological specialty. This occurrence, like that for forensic psychology not long ago, has dramatic implications, such as coming graduate programs in police psychology, postgraduate training in police psychology, APA accreditation, and future ABPP examinations and issuance of the ABPP diploma in police psychology. In many ways, by establishing these 57 areas of core competencies and by gaining APA recognition, the horizons for the practice of police psychology are truly unlimited!

REFERENCES

Aamodt, M. G. (2004). *Research in law enforcement selection*. Boca Raton, FL: Brown Walker.
ABAnet. Litigation. Retrieved August 8, 2007, from http://abanet.org/litigation/tips/
Abel, G. G., & Becker, J. V. (1979). *The sexual interest card sort*. Unpublished manuscript.
Abelson, R. P. 1982. The psychological status of the script concept. *American Psychologist, 36*, 715–712.

Abshire, J., & Bornstein, B. H. (2003). Juror sensitivity to the cross-race effect. *Law and Human Behavior*, *27*(5), 471–480.

Acton, R. G., & During, S. M. (1992). Preliminary results of aggression management training for aggressive parents. *Journal of Interpersonal Violence*, *7*, 410–417.

Adelmann, H. (1966). *Marcello Malpighi and the evolution of embryology*. Ithaca, NY: Cornell University Press.

Adorno, T., Frenkel-Brunswik, E., Levinson. D., & Sanford, N. (1950a). *The authoritarian personality*. New York: Harper.

Adorno, T., Frenkel-Brunswik, E., Levinson. D., & Sanford, N. (1950b). The adults: A review of social scientific research. *Aggression & Violent Behavior*, *12*, 300–314.

Akhtar, A. (1999). The psychodynamic dimension of terrorism. *Psychiatric Annals*, *29*(6), 350–355.

Akiskal, H. S., Kilzieh, N., Maser, J. D., Clayton, P. J., Schettler, P. J., Shea, M. T., et al. (2006). The distinct temperament profiles of bipolar I, bipolar II, and unipolar patients. *Journal of Affective Disorders*, *92*, 19–33.

Alarcon, R. D. (1999). The cascade model: An alternative to comorbidity in the pathogenesis of posttraumatic stress disorder. *Psychiatry*, *62*, 114–124.

Albrecht, S. (1996). *Crisis management for corporate self-defense*. New York: Amacom.

Albrecht, S. (1997). *Fear and violence on the job: Prevention solutions for the dangerous workplace*. Durham, NC: Carolina Academic Press.

Alder, C., & Polk, K. (2001). *Child victims of homicide*. Cambridge, UK: Cambridge University Press.

Alexander, D. A. (1994a). Police stress: An inside job. In J. T. Reese & R. Solomon (Eds.), *Organizational issues* (pp. 3–16). Washington, DC: Federal Bureau of Investigation.

Alexander, D. A. (1994b). The impact of police work on police officers' spouses and families. In J. T. Reese & E. Scrivner (Eds.), *Law enforcement families* (pp. 9–17). Washington, DC: Federal Bureau of Investigation.

Alexander, M. A. (1997). Sex offender treatment probed anew. In B. A. Arrigo & S. L. Shipley (Eds.), *Forensic psychology* (pp. 391–395). Burlington, MA: Elsevier.

Alexander, Y., & Brenner, E. H. (Eds.). (2001). *Terrorism and law*. Ardsley, NY: Transnational.

Allen, R. F., & Pilnick, S. (1973). Confronting the shadow organization: How to detect and defeat negative norms. *Organizational Dynamics*, *1*, 2–18.

Allen, J. J. B. (2002). The role of psychophysiology in clinical assessment: ERPs in the evaluation of memory. *Psychophysiology*, *39*, 261–280.

Allen, J. J. B., & Iacono, W. G. (2001). Assessing the validity of amnesia in dissociative identity disorder: A dilemma for the DSM and the courts. *Psychology, Public Policy, and Law*, *7*, 311–344.

Allen, S. G. (1983). How much does absenteeism cost? *Journal of Human Resources*, *18*, 379–393.

Allison, D. B., & Roberts, M. S. (1998). *Disordered mother or disordered diagnosis? Munchausen by Proxy Syndrome*. Hillsdale, NJ: The Analytic Press.

Allison, R. B. (1984). Difficulties diagnosing the multiple personality syndrome. *The International Journal of Clinical and Experimental Hypnosis*, *32*(2), 102–117.

Alpert, J. (Ed.). (1995). *Sexual abuse recalled: Treating trauma in the era of the recovered memory debate*. Northvale, NJ: Jason Aronson.

Altemeyer, R. (1988). *Enemies of freedom: Understanding right-wing authoritarianism*. San Francisco: Jossey-Bass.

Altemeyer, R. A. (2007). The other authoritarian personality. In J. Crouse & D. Stalker (Eds.), Do right-wing authoritarian beliefs originate from psychological conflict? *Psychoanalytic Psychology*, *24*, 25–4491.

American Board of Forensic Psychology (home page). Retrieved February 6, 2008, from http://www.abpp.org

American Psychiatric Association. (2000). *Diagnostic and statistical manual of mental disorders* (4th ed., text revision). Washington, DC: Author.

American Psychological Association. (1978). Report of the task force on the role of psychology in the criminal justice system. *American Psychologist*, *33*, 1099–1113.

American Psychological Association. (2002). *Ethical principles of psychologists and code of conduct*. Retrieved February 26, 2008, from http://www.apa.org/ethics/code/index.aspx

American Psychological Association. (n.d.). Elder abuse and neglect: In search of solutions. *APA Online*. Retrieved March 11, 2008, from http://www.apa.org/pi/aging/resources/guides/elder-abuse.aspx

Ammerman, R. T., & Hersen, M. (1991). *Case studies in family violence*. New York: Plenum.

Anastasi, A. (1976). *Psychological testing* (4th ed.). New York: Macmillan.

Andersson, L. M., & Pearson, C. M. (1999). Tit for tat? The spiraling effect of incivility in the workplace. *Academy of Management Review*, *24*, 452–471.

Andersen, S. M., & Zimbardo, P. G. (1984). On resisting social influence. *Cultic Studies Journal*, *1*(2), 196–219.

Anfang, S., & Appelbaum, P. S. (1996). Twenty years after *Tarasoff*: Reviewing the duty to protect. *Harvard Review of Psychiatry*, *4*(2), 67–76.

Anson, R. H., & Bloom, M. E. (1988). Police stress in occupational context. *Journal of Police Science and Administration*, *16*, 229–233.

Appleman, J. (2007). Successful jury trials. In J. D. Lieberman & B. D. Sales (Eds.), *Scientific jury selection*. Washington, DC: American Psychological Association.

Arbisi, P. A., & Butcher, J. N. (2004a). Psychometric perspectives on detection of malingering of pain: Use of the Minnesota Multiphasic Personality Inventory-2. *Clinical Journal of Pain*, *20*, 383–391.

Archer, J. (1991). The influence of testosterone on human aggression. *British Journal of Psychology*, *82*, 1–28.

Arito, H., Sudo, A., & Suzuki, Y. (1981). Aggressive behavior of the rat induced by repeated administration of cadmium. *Toxicology Letters*, *7*, 457–461.

Armstrong, K. R., Lund, P. E., McWright, L. T., & Tichenor, V. (1995). Multiple stressor debriefing and the American Red Cross: The East Bay Hills fire experience. *Social Work*, *40*(1), 83–90.

Arnson, E. (1995). *The social animal*. New York: W. H. Freeman.

Aronson, E., Wilson, T. D., & Akert, R. M. (2002). *Social psychology: The heart and the mind*. New York: HarperCollins.

Arrigo, B. A., & Shipley, S. L. (2000). *Forensic psychology*. Burlington, MA: Elsevier.

Arrigo, B. A., & Shipley, S. L. (2005). *Forensic psychology* (2nd ed.). Burlington, MA: Elsevier.

Artwohl, A., & Christensen, L. W. (1977). *Deadly force encounters: What cops need to know to mentally and physically prepare for and survive a gunfight*. Boulder, CO: Paladin Press.

Asch, S. E. (1956). Studies of independence and conformity: A minority of one against a unanimous majority. *Psychological Monographs*, *70*(Whole no. 416).

Ash, P., Slora, K. B., & Britton, C .F. (1990). Police agency officer selection practices. *Journal of Police Science and Administration*, *17*(4), 258–269.

Ashforth, B. E., & Humphrey, R. H. (1993). Emotional labor in service roles: The influence of identity. *Academy of Management Review*, *18*, 88–115.

Åström, P. (2007). The study of ancient fingerprints. *Journal of Ancient Fingerprints*, *1*, 2–3.

Aumiller, G. S., & Corey, D. (2007). Defining the field of police psychology: Core domains & proficiencies. *Journal of Police and Criminal Psychology*, *23*(1), 23–48.

Austin, E. J., & Deary, I. J. (2000). The 'four As': A common framework for normal and abnormal personality? *Personality and Individual Differences*, *28*, 977–995.

Autopsy shows teen died from "neck compression" (2007, December 12). *CTV.ca*. Retrieved March 21, 2009, from http://www.ctv.ca/servlet/ArticleNews/story/CTVNews/20071211/muslim_dad_071212/20071212?hub=TopStories

Avolio, B. J., Bass, B. M., & Jung, D. I. (1995). *Multifactor Leadership Questionnaire technical report*. Redwood City, CA: Mind Garden.

Azen, S. P. (1974). Predictors of resignation and performance of law enforcement officers. *American Journal of Community Psychology*, *2*, 79–86.

Azen, S. P., Snibbe, H. M., & Montgomery, H. R. (1973). A longitudinal predictive study of success and performance of law enforcement officers. *Journal of Applied Psychology*, *57*, 190–192.

Balch, R. (1977). The police personality: Fact or fiction. In D. B. Kennedy (Ed.), *The dysfunctional alliance: Emotion and reason in justice administration* (pp. 10–25). Cincinnati, OH: Anderson.

Barland, G. H., & Raskin, D. C. (1976). Validity and reliability of polygraph examinations of criminal suspects. In (Contract No. 75-N1-99-0001). Washington, DC: National Institute of Justice, Department of Justice.

Bartol, C. R. (1982). Psychological characteristics of small-town police officers. *Journal of Police Science and Administration*, *10*, 58–63.

Bartol, C. R. (1991). Predictive validation of the MMPI for small-town police officers who fail. *Professional Psychology: Research and Practice*, *22*, 127–132.

Bartol, C. (1996). Police psychology: Then, now, and beyond. *Criminal Justice and Behavior*, *23*, 70.

Bartol, C. (2004). *Introduction to forensic psychology*. Thousand Oaks, CA: Sage.

Beijen, D. J. (1995a). *Police seeking counsel*. Unpublished manuscript.

Beijen, D. J. (1995b). *Police suicide: Its reasons, and training to prevent it*. Unpublished manuscript.

Bell, J. L. (1995). Traumatic event debriefing: service delivery designs and the role of social work. *Social Work*, *40*(1), 36–43.

Ben-Porath, Y. S. (2006). Differentiating normal from abnormal personality with the MMPI. In S. Strack (Ed.), *Differentiating normal from abnormal personality* (2nd ed., pp. 337–381). New York: Springer.

Ben-Porath, Y. S., & Tellegen, A. (2008). *The Minnesota Multiphasic Personality Inventory-2 Restructured Form: Manual for administration, scoring, and interpretation.* Minneapolis: University of Minnesota Press.

Ben-Shakhar, G. (2008). Effective policing: Understanding how polygraph tests work and are used. *Criminal Justice and Behavior, 35,* 1295–1308.

Ben-Shakhar, G., & Dolev, K. (1996). Psychophysiological detection through the guilty knowledge technique: The effects of mental countermeasures. *Journal of Applied Psychology, 81,* 273–281.

Benner, A. (1982). *Concerns cops have about shrinks.* Paper presented at the meeting of the American Psychological Association, San Francisco.

Benner, A. (1994). The challenge for police psychology in the twenty first century: Moving beyond efficient to effective. In J. T. Reese & R. Solomon (Eds.), *Organizational issues* (pp. 363–374). Washington, DC: Federal Bureau of Investigation.

Benner, A. (1997). *Class lecture on critical incident stress debriefing training.* Critical Incident Debriefing Training, San Francisco Police Department.

Benner, A., & Quinn, V. (1993). *Critical incident stress debriefing manual.* Unpublished training manual, San Francisco Police Department.

Bernstein, I. H., Schoenfeld, L. S., & Costello, R. M. (1982). Truncated component regression, multicolinearity and the MMPIs use in a police officer selection setting. *Multivariate Behavior Research, 17,* 99–116.

Berry, C. O. (2007). Interpersonal deviance, organizational deviance, and their common correlates: A review and meta-analysis. *Journal of Applied Psychology, 92,* 410–424.

Beutler, L. E., Storm, A., Kirkish, P., Scogin, F., & Gaines, J. A. (1985). Parameters in the prediction of police officer performance. *Professional Psychology Research and Practice, 16,* 324–335.

Bison, J. I., & Deahl, M. P. (1994). Psychological debriefing and prevention of posttraumatic stress, more research is needed. *British Journal of Psychiatry, 165,* 717–720.

Blak, R. A. (1990). Critical incident debriefing for law enforcement personnel: A model. In J. T. Reese, J. M. Horn, & C. Dunning (Eds.), *Critical incidents in policing* (pp. 23–30). Washington, DC: Government Printing Office.

Blau, P. M. (1994). *The organization of academic work* (2nd ed.). New York: Transaction.

Blau, T. (1994). *Psychological services for law enforcement.* New York: John Wiley.

Blau, T. H., & Super, J. T. (1997). Survey of psychological services general orders in law enforcement. *Journal of Police and Criminal Psychology, 12*(1), 7–12.

Blau, T. H., Super, J. T., & Brady, L. (1993). The MMPI good cop/bad cop profile in identifying dysfunctional law enforcement personnel. *Journal of Police and Criminal Psychology, 9,* 2–4.

Board of Trustees of the Society for Personality Assessment. (2005). The status of the Rorschach in clinical and forensic practice: An official statement by the Board of Trustees of the Society for Personality Assessment. *Journal of Personality Assessment, 85*(2), 219–237.

Boes, J. O., Chandler, C. J., & Timm, H. W. (1997). *Police integrity: Use of personality measures to identify corruption-prone officers.* Monterey, CA: Defense Personnel Security Research Center.

Bohl, N. (1990). The effectiveness of brief psychological interventions in police officers after critical incidents. In J. T. Reese, J. M. Horn, & C. Dunning (Eds.), *Critical incidents in policing* (pp. 31–38). Washington DC: U.S. Government Printing Office.

Bohl, N. (1995). Professionally administered critical incident debriefings for police officers. In M. Kurke (Ed.), *Police psychology into the 21st century* (pp. 169–188). Washington, DC: American Psychological Association.

Bradstreet, R. (1994). Cultural hurdles to healthy police families. In J. T. Reese & E. Scrivner (Eds.), *Law enforcement families* (pp. 19–26). Washington, DC: Federal Bureau of Investigation.

Braverman, M. (1992). Posttrauma crisis intervention in the workplace. In J. Quick & L. Murphy (Eds.), *Stress and well being at work* (pp. 299–316). Washington, DC: American Psychological Association.

Brewster, J. (1996). Hypervigilance and cynicism in police officers. *Journal of Police and Criminal Psychology, 10*(4), 7–9.

Britt, J. M. (1990). U.S. secret service critical incident peer support team. In J. T. Reese, J. M. Horn, & C. Dunning (Eds.), *Critical incidents in policing* (pp. 55–62). Washington, DC: U.S. Government Printing Office.

Bruner, E. (1986). Ethnography as narrative. In V. Turner & E. Bruner (Eds.), *The anthropology of experience* (pp. 139–155). Chicago: University of Illinois Press.

Bruner, J. (1986). *Actual minds, possible worlds.* Cambridge, MA: Harvard University Press.

Busch, K. A., & Cavanaugh, J. L. (1986). The study of multiple murder: Preliminary examination of the interface between epistemology and methodology. *Journal of Interpersonal Violence, 1*(1), 5–23.

Bush, J. P. (1990). The development of a crisis care unit. In J. T. Reese, J. M. Horn, & C. Dunning (Eds.), *Critical incidents in policing* (pp. 63–66). Washington, DC: U.S. Government Printing Office.

Burgess, A., Douglas, J., & Ressler, R. (1988). *Sexual homicide: Patterns and motives.* New York: Lexington Books.

Butcher, J. N., Graham, J. R., Ben-Porath, Y. S., Tellegen, A., Dahlstom, W. G., & Kaemmer, B. (2001). *MMPI-2: Manual for administration, scoring, and interpretation, revised edition.* Minneapolis: University of Minnesota Press.

Carroll, D. (1988). How accurate is polygraph lie detection? In A. Gale (Ed.), *The polygraph test: Lies, truth and science* (pp. 19–28). London: Sage.

Carter, D., & Radelet, L. (1999). *The police and the community* (6th ed.). New York: Prentice-Hall.

Catherall, D. R. (1995). Preventing institutional secondary traumatic stress disorder. In C. Figley (Ed.), *Compassion fatigue: Coping with secondary traumatic stress* (pp. 232–247). New York: Brunner Mazel.

Cattell, J. M. (1895). Measurements of the accuracy of recollection. *Science, 2*, 761–766.

Catell, R. B., Eber, H. W., & Tatsuoka, M. M. (1970). *Handbook for the 16PF.* Champaign, IL: Institute for Personality and Ability Testing.

Cattell, R. B., & Jaspers, J. (1967). A general plasmode (No. 30–10–5–2) for factor analytic exercises and research. *Multivariate Behavioral Research Monographs, 67*(3), 251–259.

Cattell, R. B., & Vogelmann, S. (1977). A comprehensive trial of the scree and KG criteria for determining the number of factors. *Multivariate Behavioral Research, 12*, 289–325.

Chantler, L., & Heseltine, K. (2007). Fitness: What is the role of psychometric assessment? *Psychiatry, Psychology and Law, 14*(2), 350–358.

Chibnall, J. T., & Detrick, P. (2003). The NEO PI-R, Inwald Personality Inventory, and MMPI-2 in the prediction of police academy performance: A case of incremental validity. *American Journal of Criminal Justice, 27*(2), 224–233.

Clark, M., & Friedman, D. (1992). Pulling together: Building a community debriefing team. *Journal of Psychosocial Nursing, 30*(7), 27–32.

Clark, M. E. (1994). Interpretive limitations of the MMPI-2 Anger and Cynicism content scales. *Journal of Personality Assessment, 49*, 523–527.

Cobb, S. (1974). Social support as a moderator of life stress. *Psychosomatic Medicine, 38,* 300–314.

Corey, D. M., & Wolf, G. D. (1992). An integrated approach to reducing stress injuries. In J. Quick & L. Murphy (Eds.), *Stress and well being at work* (pp. 65–78). Washington, DC: American Psychological Association.

Costello, R. M., Schneider, S. L., & Schoenfeld, L. S. (1996). Validation of a preemployment MMPI index correlated with disciplinary suspension days of police officers. *Psychology, Crime and Law, 2*, 299–306.

Daniels, S., & King, E. (2002). The predictive validity of MMPI-2 content scales for small-town police officer performance. *Journal of Police & Criminal Psychology, 17*(2), 54.

Davis, R. (2003). Relationship between cognitive and background variables and disciplinary problems in law enforcement. *Applied H.R.M. Research, 80*(2), 77–80.

Davis, R. C. (1998). *SWAT plots: A practical training manual for tactical units.* Washington, DC: U.S. Government Printing Office.

Detrick, P. (2002). Prediction of police officer performance with the Inwald Personality Inventory. *Journal of Police and Criminal Psychology, 17*(2), 9–17.

Detrick, P., Chibnall, J. T., & Rosso, M. (2001). Minnesota Multiphasic Personality Inventory-2 in police officer selection: Normative data and relation to the Inwald Personality Inventory. *Professional Psychology: Research and Practice, 32*, 484–490.

Dietrich, J., & Smith, J. (1986). The non-medical use of drugs including alcohol among police personnel: A critical literature review. *Journal of Police Science and Administration, 14*(4), 300–306.

Dodrill, C. B. (1981). An economical method for the evaluation of general intelligence in adults. *Journal of Consulting and Clinical Psychology, 49*, 668–673.

Dodrill, C. B., & Warner, M. H. (1988). Further studies of the Wonderlic Personnel Test as a brief measure of intelligence, *Journal of Consulting and Clinical Psychology, 56*, 145–147.

DuBois, P. H., & Watson, R. I. (1950). The selection of patrolmen. *Journal of Applied Psychology, 34*, 90–95.

Dunne, J. A. (1990). Police counseling unit to deal with critical incidents. In J. T. Reese, J. M. Horn, & C. Dunning (Eds.), *Critical incidents in policing* (pp. 67–72). Washington, DC: U.S. Government Printing Office.

Dunning, C. (1990). Mitigating the impact of work trauma: Administrative issues concerning intervention. In J. T. Reese, J. M. Horn, & C. Dunning (Eds.), *Critical incidents in policing* (pp. 73–82). Washington, DC: U.S. Government Printing Office.

Endler, N. S., Parker, J. D., & Butcher, J. N. (1993). A factor analytic study of coping styles and the MMPI-2 content scales. *Journal of Clinical Psychology, 49*, 523–527.

Ellison, K. W., & Genz, J. L. (1983). *Stress and the police officer.* Springfield, IL: Charles C Thomas.

Evans, B. J., Coman, G., Stanley, R. O., & Burrows, G. D. (1993). Police officers coping strategies: An Australian police survey. *Stress Medicine, 9,* 237–246.

Everly, G. S. (1994a). Familial psychotraumatology: An analysis of the impact of traumatic stress upon the law enforcement family via destruction of the familial weltanschauung. In J. Y. Reese & E. Scrivner (Eds.), *Law enforcement families* (pp. 177–184). Washington, DC: U.S. Government Printing Office.

Everly, G. S. (1994b). A rapid crisis intervention technique for law enforcement: The SAFE-R model. In J. T. Reese & R. Solomon (Eds.), *Organizational issues* (pp. 183–191). Washington, DC: Federal Bureau of Investigation.

Everly, G. S. (1995a). An integrative two-factor model of post-traumatic stress. In G. S. Everly (Ed.), *Psychotraumatology: Key papers and core concepts in post traumatic stress* (pp. 27–47). New York: Plenum.

Everly, G. S. (1995b). The role of the critical incident stress debriefing process in disaster counseling. *Journal of Mental Health Counseling, 17*(3), 278–290.

Everly, G. S., & Mitchell J. T. (1997). *Critical incident stress management.* Ellicott City, MD: Chevron.

Everstine, D., with L. Everstine. (1993). *The trauma response: Treatment for emotional injury.* New York: W.W. Norton.

Exner, J. E. (1974). The self focus sentence completion: A study of egocentricity. *Journal of Personality Assessment, 37,* 437–455.

Exner, J. E. (1978). *The Rorschach: A comprehensive system: Vol. 2. Current research and advanced interpretation.* New York: Wiley.

Exner, J. E. (1993). *The Rorschach: A comprehensive system: Vol. 1. Basic foundations* (3rd ed.). New York: John Wiley.

Exner, J. E. (2003). *The Rorschach: A comprehensive system* (4th ed.). New York: John Wiley.

Exner, J. E., & Weiner, I. B. (1994). *The Rorschach: A comprehensive system: Vol. 3. Assessment of children and adolescents* (2nd ed.). New York: John Wiley.

Farr, J. L., & Landy, F. J. (1979). The development and use of supervisory and peer scale for police performance appraisal. In C. D. Spilberger (Ed.), *Police selection and evaluation: Issues and techniques* (pp. 61–76). Washington, DC: Hemisphere.

Fay, J. (2000). *A narrative approach to critical and sub-critical incident debriefings.* Unpublished dissertation. Retrieved April 14, 2010, from http://www.narrativeapproaches.com/narrative%20papers%20folder/narrativepolicing2.htm

Federal Bureau of Investigation. (1996). Critical incident stress in law enforcement. *Law Enforcement Bulletin,* February.

Fischler, G. L. (n. d.) *Psychological fitness-for-duty examinations: practical considerations for public safety departments.* Retrieved September 29, 2010, from http://edpdlaw.com/FitnessforDuty.pdf

Fischler, G. L. (n. d.) *Psychological guidelines for issues in law enforcement.* Retrieved August 12, 2010, from http://www.psycheval.com/issues_in_law_enforcement.shtml

Folkman, S., & Lazarus, R. S. (1980). An analysis of coping in a middle age community sample. *Journal of Health and Social Behavior, 21,* 219–239.

Forbey, J. D., & Ben-Porath, Y. S. (2007). Computerized adaptive personality testing: A review and illustration with the MMPI-2 Computerized Adaptive Version. *Psychological Assessment, 19,* 14–24.

Foreman, C. (1994). Immediate post disaster treatment of trauma. In M. B. Williams & J. F. Sommer (Eds.), *Handbook of post traumatic therapy* (pp. 268–282). Westport, CT: Greenwood.

Frankl, V. (1959). *Man's search for meaning.* Boston: Beacon.

Freedman, J., & Combs, G. (1996). *Narrative therapy: The social construction of reality.* New York: W. W. Norton.

Freedy, J. R., Resnick, H. S., Kilpatrick, D. G., Dansky, B. S., & Tidwell, R. P. (1994). The psychological adjustment of recent crime victims in the criminal justice system. *Journal of Interpersonal Violence, 9*(4), 450–468.

Fuller, R. A. (1990). An overview of the process of peer support team development. In J. T. Reese, J. M. Horn, & C. Dunning (Eds.), *Critical incidents in policing* (pp. 99–106). Washington DC: U.S. Government Printing Office.

Fullerton, C. S., McCarroll, J. E., Ursano, R. J., & Wright, K. M. (1992). Psychological responses of rescue workers: Fire fighters and trauma. *American Journal of Orthopsychiatry, 62*(3), 371–378.

Ganellen, R. J. (1996). *Integrating Rorschach and the MMPI-2 in personality assessment.* Mahwah, NJ: Lawrence Erlbaum.

Garrison, W. E. (1990). *Modeling inoculation training for traumatic incident exposure*. In J. T. Reese, J. M. Horn, & C. Dunning (Eds.), *Critical incidents in policing* (pp. 107–117). Washington DC: U.S. Government Printing Office.

Gentz, D. (1990). *The psychological impact of critical incidents on police officers*. In J. T. Reese, J. M. Horn, & C. Dunning (Eds.), *Critical incidents in policing* (pp. 119–122). Washington DC: U.S. Government Printing Office.

Gergen, K. J. (1985). The social constructionist movement in modern psychology. *American Psychologist, 40*(3), 266–275.

Gersons, B. P. R., & Carlier, I. V. E. (1994). Treatment of work-related trauma in police officers: Post traumatic stress disorder and the post traumatic decline. In M. B. Williams & J. F. Sommer (Eds.), *Handbook of post traumatic therapy* (pp. 21–33). Westport, CT: Greenwood.

Gibbs, N. (1994, September 26). Officers on the edge. *Time, 144*(13), 62.

Goldfarb, D. A., & Aumiller, G. S. *The heavy badge*. Retrieved August 10, 2010, from http://www.heavybadge.com

Graff, F. A. (1986). The relationship between social support and occupation stress among police officers. *Journal of Police Science and Administration, 14*(3), 178–186.

Graham, J. R. (1993). *MMPI-2 assessing personality and psychopathology* (2nd ed.). New York: Oxford University Press.

Gund, N., & Elliott, B. (1995). Employee assistance programs in police organizations. In M. Kurke (Ed), *Police psychology into the 21st century* (pp. 149–167). Washington, DC: American Psychological Association.

Hanscom, K. L. (2001). Treating survivors of war trauma and torture. *American Psychologist, 56,* 1032–1039.

Hargrave, G. (1987). Law enforcement selection with the interview, MMPI, and CPI: A study of reliability and validity. *Journal of Police Science and Administration, 15*(2), 25–28.

Hargrave, G. E., Hiatt, D., & Gaffney, T. W. (1986). A comparison of MMPI and CPI test profiles for traffic officers and deputy sheriffs. *Journal of Police Science and Administration, 14,* 250–258.

Hargrave, G. E., Hiatt, D., & Gaffney, T. W. (1988). F+4+9+Cn: An MMPI measure of aggression in law enforcement officers and applicants. *Journal of Police Science and Administration, 16*(3), 268–273.

Harris, C. J. (1995). Sensory based therapy for crisis counselors. In C. Figley (Ed.), *Compassion fatigue: Coping with secondary traumatic stress* (pp. 101–114). New York: Brunner Mazel.

Hart, P. M., Wearing, A. J., & Heady, B. (1994). Police stress and well-being: Integrating personality, coping, and daily work experiences. *Journal of Occupational and Organization Psychology, 68*(2), 133–157.

Hartsough, D. M. (1995). *Stresses, spouses and law enforcement: A step beyond*. In J. T. Reese, J. M. Horn, & C. Dunning (Eds.), *Critical incidents in policing* (pp. 131–138). Washington, DC: U.S. Government Printing Office.

Havassy, V. (1994). Police stress in the 90's and its impact on the family. In J. T. Reese & E. Scrivner (Eds.), *Law enforcement families* (pp. 27–34). Washington, DC: Federal Bureau of Investigation.

Hays, G. (1994). Police couples: Breaking the security access code. In J. T. Reese & E. Scrivner (Eds.), *Law enforcement families* (pp. 337–343). Washington, DC: Federal Bureau of Investigation.

Herndon, J. (1998, October). *Correlates of MMPI-2 L scale: Elevations in an LEO selection test battery*. Paper presented at the 27th annual meeting of the Society of Police and Criminal Psychology, Portland, OR.

Hiatt, D., & Hargrave, G. (1988a). Predicting job performance problems with psychological screening. *Journal of Police Science and Administration, 16,* 122–125.

Hiatt, D., & Hargrave, G. (1988b). MMPI profiles of problem peace officers. *Journal of Personality Assessment, 52,* 722–731.

Hogan, R. (1971). Personality characteristics of highly rated policeman. *Personnel Psychology, 24,* 679–686.

Hooper, J. (1996, Fall). Targeting the brain. *Time,* 47–50.

Horn, J. M. (1990). *Critical incidents for law enforcement officers*. In J. T. Reese, J. M. Horn, & C. Dunning (Eds.), *Critical incidents in policing* (pp. 143–148). Washington, DC: U.S. Government Printing Office.

Horowitz, M. J., & Kaltreider, N. B. (1995). *Brief therapy of the stress response syndrome*. In G. S. Everly (Ed.), *Psychotraumatology: Key papers and core concepts in post traumatic stress* (pp. 231–243). New York: Plenum.

Iacono, W. G., & Patrick, C. J. (1999). Polygraph ("lie detector") testing: The state of the art. In A. K. Hess & I. B. Weiner (Ed.), *The handbook of forensic psychology*. New York: John Wiley.

Initial Application for ABPP Affiliation of Police & Public Safety Psychology as a Specialty Board. Retrieved September 25, 2010, from http://library.constantcontact.com/doc209/1101925593050/doc/hICWPTSiECnMjTtq.pdf

International Association of Chiefs of Police: Officer-involved shooting guidelines. Retrieved September 29, 2010, from http://theiacp.org/psych_services_section/pdfs/Psych-OfficerInvolvedShooting.pdfnver, Colorado, 2009

International Association of Chiefs of Police: Peer support guidelines. Retrieved September 29, 2010, from http://theiacp.org/psych_services_section/pdfs/Psych-PeerSupportGuidelines.pdf

International Association of Chiefs of Police: Pre-employment psychological evaluation guidelines. Retrieved September 29, 2010, from http://theiacp.org/psych_services_section/pdfs/Psych-PreemploymentPsych Eval.pdf.

International Association of Chiefs of Police: Psychological fitness-for-duty evaluation guidelines. Retrieved September 29, 2010, from http://theiacp.org/psych_services_section/pdfs/Psych-FitnessforDuty Evaluation.pdf

Inwald, R. (1990). *Fitness-for-duty evaluation guidelines: A survey for police/public safety administrators and mental health professionals.* Paper presented at the meeting of the American Psychological Association, Boston.

Inwald, R. (1984a). *Issues & guidelines for mental health professionals conducting pre-employment psychological screening programs in law enforcement agencies.* Paper presented at the National Symposium on Police Psychological Services, FBI Academy, Quantico, VA, September 17–21.

Inwald, R. (1984b). *Law enforcement officer screening: A description of one pre-employment psychological testing program.* Submitted to the National Symposium on Police Psychological Services FBI Academy, Quantico, VA. September 17–21.

Inwald, R. E. (1988). Five year follow up study of departmental terminations as predicted by 16 pre-employment psychological indicators. *Journal of Applied Psychology, 4,* 703–710.

Inwald, R. (1992). *Inwald Personality Inventory technical manual* (Rev. ed.). Kew Gardens, NY: Hilson Research.

Inwald, R. (1993). Hilson Relationships Inventory for public safety personnel and Hilson/Spouse Mate Inventory. New York: Hilson Research.

Inwald, R. (1995). *Hilson Safety/Security Risk Inventory (HSRI) technical manual.* New York: Hilson Research.

Inwald, R. (1998). *Psychological profiles of police and public safety officers involved with domestic violence.* Paper presented at the Domestic Violence by Police Officers Conference, FBI Academy, Quantico, VA, September 17–18.

Inwald, R. E. (2004). Personality testing in law enforcement employment settings: A metaanalytic review. *Criminal Justice and Behavior, 31,* 649–675.

Inwald, R. E. (2006). *Use of a customized Hilson Research test battery to identify stress susceptibility in returning military veterans.* Paper presented at the Annual Conference of the International Association of Chiefs of Police, Boston, October 15.

Inwald, R. E. (2008). The Inwald Personality Inventory (IPI) and Hilson Research Inventories: Development and rationale. *Journal of Aggression and Violent Behavior, 13,* 298–327.

Inwald, R., & Brobst, K. E. (1988). *Hilson Personnel Profile/Success Quotient (HPP/SQ) technical manual.* New York: Hilson Research.

Inwald, R., & Brockwell, A. (1988). *Success quotient profiles of law enforcement administrators.* New York: Hilson Research.

Inwald, R. E., & Gebbia, M. I. (1992). *Inwald Survey 5 (IS5) technical manual.* New York: Hilson Research.

Inwald, R., & Gebbia, M. (1997). *Hilson Spouse/Mate Inventory and Hilson Relationship Inventory technical manual.* Kew Gardens, NJ: Hilson Research.

Inwald, R., Gebbia, M., & Resko, J. (1993). Three studies of police/spouse mate relationships using the Hilson Spouse/Mate Inventory. In E. Scrivner (Ed.), *Law enforcement families: Issues and answers.* Washington DC: U.S. Government Publishing Office.

Inwald, R., & Kaufman, J. C. (1989). *Hilson Career Satisfaction Index (HCSI) technical manual.* New York: Hilson Research.

Inwald, R., Kaufman, J., & Roberts, M. (1991). Alcohol use, drug use, and past psychiatric history. *Criminal Justice Digest, 10*(7), 1–8.

Inwald, R., Resko, J. A., & Favuzza, V. (1996). *Hilson Life Adjustment Profile (HLAP) technical manual.* New York: Hilson Research.

Inwald, R., Resko, J. A., & Favuzza, V. (1996). *Inwald Survey 2 (IS2) & Inwald Survey 8 (IS8) technical manual.* New York: Hilson Research.

Inwald, R. E., & Shusman, E. J. (1984). The IPI and MMPI as predictors of academy performance for police recruits. *Journal of Police Science and Administration, 12,* 1–11.

Inwald, R., Traynor, W., & Favuzza, V. (2000). Psychological profiles of police and public safety officers accused of domestic violence. In D. C. Sheehan (Ed.). *Domestic violence by police officers* (pp. 209–224). Washington, DC: U.S. Department of Justice.

Janik, J. (1990). What value are cognitive defenses in critical incident stress. In J. T. Reese, J. M. Horn, & C. Dunning (Eds.), *Critical incidents in policing* (pp. 149–158). Washington, DC: U.S. Government Printing Office.

Janik, J. (1993, August). *Preemployment interviews of law enforcement officer candidates*. Paper presented at the meeting of the American Psychological Association, Toronto.

Janoff-Bulman, R. (1985). The aftermath of victimization: Rebuilding shattered assumptions. In C. R. Figley (Ed.), *Trauma and its wake: The study and treatment of post-traumatic stress disorder* (pp. 15–35). New York: Brunner/Mazel.

Kates, S. (1950). Rorschach responses, strong blank scales, and job satisfaction among policemen. *Journal of Applied Psychology, 34*(4), 249–254.

Kaufmann, G. M., & Beehr, T. A. (1989). Occupational stressors, individual strains, and social support among police officers. *Human Relations, 42*(2), 185–197.

Kilpatrick, D. G., Best, C. L., Veronen, L. J., Amick, A. E., Villeponteaux, L. A., & Ruff, G. A. (1985). Mental health correlates of criminal victimization: A random community survey. *Journal of Counseling and Clinical Psychology, 53*(6), 866–873.

Kilpatrick, D. G., Edmunds, C. N., & Seymour, A. K. (1992). *Rape in America: A report to the nation*. Arlington, VA, and Charleston, SC: National Victim Center and Medical University of South Carolina.

Kilpatrick, D. G., & Resnick, H. S. (1993). PTSD associated with exposure to criminal victimization in clinical and community populations. In J. R. T. Davidson & E. B. Foa (Eds.), *PTSD in review: Recent research and future directions* (pp. 123–143). Washington, DC: American Psychiatric Press.

Kilpatrick, D. G., Seymour, A., & Boyle, J. (1991). *America speaks out: Citizens' attitudes about victims' rights and violence*. Arlington, VA: National Victim Center.

King, P., Norrell, G., & Erlandson, F. L. (1959). The prediction of academic success in a police administration curriculum. *Educational and Psychological Measurement, 19*, 649–651.

Kirkcaldy, B., Cooper, C. L., & Ruffalo, P. (1995). Work stress and health in a sample of U.S. police. *Psychology Reports, 76*, 700–702.

Kirschman, E., Scrivner, E., Ellison, K., & Marcy, C. (1992). Work and well-being: Lessons from law enforcement. In J. Quick & L. Murphy (Eds.), *Stress and well being at work* (pp. 178–191). Washington, DC: American Psychological Association.

Kitaeff, J. (2006a). *Jews in blue*. Youngstown, NY: Cambria Press.

Kitaeff, J. (2006b). *Selected readings in forensic psychology*. Upper Saddle River, NJ: Pearson.

Kitaeff, J. (2007). *Malingering, lies, and junk science in the courtroom*. Youngstown, NY: Cambria Press.

Kitaeff, J. (2010). *Forensic psychology*. Upper Saddle River, NJ: Prentice-Hall.

Klein, R. (1990). *The utilization of police peer counselors in critical incidents*. In J. T. Reese, J. M. Horn, & C. Dunning (Eds.), *Critical incidents in policing* (pp. 159–168). Washington, DC: U.S. Government Printing Office.

Kolbell, R. M. (1995). When relaxation is not enough. In L. Murphy (Ed), *Job stress interventions* (pp. 31–43). New York: Plenum.

Kornfeld, A. D. (1995). Police officer candidate MMPI-2 performance: Gender, ethnic, and normative factors. *Journal of Clinical Psychology, 51*(4), 536–540.

Kuder, G. F. (1985). *Kuder occupational interest survey*. Chicago: Science Research Associates.

Kureczka, A. W. (1996). Critical incident stress in law enforcement. *FBI Law Enforcement Magazine, 65*, 2–3.

Kurke, M. I. (1995). Organizational management of stress and human reliability. In M. I. Kurke (Ed.), *Police psychology into the 21st century* (pp. 391–415). Washington, DC: American Psychological Association.

Kurke, M. I., & Scrivner, E. M. (1995). *Police psychology into the 21st century*. Hillsdale, NJ: Lawrence Erlbaum.

Larson, J. (1969). *Lying and its detection: A study of deception and deception tests*. Montclair, NJ: Patterson Smith.

Lawrence, R. A. (1984). Police stress and personality factors: A conceptual model. *Journal of Criminal Justice, 12*, 247–263.

Linden, J., & Klein, R. (1988). *Police peer counseling: An expanded perspective*. In J. T. Reese & J. Horn (Eds.), *Police psychology: Operation assistance* (pp. 241–244). Washington, DC: Federal Bureau of Investigation.

Linton, J. C. (1993). Helping the helpers: The development of a critical incident stress management team through university/community cooperation. *Annals of Emergency Medicine, 22*(4), 663–668.

Lippert, W. W. (1990). *Police officer suicide or homicide: Treating the affected department.* In J. T. Reese, J. M. Horn, & C. Dunning (Eds.), *Critical incidents in policing* (pp. 179–190). Washington, DC: Government Printing Office.

Litz, B. T., & Weathers, F. W. (1994). *The diagnosis and assessment of post-traumatic stress disorder in adults.* In M. B. Williams & J. F. Sommer (Ed.), *Handbook of post-traumatic therapy* (pp. 19–37). Westport, CT: Greenwood.

Lykken, D. (1988). The case against polygraph testing. In A. Gale (Ed.), *The polygraph test: Lies and science.* London: Sage.

Markesteyn, T. (1992). *The psychological impact of nonsexual criminal offenses on victims.* Retrieved August 12, 2010, from http://ww2.psepcsppcc.gc.ca/publications/corrections/199221_e.asp

McCafferty, F. L., McCafferty, E., & McCafferty, M. A. (1992). Stress and suicide in police officers. *Southern Medical Journal, 85*(3), 233–243.

McCammon, S., & Allison, E. J. (1995). Debriefing and treating emergency workers. In C. Figley (Ed.), *Compassion fatigue: Coping with secondary traumatic stress* (pp. 151–130). New York: Brunner Mazel.

McCunn, L., & Pearlman, L. A. (1990). Vicarious traumatization: A framework for understanding the psychological effects of working with victims. *Journal of Traumatic Stress, 3*(1), 131–149.

McKelvie, S. (1989). The Wonderlic Personality test: Reliability and validity in the academic setting. *Psychological Reports, 65,* 161–162.

McKenzie, J. (1986). Preface. In J. T. Reese & H. A. Goldstein (Eds.), *Psychological services for law enforcement.* Washington, DC: U.S. Department of Justice.

McMains, M. J. (1990). The management and treatment of post-shooting trauma: Administration and programs. In J. T. Reese, J. M. Horn, & C. Dunning (Eds.), *Critical incidents in policing* (pp. 191–198). Washington, DC: U.S. Government Printing Office.

Mesnick, S. L. (2001). Genetic relatedness in sperm whales: Evidence and cultural implications. *Behavioural and Brain Science, 24,* 2346–2347.

Mesnick, S. L., Evans, K., Taylor, B. L., Hyde, J., Escorza-Treviño, S., & Dizon, A. E. (2003). Sperm whale social structure: Why it takes a village to raise a child. In B. M. de Waal & P. L. Tyack (Eds.), *Animal social complexity: Intelligence, culture and individualized societies* (pp. 170–174). Cambridge, MA: Harvard University Press.

Meyer, G. J. (2004). The reliability and validity of the Rorschach and TAT compared to other psychological and medical procedures: An analysis of systematically gathered evidence. In M. J. Hilsenroth & D. Segal (Eds.), *Personality assessment: Vol. 2. Comprehensive handbook of psychological assessment* (pp. 315–342). Hoboken, NJ: Wiley.

Meyer, G. J., Mihura, J. L., & Smith, B. L. (2005). The interclinician reliability of Rorschach interpretation in four data sets. *Journal of Personality Assessment, 84,* 296–314.

Miller, L. (1998). *Shocks to the system.* New York: W. W. Norton.

Miller, L. (1999). Workplace violence: Prevention, response, and recovery. *Psychotherapy, 36,* 160–169.

Miller, L. (2001a). Workplace violence and psychological trauma: Clinical disability, legal liability, and corporate policy. Part I. *Neurolaw Letter, 11,* 1–5.

Miller, L. (2001b). Workplace violence and psychological trauma: Clinical disability, legal liability, and corporate policy. Part II. *Neurolaw Letter, 11,* 7–13.

Miller, L. (2002a). How safe is your job? The threat of workplace violence. *USA Today Magazine,* March, pp. 52–54.

Miller, L. (2002b). Posttraumatic stress disorder in school violence: Risk management lessons from the workplace. *Neurolaw Letter, 11*(33), 36–40.

Miller, L. (2002c). Psychological interventions for terroristic trauma: Symptoms, syndromes, and treatment strategies. *Psychotherapy: Theory, Research, Practice, Training, 39*(4), 283–296.

Miller, L. (2006). *Practical police psychology: Stress management and crisis intervention for law enforcement.* Springfield, IL: Charles C Thomas.

Mills, M. C., & Stratton, J. G. (1982, February). The MMPI and the prediction of police job performance. *FBI Law Enforcement Bulletin,* 10–15.

Mitchell, J., & Bray, G. (1990). *Emergency services stress: Guidelines for preserving the health and careers of emergency services personnel.* Englewood Cliffs, NJ: Prentice Hall.

Mitchell, J., & Everly, G. S. (1995a). Prevention of work-related posttraumatic stress: The critical incident stress debriefing process. In L. Murphy (Ed.), *Job stress interventions* (pp. 173–183). New York: Plenum.

Mitchell, J., & Everly, G. S. (1995b). Of work-related traumatic stress among high risk occupational groups. In G. S. Everly & J. M. Lating (Eds.), *Psychotraumatology* (pp. 267–280). New York: Plenum.

Mitchell, J., & Everly, G. S. (1996). *Critical incident stress debriefing: An operations manual for the prevention of PTSD among emergency services and disaster workers.* Ellicott City, MD: Chevron

Mitchell, J. T. (1983). When disaster strikes: The critical incident debriefing process. *Journal of Emergency Medical Services, 8,* 36–39.

Mitchell, J. T. (1990). *Law enforcement applications of critical incident stress teams.* In J. T. Reese, J. M. Horn, & C. Dunning (Eds.), *Critical incidents in policing* (pp. 201–212). Washington, DC: U.S. Government Printing Office.

Mitchell, J. T. (1994a). Critical incident stress interventions with families and significant others. In J. T. Reese & E. Scrivner (Eds.), *Law enforcement families: Issues and answers* (pp. 195–204). Washington, DC: U.S. Government Printing Office.

Mitchell, J. T. (1994b). *Systematic approach to critical incident stress management in law enforcement organizations.* In J. T. Reese & R. Solomon (Eds.), *Organization issues* (pp. 215–222). Washington, DC: Federal Bureau of Investigation.

Monat, A., & Lazarus, R. S. (1977). Stress and coping: Some current issues and controversies. In A. Monat & R. S. Lazarus (Eds.), *Stress and coping: An anthology* (pp. 1–15). New York: Columbia University Press.

Mufson, L., Moreau, D., Weissman, M. M., Wickramaratne, P., Martin, J., & Samoilov, A. (1994). Modification of interpersonal psychotherapy with depressed adolescents (IPT-A): Phase I and II studies. *Journal of the American Academy of Child and Adolescent Psychiatry, 33,* 695–705.

Mullins, W. C. (1994). Peer support team training and intervention for the police family. In J. T. Reese & E. Scrivner (Eds.), *Law enforcement families: Issues and answers* (pp. 205–216). Washington, DC: Federal Bureau of Investigation.

Mullins, W. C., & McMains, M. J. (1995). Predicting patrol officer performance from a psychological assessment battery: A predictive validity study. *Journal of Police and Criminal Psychology, 10*(4), 15–25.

Munroe, J. F., Shay, J., Fisher, L., Makary, C., Rapperport, K., & Zimering, R. (1995). Preventing compassion fatigue: A team treatment model. In C. Figley (Ed.), *Compassion fatigue: Coping with secondary traumatic stress* (pp. 209–231). New York: Brunner Mazel.

Münsterberg, H. (1909). *On the witness stand.* Garden City, NY: Doubleday

Murphy, J. J. (1972). Current practices in the use of psychological testing by police agencies. *Journal of Criminal Law, Criminology, & Police Science, 63,* 570.

National Security Institute. (n.d.). *An assessment of the Aldrich H. Ames espionage case.* Abstract of report of investigation. Retrieved March 2, 2007, from http://nsi.org/Library/Espionage/Hitzreport.html

Nemoto, T., Okiyama, M., & Takahashi, M. (1985). Aspects of the roles of squid in food chains of marine Antarctic ecosystems. In W. R. Seigfried, P. R. Condy, & R. M. Laws (Eds.), *Antarctic nutrient cycles and food webs* (pp. 415–420). Berlin: Springer-Verlag.

Nesis, K. N. (1972). Oceanic cephalopods of the Peru current: Horizontal and vertical distribution. *Oceanology, 12,* 3426–3437.

Nesis, K. N. (1987). *Cephalopods of the world: Squids, cuttlefishes, octopuses and allies.* Neptune City, FL: T.F.H. Publications.

Nielsen, E. (1986). Understanding and assessing traumatic stress reactions. In J. Reese & H. A. Goldstein (Eds.), *Psychological services for law enforcement* (pp. 369–374). Washington, DC: U.S. Department of Justice.

Niles, D. P. (1994). *Traumatology: Implications for training, education and development programs.* In M. B. Williams (Ed.), *Handbook of post-traumatic therapy* (pp. 510–519). Westport, CT: Greenwood.

Ochberg, F. M. (1995). Post-traumatic therapy. In G. S. Everly (Ed.), *Psychotraumatology: Key papers and core concepts in post traumatic stress* (pp. 245–264). New York: Plenum.

Oksol, E. M., & O'Donohue, W. T. (2003). A critical analysis of the polygraph. In W. T. O'Donohue, & E. R. Levensky (Eds.), *Handbook of forensic psychology: Resource for mental health and legal professionals* (pp. 601–634). San Diego, CA: Academic Press.

Ones, D. S. (2003). Comprehensive meta-analysis of integrity test variables: Findings and implications for personnel selection and theories of job performance. *Journal of Applied Psychology, 78,* 679–703.

Ostrov, E. (1990). Critical incident psychological casualties among police officers: A critical review. In J. T. Reese, J. M. Horn, & C. Dunning (Eds.), *Critical incidents in policing* (pp. 251–256). Washington, DC: U.S. Government Printing Office.

Ozer, E., et al. (2003). Predictors of posttraumatic stress disorder and symptoms in adults: A meta-analysis. *Psychological Bulletin, 129*(1), 52–73.

Pastorella, R. (1990). Posttraumatic stress disorder and the police experience. In J. T. Reese, J. M. Horn, & C. Dunning (Eds.), *Critical incidents in policing* (pp. 269–276). Washington, DC: U.S. Government Printing Office.

Patton, D., & Violanti, J. M. (1996). *Traumatic stress in critical incidents: Recognition, consequences, and treatment.* Springfield, IL: Thomas.

Poehlman, M. (1988). *Peer support programs that deal with traumatic field events in California law enforcement* (Command College paper). Sacramento, CA: Peace Officers Standards and Training.

Quinn, V. (1994). *More about police suicides.* San Francisco: Peer Perspective, San Francisco Police Department.

Ragaisis, K. M. (1994). Critical incident stress debriefing: A family nursing intervention. *Archives of Psychiatric Nursing, 8*(1), 38–32.

Raza, S. M., & Carpenter, B. N. (1987, August). *Piecemeal or through a model: An examination of employment interviews.* Paper presented at the annual meeting of the American Psychological Association, New York.

Reese, J. T. (1984). A cop's best hopes are his family and colleagues. In *Behavioral Science in Law Enforcement.* Quantico, VA: Federal Bureau of Investigation.

Reese, J. T. (1987a). A prescription for burn-out. In *Behavioral Science in Law Enforcement.* Quantico, VA: Federal Bureau of Investigation.

Reese, J. T. (1987b). Coping with stress: It's your job. In *Behavioral Science in Law Enforcement.* Quantico, VA: Federal Bureau of Investigation.

Reese, J. T. (1991). Justifications for mandating critical incident aftercare. In J. T. Reese, J. M. Horn, & C. Dunning (Eds.), *Critical incidents in policing* (rev. ed., pp. 213–220). Washington DC: U.S. Government Printing Office.

Reese, J. T. (1995). A history of police psychological services. In M. Kurke & E. Scrivner (Eds.), *Police psychology into the 21st century* (pp. 31–44). Hillsdale, NJ: Lawrence Erlbaum.

Reese, J. T., & Goldstein, H. A. (Eds.). (1986). *Psychological services for law enforcement.* Washington, DC: U.S. Government Printing Office.

Reese, J. T., & Hodinko, B. M. (1990). Police psychological services: A history. In J. T. Reese, J. M. Horn, & C. Dunning (Eds.), *Critical incidents in policing* (pp. 297–310). Washington, DC: U.S. Government Printing Office.

Reese, J. T., Horn, J. M., & Dunning, C. (Eds.). (1990). *Critical incidents in policing.* Washington, DC: U.S. Government Printing Office.

Ressler, R., Burgess, A., & Douglas, J. (1983). Rape and rape murder: One offender and twelve victims. *American Journal of Psychiatry, 140*(1), 36–40.

Rose, J. (1995). *Consolidation of law enforecment basic training academies: An evaluation of pilot projects.* Flagstaff: Northern Arizona University.

Rudofossi, D. (2007). *Working with traumatized police officer-patients: A clinician's guide to complex PTSD syndromes in public safety populations.* New York: Baywood Press.

Ryan, A. H. (2005). *Assessment resources and Interquest, LLC.* Retrieved August 10, 2010, from https://www.rpiq.com/arpiq/bio.asp

Ryan, A. H., & Brewster, M. E. (1994). PTSD and related symptoms in traumatized police officers and their spouse/mates. In J. T. Reese & E. Scrivner (Eds.), *Law enforcement families* (pp. 217–226). Washington, DC: Federal Bureau of Investigation.

Saccuzzo, D. P., Higgins, G., & Lewandowski, D. (1974).Program for psychological assessment of law enforcement officers: Initial evaluation. *Psychological Reports, 35,* 651–654.

Sackett, P. R., & Harris, M. M. (1984). Honesty testing for personnel selection: A review and critique. *Personnel Psychology, 17,* 221–245.

Sackett, P. R., Burris, L. R., & Callahan, C. (1989). Integrity testing for personnel selection: An update. *Personnel Psychology, 42,* 491–529.

Sackett, P. R., & Harris, M. M. (1984). Honesty testing for personnel selection: A review and critique. *Personnel Psychology, 37,* 221–246.

Sarchione, C. D., Cuttler, M. J., Muchinsky, P. M., & Nelson-Gray, R. O. (1998). Prediction of dysfunctional job behaviors among law enforcement officers. *Journal of Applied Psychology, 83,* 904–912.

Saxe, L., Dougherty, D., & Cross, T. (1985). The validity of polygraph testing: Scientific analysis and public controversy. *American Psychologist, 40,* 355–366.

Saxe, S. J., & Reiser, M. (1976). A comparison of three police applicant groups using the MMPI. *Journal of Police Science and Administration, 4,* 419–425.

Scogin, F., & Beutler, L. (1986). Psychological screening of law enforcement candidates. In P. Keller & L. G. Ritt (Eds.), *Innovations in clinical practice: A source book* (pp. 317–330). Sarasota, FL: Professional Resource Exchange.

Scogin, F., Schumacher, J., Gardner, J., & Chaplin, W. (1995). Predictive validity of psychological testing in law enforcement settings. *Professional Psychology, Research and Practice, 26*(1), 68–71.

Schlossberg, H. (1974). *Psychologist with a gun*. New York: Coward, McCann & Geoghegan.

Schumacher J., Scogin, F., Howland, K., & McGee J. (1992). The relation of peer assessment to future law enforcement performance. *Criminal Justice and Behavior, 19,* 286–293.

Scogin, F., Schumacher, J., Gardner, J., & Chaplin, W. (1995). Predictive validity of psychological testing in law enforcement settings. *Professional Psychology Research and Practice, 26,* 68–71.

Sellbom, M., Ben-Porath, Y. S., & Bagby, R. M. (2008). On the hierarchical structure of mood and anxiety disorders: Confirmatory evidence and elaboration of a model of temperament markers. *Journal of Abnormal Psychology, 117,* 576–590.

Sellbom, M., Ben-Porath, Y. S. & Stafford, K. P. (2007). A comparison of MMPI-2 measures of psychopathic deviance in a forensic setting. *Psychological Assessment, 19,* 430–436.

Seligmann, J. (1994, September 26). Cops who kill themselves. *Newsweek,* 58.

Seligman, M., & Buchanan, G. M. (Eds.). (1995). *Explanatory style.* Hillsdale, NJ: Lawrence Erlbaum.

Selye, H. (1979a). Stress, cancer, and the mind. In J. Tache, H. Selye, & S. B. Day (Eds.), *Cancer, stress, and death* (pp. 11–27). New York: Plenum.

Selye, H. (1979b) *The stress of my life.* New York: Van Nostrand Reinhold.

Shalev, A. (2007, December 9). Psychotherapy useful in treating post-traumatic stress disorder in early stages. *Science Daily.* Retrieved May 12, 2009, from http://www.sciencedaily.com

Sheehan, P. L. (1995). Critical incident trauma and intimacy. In J. T. Reese, J. M. Horn, & C. Dunning (Eds.), *Critical incidents in policing* (pp. 331–334). Washington, DC: U.S. Government Printing Office.

Shusman, E. J., & Inwald, R. E. (1991). A longitudinal validation study of correctional officer job performance as predicted by the IPI and MMPI. *Journal of Criminal Justice, 19*(2), 173–180.

Shusman, E. J., Inwald, R. E., & Knatz, H. F. (1987). A cross-validation study of police recruit performance as predicted by the IPI and MMPI. *Journal of Police Science and Administration, 15*(2), 162–169.

Silva, M. N. (1990). The delivery of mental health services to law enforcement officers. In J. T. Reese, J. M. Horn, & C. Dunning (Eds.), *Critical incidents in policing* (pp. 335–341). Washington, DC: U.S. Government Printing Office.

Sloan, I. H., Rozensky, R. H., Kaplan, L., & Saunders, S. (1994). A shooting incident in an elementary school: Effects of worker stress on public safety, mental health and medical personnel. *Journal of Traumatic Stress, 7*(4), 565–674.

Smith, C. (1997). Comparing traditional therapies with narrative approaches. In C. Smith & D. Nylund (Eds.), *In narrative therapy with children and adolescents.* New York: Guilford.

Smith, C. L., & Chesnay, M. D. (1994). Critical incident stress debriefings for crisis management in post-traumatic stress disorders. *Medicine and Law, 13,* 185–191.

Solomon, R. M. (1990). *The dynamics of fear in critical incidents: implications for training and treatment.* In J. T. Reese, J. M. Horn, & C. Dunning (Eds.), *Critical incidents in policing* (pp. 347–358). Washington, DC: U.S. Government Printing Office.

Solomon, R. M. (1996, October). Post shooting trauma. *The Police Chief,* 40–44.

Spielberger, C. D. (1979). *Understanding stress and anxiety.* New York: Harper & Row.

Sprang, G., & McNeil, J. (1995). *The many faces of bereavement: The nature and treatment of natural, traumatic, and stigmatized grief.* New York: Brunner/Mazel.

Spungen, D. (1998). *Homicide: The hidden victims.* Thousand Oaks, CA: Sage.

Stern, W. (1912). *The psychological methods of intelligence testing* (G. Whipple, Trans.). Baltimore: Warwick and York.

Stern, W. (n. d.). *Human intelligence.* Retrieved October 31, 2010, from http://www.indiana.edu/~intell/stern.shtml

Stevens, D. J. (1998). What do law enforcement officers think about their work? *The Journal, 47*(1).

Stevens, D. J. (1999a). Do college educated officers provide quality police service? *Law and Order, 47*(12), 37–41.

Stevens, D. J. (1999b). Corruption among narcotic officers: A study of innocence and integrity. *Journal of Police and Criminal Psychology, 14*(2), 1–11.

Stevens, D. J. (1999c). Stress and the American police officer. *Police Journal, 72*(3), 247–259.

Stevens, D. J. (1999d). Police officer stress. *Law and Order, 47*(9), 77–81.

Stevens, D. J. (2001a). *Case studies in community policing.* New York: Prentice Hall.

Stevens, D. J. (2001b). Community policing and managerial techniques: Total quality management techniques. *The Police Journal, 74*(1), 26–61.

Super, J. T., & Blau, T. H. (1997). Survey of psychological services general orders in law enforcement. *Journal of Police and Criminal Psychology, 12*(1), 7–12.

Surrette, M. A., Aamodt, M. G., & Serafino, G. (1990). *Validity of the New Mexico police selection battery.* Paper presented at the annual meeting of the Society of Police and Criminal *Critical incident trauma and intimacy* Psychology, Albuquerque, NM.

Swann, G. B., & D'Agostino, C. (1994). Post-shooting trauma and domestic violence: Clinical observation and preliminary data. In J. T. Reese & E. Scrivner (Eds.), *Law enforcement families: Issues and answers* (pp. 227–232). Washington, DC: U.S. Government Printing Office.

Tellegen, A., & Ben-Porath, Y. S. (2008). *The Minnesota Multiphasic Personality Inventory-2 restructured form: Technical manual.* Minneapolis: University of Minnesota Press.

Terman, L. M. (1916). *The measurement of intelligence.* Boston: Houghton Mifflin.

Terman, L. M., et al. (1925). *Genetic studies of genius: Vol. 1. Mental and physical traits of a thousand gifted children.* Stanford, CA: Stanford University Press.

Terman, L. M., et al. (1938). *Psychological factors in marital happiness.* New York: McGraw-Hill.

Thurstone, L. L. (1952). L. L. Thurstone. In E. G. Boring, H. S. Langfeld, H. Werner, & R. M. Yerkes (Eds.), *A history of psychology in autobiography* (pp. 295–321). Worcester, MA: Clark University Press.

Ursano, R. J., Fullerton, C. S., & Norwood, A. E. (Eds.). (2003). *Terrorism and disaster: Individual and community mental health interventions.* New York: Cambridge University Press.

U.S. Office of Personnel Management. *Alternate dispute resolution resource guide. U.S. Office of Personnel Management.* Retrieved July 19, 2007, from http://www.opm.gov/er/adrguide

Van der Kolk, B. A. (1990). The psychological processing of traumatic events: The personal experience of posttraumatic stress disorder. In J. T. Reese, J. M. Horn, & C. Dunning (Eds.), *Critical incidents in policing* (pp. 359–364). Washington, DC: Government Printing Office.

Violanti, J. M. (1990). *Posttrauma vulnerability: A proposed model.* In J. T. Reese, J. M. Horn, & C. Dunning (Eds.), *Critical incidents in policing* (pp. 365–372). Washington, DC: U.S. Government Printing Office.

Violanti, J. M. (1995). The mystery within: Understanding police suicides. *FBI Law Enforcement Bulletin,* 19–23.

Violanti, J. M., Marshall, J. R., & Howe, B. (1985). Stress coping and alcohol use: The police connection. *Journal of Police Science and Administration, 12*(2), 106–110.

Wambaugh, J. (1973). *The onion field.* New York: Delacort.

Wambaugh, J. (1987). *Echoes in the darkness.* New York: Delacort.

Wechsler, D. (1939). *The measurement of adult intelligence.* Baltimore: Williams & Wilkins.

Weiss, P. A. (2002). Potential uses of the Rorschach in the selection of police officers. *Journal of Police and Criminal Psychology, 17*(2), 63–70.

Weiss, P. A., Weiss, W. U., & Gacono, C. B. (2008). The use of the Rorschach in police psychology: Some preliminary thoughts. In C. B. Gacono & F. B. Evans (Eds.), *Handbook of forensic Rorschach assessment* (pp. 527–542). New York: Routledge.

Weiss, W., Zehner, S. N., Davis, R. D., & Rostow, C. D. (2005). Problematic police performance and the Personality Assessment Inventory. *Journal of Police and Criminal Psychology, 20*(1), 16–21.

Weiss, W. U., Buehler, K., & Yates, D. (1996). The psychopathic deviate scale of the MMPI in police selection. *Journal of Police and Criminal Psychology, 10*(4), 57–60.

Weiss, W. U., Davis, R., Rostow, C., & Kinsman, S. (2003). The MMPI-2 L scale as a tool in police selection. *Journal of Police and Criminal Psychology, 18*(1), 57–60.

Weiss, W., Rostow, C. D., & Davis, R. D. (2004). The Personality Assessment Inventory as a selection device for law enforcement personnel. *Journal of Police and Criminal Psychology, 19*(2), 23–29.

Weiss, W. U., Serafino, G., Serafino, A., Wilson, W., & Knoll, S. (1998). Performance ratings of recently hired police officers. *Journal of Police and Criminal Psychology, 13*(1), 40–44.

White, M. (1989). *Saying hullo again: The incorporation of the lost relationship in the resolution of grief* (Selected papers, pp. 29–36). Adelaide, Australia: Dulwich Centre Publications.

White, M., & Epston, D. (1990). *Narrative means to therapeutic ends.* New York: Norton.

Wilson, J. P. (1995). The historical evolution of PTSD diagnostic criteria. In G. S. Everly (Ed.), *Psychotraumatology* (pp. 9–26). New York: Plenum.

Wollman, D. (1993). Critical incident stress debriefing and crisis groups: A review of the literature. *Group, 17*(2), 70–83.

Wonderlic. (2010). *Wonderlic human resource solutions: Our history.* Retrieved August 8, 2010, from http://www.wonderlic.com/hiring-solutions/about-us.aspx

Wygant, D. B., et al. (2007). The relation between symptom validity testing and MMPI-2 scores as a function of forensic evaluation context. *Archives of Clinical Neuropsychology, 22,* 488–499.

Yassen, J. (1995). Preventing secondary traumatic stress disorder. In C. Figley (Ed.), *Compassion fatigue: Coping with secondary traumatic stress* (pp. 178–208). New York: Brunner Mazel.
Young, M. (1991). *Community crisis response team training manual.* Washington, DC: National Organization for Victim Assistance.
Zacker, J. (1997). Rorschach responses of police applicants. *Psychological Reports, 80*, 523–528.

CASES CONSULTED

Bonsignore v. City of New York, 521F. Supp. 394, affirmed 683 F.2d 635 (2nd Cir. 1982).
Cannice v. Norwest Bank Iowa N.A., 189 F. 3d 723 (1999).
City of Greenwood v. Dowler, 492 NE.2d 1081 (Ind. App. 1986).
Colon v. Colon, 2006 WL 2318250 (App. Div. 2006).
Conte v. Harcher, 365 N.E. 2d.257 (Ill. App. 1977).
Davis v. Hennepin County, 559 N.W. 2d 117 (MN App. 1997).
Deen v. Darosa, #4-2072, 414F.rd, 731 (2005).
Denhof v. City of Grand Rapids, 494 F.3d 534,57 n.4 (16th Cir. 2007).
Flynn v. Sandahl, 58 F.3d 283 (7th Cir. 1995).
Garrity v. New Jersey, 385 U.S. 493 (1987).
Geidel v. City Bradenton Beach, 56 F. Supp. 2d 1359 (M.D. FL. 1999).
Guice-Mills v. Derwinski, 987 F.2d 794,797 (2nd. Cir. 1992).
Hardy Town of Hayneville, 50 Supp. 2d 1176 (M.D. Ala. 1999).
Hild v. Bruner, 496 F. Supp. 93 (G=D.N.J. 1980).
Holst v. Veterans Affairs, #2008-3012, 2008 U.S. App. Lexis 22998 (Unpub. Fed Cir. 2008).
Jackson v. Lake County, 790 N.E.2d. 448,451 (Ind. 2003).
Kraft v. Police Commissioner of Boston, 417 Mass. 235 at 242, 629 NE.2d. 995 at 999 (1994).
Larson v. Koch Refining Co., 11 S.W. 3d 158 (Texas, 1997).
McKnight v. Monroe Co. Sheriff's Dept., #IP00-1880-C-B, U.S. Dist. Lexis 18148 (2002).
Miller v. City of Springfield, 146 F.3d 612 (1998).
National Treasury Employees Union v. Von Raab, 385 U.S.493 (1989).
Policemen's Benevolent Association of New Jersey v. Township of Washington, D.N.J. No. 86-3525 (October 19, 1988).
PBA L-319 v. Township of Plainsboro, #C-173-98 Middlesex Co. (NJ Superior Court Unreported 1998).
Richardson v. City of Pasadena, 175 Cal. 3666 (1973-1974).
Risner v. U.S. Department of Transportation, 677 F.2d 36 (8th Cir. 1982).
Sehie v. City of Aurora, 432 F.3d 749 (7th Cir. 2005).
Tingler v. City of Tampa, 400 So. Sd,146, 149-150 (Fla. App. 1981).
Watson v. City of Miami Beach, 177 F.3d 932 (11th Cir. 1999).

Part I

General Practice

2 Police-Specific Psychological Services
Using Behavioral Scientists as Consultants to Public Safety

Joseph A. Davis

POLICE PSYCHOLOGICAL SERVICES

Behavioral scientists, specifically police psychologists, play an integral role in law enforcement today. Large metropolitan law enforcement agencies like the Dallas, Boston, and Los Angeles Police Departments staff behavioral scientists in the capacity of police psychologists and organizational development and human factors/human performance consultants (Davis, 1995; Reiser, 1972a). Many behavioral scientists who possess specialized training beyond their traditional clinical training can effectively assist law enforcement management and various other personnel, such as directors of police training academies, to enhance their day-to-day operations and performances of each department and staff member.

The scope in which police psychologists or behavioral scientists are used in modern law enforcement departments today is diverse. Consultations often range from individual to group consultation, officer candidate assessment and evaluation, police officer selection, hostage negotiation, stress management, and the counseling of police officers and their families (Davis, 1993; Depue, 1979; Reiser, 1972b). Additionally, consultations include police management and supervisory training; police academy teaching and instruction; research and development; police or community critical incident debriefing; urban crime prevention programs; advanced officer training; and diagnosing and solving organizational, managerial, or supervisory problems. Furthermore, implementing the use of employee assistance programs (EAPs), and burn-out prevention programs are fundamentally sound policies, procedures, and administrative decisions in terms of planning for the department's overall future growth and for the wellness of its personnel who operate within it (Hargrave & Berner, 1984).

Typically, police psychologists work with departments in one of two ways: They provide services, consultation, and training as an "in-house" service, that is, as an actual department staff member, or as an outside consultant who provides services under contract departmentwide. There are advantages as well as limitations to both; however, both arrangements have merit and should be set up according to agency size, number of personnel, specialized needs, and budgets of each department and division. Regardless of the arrangement, police psychologists should generally be connected to the highest level of the department's administrative and managerial structure and, if possible, as close in proximity to the chief of police as possible for the purposes of "direct line" consultation and communication (Lefkowitz, 1977).

The issue of confidentiality also has its place in the police psychologist's office when working with sworn or support personnel, especially when services such as psychotherapy, counseling, assessment, fitness-for-duty evaluation, and research are conducted (Davis, 1993). Depending on the issue or referral question, range of confidentiality can be complete, limited, restricted, or open and upfront, which is told to the officer or employee seeking or being referred for psychological services once contact with a supervisor or commanding officer is made. An example of a nonrestrictive disclosure or breach of confidentiality is when a question of officer dangerousness or an issue involving fitness for duty is of major concern (Davis, 1995; Reiser, 1972b; Somodeville, 1978).

Victimization, misuse, or abuse of police powers or officer misconduct is an area typically open and upfront in terms of disclosure that is not protected by confidentiality. Areas of confidentiality include when (1) the direct counseling and treatment of officers, their families, and various civilian personnel for job-related problems are the issue; and when (2) a critical consideration is given to privileged communications between the police psychologist, the employee, and a third party such as a supervisor or family member (Davis, 1993).

When possible, if the police psychologist is a contract provider, the office should be at a location physically outside the department to ensure confidentiality and officer comfort. If the police psychologist is an "in-house" service provider, a department representative, or an extension of the department, an office should be made available geographically within the premises that is secluded enough to promote utilization of services, confidentiality, and employee receptability (Reiser, 1972b; Somodeville, 1978).

In a unique "forensic" role utilized by some departments, the expertise of the police psychologist can play an important part as an objective scientist in major case consultation or when a crime investigation is underway, especially when the crime committed by a perpetrator or offender is a "stranger-to-stranger" crime; in cases where the crime seemed senseless, sexually sadistic, and motiveless; or when the perpetrator is unknown and cannot be identified (Davis, 1995).

Requests may come from specific investigative units within the department such as the homicide unit, sex crimes unit, or "violent crimes committed against persons" division for the purposes of "criminal investigative analysis" or "criminal-psychological personality profiling." Crime scene analysis, criminal investigative analysis, or what is often referred to as "profiling" is derived by carefully detailing the crime scene area identified by officers, detectives, coroners, medical examiners, criminalists, forensic scientists, and evidence technicians (Davis, 1993; Geberth, 1981). Along with talking to forensic crime scene photographers and by examining crime scene or victim photographs afterward, the police psychologist (especially when trained in the forensic sciences) can give many investigators sound, objective scientific support when evaluating and examining the critical elements connecting physical, mental, or circumstantial evidence during intense crime scene analysis. A profile generated at times can yield important psychological, forensic, and behavioral data or associated variables as to the offender's *modus operandi* (method of operation, or M.O.) and so-called individual *signature* in terms of *antecedent criminal behavior,* or how the individual organized and showed planning (or lack of it) for, carried out, and staged a crime, and possibly even selected the victim in some cases (Davis, 1993; Geberth, 1981).

Typically, the criminal does not commit certain types of crimes such as sexually motivated homicide overnight. These types of crimes evolve over time and can involve an organized offender type that plans a very methodical approach to victim selection and abduction such as was seen in the Ted Bundy case. Conversely, a disorganized offender type can carry out the same crime or similar crimes without such meticulous and methodical approaches to detail and victim selection such as was seen in the Richard Trenton Chase case (Davis, 1995). To complicate matters even more, the offender can possess both organized and disorganized approaches to committing violent crimes, suggesting and presenting a mixed offender type to investigators or profilers. It must be recognized even by the most experienced investigator that a criminal's M.O. can change from one crime to the next; however, the same criminal's "signature" will remain unchanged and always consistent (Cooke, 1980; Davis, 1994; Geberth, 1981). Additionally, in terms of a homicide case, the crime scene can yield significant clues regarding pre– and post–crime scene behavior as to whether the perpetrator was an organized, mixed, or otherwise disorganized type of offender, and whether injuries or sexual and physical assaults sustained to the victim's body were inflicted ante mortem (when the victim was alive) or post mortem (after the victim was already dead).

The crime scene, along with additional inspection at the "morgue scene," typically held at the coroner or medical examiner's office (some states have either a dedicated medical examiner or coroner system; however, California has a system designated by county jurisdiction as either a ME or coroner system; for example, San Diego County has a ME system and Los Angeles County has a coroner system), can also render information regarding the degree and type of violence exerted by the criminal toward the victim, especially when examining the various types of trauma inflicted to the victim such as blunt force, sharp force, asphyxia, "tight" contact, or close-range gunshot wounds (Davis, 1994; Geberth, 1981).

Many crimes have motives; however, some crimes can appear senseless or even motiveless. Evidence of sadistic torture, trauma to the face or personal areas, binding of the victim's hands and feet (ligature), the type of binding used (duct tape, rope, wire, electrical cord), disposition of the body, location of the body (i.e., in an open area or secluded area, hidden or covered, and buried or dumped in a culvert or alongside a highway or back road), along with specialized positioning of the body (undressed, dressed, in a provocative pose, or otherwise) can all reveal the killer's organization (or lack thereof), planning, and thought processes before, during, and after the act of violence was committed. Police psychologists trained in criminal investigative analyses on psychological profiling can also give evidence of *connecting* elements of the crime as well as the signature and profile of whoever carried out the heinous act of violence, no matter how organized, disorganized, sexually sadistic, or ritualistic, will in most cases typically surface (Cooke, 1980; Davis, 1994).

In addition to providing and supporting investigators with valuable antecedent criminal profile information and data, the police psychologist can be a valuable asset to the department directly when the community or even police personnel have witnessed an act of violence, a crime, or a tragedy so bizarre, unusual, brutal, or heinous that critical incident debriefing or consultation and subsequent counseling for post-traumatic stress disorder (PTSD) occur. An example would be the unforgettable massacre and mass homicide of 21 innocent and unsuspecting men, women, and children (the youngest victim was 8 months old) involving James Oliver Huberty that occurred at a McDonald's restaurant in San Ysidro, California, in July 1984. Included here would also be the mass homicide of 23 victims, October 16, 1991 at Luby's Cafeteria in Killeen, Texas, by solo gunman George "Jo Jo" Hennard. His murderous actions at the time remained the largest single incident of mass homicide in the United States until the Virginia Tech mass murder on April 16, 2007 by undergraduate student Seung-Hui Cho, or the brutal serial homicides in 1990 that effectively terrified the residential suburbs of Clairemont and University City areas of San Diego and took the lives of six women, one of which was this author's former student (Davis, 1995).

The San Diego Police Department (SDPD) and Homicide Division received thousands of calls and more than 1,100 leads or tips from the public regarding the six San Diego murder cases. Top police administrators and supervisors subsequently assigned 44 investigators to the case, which eventually turned out to be the largest serial murder manhunt in San Diego Police Department history. The FBI was also involved in the case from a psychological profiling standpoint. Other examples where critical incident debriefing can be useful are when the abduction and murder of a local child is discovered, such as the Laura Arroyo child murder case in Chula Vista, California, a suburb in San Diego County, or in the death following a shooting of a fellow officer or partner in the line of duty such as the one that took the life of SDPD Patrol Officer Ron Davis. Still other countless examples can be cited such as when a bomb explosion occurs and both police and civilians are killed (Davis, 1993).

Other examples include the death of a hostage or hostages during negotiating, or in a man-made disaster such as the PSA Flight 182 air traffic fatality in 1978 in the North Park suburb area of San Diego where approximately 160 victims died traumatically. Yet other examples are the Pan Am 103 disaster over Lockerbie, Scotland in 1988 where 270 people died, or the USAir Flight 427 where 132 died in 1994. Finally, let's never forget the tragedies and lessons that the Oklahoma City bombing in 1995 or the World Trade Center event in 2001 left behind. Of the 144 PSA victims, 4 were never identified even though dental identification teams utilizing forensic odontology (dentistry) were used. The PSA 182 flight utilized the FBI's Disaster Identification Squad, and hundreds of police, medical, fire, and civilian personnel took weeks to identify bodies from the wreckage and carnage. The identification teams worked 12-hour days. Many of the bodies and remaining carnage were beyond conventional identification and could only be identified by specialized forensic techniques used by highly trained forensic dentists. The plane crash of Reba McEntyre's country and western band also required similar action from forensic and law enforcement personnel. In similar fashion, the State of Pennsylvania mobilized its Dental Identification Team (PADIT) to work the USAir Flight 427 crash. Overall, the police psychologist or behavioral-forensic scientist can effectively provide information and feedback to the chief of police, police public relations officer, or crime prevention specialists in times when a call to action is in order by citizens of the community, especially when an increase in residential burglary takes place or when a series of violent personal crimes occur such as serial rape in the immediate area (Davis, 1993; Depue, 1979; Reiser, 1972b).

In times of public outcry or citizen unrest, a police psychologist can be of valuable assistance. Supporting the chief of police or sheriff as an organizational and human factors advisor, the psychologist or behavioral scientists can effectively establish or chair a task force to evaluate specific problems facing police and the community (Davis, 1993; Lefkowitz, 1977; Reiser, 1972b). In general, integrating the expertise and support of behavioral scientists or police psychologists into the structure and daily operation of the police department as service, management, and supervisory personnel can ensure the maintenance of productive functioning; the quality of the day-by-day performances of their sworn and nonsworn personnel; and the overall wellness, mental health, and effectiveness of their entire organization (Reiser, 1972b).

Large metropolitan police departments utilize police psychologists and behavioral-forensic scientists in various roles, especially in the areas of counseling, psychotherapy, training, critical incident stress debriefings, consultation, and research. Each department uses police psychologists differently depending on department need. The use of police psychologists has proven to be an extremely valuable asset and is cost-effective (Davis, 1993).

Overall, the services provided by the behavioral sciences or psychological services division of any police department or law enforcement agency can ultimately prove to be an excellent police management decision in terms of the overall welfare, function, wellness, happiness, and future of the department, focusing on its key sworn, nonsworn, and support personnel (Davis, 1995; Depue, 1979; Lefkowitz, 1977; Reiser, 1972b; Somodeville, 1978).

The time has come when law enforcement departments can no longer afford *not* to borrow the expertise from the behavioral and forensic sciences (Davis, 1993).

REFERENCES

Cooke, G. (1980). *The role of the forensic psychologist.* Springfield, IL: Charles C Thomas.
Davis, J. A. (1993, January). The use of behavioral scientists in law enforcement. *The Law Enforcement Quarterly,* 20–28.
Davis, J. A. (1994). *The art and science of psychological profiling: Selected readings in forensic profile analysis.* Course Workshop Training Manual, San Diego, California.
Davis, J. A. (1995). The police psychologist in today's law enforcement. *The Police Chief Magazine, 62*(11), 36–38.
Depue, R. (1979). Turning inward: The police counselor. *FBI Law Enforcement Bulletin,* 8–12.
Geberth, V. (1981). Psychological profiling. *Law and Order,* 46–52.
Hargrave, G. E., & Berner, J. G. (1984). *POST psychological screening manual.* Sacramento: California Commission on Police Officers Standards and Training.
Lefkowitz, J. (1977). Industrial-organizational psychology and the police. *American Psychologist, 32,* 346–364.
Reiser, M. (1972a). *The police department psychologist.* Springfield, IL: Charles C Thomas.
Reiser, M. (1972b). *Practical psychology for police officers.* Springfield, IL: Charles C Thomas.
Somodeville, S. (1978). The psychologist's role in the police department. *The Police Chief,* 21–23.

3 Legal Issues in Hiring and Promotion of Police Officers

Arthur Gutman

INTRODUCTION

Allegations of discrimination against police departments span a variety of issues, including refusal to hire minorities and females (i.e., facial discrimination), adverse impact of facially neutral selection criteria on minorities (e.g., cognitive tests) and females (e.g., physical requirements), racial and sexual harassment, diversity as a compelling government interest under the 14th Amendment of the Constitution, age limits for hiring and forced retirement of police officers, illegal medical and psychological inquiries prior to a conditional job offer, and more. Comprehensive coverage of these and related issues is provided by Gutman, Koppes, and Vodanovich (2010). The main focus of this chapter is on what is arguably the most important issue facing police forces today: adverse impact in hiring and promotion related to tests and other selection criteria on minorities and, to some extent, females.

As a starting point, adverse impact based on race, sex, religion, or national origin is uniquely associated with Title VII of the Civil Rights Act of 1964 (or simply Title VII).* There are three phases in the Title VII adverse impact judicial scenario. As depicted in Table 3.1, the plaintiff must identify a selection practice that disproportionately excludes one group (e.g., African Americans) relative to another group (e.g., Caucasians) in Phase 1. If the plaintiff succeeds, the defendant must prove that the challenged practice is job related and consistent with business necessity in Phase 2. Then, if the defendant succeeds, the plaintiff must prove that there is an equally valid alternative practice that produces less or no adverse impact in Phase 3.

In general, the most frequent method for assessing knowledge, skills, and abilities (or KSAs) related to police work are written multiple-choice tests because they can be administered to large groups and are easy to score. However, there are other methods of assessing these KSAs, including oral interviews, situational judgment tests, and assessment center methodology, to name a few. These other methods are often used in conjunction with written tests. Indeed, a common claim in adverse impact cases is that nonwritten tests, or different weightings among written versus nonwritten components, are as valid as the actual method(s) used. The discussion below treats all methods of assessing KSAs as a "test" subject to adverse impact analyses.

An additional point to note is that there are common issues relating to hiring and promotion of police officers as there are with firefighters. Although the focus of this chapter is on police hiring and promotion, firefighter cases will be discussed when relevant to police issues. For example, as we will witness below, the U.S. Supreme Court's 2009 ruling in *Ricci v. DeStefano* relates to promotion of firefighters. Nevertheless, this ruling has equally important implications for police departments and other entities as well.

There are six sections below. The first section reviews major Supreme Court rulings on adverse impact between 1971 and 1989, and the second section reviews early lower court rulings that were

---

* Adverse impact is also a valid claim in the Age Discrimination in Employment Act of 1967 (ADEA) based on Supreme Court rulings in *Smith v. City of Jackson* (2005) and *Meacham v. KAPL* (2008). However, the rules for deciding ADEA cases are dramatically different as compared to those for Title VII cases.

TABLE 3.1
The Title VII Adverse Impact Judicial Scenario

Phase 1   Prima facie phase requiring statistical evidence that an identified employment practice disproportionately
           excludes protected group members
Phase 2   Defense phase requiring proof that the challenged practice is job related and consistent with business necessity
Phase 3   Pretext phase requiring proof there is an alternative equally valid practice (or practices) that are equally job
           related, but that produce less or no adverse impact

based on early Supreme Court rulings. The third section features more recent rulings on cutoff scores and related issues, the fourth section features methods of reducing or eliminating adverse impact, the fifth section focuses on the Supreme Court's recent ruling in *Ricci v. DeStefano* (2009), and the sixth section offers conclusions and recommendations.

OVERVIEW OF SUPREME COURT ADVERSE IMPACT RULINGS

Table 3.2 depicts nine landmark Supreme Court rulings between 1971 (*Griggs v. Duke Power*) and 2009 (*Ricci v. DeStefano*). Five of the nine cases feature objectively scored written tests, and four of them feature other causes of adverse impact. These topics will be discussed in turn immediately below. For purposes of exposition, *Ricci v. DeStefano* (2009) will be reserved for discussion in the fifth section of this chapter.

ADVERSE IMPACT AND WRITTEN TESTS

Early precedents for written tests were established in *Griggs v. Duke Power* (1971) and *Albemarle v. Moody* (1975), and the principal rulings in these two cases served as the basis for the *Uniform Guidelines on Employee Selection Procedures* (UGESP) in 1978. *Washington v. Davis* (1976),

TABLE 3.2
Landmark Supreme Court Adverse Impact Rulings

Challenges to Written Exams	
Griggs v. Duke Power (**1971**)	Challenge to use of cognitive tests and high school diploma for upper-level coal-mining jobs in a private company
Albemarle v. Moody (**1975**)	Challenge to use of cognitive tests and high school diploma for entry-level paper mill jobs in a private company
Washington v. Davis (**1976**)	Challenge to civil service exam for entry-level jobs in the Washington, D.C., police force
Connecticut v. Teal (**1982**)	Challenge to first hurdle (a written test) in a multiple-hurdle selection procedure for state administrator jobs
Ricci v. DeStefano (**2009**)	Challenge to discarding promotion exams in a fire department after they were administered and scored
Challenges to Other Selection Criteria	
Dothard v. Rawlinson (**1977**)	Challenge to height and weight requirements for prison guards in an all-male maximum security prison
NYC v. Beazer (**1979**)	Challenge to policy of excluding methadone users for entry-level transit authority police officers
Watson v. Fort Worth Bank (**1988**)	Challenge to subjective selection procedures in promotion of bank tellers
Wards Cove v. Atonio (**1989**)	Challenge to disproportionate exclusion of Eskimos and Filipinos from higher-level jobs in a fish packing company

the first Supreme Court adverse impact ruling involving police officers, addressed the question of whether adverse impact is a valid claim under the 5th or 14th Amendments of the Constitution. *Connecticut v. Teal* (1982), the first Supreme Court Title VII claim against a government agency, addressed the question of whether a Phase 2 defense to adverse impact is required for individual steps in a multiple-hurdle selection procedure when there is no bottom-line adverse impact for the total selection process.

The *Griggs* and *Albemarle* Rulings

Griggs and *Albemarle* featured private sector employers that used cognitive tests and a high school diploma requirement in their selection process. The facts in *Griggs* were that prior to Title VII, Duke Power facially excluded African Americans from upper-level jobs. The company then initiated the testing and diploma requirements for these upper-level jobs on July 2, 1965, the very day that Title VII took effect. The prima facie case featured statistical evidence that the cognitive tests excluded 94% of African American applicants as compared to only 42% of Caucasian applicants. Additionally, the high school diploma requirement was deemed to disproportionately "chill" prospective African American applicants because the graduation rate in North Carolina at that time was 34% for Caucasians as compared to only 12% for African Americans.

Speaking for a unanimous Supreme Court, Justice Burger ruled that Title VII covers the "consequences of employment practices, not simply the motivation" of employers. He then wrote what arguably are the two most important phrases in adverse impact case law: that if the plaintiff proves adverse impact, the defendant must prove there is a *manifest relationship* between the challenged practice and the *employment in question*. There was no evidence to prove the cognitive tests and high school diploma were job related, and Duke Power lost the case.

Aware of the *Griggs* ruling, the Albemarle Paper Company tried to prove that their cognitive tests were significantly and positively correlated with job performance (i.e., using a criterion validity study). However, it was a poor study conducted a month prior to the trial. The Supreme Court struck down the study on four grounds: (1) a lack of quality, or "odd patchwork"; (2) unknown job-performance criteria and subjective supervisory rankings; (3) a focus on high-level jobs rather than the "entering low-level jobs" at issue; and (4) a validation sample that included only "job-experienced white workers." Relying on the then applicable 1970 *Guidelines on Employee Selection Procedures* by the Equal Employment Opportunity Commission (EEOC), the Supreme Court defined how a manifest relationship should be proven. Accordingly:

> The message of these Guidelines is the same as that of the Griggs case—that discriminatory tests are impermissible unless shown, by *professionally acceptable methods*[,] to be predictive of or significantly correlated with important elements of work behavior which comprise or are relevant to the job or jobs for which candidates are evaluated. [emphasis by author]

The *Albemarle* Court then created the third phase of the adverse impact scenario, permitting proof of equally valid alternatives with less or no adverse impact.

The Immediate Aftermath of *Griggs* and *Albemarle*

The *Griggs* and *Albemarle* rulings were then codified into regulatory law in the UGESP in 1978. The UGESP are still the most important regulatory authority used by courts in adverse impact cases. However, as noted by several authors,* the UGESP were based primarily on the first edition of the *Standards for Educational and Psychological Testing* (or Standards) (1974), and therefore are now outdated. Critically, this was anticipated, and is reflected in Section 1607.5(A) of the UGESP, which states, "New strategies for showing the validity of selection procedures will be evaluated as they become accepted by the psychological profession."

---

* See, for example, Landy (1986) and Binning and Barrett (1989).

As expected, new strategies in validity research have been developed since 1978, as documented in the fifth edition of the Standards (1999) and the fourth edition of the *Principles for the Validation and Use of Personnel Selection Procedures* (or Principles) published by the Society for Industrial and Organization Psychology (SIOP) (2003). Courts have cited both of these authorities with increasing frequency in recent years. Therefore, test developers and consumers should be equally as familiar with the Standards and Principles as they are with the UGESP.*

The *Davis* and *Teal* Rulings

Prior to 1972, Title VII covered only private entities. Coverage of public entities was added in the Equal Employment Act of 1972 (or EEO-72). Consequently, for the plaintiffs in *Washington v. Davis* (1976), the 5th Amendment was the only basis for challenging Civil Service Test 21, a verbal skills test first used in 1970 by the Washington, D.C., Police Department for entry-level police jobs. The Supreme Court ruled that adverse impact is *not* a valid claim under the 5th Amendment, or other Constitutional amendments.[†] Nevertheless, the Supreme Court evaluated Test 21 and ruled it was valid because it (1) measured minimum skills necessary for completing police training school, and (2) criterion validity was established with proof that scores on Test 21 were significantly and positively correlated with scores on written exams given during police training. Also of interest, a high school diploma requirement, deemed invalid for coal-mining and paper mill jobs in the *Griggs* and *Albemarle* cases, was deemed valid for police officer jobs in the *Washington v. Davis* case.

In *Connecticut v. Teal* (1982), a written test was the first of several hurdles for promotion. After all hurdles were completed, the promotion rate was higher for African Americans (22.9%) than Caucasians (13.5%). However, there was adverse impact for African Americans on the first hurdle. In its defense, the State of Connecticut relied on a provision in Section 1607.4(C) of the UGESP relating to adverse impact of the "total selection process":

> If...the *total selection process does not have an adverse impact, the [EEOC]...will not expect a user to evaluate the individual components for adverse impact*, or to validate such individual components, and will not take enforcement action based upon adverse impact in any component of that process. [emphasis by author]

Rejecting this guidance in a closely divided 5–4 ruling, the Supreme Court favored the plaintiffs on grounds that "Congress never intended to give an employer license to discriminate against some employees on the basis of race or sex merely because he favorably treats other members of the employee's group." This remains a critical ruling for police departments because multiple selection criteria are often used in both entry-level and promotion processes.

Adverse Impact and Other Selection Practices

Among the four cases in Table 3.2 featuring causes of adverse impact other than written tests, *Dothard v. Rawlinson* (1977) addressed height and weight requirements for prison guards, and *New York City v. Beazer* (1979) addressed exclusion of transit authority police officers based on past methadone use. The other two cases, *Watson v. Fort Worth Bank* (1988) and *Wards Cove Packing Co. v. Atonio* (1989), addressed subjective cause of adverse impact. As important, *Watson* and *Wards Cove* were closely connected to each other and led to a temporary alteration of the Phase 2 defense to adverse impact that was subsequently resolved in the Civil Rights Act of 1991 (or CRA-91).

---

* Readers interested in test validation developments are referred to a comprehensive discussion of the UGESP, Standards, and Principles by Jeanneret (2005).

† The Supreme Court subsequently ruled that adverse impact is not a valid claim under the Equal Protection Clause of the 14th Amendment in *Arlington Heights v. Metropolitan Housing Corp.* (1977) and *Personnel Administrator v. Feeney* (1979).

The *Dothard* and *Beazer* Rulings

In *Dothard v. Rawlinson* (1977), minimum height and weight criteria for selection of prison guards adversely impacted female applicants. The State of Alabama argued that these criteria were indicators of strength, an important job-related KSA. However, the Supreme Court struck down the requirement, ruling, "If the job-related quality that the appellants identify is bona fide, their purpose could be achieved by adopting and validating a test for applicants that measures strength directly."[*]

The *Dothard* ruling has directly affected police departments. For example, in *Horace v. Pontiac* (1980), featuring a height requirement, the city of Pontiac, Michigan, asserted, among other things, that taller police officers meet "less resistance" and gain "greater respect ... from the general public." However, the 6th Circuit ruled that "there were acceptable alternative policies which would have accomplished the desired purposes other than the obviously arbitrary 5′ 8″ height standard." Based on *Dothard*, municipalities, including the city of Pontiac, subsequently turned to other selection criteria to assess strength and agility.

In *New York City v. Beazer* (1979), the Supreme Court supported exclusion of methadone users from employment as transit authority officers because it is "obvious" that drug addiction threatens the "legitimate employment goals of safety and efficiency." Coupled with earlier lower court rulings involving public safety concerns (e.g., *Spurlock v. United Airlines*, 1972), the *Beazer* ruling made it easier for police departments to defend minimum requirements relating to educational requirements, driving records, and prior drug convictions.

For example, in *Davis v. Dallas* (1985), the 5th Circuit found it was necessary for the Dallas police department to exclude recent drug users from police work on grounds that recent drug use shows a disregard for the law. Additionally, exclusion based on poor driving records was supported based on research indicating that past driving habits predict future driving habits, and a requirement of 45 college credits with C or better grades was supported based on federal commission reports in the 1960s that "a high school education is a bare minimum requirement for successful performance of the policeman's responsibilities."

The *Watson* and *Wards Cove* Rulings

In *Watson v. Fort Worth Bank* (1988), an African American woman was passed over for promotion four times, each time in favor of a Caucasian applicant, and each time based on subjective ratings by Caucasian supervisors of (1) job performance, (2) interview performance, and (3) past experience. It was not clear how these ratings were scored or combined, but there was clearly "bottom-line" adverse impact for the "total selection process." Only eight justices heard this case, and they unanimously agreed that adverse impact based on subjective selection criteria is a valid claim.[†] However, speaking for herself and three other justices, Justice O'Connor proposed changes in the adverse impact scenario. The most important proposal was to weaken the defense burden in Phase 2 so that the defendant need only articulate (or explain) a legitimate business reason for the challenged practices, instead having to prove that they are job related.[‡]

In *Wards Cove v. Atonio* (1989), two Pacific Northwest salmon packing companies had a hiring-hall arrangement for selection of unskilled salmon packers, but used word-of-mouth to hire workers

---

[*] Interestingly, although the State of Alabama could not defend on height and weight criteria in the adverse impact challenge, it succeeded with a BFOQ (Bona Fide Occupational Qualification) defense in excluding all females on grounds that 20% of the population were sex offenders, and it was reasonably necessary to exclude all females because of potential danger to the prison environment.

[†] At the time, Anthony Kennedy's nomination to the Supreme Court was affirmed, but he was not yet seated for the *Watson* case.

[‡] The burden to articulate (or explain) without having to prove is termed a burden of "production" and is characteristic of disparate treatment cases such as *McDonnell Douglas v. Green* (1973). It is generally easier to explain a legitimate business reason than to prove job relatedness. These are complex issues, and the reader is referred to a more comprehensive discussion of these issues by Gutman et al. (2010).

for more skilled positions. As a result, Eskimos and Filipinos were overrepresented in the unskilled jobs and underrepresented in the skilled jobs. It is arguable that *Wards Cove* was more of a pattern or practice case than it was an adverse impact case.* More important for present purposes, with the addition of Anthony Kennedy to the Supreme Court, there was now a majority of five justices that turned O'Connor's proposal in the *Watson* case into case law.

The Aftermath of *Wards Cove*

Congress attempted to overturn *Wards Cove* (and five other 1989 Supreme Court rulings) in the Civil Rights Restoration Act of 1990 (CRRA-90). However, President George H. W. Bush vetoed CRRA-90, and his veto was nearly overridden. The main reason for the veto was failure by the Democrats and Republicans to agree on the Phase 2 defense burden in *Wards Cove*. Given the close call in CRRA-90, the two parties compromised in CRA-91, restoring the defense burden originally established in the *Griggs* and *Albemarle* cases so that if an identified practice is proven to cause adverse impact in Phase 1, the defendant must proved that the practice is "*job related and consistent with business necessity*" in Phase 2. Although seemingly a recovery of the original *Griggs* and *Albemarle* precedents, as we will witness later in this chapter, at least two circuit courts have parsed the phrases *job related* and *consistent with business necessity* so that more is needed than proof of test validity to establish cutoff scores.

EARLY LOWER COURT RULINGS ON ADVERSE IMPACT

The *Griggs* ruling was rendered prior to the extension of Title VII coverage to public entities in EEO-72. Having no other avenue for lawsuits prior to 1972, plaintiffs in municipal jobs challenged adverse impact via the Equal Protection Clause of the 14th Amendment. There were several lower court rulings in police and firefighter cases in which *Griggs* was affirmed under the 14th Amendment. Although the Supreme Court ultimately ruled that adverse impact is *not* a valid constitutional claim in *Washington v. Davis*, these pre-*Davis* rulings established important precedents for adverse impact challenges that influenced post-*Davis* Title VII rulings. Table 3.3 samples five pre-*Davis* 14th Amendment rulings and three post-*Davis* Title VII rulings.

Pre-*Davis* 14th Amendment Rulings

Among the pre-*Davis* rulings sampled in Table 3.3, two featured fire departments, two featured police departments, and one featured a correctional institution. All but one of these cases (*Kirkland*) originated prior to EEO-72. The circuit courts supported the plaintiff's 14th Amendment claims based on *Griggs* in each case.

Carter v. Gallagher (1971)

Carter v. Gallagher was the first post-*Griggs* 14th Amendment ruling. The plaintiffs argued that historical discriminatory practices in Minneapolis, Minnesota, created a nearly all-white fire department. Nested within this claim was an adverse impact charge focused on an entrance exam administered to 2,404 applicants over a 20-year period. Historically, Caucasians passed at rates varying from 40% to 64.7%. Although there were only 22 identifiable minority applicants over that period (six of whom passed), the district court trial judge ruled that minority applicants did "substantially less well" than Caucasians, and there were many minority applicants who took the exam

---

* For example, in *International Teamsters v. United States* (1977), a landmark pattern or practice case, African Americans and Hispanics were congregated in lower paying (short distance) bus-driving jobs and Caucasians were congregated in higher paying (longer distance) bus-driving jobs. Gutman et al. (2010) suggest that pattern or practice rules were also applicable to *Wards Cove*, because minorities were congregated in the salmon-packing jobs and Caucasians were congregated in the more professional jobs.

TABLE 3.3
Critical Lower Court Adverse Impact Rulings Between 1971 and 1980

Pre-Davis 14th Amendment Rulings	
Carter v. Gallagher (1971)	First 14th Amendment challenge to firefighter hiring exam; 8th Circuit upholds challenge, citing absence of job analysis data.
Castro v. Beecher (1972)	First 14th Amendment challenge to police hiring exam; 1st Circuit upholds challenge, citing failure to measure job-related KSAs.
Bridgeport Guardians v. Bridgeport CSC (1973)	14th Amendment challenge to police entry/promotion exams upheld by 2nd Circuit based on faulty test items.
Vulcan Society v. CSC of New York City (1973)	14th Amendment challenge to entry-level firefighter exam upheld by 2nd Circuit based on then applicable EEOC guidelines.
Kirkland v. New York State Correctional Services (1975)	14th Amendment challenge to civil service exam upheld by 2nd Circuit on "constitutionally acceptable grounds."
Post-Davis Title VII Rulings	
NAACP v. Seibels (1980)	Title VII challenge to entry-level police/firefighter exams upheld by 5th Circuit due to faulty criterion validity data.
Guardians v. CSC (1980)	Title VII challenge to entry-level police exam upheld, but important rules for content validity are established.
Gillespie v. Wisconsin (1985)	Title VII challenge to state administrator jobs is defeated based on rules established in *Guardians v. CSC*.

but could not be identified. The judge struck down the exam, saying, "No effort was ever made prior to the current examination period to analyze the fire fighter examinations to determine whether they were culturally biased or whether they were valid predictive instruments for use in selecting fire fighters."

The 8th Circuit affirmed this ruling, citing a passage from *Griggs* that states "what is required by Congress is the removal of artificial, arbitrary, and unnecessary barriers to employment when the barriers operate invidiously to discriminate on the basis of racial or other impermissible classification."

Castro v. Beecher (1972)

Castro v. Beecher was the first post-*Griggs* police case. The case featured a 100-item multiple-choice hiring test measuring word knowledge, numerical sequence, reading comprehension, reasoning, arithmetic, and analogy. The test had a passing score of 70, and the passing rate was 65% for Caucasians as compared to 25% for African Americans and 10% for Hispanics. The trial judge ruled that the passing score was arbitrary and the test's "emphasis on academic and verbal skills [had] little relation to a policeman's job." The judge also ruled:

> There is almost no effort to test the particular types of observation, memory, statement, and judgment which are useful in connection with the exercise of authority of all kinds, and which are necessary for policemen as guardians, administrators, witnesses, community counselors, social welfare aids, and representatives of a regime of law and order.

Consistent with the 8th Circuit ruling in *Gallagher*, the 1st Circuit supported the trial judge based on *Griggs*, ruling that a test that causes adverse impact must be "substantially related to job performance."

Bridgeport Guardians v. Bridgeport CSC (1973)

Bridgeport Guardians v. Bridgeport CSC featured challenges to written exams for hiring and promotion of police officers. The test was developed years earlier by a private company. The trial judge ruled that there was adverse impact for the hiring exam but not the promotion exam. The trial judge struck down the hiring exam based on *Griggs* and the 8th Circuit's ruling in *Beecher*, and the 2nd Circuit affirmed, ruling that the biggest problem with the hiring exam was that "many of the vocabulary and arithmetic questions [were] only superficially or peripherally related to police activity."

Vulcan Society v. CSC (1973)

Vulcan Society v. CSC featured a 100-item entry-level test for firefighters that was deemed flawed by the 2nd Circuit based on the EEOC's then applicable *Guidelines on Employee Selection Procedures*. Although there were other issues in this case,* the primary focus was on failure to establish *content validity* in accordance with the EEOC Guidelines. The 2nd Circuit ruled that the test was developed in an "unprofessional manner." Among the criticisms noted was that the CSC failed to do a job analysis, the test contained 20 items on civics-related issues that were deemed unrelated to firefighting, and the CSC eliminated a physical exam that was used in prior selection procedures. As we will witness shortly, the *Vulcan* ruling was a precursor to *Guardians v. Civil Service* (1980), in which the 2nd Circuit established important precedents for content validity.

Kirkland v. NY State Corrections (1975)

Kirkland v. NY State Corrections featured Test 34-944, used by the New York State Department of Civil Service for promotion of correctional officers to sergeant. There were 1,389 applicants across the state, and the passing rate was 30.8% for Caucasians as compared to 7.7% for African Americans and 12.5% for Hispanics. As in its prior rulings in the *Bridgeport Guardians* and *Vulcan* cases, the 2nd Circuit, citing *Griggs*, ruled:

> Proof in employment discrimination cases proceeds from effect to cause. Plaintiffs establish the racially disparate consequences of defendants' employment practices, and defendants must then justify such consequences on *constitutionally acceptable grounds*. [emphasis added]

Thus, the 2nd Circuit treated the Phase 2 defense outlined in *Griggs* as the "constitutionally acceptable grounds" for defending adverse impact.

POST-*DAVIS* TITLE VII RULINGS

Among the post-*Davis* cases featured in Table 3.3, *NAACP v. Seibels* (1980) established important precedents for criterion validity studies, and *Guardians v. CSC* (1980) and *Gillespie v. Wisconsin* (1985) established important precedents for content validity studies.

NAACP v. Seibels (1980)

In *NAACP v. Seibels*, written exams were used for entry-level police and firefighter jobs. The exams were correlated with three criteria, most notably training academy performance, for which there were positive and statistically significant correlation coefficients as in *Washington v. Davis*. However, the test in *Davis* was designed to measure *minimum skills* for succeeding in academy school, whereas the test in *Seibel* was used for strict rank for actual hiring decisions. The 5th Circuit struck down the *Davis* defense, ruling:

> We do not believe the Davis rationale can be extended, as the Board urges, to the general proposition that any test can be validated by showing a relationship to training. More specifically, we reject the Board's suggested extension of the Davis holding to this case, where the tests were *not used to ascertain the minimum skills necessary to complete job-relevant training, but rather were used to rank job applicants according to their test scores and to select only the highest test scorers for job placement.* [emphasis added]

---

* The CSC argued that content validity was unnecessary because their test predicted training school performance. However, there was no evidence of statistical correlations to prove the relationship, as there was subsequently in *Washington v. Davis* (1976).

As important for later cases, the correlations for the other two criteria (efficiency ratings and experimental ratings) were either mixed (i.e., both positive and negative correlations) or not statistically significant. Critically, one of the tests (10-C for firefighters) was rejected even though the correlation was positive (+.21) and statistically significant because it lacked *practical significance*. Accordingly:

> With respect to the 10-C test, the court found that there is a statistically significant correlation between test scores and experimental ratings, *but that the correlation is of very low magnitude and lacks practical significance.* [emphasis added]

Other courts have since affirmed the need for practical significance in criterion validity studies, requiring, in many cases, correlation coefficients of +.30 or higher.[*]

Guardians v. Civil Service Commission (CSC) (1980)

Guardians v. CSC was a landmark case that addressed content validity as a basis for strict rank ordering and cutoff scores. In-house personnel in the New York City CSC developed an entry-level police test, and based on test scores, applicants were rank ordered, and a passing score sufficient to generate the required number of potential trainees was established. The plaintiffs challenged content validity as a basis for rank ordering, as well as the cutoff score chosen. The fact that the test was developed in-house ultimately worked to the disadvantage of the CSC.

The challenge to content validity and rank ordering was based on Section 1607C(1) and Section 14(C)(9) of the UGESP. Section 1607C(1) contains the following warning with respect to relying "solely or primarily" on content validity to support "mental processes":

> A selection procedure based on inferences about *mental processes* cannot be supported *solely or primarily* on the basis of *content validity*. Thus, a content strategy is not appropriate for demonstrating the validity of selection procedures which purport to measure traits or constructs such as intelligence, aptitude, personality, common sense, judgment, leadership and spatial ability. [emphasis added]

Additionally, Section 14(C)(9) of the UGESP contains a passage stating that "rank-ordering should be used only if it can be shown that a higher score is likely to result in better job performance."

The 2nd Circuit ruled that content validity is appropriate for validating tests of "mental processes," and outlined the five requirements for proving job relatedness and using rank ordering based on content validity:

1. suitable job analysis
2. reasonable competence in test construction
3. test content related to job content
4. test content representative of job content
5. scoring systems selecting applicants that are better job performers

On the issue of cutoff scores, the 2nd Circuit addressed a passage from Section 1607.5H of the UGESP, stating:

> Where cutoff scores are used, they should normally be set so as to be reasonable and consistent with normal expectations of acceptable proficiency within the workforce. Where applicants are *ranked on the basis of properly validated selection procedures* and those applicants scoring below a higher *cutoff score* than appropriate in light of such expectations have little or no chance of being selected for

---

[*] The r = +.30 standard for practical significance was actually established in *NAACP v. Beecher* (1974), a pre-*Davis* case (see, for example, Landy, Outtz, & Gutman, 2010). However, cases supporting this standard emerged in larger numbers after the *Seibels* ruling, including *Clady v. Los Angeles* (1985), *Zamien v. City of Cleveland*, (1988), and *Hamer v. Atlanta* (1989) in the 1980s, and more recent rulings such as *Williams v. Ford Motor Company* (1999) and *U.S. v. Delaware* (2004).

employment, the higher cutoff score may be appropriate, but the degree of adverse impact should be considered. [emphasis added]

In interpreting this passage, the 2nd Circuit emphasized the importance of professional expertise and logical breakpoints to establish cutoff scores. Accordingly:

As with rank-ordering, a criterion-related study is not necessarily required; the employer might establish a valid cutoff score by using a *professional estimate of the requisite ability* levels, or, at the very least, by analyzing the test results to locate a logical *"break-point"* in the distribution of scores. [emphasis added]

Ultimately, the CSC failed on all counts because the in-house test constructors were deemed to lack competence in test construction. However, other defendants profited from the *Guardians* ruling, most notably the State of Wisconsin.

Gillespie v. Wisconsin (1985)

Gillespie v. Wisconsin featured state personnel jobs, but it is as relevant to police selection as any other early lower court ruling. Relying on the 1974 *Standards for Educational and Psychological Tests* and Anastasi's (1982) *Psychological Testing* text, the 7th Circuit opined that criterion validity is often difficult to accomplish because of technical factors.[*] Accordingly, criterion-related validation is often impracticable because of the limited numbers of employees available for test development and several measurement errors (APA Standards at 27; Anastasi at 433). Thus, neither the Uniform Guidelines nor the psychological literature expresses a blanket preference for criterion-related validity.

Following the lead of the 2nd Circuit, the 7th Circuit supported the cutoff score used by the state of Wisconsin based on professional expertise, as two qualified experts in test construction testified that the cutoff score was chosen so as to "interview as many minority candidates as possible" while "assuring that the candidates possessed the minimal skills" needed to perform the job in question.

Subsequently, the *Guardians* and *Gillespie* rulings were supported in other cases (e.g., *Police Officers v. City of Columbus*, 1990; *Brunet v. City of Columbus*, 1995; and *Williams v. Ford Motors*, 1999). However, as we will witness shortly, agreement among circuit courts on cutoff scores was disrupted by the 3rd Circuit in *Lanning v. Southeastern Pennsylvania Transportation Authority (SEPTA)* (1999).

RECENT RULINGS ON CUTOFF SCORES AND RELATED ISSUES

Guardians v. CSC and *Gillespie v. Wisconsin* established two important rules: (1) if a test is content and/or criterion valid, employers may hire or promote in strict rank order until positions are exhausted; and (2) if strict rank ordering is justified, professional expertise may be used to determine if cutoff scores are "reasonable and consistent with normal expectations of acceptable proficiency within the workforce" in accordance with Section 1607.5(H) of the UGESP. Rule 1 is still applicable across all circuit courts. However, Rule 2 is currently in question based on the 3rd Circuit's ruling in *Lanning v. SEPTA* (1999), particularly as it applies to initial steps in multiple-hurdle selection systems.

As depicted in Table 3.4, there were four rulings in the *Lanning* case. Subsequently, the 3rd Circuit's opinion in Lanning II (*Lanning v. SEPTA*, 1999) was rejected by the 7th Circuit in *Bew v. City of Chicago* (2001) and accepted by the 6th in *Isabel v. City of Memphis* (2005). Additionally,

---

[*] Technical difficulties associated with criterion validity studies are also discussed by Landy (1986) and Binning and Barrett (1989).

TABLE 3.4
Important Recent Rulings on Cutoff Scores

	Lanning Rulings
Lanning v. SEPTA **(1998) (Lanning I)**	District court supports 1.5-mile run in first step of a multiple hurdle for entry-level transit authority police.
Lanning v. SEPTA **(1999) (Lanning II)**	3rd Circuit remands to determine if 1.5-mile run reflects a minimum qualification for transit authority jobs.
Lanning v. SEPTA **(2000) (Lanning III)**	District court rules the 1.5-mile criterion does reflect a minimum qualification for transit authority jobs.
Lanning v. SEPTA **(2002) (Lanning IV)**	3rd Circuit affirms the district court's support of the 1.5-mile run in Lanning.
	Post-Lanning Rulings
Bew v. City of Chicago **(2001)**	7th Circuit disagrees with Lanning II ruling as it applies to full-time appointments for probationary police, and rejects the 80% rule as sole basis for proving adverse impact.
Isabel v. City of Memphis **(2005)**	6th Circuit agrees with Lanning II ruling as it applies to promotion to police sergeant, and rejects the 80% rule as sole basis for proving adverse impact.

both the *Bew* and *Isabel* rulings addressed important questions relating to the so-called 80% rule for proving adverse impact in Section 1607.4(D) of the UGESP.

THE *LANNING* RULINGS

The *Lanning* case featured a 1.5-mile run as the first step in a multiple hurdle for entry-level transit authority officers. Applicants were required to make the run (in full gear) in 12 minutes or less. Those who passed completed additional physical fitness tests and those who failed were excluded. There was no question of adverse impact in this case; the pass rate on the 12-minute criterion was 60% for males and only 12% for females. The only major issue in this case was the validity of the 12-minute criterion.

In *Lanning I* (*Lanning v. SEPTA*, 1998), the trial judge favored SETPA based on job analysis data relating to the importance of aerobic capacity for both officer safety and public safety, and also on criterion validity data on the relationship between aerobic capacity and both successful criminal arrests and commendations for field work. Consistent with the rulings in *Guardians v. CSC* (1980) and *Gillespie v. Wisconsin* (1985), the trial judge supported the 12-minute cutoff.

Then, in *Lanning II* (*Lanning v. SEPTA*, 1999), the 3rd Circuit opined that CRA-91 established new rules for supporting cutoff scores. As written in statutory language in CRA-91, causes of adverse impact must be "job related for the job in question" and "consistent with business necessity." The 3rd Circuit ruled that proof of test validity is sufficient for job relatedness, and that the defendant succeeded in this respect. However, the 3rd Circuit also ruled that to be consistent with business necessity, a cutoff score must reflect "minimum qualifications necessary for successful performance of the job in question." Accordingly:

> With respect to a discriminatory cutoff score, the business necessity prong of the Civil Rights Act of 1991, 105 Stat. 1071 (1992) must be read to demand an inquiry into whether the score reflects the *minimum qualifications necessary to perform successfully the job in question*. [emphasis added]

However, the 3rd Circuit did not strike down the 12-minute criterion, but rather remanded to the district court with instruction to evaluate the 12-minute criterion based on the newly adopted

Lanning II standard. Thereafter, in *Lanning III* (*Lanning v. SEPTA*, 2000), the trial judge supported SETPA on the *Lanning II* standard based on evidence that (a) a lower cutoff would endanger officer and public safety; (b) officers who passed the 12-minute criterion made more successful arrests; and, overall, (c) aerobic capacity, the main reason for using the 1.5-mile run, was not overrepresented for the job of transit authority officer. The 3rd Circuit then affirmed district court ruling from *Lanning III* in *Lanning IV* (*Lanning v. SEPTA*, 2002).

The *Bew* and *Isabel* Rulings

Unlike *Lanning*, where adverse impact was clearly established, there were questions in *Bew v. Chicago* and *Isabel v. Memphis* relating to the 80% rule for proving adverse impact. As written in Section 1607.4(D) of the UGESP, the 80% rule states:

> A selection rate for any race, sex, or ethnic group which is less than four-fifths ($\frac{4}{5}$) (or eighty percent) of the rate for the group with the highest rate will generally be regarded by the Federal enforcement agencies as evidence of adverse impact, while a greater than four-fifths rate will generally not be regarded by Federal enforcement agencies as evidence of adverse impact.

For example, a selection rate for Caucasians at 70% (e.g., 70 out of 100), requires a selection rate minorities or women at 80% × 70% = 56% (or 56 out of 100 or higher).

However, in a second part of Section 1607.4(D), the UGESP terms the 80% rule a "rule of thumb," and warns employers not to use it in lieu of other important factors[*]. Accordingly:

> Smaller differences in selection rate may nevertheless constitute adverse impact, where they are significant in both statistical and practical terms or where a user's actions have discouraged applicants disproportionately on grounds of race, sex, or ethnic group. Greater differences in selection rate may not constitute adverse impact where the differences are based on small numbers and are not statistically significant.

It was the second part of Section 1607.4(D) that was prominently featured in both the *Bew* and *Isabel* cases.

In *Bew v. City of Chicago*, 5,181 probationary police officers were required to pass a written test with a 66% score or higher in order to graduate to full-time appointments. Applicants were given three chances to pass. Only 33 applicants failed three times (less than 1%), and the pass rates for African Americans (98.24%) and Caucasians (99.96%) were within the 80% boundary. However, 32 of the 33 failures were African American applicants, and a test of independent proportions yielded a Z-score of more than five standard deviations, prompting the 7th Circuit to rule that adverse impact was established.[†] However, as critical for the present discussion, the 7th Circuit supported the 66% cutoff score, ruling that CRA-91 did "not distinguish business necessity and job relatedness as two separate standards."

In *Isabel v. City of Memphis*, a written test was the first hurdle for promotion for 120 applicants for police lieutenant. The original cutoff score of 70% would have violated the 80% rule, so the city reduced the cutoff score to 66%, yielding pass rates for African Americans (46 of 63 = 74.6%) and Caucasians (51 of 57 = 89.5%) that were within the boundaries of the 80% rule. The city argued

---

[*] Comprehensive discussions of the 80% rule compared to statistical and practical significance for small and large sample sizes are provided by Morris and Lobsenz (2000) and Siskin and Trippi (2005).

[†] In *Castaneda v. Partida* (1977), plaintiffs charged there was underrepresentation of Mexican Americans in a jury pool where the percentage of Mexican Americans chosen was 39% as compared to 79% in the county as a whole. The Supreme Court, based on testimony from social scientists, ruled that a Z-score difference of two standard deviations or higher constitutes a "gross disparity." This deviation rule was then applied in *Hazelwood v. United States* (1977) and was subsequently transported into adverse impact cases as the criterion for proving adverse impact.

that there was no adverse impact, but the plaintiffs prevailed based on (a) a significant difference on mean scores for African Americans (69.17) versus Caucasians (75.59), (b) an effect size of D = .9 (which is very large), and (c) a test of independent proportions that resulted in a Z-test difference of 2.35 standard deviations. The trial judge in this case (*Isabel v. City of Memphis, 2003*) also rejected the defense of the cutoff score based on *Lanning II*. Accordingly:

> The Third Circuit has held that "taken together, Griggs, Albemarle and Dothard teach that in order to show the business necessity of a discriminatory cutoff score an employer must demonstrate that its cut-off measures the minimum qualifications necessary for successful performance of the job in question." Lanning v. SEPTA, 181 F.3d 478 (3d Cir. 1999). In order to be valid, therefore, the cutoff score of 66 must appropriately measure the minimum qualifications necessary for successful performance of the job of lieutenant in the Memphis Police Department.

The 6th Circuit then affirmed the district court ruling, including the portion relating to *Lanning II* in its 2005 ruling.

Interestingly, the *Lanning II* ruling was not that critical to the *Isabel* ruling. The expert who designed the test for the City of Memphis admitted in open court that the job knowledge component of the test did not represent the full job domain for police lieutenant. Thus, his content validity study was suspect under requirement 4 of *Guardians v. CSC* (1980) (that test content must be representative of job content). As critical, the expert admitted he "did not condone the usage of a cutoff score" for the promotion process, that he was pressured to do so by the police union, and that the cutoff score adopted was "totally inappropriate," a "logical absurdity," and "ludicrous."[*]

In short, it is relatively clear that employers should not rely solely on the 80% rule to determine if there is adverse impact. However, unless and until the Supreme Court decides the issue, it is an open question as to whether CRA-91 established a new rule for assessing the validity of cutoff scores.

METHODS FOR REDUCING OR ELIMINATING ADVERSE IMPACT

Table 3.5 depicts four methods for reducing and/or eliminating adverse impact. Methods 1 and 2 (subgroup norming and banding) use statistical manipulations, Method 3 (alternative tests or combination of tests) was endorsed in two recent district court rulings, and Method 4 (manipulating test content) was endorsed in a controversial ruling in *Hayden v. Nassau County* (1999).

SUBGROUP NORMING

Subgroup norming eliminates adverse impact, but does so by using lower cutoff scores for minorities than Caucasians. Subgroup norming was used routinely in the early 1980s by the U.S. Employment Service (USES) for job referrals based on General Aptitude Test Battery (GATB) test scores.[†] At the time, subgroup norming was supported by the National Academy of Sciences, but opposed by the Department of Justice (DOJ). However, the debate was abruptly ended by the race-norming provision in Section 106(1) of CRA-91, which makes it unlawful to "adjust the scores of, use different cutoff scores for, or otherwise alter the results of, employment-related tests on the basis of race, color, religion, sex or national origin."

---

[*] The city made the mistake of administering the second component of the multiple hurdle, and when both hurdles were complete, one of the African American applicants who finished below the cutoff on hurdle 1 ultimately recorded the second-best score on both hurdles combined.

[†] Readers interested in a detailed account of the USES procedures are referred to Hartigan and Wigdor (1989) and Sackett and Wilk (1994).

TABLE 3.5
Methods for Reducing Adverse Impact

1. Subgroup Norming	Use of different norms for minority and nonminority groups; outlawed in the race-norming proscription in CRA-91.
2. Banding	Arranging scores in bands as an alternative to strict rank ordering. Race-neutral banding has been supported in the courts, but race-conscious banding has been limited at best.
3. Alternative Tests or Combinations	Valid alternatives with less adverse impact was supported in two district rulings: *Bradley v. City of Lynn* (2006) and *Johnson v. City of Memphis* (2006).
4. Manipulating Test Content	Elimination of 17 of 25 components on a test supported by the 2nd Circuit in *Hayden v. Nassau County* (1999).

Banding

Bands are ranges (or bandwidths) in which test scores are treated as being statistically equal.[*] There are two types of banding: race neutral and race conscious. In race-neutral banding, selections are made randomly within bands. Race-neutral banding is generally legal, even if it increases the percentage of minorities relative to strict rank ordering. This occurred, for example, in *Chicago Firefighters Local 2 v. City of Chicago* (2001) for promotion of firefighters, where the 7th Circuit ruled that random selection within bands is *not* a form of race norming. Accordingly:

> If banding were adopted in order *to make lower black scores seem higher*, it would indeed be a form of race norming, and therefore forbidden. But it is not race norming per se. In fact it's a universal and normally an unquestioned method of simplifying scoring by eliminating meaningless gradations. [emphasis added]

That said, race-neutral banding rarely results in meaningful increases in minority selection as occurred in the *Chicago Firefighters* case.

Race-conscious banding was originally proposed by Cascio, Outtz, Zedeck, and Goldstein (1991) (see also Cascio, Goldstein, Outtz, & Zedeck, 1995). Proponents of race-conscious banding contend it significantly reduces adverse impact with minimal loss in test utility.[†] Opposing viewpoints have been expressed by several authors (e.g., Gottfredson, 1994; Sackett & Roth, 1991, Sackett & Wilk, 1994; Schmidt, 1991). The psychometric issues in this debate are complex. For present purposes, it is critical to note that only limited forms of race-conscious banding have been supported in the courts.

Most notably, in *Bridgeport Guardians v. City of Bridgeport* (1991), the 2nd Circuit supported minority preference within bands, but only as one of nine equally weighted criteria. Then, based on the *Bridgeport Guardians* ruling, the 9th Circuit supported minority preference within bands as one of four equally weighted criteria in *Officers for Justice v. Civil Service Commission* (1992).[‡]

---

[*] The most common method of computing bandwidth is to compute the Standard Error of measurement (SEM) and multiply it by the square root of 2 to obtain the standard error of difference (SED). Then the SED is multiplied by 1.96 (Z-score associated with 95% of variance in a two-tailed statistical test on the normal curve). For example, assuming an SEM of 3.0, the SED = 4.24 equates to bandwidth of 8.31.

[†] There are three major methods for race-conscious banding: (1) top-down selection of minorities followed by top-down selection of nonminorities until the band is exhausted; (2) random selection for minorities until either minority candidates are exhausted or the proportion of minorities equals the proportion in the applicant pool, after which nonminority candidates are randomly selected; and (3) the bandwidth slides down after the top-scoring minority and nonminority candidates are chosen.

[‡] The eight factors other than minority preference in the *Bridgeport* case were departmental needs, job dependability, assignment history and job experience in the department, departmental or special skills training, participation in law enforcement/management seminars and courses, formal university education in law enforcement/management, ability to interact with persons of diverse backgrounds, and overall job performance. The three factors other than minority preference in the *Officers* case were professional conduct, education and training, and experience.

Critically, neither court supported minority preference as the sole basis for selection, and in the *Officers* case, race-conscious banding was limited to the last 15 of 115 promotions.

In *Boston Police Superior Officers v. City of Boston* (1998), another notable case, the 1st Circuit upheld promotion of an African American applicant who scored one point less than three higher-scoring Caucasians because it was consistent with the demands of a consent decree. The Caucasian officers challenged the consent decree under the 14th Amendment and lost.

In short, there are some instances in which limited forms of race-conscious banding have been supported by the courts, particularly when there were consent decrees to resolve past instances of discrimination. However, race as the sole basis for selection within bands has never been supported in any court (see Henle, 2004), and it is highly doubtful that race can serve as the sole basis for large-scale selection in view of the race-norming proscription in CR-91, even under consent decrees.

ALTERNATIVE SELECTION PROCEDURES

Unlike subgroup norming and race-conscious banding, valid alternative selection procedures with less or no adverse impact have a strong legal basis. As noted earlier in this chapter, the Supreme Court created this standard as Phase 3 of the adverse impact scenario in *Albemarle v. Moody* (1975). It was then adopted as regulatory law in the UGESP, and written into statutory law in CRA-91. As depicted in Table 3.4, plaintiffs in have succeeded with Phase 3 proof in two recent district court rulings.

In *Bradley v. City of Lynn* (2006), a written test was used for entry-level firefighters. The trial judge ruled there was adverse impact and insufficient evidence of job-relatedness. The judge also cited two valid alternatives: (1) a combination of cognitive tests and physical abilities, and (2) a combination of cognitive tests, personality tests, and biodata. The judge ruled that "while none of these approaches alone provides the silver bullet, these other non-cognitive tests operate to reduce the disparate impact of the written cognitive examination."

Arguably, the City of Lynn was a likely loser in Phase 2 absent the Phase 3 argument. Not so in *Johnson v. City of Memphis* (2006), where the trial judge ruled that a promotion exam (for police sergeant) was valid, but the plaintiffs prevailed in Phase 3. The ruling was based on the prior development of a valid promotion test in 1996 that resulted in less adverse impact relative to the current exam. The judge ruled, "It is of considerable significance that the City had achieved a successful promotional program in 1996 and yet failed to build upon that success."

It is unclear how much weight should be placed on district court rulings absent circuit court appeals. However, it is clear that there is sufficient case law, regulatory law, and statutory law to instruct employers to consider alternative selection procedures with less adverse impact as they commission and/or develop selection tests.

MANIPULATING TEST CONTENT

The events preceding *Hayden v. Nassau County* (1996) were that in 1977, the DOJ sued Nassau County for adverse impact in an entry-level police exam, and the end result was a consent decree in 1982 to construct an exam that produces no adverse impact, or is valid "in accordance with Title VII and the Uniform Guidelines." However, exams developed in 1983 and 1987 again resulted in adverse impact (and two new consent decrees). Then, in 1990, the DOJ and Nassau appointed a Technical Design Advisory Committee (TADC) to develop a new exam.

The TADC developed and administered a 25-component test to 25,000 candidates. There was "severe" adverse impact after all 25 components were scored. The TADC attempted to eliminate adverse impact completely, but considered the end result invalid. In the exam ultimately adopted, 16 of the 25 components were eliminated, resulting in less adverse impact. However, the subsequent nine-component test was challenged by 68 unsuccessful candidates alleging that they would have been selected if all 25 components were used.

The 2nd Circuit ruled "the intent to remedy the disparate impact of the prior exams is *not* equivalent to an intent to discriminate against non-minority applicants." The court acknowledged that the decision to "redesign the exam" was race conscious. However, the court reasoned that the exam was "scored in a wholly race-neutral fashion" and ruled that the plaintiffs failed to state a claim under the Equal Protection Clause of the 14th Amendment, Title VII, or the race-norming proscription in CRA-91.

The *Hayden* ruling is difficult to interpret, particularly in view of the Supreme Court's ruling in *Ricci v. DeStefano* (2009). At the time, Nassau County had the benefit of a court-sanctioned consent degree with the DOJ to resolve multiple lawsuits over a 20-year period. Therefore, at least in the author's opinion, it is not advisable to use the *Hayden* procedure absent court approval.

THE SUPREME COURT'S RULING IN THE *RICCI* CASE

In *Ricci v. DeStefano* (2009), the New Haven Civil Service Board (CSB) refused to certify promotion exams for firefighter captain and lieutenant, thereby effectively discarding the exam. The CSB argued it had a good faith belief that it would lose an adverse impact challenge to minorities. Subsequently, 17 Caucasians and 1 Hispanic sued and ultimately won at the Supreme Court level on grounds that the CSB decision to not certify constituted illegal disparate treatment under Title VII because there was no strong basis in evidence for believing the minority firefighters would prevail.[*]

There were 41 applicants and 7 vacancies for captain and 77 applicants and 8 vacancies for lieutenant. The CSB used a "rule of three" in which any of the 3 highest scoring applicants could be promoted for a given vacancy. This left 9 applicants eligible for captain and 10 applicants eligible for lieutenant. As depicted in Table 3.6, there were racial differences on passing rates (a score of 70 or higher). More important, no African Americans and two Hispanics were eligible for promotion to captain, and no African Americans or Hispanics were eligible for promotion to lieutenant.

The exams were developed by Industrial-Organizational Solutions (IOS) using a content validity strategy. The CSB sought input from several sources, but relied primarily on one of them (Dr. Hornick) for their good faith belief that they would lose an adverse impact challenge. Dr. Hornick,

---

TABLE 3.6
Projected Promotions in the Ricci Case

Captain Exam (7 Vacancies)			
	Caucasians	African Americans	Hispanics
Applicants	25	8	8
Passing Score	16	3	3
Top 9 Scores	7	0	2

Lieutenant Exam (8 Vacancies)			
	Caucasians	African Americans	Hispanics
Applicants	43	19	15
Passing Score	25	6	3
Top 10 Scores	10	0	0

---

[*] The facts in this case are very complex and are only summarized here. Readers interested in a more detailed account of the *Ricci* case are referred to Gutman and Dunleavy (2009).

a competitor to IOS, testified by telephone. He never reviewed the actual exams. Furthermore, he opined that the IOS exams were valid. However, he also opined that he generally found less adverse impact as compared with the IOS tests using an assessment center approach. The CSB ultimately discarded the exams without requesting a validity report by IOS. They also hired Dr. Hornick to create and validate new exams.

In court, the CSB argued that they "cannot be held liable under Title VII's disparate-treatment provision for attempting to comply with Title VII's disparate-impact bar." The plaintiffs, on the other hand, argued that a "good-faith belief was not a valid defense to allegations of disparate treatment and unconstitutional discrimination." Critically, the Supreme Court never evaluated written tests versus assessment centers in reaching its ruling.

At the district court level, the trial judge (Janet Bond Arterton) acknowledged that the CSB's decision was race conscious. Nevertheless, based on *Hayden v. Nassau County* (1996), Judge Arterton ruled that the noncertification decision was "race neutral." She ruled further that the "intent to remedy disparate impact of the prior exams is not equivalent to an intent to discriminate against non-minority applicants." A three-judge panel of the 2nd Circuit then affirmed Judge Arterton's ruling in a short per curium ruling. Subsequently, a 13-judge panel of the 2nd Circuit refused to further review the case in a close 7–6 ruling. The Supreme Court then agreed to review the case based on a written opinion by the six dissenters.

The Supreme Court's ruling was 5–4, with Justice Kennedy speaking for Justices Alito, Roberts, Scalia, and Thomas. Kennedy ruled there was a race-conscious motive for discarding the test, and strongly suggested that the CSB would have certified the tests if the results were more favorable for minorities. Accordingly:

> Whatever the City's ultimate aim—however well intentioned or benevolent it might have seemed—the City made its employment decision *because of race*. The City rejected the test results solely because the higher scoring candidates were Caucasian. *The question is not whether that conduct was discriminatory but whether the City had a lawful justification for its race-based action.* [emphasis added]

Nevertheless, this was not the sole basis for the majority ruling, as Kennedy ruled further that it is necessary to balance the "tension" between disparate treatment and adverse impact. He rejected a *certainty* criterion for losing on adverse impact. Accordingly:

> Forbidding employers to act unless they know, *with certainty, that a practice violates the disparate-impact provision* would bring compliance efforts to a near standstill. Even in the limited situations when this restricted standard could be met, employers likely would hesitate before taking voluntary action for fear of later being proven wrong in the course of litigation and then held to account for disparate treatment. [emphasis added]

Kennedy also rejected a good-faith belief on grounds that it was too *minimal*, ruling:

> Allowing employers to violate the disparate-treatment prohibition *based on a mere good-faith fear of disparate-impact liability would encourage race-based action at the slightest hint of disparate impact.* A *minimal* standard could cause employers to discard the results of lawful and beneficial promotional examinations even where there is little if any evidence of disparate-impact discrimination. That would amount to a de facto quota system, in which a "focus on statistics … could put undue pressure on employers to adopt inappropriate prophylactic measures. [emphasis added]

Borrowing from Title VII and 14th Amendment case law from reverse discrimination rulings (e.g., *Wygant v. Jackson*, 1986; *City of Richmond v. Croson*, 1989) and invoking the race-norming provision in CRA-91, Kennedy ruled it would be legal to discard an exam if there is a strong basis in evidence for believing an employer would lose on adverse impact. Accordingly:

If an employer *cannot rescore a test based on the candidates' race, §2000e-2(l), then it follows a fortiori that it may not take the greater step of discarding the test altogether to achieve a more desirable racial distribution of promotion-eligible candidates—absent a strong basis in evidence that the test was deficient and that discarding the results is necessary to avoid violating the disparate-impact provision....* For the foregoing reasons, we adopt the strong-basis-in-evidence standard as a matter of statutory construction to resolve any conflict between the disparate-treatment and disparate-impact provisions of Title VII. [emphasis added]

Ultimately, reasoning that the CSB did not pass the strong-basis-in-evidence test, Kennedy overturned both lower courts and granted summary judgment for the plaintiffs, thus ending the case.

In the dissenting opinion, Justice Ginsburg, speaking for Justices Breyer, Souter, and Stevens, criticized the strong-basis-in-evidence standard on grounds that it was inappropriately incorporated into Title VII adverse impact law based on 14th Amendment reverse discrimination affirmative action cases (*Wygant v. Jackson*, 1986; *Richmond v. Croson*, 1988). Accordingly:

The cases from which the Court draws its *strong-basis in-evidence* standard are particularly inapt; they concern the constitutionality of absolute racial preferences. See Wygant v. Jackson Bd. of Ed., 476 U. S. 267, 277 (1986) (plurality opinion) (invalidating a school district's plan to lay off nonminority teachers while retaining minority teachers with less seniority); Croson, 488 U. S., at 499–500 22 (rejecting a set-aside program for minority contractors that operated as "an unyielding racial quota"). An employer's effort to avoid Title VII liability by repudiating a suspect selection method scarcely resembles those cases. Race was not merely a relevant consideration in Wygant and Croson; it was the decisive factor. *Observance of Title VII's disparate-impact provision, in contrast, calls for no racial preference, absolute or otherwise.* [emphasis added]

Ginsburg endorsed a lighter *reasonableness* standard, under which the CSB's "good faith" belief would be acceptable for discarding the test under disparate treatment rules.

It is critical to remember that Kennedy's majority ruling was based *entirely* on Title VII. No precedents were established for the Equal Protection Clause of the 14th Amendment. Indeed, Kennedy suggested that a favorable Title VII ruling on strong-basis-in-evidence standard could at a later time fail under constitutional law. Accordingly:

Our statutory holding *does not address the constitutionality of the measures taken here in purported compliance with Title VII.* We also do not hold that meeting the strong-basis-in-evidence standard would satisfy the *Equal Protection Clause* in a future case. As we explain below, because respondents have not met their burden under Title VII, we need not decide whether a legitimate fear of disparate impact is ever sufficient to justify discriminatory treatment under the Constitution. [emphasis added]

In short, much uncertainty remains related to the strong-basis-in-evidence standard advocated by the Supreme Court.

It should be noted that the Office of Contract Compliance Programs (OFCCP) of the Department of Labor, which monitors compliance with Executive Order 11246 on affirmative action, has released guidance that states, among other things, that *Ricci* will not alter the affirmative action obligations of contractors, and that the OFCCP will continue to use the UGESP to assess adverse impact cases, particularly as it relates to job analysis and test validation procedures. The OFCCP added, however, that it would examine refusals to use tests in accordance with the strong-basis-in-evidence standard.*

An additional point to note is that as this chapter was going to press, the Chicago Police Department was considering scrapping its entry tests. According to an article written on January 6, 2010, in the *Chicago Sun Times*, this action would "bolster minority hiring, save millions on test

---

* The full OFCCP report is available at http://www.dol.gov/ofccp/regs/compliance/faqs/Ricci_FAQ.htm

preparation and avert costly legal battles that have dogged the exam process for decades."* While it is unclear how much weight should be given to this newspaper report, the notion that all legal problems are averted by simply eliminating testing procedures is, for reasons to be discussed shortly, not necessarily true.

CONCLUSIONS AND RECOMMENDATIONS

The case law surveyed in this chapter reveals that municipalities face a variety of Hobson's choices with respect to development and defense of cognitive tests. By the author's count, there are four ways for a municipality to be sued relating to adverse impact:

1. Adverse impact is proven by minority plaintiffs, and the municipality fails to prove that a challenged test or other selection criterion is job related.
2. The municipality proves job relatedness, but minority plaintiffs prove that a rank cutoff score for selection decisions is unjustified by the evidence offered.
3. The municipality can successfully defend its cutoff score, but minority plaintiffs prove there are other equally valid methods that produce less or no adverse impact to accomplish the same goals.
4. The municipality uses what it believes is the most valid methods with the least amount of adverse impact, but nonminority plaintiffs challenge these methods on grounds of "reverse discrimination" based on preference for minority candidates.

Additionally, there is potential liability if a municipality scraps the testing process altogether or reduces adverse impact by other questionable means, and the selection process used results in less-qualified police officers. For example, if, because of negligence or intent, an unqualified officer injures or kills a citizen, the municipality could be liable for remedies associated with wrongful death based on its failure to select only the most qualified applicants for police work.

In short, there are good reasons for relying on objective tests and related procedures for hiring and promoting police officers. They represent the best way to make decisions when there are large numbers of applicants. Additionally, many municipalities require such testing. That said, municipalities must be prepared to prove three things: (1) that the tests or other selection criteria used are job related, (2) that there is sufficient evidence for use of rank ordering and/or a specific cutoff score, and (3) that they have examined potentially valid alternative methods that produce less adverse impact before adopting their test strategy.

As discussed by Gutman and Dunleavy (2009), the correct reaction to *Ricci* is to take a proactive approach when developing selection tests. The *Ricci* ruling had little to do with whether, for example, written tests are better than assessment centers. That question would have been relevant had the New Haven CSB stood by its tests and offered a content validity defense (which likely would have succeeded), and minority plaintiffs launched a Phase 3 proof on valid alternatives with less or no adverse impact. But that did not happen. However, that is precisely the scenario that municipalities must prepare for regardless of which selection procedures are used.

What Gutman and Dunleavy (2009) recommend is to establish an advisory committee that includes experts in job analysis and test validation prior to issuing an RFP. The advisory committee should then play a key role in awarding a contract and work with the contractor(s) to ensure that tests and other selection procedures are administered and scored in accordance with the UGESP, and authorities such as the Standards and the SIOP Principles. That would represent an ideal way to establish a strong basis in evidence for discarding a test. Of course, if there is a strong basis for

---

* The article may be found at http://www.policeone.com/patrol-issues/articles/1986463-Chicago-police-may-scrap-entrance-exam. See http://www.suntimes.com/news/steinberg/1979744,CST-NWS-stein08.article and http://www.suntimes.com/news/commentary/letters/1990161,CST-EDT-vox14.articl for follow-up articles.

discarding a test, there is no reason to administer and score the test to begin with, and wait to see the results to determine if it is acceptable.

REFERENCES

American Educational Research Association, American Psychological Association, & National Council on Measurement in Education. (1974). *Standards for educational and psychological testing*. Washington, DC: American Educational Research Association.

American Educational Research Association, American Psychological Association, & National Council on Measurement in Education. (1999). *Standards for educational and psychological testing*. Washington, DC: American Educational Research Association.

Anastasi, A. (1982). *Psychological testing* (5th ed.). New York: Macmillan.

Bining, J. F., & Barrett, G. V. (1989).Validity of personnel decisions: A conceptual analysis of T. *Journal of Applied Psychology*, *74*(3) 478–494.

Cascio, W. F., Goldstein, I. L., Outtz, J., & Zedeck, S. (1995). Twenty issues and answers about sliding bands. *Human Performance*, *8*, 227–242.

Cascio, W. F., Outtz, J., Zedeck, S., & Goldstein, I. L. (1991). Statistical implications of six methods of test score use in personnel selection. *Human Performance*, *4*, 233–264.

Gottfredson, L. S. (1994). The science and politics of race norming. *American Psychologist*, *49*, 955–963.

Gutman, A. (2005). Adverse impact: Judicial, regulatory, and statutory authority. In F. J. Landy (Ed.), *Employment discrimination litigation: Behavioral, quantitative, and legal perspectives* (pp. 20–46). San Francisco: Jossey-Bass.

Gutman, A., & Dunleavy, E. (2009). The Supreme Court ruling in *Ricci v. DeStefano*. *The Industrial-Organizational Psychologist*, *47*(2), 57–71.

Gutman, A., Koppes, L. L., & Vodanovich, S. J. (2010). *EEO law and personnel practices* (3rd ed.). New York: Taylor & Francis.

Hartigan, J. A., & Wigdor, A. K. (Eds.) (1989). *Fairness in employment testing*. Washington, DC: National Academy Press.

Henle, C.A. (2004). Case review of the legal status of banding. *Human Performance*, *17*(4), 415–432.

Jeanneret, A. (2005). Professional and technical authorities and guidelines. In F. J. Landy (Ed.), *Employment discrimination litigation: Behavioral, quantitative, and legal perspectives* (pp. 47–100). San Francisco: Jossey-Bass.

Landy, F. J. (1986). Stamp collecting versus science: Validation as hypothesis testing. *American Psychologist*, *41*(11), 1183–1192.

Landy F. J., Gutman, A., & Outtz, J. (2010). A sampler of legal principles in employment selection. In J. L. Farr & N. T. Tippins (Eds.), *The handbook of employee selection* (pp. 627–650). New York: Taylor & Francis.

Morris, S. B., & Lobsenz, R. E. (2000). Significance tests and confidence intervals for the adverse impact ratio. *Personnel Psychology*, *53*, 89–111.

Sackett, P. R., & Roth, L. (1991). A Monte Carlo examination of banding and rank order methods of test scores used in personnel selection. *Human Performance*, *4*(4), 279–295.

Sackett, P. R., & Wilk, S. L. (1994).Within group norming and other forms of score adjustment in pre-employment testing. *American Psychologist*, *49*, 929–954.

Schmidt, F. L. (1991). Why all banding procedures are logically flawed. *Human Performance*, *4*, 265–278.

Schneider, J.R., & Schmidt, N. (1992). An exercise design approach to understanding assessment center dimension and exercise constructs. *Journal of Applied Psychology*, *77*(1), 32–41.

Siskin, B. R., & Trippi, J. (2005). Statistical issues in litigation. In F. J. Landy (Ed.), *Employment discrimination litigation: Behavioral, quantitative, and legal perspectives* (pp. 132–166). San Francisco: Jossey-Bass.

Society for Industrial and Organizational Psychology. (2003). *Principles for the validation and use of personnel selection procedures* (4th ed.). Bowling Green, OH: Author.

CASES CITED

Albemarle Paper Co. v. Moody (1975) 422 US 405.

Arlington Heights v. Metropolitan Housing Corp. (1977) 429 US 252.

Bew v. City of Chicago (2001) 252 F.3d 891.

Boston Police v. City of Boston (CA1 1998) 147 F.3d 13.

Bradley v. City of Lynn (2006) 433 F. Supp. 2d 157.
Bridgeport Guardians v. Bridgeport *CSC* (CA2 1973) 482 F.3d. 1333.
Bridgeport Guardians, Inc. v. City of Bridgeport (CA2 1991) 933 F.2d 1140.
Brunet v. City of Columbus (CA6 1995) 58 F.2d 251.
Carter v. Gallagher (CA8 1971) 452 F.2d 315.
Castaneda v. Partida (1977) 430 US 482.
Castro v. Beecher (CA1 1972) 459 F.2d 725.
Chicago Firefighters Local Union 2 v. City of Chicago (CA 7 2001) 49 F.3d 649.
City of Richmond v. Croson (1989) 488 US 469.
Clady v. Los Angeles (CA 9 1985) 770 F.2d 1421.
Connecticut v. Teal (1982) 457 US 440.
Davis v. Dallas (CA5 1985) 777 F.2d 205.
Dothard v. Rawlinson (1977) 433 US 321.
Gillespie v. State of Wisconsin (CA7 1985) 771 F.2d 1035.
Griggs v. Duke Power Co. (1971) 401 US 424.
Guardians of NY v. Civil Service Commission (CA2 1980) 630 F.2d 79.
Hamer v. City of Atlanta (CA11 1989) 872 F.2d 1521.
Hayden v. Nassau County (CA2 1999) 180 F.3d 42.
Hazelwood School Dist. v. United States (1977) 433 US 299.
Horace v. Pontiac (CA6 1980) 624 F.2d 765.
International Brotherhood of Teamsters v. United States (1977) 431 US 324.
Isabel v. City of Memphis (W.D. Tenn. 2003) U.S. Dist. Lexis.
Isabel v. City of Memphis (CA6 2005) 404 F.3d 404.
Johnson v. City of Memphis (2006) 355 F. Supp. 2d 911.
Kirkland v. New York State CSC (CA2 1975) 520 F.2d 420.
Lanning v. Southeastern Trans. Auth. (SEPTA) (E.D.Pa. 1998) WL 341605.
Lanning v. Southeastern Trans. Auth. (SEPTA) (1999) 181 F.3d 478.
Lanning v. Southeastern Trans. Auth. (SEPTA) (E.D.Pa. 2000) U.S. Dist. Lexis 17612.
Lanning v. Southeastern Trans. Auth. (SEPTA) (CA3 2002) 308 F.3d 286.
McDonnell Douglas v. Green (1973) 411 US 792.
Meacham v. Knolls Atomic Power Laboratory (KAPL) (2008) 128 S. Ct. 2395.
NAACP v. Seibels (CA5 1980) 616 F.2d 812.
New York City v. Beazer (1979) 440 US 568.
Officers for Justice v. Civil Service Commission (CA9 1992) 979 F.2d 721.
Personnel Administrator v. Feeney (1979) 442 US 256.
Police Officers for Equal Rights v. City of Columbus (CA6 1990) 916 F.2d 1092.
Ricci v. DeStefano (2009) 129 S. Ct. 2658.
Smith v. City of Jackson (2005) 544 US 228.
Spurlock v. United Airlines, Inc. (CA10 1972) 475 F.2d 216.
United States v. Delaware (D.Del 2004) Lexis 4560.
Vulcan Society v. CSC of New York City (CA2 1973) 490 F.2d 387.
Wards Cove Packing Co. v. Atonio (1989) 490 US 642.
Washington (Mayor, DC) v. Davis (1976) 426 US 229.
Watson v. Fort Worth Bank & Trust (1988) 487 US 977.
Williams v. Ford Motor Company (1999) 187 F.3d 533.
Wygant v. Jackson Board of Education (1986) 476 US 267.
Zamien v. City of Cleveland (CA6 1988) 906 F.2d 209.

4 Ethical Issues in Police Psychology

Challenges and Decision-Making Models to Resolve Ethical Dilemmas

Jeni L. McCutcheon

Ethical issues abound in the specialty area of police psychology. These issues bring challenges if not daily, at least regularly, for psychologists who perform work in this growing area. This chapter will look at select ethical dilemmas police psychologists encounter as well as topics of interest and relevance in resolving such dilemmas. Guidance in how to resolve ethical dilemmas will be covered, including identification of various systematic problem-solving models.

RESOURCES TO GUIDE ETHICAL PRACTICE

Ethical dilemmas arise in the practice of police psychology and there are applicable ethical codes of conduct and practice guidelines relevant to practice in the area of police psychology. These are the APA *Ethical Principles of Psychologists and Code of Conduct* (2002),[*] *Specialty Guidelines for Forensic Psychologists* (1991), other standards, and various guidelines put forth by the Police Psychology Services Section of the International Association of Chiefs of Police (2004, 2006, 2009).

The APA *Ethical Principles of Psychologists and Code of Conduct* is certainly the most widely used and authoritative reference in recognizing and being aware of expectations for ethical practice as a psychologist. The current version of this code was published in 2002 and came into effect in June 2003. This code appears to be here to stay, though there was an amendment of specific codes (1.02 and 1.03) within Standard 1, Resolving Ethical Issues (APA, 2010). This change was approved in February 2010 by the American Psychological Association Executive Council and became effective June 1, 2010, in order to provide greater clarity for and guidance to psychologists in resolving conflicts between ethics and law, regulations, or other governing legal authority, and conflicts between ethics and organizational demands (APA, 2010). In considering the *Ethical Principles of Psychologists and Code of Conduct* and the specialty area of police psychology, there are general principles to keep in mind. Although not enforceable, these "aspirational" principles are certainly relevant and important, as they represent the highest standards of thinking and conduct to strive for in providing services. In regard to provision of police psychology services, Principle A, Beneficence and Nonmaleficence, means that psychologists seek to do good, attempt to avoid doing harm, look out for the welfare of those with whom they work, and are aware of

---

[*] © 2002 by the American Psychological Association. Adapted with permission. The official citation that should be used in referencing this material is American Psychological Association. (2002). Ethical principles of psychologists and code of conduct. *American Psychologist, 57*, 1060–1073.

their influence. Principle B, Fidelity and Responsibility, speaks to psychologists needing to estab-lish trust, loyalty, and an awareness of their professional responsibilities, and work cooperatively with others. Principle C, Integrity, refers to the need for psychologists to be honest in their deal-ings, truthful in their duties, accurate in their work product, honorable in their commitments, and considerate in enumerating and taking responsibility for possible harmful effects of their work. Principle D, Justice, seeks to inspire in psychologists the need to be fair, exercise sound judg-ment, and recognize their own biases and limits of their competence. Last, Principle E, Respect for People's Rights and Dignity, promotes respect and dignity for others, awareness and positive regard for diversity, and an avoidance of going along with or participating in activities that are based on prejudices and may result in harm to others (APA, 2002).

Another source of information and guidance in identifying and resolving ethical issues are the *Specialty Guidelines for Forensic Psychologists*. These guidelines were created by the Committee on Ethical Guidelines for Forensic Psychologists (1991) and are frequently applicable to this area of practice. These guidelines are currently in revision and have been for several years. The *Standards for Educational and Psychological Testing* (AERA, 1999) also provide guidance about the con-struction, selection, application, and fair and ethical use of psychological testing in employment situations.

Though not ethical codes per se, there are other documents that guide the police psychologist toward ethical practice. There are guidelines developed by the Police Psychological Services Section of the International Chiefs of Police (International Association of Chiefs of Police, 2004a, 2004b, 2006a, 2006b, 2009). After extensive work in creating new guidelines, and revising existing guide-lines within the section by section psychologists, they are offered to and approved by the Executive Council of Chiefs of Police. The purpose of the guidelines is to assist law enforcement agencies and their psychologists in handling certain types of occurrences and practices within law enforcement agencies. These guidelines help to establish the current and evolving standard of practice in police psychology service provision; they reflect the end result of police psychologists discussing, often working in collaboration with police chiefs and setting forth desirable courses of action for ethical practice in this area. The following guidelines exist: Fitness for Duty Evaluation Guidelines (2009), Officer-Involved Shooting Guidelines (2004), Peer Support Guidelines (2006), Pre-Employment Psychological Evaluation Guidelines (2004), and Guidelines for Consulting Police Psychologists (2006).

The legal aspects of police psychology practice are extensive and complex. Many federal laws impact police psychology practice. Some of these are the Americans with Disabilities Act (ADA), the Health Insurance Portability and Accountability Act (HIPAA), and recently the Genetic Information Nondiscrimination Act (GINA), which limits inquiry regarding family medical history and genetic information. Additionally, various tort and case laws such as *Pettus v. Cole* (1996) and *Jaffee v. Redmond* (1996) influence police psychology practice.

Although employing knowledge of both ethics and legal issues often goes hand-in-hand in choos-ing a best course of action in handling ethical questions, legal issues relevant to police psychol-ogy practice are not specifically addressed in this chapter. Another chapter within this handbook provides thorough coverage of the extensive statutes, laws, and regulations that affect this area of practice. When mentioned in this chapter, laws are referenced only to make ethical examples richer for the reader. Relatedly, while good ethical practice is a step toward risk management, it should be noted that this chapter is aimed specifically at discussing ethical issues in police psychology rather than being a risk management practice "how-to" guide.

COMMON ETHICAL DILEMMAS

Research regarding ethical dilemmas encountered by police psychologists is scarce. Zelig (1988) surveyed police psychologists and found that dilemmas commonly involved six often-overlapping categories: confidentiality, resolving conflicts between professional standards and the needs of the organization, dual relationships, use and administration of psychological tests, problems with the agency overruling the psychologist's recommendations, and "other" dilemmas. In Zelig's study, "confidentiality" was the most commonly cited ethical dilemma, with "managing conflicts between the psychologist's professional standards and the needs of the organization" and "dual relationships" rounding out the top three most commonly cited dilemmas. Some psychologists reported that they did not encounter any ethical dilemmas.

Zelig's findings are consistent with psychologist-identified ethical dilemmas as a whole. Pope and Vetter (1992) surveyed members of the American Psychological Association. Their survey revealed that the top two ethical dilemmas experienced by psychologists involved "confidentiality" and "dual relationships." This study was replicated in Sweden with the same findings; the top two ethical dilemmas encountered by Swedish psychologists were confidentiality and blurred, dual, or conflictual relationships (Colnerud, 1997). Slack and Wassenaar (1999) found the same results in surveying South African clinical psychologists. Pettifor and Sawchuk (2006) reviewed other research and similar studies internationally and ascertained that among nine primarily western countries—the United States, United Kingdom, Norway, Finland, Canada, Sweden, New Zealand, South Africa, and Mexico—confidentiality and dual relationships were among the most often-cited areas of ethical dilemmas encountered by psychologists.

Despite the scarcity of research, it is reasonable to believe that a majority of police psychologists would cite ethical dilemmas as an ongoing and routine challenge. Stemming back 25-plus years, articles and texts in the area of police psychology have cited ethical concerns as important to consider. Attention to ethical issues and resolving ethical dilemmas are certainly far from new and novel concepts (Dietz & Reese, 1986; Inwald, 1984; Reese, 1987; Reese & Goldstein, 1986). At police conferences, ethical aspects of police psychology have been addressed through interactive ethical case scenario exercises (Corey & Trompetter, 2009) and at formal conference presentations (Corey & Trompetter, 2009; Gelles, Morgan, & Moorehead, 2006). Also, in the creation and revisions of the guidelines for police psychologists through the International Association of Chiefs of Police, there has been attention paid toward ethical practice. As an example, Section 8.2 of the Fitness for Duty Evaluation Guidelines (2009) reads:

> As part of the informed consent process, the examiner clarifies who the client is and communicates this to all involved parties at the outset of the evaluation. Regardless of who is identified as the client, the examiner owes an ethical duty to both parties to be fair, impartial, accurate and objective, and to honor the parties' respective legal rights and interests. (p. 4)

ETHICAL DILEMMAS AND CHALLENGES

COMPETENCE

Several areas of the APA *Ethical Principles of Psychologists and Code of Conduct* (2002), such as Standard 2: Competence, apply to police psychologists. As examples:

2.03 *Maintaining Competence*
   Psychologists undertake ongoing efforts to develop and maintain their competence.
2.04 *Bases for Scientific and Professional Judgments*
   Psychologists' work is based on established scientific and professional knowledge of the discipline.
2.05 *Delegation of Work to Others*
   Psychologists who delegate work to employees, supervisees, or research or teaching assistants or who use the services of others, such as interpreters, take reasonable steps to (1) avoid delegating such work to persons who have a multiple relationship with those being served that would likely lead to exploitation or loss of objectivity; (2) authorize only those

responsibilities that such persons can be expected to perform competently on the basis of their education, training, or experience, either independently or with the level of supervision provided; and (3) see that such persons perform these services competently.

These standards speak to the need for police psychologists to receive adequate training in this practice area. Police psychologists need to keep up with advancements in their field, stay apprised of pertinent research and literature, and be aware of revised guidelines specific to the area of police psychology as well as be knowledgeable of federal and state laws and case laws that impact police psychology practice. The ethical codes and laws also speak to the need to assume full responsibility for those working under the police psychologist's license, such as where allowed for by law, when practicum students and predoctoral interns and postdoctoral residents are volunteers or employees of contract psychologists or of police agencies.

Potential ethical dilemmas in this area can arise in a multitude of ways. Consider the self-identified police psychologist who does not belong to or attend any of the annual conferences of the three major police psychologist organizations: the International Association of Chiefs of Police, Police Psychological Services Section (IACP PPSS); the Society for Police and Criminal Psychology (SPCP); and the American Psychological Association (APA), Division 18, Police & Public Safety Section. Consider the psychologist who uses outdated psychological tests or employs assessment measures not typically used in assessment of police populations for pre-employment evaluations (and are not validated or normed based on these populations). Consider the intern who does not keep up in a timely manner on report-writing tasks and updating clinical notes. Consider the psychologist who performs unwarranted fitness-for-duty evaluations on returning veterans simply because the agency thinks this would be a good idea. As with most competence issues, these likely are not purposeful deviations from the standard of practice, but actions taken based on a lack of education and knowledge.

CONFIDENTIALITY

Several areas of the APA Ethical Principles of Psychologists and Code of Conduct (2002), such as Standard 4: Privacy and Confidentiality, are applicable to police psychology:

4.01 *Maintaining Confidentiality*
Psychologists have a primary obligation and take reasonable precautions to protect confidential information obtained through or stored in any medium, recognizing that the extent and limits of confidentiality may be regulated by law or established by institutional rules or professional or scientific relationship.

4.02 *Discussing the Limits of Confidentiality*
(a) Psychologists discuss with persons (including, to the extent feasible, those legally incapable of giving informed consent and their legal representatives) and organizations with whom they establish a scientific or professional relationship (1) the relevant limits of confidentiality and (2) the foreseeable uses of the information generated through their psychological activities.
(b) Unless it is not feasible or contraindicated, the discussion of confidentiality occurs at the outset of the relationship and thereafter as new circumstances may warrant.
(c) Psychologists who offer services, products, or information via electronic transmission inform clients/patients of the risks to privacy and limits of confidentiality.

4.04 *Minimizing Intrusions on Privacy*
(a) Psychologists include in written and oral reports and consultations, only information germane to the purpose for which the communication is made.
(b) Psychologists discuss confidential information obtained in their work only for appropriate scientific or professional purposes and only with persons clearly concerned with such matters.

4.05 *Disclosures*

    (a) Psychologists may disclose confidential information with the appropriate consent of the organizational client, the individual client/patient, or another legally authorized person on behalf of the client/patient unless prohibited by law.

    (b) Psychologists disclose confidential information without the consent of the individual only as mandated by law, or where permitted by law for a valid purpose such as to (1) provide needed professional services; (2) obtain appropriate professional consultations; (3) protect the client/patient, psychologist, or others from harm; or (4) obtain payment for services from a client/patient, in which instance disclosure is limited to the minimum that is necessary to achieve the purpose.

These codes point to the need for the police psychologist to keep confidences, define who the client is, and obtain informed consent. It is vital not only for ethical practice but also for the credibility of the police psychologist to keep private (except as otherwise mandated by law) the information and disclosures shared within the context of a relationship.

Trouble can arise in this area when the relationship between the psychologist and the client is unclear, never really identified or clarified, and/or not made explicit and transparent to the involved parties. Consider, for example, the applicant who shows up for a pre-employment evaluation thinking he or she already has the job and "because you are a psychologist, I thought what I tell you is private." Other ethical dilemmas can arise in related areas, when there are questions of who owns the records, who gets the report(s), what is private and what is not as far as what is said in the course of an evaluation, and, more to the point, what sensitive and private disclosures are germane and end up in a report, and which are screened out with only general comments made.

To elaborate, ponder that in the process of pre-employment evaluations, applicants are routinely asked highly personal questions about their background, substance abuse, mental health and medical histories, but (unless required by state statute) are not at all privy to how they performed in these evaluations. To psychologists not skilled in police psychology or in forensic evaluative areas, the idea that you do not provide feedback to the very person who spent time and effort taking these tests seems counterintuitive. In this case, the agency holds the confidentiality because they are the client agency and the applicant is the subject of the evaluation. In concert with the obligation to provide relevant information to the agency so that they can make an informed hiring decision, it is also the psychologist's ethical responsibility to provide only germane, salient data in the report and to the hiring authority. As stated previously, the ethical codes guard against invasion of privacy. As an example, the fact that an applicant engaged in a sex act at work is a relevant detail. Additionally, that he or she engaged in a sex act with a coworker at work is also pertinent. However, the fact that he or she sex act involved a coworker and that both he or she and the coworker are married but not to each other does not need to be included in the report details. It is becoming more the case that psychologists recognizing that only relevant, job-related behaviors be included in reports include only relevant data, observations, and test results. Typically therefore, long histories such as those routinely included in the psychosocial history section of traditional psychological full-battery reports are not included. "Superfluous data which are not reasonably tied to the purpose for which the evaluation was conducted, such as diagnostic impressions or the inclusion of lengthy personal, social and family histories[,] should not be routinely included in pre-employment psychological evaluation reports" (Super, 1997, p. 4). As the development of laws are often reactive from ethical issues that arise, the introduction of the Genetic Information Nondiscrimination Act (GINA) seems to reinforce that not only is it ethically the trend to include only the most relevant job-related details in report, but also now specific details about an applicant's personal family history are also not to be included in reports and cannot be part of the inquiry in employment-related testing and evaluations.

In regard to how to handle confidentiality in police psychology practice, it is this author's beginning stance that as far as clinical contacts and services, unless there is a mandated treatment referral situation or an exception to confidentiality by law, all contacts are confidential. As an example, the fact that someone called to inquire about services is confidential even if he or she never follows through and seeks therapy. Similarly, any disclosures made during ride-alongs, facility visits, or briefings are considered confidential. Whenever evaluation, crisis intervention, and formal therapy services are provided, it is good practice to provide and obtain verbal and written informed consent. And, in situations where there is a lack of guaranteed confidentiality such as the psychologist keeping confidentiality but peer-support attendees perhaps having to report a policy-violation disclosure up their chain of command in a critical incident stress management team intervention, proceeding with caution is important. Specifically, because peer support and group debriefing services are not guaranteed to be confidential and considered a privileged communication (in most states), it is prudent for the psychologist to share these limitations, but then to ask attendees to maintain confidentiality. Where there are limited aspects of confidentiality, such as in confirming attendance at a post-officer-involved shooting one-to-one meeting or in cases of mandated therapy treatment, it is important to be open and transparent about these limitations. Similarly, in the course of evaluations, it is vital to share openly when, and if, there is confidentiality.

A point to bear in mind is not just the psychologist's personal actions, but the environment in which the psychologist works. When one works as an in-house police psychologist, it may be the case that they will encounter past, current, and future clients and evaluation subjects each day. It is vital in situations like these that what is known about these individuals is kept compartmentalized and private. Stating this at the first contact and asking for feedback is often helpful. Additionally, if working within an in-house unit, other nonpsychologists may need encouragement and education to value privacy and confidentiality as well. For instance, when a friendly and sociable lieutenant comes to visit and say hello, he or she may have to be gently reminded to avoid greeting coworkers who are visiting your unit seeking professional services with a loud, "Hey, hello, Sergeant! What are you doing here?!"

DUAL RELATIONSHIPS, ROLE CONFLICT, AND BOUNDARY ISSUES

Multiple areas of the *Ethical Principles of Psychologists and Code of Conduct* (2002) Standard 3: Human Relations are relevant. These include:

   3.04 *Avoiding Harm*
      Psychologists take reasonable steps to avoid harming their clients/patients, students, supervisees, research participants, organizational clients, and others with whom they work and to minimize harm where it is foreseeable and unavoidable.
   3.05 *Multiple Relationships*
      (a) A multiple relationship occurs when a psychologist is in a professional role with a person and (1) at the same time is in another role with the same person, (2) at the same time is in a relationship with a person closely associated with or related to the person with whom the psychologist has the professional relationship, or (3) promises to enter into another relationship in the future with the person or a person closely associated with or related to the person. A psychologist refrains from entering into a multiple relationship if the multiple relationship could reasonably be expected to impair the psychologist's objectivity, competence, or effectiveness in performing his or her functions as a psychologist or otherwise risks exploitation or harm to the person with whom the professional relationship exists. Multiple relationships that would not reasonably be expected to cause impairment or risk exploitation or harm are not unethical.
      (b) If a psychologist finds that, due to unforeseen factors, a potentially harmful multiple relationship has arisen, the psychologist takes reasonable steps to resolve it with due regard for the best interests of the affected person and maximal compliance with the Ethics Code.

(c) When psychologists are required by law, institutional policy, or extraordinary circumstances to serve in more than one role in judicial or administrative proceedings, at the outset they clarify role expectations and the extent of confidentiality and thereafter as changes occur.

3.06 *Conflict of Interest*

Psychologists refrain from taking on a professional role when personal, scientific, professional, legal, financial, or other interests or relationships could reasonably be expected to (1) impair their objectivity, competence, or effectiveness in performing their functions as psychologists or (2) expose the person or organization with whom the professional relationship exists to harm or exploitation.

3.07 *Third-Party Requests for Services*

When psychologists agree to provide services to a person or entity at the request of a third party, psychologists attempt to clarify at the outset of the service the nature of the relationship with all individuals or organizations involved. This clarification includes the role of the psychologist (e.g., therapist, consultant, diagnostician, or expert witness), an identification of who is the client, the probable uses of the services provided or the information obtained, and the fact that there may be limits to confidentiality.

3.08 *Exploitative Relationships*

Psychologists do not exploit persons over whom they have supervisory, evaluative, or other authority such as clients/patients, students, supervisees, research participants, and employees.

3.09 *Cooperation With Other Professionals*

Where indicated and professionally appropriate, psychologists cooperate with other professionals in order to serve their clients/patients effectively and appropriately.

3.10 *Informed Consent*

(a) When psychologists conduct research or provide assessment, therapy, counseling, or consulting services in person or via electronic transmission or other forms of communication, they obtain the informed consent of the individual or individuals using language that is reasonably understandable to that person or persons except when conducting such activities without consent is mandated by law or governmental regulation or as otherwise provided in this Ethics Code.

(b) For persons who are legally incapable of giving informed consent, psychologists nevertheless (1) provide an appropriate explanation, (2) seek the individual's assent, (3) consider such persons' preferences and best interests, and (4) obtain appropriate permission from a legally authorized person, if such substitute consent is permitted or required by law. When consent by a legally authorized person is not permitted or required by law, psychologists take reasonable steps to protect the individual's rights and welfare.

(c) When psychological services are court ordered or otherwise mandated, psychologists inform the individual of the nature of the anticipated services, including whether the services are court ordered or mandated and any limits of confidentiality, before proceeding.

(d) Psychologists appropriately document written or oral consent, permission, and assent.

3.11 *Psychological Services Delivered to or Through Organizations*

(a) Psychologists delivering services to or through organizations provide information beforehand to clients and when appropriate those directly affected by the services about (1) the nature and objectives of the services, (2) the intended recipients, (3) which of the individuals are clients, (4) the relationship the psychologist will have with each person and the organization, (5) the probable uses of services provided and information obtained, (6) who will have access to the information, and (7) limits of confidentiality. As soon as feasible, they provide information about the results and conclusions of such services to appropriate persons.

(b) If psychologists will be precluded by law or by organizational roles from providing such information to particular individuals or groups, they so inform those individuals or groups at the outset of the service.

Entire books have been written on the subject of multiple relationships, often because they have been a controversial topic for psychologists and are often tricky to navigate. Multiple relationships occur when the psychologist has more than one relationship with a client. They can also occur when the psychologist is placed in another role where he or she has a relationship with a client as well as a relationship with someone the client is close to or associated with. Additionally, multiple relationships can occur when the psychologist initially has one role or relationship with a client and then enters into a different or new relationship involving the client.

The concern with multiple relationships is that they can become problematic when they risk the possibility of harm or exploitation to the client. Traditionally, in psychology and in past ethical codes for psychologists, there has been a push for psychologists to entirely avoid multiple relationships (previously called *dual relationships*). Thinking is changing slightly in this area such that not all multiple relationships are automatically viewed as harmful and to be avoided. Instead, the likelihood of psychologists developing multiple relationships is increasingly recognized as commonplace if not inevitable. This evolving perspective is much the case in the area of police psychology. Nonetheless, the burden of proof is always on the psychologist that any multiple relationship is in the best interest of the client and that the client is free from undue influence, exploitation, and harm because of their involvement in this relationship.

Multiple relationships in police psychology would be difficult to avoid even if one tried, and typically are commonplace and part and parcel of the daily practice of police psychology. These relationships often naturally evolve in the police agency setting, particularly if one is an in-house police psychologist, because of frequent contact and sometimes even daily contact with their clients and patients. Consider the therapy patient who is selling raffle tickets for an office event, or the past therapy patient that you work out next to and exchange pleasantries with in the agency gym, or the person you provided crisis intervention services coincidentally being the designated person when you are out of the office on a facility or district tour. Consider the person who was a subject in a fitness-for-duty evaluation you performed who now works in a division and is the person contracting your consultation services about how to handle a personnel action.

Though not all police psychologists may share this view, it is this author's opinion that with careful regard to avoid harm and exploitation, multiple relationships with clients within a police agency may actually be a positive influence not only for the client involved, but for the psychologist and his or her credibility as well. Word-of-mouth referrals indicate trust. Positive interactions with agency personnel lead to more referrals, not just because people want to send work your way, but also because you have earned their trust. This is not so different from the mindset of the psychologist who works in small or rural communities where your grocer, dentist, and neighbor may all share personal and professional relationships with you, and your lives routinely intersect.

Think about the following example. Your unit of police psychologists spends an evening with the K-9 squad for an outreach and education experience. Here you shadow the squad, spend time learning what they do firsthand, and participate in training with them, even donning a bite-suit and being a decoy for the dogs in a training exercise. The psychologist role was that of learner and participant. In the course of spending time with this squad, familiarity ensued, and jokes about the psychologists' toughness (or lack thereof, really, as the dogs yanked us to the ground) were exchanged. Part of that night involved being a passenger in high-speed driving exercises for pursuit practice for both the officers and the handling of their dogs. As the night progressed, several of the officers opened up about their thoughts and personal issues. Although there was not any sort of patient–psychologist privileged relationship, it could be considered therapeutic, and certainly the details of their disclosures were kept confidential. What happened next is that members of this squad sought out police psychologists for consultation several times over the next year in regard to behavioral and psychological issues. Additionally, when there was an officer-involved shooting incident and many of these officers came for their mandated one-to-one meeting, they felt comfortable and familiar with the psychologists and talked freely. In the context of each relationship, it was important to clarify our role, acknowledge past contact, and invite feedback. To offer more role confusion to ponder, consider that when these officers rise in the ranks, as is typical in law enforcement agencies, it is conceivable that these officers, the past teachers and trainers in one setting who then become seekers of consultation and then akin to clinical patients protected by privilege after a shooting incident, could then become the psychologist's nonpsychologist commander when they assume command of a division the unit is organized under.

Other examples that bring to light the intricacies of multiple relationships in police psychology are as follows. Consider an example where a police psychologist goes on a ride-along with an officer and this officer later becomes a clinical client seeking therapy services. Or, when a police psychologist goes on a ride-along with an officer previously unknown to them, and then the entire squad gets together at a restaurant to eat dinner and the psychologist ends up sitting face-to-face with one of her current or recent clinical therapy patients or someone she performed a fitness-for-duty evaluation on several years ago. In such situations, it is important that the psychologist be adaptable and willing to flex roles. It is also important that the psychologist be aware, look for, and be considerate of what is in the best interest of the client. This means safeguarding and maintaining confidentiality, clarifying roles as much as possible, and finding ways to remove oneself when it appears or it is revealed that a client is uncomfortable. There are a myriad of ways to politely and expediently avoid such multiple relationship situations; it is this author's stance that such measures should be taken if contact by the psychologist appears at all detrimental to the client.

As a counterpoint, an alternative view is presented. In the absence of the multiple relationships causing harm to the client, one might consider it inappropriate in police culture, or possibly viewed as self-serving and disrespectful, to suddenly say in any of these situations something to the effect of "I need to avoid having another sort of professional relationship with you since we already have met in one context or already have just one established relationship and it needs to stay that way." One could wonder whether it is the existence of multiple relationships in some circumstances that leads to greater comfort, greater collegiality, and greater ease for clients in dealing with a police psychologist. Perhaps such connections may be something to seek out and to nurture, instead of avoid. Gelber (2003) stated this well:

> Although the traditional professional ethics code for the psychologist discourages "dual relationships," contemporary revisions have recognized not only the inevitability but also the necessity of psychologists' working with both line officers and managers. Whether they are participating in supervisor's meetings or celebrating at promotional dinners, the bureau psychologists are viewed as an integral part of the division and must adapt to the multifaceted nature of their relationships with department personnel. ("LAPD Psychologists Hit the Streets," para. 16)

Additional commentary on out-of-office experiences and multiple relationships is reflected on by Zur (2001). He describes contact with clients out of the office as either carried out as part of a treatment plan or where the experience is "geared to enhance therapeutic effectiveness." This author's examples of contact as part of a treatment plan include: (1) having a cup of coffee with a police officer clinical client just prior to his oral advancement board examination to provide last-minute support after a series of therapy sessions aimed at improving confidence and decreasing anxiety related to his board examination; and (2) at the agency's workout facility, meeting with officers to practice positive self-talk and teach "what-if" thinking skills prior to law enforcement training academy exercises such as a defensive tactics exercise, or a capsaicin spray/foam exposure exercise to help decrease dropout from the academy. This author's examples of contact to enhance therapeutic effectiveness include: (1) attending the funeral of a police staff member you did not know, to support the therapy you are doing with his surviving family members; and (2) responding to the scene of an officer-involved shooting incident where one of your patients is having a hard time and upon arrival to the scene you provide support to the employee and his squad members. Zur also details a third-type of out-of-office experiences and multiple relationships as encounters that naturally occur as a matter of course of being part of the same community and truly are dual relationships. This author's examples include: (1) running into a client at the private gym where you both live and work out; (2) learning that a friend in your circle of friends is related to a past therapy patient.

In managing role conflicts, a timeless set of suggestions come from Dietz and Reese (1986). Among their suggestions are to provide their agencies with a copy of the ethical principles of psychologists and code of conduct, always identify your profession and client in your work in police psychology settings, obtain fully informed consent, be mindful of confidentiality as it applies to each situation based on who the client, avoid overidentifying with law enforcement, and stay grounded in "one's parent discipline to avoid over-identification with law enforcement" (p. 95). Janik (1994) stressed also the need for the police psychologist to be highly involved with the police agency and to avoid overidentifying, which may led to a blurring of professional boundaries.

In figuring out how to resolve multiple relationship dilemmas, there is often no clear, correct answer about how to proceed. Considering what is in the best interest of the client is surely the foremost concern. This ought to involve considering always, if known or able to be queried, the client's take on the situation, and whether an honest and open relationship exists or a difference in real or perceived power that will result in less than a forthcoming answer from the client. It may also be helpful to consider the nature and quality of the previous relationship, how the relationship ended or terminated, and whether it is still going on. A best practice approach seems to be to discuss, share openly, and invite feedback and reactions from the client about how the role and relationship are changing.

Finally, when able, keeping boundaries as clear as possible is often the best move. It is desirable and wise to try to structure the relationship as early on as possible, preferably at the first contact. When you can refer somebody to another professional and avoid a multiple relationship, this may be something to seriously consider. And, another simple step is to practice what appears to be a commonsense move: to always define and try to state aloud the role you are being asked to assume to those involved. This might look like saying aloud, "I hear you have concerns about Officer A and you are trying to figure out if you need an evaluation to determine his fitness for duty?" or instead inquiring, "I hear you saying that you are worried about Officer A. Would you like to refer him to me for therapy services?" Or, this might look like saying something to the effect of, "So, Chief, what I hear you saying is that you have such-and-such situation and you would like my input, as far as consultation about how you might consider proceeding regarding your concern about Officer A. Does that sound right?" In doing so, there is room for clarification and questions, so that a role is discussed and agreed on before proceeding. As discussed in previous examples, there also needs to be an awareness and flexibility with the fact that previously designated roles might change.

IDENTIFYING THE CLIENT

Hand in hand with the issues of dual relationships, role conflict, and boundary issues is recognizing who the client is in the course of police psychology practice. This is important in order to figure out where the psychologist's loyalties lie, who services are being provided to, and how confidentiality is to be held. As a long-ago task force in looking at the role of psychology in the criminal justice system eloquently stated, without likely the prescience that over 40 years later this would still be a pertinent issue:

> When psychologists do try seriously to articulate who their client is—where their loyalties are to be given—in criminal justice, they sometimes appear to be under the impression that they are constrained to a multiple-choice answer, with the alternatives being (a) the "system" (or "society") and (b) the offender (or police officer or defendant, as the case may be). It appears to us that there is no need for psychologists to impale themselves on the horns of this dilemma, since "Who is the client? is not a

multiple-choice question. It requires an essay answer. (Task Force on the Role of Psychology in the Criminal Justice System, 1978, p. 1102)

Police psychology is not the only area that struggles with multiple pulls regarding "Who is the client?" Kennedy and Johnson (2009) report that ethical dilemmas where there are multiple and sometimes competing obligations are common for psychologists in managed care, educational, governmental, and correctional settings. Because of such competing demands, military psychology has a similar concept that may be applicable to police psychology. They use the term *mixed agency*. In military psychology, the concept of mixed agency is "the simultaneous commitment to two or more entities" and is described as "a day-to-day matter" that military psychologists grapple (Kennedy & Johnson, 2009, p. 22). Such instances include fitness-for-duty evaluations, working with detainees, and providing consultation in regard to interrogation and counterintelligence issues. A survey of U.S. Air Force psychologists found, consistent with police and general psychology research, that the top ethical dilemmas encountered by these military psychologists involved conflicts between ethics and organizational demands, maintaining confidentiality, and multiple relationships (Orme & Doerman, 2001).

Kennedy and Johnson (2009) identify three ways to solve mixed agency dilemmas. The first involves following procedures exactly such that "one adheres strictly to the letter of the law" (p. 24). The second method involves a stealth approach where the "psychologist attempts to resolve mixed-agency quandaries by quietly thwarting ethically problematic legal requirements in favor of full adherence to the APA Ethics Code" (p. 24). The authors credit Johnson and Wilson (1993) for this approach. The third strategy detailed to manage mixed-agency dilemmas is the "best interest approach," whereby the psychologist attempts to promote the best interests of each person or organization with the idea that this approach "may offer the greatest hope of avoiding harm to any person or organizational entity while balancing obligations to both the Ethics Code and federal regulations" (p. 24). Certainly whether these strategies, particularly the second and third, are applicable to police psychology remains to be seen, but they are offered here as another way one might go about trying to wrap his or her mind around how to negotiate complex ethical dilemmas in police psychology.

DEALING WITH ORGANIZATIONAL DEMANDS

Two areas of the APA *Ethical Principles of Psychologists and Code of Conduct* (2002) are pertinent here:

1.03 *Conflicts Between Ethics and Organizational Demands*
If the demands of an organization with which psychologists are affiliated or for whom they are working are in conflict with this Ethics Code, psychologists clarify the nature of the conflict, make known their commitment to the Ethics Code, and take reasonable steps to resolve the conflict consistent with the General Principles and Ethical Standards of the Ethics Code. Under no circumstances may this standard be used to justify or defend violating human rights.

3.09 *Cooperation With Other Professionals*
When indicated and professionally appropriate, psychologists cooperate with other professionals in order to serve their clients/patients effectively and appropriately.

Dealing with organizational demands can be challenging work as a police psychologist. Ethical conflicts can arise when the psychologist runs up against conflicts between the psychologist's standard of practice, his or her codes of conduct, and the needs of the organization. Often, what the agency asks for or needs collides with something the psychologist feels is outside what is appropriate to provide and in many cases may actually constitute unethical practice if the psychologist acquiesces. Consider the possibility of a police commander first identifying an officer as a problem employee and directs that a fitness-for-duty evaluation be performed on the basis that the officer is prescribed an antidepressant medication (without any personal or workplace behaviors present that might suggest the need for such an evaluation). Consider requests that psychologists sometimes receive to break confidentiality. Or, the idea of perhaps a change in the rating of a pre-employment candidate. Ponder the idea of a new psychologist who has never been trained in or performed a fitness-for-duty evaluation being told that this is now one of his or her new job duties, to start immediately. Consider the reality of being directed to write a letter stating that an officer seen for a one-to-one post-officer-involved shooting situation is "fit" to return to work (when the standard of practice defined by IACP guidelines is that these are not fitness evaluations but instead supportive interventions). Imagine that in regard to all the previous situations, the psychologist is told, "Well, the last psychologist we used had no problem with these requests." In each of these situations, competent police psychologists will know what the appropriate response is, namely, resisting and finding a workable solution based on sound police psychology practice. But the matter of how to do this professionally, without being perceived as insubordinate and in trying to be helpful in educating about what you can provide and why you may not be able to meet the request as it currently stands—well, this is a much more complex matter.

Though no police psychologist is immune to dealing with organizational demands, there may be slight differences between psychologists who work as employees within police agencies and those who work outside the agency as consulting or contract psychologists. In-house psychologists, by virtue of being there for daily operations, may have more influence on processes and more opportunities to educate and build trust with personnel and command staff, which may in turn diminish the frequency and intensity of these organizational and ethical conflicts. On the other hand, if a psychologist works in-house and the conflicts are not regarded with sensitivity toward the psychologist needing to maintain ethical practice, life can be very difficult for that police psychologist. Psychologists working outside the police agency may be freer from daily conflict, depending on their level of involvement with the agency, but may also have less exposure to personnel and be afforded less influence in helping shape policies and practice so that psychological services are in line with current standards of practice.

RESOLVING ETHICAL DILEMMAS

There exist multiple ways of identifying, working through, and resolving ethical dilemmas. One should first ask, "Is this really an ethical dilemma, or is it some other (moral, business, or other problem-type) dilemma?" When ethical problems or dilemmas exist, a systematic problem-solving model may be of help. Another problem-solving method is to expand more abstractly the way we approach and solve problems. For instance, there is the idea that we have more than one party we are serving, and that is in contrast to the idea that we have always just one defined client. We may actually have responsibilities to multiple parties. Additionally, there is the idea of considering the culture we are working with and what is normative for that culture as an important factor in resolving ethical dilemmas. Finally, ethical practice can be promoted by attention to other methods that lead toward ethical practice. These include seeking consultation, and being aware of and adhering to professional standards and guidelines by recognizing commonly held standards of practice. These are all methods to employ toward ethical practice in the area of police psychology.

SYSTEMATIC ETHICAL DECISION-MAKING MODELS

It seems prudent to have in mind and be able to employ a systematic process through utilization of an ethical decision-making model. Having a systematic method allows for consistency as well as a plan to follow when challenged or genuinely stumped in an ethical dilemma when one needs to weigh options and is unsure how to proceed. It is important to note that even after reviewing relevant codes, guidelines, and seeking consultation, there may be no one clear "right" way to proceed to provide resolution.

One method of problem solving when ethical dilemmas exist is to employ a systematic process through utilization of an ethical decision-making model. Many decision-making models exist. The reader with interest in these models may want to refer to Cottone and Claus (2000) for a thorough review of the history of ethical decision-making models as well as a list of popular models. Several select models that this author finds helpful are mentioned here.

This author's preferred model because of familiarity and years of helpful use is Corey, Corey, and Callanan's (2007) eight-step ethical decision-making model:

1. Identify the problem or dilemma.
2. Identify the potential issues involved.
3. Review the relevant ethical codes.
4. Know the applicable laws and regulations.
5. Obtain consultation.
6. Consider possible and probable courses of action.
7. Enumerate the consequences of various decisions.
8. Decide on what appears to be the best course of action. (p. 23)

Pope and Vasquez (2007) propose a lengthier ethical decision-making model, drawing from the Canadian Psychological Associations ethics codes (2000). They caution that not all of the following steps are relevant to each ethical dilemma and that some steps may be omitted or adapted depending on the situation:

1. Identify the situation that requires ethical consideration and decision making.
2. Anticipate who will be affected by your decision.
3. Figure out who, if anyone, is the client.
4. Assess your relevant areas of competence—and of missing knowledge, skills, experience, or expertise—in regard to the relevant aspects of this situation.
5. Review relevant formal ethical standards.
6. Review relevant legal standards.
7. Review the relevant research and theory.
8. Consider how, if at all, your personal feelings, biases, or self-interest might affect your ethical judgment and reasoning.
9. Consider what effects, if any, that social, cultural, religious, or similar factors may have on the situation and in identifying ethical responses.
10. Consider consultation.
11. Develop alternative courses of action.
12. Evaluate the alternative courses of actions.
13. Try to adopt the perspective of each person who will be affected.
14. Decide what to do, and then review or reconsider it.
15. Act on and assume personal responsibility for your decision.
16. Evaluate the results.
17. Assume personal responsibility for the consequences of your actions.
18. Consider implications for preparation, planning, and prevention. (pp. 111–118)

Zur (2007) presents a seven-step decision-making model, provided here in abbreviated form:

1. Identify the issues.
2. Identify the relevant moral, ethical, clinical, legal, professional, communal, and other issues and conflicts involved.
3. Develop a series of alternative courses of action.
4. Conduct an analysis of the likely short-term, ongoing, and long-term risks and benefits of each course of action for anyone or anything involved or likely to be affected.
5. First, separately weigh the risks against the benefits within each option, then compare them and choose a course of action.
6. Implement the course of action chosen through the risk-benefit analysis.
7. Develop ways to assess the success or effectiveness of the plan and respond to the results of the assessment by either continuing with it if it has proved successful or modifying or discontinuing it if it has failed to accomplish some or all of its objectives.

These models appear to be well suited for clinical and consultation situations, though it is likely that each model could be applied to some or greater extent to assessment, operational, and educational psychology tasks. Bush, Connell, and Denney (2006) offer an eight-step systematic model for decision making in forensic psychology:

1. Identify the problem.
2. Consider the significance of the context and setting.
3. Identify and use ethics and legal resources.
4. Consider personal beliefs and values.
5. Develop possible solutions to the problem.
6. Consider the potential consequences of various solutions.
7. Choose and implement a course of action.
8. Assess the outcome and implement changes as needed. (pp. 28–35)

Corey and Trompetter (2009) propose a systematic decision-making model for law enforcement psychologists to resolve ethical dilemmas. Their model involves the acronym C.L.E.A.R:

C: Clinical considerations. Will the action I'm taking improve, complicate, or have a neutral effect on my clinical work in this matter (treatment or evaluation)? Note that this can be thought of in the psychologist's operational or consulting work, too.

L: Legal considerations. What does the law say about this issue? Do I know? Are there competing laws?

E: Ethical considerations. These involve the ethical principles and standards delineated in the *Ethical Principles and Code of Conduct for Psychologists* (APA, 2002).

A: Administrative considerations. What contractual obligations do I have? What commitments have I made in my disclosures, authorization forms, or informed consent procedures? What agency policy issues or rules need to be considered? What effect will my decision have on my office practices or on my staff?

R: Risk management considerations. How might my licensing board view my decision? Will it pass the "sniff" test or the "headline test"? How would similarly situated colleagues see it? What do the practice guidelines say about it?

Other Ethical Dilemma Resolution Strategies

Aside from systematic decision-making models, there are other methods to guide ethical decision making and practice. These may be helpful to psychologists who are still left without clear answers about how to proceed after employing one or more of the systematic ethical decision-making models.

Reconsidering the Definition of the Client

One way is to expand more abstractly the way we approach and solve problems. For instance, instead of focusing on just having one single client, as this is often not the case in police psychology where there may be more than one client, there is the idea that we have more than one party we are serving, even with a defined client. Fisher (2009) detailed a method of thinking about "the fact that psychologists have ethical obligations to all parties in every case, regardless of the number or nature of the relationships" (p. 1). She provides examples of how third-party requests, and providing services to or through organizations, are examples where such considerations exist. She encourages that such situations need to be pondered, the relationships need to be clarified, and the psychologist needs to be planful in his or her approach.

For police psychologists, there are numerous situations where we may have one such "master" or primary client (typically, the police agency) but actually have many parties to recognize and to be responsible for. Consider, for example, the police officer client who is referred by the police agency for mandated anger management therapy. The primary client could be considered to be the police agency; the agency made the referral and wants information regarding attendance in treatment. But then there is the other client, the person seeking therapy, and as outlined in an informed consent, his or her private disclosures and the details of the treatment are kept confidential. Consider also the work of a police psychologist as part of a crisis negotiation callout. Their client in this case is the police agency. Their client is not the subject on scene, such as a hostage taker. Though not a client per se, an interested party may be the public as a whole, who is expecting the police agency to end the situation and maintain the safety of the environment where the incident is taking place, and the police psychologist is now involved in this as well.

Additionally, the idea that we have changing responsibilities to others in evolving situations is relevant to consider. Do we have a duty or responsibility to more than just the client in performing police psychology functions? The answer can sometimes be a surprising "yes."

Consider the case of a pre-employment evaluation where police psychologists may have a responsibility to more than just the client agency. One recent Arizona case could provide food-for-thought in considering different responsibilities in evaluations. *Stanley v. McCarver* (2003) involved holding negligent a radiologist who interpreted Christine Stanley's chest X-ray that was administered as part of a pre-employment evaluation. This X-ray revealed lung nodule densities that Stanley believes would have led to a quicker diagnosis of the lung cancer she was eventually diagnosed with 10 months later. In the initial case, the court found that Dr. McCarver had not acted negligently because there was not a physician–patient relationship with Stanley. Upon appeal, this decision was reversed in part and the court found that "a physician has a duty to exercise reasonable care in conducting the examination and this duty includes communicating about the examination directly to the person examined" (para. 21).

As an Arizona psychologist, the case has altered this author's response in several pre-employment situations. As an example, consider the case of a pre-employment evaluation where a client presents as emotionally unstable. Though this is a very rare occurrence in pre-employment evaluations, it does occasionally happen. When an applicant has expressed recent and/or current suicidal ideation for instance and/or is clearly majorly depressed, this psychologist has stopped the evaluation. The focus is then on sharing the concerning findings, expressing a strong recommendation that the person seek prompt or immediate (depending on the level of dangerousness) medical and/or mental health treatment, and, last, identifying referrals for the applicant. It goes without saying that applicants quickly figure out they likely did not receive a "pass," positive rating, or "hire" recommendation. The incident is documented on a separate form and placed within the applicant's pre-employment psychological record. The police agency then gets a report with a "no-hire" recommendation. In circumstances such as this case, there are multiple parties the psychologist must exercise responsibility toward.

What About the Culture?

Another method to guide ethical decision making and practice is to consider the context and cultural variables of the culture we work in. In this case, this is the law enforcement culture as a whole, and specifically the culture of the police agency where the psychologist works. Traditionally, law enforcement culture values loyalty and collegiality, often regards officers as family, values being helpful, and consists of heroic individuals who value strength. There is also typically respect for rules and policies and structure, and an acquiescence to dealing with issues within a hierarchical setting. At times, there can be rigidity and a black-and-white thinking style (which, of course, helps maintain order and structure within the system). If, as a police psychologist, you are aware and respectful of this culture and work at resolving ethical dilemmas within this framework, then working in a police agency can often become a much easier task. As an example, in this psychologist's pre-employment evaluation experience, a common situation occurred. This involved processing public safety applicants within a state where 18-year-old applicants commonly reported in their personal life having sexual intercourse with minors, say, typically 17-year-olds. The law in this particular state, by its letter, does not allow consent for such sexual relations. Because of this, in each case, a mandated report of possible child abuse was required by the psychologist.

This situation was understandably concerning from a hiring perspective (as well as tedious, but required, for the psychologists). It led to a valid point on the part of the police agency in questioning along the lines of how we can have you make mandated reports and then we turn around and hire this person for work within our agency. From the psychologist's point of view, this situation presented the ethical issue of dealing with organizational demands and the legal issue of not being able to ignore or discharge a legal and mandated duty to report.

How you approach a dilemma is sometimes everything. What was not successful in this situation was any sort of insistence that this psychologist had an ethical dilemma that needed resolving. It was important to keep in mind that the police agency is not beholden to the APA *Ethical Principles of Psychologists and Code of Conduct*. Resolution came from discussing with supportive command staff the needs and wants of the agency; the ethical, legal and hiring issues; the conflicts; the pros and cons of taking different courses of actions; and sharing the consultation feedback this psychologist had thus far gathered in looking at this issue. Ultimately, what led to a successful resolution was talking about a mutual respect and regard for following the law, which in this case meant the psychologist making reports as required. A clear statement was made that was the starting point for a resolution. A member of command staff said, "Well, it's as simple as we can't have you breaking the law, Doc. You've got to follow the law." A discussion ensued about how while a duty to report exists, with 99% of the applicants evaluated that present with this circumstance, there was not a clinical concern such that this reporting mandate led to a no-hire recommendation in the pre-employment evaluation report. Based on this discussion, new wording was incorporated into the pre-employment report to explain this, a specific reporting system was implemented to keep the law enforcement agency the primary reporting source when possible, and both parties walked away feeling the issue was well resolved. Without an appreciation of resolving this dilemma within and having respect for the police culture, it is unlikely this situation would have been resolved positively.

The Role of Consultation

A final way to resolve ethical dilemmas is to have a process in place to seek consultation from other police psychologists. Reliance on previous experience and the opinions of peers may be paramount in solving ethical dilemmas (Osborn, Day, Komesaroff, & Mant, 2009). Seeing ethical behavior of peers is also influential in promoting ethical behavior (Deshpande & Prasad, 2006). Having experienced colleagues who can help one to think aloud about the importance of adherence to professional standards, assist in considering standards of practice, and provide a sounding board to contemplate how to proceed are other ways of maintaining ethical police psychology practice. To this end, there are various professional police psychology organizations (previously identified and referred to) to join. There are also committees to call on for consultation such as the American Psychological Association; the Division 18 (Psychologists in Public Service) mentoring program; and the newly formed International Association of Chiefs of Police, Police Psychological Services Section Early Career Psychologists Committee, and International Association of Chiefs of Police, Police Psychological Services Section Ethics Committee. Additionally, peers may be identified for individualized consultation through posts on the listservs for the American Psychological Association (APA), Division 18, Police & Public Safety Section; and the International Association of Chiefs of Police, Police Psychological Services Section (IACP PPSS).

PROFICIENCIES AND SPECIALTY ETHICAL GUIDELINES FOR POLICE PSYCHOLOGISTS

Police psychology is an emerging and evolving practice area. Though there have long been efforts to define the roles and scope of practice of police psychologists (Aamodt, 2000; Blau, 1994; Dietz, 2000; Kurke & Scrivner, 1995; Ostrov, 1986), the greatest effort perhaps toward defining the work police psychologists perform was defined by the Police Psychology Core Domains & Proficiencies

Joint Committee on Police Psychology Competencies, which met in the fall of 2007. This committee was a joint effort between members of the International Association of Chiefs of Police, Police Psychological Services Section (IACP PPSS); members of the Society for Police and Criminal Psychology (SPCP); and members of the American Psychological Association (APA), Division 18, Police & Public Safety Section. They identified 57 distinct tasks and proficiencies of police psychologists that were then separated into four core domains: assessment, intervention, operational, and consulting (Aumiller & Corey, 2007). Aumiller and Corey's extensive document listing and defining these domains and proficiencies are "now the accepted definition of the field of police psychology as defined by members of the profession" (2007, p. 65). Additionally, in 2008, police psychology was recognized as a proficiency area by APA.

Police psychology is a compilation of different types of psychology practice. Police psychology is often regarded as part of forensic psychology (Falkenbach, 2008). Certainly many of the assessment tasks of police psychology are forensic in nature. However, many aspects of police psychology practice, such as providing psychotherapy, are more clinical or counseling in nature. Additionally, some police psychologists come from an industrial-organizational background and perspective. Research, personnel selection, and organizational consultation come strongly from this tradition.

Provision of police psychological services stems back to psychological tests used in police selection in 1916 (Dietz & Reese, 1986), then it picked up momentum in the 1950s (Zelig, 1987) and really took off in the 1980s, when police psychology started to be recognized as a distinct field and area of practice (Scrivner, 1994). Since that time, it has not stopped progressing at a very steady pace as both an identity for psychologists and in scope of the services provided. Because of this, increasingly, police psychologists run into ethical dilemmas that are not adequately resolved through reliance on current ethical guidelines and codes. This is in part because police psychology practice is not all clinical and counseling in nature, just as it is not all industrial-organizational in nature.

It is this psychologist's opinion that there is a need for specialty ethical guidelines for police psychology. If we rest on the idea that we are a relatively new and emerging field and stay silent, it is likely that our field and scope of practice will be defined for us by others. We then risk having our practice dictated to us and judged by standards that do not fit us well or address some of our unique ways of practicing, based on not only the work we do but also the unique population we serve.

Obviously, there are arguments against a set of specialty ethical guidelines for police psychology. First, there is the issue of redundancy and how to manage likely conflicts between a new specialty guideline and the existing APA *Ethical Principles of Psychologists and Code of Conduct*. There is also a relevant consideration of one more document for police psychologists to consider and try to follow, which some may consider onerous and burdensome. Additionally, there is the idea that perhaps advocating as a group to influence future revisions of the *Ethical Principles of Psychologists and Code of Conduct* is a preferred course of action instead of creating specialty guidelines.

An impetus to consider as a profession developing specialty guidelines may be that we have proficiencies as police psychologists that are currently starting to become out of line or at least risky, within the current ethical standards of our profession as a whole. However, this does not mean that we are unethical psychologists, rather that the codes as they exist may need some fine-tuning to be more applicable to the changing work that we do. Examples of where we may not be currently adequately represented in the current psychological professional culture and *Ethical Principles of Psychologists and Code of Conduct* are when police psychologists work as consultants with agencies and in crisis negotiation situations. In the last several years, there have been heated debates among psychologists and mental health professionals, with many arguing that psychologists need not be involved in any way with actions that could lead to the harm, serious injury, or death of individuals. Any police psychologist involved in crisis negotiation training or operational support knows that based on the opinions and misunderstandings of what we do by many, police psychologists may soon have mandates placed on them that drastically shape and/or limit their proficiencies and ability to provide such services. We are also somewhat unique as a field in how we engage in multiple relationships, and it is possible that a stronger stance in recognizing and even in some cases advocating the positive benefits of such relationships is warranted. Examples such as these, and likely there are others, necessitate that we have our practices reflected in ethical codes that are specific to our area of practice.

If developed, perhaps a set of specialty guidelines for police psychology practice can be modeled after existing specialty guidelines. For instance, the specialty guidelines for forensic psychologists are aspirational in nature. They do not set a mandate for appropriate professional conduct. Specialty guidelines are meant to be used together with other relevant ethical codes, such as the *Ethical Principles of Psychologists and Code of Conduct*, and in conjunction with relevant laws and regulations. Perhaps specialty ethical guidelines for police psychologists can be used in much the same spirit and practice. While aspirational, they would provide a sort of set of directions for ideal conduct and actions by police psychologists. Such a guideline would also help establish and expand the literature base of the current standard of practice in police psychology.

DIRECTIONS FOR FUTURE RESEARCH

Further research and study is needed. First, along the lines of Zelig's (1988) study, there is a need for ongoing research to identify the most prevalent ethical dilemmas that police psychologists encounter. Frequency of these dilemmas' occurrence would also be enlightening. Surveying about not only police psychology practice but also the wider domain of public safety psychology practice may be helpful as many police psychologists also work with fire, corrections, and detention personnel. It is likely that the ethical dilemmas encountered by police psychologists are similar if not identical to the types of dilemmas encountered by psychologists who work with these other related professions. This is a supposition and therefore research needs to bear out what differences, if any, arise in the types and frequencies of ethical dilemmas psychologists encounter in working with these different professional groups.

Research about the methods police psychologists most commonly utilize to resolve ethical dilemmas are also suggested. It would be interesting to learn how police psychologists resolve the ethical dilemmas they encounter as well as to see if there are differences between those psychologists who are longstanding in the fields; newer to this specialized area of work; and clinical, counseling, forensic, academic, or industrial-organizational in training and affiliation; as well as whether there are other relevant variables. Additionally, ethical casebooks and workbooks can be helpful (Kenyon, 1999; Nagy, 2005; Pope, Sonne, & Greene, 2006; Steinman, Richardson, & McEnroe, 1998), and such books aimed specifically at police psychology practice seem warranted. A final area for future study is in arriving at whether there is a need for specialty ethical guidelines for police psychology. Surveying police psychologists would be helpful to answer these questions, as well as then proceed toward creating such a code.

REFERENCES

Aamodt, M. G. (2000). The role of the I/O psychologist in police psychology. *Journal of Police and Criminal Psychology, 15*(2), 8–10.

American Educational Research Association, American Psychological Association, National Council on Research in Education. (1999). *Standards for educational and psychological testing* (2nd ed.). Washington, DC: American Educational Research Association.

American Psychological Association. (2010). American Psychological Association amends ethics code to address potential conflicts among professional ethics, legal authority and organizational demands. Retrieved April 3, 2010, from http://www.apa.org/news/press/releases/2010/02/ethics-code.aspx

American Psychological Association. (2002). Ethical principles of psychologists and code of conduct. *American Psychologist, 57,* 1060–1073.

Aumiller, G. S., & Corey, D. (2007). Defining the field of police psychology: Core domains & proficiencies. *Journal of Police and Criminal Psychology, 22,* 65–76. doi: 10.1007/s11896-007-9013-4

Blau, T. H. (1994). *Psychological services for law enforcement.* New York: John Wiley.

Bush, S. S., Connell, M. A., & Denney, R. L. (2006). *Ethical practice in forensic psychology: A systematic model for decision-making.* Washington, DC: American Psychological Association.

Canadian Psychological Association. (2000). *Canadian code of ethics for psychologists.* Ottawa: Author.

Cohen, E. D., & Cohen, G. S. (1999). *The virtuous therapist: Ethical practice of counseling and psychotherapy.* Belmont, CA: Wadsworth.

Colnerud, G. (1997). Ethical dilemmas of psychologists: A Swedish example in an international perspective. *European Psychologist, 2*(2), 164–170.

Committee on Ethical Guidelines for Forensic Psychologists. (1991). Specialty guidelines for forensic psychologists. *Law and Human Behavior, 15,* 655–665.

Corey, G., Corey, M. S., & Callanan, P. (2007). *Issues and ethics in the helping professions.* Belmont, CA: Thomson Brooks/Cole.

Corey, D., & Trompetter, P. S. (2009, October). *Ethical dilemmas for law enforcement psychologists: A systematic model for decision-making.* Paper presented at the International Association of Chiefs of Police, Police Psychological Services Section Conference, Denver, CO.

Cottone, R. R., & Claus, R. E. (2000). Ethical decision-making models: A review of the literature. *Journal of Counseling & Development, 78,* 275–283.

Deshpande, S. P., Joseph, J., & Prasad, R. (2006). Factors Impacting Ethical Behavior in Hospitals. *Journal of Business Ethics, 69*(2), 207–216.

Dietz, A. S. (2000). The role of the I/O psychologist in police psychology. *Journal of Police and Criminal Psychology, 15*(2), 1–7.

Dietz, P. E., and Reese, J. T. (1986). The perils of police psychology: 10 strategies for minimizing role conflicts when providing mental health service and consultation to law enforcement agencies. *Behavioral Sciences & the Law, 4*(4), 385–400.

Falkenbach, D. M. (2008). Forensic psychology. In G. Madhavan, B. Oakley, & L. Kun (Eds.), *Career development in bioengineering and biotechnology* (pp. 214–221). New York: Springer.

Fisher, M. A. (2009). Replacing "Who is the client?" with a different ethical question. *Professional Psychology Research and Practice, 40*(1), 1–7. doi: 10.137/a0014011

Gelber, C. (2003). LAPD bureau psychologists hit the streets. *Police Chief,* September. Retrieved April 3, 2010, from http://policechiefmagazine.org

Gelles, M. G., Morgan, C. A., & Moorehead, O. (2006, October). Ethical challenges for police psychologists in consultation to police operations. Paper presented at the International Association of Chiefs of Police, Police Psychological Services Section Conference, Boston.

International Association of Chiefs of Police. (2004a). *Officer-involved shooting guidelines.* Arlington, VA. Retrieved April 3, 2010, from http://www.theiacp.org/psych_services_section/

International Association of Chiefs of Police. (2004b). *Pre-employment psychological evaluation guidelines.* Arlington, VA. Retrieved April 3, 2010, from http://www.theiacp.org/psych_services_section/

International Association of Chiefs of Police. (2006a). *Peer support guidelines.* Arlington, VA. Retrieved April 3, 2010, from http://www.theiacp.org/psych_services_section/

International Association of Chiefs of Police. (2006b). *Guidelines for consulting police psychologists.* Arlington, VA. Retrieved April 3, 2010, from http://www.theiacp.org/psych_services_section/

International Association of Chiefs of Police. (2009). *Fitness for duty evaluation guidelines.* Arlington, VA. Retrieved April 3, 2010, from http://www.theiacp.org/psych_services_section/

Inwald, R. E. (1984). Psychological screening: Legal, ethical, and administrative questions. *Police Chief,* January.

Janik, J. (1994). Desirable qualifications in a police psychologist. *Journal of Police and Criminal Psychology, 10*(2), 24–31.

Johnson, W. B., & Wilson, K. (1993). The military internship: A retrospective analysis. *Professional Psychology Research and Practice, 24,* 312–318.

Kennedy, C. H., & Johnson, W. B. (2009). Mixed agency in military psychology: Applying the American Psychological Association Ethics Code. *Psychological Services, 6*(1), 22–31.

Kenyon, P. (1999). *What would you do? An ethical case workbook for human service professionals.* Pacific Grove, CA: Brooks/Cole.

Kurke, M. I., & Scrivner, E. M. (Eds.). (1995). *Police psychology into the 21st century.* Hillsdale, NJ: Lawrence Erlbaum.

Nagy, T. F. (2005). *Ethics in plain English: An illustrative casebook for psychologists* (2nd ed.). Washington, DC: American Psychological Association.

Orme, D. R., & Doerman, A. L. (2001). Ethical dilemmas and U.S. Air Force clinical psychologists: A survey. *Professional Psychology Research and Practice, 32*(3), 305–311.

Osborn, M., Day, R., Komesaroff, P., & Mant, A. (2009). Do ethical guidelines make a difference to decision-making? *Internal Medicine Journal, 39*, 800–805.

Ostrov, E. (1986). Police/law enforcement psychology. *Behavioral Sciences & the Law, 4*(4), 353–370.

Pettifor, J. L., & Sawchuk, T. R. (2006). Psychologists' perceptions of ethically troubling incidents across international borders. *International Journal of Psychology, 41*(3), 216–225.

Pope, K. S., Sonne, J. L., & Greene, B. (2006). *What therapists don't talk about and why: Understanding taboos that hurt us and our clients.* Washington, DC: American Psychological Association.

Pope, K. S., & Vasquez, M. J. (2007). *Ethics in psychotherapy and counseling.* San Francisco, CA: John Wiley.

Pope, K. S., & Vetter, V. A. (1992). Ethical dilemmas encountered by members of the American Psychological Association: A national survey. *American Psychologist, 47*(3), 387–411.

Reese, J. T. (1987). *A history of police psychological services.* Washington, DC: U.S. Government Printing Office.

Reese, J. T., & Goldstein, H. A. (Eds.). (1986). *Psychological services for law enforcement: A compilation of papers submitted to the National Symposium on Police Psychological Services (at the FBI Academy, Quantico, VA).* Washington, DC: U.S. Government Printing Office.

Schank, J. A., & Skovholt, T. M. (1997). Dual-relationship dilemmas of rural and small-community psychologists. *Professional Psychology, 28*(1), 44–49. doi: 0.1037/0735-7028.28.1.44

Scrivner, E.M. (1994). *Controlling police use of excessive force: The role of the police psychologist* Retrieved April 3, 2010, from http://www.ncjrs.gov/?txtfiles/ppsyc.txt

Slack, C. M., & Wassenaar, D. R. (1999). Ethical dilemmas of South African clinical psychologists: International comparisons. *European Psychologist, 4*(3), 179–186.

Stanley v. McCarver and Osborn, Nelson & Carr Portable X-Ray, Inc. 1 CA-CV 02-0328 (Superior Court in Maricopa County, AZ 2003).

Steinman, S. O., Richardson, N. F., & McEnroe, T. (1998). *The ethical decision-making manual for helping professionals.* Belmont, CA: Brooks/Cole.

Super, J. T. (1997). *Select legal and ethical aspects of pre-employment psychological evaluations, 12*(2), 1–6.

Task Force on the Role of Psychology in the Criminal Justice System, American Psychological Association. (1978). Report of the task force on the role of psychology in the criminal justice system. *American Psychologist, 33*(12), 1099–1113.

Zelig, M. (1987). Clinical services and demographic characteristics of police psychologists. *Professional Psychology Research and Practice, 18*(3), 269–275.

Zelig, M. (1988). Ethical dilemmas in police psychology. *Professional Psychology Research and Practice, 19*(3), 336–338.

Zur, O. (2001). Out-of-office experience: When crossing office boundaries and engaging in dual relationships are clinically beneficial and ethically sound. *The Independent Practitioner, 21*(1), 96–100.

Zur, O. (2007). *Boundaries in psychotherapy.* Washington, DC: American Psychological Association.

CASES CITED

Jaffee v. Redmond, 518 U.S. 1 (1996).

Pettus v. Cole, 49 Cal. App. 4th 402, 57 Cal.Rptr. 2d 46 (1996).

5 Probation and Surveillance Officer Candidates

Similarities and Differences With Police Personnel

D. Scott Herrmann

Barbara Broderick

As discussed in Chapter 1 of this book, the use of psychological tests to aid in the evaluation and selection of police candidates is well established in the United States, with the foundation of such assessment dating back to the turn of the 20th century (Maloney & Ward, 1976). Lewis Terman of Stanford University was one of the field's earliest pioneers, and conducted one of the first documented studies of police selection in the United States (Reese, 1995; Terman & Otis, 1917). However, it was not until the 1967 President's Commission on Law Enforcement and Administration of Justice that the psychological assessment and selection of law enforcement candidates became solidified in the United States (Benner, 1986; Reese, 1995). In the decades that followed, many changes occurred in the psychological tools that were developed for the selection of law enforcement candidates, the evaluation methods employed, and the laws governing the selection process. Now, as law enforcement psychology (i.e., the application of professional psychology with police and allied law enforcement groups) continues to develop and expand into the 21st century, evolutionary changes continue to punctuate this unique area of psychological practice in new and previously unforeseen ways.

One area of change that represents a truly burgeoning area of growth and opportunity for law enforcement psychologists is the provision of psychological services to *nontraditional* law enforcement agencies. Specifically, these are agencies that fall outside the umbrella cast by the U.S. Department of Justice and state/local law enforcement, but that nevertheless assume quasi–law enforcement functions in communities and neighborhoods. One example of a nontraditional law enforcement agency is that of a probation department, where court-appointed officers function in a hybrid capacity that often involves both law enforcement and social work functions.

Currently, there are more than 2,000 separate probation agencies in the United States that fall under the jurisdiction of the courts (Abadinsky, 2009), many of which employ a combination of both probation officers and surveillance officers. While probation and surveillance officers' job functions tend to be multifaceted and are described in detail later in this chapter, the primary role of a probation officer is to ensure that court-mandated "conditions of probation" are followed and adhered to by convicted offenders, while surveillance officers' primary job duty is to assist the probation officer in ensuring such conditions are met. In addition to probation departments at the federal, state, county, and municipal levels, there are also private companies and nonprofit organizations providing probation services throughout the United States (Burrell, 2005). Indeed, with courts and allied criminal justice agencies growing at a rapid pace, and with the employment of probation officers expected to increase by 11% between 2006 and 2016 (U.S. Department of

Labor, 2008), practice opportunities are abundant for law enforcement psychologists seeking to expand their services into this adjunctive area of practice.

However, while the practice opportunities are plentiful, psychological evaluations of probation/ surveillance candidates *should not* be construed as simply synonymous with police psychological evaluations because there are a number of important and noteworthy distinctions that exist between these vocational cohorts. For example, there are important differences in essential job functions, in the philosophical orientation of departments, and in background and training requirements of the involved officers. Moreover, in most jurisdictions, police officers are required to be certified under a state's Police Officer Standards & Training Board (POST), while probation officers may or may not be required to be POST-certified. Additionally in some jurisdictions, probation officers are formally recognized as "peace officers," while in other jurisdictions they are not. According to a recent survey by the American Probation and Parole Association (2006), 25 of 56 states and territories have formally recognized adult probation officers with peace officer status, and 17 of 56 states and territories have recognized juvenile probation officers with such status. Other areas of distinction include those related to essential job functions. While a police officer's primary job function is often defined as "protecting and serving the community," a probation officers' job function usually entails providing both enforcement *and* rehabilitative services to convicted felons under the auspices of the courts. Each probation department is therefore in the unique position of articulating whether "rehabilitation," "enforcement," or a combination of both perspectives is to be emphasized in a probation agency's mission statement and philosophical outlook (see Burton, Latessa, & Barker, 1992; Small & Torres, 2001, for a thorough discussion of this topic).

While these are but a few examples that demonstrate how probation departments are not one-in-the-same with police agencies, there are nevertheless important areas of similarity and overlap between these entities as well. For example, many probation/surveillance officers in the 21st century carry firearms while performing their duties. They are also empowered with arrest authority, wear body armor in the field, function within "chain-of-command" organizations, and are subject to many of the same occupational hazards and stressors encountered by police officers. One specific example of the overlapping function between probation and police can be found in Arizona, where the Maricopa County Adult Probation Department (MCAPD) received nearly $700,000 in federal stimulus funding in 2009 for its fugitive apprehension unit in order to combat illegal narcotics activity and drug trafficking within the state. Because MCAPD serves more warrants than any other law enforcement agency within the nation's fourth most populous county, the Department of Justice recognized MCAPD as uniquely positioned to receive and apply such funding to further the DOJ's law enforcement objectives. Thus, while it cannot be assumed that police and probation are merely synonymous vocational cohorts, there are important areas of overlap regarding police-oriented job functions that should be recognized.

Consequently, before stepping into this unique area of practice by providing psychological services to probation departments, law enforcement psychologists must have a good working knowledge of what the specific similarities and differences are between police and probation cohorts. They must know what the different types of probation departments are (e.g., adult versus juvenile, federal versus local, and so forth), what the differences are in terms of agency mission and values, and what the historical factors are that gave rise to the "probation movement" to begin with. The purpose of this chapter is therefore to highlight some of these important distinctions for law enforcement psychologists who may not have been otherwise exposed to this information. It is incumbent on those interested in working in this area to have a solid grounding and knowledge of the important nuances that exist *prior* to performing psychological evaluations of probation/surveillance officer candidates. Only this way will the most thoughtful and defensible psychological evaluations for probation department organizations and consumers result.

PROBATION/SURVEILLANCE OVERVIEW

HISTORY OF PROBATION MOVEMENT IN THE UNITED STATES

The probation movement in the United States can be traced back to John Augustus of Boston, Massachusetts, widely recognized as the "first probation officer" in the United States. In the late 1800s, Augustus was a shoemaker in Boston who took it upon himself to bail out a man charged with being a vagrant and common drunkard. Successful rehabilitation with this first case led Augustus to bail out other defendants in an effort to attempt rehabilitation with them, which commonly included vocational assistance and help establishing a residence. In his capacity as a volunteer, Augustus would also make frequent returns to the court to provide progress updates on his charges and to make recommendations regarding case dispositions.

Augustus reportedly worked in this manner for nearly 18 years, and generally received strong support from judges regarding his efforts. Between 1841 and 1859, nearly 2,000 men and women were spared incarceration because of Augustus's intervention and supervision efforts (Champion, 2008). Interestingly, however, many policemen were said to oppose Augustus's rehabilitation efforts because they were unable to collect their customary fee for each rehabilitated case that did not result in a commitment to the House of Corrections (Abadinsky, 2009).

After Augustus's death in 1859, supporters successfully lobbied the Massachusetts legislature to enact the first probation statute in 1878, which authorized the Boston mayor to hire a probation officer who would be supervised under the superintendent of police. Thereafter, the second state to adopt an official probation statute was Vermont in 1898, with other states quickly following suit. Although most early probation officers were unpaid, voluntary positions, many of the earliest paid probation officers worked simultaneously as police officers, deputies, or clerks in district attorney's offices (Champion, 2008). By 1919, the Illinois legislature enacted a law providing that counties pay salaries and expenses of probation officers, and in each police district, a police officer spent part of his time out of uniform performing the duties of a probation officer (Schultz, 1973). In 1925, Congress enacted legislation establishing the Federal Probation System, and in 1929 the first paid United States Probation Officer (USPO) was appointed under the Department of Justice. Thereafter, in 1939, federal probation administration was shifted to the newly created Administrative Office of the United States Courts. In the 21st century, probation departments exist at the federal, state, and county levels. Probation in the United States is administered by more than 2,000 separate agencies supervising in excess of 3 million adult offenders on probation for felonies and misdemeanors (Abadinsky, 2009).

With regard to juvenile probation, the first juvenile court was established in Chicago in July 1899 by way of the Juvenile Court Act introduced by the Illinois legislature. Prior to this date, Massachusetts, New York, and certain other states had statutes providing for the separate hearings of children's cases apart from adult cases, but it was not until 1899 that the first juvenile court in the United States was officially established (Flexner & Baldwin, 1916). Between 1900 and 1920, 20 states passed similar acts to establish juvenile courts, and by the end of World War II, all states had created juvenile court systems (Champion, 2008). The development of juvenile probation followed closely thereafter, although some historical accounts have indicated that some form of juvenile probation was provided by a private society in the central district of Boston as early as 1888 (Flexner & Baldwin, 1916). In short, juvenile courts and juvenile probation agencies emerged as an outgrowth of the notion that juveniles deserve enhanced reform and rehabilitative efforts as compared to adult offenders, and juvenile courts have traditionally had considerable latitude in managing the affairs of juveniles. Another important distinction is that juvenile court and probation records in most states are routinely expunged and/or sealed once the offender reaches a certain age. The purpose of these laws is to allow a minor who has committed delinquent acts to erase his or her record permanently and begin with a "clean slate" upon entering adulthood.

Essential Functions of Probation/Surveillance Work

Among probation officers' many duties, the most primary job responsibility is to serve as the "eyes and ears of the court." Beyond this general description, however, probation work may entail a wide array of different responsibilities and duties, and there may be wide fluctuation across probation agencies in terms of the duties assigned to probation officers. Not infrequently, some probation officer duties may appear contradictory, for example, (1) to rehabilitate and treat offenders who are amenable to treatment, and (2) to protect society from those individuals who pose a risk to the community (Colley, Culbertson, & Latessa, 1986). These kinds of multiple role expectations present a true dilemma for probation administrators charged with balancing these often contradictory agendas when there is disagreement about whether a "law enforcement" or "social work" approach should be emphasized. Nevertheless, some common probation officer duties found in most departments often include directing and counseling probationers regarding the terms of their probation, conducting field visits (home, work, treatment facilities or jail), investigating alleged violations of probation, administering breathalyzer/urinalysis tests, assessing social history and risk to the community, directing probationers to community resources, conducting investigations and preparing a variety of electronic and written reports for the court, coordinating services with other social and law enforcement agencies, testifying at court hearings, and, in some jurisdictions, conducting searches and effecting arrests.

Surveillance officers, on the other hand, typically perform "journey-level" probation officer functions and assist probation officers in enforcing the terms and conditions of probation. While in general parlance the word *surveillance* often conjures up ideas of surreptitious undercover investigations or cloak-and-dagger operations (Lyon, 2007), when used by probation departments, it has an altogether different meaning. Surveillance within probation departments typically involves focused, systematic attention to the personal details and behaviors of those who are under direct supervision of the court. Surveillance officer duties often involve considerable fieldwork and are similar to those of probation officers but are not performed with the same degree of independence or autonomy as that of probation officers. Some essential surveillance officer functions typically include providing ongoing surveillance to a caseload of probationers, assisting in the enforcement of mandated curfews, conducting telephone contacts, performing work-site or school visits during day and evening hours, maintaining chronological logs and records of probationer activity, responding to inquires by family members or law enforcement officers, assisting with rehabilitation functions by providing counseling, evaluation of living arrangements, administering alcohol and drug tests, appearing in court with a probation officer, and, in some jurisdictions, conducting searches and making arrests. While there is substantial overlap between probation officer and surveillance officer functions, the critical difference between the two is that probation officers function in a more independent and autonomous capacity and are viewed as operating with a higher degree of professionalism. Probation officers are frequently viewed as the eyes and ears of the "court," but surveillance officers are more often viewed as the eyes and ears of the "probation officer."

To Arm or Not to Arm: Not all POs/SOs Carry Firearms

Although important distinctions exist between police and probation/surveillance functions, one factor causing these distinctions to blur—especially in the public's eye—is when probation/surveillance officers carry firearms. In the 21st century there is a growing trend within probation departments to arm their officers (Roscoe, Duffee, Rivera, & Smith, 2005; Small & Torres, 2001), with many probation departments additionally empowering their officers with full arrest authority. As of this writing, all but 11 of the 94 federal judicial districts permit U.S. probation officers to carry firearms (Small & Torres, 2001). Similar trends are taking place at the state and county levels. Accordingly, probation agencies are now providing tactical training to their officers and establishing policies and procedures for firearm certification (and decertification when necessary) for their officers who carry firearms. With the enhanced function of carrying firearms comes increased risks, not only to probation officers but also to probation departments and the community as a whole.

VALUED CHARACTERISTICS OF PROBATION/SURVEILLANCE OFFICERS

As a rule of thumb, probation departments generally maintain higher educational standards for entry-level officer positions compared to police agencies. A bachelor's degree is usually required to work as a probation officer, with some jurisdictions requiring a master's degree for an entry-level position. Entry-level surveillance officers are usually required to possess only an associate's degree or a high school diploma/GED. Entry-level probation officers are often recruited into the field from college and university based criminal justice departments as well as from social work, counseling, and psychology departments. Clearly, one of the ways that probation departments differ from police departments is that probation tends to draw officers from a much more diverse educational/vocational background. As Colley et al. (1986) note, "When different professional backgrounds are brought to the same job, friction may arise as to the 'right way' of doing the job." (p. 67). This friction is clearly evident in some probation departments and even across certain specialized probation units, simply due to the diversity of backgrounds and perspectives represented within an agency.

Regarding a philosophical approach to probation work, some empirical research has begun to emerge that sheds light on how the majority of probation officers tend to view their job functions and what sort of professional roles they most value. An early study on how probation officers perceive their roles was conducted by Van Landingham, Taber, and Dimants (1977). In this study, several hundred probation officers in the state of Ohio were surveyed regarding their perceived essential job functions. Results indicated that officers tended to favor "advice/guidance" services and "referral/court consultation" services the most, but there was considerable disagreement regarding law enforcement–related functions. Some officers embraced law enforcement functions, while others did not. In a related study, Wright (1997) found that probation officers in Delaware were much more inclined toward offender reform than offender control and cited overwhelming support for probation officers embracing a "casework strategy" as opposed to a "law enforcement mentality" (p. 77). While these findings do emphasize a social work over law enforcement orientation, we contend that given the multifaceted functions and duties that currently exist within probation departments, there is adequate room for *both* philosophical perspectives within probation departments in the 21st century. However, it is incumbent on the law enforcement psychologist and probation department administration to ensure that a probation officer's unique philosophical and psychological characteristics truly match his or her duty assignment within a department. It is also imperative that probation agencies have a well-articulated set of competencies that clearly spell out the traits and characteristics an agency most values among its officers and that a mission statement has been adopted that supports and reinforces the competencies and characteristics identified.

An example of such a competency set can be found in Arizona, where in 2008/2009 the Maricopa County Adult Probation Department (MCAPD), the nation's fifth largest probation department with more than 1,150 employees, undertook a yearlong effort to identify and define the specific traits and characteristics most valued within its adult probation officers. In collaboration with the consulting agency CPS Human Resource Services, focus groups were established, comprised of probation officer supervisors, division directors, human resource managers, and a psychologist, in order to identify core competencies and traits that best distinguish the department's top probation officer performers from lesser performers. Thereafter, a second focus group further narrowed the list of core competencies to a list of 14 "must-have" traits and characteristics that define the agency's top probation officer performers. As a final procedural step, executive-level review and fine tuning was also conducted to ensure the core competencies and traits were congruent and synonymous with the agency's fundamental mission statement. While this process focused specifically on Maricopa County adult probation officers, the characteristics and traits identified through this process have broad generalizability to other probation departments throughout the United States given the rigorous and comprehensive methodology employed. Consequently, the final competency list (see Table 5.1) is reproduced here for use by law enforcement psychologists and other evaluators seeking to identify which core traits and characteristics of standard adult probation officers tend to be most valued within probation agencies in the early 21st century.

Specialized Units Within Probation Departments

Beyond these core traits and competencies, however, probation departments in the 21st century are increasingly multifaceted in nature, and frequently contain specialized units that perform highly unique functions with different offender populations. In some instances, it may therefore be necessary to select and screen for probation/surveillance candidates who possess additional sets of specialized characteristics and traits that facilitate the performance of such work. Regarding these specialized functions, some of the most common specialized units within probation departments include intensive probation units, sex offender units, and warrants units, each of which require a specialized set of competencies and attributes from the probation/surveillance officers who perform such work. Consequently, law enforcement psychologists must be aware of the specialized requirements and competencies needed to serve within these specialty areas and must tailor their assessment and selection procedures accordingly. While no comprehensive methodology has yet been employed to identify discrete competencies and traits needed by those who perform work within these specialized units, a brief description of the unique job functions is provided here to help illuminate some of the specific job demands faced by those who work within these positions.

Intensive Probation Units

Intensive Supervised Probation (ISP) programs have become increasingly popular since the 1960s for managing high-risk nonincarcerated offender populations. ISP programs function as an alternative to incarceration for both adult and juvenile offenders while providing an acceptable level of public safety (Champion, 2008). While less prevalent than adult ISP programs, juvenile ISP programs are currently operating in about one-third to one-half of all U.S. jurisdictions (Champion, 2008). ISP programs often require more frequent face-to-face officer/client contacts than is normally afforded to probationers. Also probationers in ISP units are often subject to a higher level of scrutiny by way of electronic monitoring devices, offender participation in regular drug screens, and so forth.

Sex Offender Units

There is general agreement in the probation field that sex offenders require specialized supervision because they share unique characteristics that often include maintaining secretive and manipulative lives, often planning their crimes with considerable forethought, committing a wide range and large number of offense behaviors, and showing a continued propensity to reoffend (Abadinsky, 2009; English, Pullen, & Jones, 1997). Sex offenders, and especially those who prey on children, represent a significant risk to the communities in which they live and to probation agencies responsible for supervising them (Abadinsky, 2009). Child sex offenders often end up on probation because of prison overcrowding (Lurigio, Jones, & Smith, 1995) or because plea agreements are accepted that stem from weak incriminating evidence or the prosecution's unwillingness to place victimized children through the trauma of a trial (Stalans, 2004). For these reasons, sex offenders require specialized probation/surveillance services, and many agencies have developed specialized sex

TABLE 5.1
Competency Model for Standard Adult Probation Officer

Building Trust	Interact with others in a way that gives them confidence in one's motives and representations and those of the organization; is respectful and seen as positive, direct, and truthful; keeps confidences, promises, and commitments.
Collaboration	Builds constructive working relationships with clients/customers, other work units, community organizations, and others to meet mutual goals and objectives; participates as an enthusiastic, active, and contributing member of a team to achieve team goals; works positively and cooperatively with other team members; involves others; shares information as appropriate; shares credit for team accomplishments.
Communications	Clearly conveys and receives information and ideas through a variety of media to individuals or groups in a manner that engages the listener; helps them understand and retain the messages, and invites response and feedback; keeps others informed as appropriate; demonstrates good writing, verbal, and listening skills.
Conflict Management	Uses appropriate interpersonal styles and techniques to reduce tension and/or conflict between two or more people; able to size up situations quickly; able to identify common interests; facilitates resolution.
Continuous Learning and Professional Development	Is committed to developing professionally; attends professional conferences; focuses on best practices; values cutting edge practices and approaches; takes advantage of a variety of learning activities; introduces newly gained knowledge and skills on the job.
Cultural Competency	Cultivates opportunities through diverse people; respects and relates well to people from varied backgrounds, understands diverse worldviews, and is sensitive to group differences; sees diversity as an opportunity; challenges bias and intolerance.
Customer/Client Focus	Makes customers/clients/victims and their needs a primary focus of one's actions; builds appropriate customer/client relationships; shows interest in, empathy for, and understanding of the needs and expectations of internal and external customers; gains customer trust and respect; is caring and compassionate; meets or exceeds customer expectations.
Decision Making / Problem Solving	Breaks down problems into components and recognizes interrelationships; makes sound, well informed, and objective decisions; compares data, information, and input from a variety of sources to draw conclusions; takes action that is consistent with available facts, constraints, and probable consequences.
Facilitating Change	Facilitates the implementation and acceptance of change within the workplace; encourages others to seek opportunities for different and innovative approaches to addressing problems and opportunities.
Influence	Uses appropriate interpersonal skills and techniques to gain acceptance for ideas or solutions; uses influencing strategies to gain genuine agreements; seeks to persuade rather than force solutions or impose decisions or regulations; supports building personal autonomy.
Planning and Organizing	Organizes work, sets priorities, and determines resources requirements; determines necessary sequence of activities needed to achieve goals.
Stress Tolerance	Maintains effective performance under pressure; handles stress in a manner that is acceptable to others and to the organization.
Teamwork	Builds constructive working relationships with interested parties dealing with criminal justice matters, i.e., court, attorneys, treatment providers, police, other work units, community organizations, and others to identify and meet mutual goals and objectives; participates as an active and contributing member of teams with a focus on improving offender outcomes and department goals; works cooperatively with other team members, involves others, shares information as appropriate, and shares credit for team accomplishments.
Technical/Professional Knowledge and Skill	Possesses, acquires, and maintains the technical/professional expertise required to do the job effectively and to create client/customer solutions; technical/professional expertise is demonstrated through problem solving, applying professional judgment, and competent performance.

offender units to aggregate personnel who possess the unique traits and characteristics necessary to work effectively with this specialized population. Research has shown that such specialized sex offender units provide clear advantages for supervision staff and for probation departments as a whole (Gilligan & Talbot, 2000).

Warrants Units

Of all the specialized units within probation departments, warrants units are probably the most closely aligned with traditional police functions. The primary purpose of a warrants unit is to investigate, locate, and apprehend fugitive probationers who have had a bench warrant or other arrest warrant issued. Not surprisingly, most departments require probation officers in warrants units to carry firearms, in addition to issuing identification jackets, bullet-proof vests, and other tactical equipment. Warrants units also assist other probation department units with special operations such as executing search orders, effecting home visits of potentially dangerous probationers, and other specialized "law enforcement–oriented" operations.

EMPIRICAL RESEARCH FINDINGS REGARDING THE PSYCHOLOGICAL ASSESSMENT OF PROBATION/SURVEILLANCE OFFICER CANDIDATES

To date, very little scientific work has been done regarding the psychological evaluation and selection of candidates who occupy probation or surveillance officer positions, and the area has been largely ignored by those who work within the realm of law enforcement psychology. For example, an Advanced EBSCO host search of the PsychARTICLES and PsychINFO databases in April 2009 for the Boolean terms *probation, surveillance, psychological, screening, evaluation,* and *selection* yielded zero on-point hits. While the psychological literature is replete with empirical studies assessing the efficacy of selection tools for predicting police officer performance (e.g., Cortina, Doherty, Schmitt, Kaufman, & Smith, 1992; Inwald & Shusman, 1984; Sarchione, Cuttler, Muchinsky, & Nelson-Gray, 1998; Scogin, Schumacher, Gardner, & Chaplin, 1995), the literature is barren regarding the psychological assessment and selection of probation and surveillance officer candidates. Only one tangentially related dissertation study by Hamill (2001) was found in the literature seeking to determine if cultural sensitivity differences existed among a cohort of probation officer candidates when compared to general community norms. Specifically, in this study probation officer candidates were psychologically assessed by way of the MMPI or MMPI-2 as part of a standard pre-employment screening procedure, and a subset of hired probation officers later completed additional measures after an initial period of employment. While some cultural sensitivity differences related to race, age, and length of employment were found at the pre-employment stage, the differences later diminished as a function of time working within the probation department. Although MMPI and/or MMPI-2 data were systematically collected as part of this exploratory study of probation officer candidates, the data were *not* systematically analyzed beyond generating supplementary prejudice scale score calculations as a measure of cultural sensitivity (see Duckworth & Anderson, 1995; Dunbar, 1995).

AGGREGATE LAW ENFORCEMENT NORMS

When psychological instruments are used to assess law enforcement candidates, the current pre-employment psychological evaluation guidelines of the International Association of Chiefs of Police (IACP) Police Psychological Services Section dictate "tests should have a substantial research base for interpretation with normal range populations in general and public safety applicants in particular" (IACP Police Psychological Services Section, 2009). At present, however, not every psychological instrument that would appear useful for screening police or probation/

surveillance candidates has public safety norms available. Moreover, even fewer instruments have "position specific" norms available. Currently, some psychological instruments lump together normative data from different law enforcement occupations under a common rubric of "public safety officers" (e.g., the PAI Law Enforcement, Corrections and Public Safety Selection Report [PAI]; (Roberts, Thompson, & Johnson, 2000), and allow for comparisons to be made between an individual and a pool of literally thousands of police and other public safety applicants (see Roberts et al., 2000). While this practice may allow for comparisons across occupational cohorts where no specific comparison group data is available, we maintain that by doing so important distinctions between vocational cohorts may be minimized. Even though a thread of commonality may run through several related law enforcement occupational groups, aggregating norms in this fashion has a homogenizing effect that may gloss over important distinctions and differences between vocational cohorts. By extension, we also believe it is of utmost importance to know whether psychological screening instruments and procedures historically used and validated with police officer candidates are equally valid and useful for evaluating and selecting probation/surveillance officer candidates. It is sometimes assumed that assessment devices will have equivalent validity with police and probation officer candidates, but predictive validity *must* be established and cannot be assumed.

EMERGING RESEARCH SPECIFIC TO PROBATION/SURVEILLANCE SELECTION

While there is a dearth of published empirical studies on the psychological assessment of probation/surveillance candidates, the tide is beginning to turn. An in-house study (currently unpublished) conducted by the Superior Court of Arizona's Personnel Psychological Services Unit examined the predictive validity of Institute of Personality and Ability Assessment's (IPAT) PsychEval Personality Questionnaire/Protective Services Report Plus (PEPQ/PSR Plus) in its ability to successfully predict job performance among probation officers. The PEPQ/PSR Plus is a psychological composite intended to provide a global view of protective services candidates (e.g., police officer, fire fighter, security guard, EMT, corrections officer, and other similar occupations) by assessing 16 "normal" personality dimensions as well as 12 "pathology-oriented" dimensions. The PEPQ/PSR Plus specifically contains information about a test taker's response style, an interpretive section regarding four protective services dimensions, a profile summary of 5 global factor scales, 16 primary factor scales, 12 pathology-oriented scale scores, and a pathology-oriented index providing a snapshot of a test taker's psychological health in four critical composite dimensions. In this study, the ability to predict job-related "critical incidents" among probation officers was examined in a group of 203 pre-employment and 60 incumbent probation officer candidates who completed the PEPQ/PSR Plus instrument as part of either a standard pre-employment screening or a pre-arming psychological screening process. Following their evaluation, involvement in subsequent work-related critical incidents (e.g., gross misconduct, demotion, involuntary termination, and so on) was monitored by the employer agency for a period of 1 year. For pre-employment candidates, this monitoring took place during their initial probationary period of employment, while incumbent officers were not considered on probationary status during this time frame. Through a logistic regression modeling procedure, it was found that (1) a one-unit increase on the PEPQ/PSR Plus Alienation/Perceptual Distortion scale resulted in the odds of a critical incident increasing by 53%, (2) a one-unit increase on the PEPQ/PSR Plus Interpersonal Relations scale resulted in a decrease in the odds of a critical incident by 3.5 times, and (3) a one-unit increase on the PEPQ/PSR Plus Intellectual Efficiency composite resulted in a decrease in the odds of involvement in a critical incident by 2.87, controlling for the other variables (Herrmann & Bidwell, 2009). While these findings should be viewed as preliminary at the time of this writing, the PEPQ/PSR Plus is one instrument that has demonstrated some measure of predictive validity when used as an assessment/selection device with probation officer candidates.

RECOMMENDATIONS FOR PSYCHOLOGISTS EVALUATING PROBATION/SURVEILLANCE CANDIDATES

For law enforcement psychologists wishing to conduct psychological evaluations on probation/ surveillance candidates, one of the first orders of business is to clearly understand the philosophical outlook of the department for whom the evaluations are conducted. Does the department emphasize a social work perspective, a law enforcement perspective, or a hybrid approach to probation work? Also, what specific duty assignment is the probation/surveillance officer being evaluated for (e.g., standard line officer, specialized unit, and so on)? Is the evaluation for an adult probation department or a juvenile probation department? Once these questions have been answered, the evaluating psychologist must include a number of clinical interview questions to elicit relevant information to determine "goodness of fit" with a specific department and/or duty assignment. Such questions and responses will help determine the degree to which a candidate's philosophical approach fits within a particular probation department's culture and the area of assignment a probation/surveillance officer might be best suited for.

PSYCHOLOGICAL/PERSONALITY VARIABLES TO EMPHASIZE

In addition to clinical interview data, law enforcement psychologists must determine which personality variables and characteristics to emphasize in a written test protocol to screen for "goodness of fit," and which tests best illuminate the personality variables of interest. As previously noted, the limited research in this area involving probation officers has consistently favored a "rehabilitative perspective" rather than an "enforcement perspective" (Van Landingham et al., 1977; Wright, 1997). Consequently, personality variables such as interpersonal warmth, openness to change, interpersonal sensitivity, and tolerance should be prominently emphasized in most psychological evaluations of probation officer candidates.

In calling for such prominence to be placed on personality variables related to the helping/ caring aspects of probation work, it is important to note that such is *entirely congruent* with the personality variable literature involving the selection of traditional police/law enforcement officers. For example, in his extensive meta-analytic review of law enforcement selection studies, Aamodt (2004) found that the personality variable "tolerance" was the single best predictor of performance when compared against all other personality variables. In related research, "conscientiousness" has also emerged as an important personality variable predictor of job performance and work behavior in general (Miller, Griffin, & Hart, 1999; Sarchione et al., 1998; Tett, Jackson, & Rothstein, 1991).

Conscientiousness is considered one of the five core dimensions of personality that have recently become known as the "Big Five" dimensions of personality. In short, the Big Five represent broad categories of personality traits that have been empirically shown to largely define human personality. The five overarching dimensions of the Big Five have been identified as extraversion, agreeableness, conscientiousness, neuroticism, and openness. Several instruments have been developed or revised to provide measures of the Big Five personality dimensions among which "conscientiousness is one of the core dimensions (e.g., the California Psychological Inventory [CPI; Gough, 1995]; the NEO Personality Inventory-Revised [NEO-PI-R; Costa & McCrae, 1992]; the PsychEval Personality Questionnaire/Protective Services Report [PEPQ/ PSR; Cattell, Cattell, Catell, Russel, & Bedwell, 2003]). While some authors have cited a preference for the NEO-PI-R as the most comprehensive and satisfactory measure of conscientiousness (Claussen-Rogers & Arrigo, 2005; Schinka, Kinder, & Kremer, 1997), we maintain that regardless of specific instrumentation choice, law enforcement psychologists should necessarily include at least one validated measure of "conscientiousness" and one validated measure of "tolerance" because both have been consistently linked to performance outcomes in law enforcement groups.

INSTRUMENTATION SELECTION

In the 21st century, many psychological instruments are available to the law enforcement psychologist wishing to conduct evaluations of police candidates, with many offering specific law enforcement norms and report options. While far fewer options are specifically targeted toward probation/surveillance candidates, some instrument authors have begun to recognize the important distinctions that exist between police and probation/surveillance cohorts and have recognized the need for specialized instrumentation. Among the instrument options that stand out as most relevant to probation/surveillance screening are (1) the Behavioral Personnel Assessment Device (B-PAD) (The B-PAD Group, 2001), (2) the PsychEval Personality Questionnaire/Protective Services Report Plus (PEPQ/PSR Plus) (Institute of Personality Ability Testing, 2003), and (3) the California Psychological Inventory (CPI) Police and Public Safety Selection Report (Roberts & Johnson, 2001). We feel that each of these instruments should be given serious consideration for inclusion in a comprehensive assessment battery for probation/surveillance officer assessment, since each makes a unique contribution in the ability to evaluate variables and characteristics relevant to probation/surveillance work.

The B-PAD

First, the B-PAD is a video-based behavioral demand test that assesses an applicant's interpersonal skills and judgments and is based on a rationale and model of test construction called the Behavioral-Analytic Model of Assessing Competence (Goldfried & D'Zurilla, 1969). According to this model, the preferred goal of assessment is the appraisal of competence rather than the presence or absence of global attributes or traits. The B-PAD contains different scenarios portraying difficult interpersonal challenges that are presented to a candidate who is then video recorded as he or she responds to the different scenes. Eight scenarios are presented to ensure that each applicant's competence is assessed across an appropriate range of situations. What makes this test relevant to probation/surveillance officers is that scene catalogs have been developed for both juvenile and adult probation/surveillance officer candidates, with job-relevant scenes reflecting the unique challenges that each position might encounter in the field. While validation studies of probation/surveillance versions of the B-PAD have yet to be conducted, multiple outcome studies have assessed the utility of the B-PAD test using police-specific scenes with police officer candidates and have cited support for this instrument's reliability and validity (e.g., Doerner & Nowell, 1999; Rand, 1987; Stein, 1995; Young, 1992).

The PEPQ/PSR-Plus

As previously noted, the PEPQ/PSR Plus is one of the few instruments that has been subject to some level of empirical scrutiny regarding its ability to predict performance among probation officers (Herrmann & Bidwell, 2009). It also includes the assessment of a number of normal personality variables thought to be specifically relevant and of interest to probation department employers (e.g., interpersonal warmth, openness to change, interpersonal sensitivity, and rule consciousness [i.e., conscientiousness]). For these reasons, it is also recommended for inclusion in a comprehensive assessment battery, which at a minimum should necessarily include measures of both normal personality variables as well as measures of psychopathologic dysfunction. The Institute for Personality and Ability Testing (IPAT) continues to be involved in active research efforts to provide validity evidence for its public safety screening tools such as the PEPQ/PSR Plus and intends to broaden the scope of its validity efforts to include probation/surveillance officer studies in the years to come (S. Bidwell, IPAT, personal communication, March 24, 2009).

The California Psychological Inventory (CPI) Police and Public Safety Selection Report

The CPI Police and Public Safety Selection Report (CPI; Roberts & Johnson, 2001) is currently the *only* assessment instrument available to law enforcement psychologists whereby an applicant's scores can be compared against probation officer norms. Specifically, a probation applicant's scores can be compared against a sample of 1,174 probation officer applicants, 83 incumbent probation officers, and 6,000 general community member norms. While both the applicant and incumbent probation officer norms are not robust, the instrument is the only psychometric option available to law enforcement psychologists who wish to compare "apples to apples" when screening probation officer candidates as opposed to the more common approach of comparing "apples to oranges" when police officer norms are used as a reference group. However, the downside of this interpretive report is that law enforcement psychologists are forced to choose between norm options that include "Probation Department Officer-Counselor (nonweapon carrying)," and "Weapon Carrying Screening for Nonsworn Position." No current option is available for "Probation Department Officer-Counselor (weapon carrying)."

Nevertheless, by having specific probation officer norms available, the CPI interpretive report by Roberts and Johnson (2001) clearly distinguishes itself as a logical pick among the top-tier choices available for probation/surveillance officer screening. The authors of this interpretive report also allude to their intentions to continue developing probation specific norms in the future. For example, in their *CPI Police and Public Safety Selection Report Technical Manual* (5th edition), Roberts and Johnson (2001) note that they "intend to provide future updates that will continually expand the value of this report for screening psychologists," "would like to include larger normative samples of hired, post-probation employees in each job category," and "intend to add a new profile for probation department juvenile counselors" (p. 39). These intentions were again echoed by report author and statistician Mike Johnson (personal communication, October 14, 2009), who expressed intent to "build this out in the future" by increasing the size and heterogeneity of probation officer norms.

EMERGING TRENDS

In addition to the assessment options noted above, the Minnesota Multiphasic Personality Inventory-2–Revised Format (MMPI-2-RF; Ben-Porath & Tellegen, 2008) is an additional instrument expected to have appeal for screening probation/surveillance officers because of the anticipated ability to generate "local norms" within the next few years. Currently, the MMPI-2-RF allows for scoring options that include separate comparison group data for both law enforcement and corrections officers, but currently does not have any direct comparison groups for probation officers. However, as reported by this instrument's lead author, Yossef Ben-Porath (personal communication, April 29, 2009), the MMPI-2-RF scoring software will soon allow users to create their own comparison group norms by aggregating any MMPI-2-RF data they have accumulated on their individual computer systems, with this functionality expected to be available beginning 2010 or 2011. The ability to easily and efficiently generate local comparison group norms for probation/surveillance cohorts is expected to be a highly useful addition for many users including law enforcement psychologists who routinely work with probation/surveillance candidates where limited normative data currently exist.

CONCLUSION

In summary, the work of probation/surveillance officers is multifaceted and involves a complex blend of both rehabilitative and enforcement functions. Because the area of conducting psychological evaluations and screenings of probation/surveillance officer candidates is evolving rapidly, law enforcement psychologists who perform this work are urged to regularly return to the empirical literature over the next several years to keep abreast of new and emerging trends. Many methodological advancements are currently underway, and more are anticipated, as psychologists become increasingly aware of the abundant practice opportunities that exist within and for probation departments. While the models and templates developed to psychologically evaluate police officer candidates often lend themselves to the task of performing psychological evaluations of probation/ surveillance officer candidates, important distinctions between these vocational cohorts require nuanced approaches, methodologies, and perspectives. Probation/surveillance officers should be recognized by the law enforcement psychologist as a distinct but related vocational entity within the law enforcement community—one that possesses its own unique vocational history, mission, culture, and values. As this chapter has attempted to illuminate, it is incumbent on the law enforcement psychologist to be knowledgeable of where the important differences and nuances lie. "Off-the-rack" or "one-size-fits-all" approaches to psychological assessment that too closely approximate standard police psychological evaluation methodologies are likely to miss the mark by failing to recognize important distinctions that do exist.

REFERENCES

Aamodt, M. G. (2004). *Research in law enforcement selection.* Boca Raton, FL: Brown-Walker.

Abadinsky, H. (2009). *Probation and parole: Theory and practice* (10th ed.). Upper Saddle River, NJ: Prentice Hall.

American Probation and Parole Association. (2006). *Adult and juvenile probation and parole national firearm survey* (2nd ed.) Retrieved November 12, 2009, from http://www.appa-net.org/eweb/DynamicPage. aspx?WebCode= VB_SurveyFirearms

Ben-Porath, Y. S., & Tellegen, A. (2008). *MMPI-2-RF (Minnesota Multiphasic Personality Inventory-2-RF): Manual for administration, scoring and interpretation.* Minneapolis: University of Minnesota Press.

Benner, A. W. (1986). Psychological screening of police applicants. In J. T. Reece & H. A. Goldstein (Eds.), *Psychological services for law enforcement* (pp. 11–19). Washington, DC: U.S. Department of Justice, Federal Bureau of Investigation.

Burrell, W. D. (2005). Trends in probation and parole in the states. In K. S. Chi, A. S. Wall, & H. M. Perkins (Eds.), *The book of states* (37th ed., pp. 595–600). Lexington, KY: Council of State Governments.

Burton, V. S., Latessa, E. J., & Barker, T. (1992). The role of probation officers: An examination of statutory requirements. *Journal of Contemporary Criminal Justice, 8*(4), 273–282.

Cattell, R. B., Cattell, A. K., Cattell, H. E. P., Russel, M. T., & Bedwell, S. (2003). *The PsychEval Personality Questionnaire.* Champaign, IL: Institute for Personality and Ability Testing.

Champion, D. J. (2008). *Probation, parole and community corrections in the United States* (6th ed.). Upper Saddle River, NJ: Prentice Hall.

Claussen-Rogers, N. L., & Arrigo, B. A. (2005). *Police corruption and psychological testing: A strategy for preemployment screening.* Durham, NC: Carolina Academic Press.

Colley, L. L, Culbertson, R. G., & Latessa, E. (1986). Probation officer job analysis: Rural-urban differences. *Federal Probation, 50*(4), 67–71.

Cortina, J. M., Doherty, M. I., Schmitt, N., Kaufman, G., and Smith, R. G. (1992). The "Big Five" personality factors in the IPI and MMPI: Predictors of police performance. *Personnel Psychology, 45,* 119–130.

Costa, P. T., Jr., & McCrae, R. R. (1992). *Professional manual for the Revised NEO Personality Inventory.* Odessa, FL: Psychological Assessment Resources.

Doerner, W. G., & Nowell, T. M. (1999). The reliability of the behavioral-personnel assessment device (B-PAD) in selecting police recruits. *Policing: An International Journal of Police Strategies & Management, 22*(3), 343–352.

Duckworth, J. C., & Anderson, W. P. (1995). *MMPI and MMPI-2: Interpretation for counselors and clinicians* (4th ed.). Bristol, PA: Accelerated Development.

Dunbar, E. (1995). The prejudiced personality, racism, and anti-Semitism: The PR scale forty years later. *Journal of Personality Assessment, 65,* 270–277.

English, K., Pullen, S., & Jones, L. (1997). *Managing adult sex offenders in the community: A containment approach.* Washington, DC: National Institute of Justice.

Flexner, B., & Baldwin, R. N. (1916). *Juvenile courts and probation.* New York: Century Company.

Gilligan, L., & Talbot, T. (2000).*Community supervision of the sex offender: An overview of current and promising practices.* Silver Spring, MD: Center for Sex Offender Management.

Goldfried, M., & D'Zurilla, T. (1969). A behavioral-analytic model for assessing competence. In C. D. Spielberger (Ed.), *Current topics in clinical community psychology* (pp.151–169). New York: Academic Press.

Gough, H. G. (1995). *California Psychological Inventory: 434 professional manual.* Palo Alto, CA: Consulting Psychologists Press.

Hamill, M. A. (2001). *Cultural sensitivity of probation officers as a measure for preemployment screening.* Unpublished doctoral dissertation, California School of Professional Psychology, Fresno.

Herrmann, D. S., & Bidwell, S. (2009). *The PEPQ/PSR Plus and the selection of probation officers: A predictive validity analysis.* Manuscript in preparation.

IACP Police Psychological Services Section (2009). *Pre-Employment Psychological Evaluation Guidelines.* Retrieved January 25, 2010, from http://www.theiacp.org/psych_services_section/

Institute for Personality and Ability Testing. (2003). *PsychEval Personality Questionnaire/Protective Services Report Plus (PEPQ / PSR Plus).* Champaign, IL: Author. (Available from http://www.ipat.com)

Inwald, R. E., & Shusman, E. J. (1984). The IPI and MMPI as predictors of academy performance for police recruits. *Journal of Police Science and Administration, 12,* 1–11.

Lurigio, A. J., Jones, M., & Smith, B. E. (1995). Child sexual abuse: Its causes, consequences and implications for probation practice. *Federal Probation, 69,* 69–76.

Lyon, D. (2007). *Surveillance studies: An overview.* Malden, MA: Polity.

Maloney, M. P., & Ward, M. P. (1976). *Psychological assessment: A conceptual approach.* New York: Oxford University Press.

Miller, R. L., Griffin, M. A., & Hart, P. M. (1999). Personality and organized health: The role of conscientiousness. *Work and Stress, 13*(1), 7–19.

Rand, R. R. (1987). Behavioral police assessment device: The development and validation of an interactive, pre-employment, job related, video psychological test. *Dissertation Abstracts International, 48*(3-A), 610–611. (UMI No. 8713282)

Reese, J. T. (1995). A history of police psychological services. In M. I. Kurke & E. M. Scrivner (Eds.), *Police psychology into the 21st century* (pp. 31–44). Hillsdale, NJ: Lawrence Erlbaum.

Roberts, M. D., & Johnson, M. (2001). *CPI police and public safety selection report technical manual.* Los Gatos, CA: Law Enforcement Psychological Services.

Roberts, M. D., Thompson, J. A., and Johnson, M. (2000). *PAI law enforcement, corrections and public safety selection report module manual.* Lutz, FL: Psychological Assessment Resources.

Roscoe, T., Duffee, D., Rivera, C., & Smith, T. (2005, November). *Factors associated with the arming of probation officers: An empirical examination.* Paper presented at the annual meeting of the American Society of Criminology, Royal York, Toronto.

Sarchione, C. D., Cuttler, M. J., Muchinsky, P. M., & Nelson-Gray, R. O. (1998). Prediction of dysfunctional job behaviors among law enforcement officers. *Journal of Applied Psychology, 83*(6), 904–912.

Scogin, F., Schumacher, J., Gardner, J., & Chaplin, W. (1995). Predictive validity of psychological testing in law enforcement settings. *Professional Psychology: Research and Practice, 26*(1), 68–71.

Schinka, J. A., Kinder, B. N., & Kremer, T. (1997). Research validity scales for the NEO-PI-R: Development and initial validation. *Journal of Personality Assessment, 68,* 127–138.

Schultz, J. L. (1973). The cycle of juvenile court history. *Crime and Delinquency, 19*(4), 457–476.

Small, S., & Torres, S. (2001). Arming probation officers: Enhancing public confidence and officer safety. *Federal Probation, 65*(3), 24–28.

Stalans, L. J. (2004). Adult sex offenders on community supervision: A review of recent assessment strategies and treatment. *Criminal Justice and Behavior, 31,* 564–608.

Stein, S. (1995). Police officer selection: An inquiry into the scoring criteria of the Behavioral Personnel Assessment Device for police. *Dissertation Abstracts International: Section B: The Sciences and Engineering, 56*(3-B), 1741.

Terman, L., & Otis, A. (1917). A trial of mental and pedagogical tests in a civil service examination for policemen and firemen. *Journal of Applied Psychology, 1,* 17–29.

Tett, R. P., Jackson, D. N., & Rothstein, M. (1991). Personality measures as predictors of job performance: a meta-analytic review. *Personnel Psychology, 44,* 703–741.

The B-PAD Group. (2001). *Behavioral Personnel Assessment Devices: B-PAD.* Sonoma, CA: Author. (Available from http://www.bpad.com)

U.S. Department of Labor. (2008). *Occupational outlook handbook* (2008–2009 ed.) Washington, DC: Author.

Van Landignham, D. E., Taber, M., & Dimants, E. R. (1977). How probation officers view their job responsibilities. In D. B. Kennedy (Ed.), *The dysfunctional alliance: Emotion and reason in justice administration.* Cincinnati, OH: Anderson Press.

Wright, C. E. (1997). *The relationship of case management strategies to probation officer personality types.* Unpublished doctoral dissertation, Wilmington College. (UMI No. 9728590)

Young, T. (1992). *Use of the Behavioral Police Assessment Device in the selection of law enforcement officers.* Unpublished doctoral dissertation, The Professional School of Psychology. (UMI No. LD02540)

Part II

Pre-Employment Psychological Screening

6 Criterion-Related Validity in Police Psychological Evaluations

Peter A. Weiss

William U. Weiss

INTRODUCTION

Use of psychological assessment instruments such as the Minnesota Multiphasic Personality Inventory-2 (MMPI-2), Personality Assessment Inventory (PAI), and California Psychological Inventory (CPI) has become a frequent practice in police psychological evaluations in recent years. Such instruments are often used in conditional pre-employment psychological evaluations as well as for other purposes such as fitness-for-duty (FFDE) evaluations (Weiss, 2010; Weiss, Weiss, & Gacono, 2008). A major issue with such assessment instruments is that many of these tests were originally designed for purposes of clinical diagnosis and treatment planning and are not in fact instruments originally designed for use in employment settings. While certain newer instruments, such as the M-PULSE (Davis & Rostow, 2008), were designed especially for purposes of police psychological evaluations and were originally validated with law enforcement populations, most of these instruments were not, and validity studies had to be performed to make these instruments (particularly personality inventories such as the MMPI-2 and PAI) acceptable for use in law enforcement evaluations. As a result of the current emphasis by the American Psychological Association (APA) on promoting evidence-based practice, it is important for psychologists using such instruments in their practice of police psychology to have an understanding of the validity of these tests for applications in police work. The purpose of this chapter is (1) to better acquaint the practicing police psychologist with the validity issues applicable to the use of such assessment instruments, and then (2) to review the evidence supporting the validity of the most popular instruments.

TEST VALIDITY ISSUES IN POLICE PSYCHOLOGICAL EVALUATIONS

In teaching about the validity of psychological tests, the present authors have divided it into three components. The first may be termed *rational validity*, which may be further broken down into face validity and content validity. Essentially, rational validity is the degree to which an assessment instrument makes sense during an inspection process; in other words, whether the test items appear to measure what the test developers say they should measure. Face validity is whether or not test items obviously measure the characteristic the test developer is attempting to measure. According to Kazdin (1998), this is not typically part of the psychometric development of a measure but rather an informal evaluation of its usefulness. Content validity is evidence that the items on a test or measure relate to the concept underlying the measure. It asks the question: Does the test appropriately sample the universe of items associated with the concept? Problems with face or content validity are rarely a problem in contemporary psychological testing; tests that are ultimately validated from predictive, construct, and criterion points of view also have good face and content validity. However, this is an important first question to ask in establishing the validity of a measure for any purpose: Does this instrument at least *appear* to measure what it claims to measure on the surface?

The second type of validity is *construct validity*, which relates to the degree to which a test supposedly measures the construct, or concept, that it claims to measure. For example, does this test actually measure a concept such as depression, locus of control, or self-esteem? The concept of construct validity has been extensively explored by Campbell and Fiske (1959), who proposed the multitrait-multimethod matrix for establishing the construct validity of a measure.

The kind of test validity that is perhaps the most important for police psychologists and other mental health practitioners, however, is the third kind, which is commonly referred to as *criterion-related validity*. This is the degree to which a particular measure can be used to predict some external criterion. For example, if scores on the MMPI-2 could be used to accurately predict termination for cause within police departments, then the MMPI-2 would be said to have criterion-related validity for that purpose. According to Kazdin (1998) psychologists use both concurrent validity (correlation with a measure at one point in time) and predictive validity (correlation with a measure at some point in the future) as ways of establishing the criterion-related validity of an instrument. Most police psychologists are concerned with the degree to which assessment instruments used as part of a psychological evaluation can be used to predict performance—either good or bad—at some point in the future, so predictive validity is the aspect of criterion-related validity most often explored by police psychologists. However, there are special issues with validating tests used for law enforcement purposes that make establishing their criterion-related (especially predictive) validity difficult.

PROBLEMS AND LIMITATIONS IN LAW ENFORCEMENT TEST RESEARCH

While tests used in psychological evaluations in law enforcement need to be validated for their predictive validity, particularly in the area of police selection, there are a number of limitations to research that must be overcome. A major limitation of such research is that pure predictive validity studies are not practical. A pure predictive validity study in the area of law enforcement would be one in which a wide variety of individuals obtained through random sampling are given a test and then hired as police officers; next, the data would be analyzed to determine if the test predicted either poor or good performance. However, such a procedure would undoubtedly expose police departments to lawsuits because hiring applicants using a random sampling procedure would result in individuals becoming police officers who exhibited performance problems. Given that law enforcement is a sensitive, high-risk profession in which officers have the right, under certain circumstances, to take life and liberty, such an approach to research would be highly impractical.

Another related limitation is that psychological evaluations are the last thing considered in making law enforcement hiring decisions. According to the Americans with Disabilities Act (ADA), such evaluations—even if mandated by law—can only be performed after all other factors have been considered and a conditional offer of employment has been extended to the candidate (Weiss, Weiss, & Gacono, 2008). While certain kinds of psychological tests can be given on a pre-offer basis (see, for example, Jones, Cunningham, & Dages, 2010), most psychological tests fall into the category of "medical tests" and therefore can only be used postoffer. While this restriction is obviously necessary to prevent discrimination, it also presents a challenge to law enforcement researchers because subjects who find their way into police validity studies tend to be more psychologically healthy than the rest of the general population (Weiss, Hitchcock, Weiss, Rostow, & Davis, 2008).

These problems, while unavoidable, create a situation in which criterion-related validity studies in police psychology lose power. Most data samples for research on police psychological evaluations consist of assessment data collected during the course of routine evaluations. As stated earlier, this means the sample has been highly preselected, and most individuals with unusual behavioral or personality characteristics are already eliminated from the sample at earlier stages of the process. Therefore, the researcher must work with data samples that have extreme restrictions on predictor variables. As an example, the sample in the Weiss, Hitchcock, et al. (2008) study had mean PAI clinical scale scores that were a half standard deviation below the population mean, and most other criterion-related studies of police evaluations have similar sets of descriptive statistics. In addition, in making these preselections, we also limit the range of the criterion variables because most individuals in the sample wind up being excellent candidates for police work. For example, few candidates who are eventually hired will be terminated for cause, or engage in seriously problematic on-the-job behaviors because of the rigor of modern police-screening procedures. As a result of the truncation of range of both criterion and predictor variables, validation studies in police psychology lose a great deal of power, and effect sizes tend to be small.

The Issue of Effect in Criterion Validity Police Studies

The issues described above make it clear that researchers, and consumers of research, must keep an open mind when reading and interpreting validity studies of police psychological evaluations. Moreover, small effect sizes in research can be highly significant when the stakes are high, as they are in police psychological evaluations. Making an error in a pre-employment psychological evaluation can result in serious departmental liability problems—or even loss of life. Therefore, the researcher and consumer must carefully weigh results to determine the true significance of the findings. High correlations are rarely found in this kind of validation research, yet this does not mean that the tests discussed above have no predictive power. Rather, most studies suffer from truncation of range, and small effects can be highly important. A more thorough discussion of these issues can be found in Hitchcock, O'Conner, and Weiss (2010).

Evidence for the Validity of Tests in Police Psychological Evaluations

Ethically, psychologists should not be using instruments in their evaluations that have no predictive power. According to APA guidelines, psychologists should follow the basic principles of evidence-based practice (American Psychological Association, 2002). For police psychological evaluations, what this means for the practitioner is that the tests used as part of the evaluation procedure have been proven to work for the purposes for which they are used. This emphasis is particularly important when using tests relating to personality and psychopathology, because in most cases (for example, the MMPI-2 and PAI), these tests were not originally developed for use with police populations. In such cases, being able to present evidence for the usefulness of such tests for police evaluations is crucial.

As stated earlier, although effect sizes in research on police psychological evaluations are small, in most cases these effects are small but significant. There are a number of measures for which extensive validation research exists and justifies their use. The remainder of this chapter is devoted to a discussion of the evidence for the validity of some of the most popular measures used in pre-employment police psychological evaluations. The authors hope readers will find this summary useful for justifying their own evidence-based practice. It should be noted that instruments originally developed as measures of personality and psychopathology will be dealt with separately from instruments originally designed for use with, and normed on police populations, as differences exist in how such instruments may be used and interpreted.

Tests of Personality and Psychopathology

The MMPI-2

The MMPI-2 and its predecessor, the MMPI, have been used for years in the field of police psychology. In 1959, King, Norrell, and Erlandson published an article in which they attempted to use the original MMPI to predict police academy grades. This article represents the first attempt to validate this test for personnel selection. Since that time, numerous validation articles have been published on the MMPI and MMPI-2 in police psychological evaluations (Weiss & Weiss, 2010). The MMPI was restandardized in 1989, and the resultant version, the MMPI-2, is the one in use today. It is similar to the original MMPI, but it has a more representative standardization sample, and item content has been revised so that objectionable items were deleted and archaic language updated. The test is interpreted using standard (T) scores, which have a mean of 50 and a standard deviation of 10. Any T score greater than 65 on the MMPI-2 is considered clinically significant and therefore noteworthy.

The main purpose of the MMPI-2 is the detection of psychopathology. Therefore, in accordance with the Americans with Disabilities Act, it is considered a *medical test* and is only considered appropriate for use in police selection after all other factors have been considered. However, its criterion validity for use as a postoffer screening measure has been relatively well established, particularly with regard to the validity scales. The use of the L (Lie) scale as a tool in postoffer police selection has been investigated by Weiss, Davis, Rostow, and Kinsman (2003). The hypotheses for the Weiss et al. (2003) study were taken primarily from earlier work by Herndon (1998) and Boes, Chandler, and Timm (1997), which suggested that individuals who obtain elevated L scale scores on the MMPI-2 tend to engage in problem behaviors if hired by police departments. In this study, which used a sample of 1,347 officers, it was discovered that high L scale scores were associated with future performance problems such as termination for cause, knowledge mistakes, failure to complete the requirements for traditional hire, and insubordination. While such candidates appear normal in a clinical interview, their denial, excessive sense of virtue, and lack of a sense of their own shortcomings make them poor candidates for a high-stress occupation such as police work. In addition, their high-L presentation may in part be due to attempts to conceal psychological adjustment problems. Weiss et al. (2003) recommend a raw score cutoff of eight for psychological screening. A follow-up study (Weiss, Weiss, Davis, & Rostow, 2010) has confirmed the usefulness of this cutoff score.

While research on the L scale as a tool in police selection has shown the usefulness of the scale, the clinical scales have presented a more mixed picture. A full review of the evidence for the use of the MMPI-2 Basic Scales, as well as other subscales and scales, can be found in Weiss and Weiss (2010) and is beyond the scope of the present chapter. However, Brewster and Stoloff (1999) have made the argument based on prior MMPI-2 research that any applicant obtaining a T score greater than 65 on any of the MMPI-2 Basic Scales (with the possible exception of scale 5) can be justifiably removed from the applicant pool. In addition, other studies—particularly that of Sellbom, Fischler, and Ben-Porath (2007)—have suggested the usefulness of the Basic Scales in the psychological screening of law enforcement officers.

Aamodt (2004), in his meta-analysis of test results in law enforcement selection, has presented a more modest picture of the ability of the MMPI-2 to discriminate between good and bad applicants. Aamodt states that Scale 9 (Ma) is significantly correlated but at a low level, with poor supervisor ratings of performance and poorer police academy grades as a law enforcement officer. Aamodt states that other Basic Scales produced insignificant results for a number of criterion variables in his meta-analysis. However, it should be noted that the truncation-of-range problems discussed earlier in the chapter are likely to be problems in such a meta-analysis; very few hired applicants actually develop performance problems, and very few applicants with extreme scores on the MMPI-2 even make it to the psychological evaluation phase due to ADA regulations. However, it does seem a relatively safe practice to eliminate individuals with extreme MMPI-2 clinical scale scores from the applicant pool, although such individuals are rare because of contemporary assessment practices. As stated earlier, most applicants with personality problems or levels of psychopathology that would cause elevated scores on MMPI-2 clinical scales are eliminated from the applicant pool at earlier stages of the hiring process. Those individuals given a psychological evaluation (the last procedure in the hiring process) typically produce clinical (but not necessarily validity) scale scores that are within the normative range.

The Personality Assessment Inventory (PAI)

The Personality Assessment Inventory, or PAI (Morey, 2007), has been the subject of fairly extensive criterion-related validity research by the present authors in recent years. For the last 10 years, we have researched all of the validity scales as well as a number of the clinical scales that appeared related to law enforcement work. The PAI, like the MMPI-2, is a personality inventory oriented around measuring psychopathology, and it has several features that have made it generally appealing to most psychologists doing self-report evaluations. These features have caught the attention of police psychologists as well. It is shorter (344 as opposed to 567 items) and easier to read, and it has a 4-point scale for each item as opposed to a forced-choice true/false format. It also has scales that provide general diagnostic information—such as those measuring certain personality disorders—not generally in use on the MMPI-2.

The PAI takes a somewhat different approach to the assessment of profile validity than the MMPI-2. Two of its scales, Inconsistency (ICN) and Infrequency (INF), measure not a response style but rather whether an individual is paying attention to item content when taking the test. These are similar in function to the VRIN and TRIN scales on the MMPI-2. The VRIN scale on the MMPI-2 is a measure of random responding that compares a series of similar item pairs. Individuals who respond randomly to the MMPI-2 typically endorse these similar items in opposite directions due to inattention. The TRIN scale is a measure of all-true and all-false responding that compares items with similar content typically endorsed by subjects in opposite directions. The ICN scale also works by comparing item pairs with similar content, but INF is derived in a different manner from VRIN and TRIN. The INF scale consists of items infrequently endorsed by all subjects regardless of psychopathology. Individuals scoring high on these scales (ICN and INF) have generally produced PAI profiles that are invalid and are not interpretable, because they have answered randomly, or have trouble with attention or reading comprehension.

However, the two other validity scales on the PAI, Negative Impression (NIM) and Positive Impression (PIM), have been of much more interest to researchers. Studies by Weiss, Rostow, Davis, and Decoster-Martin (2004), and Weiss, Zehner, Davis, Rostow, and Decoster-Martin (2005) showed that elevated NIM scores are modestly correlated with problem performance as a police officer after hire. These studies discovered that high NIM officers engaged in neglect of duty, made conduct mistakes, and were more likely than other officers to receive reprimands from supervisors. While part of the NIM effect may have been due to associated elevations in clinical scales, these findings are interesting and useful for the police psychologist and suggest that high NIM scorers can be excluded from applicant pools.

Unlike the MMPI-2, in which the L-scale, a measure of positive impression management, has been associated with poor performance as a law enforcement officer, such findings have not been confirmed on the PAI with PIM. In fact, in the study by Weiss et al. (2004), higher scores on PIM were very modestly correlated with good performance as a police officer for some outcome variables. This finding is probably because research has shown that PIM measures a different aspect of impression management than the MMPI-2 L scale (Weiss, Serafino, & Serafino, 2000). PIM probably is a good measure of positive impression management; however, L is more a measure of deceptiveness.

Some criterion-related research has also been performed on the PAI clinical scales for purposes of law enforcement selection. The Antisocial (ANT) scales on the PAI have been relatively well researched for their ability to predict performance as a police officer. The Weiss et al. (2004) and Weiss et al. (2005) studies showed that the ANT full scale and its subscales (ANT-A/Antisocial Behaviors, ANT-E/Egocentricity, ANT-S/Stimulus Seeking) were associated with problem behaviors such as insubordination, excessive citizen complaints, neglect of duty, conduct mistakes, and termination for cause. Further investigation using a multiple regression format (Weiss et al., 2005) showed that these scales can be used together to predict the performance of law enforcement personnel. This research evidence suggests that a case could be made to eliminate such individuals with high scores (T ≥ 70) from the applicant pool in police selection work. Similarly, support for the criterion-related validity of the Aggression (AGG) scale and its subscales also exists due to the Weiss et al. (2004) study. This study suggested that clinically elevated scores on the AGG scale and its subscales (Physical Aggression/AGG-P, Aggressive Attitude/AGG-A, and Verbal Aggression/AGG-V) are associated with a number of negative performance characteristics.

As of this writing, one major study (Weiss, Hitchcock, et al., 2008) has been conducted on the PAI Borderline scales. This study also included the Drug and Alcohol scales as predictor variables as well. A total performance score that summed performance errors across 32 performance variables was used as the criterion variable. This study did not obtain significant results with the entire sample, but when a subsample of the 132 officers who exhibited the most on-the-job performance problems was used, significant correlations with poor performance were found for the Borderline Full Scale (BOR), BOR-N (Negative Relations), and DRG (Drug Use) scales. This study provides further support for the use of the PAI in the pre-employment screening of law enforcement officers.

Despite the extensive research on scales measuring validity, problem behaviors, personality disorders, and alcohol/drug use, virtually no peer-reviewed research exists supporting the criterion-related validity of the PAI scales that measure primarily Axis I psychopathology. However, this is not likely due to problems with the validity of these scales; rather, it is probably due to the issue, discussed earlier, of few individuals exhibiting such psychopathology ever getting to the psychological evaluation part of the hiring process in the first place. Weiss, Hitchcock, et al. (2008) comment on the fact that law enforcement candidates tend to produce profiles on self-report tests of psychopathology that have lower means than those found in normative samples, and very few individuals produce scale elevations. While new research should be conducted, this lack of research evidence speaks to the problems with criterion-related validity research discussed earlier.

The California Psychological Inventory (CPI)

The California Psychological Inventory (CPI) has become a popular pre-employment screening measure in recent years because it can be used alongside a test of psychopathology as a measure of more ordinary, commonplace personality characteristics. The CPI has 434 items and measures 20 dimensions of personality over four major areas of personality: measures of poise, measures of normative orientation and values, measures of cognitive and intellectual functioning, and measures of role and interpersonal style. Over the years, the CPI has proven to be one of the more popular measures used in pre-employment screening for police and security personnel. It was the second most widely used test for pre-employment screening in Super's (2006) survey of pre-employment screening instruments. Although this study was limited geographically (it mainly included departments in the southeastern United States), there is little question that it is popular because it is not a test of psychopathology and has been shown to be useful for pre-employment purposes. It has been frequently used in conjunction with tests of psychopathology so that psychologists will have one test oriented toward psychopathology (such as the PAI or MMPI-2) and one oriented toward more commonplace personality characteristics.

There have been multiple validation studies on the CPI. However, Aamodt (2004) ran a meta-analysis of studies of the CPI in predicting the criterion variables of performance ratings, academy performance, and discipline problems. This meta-analysis is probably the best overall summary of the efficacy of the CPI for police work. The meta-analysis for performance ratings was a rather large study as it involved between 13 and 17 studies, with overall N's of between 1,072 and 1,400 participants. While most of the r's in Aamodt's meta-analysis were small, as with most criterion-related police research, moderate correlations were found for the Tolerance and Intellectual Efficiency Scales, which produced some correlations above .20, which are fairly large effects in this type of research. According to Aamodt (2004), individuals scoring high in tolerance are tolerant, nonjudgmental, and resourceful; those scoring high in Intellectual Efficiency are intelligent, clear thinking, and capable. According to Aamodt (2004), these are desirable characteristics in law enforcement officers, and low scorers on these scales at times have performance problems; similarly, officers high in these characteristics tend to do well on the job and are well liked by supervisors. Certainly, a case can be made for using the CPI—particularly these two scales—in the pre-employment screening of law enforcement officers.

TESTS DESIGNED FOR LAW ENFORCEMENT POPULATIONS

The Inwald Personality Inventory (IPI)

The Inwald Personality Inventory (Inwald, 1982) was the first test developed and validated for the psychological screening of applicants for high-risk occupations. Inwald (2008) has extensively documented the process of development and validation of the IPI, so users of this test are strongly encouraged to consult her article for a thorough understanding of the criterion-related validity of the IPI. However, a brief description of the validity of the IPI is presented here. The IPI is a 310-item true/false self-report inventory that focuses mainly on admitted past behavior patterns in an attempt to predict future job-related behaviors (Inwald, 2008). Particular emphasis was placed on admissions of past antisocial behaviors during the development of this test. When initially published, the test had the advantage of a very large normative sample of more than 2,500 law enforcement candidates, and early research on the IPI showed considerable promise. According to Inwald (2008), an independent meta-analysis conducted using the IPI studies available in 1991 (Ones, Viswesveran, Schmidt, & Schultz, 1991; Ones, Viswesveran, & Schmidt, 1993) revealed a very respectable validity coefficient of .37 for prediction of future job performance.

Since the early 1990s, multiple validity studies have been conducted on the IPI. Because of space concerns, we will not list all of these studies here. However, the police psychologist interested in gaining a thorough understanding of the validity behind the IPI is strongly encouraged to consult Inwald's (2008) article, which contains a thorough list of abstracts related to validity research on the IPI. In addition, Inwald has developed multiple other measures that are often used in police psychology, and a thorough discussion of these can be found in this article as well. The IPI continues to be the most popular of the Inwald–Hilson measures for police psychological assessment (see, for example, Super, 2006).

The Matrix-Predictive Uniform Law Enforcement
Selection Evaluation Inventory (M-PULSE)

An exciting new addition to the battery of tests available to the police psychologist is the Matrix-Predictive Uniform Law Enforcement Selection Evaluation Inventory, commonly known as the M-PULSE (Davis & Rostow, 2008).

The M-PULSE is a 455-item inventory scored on a four-point scale that focuses primarily on identifying law enforcement officer candidates at risk for specific liabilities most frequently associated with performance problems as a law enforcement officer. The M-PULSE consists of 18 liability scales that focus on these specific areas such as Potential for Termination and Criminal Conduct. It also has four empirical scales, each with a series of subscales, that assess personality characteristics and attitudes that could negatively influence law enforcement work. These are Negative Self-Issues, Negative Perceptions Related to Law Enforcement, Unethical Behavior, and Unpredictability. The M-PULSE also has two validity scales to assess the degree to which the examinee responds in an open and honest fashion. While the M-PULSE is a new instrument in the field of police selection, the results for correct classification of various future performance problems as a law enforcement officer using the liability scales have been particularly impressive. The classification rates for each performance problem using these scales are presented in detail in the M-PULSE manual (Davis &

Rostow, 2008) based on the norming sample of 2,000 officers. While further validation research on the M-PULSE is currently conducted, this test appears to present an actuarial method for identifying officer candidates who are at risk for potential performance problems.

Other Measures

This review has attempted to take into account the most popular and recent measures used for police evaluations and to provide the reader with some understanding of the basis for their criterion validity. However, many measures have been used in the psychological assessment of law enforcement officers. For example, other tests such as the 16PF and Wonderlic Personnel Test have sometimes been used, but probably not with the frequency of the tests reviewed above. In recent years, there has been some discussion in the literature regarding the potential use of the Rorschach Comprehensive System in police psychological evaluations, mainly due to the fact that it is less susceptible to attempts at impression management than most other self-report tests (Brewster, Wickline, & Stoloff, 2010; Weiss, 2002; Weiss, Weiss, & Gacono, 2008). While the Rorschach certainly has a great deal of potential, the process of conducting validation research has been slow, and much research needs to be performed to establish its criterion validity in police psychological evaluations. The psychologist wishing to use tests for evaluations should be aware of their established validity for the type of evaluation that he or she is conducting, especially with those instruments encountered less frequently in police work.

CONCLUSION

In this chapter, we discussed the importance of criterion-related validity in police psychological evaluations. Clearly, in making decisions regarding such issues as selection of law enforcement personnel, the psychologist should be aware of the ability of a chosen test to perform a particular function. Fortunately, criterion-related validity studies exist for the vast majority of tests currently used in police psychological evaluations. A brief review of the criterion-related validity data for a number of the most popular and recent tests is presented here. However, we encourage readers to investigate these issues further and to become knowledgeable consumers of research on the tests they utilize in clinical practice.

REFERENCES

Aamodt, M. G. (2004). *Research in law enforcement selection*. Boca Raton, FL: Brown Walker.
American Psychological Association. (2002). Ethical principles of examiners and code of conduct. *American Psychologist, 57*, 1060–1073.
Boes, J. O., Chandler, C. J., & Timm, H. W. (1997). *Police integrity: Use of personality measures to identify corruption-prone officers*. Monterey, CA: Defense Personnel Security Research Center.
Brewster, J., & Stoloff, M. L. (1999). Using the good cop/bad cop profile with the MMPI-2. *Journal of Police and Criminal Psychology, 14*(2), 29–34.
Brewster, J., Wickline, P. W., & Stoloff, M. L. (2010). Using the Rorschach Comprehensive System in police psychology. In P. A. Weiss (Ed.), *Personality assessment in police psychology: A 21st century perspective* (pp. 188–226). Springfield, IL: Charles C Thomas.
Campbell, D. T., & Fiske, D. W. (1959). Convergent and discriminant validation by the multitrait multimethod matrix. *Psychological Bulletin, 56*, 81–105.
Davis, R. D., & Rostow, C. D. (2008). *M-PULSE Inventory: Matrix-Predictive Uniform Law Enforcement Selection Evaluation Inventory Technical*. Toronto: MHS.
Herndon, J. (1998, October). *Correlates of the MMPI-2 L Scale: Elevations in an LEO selection test battery*. Paper presented at the 27th annual meeting of the Society for Police and Criminal Psychology, Portland, OR.
Hitchcock, J. H., O'Conner, R., & Weiss, P. A. (2010). Effect sizes in police psychology personality assessment research: A primer. In P. A. Weiss (Ed.), *Personality assessment in police psychology: A 21st century perspective* (pp. 250–278). Springfield, IL: Charles C Thomas.

Inwald, R. E. (1982). *Inwald Personality Inventory (IPI) technical manual*. New York: Hilson Research, Inc. (Reprinted [2008], Chicago IL: IPAT, Inc., a subsidiary of OPP Ltd.)

Inwald, R. E. (2008). The Inwald Personality Inventory (IPI) and Hilson Research inventories: Development & rationale. *Journal of Aggression and Violent Behavior, 13,* 298–327.

Jones, J. W., Cunningham, M. R., & Dages, K. D. (2010). Pre-offer police integrity testing: Scientific foundation and professional issues (pp. 159–187). In P. A. Weiss (Ed.), *Personality assessment in police psychology: A 21st century perspective*. Springfield, IL: Charles C Thomas.

Kazdin, A. (1998). *Research design in clinical psychology* (3rd ed.). Needham Heights, MA: Allyn & Bacon.

King, P., Norrell, G., & Erlandson, F. L. (1959). The prediction of academic success in a police administration curriculum. *Educational and Psychological Measurement, 19,* 649–651.

Morey, L. C. (2007). *Personality Assessment Inventory: Professional manual* (2nd ed.). Lutz, FL: Psychological Assessment Resources.

Ones, D. S., Viswesveran, C., & Schmidt, F. L. (1993). Comprehensive meta-analysis of integrity test validation: Findings and implications for personnel selection and theories of job performance. *Journal of Applied Psychology, 78,* 679–703.

Ones, D. S., Viswesveran, C., Schmidt, F. L., & Schultz, S. D. (1991). *Meta-analysis results for criterion-related validity of the Inwald Personality Inventory*. Unpublished manuscript, University of Iowa, Department of Management and Organizations.

Sellbom, M., Fischler, G. L., & Ben-Porath, Y. S. (2007). Identifying MMPI-2 predictors of police officer integrity and misconduct. *Criminal Justice and Behavior, 34,* 985–1004.

Super, J. T. (2006). A survey of pre-employment psychological evaluation tests and procedures. *Journal of Police and Criminal Psychology, 21*(2), 83–90.

Weiss, P. A. (2002). Potential uses of the Rorschach in the selection of police officers. *Journal of Police and Criminal Psychology, 17*(2), 63–70.

Weiss, P. A., Hitchcock, J. H., Weiss, W. U., Rostow, C., & Davis, R. (2008). The Personality Assessment Inventory borderline, drug, and alcohol scales as predictors of overall performance in police officers: A series of exploratory analyses. *Policing and Society, 18,* 301–310.

Weiss, P. A., & Weiss, W. U. (2010). Using the MMPI-2 in police psychological assessment. In P. A. Weiss (Ed.), *Personality assessment in police psychology: A 21st century perspective* (pp. 59–71). Springfield, IL: Charles C Thomas.

Weiss, P. A., Weiss, W. U., & Gacono, C. B. (2008). The use of the Rorschach in police psychology: Some preliminary thoughts. In C. B. Gacono & F. B. Evans (Eds.), *The handbook of forensic Rorschach assessment* (pp. 527–542). Mahwah, NJ: Lawrence Erlbaum.

Weiss, W. U. (2010). Procedural considerations in security personnel selection. In P. A. Weiss (Ed.), *Personality assessment in police psychology: A 21st century perspective* (pp. 299–316). Springfield, IL: Charles C Thomas.

Weiss, W. U., Davis, R., Rostow, C., & Kinsman, S. (2003). The MMPI-2 L scale as a tool in police selection. *Journal of Police and Criminal Psychology, 18*(1), 57–60.

Weiss, W. U., Rostow, C., Davis, R., & Decoster-Martin, E. (2004). The Personality Assessment Inventory as a selection device for law enforcement personnel. *Journal of Police and Criminal Psychology, 19*(2), 23–29.

Weiss, W. U., Serafino, G., & Serafino, A. (2000). A study of the interrelationships of several validity scales used in police selection. *Journal of Police and Criminal Psychology, 15*(1), 41–44.

Weiss, W. U., Weiss, P. A., Davis, R. D., & Rostow, C. D. (2010, March). *Exploring the MMPI-2 L scale cutoff in police selection*. Paper presented at the annual meeting of the Society for Personality Assessment, San Jose, CA.

Weiss, W. U., Zehner, S. N., Davis, R. D., Rostow, C., & Decoster-Martin, E. (2005). Problematic police performance and the Personality Assessment Inventory. *Journal of Police and Criminal Psychology, 20*(1), 16–21.

7 Pre-Employment Screening of Police Officers

Integrating Actuarial Prediction Models With Practice

Michael J. Cuttler

INTRODUCTION

Psychological assessment of candidates for employment as police officers has become a widespread practice in the United States and most, if not all, police psychologists are either familiar with or directly involved in this practice. In a recent national survey, Cochrane, Tett, and Vandecreek (2003) surveyed a cross-section of small, medium, and large police agencies and found that as many as 90% of the departments surveyed currently use psychological testing in their pre-employment selection. Bartol (1996) surveyed police psychologists in regard to their activities and reported that pre-employment assessment accounts for the highest percentage of time expended (34.3%) among this group of practitioners. Scrivner and Kurke (1996) surveyed police psychologists employed by the 50 largest U.S. police agencies and found that 71% of this sample reported performing pre-employment psychological evaluations as part of their regular activities. Based on employment figures published by the U.S. Department of Justice (2007), it's been estimated that as many as 100,000 pre-employment assessments of police officers are performed each year by as many as 4,500 psychologists (Corey, Cuttler, & Moss, 2009).

The earliest research in pre-employment assessment/selection of police officers developed within the disciplines of I/O and clinical psychology, albeit without evidence of significant interdisciplinary interaction. After 1980, a number of professional presentations and publications also appeared in conjunction with the emergence of forensic psychology as a distinct specialty (Monahan, 1981; Shapiro, 1983; Ziskin, 1981). Subsequently, societal, legal and technological developments (e.g., the Americans With Disabilities Act, 1990; the Civil Rights Act, 1991; and the Equal Employment Opportunity Commission's Uniform Guidelines on Employee Selection, 1978, as cited in Equal Employment Opportunity Commission, 1995) encouraged convergence of research, practice, and perspectives within these disciplines. Convergence of research in this regard is reflected in the literature, particularly through a number of retrospective validity studies and meta-analyses, while convergence in practice is seen through development of specialized test instruments, scales, and other techniques. However, although instrument design and supporting research have converged across clinical, industrial, and forensic disciplines, there has been considerably less discussion in the literature regarding interpretive strategy from the practitioner perspective. From this perspective, consideration of the research in regard to actuarial prediction vs. clinical judgment is particularly apropos.[*] The actuarial assessment literature can also serve as a conceptual bridge between these disciplines. Such is the purpose, focus, and organization of this chapter.

---

[*] *Clinical prediction* refers to the use of an individual (an expert, a clinician) to predict an event. *Actuarial prediction* refers to the use of an actuarial formula to predict the same event (Westen & Weinberger, 2004).

HISTORY*

Dawes (2005), in her article "The Ethical Implications of Paul Meehl's Work on Comparing Clinical Versus Actuarial Prediction Methods," describes a lake in Massachusetts (Webster) that historically had a long Native American name (Chargoggaggoggmanchargagoggcharbunagungamaug) which, according to Dawes, translates to "I fish on my side, you fish on your side, and no one fishes in the middle" (p. 1245). Assessment of police officer candidates has historical roots in both the clinical and the I/O literature, but until the early 1980s, few (if any) fished in the middle of the lake.

Drees, Ones, Cullen, Spilberg, and Viswesvaran (2003) suggest the practice of screening police officers for critical traits may be traced back to 1829 London (see also Chenoweth, 1961; Matarazzo, Allen, Saslow, & Wiens, 1964). Cochrane et al. (2003) and cite the President's Commission on Law Enforcement and the Administration of Justice (1967) which recommended screening of all potential officers at that time. Subsequently, the National Advisory Commission on Criminal Justice Standards and Goals Task Force on Police (1973) recommended a standard screening procedure to include (a) a written test of mental ability or aptitude, (b) an oral interview, (c) a psychological examination, and (d) a background investigation.

These reports are identified in the I/O literature as the primary antecedents of a number of studies published during that time frame which focused on operational definition of job success in police work as well as linkages to skill and ability measures (Cohen & Chaiken, 1973; Dunnette & Motowidlo, 1976; Gordon & Kleiman, 1976; Kent & Eisenberg, 1972; Landy, 1976; Smith & Stotland, 1973).

In contrast to activity in the I/O area, examination of the clinical literature during the 1960s and 1970s supports the impression that the early state of the art in regard to clinical psychological testing and assessment of police officer candidates was characterized by not only a preponderance of descriptive information regarding the psychological characteristics of officers but also a dearth of objective data and/or testable hypotheses regarding personality and psychological findings.

Lefkowitz (1977), in his review of police selection procedures titled "Industrial organizational psychology and the police," cited evidence that the use of psychological/psychiatric inquiry began to emerge as early as 1938 and had been adopted by a number of large municipalities by the mid-1950s (see also Matarazzo et al., 1964). However, Lefkowitz further noted that although psychological tests and interviews were increasingly included in published investigations of police selection during the 1960s and 1970s, substantive findings in the clinical literature were sparse. Contrasting the clinical literature of the time to the I/O studies noted above, he asserts that the results of psychological tests and clinical interviews were rarely, if ever, directly linked to job performance or designed in such a way as to facilitate cross validation and/or other forms of scientific inquiry.

> The published reports of clinical evaluations of police candidates' emotional fitness usually contain rich descriptive accounts of typical personality and mental functioning. However, they are often devoid of data other than the clinician's personal impressions.... This is often a function of the fact that the clinicians are assessing qualities for which few objective or standardized measuring instruments exist. (Lefkowitz, 1977, p. 354)

Similarly, Cuttler and Muchinsky (2006) note that interest in pre-employment testing of police officers was limited primarily to physical ability, mental ability, and aptitude predictors (i.e., I/O psychology) until the work of Ogelsby (1957), who suggested that screening of police applicants would be enhanced by evaluation of personality factors. Matarazzo et al. (1964) published one of the few early attempts at clinical evaluation of police applicants that contained

---

* Robin Inwald, PhD, provided substantive input to this section in regard to historical context, events, unpublished studies, and other professional activities.

objective empirical data (10 clinical instruments including the WAIS, MMPI, Edwards Personal Preference Inventory, Rorschach, Taylor Manifest Anxiety Inventory, and five other tests, as well as a clinical interview), derived from 243 police and fire applicants evaluated within a 3-year period. The study reported descriptive statistics obtained from this applicant pool and concluded that the police and fire departments in Portland, Oregon, were recruiting "superior young men" defined as those with above average intelligence and excellent social adjustment. Although the authors included the finding that these (test) scores did not differ significantly from scores developed from incumbent officers, the study also did not include longitudinal, comparative, or criterion outcome measures. Similarly, no attempts to cross validate or replicate these findings were attempted or appeared in the early literature. As such, the authors were limited in their conclusions in regard to the broader applicability of these findings, beyond noting that the attrition rate of those hired was similar to that reported in another earlier study in St. Louis (Dubois & Watson, 1950), that is, inasmuch as different measures were used in these studies, not much else could be said.

In their review of the history of personality assessment in police psychology, Weiss and Inwald (2010) report increased interest and practice of pre-employment assessment by both police agencies and psychologists during the 1970s and cite a few empirical studies using personality tests in the time period between 1964 and 1979. However, in this regard, the few 1970s studies cited by Weiss and Inwald (Azen, 1974; Azen, Saccuzo, Higgins, & Lewandowski, 1974; Saxe & Reiser, 1976; Snibbe & Montgomery, 1973) were primarily based on the MMPI, and their results were descriptive rather than predictive.

The first cross-validation studies for public safety officers, using the MMPI and the Inwald Personality Inventory (IPI) to predict police job performance, were presented at the 1983 American Psychological Association convention and subsequently published (Inwald, 1983; Inwald, 1988; Shusman, Inwald, & Knatz, 1987; Shusman, Inwald, & Landa, 1984). In addition, from 1979 through 1984, Inwald, with several of her colleagues, reports making over three dozen presentations at state and national conferences that included data from longitudinal prediction research (personal communication, May 14, 2010). In addition to these early efforts, Inwald's subsequent work has advocated for and supported clear validation guidelines and actuarial prediction techniques as well as increased accountability of police psychologists for their pre-employment evaluations (Inwald, 1980, 1982a, 1984a; Inwald & Sakales, 1982; Sakales & Inwald, 1982).

Cochrane et al. (2003) and Varela et al. (2004) cite two large meta-analytic studies that appeared in the early 1990s (Barick & Mount, 1991; Tett, Jackson, & Rothstein, 1991), demonstrating modest relationships between personality test scores and police officer performance which included a number of outcome studies published in the late 1980s (Bartol, 1991; Hiatt & Hargrove, 1988; Inwald & Knatz, 1988; Scogin, Schumacher, Howland, & McGee, 1989; Shusman, Inwald, & Knatz, 1987).

In their review, Weiss and Inwald (2010) suggest that research results in the 1970s were a function of the design, focus, and standardization of the instruments available at the time that were primarily designed for clinical diagnostic use (e.g., the MMPI and clinical diagnosis based on psychiatric patient norms). The authors further attribute this limitation of existing instruments as the impetus for subsequent development of instruments specifically designed and standardized for use in law enforcement populations (IPI, Inwald, 1982b) as well as normative studies, specialized scales (Inwald, 2008), and adaptations of other tests commonly used for this purpose (CPI, Roberts & Johnson, 2001).

While Weiss and Inwald (2010) attributed the lack of empirical findings during the earlier time period to limitations of the instruments, Lefkowitz (1977), in the I/O literature of that time, attributed the absence of empirical work in personality assessment of police officers to a conceptual distinction between *screening* and *prediction*, the former characterizing clinical inquiry and the latter attributed to I/O research. According to Lefkowitz (1977), clinical inquiry of the time was focused on elimination of those judged to be emotionally unfit... [while making] few attempts to ascertain either the validity of those assessments or the degree to which specific clinical attributes may or may not be related to the job performance of those who pass the screening. (p. 354)

Fishing on the I/O side of the lake, Lefkowitz (1977) went on to describe this distinction as a fundamental difference between the nature of clinical vs. industrial inquiry, that is, "the traditional psychiatric model practiced by clinical psychologists and psychiatrists" (screening/clinical) vs. "procedures which attempt to predict job success as defined by a variety of operational criteria" (prediction/industrial) (p. 354). However, it is interesting that this clinical vs. industrial distinction occurred within the context of another important discussion in the history of clinical psychology and the science of psychological assessment— clinical vs. actuarial prediction.

At roughly the same time that Ogelsby (1957), Matarazzo et al. (1964), and others were publishing early descriptive work on psychological attributes of police officers and—on the other side of the lake—Lefkowitz was noting the scarcity of attempts to investigate or document the relationship of personality test findings and/or specific clinical attributes to job performance, Paul Meehl, a clinical psychologist, professor of psychology, and practicing psychotherapist was defending his "disturbing little book" *Clinical Versus Statistical Prediction* (Meehl, 1954/1996).

Although his work spans a lifetime and his productivity and contribution to the field are legendary, the majority of Meehl's work in identifying conditions and components of actuarial prediction as well as the consistent, unvarying superiority of this statistical/actuarial approach in virtually all circumstances when compared to clinical judgment, occurred during roughly the same time period that psychological tests were initially used to *screen* police officer candidates. This occurred while reporting results in clinical rather than performance linked terms and during the same time period in which this lack of empirical findings was reported in the I/O literature.

As noted earlier, prior to the mid-1980s, it was common among police psychologists to gather information about employment candidates using primarily clinical instruments and to interpret this information *clinically* (i.e., apply observational, theoretical, and experiential perspectives to synthesize predictive hypotheses) while reporting findings and making recommendations in terms that might—or might not—have relevance to future job performance as a law enforcement officer. However, although it is not surprising that industrial psychologists of the time described these clinical evaluations of police officer candidates as "devoid of data other than the clinician's personal impressions" (Lefkowitz, 1977, p. 354), it should be remembered that this practice was, in fact, characteristic of the entire (broader) field of clinical psychological assessment at the time, that is, police psychologists in the 1970s and early 1980s were performing assessments (and making predictions) following the same manner of practice as most other clinical psychologists performing assessments in other fields. Borrowing from Dawes (2005), the clinicians were fishing on their side of the lake, while I/O psychologists were fishing on their side (and few, if any, clinical or I/O psychologists were "fishing in the middle of the lake"). Within this context, Meehl's work in actuarial vs. clinical prediction appeared; subsequently, this was also the context into which specialized assessment instruments, practices, and empirical studies of predictive validity in law enforcement selection emerged.

CLINICAL VS. ACTUARIAL PREDICTION

In 1954, Paul Meehl published his classic book *Clinical Versus Statistical Prediction*. According to Meehl, *clinical prediction* referred to the use of an individual—an expert, a clinician—to predict an event. *Statistical prediction* referred to the use of an actuarial formula to predict the same event (Westen & Weinberger, 2004).

There is a wealth of research, historical review, and commentary dealing with actuarial vs. clinical prediction and associated areas, for example, Grove and Lloyd (2006), Grove (2005), Grove and Meehl (1996), and Dawes, Faust, and Meehl (1989). Summarizing this entire field is beyond the scope of this chapter. However, it is also well known that Meehl initially examined 20 empirical studies comparing clinical judgment to statistical (actuarial) prediction and found clear-cut and consistent superiority of statistical prediction over clinical judgment. In addition, this finding has been replicated numerous times across multiple studies by Meehl and others over the years, within many contexts, using many instruments with essentially the same findings (Dawes, Faust, & Meehl, 1989; Grove, Zald, Lebow, Snitz, & Nelson, 2000).

In reviewing Meehl's work, Grove and Lloyd (2006) summarized:

> Meehl's (1954/1996) conclusion that statistical prediction consistently outperforms clinical judgment has stood up extremely well for half a century. His conceptual analyses have not been significantly improved since he published them in the 1950s and 1960s. His work in this area contains several citation classics, which are part of the working knowledge of all competent applied psychologists today. (p. 192)

It should also be noted, however, that in spite of what amounts to overwhelming evidence in support of actuarial prediction techniques over clinical judgment in virtually all circumstances, Meehl's findings were not universally accepted in practice when first published nor are they universally accepted and incorporated within the broader field of psychological assessment practice today.

Through the years, Dawes, Faust, and Meehl (1989), Meehl (1954/1996), Grove and Lloyd (2006), Grove (2005), and others have described and evaluated a host of arguments asserting the equality and/or superiority of clinical (over actuarial) prediction and have meticulously refuted them. That said, when asked to describe their interpretive strategy, many clinical psychologists respond that they do not routinely make predictions based on actuarial interpretation. Similarly, many police psychologists (a specific subset of "most clinical psychologists") performing pre-employment assessments report use of *actuarially guided* or *hybrid* decision-making practices consisting of routine review, consideration, and aggregation of statistical data (e.g., specialized test scores), followed by intervening expert judgment. Nonetheless, however mainstream, modal, and/or representative of common practice the hybrid assertion may be, it should also be noted that this point of view is neither logically nor scientifically consistent. Statistical and clinical interpretations are mutually exclusive by definition. A decision/prediction can be either actuarial (rule based) or clinical (results modified/enhanced/synthesized by professional interpretation); it cannot be both. There are no true hybrids:

> [C]linical and statistical prediction (are) mutually exclusive. If actuarial predictions are synthesized clinically, this is clinical prediction; if clinical predictions are synthesized statistically, this is statistical prediction. There is no such thing as a true hybrid. This point has been repeatedly misunderstood, and in my opinion, often tendentiously and misleadingly argued by some psychologists. (Grove, 2005, p. 1234)

The defining component of actuarial judgment is that actuarial predictions occur *mechanically* as a function of predetermined rules, that is, there is no intervening professional judgment or mediation of any kind, and no other data are considered. Clinical prediction occurs when data are interpreted and predictions are synthesized by an expert using experience, perspective, and/or other clinically mediated processes. Once predictions based on statistical rules are modified by a clinician, they become clinical predictions. The *hybrid* or *actuarially guided* strategy described above (statistical aggregation mediated by expert judgment) is, in fact, clinical prediction and has been so described by Meehl (1986) as "clinical data combination" (Grove, 2005, p. 1234). In the case of police psychology, although the clinician may take advantage of information that is statistically aggregated and/or actuarially derived—for example, specialized test scores—once judgment is applied, the final decision is nonetheless clinical. According to more than 50 years of research, these statistically aggregated clinical predictions are not likely to be as accurate as predictions arrived at actuarially. In addition, it also should be noted that this same body of research has found that making additional information and/or experience that is not part of the prediction model available to clinical judges is not likely to alter this finding nor improve clinical accuracy in any way. (Dawes, Faust, & Meehl, 1989; Goldberg, 1991).

This confusion regarding hybrid practice may be due to a misperception among some clinicians that actuarial prediction always requires aggregation of quantitative data followed by sophisticated statistical analysis. This is not necessarily the case. According to Meehl (1954/1996), when considering statistical prediction (as opposed to clinical judgment):

> [The] distinction is that between the source or type of information employed in making predictions and the manner in which this information is combined for predictive purposes. (p. 15)

The primary clinical vs. actuarial distinction lies between uniform application of structured rules (actuarial) vs. judgment based decision making (clinical), whatever the form of data gathered. Most objective psychological tests yield statistical data, while interviews yield observational data, and personal history questionnaires yield descriptive data. However, observational and descriptive data also can be aggregated statistically just as statistical data (e.g., scores on psychological tests) can be interpreted clinically. The distinction is in the judgment technique, not in the type of data judged. Actuarial models often include *expert rules* derived from experience, albeit applied mechanically, just as clinical models often include statistical data, for example, test scores applied or weighted at the discretion of the clinician. In either event, the *practice activity* of a psychologist utilizing actuarial prediction and the practice activity of a psychologist utilizing clinical prediction are more or less identical, that is, both gather and aggregate the same data protocols (responses to test items and interview questions, review of background information, and so on). The distinction lies in what happens after the data are gathered (the decision/prediction-making process).

Objective test and questionnaire items lend themselves reasonably well to statistical prediction, but these same data can be (and most often are) interpreted clinically. In the same way, responses to structured interview questions, such as those dealing with life history and background information, may be coded and scored (aggregated) for use in statistical prediction models, but they may also be (and often are) interpreted clinically. In actuarial models, scores derived from psychological tests and life history inquiries may be inserted into a series of prediction routines and equations derived from comparison of problem officers with controls (nonproblem officers), resulting in a classification prediction (e.g., problem/nonproblem). In a clinical model, this same information (high/low scores, interview responses) is reviewed and interpreted by a clinician who may code it and apply some *rules of thumb* derived from education, experience, and judgment or from the results of a specialized test. However, unless these *rules of thumb* and coded information constitute 100% of the judgment equation and are completely, consistently, and/or *mechanically* applied in all cases—that is, the clinician does not decide which rules apply and/or with what degree of weight—the prediction process is clinical. Once again, and as noted above, based on the results of multiple studies over the past 50 years, the latter prediction (clinical) when aggregated across multiple cases will not be as accurate as the former (actuarial) (Dawes, Faust, & Meehl, 1989; Grove et al., 2000).

With regard to interview data, both Meehl (1959) and Westin and Weinberger (2004) have presented evidence that structured interview and/or structured scoring techniques that convert (aggregate) clinically derived nonstandardized data into structured scored form may be incorporated into actuarial models.

> It is also possible that interview-based judgments at a minimally inferential level—if recorded in standard form (for example, Qsort) and treated statistically—can be made more powerful than such data treated impressionistically as is currently the practice. (Meehl, 1959, p. 124)

Similarly, Shedler and Westin (2004) reported development and use of a structured scoring technique similar to Qsort (SWAP-200), completed by clinicians observing psychiatric patients that demonstrated predictive validity superior to psychological tests when the results were calculated actuarially. In this case, clinicians, described as "expert observers," generated data that were subsequently used actuarially, that is, data created by clinical observation when applied actuarially were found to be superior to statistical data aggregated clinically.

On the other hand, responses to *semi structured* interviews and other nonstandardized, nonobjective instruments of inquiry are more problematic for use in actuarial prediction since the responses are not necessarily uniform across all applicants and the resultant data often require some form of interpretive intervention, for example, scoring, coding, and interpretation. However, semistructured interview formats are reported to be in use in a large percentage of law enforcement agencies using pre-employment assessment (Cochrane et al. 2003), and this technique (semistructured interview) is currently specified as a required component of pre-employment assessment in practice guidelines published by the Police Psychological Services Section of the International Association of Chiefs of Police (2009).

As noted earlier, it is estimated that as many as 4,500 psychologists perform as many as 100,000 pre-employment assessments each year (Corey et al., 2009). Because it can be expected that these psychologists are representative of the broader field of clinical practice, it is probably fair to say that, in spite of research evidence to the contrary, a substantial cohort of the psychologists who perform police officer pre-employment assessments each year are making predictions clinically, albeit statistically enhanced by psychological test data. Although many are gathering all the information needed for actuarial assessment, incorporating actuarially derived information (test scores) in their decision-making process, and operating well within the mainstream of accepted practice, on the whole, these predictions are ultimately clinical, not as accurate as they could be, and also not strictly consistent with a substantial body of scientific evidence.

In this regard, Grove and Lloyd (2006) found that many clinicians were actually unaware of these issues and/or untrained in actuarial prediction:

> We surveyed a 10% random sample of American Psychological Association Division 12 (clinical) psychologists to learn how familiar they were with the controversy, their views on the matter, and their clinical practices. Of 183 responders (28% response rate), more than 15% had never heard of the controversy or had merely heard that it existed; only 42% had covered the controversy in detail during their training; 10% had not been taught that there were any available statistical prediction methods, let alone what they were or how to use them, and another 6% had only had the existence of such methods mentioned. (p. 194)

Dawes et al. (1989) speculated as to why so few practitioners seemed to have changed practice habits in the face of such consistent evidence and concluded:

> Failure to accept a large and consistent body of scientific evidence over unvalidated personal observation may be described as a normal human failing or, in the case of professionals who identify themselves as scientific, plainly irrational. (p. 1673)

In a later article, Dawes (2005) goes even further:

> Providing service that assumes that clinicians "can do better" simply based on self-confidence or plausibility in the absence of evidence that they can actually do so is simply unethical. (p. 1245)

However, although clinical interpretation of pre-employment assessment data may or may not be unethical (Dawes, 2005), clinical rather than (actuarial) interpretation of pre- employment assessment data is arguably not consistent with evidence available in the literature, particularly when predicting training performance and/or overall suitability where screen-out baselines of occurrence exceed 20%.

Pre-employment assessment of police officers is a *high stakes* activity for all involved (applicant, employer, psychologist, and community). In addition to the likelihood that these assessments will have a direct and immediate impact on the future employment prospects of the applicant, these assessments are also typically performed within the civil service/public employment arena where financial loss and/or substantial harm may accrue to an employer as well as to the community at large for wrongful employment, wrongful rejection, and/or failing to properly screen. As such, a higher level of legal scrutiny (and jeopardy) is associated with this activity than may be associated with other assessment activities within clinical psychology.

In addition, various legal and professional mandates have emerged since 1978 that have directly impacted the practice of pre-employment assessment (EEOC Uniform Guidelines on Employee Selection, 1978), principles for validation and use of personnel selection procedures (Society for Industrial and Organizational Psychology, 2003), the Civil Rights Act of 1991, and the Americans With Disabilities Act (1990).

These developments (increased demand, high-stakes scrutiny, and statutory requirements) have created a practice climate favoring actuarial assessment, or at least statistical documentation of baselines, validity, and outcome that is more pronounced than in many other fields of clinical psychology endeavor. As such, the past 20 years have seen a *paradigm shift* within police psychology, encouraging convergence of clinical, I/O, and forensic inquiry (pushing us into *the middle of the lake*).

As noted by Grove and Lloyd (2006), Meehl's primary contribution to the field was putting this controversy center stage as well as clarifying the concepts underlying the debate. With regard to police psychology, Meehl's work occurred within the context of legal and societal changes that were placing increasing demands on the practice of pre-employment psychological assessment with regard to job related validity. As a result, police psychologists were driven to examine their techniques and practices in a more quantitative and empirical light than previously, thus setting the stage for research, the creation of new instruments, documentation of the predictive validity of pre-employment assessment, and a general convergence of clinical, I/O, and forensic inquiry.

RETROSPECTIVE RESEARCH

Starting in the mid-1980s, meta-analytic studies emerged that reviewed the available research linking personality tests to job performance and established consensus in regard to the predictive validity of these instruments (Barrick & Mount, 1991; O'Brien, 1996; Schmitt, Gooding, Noe, & Kirsch, 1984; Tett, Jackson, & Rothstein, 1991; Tett, Jackson, Rothstein, & Reddon, 1994). During this time, a number of tests and other instruments specifically designed for use in screening police officers also emerged. Studies of the predictive validity of these tests formed the foundation of validation evidence for use of these instruments in pre-employment screening. According to Varela et al. (2004), these earlier studies found evidence of modest but significant validity predicting police officer performance with personality measures. In general, validity coefficients were in the range of .12 to .25 for independent variables related to a number of scales on a number of tests, most commonly MMPI/2 (Minnesota Multiphasic Personality Inventory), CPI (California Psychological Inventory), and IPI (Inwald Personality Inventory), as well as a wide variety of dependent variables, ranging from job performance outcomes (e.g., training performance, turnover, and retention) to subjective ratings on personality constructs. Varela's study incorporated results from a considerably larger number of studies than previous meta-analyses (78), reported results linked to both objective performance and construct ratings, and found similar validity coefficients (.09–.23) with differential findings grouped by test (MMPI/2, CPI, IPI), study design, and character of the dependent (outcome, criterion) variables.

Another interesting and thorough study was performed by Ones, Viswesvaran, and Dilchert (2004) in conjunction with a project initiated by the California Peace Officer Training and

Standard Commission (POST) and led by Spilberg (2003). The focus of this project was development of a revised psychological screening manual to guide and inform law enforcement agencies in California in proper use of mandated pre-employment psychological screening. As part of this project, Spilberg (an I/O psychologist; 2003) performed a comprehensive job analysis, surveying police agency executives and police psychologists (primarily clinical psychologists) yielding a set of 10 content-linked peace officer psychological attributes. These attributes (constructs) became the psychological screening dimensions that California agencies were advised to incorporate in pre-employment screening. These constructs also became the dependent variables in the meta-analysis performed by Ones et al. (2004). Next, a panel of police psychologists linked these constructs to specific scales on various psychological tests, and these scales became the independent (predictor) variables for the meta-analysis. This study found a somewhat wider range of validity coefficients than reported by previous meta-analyses (0.10–0.40) due, in part, to the careful attention that was paid to development and standardization of constructs and predictor variables. These results also reflected an unusually comprehensive range of police behavior as opposed to earlier meta-analytic studies that aggregated studies with less comprehensive outcome variables. In addition, the study is an excellent example of clinical/IO convergence as I/O techniques such as critical incident review and job analysis were integrated with clinical expertise. These findings further documented the validity and utility of psychological testing in this setting as well.

When reviewing this body of research, it is important to note that although the independent predictor variables (psychological test scores, typically, MMPI/2, CPI, IPI, 16PF, and a few others) were quite similar across most studies, the dependent outcome variables varied substantially. Some studies used objective job performance as outcomes (e.g., retention and turnover, attendance, training performance, disciplinary action, and so on), while others used ratings of behavior based on constructs (e.g., Big 5 personality constructs as in Barrick & Mount, 1991; California POST 10 as in Ones et al., 2004) that were subsequently linked to job performance. This distinction was noted by Varela et al. (2004), who further found that validity coefficients for construct ratings, which he called "soft" ratings, were somewhat higher than validity coefficients for objective performance.

In as much as the predictor variables in these studies were, in fact, components of test instruments designed to measure psychological constructs in the first place, it would seem that this finding (personality tests are better predictors of construct ratings than actual performance) is not particularly surprising, that is, documenting predictive validity using dependent variables linked to personality may maximize the observed validity coefficient of a test but may not necessarily provide an accurate view of the overall utility of the instrument in question since both the predictor variables and the outcome variables are drawn from the same domain (personality) and hence subject to similar sources of error. This is an important item to remember when considering validation evidence supporting specific personality tests for use in a pre-employment assessment protocol.

PRACTICE GUIDELINES

Of the estimated 4,500 psychologists assumed to be performing some kind of police psychology service, about 200–300 have dedicated a substantial proportion of their practice activities primarily to police psychology and are members of national professional organizations (Corey et al., 2009). One such organization, the Police Psychological Services Section of the International Association of Chiefs of Police (IACP_PPSS), is a group of approximately 200 psychologists whose practice is substantially focused on police psychology. Founded in the mid-1980s, this group publishes a number of practice guidelines, including guidelines for practice of pre-employment assessment. These guidelines have come to be viewed as an expression of "best practice" in this area. First published in 1986, they have been periodically reviewed and rewritten (IACP_PPSS, 1992, 1998, 2004,

2009). The comparative content of each version of these practice guidelines represents a series of interesting *snapshots* of the state of the art of pre-employment assessment in the past 20 years and also reflects the paradigm shift that has occurred regarding validation, performance prediction, and outcome research (and migration to the *middle of the lake*).

The original (pre-employment) guidelines were developed by Inwald (1984a, 1985c, 1986b) and formally adopted by the IACP's Police Psychological Services Section after discussions and modifications at the 1986 IACP convention. In addition to a number of basic practice considerations (choice of tests, qualification of examiners, confidentiality of results, and so on), Inwald's original proposed guidelines also contained a number of direct references to program components necessary to support validation and actuarial assessment. These components included surveys to identify critical job performance attributes, development of specific behavioral outcomes to be predicted, identification of base rates of occurrence of outcomes (to assess "cost of selection" and efficiency of tests over chance prediction), and development of behaviorally based structured (scorable) interview protocols. As such, these components were included in the original published guidelines (Inwald, 1986b); however, with the exception of a general reference to base rates, most of these components supporting research and validation were dropped from revised 1992 guidelines (Inwald, personal communication, December 29, 2009).

The 1992 guidelines did note that tests should be "validated" and assessment results should be expressed in job-related (rather than medical or psychopathological) terms and linked to a "psychological job analysis." In 1998, the term *psychological job analysis*—a term coined by Inwald (1998)—was replaced with more precise terminology:

> Data on attributes considered most important for effective performance in a particular position should be obtained from job analysis, interview, surveys, or other appropriate sources. (IACP_PPSS, 1998, p. 1, item 4)

Although the Americans With Disabilities Act (ADA, 1990) was enacted prior to 1992, the 1992 version of the guidelines was silent on the issue of pre/post offer assessment, probably because the Act did not go into effect until 1994. In 1998, specific reference to ADA was added to the guidelines without very much elaboration beyond the admonishment that psychological evaluations should be performed subsequent to conditional offers of employment.

By 2004, the guidelines had become considerably more detailed on the subject of ADA, particularly in regard to "medical" vs. "nonmedical" evaluations, instruments, and methods of inquiry which could be conducted prior to conditional offers of employment. Perhaps reflecting the growing practice of "bifurcation" (nonmedical assessment pre-offer followed by mental health inquiry post-offer):

> Personality tests and other methods of inquiry that are not medical by the above definition and that do not include specific prohibited topics or inquiries may be conducted at the pre-offer stage. However, these assessments are alone not capable of determining a candidate's emotional stability and therefore would not constitute an adequate pre-employment psychological evaluation. (IACP_PPSS, 2004, p. 2, item 11)

The 2004 guidelines also contained specific reference to ADA regarding post-offer inquiry:

> A psychological evaluation is considered "medical" if it provides evidence that could lead to identifying a mental or emotional disorder or impairment as listed in the DSM-IV, and therefore must only be conducted after the applicant has been tendered a conditional offer of employment. (IACP_PPSS, 2004, p. 2, item 11)

However, beyond asserting that test instruments and the selection processes should be validated in some way, the 2004 version of the guidelines was almost silent about the documentation of validity and/or the process through which this validation should occur.

A test battery including objective, job-related, validated psychological instruments should be administered to the applicant. Written tests selected should be validated for use with public safety candidates. Continuing collaborative efforts by the hiring agency and evaluating psychologist should be made to validate final suitability ratings using behavioral criteria measures. (IACP_PPSS, 2004, p. 2, item 11)

In this regard, it seems the authors of the 2004 guidelines emphasized legal parameters of the pre- and post-offer distinction over technical requirements. However, as noted earlier, each of these guideline versions represent a snapshot of the professional climate at the time of draft. In 2003–2004, the field was just beginning to come to terms with implications of the ADA, particularly as it impacted practice requirements. More practitioners were expanding practice to include bifurcated pre-offer vs. post-offer assessments, and these developments were reflected in the focus of the 2004 guideline version.

As more police psychologists embraced the bifurcated assessment format, a number of new instruments and supporting research emerged. These developments were reflected in the 2009 guidelines, which are considerably more forthcoming in regard to instrument development, validation, and technical issues. As such, this most recent version of the guidelines is another snapshot reflecting the current state of interest and focus in the field.

Starting from one side of the lake and moving toward the middle, in some ways, the 2009 guidelines return full circle to the original version drafted more than 20 years ago (Inwald, 1986b). Since 1992, emphasis in the field has transitioned from defining what should be addressed in a report and the type of tests to be used, to revising the process of assessment to conform to ADA, and finally to development of instruments and processes demonstrably linked to job performance and prediction of suitability in the most accurate and efficient manner. Certainly, the early criticism of clinical assessment without actuarial evidence by I/O psychologists and early forensic psychologists (e.g., Levy, 1967; Shapiro, 1983; Ziskin, 1981) has been resolved:

[They] have not determined what constitutes "emotional suitability" for law enforcement; … (and) hence, psychological tests and psychiatric interviews have not demonstrated much predictive value. (Levy, 1967 as quoted in Lefkowitz, 1977, p. 354)

The 2009 guidelines reflect specific developments in the field addressing, among other things, *research and development of new instruments*:

Nothing in these guidelines should be construed to discourage scientifically legitimate research, innovation, and/or use of new techniques that show promise for helping hiring agencies identify, screen, and select qualified candidates. (IACP_PPSS, 2009, p. 1, item 2.3)

documentation of job relatedness:

Information about duties, powers, demands, working conditions, and other job-analytic information relevant to the intended position, should be obtained by the psychologist before beginning the evaluation process. This information should be directed toward identifying behaviors and attributes that underlie effective and counterproductive job performance. (IACP_PPSS, 2009, p. 2, item 5.1)

validation:

Tests should have a substantial research base for interpretation with normal range populations in general and public safety applicants in particular. Validation evidence should be consistent with *Principles for the Validation and Use of Personnel Selection Procedures* (SIOP, 2003). (IACP_PPSS, 2009, p. 3, item 7.2.1) *integration of predictive information from other domains (e.g., life history):*

> Information regarding the applicant's relevant history (e.g., school, work, interpersonal, family, legal, financial, substance use, mental health, and so on) should be collected and integrated with psychological test and interview data. (IACP_PPSS, 2009, p. 4, item 9.1)

and *use/utility of pre-employment assessment in both nonmedical (pre-offer) and medical (post-offer) contexts*:

> A pre-employment psychological evaluation may include procedures or tests that are not medical in nature (i.e., designed and used to measure personality traits, behaviors, or characteristics such as judgment, stress resilience, anger management, integrity, conscientiousness, teamwork, and social competence). However, these nonmedical procedures alone would not constitute a complete pre-employment psychological evaluation since they do not include the medical element. (IACP_PPSS, 2009, p. 2, item 3.4)

SPECIALIZED TEST INSTRUMENTS

In addition to research documenting the validity of psychological tests in pre-employment settings and guidelines reflecting best practices to include research and validation, a number of specialized tests and new scales of existing tests designed for specific use in police pre-employment screening emerged during this period. The Inwald Personality Inventory (IPI), originally constructed in 1979 and published in 1982, was the first comprehensive personality inventory designed and validated specifically for public safety officer selection (Weiss & Inwald, 2010) and, as such, was unique in the field of public safety officer screening at that time. In addition to including standard scales identifying psychopathology, the IPI also included scales containing items related to past job difficulties, trouble with the law, absence, lateness tendencies, and alcohol/drug use, among other behavior patterns. The test also reported scores based on public safety officer norms as opposed to general population norms and included capabilities for generating local agency norms and/or those of related job classifications such as hostage negotiators, dispatchers, and so on (Inwald, 1982b). In addition, the report included actuarial prediction equations derived from systematic follow-up data, providing practitioners with predictions of risk for specific performance difficulties (Inwald, 1982b, 1988, 2008).

In this same time frame, the tests most widely in use to screen law enforcement officers were the Minnesota Multiphasic Personality Inventory (MMPI; Hathaway & McKinnley, 1940), the California Psychological Inventory (CPI; Gough, 1956, 1987), and the 16PF (Cattell, 1949). Specialized narrative reports for law enforcement selection based on these instruments were also developed and marketed for these instruments during this time, but the scores were based on general population norms and not specifically linked to job performance attributes specific to law enforcement. In 1981, the Law Enforcement Assessment and Development Report (LEADR) was published, a derivative of Raymond Cattell's 16PF (1949) published by IPAT, with a public-safety-related narrative report (Dee-Burnett, Johns, & Krug, 1981), and in 1984, the Minnesota Report: Personnel Selection System appeared based on the MMPI. For the most part, these tests reported findings in terms of sets of constructs based on conventional clinical interpretations of personality and did not contain direct linkages to specific law enforcement performance attributes.

From 1987 to 1997, several specialized tests were developed by Inwald and her colleagues that focused on specific traits and behaviors germane to law enforcement officer job performance. These instruments also reported public safety candidate norms and utilized actuarial prediction equations. The instruments included the Hilson Personnel Profile/Success Quotient (HPP/SQ, social/emotional intelligence issues; Inwald & Brobst, 1988), the Inwald Survey 5 (IS5, integrity, and domestic violence issues), the Hilson Safety/Security Risk Inventory (HSRI, unsafe behavior in the workplace; Inwald, 1995), the Inwald Survey 2 (IS2, violence potential; Inwald, Resko, & Favuzza, 1994), and the Hilson Life Adjustment Profile (HLAP, psychopathology; Inwald, Resko, & Favuzza, 1996).

In 1995, a specialized report for the CPI used police applicant norms (Roberts & Johnson, 2001) as a comparison base. This report contained several specialized scales as well as actuarially calculated risk predictions based on comparison of applicant groups (problem officers vs. controls) that were directly germane to law enforcement performance. In most cases, the dependent variables (those that defined problem officers) were based on identification of what the authors described as "selection relevant items" as defined by pre-employment personal history and background findings. Subsequently, however, Roberts and Johnson (2001) enhanced this report to include "true outcome performance measures" such as criterion groups of applicants that lied about illegal drug use during the pre-employment screening process and, subsequently, officers who had experienced "involuntary departures" as well as supervisory issues and other negative job performance events (Roberts, personal communication, December 9, 2009).

Roberts, Thompson, and Johnson (2000) created a special report for the Personality Assessment Inventory (Morey, 2007) contrasting current applicants applying for public safety jobs with norms from a group of applicants in four job classifications (police officer, communications dispatcher, corrections officer, and firefighter/EMT) who successfully completed the job-screening procedures for the same position, were hired, and completed at least 1 year in that position. Like the IPI, the report also contains risk statements in regard to ratings of job suitability made by experienced psychologists conducting psychological evaluations of job applicants for specific public safety positions (e.g., police officer or corrections officer), and added specific types of background problems identified on personal history questionnaires.

In as much as the primary purpose of pre-employment assessment is prediction of on-the- job behavior, predictor domains (in this case test scores/scales) should be independent, since correlation between predictor domains is known to be a source of error in psychometric tests. Similarly, it has also been noted that multiple predictor models containing correlated scores can be expected to have higher standard error values (Campbell & Fiske, 1959; Cureton et al., 1996). As noted earlier in the discussion of retrospective research, prediction error can be expected from any personality test—regardless of the outcome to which it is linked. However, when a test is linked to construct ratings, both the predictors (scores) and the outcomes (constructs) are open to similar sources of error. When personality constructs are subsequently linked to job outcomes they become vulnerable yet again to the same source of error. As such, the observed validity coefficient between test and construct may be greater than a validity coefficient derived from a direct link between test score and job outcome. Similarly, intercorrelation of personality test scales will inflate the apparent validity of a test and/or a prediction model since the correlated scales are vulnerable to similar sources of error.

Apropos to the question of error associated with correlated scales, the Institute for Personality Assessment and Ability Testing (IPAT) has constructed several specialized law enforcement reports based on the 16PF (Cattell, Cattell, & Cattel, 1993) and the PEPQ (PsychEval Personality Questionnaire, Cattell, Cattell, Cattell, Russell, & Bedwell, 2003). Both the fundamental design and the scales of these instruments were derived from factor analysis; hence, these scores are minimally intercorrelated. Due to their independence, such scales are particularly well suited for construction of prediction models. The most recent edition of the 16PF (2003), which assesses normal personality, was redesigned in light of ADA requirements to be nonmedical and can be administered prior to a conditional offer of employment as well as in bifurcated processes (normal assessment pre-offer, mental health assessment post-offer). The PEPQ assesses both normal personality and psychopathology and is designed for use post-offer, and/or in the second phase of bifurcation. Both instruments report scores on four "Protective Service Dimensions" derived from content analysis of the law enforcement literature as well as linkage to Cattell's original 16-factor analytically derived personality scales (Cattell, 1949), and the "Big 5 factors of personality" (Goldberg, 1993).[*] Scores on these resultant constructs are significantly related to job outcome, with effect sizes ranging from .08 to .87, and intercorrelations of the scores are minimal (Cattell, Cattell, Cattell, Russell, & Bedwell, 2003).

Similarly, Tellegen et al. (2003), noting that the clinical scales in the MMPI-2 were intercorrelated (and hence a potential source for error in both diagnostic and selection contexts), factor analyzed the MMPI-2 clinical scales and derived a set of nine restructured clinical scales (RC scales) that were not significantly correlated yet, at least as valid in regard to prediction (Tellegen, 2009). Subsequently, Ben-Porath and Tellegen constructed the MMPI-2-RF (restructured form), consisting of a subset of 338 items derived from the original 587 item MMPI-2, incorporating these factor analytic scales along with several higher order scales. Recent outcome research based on objective performance outcomes has been encouraging. Sellbom, Fischler, and Ben-Porath (2007) found that the RC Scales were better at predicting specific behavioral misconduct in peace officers. As such, it would seem the MMPI-2-RF addresses several of the limitations of other personality tests described above (tests linked to constructs not direct outcomes, tests yielding correlated measures). It should also be noted, however, that the MMPI-2-RF contains items that measure emotional stability, and, similar to the PEPQ (Cattell et al., 2003), this test is considered medical under the ADA and must be administered after a conditional offer of employment has occurred and where significant range restriction is likely.

Unlike other specialized reports (e.g., CPI, IPI, Roberts et al., 2001), the MMPI-2-RF reports scores in terms of general population norms rather than law enforcement applicant norms. As noted earlier, incorporation of applicant norms can be useful in interpreting test results primarily due to the fact that substantial differences are likely between responses of police job applicants vs. the general population (Bartol, 1982; Carpenter & Raza, 1987; Hargrave, Hiatt, & Gaffney, 1986, Varela et al., 2004). However, Ben-Porath (2009) points out that these data can also be misleading in that they can mask genuine differences between peace officer candidates and members of the general population, hence facilitating *false negative* predictions (passed when not suitable) based on information that may have been identified upon further probing. Therefore, the MMPI-2-RF reports scores in general population terms while providing descriptive information regarding the range of law enforcement applicant population scores for comparative purposes.

OTHER PREDICTIVE DOMAINS AND INSTRUMENTS; INCREMENTAL/CONVERGENT VALIDITY AND MERGED PROCESSES

In addition to personality tests, several other classes (domains) of independent variables have been found to be predictive of job performance in police officers. The most common of these measures are cognitive ability and life history. Variables from these predictor domains are commonly incorporated into assessment protocols performed by police psychologists. In addition, there is evidence that each of these predictor domains are independent (noncorrelated) and linked to objective performance outcomes.

With regard to general mental ability, Schmitt et al. (1984) conducted a meta-analysis of 99 employees in a variety of occupations, including law enforcement, and reported that mental ability is a significant predictor of success in these occupations. Similarly, in a meta-analytic investigation limited to law enforcement occupations, Aamodt (2004) reported an average correlation of r = .41 between mental ability and various measures of academic performance. Likewise, Hirsch, Northrup, and Schmidt (1986) reported an average correlation of r = .34 between mental ability and

---

[*] The "Big 5 factors of personality" are five broad domains or dimensions of personality that have been identified and documented through extensive research. These factors are considered one of the most comprehensive, empirical, data-driven research findings in the history of personality psychology. The Big 5 factors are openness, conscientiousness, extroversion, agreeableness, and neuroticism. (Neuroticism is also referred to as *emotional stability*.) For detailed information, see Goldberg (1993).

academy training. As such, there is general consensus that cognitive ability is a primary predictor of suitability in law enforcement. Use of this predictor, however, is limited by the fact that scores on many tests measuring mental ability also often questioned in regard to disparate impact* on specific racial groups (Equal Employment Opportunity Commission, 1995); as such, their utility as unilateral predictors can be limited.

Life history events are routinely gathered and evaluated by police psychologists during the assessment process as well. In addition to their relationship to personality information, evidence suggests that these data are not particularly subject to disparate impact on racial or gender groups and can also be a robust and independent predictor of police performance. According to Tenopyr (1994), there is substantial evidence for convergence between life history and personality constructs. In similar fashion, Mumford, Snell, and Reiter-Palmon (1994) stated:

> Perhaps the most straightforward answer to the question we have posed covering the relationship between background data and personality is to argue that background data represent little more than an alternative format for personality assessment. (pp. 584–585)

There are basically two ways to report and use life history events in pre-employment prediction. One approach is to identify the occurrence of defined life events in the history of an applicant and measure the degree to which these discrete events (e.g., job terminations) are predictive of a specific outcome (e.g., problem performance as a police officer). A second approach is to link defined life events to personality constructs (e.g., job termination linked to conscientiousness), the latter (construct ratings) becoming the outcome variable. Both approaches are convergent valid predictors of outcome and independent of personality measures (Cuttler & Muchinsky, 2006; Sarchione, Cuttler, Muchinsky, & Nelson-Gray, 1998; Tenopyr, 1994).

As mentioned earlier, the IPI, first published in 1979, was the first personality assessment instrument that included biographical/behavioral data items such as arrest history, driving record, work history, and substance use as well as scales identifying the presence of psychopathology and antisocial attitudes. These inquiries were presented as true/false test items and were linked to constructs in the context of a personality inventory rather than in an instrument designed to develop discrete descriptive detail about life events such as a personal history questionnaire. As noted, although responses to individual items (e.g., "I received good grades in school") were qualitatively reported (i.e., in a critical items listing), the responses were quantitatively linked to personality-based construct scales (e.g., conscientiousness) and these construct scores were the primary variables in the subsequent validation studies (Inwald, 1982b, 2008).

Similar to the preceding discussion, but taking a more clinical approach to use of life history information, Johnson and Roberts (2006) constructed the PsyQ, which they describe as a self-report questionnaire that provides life history information pertinent to the evaluation of applicants for public safety positions. The questionnaire contains 340 questions presented in multiple-choice formats, containing a varying number of response categories, as required to reflect the full range of relevant responses to each question. The results (responses by applicant to multiple-choice questions) are organized into problem categories developed by a panel of psychologists. The scores of these items are aggregated into these categories and are reported in relative frequency terms, comparing an applicant's response to frequencies in a database of previous applicants. According to the authors, the information developed by this questionnaire is primarily intended to help clinicians determine the extent to which the findings from psychological testing are corroborated by actual behavior. As such, although likely to provide utility as a guide to a psychologist in conducting interviews, the

---

* In U.S. employment law, *adverse impact* is also known as *disparate impact* and is defined as a "substantially different rate of selection in hiring, promotion, or other employment decision which works to the disadvantage of members of a race, sex, or ethnic group" (EEOC Uniform Employee Selection Guidelines; Questions and Answers; Section 16. http://www.uniformguidelines.com/uniformguidelines.html#129).

questionnaire's utility and/or potential for convergent validity or as an independent predictor of outcome in an actuarial model has not yet been investigated.

With regard to use of discrete life history events as an independent outcome predictor, Sarchione et al. (1998) constructed a list of critical life events identified by subject matter experts (background investigators). These subject matter experts also weighted these items in terms of criticality and predictive value when reviewing police applicant backgrounds, creating quantitative scales for employment, criminal, and substance-related items. The investigators then examined personnel records and internal affairs files and identified groups of problem officers (who experienced discipline, or were terminated). After correction for range restriction, the study found effect sizes from 0.40 to 0.74 for specific life event scales as predictors of various on-the-job disciplinary actions. The study also included CPI scores that yielded effect sizes from 0.48 to 0.67 as predictors of these outcomes as well. Cuttler and Muchinsky (2006) cross-validated these findings and added a fourth scale (veracity) corresponding to omissions, errors, and discrepancies in reported information as well as documenting predictive validity for a broader range of outcomes (failure to complete training, termination, selection failure). These studies found consistent evidence that the life history scales were essentially independent of (not correlated with) personality tests and/or cognitive ability measures, nor were these life history scales (employment, criminal, substance, veracity) correlated with each other. As such, the authors suggested that substantial incremental validity may be derived from combining life history and personality test scores.

Achievement of incremental validity though use of scored life events requires gathering and aggregating life history data in a reliable and efficient manner. However, unlike psychological tests to which subjects usually respond in a yes/no, true/false, or multiple-choice manner, a number of unique intervening variables impacting the practice and quality of life history assessment are not necessarily present in personality measurement. Cuttler (2007) notes that the accuracy and utility of a life history questionnaire are affected by the way the questions are formulated and presented, the manner in which the responses are scored, and the attitude or bias of the respondent who completes the questionnaire.

According to Cuttler (2007), there is also likely to be considerable and understandable (conscious and unconscious) motivation on the part of job applicants to present themselves in as favorable a light as possible. The effect of this motivation in regard to psychological tests is also well known and documented (Anastasi, 1988). However, although it has been suggested that this *impression management* effect does not necessarily alter the fundamental findings of psychological tests, particularly in *normal* populations (Ben-Porath, 2009) and/or when interpreting test results actuarially (Grove, 2005; Grove & Meehl, 1996), the *transparency* of life history questions is such as to render this (bias) effect considerably more critical when aggregating life history information.

Direct questions regarding life history are considerably more *transparent* to an applicant than personality items, and this transparency is likely to affect applicant response. For example, the scoring, interpretation, and/or implication of a true/false item—such as "From time to time I go to the movies by myself"—is probably not as apparent to a job applicant as "Have you ever been fired from a job"? As a function of this transparency, bias, and/or impression management motivation, the quality of life history data derived through self-report questionnaires is fundamentally dependent on the design of the instrument used to collect this data as well as its ability to minimize response bias. In this regard, the simplest and most straightforward life history questionnaires can also be the most open to bias (Cuttler, 2007).

The simplest way to gather life history information is to construct a series of questions to which an applicant responds in a binary (yes/no; true/false) format similar to that of a psychological test. This approach has the advantage of being easily machine scored and aggregated. Some more sophisticated versions of these questionnaires may present these items in conditional *branch/stem* format (e.g., have you ever been fired from a job? <if yes> how many times?). However, response to these items will also depend on the applicant's interpretations, of the questions, for example, an applicant might respond *no* to the question above because "I was not fired, but after I showed up late for the third time, I agreed with my boss that it was best that I resign." Even in a more sophisticated questionnaire that allows for text entry of an explanation such as this, in order to assign an accurate score, the response must be read and interpreted. Although these omissions, interpretations, and discrepancies will usually be identified and reconciled later in the selection process (i.e., a background investigation and/or upon post-offer interview with a psychologist), these limitations are also likely to effect the reliability and utility of the life history data, particularly if these data are derived from a questionnaire and, in conjunction with psychological test data, placed in an actuarial model for screening purposes.

Another way to develop life history information is to create a set of critical items and then manually review a comprehensive personal history questionnaire (similar to those used in most background investigations) that has been previously submitted by the applicant. The life history data are then derived and/or extracted from narrative information rather than directly solicited from the applicant. This approach has the advantage of being *passive*, that is, not requiring or depending on interaction with the applicant. However, this approach has two major drawbacks. First, it is tedious and time consuming, requires considerable human intervention, is open to error and, as such, is of questionable utility when screening larger applicant pools. Second, although there are fewer direct transparent questions, this approach is still open to the sources of response bias described above (interpretations, omissions, and discrepancies) on the primary document (the personal history questionnaire).

Electronic (online) administration of personal history questionnaires can mediate a number of these drawbacks. Specifically, omissions can be easily eliminated by requiring responses. Through simple programming, *branch* questions can be conditionally presented based on applicant responses to stem questions and applicants can be constrained from *cruising* the questionnaire and/or anticipating questions and changing responses. Similarly, additional and clarifying information can be elicited during online administration that can be stored in a database and/or easily read. However, aggregating and interpreting this information would still require human intervention.

In 2001, Cuttler developed an online personal history questionnaire using patented technology that addressed these issues (Cuttler, Cuttler, & Seddon, 2008). The questionnaire also addressed the more fundamental issues of response bias by automating the process by which scored life history information was extracted from applicant-entered personal history information without asking direct questions. In addition to stem/branch conditional question presentation, programming was included that parsed and organized data into defined units (called life events) which were then linked together by logic to create scored items. The application could also intelligently scan text responses as well as report veracity, that is, discrepancies both within the questionnaire and when responses are compared to previous administrations. Inasmuch as this questionnaire reports both quantitative scores based on weighted life history events as well as detailed descriptive information input by applicants and stored in a database, the results are useful for both actuarial decision making and for facilitating background investigations. Cuttler (2000) also developed a series of five actuarial prediction equations using combinations of life history and psychological test data (CPI). This merged process, called the Multi Domain Assessment report, is an actuarially scored report that takes advantage of the opportunities for incremental validity available from combining these noncorrelated predictors derived from multiple domains (life history, personality, and cognitive/educational).[*]

PRACTICAL CONSIDERATIONS FOR DEVELOPMENT AND USE OF ACTUARIAL PREDICTION MODELS

Pre-employment assessment of police officer candidates is particularly well suited for development and use of actuarial prediction models. In this regard, the demographic characteristics of the applicant pool, training requirements, duties, and critical performance attributes of police and public

---

[*] The author (Michael J. Cuttler, PhD) is a principal owner of LESI® (Law Enforcement Services, Inc.), publisher of onlinePHQ® and Multi Domain™ Screening Report, as well as owner and primary named inventor in U.S. Patent 7,346,541 relating to these instruments.

safety jobs are reasonably common across employing agencies. Similarly, operational definition of dependent variables (specific negative selection and job outcomes), cross-validation, and follow-up are greatly facilitated within this population since policies and practices across police agencies are often required by statute and/or traditional sense of standard operating procedure. Finally, the emerging practice of *bifurcated assessment* (nonmedical ability/personality screening performed pre-offer; emotional stability assessment performed post-offer) is also particularly well-suited for actuarial prediction since in the pre-offer stage, larger applicant pools must be screened efficiently and inexpensively, and negative outcomes (e.g., failing to complete components of the selection process) occur at substantially higher base rates while smaller groups are screened for mental health issues (which occur at substantially lower base rates) on a post–conditional offer basis.

Actuarial assessment is a process by which predictor and outcome variables are identified, rules are applied, predictions are made, outcomes are recorded, and rules are modified based on these observed outcomes. Although identification/development of replicable empirical predictors/models, identification of criterion variables, and valid evaluative research designs are required to incorporate actuarial prediction techniques into practice, psychologists do not necessarily have to create new assessment protocols, that is (and as noted earlier), in many cases the activity of the psychologist need not change—simply the prediction (aggregation) technique would be modified. For identification of variables, the choice of outcome (dependent) variable should be made with reference to the independent (predictor) variables chosen and the manner in which the results and predictions will be reported to the agency. Specifically, when choosing test instruments, if the psychologist chooses to report results and make predictions based on construct ratings (e.g., Psychological Performance Dimensions similar to those described such as POST 10 [Spilberg, 2003] or Big 5 [Goldberg, 1993]), then test instruments might be chosen that, according to their technical manuals, have been designed and validated with primary reference to these construct ratings (e.g., 16PF Protective Service Reports, MMPI-2-RF, and PAI). If the psychologist chooses to make predictions and reports based on actual job outcomes, then instruments designed and validated primarily against these criteria should be included in the battery (e.g., IPI, CPI Public Safety Report, Multi Domain Screening Report, and MMPI-2-RF).

However, it is also important to note that construct-based predictions can certainly be derived from scores on tests primarily identified with objective outcome. Similarly, direct performance predictions can also be made based on construct-linked test scores. This practice is indeed common, is supported by independent research findings (e.g., Ones et al., 2004), and is even recommended by some training and standards groups (Spilberg, 2004). However, doing so (creating construct-based predictions rather than specific job outcome predictions) from scores on instruments based on general personality constructs also requires that the psychologist then create or adopt rules for converting those scores to job-related construct ratings. Similarly, when used in actuarial prediction, these conversion rules (from general personality constructs to job-specific outcomes) must be *mechanical*, that is, applied to all cases equally and not modified by discretion or judgment of the psychologist.

As stated in the current IACP-PPSS guidelines:

> 5.1. Information about duties, powers, demands, working conditions, and other job-analytic information relevant to the intended position, should be obtained by the psychologist before beginning the evaluation process. This information should be directed toward identifying behaviors and attributes that underlie effective and counterproductive job performance.
>
> 5.2. The psychologist should consult with the hiring agency to establish selection criteria and the agency's level of acceptable risk for problematic behaviors. (sections 5.1, 5.2, pp. 3–4)

And the guidelines further stated:

> 10.2 Rating and/or recommendation for employment based upon the results of the evaluation should be expressly linked to the job-analytic information referenced in paragraphs 5.1 and 5.2. (section 10.2, p. 5)

Many hiring authorities (indeed, many state statutes) also require that the psychologist provide a specific hiring recommendation. Other authorities require an overall score or rating and then set their own hiring policy (the score at which they will hire/reject). In any event, the primary components to be determined for any prediction model are the nature of the outcome (construct vs. specific), the instruments to be used, and the rules to be applied. However, in actuarial decision making, the overall rating will always be the result of a rule set that is uniformly and *mechanically* applied.

As noted earlier, the actuarial rules constructed and applied need not be statistically sophisticated. Rather, they can be *expert* rules derived by the clinician based on experience, quantitative review of past cases, or both. If applied in an actuarial manner, these predictions are still quite likely superior to clinical predictions (Grove & Meehl, 1996). The critical point is that once established, these rules must be applied uniformly rather than based on the discretion of the clinician. Psychologists applying these rules should carefully gather outcome information. Once outcomes are observed, rules can be modified at reasonable intervals to increase accuracy.

Although the evidence shows that actuarial prediction models are superior to clinical predictions in most situations, it is also important to remember that no predictor, rule, or model is perfect. Some level of error is always expected to be associated with any predictor or prediction model, including well-constructed models using independent noncorrelated predictors. In some situations (e.g., prediction of events with low baseline of occurrence), no prediction model—neither clinical nor actuarial—will operate efficiently. The validation coefficients and effect sizes reported in the earlier sections of this chapter account for only a fraction (albeit a statistically significant fraction) of the variance observed on outcome, and the acceptance of error is implied when designing any selection process. In accepting the existence of error, it is further implied that the consequences of not screening should be greater than the consequences of screening. This assumption is certainly apropos to law enforcement where the possibility of harm to others is directly apparent; hence, screening is justified. In addition to correlated measures, other sources of error associated with pre-employment prediction are functions of the design of the test or assessment instrument, the nature of the population assessed, and the base rate of occurrence of the outcome to be predicted.

Regarding base rate of occurrence, Meehl (1954/1996) and others (Finn, 2009; Westen & Weinberger, 2004) note that actuarial prediction is most accurate when baseline of occurrence approaches 50% (each alternative in the prediction model is equally probable). Unfortunately, this is rarely the case in law enforcement, as the frequency of occurrence of the negative behaviors and outcomes to be predicted usually range from below 5% for serious violations (e.g., integrity, sexual misconduct, and termination for cause) to above 20% for training failure and minor discipline to above 35% for selection process failures (Cuttler & Muchinsky, 2006). In this regard, Streiner (2003), when comparing accuracy of actuarial models that *screen out* negative outcomes to those that *screen in* positives, found that the former (screen-out-negatives model) is likely to be more accurate in low-baseline settings (occurrence < 50%) and the latter (screen-in-positives model) is more effective in high-baseline settings (where occurrence > 50%). This finding is consistent with pre-employment screening models in police psychology designed primarily to identify problem officers (i.e., screen out) via actuarial prediction. However, it is also likely that this approach will be less accurate in models that attempt to screen in positive traits (e.g. leadership).

In a prediction model used for pre-employment screening, the prediction is usually expressed in terms of a binary classification (suitable/not suitable; problem/nonproblem; pass/fail training, and so forth). The overall utility of the prediction model is a function of the total number of accurate classifications that result as well as number of errors that are made, particularly in regard to screening out otherwise qualified applicants. Accurate classification includes true positives (targeted outcome predicted and occurs), true negatives (target outcome not predicted and does not occur), false positives (target outcome is predicted but does not occur), and false negatives (targeted outcome occurs but is not predicted). The base rate of occurrence of the targeted outcome directly affects the rate at which each of these classifications occurs. In general, the efficiency of a prediction model is a function of the ratio of false positives to true positives as compared to the ratio of targeted occurrence to nonoccurrence (Meehl & Rosen, 1955). In low-baseline situations, a test or set of rules can easily seem accurate in identifying true positives but will nonetheless be worse than, or no better than, chance in terms of overall accuracy.

The goal of a screen out selection model is to maximize the hit rate (prediction of targeted outcome or true positives) while minimizing the rate at which otherwise qualified applicants are screened out (false positive). The rate at which otherwise qualified applicants are screened out due to error is also known as the *cost* of selection. Given the critical responsibilities of the law enforcement job and the potential harm to society that can accrue in the absence of screening, some level of error (or cost of selection) is usually seen as acceptable. However, this issue is also often the subject of debate when screening decisions are challenged legally, particularly in regard to EEOC requirements. Whether creating a set of actuarial assessment rules or considering information for clinical judgment, the base rate of occurrence of the targeted attribute plays a major mediating role in the overall accuracy of the screening instruments, model, and/or decision.

As noted above, predictions in pre-employment assessment are fundamentally classification problems in which one of two conditions are predicted (e.g., problem/no problem). As shown in Table 7.1, two condition classifications yield four outcomes: correct prediction of problem (true positive), correct prediction of no problem (true negative), incorrect prediction of problem (false positive), and incorrect prediction of no problem (false negative). To appreciate the effects of baseline on classification, one must consider the ratio of true positives (hits) to false positives (cost) in light of base rate of occurrence, and results must be compared to the overall accuracy of what would occur by chance (without screening or testing; Finn, 2009).

Table 7.2 illustrates an example of classification in a low-baseline situation: predicting integrity violations whose base rate is thought to be 5% or lower among police officers (Boes, Chandler, & Timm, 1997). In Table 7.2a, 1,200 applicants are randomly assigned to cells based on this base rate; that is, 60 applicants are randomly predicted to be violators. Given the 5% base rate, only 3 (.25%) will be true positives or actual violators, 57 (4.75%) will be false positives and potentially screened out, while 57 (4.75%) actual violators will be screened in (false negatives). In addition, 1,083 (90.25%) true negatives will be predicted, making the overall accuracy of random selection 90.5% and the cost of selection using this random procedure instrument 4.75% of qualified applicants screened out (false positives).

A test or a model can claim to be very accurate in identifying true positives, but identification of true positives alone does not indicate that the test is more accurate than chance (or not screening) in terms of overall accuracy and cost. Table 7.2b represents the results of a hypothetical test (or rule) that claims to be 90% accurate in identifying violators correctly in terms of true positive. As such,

TABLE 7.1
Classifications of Predictions and Outcomes

	Predicted	Not Predicted
Observed	True positive	False negative
Not observed	False positive	True negative

Note: A predicted outcome (e.g., integrity violation) may be observed to be true (true positive) or false (false positive). Similarly, a prediction of no outcome (e.g., not a violator) may be observed as false (false negative) or true (true negative). In general, the efficiency of a prediction model is a function of the ratio of false positives to true positives as compared to the ratio of occurrence to nonoccurrence (Meehl & Rosen, 1955).

TABLE 7.2
1,200 Officers Integrity Violations (Base Rate = 5%)

(a) Randomly assign (base rate = 5%)

	Predicted integrity violators	Predicted nonviolators
Actual integrity violators	3 (true positives) or 0.25%	57 (false negatives) or 4.75%
Actual nonviolators	57 (false positives) or 4.75%	1083 (true negatives) or 90.25%
	60 (5%)	1140 (95%)

Chance assignment is 90.5% accurate (1086/1200).

(b) Test for predicting integrity violators (90% accurate for true positive) (base rate = 5%)

	Predicted integrity violators	Predicted nonviolators
Actual integrity violators	54 (true positives) or 4.5%	6 (false negatives) or 0.5%
Actual nonviolators	118 (false positives) or 10.4%	1022 (true negatives) or 85.1%
	172 (14.3%)	1028 (85.7%)

Test is 89.7% accurate (1076/1200).

Note: In this case, the test is slightly less accurate than chance, but has more than twice as many false positives. Even if the test identified all violators (true positives = 60, false negatives = 0), overall accuracy would be 90.2—still less than chance with twice as many excluded due to the false positive rate.

57 of the 60 violators (90%) are identified (true positives); however, this test/rule actually identifies a total of 172 applicants (14.3%) as violators, erroneously classifying 118 nonviolators (10.4%; false positives). The overall accuracy of this test is actually slightly *less* than chance (89.7%), and the *cost of selection* represented by this test is 10.4% (118/1,200) or more than *twice as high* as would be expected by chance (4.75%). Given this rate of false positives (and the low base rate), this would hold true even if the test were 100% accurate in identifying violators, that is, its cost of 10.4% would be twice as high, while its overall accuracy would improve only slightly to 90.2% and still be less than chance (90.5%). In short, given the low base rate of occurrence of integrity violators (5%), a test/rule must produce significantly less than 4.5% false positives to improve over chance.

Before using a test that claims to have high accuracy in identifying negative performers, psychologists and hiring authorities would be well advised to carefully review complete data in regard to both false positives and false negatives in the test's technical manual prior to building decision rules based on specific test scores. This is particularly salient given the current legal environment (EEOC, 1995) which stresses minimizing cost or false positives (screening out otherwise qualified applicants) since even if the test were perfect in identifying true positives, the hiring authority would also be responsible for minimizing the rate of false positives (cost).

When predicting events with higher baseline, tests and models can be considerably more accurate than chance. In this regard, Table 7.3 represents predictions of events with somewhat higher base rates—for example, incidents of on-the-job discipline to include relatively minor reprimands as well as serious incidents—known to be around 20% (Sarchione et al., 1998). Table 7.3a represents a *chance* assignment matrix of the same 1,200 officers whereby 240 (20%) are randomly predicted to experience some form of disciplinary action. Given a 20% base rate, 48 of the random assignments will be true positives and 192 (16%) will be false positives. Similarly, 192 disciplined officers (16%) will be randomly assigned as false negatives and the remaining 768 (64%) will be true negatives. The overall accuracy of this (random) classification procedure (68%) is significantly less, and the cost (16% false positive) significantly higher than what was observed in the earlier situation when the base rate was 5%. The difference in accuracy of random assignment is a function of the higher base rate and, consequently, the higher number of false positives.

Table 7.3b represents the classification results that would be obtained from the same test described earlier that claimed 90% accuracy in true positives when predicting a 20% baseline outcome. Now

TABLE 7.3
1,200 Officers Minor Discipline (Base Rate = 20%)

(a) Randomly assign (base rate = 20%)

	Predicted integrity violators	Predicted nonviolators
Actual integrity violators	48 (true positives) or 4%	192 (false negatives) or 16.0%
Actual nonviolators	192 (false positives) or 16.0%	768 (true negatives) or 64.0%
	240 (20%)	960 (80%)

Chance assignment is 68% accurate (816/1200).

(b) Test for predicting integrity violators (90% accurate for true positive) (base rate = 20%)

	Predicted integrity violators	Predicted nonviolators
Actual integrity violators	216 (true positives) or 18%	24 (false negatives) or 2%
Actual nonviolators	118 (false positives) or 9.8%	842 (true negatives) or 70.2%
	334 (27.8%)	866 (70.4%)

Test is 88.1% accurate (1058/1200).

Note: Due to the higher base rate, the test is now significantly better than chance in terms of both accuracy and false positives. A change in the base rate of occurrence of the dependent (outcome) variable from 5% (integrity violators) to 20% (minor discipline) has a substantial effect on the accuracy of a test that identifies 90% of true positives as well as on the cost of selection (false positives).

the test identifies 216 true positives (90% of 240) and the same 118 false positives as were identified in the earlier condition. In this case, the overall accuracy is 88.1%, which is substantially greater than the chance model, while the false positives (cost) represent only 9.8% or slightly more than half the rate expected by chance (16%). These data illustrate the importance of base rate when evaluating instruments as well as when selecting outcomes. In the case of low-base-rate outcomes such as discipline for integrity, violence, sexual misconduct, and so forth, the utility of attempting to screen applicants in order to predict these specific outcomes is questionable. However, accurate prediction of higher base rate occurrences—such as failing background investigation, failing to complete training, recycling in field training, and/or expanding the definition of discipline to include less serious infractions—is considerably more practical, particularly for use in pre-offer screening, given properly designed instruments, uncorrelated predictors, and models.

In addition to correlations between measures and base rates of occurrence, a third related issue affecting the validity of questionnaires, tests, and prediction models involves characteristics of the applicant pool when compared to the general population. Although the pool of individuals that apply to law enforcement agencies is in many ways similar to the general population, given the general requirements of the job, a certain degree of range restriction is to be expected within the sample due to educational requirements, credit, and criminal history requirements, illegal drug use, and so on. As noted by Ben-Porath (2009), range restriction may also effect test and questionnaire interpretation when using instruments that report scores in relative frequency terms, for example, some personal history questionnaires and some test instruments that calculate scaled scores from applicant norms without reference to general population norms.

Failure to take range restriction into account can cause misleading results, particularly in regard to disregarding or eliminating potentially useful predictors as well as to inflate the apparent validity of a particular test and/or overstate (or understate) the significance of a score that deviates from population norms. Similarly, correction for range restriction is particularly important when considering studies that use concurrent designs (study of applicants who were hired as opposed to all who applied). In this regard, there is likely to be significant differences in range between a group of applicants who have been hired after successfully completing a screening procedure that includes testing, background investigation, interviews, and so on, as well as the larger group of applicants who either failed to successfully complete or dropped out of the hiring process.

Given reliable quantitative measures, correcting for range restriction effects is a relatively straightforward statistical procedure that requires comparison of general population descriptive statistics for an instrument or measure to applicant pool statistics (Hunter & Schmidt, 1990). Range restriction within the law enforcement pre-employment assessment literature has been reported and corrected in the work of several researchers in this area (Cuttler & Muchinsky, 2006; Ones et al., 2004; Sarchione et al., 1998; Sellbom et al., 2007; Varela et al., 2004). However, when considering validation evidence and/or research conclusions regarding specific instruments, psychologists and other hiring authorities should carefully review the degree to which range restriction may have affected results.

SUMMARY AND CONCLUSIONS

Research supporting the practice of pre-employment psychological assessment of police officer candidates has its historical roots in clinical, I/O, and forensic psychology. The development of this area mirrors the field of assessment in general and is characterized by a convergence of these disciplines as well as the mediating effect of societal conditions and legal developments. In the past two decades, pre-employment assessment of law enforcement officers as an area of interest, inquiry, and professional practice has emerged from its historical roots to become a broadly regarded and relatively popular area of both practice and research. Proficiency in this area calls for a broad understanding of clinical, forensic, and I/O psychology principles. In addition, the work of Paul Meehl and others in regard to actuarial vs. clinical prediction is particularly relevant.

The fundamental distinction between actuarial and clinical prediction is not necessarily the data developed or the practice protocol (almost always test scores, life history data, and interview responses). Rather, the primary distinction is that the latter (clinical) involves intervention by professional judgment, while the former (actuarial) involves consistent application of rules in all cases. Actuarial prediction rules may be quantitatively sophisticated, they may be constructed as a set of expert rules derived from professional experience and review of the literature, or they may be a combination of the two. In any event, when using any reasonably developed model, a substantial body of research documents the superior accuracy of this (actuarial) approach over clinical prediction, particularly when base rates of occurrence for targeted outcomes exceed 20% as is the case with background/selection failure, training failure, and disciplinary action (Cuttler & Muchinsky, 2006).

Development of an actuarial model does not necessarily require amassing large amounts of data or incorporating sophisticated statistical techniques. Test instruments and personal history questionnaires designed to support actuarial assessment are widely available and simple models can be built by consistently applying expert rules to actuarially derived data. Practice protocols need not be changed—simply the process by which the data is aggregated. Practitioners need only develop rules, consistently apply them, conscientiously follow up with results, and modify the rules if indicated.

No predictor or prediction model is perfect: all are subject to error, and all are sensitive to and affected by error sources such as correlation between predictors, population range restriction, and base rate of occurrence. Certainly, there are some situations—for example, low-base-rate outcomes such as integrity violation, sexual misconduct, and so forth—in which neither actuarial nor clinical models are likely to predict at levels greater than chance. There are also rare situations such as Meehl's *broken leg* case (Meehl, 1954/1996), where additional information will trump actuarial models.* However, these situations are few and far between (Grove & Lloyd, 2004). All things

---

* Meehl (1954/1996) presented his classic *broken leg case* as an example of one of the few times clinical prediction would outperform an actuarial model. In this case, Professor A is known to have gone to the movies every Tuesday night for the past year. The actuarial model would therefore predict that Professor A would go to the movies next Tuesday. However, on Monday, Professor A has broken his leg and is forced to wear a cast that does not allow him to sit in a theater seat. The "clinician" observes this fact; the model cannot.

being equal, and in most settings associated with pre-employment assessment, research findings consistently report superiority of actuarial prediction over clinical judgment.

In the past two decades, legal regulations and professional guidelines have emerged that have clarified the need for scientifically prudent practice and supported use of new and more efficient assessment protocols (e.g., bifurcated assessment) and, as such, encouraged the emergence of a substantial body of scientific knowledge. Similarly, consensus has emerged in regard to the predictive validity of various psychological tests, and research has been performed documenting the relevance of various outcome criteria both in terms of performance-linked personality constructs and actual job outcome. There have also been several new instruments developed using other predictor domains (e.g., life history and merged processes) that have yielded evidence of convergent validity. All of these developments are consistent with the use of actuarial models. The distinctions between I/O and clinical practice and research have largely evaporated (we are all pretty much fishing in the middle of the lake these days), and the current economic situation within the public sector has created the need to perform these services in an efficient manner. Given the emergence of bifurcated assessment processes and the higher base rates associated with well-defined outcomes, as well as the existing body of knowledge regarding the superior accuracy of rule-based (actuarial) assessment, the state of the art at the present time begs the adoption of actuarial assessment principles into the practice of pre-employment assessment.

REFERENCES

Aamodt, M. G. (2004). *Research in law enforcement selection*. Boca Raton, FL: Brown Walker.

American Psychological Association. (1985). *Standards for educational and psychological testing*. Washington, DC: Author.

Americans With Disabilities Act, 42 U.S.C.A. § 12101 et seq. (1990).

Anastasi, A. (1988). *Psychological testing* (6th ed.). New York: Macmillan.

Azen, S. P. (1974). Predictors of resignation and performance of law enforcement officers. *American Journal of Community Psychology, 2*, 79–86.

Azen, S. P., Snibbe, H. M., & Montgomery, H. R. (1973). A longitudinal predictive study of success and performance of law enforcement officers. *Journal of Applied Psychology, 57*, 190–192.

Barrick, M. R., & Mount, M. D. (1991). The big five personality dimensions and job performance: A meta-analysis. *Personnel Psychology, 44*, 1–26.

Bartol, C. R. (1982). Psychological characteristics of small town police officers. *Journal of Police Science and Administration, 10*, 58–63.

Bartol, C. R. (1991). Predictive validation of the MMPI for small-town police officers who fail. *Professional Psychology: Research and Practice, 22*, 127–132.

Bartol, C. R. (1996). Police psychology: Then, now, and beyond. *Criminal Justice and Behavior, 23*, 70–89.

Ben-Porath, Y. S. (2007, October). *Use of the MMPI-2 Restructured Form in assessing law enforcement candidates*. Paper presented at the meeting of the Police Psychological Services Section of the International Association of Chiefs of Police, New Orleans, LA.

Ben-Porath, Y. S. (2009). *The MMPI-2 and the MMPI-2-RF*. Manuscript submitted for publication to Spilberg, S., California Peace Officer Standards and Training Commission, Sacramento, CA.

Ben-Porath, Y. S., & Tellegen, A. (2008). *The Minnesota Multiphasic Personality Inventory—2 restructured form: Manual for administration, scoring, and interpretation*. Minneapolis University of Minnesota Press.

Boes, J. O., Chandler, C. J., & Timm, H. W. (1997). *Police integrity: Use of personality measures to identify corruption-prone officers*. Monterey, CA: Defense Personnel Security Research and Education Center.

Bolte, M. E., & Smith, E. H. (2001). *Psychological screening standards: State-by-state survey*. Columbia: South Carolina Criminal Justice Academy, Law Enforcement Assessment and Psychological Services Unit.

Campbell, D. T., & Fiske, D. W. (1959). Convergent and discriminant validation by the multitrait-multimethod matrix. *Psychological Bulletin, 56*, 81–105.

Carpenter, B. N., & Raza, S. M. (1987). Personality characteristics of police applicants: Comparisons across subgroups and with other populations. *Journal of Police Science and Administration, 15*, 10–17.

Cattell, R. B. (1949). *16PF questionnaire*. Champaign, IL: Institute for Personality and Ability Testing.

Cattell, A. K., & Cattell, H. E. P. (1993). *Sixteen Personality Factor fifth edition questionnaire.* Champaign, IL: Institute for Personality and Ability Testing.

Cattell, R. B., Cattell, A. K., Cattell, H. E. P., Russell, M. T., & Bedwell, S. (2003). *The PsychEval personality questionnaire.* Champaign, IL: Institute for Personality and Ability Testing.

Chenoweth, J. H. (1961). Situational tests: A new attempt at assessing police candidates. *Journal of Criminal Law, Criminology, and Police Science, 52*, 232–238.

Cochrane, R. E., Tett, R. P., & Vandecreek, L. (2003). Psychological testing and the selection of police officers: A national survey. *Criminal Justice and Behavior, 30*, 511.

Cohen, B., & Chaiken, J. M. (1973). *Police background characteristics and performance.* Lexington, MA: Lexington Books.

Corey, D. M., Cuttler, M. J., & Moss, J. A. (2009, December). *Pre-application discussion with the ABPP Board of Trustees regarding a proposed Specialty Board in police and public safety psychology.* Presentation made to Board of Trustees American Board of Professional Psychology, Chapel Hill, NC.

Cureton, E. E., Cronbach, L. J., Meehl, P. E., Ebel, R. L., & Ward, A. (1996). Validity. In A. W. Ward, H. W. Stoker, & M. Murray-Ward (Eds), *Educational measurement: Origins, theories, and explications, Vol. 1: Basic concepts and theories* (pp. 125–243). Lanham, MD: University Press of America.

Cuttler, M. J. (2000). *Multi domain screening report.* Greensboro, NC: Law Enforcement Services.

Cuttler, M. J. (2007). *Minimizing response bias, enhancing veracity, and improving accuracy of predictions based on biodata* [White paper]. IPAT 2007 LESI 2001.

Cuttler, M., Cuttler, E., & Seddon T. (2008). *U.S. Patent No. 7,346,541. System, method and computer readable medium for acquiring and analyzing personal history information.* Washington, DC: U.S. Patent and Trademark Office.

Cuttler, M. J., & Muchinsky, P. M. (2006). Prediction of law enforcement training performance and dysfunctional job performance with general mental ability, personality and life history variables. *Criminal Justice and Behavior, 33*(1), 3–25.

Dawes, R. M. (2005). The ethical implications of Paul Meehl's work on comparing clinical versus actuarial prediction methods. *Journal of Clinical Psychology, 61*(10), 1245–1255.

Dawes, R. M., Faust, D., & Meehl, P. E. (1989). Clinical versus actuarial judgment. *Science, 243*, 1668–1674.

Dee-Burnett, R., Johns, E. F., & Krug, S. E. (1981). *Law enforcement assessment and development report (LEADR)–manual.* Chicago: IPAT.

Delprino, R. P., & Bahn, C. (1988). National survey of the extent and nature of psychological services in police departments. *Professional Psychology: Research and Practice, 19*, 421–425.

Drees, S. A., Ones, D. S., Cullen, M. J., Spilberg, S. W., & Viswesvaran, C. (2003, April 11). Personality assessment in police officer screening: Mandates and practices. In S.W. Spilberg & D. S. Ones (Chairs), *Personality and work behaviors of police officers.* Symposium conducted at the 18th annual meeting of the Society for Industrial and Organizational Psychology, Orlando, FL.

DuBois, P. H., & Watson, R. I. (1950). The selection of patrolmen. *Journal of Applied Psychology, 34*, 90–95.

Dunnette, M. D., & Motowidlo, S. J. (1976) *Police selection and career assessment.* Washington, DC: Law Enforcement Assistance Administration, U.S. Department of Justice, U.S. Government Printing Office.

Equal Employment Opportunity Commission, Uniform Employee Selection Guidelines; Questions and Answers; Section 16. http://www.uniformguidelines.com/uniformguidelines.html#129

Equal Employment Opportunity Commission, ADA Division, Office of Legal Counsel. (1995). *Enforcement guidance: Pre-employment disability-related inquiries and medical examinations under the Americans With Disabilities Act of 1990.* Washington, DC: Equal Employment Opportunity Commission.

Finn, S. E. (2009). Incorporating base rate information in daily clinical decision making. In J. N. Butcher (Ed.), *Oxford handbook of personality assessment* (pp. 140–149). New York: Oxford University Press.

Goldberg, L. R. (1991). Human mind versus regression equation: Five contrasts. In W. M. Grove & D. Cicchetti (Eds.), *Thinking clearly about psychology: Vol. 1. Matters of public interest* (pp. 173–184). Minneapolis: University of Minnesota Press.

Goldberg, L. R. (1993). The structure of phenotypic personality traits. *American Psychologist, 48*, 26–34.

Gordon, M. E., & Kleiman, L. S. (1976).The prediction of trainability using a work sample test and an aptitude test: A direct comparison. *Personnel Psychology, 29*, 243–253.

Gough, H. G. (1956). *California psychological inventory.* Palo Alto, CA: Consulting Psychologists Press.

Gough, H. G. (1987). *California Psychological Inventory administrator's guide.* Palo Alto, CA: Consulting Psychologists Press.

Grove, W. M. (2005). Clinical versus statistical prediction: The contribution of Paul E. Meehl. *Journal of Clinical Psychology, 61*(10), 1233–1243.

Grove, W. M., & Lloyd, M. (2006). Meehl's contribution to clinical versus statistical prediction. *Journal of Abnormal Psychology, 115*(2), 192–194.

Grove, W. M., & Meehl, P. E. (1996). Comparative efficiency of informal (subjective, impressionistic) and formal (mechanical algorithmic) prediction procedures: The clinical-statistical controversy. *Psychology, Public Policy, and Law, 2*(2), 293–323.

Grove, W. M., Zald, D. H., Lebow, B. S., Snitz, B. E., & Nelson, C. (2000). Clinical versus mechanical prediction: A meta-analysis. *Psychological Assessment, 12*, 19–30.

Hargrave, G. E., Hiatt, D., & Gaffney, T. W. (1986). A comparison of MMPI and CPI test profiles for traffic and deputy sheriffs. *Journal of Police Science and Administration, 14*, 250–258.

Harville, L. M. (1991). *An NCME instructional module on standard error of measurement; in ITEMS, Instructional Topics in Educational Measurement.* Madison, WI: National Council on Measurement in Education.

Hathaway, S. R., & McKinley, J. C. (1940). *The MMPI manual.* New York: Psychological Corporation.

Hiatt, D., & Hargrove, G. E. (1988). Predicting job performance problems with psychological screening. *Journal of Police Science and Administration, 16*, 122–125.

Hirsch, H. R., Northrup, L. C., & Schmidt, F. L. (1986). Validity generalization results for law enforcement occupations. *Personnel Psychology, 39*, 399–420.

Inwald, R. (1980, September). *Personality characteristics of law enforcement applicants and development of assessment instruments.* Paper presented at the meeting of the American Psychological Association, Montreal, Canada.

Inwald, R. (1982a, August). *Conducting testing programs within law enforcement agencies: ethical/legal issues.* Paper presented at the meeting of the American Psychological Association, Washington, DC.

Inwald, R. (1982b). *Inwald Personality Inventory (IPI) technical manual.* New York: Hilson Research, Inc. (Reprinted [2008], Chicago: IPAT, Inc., a subsidiary of OPP Ltd.)

Inwald, R. (1983, August). *Cross-validation of job performance prediction for law enforcement officers.* Paper presented at the meeting of the American Psychological Association, Anaheim, CA.

Inwald, R. (1984a, August). *Ethical guidelines for screening for high risk occupations.* Paper presented at the meeting of the American Psychological Association, Toronto, Canada.

Inwald, R. (1984b). Pre-employment psychological testing for law enforcement: ethical and procedural issues: what should administrators do? *Training Aids Digest, 9*(6), 1–7.

Inwald, R. (1984c). *Proposed guidelines for providers of pre-employment psychological testing services to law enforcement agencies, version III.* Manuscript submitted to APA Task Force of Division 18, Section of Police and Public Safety Psychology.

Inwald, R. (1985a). Professional opinions on a set of proposed guidelines for mental health practitioners conducting pre-employment psychological screening programs in law enforcement agencies. *Corrections Digest, 16*(7), 1–2.

Inwald, R. (1985b). Proposed guidelines for conducting pre-employment psychological screening programs. *Crime Control Digest, 19*(11), 1–6.

Inwald, R. (1985c, December). *Establishing standards for psychological screening.* Presentation at the FBI-sponsored World Conference on Police Psychology, Quantico, VA.

Inwald, R. (1986a). Why include individual interviews for all law enforcement candidates? *Criminal Justice Digest, 5*(3), 1–3.

Inwald, R. (1986b). The development of guidelines for psychological screening in law enforcement agencies. In J. T. Reese and J. M. Horn (Eds.), *Police psychology: Operational assistance* (pp. 233–240). Washington, DC: U.S. Department of Justice, FBI. (Reprinted in *Crime Control Digest, 20*(36), 6–9.)

Inwald, R. (1988). Five year follow-up study of departmental terminations as predicted by 16 pre-employment psychological indicators. *Journal of Applied Psychology, 73*(4), 703–710.

Inwald, R. (1995). *Hilson Safety/Security Risk Inventory (HSRI) technical manual.* New York: Hilson Research, Inc. (Reprinted [2008], Chicago: IPAT, Inc., a subsidiary of OPP Ltd.)

Inwald, R. (1998). *Hilson Job Analysis Questionnaire (HJAQ) technical manual.* New York: Hilson Research, Inc. (Reprinted [2008], Chicago: IPAT, Inc., a subsidiary of OPP Ltd.)

Inwald, R. (2008). The Inwald Personality Inventory (IPI) and Hilson Research inventories: Development and rationale. *Aggression and Violent Behavior, 13*(4), 298–327.

Inwald, R., & Brobst, K. E. (1988). *Hilson Personnel Profile/Success Quotient (HPP/SQ) technical manual.* New York: Hilson Research, Inc. (Reprinted [2008], Chicago: IPAT, Inc., a subsidiary of OPP Ltd.)

Inwald, R., & Gebbia, M. I. (1992). *Inwald Survey 5 (IS5) technical manual.* New York: Hilson Research, Inc. (Reprinted [2008], Chicago: IPAT, Inc., a subsidiary of OPP Ltd.)

Inwald, R., & Kaufman, J. C. (1989). *Hilson Career Satisfaction Index (HCSI) technical manual.* New York: Hilson Research, Inc. (Reprinted [2008], Chicago: IPAT, Inc., a subsidiary of OPP Ltd.)

Inwald, R., & Knatz, H. (1988, August). *Seven-year follow-up of officer terminations predicted by psychological testing.* Paper presented at the annual meeting of the American Psychological Association, Atlanta, GA.

Inwald, R., Resko, J. A., & Favuzza, V. (1994). *Inwald Survey 2 (IS2) & Inwald Survey 8 (IS8) technical manual.* New York: Hilson Research, Inc. (Reprinted [2008], Chicago: IPAT, Inc., a subsidiary of OPP Ltd.)

Inwald, R., Resko, J. A., & Favuzza, V. (1996). *Hilson Life Adjustment Profile (HLAP) technical manual.* New York: Hilson Research, Inc. (Reprinted [2008], Chicago: IPAT, Inc., a subsidiary of OPP Ltd.)

Inwald, R., & Sakales, S. (1982, August). *Predicting negative behaviors of officer recruits using the MMPI and IPI.* Paper presented at the meeting of the American Psychological Association, Washington, DC.

Inwald, R., Traynor, B., & Favuzza, V. A. (1998). *Hilson Management Survey (HMS) technical manual.* New York: Hilson Research, Inc. (Reprinted [2007], Chicago: IPAT, Inc., a subsidiary of OPP Ltd.)

Johnson, M., & Roberts, M. (2006, October). PsyQ report and test scoring system. JR&A Users Conference.

Kent, D. A., & Eisenberg, T. (1972). The selection and promotion of police officers. *The Police Chief, 39*(2), 20–29.

Landy, F. J. (1976). The validity of the interview in police officer selection. *Journal of Applied Psychology, 61,* 193–198.

Lefkowitz, J. (1977). Industrial-organizational psychology and the police. *American Psychologist, 32*(5), 346–364.

Levy, R. J. (1967). Predicting police failures. *Journal of Criminal Law, Criminology and Police Science, 58,* 265–275.

Levy, R. J. (1973). A method for the identification of the high risk police applicant. In J. R. Snibbe & R. M. Snibbe (Eds.), *The urban policeman in transition.* Springfield, IL: Charles C Thomas.

Matarazzo, J. D., Allen, B. V., Saslow, G., & Wiens, A. N. (1964). Characteristics of successful policeman and fireman applicants. *Journal of Applied Psychology, 48,* 123–133.

Meehl, P. E. (1996). *Clinical vs. statistical prediction.* Minneapolis: University of Minnesota Press. (Original work published 1954)

Meehl, P. E. (1959). Some ruminations on the validation of clinical procedures. *Canadian Journal of Psychology, 13,* 106–128.

Meehl, P. E. (1978). Theoretical risks and tabular asterisks: Sir Karl, Sir Ronald, and the slow progress of soft psychology. *Journal of Consulting and Clinical Psychology, 46,* 806–834.

Meehl, P. E. (1986). Causes and effects of my disturbing little book. *Journal of Personality Assessment, 50*(3), 370–375.

Meehl, P. E., & Rosen, A. (1955). Antecedent probability and the efficiency of psychometric signs, patterns, or cutting scores. *Psychological Bulletin, 52,* 194–216.

Monahan, J. (1981). *The Clinical Prediction of Violent Behavior.* Washington, DC: National Institute of Mental Health. (Reprinted as *Predicting violent behavior: An assessment of clinical techniques.* [1981]. Thousand Oaks, CA: Sage. Excerpts reprinted in L. J. Hertzberg, et al., Eds., [1990]. *Violent behavior* [pp. 125–150, 259–279]. Manhattan Beach, CA: PMA.)

Morey, L. C. (2007). *Personality Assessment Inventory professional manual* (2nd ed.). Lutz, FL: Psychological Assessment Resources.

Mumford, M. D., Costanza, D. P., Connelly, M. S., & Johnson, F. F. (1996). Item generation procedures and background data scales: Implications for construct and criterion-related validity. *Personnel Psychology, 49,* 361–398.

National Advisory Commission on Criminal Justice Standards and Goals. (1973). *Task force on police.* Washington, DC: U.S. Government Printing Office.

O'Brien, S. G. (1996). *The predictive validity of personality testing in police selection: A meta-analysis* (Unpublished master's thesis). University of Guelph, Guelph, Canada.

Oglesby, T. W. (1957). Use of emotional screening in the selection of police applicants. *Public Personnel Review, 18,* 228–231.

Ones, D. S., Viswesvaran, C., Cullen, M. J., Drees, S. A., & Langkamp, K. (2003, April). Personality and police officer behaviors: A comprehensive meta-analysis. In S. W. Spilberg & D. S. Ones (Chairs), *Personality work behaviors of police officers.* Symposium conducted at the 18th annual meeting of the Society for Industrial and Organizational Psychology, Orlando, FL.

Ones, D. S., Viswesvaran, C., & Dilchert, S. (2004, November). A *construct-based, comprehensive meta-analysis and implications for pre-offer screening and psychological evaluations.* Paper presented at the annual meeting of the International Association of Chiefs of Police (IACP), Los Angeles, CA.

Police Psychological Services Section of the International Association of Chiefs of Police. (1992, 1998, 2004, 2009). *Pre-employment psychological evaluation guidelines*. Retrieved from http://psych.iacp.org

Roberts, M., & Johnson, M. (2001). *CPI police and public safety selection report, technical manual*. Los Gatos, CA: Law Enforcement Psychological Services.

Roberts, M. D., Thompson, J. A., & Johnson, M. (2000). *PAI law enforcement, corrections, and public safety selection report manual*. Odessa, FL: Psychological Assessment Resources.

Saccuzzo, D. P., Higgins, G., & Lewandowski, D. (1974). Program for psychological assessment of law enforcement officers: Initial evaluation. *Psychological Reports, 35*, 651–654.

Sakales, S., & Inwald, R. (1982, August). *Prediction of police academy performance for transit police officer candidates: Role of two personality screening measures to identify on-the-job behavior problems of law enforcement officer recruits*. Paper presented at the meeting of the American Psychological Association, Washington, DC.

Sarchione, C. D., Cuttler, M. J., Muchinsky, P. M., & Nelson-Gray, R. O. (1998). Prediction of dysfunctional job behaviors among law enforcement officers. *Journal of Applied Psychology, 83*, 904–912.

Saxe, S. J., & Reiser, M. (1976). A comparison of three police applicant groups using the MMPI. *Journal of Police Science and Administration, 4*, 419–425.

Schmitt, N., Gooding, R. Z., Noe, R. A., & Kirsch, M. (1984). Metaanalyses of validity studies published between 1964 and 1982 and the investigation of study characteristics. *Personnel Psychology, 37*, 407–422.

Scogin, F., Schumacher, J., Howland, K., & McGee, J. (1989, August). *The predictive validity of psychological testing and peer evaluation in law enforcement settings*. Paper presented at the American Psychological Association Convention, New Orleans, LA.

Scrivner, E. M., & Kurke, M. I. (1995). Police psychology at the dawn of the 21st century. In M. I. Kurke & E. M. Scrivner (Eds.), *Police psychology into the 21st century*. Hillsdale, NJ: Lawrence Erlbaum.

Sellbom, M., Fischler, G. L., & Ben-Porath, Y. S. (2007). Identifying MMPI-2 predictors of police officer integrity and misconduct. *Criminal Justice and Behavior, 34*, 985–1004.

Shapiro, D. L. (1983). *Psychological evaluation and expert testimony*. New York: Van Nostrand Reinhold.

Shedler, J., & Westen, D. (2004). Refining personality disorder diagnosis: Integrating science and practice. *American Journal of Psychiatry, 161*, 1350–1365.

Shusman, E. J., Inwald, R. E., & Knatz, H. F. (1987). A cross-validation study of police recruit performance as predicted by the IPI and MMPI. *Journal of Police Science and Administration, 15*, 162–168.

Shusman, E. J., Inwald, R. E., & Landa, B. (1984). Correction officer job performance as predicted by the IPI and MMPI: A cross-validation study. *Criminal Justice and Behavior, 11*(3), 309–329.

Society for Industrial and Organizational Psychology. (2003). *Principles for validation and use of personnel selection procedures* (4th ed.). Washington, DC: American Psychological Association.

Smith, D. H., & Stotland, E. (1973). A new look at police officer selection. In J. R. Snibbe & H. M. Snibbe (Eds.), *The urban policeman in transition*. Springfield, IL: Charles C Thomas.

Spilberg, S. W. (2003, April). Development of psychological screening guidelines for police officers: Background and development of essential traits. In S. W. Spilberg & D. S. Ones (Chairs), *Personality work behaviors of police officers*. Symposium conducted at the 18th annual meeting of the Society for Industrial and Organizational Psychology, Orlando, FL.

Streiner, D. L. (2003). Diagnosing tests: Using and misusing diagnostic and screening tests. *Journal of Personality Assessment, 81*(3), 209–219.

Tenopyr, M. L. (1994). Big five, structural modeling, and item response theory. In G. S. Stokes, M. D. Mumford, & W. A. Owens (Eds.), *Biodata handbook: Theory, research, and use of biographical information in selection and performance prediction* (pp. 519–534). Palo Alto, CA: Consulting Psychologists Press.

Tett, R. P., Jackson, D. N., & Rothstein, M. (1991). Personality measures as predictors of job performance: A meta-analytic review. *Personnel Psychology, 44*, 703–740.

Tett, R. P., Jackson, D. N., Rothstein, M., & Reddon, J. R. (1994). Meta-analysis of personality job performance relations: A reply to Ones, Mount, Barrick, and Hunter (1994). *Personnel Psychology, 47*, 157–172.

U.S. Department of Justice. (n.d.) *Bureau of Justice statistics*. Retrieved November 20, 2009, from http://www.ojp.usdoj.gov/bjs/lawenf.htm

Varela, J. G., Boccaccini, M. T., Scogin, F., Stump, J., and Caputo, A. (2004). Personality testing in law enforcement employment settings: A meta-analytic review. *Criminal Justice and Behavior, 31*, 649.

Weiss, P. A., & Inwald, R. (2010). A brief history of personality assessment in police psychology. In P. A. Weiss (Ed.) *Personality assessment in police psychology: A 21st century perspective* (pp. 5–28). Springfield, IL: Charles C Thomas.

Westen, D. (2002). *Clinical diagnostic interview*. Unpublished manuscript, Emory University. Available from www.psychsystems.net/lab

Westen, D., & Rosenthal R. (2005). Improving construct validity: Cronbach, Meehl, and Neurath's ship. *Psychological Assessment, 17*(4), 409–412.

Westen, D., & Weinberger, J. (2004). When clinical description becomes statistical prediction. *American Psychologist, 59*(7), 595–613.

Westen, D., & Weinberger, J. (in press). In praise of clinical judgment: Meehl's forgotten legacy. *Journal of Clinical Psychology*.

Ziskin, J. (1981). *Coping with psychiatric and psychological testimony.* Los Angeles: Law and Psychology Press.

8 Appraising and Managing Police Officer Performance

Rick Jacobs

Christian Thoroughgood

Katina Sawyer

OVERVIEW OF PERFORMANCE APPRAISAL IN ORGANIZATIONS

In the classic book *Good to Great*, Jim Collins notes that successful organizations and teams have one critical thing in common: they get the right people on the bus (Collins, 2001). Truth be told, selecting and promoting the right people in organizations remain critical first steps in creating a highly effective and efficient workforce. In general this is true, but nowhere is it more the case than in a police department, especially when it comes to selection of new officers. Consider the fact that in almost every other type of organization, deficiencies in selection can at least be partially made up by successful introduction of supervisors and other leaders in various positions throughout the company. In police departments, it is rare—in fact, highly unlikely—that supervisors and leaders come from anywhere else except those who joined the force as new officers. The pool of applicants for promotions is almost exclusively made up of individuals who have come up through the ranks. Ineffective selection programs and the inevitable hiring mistakes that occur even with the best selection processes result in limitations in terms of candidates for promotions (these ideas are further developed in Chapter 11).

While getting the right people on the bus or, in the present case, into the patrol vehicle is vital to organizational success, it is equally important that organizations possess well-developed performance appraisal systems to (1) make informed administrative decisions regarding promotions, (2) help facilitate training, and (3) ensure we are doing all we can to motivate and improve the performance of those already on the force. Such systems are essential to providing developmental feedback to officers, helping organizations increase the readiness of officers for their current assignments as well as future positions, and understanding where the department's strengths and developmental opportunities exist. As such, it remains a priority of most departments to seek out and identify those systems that have the capacity to accurately measure officer performance and provide important performance based information. Needless to say, the ability to make important personnel decisions that benefit the department and its officers hinges on the quality of the performance evaluation system utilized. In many departments, the performance evaluation and management system is a major weakness and a missed opportunity when it comes to improving individual officer performance and the overall effectiveness of the agency.

In the following review, we address what role performance appraisal research plays in the evaluation of police officer performance specifically. In so doing, we first summarize key areas of research on performance appraisal in organizations, pointing out related theory, goals, and other traditional issues found in the research and practice literature. Next, we discuss those system elements that lead to effective performance appraisal and management programs, offer information on where programs can get off track, and document the evidence for performance improvement as a result of performance management. The process of system implementation is also discussed, including best practices for preparing officers for performance evaluations, steps that departments can take to create a positive environment for launching the process, proper training of supervisors who will be the evaluators of performance, departmental requirements for monitoring and evaluating the rating process, and ideas on utilizing performance data effectively.

The chapter also addresses issues related to feedback to officers, including who should deliver feedback, what feedback should be given, and how often feedback should be conveyed. We also highlight the critical role of trust in the feedback process and the creation of a climate conducive to feedback. Finally, we conclude the chapter by discussing the future of performance appraisal and management, including the role of online appraisals, performance improvement initiatives, and self-evaluation.

THEORY, GOALS, AND TRADITIONAL ISSUES

DEFINING PERFORMANCE

Industrial-organizational psychologists have long since debated the definition of job performance. Austin and Villanova (1992) famously referred to this issue as the "criterion-problem," suggesting that traditional measures of job performance fail to conceptualize and measure performance constructs that are multidimensional in nature. Specifically, such measures often suffer from criterion deficiency and contamination. While the former refers to aspects of the performance domain not measured by the appraisal instrument (leaving out of the evaluation critical performance factors), the latter refers to specific measurement error created by including in the assessment performance either measures that are not part of the job requirements or things out of the control of the officer being evaluated (i.e., unrelated elements unintentionally measured as a part of the performance domain). Examples of criterion contamination include inherent rater biases (e.g., halo, leniency, and so forth, which are tied to the assessor—not the assessee), external factors outside the ratee's control (resource deficiencies such as poor or no training programs, understaffing, and/or inadequate equipment), and/or behaviors not identified through job analysis but that nonetheless influence ratings (e.g., specific indicators of personality that have no obvious link to required job behaviors). As such, work psychologists have underscored the importance of conducting a thorough job analysis to fully define the performance domain, develop a holistic understanding of key job-related behaviors, and thereby develop a valid appraisal system (Viswesvaran & Ones, 2000).

Before conducting a job analysis, however, it is important to have a general understanding of what performance entails. Campbell (1999) defined performance as "behavior or action that is relevant for the organization's goals and that can be scaled (measured) in terms of the level of proficiency (or contribution to goals) that is represented by a particular action or set of actions" (pp. 402–403). Furthermore, Motowidlo (2003) defined performance as "the total expected value to the organization of the discrete behavioral episodes that an individual carries out over a standard period of time" (p. 51). In short, performance is what employers pay employees to do (Campbell, 1999) and, in the context of police performance, it is not only what the department expects from the officer but also what the public demands—and it represents those behaviors associated with preserving life and property.

Additionally, scholars have distinguished between task and contextual performance (Arvey & Murphy, 1998). Borman and Motowidlo (1993) suggested that task performance revolves primarily around the organization's "technical core," where raw materials are processed and transformed into their final products. As such, they defined task performance as "the proficiency with which job incumbents perform activities that are formally recognized as part of their jobs, activities that contribute to the organization's technical core either directly by implementing a part of its technological process, or indirectly by providing it with needed materials or services" (p. 73). Contextual performance, on the other hand, does not support the technical core itself as much as it supports the "organizational, social, and psychological environment in which the technical core must function" (Borman & Motowidlo, 1993, p. 73).

For example, while task performance for police officers might include monthly documentation of traffic stops, creating accurate reports, and listening carefully to citizens while they describe events, contextual performance might include behaviors related to boosting squad morale or being available for additional assignments. In fact, Motowidlo and Van Scotter (1994) found that both factors contribute independently to overall performance ratings, with personality variables predicting contextual performance more than task performance. Thus, it appears that raters take into account both task and contextual elements when evaluating subordinates. This suggests cognitive ability tends to predict task performance, while personality may better predict contextual performance (Arvey & Murphy, 1998). As such, it is possible that different predictors may be required depending on the performance domain in question.

Previous Research

Much of the research on performance appraisal prior to 1980 was dominated by measurement issues and the search for a perfect rating format. Such research focused on comparing various rating formats, including graphic ratings scales, behaviorally anchored ratings scales, traditional Likert scales, behavioral checklists, and other formats (Arvey & Murphy, 1998; Jacobs, Kafry, & Zedeck, 1980; Landy & Farr, 1980). However, after 30 years of research on the topic, Landy and Farr (1980) called a moratorium on research related to rating formats, concluding that although raters may have a preference for one format over another, differences in ratings due to format are minimal and overall inconsequential when it comes to the overall performance information provided to the individual and the organization. They did, however, note that behavioral anchors are superior to simple numerical scales or those that rely on common adjectives and that anchoring should be based on methods grounded in firm psychometric theory. In fact, right now any organization—police or other—can find a variety of tools for measuring performance and be ready to launch a program without the burden of creating a site-specific rating form. With respect to police officer performance, the reader of this chapter can contact the senior author and receive a set of scales to be used for officers, supervisors, or command personnel. Suffice it to say, the scales themselves are critical for a successful system, but are available from many sources.

Moving beyond issues related to the rating format, Landy and Farr (1980) urged researchers to consider the role of rater cognition in the performance appraisal process, which subsequently led to a flurry of research on the topic during the 1980s. During this time, increased attention was paid toward understanding *how* raters reach their judgments of employee performance. Such research targeted various cognitive processes of raters including observation and information acquisition, encoding and categorization, storage, retrieval, integration, and evaluation (DeNisi, Cafferty, & Meglino, 1984; DeNisi & Williams, 1988; Murphy & Cleveland, 1995). Moreover, one of several themes to emerge from this body of research was the effects of raters' implicit theories on ratings, including the tendency for raters to commit various rating errors including halo, leniency, and systematic distortion based on assumed rather than actual ratee behavior (Ostroff & Ilgen, 1992). Among other important findings, it was suggested that characteristics of the rater and ratee (e.g., sex, race, age, tenure, cognitive complexity, leadership style, rater–ratee relationship, and so on) activate inherent rater biases, leading to distorted ratings (Landy & Farr, 1980). Other findings emphasized that raters tend to utilize more global judgments of employees when they are aware of their need to provide a rating, but must reprocess information from an appraisal perspective (thereby potentially introducing bias) when they are not aware of their need to ultimately provide a rating (Hastie & Park, 1986).

Despite such findings, much of the research on rater cognition has not been tested in the field, with the overwhelming majority of studies being experimental in nature and lacking all of the real-world cues that are part of performance assessment in ongoing organizations. In one of the few field studies to date conducted in the field and designed to evaluate processing issues, DeNisi and Peters (1996) found structured diary keeping (a method that allows appraisers to more effectively document employee performance information over time and makes such information more easily accessible to raters) lowered rating elevation (i.e., improved accuracy) and increased raters' ability to discriminate between and within persons. This finding suggested that structure in the rating process is important for accurate recall of performance information. Unfortunately, the cognitive approach to performance appraisal failed to have lasting effects on informing practice. In fact, such research served to create a major schism between researchers and practitioners during the 1980s. While the cognitive revolution certainly struck a chord in researchers interested in unlocking the mysteries of rater's thought processes when making performance ratings, those in the field were left wondering how such research informed the practice of performance appraisal in organizations.

As a result of this division, the 1990s brought with it an emphasis on performance appraisal as embedded within the larger social-organizational context (Bretz, Milkovich, & Read, 1992; Ilgen, Barnes-Farrell, & McKellin, 1993). Specifically, Ilgen and colleagues (1993) suggested the appraisal process as entrenched within a rating environment or *social milieu* that raters and ratees occupy during the process. However, it was Murphy and Cleveland (1991, 1995) who brought considerations of the social-organizational context to the forefront of the performance appraisal discussion. In their seminal work, they argued for a social-psychological approach to performance appraisal, emphasizing a variety of contextual influences on performance ratings. Specifically, they suggested that ratings are a function of several different categories of environmental factors, including distal variables (e.g., organizational climate, culture, economic conditions, and so forth), process proximal variables (rater accountability, feedback environment, and so on), structural proximal variables (appraisal goals and purpose, appraisal training, and so on), and rater and ratee behavior (e.g., rater–ratee attitudinal reactions, cognitive reactions, perceptions of justice, and so forth). As such, while cognitive research during the 1980s served to shed light on the limits of raters to make accurate ratings, the social-organizational approach expanded our view of the appraisal process by incorporating issues of rating context into the discussion.

A brief review of the social-organizational literature suggests that while little systematic research has investigated the role of distal variables, a good deal of work has been done on the influence of proximal (both process and structural) variables (Levy & Williams, 2004). Levy and Williams (2004) refer to process proximal variables as those factors that have a "direct impact on how the appraisal process is conducted" (p. 885). With regard to raters, research demonstrates that rater–ratee similarity is related to performance ratings and specifically that positive affective regard for subordinates is related to higher ratings, a lower penchant to punish, more favorable leader-subordinate relationships, stronger halo effects, and decreased rating accuracy (Lefkowitz, 2000). Other research suggests that certain individual differences, and in particular high rater agreeableness and low conscientiousness, are associated with higher performance ratings (Bernardin, Cooke, & Villanova, 2000). Further, evidence suggests that attributions about ratee behavior (e.g., whether due to ability or effort) may influence raters' reactions and ratings (Johnson, Erez, Kiker, & Motowidlo, 2002), and the extent to which raters are held accountable for the ratings they provide have the potential to distort ratings—with more accountability leading to inflated ratings (Klimoski & Inks, 1990).

On the ratee side, research has tended to focus on motivation and reactions to appraisal processes (Levy & Williams, 2004). In terms of motivation, while little support has been found for the effectiveness of merit pay systems (e.g., Pay for Performance, Performance Pay, etc.) (Campbell, Campbell, & Chia, 1998; Goss, 2001), it appears that participation in the appraisal process is critical to motivating employees, who must perceive the appraisal system as fair and ethical (Pettijohn, Pettijohn, & d'Amico, 2001; Roberts, 2003; Roberts & Reed, 1996; Shah & Murphy, 1995). With regard to ratee reactions, research has tended to focus on system and session satisfaction; perceived utility and accuracy; procedural, distributive, and interactional justice; feedback and acceptability; and due process (Erdogan, Kraimer, & Liden, 2001; Folger, Konovsky, & Cropanzano, 1992; Levy & Williams, 2004; Taylor, Masterson, Renard, & Tracy,

1998). One important piece of work by Folger and colleagues (1992), in particular, suggests that perceptions of fairness are achieved when adequate notice, fair hearing, and judgment based on evidence are present in the appraisal system. In general, it appears that fair appraisal systems lead to a wide array of positive rater and ratee outcomes, including less emotional exhaustion, increased ratee acceptance of feedback, more positive reactions to one's supervisor and the organization, and more satisfaction with the appraisal system and the job by the rater and ratee (Brown & Benson, 2003; Flint, 1999; Leung, Su, & Morris, 2001; Levy & Williams, 1998; Taylor et al., 1998). Moreover, ratee reactions seem strongly tied to the opportunity to participate in the appraisal process and the amount of information provided about the process (Cawley, Keeping, & Levy, 1998; Levy & Williams, 1998; Williams & Levy, 2000).

Research on ratee reactions to various appraisal structures and formats also suggests that ratees (and raters) react most favorably to behavior observation scales (BOS) in comparison to other scales—although these differences are sometimes quite small (Tziner & Kopelman, 2002; Tziner, Kopelman, & Joanis, 1997). Further, DeNisi and Peters (1996) suggest that raters react more positively to appraisal systems that employ performance diaries despite such techniques requiring more work. These positive reactions stem from the ability to better recall performance information and thus better differentiate between ratees.

Other research suggests that aspects of the leader-member relationship may impact ratee evaluations. In particular, ratee trust, and specifically trust in one's supervisor, seem particularly important in predicting both incumbents' and supervisors' acceptance of their appraisal and satisfaction with the appraisal system (Hedge & Teachout, 2000; Mani, 2002). Moreover, subordinates who are a part of a leader's *in* group may be allocated higher performance ratings than those designated in the leader's *out* group (Duarte, Goodson, & Klich, 1993; Kacmar, Witt, Zivnuska, & Gully, 2003).

Further, research suggests that group and organizational dynamics may also impact performance ratings. Empirical evidence supports the effects of impression management on the appraisal process. For example, Gendersen and Tinsley (1996) found that assertive impression management techniques (e.g., ingratiation and self-promotion) led to higher performance ratings than defensive techniques (e.g., excuse making and justifications). Additionally, several authors have suggested the importance of a feedback culture (London, 2003; London & Smither, 2002) in which managers and employees feel comfortable both giving and receiving feedback. Feedback culture has been found to be related to satisfaction with feedback, motivation to use feedback, and feedback seeking (Norris-Watts & Levy, 2004; Steelman, Levy, & Snell, 2004).

While process proximal variables directly impact both rater and ratee behavior during the appraisal process, structural proximal variables refer to system elements that comprise the organization or design of the performance management process such as the types and number of performance dimensions, the frequency of appraisals, and the purpose of the appraisal (Levy & Williams, 2004). For example, preliminary evidence on multisource feedback systems suggests that rater and ratee acceptance of such feedback and other positive reactions depend on the organizational culture, credibility of raters, high rates of participation, anonymity of ratings, knowledge of and experience with the multi source system, social support, and individual self-efficacy (Maurer, Mitchell, & Barbeite, 2002; Waldman & Bowen, 1998; Williams & Lueke, 1999). Moreover, inconclusive evidence remains as to whether such systems lead to performance improvements (Kluger & DeNisi, 1996; Seifert, Yuki, & McDonald, 2003).

Additionally, many researchers continue to investigate how ratings are influenced by the purpose of the appraisal. Consistent with Taylor and Wherry's (1951) original hypotheses, Jawahar and Williams (1997), in their review of 22 studies on the effects of rating purpose, found that ratings that were made for administrative purposes were more lenient than those made for research or developmental purposes. Finally, a considerable amount of work has addressed the role of rater training in the appraisal process (Bernardin & Buckely, 1981; Pulakos, 1984). Woehr and Huffcutt (1994) conducted a meta-analysis, which provided support for frame-of-reference (FOR) training (a method that seeks to standardize raters' perceptions of performance by facilitating agreement on what specific behaviors define the spectrum of performance), and subsequent research has corroborated the efficacy of this form of training (Sulsky & Day, 1992; Sulsky & Keown, 1998; Sulsky, Skarlicki, & Keown, 2002).

No doubt the performance appraisal literature has come a long way in the past 60 years. What began with research primarily dedicated to measurement issues and the search for the perfect rating format was accompanied by two subsequent shifts in the research literature, the cognitive approach of the 1980s and the social-organizational perspective of the 1990s. Moreover, this rich research history has provided us with a strong empirical framework for designing performance appraisal systems today. Given this historical backdrop, in the next section, we discuss specifically those system elements that lead to effective programs, where programs can get off track, and evidence for performance improvement as a result of such systems.

IMPLEMENTING PERFORMANCE APPRAISAL PROGRAMS

SETTING THE STAGE

As discussed in the previous section, defining which competencies are required to effectively perform as a police officer is the first step in providing a framework for a useful performance appraisal system. However, once these competencies are in place, the question remains of how to best create a system which accurately measures these competencies. A variety of aspects can be considered when implementing a performance appraisal system. From training the raters to using the resulting data to make administrative decisions, many pieces of the performance appraisal puzzle must be in place to ensure success.

Although often overlooked, some of the most important parts of the performance appraisal process take place even before the system is put in motion. Before beginning to use any performance appraisal system, departments need to be sure that officers are aware of the competencies evaluated, how they are linked to the job, and why they are important. As referenced previously, this method of performance appraisal implementation is called *due process* (Folger et al., 1992). Due process refers to a lifecycle approach to performance appraisal—one in which officers are informed from the start which competencies are important in defining job performance and which behaviors are viewed as effective and which are seen as ineffective. As such, officers are provided with a clear understanding of how performance ratings will be derived (Folger et al., 1992). Ensuring that officers are *on board* with the way in which performance is defined, as well as the key features of the system, will result in an environment of trust surrounding appraisal, as opposed to suspicion (Farr & Jacobs, 2006). One common finding from both research and practice is that employees do not like being evaluated. Thus, creating clear guidelines for performance from the start allows organizations to avoid the potential for surprise during the evaluation process and enhances the overall perceptions of system fairness. Latham, Almost, Mann, and Moore (2005) also note that performance appraisal should be based on a sound job analysis, along with a behaviorally based criterion to ensure that employees are evaluated on the core tenets of the job in an objective and fair manner. Rosen, Levy, and Hall (2006) reiterate this point by demonstrating that employees who perceive political motives underlying the performance appraisal process were likely to have lower job satisfaction and affective commitment, which were both found to be negatively related to job performance. Therefore, ensuring that the performance appraisal process is perceived as valid and worthwhile by employees is important for maintaining a productive and satisfied workforce. Table 8.1 reflects a list of areas of responsibility for police officers and the basics on which a system can be built for evaluating the performance of police officers. As can be seen, the areas of performance are specific and clearly a part of a police officers' job. The performance evaluation process is further enhanced by specific performance assessment scales for each of the areas. Table 8.2 is a similar list, but in this case represents a police supervisor/ sergeant. Again, these types of definitions can be used to define scales for rating performance. Scales based on this type of approach are available by contacting the senior author of this chapter.

TABLE 8.1
List of Performance Evaluation Dimensions for Police Officer Assessment

A. **Patrol Preparation and Relief:** Activities performed at the beginning and end of a shift during shift changes. This includes safeguarding and accounting for all agency property and equipment.

B. **Patrol/Guard Duties and Responsibilities:** Activities involving observing assigned area to detect unusual activities or violations of the law and preserving the safety of individuals and security of property in assigned area.

C. **Vehicle Enforcement and Control:** Activities involving the safe and legal operation of vehicles. This includes enforcing laws, handling accidents, assisting accident victims, and eliminating public safety hazards.

D. **Responding to Crimes and/or Disturbances:** Activities performed while responding to all types of offenses, including crimes in progress, civil matters and domestic disputes, property crimes, serious crimes, and so on. This includes the initial investigation of crimes and/or disturbances.

E. **Apprehension and Control of Suspects, Prisoners/Inmates:** Activities involving pursuit, isolation, containment, apprehension, and control of suspects or prisoners/inmates. This also includes activities performed in the process of searching to locate suspects, prisoners/inmates, or missing persons.

F. **Search:** Activities involving searches of suspects, prisoners/inmates, or crime scene/facility to locate physical evidence or contraband.

G. **Arrest and Detention:** Activities involving arrest processing procedures, transporting, detention, and lodging of prisoners/inmates or juveniles.

H. **Evidence/Property:** Activities involving the safeguarding, storing, and accounting for evidence and nonagency property.

I. **Emergency Situations:** Activities involving responding to emergency situations (e.g., natural disasters, riots, hostage situations, fires, escapes, floods/high water, and so forth), maintaining order, and notifying appropriate agencies to secure assistance.

J. **Care of Victim, Prison/Inmate Welfare:** Activities involving attending to medical and emotional needs of victims, agency personnel, other citizens, or prisoners/inmates.

K. **Inmate Supervision:** Activities involving supervising or controlling inmates during daily activities to maintain safety and security of inmates and staff. This includes communicating with inmates, overseeing the visitation of inmates, and maintaining a clean and safe environment during work, meals, showers, and so on.

L. **Notifications/Communications/Administration:** Activities involving distribution of information regarding incidents and conditions. This also includes communications with superiors, other personnel, and individuals from other agencies to coordinate activities.

M. **Reports, Forms, and Memo Books:** Activities involving the preparation of written forms, reports, photo/video records, or memo books. Forms and reports may be of a variety of types such as captioned (fill-in-the-blank), written narrative, or a combination of these types.

N. **Court Activities:** Activities involving providing assistance with court procedures including appearing in court and presenting testimony.

O. **Public Interaction:** Activities involving interactions with members of the public. This includes answering questions about community conditions and problems.

P. **Agency Policies, Procedures, Rules, and Laws:** Activities involving keeping current with agency policies and rules, and city, state, and federal laws that govern the activities of officers and applying/enforcing them correctly.

Q. **Professional Development:** Activities performed to improve one's skills or to improve the agency. This includes participating in specific training or education and participating in professional organizations or conferences.

In addition to presenting employees with clear and relevant criteria, it should also be noted that it is possible for employees to voice their opinion if a part of the system appears unfair or unclear. The ability to participate in the appraisal process by respectfully questioning the system is also a part of due process (Folger et al., 1992). In line with this idea, Cawley and colleagues (1998) empirically demonstrated the effects of employee participation in the appraisal process. The authors found that employees had more favorable reactions to a performance appraisal system in which they could voice their opinion about the accuracy of their performance ratings and the system in general, regardless of whether or not their feedback would have an impact on organizational practice in the future. Thus, it is clear that employees are more comfortable with appraisal when they feel they have the opportunity to provide input about the system.

TABLE 8.2
Performance Evaluation Dimensions for Police Sergeant

I. Supervision of Field/Case Work

A. Incident Supervision: This duty involves assuming responsibility for incidents or special operations to ensure the efficient and safe handling of the incident/operation and the preservation of life and property.

B. Case Management: This duty involves assuming responsibility for investigations coming under the sergeant's supervision to ensure the productive and appropriate handling of all investigative matters and to preserve the integrity of these investigations.

II. Personnel Management

C. Personnel Assignment and Coordination: This duty involves assigning or allocating personnel so as to ensure sufficient personnel resources are available to handle the workload. This area also involves planning and preparing for special circumstances such as sporting events and emergencies.

D. Personnel Evaluation: This duty involves observing subordinate performance to identify strengths and areas of needed improvement. It also includes conducting formal performance evaluation sessions and informal counseling sessions with subordinates to recognize performance strengths and discuss and resolve performance problems.

E. Policy Implementation and Performance: This duty involves interpreting, enforcing, and explaining the rules and regulations that govern the activities of department personnel.

F. Training: This duty involves ensuring that personnel are properly trained to carry out their assigned duties. This includes planning, developing, conducting, monitoring, and evaluating formal and informal training programs. The training context can be the academy or the field. The trainees may be department personnel at any level, personnel from other agencies, or civilians.

III. Administrative Activities

G. Record and Report Management: This duty involves reviewing, preparing, and/or maintaining logs, records, forms, memos, reports, and other field and administrative documents and correspondence used in the course of performing the job. This includes reviewing documents prepared by subordinate or other personnel for completeness and accuracy, reviewing and authorizing personnel requests, and integrating information from multiple sources into summary documents.

H. Internal/External Communication and Coordination: This duty involves communicating or coordinating activities with department personnel and individuals from other agencies to accomplish work objectives and discuss issues of mutual concern.

I. General Administration: This duty involves participating in the development, implementation, and evaluation of division/department programs, policies, procedures, and objectives.

IV. Hands-On Field/Case Work

J. Traffic Observation, Enforcement, and Control: This duty involves all activities conducted to ensure the safe and legal operation of vehicles on the road. This includes performing or supervising others in performing tasks such as assisting motorists, enforcing traffic laws, handling accidents, assisting accident victims, and identifying and eliminating public safety hazards.

K. Responding to Crimes and Disturbances: This duty involves the activities performed while responding to all types of offenses including crimes in progress, civil matters and domestic disputes, property crimes, serious crimes, and so on.

L. Investigation: This duty involves all activities performed as part of internal or criminal investigations. This includes performing or supervising others in performing tasks such as obtaining and analyzing information, collecting physical evidence, and participating in the judicial/administrative process.

M. Arrest-Related Activities: This duty involves activities performed for the purpose of apprehending, restraining, arresting, transporting, and detaining suspects to be taken into custody according to the law and department guidelines. It also includes activities performed or supervised in the process of searching vehicles, persons, and/or premises for weapons, fruits of a crime, or contraband in order to effect arrest, protect self and the public, and/or obtain evidence.

TABLE 8.2 (CONTINUED)
Performance Evaluation Dimensions for Police Sergeant

V. Public and Community Relations

N. Public and Community Relations: This duty involves activities that have an impact on the department's image in the community by virtue of the subordinate's interactions with individual members of the public, community organizations, and the media.

VI. Professional Development

O. Professional Development: This duty involves participating in activities to keep apprised of job-related developments in laws, technology, policies, and procedures as well as to enhance job-related knowledge, skills, and abilities. This can include reading internal memos and bulletins; reading external publications; participating in training or certification drills and classes; and/or attending outside conferences, seminars, and courses.

Kozlowski, Chao, and Morrison (1998) recommend that, in addition to clear and relevant criteria, appraisals should be frequent and appropriate. Therefore, it may be useful to determine up front how often appraisals will take place and to consider how these appraisals align with organizational activities and strategy. Providing employees with a clear idea of what the performance criteria are, why they are important to the job, how often they will be assessed, and how assessment aligns with organizational strategy will all help to set the stage for a smooth and effective performance appraisal process.

TRAINING RATERS

Once the performance appraisal system has been rolled out, it is important to identify those individuals who will be responsible for providing ratings and to properly train them to use the system successfully. As discussed previously, raters without proper training may fall prey to a variety of rating biases such as halo (employees are either all good or all bad) or leniency (every employee is great) (Ostroff & Ilgen, 1992). Further, raters may pursue personal goals when providing ratings for their officers (e.g., providing low ratings to an exemplary officer as a motivator for even better performance or providing high ratings to a poor performing officer to get them out of a particular unit and under someone else's command) (Murphy & Cleveland, 1995). Further, Wong and Kwong (2007) tested these assumptions empirically, demonstrating that in a sample of students, those who were given the goals of promoting harmony and fairness in their ratings tended to provide less discriminating ratings between candidates and higher ratings for candidates in general. This provides support for the notion that when raters have a goal in mind, they can paint a picture of performance in alignment with that goal but not necessarily consistent with what they observe.

In the end, a system is only as good as the people who use it. Thus, it is completely possible for an organization to have a fantastic performance appraisal system in place and still achieve mediocre or even disastrous results. As such, it is helpful to view the performance appraisal system as a vehicle: all of the parts may be in place but, without a properly trained driver and periodic servicing, the car does not function properly and is at risk for a crash. However, providing rater training is clearly a key component of a successful performance appraisal process.

One type of rater training has been touted as particularly effective in driving an accurate performance system: Frame of Reference (FOR) training (Schleicher, Day, Mayes, & Riggio, 2002; Woehr, 1994). FOR training consists of a variety of components (as outlined in Schleicher et al., 2002), which all help to make certain that raters will be able to accurately assess officer behavior. The first step in FOR training is to communicate the important dimensions of the job as well as the behaviors that comprise effective performance for each role. This is clearly important because raters need to be aware of what performance means, as well as what it looks like when an officer is performing well. What is important to note here is that many systems carry with them an implicit assumption when rater training is minimal or nonexistent (as is often the case) that since a supervisor/sergeant was once a police officer, he or she knows about performance and can appropriately observe and rate the performance of others. Everything we have discussed up to this point shows that, in many cases, this assumption is simply not true. Performance appraisal training helps create a unified definition of performance across raters so that officers will receive similar ratings regardless of their rater. The second step of FOR training is to allow raters to discuss which behaviors are indicative of each level of performance. For example, while it may be useful to know that police officers should call for help when arriving to the scene of an armed robbery, it is also useful to know that high-performing officers call for help on the way to the scene, while mid range performers would call within 10 seconds of arrival, and low performers would call within 30 seconds of arrival or whenever they find it convenient. This implies that raters should be aware of not only what good performance entails but also what this means when determining whether the behavior of an employee is high, medium, or low for a particular competency. Finally, raters should be able to provide practice evaluations and discuss these evaluations with one another in order to calibrate ratings. This final step gives raters the opportunity to practice assessing behavior and then to compare ratings with other raters in order to provide a consistent and clear basis for which raters should be formulating performance ratings. After completing all of the steps of FOR training, raters should be ready to use the system properly, resulting in ratings as precise and consistent as possible. One important point to take away from this is that training raters can only help. Raters who can effectively evaluate officers will gain additional insights from the training and will find the information reinforcing, while those officers not quite as accomplished as performance evaluators will learn important skills and gain confidence in their ability to do things properly.

The effects of FOR training have been empirically demonstrated as well. Woehr and Huffcutt (1994) found an effect size of .83 on rating accuracy for FOR training when compared to either a control group or a no training group. Day and Sulsky (1995) also demonstrated that FOR training had a significant main effect on performance rating accuracy. Further, Schleicher and associates (2002) empirically demonstrated that FOR training improved the reliability, accuracy, and discriminant validity of ratings in an assessment center. In addition, FOR training significantly improved the criterion-related validity of the assessment center for predicting supervisors' ratings of job performance (Schleicher et al., 2002). Thus, FOR training is an extremely valuable tool for increasing the validity and predictive capabilities of performance ratings. This type of training should, therefore, be considered best practice in preparing raters for providing performance ratings for employees. Systems that fail to provide rater training will be far less effective.

Monitoring the Rating Process

After raters are trained, they are ready to begin conducting appraisals and the department must be prepared to effectively store, evaluate, and provide feedback on the rating process. As one can see, the performance management process does not begin and end with the rating of officer performance; it is far more involved. Performance appraisal systems must be monitored throughout the lifecycle to ensure they are used properly. Not only must raters be retrained as time passes, but also the system must be evaluated to arrive at correct conclusions about what is needed for the system to function efficiently. In other words, no performance appraisal and management process is perfect from the beginning, and systematic evaluation and updating are critical to meet the needs of the department.

For example, even if raters are trained, they might find it difficult to keep track of performance appraisal information over time, particularly if they supervise many employees. Thus, it may be necessary to implement a structured way for raters to keep track of performance information. Structured diary keeping may provide a way for raters to continue making the best use of a performance system by offering a coherent framework within which to organize employee performance data. It has been demonstrated that those who used structured diaries (diaries that keep track of how the employee is performing on a day-to-day basis and are kept for future reference) had more positive reactions to the appraisal system, recalled performance information more effectively, and produced less biased and more discriminating ratings—both between and within employees; DeNisi et al., 1989; DeNisi & Peters, 1996. This may also help to alleviate issues that arise when raters make judgments based on recent performance, discounting prior performance. For example, Reb and Cropanzano (2007) demonstrated in a lab study that raters gave higher ratings to those with increasing performance than those who had consistent or decreasing performance, regardless of whether or not the ending point was the same. The same was true for decreasing performance, which resulted in lower ratings than consistently poor performance. In this case, structured diary keeping may help raters to recall a more accurate portrait of performance—one that is dynamic and takes the entire spectrum of performance into account. Thus, if ratings appear inflated, if there are only fine distinctions made between employees, or if supervisors are having difficulty taking into account the full range of performance, organizations may want to consider implementing a structured diary technique.

In addition, it is possible that performance data are biased in other ways, namely, that the data are results in group differences for protected classes. For example, Stauffer and Buckley (2005) re-examined Sackett and Dubois (1991), finding that both black and white raters give higher ratings to white ratees, reporting similar results. However, in both papers, the gap between ratings for white and black ratees was much higher for white raters than for black raters, creating a larger advantage for white ratees when the rater is white than when the rater is black. Thus, it is possible that racial differences may be found in performance appraisal ratings. Similarly, Lyness and Heilman (2006) found that female managers in masculine-stereotyped jobs (line manager) were rated lower than female managers in female-stereotyped jobs (staff jobs) (both groups were rated lower than male managers in both line and staff jobs). Further, women who had been promoted received higher performance ratings than men who had been promoted, demonstrating that women had to be clearly better than their counterparts to make it to the next level. Thus, because the risk for group differences exists, it is in the organization's best interest to monitor resultant ratings for bias. Although group differences do not necessarily imply foul play, they should be made subject to inquiry and examination. The possibility that ratings could have adverse impact is another reason to use a valid and well-researched performance appraisal system. If ratings result in bias, but the system is valid and job related, the organization can defend itself. Without a well-founded system, however, the organization is subject to litigation and in the current environment organizations must be cognizant of this possibility.

UTILIZING THE PERFORMANCE EVALUATION DATA

Once a system is in place, raters have been trained, and the system is consistently monitored, the next step is to use the ratings properly. Ratings are normally used for two purposes: (1) to make administrative decisions, such as firing or promotion or salary adjustments, and/or (2) for development, through developmental feedback and the potential to create an action plan for the future. In most police agencies, performance assessment is an annual event that has little impact on salary, promotion opportunity, or developmental planning. Most often, it is an event that officers and supervisors are required to conduct and only in rare instances does it lead to anything more than documenting poor performance for a few officers who, after several years of repeated poor performance, might be transferred or terminated. That is an unfortunate *lack of use* of what can be extremely important information. It is our belief that a culture must be created that focuses on the potential benefits of a strong performance appraisal and management process. Key to creating this culture is a clear statement of how performance evaluation information will be used and what systems will be in place to act on the results.

The way in which data is utilized can actually have an effect on the ratings themselves. For example, Greguras, Robie, Schleicher, and Goff (2002) found that subordinate ratings are of better quality when they are used for developmental purposes. This suggests that subordinates may not feel comfortable providing accurate ratings for their supervisor when it is clear that their ratings may have an impact on job outcomes. Further, it suggests that subordinates may fear the consequences of painting an accurate picture of their supervisors' behavior. In the same study, however, peer ratings were of good quality when used for administrative or for developmental purposes (Greguras et al., 2002). Atkins and Wood (2002) also note that the best predictor of assessment center performance is the average of peer, supervisor, subordinate, and self-ratings. This may demonstrate that different members of the organization may be exposed to different aspects of an employee or, on the other hand, it may point to the unwillingness of various employee contacts to share certain performance information. Thus, it is important to think about the purpose of the rating, as well as the source of the rating, when determining how best to use performance data. These findings may also suggest that organizations may want to keep the two processes separate according to their final use (Murphy & Cleveland, 1995).

Murphy and Cleveland (1995) offer three best practices for the use of performance information. The authors note that it may be necessary to change the underlying value of and rewards linked to the performance appraisal system, as opposed to attempting to coerce raters to avoid bias. Thus, it is more important to convince raters that rating is personally instrumental and helpful to the organization at the same time, rather than pushing for accuracy without a clear reason why. In order to do this, Murphy and Cleveland (1995) first suggest that rewards should be tied to rating behavior. In order to increase rating accuracy, organizations should demonstrate that they are willing to reward proper rating behavior. If the organization demonstrates that accurate rating is important through the use of rewards, then raters will be more likely to provide accurate ratings. Further, if raters know that the organization is serious about rating, they may be less likely to treat rating like a chore.

Second, Murphy and Cleveland (1995) suggest that making sure the effects of negative ratings are reduced may make it more likely that accurate ratings will be provided. For example, if a rater knows that a poor rating will result in job loss for the ratee, he or she may be unwilling to provide negative information. While meta-analyses have shown that pay-for-performance increases performance, Murphy and Cleveland (1995) suggest that this strategy may take a negative toll on performance appraisal accuracy. This suggestion may be especially helpful when subordinates provide ratings for their supervisors, given that they may fear backlash from supervisors if the rating is negative (Greguras et al., 2002). Thus, it is helpful to create a system in which performance ratings are not directly linked to negative outcomes for ratees.

Finally, Murphy and Cleveland (1995) suggest that, while performance ratings should not be directly tied to negative sanction for ratees, raters should see a clear link between rating behavior and rewards. Making the process more visible creates a motivational environment for rating accuracy, similar to the positive effects of pay for performance that Rynes, Gerhart, and Parks (2005) discussed in their meta-analysis. Taken together, organizations should make sure to create a reward structure for raters, with clear links to benefits as the result of accurate rating behavior. Further, organizations should make the links between ratings and negative sanctions for ratees less clear, so that raters do not feel personally responsible for the downfall of fellow employees. What all this points to is the promotion of a culture in which individuals understand how performance information will be used, are motivated to positively participate in the system, and trust the system to benefit the organization and the employees that comprise it.

One of the primary ways raters can use performance information, moreover, is to provide officers with feedback about their performance. Feedback is often misused and improperly delivered, creating anxiety and lower levels of motivation in ratees. In the next section, proper feedback delivery and environment will be discussed, in order to ensure that organizations are making the best possible use of performance information. As should be obvious, any rater training process must include information on the proper conduct of the feedback process.

FEEDBACK IN PERFORMANCE APPRAISAL

Reference different fields of study, and you will find various ways in which the term *feedback* has been conceptualized and defined. Industrial-organizational psychologists generally refer to feedback as information provided to an individual that clarifies expectations of their job and alerts them to how well their current performance meets such expectations (Spector, 2006). Although it was long assumed that employee feedback resulted in positive gains in performance, a meta-analysis by Kluger and DeNisi (1996) exposed the reality that feedback has the potential to produce not only performance gains but also performance declines. Indeed, as Taylor, Fisher, and Ilgen (1984) note, "Feedback may have no impact on the recipient at all, it may cause the individual to lash out angrily, or it may result in a response quite different from that desired by the source" (p. 82). Ilgen, Fisher, and Taylor (1979) suggested that variability in response to feedback might be due to a series of psychological or cognitive processes elicited by the feedback process.

As such, many studies have sought to determine what characteristics of the feedback process contribute to its effectiveness or lack thereof (Fedor, Rensvold, & Adams, 1992; Gaddis, Connelly, & Mumford, 2004; Kluger & DeNisi, 1996; Moss, Valenzi, & Taggart, 2003). Before considering such characteristics, it is important to understand that the effectiveness of any feedback system hinges on recipients' acceptance of such feedback (Ilgen et al., 1979). Ilgen and colleagues (1979) defined feedback acceptance as "the recipient's belief that the feedback is an accurate portrayal of his or her performance" (Ilgen et al., 1979). Further, research suggests that feedback acceptance acts as a gatekeeper or moderator between feedback delivery and effectiveness (Anseel & Lievens, 2007). Using self-consistency theory, Korman (1970) argued that "individuals will be motivated to perform on a task or job in a manner which is consistent with the self-image with which they approach the task or job situation" (p. 32). Thus, one's response to performance feedback is expected to be congruent to his or her acceptance of such feedback. As such, positive or negative feedback, which is perceived as accurate and therefore accepted by the recipient, is more likely to motivate one to respond than feedback perceived as inaccurate (Kinicki, Prussia, Wu, & McKee-Ryan, 2004).

In support of this proposition, Brett and Atwater (2001) found that perceptions of feedback accuracy from peers and direct reports were positively related to individuals' reactions to feedback. Moreover, Kinicki and colleagues (2004) tested a path model, which found that perceived accuracy was positively associated with recipients' desire to respond to feedback. Additionally, other findings suggest that positive reactions to feedback have significant links with other important organizational outcomes. Jawahar (2006), for instance, found that satisfaction with feedback was positively related to organizational commitment, job satisfaction, and commitment toward and satisfaction with one's managers, and negatively related to turnover intentions. As such, it seems clear that before any performance changes can occur, feedback recipients must decide whether to lend any credence to the feedback they have been given (Ashford, 1986).

Given the crucial role that feedback acceptance appears to play in the feedback delivery–performance relationship, what factors might predispose recipients from perceiving feedback as accurate and acceptable, and what can organizations do to foster such acceptance? In the following sections, we consider the effects of feedback content, specificity, frequency, delivery, and source on individuals' willingness to accept and utilize performance feedback. Moreover, we explore the role of trust in the feedback process and discuss how organizations can create environments conducive to feedback.

FEEDBACK CONTENT

Given the sensitive and anxiety-inducing nature of feedback in organizations (Cleveland et al., 2007), it is no surprise that the content of feedback may have a substantial impact on the likelihood of feedback acceptance. In general, research suggests that individuals are more accepting of positive feedback (Brett & Atwater, 2001), which likely stems from the motivation to preserve one's self-esteem from the perceived failure resulting from negative feedback (Anseel & Lievens, 2007). More precisely, it has been suggested that individuals are more likely to reject feedback that results in a negative sign (Ilgen et al., 1979), which refers to performance discrepancies in which one's actual performance, relayed through feedback, is lower than one's perceived performance (perceived overestimation of performance). In contrast, positive signs refer to discrepancies in which actual performance is higher than perceived performance (perceived underestimation of performance).

These findings do not necessarily indicate that individuals wholly reject negative feedback. They do indicate, however, that when performance discrepancies exist, individuals prefer positive feedback signs that portray them in a positive light and confirm their own self-perceptions (Aronson, Wilson, & Akert, 2007; Nease, Mudgett, & Quiñones, 1999). Moreover, they suggest that feedback providers ought to balance their negative feedback with positive feedback in order to reduce perceived performance overestimations as much as possible. By narrowing the perceived gap between one's actual performance and perceived performance, feedback providers may be more likely to gain feedback acceptance, which in turn may lead to performance improvements on the part of feedback recipient. Additionally, Smither and Walker (2004) showed that providing a small amount of negative feedback is related to enhanced performance, but that a large amount of negative feedback impairs future performance. Atwater and Brett (2006) further suggest that feedback sessions should begin with positive feedback in order to spur feedback acceptance. Thus, feedback providers should be aware of the amount of negative feedback they provide, making sure to buffer it with positive feedback at the beginning of the feedback session and ensuring that subordinates are not overwhelmed by too much negative feedback during the process.

Other research indicates that feedback is perceived as valuable when it helps employees reduce uncertainty, provides recipients information regarding their goal progress, and indicates how one's performance is evaluated by others (Ashford & Cummings, 1983; Steelman & Rutkowski, 2004). Ilgen and associates (1979) further suggested that feedback is more likely to be accepted and used when it is perceived as valid, accurate, and reliable. Thus, feedback providers should always err on the side of providing higher quality feedback during feedback sessions (Ilgen et al., 1979).

Kluger and DeNisi (1996), however, note that such feedback ought to be focused more on the performed task than the person receiving the feedback. In their influential meta-analysis, they found that feedback intervention (FI) effectiveness decreased as feedback became more directed toward the feedback recipient than the task. This is consistent with other research that supports the idea that individuals are more likely to accept feedback that compares them to a neutral standard, rather than to their peers. It is believed that such comparisons can hurt recipients' self-concept and reduce their likelihood of accepting feedback (Atwater & Brett, 2006) as well as focus attention on recipients' weaknesses—potentially eliciting negative emotional reactions instead of internalization of feedback (Smither & Walker, 2004). This suggests that recipients may be less likely to accept and ultimately use feedback they perceive as a personal attack rather than an honest assessment of performance on the task. Thus, feedback providers should be careful that their feedback not be directed toward personal characteristics or compare recipients to their peers, but rather should focus on specific performance aspects related to the task.

Feedback Specificity

To date, feedback specificity, or the level of information presented in feedback messages, has received quite a bit of attention in the performance appraisal literature (Annett, 1969; Goldstein, Emanuel, & Howell, 1968). Generally speaking, it is believed that effective feedback includes specific information about behaviors performed incorrectly and how to correct them, rather than generalized or ambiguous statements (Bernardin & Beatty, 1984; Goodman, Wood, & Hendickx, 2004; Kirk & MacDonald, 1989). Such feedback provides a rich source of information about explicit behaviors that are appropriate or inappropriate for effective performance, thereby allowing recipients to learn from and correct their behavior (Adams, 1987; Anderson, 1982; Annet, 1969; Ilgen et al., 1979). In so doing, feedback specificity is thought to decrease information-processing activities, such as error diagnosis, encoding, and retrieval (Christina & Bjork, 1991; Schmidt, 1991), which subsequently reduce the cognitive load required to make links between actions and outcomes (Goodman & Wood, 2004). Moreover, specific feedback provides information on how individuals are progressing toward their goals and informs them about how their job performance is evaluated (Ashford & Cummings, 1983).

In fact, empirical evidence suggests that specific, objective feedback consistent with actual performance leads to higher performance than less specific, more subjective feedback (Kopelman, 1986). Moreover, feedback interventions that are supplemented with information regarding tasks, strategies, and appropriate behaviors have been found to result in increased short-term performance during practice and training (Goodman & Wood, 2004; Kluger & DeNisi, 1996). In an interesting study conducted by Steelman and Rutkowski (2004), the authors found that feedback quality moderated the relationship between unfavorable feedback and motivation to use feedback. This finding suggests that employees are more highly motivated to use negative feedback when that feedback is perceived to be of high quality and directed toward improving their performance than similar feedback of lower quality.

Despite such findings, overly specific narrative feedback may also introduce excessive cognitive load on recipients, hindering their understanding of the feedback (Atkins, Wood, & Rutgers, 2002). For example, Atkins et al. (2002) conducted an experiment, which found that participants who received feedback in a graphical format outperformed participants who received feedback in a tabular format on an inventory management task. Findings indicated that the portrayal of relationships between variables visually in the graphical format facilitated quicker decision making than the more detailed derivation of relationships from data provided in the tabular format. Interestingly, however, the tabular format produced the strongest evidence of learning. Atkins et al. (2002) reasoned that while graphical feedback formats may reduce processing and interpretation costs inherent to tabular formats, it is the lack of such processing and detailed analyses that handicap learning—which is critical for long-term performance improvement and development.

In a similar vein, Goodman and Wood (2004) further suggested that while feedback specificity is generally advantageous for improving immediate performance, it may undermine certain aspects of the learning process necessary for independent performance at a later time. In particular, they found that specific feedback improved recipients' ability to learn from good performance but produced deleterious effects on learning how to respond to poor performance. They reasoned that it is important that feedback providers consider what exactly they want recipients to learn with regard to the task. That is, if the feedback provider wants the recipient to learn how to respond to both good and poor performance, feedback must be supported by sufficient opportunities for the recipient to test and learn the local response rules for different aspects of a task. For example, if we wanted a car mechanic to learn how to respond when a carburetor functions properly and when it malfunctions, feedback should not be so specific that it ensures the carburetor functions properly. Rather, feedback should be less specific so that recipients commit errors and learn which behaviors will lead to proper carburetor functioning.

In general, these findings suggest that specific feedback is more beneficial than vague, generalized feedback. Employees must learn which specific behaviors are indicative of good and poor performance, not only so that they can correct such behaviors but also in order to protect against perceptions of arbitrariness in the feedback process. However, it also important that feedback providers consider what they want recipients to learn regarding the task. In order to promote long-term learning, less specific feedback may be more beneficial to promoting experimentation and richer, more effective response patterns on the part of employees. In fact, research on error management training (EMT), a method that involves active exploration and explicit encouragement for trainees to commit errors in order to promote learning, suggests increased training transfer on novel tasks (Keith & Frese, 2008).

Feedback Frequency

Feedback frequency has also been explored as a potential factor influencing feedback acceptance and perceived utility (Fedor & Buckley, 1987; Fulk, Brief, & Barr, 1985; Landy, Barnes, & Murphy, 1978). In general, it is thought that frequently delivered feedback is more effective in promoting employee performance improvements than less frequent feedback (Fedor & Buckley, 1987; Ilgen et al., 1979). In a review of the PA literature, Ilgen et al. (1979) concluded that the close temporal pairing of feedback with employee performance behavior has an overall positive effect on future performance. They reasoned that frequently delivered feedback reduces the chances that interference will occur in the periods between behavior and the feedback, which have the potential to distort feedback effectiveness.

In fact, research suggests that frequency of feedback is positively related to recipients' perceived accuracy and fairness of feedback (Fulk, Brief, & Barr, 1985; Landy et al., 1978). Because feedback tends to not be delivered as frequently as it should in today's organizations, recipients may view feedback as a scarce, valuable resource that decreases role ambiguity by continually informing employees about where they stand with regard to their performance levels (Beehr & Love, 1983; Fedor & Buckley, 1987). Thus, increasing the frequency of feedback may facilitate more positive employee reactions and outcomes during the feedback process. However, Fedor and Buckley (1987) warn that more may not always be better when it comes to feedback, and that other factors must be taken into consideration when deciding whether to provide more frequent feedback or not. For example, instituting more frequent feedback sessions may send implicit messages to employees that supervisors do not trust them as competent and capable of carrying out their tasks without increased micromanagement. Moreover, Fedor and Buckley (1987) suggest that because negative feedback is typically perceived as less accurate and more controlling, providing such feedback more regularly may in fact lead to decreased feedback acceptance. In fact, it has been shown that while positive feedback provided immediately promotes a strengthening of previous behavioral responses, negative feedback is more effective after a time lag, which allows for decomposition in the strength of the previous incorrect behavioral response (Buchwals & Meager, 1974; Fedor & Buckley, 1987). As such, it stands to reason that while providing feedback on how to do a job may be perceived positively when done once or twice, such feedback may be reacted to more negatively when delivered in excess (Fedor & Buckley, 1987).

Similar to the case of feedback specificity, it may also be the case that more frequent feedback is not necessarily conducive to long-term sustained maintenance of learned behavior (Fedor & Buckley, 1987). Research on error management training (EMT) suggests that individuals must engage in active exploration of a task and make consistent errors in order to promote a long-term structured understanding of how to perform it well (Keith & Frese, 2008). As such, these findings suggest that while supervisors should seek to provide regular feedback to employees, they should also recognize that more is not always better. Specifically, because recipients' feedback perceptions are crucial to its acceptance, supervisors should be aware that the intent behind providing increased amounts of feedback may not be perceived accurately by those receiving such feedback, that is, what may be intended as supportive may in actuality be perceived as controlling (Fedor & Buckley, 1987). Moreover, too frequent feedback may hinder long-term learning, an outcome all managers want to avoid. As such, Fedor and Buckley (1987) recommend that supervisors find out how often their employees desire feedback, while also minimizing the perceived costs of asking for feedback.

Feedback Delivery

It is also important that feedback providers take active steps to preserve and respect recipients' self-esteem by being sensitive and understanding in order to obtain feedback acceptance, rather than simply viewing their role as a provider of information. Research suggests that the manner in which feedback is delivered may significantly impact employees' acceptance and perceived utility of the feedback (Steelman & Rutkowski, 2004). For example, it has been found that a supportive, constructive attitude on the part of feedback providers contributes to increased recipient satisfaction, perceptions of fairness, and motivation to improve job performance (Burke et al., 1978). Furthermore, feedback consisting of greater interpersonal fairness has been found to be related to more favorable attributions toward the feedback provider, more acceptance of the feedback provider, and more favorable reactions to the organization (Leung et al., 2001). Steelman and Rutkowski (2004), for example, found that employees were more motivated to improve their job performance following negative feedback when feedback is delivered in a considerate manner.

FEEDBACK SOURCE

Not surprisingly, much research has also investigated whether feedback acceptance depends on who provides such feedback. This research has often investigated the feedback source's credibility, which refers to one's expertise and trustworthiness in providing feedback (Giffin, 1967; Kinicki et al., 2004). According to Steelman and Rutkowski (2004), expertise includes "knowledge of the recipient's job requirements, knowledge of the recipient's actual job performance and the ability to evaluate that performance in an accurate manner," while trustworthiness represents "whether or not the individual trusts the feedback source to provide accurate performance information" (p. 8). As such, credible feedback providers are seen as possessing expertise relative to the specific tasks evaluated and are trusted to provide objective feedback, free from outside biasing factors (e.g., political considerations, feedback source's mood at the time of feedback, and so on) (Ilgen et al., 1979; Steelman & Rutkowski, 2004).

For example, Bannister (1986) conducted an experimental study in which it was found that source credibility had a significant effect on feedback recipients' intentions to use suggestions given during feedback. Bannister (1986) concluded that the individual's perceptions of the feedback provider's qualifications to provide feedback are critical in determining an individual's intent to use feedback or not. Consistent with these findings, Collins and Stukas (2006) found that individuals were more likely to accept self-inconsistent feedback from a high-status therapist than a low-status therapist. Moreover, such findings seem to generalize to the field as well. Steelman and Rutkowski (2004) surveyed 698 employees at two different manufacturing companies and found that employees were more motivated to improve their job performance when they perceived the feedback provider to be credible. Finally, Podsakoff and Farh (1989) found that individuals who received more credible negative feedback set higher goals and performed better than individuals who received less credible negative feedback.

In short, these findings provide strong support for the credibility and status of the feedback provider in the feedback process. It appears that feedback recipients make strong attributions regarding the validity of feedback based on the perceived credibility and status of the feedback source. Thus, organizations should make a strong effort to make sure that feedback is delivered by highly qualified individuals with experience on the task evaluated and professional status that is greater than the feedback recipient's. In so doing, recipients may be more likely to both accept and use feedback in order to improve their future performance.

THE ROLE OF TRUST IN FEEDBACK

Further examination of the feedback process highlights the importance of recognizing that feedback does not exist within a vacuum, but rather is embedded within the larger social-organizational context or *social milieu*, as referred to by Bretz and colleagues (1992). As such, research suggests that context plays a potentially pivotal role in shaping aspects of the appraisal process, including feedback, and the ways in which employees react to such processes (Farr & Jacobs, 2006; Murphy

& Cleveland, 1995). Specifically, Folger et al. (1992) discussed performance appraisal as process in which individuals at all organizational levels (including subordinates, supervisors, and upper management) have a stake, leading to potentially conflicting interests regarding the results of a given performance appraisal or feedback session. Thus, feedback providers, in such contexts, are believed to hold power over subordinates, who inevitably make themselves vulnerable during such sessions (Mayer, Davis, & Schoorman, 1995). Therefore, in order for feedback sessions, and performance appraisal processes in general, to be effective, those engaged in the process must trust in it. For feedback recipients, this means trusting their supervisors, and the system used to evaluate them. For supervisors, this means having faith in the quality of their feedback and the appraisal system that informs it.

Jablin (1979), for example, suggested that an employee's trust in their supervisor influences the communication link between the two. As trust fades, it is argued that information fails to make a substantive impact during communication (Ilgen et al., 1979; Jablin, 1979). Thus, it stands to reason that when trust decreases, so does the impact of supervisory feedback on subordinates' behavior. Providing empirical support for this idea, Herold and Greller (1977) found that supervisors who were more "psychologically close" with their subordinates had a greater impact in terms of feedback than those who were more psychologically distant. In addition, Earley (1986) found that workers' trust in the feedback source partially mediated the relationship between feedback and workers' response to and value attached to praise and criticism.

In sum, these findings suggest that trust plays a crucial role in individuals' willingness to accept and respond to feedback. Thus, supervisors should actively try to promote trust among their subordinates by educating subordinates about the performance appraisal and feedback process, showing how the feedback process may be used to promote employee development, demonstrating consideration for employees' work and well-being, exhibiting dependability on a regular basis, and communicating a sense of honesty and forthrightness in daily activities, among other things. In so doing, it may be possible to promote a climate of trust surrounding the feedback process, which will work to facilitate feedback acceptance and ultimately improved job performance.

Feedback Environments and Effort Costs

Continuing on with the role of context in the feedback process, increased attention has been paid to creating organizational environments conducive to feedback. While much of the feedback literature has examined feedback through a relatively narrow lens, several researchers have suggested that organizations can facilitate the creation of feedback-oriented cultures by improving feedback quality, emphasizing the importance of feedback, and supporting its use by employees (London, 2003; Rosen et al., 2006). According to Rosen and colleagues (2006), in such cultures, feedback is "easily accessible, salient, and thus likely to influence employee beliefs and behaviors on a day-to-day basis" (p. 212). As such, many researchers have begun to examine what aspects of the organizational environment encourage and support the use of feedback in improving employee performance (Levy, Albright, Cawley, & Williams, 1995; Steelman et al., 2004; Williams, Miller, Steelman, & Levy, 1999).

In particular, such research has surrounded contextual elements that contribute to employees' willingness to seek out feedback from their employer (Ashford & Cummings, 1983; Whitaker, Dahlin, & Levy, 2007). *Feedback seeking* has been defined as the efforts demonstrated by individuals in an organization to reduce uncertainty regarding the acceptability of their performance (Ashford, 1986; Ashford & Cummings, 1983). In particular, the literature has predominantly centered on *inquiry*, which Ashford and Cummings (1983) referred to as the active request for feedback. Such feedback seeking behavior, moreover, has been shown to be related to important organizational outcomes, including employee learning, job satisfaction, and motivation (Anseel & Lievens, 2007; Hackman & Oldham, 1976; Mignerey, Rubin, & Gordon, 1995; Murphy & Cleveland, 1995).

Further, research on contextual predictors of feedback seeking has primarily focused on perceived effort costs (Ashford & Cummings, 1983) and the feedback environment (Steelman et al., 2004). While *effort costs* refer to the perceived amount of effort employees believe they must expend to obtain feedback, a *feedback environment* refers to the extent to which workplace characteristics promote active use of feedback inquiry (Whitaker et al., 2007). The idea of a feedback environment is similar to what other researchers have termed an *active learning climate*, in which the organizational environment plays an active role in facilitating "new knowledge acquisition by encouraging employees to ask questions, seek feedback, reflect on potential results, explore, and experiment" (Katz-Navon, Naveh, & Stern, 2009, p. 1200). Moreover, it is believed that feedback seeking decreases as a function of higher effort costs (Ashford, 1986; Ashford & Cummings, 1983) and increases with the supportiveness of a feedback environment (Steelman et al., 2004). In fact, Whitaker and colleagues (2007) found that among 170 subordinate–supervisor dyads, subordinates who perceived a supportive feedback environment demonstrated increased feedback-seeking behavior, higher role clarity, and higher job performance. Recently, Steelman and colleagues (2004) developed and validated a measure of feedback environment that includes seven factors of the feedback process, including many of the factors previously mentioned such as source credibility, feedback quality, feedback delivery, frequency of favorable feedback, frequency of unfavorable feedback, feedback availability, and support of feedback seeking. Moreover, empirical evidence suggests that higher levels of perceived feedback environment are related to increased affective commitment, job satisfaction, and organizational citizenship behaviors, in addition to decreased absenteeism (Norris-Watts & Levy, 2004; Steelman & Levy, 2001).

Given such findings, it is important that supervisors and the broader organization work to decrease effort costs associated with feedback seeking. Research by authors such as Whitaker and colleagues (2007) suggest that employees may not be obtaining feedback even from supportive coworkers if a substantial amount of effort is required to do so. As such, organizations should put forth extra effort to make sure all barriers to the effective exchange of information between feedback recipients and providers are removed. Such research also suggests that by promoting feedback seeking, organizations may indirectly encourage employees to seek development-related feedback more consistently (London, 2003; London & Smither, 2002), leading to increased role clarity and improved performance (Whitaker et al., 2007). Finally, empirical evidence indicates that organizations, which promote environments that are supportive of employee efforts to seek out feedback, demonstrate a variety of positive outcomes. As such, organizations can promote such environments by encouraging both supervisors and employees to express openness to the feedback process and by openly rewarding such behavior.

SUMMARY

We have provided a lot of information regarding research and practice as it pertains to performance assessment and management. Much has been done in this area, and over the decades of theory building and practical application, we have learned quite a bit. While we believe in the importance of being very specific about what has been done in the past, it is often important to step back and simply summarize what we know and what it means in terms of creating a successful performance management program. Here is our perspective.

DEFINING PERFORMANCE

Without a doubt, nothing works unless time is spent and effort is expended to accurately define the key responsibilities and expected behaviors of those evaluated. Traditionally, this starts with a job analysis or a very comprehensive job description. We know this step helps rater and ratee when it comes to understanding performance expectations and accepting the accuracy of performance evaluations when they are conducted. We also know that from a fairness and legal perspective, a system of performance management will never be seen as reasonable unless the agency has done its homework and clearly documented what is required by the job. These descriptions should be multidimensional, covering critical areas of job performance and behavioral specifying the types of actions that represent poor, average and strong job performance.

SETTING THE STAGE

Performance management is not just an organizational requirement—it is an organizational event. In police agencies and other organizations, the process of evaluating performance is often approached with dread. Evaluators do not enjoy conducting evaluations; those evaluated feel like they are unnecessarily put under the microscope, and those responsible for the process within the HR organization often feel they have to harass and cajole individuals just to do what needs to be done. It is not a happy time of the year for many members of the organization. With this backdrop, it is important that a more positive environment is created by focusing on the process and potential positive outcomes that will result from effective performance management. This requires a campaign initiated by the agency and supported from the top down. Without this kind of effort, the process will wallow in apathy and the benefits will never emerge.

TRAINING, TRAINING, AND MORE TRAINING

We make a faulty assumption when it comes to performance management. We often assume that because someone has become a supervisor, they *can* and *will* be competent in the evaluation of others. Many supervisors and command personnel are good at reviewing the work of others and may enjoy the process, but not all. The role of training evaluators on the how to's and why's of performance evaluation is critical. Even for those positively disposed to the activity, training helps. An essential part of any performance management system is the training of raters on all aspects of the system.

It is also critical that those evaluated are informed regarding the process. This is an often neglected area and is part of what we describe above in setting the stage. While it may be an annual agency requirement that performance reviews will occur, it is not necessarily clear to evaluated individuals exactly how the evaluations will be conducted, what is being measured, and how the data will be used. All these topics should be explained in advance of system implementation.

KEEPING TRACK/MONITORING THE SYSTEM

The most effective processes do not stop at the collection of data and the checking off of yet another organizational event required by the agency. The best systems review results, hold raters accountable for doing the evaluations in a timely fashion, analyze data for potential problems (bias, halo, and missing information as examples), and use this information to enhance the future system implementations.

USING THE DATA

Traditionally, data from performance evaluations are used to understand individual performance, to provide feedback to the person evaluated, and/or to trigger personnel actions such as administering rewards or reprimands. While these are clearly important uses for the data, organizations are missing opportunities unless they look across individuals to understand where the agency may have repeated performance decrements indicating needed training programs or where the department is truly excelling and how that information can be leveraged for future motivational programs. Suffice it to say that the best run performance management programs continue beyond the individual level of analysis and look at groups, departments, and agencywide data to better understand performance.

Feedback—"Don't Ask if You Aren't Going to Tell"

Over the years, we have learned quite a bit about how we can move from performance appraisal to using that information to drive future performance. It begins with a well-developed feedback process that brings supervisor and officer together to talk about the past and to plan for the future. Feedback does not happen automatically, and many involved in the process of delivering and receiving feedback need guidance to effectively turn observations of performance into performance improvements.

THE FUTURE OF PERFORMANCE APPRAISAL AND WHAT IT MEANS FOR POLICE DEPARTMENTS

Thus far, this chapter has outlined best practices for performance appraisal in organizations—from traditional issues regarding instrumentation to how to deliver performance feedback. However, performance appraisal methodology has never been stagnant. We have seen changes in research emphasis and practice over the past five decades. The future will bring improvements and updates to best practice as it stands today. Although it is impossible to predict exactly what the future will hold, there are a few areas that have already begun to show promise and that we believe will allow police departments to enhance the effectiveness of their performance assessment processes.

The first of these areas lies in the realm of online assessment. Online assessment is quick and easy, and fits in well with today's demand for technology-driven solutions. For example, e-learning has become very popular in organizational training because it is easy to use and can be completed by employees at any time. The same is true for online performance appraisal systems. Supervisors can complete surveys about officer behavior at a convenient time and in a quick, easy fashion. As the computerization of police work marches forward, more and more systems will be available for documenting and evaluating police officer performance. The use of online performance appraisal also facilitates self-evaluation and lends itself to automated comparisons between subordinate and supervisor that can form the basis of performance discussions and goal setting. As such, online assessments are also extremely useful tools for organizations because they save time and energy, and allow for the automated collection and storage of performance assessment data. Making performance appraisal systems more user-friendly and more efficient is undoubtedly in the best interest of the organization, and online appraisals certainly help to propel these goals forward.

Second, there has been a recent upswing in the use of self-assessment for performance appraisal. In this case, employees are able to provide ratings regarding their own performance. However, the literature suggests that self-appraisals are ridden with bias. For example, Atkins and Wood (2002) demonstrated that self-ratings were negatively and nonlinearly related to assessment center performance. In addition, those with the highest self-ratings were those with the lowest actual performance. Overcompensating for poor performance, the worst employees may likely report that they are doing the best. Further, the negative relationship between self-rating and actual performance also indicates that high performers may be hard on themselves, creating a performance profile much lower than in reality. It has also been demonstrated that self-ratings tend to be less variable than supervisor, peer, or subordinate ratings, suggesting possible halo or leniency errors (Scullen, Mount, & Judge, 2003). Thus, while self-evaluations may provide interesting information, it is not suggested for use in making administrative decisions. Organizations should be aware of employees' intent to distort self-ratings and should proceed with caution when determining how to make use of self-report performance data.

Finally, organizations falling behind industry standards may choose to implement performance improvement initiatives. In this case, the organization may need to change or increase current performance standards. This may require an overhaul of the existing performance system in order to reflect the new vision of employee performance. However, in terms of validity, this may be dangerous. Using *visionary* performance standards to create a new appraisal system is possible; however, it is necessary to make sure that employees chosen to fulfill newly envisioned roles are selected into this role based on predictors that indicate high performance using the new appraisal system. For example, selecting an employee into a new role based on old standards and then appraising them according to new standards creates a situation in which employee characteristics may not fit the new tenets of the job. This may lead to a low correlation between predictors, job behaviors, and performance ratings—a recipe for legal disaster. Thus, when attempting to improve performance, organizations should attempt to make changes throughout the entire system, from selection to appraisal to reward structures. In this way, performance appraisal can become an integral part of the organization's strategy, while still ensuring validity in the process.

REFERENCES

Adams J. A. (1987). Historical review and appraisal of research on the learning, retention, and transfer of human motor skills. *Psychological Bulletin, 101*, 41–74.
Anderson, J. R. (1982). Acquisition of cognitive skill. *Psychological Review, 89*, 369–406.
Annett, J. (1969). *Feedback and human behavior*. Hammondsworth, UK: Penguin.
Anseel, F., & Lievens, F. (2007). Long-term impact of the feedback environment on job satisfaction: A field study in a Belgian context. *Applied Psychology, 56*, 254–266.
Aronson, E., Wilson, T. D., & Akert, R. M. (2007). *Social psychology*. Upper Saddle River, NJ: Pearson Education.
Arvey, R. D., & Murphy, K. R. (1998). Performance evaluation in work settings. *Annual Review of Psychology, 49*, 141–168.
Ashford, S. J. (1986). Feedback-seeking in individual adaptation: A resource perspective. *Academy of Management Journal, 29*, 465–487.
Ashford, S. J., & Cummings, L. L. (1983). Feedback as an individual resource: Personal strategies of creating information. *Organizational Behavior & Human Performance, 32*, 370–398.
Atkins, P. W. B., & Wood, R. E. (2002). Self-versus others' ratings as predictors of assessment center ratings: Validation evidence for 360-degree feedback programs. *Personnel Psychology, 55*, 871–904.
Atkins, P. W. B., Wood, R. E., & Rutgers, P. J. (2002). The effects of feedback format on dynamic decision making. *Organizational Behavior and Human Decision Processes, 88*, 587–604.
Atwater, L., & Brett, J. (2006). Feedback format: Does it influence manager's reactions to feedback? *Journal of Occupational Psychology, 79*, 517–532.
Austin, J. T., & Villanova, P. (1992). The criterion problem: 1917–1992. *Journal of Applied Psychology, 77*, 836–874.
Bannister, B. D. (1986). Performance outcome feedback and attributional feedback: Interactive effects on recipient responses. *Journal of Applied Psychology, 71*, 203–210.
Beehr, T. A., & Love, K. G. (1983). A meta-model of the effects of goal characteristics, feedback, and role characteristics in human organizations. *Human Relations, 36*, 151–166.
Bernardin, H. J., & Beatty, R. W. (1984). *Performance appraisal: Assessing human behavior at work*. Boston: PWS-Kent.
Bernardin, H. J., & Buckley, M. R. (1981). A consideration of strategies in rater training. *Academy of Management Review, 6*, 205–212.
Bernardin, J. H., Cooke, D. K., & Villanova, P. (2000). Conscientiousness and agreeableness as predictors of rating leniency. *Journal of Applied Psychology, 85*, 232–236.
Borman, W., & Motowidlo, S. (1993). Expanding the criterion domain to include elements of contextual performance. In N. Schmitt & W.C. Borman (Eds.), *Personnel selection in organizations* (pp. 71–98). San Francisco: Jossey-Bass.
Brett, J. F., & Atwater, L. E. (2001). 360 degree feedback: Accuracy, reactions, and perceptions of usefulness. *Journal of Applied Psychology, 86*, 930–942.
Bretz, R. D., Milkovich, G. T., & Read, W. (1992). The current state of performance appraisal research and practice: Concerns, directions, and implications. *Journal of Management, 18*, 321–352.
Brown, M., & Benson, J. (2003). Rated to exhaustion? Reactions to performance appraisal processes. *Industrial Relations Journal, 34*, 67.
Buchwals, A. M., & Meager, R. B. (1974). Immediate and delayed outcomes: Learning and the recall of responses. *Journal of Experimental Psychology, 103*, 758–767.

Burke, R. J., Weitzel, W., & Weir, T. (1978). Characteristics of effective employee performance review and development interviews: Replication and extension. *Personnel Psychology, 31*, 903–919.

Campbell, D. J., Campbell, K. M., & Chia, H.-B. (1998). Merit pay, performance appraisal, and individual motivation: An analysis and alternative. *Human Resource Management, 37*, 131.

Campbell, J. P. (1999). The definition and measurement of performance in the new Age. In D. R. Ilgen & E. Pulakos (Eds.), *The changing nature of performance* (pp. 399–430). San Francisco: Jossey-Bass.

Cawley, B. D., Keeping, L. M., & Levy, P. E. (1998). Participation in the performance appraisal process and employee reactions: A meta-analytic review of field investigations. *Journal of Applied Psychology, 83*, 615–633.

Christina, R. W., & Bjork, R. A. (1991). Optimizing long-term retention and transfer. In D. Druckman & R. A. Bjork (Eds.), *In the mind's eye: Enhancing human performance* (pp. 23–55). Washington, DC: National Academy Press.

Cleveland, J. N., Lim, A. S., & Murphy, K. R. (2007). Feedback phobia? Why employees do not want to give or receive performance feedback. In J. Langan-Fox, C. L. Cooper, & R. J. Klimoski (Eds.), *Research companion to the dysfunctional workplace: Management challenges and symptoms*. Cheltenham, UK: Edward Elgar.

Collins, D. R., & Stukas, A. A. (2006). The effects of feedback self-consistency, therapist status, and attitude toward therapy on reaction to personality feedback. *The Journal of Social Psychology, 146*, 463–483.

Collins, J. (2001). *Good to great*. New York: HarperCollins.

Day, D. V., & Sulsky, L. M. (1995). Effects of frame-of-reference training and information configuration on memory organization and rating accuracy. *Journal of Applied Psychology, 80*, 158–167.

DeNisi, A. S., Cafferty, T. P., & Meglino, B. M. (1984). A cognitive view of the performance appraisal process: A model and research propositions. *Organizational Behavior & Human Performance, 33*, 360–396.

DeNisi, A. S., & Peters, L. H. (1996). Organization of information in memory and the performance appraisal process: Evidence from the field. *Journal of Applied Psychology, 81*, 717–737.

DeNisi, A. S., & Williams, K. J. (1988). Cognitive approaches to performance appraisal. *Research in Personnel and Human Resources Management, 6*, 109–155.

Duarte, N. T., Goodson, J. R., & Klich, N. R. (1993). How do I like thee? Let me appraise the ways. *Journal of Organizational Behavior, 14*, 239.

Earley, P. C. (1986). Trust, perceived importance of praise and criticism, and work performance. An examination of feedback in the United States and England. *Journal of Management, 12*, 457–473.

Erdogan, B., Kraimer, M. L., & Liden, R. C. (2001). Procedural justice as a two-dimensional construct: An examination in the performance appraisal account. *Journal of Applied Behavioral Science, 37*, 205–222.

Farr, J. L., & Jacobs, R. (2006). Unifying perspectives: The criterion problem today and into the 21st century. In W. Bennett, C. Lance, & D. Woehr (Eds.), *Performance measurement: Current perspectives and future challenges* (pp. 321–337). Mahwah, NJ: Lawrence Erlbaum.

Fedor, D. B., & Buckley, R. M. (1987). Providing feedback to organizational members: A reconsideration. *Journal of Business and Psychology, 2*, 171–181.

Fedor, D. B., Rensvold, R. B., & Adams, S. M. (1992). An investigation of factors expected to affect feedback seeking: A longitudinal field study. *Personnel Psychology, 45*, 779–805.

Flint, D. H. (1999). The role of organizational justice in multi-source performance appraisal: Theory-based applications and directions for research. *Human Resource Management Review, 9*, 1–20.

Folger, R., Konovsky, M. A., & Cropanzano, R. (1992). A due process metaphor for performance appraisal. *Research in Organizational Behavior, 14*, 129–177.

Fulk, J., Brief, A. P., & Barr, S. H. (1985). Trust-in-supervisor and perceived fairness and accuracy of performance evaluations. *Journal of Business Research, 13*, 301–313.

Gaddis, B., Connelly, S., & Mumford, M. D. (2004). Failure feedback as an affective event: Influences of leader affect on subordinate attitudes and performance. *The Leadership Quarterly, 15*, 663–686.

Gendersen, D. E., & Tinsley, D. B. (1996). Empirical assessment of impression management biases: The potential for performance appraisal error. *Journal of Social Behavior and Personality, 11*, 57–77.

Goldstein, I. L., Emanuel, J. T., & Howell, W. C. (1968). Effect of percentage and specificity of feedback on choice behavior in a probabilistic information-processing task. *Journal of Applied Psychology, 52*, 163–168.

Goodman, J. S., & Wood, R. E. (2004). Feedback specificity, learning opportunities, and learning. *Journal of Applied Psychology, 89*, 809–821.

Goodman, J. S., Wood, R. E., & Hendickx, M. (2004). Feedback specificity, exploration, and learning. *Journal of Applied Psychology, 89*, 248–262.

Goss, W. (2001). Managing for results—Appraisals and rewards. *Australian Journal of Public Administration*, *60*, 3.

Greguras, G. J., Robie, C., Schleicher, D. J., & Goff, M. (2003). A field study of the effects of rating purpose on the quality of multisource ratings. *Personnel Psychology*, *56*, 1–21.

Hackman, R. J., & Oldham, G.R. (1976). Motivation through the design of work: Test of a theory. *Organizational Behavior & Human Performance*, *16*, 250–279.

Hastie, R., & Park, B. (1986). The relationship between memory and judgment depends on whether the judgment task is memory-based or on-line. *Psychological Review*, *93*, 258–268.

Hedge, J. W., & Teachout, M. S. (2000). Exploring the concept of acceptability as a criterion for evaluating performance measures. *Group & Organization Management*, *25*, 22–44.

Herold, D. M., & Greller, M. M. (1977). Feedback: The definition of a construct. *Academy of Management Journal*, *20*, 142–147.

Ilgen, D. R., Barnes-Farrell, J. L., & McKellin, D. B. (1993). Performance appraisal process research in the 1980s: What has it contributed to appraisals in use? *Organizational Behavior and Human Decision Processes*, *54*, 321–368.

Ilgen, D. R., Fisher, C. D., & Taylor, M. S. (1979). Consequences of individual feedback on behavior in organizations. *Journal of Applied Psychology*, *64*, 349–371.

Jablin, F. M. (1979). Superior-subordinate communication: The state of the art. *Psychological Bulletin*, *86*, 1201–1222.

Jacobs, R. R., Kafry, D., & Zedeck, S. (1980). Expectations of behavioral rating scales. *Personnel Psychology*, *33*, 595–640.

Jawahar, I. M. (2006). An investigation of potential consequences of satisfaction with appraisal feedback. *Journal of Leadership & Organizational Studies*, *13*, 14–28.

Jawahar, I. M., & Williams, C. R. (1997). Where all the children are above average: The performance appraisal purpose effect. *Personnel Psychology*, *50*, 905–925.

Johnson, D. E., Erez, A., Kiker, S. D., & Motowidlo, S. J. (2002). Liking and attributions of motives as mediators of the relationships between individuals' reputations, helpful behaviors, and raters' reward decisions. *Journal of Applied Psychology*, *87*, 808–815.

Kacmar, K. M., Witt, L. A., Zivnuska, S., & Gully, S. M. (2003). The interactive effect of leader–member exchange and communication frequency on performance ratings. *Journal of Applied Psychology*, *88*, 764–772.

Katz-Navon, T., Naveh, E., & Stern, Z. (2009). Active learning: When is more better? The case of resident physicians' medical errors. *Journal of Applied Psychology*, *94*, 1200–1209.

Keith, N., & Frese, M. (2008). Effectiveness of error management training: A meta-analysis. *Journal of Applied Psychology*, *93*, 59–69.

Kinicki, A. J., Prussia, G. E., Wu, B., & McKee-Ryan, F. M. (2004). A covariance structure analysis of employees' response to performance feedback. *Journal of Applied Psychology*, *89*, 1057–1069.

Kirk, P., & MacDonald, I. (1989). The role of feedback in management learning. *Management Education & Development*, *20*, 9–19.

Klimoski, R., & Inks, L. (1990). Accountability forces in performance appraisal. *Organizational Behavior and Human Decision Processes*, *45*, 194–208.

Kluger, A. N., & DeNisi, A. (1996). Effects of feedback intervention on performance: A historical review, a meta-analysis, and a preliminary feedback intervention theory. *Psychological Bulletin*, *119*, 254–284.

Kopelman, R. E. (1986). Objective feedback. In E. A. Locke (Ed.), *Generalizing from laboratory to field settings* (pp. 119–145). Lexington, MA: D. C. Heath.

Korman, A. K. (1970). The prediction of managerial performance: A preview. *Studies in Personnel Psychology*, *2*, 4–26.

Kozlowski, S. W. J., Chao, G. T., & Morrison, R. F. (1998). Games raters play: Politics strategies, and impression management in performance appraisal. In J. W. Smither (Ed.), *Performance appraisal: State of the art in practice* (pp. 163–208). San Francisco: Jossey-Bass.

Landy, F. J., Barnes, J. L., & Murphy, K. R. (1978). Correlates of perceived fairness and accuracy of performance evaluation. *Journal of Applied Psychology*, *63*, 751–754.

Landy, F. J., & Farr, J. L. (1980). Performance rating. *Psychological Bulletin*, *87*, 72–107.

Latham, G. P., Almost, J., Mann, S., & Moore, C. (2005). New developments in performance management. *Organizational Dynamics*, *34*, 77–87.

Lefkowitz, J. (2000). The role of interpersonal affective regard in supervisory performance ratings: A literature review and proposed causal model. *Journal of Occupational and Organizational Psychology*, *73*, 67–85.

Leung, K., Su, S., & Morris, M. W. (2001). When is criticism not constructive? The roles of fairness perceptions and dispositional attributions in employee acceptance of critical supervisory feedback. *Human
Relations*, *54*, 1155–1187.

Levy, P. E., Albright, M. D., Cawley, B. D., & Williams, J. R. (1995). Situational and individual determinants of
feedback seeking: A closer look at the process. *Organizational Behavior and Human Decision Processes*,
62, 23–37.

Levy, P. E. & Williams, J. R. (1998). The role of perceived system knowledge in predicting appraisal reactions, job satisfaction, and organizational commitment. *Journal of Organizational Behavior*, *19*,
53–65.

Levy, P. E., & Williams, J. R. (2004). The social context of performance appraisal: A review and framework for
the future. *Journal of Management*, *30*, 881–905.

London, M. (2003). *Job feedback: Giving, seeking, and using feedback for performance improvement*. Mahwah,
NJ: Lawrence Erlbaum.

London, M., & Smither, J. (2002). Can working with an executive coach improve multisource feedback ratings
over time? A quasi-experimental field study. *Personnel Psychology*, *56*, 23–46.

Lyness, K. S., & Heilman, M. E. (2006). When fit is fundamental: Performance evaluations and promotions of
upper-level female and male managers. *Journal of Applied Psychology*, *91*, 777–785.

Mani, B. G. (2002). Performance appraisal systems, productivity, and motivation: A case study. *Public
Personnel Management*, *31*, 141–159.

Maurer, T. J., Mitchell, D. R. D., & Barbeite, F. G. (2002). Predictors of attitudes toward a 360-degree feedback
system and involvement in post-feedback management development activity. *Journal of Occupational &
Organizational Psychology*, *75*, 87–107.

Mayer, R. C., Davis, J. H., & Schoorman, F. D. (1995). An integrative model of organizational trust. *Academy
of Management Review*, *20*, 709–734.

Mignerey, J. T., Rubin, R. B., & Gorden, W. I. (1995). Organizational entry: An investigation of newcomer
communication behavior and uncertainty. *Communication Research*, *22*, 54–85.

Moss, S. E., Valenzi, E. R., & Taggart, W. (2003). Are you hiding from your boss? The development of a
taxonomy and instrument to assess the feedback management behaviors of good and bad performers.
Journal of Management, *29*, 487–510.

Motowidlo, S. J. (2003). Job performance. In W. C. Borman, D. R. Ilgen, & R. J. Klimoski (Eds.), *Handbook of
psychology: Industrial and organizational psychology* (pp. 39–53). Hoboken, NJ: John Wiley.

Motowidlo, S. J., & Van Scotter, J. R. (1994). Evidence that task performance should be distinguished from
contextual performance. *Journal of Applied Psychology*, *79*, 475–480.

Murphy, K. R., & Cleveland, J. N. (1991). *Performance appraisal: An organizational perspective*. Needham
Heights, MA: Allyn & Bacon.

Murphy, K. R., & Cleveland, J. N. (1995). *Understanding performance appraisal: Social, organizational, and
goal-based perspectives*. Thousand Oaks, CA: Sage.

Nease, A. A., Mudgett, B. O., & Quiñones, M. A. (1999). Relationships among feedback sign, self-efficacy, and
acceptance of performance feedback. *Journal of Applied Psychology*, *84*, 806–814.

Norris-Watts, C., & Levy, P. E. (2004). The mediating role of affective commitment in the relation of the feedback environment to work outcomes. *Journal of Vocational Behavior*, *65*, 351–365.

Ostroff, C., & Ilgen, D. R. (1992). Cognitive categories of raters and rating accuracy. *Journal of Business and
Psychology*, *7*, 3–26.

Pettijohn, C. E., Pettijohn, L. S., & d'Amico, M. (2001). Characteristics of performance appraisals and their
impact on sales force satisfaction. *Human Resource Development Quarterly*, *12*, 127–146.

Podsakoff, P. M., & Farh, J. (1989). Effects of feedback sign and credibility on goal setting and task performance. *Organizational Behavior and Human Decision Processes*, *44*, 45–67.

Pulakos, E. D. (1984). A comparison of rater training programs: Error training and accuracy training. *Journal
of Applied Psychology*, *69*, 581–588.

Reb, J., & Cropanzano, R. (2007). Evaluating dynamic performance: The influence of salient Gestalt characteristics on performance ratings. *Journal of Applied Psychology*, *92*, 490–499.

Roberts, G. E. (2003). Employee performance appraisal system participation: A technique that works. *Public
Personnel Management*, *32*, 89.

Roberts, G. E., & Reed, T. (1996). Performance appraisal participation, goal setting and feedback. *Review of
Public Personnel Administration*, *16*, 29.

Rosen, C. C., Levy, P. E., & Hall, R. J. (2006). Placing perceptions of politics in the context of the feedback environment, employee attitudes, and job performance. *Journal of Applied Psychology*, *91*,
211–220.

Rynes, S. L., Gerhart, B., & Parks, L. (2005). Personnel psychology: Performance evaluation and pay for performance. *Annual Review of Psychology, 56,* 571–600.

Sackett, P. R., & Dubois, C. L. (1991). Rater-ratee race effects on performance evaluation: Challenging meta-
analytic conclusions. *Journal of Applied Psychology, 76,* 873–877.

Schleicher, D. J., Day, D. V., Mayes, B. T., & Riggio, R. E. (1992). A new frame for frame of reference training:
Enhancing the construct validity of assessment centers. *Journal of Applied Psychology, 87,* 735–746.

Schmidt, R. A. (1991). Frequent augmented feedback can degrade learning: Evidence and interpretations. In
J. Requin & G. E. Steimach (Eds.), *Tutorials in motor neuroscience* (pp. 59–75). London: Kluwer.

Scullen, S. E., Mount, M. K., & Judge, T. A. (2003). Evidence of the construct validity of developmental ratings
of managerial performance. *Journal of Applied Psychology, 88,* 50–66.

Seifert, C. F., Yuki, G., & McDonald, R. A. (2003). Effects of multisource feedback and a feedback facilitator on
the influence behavior of managers toward subordinates. *Journal of Applied Psychology, 88,* 561–569.

Shah, J. B., & Murphy, J. (1995). Performance appraisals for improved productivity. *Journal of Management
in Engineering, 11,* 26.

Smither, J. W., & Walker, A. G. (2004). Are the characteristics of narrative comments related to improvement
in multirater feedback ratings over time? *Journal of Applied Psychology, 89,* 575–581.

Spector, P. E. (2006). *Industrial and organizational psychology: Research and practice.* Hoboken, NJ: John
Wiley.

Stauffer, J. M., & Buckley, R. M. (2005). The existence and nature of racial bias in supervisory ratings. *Journal
of Applied Psychology, 90,* 586–591.

Steelman, L. A., & Levy, P. E. (2001, April). The feedback environment and its potential role in 360-degree
feedback. In J. R. Williams (Chair), *Has 360-degree feedback really gone amok? New empirical data.*
Symposium conducted at the 16th annual meeting of the Society for Industrial and Organizational
Psychology, San Diego, CA.

Steelman, L. A., Levy, P. E., & Snell, A. F. (2004). The feedback environment scale: Construct definition, measurement, and validation. *Educational and Psychological Measurement, 64,* 165–184.

Steelman, L. A., & Rutkowski, K. A. (2004). Moderators of employee reactions to negative feedback. *Journal
of Managerial Psychology, 19,* 6–18.

Sulsky, L. M., & Day, D. V. (1992). Frame-of-reference training and cognitive categorization: An empirical
investigation of rater memory issues. *Journal of Applied Psychology, 77,* 501–510.

Sulsky, L. M., & Keown, J. L. (1998). Performance appraisal in the changing world of work: Implications for
the meaning and measurement of work performance. *Canadian Psychology, 39,* 52–59.

Sulsky, L. M., Skarlicki, D. P., & Keown, J. L. (2002). Frame-of-reference-training: Overcoming the effects
of organizational citizenship behavior on performance rating accuracy. *Journal of Applied Social
Psychology, 32,* 1224–1240.

Taylor, E. K., & Wherry, R. J. (1951). A study of leniency in two rating systems. *Personnel Psychology, 4,*
39–47.

Taylor, M. S., Fisher, C., & Ilgen, D. (1984). Individuals reactions to performance feedback in organizations:
Control theory perspective. In K. Rowland & G. Ferris (Eds.), *Research in personnel and human resource
management* (pp. 81–124). Greenwich, CT: JAI.

Taylor, M. S., Masterson, S. S., Renard, M. K., & Tracy, K. B. (1998). Managers' reactions to procedurally just
performance management systems. *Academy of Management Journal, 41,* 568–579.

Tziner, A., & Kopelman, R. E. (2002). Is there a preferred performance rating format? A non-psychometric
perspective. *Applied Psychology: An International Review, 51,* 479–503.

Tziner, A., Kopelman, R., & Joanis, C. (1997). Investigation of raters' and ratees' reactions to three methods
of performance appraisal: BOS, BARS, and GRS. *Canadian Journal of Administrative Sciences, 14,*
396.

Viswesvaran, C., & Ones, D. S. (2000). Perspectives on models of job performance. *International Journal of
Selection and Assessment, 8,* 216–226.

Waldman, D. A., & Bowen, D. E. (1998). The acceptability of 360 degree appraisals: A customer-supplier
relationship perspective. *Human Resource Management, 37,* 117.

Whitaker, B. G., Dahling, J. J., & Levy, P. (2007). The development of a feedback environment and role clarity
model of job performance. *Journal of Management, 33,* 570–591.

Williams, J. R., & Levy, P. E. (2000). Investigating some neglected criteria: The influence of organizational
level and perceived system knowledge on appraisal reactions. *Journal of Business and Psychology, 14,*
501–513.

Williams, J. R., & Lueke, S. B. (1999). 360 degrees feedback system effectiveness: Test of a model in a field
setting. *Journal of Quality Management, 4,* 23.

Williams, J. R., Miller, C. E., Steelman, L. A., & Levy, P. E. (1999). Increasing feedback seeking in public context: It takes two (or more) to tango. *Journal of Applied Psychology, 84*, 969–976.

Woehr, D. J. (1994). Understanding frame of reference training: The impact of training on the recall of performance information. *Journal of Applied Psychology, 79*, 525–534.

Woehr, D. J., & Huffcutt, A. I. (1994). Rater training for performance appraisal: A quantitative review. *Journal of Occupational and Organizational Psychology, 67*, 189–205.

Wong, K. F. E., & Kwong, J. Y. Y. (2007). Effect of rater goals on rating patterns: Evidence from an experimental field study. *Journal of Applied Psychology, 92*, 577–585.

9 Assessments for Selection and Promotion of Police Officers

Rick Jacobs

Lily Cushenbery

Patricia Grabarek

This chapter provides perspective on assessments used for selecting and advancing/promoting employees. We start with a broad overview of how employees are selected, then focus on what is going on in today's police departments. The same strategy is used in our presentation on promotion systems before we move on to specific issues confronted when organizations engage in assessment and use the information to make employment decisions. The chapter concludes with a brief overview of legal issues facing police agencies as they attempt to identify talent to join the organization or to move up the rank structure and how we can successfully design and implement programs that encompass best practices and avoid legal complications.

SELECTING EMPLOYEES: A BRIEF OVERVIEW

Selecting the best candidates for a job is critical for all organizations, but in few settings is it more important than law enforcement. In valid selection systems, those who do well on the tests and other instruments used in the screening and selection process become the high performers once they are integrated into the organization. Conversely, those who do poorly in the selection process would have likely been poor performers had they been given the job. That is the essence of validity; something we find out about the individual in the pre-employment assessments accurately forecasts subsequent job performance.

THEORY AND TOOLS

Several important assumptions are made when creating selection systems. Many are obvious, but it helps to make sure we understand the science behind selection. According to Guion (1998), selection systems rely on the following basic assumptions:

- People have a variety of abilities.
- People differ in one or more of these abilities.
- These differences can be measured.
- These differences remain stable over time.
- Different jobs require different abilities.

It is the match between the required abilities of the job and the measured abilities of job applicants that helps us create valid selection systems.

Tests and Test Batteries

Employers often use single tests or a combination of multiple tests to predict performance. For many years, civil service testing relied on multiple-choice tests that had one correct answer and three or four incorrect answers. Traditionally, these tests had 100 items, and a candidate's fitness for the job was based on his or her performance on the test. Those candidates with high scores were selected with the assumption that their high test scores were indicative of future job performance. This logic works, provided a link exists between what is required to perform well on the test and the actual requirements of the job. When an employer creates a selection test or system that includes multiple tests, the key to successful selection is ensuring that the tests and the job have commonality. For years, employers relied solely on tests of cognitive abilities to select employees. The logic here is that those who are smarter and more cognitively complex would become the best performing employees. While many still argue this to be true, the broader reality is that jobs are multifaceted and require a variety of knowledge, skills, abilities, and personal characteristics. Attempting to predict performance with a single test will likely result in partial success at best.

Many selection systems are created by assembling a group of tests, often referred to as a *test battery*. Frequently, these batteries include cognitive ability tests along with one or more distinctive types of tests such as a personality assessment measuring one or more dimensions of personality believed to be related to performance on the job. These systems adopt the perspective that the job in question is a collection of requirements: some involve thinking, some involve how individuals approach tasks, and some involve individuals' ability to work with others. The goal here is to assemble a group of tests that matches the various requirements of the job. In many of these systems, we see assessments that tap candidates with respect to cognitive ability, personality, background, and more. Hough (2003) and McHenry, Hough, Toquam, Hanson, and Ashworth (1990) provide a nice perspective on the value of test batteries. They concluded that cognitive ability tests are better when predicting certain performance criteria (*can-do*) and personality scales are better at predicting others (*will-do*). The accuracy of predicting performance increases when using test batteries because of the combination of different types of tests as well as the more thorough assessment of candidates relative to the critical performance areas required by the job. Many selection systems adopt this test battery approach.

Interviews

Interviews are the most frequently used assessment tool and are believed to assess multiple aspects of the applicant, allowing an accurate forecasting of job relevant skills and abilities. Personality is the most frequently assessed set of characteristics, and 35% of interviews are believed to include some assessment of personality. Other characteristics that interviewers typically assess are applied social skills (28%), mental ability (16%), and specific job-related knowledge and skills (10%) (Huffcutt, Conway, Roth, & Stone, 2001). Interviewers first attempt to assess applicant values and personality before matching them with specific job requirements or organization characteristics (Posthuma, Moregeson, & Campion, 2002).

Interviews have historically been one of the most researched selection tools used by organizations. In early studies, interviews were found to be relatively unreliable due to fluctuations in the questions asked and how conclusions were drawn by individual interviewers. Since the early 1960s, interviews have steadily improved with the addition of structure. Structure helped minimize the unwanted variations in what was asked and how interviewers reached conclusions about the applicants.

The research literature has presented mixed findings on the overall utility or usefulness of interviewing during the selection process. Some studies have found no incremental validity, or increased predictability of performance, with the use of interviews above and beyond other information such as test scores. Consequently, some argue that interviews should be eliminated because they require vast resources in terms of personnel and time but do not contribute additional information.

Additionally, some concern exists that interviewees can be coached and their performance in the interview is not indicative of what truly defines the candidate (Maurer, Solamon, & Troxtel, 1998). In contrast, other studies have found that tests such as cognitive ability and personality only add 4% of new information beyond what the interview provides, and therefore the interview should be the tool of choice and other selection tools are not required.

Modern interview practices treat the interview more like a traditional test rather than an unstructured conversation. Today, selection systems include interviews that tie individual questions to key requirements of the job. In addition, careful attention is paid to how interviewers are trained in things such as the ideal interview environment, interviewer tone of voice, and factors that affect interviewer judgment. Finally, when interviewers use measures that have been developed for the specific purpose of summarizing what was discussed once the interview is completed, accuracy is enhanced. All of these features help increase the reliability of the interview and the ability to predict future performance from the interview evaluations (Chapman & Zweig, 2005). Given that interviews will continue to be used in most selection settings, it is important to understand best practices in creating and conducting interviews.

Work Sample Tests

In work sample tests, applicants complete tasks that are very similar to those found in the job. The idea behind this type of test is that performance on *job-similar tasks* is highly predictive of performance on those same tasks once the applicant is on the job (Bobko, Roth, & Buster, 2005; Schmidt & Hunter, 1998). Many examples of work sample tests are used for selection. For example, in physical ability tests, candidates are asked to engage in a series of tasks very similar to tasks that they would encounter on the job. Such tasks include pushing a stopped vehicle, separating two individuals engaged in an argument, and/or carrying or dragging a dummy over a specified distance. Similarly, written and oral work simulations—such as asking an individual to fill out paperwork, respond to phone inquiries, or deal with an irate citizen—represent real tasks often performed by police officers. The important characteristic of a work sample is that it replicates the job in a meaningful way so that most individuals would conclude that a direct relationship exists between performance on the work sample and performance on the job. Work sample tests are perceived as fair and valid, which results in positive applicant reactions (Bobko et al., 2005).

While work sample tests can be a valuable addition to any selection system, they can also be expensive to develop and implement. They require a great deal of specificity and therefore often require full customization for each individual job. Further, work sample tests often require specific information from the job and therefore cannot be used in entry-level testing since candidates will likely gain information and/or skills once they are hired and receive training. Work sample tests can be valuable in selecting employees, but there is a delicate balance between what the test can contain and what candidates come to the test already knowing about the job.

Situational Judgment Tests

Situational judgment tests (SJTs) are a series of job-related scenarios presented in written, oral, or visual (video) formats where an applicant is asked to present a written or oral description of how they would react to a hypothetical situation (Clevenger, Pereira, Wiechmann, Schmitt, & Harvey, 2001; McDaniel, Morgeson, Finnegan, Campion, & Braverman, 2001). They are designed to measure judgment in work settings. Some tests ask for applicants to choose a response among a set of alternative responses while others ask for a rating of agreement with various responses (McDaniel et al., 2001).

There are many advantages of these types of tests. SJTs have good predictive validity and are moderately correlated with cognitive ability. They also have incremental validity above cognitive ability testing (McDaniel et al., 2001). In addition, situational judgment tests have high face validity, meaning they appear to test what they are actually testing (Clevenger et al., 2001). Applicants tend to have positive reactions to these types of tests because of their obvious relationship to the job for which the applicants are competing. Furthermore, these tests are relatively easy and often inexpensive to create, although this is less true for video-based versions. Racial group biases are also smaller in situational judgment tests than in cognitive ability tests. However, the racial group differences for situational judgment tests still exist and are bigger than those found in personality measures (Clevenger et al., 2001).

Integrity Tests

Integrity tests are very widely used in selection of employees (Alliger & Dwight, 2000). They are used to identify individual characteristics that increase the likelihood to engage in counterproductive work behaviors such as theft, undermining, and absenteeism. There are two types of integrity tests: overt and personality. Overt integrity tests measure attitudes toward dishonest behavior and ask about previous illegal activity (Sackett, Burris, & Callahan, 1989). Personality integrity tests measure attitudes and dispositions related to integrity, including reliability and conscientiousness (Hogan & Brinkmeyer, 1997; Neuman & Baydoun, 1998).

Many employers prefer to use integrity tests to predict applicants who are likely to engage in these negative work behaviors and remove them from the selection pool instead of waiting to discover these behaviors later (Camara & Schneider, 1995; Mikulay & Goffin, 1998). Integrity tests are successful at predicting counterproductive work behaviors because individuals perceive their work environment differently (Murphy, 1993). For example, some individuals do not see a problem with taking some resources home from work (such as pens), while others believe this is wrong. Although integrity tests are often shown to be predictive of subsequent job performance in a broad context, the use of these tests is not without criticism and can be seen as beginning the employment process from a position of distrust.

Personal History Assessment

A personal history assessment requires applicants to fill out questions about educational background, prior work experience, and other previous activities. These include what psychologists like to call *biodata*—historical, external actions or objective and discrete events that people have control over. As the name implies, the focus of personal history assessment is past actions and behaviors and almost always emphasizes specific events (Mael, Connerley, & Morath, 1996). The content of the actual assessment attempts to tie job requirements to indicators from past behaviors that reflect favorably on the candidate's ability to perform the tasks of the job. For example, personal history data are often collected to select people for overseas assignments. Since this type of work requires interactions with people from different cultures, one indicator of future success is an individual's interest in other cultures prior to working overseas. Questions on a personal history assessment in this context would include asking about foreign language competency, attending foreign film festivals, and even interest in sampling foods from ethnic restaurants. The logic here is that those who will succeed in the assignment already have an interest in exploring other cultures and these items help define past behaviors reflecting that interest.

Assessment Centers

Assessment centers are categorized by multiple assessors, multiple exercises, and multiple competencies (Thornton & Rupp, 2006). They are used to select employees by gathering the opinions of multiple evaluators (assessors) across a variety of work-related tasks (exercises) and simultaneously measuring a series of job-relevant dimensions (competencies). Assessment centers are typically used in selection by diagnosing individuals' strengths and weaknesses that are relevant to the organization's requirements for the job. The exercises range from oral presentations to written reports to role-plays of job relevant situations, each providing opportunities for applicants to display behaviors that showcase their abilities and potential in the different competencies. Several assessors, or raters, observe the applicants complete these exercises and rate the observed behaviors to create competency scores and an overall assessment rating (OAR).

Assessment centers have many advantages and disadvantages when it comes to selecting employees. They have criterion-related validity, which means scores from assessment centers predict on-the-job performance (e.g., Haaland & Christiansen, 2002; Thornton & Rupp, 2006). They can also include traditional tests such as cognitive ability and personality inventories (Guion, 1998) in addition to the exercises in the assessment center. Even when these more traditional tests are used, assessment centers still have incremental validity, or provide new information above and beyond the other tests.

In addition, many applicants perceive assessment centers positively. Applicants can see how the assessment relates to the job and are more likely to view assessment centers as fair in terms of the employment decision (Thornton & Rupp, 2006). Further, assessment centers have lower levels of racial group differences than tests such as cognitive ability and therefore can enhance the diversity of the selected group. Assessment centers can be seen as the ultimate form of *test batteries* because they include a wide variety of assessment tools from traditional tests to interviews to more interactive tools where assessors evaluate candidates during the performance of job simulations. Assessment centers provide rich data about each applicant, and as such have a correspondingly high cost in terms of both development and implementation. Many organizations lack the resources to create assessment centers, while others simply find it difficult to assemble the finances and people to put them into practice.

GOALS OF SELECTION

When creating a selection system, the primary goal is to sort candidates in a way that identifies their job-related skills and abilities. When done correctly, the system will allow organizations to select those capable of doing the job and reject those less likely to succeed. This is far from the only goal of selection. A good selection system should have other positive outcomes such as creating favorable impressions among job applicants (Barrick & Zimmerman, 2005), ensuring that those selected are retained by the organization (Hausknecht, Day, & Thomas, 2004), and helping to achieve diversity in the selected group at a rate representative of the diversity seen in the applicant pool (Guion, 1998). However, among these additional goals, achieving racial diversity and avoiding adverse impact have received the most attention in selection. This is particularly true in the police context.

Most organizations take a great deal of care to avoid hiring employees using a process that has an adverse impact for a protected class. Title VII of the Civil Rights Act prohibits discrimination by employers on the basis of race, color, religion, sex, or national origin. Actual or implied selection rates are the sources of adverse impact defined by law (Gutman, 2004). If adverse impact exists, an organization must prove job relatedness and business necessity of the selection process via validity evidence that shows that performance on the test is systematically related to performance on the job. Such evidence can be presented by criterion-related validity (test scores are related to job performance measures), construct validity (the test is measuring what it should be), and content validity (the content of the test is relevant to the job) (Sackett & Wilk, 1994).

Unfortunately, many valid tests commonly used for selection have racial group differences (Campion et al., 2001) that result in disproportionate selection as a function of race. For example, cognitive ability tests have documented validity for a wide variety of jobs, but they also show significant group differences with white candidates outperforming black and Hispanic candidates. Thus, cognitive ability tests are known to create adverse impact in selection systems (Berry, Gruys, & Sackett, 2006). This presents a significant challenge to those designing selection systems where the goals are not only valid selection but also relative equality of outcomes across groups (Sackett, De Corte, & Lievens, 2010). Several potential solutions have been suggested, including alternative tests such as work samples (Bobko et al., 2005) and personality assessments (Sackett, Schmitt, Ellingson, & Kabin, 2001). While both of these have been shown to reduce adverse impact, the decrease is less than anticipated given that many of these indicators have been shown to be related to cognitive ability, at least for the types of job applicants that predominate in police officer selection (Cascio, Jacobs, & Silva, 2010).

SELECTING POLICE OFFICERS

Selection systems created for police departments are based on the broader research but also have several unique aspects such as the need to incorporate assessment of physical fitness, the need to ensure high levels of personal integrity, and the need to have a workforce representative of the people it serves. Currently, a variety of selection programs are used to identify police officers who can perform the complicated tasks and assume the heavy responsibilities inherent in the job. The following section discusses the types of assessment tools used specifically in police departments.

The majority of police departments use a battery of tests and assessment devices to determine the applicants best suited for the job. This process involves both selection testing and assessments that occur after the initial decision regarding job suitability. It is important to keep the sequence of the selection process in perspective. More than 90% of departments use a combination of an application, job-related ability tests, interviews, medical exams, psychological exams (pathology assessment), and background investigations (Cochrane, Tett, & Vandecreek, 2003). In addition, more than 50% of departments require drug screening, physical fitness assessment, and polygraph testing. Only 8% of police departments use formal assessment centers for officer selection (Cochrane et al., 2003), but the technique is more widely used in police promotional exams. According to Dayan, Kasten, and Fox (2002), it is possible that assessment centers are more prevalent in police officer selection but are underreported.

Ability Testing

Virtually every police officer selection process begins with an application, a determination of eligibility (minimum age, limited or no arrest record, driver's license, and so on), and an ability test. The determination of eligibility is a dichotomous decision that results in either allowing the candidate to move on to the next phase of the process or an early exit from a career in law enforcement with that agency and perhaps with others as well. Those eligible to test are given a time to report for testing, which takes place at a specified location. A majority of these tests are paper and pencil in format with candidates responding to a series of questions and choosing the best response from four or five alternatives. Some agencies have moved from paper-and-pencil to computer-based tests, but the underlying assessment is very much the same and answers the question: Does the candidate possess the cognitive ability to perform as a police officer?

The tests include items designed to assess such thinking skills as written comprehension, inductive reasoning, deductive reasoning, information ordering, and problem sensitivity. This type of testing has been shown to be valid in a variety of settings, including the selection of law enforcement officers. The major drawback is that these types of tests are often associated with adverse impact, resulting in fewer minority group members making it into the final pool of selected candidates. In spite of this undesirable outcome, there is a need for assessing thinking skills as the cognitive demand of the job is substantial, beginning with learning relevant laws, policies, and procedures and culminating with the thought processes required to perform on the street in real time.

Many departments have moved to a selection system that uses cognitive abilities to set minimum qualifications based on test results and then moves candidates through to other assessments (personality, biodata, and interview) where those scores are then combined with the cognitive assessment to form a total selection score.

Personality Assessments

Personality testing has two distinct purposes in law enforcement selection systems. First, personality testing is often used to identify those candidates likely to be strong performers on the job and to help avoid hiring those who have personality scores/profiles that are predictive of poor performance. In this way, personality tests are used much like cognitive ability tests simply as a means to identify talent. The second way we see personality assessments entering in the employment process is further down the line when departments have identified who to hire and are concerned with avoiding hiring an individual who demonstrates signs of pathology. If the personality test indicates a potential pathology, it is necessary to follow up with a clinical interview.

Approximately 90% of police departments use personality assessments somewhere in their selection process (Cochrane et al., 2003) with the dual goals of identifying applicants who are well adjusted and possess the skills necessary to do the job (Detrick, Chibnall, & Luebbert, 2004). A number of different personality inventories have been successfully deployed by police departments, including, but not limited to, the Minnesota Multiphasic Personality Inventory (MMPI), the Inwald Personality Inventory (IPI), the NEO Personality Inventory, and the Sixteen Personality Factor Questionnaire (16PF).

The MMPI is the most commonly used inventory in police departments (Detrick et al., 2004), but it is not without criticism. The MMPI seems more of a general measure of psychopathology and is not particularly good at predicting performance in law enforcement (Scogin, Schumacher, Gardner, & Chaplin, 1995). This highlights the point made previously regarding the dual purpose of personality testing. It should always be clear to both the police agency and the candidate the exact purpose of any assessment. Perhaps the MMPI should be restricted to identifying potential pathology and not for identifying performance-related attributes. Much of the MMPI's widespread use came from its reputation in excluding candidates with problems rather than in selecting those likely to be excellent performers on the job (Scrivner, 2001). The IPI is another popular tool used by police departments and was created specifically for police officer selection. Performance on the job has been shown to be significantly related to the IPI (Detrick & Chibnall, 2002; Inwald, 1988, 1992). The NEO Personality Inventory (Costa & McRae, 1992; Detrick et al., 2004) has also been supported in its use for selecting police officers. Finally, the 16PF is frequently used in police selection (Cochrane et al., 2003) and has been supported in its ability to predict turnover (Drew, Carless, & Thompson, 2008).

Recently, Cascio et al. (2010) have made a strong argument for the use of personality testing in conjunction with cognitive ability assessment. These authors have demonstrated that personality information, when added to information about candidate's thinking skills, can not only add to the prediction of job performance but can simultaneously reduce the level of adverse impact in the final selection pool when compared to selection systems based solely on cognitive assessment. In many ways this work highlights the importance of assessing many different aspects of the candidate with greater validity and lower levels of adverse impact. This approach remains promising as we attempt to build more effective police officer selection programs.

Faking on Personality Tests and Distortion on Other Types of Assessments

Despite the extensive research on selection testing and the substantial progress made over the past five decades in creating and implementing valid tests, some issues remain unresolved. There are problems in maximizing the effectiveness of our tools and a clear need for ongoing research. Organizations, especially within law enforcement, tend to fear that applicants fake personality tests to appear more socially desirable or more consistent with the requirements of the job. For example, a person who is chronically late may know that punctuality is a desirable trait and would indicate that they are always on time. If a personality test is used, the candidate would indicate that they have a high awareness of being on time or conscientious. While these statements are not true, the candidate can easily disguise their tendencies by answering in a way that is consistent with their vision of what the organization hopes to hear. Psychologists refer to this specific problem as *test transparency*, meaning that the candidate can "see the correct or best answer." In contrast, a cognitive ability test has a right or wrong answer, and the candidate either knows the answer or doesn't; it is not easy to *fake* smart.

While several researchers have indicated that faking may be less problematic than originally thought (Ellingson, Sackett, & Connelly, 2007; Hogan, Barrett, & Hogan, 2007; Hough, Eaton, Dunnette, Kamp, & McCloy, 1990), in high-stakes testing many individuals will distort their responses. Given that many tests are both potentially useful for selection while simultaneously allowing for faking a selection system, more needs to be done to ensure that those identified via tests are not just those who successfully *game* the testing process. There are at least four avenues available to help us with the issue.

- Know who is likely to fake—research exists that indicates who is most likely to fake or distort their responses. Applicants with high social skills and/or those who score high on social desirability are associated with improving their scores, while those high on integrity are less likely (Hough et al., 1990). There has been some evidence that faking occurs even on integrity tests; integrity tests are the easiest to fake (McFarland & Ryan, 2000), and they often do not include lie scales (Lilienfeld, Alliger, & Mitchell, 1995).
- Use validity (lie) scales—these scales indicate whether or not a candidate is likely to engage in response distortions to improve their scores.
- Verify responses—in the context of police testing, it is possible to ask questions on a test, print out responses for each candidate, and then verify the response during background investigation or another step in the process.
- Use multiple gates or hurdles in selection—using the polygraph, background investigation, or other hurdles, eliminate those not responding truthfully during earlier stages of selection.

Despite the low base rate of faking, utilizing the research to prevent it is comforting for the organizations that fear its occurrence and can help eliminate the occasional problem candidate.

Interviews

One logical perspective pervasive in selection system development is to place the less expensive, less labor-intensive procedures at the beginning of the process and hold those that require more resources for later when we have eliminated candidates and therefore have fewer in the pipeline. The interview can be seen in this context. Law enforcement agencies interview police officer candidates once the pool has been evaluated via the application for minimum qualifications and the absence of disqualifiers (conviction of a felony as an example), along with certain qualifying information such as sufficiently high scores on entry level tests including cognitive ability, personality, and/or biodata assessment. With this "partially qualified" group, agencies often create an interview process that will allow them to make additional judgments regarding suitability. Police officer interviews run the range from informal conversations with the chief in smaller departments to formalized processes with multiple assessors in some of the larger and more administratively capable departments. Best practices in police officer interviewing include:

- Prequalifying those interviewed to minimize spending time with poorer candidates
- Providing training for interviewers
- Interviewing in teams of two or preferably three people
- Developing interview questions around specific dimensions such as empathy, oral communication, interpersonal sensitivity, and the ability to listen
- Providing interviewers with a structured format for evaluations

These interviews are often the last step in the pretesting selection process, and successful candidates move on to the remaining steps such as psychological screening, medical evaluation, and a background check.

Finally, interviews may be useful in decreasing race and gender bias in the selection process. Racial and gender-related group differences are lower in interviews than what is traditionally found in using cognitive ability tests for selection (Huffcutt et al., 2001; Sacco, Scheu, Ryan, & Schmitt, 2003). This is important to consider because including a well-constructed interview in the selection process can enhance validity while simultaneously reducing adverse impact.

Assessment Centers

The use of assessment centers for selecting police officers is gaining in popularity, but its rise is limited by the tremendous resource demands of the technique. Assessment center ratings have been found to be valid predictors of training and job performance. These police assessment centers, combined with cognitive ability tests and personality tests, can predict on-the-job police performance better than cognitive ability and personality alone (Dayan et al., 2002). Thus, assessment center performance shows a unique contribution to the prediction of good police performance, above that of cognitive ability. Furthermore, assessment centers have been shown to have less adverse impact than cognitive ability testing in police selection (Pynes & Bernardin, 1992) and therefore may be a viable alternative or addition to cognitive ability testing. In reality, many departments create an assessment center when they piece together the various elements in a series of steps the candidates must follow to gain employment. In addition to having these multiple exercises and multiple assessors evaluating candidates on multiple dimensions, assessment centers generally try to do all steps in a fixed period of time. Many systems exist that have a great deal of overlap with assessment centers and can be considered highly similar in process and tend to have highly similar outcomes.

Physical Fitness

Many agencies use physical fitness testing for selection (Cochrane et al., 2003; Lonsway, 2003). This type of work samples testing seems intuitive since police officers often have to engage in strenuous physical activity on the job. However, there is a weak relationship between physical test performance and on-the-job performance in incidents involving physical activity (Wiener, 1994). Because of this and due to the substantial gender differences found in this type of testing, this selection tool is often challenged regarding job relatedness (Lonsway, 2003). Women perform as successfully as men on the job (Martin & Jurik, 1996), so the use of physical testing that systematically excludes women from consideration at the beginning of the selection process is often questioned.

What is important to know about physical ability testing in police is that there are two categorically different approaches when such tests are deployed. First, some tests actually replicate the activities of the job. These are job simulations, or what we described earlier as work samples. Here, activities such as running a specified distance, negotiating an obstacle course, moving a stalled vehicle, and separating two arguing parties (usually simulated using equipment rather than people) are put together as a course the candidate must follow. Each event is timed, and the set of events is then scored either by awarding points for each event or as a pass/fail for the set of events. Scoring is usually developed by running incumbent officers through the course and determining appropriate minimum performance standards for each event and for the set of events. This type of testing can be contrasted to what is referred to as surrogate testing. In surrogate testing, exercises such as push-ups, sit-ups, and step-ups are used to measure the fitness levels of the candidates. Scoring is often referenced to norms created by gender and age so that someone older is not required to do as much as someone younger. This age/gender norming is highly controversial since the job requires all officers regardless of age or gender to perform similarly when they arrive on the scene. Having some form of physical testing in a selection program does provide assurance that the incoming class of officers is ready to assume the duties of the job. In some cases, physical ability/fitness testing occurs after the fact rather than during the selection process. For many departments, the training academy has a fitness program and graduation is predicated on meeting standards (Lonsway, 2003).

Polygraphs

Polygraphs are used in more than 50% of police departments (Cochrane et al., 2003). They are intended to add incremental predictive validity to the selection process (Handler, Honts, Krapohl,

Nelson, & Griffin, 2009) by providing information that has not hitherto been part of the process. Polygraph tests are intended to be used as a screening tool to identify unacceptable behaviors that are a risk to the integrity of the position of a police officer. However, polygraphs are controversial and not legal in certain contexts. Within law enforcement and due to the safety sensitive nature of the work, police departments continue to use polygraphs but often do not use them as the sole determinant for disqualifying an applicant (Handler et al., 2009). Polygraph tests are frequently used as *decision support* or as an extra source of information in the selection process. In addition, polygraph tests tend to deter unsuitable applicants from applying because they are uncomfortable with the idea of the test (Handler et al., 2009).

However, there are some potential problems with the tool. Polygraphs often result in a false positive, identifying someone as lying when in fact they are telling the truth. To a lesser degree, polygraphs result in false negatives, identifying someone as telling the truth when they are falsifying information.

To ensure that the polygraph test is helping the selection system and not creating issues, some have recommended that polygraph examiners be well trained, have a strict protocol, and be observed and evaluated frequently (Handler et al., 2009). Also, only issues relevant to police selection should be discussed in these types of interviews, such as tolerance-related issues, past criminal conduct, illegal drug use, and formal disciplinary actions from previous employers. The information gathered from these types of questions is critical to selecting police officers but is easily falsified using other selection tools. Thus, a polygraph may be useful for gathering this type of specific information.

Creating a selection process that will result in the desired outcomes for a police department is a daunting task. It requires a thorough understanding of the job as it is performed in that department, a clear set of tests/exercises/hurdles that candidates must pass, and consistency in the administration of all tests to all candidates. It further requires a great deal of expertise and the use of tools that have proven effectiveness in terms of validity. In addition, modern police departments seek to be representative of the people they serve so any selection system must result in a diverse set of officers. Over the past several decades, police agencies have created successful systems that incorporate a variety of tests and other assessment procedures. Departments wishing to build a system or revamp the one currently in use have opportunities to learn from the science and practice of police officer selection.

PROMOTIONAL TESTING: A BRIEF OVERVIEW

Organizations create structure by moving individuals from lower level jobs into positions of supervision and management. In so doing, they use a variety of strategies including hiring leaders from other organizations and moving individuals within the organization up to positions of greater responsibility. In most settings, although not often in police departments, a combination of external and internal candidates become leaders. Regardless of who makes up the candidate pool, the success of the promotional process will determine the success of the organization as a whole.

Promotions represent an opportunity to enhance the skills and abilities of individuals, put people in positions where they can do the same for those reporting to them, and help the organization grow and prosper. Conversely, poor promotional systems can run the risk of identifying the people not capable of performing the job. Worse, these wrongly promoted individuals can poison the well, making capable participants who were not promoted look at the outcome with contempt and cause such unwanted consequences as negative job attitudes, insubordination, lower levels of work motivation, and ultimately higher levels of employee turnover.

Formal promotions procedures serve to create a more salient link between employee performance and organizational rewards (Greenberg, 1986). For employees who have long-term plans to be in an organization, the expectation for promotion can have positive effects on performance. For example, one study shows that employees are more willing to forgive instances of inequity in an organization if they believe the long-term rewards of organizational membership outweigh the costs (Kaplan & Ferris, 2001). The opposite can also occur, as individuals who had initially expected promotions become disenchanted with the system within their organization, develop the perception that they are working in a dead-end job, and thus decrease effort (Kaplan & Ferris, 2001). Thus, even how a worker is considered for promotion can have important organizational outcomes.

An important point about promotions is their limited quantity. The likelihood of promotion is often less predictable than other outcomes such as annual salary increases and places greater importance on each promotion since the next opportunity will occur at an unspecified future time (Kaplan & Ferris, 2001). For example, in a study of nonacademic employees in a large university, the greater the amount of time between promotion availability, the more organizational politics and job-related stress occurred (Ferris et al., 1996). Moreover, the pay structure in most organizations flattens out after a few years, and individuals may see promotions as a way to increase their incomes. However, employees considered for promotion should be interested in the new job duties and responsibilities that come with the promotion instead of focusing on the rewards (Scarborough, Van Tubergen, Gaines, & Whitlow, 1999). The limited quantity of promotions can sometimes create competition and animosity within an organization.

For all of the above reasons, promotions are a key ingredient to the successful operation of any organization. A well-developed system of promotions can add to the capability of the organization not only at the level of the promotion but also for all those who interact with the promoted individuals. On the opposite end of the spectrum, substandard promotion systems can threaten the well-being of an organization in terms of future performance and in the way individuals evaluate the quality of their organization.

POLICE PROMOTIONS

The promotions process in law enforcement has many similarities to selecting new officers in that some individuals receive the new job while others do not. Like selection, there are two desired or correct outcomes when it comes to promotions; those who are qualified get the new, higher level job and those who are not qualified do not. Similarly, two potential errors exist. We can promote an unqualified person to a position of greater authority or reject someone who would be successful in that new position. The quality of our system is dependent on the degree to which we maximize the first two and minimize the second two. What distinguishes promotional systems from selection systems designed to add new employees to the organization is the following:

- Applicants for promotions already work within the organization (almost always).
- A great deal more information about each candidate is available.
- Testing for more of the knowledge, skills, and abilities of the job is possible.
- Unsuccessful candidates remain part of the organization and require attention.

These differences create unique opportunities and challenges for departments when it comes to the tricky business of making promotions (Scarborough et al., 1992). For police departments, a variety of tools and techniques have been created over the years from such diverse influences as the research literature on promotions to union–management agreements that specify the use of certain types of tests or ban the use of others. The challenge lies in putting tools into practice that result in the identification of those truly ready for advancement, the perception of justice by participating officers, and the fair inclusion of all.

Current Programs in Use

Many promotional procedures currently in use in today's police department start with a detailed understanding of the positions considered via a job analysis, which typically includes (1) a review of the job tasks frequently performed or considered very important even if they are not encountered often, (2) the required abilities that allow individuals to perform these tasks, and (3) the knowledge associated with performance of these tasks. Departments approach the development of promotional systems from a content validity perspective where the goal is to create a system in which the test components match up closely with the actual job requirements. Typically, applicants are given a job knowledge test assessing their expertise on laws, rules, and procedures. This test is often followed by a formalized panel interview in which candidates are asked to respond to situations typical of what they would find should they assume the next-level position. The job knowledge test is usually presented in a written format with multiple-choice questions. The panel interview is conducted by a team of assessors and often involves responding to two or more simulated situations. Scores on the two phases are combined to form the promotion score. The method of combining the information varies from one department to another.

Interestingly enough, one piece of potentially valuable information rarely sees its way into the promotional process. Officers considered for promotion are almost always in the rank immediately lower than the one where the competition is taking place. In some instances, departments allow officers to *skip* ranks but this is the exception and not the rule (Maurer, Solomon, & Troxtel, 1998). Departments have a tremendous amount of relevant job performance information on virtually everyone considered for promotion in the form of what those officers have been doing in their current job or role (Harvey, 1999). Since in most police organizations the move from one position (police officer) to the next (police sergeant) often involved many of the same responsibilities and tasks, using past performance makes sense because it gives a clear indication on how the officer will perform on part of the new job if promoted. It is important to note that this is an untapped information pool for most promotional systems. It remains untapped because of the difficulty in extracting that information in what would be perceived by all as an accurate and fair manner.

Still, in some systems performance appraisal does play a role, and it is important to cite not only the usefulness of these types of data but also how we might incorporate them into the promotion process. As an example, one jurisdiction we have worked with for over a decade uses past performance as a qualifier for admission to the promotion process. This system is designed to keep those who the department feels are undeserving of promotion out of the process. At the outset, when promotion opportunities are announced, all interested officers apply. Once the applications are closed, all those who have applied are evaluated by their immediate supervisors, and that rating is further evaluated/approved by a second-level supervisor. If a promotion candidate is seen as problematic based on past performance, the candidate is notified that he or she will not receive further consideration for promotion. This seems to be the best way to incorporate some form of past performance into the process, although it certainly does not take full advantage of all we know about those working for us. Alternatives such as gathering performance scores and entering them into the combination of scores that result in an overall promotion ranking are possible. However, given the suspicion associated with how those performance scores are determined, the bias that may be inherent in them, and issues surrounding supervisor–subordinate interactions all conspire to make such a plan problematic and seldom used.

Applicant Reactions to Promotional Systems

Applicant reactions to the promotion process can be categorized into two different types of perceptions of fairness: satisfaction with the fairness of the promotions process and system (procedural justice) and satisfaction with the fairness of the decision or outcome (distributive justice). Of the two types of potential injustice perceptions, the latter is far more frequent than the former. In many departments, the promotions system procedures either have been well accepted over time or have been the result of union–management negotiations and therefore have been created with an eye toward what is acceptable to participants. An example of distributive justice in this context is an officer who believes the promotion system is fair while he or she is going through the promotions process, but no longer believes in the system because his or her name is not on the list of those to be promoted. This is often the case because we hear very few complaints about the process when it is underway and immediately following the actual tests, but many issues are brought to the surface once the list of promotions is published. Perceptions of justice are critical as they can influence future job satisfaction of officers, self-esteem for those unsuccessful in getting promoted, and organizational climate for all involved (Truxillo & Bauer, 1999).

These perceptions of promotion system fairness do not occur in a vacuum. Previous encounters with organizational human resource functions, such as performance appraisals, will influence officer reactions to promotion decisions (Kaplan & Ferris, 2001). For example, if an officer received an unfairly harsh evaluation that year, she may have less faith in the organizational leadership. The opposite is also possible; an officer who received a steady stream of positive feedback may have higher expectations of organizational rewards. These perceptions serve as a backdrop when it comes to evaluating how fair the promotion system was in identifying the truly talented officers under consideration.

Consequently, it may be very hard to create a promotion program seen as fair when other processes within the department are viewed as lacking in credibility. The importance of these perceptions cannot be overstated. A key difference in promotion—compared to selection—is that the unsuccessful candidate continues to work in the organization. Departments around the world have experiences with those who wanted to be promoted and were not. When officers feel the system is fair both in terms of procedure and outcome, there are relatively few issues once promotions are made; however, when the procedure and/or outcomes are seen as unfair, many dysfunctional behaviors follow for officers who were unsuccessful. These include lower levels of job satisfaction, disengagement from the job in the form of poor subsequent performance, increased use of time off, and insubordination toward those who were promoted and seen as unworthy.

Validation

One step that is critical from both a logical and a legal perspective is the validation of the individual tests that make up the promotion system and the total system as a decision-making process. As indicated in the preceding discussion, promotion systems in law enforcement almost always involve a content validation strategy. This process of validating the tests and the system requires those associated with creating the system to show the job-relatedness of each step in the process by linking what is required on the test to what is required on the job. While using a strong content validity approach helps to enhance the quality of the individual assessment tools and ultimately the quality of the promotion decisions that result from using the system, content validation also can be an important step in building trust in the system by those participating. The validation process is beyond the scope of this chapter, but it is clearly a major consideration in building and evaluating an effective promotion system.

Affirmative Action and Promotions

There are many misperceptions about affirmative action, but in its truest form it basically states that when two candidates are equal in every way, an organization will take affirmative steps to hire and promote those from underrepresented groups. This puts quite a burden on a promotion system because it requires a conclusion that two candidates are identical in terms of their qualifications. Most police departments rely on promotion scores that result in very fine discriminations so that they do not have to use such things as race or gender as *tie breakers* as many perceive such a process unfair or biased to a particular group.

In contrast, many departments have been under consent decrees or are currently under such mechanisms designed to create greater minority representation among those in promoted positions. Consent decrees are agreements departments make through the legal process to make up for past unfair practices that resulted in lower levels of diversity by promoting individuals who are qualified but may not be quite as qualified as other participants in the system. While these decrees serve a specific important purpose, they also can have the unwanted consequence of decreasing the perceptions of fairness in the overall promotion process.

There have been some suggestions for mitigating the perceptions of unfairness with regard to promotion decisions influenced by affirmative action. Previous work by Heilman and colleagues (Heilman, Lucas, & Kaplow, 1990; Heilman, Simon, & Repper, 1987) has suggested that negative reactions to promotional decisions based on affirmative actions can be mitigated by emphasizing the promoted employee's merits rather than group identity. This would require a follow-up process to the publishing of a promotion list and should include all those who are promoted and not just those who may have received special consideration.

In addition, Bobocel and Farrell (1996) suggest that the way in which information about the system is transmitted to participants and future promotional candidates may be more important than how the decision was made. In a study of people's perceptions of fairness about affirmative action promotion decisions in police department scenarios, explanations of promotional decisions were perceived as most fair when the leadership provided justifications for promotions decisions. More specifically, participants rated an explanation that "diversifying the workplace would make it more effective" as less fair than an explanation where the woman was promoted over the man because "historically, qualified women did not have the same access to jobs and promotions and we should attempt to reduce this disparity whenever the opportunity is present." It is possible to increase perceptions of fairness in affirmative action promotion decisions by providing detailed information about the process. Saal and Moore (1993) studied reactions to affirmative action promotions and concluded that the process is problematic and often results in conclusions of unfairness that are difficult to overcome. Their work looked specifically at gender effects and highlight potential issues facing police departments as they move to better represent women in leadership positions. While the creation of a fair promotion process is difficult, dealing with the outcomes of the system represents additional challenges as we seek to not only promote the right people but also make sure they can do their jobs once promotions are made.

Considerations After Promotions

Changes in roles, while most often seen as a very positive step, can be a source of stress for newly promoted officers. Promoted officers need some guidance and support from their superior officers as they make the transition from officer to sergeant or from lieutenant to captain. The interpersonal dynamics in the department will change when an officer is suddenly in a supervisory or leadership position above his or her previous peers or cohorts during academy days. The promotion system can help identify the most talented, but it does not fully prepare them for the new responsibilities and social situations. In many ways, testing is asked to do too much and we ignore the fact that other opportunities exist to enhance the process of successfully moving people into the promoted position. While the test does supply the right people, providing training for the newly promoted officers is an important part of the promotions process and not always the focus of evaluating its overall success.

Gaston and King's (1995) survey of police officers in the United Kingdom revealed recently promoted officers' views on their formal promotion training. When asked which topics were most useful for training, 90% answered "developing managerial skills," which included people management, time management, team building and leadership, interpersonal and communication skills, motivation, and appraisal of subordinates. Two-thirds of respondents believed an external management training program, which would cover these broad topics rather than those specific to police work, would be useful because it would bring a wider perspective for their duties. In addition, 78% of respondents had experienced stress in the process, with role ambiguity cited as the most frequent stressor. Many department neglect this step in their promotion planning and simply *sew on the stripes* hoping that the required behaviors for the new position will suddenly appear or have been guaranteed through the testing process. Most departments lack the internal training programs or the financial resources to make them available to newly promoted officers.

Mentoring programs may also help newly promoted officers cope with their expanded roles. A mentoring program could consist of a more experienced sergeant reviewing the newly promoted sergeant's performance on a regular basis or being available to answer questions and provide perspective. Within police work, there is a precedent for such activities as most departments have a Field Training Officer assigned to new officers. Mentoring simply moves the process up the organizational hierarchy. The program can be structured by the department, with formally recognized meetings and evaluations, or it can be a more informal process where new sergeants seek out help from those with greater levels of experience as supervisors and leaders. The department may even wish to implement training programs for mentors to support their progress.

There are several positive outcomes that can follow from a well-developed and properly implemented promotion process. Officers who receive promotions may have more positive reactions to their work environment. Their new role will provide challenges and opportunities for personal and professional growth. A promotion is also an indication that the officer is no longer entry level within the department, and it is a public acknowledgement that he or she has increased value to the organization as well as an affirmation of their leadership qualities.

Well-developed promotional systems can have positive consequences for all participants, even those who do not succeed. When officers are required to study materials critical to successful job performance, they increase their job-related abilities. The very nature of studying for the promotion exam can enhance performance of individuals and raise the level of performance for the entire department. For example, officers studying for exams often identify departmental rules and regulations no longer practiced and accordingly update the documentation of operations. Finally, in the best promotional exams, both successful and unsuccessful candidates receive feedback regarding their performance. When properly done, this feedback improves subsequent job performance and can better prepare candidates who wish to compete next time around.

Selecting the best officers for promotion is clearly critical to the organization's future success, but it should not be the only goal of the promotions process. The perceived fairness of the process can have important outcomes for the department. Since the applicants who were not selected will still be members of the department, those who are not selected for promotions may be just as impactful to the organizations as those selected. Unlike other rewards that can be distributed equally to several employees, the difference between a person who receives a promotion and a person who does not can be substantial (Kaplan & Ferris, 2001). Thus, the department has a responsibility to make the promotions system as fair, transparent, and valid as possible.

Gaining Support From System Participants

Applicant reactions to any personnel decision-making system are important to consider for multiple reasons. Applicants who react positively to a promotion system tend to view the organization more positively and are more likely to adapt to the new job more quickly. They are also more likely to speak to others about the department in positive terms (Hausknecht et al., 2004). In addition, candidate reactions may be related to filing legal complaints, such that those that perceive the selection or promotion system as being invalid or negative in some way are more likely to file complaints (Hausknecht, et al., 2004). From a more cynical perspective, we have often described the outcomes of a poorly developed and implemented sergeant promotion process as resulting in two groups of individuals, new sergeants and plaintiffs. Clearly this overstates the point, but it should be noted that spending time gaining support for the promotion process can have positive outcomes once the list of promotions is made public. While applicants' reactions are often determined by their outcome in the process (Ryan & Ployhart, 2000), it is possible for applicants to focus attention away from the exclusive consideration of whether they were promoted to the broader and more inclusive perspective of whether the process was fair to all who participated (Truxillo & Bauer, 1999; Truxillo, Bauer, Campion, & Paronto, 2002).

CONCLUDING THOUGHTS

It is simply impossible to overstate the importance of selection and promotion systems in contributing to the effectiveness of a police department. Unlike many other organizations, most if not all of the talent that comes into a police department enters during the selection process for new officers. This puts a premium on the accurate identification of individuals who can perform the difficult and demanding duties of a police officer and develop the skills and abilities necessary to move up the ranks. The same is true of promotions since most departments rely on some form of successful performance at a lower rank as eligibility to move into the next position in the hierarchy. This chapter discussed the importance of treating selection and promotion as processes that have more than the single objective of accurate assessment of individuals so that employment decision making is based on sound information. Readers thinking about promotion systems in their organizations should consider that in addition to picking the right people for future performance, selection and promotion systems must be acceptable to the participants, help in building the skills and abilities of all individuals participating, and should result in a pool of selected individuals who reflect the department and more broadly the diverse community it serves. The road to success in human resources decision making is filled with potholes that need to be effectively navigated while balancing desired outcomes with best practices to fulfill the needs of the police department.

REFERENCES

Alliger, G. M., & Dwight, S. A. (2000). A meta-analytic investigation of the susceptibility of integrity tests to faking and coaching. *Educational and Psychological Measurement, 60*, 59–72.

Barrick, M. R., & Zimmerman, R. D. (2005). Reducing voluntary, avoidable turnover through selection. *Journal of Applied Psychology, 90*, 159–166.

Berry, C. M., Gruys, M. L., & Sackett, P. R. (2006). Educational attainment as proxy for cognitive ability in selection: Effects on levels of cognitive ability and adverse impact. *Journal of Applied Psychology, 91*, 696–705.

Bobko, P., Roth, P. L., & Buster, M. A. (2005). Work sample selection tests and expected reduction in adverse impact: A cautionary note. *International Journal of Selection and Assessment, 13*, 1–10.

Bobocel, D. R., & Farrell, A. C. (1996). Sex-based promotion decisions and interactional fairness: Investigating the influence of managerial accounts. *Journal of Applied Psychology, 81*, 22–35.

Camara, W. J., & Schneider, D. L. (1995). Questions of construct breadth and openness of research in integrity testing. *American Psychologist, 50*, 459–460.

Campion, M. A., Outtz, J. L., Zedeck, S., Schmidt, F. L., Kehoe, J. F., Murphy, K. R., & Guion, R. M. (2001). The controversy over score banding in personnel selection: Answers to 10 key questions. *Personnel Psychology, 54*, 149–185.

Cascio, W. F., Jacobs, R. R., & Silva, J. (2010). Validity, utility and adverse impact: Practical implications from 30 years of data. In J. Outtz (Ed.), *Adverse impact*. Hoboken, NJ: Lawrence Erlbaum.

Chapman, D. S., & Zweig, D. I. (2005). Developing a nomological network for interview structure: Antecedents and consequences of the structured selection interview. *Personnel Psychology, 58*, 673–702.

Clevenger, J., Pereira, G. M., Wiechmann, D., Schmitt, N., & Harvey, V. S. (2001). Incremental validity of situational judgment tests. *Journal of Applied Psychology, 86*, 41–417.

Cochrane, R. E., Tett, R. P., & Vandecreek, L. (2003). Psychological testing and the selection of police officers. *Criminal Justice and Behavior, 30*, 511–537.

Costa, P. T., Jr., & McRae, R. R. (1992). *NEO-PI-R professional manual*. Odessa, FL: Psychological Assessment Resources.

Dayan, K., Kasten, R., & Fox, S. (2002). Entry-level police candidate assessment center: An efficient tool or a hammer to kill a fly? *Personnel Psychology, 55*, 827–849.

Detrick, P., & Chibnall, J. T. (2002). Prediction of police officer performance with the Inwald Personality Inventory. *Journal of Police and Criminal Psychology, 17*, 9–17.

Detrick, P., Chibnall, J. T., & Luebbert, M. C. (2004). The revised NEO personality inventory as predictor of police academy performance. *Criminal Justice and Behavior, 31*, 676–694.

Drew, J., Carless, S. A., & Thompson, B. M. (2008). Predicting turnover of police officers using sixteen personality factor questionnaire. *Journal of Criminal Justice, 36*, 326–331.

Ellingson, J. E., Sackett, P. R., & Connelly, B. S. (2007). Personality assessment across selection and development contexts: Insights into response distortion. *Journal of Applied Psychology*, *92*, 386–395.

Ferris, G. R., Frink, D. D., Galang, M. C., Zhou, J., Kacmar, K. M., & Howard, J. L. (1996). Perceptions of organizational politics: Prediction, stress-related implications, and outcomes. *Human Relations*, *49*, 233–266.

Gaston, K., & King, L. (1995). Management development and training in the police: a survey of the promotion process. *Journal of European Industrial Training*, *19*, 20–25.

Gilliland, S. W. (1993). The perceived fairness of selection systems: An organizational justice perspective. *Academy of Management Review*, *18*, 694–734.

Greenberg, J. (1986). Determinants of perceived fairness of performance evaluations. *Journal of Applied Psychology*, *71*, 340–342.

Guion, R. M. (1998). *Assessment, measurement, and prediction for personnel decisions*. Mahwah, NJ: Lawrence Erlbaum.

Gutman, A. (2004). Ground rules for adverse impact. *The Industrial-Organizational Psychologist*, *41*, 109–119.

Haaland, S., & Christiansen, N. D. (2002). Implications of trait-activation theory for evaluating the construct validity of assessment centre ratings. *Personnel Psychology*, *55*, 137–163.

Handler, M., Honts, C. R., Krapohl, D. J., Nelson, R., & Griffin, S. (2009). Integration of pre-employment polygraph screening into the police selection process. *Journal of Police and Criminal Psychology*, *24*, 69–86.

Harvey, A. J. (1999). Promotion time: 10 questions to ask yourself before taking the plunge. *The Police Chief*, *66*, 84–87.

Hausknecht, J., Day, D., & Thomas, S. (2004). Applicant reactions to selection procedures: An updated model and meta-analysis. *Personnel Psychology*, *57*, 1–45.

Heilman, M. E., Lucas, J. A., & Kaplow, S. R. (1990). Self-derogating consequences of sex-based preferential selection: The moderating role of initial self-confidence. *Organizational Behavior and Human Decision Processes*, *46*, 202–216.

Heilman, M. E., Simon, M. C., & Repper, D. P. (1987). Intentionally favored, unintentionally harmed? Impact of sex based preferential selection on self-perceptions and self-evaluations. *Journal of Applied Psychology*, *72*, 62–68.

Hogan, J., Barrett, P., & Hogan, R. (2007). Personality measurement, faking, and employment selection. *Journal of Applied Psychology*, *92*, 1270–1285.

Hogan, J., & Brinkmeyer, K. (1997). Bridging the gap between overt and personality-based integrity tests. *Personnel Psychology*, *50*, 587–599.

Hough, L. M. (2003). Emerging trends and needs in personality research and practice beyond main effects. In M. B. Barrick & A. M. Ryan (Eds.), *Personality and work: Reconsidering the role of personality in organizations* (pp. 289–325). San Francisco: Jossey-Bass.

Hough, L. M., Eaton, N. K., Dunnette, M. D., Kamp, J. D., & McCloy, R. A. (1990). Criterion-related validity of personality constructs and the effect of response distortion on those validities. *Journal of Applied Psychology*, *75*, 581–895.

Huffcutt, A. I., Conway, J. M., Roth, P. L., & Stone, N. J. (2001). Identification and meta-analytic assessment of psychological constructs measured in employment interviews. *Journal of Applied Psychology*, *86*, 897–913.

Inwald, R. (1988). Five-year follow-up study of department terminations as predicted by 16 pre-employment psychological indicators. *Journal of Applied Psychology*, *73*, 703–710.

Inwald, R. (1992). *Inwald Personality Inventory technical manual (revised)*. New York: Hilson Research.

Kaplan, D. M., & Ferris, G. R. (2001). Fairness perceptions of employee promotion systems: A two-study investigation of antecedents and mediators. *Journal of Applied Social Psychology*, *31*, 1204–1222.

Lilienfeld, S. O., Alliger, G., & Mitchell, K. (1995). Why integrity testing remains controversial. *American Psychologist*, *50*, 457–458.

Lonsway, K. A. (2003). Tearing down the wall: Problems with consistency, validity, and adverse impact of physical agility testing in police selection. *Police Quarterly*, *6*, 237–277.

Mael, F., Connerley, M., & Morath, R. A. (1996). None of your business: Parameters of biodata invasiveness. *Personnel Psychology*, *49*, 613–650.

Martin, S. E., & Jurik, N. C. (1996). *Doing justice, doing gender: Women in law and criminal justice occupations*. Thousand Oaks, CA: Sage.

Maurer, T., Solomon, J., & Troxtel, D. (1998). Relationship of coaching with performance in situational employment interviews. *Journal of Applied Psychology*, *83*, 128–136.

McDaniel, M. A., Morgeson, F. P, Finnegan, E. B., Campion, M. A., & Braverman, E. P. (2001). Use of situational judgment tests to predict job performance: A clarification of the literature. *Journal of Applied Psychology, 86,* 730–740.

McFarland, L. A., & Ryan, A. M. (2000). Variance in faking across noncognitive measures. *Journal of Applied Psychology, 85,* 812–821.

McHenry, J. J., Hough, L. M., Toquam, J. L., Hanson, M. A., & Ashworth, S. (1990). Project A validity results: The relationship between predictor and criterion domains. *Personnel Psychology, 43,* 335–355.

Mikulay, S. M., & Goffin, R. D. (1998). Measuring and predicting counterproductivity in the laboratory using integrity and personality testing. *Educational and Psychological Measurement, 58,* 768–790.

Murphy, K. R. (1993). *Honesty in the workplace.* Pacific Grove, CA: Brooks/Cole.

Neuman, G. A., & Baydoun, R. (1998). An empirical examination of overt and covert integrity tests. *Journal of Business and Psychology, 13,* 65–79.

Posthuma, R. A., Morgeson, F. P., & Campion, M. A. (2002). Beyond employment interview validity: A comprehensive narrative review of recent research and trends over time. *Personnel Psychology, 55,* 1–81.

Pynes, J., & Bernardin, H. J. (1992). Entry-level police selection: The assessment center is an alternative. *Journal of Criminal Justice, 20,* 41–52.

Ryan, A. M., & Ployhart, R. E. (2000). Applicants' perceptions of selection procedures and decisions: A critical review and agenda for the future. *Journal of Management, 26,* 565–606.

Saal, F. E., & Moore, S. C. (1993). Perceptions of promotion fairness and promotion candidates' qualifications. *Journal of Applied Psychology, 78,* 105–110.

Sacco, J. M., Scheu, C. R., Ryan, A. M., & Schmitt, N. (2003). An investigation of race and sex similarity effects in interviews: A multilevel approach to relational demography. *Journal of Applied Psychology, 88,* 852–865.

Sackett, P. R., Burris, L. R., & Callahan, C. (1989). Integrity testing for personnel selection: An update. *Personnel Psychology, 42,* 491–529.

Sackett, P. R., De Corte, W., & Lievens, F. (2010). Decision aids for addressing the validity-adverse impact trade-off. In J. L. Outtz (Ed.), *Adverse impact: Implications for organizational staffing and high stakes selection* (pp. 453–472). New York: Routledge.

Sackett, P. R., Schmitt, N., Ellingson, J. E., & Kabin, M. B. (2001). High-stakes testing in employment, credentialing, and higher education: Prospects in a post-affirmative action world. *American Psychologist, 56,* 302–318.

Sackett, P. R., & Wilk, S. L. (1994). Within-group norming and other forms of score adjustment in preemployment testing. *American Psychologist, 49,* 929–954.

Scarborough, K. E., Van Tubergen, G. N., Gaines, L. K., & Whitlow, S. S. (1999). An examination of police officers' motivation to participate in the promotional process. *Police Quarterly, 2,* 302–320.

Schmidt, F. L., & Hunter, J. E. (1998). The validity and utility of selection methods in personnel psychology: Practical and theoretical implications of 85 years or research findings. *Psychological Bulletin, 124,* 262–274.

Scogin, F., Schumacher, J., Gardner, J., & Chaplin, W. (1995). Predictive validity of psychological testing in law enforcement settings. *Professional Psychological Research and Practice, 26,* 68–71.

Scrivner, E. (2001). *Innovations in police recruitment and hiring: Hiring in the spirit of service.* Washington, DC: Community of Oriented Police Service, U.S. Department of Justice.

Thornton, G. C., III, & Rupp, D. E. (2006). *Assessment centers in human resource management: Strategies for prediction, diagnosis, and development.* Mahwah, NJ: Lawrence Erlbaum.

Truxillo, D. M., & Bauer, T. N. (1999). Applicant reactions to test score banding in entry-level and promotional contexts. *Journal of Applied Psychology, 84,* 322–339.

Truxillo, D. M., Bauer, T. N., Campion, M. A., & Paronto, M. E. (2002). Selection fairness information and applicant reactions: A longitudinal field study. *Journal of Applied Psychology, 87,* 1020–1031.

Wiener, J. (1994). *Physical abilities test: Follow-up validation study.* Sacramento, CA: POST.

10 The Integration Section of Forensic Psychological Evaluation Reports in Law Enforcement
Culturally Responsive Ending Words

Ronn Johnson

INTRODUCTION

The integration section (I-Section) is a critical part of most forensic psychological evaluation reports. This is especially true for reports written for law enforcement personnel. The I-Section refers to that portion of the report in which the examiner analyzes, prioritizes, and synthesizes significant elements of the evaluation data in order to render opinions leading to recommendations (Melton et al., 2007; Sattler, 1988). In general, writing the I-Section involves crafting a conceptual model of the examinee that addresses questions about the individual's functioning in a number of different domains. The I-Section relies on various sources to support the examiner's opinions and recommendations (Ackerman, 2006). Multiple data sources are used in the I-Section to support evidence-based explanations for findings that might otherwise appear vague or weakly supported (Cates, 1999). Integrated reports rely on good clinical judgment skills (Groth-Marnat & Horvath, 2006), and the I-Section is a measure of the standard of practice used by forensic psychologists when conducting psychological interviews, for example, pre-employment evaluations, special unit assignments, and fitness-for-duty (FFD) examinations. For instance, did the examiner adhere to the ethical demands of forensic assessments, for example, providing notification to the examinee regarding the purposes of the evaluation and any limitations on confidentiality? The I-Section is not, however, the final word. One important objective of the I-Section is to provide clear and convincing evidence that persuasively communicates the examiner's "culturally responsive ending words" represented in her or his opinions and recommendations (Melton et al., 2007). This objective is best achieved by establishing an evidence-based (i.e., data-driven) foundation in the report (Goodheart, Kazdin, & Sternberg, 2006).

The I-Section is written in a conclusory framework. It is used to help agency/departmental decision makers or legal authorities become more fully informed and knowledgeable consumers of forensic psychological evaluations (International Association of Chiefs of Police [IACP], 1998). Several factors underscore the importance of the I-Section. Agency/departmental decision makers must be able to (1) understand the importance of the psychologist's opinions and recommendations, (2) understand the basic principles of the forensic psychological evaluation process and the specific role of the I-Section, and (3) evaluate the quality of the written psychological report via the I-Section. The I-Section is thus an extension of applicable laws and codes or relevant departmental policies.

Special care must be taken when writing the I-Section. First, the ethical principles and guidelines for forensic psychologists (American Psychiatric Association, 2000) speak to issues relevant to the I-Section. APA codes direct psychologists to base their opinions on information and techniques sufficient to substantiate their findings. Psychologists provide such opinions only after they have conducted a thorough examination of the examinee adequate to support their final conclusions (i.e., *ending words*) in the I-Section. The ending words of the I-Section must be communicated in ways that promote understanding through a forceful presentation of the data on which the conclusion is based (Melton et al., 2007). The specific content, structure, format, and substance are determined by the relevant psycho-legal issue(s) at hand as well as the laws or rules in the jurisdiction in which the work was completed (American Board of Forensic Psychology [ABFP], 2009).

Second, the assessment points for I-Section content are best anchored to a widely recognized system of job relevant domains, for example, the California Commission on Peace Officer Standards and Training (POST). Thus, the psychological screening dimensions for a patrol officer should include positive and counterproductive behaviors that must be included as the foundation for recommendations in the I-Section. Aamodt (2004b) reviewed investigations using personality variables to assess different police performance outcomes and stressed the importance of personal dispositions for predicting performance in these contexts. POST facilitates the psychologist's use of job-relevant dimensions when crafting the I-Section.

Third, concerns about negligent hire or retention issues later manifest themselves through officer-involved shootings, excessive use-of-force charges, collateral injuries or death secondary to pursuit chases, inattention to detail, off-duty misconduct, or otherwise rude behaviors. For example, the I-Section assumes the added burden of trying to avoid a potential negligent hire or retention; the impact may not surface until 5 years after the report is written (Johnson & Scott, 2009). Regardless of the specific standard a forensic psychologist may elect to use, legal consequences to examinees' behavior can be traced back to the psychological component of the hiring process.

Any perceived officer misconduct can serve as a basis for a lawsuit. Legal pitfalls or the threat of liability underscore the pivotal role the I-Section can play (Melton et al., 2007; Davis & Rostow, 2004). The I-Section outlines the basis of psychological decisions and recommendations made by forensic psychologists when evaluating personnel for safety sensitive positions. In the end, an agency/department relies on the opinions and recommendations made in the I-Section, which can point to aggressive behavior, poor judgment, or other dangerous propensities. An agency/department may be liable for negligent hiring if it knew (or should have known) that the officer posed a threat to others at the post–job offer phase, at the FTO phase, or later. Likewise, an agency/department can be held liable for negligent retention if it continues to employ an officer knowing of his or her problematic behavioral characteristics. In the end, the I-Section should be written as if it is a legal document that will be read in open court (Melton et al., 2007).

Forensic psychologists writing I-Sections must keep an eye on the elements that play a role in reducing negligent hiring issues. An awareness of negligent hiring and retention can be enhanced through several ethically based factors. First, there is a duty owed by the agency/department in selecting or retaining an officer; second, a breach of that duty can occur as a consequence of an officer's on- or off-duty behavior; and third, that breach of duty could result in an injury to a third party, and the agency/department and psychologist could be liable for damages (Knapp & VandeCreek, 2006). The examiner's opinions, recommendations, suitability ratings, and reservations must be presented in the I-Section in a transparent way. There is cause for some relief when we note that only a relatively low percentage of problem officers, as the Christopher Commission found in an investigation of the Los Angeles Police Department (LAPD) after the 1991 beating of Rodney King. The Commission noted that fewer than one-half of 1% of LAPD officers accounted for 15% of citizen complaints of excessive force or improper tactics. Moreover, the Commission noted that this disproportion could not be explained by assignment or arrest rates, implying these problem officers simply had a proclivity toward deviance (Independent Commission on the Los Angeles Police Department, 1991).

Police misconduct is, however, low in comparison to the general population. The controversy over peace officer misconduct is fueled by the high-profile nature of the resulting media coverage due to the perceived breach of public trust. As we will discuss in more detail, forensic psychologists must remain attentive to cultural, ethnic, gender, race, and sexual orientation issues as they conduct evaluations and craft the I-Section. Cross-culturally, the standards for peace officers are much higher than that for civilians (Borum, Super, & Rand, 2003; Rostow & Davis, 2004).

The I-Section must be crafted in a way that reflects the advanced clinical judgment of the psychologist and represents a convergence of practice and science. It is the most analytically complex portion of the pre-employment psychological report. The assessment is usually accomplished through an examination of the examinee's attitudes, emotions, overt behaviors, and personal disposition considered relevant for the position. The I-Section functions like a report (within a report) on risk assessment issues, but it is not a summary of the main report (Johnson, 2009; Tallent, 1988). General factors are examined to strengthen the psychologist's conclusions and recommendations in the I-Section. It should be noted that it is wise to never stitch together hunches and speculation, which serve only to weaken the credibility of the examiner's recommendations. Nietzel and Hartung (1993) stress that an officer's ability to perform his or her various job duties, as well as handle the interpersonal demands, must be presented through convincing, evidenced-based arguments. The examiner's skill in synthesizing, analyzing, accepting, and rejecting hypotheses while offering a clear and convincing rationale for opinions offered is a *sine qua non* of the I-Section.

Challenges to the examiners' opinions can originate from any number of sources. For instance, applicant appeals, internal departmental reviews, and even possible litigation stem from the actions taken by an officer recommended by a forensic psychologist (Borum et al., 2003). An examiner must assume that the I-Section may serve as the basis for a script outline used by an opposing attorney while scrutinizing the work of the examiner (Melton et al., 2007). The format and scope of the I-Section may be the subject of debate and widespread variation, depending on the skills set of the examiner, the purpose of the report, and departmental needs. The forensic psychologist must operate in a system when a nonpsychologist/nonadministrator dictates the scope of work in the report area. The goal of this chapter is to offer guidance to qualified police psychologists on how to approach crafting the I-Section.

The clinical judgment of the psychologist working in this context of report writing cannot be ethically abandoned through the clerical expediency of a non-research-based report template. Nor should computerized reports that identify large samples be used in the absence of independent review through exhaustive studies in peer-reviewed journals for those computer-based reports (Johnson, 2009). Each I-Section must be individualized for the examinee based on the parameters of POST, IACP, relevant code/statutes, culturally responsive assessment techniques, and evidence-based, structured clinical judgment (Melton et al., 2007).

This chapter is organized into three sections. The first section discusses the cultural context in which the I-Section is crafted. The second section provides information on the basic principles and a forensic decision-making model (FDM) for the I-Section. Finally, conclusions and implications for training and research are discussed.

CULTURAL ISSUES AND THE I-SECTION

Culture matters in police and peace officer work. Current psychometric practice must be culturally responsive for several reasons. First, APA ethical standards, ethnic minority standards, and ABFP guidelines stress culture as a core examiner competency, and cultural responsiveness should be exercised through the preparation of a I-Section of pre-employment examinations and FFDEs (APA, 2002; Rostow & Davis, 2004). Second, despite efforts to objectify and standardize the evaluation process, examiners are not immune from attitudes or biases in their work with diverse cultural

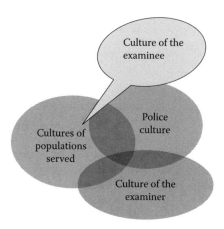

FIGURE 10.1 Overlapping cultures in forensic evaluations.

groups. For instance, research has revealed evidence that blacks are misdiagnosed by being evaluated as paranoid and dangerous (Adebimpe, 1981; Levinson & York, 1974). Third, there is a paucity of literature that examines culture and decision making in forensic psychology. Finally, it cannot be assumed that diversity and multicultural training is widespread in forensic psychology. Some examiners confuse their exposure to diverse groups with diversity credibility and cross-cultural competence that could not be impeached when dealing with ethnoracial issues (Ridley, 2005).

The I-Section must be written with a firm understanding of at least four overlapping cultures. These cultures include the police, the diverse populations served, and the examinee's culture as well as that of the examiner (see Figure 10.1).

POLICE CULTURAL FACTORS AS A PSYCHOLOGICAL FILTER FOR POLICE WORK

The I-Section highlights the known cultural and racial factors to which the examinee will need to respond in the scope of her or his police work (Covington, 2001; Russell, 2001; Weitzer & Tuch, 2002, 2004). The police—or *blue*—culture (Woody, 2005) is dominated by a white male heterosexual ethos. A police environment plays an important role in shaping the attitudes of recruits. However, it is probably not rational to expect academy or FTO experiences to somehow program police to remain unaffected by the diversity of the communities where they serve.

Figures on diversity suggest noticeable increases in the ethnic/racial, sexual orientation, and number of women in police departments in cities of more than 250,000 people (Doss, 1990; Messerschmidt, 1993; Sklanksy, 2006). From a culturally relevant risk assessment standpoint, the questions become, "To what extent does an examinee identify with police culture?" and "To what extent has—or can—an examinee acculturated (or will acculturate) as needed for work in law enforcement?" For example, a pre-employment applicant applying for a highway patrol position with excessive speeding tickets may be identified as someone who has failed to internalize the value of compliance with the law. The I-Section may report that an applicant's decisions may convert values held into behaviors that may function to the benefit or detriment to individuals of a particular group (Sue & Sue, 2008). The larger issue for the police culture may be the extent to which there could be conflict between the police culture and an examinee's gender, sexual orientation, and/or ethnic/racial group (Rostow & Davis, 2004). The latter point is reinforced by high-profile incidents involving police, as reflected in Table 10.1.

The net effect of incidents such as those in Table 10.1 reveal problematic behaviors with strong cultural, gender, and racial overtones. Forensic mental health examiners must be able to justify how these cultural matters were assessed.

TABLE 10.1
High-Profile Cross-Cultural, Race, and Gender Incidents in Police Work

- A police chief was ordered held without bail on charges that he tried to cover up the fatal beating of a Mexican immigrant by a group of white teenagers. One of the officers involved in the incident dated the mother of one of the accused and another officer's son played on the football team. Another officer was indicted separately in a scheme to extort money from illegal gambling operations.

- Several female officers were sexually harassed by male police personnel over the course of many years. Four sergeants and an officer made sexually explicit remarks and unwanted sexual advances toward the women, including fondling and rubbing against them. Pornographic videos were allegedly shown in the workplace. Each woman suffered emotional distress and related symptoms.

- A lawsuit was filed by a gay police officer who alleged that his peers harassed him, including placing a gay escort ad in his locker, stating that he only handles gay sex crimes, and suggesting that he was infected with HIV.

- In a suit, a white police officer asserted that he was the victim of a years-long police department practice of *racial set-asides* for the position of assistant chief for which he had applied. He went on to state that he was "the most qualified person in the department for the job last year but that the position was given to an officer who is Hispanic." The plaintiff had been with the department since 1979, 3 years longer than the Hispanic officer selected.

- While in police custody, a suspect of Puerto Rican descent was beaten to death and then hung from the bars of a holding cell to make it appear as if he had committed suicide. The coroner accepted the chief's explanation that bruises had occurred when he resisted arrest. An autopsy arranged by the family of the deceased confirmed that he had "suffered extensive, massive injuries consistent with a profound beating. The defendant did not die of hanging," the civil lawsuit claimed.

- Ethnic minority officers complained about being harshly disciplined and receiving fewer promotions. Officers who used racial slurs against blacks were not disciplined by the chief. After lodging their complaints, they were sent for psychological exams. Each officer had previously passed their routine annual psychological evaluations. One of the complaining officers had passed his exam just 1 month earlier. This time, they all failed the psychological exam and lost their jobs as police officers. The same psychologist who had repeatedly passed them for years now failed them.

- A mounting pile of lawsuits alleged there were falsified arrests, harassment, and targeting of LGBT (lesbian, gay, bisexual, and transgender) drivers. An officer was accused of civil rights violations by falsifying DUI (driving under the influence) charges and other traffic violations. The same officer also allegedly used excessive force and verbally harassed those he reportedly targeted, which were motivated to falsify charges by the hope to gain more overtime pay for time spent in court. The officer had reportedly made nearly 600 DUI arrests since 2006.

CULTURES OF POLICE EXAMINEES

There may be hidden bias and hostility among some police officers, which place all officers at risk while undermining public trust (Weitzer & Tuch, 2002; Woody, 2005). For example, how does a young Latino male encountering the police for the first time know if he has met a good officer or a closet racist? It is this uncertainty that creates so many cultural collisions and mishaps (Weitzer & Tuch, 2006). If the high-profile cases presented in Table 10.1 reflect the true feelings of some officers in a department, then it is likely that these biases/prejudices could seep out while officers are on the job. In terms of the police culture, the I-Section asks what process is used to assess an officer's biases and measure its potential impact on the performance of job-relevant duties (Woody, 2005). The I-Section may offer information regarding the question "Do individual from different cultures execute police duties differently?" The culture of the examinee may overlap with the police culture in that it could be an FFDE, a lateral transfer, or the individual might have grown up in a law enforcement family. In sum, an examiner must remain aware of police culture when crafting the I-Section (Rostow & Davis, 2004; Woody, 2005).

CULTURES OF DIVERSE POPULATIONS SERVED AND THE I-SECTION

The suitability criteria of police officers require that they have the ability to effectively communicate with the diverse populations served (Scrivner, 2006). For example, an investigation involving Boston's 10-Point Coalition, Winship and Berrien (1999, p. 67) found that the Boston Police Department (BPD) could secure support from African American churches during gang crackdowns. Ethnoracial credibility was established by the BPD through behaviors consistent with fairness and respect previously agreed upon with church elders.

The I-Section should contain a projected risk assessment as to how an examinee can be expected to interact with the diverse groups served by the agency/department. The examinee's cross-cultural experiences, competencies, diversity conflicts, and dispositions must be highlighted (Ridley, 2005; Sue & Sue, 2008). For example, the Cambridge police officer who arrested a college professor at his residence under the assumption that breaking and entering occurred had the perception of a verbally aggressive suspect. How would a psychologist assess such an officer (assuming this same officer would have been referred for a FFDE in the aftermath of such an incident)?

High-profile incidents such as the Cambridge case raise concerns about police–community relations and ethnoracial attitudes toward the police and police behavior. These incidents contain a racial flavor due in large part to preexisting tensions between the police and citizens. A history of differential treatment of African Americans has fueled more negative attitudes toward the police among African Americans than whites (Jordan, Gabbidon, & Higgins, 2009). The psychosocial basis is both historical and recent and has its origins in the role of the police in enforcing the rule of law as well as African Americans' ethnoracial status. Historically, the relationship between African Americans and the police has been problematic, ranging from tense to openly oppositional (Howell, Perry, & Vile, 2004). The I-Section can offer insights into the ethnoracial window of the examinee as it relates to either issues brought about by the need for an evaluation or factors likely to have an unwanted impact on interracial exchanges (Gabbidon & Higgins, 2009; Woody, 2005). The cross-cultural objective of the I-Section is to provide sufficient coverage and support for the ethnoracial or gender-related opinions of the examiner.

CULTURE OF THE EXAMINER AND THE I-SECTION

Race is an important predictor of perceptions, and it is it implicitly discriminatory to ignore this reality during an evaluation (Weitzer & Tuch, 2004). Each examiner must assume a nondefensive posture and remain receptive to the possibility that ethnoracial factors are operating during the forensic evaluations. For example, findings that suggest that health professionals may hold unconscious preferences and stereotypes that, in turn, sway clinical decisions (Green et al., 2007). These types of factors should prompt the examiner to explore biases or other ethnoracially conscious behaviors that could affect his or her decisions about an examinee (Sue & Sue, 2008). Culturally informed examiners remain aware of the potential for unintentional behaviors that can lead to decisions that could have inequitable outcomes for examinees (Ridley, 2005). Probably the most ill-advised action, on the part of the examiner, would be to discount or marginalize the relevance of these issues in the structured decision-making process. The examiner may need to confront a range of referral issues with ethnoracial elements. These ethnoracial and job-relevant factors must be communicated in the I-Section in a way that assists decision makers. The strength of the I-Section is contingent on the use of several data sources through a self-imposed ethnoracial filter (Ridley, 2005; Sue & Sue, 2008).

The level of detail and amount of attention in the I-Section devoted to this area should be sufficient to cover an applicant's/examinee's cultural issues as they would affect her or his anticipated duties. At a minimum, the forensic psychologist must acknowledge—and be able to defend—attention to relevant cultural factors. It is unethical to write a statement such as "The examiner or evaluation did not reveal any cultural or racial factors relevant to this examinee." This or similarly worded statements leave the examiner open to having to explain why he or she failed to consider cultural factors brought up in any appeal or legal hearing.

DECISION-MAKING MODEL FOR WRITING THE I-SECTION

After an examiner has gathered large amounts of data on an examinees, she or he should ask the question, "What do I do to make sense of this information in order to make the best recommendations?" To answer this question, an examiner must have a precise understanding of the purpose of the evaluation. Moreover, an examiner must combine knowledge of police culture, clinical problem solving, and her or his understanding of several accepted standards in order to craft a useful I-Section (AAFP, 2010; Bersoff, 1995). A few forensic psychology ethical decision-making models help clarify the reasoning process from a forensic psychological context. APA, IACP, and AAFP stress the integration of culture to buttress the defensibility of the decision-making steps when applied to diverse examinees.

The following is a description of 10 chief considerations (i.e., interrelated FDM sources) that can be used when writing the I-Section. Use of the FDM allows the examiner to ask the most fundamental I-Section question: What types and sources of data did the examiner use during the process of developing the recommendations? It is worth noting that the majority of these domains allow for the incorporation of cultural factors. This is especially relevant for examiners with limited diversity and cross-cultural training. Figure 10.2 provides an FDM for the I-Section.

These components include data that address the significant content and quality of the recommendations made. The decision-making process can be broken down into the above domains. Although not all of these 10 FDM domains are always available, if accessed, they allow for a more structured judgment. It is important to remember that the I-Section is not a summary of the report but sharply focused responses to the reasons for the referral. The FDM is designed to guide the examiner when considering data relevant to the evaluation demands (Melton et al., 2007; Simon & Shuman, 2002).

STEP 1. FFDE OR OTHER REFERRAL QUESTIONS ABOUT THE EXAMINEE

This first step is included because the approach and organization of the evaluation are largely determined by the nature of the referral question(s) (i.e., references). For pre-employment evaluations, the question is usually based on suitability and stability. Other forensic evaluations and FFDEs have more complicated psycho-legal questions that must be clearly spelled out and understood by the examiner as they are communicated back to authorized stakeholders. An examiner must assess any cultural or gender factors relevant to the referral questions (APA, 2002; Melton et al., 2007; Sattler, 1988).

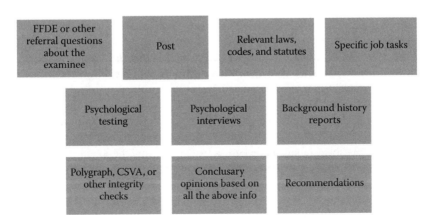

FIGURE 10.2 Forensic decision-making model (FDM) for the I-Section.

Step 2. Identify All Relevant POST Standards

POST is probably the first reference standard for most police personnel evaluations (POST, 2008). POST is cited by IACP and is widely used by experienced forensic psychologists working in law enforcement. Several areas of work-related psychological functioning should be reviewed in light of several domains in this model. These psychological POST dimensions often include social competence/teamwork, adaptability/flexibility, conscientiousness/dependability, impulse control/attention to safety, integrity/ethics, emotional regulation/stress tolerance, decision making/judgment, assertiveness/persuasiveness, and avoiding substance abuse and other risk-taking behavior (POST, 2008; Trompetter, 1998). For a problematic examinee, usually several POST elements should be considered for their applicability. Police officers encounter job-specific operational stressors such as exposure to danger, threats, and trauma (e.g., accident scenes and dealing with death), and dealing with violence and abusive members of the public (Anshel & Kaissidis, 1997; Thompson, Kirk, & Brown, 2001). Management stressors reflect more common organizational stressors, for example work overload, staff shortages, poor communication, and perceived lack of support (Finn, Talucci, & Wood, 2000). An examiner must assess any cultural or gender factors relevant to the POST issues as well as personal stress and work-related stress boundaries.

Step 3. Identify All Relevant Laws, Codes, and Statutes

As previously noted, the evaluation has possible psycho-legal implications and the I-Section must be addressed in the pre-employment, FFDE, or special-unit assignment evaluations (Rostow & Davis, 2004). For example, departments operating under some type of POST mandate have the authority to establish minimum selection standards for peace officers employed by agencies that participate in the POST program (reference). It is essential for the psychologist writing the report to know the department's statutory requirements (Rostow & Davis, 2004). Interpreted properly, the data presented in these codes or statutes usually specify competence domains. Awareness of such codes or statutes can probably increase the frequency with which the components of competence are cited by evaluators in the I-Section (Goldstein, Morse, & Shapiro, 2003).

Step 4. Specific Job Tasks

All of the examiner's opinions and recommendations should be linked to departmental job tasks (Borum et al., 2003). All departments have written job descriptions that outline the specific duties of a particular position (Rostow & Davis, 2004). The human resources department's written policies may spell out in detail the job tasks. These written job tasks are critical assessment areas for use in the I-Section. The examiner must highlight all job tasks relevant to the evaluation as well as explain why the actions—or lack thereof—of the examinee have been called into question (as in the case of an FFDE). These job tasks may also be referenced in the I-Section by a psychologist in FFDEs in order to anchor concerns about an officer evaluated as being *not fit for duty*.

For example, police officers regularly work in highly stressful conditions. Therefore, an assessment review would speak to how the examinee anticipates job stress or how job stress could affect the examinee's performance. Signs of vulnerability to stress may be reflected in a number of data sources, for example, psychological testing or financial stress (Berkun, 2000; Lieberman, Tharion, Shukitt-Hale, Speckman, & Tulley, 2002). In such a case, the examiner could question the extent to which an examinee is able to manage the stress from home and the job or if they can be restored to full functioning with mandatory treatment (in the case of an FFDE). An examiner would highlight the reaction of an examinee to prolonged exposure to stress stemming from police work. For example, an officer was referred for an FFDE because of an incident in which he pointed his service revolver at a sergeant in a glass-enclosed communication center because he thought the dispatcher did not provide him with enough information on a man with a gun call. When asked about this incident during an FFDE, the officer replied, "I yelled at him. 'You son-of-a-bitch. You could have got me killed.'" In this case, the I-Section highlighted the officer's personal stress (from financial issues) that was the result of him working security at several off-duty events. Sanders, Hughes, and Langworthy (1995) report that police officers must be psychologically fit to cope with various stressors. The I-Section would be further strengthened by citing relevant literature on psychological concerns related to any examinee.

STEP 5. PSYCHOLOGICAL TESTING

The I-Section must provide a focused discussion of the results of psychological tests used by the examiner (Curran, 1998; IACP, 1998; Rostow & Davis, 2004;). Several tests have been used in police personnel work. An examiner may need to use additional tests to address the unique requirements of some departments or positions, or various FFDE referral issues. The tests most commonly used include MMPI-2, MMPI-2-RF, 16PF, CPI, PAI, and IPI.

In practice, the I-Section would highlight relevant elevations and de-elevations to address relevant psycho-legal questions concerning why the examinee was referred. The I-Section requires the examiner to link the psychological testing with corresponding behaviors, interviews, and job tasks (Melton et al., 2007; Sattler, 1988). The discussion of the test results would be strengthened by references to research-based interpretations (i.e., independent peer reviewed journals). The I-Section also requires some discussion of *miss rates* for various tests when they are used with various ethnic, gender, and racial groups (Johnson, 2009). In this case, an examiner would need to be prepared to defend her or his choice of such instruments, to demonstrate that the instruments chosen are valid predictors of job performance, and that the instruments chosen do not adversely affect minority groups protected by federal legislation (Inwald, 1988).

Each test and its resulting score must be examined for its relevance for use with a particular examinee, for example, use of nongendered norms for the MMPI-2 (Graham, 2006). The I-Section discusses opinions drawn from the psychological testing. Special attention should be devoted to any ethnoracial factor that attenuates a more traditional interpretation of the test results. In sum, psychological testing is a major evidence-based source when linked to other elements in the FDM, such as psychological interviews.

STEP 6. PSYCHOLOGICAL INTERVIEWS

Interviews are one of the primary *in vivo* data sources for the I-Section. FFDEs may rely on third-party information from coworkers, supervisors, other mental professionals, relatives, or spouses in order to formulate opinions and recommendation (Heilbrun, Rosenfeld, Warren, & Collins, 1994; Melton et al., 2007; Rostow & Davis, 2004). The I-Section should include relevant interview data and observations that pertain to the referral questions or the reasons for the evaluation. Examiners may tailor questions for interview subjects that relate to a specific psychological concern such as anger problems or harsh treatment to certain diverse groups, for example, "Tell me about the times you have observed John lose his temper." Cultural information that may affect the evaluation must be explained in the I-Section (Weiner, 2006).

The examiner should note any significant unsolicited disclosures, comments, or questions from the examinee that are relevant to the evaluation. After the examiner reviews negative history, any details pertinent to the evaluation should be noted in the I-Section. The examinee's reactions and statements made when confronted with discrepancies or self-serving efforts to soften the impact of negative information should also be noted (Melton et al., 2007).

Cross-cultural and other communication issues stemming from questioning techniques affect the examiner's perceptions of the examinee's interview style. The I-Section can be used to reveal behavioral characteristics that may point to attitudinal clashes (Scrivner, 2006). And, as noted above, the examiner must have insight into her or his own unexamined cultural assumptions

(Ridley, 2005; Sue & Sue, 2008), which can alter the examiner's perceptions of the examinee. For example, interview behavior noted in the I-Section must be first decoded by the examiner in a culturally responsive way (Matsumoto, 1989; Ridley, 2005). An examiner who is cross-culturally competent in working this domain of the FDM could have advantages over an examiner who is not (Matsumoto, 2002).

STEP 7. BACKGROUND HISTORY REPORTS

An accurate and comprehensive background history report usually offers a more longitudinal view of the examinee (Owens, 1976). Studies have demonstrated that background data are effective predictors for a variety of human performance domains (Owens, 1976; Reilly & Chao, 1982). The department may use some type of computerized form for collecting the relevant history, through either a personal history questionnaire (PHQ) or a personal history statement (PHS).

This I-Section domain also functions as a foundation for opinions and recommendations. The same background report may also allow the examiner to link the I-Section to psychological testing and POST. For FFDEs, performance reviews and FTO evaluations may also be useful (Rostow & Davis, 2004). Again, the I-Section is not a summary, and the examinee's history must be analyzed for details that inform the opinions of the examiner. The I-Section is also where history that challenges or contradicts the examiner's opinions should be reported. This review includes inaccuracies or inconsistencies in the background history report, which must, of course, be discussed as well. In this case, the significant history contained in the I-Section must be communicated in a way that addresses the purpose of the evaluation while offering a justification for giving more or less decision-making weight to some information (Melton et al., 2007).

STEP 8. POLYGRAPH, CSVA, OR OTHER INTEGRITY CHECK

Forensic psychologists encounter referral evaluation questions that require integrity to be addressed (Melton et al., 2007; Simon & Shuman, 2002). Integrity is a critical component in law enforcement personnel selection as well. The polygraph or other integrity measures (e.g., CSVA) are used by departments during the pre-employment phase of the hiring process. There is considerable controversy about the use of the polygraph, which has resulted in some states limiting its use (Employee Polygraph Protection Act of 1988; Lykken, 1981; Sackett & Decker, 1979; Saxe, Dougherty, & Cross 1985). Although national security concerns have resulted in some federal exemptions for the use of the polygraph, polygraphs do not have strong support based on Daubert and Frye considerations (*Daubert* v. *Merrill Dow Pharmaceuticals*, 1993). Nevertheless, despite concerns about its use, polygraphs are used in law enforcement and national security situations. In terms of the I-Section, the examiner may use issues identified in the polygraph or CSVA as cautionary points. These issues must, however, be yoked to evidence that substantiates the integrity issue. No examiner should base his or her opinions or recommendations relying primarily on results from these integrity measures.

STEP 9. CONCLUSORY OPINIONS BASED ON ALL THE ABOVE INFORMATION

The information gathered during the evaluation process is analyzed and broken down into reasonable conclusions, usually stated as opinions (Kellerman & Burry, 1981). These opinions are not data (Shapiro, 1991): the strength of the opinion(s) is based on psychologically relevant facts that eventually led to the examiner's recommendation(s). Any weakness in the methods used, such as questionable psychometric properties of tests, will weaken the examiner's opinions. The examiner's ending words are not the last word in the process because examinee may hire her or his own experts, or a department-ordered internal second (and third) opinion may come into play. Conclusory opinions must have a traceable connection to the body of the report. In other words, one of the ways of evaluating the quality of the I-Section is the extent to which it explains the reasoning that forms the basis for an examiner's opinion (Skeem, Golding, Cohen, & Berge, 1998). I-Section opinions must offer full acknowledgement of the original reason(s) for the evaluation such as circumscribed stated intent of FFDEs, pre-employment, or special unit assignments (APA, 2002; Committee on Ethical Guidelines for Forensic Psychologists, 1991). Weiner (2006) offers cogent guidance that is particularly relevant for the I-Section when he recommends the conclusions should be written in a "clear, relevant, informative, and defensible manner." An examiner should also avoid offering expansive opinions in the I-Section that are not within the scope of the original referral circumstance (Melton et al., 2007).

In terms of the format of the conclusory opinions, the I-Section might include a brief statement about the standards (e.g., POST, psycho-legal, or job descriptions) used in pre-employment or the listed concerns resulting in a FFDE. A failure to focus on a narrowly defined scope for the evaluation may result in the report assessed as insufficient (Melton et al., 2007). Another approach could include a breakdown of each referral question followed by the examiner's opinion regarding that particular issue. The examiner's analysis of the data contained in the report must offer a cogent description of the relationship between the findings and opinions (Melton et al., 2007). The opinion should contain a brief evidence-based rationale that would be discoverable through an independent report review. Self-imposed questions could include "What were the key single-themed questions about this examinee?" or "Considering the issues resulting in this evaluation and the data you collected, what are your opinions regarding this examinee?" Each opinion should have a risk assessment rating (e.g., low risk, medium risk, or high risk) for problematic issues identified in the opinions. The risk assessment should include a cultural risk assessment rating as appropriate. I-Section conclusions will be strengthened by actual quotes from the research used to support the opinions presented (Ackerman, 2006). It is assumed that the examiner has adequate data on which she or he can base opinions and has addressed the issues emerging from data that are inconsistent with the examiner's views (Sattler, 1988).

STEP 10. RECOMMENDATIONS

Recommendations are the final part of the I-Section. Rucker (1967) found that the usefulness of a report is based largely on the strength of the recommendations. Recommendations and interventions must be presented with enough detail that the intended audience is persuaded that the recommendations are relevant and achievable without extraordinary measures. For example, in the case of FFDEs, clear and convincing recommendations for restoring function should not significantly exceed reasonable resources available to assist an examinee (Brenner, 2003; Whitaker, 1994). The recommendations must clarify questions related to findings as they pertain to the evaluation. FFDEs can have at least four broad categories of recommendations based on the opinions rendered by the examiner. These recommendations include:

- Not psychologically fit for duty
- Not psychologically fit but restorable to minimal level of required functioning (with mandatory treatment) in the current position, other, or modified duty assignment
- Fit with no significant impairment in psychological functioning
- Serious reservations based on examinee's approach to the evaluation process

For pre-employment evaluations, recommendation ratings may be presented in several ways. The pre-employment recommendations may include:

- Recommend
- Recommend with reservations
- Not recommended

- Letter grade ratings such as A, B, C, D, or F
- "Meets" minimum psychological standards (based on some referenced and applicable code, law, or statute)
- "Does not meet" minimum psychological standards (based on some referenced and applicable code, law, or statute)

Whatever categories an examiner may use when making recommendations, they must be made in a way that promotes full understanding of how they are to be used by the department or legal authority (Harvey, 1997). Each of the preceding decision-making elements must address issues specific to the reasons (i.e., questions) resulting in the evaluation and issues that emerge during the evaluation that are specific to the person being evaluated.

CONCLUSIONS

The most challenging demand for a forensic psychologist undertaking an evaluation is integrating data from a variety of sources (Gacono & Hutten, 1994; Meloy, 1991; Sattler, 2001). An effective I-Section is focused on providing information that promotes an understanding of issues or questions raised about the person being evaluated within the context of various law enforcement settings. There are a wide range of referral questions for pre-employment and special unit assignments evaluations and FFDEs. The I-Section should be crafted in a way that allows a diverse group of decision makers to read and understand the recommendations. Crafting the I-Section is a complex task involving multiple comparisons and weighing psychological data in relation to the referral question. The process of writing the report requires a substantial amount of time; the I-Section pulls together what can seem like an unending stream of raw data (Harvey, 1997; Whitaker, 1994), which can be daunting for inexperienced examiners. The I-Section is a triage-oriented process of excluding and including information, keeping only what is relevant to the questions under consideration. There is wide variation in the way reports pull together the information from psychologically relevant sources.

The examiner must offer explanations for why (or why not) certain information was handled in formulating the ending words formulated in the I-Section (Kamphaus, 1993; Ownby, 1997; Sattler, 2001; Tallent, 1993). Contradictions and inconsistencies in the findings must be discussed so that the report offers a reasonable basis for the decisions made about the data used or not used. The examiner has a particular burden to explain the meaning of the findings as they pertain to the opinions rendered (Beutler, Groth-Marnat, & Rosner, 2003; Lewak & Hogan, 2003). Considering the comprehensive amount of data involved in pulling together the I-Section, this must be done in a practical format. Establishing a foundation for the opinions and recommendations offered can be easier said than done. Overreliance on one data source (e.g., testing) can reduce confidence in the recommendations. This is especially true if the testing is not linked to job-specific psychopathology or the absence thereof (Cates, 1999). Each data source used in the I-Section has reliability and validity issues that should be identified and discussed in a way that communicates the examiner's awareness of how they affected her or his opinions and recommendations. Cross-cultural and international issues are especially relevant. Examiners cannot assume all data will be useful or point in the same direction (Melton et al., 2007; Sattler, 2001).

Cultural cautions in the I-Section include being sensitive to an overreliance on data from computerized reporting systems that may identify what appear to be large ethnic/racial groups. Yet, the examiner remains responsible for convincingly articulating his or her awareness of independent, peer-reviewed journal reviews of the data in those computerized reports. Similar concerns are raised by examiners using tightly scripted template reports that have been stripped of cultural factors that could be of particular relevance in formulating I-Section opinions.

The purpose of the I-Section is to increase the forensic conceptualization of an examinee through the communication of opinions and recommendations in such a way that personnel action can be taken by department decision makers. Reports written with strong I-Sections weave together multiple relevant data sources as a by-product of forensically relevant judgments.

REFERENCES

Aamodt, M. G. (2004). *Research in law enforcement selection.* Boca Raton, FL: Brown/Walker Press.

Ackerman, M. J. (2006). Forensic report writing. *Journal of Clinical Psychology, 62*(1), 59–72.

Adebimpe, V. R. (1981). Overview: White norms and psychiatric diagnostic of black patients. *American Journal of Psychiatry, 138,* 279–285.

American Board of Forensic Psychology. (2009). *Specialty guidelines for forensic psychology.* Committee on the Revision of the Specialty Guidelines for Forensic Psychology.

American Board of Forensic Psychology. (2010). *Specialty guidelines for forensic psychologists.* Chapel Hill, NC: Author.

American Educational Research Association (AERA). (1999). *Standards for educational and psychological testing.* Washington, DC: Author.

American Psychiatric Association. (1998). *Position statement: Psychiatric treatment and sexual orientation.* Washington, DC: Author.

American Psychiatric Association. (2000). *Diagnostic and statistical manual of mental disorders* (4th ed., text rev.). Washington, DC: Author.

American Psychological Association (APA). (1992). Ethical principles of psychologists and code of conduct. *American Psychologist, 47,* 1597–1611.

American Psychological Association (APA). (1998). *Answers to your questions about sexual orientation and homosexuality.* Washington, DC: Author.

American Psychological Association (APA). (2002). Ethical principles of psychologists and code of conduct. *American Psychologist, 58,* 650–659.

American Psychological Association Committee on Professional Practice & Standards. (1998). *Guidelines for psychological evaluations in child protection matters.* Washington, DC: American Psychological Association.

Anshel, M. H., & Kaissidis, A. N. (1997). Coping style and situational appraisals as predictors of coping strategies following stressful events in sport as a function of gender and skill level. *British Journal of Psychology, 88,* 263–276.

Berkun, M. (2000). Performance decrement under psychological stress. *Performance in Extreme Human Environments, 5,* 92–97.

Bersoff, D. N. (1995). *Ethical conflicts in psychology.* Washington, DC: American Psychological Association.

Beutler, L. E., Groth-Marnat, G., & Rosner, R. (2003). Introduction to integrated assessment of adult personality. In L. E. Beutler & G. Marnat (Eds.), *Integrative assessment of adult personality* (2nd ed., pp. 1–36). New York: Guilford.

Borum. R., Super, J., & Rand, M. (2003). Forensic assessment for high-risk occupations. In A. Goldstein (Ed.), *Handbook of psychology* (Vol. 11, Forensic psychology). Hoboken, NJ: John Wiley.

Brenner, E. (2003). Consumer-focused psychological assessment. *Professional Psychology: Research & Practice, 34,* 240–247.

California Police Officers Standard and Training Commission. (2008). *Administrative progress report.* Retrieved from http://www.post.ca.gov/bulletin/APRS/January_2008_apr.pdf

Cates, J. A. (1999). The art of assessment in psychology: Ethics, expertise, and validity. *Journal of Clinical Psychology, 55*(5), 631–641.

Committee on Ethical Guidelines for Forensic Psychologists. (1991). Specialty guidelines for forensic psychologists. *Law and Human Behavior, 15.*

Covington, J. (2001). Round up the usual suspects: Racial profiling and the war on drugs. In D. Milovanovic & K. K. Russell (Eds.), *Petit apartheid in the U.S. criminal justice system: The dark figure of racism* (pp. 27–42). Durham, NC: Carolina Academic Press.

Curran, S. F. (1998). Pre-employment psychological evaluation of law enforcement applicants. *Police Chief, 65*(10), 88–95.

Davis, R. D., & Rostow, C. D. (2004). Using the MMPI special scale configurations of predict law enforcement officers fired for cause. *Applied HRM Research, 9*(2), 57–58.

Donders, J. (2001). A survey of report writing by neuropsychologists: II. Test data, report format, and document length. *Clinical Neuropsychologist, 15,* 150–161.

Doss, M. T., Jr. (1990). Police management: Sexual misconduct and the right to privacy. *Journal of Police Science and Administration, 17,* 194–204.

Employee Polygraph Protection Act of 1988, Pub. L. No. 100-347 (H.R. 1212, 29 USC 2001).

Finn P., Talucci, V., & Wood, J. (2000, January). On the job stress in policing: Reducing it, preventing it. *National Institute of Justice Journal,* 19–24.

Gabbidon, S. L., & Marzette L. N. (2007). Racial profiling and the courts: An empirical analysis of federal litigation, 1991–2006. *Journal of Contemporary Criminal Justice, 23*(3), 226–238.

Gagliardi, G. J., & Miller, A. K. (2007). Writing forensic psychological reports. In B. Jackson (Ed.), *Learning forensic assessment.* Mahwah, NJ: Lawrence Erlbaum.

Gancono, C. B., & Hutton, H. E. (1994). *The Hare PCL-R: Clinical interview schedule (Adult form).* Unpublished manuscript.

Goldstein, A. M., Morse, S. J., & Shapiro, D. L. (2003). Evaluation of criminal responsibility. In A. M. Goldstein (Ed.), *Forensic psychology* (pp. 381–406). Hoboken, NJ: John Wiley.

Goodheart, C. D., Kazdin, A. E., Sternberg, R. J. (Eds). (2006). *Evidence-based psychotherapy: Where practice and research meet.* Washington DC: American Psychological Association.

Graham, J. R. (2006). *MMPI-2: Assessing personality and psychopathology* (4th ed.). New York: Oxford University Press.

Green, A., Carney, D., Pallin, D., Ngo, L. H., Raymond K. L., Iezzoni L. I., et al. (2007). Implicit bias among physicians and its prediction of thrombolysis decisions for black and white patients. *Journal of General Internal Medicine, 22*(9), 1231–1238.

Green, D., Callands, T. A., Radcliffe, A. M., Luebbe, A. M., & Klonoff, E. A. (2009). Clinical psychology students' perceptions of diversity training: A study of exposure and satisfaction. *Journal of Clinical Psychology, 65*(10), 1056–1070.

Groth-Marnat, G. (1999). Current status and future directions of psychological assessment: Introduction. *Journal of Clinical Psychology, 55,* 781–785.

Groth-Marnat, G., & Horvath, L. S. (2006). The psychological report: A review of current controversies. *Journal of Clinical Psychology, 62*(1), 73–81.

Harvey, V. S. (1997). Improving readability of psychological reports. *Professional Psychology: Research & Practice, 28*(3), 271–274.

Harvey, V. S. (2006). Variables affecting the clarity of psychological reports. *Journal of Clinical Psychology, 62*(1), 5–18.

Heilbrun, K., Rosenfeld, B., Warren, J., & Collins, S. (1994). The use of third party information in forensic assessments. *Bulletin of the American Academy of Psychiatry and Law, 22,* 399–406.

Howell, S. E., Perry, H. L., & Vile, M. (2004). Black cities/white cities: Evaluating the police. *Political Behavior, 26*(1), 45–68.

Independent Commission on the Los Angeles Police Department. (1991). *Report of the Independent Commission on the Los Angeles Police Department.* Los Angeles: Author.

International Association of Chiefs of Police, Police Psychological Services. (1998). *Fitness-for-duty evaluations.* Alexandria, VA: Author

Inwald, R. (1988). Five year follow-up study of departmental terminations as predicted by 16 pre-employment psychological indicators. *Journal of Applied Psychology, 73,* 703–710.

Johnson, R., & Scott, M. (2009). *Smelling alcohol in the evaluation of police recruits and fitness for duty evaluations.* Paper presented at the IACP 116th Annual Meeting, Law Enforcement and Technology Conference, Police Physicians Section Meeting, Denver, CO.

Jordan, K. L., Gabbidon, S. L., & Higgins G. E. (2009). Exploring the perceived extent of and citizens' support for consumer racial profiling: Results from a national poll. *Journal of Criminal Justice, 37*(4), 353–359.

Kamphaus, R. W. (1993). *Clinical assessment of children's intelligence.* Boston: Allyn & Bacon.

Kellerman, H., & Burry, A. (1981). *Handbook of psychodiagnostic testing: Personality analysis and report writing.* New York: Grune & Stratton.

Kellerman, H., & Burry, A. (2007). *Handbook of psychodiagnostic testing: Analysis of personality in the psychological report* (4th ed.). New York: Springer.

Knapp, S., & VandeCreek, L. (2006). *Practical ethics for psychologists: A positive approach.* Washington, DC: American Psychological Association.

Levinson, R. M., & York, M. Z. (1974). The attribution of dangerousness in mental health. *Journal of Health & Social Behavior, 15,* 328–335.

Lewak, R. W., & Hogan, R. S. (2003). Integrating and applying assessment information: Decisionmaking, patient feedback, and consultation. In L. E. Beutler & G. Groth-Marnat (Eds.), *Integrative assessment of adult personality* (pp. 356–397). New York: Guilford.

Lichtenberger, E. O. (2006). Computer utilization and clinical judgment in psychological assessment reports. *Journal of Clinical Psychology, 62*(1), 19–32.

Lieberman, H. R., Tharion, W. J., Shukitt-Hale, B., Speckman K. L., & Tulley, R. (2002). Effects of caffeine, sleep loss, and stress on cognitive performance and mood during U.S. Navy SEAL training. *Psychopharmacology, 164*(3), 250–261.

Lykken, D. T. (1981). *A tremor in the blood.* New York: McGraw-Hill.

Matsumoto, D. (1989) Cultural influences on the perception of emotion. *Journal of Cross-cultural Psychology, 20,* 92–105.

Matsumoto, D. (2002). Methodological requirements to test a possible in group advantage in judging emotions across cultures: Comments on Elfenbein and Ambady and evidence. *Psychological Bulletin, 128,* 236–242.

Messerschmidt, J. W. (1993). *Masculinities and crime: Critique and reconceptualization of theory.* Lanham, MD: Rowman & Littlefield.

Meloy, J. R. (1991). The blurring of ego boundary in projective identification [Letter to the editor]. *American Journal of Psychiatry, 148,* 1761–1762.

Melton, G. B., Petrila, J., Polythress, N. G., & Slobogin, C. (2007). *Psychological evaluations for the courts: A handbook for mental health professionals and lawyers* (3rd ed.). New York: Guilford.

Michaels, M. H. (2006). Ethical considerations in writing psychological assessment reports. *Journal of Clinical Psychology, 62*(1), 47–58.

Nietzel, M. T., & Hartung, C. M. (1993). Psychological research on the police: An introduction to a special section on the psychology of law enforcement. *Law & Human Behavior, 17*(2), 151–155.

Owens, W. A. (1976). Background data. In M. D. Dunnette (Ed.), *Handbook of industrial and organizational psychology.* Chicago: Rand McNally.

Ownby, R. L. (1997). *Psychological reports: A guide to report writing in professional psychology* (3rd ed.). New York: John Wiley.

Reilly, R. R., & Chao, G. T. (1982). Validity and fairness of some alternative employee selection procedures. *Personnel Psychology, 35*(1), 1–62.

Ridley, C. R. (2005). *Overcoming unintentional racism: A practitioner's guide to intentional interviewing* (2nd ed.). Thousands Oaks, CA: Sage.

Rostow, C. D., & Davis R. D. (2004). *A handbook for psychological fitness-for-duty evaluations in law enforcement.* Binghampton, NY: Haworth Clinical Practice Press.

Rucker, C. M. (1967). Technical language in the school psychologist's report. *Psychology in the Schools, 4,* 146–150.

Russell, K. K. (1998). *The color of crime: Racial hoaxes, white fear, black protectionism, police harassment, and other macroaggressions.* New York: New York University Press.

Russell, K. K. (2001). Racial profiling: A status report of the legal, legislative, and empirical literature. *Rutgers Race and the Law Review, 61,* 1–16.

Sackett, P. R., & Decker, P. J. (1979). The detection of deception in the employment context: A review and critical analysis. *Personnel Psychology, 32,* 487–506.

Sanders, B., Hughes, T., & Langworthy, R. (1995). Police officer recruitment and selection: A survey of major police departments in the U.S. *Police Forum, 5,* 1–4.

Sattler, J.M. (1988). *Assessment of children.* San Diego, CA: Author.

Sattler, J. M. (1991). *Assessment of children* (3rd ed.). San Diego, CA: Author.

Sattler, J. M. (1998). *Clinical and forensic interviewing of children and families: Guidelines for mental health, education, pediatric, and child maltreatment fields.* San Diego, CA: Author.

Sattler, J. M. (2001). *Assessment of children: Cognitive applications* (4th ed.). San Diego, CA: Author.

Saxe, L., Dougherty, D., & Cross, T. (1985). The validity of polygraph testing: Scientific analysis and public controversy. *American Psychologist, 40,* 355–366.

Scrivner, E. (2006). Psychology and law enforcement. In I. B. Weiner & A. K. Hess (Eds.), *The handbook of forensic psychology.* Hoboken, NJ: John Wiley.

Shapiro, D. L. (1991). *Forensic psychological assessment.* Boston: Allyn & Bacon.

Simon, R. I., & Shuman, D. W. (Eds.). (2002). *Retrospective assessment of mental states in litigation predicting the past.* Washington, DC: American Psychiatric Association.

Skeem, J., Golding, S. L., Cohen, N., & Berge, G. (1998). Logic and reliability of evaluations of competence to stand trial. *Law & Human Behavior, 22,* 519–547.

Sklansky, D. (2006). Sexual orientation and workplace rights: A potential land mine for employers? *Employee Relations Law Journal, 18*(1), 29–60.

Snyder, C. R., Ritschel, L. A., Rand, K. L., & Berg, C. J. (2006). Balancing psychological assessments: Including strengths and hope in client reports. *Journal of Clinical Psychology, 62*(1), 33–46.

Sue, D. W., & Sue, D. (2008). *Counseling the culturally diverse: Theory and practice* (5th ed.). Hoboken, NJ: John Wiley.

Tallent, N. (1988). *Psychological report writing*. Englewood Cliffs, NJ: Prentice Hall.

Tallent, N. (1993). *Psychological report writing* (4th ed.). Englewood Cliffs, NJ: Prentice Hall.

Tallent, N., & Reiss, R. J. (1959). Multidisciplinary views on the preparation of written psychological reports: III. The trouble with psychological reports. *Journal of Clinical Psychology, 15*, 444–446.

Thompson, B. M., Kirk, A., & Brown, D. F. (2001). Work based support, emotional exhaustion, and spillover of work stress to the family environment: A study of policewomen. *Stress Medicine, 21*(3), 199–207.

Trompetter, P. (1998, October). Fitness-for-duty evaluations: What agencies can expect. *Police Chief, 60*, 97–105.

Weiner, I. B. (2006). Writing forensic reports. In I. B. Weiner & A. K. Hess (Eds.), *The handbook of forensic psychology*. Hoboken, NJ: John Wiley.

Weitzer, R., & Tuch, S. (2002). Perceptions of racial profiling: Race, class, and personal experience. *Criminology, 40*, 435–457.

Weitzer, R., & Tuch, S. A. (2004). Race and perceptions of police misconduct. *Social Problems, 51*, 305–325.

Weitzer, R. J., & Tuch, S. A. (2005). Racially biased policing: Determinants of citizen perceptions. *Social Forces, 3*, 1009–1030.

Weitzer, R., & Tuch, S. A. (2006). *Race and policing in America: Conflict and reform*. Cambridge, UK: Cambridge University Press

Winship, C., & Berrien, J. (1999). Boston cops and black churches: New approaches to fighting crime. *Public Interest, 136*, 52–68.

Whitaker, D. (1994). *How school psychology trainees learn to communicate through the school psychological report* (Unpublished Ph.D. dissertation). University of Washington, Seattle.

Woody, R. H. (2005). The police culture: Research implications for psychological services. *Professional Psychology: Research & Practice, 36*(5), 525–529.

CASE CITED

Daubert v. Merrell Dow Pharmaceuticals, Inc., 509 US 579, 589 (1993).

11 Challenging the Police De-Selection Process During the Psychological Interview
How Gullibility Spells Hiring Doom for the Unwary

Jose M. Arcaya

> *And I wept both night and day,*
> *And he wip'd my tears away,*
> *And I wept both day and night,*
> *And hid from him my heart's delight,*
>
> *So he took his wings and fled;*
> *Then the morn blushe'd rosy red;*
> *I dried my tears, & arm'd my fears*
> *With ten thousand shields and spears.*
>
> **William Blake**
> *Songs of Innocence*

INTRODUCTION

As central parties responsible for selecting prospective police officers and other law enforcement employees to work in municipal or governmental agencies, psychologists are charged with screening out applicants showing instability, bad judgment, addictive tendencies, and other traits incompatible with successful functioning as peace officers. Apart from administering standardized tests and reviewing applicants' background records, they must employ face-to-face interviews to assess the demeanor, candor, and intelligences of those potential police officers. That portion of the evaluative process—where the applicant provides unexpected or spontaneous revelations during the oral interview—is this chapter's principal concern.

Specifically, we will argue that police psychologists—those working on behalf of law enforcement departments as evaluators—often use the applicants' revelations of past indiscretions to disqualify them unfairly. Here, the terms *personal information*, *disclosures*, or *admissions* will refer to adverse data the candidate had not previously mentioned in his or her written, pre-interview application.

The applicant tends to provide it trustingly in an attempt to be transparent to the police examiner as well as to demonstrate that the behavior(s) in question (e.g., speeding, excessive drinking, or shoplifting) no longer play a part in the applicant's life. Despite this open renunciation of that conduct or lifestyle, the admission in question is still used as the basis for disqualifying the candidate as a police officer. Finally, those kinds of revelations are almost always instigated by the

227

police psychologist's mode of questioning and the institutional forces operating in the assessment environment, not by the applicant. In short, admissions tend to be extracted externally rather than by free will.

Such confessions, it will be argued, are too quickly incorporated into a *reject* narrative rather than contextualized in terms of the spirit in which they were made (e.g., "I used to smoke marijuana a lot in high school, but stopped after my first year in college") because of preexisting biases favoring a suspicious outlook toward all police applicants. They are seen as stable personality characteristics rather than reports of transcended difficulties, cured negative habits, or worked-through issues. Almost always, admissions never receive credit as instances of honesty or integrity but as problems cleverly uncovered by the police psychologist. Moreover, those engaged in police hiring evaluations tend to be influenced by the prevailing job culture, encouraging the commission of false negative errors over false positive ones (i.e., it is better to be safe than sorry). Thus, revelations of impropriety made against one's own interests are likely to be viewed as free evidence for an easy turn-down, not instances of goodwill behavior.

As a professional psychologist who is frequently asked to appeal turn-downs, I have noted repeatedly that admissions not only are not accorded the credit they deserve, but also tend unduly to cancel out or diminish the applicant's other positive accomplishments. The fact that the candidate had secrets or unrevealed information (because, perhaps, it was no longer relevant to his or her ongoing life) serves to detract from the job seeker's positive history. Instead, past misdeeds take center stage as a result of being induced during the oral examination and push out current accomplishments from meaningful consideration. Once job applicants admit to something that should have been kept to themselves, police examiners then tend to hold the job applicant's feet to the fire.

This is often done by forcing candidates into acknowledging more serious misbehaviors than the ones admitted, sometimes to the point of extracting false information. Even though the applicant's intent in disclosing that data in the first place (e.g., having smoked marijuana, stolen a small amount of money, or been drunk behind the wheel) might have been to show a current change in character or behavior by contrasting it to the past, the admission itself now becomes an object of intense interest, close inspection, and skeptical questioning (e.g., "Are you sure? Tell me when you really stopped. How much had you been consuming? What made you stop?"). As is often the case with people trying to explain their way out of misunderstandings, candidates are then likely to make matters worse by trying to clarify what they believe was misrepresented (e.g., "I meant to say that I no longer smoke marijuana, but I have friends who still do"). That sort of reaction sweeps them into an ever deepening whirlpool of disbelief driven by the examiner's confirmation bias;* only a guilty individual would act so defensively.

As a cautionary note, we assert that not all police candidate selections or determinations are inaccurate or wrong. We only challenge the ones that base their determinations primarily on admissions rather than real information derived from the applicants' factual histories. We claim that when police candidate evaluators employ browbeating and mental coercion to extract disqualifying evidence, the ensuing rejection is questionable. That information becomes doubly suspect not only because it often refers to matters of the distant past (e.g., "Five years ago or so, I got into a shoving match with my roommate"), but also because it was produced to placate examiner's expectations. Admissions are never about the here and now, only about recalled conduct.

After exploring this phenomenon further, discussing similarities between its conundrums and the reason for the Fifth Amendment's presence in the Constitution, we discuss ethical conflicts associated with advising prospective police candidates about the dangers they encounter by making inadvertent admissions. Finally, we make recommendations for improving the police selection procedure with respect to the oral interview.

---

* *Confirmation bias* is selective thinking characterized by a tendency to notice and to look for what confirms one's beliefs while ignoring or undervaluing the relevance of what contradicts that viewpoint (Nickerson, 1996).

THE POLICE HIRING PROCEDURE

The oral examination is one part within the larger hiring process. While approaches for picking job candidates vary notably among jurisdictions (e.g., some require a college degree, others only a few post–high school credits; some demand paramilitary experience, others none; some administer the MMPI-2, others the Inwald Personality Inventory; see Taylor et al., 2006), all demand applicants to submit written applications containing extensive background information, subject themselves to formal psychological testing, and partake in personal interviews with psychological evaluators.

Police applicants generally get rejected in one of three ways: by record, by perjury, and/or by admission. The first arises from an objective, problematical record characterized by significant mis-behaviors or infractions (e.g., moving violations, firings, bankruptcies, dishonorable military discharges, domestic incidents, and serious juvenile misbehaviors). In this instance, disqualification is directly proportional to the number of identified problems, the severity of the issues concerning those problems, and the vintage of the misconduct in question (i.e., the more recent the problem, the worse its impact on the candidacy). Needless to say, if all three variables are pointing negatively, the police psychologist's job is made relatively easy and little thinking is involved in making the rejection.

On the other hand, if the fact pattern points toward the opposite direction (i.e., the offenses are few in number, relatively minor, and distant in time), the candidate's chances for being hired improve notably. When that kind of pattern appears, the police psychologist's job becomes harder because it demands more machinations to justify the candidate's rejection. The professional must explain how he or she weighed the examinee's strengths and weaknesses in getting to the disqualification.

For example, consider the fact pattern involving an applicant with a checkered past. He has had two arrests; the last one (a disorderly conduct charge for being with a group of people who were fighting others) occurred 5 years ago and is deemed to be of medium severity. The first arrest was for riding in a stolen car as a juvenile (7 years previously). Today, the applicant works responsibly, has had no other legal issues since the last arrest, is close to graduating from college, and would probably challenge the police psychologist's decision-making capacity. Because no clear calculus for combining such a group of complex elements exists to justify either a hire or a fire decision, the police psychologist is left with little more than guessing. However, regardless of the decision, at least the situation contains objective evidence. Although the examiner could be accused of being excessively rigid in deciding against the applicant, at least objective information was used in arriving at the determination. The data were transparent, not conjured in the examiner's mind.

Similarly, perjury, the second type of rejection, is also rooted in hard evidence. It emerges when the candidate provides information that contradicts the written record. The opposing data could have come from the written pre-examination or employment questionnaire or because a departmental investigator dug up background facts not previously known to the police psychologist. In either case, the result is that an attempt was made to downplay or omit past bad behavior.[*] The lying, of course, is aimed at burnishing an applicant's job profile, knowing that telling the truth would likely lessen his or her hiring possibilities (e.g., admitting only one juvenile arrest when three was the real number; denying having ever been fired, yet one firing is uncovered when past employers are questioned during a background check).

The common issue for the police psychologist to consider is whether the inconsistency was willful lying or the product of simply forgetting (the defense which the candidate almost always invokes). Whatever the eventual decision, the facts under consideration are clear to an external reader of the case as they would be if personality test findings (e.g., MMPI-2, Inwald Personality Inventory, CP) are included to arrive at the final decision (i.e., "Did the applicant also demonstrate propensities toward lying on the objective testing?"). While the disqualification might be debated, the outcome emerged from verifiable information.

---

[*] I should note that I have never encountered the opposite: a candidate who depicts a problem worse than it really was.

As already suggested, the validity of an admissions rejection is the most problematic. It is centered on what candidates said, independent of the objective record. It also can be a product of induction by the very circumstances of the oral interview. Because only the candidate really knows the facts of the matter—they cannot be confirmed by a third party—only the police examiner's conjectures remain to determine how much importance to place on the disclosure. At work is not only what the applicant has verbalized, but also the police examiners' suspicions, biases, and need to play detective.

Indeed, it is not unusual for police psychologists to provoke examinees into repudiating or revising sanguine versions of the past because they are deemed unconvincing or questionable, encouraging instead what is believed to be a more realistic (i.e., negative) account of the occurrence. For example, the examiner might remark, "It would not be unusual for a young man in this day and age to have used marijuana on more than one occasion. Was that the case for you?" or "You indicate never having received any moving violation yet you've been driving for 5 years. Didn't you ever drive recklessly without being caught?" The result would be that an examinee would provide self-damning data, believing that everyone else going through the hiring process is doing the same thing. Such is the power of suggestion that I have even known candidates who have made up examples of misconduct just to avoid seeming *fake* by the interviewing psychologist. In short, they did not want to disappoint the examiner's explicitly stated assumption that "boys will be boys."

On the other hand, police psychologists tend not to delve as deeply into applicants' positive accomplishments (e.g., that he or she won an academic excellence award, or was approved for advanced military training while in the U.S. Marine Corps) as they do the problematic material. The unacknowledged reason is that police psychologists tend see their primary job as keeping out "bad apples" rather than acquiring good ones. As someone once said, a rejected candidate will never threaten a department, but a hired one can always disappoint. From the trusting viewpoint of the applicant, the selection process is fair, professionally administered, and open-minded. Therefore, they think the open-hearted (i.e., sincere) nature of their revelations will be sensitively understood as a closed episode of their life. They also think they will be given due credit for having voluntarily shared disavowed episodes of fighting, drinking, speeding, and experimental drug use.

More often than not, those admissions are about youthful misconduct (e.g., "I had several fights during my first semester in college," "I was part of fraternity drinking contest and won," or "My girlfriends and I raced other cars when we first got our licenses") or one-time personal problems ("When I graduated from high school, I visited a therapist at my mother's request because I didn't feel like doing much"; or "After breaking up with my boyfriend, I was prescribed Elavil for my depression") that they believe have been transcended. The statements are not intended as reflective of ongoing adjustment issues (e.g., "I have just separated from my wife," "Although I didn't want to declare bankruptcy, I just did because of my many pressing debts"). Thus, had the applicants kept such data to themselves, based on their otherwise acceptable backgrounds, they would have probably been hired. At the same time, they want to show their honest side. Thus, admissions are often provided as symbols of good faith—to indicate that the candidate has nothing to hide from the department and can be trusted to fess up if he or she makes mistakes. They are advertisements for sincerity.

Yet applicants do not get the expected response for such truthfulness; instead, it is cynically received by the examiner with silent gratitude (i.e., "Thanks, you've just made my job easier.") Now, the police psychologist is able to write a fairly straightforward rejection (e.g., "The candidate admitted to… getting drunk at several college parties … stealing clothes from the shopping mall 5 years ago… driving while intoxicated 2 weeks after getting her driver's license.") On the other hand, upon learning of the consequences created by their candor, candidates lament with the typical statement, "Boy! Was I stupid to have trusted the doctor!"

They see themselves as having been fools, thinking that had they been clearer in what they acknowledged, the rejection could have been averted. Yet, had they known at the time that their words were interpreted in an opposite manner than intended (which does not normally happen

because the police psychologists are experts at hiding their real opinions during hiring interviews), any attempts to revise those misspoken words (e.g., "I now only drink on very few occasions," "I had financial problems 2 years ago, but now I have almost paid off my debts") would still
have been met by objections and disapproval. Then, the candidates would have been described in
the rejection report as uncooperative, defensive, and argumentative.

FIFTH AMENDMENT PARALLELS

The impulse toward sincerity and candor in an effort to show good moral character through self-
transparency and untempered self-disclosure, but that causes legal difficulties later, is exactly why
the Fifth Amendment was included in the Constitution. It provides the right of silence to govern-
mentally detained individuals in order to avoid self-incrimination. The drafters knew that state powers are much greater than the citizen's ability to defend against imprisonment. Moreover, they were
also aware that, without external restraints, government would likely resort to force, coercion, or
deception to acquire sought-after confessions.

Although criminal interrogations and employment interviews are conducted for very different
purposes (i.e., to determine criminal culpability versus job fitness), of relevance for this discussion
are the similar psychological dynamics driving both, which explain why examinees admit more
negative information than is necessary. Here, we discuss four of these psychological dynamics.

First, admissions are produced in the context of social pressure. Both the interrogation and the
hiring are conducted in private and in the face of powerful others. Like a police interrogation, the
selection interview is open to the use of entrapment, manipulation, or enticement to acquire self-
incriminating information. Since police examiners tend to be older than the applicants, they can
seem more intimidating when expressing skepticism about the candidate's degree of candor (e.g.,
"Are you sure you never got into any fights after turning 18?" "Tell me the truth: how much marijuana have you *really* smoked?" "Everyone steals. When did you last take something that didn't
belong to you?").

Second, those applying for law enforcement work tend to be young, idealistic, and, besides desir-
ing to help others, committed to the rule of law. They also tend to be respectful of authority—why
else would they be seeking employment with a paramilitary organization such as a police department? Thus, lacking the cynicism that they are likely to acquire after becoming seasoned officers,
applicants typically come into the hiring situation programmed to tell the truth. Unfortunately, this
predilection is very compatible with the police psychologist's need to acquire *rejecting* evidence. It
propels the applicant to trust and admit. Without such an impulse for honesty, the interviewer would
be left with little (assuming there are no skeletons in the closet) to criticize. The police psychologist
would be left with the default position of hiring the examinee, not his or her first impulse. As noted
earlier, they believe it is safer to reject than to hire.

Third, police applicants frequently arrive with the naïve belief that the hiring agency somehow has supernatural powers or uncanny detection capabilities to find out about their personal pasts.
Therefore, it would be futile for anyone to lie since it would be detected anyway. Facing the scrutiny of a professional psychologist whom these young and impressionable applicants likely endow
with all-knowing powers, they sense themselves as transparent or otherwise psychologically naked.
Thus, they are vulnerable to altering their statements at the behest of the interviewer, acceding to
his or her authority, or shifting positions if it is so suggested (e.g., "The police examiner claimed
that, because I had been stopped 4 years ago for drunken driving, I had probably drunk more than
the five beers I had that night. I went along with his number since he seemed to know what he was
talking about").

Last, candidates are not just encouraged but also generally ordered to be honest during every
step of the admission process. They continuously hear that truth telling is the hallmark of a good
law enforcement officer (e.g., "Honesty is the best policy," or "Don't lie—you will be found out if
you do") and lectured that sincerity is compatible with good recruit behavior. Moreover, they are

also encouraged to believe—although not explicitly reassured—that they will receive admiration, respect, or esteem if they courageously divulge unflattering information that had not already been disclosed in the pre-interview application. Embodying Lerner's (1980) famous just-world thesis— that most people believe that bad things tend to happen to the bad while good to the just—police candidates think freely provided negative revelations will show they're good and definable. The candor will protect them from the consequences of what they have disclosed.

Kassin (2005) notes this same thinking guiding the actions of innocent people who, despite awareness of their Fifth Amendment Miranda warnings, still go on to divulge and even confess false information, believing they will be treated better than if they kept quiet. That travesty occurs because the interrogator fools the suspect into believing that he or she has the suspect's interests in mind (i.e., is a friend) and can mitigate charges if cooperation is forthcoming. *Cooperation*, of course, means providing on-the-record statements or admissions, which the investigator can cite to the judge as indications of good-heartedness. Under the stress of detention, the offer is enough to induce the self-damaging revelations (i.e., "Look how innocent I am: I didn't hide behind silence"). After all, wouldn't a guilty person remain quiet, knowing that otherwise he or she would worsen a bad situation? Kassin (2005) explains the dynamics of such behavior in the following way:

> The phenomenology of innocence may be rooted in a generalized and perhaps motivated belief in a just world in which human beings get what they deserve and deserve what they get (Lerner, 1980). It may also stem from of an "illusion of transparency," a tendency for people to overestimate the extent to which their true [positive] thoughts, emotions, and other inner states can be seen by others (Gilovich et al., 1998; Miller & McFarland, 1987). (Kassin, 2005, p. 218)

Negative admissions (e.g., "Yes, I got into a fist fight during a fraternity initiation," "I *did* try marijuana in high school") tend to erase all the good that the examinee has brought to the table, diminishing disproportionately the impact of the applicant's positive accomplishments. Since it is harder to take back what has been said than never to have said it in the first place, the applicant often then finds himself or herself in the untenable situation of trying to prove that he or she is not *guilty*. The subsequent rejection that follows is a robotic, canned, or formulaic action—applied in this instance as it has in many other situations. Typically, it questions an applicant's integrity while implicitly lauding the examiner's perceptiveness in extracting the negative data (e.g., "The candidate didn't realize the implications of what he was saying when admitting that he brought a knife to school"). Without any objective "anchor" to determine the context or seriousness of the information, the police examiner is left relying on his or her word or speculations (e.g., "He told me that the knife was in the pocket because he had forgotten to leave it at home after having used it on a fishing trip; the story didn't sound credible"). The examiner then creates a *reject* story or narrative in which the admission is placed.

Spence (1982) has noted in the psychoanalytic therapy situation a propensity for analysts to "smooth" the patient's account of his or her life, omitting some details and magnifying others, to establish a coherent—but not necessarily correct— account of the past. That transformation is not done against the patient's will, but in cooperation with it, providing the latter with a better account of his or her childhood and background than had previously been the case. However, the result is a narrative, not necessarily the truth of what really went on.

AFTERMATH IN THE POLICE HIRING SITUATION

In most cities and jurisdictions, rejected police candidates can appeal their rejections in front of hearing boards or administrative courts. Beyond hiring a lawyer, the appellant or the appellant's lawyer inevitably contracts a private psychologist to provide an opposing professional opinion regarding the candidate's mental fitness to accomplish the job in question.

Opposing the appeal is not only the police psychologist who made the turn-down but also the lawyers representing the department for which the police psychologist works.

The legal contest is frequently not about statutory or case law matters but about different psychological theories of the mind, for example, whether a particular test finding really represents the negative behaviors asserted by the police psychologists. Typically, the police psychologist places greater weight on past behavior, not on present conduct. Citation is made to difficulties in such objectively verified spheres of life as the applicant's work history, psychological test outcomes, driving background, academic attainments, finances, as well as inconsistencies between material contained in the applicant's written records and words uttered during the oral interview.

While the police psychologist is prone to looking at the past as the best predictor of future behavior, the defending psychologist argues that the police psychologist either misunderstood the candidate's background, misheard the interviewee's commentary, provided insufficient attention to the applicant's achievements, and/or magnified more than necessary the candidate's past mistakes. He or she will assert that current conduct (e.g., stable employment, community involvement) is indicative of compatibility with desired police character makeup. Although technically both are supposedly neutral experts, in reality, they are quasi-advocates who endow the same facts with distinctly different meanings (e.g., police psychologist: "The candidate has had four different jobs in two and a half years, suggesting instability of character"; and private psychologist: "The candidate's four jobs were in the area of restaurant work, where turnovers are quite frequent"). Thus, not unlike Spence's thesis (1982), the two psychologists are involved in a kind of storytelling contest, a narrative construction that portrays the disqualified candidate in opposite ways.

The administrative officer or judge hearing the appeal obviously must decide the version having the greatest persuasive impact (e.g., police psychologist: "The candidate shows mental instability, poor impulse control, deceptive character, untrustworthiness"; and the applicant's psychologist: "The applicant is a worthy hire because he or she meritoriously served in the armed forces, has an honorable history of employment, and serves the community through volunteer work"). It is not so much the applicant's objective history in dispute (because it cannot be challenged) but material gained during the police psychologist's oral interview, where the greatest degree of contention between the two psychologists occurs.

In this matter, the police psychologist is in the more powerful position of the two. He or she has set the mood (e.g., "The applicant was highly guarded...flip...hostile") and storyline (e.g., "She admitted to having engaged in two shoplifting incidents, the latest 2 years ago. That is proof of dishonesty"). The appeal psychologist, on the other hand, must supply a host of credible counter-explanations to contest the damning evaluation (e.g., "The applicant was apparently reactive to police psychologist's gruffness...thought the examiner wanted her to answer quickly...she felt disrespected"). If not, what is left uncontested is assumed by the court to be true.

Rejections are generally overturned in one or more of three ways: (1) challenging the accuracy of the police psychologist's claims (i.e., he or she was totally or partially mistaken about the facts used to disqualify), (2) noting the lengthy time span between the last misbehavior and the present date (the longer, the better), and (3) citing laudable conduct contradicting the assertion that the candidate is unsuitable for police work (e.g., being honorably discharged from the armed forces, working adequately as a voluntary peace officer, performing praised community service, and/or attaining advanced educational credentials).

It is rare that the rejected candidate has a spotless record. There is always some blemish (if not more) in the background that pushes him or her into the unfit category. The ultimate question for disputation in the appeal process is whether the rejection was based on reasonable assumptions that future work problems would likely arise if the applicant were hired: How much of the decision was driven by the examiner's cognitive recipes or stereotypes, relegating the candidate into the rejection category (e.g., a drunk, a liar, a hothead), rather than through objective analysis of the facts? Did the evaluator excessively simplify the applicant's history so that a more complicated truth was obscured by a simple-minded conception?

While dealing with the objective features of the case is difficult enough (e.g., reframing data and showing evidence of rehabilitation), coping with admissions demands explaining to the court the possibly coercive circumstances in which they were made and the intentions which motivated them in the first place (e.g., an attempt to show candor). It also requires casting into doubt the examiner's manner of drawing out information from the applicant and why certain implications were drawn from the adduced material and not others. A detailed account of that activity is beyond the scope of this chapter.

ETHICAL ISSUES

Should candidates be informed of the negative consequences they face by disclosing unflattering information? Must they be warned that the police psychologists are not their friends or that what they put in their pre-interview applications can be used against them in the oral interview? Would it be an implicit encouragement to lie if the consulting psychologist informs a rejected candidate that other jurisdictions would never know that he or she had been rejected by the one in question? What is the consulting psychologist's responsibility to the larger society? Should he or she give away secrets in which police psychologists disqualify candidates? Should he or she "let the cat out of the bag"?

I know of no academic discussion related to those questions. However, they are the ones commonly posed by law enforcement applicants wanting to know how to increase their chances of being hired. As for me, I believe in transparency. Applicants should know the evaluation process is laced with traps to induce the unwary into making admissions contrary to his or her interests.

The police psychologist, sometimes appearing warm and personable, will always be on the department's side, not the applicant's. By definition, as a forensic expert, he or she advocates or works for the institution that pays his or her salary, not the person being assessed. At least that much should be said. At the same time, applicants should not be encouraged to lie. Instead, the law enforcement job candidates should be educated about the hiring situation that they will be facing. It is not much different than giving them a Miranda warning.

Example

Problems arose with this candidate's application after endorsing two alcohol-related items on a particular police department's screening questionnaire (#29: "Do you believe social drinking can lead to alcoholism?"—False; #31: "Do you ever get drunk?"—True), suggesting a history of excessive imbibing. He did not have to answer in that fashion since no external record existed that he had taken excessive liberties with alcohol. During the subsequent face-to-face, the following dialogue ensued between the applicant and the examining psychologist. That information is taken directly from her notes:

> (*Number of times drunk in your life*?) "...my life! ...wow! (*approximate*?) I don't...a 100 or 150 somewhere around there...(*number of drinks for you to get drunk*?) "beer probably...4...within an hour...4 won't drive (total number?)...total...10 beers or so...Cd indicated that the last time within the last 12 months alone he had been drunk "...20 times maybe." Mr. Moculski allegedly also confessed to drinking "once a week...(*each time*?) if hanging out maybe a beer...if watching football take a beer, if party with friends coming from college 9–10 beers but I won't drive." (*He also checked "yes" to the question,* "Have you ever abused alcohol?" in the field investigator's *record form.*)

The applicant was then examined by a second psychologist, an expert in drug and alcohol addictions. He reported as follows:

> The candidate admitted to being drunk 200 times and revealed leading an "alcohol centric [life]; that [meaning] getting drunk is an important activity in his life." [This candidate] also noted, a discrepancy between the amount of drinking per occasion revealed by the candidate (2–3) in that particular interview and what he earlier stated to the other psychologist (9–10). In line with the preceding admissions, [the candidate] is pronounced to be at risk for alcohol related problems.

In later conversations, the candidate gave the following explanation for making those statements:

Yes, I circled "yes" to the [pre-oral questionnaire asking if I was a binge drinker] *because I thought that "binge drinking" meant consuming 3–5 drinks in an hour. I did drink like that while in college, but it lost its appeal. I have not done so in the past six years. I go to the gym to improve my health and also to meet the NYPD academy standards. I have also been mountain biking for about two years which demands great physical stamina. That type of behavior is not consistent with someone who values alcohol more than his wellbeing. My admission was just an attempt to be honest. I had heard on the news that binge drinking was defined as having 3–5 drinks in an hour. I went out every weekend because my friends and I turned 21 around the same time and it was something new and fun to do. But, since we did it almost every weekend, drinking lost its appeal. It is no longer part of my life going out and I am not at all dependent on drinking every time I go out. The only time I drink now is when I watch football on Sundays with my friends.*

I never claimed to have been drunk 200 times to either police psychologist. Instead, I stated I drank alcohol about 150 to 200 times in my entire life. That means one to three beers in the course of two and a half years. They were all single occasions. I certainly did not get drunk on each occasion or even "high". I have never done any type of drugs in my life and I certainly didn't drink every day. During my early undergraduate years I would drink, at most, twice a week and, on rare occasion, three times. Also, I never said that one beer would get me drunk.

The [police] psychologist asked me how many drinks I have had in my life not how many times I got drunk. I didn't think the question was a fair one: "how many drinks have I had in my whole life?" How is someone supposed to know how many drinks they have had in their life? The first also asked me to estimate the amount (as had the second) and I guessed 150 drinks. The psychologist responded with, "don't you think that's a little low" so I revised the number to 200. It was not what I really believed, but what I thought would satisfy her request to give a better response. However, I never intended my answer to mean that I was drunk on each occasion that I tasted alcohol.

Yes, the candidate could have refrained from saying all that he revealed. No one would have been the wiser because there was no contradictory data attesting otherwise. However, the candidate made his own bed by putting his foot in his mouth, believing that to tell all would show forthright of character. Now he has contracted me in an appeal action to overturn the rejection that ensued.

I do not believe the candidate is or was ever was an alcoholic. Instead, it is likely that he overdrank here and there, like many young college undergraduates. To his credit, he graduated with a B.S. in Criminal Justice in the requisite 4 years, has worked steadily, and is without untoward incident since graduating high school 8 years earlier. He also moonlights as an emergency medical technician in a large metropolitan city. However, those accomplishments were not sufficient to stop the *reject* label from being applied to his job application.

CONCLUDING THOUGHTS AND RECOMMENDATIONS

Certainly, psychologists working for police departments will do what they must to ensure that they hire the most competent applicants. That is why they veer on the false negative rather than false positive side of the decision-making spectrum. Yet, for those of us in the business of working with job rejection appeals and pre-application consultations, the duty is murkier. To repeat the earlier rhetorical questions, should we encourage silence if particular personal facts cannot be verified? If applicants were criminal suspects and we their lawyers, we would certainly advise them to remain quiet and not confess to anything. As I explain to every pre-application candidate, police departments have no universal "eye in the sky." They cannot check up on matters not in the public record or the candidate's verifiable history (e.g., schooling, work, military conduct, and criminal history). If they admit the personal, it is at their own peril.

With regard to appealing rejections that have the strong taint of "foot-in-mouth" disease (the majority of my cases), the task is much harder than mere prevention. Here, the job is rejecting and revising the storyline now imposed on the candidate by the rejecting psychologist (e.g., he or she is vulnerable to an emotional breakdown because she admitted to taking Prozac 5 years earlier, or he or she presents the risk of engaging in police brutality because he or she admitted to being a gang member in his or her early junior high school years). It is a labor of "un-smoothing" the narrative.

That can only be done by pointing out to the appealing authority that the police examiner over-stretched the credibility of his or rejection argument. It is also helped by piling on the candidate's positive accomplishments that are contrary to the psychologist's turn-down. However, the best preventive measure would have been to have said or admitted to nothing.

Finally, with respect to the recommendations for the examining police psychologist, he or she should consider the possibility that departmental or institutional biases are at play in their decision making. I also believe that they do not fully appreciate the idealism and naïveté of those whom they encounter. More often than not, when candidates are showing otherwise clean records, they are essentially children who have at times misstepped. They should also acquaint themselves with Freud's old concepts of transference and countertransference (the references to which are too numerous to detail). How much is a given disqualification a function of the applicant's shortcomings and limitations? How much of it is a projection of the police psychologist's own unexamined psychology?

REFERENCES

Blake, W. (1967). *Songs of innocence and experience*. Oxford: Oxford University Press. (Original work published 1789–1794)

Gilovich, T. K., Savitsky, K., & Medev, V. H. (1998). The illusion of transparency: Biased attempts by others to read one's emotions. *Journal of Personality and Social Psychology, 75*, 332–346.

Kassin, S. M. (2005). On the psychology of confession: Does innocence put innocents at risk? *American Psychologist, 60*, 215–228.

Lerner, M. (1966). Observer reaction to the "innocent victim": Compassion or rejection? *Journal of Personality and Social Psychology, 4*(2), 203–210.

Lerner, M. (1980). *The belief in a just world: A fundamental delusion*. New York: Plenum.

Miller, D. T., & McFarland, C. (1987). Pluralistic ignorance: When similarity is interpreted as dissimilarity. *Journal of Personality and Social Psychology, 75*, 298–305.

Nickerson, R. S. (1996). Confirmation bias: A ubiquitous phenomenon in many guises. *Review of General Psychology, 2*(2), 175–220.

Spence, D. P. (1984). *Narrative truth and historical truth: Meaning and interpretation in psychoanalysis*. New York: Basic Books.

Spence, D. P. (1986). Narrative smoothing and clinical wisdom. In T. R. Sarbin (Ed.), *Narrative psychology* (pp. 211–232). New York: Praeger.

Part III

Training and Evaluation

12 Police Couples Counseling/ Assessment and Use of the Inwald Relationship Surveys

Robin Inwald

Elizabeth Willman

Stephanie Inwald

During the last 3 decades, many professional discussions and opinions have been presented at conferences and in the literature about the potential negative effect of police work on couples and family relationships. There appears to be general consensus that training police couples, their families, and/or individual officers in the area of "police stress inoculation," along with confidential counseling as an early intervention, is appropriate in order to prevent poor work performance, domestic violence, divorce, and even suicide when at least one partner is working in the law enforcement field. However, limited data support this concept, and few research studies focus on police couples (Bartlett, 2004).

This chapter includes a literature review of available articles and books written on the subject of couples counseling and couples assessment in the police/public safety field. Survey data describing the frequency of couples counseling in the law enforcement field are presented, and methodological approaches that have been promoted as helpful in working with police couples are described. Finally, two case studies involving a comprehensive assessment of police couples using the Inwald Research Relationship Surveys are presented, one with an apparently successful relationship and one where the couple admitted to substantial relationship difficulties.

POLICE COUPLES LITERATURE REVIEW

In order to find available studies on this subject, a search through several databases was conducted using the following key words: *law enforcement personnel*, *police marriages*, and *police couples*. An independent follow-up search used the key words *police family*. In the first search, 78 journal articles and eight books were identified and reviewed from the following databases: PsychInfo, an online database for psychology and behavioral sciences with articles, summaries, and citations from journals, books, and dissertations; ProQuest, an online database containing abstracts and indexing for social and behavioral sciences; Academic Search Premier/ EBSCO, a database that contains indexing and abstracts for more than 8,450 journals; Sage Journals online, a database with more than 560 journals related to health, business, science, and behavioral and social sciences; and SocIndex, an online database for social sciences. Twenty-six articles were found that specifically mentioned work with police couples. However, only three articles (11.5%) contained research-based data obtained from evaluating police couples, each having collected these data using instruments developed by the first author of this chapter. The second search identified two additional articles on ProQuest, four from the PILOTS database, which publishes "international literature on traumatic stress," and two from Sociological Abstracts. The following review summarizes the findings of these literature searches.

During the 1970s, Rogers (1977) wrote that success in police work was best predicted by family stability and Danto (1978) reported that, in police officer suicides, marital problems were evident and may have been the precipitating factors. A number of articles were published about the impact of job stress on the family (Reiser, 1974), including a debate about police officer suicide rates (Rogers, 1977; Terry, 1981) and a call for couples' communication training and family therapy as intervention techniques (Maynard & Maynard, 1980; Reese, 1982). However, despite related comments in the literature, there were no quantitative studies found that presented research data about police couples in the 1970s or 1980s.

Borum and Philpot (1993) noted that there had been a large focus on police stress and its impact on officers but added that the "literature has not equally addressed the effects of police work on officers' relationships" (p. 122). They also noted:

> The law enforcement profession brings tremendous pressures to bear on the family relationships of those involved in this line of work. Widespread recognition of this has led to a popular notion that divorce rates for police officers are considerably higher than the national average. While empirical evidence does not support this particular idea, the variety of potential problems for these families is quite evident (p. 122).

In 1993 (July 27–30), the FBI sponsored the conference "Law Enforcement Families: Issues & Answers" at the FBI Academy in Quantico, Virginia. This conference was organized after the House of Representatives heard testimony regarding the counseling needs of law enforcement families (Bartlett, 2004). Several presentations were generated for this conference, followed by published papers in the FBI conference proceedings, thus beginning an ongoing discussion about police couples and their families by police psychologists and other interested professionals nationwide (Scrivner & Reese, 1994). Despite great interest, and a "setting of the stage" for follow-up studies, few of the presentations at that conference provided evidence-based research on police couples.

The first author presented her research at the FBI conference after developing the Hilson Spouse/Mate Inventory (HSMI) and Hilson Relationship Inventory for Public Safety Personnel (HRI-P), the first assessment instruments known by this author, which are used for evaluating relationship issues specific to police personnel and their spouses/partners (Inwald, Gebbia & Resko, 1993). These inventories focused on identifying communication/relationship difficulties, attitudes toward police issues, and stress symptoms in police couples. Two additional sets of colleagues also used these inventories to generate research papers for this conference.

Kaufmann, Smith, and Palmatier (1994) conducted a police couples' study using Inwald's HSMI and HRI-P with undercover officers in two basic narcotics officer training programs. Twenty-four undercover officers and their spouses/mates completed these two inventories. Officers reported a slight to moderate negative impact on their lives because of undercover work. However, contrary to the responses of their spouses/mates, officers reported that "rotating shifts," "politics of the job," and "spouses left alone at night" had a significant negative effect on their lives (p. 111). Additionally, spouses and mates of less senior officers reported lower stress levels compared to the spouse/mates of senior officers with longer careers in law enforcement. The researchers concluded that spouse/mate support programs and officer "transition" (p. 111) programs would be beneficial in the world of undercover policing.

Ryan and Brewster (1994) utilized Inwald's HSMI, HRI-P, a Post-Traumatic Stress Disorder subscale of the Minnesota Multiphasic Personality Inventory (MMPI), and the Beck Depression Inventory to study 12 recently traumatized police officers and their spouse/mate relationships. In this preliminary study, both relationship inventory scores and depression scores were similar for officers and their spouses/mates, suggesting that "the marital dyad may share many emotional consequences and symptoms following a traumatic event" (p. 222).

Other FBI presentations included some data about divorce, trauma, and suicide in police families. Gentz and Taylor (1994) examined attitudes about divorce among veteran law enforcement officers. The results of this study suggested a strong belief among veteran officers that their career choice and marital problems could lead to divorce. The authors concluded that further investigation regarding the impact of law enforcement careers on marriages is necessary.

Bohl and Solomon (1994) examined 30 officers and their spouses regarding postshooting reactions to determine (1) the degree to which spouses, as a group, recognize and acknowledge postshooting psychological and physical symptoms shown by their mates, and (2) the degree of agreement about these symptoms between husband–wife pairs. A 37-item questionnaire was used to identify stress symptoms typically experienced after a critical incident. Results illustrated that spouses often did not recognize and/or acknowledge the symptoms reported by their mates and, as a result, they may have failed to see problems even when the officer admitted that such problems existed. These authors called for more research on spouses and their interactions. Finally, Janik and Kravitz (1994) studied the relationship between marital discord and police suicide rates in a group of 134 police officers referred for fitness-for-duty evaluations, where 55% of them had admitted to previous suicide attempts. Results of this study indicated that complaints of marital problems "make an officer 4.8 times more likely to attempt suicide and 6.7 times more likely if they had been suspended; they were 21.7 times more likely if both complaints were present. Interestingly, complaints of being administratively harassed made officers less likely to attempt suicide" (p. 73).

Many other FBI conference-generated papers presented the view that the police family "experiences pressures typically not found in other occupations," stressing the need for additional research and interventions (Reese & Scrivner, 1994). Flater (1994), who described law enforcement family workshops, noted, "It is well documented that working in the field of law enforcement is detrimental to the functioning relationships of family life. However, by the time the law enforcement family seeks counseling, the relationship has usually reached a crisis point" (p. 329). Hays (1994) suggested that "in order to be effective in working with police couples, the therapist must have a solid understanding of the challenges of police work and…establish a nonhierarchical relationship" (p. 337). Klein (1994) recommended the use of peer counselors to help officers develop more effective communication skills with their spouses adding, "Communication that works well on the job does not work in (police) relationships" (p. 345).

During the mid-1990s, psychologists working with law enforcement agencies acted on the observation that police officers, or "tough guys, are often resistant to psychotherapy in its traditional forms and so special therapeutic approaches are required" (Miller, 1995, p. 592). Two counseling-oriented books were published specifically for law enforcement officers and their spouses/partners about police work, its particular stressors, and potential negative effect on relationships. In *Keeping It Simple: Sorting Out What Really Matters in Your Life*, Aumiller presented an instructive dialogue between a police officer and his therapist, including a series of therapeutic exercises, to teach the principle of keeping life simple, and free from alcohol/drug abuse and infidelity (Aumiller, 1995).

In the first edition of *I Love a Cop: What Police Families Need to Know*, Kirschman offered information designed to assist officers, families, and their partners in coping with the "everyday challenges facing police officers throughout their careers" (Kirschman, 2007, p. 7). This book's focus was to aid officers and their partners in creating a resilient and "supportive family environment where everyone can thrive" (Book Jacket). In a revised 2007 edition, chapters were added on substance abuse and domestic violence, along with accompanying statistics.

In the fall of 1998 (September 14–18), as the result of increasing concerns about domestic violence in police families, the FBI sponsored a "Domestic Violence by Police Officers" conference at Quantico, Virginia. As with the previous conference on law enforcement families, there were few data-based papers and much theoretical and practical information, including first-person accounts, regarding police couples and domestic violence. After the weeklong presentations and discussions on this topic concluded, the first author developed a new scale for identifying those individuals, including police officer candidates, who were most likely to become involved in domestic violence. This scale was added to the updated and renormed Inwald Survey 5-Revised (IS5-R; Inwald, Traynor, & Favuzza, 2000). While the IS5-R, with its Domestic Violence Scale, now has been used to assess thousands of police officer candidates, as well as officers who had been charged with incidents of domestic violence, no comprehensive studies of police couples or officers have been conducted using this measure prior to the occurrence of violent incidents.

During the early 2000s, psychologists continued to comment on police couples and relationships. However, despite the expressed interest in this area, little actuarial research was conducted: "While a few reports give anecdotal accounts of the role of police authoritarian style in marital interaction, a systematic examination of the relationship is virtually absent" (Sgambelluri, 2000). Bartlett (2004) wrote that "in the field of law enforcement occupational stress, the impact of a law enforcement career on the family and intimate relationships has been ignored" (as cited 10 years later in Bartlett, 2004).

The present literature search found only two assessment research studies with police couples during the 15-year period from 1995 to 2009, and both were doctoral dissertations. In 2004, Bartlett's dissertation included a construct validation study for Inwald's first two police couple's inventories, the Hilson Spouse/Mate Inventory (HSMI) and the Hilson Relationship Inventory for Public Safety Personnel (HRI-P; Inwald & Gebbia, 1997). With 60 participants, all sworn law enforcement officers and their mates, data were obtained showing a significant −.69 correlation between the communication/relationship difficulties subscale and the Dyadic Adjustment Scale (Spainer, 1976), "indicating divergent validity." Additionally, Bartlett's independent "Police Issues Interview" correlated .80 with the police issues subscale, "indicating that the HSMI and HRI-P police issues subscale is assessing a common construct pertaining to issues in the lives of law enforcement personnel and their mates" (Bartlett, 2004).

In 2005, Hirshfeld conducted a study of 33 police academy trainees and their mates that examined "secondary stress reactions among spouses and co-resident partners of newly recruited police officers, 6 and 12 months into their police service" (p. 1). Several instruments were administered in this study, including the Critical Incident History Questionnaire (CIHQ), PTSD Checklist (PCL), Symptom Checklist 90-Revised (SCL-90-R), and Beck Depression Inventory (BDI), among others. This study's goal was to "shed light on the conceptual ambiguities surrounding current discussions of secondary stress" (p. 1).

Other articles continued to highlight police family issues in the 2000s. In 2001, Roberts and Levenson commented on the connection between work and family life, stating that they are the "two major domains in our lives" (p. 1052). They further noted, "Research suggests that experiences from one domain can spill over into, or impact the other." These authors commented that police spouses "absorb" (p. 1052) much of the officer's stress and emotional distress. Kruger and Valltos (2002) added:

> Ironically, individuals who make good law enforcement officers often share some personality traits with those who batter or abuse their family members, such as the inclination to maintain control in emotional and tense circumstances, the tendency to establish a position of power and authority, and the physical presence to use weapons and other methods of physical control when needed. (pp. 2–3)

Johnson, Todd, and Subramanian (2005) discussed the theory that individuals who marry law enforcement officers "marry into the police family and are expected to adhere to the values and norms" of police culture. These authors explained:

> In exchange for the spouse's loyalty, the department promises to be there (in active duty and in death) for the officer and (his/her) family. This can become problematic when the police spouse calls 911 for protection against an abusive spouse.... While a wealth of information and resources exist for domestic violence victims ... police spouse victims are still as isolated and invisible as victims were 30 years ago. (p. 4)

In 2007, Miller stated:

> Research suggests that if police families can survive for the first three years, they have no greater risk for breaking up than other families. Furthermore, second police marriages tend to be even more stable and to endure as well or better than first or second marriages in the general population. (p. 21)

Miller's therapeutic goals stressed "(1) strengthening the demarcation line between the marriage and the police department demands; (2) reducing divided loyalties, triangulation, and jealousies between the job and the marriage; and (3) helping the couple strive towards bonding and intimacy" (Miller, 2007, p. 24).

In 2008, Davidson and Moss found that officers who disclosed insights into their traumatic experiences to their spouses did not reduce their psychological stress symptoms. These authors further noted that mental health providers need to develop new methodologies to assist officers in extracting meaning from the traumatic aspects of their work in order to reduce psychological adjustment difficulties. Finally, Violanti et al. (2008) noted that "marriage has been identified as a protective factor against suicide ideation and suicide" (p. 43).

2009 SURVEY OF POLICE PSYCHOLOGISTS AND COUPLES COUNSELING

In order to gather information about current trends in counseling, research, and assessment of police couples, a survey/interview was conducted by the first author while attending three separate national police psychology conferences in 2009. In-person interviews were conducted with participants at the annual meetings of the Police Psychological Services Section of the International Association for Chiefs of Police (IACP), the Society for Police & Criminal Psychology (SPCP), and the Consortium for Police Psychologists (COPPS). A total of 68 practicing police psychologists were interviewed directly about their work with police couples (where at least one of the partners held a position in law enforcement).

Of the 68 police psychologists interviewed, 47 (or 69%) had conducted therapy sessions with police couples during their careers. Together, these psychologists reported that they had counseled a total of 6,285 police couples (median of 24 couples per psychologist) over an average of 17 years in the field (median of 16 years per psychologist). This group of psychologists also represented the most active police psychology professionals in the United States, who regularly attend the specialized police psychology conferences and contribute articles and presentations in their field of specialization. When questioned about their theoretical orientation/approach to counseling police couples, there was little consensus. The most popular methodological approach was *cognitive-behavioral therapy* (mentioned by 18 psychologists, or 26% of those who conducted therapeutic sessions with police couples), followed by *systems approach* (mentioned by seven psychologists, or 10%), and *John Gottman's relationship research* (mentioned by four psychologists, or 6%). Eleven psychologists (16%) said they were eclectic in their approaches to counseling police couples.

Few police psychologists had used standardized assessment tools with their police couples, though 16 (23.5%) mentioned occasional use of instruments such as the HSMI/HRI-P, Myers-Briggs Type Indicator (MBTI), Minnesota Multiphasic Personality Inventory (MMPI), California Psychological Inventory (CPI), Sixteen Personality Factor Questionnaire (16PF), Inwald Personality Inventory (IPI), Symptom Checklist-90 (SCL-90), and Fundamental Interpersonal Relations Orientation (FIRO-B). Other than the research studies previously mentioned that were conducted using Inwald's HSMI and HRI-P, no additional research on police couples had been conducted by the 68 police psychologists in this survey.

TWO POLICE COUPLE CASE STUDIES

Description of Instruments Used

The Inwald Research Relationship Surveys, including the Inwald Couples Compatibility Questionnaire (ICCQ), Inwald Partner's Personality Inventory (IPPI), Inwald Personality Survey (IPS), Inwald Attitude Survey (IAS), and Inwald Trauma Recovery Inventory (ITRI), are used for the purpose of public safety officer relationship assessment and couples counseling in employee assistance programs (Inwald, 2006a, 2006b, 2006d). The IPS and the IAS, each containing under 110 true/false items, are used for self-assessment with regard to relationship issues. The IPS is a derivative of the Hilson Personnel Profile/Success Quotient (HPP/SQ), the first comprehensive personality inventory measuring "emotional intelligence" (Inwald, 2008; Inwald & Brobst, 1988; Inwald & Brockwell, 1988). The IAS is a derivative of the Inwald Survey 5 (IS5), an instrument that includes scales measuring areas of "integrity" and anger management, among others (Inwald & Gebbia, 1992).

The ICCQ and IPPI are surveys completed by individuals about their partners/spouses. The ICCQ, containing 148 true/false items, focuses on relationship compatibility; the IPPI, containing 128 true/false items, focuses on the partner's behavior patterns that may negatively affect relationships such as antisocial attitudes and substance abuse tendencies (see Appendix A for the individual scale names and descriptions of Inwald Research Relationship Surveys). All four components of the Inwald Research Relationship Surveys were developed after a series of FBI conferences provided information suggesting that relationship problems are often triggers for police officer suicides and violent behavior.

The Inwald Trauma Recovery Inventory (ITRI) was developed by the first author as a result of discussions at the 1998 FBI Conference on Domestic Violence by Police Officers and the recent influx of officers returning from overseas military duty in the Middle East (Inwald, 1998; Inwald, 2006c). This instrument, containing 111 true/false items, focuses on the assessment of reactions to traumatic events as well as the identification of an individual's current feelings of depression, anger, and/or stress. It can be administered to an individual or used as part of a comprehensive battery to evaluate a couple's coping skills.

The Inwald Research Relationship Surveys, used with or without the ITRI, are the first comprehensive partner/spouse-oriented surveys developed for use as a preventative approach, providing actuarial "relationship check-ups" (Inwald, 2010, p. 4) to assist public safety officers. An employee assistance counselor or family psychotherapist can interpret narrative results to couples and review comparative profile graphs, showing each individual how his or her admitted behavior patterns and/or personality characteristics may be affecting the relationship. Providing and explaining survey results with the aid of a tangible graph format to officers, who may be defensive about admitting to their shortcomings, can help them better understand how their behavior patterns might be improved. In addition, the therapist can use the visual documentation of the profiles, along with the printed individual item endorsements, to develop a treatment plan with the direct involvement of each couple. Finally, public safety agencies can offer the use of accessible online surveys, such as these relationship surveys, as a way to demonstrate their commitment to maintaining a preventative approach to domestic violence in police families.

Couple Case Study A

The Inwald Research Relationship Surveys, including the Inwald Couples Compatibility Questionnaire (ICCQ), Inwald Partners Personality Inventory (IPPI), Inwald Personality Survey (IPS), and the Inwald Attitude Survey (IAS) were administered to a 32-year-old public safety officer, Jim, and his 29-year-old wife, Amy (see Appendix A for each survey's scale names and descriptions). Jim has been working as a patrol officer for a small Midwestern department for 10 years, and has specialized as a K-9 Handler for the past 3½ years. Amy has been working in a dispatch center for the past 4 years. The couple has four children together.

Jim's IPS results (see Figure 12.1) showed him to be an academically-oriented (AI, Academic Interest), socially sensitive (SC, Social Approval Concerns), and driven/hardworking person (EF, Effort toward Responsibilities) with a strong work ethic (SR, Sensitivity about Responsibility). Liked by his peers (PP, Popularity with Peers), he appeared sensitive to how he is perceived by others. It was reported that, in his department, Jim takes his responsibilities as a public safety officer very seriously and is highly organized when it comes to work.

Jim's high TF score (Limited Tolerance of Frustration) on the IAS (see Figure 12.2) suggests that he may be an impatient person who tends to overreact when frustrated. Jim readily admitted

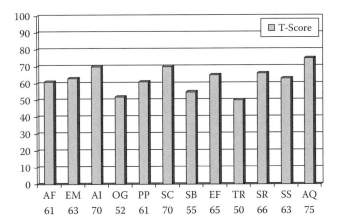

FIGURE 12.1   IPS for Jim—Couple Case Study A.

to his shortcomings (AF, Admission of Faults), including having a temper, but also endorsed items showing that he does not trust others easily (TN, Lack of Trusting Nature). Finally, Jim's high CS (Composure under Stress Difficulties) score suggests a sense of entitlement or belief that he would be able to "beat the system." Jim's elevated levels of cynicism and distrust may reflect his personal style or attitudes developed after working in the law enforcement field for over 10 years.

With regard to how he views Amy, Jim's ICCQ (see Figure 12.3) indicates that, despite several areas of admitted incompatibility, Jim wants to stay in this relationship (high BL, Bottom Line). Jim reported feeling a high level of affection and physical attraction for Amy (AF, Affection/Physical Attraction) as well as compatibility in the area of general habits (HA, Habits/Issues Compatibility). However, Jim also expressed that he feels Amy is often very jealous and controlling of him (low JE score, Lack of Jealous Behavior, and low CB score, Lack of Controlling Behavior). Finally, his ICCQ scores suggest that Jim and his wife do not share the same interests or backgrounds (CI, Interests Compatibility, IB, Interests/Background Compatibility).

Jim's IPPI (see Figure 12.4) about Amy suggests that he believes she is a moderate drinker (AU, Alcohol Use Patterns) with some past work adjustment difficulties (LR, Reliability).

Amy's IPS results (see Figure 12.5) indicated that, like her husband, she was candid on the survey and readily admitted to her flaws and/or shortcomings (AF, Admission of Faults). Somewhat extroverted (OG, "Outgoing" Personality) and liked by her peers (PP, Popularity with Peers), Amy appears to have a strong need for obtaining the approval of others, and she also may tend to be

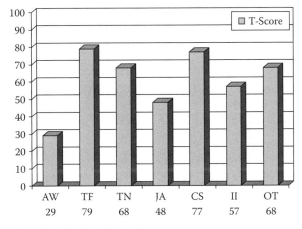

FIGURE 12.2   IAS for Jim—Couple Case Study A.

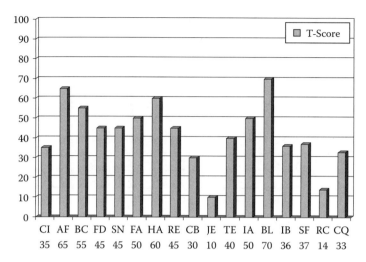

FIGURE 12.3   ICCQ for Jim—Couple Case Study A.

highly sensitive to criticism (SC, Social Approval Concerns). However, unlike her husband, she is a procrastinator (TR, Timeliness about Responsibilities) and is not particularly driven or motivated at work (EF, Effort toward Responsibilities). She cares about helping others (EM, Empathy/Helping Others) and may use her social skills to counsel those who come to her for advice/support.

Results on the IAS (see Figure 12.6) suggest that Amy has had some difficulties in the area of work, such as a history of absence and/or lateness (JA, Job/Career Adjustment Difficulties). This was corroborated by Jim's IPPI about Amy, suggesting past work adjustment difficulties. Amy also appeared to be somewhat suspicious of the motives of others (TN, Lack of Trusting Nature) and showed a tendency to become easily frustrated (TF, Limited Tolerance of Frustration). These characteristics may cause some difficulties in Amy's marriage because she may tend to be overly sensitive (IPS results above), suspicious, and somewhat rebellious (IAS results) at times. Amy's admissions on the IAS are corroborated by Jim's ICCQ results above, where he reported that Amy was both jealous and controlling in their relationship.

Amy's ICCQ (see Figure 12.7) suggests that she, like Jim, feels a strong physical affection/attraction to her spouse (AF, Affection/Physical Attraction) and wants their relationship to continue (BL, Bottom Line), despite some family differences (FA, Family Compatibility). While generally content with her marriage, Amy endorsed items indicating that Jim may tend to be a somewhat jealous person (JE, Lack of Jealousy) who loses his temper under stress (TE, Temper Control) and

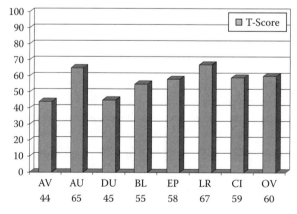

FIGURE 12.4   IPPI for Jim—Couple Case Study A.

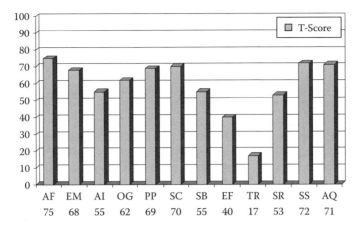

FIGURE 12.5   IPS for Amy—Couple Case Study A.

is very assertive with her (IA, Interpersonal Assertiveness). According to Amy, financial issues have negatively affected this relationship (FD, Financial/Functional Compatibility). Amy's ICCQ suggests that this couple shares more interests in common than were reported by her husband (CI, Interests Compatibility).

It is interesting to note that Amy's IPPI results (see Figure 12.8) about Jim are very similar to his views about her on the same issues. Amy indicated that she believes Jim has a moderate to high tolerance/use of alcohol (AU, Alcohol Use) and that he also has a history of absence abuse (e.g., taking sick time from work when not really ill: LR, Reliability).

In an interview with the second author, Jim reported it was not surprising to him that the survey results suggested a high level of jealousy in the relationship because both he and Amy are working in law enforcement. Jim mentioned that he often hears about police officers from different departments exchanging stories about other officers and their relationships with the dispatchers. He admitted, "It bothers me from time to time that they are always talking a lot with the dispatchers, especially with Amy." Jim stated that he feels Amy is often "controlling and unreliable in certain areas" and that he is annoyed when she questions him, from time to time, about the messages he sends to other dispatchers, regardless of their content. Jim admitted that he becomes upset when questioned, causing both partners to struggle with the issue of jealousy.

This couple also expressed a strong commitment to police work, mentioning that having different schedules was helpful in allowing individual time with their four children and then time with each other while the children were at school. Jim and Amy felt that this was beneficial in raising

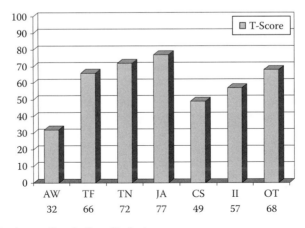

FIGURE 12.6   IAS for Amy—Couple Case Study A.

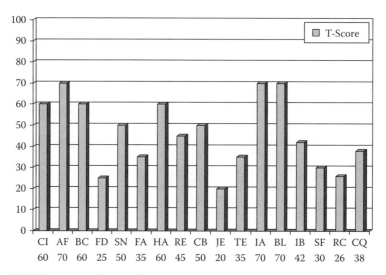

FIGURE 12.7   ICCQ for Amy—Couple Case Study A.

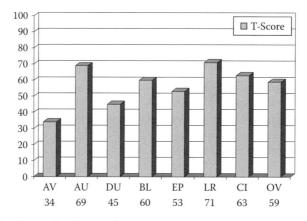

FIGURE 12.8   IPPI for Amy—Couple Case Study A.

their family because at least one parent always was home to supervise the children. Finally, Jim reported that he and Amy found the feedback from the Inwald Research Relationship Surveys to be very helpful and remarked that the information gave them "something to work on." Despite some differences, Amy and Jim appeared firmly committed to their marriage, with each partner presenting a candid and realistic evaluation of the positive and negative characteristics defining their relationship.

Couple Case Study B

The Inwald Research Relationship Surveys, including the Inwald Couples Compatibility Questionnaire (ICCQ), Inwald Partners Personality Inventory (IPPI), Inwald Personality Survey (IPS), and Inwald Attitude Survey (IAS), along with the Inwald Trauma Recovery Inventory (ITRI), were administered to a 27-year-old male public safety officer, Peter, and his 28-year-old wife, Stacy (see Appendices A and B for each survey's scale names and descriptions). Peter began working in the law enforcement field when he was 19, first as a dispatcher for 3 years and then as a crime scene technician for 2 years. He had worked for 1 year as a part-time patrol officer and had been working for 1 year as a full-time officer in a small southern police agency when he shot and killed a mentally ill man who was shooting at him. Although later cleared by his department, Peter fired 10 shots at

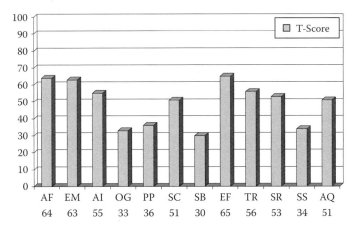

FIGURE 12.9   IPS for Peter—Couple Case Study B.

the man, hitting him eight times. Peter began counseling approximately 1 month after this deadly force incident. After meeting through the Internet, Peter and Stacy were married for 8 years and had three children together. They separated 1 month prior to testing.

Peter's high score on the EM (Empathy/Helping Others) scale of the IPS (see Figure 12.9) suggests that he has a strong interest in coaching or counseling others and that he is the type of person others may seek out for advice. His relatively high EF (Efforts toward Responsibility) score suggests that this officer is a dedicated worker who will put in extra time to meet his responsibilities. Peter recently worked to develop a peer-counseling network in his law enforcement community. This officer appears to set very high standards for himself and, at times, can be highly self-critical as indicated by his high AF (Admission of Faults) score and low SB (Self-Belief) score. An introverted person, as indicated by a low OG (Outgoing Personality) score, he may lack self-confidence at times (low SB score) and have some difficulties communicating his needs to others.

Peter's relatively high TF (Limited Tolerance of Frustration) score on the IAS (see Figure 12.10) suggests that he may be a somewhat impatient person who has difficulty tolerating frustration. He may tend to overreact or become argumentative in situations where he feels misunderstood.

Peter's ITRI scores (see Figure 12.11) show evidence of depression, as indicated by his elevated LS (Lack of Satisfaction with Life) score and individual item endorsements, suggesting suicidal thoughts. In addition, elevations on both SN (Lack of Social Network) and FS (Lack of Family Support) reflect his belief that he lacks a significant social network and family support. Finally,

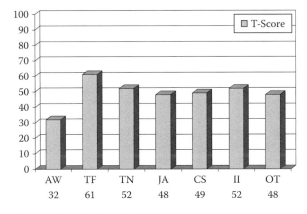

FIGURE 12.10   IAS for Peter—Couple Case Study B.

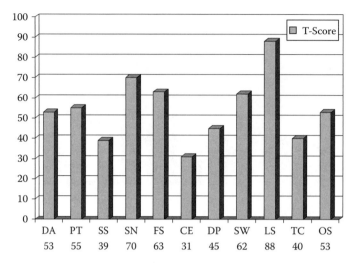

FIGURE 12.11   ITRI for Peter—Couple Case Study B.

Peter's elevated SW (Lack of Self-Worth) score suggests a low level of self-esteem, in agreement with his IPS results. Several ITRI item endorsements verify that he believes his deadly force incident had a serious negative effect, resulting in increased frustration, temper outbursts, and feelings of being out of control.

With regard to how he views Stacy, Peter's ICCQ (see Figure 12.12) indicates serious difficulties in the overall relationship, as demonstrated by a low BL (Bottom Line) and CQ (Compatibility Quotient). Peter's low scores on his ICCQ suggest that, other than agreeing that they do not have a problem with jealousy (JE), Peter feels they do not have compatible interests (CI), habits (HA), or compatible financial attitudes (FD). Coming from different backgrounds (BC), he also feels that Stacy lacks a respectful attitude toward him (RE), loses her temper frequently (TE), and has a drinking habit (individual items).

Peter's IPPI about Stacy (see Figure 12.13) verifies his belief that she is a high risk for alcohol abuse (AU = 83t); has shown a history of work adjustment difficulties, confirmed by an elevated EP (Employment Problems) score; and shows evidence of depression (individual Critical Items—CI).

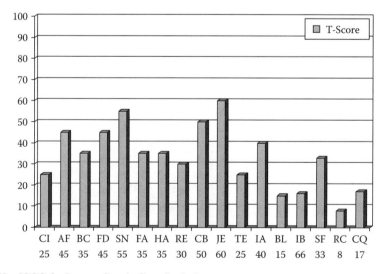

FIGURE 12.12   ICCQ for Peter—Couple Case Study B.

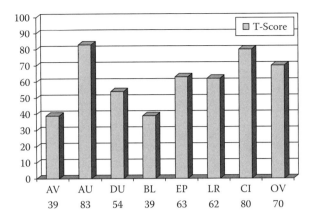

FIGURE 12.13   IPPI for Peter—Couple Case Study B.

Stacy's IPS results (see Figure 12.14) were similar to Peter's in that they were both candid on the test (AF), introverted (OG), lacked self-esteem (SB), and demonstrated a desire to help others (EM). Stacy's IPS also showed her tendency to procrastinate (TR), seek the approval of others, and be overly sensitive to criticism (SC).

Stacy had unusually high scores on the IAS (see Figure 12.15), indicating very poor frustration tolerance and temper control (TF = 82t), distrust of others (TN), job adjustment difficulties (JA), and integrity concerns (II). Her adjustment difficulties admitted on the IAS corroborated Peter's view of her on the ICCQ and IPPI.

ITRI results for Stacy (see Figure 12.16) indicated that a traumatic event has been significant in her life (PT). Suicidal thoughts and depression (LS = 100t and 28 Critical Items) were admitted along with difficulties with temper control (TC) and low self-worth (SW). Peter reported to his therapist that Stacy had come from an abusive family background and had "cut herself" in a bid for attention on several occasions.

With regard to how Stacy viewed Peter, Stacy's ICCQ (see Figure 12.17) also indicated serious difficulties in the relationship (low RC and CQ). However, she had higher overall scores and reported that there was much more physical attraction/affection in the relationship than Peter had indicated in his responses (AF). Stacy's low scores on her ICCQ suggested that she felt Peter lacked a respectful attitude toward her (RE) and lost his temper frequently (TE), and that they had some significant family conflicts/incompatibility (FA).

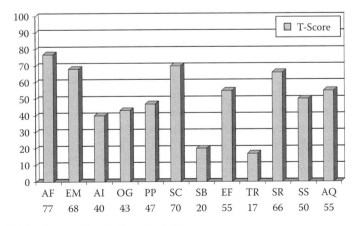

FIGURE 12.14   IPS for Stacy—Couple Case Study B.

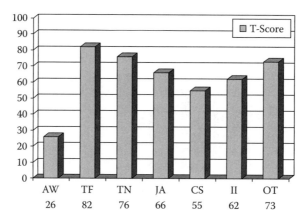

FIGURE 12.15   IAS for Stacy—Couple Case Study B.

Stacy's IPPI about Peter (see Figure 12.18) indicated that she believes he may abuse alcohol (AU), has had several incidents of antisocial behavior (BL), and has shown signs of depression and difficulty controlling his temper (Critical Items).

Peter admitted in therapy that he had been drinking more often since the deadly force incident because of his having nightmares and emotional difficulties. He also admitted to putting his fist through a wall. He acknowledged that when Stacy became pregnant, he had decided to become a police officer in order to support the family. It appeared to the therapist that, although Peter took his responsibilities seriously with regard to both the police department and his family, he also felt great stress on his job and was neither fully committed nor well suited for police work as a profession. His interest in counseling and possible goal of obtaining certification in that field was encouraged by the therapist as a future career option.

While Stacy did not want to end the marriage, this couple's unhappiness and incompatibility are evident in their combined survey results. In addition, both endorsed the ICCQ item suggesting that they have "serious differences of opinion related to children." With therapy, Peter claimed there were improvements in a few of his problem areas. However, the survey results reveal a relationship that will be difficult to salvage due to admitted alcohol use, lack of temper control, impulsive reactions, and expressed incompatibility in several key areas.

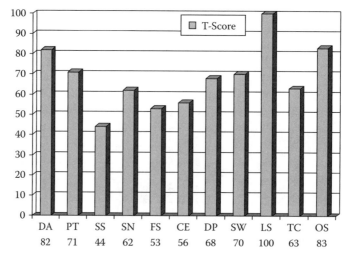

FIGURE 12.16   ITRI for Stacy—Couple Case Study B.

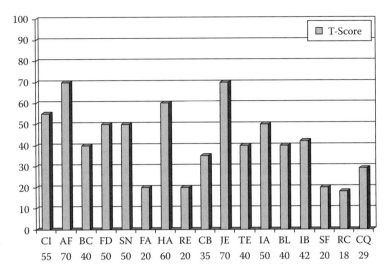

FIGURE 12.17   ICCQ for Stacy—Couple Case Study B.

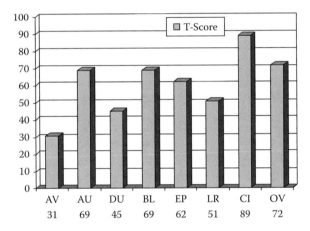

FIGURE 12.18   IPPI for Stacy—Couple Case Study B.

SUMMARY

After reviewing the available literature and surveying dozens of practicing police psychologists, it is clear that there still is much interest, though relatively little quantitative research, in the area of police couples and police marriages. At a time when public safety departments are cutting back on recruitment because of severe budget restrictions, it is especially important to care for the mental and physical health of working law enforcement officers. Also, with a reduction in pre-employment psychological screening duties, police psychologists may have more available time to attend to new areas of development, such as "police family wellness." Since it has been established that an officer's home life, along with a positive significant relationship, is a key factor in maintaining that officer's sense of well-being, a new focus on helping police couples with their individual relationship challenges may prove valuable for increasing work productivity as well. When presented in a nonjudgmental atmosphere that does not compromise the officer's work status, voluntary "relationship checkups," with reliable feedback from an experienced police psychologist or trained peer counselor, may become one standard early intervention strategy that will benefit both the individual couples and the police agencies that hire them. It is hoped that the information in this chapter, as well as the development of the Inwald Research Relationship Surveys, will be of use to police psychologists and law enforcement department administrators as they work together to support the physical and emotional health of their public safety officers.

Author Note

Inquiries about the Inwald Research Relationship Surveys presented in this chapter, including the Inwald Couples Compatibility Questionnaire (ICCQ), Inwald Partners Personality Inventory (IPPI), Inwald Personality Survey (IPS), Inwald Attitude Survey (IAS), or Inwald Trauma Recovery Inventory (ITRI), should be addressed to: Inwald Research, Inc., P.O. Box 73, Cleverdale, NY 12820; phone: 917-757-9063 or 866-508-2224.

There also are free computer administration and test-scoring services available for individuals and/or agencies interested in participating in research using this test battery with police and other couples in the public safety field. Original independent research studies are encouraged, and training will be provided for giving appropriate feedback to couples who complete the surveys. For further information, please contact the authors.

REFERENCES

Aumiller, G. (1995). *Keeping it simple: Sorting out what really matters in your life.* Avon, MA: Adams Media.

Bartlett, K.G. (2004). *A validation study of the Hilson Relationship Inventory of Public Safety Personnel (HRI-P) and the Hilson Spouse/Mate Inventory (HSMI).* Doctoral dissertation, Wright Institute Graduate School of Psychology, Berkeley, CA.

Bohl, N., & Solomon, R. M. (1994). Male law enforcement officers and their spouses' perceptions to post-shooting reactions. In E. Scrivner (Ed.), *Law enforcement families: Issues and answers* (pp. 101–109). Washington, DC: U.S. Government Printing Office.

Borum, R., & Philpot, C. (1993). Therapy with law enforcement couples: Clinical management of the high-risk lifestyle. *The American Journal of Family Therapy, 21*(2), 122–135.

Danto, B. (1978). Police stress. *Police Stress, 1*(3), 32–36.

Davidson, A. C., & Moss, S. A. (2008). Examining the trauma disclosure of police officers to their partners and officers' subsequent adjustment. *Journal of Language and Social Psychology, 27*(1), 51–70.

Flater, L. (1994). Officer/spouse workshops: A prevention and intervention technique. In E. Scrivner (Ed.), *Law enforcement families: Issues and answers* (pp. 329–336). Washington, DC: U.S. Government Printing Office.

Gentz, D., & Taylor, D. (1994). Marital status and attitude about divorce among veteran law enforcement officers. In E. Scrivner (Ed.), *Law enforcement families: Issues and answers* (pp. 67–71). Washington, DC: U.S. Government Printing Office.

Hays, G. (1994). Police couples: Breaking the security code. In E. Scrivner (Ed.), *Law enforcement families: Issues and answers* (pp. 337–344). Washington, DC: U.S. Government Printing Office.

Hirshfeld, A. (2005). *Secondary effects of traumatization among spouses and partners of newly recruited police officers.* Doctoral dissertation, Alliant International University.

Inwald, R. (1993). *Hilson Relationships Inventory for public safety personnel and Hilson/Spouse Mate Inventory.* New York: Hilson Research.

Inwald, R. (1998, September 17–18). *Psychological profiles of police and public safety officers involved with domestic violence.* Paper prepared and presented at the Domestic Violence by Police Officers Conference, FBI Academy, Quantico, VA.

Inwald, R. (2006a, May 19). Assessment of marital issues for law enforcement couples. Annual Conference of the Consortium of Police Psychologists, Fort Lauderdale, FL.

Inwald, R. (2006b, October 14). Identifying relationship difficulties in police couples using the Inwald Relationship Assessment Battery. Annual Conference of the International Association of Chiefs of Police, Boston, MA.

Inwald, R. (2006c, October 15). *Use of a customized Hilson Research test battery to identify stress susceptibility in returning military veterans.* Annual Conference of the International Association of Chiefs of Police, Boston, MA.

Inwald, R. (2006d, October 26). Inwald Couples Evaluation Program (ICEP): An evaluation of the profiles and problems of police couples. Annual Conference of the Society for Police and Criminal Psychology, Washington DC.

Inwald, R. E. (2008). The Inwald Personality Inventory (IPI) and Hilson Research Inventories: Development & rationale. *Journal of Aggression and Violent Behavior, 13*, 298–327.

Inwald, R. (2010). Use of the Inwald Personality Inventory, Hilson tests, and Inwald Surveys for selection, "fitness-for-duty" assessment, and relationship counseling. In P. A. Weiss (Ed.), *Personality assessment in police psychology* (pp. 91–131). Springfield, IL: Charles C Thomas.

Inwald, R., & Brobst, K. E. (1988). *Hilson Personnel Profile/Success Quotient (HPP/SQ) technical manual.* New York: Hilson Research.

Inwald, R., & Brockwell, A. (1988). *Success quotient profiles of law enforcement administrators.* New York: Hilson Research.

Inwald, R. E., & Gebbia, M. I. (1992). *Inwald Survey 5 (IS5) technical manual.* New York: Hilson Research.

Inwald, R., & Gebbia, M. (1997). *Hilson Spouse/Mate Inventory & Hilson Relationship Inventory technical manual.* Kew Gardens, NJ: Hilson Research.

Inwald, R., Gebbia, M., & Resko, J. (1993). Three studies of police/spouse mate relationships using the Hilson Spouse/Mate Inventory. In E. Scrivner (Ed.), *Law enforcement families: Issues and answers.* Washington, DC: U.S. Government Printing Office.

Inwald, R., Traynor, W., & Favuzza, V. (2000). Psychological profiles of police and public safety officers accused of domestic violence. *Domestic Violence by Police Officers.* Washington, DC: U.S. Government Printing Office.

Janik, J., & Kravitz, H. (1994). Police suicides: Trouble at home. In E. Scrivner (Ed.), *Law enforcement families: Issues and answers* (pp. 73–81). Washington, DC: U.S. Government Printing Office.

Johnson, L. B., Todd, M., & Subramanian, G. (2005). Violence in police families: Work-family spillover. *Journal of Family Violence, 20*(1), 3–12.

Kaufmann, G., Smith, R., & Palmatier, J. (1994). An assessment of undercover officer spouse/mate relationships. In E. Scrivner (Ed.), *Law enforcement families: Issues and answers* (pp. 111–116). Washington, DC: U.S. Government Printing Office.

Kirshman, E. (1997). *I love a cop: What police families need to know.* New York: Guilford.

Kirshman, E. (2007). *I love a cop: What police families need to know* (Rev. ed). New York: Guilford.

Klein, R. (1994). Training peer counselors to provide the initial intervention in law enforcement relationship problems. In E. Scrivner (Ed.), *Law enforcement families: Issues and answers* (pp. 345–351). Washington, DC: U.S. Government Printing Office.

Kruger, K. J., & Valltos, N. G., (2002, July). Dealing with domestic violence in law enforcement relationships. *FBI Law Enforcement Bulletin.*

Maynard, P., & Maynard, N. (1980, February). Providing police family stress through couples' communication training. *The Police Chief*, pp. 30–31.

Miller, L. (1995). Tough guys: Psychotherapeutic strategies with law enforcement and emergency personnel. *Psychotherapy, 32*(4), 592–599.

Miller, L. (2007). Police families: Stresses, syndromes and solutions. *The American Journal of Family Therapy, 35*, 21–40.

Reese, J., & Scrivner, E. (1994). Family issues with no easy answers. In E. Scrivner (Ed.), *Law enforcement families: Issues and answers* (pp. 3–7). Washington, DC: U.S. Government Printing Office.

Reese, J. T. (1982, November). Family therapy in law enforcement: A new approach to an old problem. *FBI Law Enforcement Bulletin*, pp. 1–5.

Reiser, M. (1974). Some organizational stresses on policemen. *Journal of Police Science and Administration, 2*(2), 156–159.

Roberts, N. A., & Levenson, R. W. (2001). The remains of the workday: Impact of job stress and exhaustion on marital interaction in police couples. *Journal of Marriage and Family, 63*, 1052–1067.

Rogers, K. (1977). Marriage and the police officer. *The Police College Magazine, 14*(1), 10.

Ryan, A. H., & Brewster, M. E. (1994). Post-traumatic stress disorder and related symptoms in traumatized police officers and their spouses/mates. In E. Scrivner (Ed.), *Law enforcement families: Issues and answers* (pp. 217–225). Washington, DC: U.S. Government Printing Office.

Sgambelluri, A. V. (2000). Police culture, police training, and police administration: Their impact on violence in police families. In D. Sheehan (Ed.), *Domestic violence by law enforcement officers* (pp. 309–322). Washington, DC: U.S. Government Printing Office.

Spainer, G. (1976). Measuring dyadic adjustment: New scales for assessing the quality of marriage and similar dyads. *Journal of Marriage and the Family, 38,* 15–28.

Terry, W. (1981). The empirical evidence. *Journal of Police Science and Administration, 9*(1) 61–75.

Violanti, J. M., Fekedulegn, D., Charles, L. E., Andrew, M. E., Hartley, T. A., Mnatsakanova, A., & Burchfield, C. M. (2008). Suicide in police work: Exploring potential contributing influences. *American Journal of Criminal Justice, 34*, 41–53.

APPENDIX A: INWALD RESEARCH RELATIONSHIP SURVEYS—SCALE DESCRIPTIONS

Inwald Personality Survey (IPS) Scale Descriptions

Admission of Faults (AF)

Measures degree of defensive responding on this survey. Low scores suggest a desire to appear unusually virtuous and without fault. Low scores on this scale indicate that the other test scores may be inflated due to "socially-desirable" responses.

Empathy/Helping Others (EM)

Individuals with high scores on this scale may be skilled in counseling and coaching others. Such individuals enjoy making suggestions and giving people advice regarding their problems and/ or goals.

Academic Interest/New Skills Development (AI)

Measures achievement in past jobs and school. High scores suggest excellence in academic/work history as well as past recognition for special skills and/or talents. General level of academic ability may be reflected in this scale.

SA—Social Ability Content Areas (OG, PP, SC)
Outgoing Personality (OG)

Measures tendency to be outgoing and talkative. High scores suggest an extroverted, outer-directed individual.

Popularity With Peers (PP)

Measures degree of popularity this person has enjoyed in the past. High scores suggest a charismatic individual who is liked by others and may have been frequently chosen as a leader or spokesperson.

Social Approval Concerns (SC)

Measures degree of sensitivity regarding social approval. High scorers are particularly aware of how their behavior is being judged by others and strive to gain others' approval. High scorers may become upset when they feel they have said the wrong thing or hurt someone else's feelings.

Self-Belief (SB)

Measures self-confidence and general sense of mastery over obstacles in the world. High scorers are sure of themselves and feel they can do most things well.

IN—Initiative Content Areas (EF, TR, SR)
Effort Toward Responsibilities (EF)

Measures the tendency to go the extra mile and strive for completion of tasks and excellence. High scorers may tend to work harder than their peers and may demonstrate qualities of workaholism. They may also show the ability to focus or concentrate on tasks for long periods of time.

Timeliness About Responsibilities (TR)

Measures the tendency to avoid procrastination. High scorers tend to complete work on time, to organize work when it is assigned, and to meet responsibilities in a timely fashion. Low scorers may complete their work on or close to schedule, but they tend to put it off until the last minute.

Sensitivity About Responsibilities (SR)

Measures level of concern regarding completing assigned tasks in a correct and/or timely manner. Anxiety over incomplete or unsatisfactory work is common for high scorers, who try to meet responsibilities so that they will not feel guilty or pressured.

Social Skills (SS)

Measures overall social/communication skills by combining three scales: OG + PP + SC.

Adaptability Quotient (AQ) Total Score

Measures potential for success and emotional intelligence. High scores on the combination of all IPS scales suggest higher overall potential.

INWALD ATTITUDE SURVEY (IAS) SCALE DESCRIPTIONS

Lack of Self-Awareness (AW)

Measures the degree to which the individual has been honest or candid about his/her feelings and behaviors. High scores suggest a denial of minor shortcomings in an effort to appear unusually virtuous and without fault. Elevated scores on this scale also may indicate that other tests scores may be deflated due to socially-desirable responses.

Limited Tolerance of Frustration (TF)

Identifies individuals with impulsive behavior patterns and low frustration tolerance. High scores indicate patterns of impulsive, restless behavior. High scorers on this scale may be outspoken and/or impatient with others. Elevated scores also may identify those who express hostility and anger more frequently than others who face similar situations.

Lack of Trusting Nature (TN)

High scorers may tend to distance themselves from others and may show distrust regarding the behavior of others. These individuals may be more content in situations that do not require extensive teamwork.

Job/Career Adjustment Difficulties (JA)

High scorers on this scale may tend to have job adjustment difficulties and/or difficulties holding jobs. Elevated scorers may have a history of being disciplined for counterproductive behavior.

Composure Under Stress Difficulties (CS)

Elevated scores on this scale suggest antisocial attitudes. High scorers may have more relaxed attitudes towards theft when compared with others. These individuals may feel that taking risks, or bending the rules in order to "beat the system," is justified.

Integrity Issues (II)

Elevated scores on this scale suggest a history of brushes with the law and societal norms, especially with regard to theft from employees and/or other parties. The backgrounds of these individuals may include incidents where personal integrity has been questioned.

Overall Total (Risk Score—OT)

A combination of all IAS scales measuring overall conscientiousness/reliability. Low scores suggest lower levels of overall conscientiousness/reliability.

Inwald Couples Compatibility Questionnaire (ICCQ) Scale Descriptions

Interests/Background Compatibility (IB = CI + AF + BC + FD)
Interests Compatibility (CI)

Identifies compatibility in the area of common interests such as hobbies, shared activities, time spent together, daily routines, and friends. Elevated scores indicate that, as far as the person answering the questionnaire is concerned, there is compatibility in this area.

Affection/Physical Compatibility (AF)

Identifies the level of physical attraction the person answering this questionnaire feels towards his or her mate. High scores also measure the level of satisfaction with affection received from the other person. Low scores suggest that there may not be as much affection and/or physical attraction in the relationship as the person answering the questionnaire would like.

Background Compatibility (BC)

Identifies cultural, political, religious, and age similarities for this couple. High scores suggest that both people in this relationship come from similar backgrounds and age groups. Low scores suggest potential difficulties in the relationship based on different cultural, religious, and/or political backgrounds.

Financial/Functional Compatibility (FD)

Identifies areas of conflict regarding financial matters, including concerns that the other person in the relationship has had financial difficulties and/or career problems that have caused difficulties for the couple.

Social/Family Compatibility (SF = SN + FA)
Social Network Compatibility (SN)

Identifies the compatibility of this couple with regard to each member's friends and social network. Low scores suggest that there are serious concerns about the other person's friends and/or the amount of time spent socializing with them.

Family Compatibility (FA)

Identifies the compatibility of this couple with regard to family members. Low scores suggest problems getting along with certain relatives and/or concerns about this relationship by relatives that may be a source of conflict for this couple.

Relationship Compatibility (RC = HA + RE + CB + JE + TE + IA)
Habits/Issues Compatibility (HA)

Designed to measure concerns about the other person's habits such as use of alcohol, drugs, personal care, and overeating. Low scores suggest that some habitual behaviors of this nature may be causing friction in the relationship.

Respectful Treatment (RE)

Scale results indicate whether or not the person answering this questionnaire believes that his or her mate is respectful and sensitive. High scores suggest concerns about the way he or she is treated by the other person.

Lack of Over-Controlling Behavior (CB)

Identifies the presence of over-controlling behavior on the part of the other person. Low scores suggest problems in the relationship due to the other person's overly critical, moody, or assertive nature.

Lack of Jealousy (JE)

Documents a pattern of jealous behavior on the part of the other person. A low score on this scale indicates that jealous behavior is causing some discomfort for the person answering this questionnaire.

Temper Control (TE)

Measures concerns about the other person's ability to control his or her temper. Low scores indicate that the other person may tend to overreact, may lose his or her temper, and may be unpleasant and complaining when there are conflicts in the relationship.

Interpersonal Assertiveness (IA)

Documents the respondent's concerns regarding the other person's level of assertiveness. Low scores suggest that the respondent believes his or her partner lacks assertiveness and may let others take advantage of situations.

Bottom Line Summary (BL)

Identifies doubts or insecurities about the relationship. Serious differences about the level of commitment or staying together may be expressed. Low scores suggest that the person answering the questionnaire is unsure about the other person and the possibility of a future together.

Interests/Background Compatibility (IB)

Composite score (IB = CI + AF + BC + FD)

Social/Family Compatibility (SF)

Composite score (SF = SN + FA)

Relationship Compatibility (RC)

Composite score (RC = HA + RE + CB + JE + TE + IA)

Compatibility Quotient (CQ)

The Compatibility Quotient is the total score that indicates overall compatibility in the relationship. High scores suggest high compatibility in most areas for this couple.

INWALD PARTNERS PERSONALITY INVENTORY (IPPI) SCALE DESCRIPTIONS

Avoidance of Criticism (AV)

A high score on this scale indicates that the test-taker believes his or her partner often is not candid about feelings and behaviors. He or she feels that this partner has limited insight and judgment about personal shortcomings. Individuals with high scores feel their partners may tend to give socially acceptable responses to questions.

Alcohol Use Patterns (AU)

High scores suggest that the test-taker believes his or her partner has been a habitual user of alcohol.

Drug Use Patterns (DU)

A positive score indicates that the test-taker believes his or her partner has some admitted use of drugs. A high score indicates the partner may be a habitual drug user.

Brushes With the Law & Society (BL)/Legal Problems (LP—alternate IPPI version)

A high score on this scale indicates the test-taker believes his or her partner has had a history of brushes with the law and/or with societal norms. This may include arrests and/or convictions.

Employment Problems (EP)

A high score on this scale indicates the test-taker believes his or her partner has had difficulties holding a job. The partner may have had a spotty employment record and may have a history of interpersonal difficulties at work.

Reliability (Lack of Reliability—LR)

A high score here indicates that the test-taker believes his or her partner has a tendency to contract minor illnesses that may keep the partner from working. The partner also may have difficulty meeting job responsibilities and may have a history of abusing sick leave privileges at work.

Critical Items (CI)

A list of critical items for further evaluation and discussion.

Overall Score (OV)

A combination of all IPPI scales measuring overall potential for difficulties in relationships due to a lack of conscientiousness and/or the presence of antisocial behavior patterns. High scores are suggestive of such patterns.

APPENDIX B: INWALD TRAUMA RECOVERY INVENTORY (ITRI) SCALE DESCRIPTIONS

DIFFICULTIES WITH DAILY ACTIVITIES (DA)

Measures the extent to which tested individuals believe they can take care of themselves and their families. Low scorers express confidence that they have the ability to take care of their basic needs. High scorers may show evidence of an inability to function and to provide daily necessities for themselves and their families.

PAST TRAUMATIC EVENTS (PT)

High scores on this scale suggest that the individual has perceived a specific event as traumatic. Low scores suggest that the individual has not perceived the specified event as a major life trauma.

STRESS SYMPTOMS (SS)/SYMPTOMS OF STRESS (SY—ALTERNATE ITRI VERSION)

Measures admitted physical symptoms or stress reactions that may adversely affect functioning. High scorers admit to physical symptoms that may be related to stressful events.

SOCIAL NETWORK (SN)

Measures an individual's social network and social relationships. Low scorers may be socially active people with a wide circle of friends who can provide them with support in times of stress. High scorers may be isolated individuals who do not socialize often and do not have close friends for social support.

FAMILY SUPPORT (FS)

Measures a person's family relationships with attention to the degree of closeness with family members. Low scorers may have close relationships with family members and can depend on those family members for support in times of crisis. High scorers do not express strong family ties, may have negative feelings about immediate family members, and may not be able to depend on family for support in times of crisis.

CRITICAL EVENTS (CE)

Measures the presence of recent events that may have affected the person's ability to enjoy life. Low scorers have not reported many difficulties that could affect their ability to enjoy daily routines. High scorers report that there have been recent life events that have been difficult for them, such as illness, death of a loved one, physical injuries or illness, serious accidents, or natural disasters.

DEPRESSION (DP)

High scores on this scale indicate discouragement and depression. High scorers may have difficulty coping with daily stresses and/or may show symptoms of clinical or reactive depression.

LACK OF SELF-WORTH (SW)

Measures self-confidence and general sense of mastery over obstacles in the world. High scorers may be unsure of themselves and feel they cannot do things as well as others.

LACK OF SATISFACTION WITH LIFE (LS)

Measures individuals' general satisfaction with their accomplishments in life. High scorers may feel that they have not been able to reach their goals and report dissatisfaction with their accomplishments. High scorers may also express disappointment with how their life has developed. Low scorers express contentment that they have been able to reach most goals and that they are satisfied with their accomplishments.

LACK OF TEMPER CONTROL (TC)

Measures a history of difficulty controlling angry impulses. High scorers on this scale may be outspoken and/or impatient with others.

OVERALL SCORE (OS)

Total score for all scales of the ITRI.

13 Principles of Fitness-for-Duty Evaluations for Police Psychologists

David M. Corey

INTRODUCTION

Police employers have a legal duty to ensure that police officers under their command are mentally and emotionally fit to perform their duties, and failure to do so can result in significant civil liability (*Bonsignore v. City of New York,* 1982) and serious consequences to citizens, the examinee, other officers, an employing agency's reputation, and trust in the community (Corey, 1988). Various courts have interpreted this duty to include the authority to mandate psychological fitness-for-duty (FFD) evaluations* of police officers reasonably believed to be impaired in their ability to perform their job functions because of a known or suspected psychological condition (*Colon v. City of Newark,* 2006; *Conte v. Horcher,* 1977; *Deen v. Darosa,* 2005; *Kraft v. Police Commissioner of Boston,* 1994; *McKnight v. Monroe Co. Sheriff's Dept.,* 2002; *Tingler v. City of Tampa,* 1981; *Watson v. City of Miami Beach,* 1999).

The circumstances giving rise to FFD evaluations of police officers are many and varied. They may involve suspicion of job-relevant psychopathology associated with on-duty performance (e.g., excessive force, repeated problems of judgment), off-duty conduct (e.g., domestic violence, driving while intoxicated), a suicide attempt, psychiatric hospitalization, or a disability claim. Stone (2000) reported that 26% of the cases from his own practice in the southern region of the United States resulted from suspected psychopathology (i.e., diagnosable mental condition), 19% from excessive force issues, 15% from substance abuse, 13% from behavior implicating poor judgment, and 9% from domestic violence.

Dawkins, Griffin, and Dawkins (2006) utilized an alternative classification scheme for their analysis of the FFD referrals in their own Midwestern practice. Similar to Stone, they found that 16.5% of the more than 200 referrals they analyzed involved alcohol use, but they reported more than twice as many referrals involving domestic violence (20.5%). They reported that 16.3% involved other behavioral concerns, 36.9% pertained to psychopathology or emotional distress, and 4.7% were for officers being considered for rehire following employment separation.

The right of a police employer to intrude on the medical and personal privacy of its officers derives from two special features of police work: the power of the position and the fact that police officers are public employees. Police officers are members of quasi-military organizations, "called upon for duty at all times, armed at almost all times, and exercising the most awesome and dangerous power that a democratic state possesses with respect to its residents—the power to use lawful force to arrest and detain them" (*Policemen's Benevolent Association of New Jersey v. Township of Washington,* 1988, at 141). As citizens, police officers retain their constitutional rights (e.g., *Garrity v. New Jersey,* 1967), but as public employees, they "subordinate their right to privacy as a private

---

* The term *FFD evaluation* is used throughout this chapter to avoid the more awkward abbreviation *FFDEs* in its plural form. Some authors and publications use the latter abbreviation, and they are used here when quoting from them. These terms and abbreviations are equivalent in meaning.

citizen to the superior right of the public to an efficient and credible police department" (*Richardson v. City of Pasadena,* 1973/1974, at headnote 1). In the words of the U.S. Supreme Court, "the public should not bear the risk that employees who may suffer from impaired perception and judgment will be [in] positions where they may need to employ deadly force" (*National Treasury Employees Union v. Von Raab,* 1989, at 671).

The employer's duty to ensure a psychologically fit workforce does not, however, extend an unfettered right to require such evaluations of any police officer in any instance (*Denhof et al. v. City of Grand Rapids,* 2005; *Holst v. Veterans Affairs,* 2007; *Jackson v. Lake County,* 2003; *McGreal v. Ostrov,* 2004). Instead, the employer's duty is balanced by public interests and the employee's constitutional, civil, and property rights and interests.

This chapter will explain how FFD examinations, and the findings and opinions that result from them, are shaped and restrained by six overarching considerations:

1. The threshold for determining when an employer may properly require an officer to submit to an FFD evaluation
2. The definition of unfitness
3. The nature of the examiner's role and relationship to the various parties
4. The scope of the examination and the sources of information relied upon
5. The limitations on disclosure of private information to the employer
6. The examinee's statutory procedural rights

Each of these considerations will be discussed in this chapter in the context of 15 proposed principles for conducting FFD evaluations of police officers organized under four topics: referral issues (Principles 1–7), examination and procedural issues (Principles 8–11), determining fitness (Principle 12), and communicating the results (Principles 13–15).

PRINCIPLES OF FITNESS-FOR-DUTY EVALUATIONS

Several excellent texts exist on the topic of FFD evaluations of police officers (e.g., Decker, 2006; Rostow & Davis, 2004; Stone, 2000), but these are aimed at a mixed audience of police employers and examiners. This chapter is focused solely on the practical and conceptual requirements of FFD evaluations for police psychologists, beginning with the initial referral and progressing to the examination procedures, formulating an opinion or determination of fitness, and communicating the results.

In his seminal book, *Principles of Forensic Mental Health Assessment,* Heilbrun (2001), as well as Heilbrun, Grisso, and Goldstein (2009), presented a series of established and emerging principles for conducting psychological evaluations for the courts. I have drawn from this framework to present 15 principles of FFD evaluations for police psychologists derived from the professional literature, case law, federal statutes and regulations, practice guidelines, ethical standards, and my own experience conducting more than 1,000 fitness examinations.

Referral Issues

Principle 1: Assess how the employer met the legal threshold for mandating a fitness examination

By law, an employer may require an FFD evaluation of an incumbent police officer only when objective facts pose a reasonable basis for concern about his or her fitness (Equal Employment Opportunity Commission [EEOC], 1997; McDonald, Kulick, & Creighton, 1995). This is a central distinction between FFD evaluations and pre-employment psychological evaluations of police applicants. Under the Americans with Disabilities Act of 1990, when employers require applicants to undergo pre-employment psychological screening, the evaluation must be given to all entering applicants in that job class. In addition, to the extent that the psychological evaluation constitutes a "disability-related question" (i.e., one or more questions likely to elicit information about a disability; see EEOC, 1995, p. 3) or "medical examination" (e.g., a procedure or test that seeks information about an individual's physical or mental impairments or health; see EEOC, 1995, p. 11), it may be administered only after the employer has given the applicant a conditional offer of employment (29 C.F.R. §1630.14(c); see also *Leonel v. American Airlines,* 2005).

In contrast, when making a disability inquiry or medical examination of an *incumbent employee,* the ADA requires the employer to meet a fact-specific, individualized threshold; namely, that the questions or examination are "job-related and consistent with business necessity" (42 U.S.C. §12112(d)(4)(A); 29 C.F.R. §1630.14(c)). In general, the ADA regards this threshold as having been met when an employer "has a reasonable belief, based on objective evidence, that (1) an employee's ability to perform essential job functions will be impaired by a medical condition, or (2) an employee will pose a direct threat due to a medical condition" (EEOC, 2000, Question 5, p. 7). In other words, legal justification for a compulsory mental health examination of an employee requires objective evidence of job-related performance problems or safety threats *and* a known or reasonably suspected mental condition. As Gold and Shuman (2009) point out, "One of these in the absence of the other represents an insufficient basis for an FFD" evaluation (p. 244). These threshold conditions also are reflected in the "Psychological Fitness-for-Duty Evaluation Guidelines" published by the International Association of Chiefs of Police (IACP, 2009). (Note: The IACP Guidelines are written and ratified by the members of the IACP Police Psychological Services Section, represent best practices of police psychologists who perform these examinations at the request of police employers, and "should guide the expectations of examiners, examinees, and agencies" [Borum, Super, & Rand, 2003, p. 142].)

Sometimes this threshold may be met when an employer knows about an employee's medical condition, has observed performance problems, and reasonably can attribute the problems to the medical condition. An employer also may be given reliable information by a credible third party that an employee has a medical condition, or the employer may observe symptoms indicating that an employee may have a medical condition that will impair his or her ability to perform essential job functions or will pose a direct threat. Although health problems that have had "a substantial and injurious impact on an employee's job performance" (*Yin v. California,* 1996, at 868) can justify an FFD evaluation, these are not the only circumstances that satisfy the business necessity standard.

Several courts have held that an employer may preemptively require an FFD examination without showing that an employee's job performance has suffered as a result of health problems, "particularly when the employer is engaged in dangerous work" (*Brownfield v. City of Yakima,* 2010, slip op. at 10825; see also *Cody v. CIGNA Healthcare of St. Louis, Inc.,* 1998; *Watson v. City of Miami Beach,* 1999). Although the business necessity standard "is quite high, and is not to be confused with mere expediency" (*Cripe v. City of San Jose,* 2001, at 890), this objective test may be met without either known medical problems or observed deterioration in the performance of essential job functions. In *Brownfield,* the court concluded that an officer's repeated volatile responses to co-workers and supervisors established business necessity for a series of fitness evaluations. Moreover, the court noted,

> our consideration of the FFDEs' legitimacy is heavily colored by the nature of Brownfield's employment. Police officers are likely to encounter extremely stressful and dangerous situations during the course of their work. When a police department has good reason to doubt an officer's ability to respond to these situations in an appropriate manner, an FFDE is consistent with the ADA. (slip op. at 10827)

This threshold analysis is a critically important one for the employer, but it is equally crucial for the examining psychologist who wants to avoid becoming the target of litigation where the employee has successfully shown that a disability-related inquiry or medical examination was not job related and consistent with business necessity (*Denhof et al. v. City of Grand*

Rapids, 2005). Indeed, Borum et al. (2003) regard this as "[t]he most fundamental legal issue in FFDEs" (p. 140).

IACP guidelines recommend that the employer and examiner "consult before an FFDE commences in order to ensure that an FFDE is indicated in a particular case" (IACP, 2009, Guideline 4.3). An employer's initial consultation with the examiner may provide important evidence at trial, buttressing its belief that a mental health condition prevented the employee from performing an essential function of the job (*Sullivan v. River Valley School District,* 1999).

As important as the threshold analysis is for managing litigation risk, it also serves two other valuable purposes. First, it provides an opportunity for the examiner to discuss with the employer less intrusive, nonmedical alternatives (IACP, 2009, Guideline 4.2), given that "[t]he stakes involved in an FFD evaluation for both employees and employers cannot be overstated" (Gold & Shuman, 2009, p. 238). Courts also cite the intrusive characteristics of an FFD evaluation, along with the potential adverse impact of disclosure of information gathered in the examination, when considering whether an evaluation was lawfully ordered (*Hill v. Winona,* 1990; *Stewart v. Pearce,* 1973). Thus, prereferral consultation between the employer and examiner helps to ensure that other appropriate alternatives are considered before mandating the FFD examination. As Rostow and Davis (2004) note, "In the end, the most appropriate referrals should be work related and reasonably connected to a suspicion of mental or emotional illness" (p. 149).

When a referral involves job relevant behavior reasonably linked to a possible mental health condition, this means only that the employer *may* order an FFD evaluation, but nothing in the ADA compels it. Indeed, an array of cases illustrate the appropriateness of an employer's decision to terminate an employee known to have, or reasonably suspected to have, a mental disorder when the employee's conduct, or behavioral manifestation of the disorder, was such that it rendered him or her unqualified for the position (e.g., *Marino v. U.S. Postal Service et al.,* 1994; *Mazzarella v. U.S. Postal Service,* 1994; *Palmer v. Circuit Court of Cook County,* 1997). In general, when an employer knows in advance that it would be unwilling to return an employee to the job in the event that the employee is found fit for duty, alternatives to an FFD examination should be considered. Thus, in a prereferral conference involving cases of gross misconduct, examiners may wish to discuss with the employer the option of considering termination in lieu of an FFD examination. Employers may benefit from being reminded that the ADA generally does not require an employer to tolerate violations of workplace rules and policies, including those that prohibit workplace violence or threats of it, or to retain employees who engage in such violations. Whereas police employers are permitted to mandate FFD evaluations under the conditions discussed above, they are not required to do so as an alternative or precursor to termination. On the other hand, they also may not take a more severe adverse action against an employee with a disability than against a nondisabled employee who engaged in the same misconduct.

A second reason for the importance of a prereferral conference between the prospective examiner and the employer is to better understand the employee's behavioral history, both across the full term of employment and during the recent episode that spurred the referral. This helps the psychologist begin to think about the types and sources of data that may need to be considered during the data-gathering process discussed in Principles 8–11.

Examiners should be careful to recognize the special consideration afforded return-to-work certifications when the employee is released from medical leave under the Family & Medical Leave Act (FMLA) of 1993. Under the terms of the FMLA, an employee generally may not be compelled by the employer to submit to an independent evaluation of his or her fitness for duty once certified by the treating health care provider as ready to return to work, although pre-leave or post-return behavior may justify an FFD evaluation (*Albert v. Runyon,* 1998; see also *Brumbalough v. Camelot Care Centers*, 2005). Thus, when the FFD evaluation referral results solely from information obtained from FMLA disclosures, the employer should be cautioned to consider the *Runyon* decision and to consult with legal counsel before proceeding. On the other hand, when an employer can establish that it would have ordered an FFD examination *if the employee had not taken leave*, an examination may be permissible (*Carrillo v. National Council of Churches of Christ in the USA*, 1997).

Finally, for referrals involving a federal police agency under the authority of the Office of Personnel Management, federal regulations stipulate that these agencies may not refer an employee for psychiatric or psychological examination unless it has first shown through a physical examination that there is "no physical basis to explain actions or behavior which may affect the safe and efficient performance of the individual or others," and the position has medical standards that call for a psychiatric or psychological examination (5 C.F.R. §339.301(e)(1)). Particularly when an employee is perceived to pose an imminent risk of serious harm to oneself or others, employers often work hastily to obtain an FFD evaluation in short order, and a prereferral conference helps to ensure that these requirements are satisfied before agreeing to conduct an evaluation that may ultimately be deemed invalid under the law.

Principle 2: Identify the relevant clinical and forensic questions

All mental health assessments are properly driven and constrained by the clinical, forensic, and other questions that prompt the evaluation. Because these questions determine the scope of the examination, the kinds of data that will be gathered, how the data will be analyzed, what judgments or determinations will be made, what information will be disclosed (and to whom), and how it will be communicated, it is essential that the examiner first clarify precisely what the employer wants to know. This is often accomplished by a written referral letter from the employer that specifically lists the questions to be addressed in the course of the evaluation. Alternatively, the examiner can prepare a draft letter of his or her understanding of the employer's referral questions and provide an opportunity for clarification (IACP, 2009, Guideline 7.2). Even when employers do specify their referral questions in writing, they often simply ask the psychologist to evaluate the employee's fitness for duty, without elaboration. But what exactly is the clinical meaning of *fitness for duty*? Alternatively, what does it mean to be *unfit*?

Anfang and Wall (2006) point out that fitness for duty has no consistent clinical definition. They propose a clinically operational definition of *unfitness* as "the inability to perform required occupational duties with reasonable skill and safety as a result of illness or injury" (pp. 676–677). Rostow and Davis (2004) define *unfitness* as "mental impairment that may impact upon the ability of the officer to perform his duty in a safe and effective manner" (p. 62). The IACP Guidelines conceptualize *unfitness* in a police officer as being "unable to safely and/ or effectively perform his or her duties due to a psychological condition or impairment" (IACP, 2009, Guideline 3.1).

Other authors have emphasized the importance of distinguishing problems of *unfitness* from those associated with *unsuitability* or *misconduct*. Writing about FFD evaluations in the military, Budd and Harvey (2006) observed that

> there are those individuals whose character structure and the associated attitudes, emotions, and/or behaviors are, in the opinion of the provider, the primary sources of their difficulties in the military. A recommendation for [administrative discharge] should be made when the prognosis for rehabilitation is poor and/or the potential for continued difficulty with occupational demands, misconduct or acting out is high ... and these recommendations are channeled through the command's legal department instead of the medical board. (pp. 42–43)

Decker (2006) emphasizes the role of an FFD evaluation in ascertaining whether a law enforcement officer's behavior is simply misconduct or the result of a mental disorder. "If the set of circumstances or the officer's behavior precipitating the FFD evaluation is found to be the result of misconduct, then disciplinary action is the appropriate course" (p. 4). She noted that it is "particularly important to differentiate 'simple misconduct' from bad behavior that is the result of mental illness" (p. 43). Anfang and Wall (2006) echo the importance of the FFD examiner understanding "the distinction between impairment due to psychiatric illness and inability to perform duties separate from psychiatric illness" (p. 677).

There is no more fundamental issue in an FFD evaluation than how the examiner defines unfitness. Some examiners are reluctant to restrict a definition of unfitness to one requiring a psychological impairment or condition, noting that problems such as interpersonal passivity or timidity, which may be personality based rather than caused by a mental health condition, can also lead to ineffective performance (Stone, 2000). But broadening the definition to include normal range, albeit problematic, behavior poses several risks. First, because the ADA requires a reasonable suspicion of a mental health condition to justify an FFD evaluation, it seems disingenuous to conclude from such an examination that no mental health condition exists but that the employee is unfit for duty anyway. Certainly there are instances where an employee's problematic, disruptive, inefficient, unsafe, or even illegal behavior is caused not by a mental or emotional condition but rather from maladaptive personality traits, character deficits, motivational problems, or other nonpathological factors. These employees may be ill-suited for continued employment, and an administrative decision to terminate their employment may very well be justified. But the fact that an examinee in an FFD examination is a "bad" employee, perhaps even undeserving of continued employment, does not require—legally or ethically—that it is the examining psychologist who should make that determination.[*] In general, clinical opinions about fitness for duty should rest on evidence that the layperson is not qualified to assess (e.g., signs and symptoms of psychopathology). When judgments about unfitness are based on behaviors and other evidence that an employer, layperson, and psychologist can assess with equal facility—such as in the case of an insubordinate, disruptive, or dishonest police officer whose conduct does not result from a mental health condition—they fall outside the realm of a professional, clinical or "medical" opinion because they are devoid of the special expertise required for such judgments. As Gold and Shuman (2009) note, "[E]valuators should be certain to limit opinions to questions of psychiatric impairment" (p. 261). If examiners conclude or suspect that problematic personality traits; moral turpitude; or deficits in knowledge, skill, practices, or training, unconnected to an underlying psychological condition or disorder, render an employee potentially ineffective, inefficient, or unsafe, they should report this to the referring party and defer any judgments about disposition to the employer (Gold & Shuman, 2009; see also Anfang et al., 2005).

A second risk associated with not linking the definition of unfitness to a psychological condition or impairment is that it increases the potential for the examiner to be misused by an employer with

---

[*] Under most circumstances, the examiner's fitness determination should not directly decide the employee's disposition (i.e., return to duty or not). According to the EEOC,

> A doctor who conducts medical examinations for an employer should not be responsible for making employment decisions or deciding whether or not it is possible to make a reasonable accommodation for a person with a disability. That responsibility lies with the employer. The doctor's role should be limited to advising the employer about an individual's functional abilities and limitations in relation to job functions, and about whether the individual meets the employer's health and safety requirements. (EEOC, 2002, at 6.4)

In the U.S. military, ultimate judgments about fitness are made by the service member's commanding officer, and the examiner's role is limited to providing findings and a recommendation as to whether the service member is deemed unsuitable for continued military service due to a mental health disorder (U.S. Department of Defense, 1997). Likewise, police employers retain the ultimate responsibility for making retention decisions, with proper consideration—not deference—given to the results and recommendations of the FFD evaluation. As noted by the court in *Thompson v. City of Arlington* (1993):

> City and its officials, who have special knowledge of the factors that enter into whether a particular person should serve as a police officer, are better equipped than the health care providers, or other health care experts, to determine whether plaintiff should return to regular duty. (at 1144)

illegitimate motives. Gold and Shuman (2009) point out that "forced FFD evaluations" may be used in an attempt to discredit or even terminate an employee. The authors continue:

> For example, an FFD referral may be made in an attempt to discharge a chronically underperforming employee or as a substitute for discipline, or as a way to gather information to harm the reputation of the [employee] who has brought a complaint against the employer.... Participation in such an evaluation represents a misuse of mental health expertise. (p. 244)

As noted earlier, an officer's inability to perform the essential functions of the position due to a mental or emotional impairment is but one of the two purposes for which FFD evaluations are typically sought by employers and permitted under the ADA. The other purpose is to determine whether an employee poses a "direct threat" due to a medical condition (EEOC, 1991). Employees may be referred for direct threat evaluations whether or not the employer intends to terminate the employee because questions may exist about the potential for the termination itself triggering violence, and how to minimize or manage that risk (Borum et al., 2003). The standards for determining unfitness on the basis of *impairment* or *direct threat* will be discussed under Principle 5 (Identify the legal standard for determining fitness).

The employer's referral may contain other questions that the examiner will be asked to address in the course of the FFD evaluation, and the parameters of each should be fully understood by the examining psychologist before proceeding. These may include questions about disability, industrial vs. nonindustrial causation, particular types of impairment (e.g., memory or other neuropsychological functioning), accommodation, violence risk management, treatment, effects of medications, and restricted or limited duty.*

Principle 3: Decline the referral if it falls outside your area of expertise or competence

After clarifying the precise clinical and forensic questions, the examining psychologist is better positioned to judge whether he or she has the expertise (i.e., education, training, and experience) to answer the referral questions. Professional ethical standards require that psychologists provide services "with populations and in areas only within the boundaries of their competence, based on their education, training, supervised experience, consultation, study, or professional experience" (APA, 2002, Standard 2.01(a)). These standards also stipulate that "[w]hen assuming forensic roles, psychologists are or become reasonably familiar with the judicial or administrative rules governing their roles" (Standard 2.01(f)).

IACP (2009) Guideline 5.1 contains a similar provision, recommending that examiners have the following minimum qualifications:

1. Be licensed as a psychologist or psychiatrist with education, training, and experience in the diagnostic evaluation of mental and emotional disorders
2. Possess training and experience in the evaluation of law enforcement personnel
3. Be familiar with the police psychology literature and the essential job functions of the employee being evaluated
4. Be familiar with relevant state and federal statutes and case law, as well as other legal requirements related to employment and personnel practices (e.g., disability, privacy, third-party liability)
5. Satisfy any other minimum requirements imposed by local jurisdiction or law
6. Recognize their areas of competence based on their education, training, supervised experience, consultation, study, or professional experience
7. Seek appropriate consultation to address issues outside their areas of competence that may arise during the course of an FFD evaluation

---

* *Restrictions* generally pertain to what an employee *should not* do as a result of a mental or emotional condition, whereas *limitations* refer to what an employee *cannot* do (Anfang & Wall, 2006, p. 677).

Upon fully understanding the clinical and forensic questions pertaining to the FFD evaluation referral, the examining psychologist should carefully and candidly assess whether his or her education, training, and experience are sufficient to adequately address the questions and, if not, whether the shortfalls can be remedied through additional study or consultation with a more experienced colleague. Examples include referral questions that require the psychologist to possess competency in a specialty or proficiency (e.g., forensic psychology, neuropsychology, psychopharmacology), specialized knowledge (e.g., familiarity with ADA case law related to a particular impairment, such as the ability to interact with others), or exceptional experience (e.g., a complex, contested, and/or litigated case with contradictory evidence). Lacking the requisite qualifications, the examiner should decline the referral.

FFD evaluations are often referred to as "high stakes" or "high risk" evaluations (Anfang & Wall, 2006; Borum et al., 2003), and the legal liability to both the examiner and employer can be great. In addition, the stakes are also very high for the employee, for whom an "unfit" finding may be career ending. Ethical standards require that psychologists "take reasonable steps to avoid harming their ... organizational clients, and others with whom they work, and to minimize harm where it is foreseeable and unavoidable" (APA, 2002, Standard 3.04). Meeting this ethical requirement may demand that some examiners decline the FFD evaluation referral, agree to address just a subset of the questions posed in the referral, or proceed only after obtaining appropriate consultation.

Anfang and Wall (2006) point out that "[t]he legal concepts, evaluation process, and administrative issues may be complex and unfamiliar to the nonforensic clinician.... FFD evaluations can often become the subject of administrative or legal dispute because of the significant personal, legal, and financial consequences" (p. 678), and evaluators may be asked to defend their opinions in deposition and under cross-examination during court testimony. Therefore, when accepting a referral for an FFD evaluation that is known or reasonably anticipated "to be in the context of litigation, arbitration, or another adjudicative process, the examiner should be prepared by training and experience to qualify as an expert in any related adjudicative proceeding" (IACP, 2009, Guideline 5.2). Indeed, Gold and Shuman (2009) advise clinicians performing FFD evaluations to "consider the possibility that litigation or administrative processes may arise from claims requiring mental health assessments. Thus, the specialty guidelines for forensic clinicians may be interpreted to apply to third-party evaluations of all kinds whether litigation has occurred or not" (p. 2).

Principle 4: Decline the referral if you are unable to be impartial

Standards of professional ethics require that psychologists "refrain from taking on a professional role when personal, scientific, professional, legal, financial, or other interests or relationships could reasonably be expected to (1) impair their objectivity, competence, or effectiveness in performing their functions as psychologists, or (2) expose the person or organization with whom the professional relationship exists to harm or exploitation" (APA, 2002, Standard 3.06). Similarly, IACP Guidelines state that a prospective FFD examiner should decline to conduct an FFD evaluation when his or her objectivity may be impaired (IACP, 2009, Guideline 6.1). (See also the draft revision of the *Specialty Guidelines for Forensic Psychology* (SGFP), American Psychology-Law Society, 2008, Guideline 3.02, Impartiality and Fairness.)

The necessity for impartiality in the FFD examiner also requires that the examiner have no treatment relationship with the officer being examined (cf. Gold & Shuman, 2009; IACP, 2009, Guideline 6.1.2). Anfang and Wall (2006) observed:

> For FFD evaluations, as for most forensic examinations, a comprehensive evaluation often requires review of additional information (i.e., collateral contacts; psychological testing, including validity assessment; and possible third-party or surveillance data) and a neutral objectivity that is different from the typical alliance-based, patient-centered treatment relationship. (pp. 677–678)

This is a view long championed by Greenberg and Shuman (1997, 2007), who argue that, among the salient differences between the testimony of treating psychologists and forensic psychologists, the former "is a care provider and usually supportive, accepting, and empathic; the forensic evaluator is an assessor and usually neutral, objective, and detached as to the forensic issues" (p. 53). Whereas the therapist's role is to be supportive and to advocate for the client's interests, the forensic evaluator's role is to exercise "untainted and unbiased judgment" (Greenberg & Shuman, 2007, p. 131). Indeed, these roles are "irreconcilably mutually exclusive" (p. 132).

Heilbrun (2001) defines *impartiality* as "the evaluator's freedom from significant interference from factors that can result in bias" (pp. 36–37). Some degree of even implicit bias may be unavoidable, but the "crucial test" involves whether that bias "would keep the evaluator from moving from data to whatever conclusions are best supported by such data" (Heilbrun et al., 2008, p. 102). The consequences of conducting an FFD evaluation when impartiality has been lost or compromised, or even when it appears so to an objective observer, can be significant.

In *Denhof et al. v. City of Grand Rapids* (2007), the examining psychologist, prior to conducting the FFD examination, told the police chief that the relationship between the officer and the department was like a "marriage gone bad" and they were "best off simply separating, for the good of all persons involved" (p. 9). The court concluded that the examining psychologist "was predisposed to finding Denhof unfit for duty" and concluded that it was "hard to see any possibility that [the psychologist] would yield a result other than finding that Denhof should be separated from the police force" (p. 9). This fact, the court decided, prevented the employer from claiming an honest belief in the determination of unfitness from the FFD examination, because "reliance on a doctor who had already made up his mind did not qualify as reasonable reliance" (p. 9).

The pressure to affirm the perceived or stated expectations of the referring party can be significant in these high-stakes examinations. Psychologists who receive repeated referrals from employers, labor groups, or other sources may create what Anfang and Wall (2006) call "incentive biases" to provide opinions favorable to the perceived or stated expectations of the referring party, thus requiring a decidedly vigilant awareness of, and defense against, the various sources of bias (Gold & Shuman, 2009). Conversely, Anfang and Wall point out that "when the forensic examiner is retained directly by the examinee or his attorney, high-stakes cases can potentially lead to dramatically partisan and conflicted circumstances" (p. 678).

Novice examiners sometimes scoff at the notion of impartiality in FFD evaluations, believing that the employer, as client, is the sole beneficiary of the examiner's professional duties, that no obligations extend to the officer being evaluated, and therefore there is no requirement for impartiality. Fisher (2009), however, points out that "psychologists have ethical obligations toward every party in a case, no matter how many or how named" (p. 1). Koocher (2007) agrees, noting that "both the entity requesting the service and the person undergoing evaluation hold a kind of client status in such cases" (p. 380). Writing specifically about FFD evaluations of police officers, Stone (2000) observed, "While the examination is an independent forensic evaluation conducted on behalf of the employer, the employee also has standing as a client. As such, the employee's welfare should be given substantial weight in determining whether and how to undertake the evaluation" (p. 130). The IACP Guidelines explicitly acknowledge this as well:

> Regardless of who is identified as the client, the examiner owes an ethical duty to both parties to be fair, impartial, accurate and objective, and to honor the parties' respective legal rights and interests. Other legal duties also may be owed to the examinee or agency as a result of statutory or case law unique to an employer's and/or examiner's jurisdiction. (IACP, 2009, Guideline 8.2)

Notwithstanding the assertion by many respected FFD examiners that examinees in such evaluations should be advised that they have no "doctor–patient" relationship (Rostow & Davis, 2003; Stone, 2000), several courts and other legal authorities have reached a different conclusion. In *Pettus v. Cole* (1996), the California Court of Appeals found that an employer's examining psychiatrist has a doctor–patient relationship with an employee-examinee even when the examination is performed for the benefit of the employer. Similarly, the Nevada Supreme Court held that individuals examined by a psychologist for the purpose of determining suitability for employment were "patients" within the meaning of a statute requiring health care providers to make a patient's records available on request (*Cleghorn v. Hess*, 1993). In *McGreal v. Ostrov* (2004), the court held that McGreal, a police officer who was compelled to submit to an FFD evaluation, was a "recipient of mental health services" and enjoyed the rights of confidentiality associated with personal health information. Other courts and authorities also have held that persons compelled to submit to independent medical evaluations are "patients" under the law (cf. *Arkansas Attorney General Opinion,* 2001; *Crandall v. Michaud*, 1992; *Elkins v. Syken*, 1996; *Simmons v. Rehab Xcel, Inc.*, 1999).

Principle 5: Identify the legal standard for determining fitness

Standards for State and Municipal Police Officers

Most states have statutes and/or administrative rules that impose some kind of mental requirements on police officers. The remaining 12 states are silent concerning any psychological or mental health criteria for police officer certification, leaving it to each individual agency to determine what standards to use, if any. More than half of the 38 states with these requirements use language identical, or nearly identical, to a California statute that states that any peace officer shall "[b]e found to be free from any physical, emotional, or mental condition that might adversely affect the exercise of the powers of a peace officer" (California Government Code §1031(f)). The case of *Sager v. County of Yuba* (2007) provides an instructive illustration of how these qualifying mandates for police officers can be applied in an FFD examination. In response to the argument of Sager, a deputy sheriff who was found psychologically unfit for duty, that the California Government Code §1031 standards apply only to police applicants rather than incumbent deputies, the court wrote:

> [T]he section 1031 standards must also be maintained throughout a peace officer's career.... At least two of the standards reflect fundamental law enforcement qualifications: good moral character (§ 1031, subd. (d)) and mental fitness (§ 1031, subd. (f)). If Sager's position is correct, an officer who lost his moral compass would be immune from these standards and only subject to a moral character standard if the applicable job description in that department reiterated that standard as a defined duty of that classification of officers. That absurd result highlights the flaw in Sager's position. (at 14)

Hence, the statutory and regulatory requirements in the employee's jurisdiction may also provide the examiner with important guidance regarding the standard for psychological fitness.

Standards for Federal Police Officers

When evaluating police officers in the federal system who are subject to the requirements of the Office of Personnel Management (e.g., police officers in the Federal Protective Service, Immigration and Customs Enforcement, U.S. Marshals Service, Department of Veterans Affairs), the Rehabilitation Act of 1973 (29 U.S.C.A. §706), rather than the ADA, establishes the procedural and threshold standard. Although the ADA and the Rehabilitation Act share common statutory elements, the associated regulations and case law differ substantively from the ADA in three ways pertinent to FFD evaluations: (1) the threshold for determining when a federal employee may be referred for a mental health evaluation, (2) the standard for medical disqualification of a federal employee on the basis of a medical or mental health condition alone, and (3) the standard for determining a direct threat.

As noted under Principle 1, a federal police agency under the authority of the OPM regulations may not refer an employee for psychiatric or psychological examination unless certain threshold conditions are met (OPM Medical Qualification Determinations, 1995; 5 C.F.R. §339.301). Once these requirements are satisfied, then an FFD examination conducted by a licensed psychiatrist or licensed psychologist "may only be used to make legitimate inquiry into a person's mental fitness to successfully perform the duties of his/her position without undue hazard to the individual or others" (5 C.F.R. §339.301(e)(2)). Thus, like the EEOC regulations that implement and enforce the ADA, the OPM regulations contain two prongs to the determination of fitness, either or both of which may be at issue in an FFD evaluation (EEOC, 2000, Question 5, p. 7): inability to perform essential functions or posing a direct threat.

When the first prong is at issue and behavioral evidence shows that the employee's performance is unsafe or inefficient, the OPM regulations rely on 5 C.F.R. §339.301 (OPM Medical Qualification Determinations, 1995) to show simply that the employee's medical condition is behind the employee's inability to meet the performance standard. However, when relying on the employee's medical condition *alone*, in the absence of inefficient performance, OPM relies on 5 C.F.R. §339.206, which stipulates three elements to the disqualification standard: (1) the medical condition is itself disqualifying with respect to the medical standards of the position, (2) recurrence of the condition cannot medically be ruled out, and (3) the duties of the position are such that a recurrence would pose a reasonable probability of substantial harm (*Slater v. Dept. of Homeland Security*, 2008).

Direct Threat

Under the terms of the ADA, a *direct threat* means a significant risk of substantial harm that cannot be eliminated or reduced by reasonable accommodation (29 C.F.R. §1630.2(r)). Determinations of direct threat must be based on an individualized assessment of the person's present ability to safely perform the essential functions of the job. The ADA stipulates that the determination must be based on a reasonable medical judgment relying on the most current medical knowledge and/or best available objective evidence (29 C.F.R. §1630.2(r)). Furthermore, the following factors must be considered when making the determination: (1) the duration of the risk, (2) the nature and severity of the potential harm, (3) the likelihood that potential harm will occur, and (4) the imminence of the potential harm (29 C.F.R. §1603.2(r); *Anderson v. Little League Baseball, Inc.*, 1992).

The standard for an employer to show that it has met the burden of proving that an employee poses a significant risk of substantial harm is *substantial evidence*, defined as "such relevant evidence as a reasonable mind might accept as adequate to support a conclusion" (*Universal Camera Corp. v. National Labor Relations Board*, 340 U.S. 474 (1951), at 477 [citation omitted]; see also *Knill v. Principi*, 2001). However, in assessing whether an employee can perform his or her duties without a significant risk to the safety of the individual or others, the examiner "must consider the nature of the position and the consequences should the employee fail to perform his duties properly" (*Lassiter v. Reno*, 1996/1997, at 1153). In *Lassiter*, the circuit court decided that the employer was not required to show that a U.S. Deputy Marshal with paranoid personality disorder was reasonably likely to become violent, but rather that he posed a significant risk to the safety of himself or others if he did so. The court wrote:

> Given the duties of a deputy marshal, a significant risk to the safety of others can arise not only from an inclination to strike out in violence, but also from a tendency to misperceive the true nature of events.... Placed in unfamiliar circumstances that may or may not be hostile, the deputy marshal must have the ability to decide in an instant whether the use of deadly force is warranted. If an innocent person is injured or killed because a deputy marshal "read...threatening meanings into benign remarks or events[,]" "it is not difficult to imagine the public outrage, let alone the potential liability" to which the federal government would be subjected. (at 40)

Thus, although the EEOC defines *direct threat* to mean "a significant risk of substantial harm" (29 C.F.R. §1630.2(r)), multiple courts have held that where the employee's position implicates the safety of others, and the potential harm is severe, even a low probability that the harm will occur will be sufficient to establish a direct threat (*Butler v. Thornburgh*, 1990; *Hogarth v. Thornburgh*, 1993; *Myers v. Hose*, 1995). Conversely, where the potential harm is not fatal or catastrophic, the examiner usually will be required to demonstrate that the risk is highly probable in order to establish that a direct threat exists (Mariani & Avelenda, 2009).

It is incumbent on examiners to have a "fundamental and reasonable level of knowledge and understanding of the legal standards, laws, rules, and precedents" that apply to the FFD evaluation within the parties' jurisdictions (American Psychology-Law Society, 2008, Guideline 4.04). This is especially critical with respect to the legal standard for determining fitness.

Principle 6: Determine the examinee's rights and limitations to access to the report and other personal health information

As discussed under Principle 4, it is neither an ethical truism nor a matter of law in all jurisdictions that the examiner–examinee relationship is devoid of the obligations traditionally and statutorily associated with a doctor–patient relationship. This is no less true in the context of an examinee's right to access personal health information gathered or created for purposes of an FFD evaluation (*McGreal v. Ostrov*, 2004; *Pettus v. Cole*, 1996).

The Health Insurance Portability and Accountability Act (HIPAA) Privacy Rule (2000b) gives patients the right to inspect and amend records containing their personal health information (PHI), and psychologists who meet HIPAA's definition of a health care provider are obligated to comply with the Privacy Rule's requirements for disclosure of PHI (see 45 C.F.R. §160.524 and §160.526). HIPAA defines PHI as all "individually identifiable health information held or transmitted by a covered entity or its business associates, in any form or medium, whether electronic, paper or oral" (45 C.F.R. §160.103). As noted by Gold and Shuman (2009), this definition "does not distinguish information generated by employment-related mental health evaluations from records of treatment. Nor does the Privacy Rule explicitly make the purpose for which the information was created of any consequence" (p. 37).

Some psychologists have argued with only partial accuracy that HIPAA's Privacy Rule pertaining to an examinee's right of access to PHI is exempted in an FFD examination under a provision that bars access when the PHI was "compiled in reasonable anticipation of, or for use in, a civil, criminal or administrative action or proceeding" (45 C.F.R. §164.524(a)(ii)). But under this exception, a psychologist may only "deny access to any information that relates specifically to legal preparations but may not deny access to the individual's underlying health information" (U.S. Department of Health & Human Services, 2000, p. 82554). Consequently, examiners covered under HIPAA should include in their initial disclosures to employers and examinees alike the provisions of the Privacy Rule and their own practices relevant to an examinee's access to reports and underlying PHI (Gold & Shuman, 2009). Although the Privacy Rule permits denial of an individual's access to PHI if it is judged by the examiner to be "reasonably likely to endanger the life or physical safety of the individual or another person" (45 C.F.R. §164.524(a)(3)(i)), it is important to keep in mind—and to disclose—that this decision is reviewable.

The HIPAA Privacy Rule establishes a national privacy floor rather than a ceiling, so an examinee may be afforded even more definitive access to PHI by state statutes and administrative rules, related case law, or the terms of a collective-bargaining agreement. Examiners should determine in advance of the examination what jurisdictional or agency rules may pertain to the examinee's access to PHI, including the final written report. In any event, examinees may be denied access to PHI that "was obtained from someone other than a health care provider under a promise of confidentiality and the access requested would be reasonably likely to reveal the source of the information," and the grounds for denial on this basis are unreviewable (45 C.F.R. §164.524(a)(2)(v)). A report containing such information should be redacted before giving the examinee access to it.

Principle 7: Provide appropriate disclosure to the referring party concerning fees, evaluator role, and procedures

Any medical examination compelled by the employer must be paid entirely by the employer (EEOC, 2000, Question 11, pp. 11–12). Still, the examiner's fees, including any differences in rate by type of service (e.g., evaluation versus testimony in court or other adjudicative forum), should be disclosed to the referring party in advance of the service. In addition, the examiner should clarify the nature of the services to be provided, the estimated hours and time period, the provisions if the anticipated services cannot be performed within this period, who will be responsible for payment, any special financial considerations (e.g., fees in the event of cancellations, terms of payment, and interest on delinquent balances), and anticipated work products (e.g., verbal consultation, report, and testimony)

(Heilbrun, 2001). A useful and simple form of disclosure that meets some, although not all, of these disclosure obligations may be accomplished by providing the referring party with a copy of the IACP FFDE Guidelines (2009), along with a statement that these guidelines are expected to apply to both the referring party and the examiner.

Anfang and Wall (2006) advise that it is best to clarify all terms of an FFD evaluation in a letter of engagement, with the letter signed and returned to the examiner before the examination begins. They recommend inclusion of all fees and payment arrangements; cancellation, deposition, and in-court testimony policies; the level of detail that the report will contain; and the precise nature of collateral records and other documents sought in connection with the referral (e.g., job descriptions, performance evaluations, disciplinary records, awards and commendations, complaints and suits, and documentation of previous episodes of impairment and disability). The IACP FFDE Guidelines (2009) also stipulate that the informed consent of the employer, in addition to the examinee, should be obtained (Guideline 8.1).

EXAMINATION AND PROCEDURAL ISSUES

This section describes the principles that pertain to the examination itself and apply only when the psychologist has accepted the evaluation referral and when the referring party and the psychologist have agreed to the terms. It presumes that the examiner has:

1. Assessed how the employer has met the legal threshold for mandating a fitness examination
2. Identified the relevant clinical and forensic questions
3. Determined that the referral is within his or her area of expertise
4. Determined that he or she is able to conduct the examination with impartiality
5. Identified the legal standard for determining fitness
6. Determined the examinee's rights and limitations regarding access to the report and other personal health information gathered in the course of the evaluation
7. Provided appropriate disclosure to the referring party concerning fees, the evaluator's role, and procedures

Principle 8: Provide the examinee with appropriate disclosure and obtain informed consent/authorization

It is a cornerstone of professional ethics in psychology that examiners are to be honest about the nature, purpose, intended uses, and possible outcomes of the evaluation, and this is especially true in FFD evaluations, where the consequence of an employee's failure to cooperate may be loss of employment (Anfang & Wall, 2006). Some clinicians and attorneys assert that true informed consent in FFD evaluations cannot occur because one of the necessary elements of consent—namely, voluntariness—is absent. This view, however, fails to recognize informed consent as a broad ethical obligation "that costs nothing and treats the examinee with respect" (Gold & Shuman, 2009, p. 28). Indeed, the fundamental legal principle underlying the necessity for consent "is now beyond debate" (p. 27).

APA ethical standards (APA, 2002) stipulate that even when informed consent may not be legally required, psychologists nevertheless (1) provide an appropriate explanation, (2) seek the individual's assent, and (3) consider such person's preferences and best interests (Standard 3.10(b)). Thus, whether conceptualized as consent, informed consent, assent, or disclosure, psychologists should always provide the examinee with clarification concerning important elements of the examination. At a minimum, these include:

1. A description of the nature and scope of the evaluation
2. The limits of confidentiality, including any information that may be disclosed to the employer without the examinee's authorization

3. The party or parties who will receive the FFDE report of findings, and whether the examinee will receive a report
4. The potential outcomes and probable uses of the examination, including treatment recommendations, if applicable
5. Other provisions consistent with legal and ethical standards for mental health evaluations conducted at the request of third parties (IACP, 2009, Guideline 8.1)

Although the importance of obtaining consent or, in the alternative, providing disclosure, is an established ethical and legal principle (*Schloendorff v. Society of New York Hospital*, 1914), debate surrounds the appropriate actions of the examiner in the event that an employee refuses to consent to the evaluation. Rostow and Davis (2004) contend that the examiner could proceed under some circumstances, whereas Gold and Shuman (2009) assert that the examination should not take place in the absence of written confirmation of consent, noting that "[f]ailing to obtain a consent later determined to be required cannot be remedied" (p. 28). Anfang and Wall (2006) suggest that the consent form be given to the examinee in advance of the examination in order to facilitate dialogue and consultation with other parties who may be involved with the examinee, including attorneys, union representatives, and treating clinicians. Under no circumstances, however, should an employee be required to waive all procedural rights or liability as a condition of the FFD examination (*Jackson v. Wilson,* 1979).

Even when informed consent is obtained in writing prior to the examination, it should be kept in mind that informed consent is a process, not simply an event. In the course of the examination, the examiner may need to revisit important aspects of the informed consent document in order to clarify, for example, the limits of confidentiality, the purpose of the examination, or the potential outcomes. Some clinicians request that examinees summarize key elements of the informed consent or disclosure document in their own words both to ensure that consent is given knowingly and intelligently, even if not voluntarily, and to enable documentation of that fact in the event of subsequent litigation.

Special attention to an exceptional form of disclosure may be needed in situations where a police officer examinee is asked to discuss or reveal information that could violate the officer's constitutional right to be free from compulsory self-incrimination (Aitchison, 2000). In *Garrity v. New Jersey* (1967), the U.S. Supreme Court ruled that the use of a police officer's statements in criminal proceedings violated the Fifth Amendment guarantee that citizens cannot be forced to be witnesses against themselves. The Court held that "the choice imposed on [the officers] was one between self-incrimination or job forfeiture" (at 497) and ruled that statements which a law enforcement officer is compelled to make under threat of possible forfeiture of his or her job could not subsequently be used against the officer in a criminal prosecution.

Under *Garrity* and its progeny (e.g., *Gardner v. Broderick,* 1968), before a police employer questioning a police officer can discipline the officer for refusing to answer questions, the employer must (1) order the officer to answer the questions under threat of disciplinary action; (2) ask questions that are specifically, narrowly, and directly related to the officer's duties or the officer's fitness for duty; and (3) advise the officer that the answers to the questions will not be used against the officer in criminal proceedings (*Lefkowitz v. Turley,* 1973). Because an FFD examination is a compulsory examination in which the police officer examinee is usually ordered to participate and cooperate fully under threat of discipline or termination for failure to do so, and because information obtained in the examination about the officer's self-incriminating statements could be included in an evaluation report, examiners should be careful to ensure that an employer has issued the required *Garrity* notice before inquiring into matters likely to reveal self-incriminating information.

Principle 9: Decide whether to permit third-party observers and/or recording devices into the interview

Otto and Krauss (2009) give a detailed discussion of the ethical, clinical, and legal challenges involved in contemplating the presence of third-party observers in an assessment. In particular, they note the potential impact of the third party's presence on the examinee's participation and—in cases in which psychological testing is administered—test standardization, norms, and security. For purposes of their review, they define a third-party observer as "an individual whose sole purpose is to observe (and perhaps document)—*but not affect*—the psychological evaluation" (pp. 2–3).

Otto and Krauss classified concerns about the presence of third-party observers into four categories: (1) negative effects on the examinee's responses and participation, (2) interruption of the flow of information from the examinee to the examiner, (3) threats to the validity of conclusions that can be drawn from the evaluation, and (4) threats to the security (and future utility) of psychological assessment techniques and tests. With respect to the first of these, they found little empirical evidence to support this concern outside the limited impact of observers on some memory and learning tests. Furthermore, they point out that many other factors common to the psychological evaluation (e.g., examiner and examinee demographic variables, such as race, socioeconomic status, sex; the examiner's style and expectations of the examinee; the examinee's anxiety level; the nature and purpose of the evaluation) "can have greater or similar effects on the psychological evaluation process" (p. 6) but are nonetheless well tolerated by examining clinicians. This includes invited third-party observers such as students and interns.

Concerns over interruption of the flow of information from the examinee to the examiner likewise carry little weight, given the ready availability of the less intrusive alternatives: video- or audio-recording devices. They also note that ground rules could easily be established that prohibit third-party observers from interrupting the flow of information from the examinee to the examiner.

Concerns about the threats to the validity of information that can be drawn from evaluations in which third-party observers were present were also unsupported. Otto and Krauss (2009) point out that a wide array of factors affect an examinee's performance in an assessment, and in forensic evaluation contexts, "threats to validity stemming from the presence of a third party during the assessment are likely to be overshadowed by these other factors—the most important of which being that almost all psychological and neuropsychological instruments have been normed on individuals involved in legal proceedings" (p. 7). They conclude that the presence of third-party observers, "insofar as it constitutes a deviation from standard test administration—is not nearly as well documented, and is likely a lesser threat to the validity of conclusions drawn from psychological test data, than the effects of the litigation" (p. 7).

Finally, Otto and Krauss (2009) conclude that the basis for concerns over the threats to the security and future utility of psychological assessment techniques and tests are easily overcome by "requesting that the observer be someone who is bound to protect test security or request that test administration be recorded and only made available to persons obligated to protect test security (i.e., a psychologist)" (p. 8).

Although courts have been divided on the question of third-party observers in psychological and psychiatric forensic examinations, the greater weight of opinion appears to fall on the side of not permitting their attendance when, notwithstanding the Otto and Krauss (2009) analysis, the examiner objects to it. In *Vinson v. The Superior Court of Alameda County* (1987), the court denied the employee's request to have her attorney present during the FFD examination, noting:

> We were skeptical that a lawyer, unschooled in the ways of the mental health profession, would be able to discern the psychiatric relevance of the questions. And the examiner should have the freedom to probe deeply into the plaintiff's psyche without interference by a third party.... Whatever comfort her attorney's hand-holding might afford was substantially outweighed by the distraction and potential disruption caused by the presence of a third person. (p. 412)

In *Tomlin v. Holecek et al.* (1993), the court concluded that the presence of third parties would lend a degree of artificiality to the interview that would be inconsistent with applicable professional standards and that allowing a tape-recording would be "an undesirable infusion of the adversary process into the examining room" (at 628). In *Galieti v. State Farm Mutual Automobile Insurance Co. et al.*

(1994), the court held that the employee bore the burden of proving the need to record the assessment or have an observer present. In *Ragge v. MCA/Universal Studios et al.* (1995), the court refused the employee's request for a third-party observer as meritless because of the observer's potential to interfere with, or even contaminate, the examination. These court decisions are consistent with the positions of a number of authors on the topic who advise that the presence of third parties unnecessary to the conduct of the evaluation should always be avoided (Gold & Shuman, 2009).

These considerations aside, there is at least one circumstance in which an examiner may be obligated either to permit a third party to observe the assessment or to decline the referral, and that is when the employee is represented by a labor union and is afforded *Weingarten* rights (*NLRB v. Weingarten, Inc.,* 1975). Under the *Weingarten* ruling, an employee in a collective-bargaining group who reasonably believes that an interview or examination may result in disciplinary action against the employee has a right to the presence of a union representative, if requested, although the representative may not interfere with the proceedings. Examiners who object to the presence of third-party observers should respectfully postpone the examination until the referring party has been notified and is able to make a determination to allow or oppose the request. In a case involving a federal corrections officer referred for an FFD evaluation, the examiner's unilateral decision to prevent the employee's union representative from observing the examination resulted in an adverse finding against the employer when the arbitrator determined that the employee's *Weingarten* rights were violated (*AFGE Local 596 v. Department of Justice et al.,* 2007).

Principle 10: Select multiple sources of clinical and behavioral information, using relevance and reliability as guides

Reliance on multiple sources of information and corroborating important data whenever feasible is a standard practice in forensic evaluations (American Psychology-Law Society, 2008, Guideline 11.02; Heilbrun et al., 2009). Heilbrun (2001) asserts that the use of multiple sources of information in a forensic mental health assessment is an established principle because it (1) enhances accuracy and (2) allows the examiner to check hypotheses generated by one or more of the data sources or measures. The role of third-party information, primarily consisting of documents and interviews with collateral informants, is especially important given the elevated potential in FFD evaluations for either party to provide an incomplete picture of the relevant facts.

But an FFD evaluation is not a fishing expedition wherein the examiner is free to conduct a comprehensive assessment of the employee and scrutinize, measure, and evaluate every aspect of the employee's functioning. Rather, under the terms of the ADA, "[t]he inquiries or examinations must not exceed the scope of the specific medical condition and its effect on the employee's ability, with or without reasonable accommodation, to perform essential job functions or to work without posing a direct threat" (EEOC, 1997, Question 14, p. 10). When it is not yet confirmed whether an employee actually has a medical or mental health condition—as when the referral results from a sudden, adverse change in behavior or work performance that leads to the reasonable suspicion of a mental health condition—the scope of the examination should be narrowed to those conditions reasonably linked to the problem behavior or other objective evidence giving rise to the referral. On the other hand, when an employee with a previously diagnosed condition is referred for evaluation to determine his or her readiness to return to work, the scope of the evaluation must be limited to that condition. In any case, an examination for either inability to perform essential functions of the job or possible direct threat must be narrowly tailored to seek only that information necessary to address those referral questions (Gold & Shuman, 2009).

The IACP FFDE Guidelines (IACP, 2009) provide a useful starting point for selecting sources of information. These guidelines recommend that they include, but not be limited to:

1. Performance evaluations, previous remediation efforts, commendations, testimonials, internal affairs investigations, formal citizen/public complaints, use-of-force incidents, reports related to officer-involved shootings, civil claims, disciplinary actions, incident

reports of any triggering events, medical records, prior psychological evaluations, and other supporting or relevant documentation related to the employee's psychological fitness for duty (Guideline 7.3)

2. In some cases, medical/psychological treatment records and other data (Guideline 7.3)
3. Psychological testing using assessment instruments (e.g., personality, psychopathology, cognitive, specialized) appropriate to the referral question(s) (Guideline 9.1.2)
4. A comprehensive, face-to-face clinical interview (Guideline 9.1.3)
5. Collateral interviews with relevant third parties if deemed necessary by the examiner (Guideline 9.1.4)
6. Examination by a specialist if deemed necessary by the examiner (Guideline 9.1.5)

Heilbrun (2001) cautioned that the information sought and relied on in any forensic assessment

> should be guided by relevance to the forensic issues and the validity of the different sources.... If a given source has little or no accuracy, then it cannot increase the overall accuracy of the evaluation of forensic issues, and will decrease it if given much weight. (pp. 107–108)

When evaluating whether third-party information is reliable enough to justify requiring a medical evaluation, the EEOC lists the following factors: (1) the relationship of the person providing the information to the employee about whom it is being provided, (2) the possible motivation of the person providing the information, (3) how the person learned the information (e.g., directly from the employee whose medical condition is in question or from someone else), and (4) other evidence that the employer has that bears on the reliability of the information provided (EEOC, 2000, Question 12, p. 12). These factors may also aid the examining psychologist in evaluating the reliability of third-party information. The use of multiple sources of information can bolster confidence in findings when the data reveal consistency across sources, because some individuals who might be interviewed in connection with an FFD evaluation may be biased against or in favor of the employee (Heilbrun et al., 2003).

Certainly the most important, but by no means the only, source of information about the employee's fitness for duty is the clinical interview. In addition to standard examination elements, including a mental status examination, FFD interviews should explore all standard dimensions of history: personal, familial, mental health, developmental, educational, legal, military, marital, occupational, and social. The employee's history of substance abuse, stress management, interpersonal conflict management, and occupational adaptation should be explored as well. In particular, it is essential that the examinee be provided with a full opportunity to tell his or her side of the story as it pertains to the issues underlying the referral, including alternative explanations and perspectives.

Job descriptions and job analyses also are valuable sources of information. Borum et al. (2003) point out:

> Even if the psychologist is generally familiar with the job or knows specific abilities identified from other agencies, it is often helpful to obtain a job description from the specific requesting agency to ensure that one is providing the most precise assessment of fit between the examinee's condition and the agency's requirements. (p. 142)

In the previous discussions under Principles 1 and 2, the importance of gathering the employer's objective evidence of functional impairment, performance deficits, or direct threat to the employee or others was emphasized, along with the necessity for obtaining the specific referral questions. This information, in combination with the job description or job analysis, is critical for determining the breadth and depth of other information that may be required, including collateral interviews of supervisors, coworkers, family members, or treating clinicians. As Gold and Shuman (2009) observed:

> The quality and quantity of the information upon which an FFD examination should be based is a function of the risk to which third persons may be exposed, the opportunity of those exposed to the risk

to affect it by their own actions, and the examinee's interests. For example, when serious bodily harm is a potential risk, collateral data to verify possibly partisan information is a necessary component of competent decision-making. (p. 252)

The selection of data sources will also be driven in part by the forensic decision-making model used by the examiner (Heilbrun, 2001; see also Principle 12) as well as the legal standard for determining fitness (see Principle 5). In FFD evaluations of police officers, public safety and direct threat are *always* implicated in the judgment of fitness and must *always* be a consideration when deciding on the breadth, depth, and type of information and records to gather.

This point is underscored in *Colon v. City of Newark* (2006), in which a police officer, Bazyt Bergus, assaulted Carlos Colon while Colon was detained in a Newark detention facility and Bergus was assigned to detention duties. Bergus's assignment followed a series of investigations, disciplinary actions, and subsequent appeals related to accusations of domestic assault and other violent conduct. Bergus eventually was referred for an FFD evaluation to be done by an independent psychologist. Neither the employer nor Bergus disclosed to the examiner the details of these accusations and investigations, nor was the psychologist given any information regarding Bergus's two previous pre-employment psychological evaluations. The first of these concluded that he exhibited marked animus "towards blacks as well as a tendency towards impulsivity and a history of aggressiveness" and that "if appointed as a police officer he could constitute a danger to the community" (p. 5). The second, conducted 4 years later with the same psychologist, concluded that Bergus was qualified, although with the familiar caveat that he "apparently tried to present a favorable picture by denying many normal, though not socially desirable, characteristics" (p. 6).

Colon eventually sued Bergus and the City of Newark, alleging deprivation of his civil rights, partly on the basis of the official departmental policy of withholding from evaluating psychologists complete psychological and disciplinary histories of officers referred for evaluation. The jury found both Bergus and the City of Newark liable. On appeal, the court affirmed, noting:

[W]e are satisfied, as was the trial judge, that a reasonable jury could have found … that the defendant demonstrated deliberate indifference to the civil rights of the public, including Carlos Colon, in its official policies governing the supervision and discipline of Bergus as well as the transmission of information for "fitness for duty" evaluations, and that these policies were the motivating force behind Colon's assault. (pp. 12–13)

Further, Bergus was cleared as fit for duty after a psychological evaluation that, in accordance with usual departmental practice, was rendered without benefit of a full and complete historical record of disciplinary charges and psychological profiles (p. 18).

Care should be taken to ensure that the examining psychologist requests, and documents the request for, all records and collateral information relevant to a "full and complete historical record" of the employee's behavior on and off duty.

In addition to requesting records from the employer and conducting collateral interviews of coworkers and supervisors, as may be indicated, Borum et al. (2003) advise, "To ensure a fair and balanced process, it may also be probative for the expert to ask the examinee if there are specific individuals he or she thinks should be interviewed or documents that should be reviewed as part of the evaluation" (p. 143).

As in the *Colon* matter, referrals for FFD examinations most commonly result from on- or off-duty conduct that raises reasonable concerns about an employee's psychological fitness, prompting careful review of the objective facts preceding and surrounding that conduct. Other referrals occur after an officer has requested leave for treatment or recovery from a psychological injury or condition (e.g., Posttraumatic Stress Disorder following an on-duty traumatic incident), often with the agreement of his or her personal health care provider, and subsequently seeks a return to duty. In these "return-to-work" evaluations, the examiner should gather information related to (1) the circumstances that precipitated the medical leave, (2) psychotherapy or treatment records, and (3) information about "what has happened since the declaration of unfitness and what changes have occurred in the symptoms or impairments that initially caused concern" (Borum et al., 2003, p. 144). These authors go on to note:

> Reliance on third-party information is critical to gauge any changes in thinking, mood, or behavior that may be observable by others and to assess the extent to which they are consistent with the officer's self-report. If the officer has been referred for treatment, the evaluator ordinarily should contact the treatment provider to request records (with written consent of the officer) and to gather, preferably through discussion, relevant information about specific symptoms or behaviors of concern. The treating professional may also have relevant data and opinions about the officer's prognosis. When consulting a treating professional, however, the FFDE examiner must always consider that the provider has a primary alliance with the officer, and that the applicability of any information must be considered in light of the known distinctions between therapeutic and forensic roles. (p. 144)

The ADA permits an employer to obtain only that medical information necessary to determine whether the employee can do the essential functions of the job or work without posing a direct threat (EEOC, 2000, Question 13, p. 12). "This means that, in most situations, an employer cannot request an employee's complete medical records because they are likely to contain information unrelated to whether the employee can perform his/her essential functions or work without posing a direct threat" (p. 12). However, when an employer has a reasonable belief that an employee's present ability to perform essential job functions will be impaired by a medical condition or that he or she will pose a direct threat due to a medical condition, the employer may ask the employee for additional documentation regarding his or her medications or treatment (EEOC, 2000, Question 17, p. 13).

In order for an inquiry into the private life of an employee to be upheld by the courts, it must be made as narrowly as possible; broad, sweeping requests for information are not likely to be valid (Aitchison, 2000). But where an order to produce a request for particular private information—including medical or treatment records—has a direct relationship to job performance, it is likely to be upheld as valid (*Schuman v. City of Philadelphia*, 1979).

The authority of the FFD examiner to require a review of treatment records as an element of the examination was affirmed in the case of *Thomas v. Corwin* (2007). Jana Thomas, a police officer in the Juvenile Unit of the Kansas City Police Department (KCPD), was ordered to submit to an FFD evaluation after she was placed on medical leave by her treating psychologist for work-related stress and anxiety and then was later released for duty. The examining psychologist concluded that Thomas did not appear to have any major psychological disorder, but he could not find her fit for duty in the absence of evidence of effective medical intervention for her anxiety or a change in working conditions to resolve her complaints within the Juvenile Unit. He reported that he could not issue a final report without access to Thomas's medical records. He opined that Thomas's reluctance to disclose her medical records might indicate other reasons for her alleged work-related stress and anxiety, given that her alleged stress reaction appeared to be "disproportional to the problems" (at 524) in the Juvenile Unit. Thomas refused to authorize release of the records, and KCPD fired her. She sued, alleging ADA violations, discrimination, and invasion of privacy.

The district court issued summary judgment in favor of KCPD, and the appeals court affirmed, writing, "We agree with the district court that examining Thomas was vital to operating the Juvenile Unit, and the focused request for a limited portion of Thomas's medical records was no broader or more intrusive than necessary" (at 529). The court went on to conclude:

> By refusing to provide [the examining psychologist] the opportunity to review her medical records and to discover the root of Thomas's stress and anxiety, Thomas created a stalemate in which KCPD had little choice but to terminate Thomas rather than return her to the position from which Thomas's stress and anxiety originated. Thomas's refusal to cooperate with the reasonable requirements of her FFD evaluation and her violation of KCPD's rules of conduct provided the defendants with legitimate, nondiscriminatory reasons to terminate Thomas. (at 531)

Failure of an examining psychologist to obtain psychiatric treatment records in an FFD evaluation also can lead to error and impede the employer's ability to make decisions involving officer and public safety. In *Thompson v. City of Arlington* (1993), the employer sent police officer Ann Thompson for a psychological FFD evaluation once she was released by her treating mental health care providers to return to work following a suicide attempt. The examining psychologist did not review the psychiatric records but determined Thompson fit for duty. In turn, the employer demanded a review of Thompson's psychiatric treatment records, and she refused, leading the employer to place her on indefinite restricted duty. She sued in federal court, alleging, among other things, a violation of her right to privacy. The court dismissed her suit, citing the inevitable limitations of a treating health care provider's return-to-work opinion and the need for an objective one:

> An important, if not the primary, obligation of plaintiff's doctors is to serve her needs. If those doctors were to conclude that plaintiff's return to regular police officer duty would have a beneficial effect on her mental health, their natural leaning would be to take steps to cause her to return to regular duty. They would be extremely reluctant to report to City that she remains unfit to return to regular duty if, from a medical standpoint, such a report could be a factor in delaying or preventing her recovery. (at 1147)

The court went on to distinguish the patient-centered advocacy of the treating health care provider from the independent judgment of the FFD examiner, while noting the critical importance of having access to the records underlying the treating provider's opinions:

> And, as to City's own health care expert, a self-evident fact is that such an expert is highly unlikely to obtain full and candid information if the expert is required to rely on interviews with plaintiff concerning factors that enter into her mental makeup. Common sense says that, if plaintiff has determined that she wants to return to regular police officer duty, there is a serious risk that she will limit the information she provides in an evaluation by City's expert to facts and circumstances she believes would support her claim that she is fit for such a return. If City's expert is to be able to provide a meaningful opinion to City, the expert would be required to have full information, certainly at least as much information as plaintiff's health care providers acquire. The most effective, and only reasonable, method of obtaining that degree of information would be to cause all the information in possession of plaintiff's regular doctors to be provided to City for evaluation by its own expert. (at 1147)

Principle 11: Assess response style

One of the core features of a forensic evaluation that distinguishes it from therapeutic assessments is the absence of any presumption that the examinee's self-report is accurate (Greenberg & Shuman, 1997; Heilbrun, 2001). In an FFD examination, the potential for the examinee to under- or over-report symptoms; deny, minimize, or exaggerate facts; conceal certain information; or otherwise misrepresent the truth must always be considered, due in large part to the incentives associated with the outcome. The candidate's orientation toward accuracy or inaccuracy in his or her self-report is referred to as *response style*.

Response style is conceived as including four particular styles: (1) *reliable/honest* (factual inaccuracies attributable to misunderstanding or misperception), (2) *malingering* (factual inaccuracies derived from conscious fabrication or intentional exaggeration of symptoms), (3) *defensive* (factual inaccuracies resulting from intentional denial or minimization), and (4) *irrelevant/uncooperative* (resulting from a failure to become engaged in the evaluation or from a refusal to respond fully or at all) (Heilbrun, 2001; Rogers, 1997).

There are two primary means for assessing response style: (1) third-party information and (2) psychological assessment instruments, or tests, with built-in measures of response style. In the previous discussion of Principle 10, emphasis was placed on the importance of gathering third-party information. Its utility is tied not only to the improved depth and breadth of information obtained through collateral sources, but also to its potential for detecting malingering, defensiveness, dishonesty, and uncooperativeness. Melton et al. (1997) observed that "obtaining information contradicting the client's version of events is probably the most accurate means of detecting fabrication and may be the only viable one with clients who sabotage interview and testing efforts" (pp. 57–58). This is not to say that any given collateral source should be considered more reliable than the examinee, but rather that consistencies and discrepancies across and within data sources are an important means of weighing validity.

Standardized assessment instruments with validity scales or indices, such as the MMPI-2, MMPI-2-RF, PAI, CPI, MCMI-III, and 16PF, also can serve useful roles in evaluating response style, especially when used in conjunction with third-party information. Consideration should always be given, however, to the base rates of these scales in a particular norm group, such that examinees in an FFD evaluation are not judged to be defensive or dissimulating on the basis of validity scales alone when the scale norms were derived from respondents from a decidedly different context (i.e., police applicants in a pre-employment evaluation may not be comparable on validity scales to incumbent employees in an FFD examination) (Heilbrun, 2001). Evidence of frank lying, dissimulation, falsification, or overt concealment should always be reported to the referring party along with any reservations or limitations in the reliability of the examiner's opinions as a result of the employee's response style. In general, however, when the examinee's response style, based on evidence from third-party sources and psychological testing, suggests that his or her responses are unreliable, they should be regarded as less probative than information obtained from other sources with higher reliability.

DETERMINING FITNESS

Principle 12: Use a model for determining fitness for duty

Heilbrun (2001; see also Heilbrun et al., 2009) argues for the use of a model to help guide the forensic clinician in data gathering, data interpretation, and communication of results. He cites two general models to consider: Morse (1978) and Grisso (1986, 2003). Both have compelling features and applicability to FFD evaluations, although neither was developed for this application. Morse's model offers a straightforward application to a wide range of forensic mental health assessments, including the FFD evaluation, with a focus on three broad considerations: (1) the existence of a mental disorder or condition, (2) the functional abilities relevant to the referral questions, and (3) the strength of the causal connection between the first and the second considerations.

Gold and Shuman (2009) propose an alternative model (Battista, 1988) for workplace evaluations involving questions of impairment. Like Morse's model, Battista's involves the analysis of three elements: (1) *work demand*, which consists primarily of the relevant work skills and other requirements of a particular job, and can be derived most expediently from the job description and/or job analysis; (2) *work supply*, consisting of the employee's performance and employment history, including the ability to perform work functions with or without a social or interpersonal component, but also including the ability to perform simple and repetitive tasks, perform complex or varied tasks, work under stressful versus routine conditions, and work with and without supervision; and (3) *work capacity,* meaning the balance or interaction between work demand and work supply, such that adequate work capacity results in the employee having enough work supply (ability) to satisfy work demand. Because reduced work capacity can result from either work supply falling below work demand, or work demand increasing to surpass work supply, Battista's model provides a useful framework for analyzing and locating the cause(s) for any observed decrease in work capacity.

This model also incorporates the procedural advice of Borum et al. (2003) when conducting FFD evaluations for police officers and other high-risk positions:

> [T]he psychologist must evaluate the degree of fit between the employee's current capacities or impairments and the essential requirements of the position. The assessment can be done by (a) determining if there are psychological or behavioral problems, and if so, evaluating their potential impact on the employee's ability to perform the functions of the job; and (b) determining if there are any significant impairments in the employee's ability to perform essential job functions, and if so, evaluating their cause. (p. 143)

In my own approach to determining fitness, I adopt a blended model that incorporates elements of Morse's and Battista's models, but which is framed within the context of Grisso's (2003). It consists of four analytic components:

1. *Functional Analysis:* Concerned principally with *work supply*, this analysis asks the question, What is it that the officer is able to do, and not able to do, effectively? It considers the officer's work and behavioral *history*, not merely recent or current functioning. It is concerned with both retained and impaired functioning in an effort to obtain as accurate a picture as possible of the officer's past, current, and reasonably anticipated job relevant behavior.

2. *Contextual Analysis:* Not all police work is identical; it varies depending on the nature of the assignment (e.g., patrol versus desk duty, intermittent undercover versus deep and sustained undercover, homicide versus property crime investigations); the volume of calls for service and population-to-officer ratio (i.e., urban, suburban, rural); and other factors affecting the degree of isolation, stress, risk, and other demands associated with the specific position. The contextual analysis considers these and other relevant work demand characteristics, including consideration of what Brodsky (1996) calls "tolerance limits" within which the employee must operate and that are affected by elements outside the employer's control (e.g., civil service rules, union contracts, and organizational culture). At this stage of analysis, familiarity with the demands and milieu of the position is crucial, and an adequate objective analysis may require a site visit, interviews with supervisors and/or incumbents, and review of job analyses and position descriptions.

3. *Causal Analysis:* This component addresses evidence of the existence of a mental or emotional condition that may account for any observed functional deficits. In practical terms, if no mental or emotional condition exists, the analysis of fitness ends here because the minimum requisite condition for "unfitness" is not met. As noted in the discussion of Principle 5, this does not mean the officer should be retained, but only that the officer's behavioral problems are not attributable to a mental or emotional condition and, therefore, do not implicate fitness. This information permits both the employer and employee to explore alternative means for bringing equipoise to the disparity between work supply and work demand. On the other hand, when a mental condition is found to exist, its nexus to any functional deficits must still be determined. In conducting this analysis, it is important to differentiate between work capacity deficits that (1) derive from the examinee's mental or emotional condition, and (2) are caused by factors independent of that condition (e.g., attitude, motivation, skill or knowledge deficits, interpersonal conflicts, and general medical conditions).

4. *Interactive Analysis:* This element is, as Grisso (2003) points out, an assessment of person–context fit. It is concerned with the degree of congruency or balance between *work supply* and *work demand*—what Battista (1988) calls *work capacity*. Naturally, it requires not only an understanding of the examinee's functional abilities and deficits (derived from the functional analysis), but also an awareness of the *work demands*, or the particular job and working conditions of the officer.

5. *Judgmental Analysis:* This component is concerned with the degree of person–context (i.e., work supply–work demand) incongruency required before it can be determined that the employee cannot safely or effectively perform the job. It addresses what Grisso regards as the "ultimate question" (2003, p. 36), which, in the context of an FFD evaluation, is simply, *How much incongruency is enough to warrant a finding of unfitness?* (Note: Whether this ultimate question is most properly answered by the employer or by the examiner is an issue that warrants serious debate (Heilbrun et al., 2009), although the constraints of this chapter prevent it from further exploration. Examiners who object to opining on the ultimate question should make that position known at the time of the referral (see Principle 1). For these examiners, this model would conclude after the interactive component.)

Regardless of what model is used, its usefulness is measured by its ability to bring an organizational structure that constructively guides the selection and organization of data sources and information, promotes effective analysis, and facilitates the communication of opinions and testimony. The use of a poor model, on the other hand, would likely result in a worse outcome than no model at all (Heilbrun, 2001).

COMMUNICATING THE RESULTS

The written product of the FFD evaluation is not merely an opinion or judgment about fitness. It is also an explication of that opinion within the confines of the referring party's request and/or governing conditions. Melton et al. (2007) discuss several important ways that forensically oriented reports differ from those written for traditional clinical settings. First, the recipients usually will not be other mental health professionals, but employers, human resource professionals, attorneys, labor unions, and other laypersons unfamiliar with clinical language and meaning. For this reason, Heilbrun (2001) and others recommend that examiners avoid the use of clinical jargon when writing these reports.

A second difference from traditional clinical reports is the likelihood that they will become more broadly distributed to other unanticipated persons and parties, whether through the employer's decisions, administrative procedures, or subsequent litigation. Consequently, "special care must be taken to minimize any infringement on the privacy rights of persons mentioned in the report" (Melton et al., 2007, p. 583).

A third difference is the degree of scrutiny that the report and the author are likely to receive in the course of any adjudicative proceedings or negotiations. Examiners should expect to be asked to provide testimony concerning their opinions and the bases for them, and this testimony may take place in the context of adversarial proceedings, under oath, where a well-written report will facilitate testimony and a poorly written one "may become, in the hands of a skillful lawyer, an instrument to discredit and embarrass its author" (Melton et al., 2007, p. 583).

To these important considerations must be added an essential final difference, and that is the outcomes or consequences at stake in an FFD evaluation of a police officer. In addition to the impact that the findings may have on the decision to retain or terminate the officer, the nature and content of the report could affect the employee's reputation, standing, and career even if retained in his or her position. Furthermore, an unclear and ultimately unhelpful report concerning an officer who represents a direct threat to the safety of others could result in the employer or other trier of fact ordering that the employee be returned to duty notwithstanding the findings of the examiner, thereby potentially jeopardizing safety. Thus, reports prepared in connection with FFD evaluations should reflect the seriousness of purpose, the significance of the potential consequences, the scrutiny they are almost certain to receive or should receive, and the breadth and nature of the audience, both intended and reasonably anticipated, that characterize these examinations.

Principle 13: Guard the legal and ethical limitations on report content

It is a standard of ethical practice that "[p]sychologists include in written and oral reports and consultations only information germane to the purpose for which the communication is made" (APA, 2002, Standard 4.04(a)). This ethical standard is echoed by the federal HIPAA Privacy Rule (U.S. Department of Health & Human Services, 2000), which states that a covered health care provider must make reasonable efforts to limit disclosure of protected health information to the *minimum necessary* to accomplish the intended purpose of the use, disclosure, or request (45 C.F.R. §164.502(b)(1)). Rostow and Davis (2004) make this point directly when discussing what law enforcement (LE) executives should anticipate receiving in a report from an FFD examiner:

> The LE executive must not expect a complex examination of the officer's life outside of the events connected to the reason for referral.... In general, the department will be given only the information that it must have to meet its public safety and business necessity obligations in the employment context... without revealing protected health information. (pp. 105–106)

The ADA also imposes limits on how much private information can be disclosed to an employer, stipulating that "[a]n employer is entitled only to the information necessary to determine whether the employee can do the essential functions of the job or work without posing a direct threat" (EEOC, 2000, Question 13, p. 12).

Courts have held that FFD examiners who go too far in disclosing confidential aspects of an employee's life or health may be subject to tort action for invasion of privacy. In *McGreal v. Ostrov* et al. (2004), the circuit court ruled that the chief of police and his codefendants "were not entitled to disclosure of anything other than the fitness for duty determination. They were not entitled ... to force the disclosure of the intimate and irrelevant details of McGreal's home life" (p. 53). In an earlier California case, *Pettus v. Cole* (1996), the court reached nearly the identical opinion when the FFD examiners disclosed the employee's history of an alcohol use disorder when the referring question was limited only to whether Pettus qualified for disability under the company's benefits plan. The court wrote:

> There is no reason in law or policy why an employer should be allowed access to detailed family or medical histories of its employees, or to the intricacies of its employees' mental processes, except with the individual's freely given consent to the particular disclosure or some other substantial justification. (at 99)

Although it is important for examiners to strike a balance between offering too much detail and too little (see Principle 14), there also are particular facts about an employee that should not be communicated at all. One of these involves the employee's genetic information, defined under the Genetic Information Nondiscrimination Act (GINA, 2008) as including the manifested medical conditions of family members (29 C.F.R. §1635.3(b)). Thus, for an FFD examiner who is performing the examination as an agent of the employer, both *acquiring* information about the employee's family medical history and *disclosing* that information is prohibited under GINA.

Nonforensic clinicians are generally not trained in preparing reports for the lay audience, so particular care must be taken to ensure that the FFD evaluation report does not contain information that exceeds either ethical or legal boundaries. It also is important to be vigilant to the possibility of organizational or administrative limits on the content of a fitness-for-duty report, inasmuch as many police agencies have written policies that specify the constraints on report content.

In *Pettus* (1996), the court noted that, in the absence of a specific authorization from the employee to disclose personal health information, the examining doctor must limit disclosure to a description of the "functional limitations" that may result from the employee's medical condition. As stated by Gold and Shuman (2009), "Advancing the credibility of the examination by providing all information disclosed to an employer risks unnecessary breaches of confidentiality and psychological harm to the examinee" (p. 33).

Principle 14: Avoid mere conclusory opinions unless otherwise instructed by the referring party

In an effort to avoid reporting too much private information and facing possible legal, civil, regulatory, or professional sanctions, psychologists sometimes choose to limit their reports simply to a "fit versus unfit" statement without further detail or explanation. This strategy might even be requested by the referring party, in which case it is incumbent on the examiner who accepts such a referral to comply with it. But doing so may very well undermine the usefulness of the report, and examiners should consider the consequences of this approach, as well as the alternatives, and discuss both with the retaining party at the outset of the evaluation.

In the federal environment, the Merit Systems Protection Board (*Lassiter v. Department of Justice*, 1993) held that the proper standard when assessing the probative weight of medical opinion in an FFD evaluation is (1) whether the opinion was based on a medical examination, (2) whether the opinion provided a "reasoned explanation for its findings as distinct from mere conclusory assertions" (p. 4), (3) the qualifications of the expert rendering the opinion, and (4) the extent and duration of the expert's familiarity with the condition of the employee. In *Slater v. Dept. of Homeland*

Security (2008), the Board concluded that the FFD reports that were "entirely conclusory, devoid of any medical documentation or explanation in support of their conclusions" carried less "credibility and reliability" than one that was "a thorough, detailed, and relevant medical opinion addressing the medical issues of the agency's removal action" (at paragraph 16).

Gold and Shuman (2009) argue in favor of a "reliability" standard for reports and testimony regarding workplace mental health evaluations, and they assert that reliable expert opinion in this context is characterized by four considerations. It should (1) rest on an adequate basis (e.g., dates and details of interviews and examinations; results of psychological testing; school, military, and work records); (2) clearly articulate what opinion(s) or conclusion(s) the examiner draws from the raw data; (3) clearly explain how the examiner reasoned from the raw data to the opinion offered, including the relevant science and its limits; and (4) fairly address these issues from the perspective of alternative explanations (*Gilbert v. Daimler Chrysler Corp.,* 2004; Shuman, 2005; see also American Psychology-Law Society, 2008, SGFP Guideline 13.01, Accuracy, Fairness, and Avoidance of Deception).

Preparing a report that contains these elements of reliability may also facilitate the due process rights of the employee. In the landmark case of *Cleveland Board of Education v. Loudermill* (1985), the Court held that a represented public employee may not be terminated without first giving the employee "oral or written notice of the charges against him, an explanation of the employer's evidence, and an opportunity to present his side of the story" (at 546). Subsequent cases have extended *Loudermill* due process rights to circumstances in which an officer has been dismissed as a result of an FFD evaluation, noting that the terminated employee has a right to understand the psychological "charges" against him, the evidence underlying the charges, and to be given an opportunity to refute them (cf. *Bass v. City of Albany,* 1992; *Bauschard v. Martin,* 1993; *Nuss v. Township of Falls, et al.,* 1985).

When the retaining party requires a mere conclusory opinion in spite of the inherent limitations of that approach, examiners may consider an alternative posited by Stone (2000). He suggests under such circumstances that the examiner prepare two reports: one for the referring party that conforms to the required limitations and a second for the file that explicates the rationale for the opinions and conclusions and is available for use in litigation should it later be required. Whatever approach is used, examiners should make every effort to prepare a report that conforms to the limits of the law, the explicit terms of the referring party's request and policies, and ethical considerations, while also striving to provide sufficient probative value to be useful both in the immediate employment related decisions and any reasonably anticipated adjudicative or administrative proceeding.

Principle 15: Address causation, treatment, or restoration of fitness, and/or accommodation only if requested by the referring party

The importance of clarifying the relevant clinical and forensic questions in advance of the examination was emphasized in the discussion under Principle 2. It does little to benefit the examiner or any of the involved parties if this task is postponed until after the examination is finished and the report writing begins. But even at this stage, obtaining such clarification is better done late than not at all.

As previously discussed, it is best to obtain the referral source's questions in writing. Evaluators should write their opinions framed as responses to these questions, organized by listing each question, followed by the response. "When specific questions are asked, evaluators should limit themselves to providing opinions and supporting data responsive only to these questions unless otherwise specified" (Gold & Shuman, 2009, p. 153). This is especially true on matters of causation, treatment or restoration of fitness, and accommodation. Offering opinions beyond the limits of the referral questions inappropriately extends into the *disposition* stage (cf. Grisso, 2003) of decision making, which is a matter properly left to the employer.

Causation

Examining clinicians are often tempted in FFD examination reports to address causation, if only because it is a central element of most clinical training programs and a compelling topic of interest. Clinicians generally are drawn to questions of causation, and in an effort to help explain the employee's condition or to facilitate treatment, evaluators may be inclined to discuss or opine on causation in the report, notwithstanding the lack of empirical evidence underlying many such opinions. Evaluators should be mindful that causation is not merely a clinical concept, but a legal one, as well, and the definitions and implications associated with each are quite different from one another. Furthermore, for important reasons having to do with risk management, liability exposure, collective-bargaining procedures, and other legal and administrative considerations, the referring party may want the issue of causation to be addressed at another time, by a separate examiner, or not at all. Causation in particular is a concept that carries implications of potential liability both for the employee and the employer, and each party may be differentially helped or harmed by addressing this question prematurely. (Note: *Causation* in this context refers to the etiology—proximate or remote—of the disorder. In contrast, the *causal analysis* discussed as a decision-making component under Principle 12 is concerned with the underlying cause of the employee's functional impairments (i.e., whether the impairment is due to a mental health condition or some other factor). It is not concerned with the cause of the condition itself.)

Treatment

If causation is a compelling topic for clinicians, it pales in comparison to the attraction to treatment. Clinicians generally wish to be helpful, and this is especially true when faced with an examinee that is psychologically injured, suffering, or otherwise distressed. Indeed, when an evaluator concludes that an employee is psychologically unfit for duty, the referring party often requests that the examiner address how fitness might be restored. When this is the case, evaluators should still be careful to limit their treatment recommendations, including modalities and duration, to those for which there is adequate evidence of effectiveness.

Most importantly, examiners should be careful not to *condition* a determination of fitness on an employee's participation in counseling or other therapy. When such a condition is stipulated, it typically is rationalized in one of two ways: either because the examiner believes the employee's current fitness is unlikely to be sustained without additional or ongoing treatment, or because the employee's current unfitness results from a minor impairment expected to respond quickly to treatment. In cases of the former, if the employee's current fitness is so fragile or unstable as to be undone in the foreseeable future without the benefit of ongoing treatment, the examiner should reconsider whether the *interactive analysis* (see Principle 12) justifies the fit-for-duty conclusion. Examiners need not, nor should they, be constrained in their analyses only to the employee's present symptoms and adaptation; they should also consider the known or reasonably anticipated course of the examinee's condition and fitness in light of the individualized assessment.

In cases where the employee is judged currently unfit for duty due to a remediable condition, it is usually more prudent to acknowledge the current unfit status and not address recommendations designed to restore fitness unless requested by the referring party. When an employer requires treatment as an employment condition, some jurisdictions have held that the employer is responsible for the cost of treatment and compensation to the employee for any on-duty time used to engage in treatment (*Sehie v. City of Aurora*, 2005; see also *Todd v. Lexington Fayette Urban County Government*, 2009), where the court reached a different conclusion when the mandated conditions are for the benefit of the employee and not the employer). Furthermore, employees required to engage in treatment can easily come to believe (erroneously) that treatment compliance will or should shield them from consequences for persistent problematic behavior. Unless the referring party has specifically requested the examiner to opine on treatment or restoration of fitness, the report should be silent on this question. When the employer does request treatment recommendations from the examiner, it may be useful to reference the practical guidance of the EEOC:

> Regardless of whether employers believe they are trying to help employees who have medical conditions, employers should focus instead on addressing unacceptable workplace conduct. Employer comments about the disability and its treatment could lead to potential ADA claims (e.g., the employer "regarded" the employee as having a disability or the employer engaged in disparate treatment). (EEOC, 2008, Question 12, p. 12)

Accommodation

Under the ADA, an employer "must provide a reasonable accommodation to the known physical or mental limitations of a qualified individual with a disability unless it can show that the accommodation would impose an undue hardship" (EEOC, 1997, p. 12). A reasonable accommodation is defined as "any change in the work environment or in the way things are customarily done that enables an individual with a disability to enjoy equal employment opportunities" (29 C.F.R. §1630.9). This may include job restructuring, part-time or modified work schedules, reassignment to a vacant position, and providing additional unpaid leave for necessary treatment.

Employers are only responsible, however, for providing a reasonable accommodation to a *known* limitation of a qualified individual with a disability. Even when an employee has a psychological condition that renders him or her unfit for duty, it is not *per se* legally equivalent to a disability under the terms of the ADA. Indeed, some conditions that may not meet the ADA's definition of a disability may nevertheless render an employee unfit for duty. Moreover, except in cases of obvious disabilities, it is generally the case that the employer's obligation to explore accommodation arises only "when the employee tells the employer he is disabled" (*Hammon v. DHL Airways*, 1997/1999, at 445). The employee need not use the word *disabled* or *disability* to formally initiate the accommodation exploration process (*Cannice v. Norwest Bank Iowa N.A.*, 1999); on the other hand, where the employee openly denies having a disabling condition, even an FFD examiner's finding to the contrary may not be sufficient to require accommodation efforts on the part of the employer (*Larson v. Koch Refining Co.*, 1996).

Once an employee specifically requests an accommodation for a work-impairing condition, the employer has an affirmative duty to engage in the "interactive process" to obtain relevant information about the employee's condition and the basis for requesting an accommodation (*Barnett v. U.S. Air., Inc.*, 2000). Thus, employers may prefer, and usually are best advised, to separate questions of reasonable accommodation from the FFD question. However, when in the interests of expediency and/or compassion an employer asks the examiner to make recommendations regarding accommodation, the examiner should become knowledgeable about the types of accommodation that are regarded by the courts as reasonable (e.g., an employer is not required to restructure or reallocate the essential functions of a job as a reasonable accommodation, and the essential functions may include the start and stop time of an employee's work schedule; see *Guice-Mills v. Derwinski*, 1992). Unless the examiner is familiar with the statutes, regulations, and case law pertinent to reasonable accommodation, it is best to inform the referring party that questions about accommodation will be deferred to a separate stage and examiner, even if requested. Under any circumstances, reasonable accommodation is always an employer's decision, not an examiner's.

CONCLUDING REMARKS

These 15 principles represent established practices informed by law, professional standards, the literature, and experience. In selecting these, I undoubtedly have left out other fundamental practices that seem obvious, are universally accepted, or have little consequence if not carried out. To the extent that I have overlooked a principle of importance, future editions of this *Handbook* may provide a remedy.

As a reflection of law, standards, and experience, these principles will evolve over time. They also will, and should, provoke discussion and debate. But in the interim it is my hope that they also will provide some measure of guidance to psychologists who seek to approach these high-stakes evaluations with the exacting attention to law, ethics, and practice standards that they demand and deserve. Nothing short of human lives is at stake when evaluating the psychological fitness of a police officer, and nothing less than principled work is required from those who do them.

Author Note

The author is grateful to Casey O. Stewart for his review of an earlier draft of this chapter and for his substantive advice. Thanks also go to Kirk Heilbrun for generously permitting his principles of forensic mental health assessment (Heilbrun, 2001) to be used as a foundation for this material. Finally, gratitude is extended to Yossef S. Ben-Porath, Herbert M. Gupton, Michael D. Roberts, Jim Tracy, Philip S. Trompetter, and Richard C. Wihera, whose ongoing peer consultation provided the impetus for this chapter.

REFERENCES

Aitchison, W. (2000). *The rights of law enforcement officers* (4th ed.). Portland, OR: Labor Relations Information System.

American Psychology-Law Society. (2008). *Specialty guidelines for forensic psychology* (4th draft). Retrieved December 15, 2009, from http://ap-ls.org/links/92908sgfp.pdf

Americans with Disabilities Act of 1990, 42 U.S.C. § 12101 *et seq.* (1990).

American Psychological Association. (2002). *Ethical principles for psychologists and code of conduct.* Washington, DC: Author.

Anfang, S. A., Faulkner, L. R., Fromson, J. A., & Gendel, M. H. (2005). American Psychiatric Association resource document on guidelines for psychiatric fitness-for-duty evaluations of physicians. *Journal of the American Academy of Psychiatry and the Law, 33,* 85–88.

Anfang, S. A., & Wall, B. W. (2006). Psychiatric fitness-for-duty evaluations. *Psychiatric Clinics of North America, 29,* 675–693.

Battista, M. E. (1988). Assessing work capacity. *Journal of Insurance Medicine, 20*(3), 16–22.

Borum, R., Super, J., & Rand, M. (2003). Forensic assessment for high-risk occupations. In A. M. Goldstein & I. B. Weiner (Eds.), *Forensic psychology* (Vol. 11, pp. 133–147). Hoboken, NJ: John Wiley.

Brodsky, C. M. (1996). Psychiatric aspects of fitness for duty. *Occupational Medicine, 11*(4), 719–726.

Budd, F. C., & Harvey, S. (2006). Military fitness-for-duty evaluations. In C. H. Kennedy & E. A. Zillmer (Eds.), *Military psychology* (pp. 35–60). New York: Guilford.

California Government Code §1031 (2005).

Corey, D. M. (1988). *The psychological suitability of police officer candidates.* Ph.D. dissertation, Fielding Graduate University, Santa Barbara, CA. Retrieved August 26, 2010, from *Dissertations and theses: Full text.* (Publication No. AAT8821055).

Dawkins, M., Griffin, S., & Dawkins, M. (2006, October). *Psychological fitness-for-duty examinations (FFD): Making effective use of FFD outcome data.* Paper presented at the 113th Annual Conference of the International Association of Chiefs of Police, Police Psychological Services Section, Boston, MA.

Decker, K. P. (2006). *Fit, unfit or misfit.* Springfield, IL: Charles C Thomas.

EEOC regulations to implement the equal employment provisions of the Americans With Disabilities Act, Title 29, Subtitle B, Chapter XIV, Part 1630 (1991).

Equal Employment Opportunity Commission. (1995). *ADA enforcement guidance: Preemployment disability-related questions and medical examinations* (Compliance manual, Volume II, Section 902, No. 915.002). Washington, DC: Author.

Equal Employment Opportunity Commission. (1997). *EEOC enforcement guidance on the Americans with Disabilities Act and Psychiatric Disabilities* (Compliance Manual, Volume II, Section 902, No. 915.002). Washington, DC: Author.

Equal Employment Opportunity Commission. (2000). *Enforcement guidance on disability-related inquiries and medical examinations of employees under the Americans with Disabilities Act* (Compliance Manual, Volume II, Section 902, No. 915.002). Washington, DC: Author.

Equal Employment Opportunity Commission. (2002). *ADA technical assistance manual,* January 1992. Publication EEOC-M-1A (10/29/2002 Addendum). Washington, DC: Author.

Equal Employment Opportunity Commission. (2008). *The Americans with Disabilities Act: Applying performance and conduct standards to employees with disabilities.* Retrieved January 4, 2010, from http://www.eeoc.gov/facts/performance-conduct.html

Family & Medical Leave Act, 29 U.S.C. §2601 (1993).

Fisher, M. A. (2009). Replacing "Who is the client?" with a different ethical question. *Professional Psychology: Research and Practice, 40*(1), 1–7.

Genetic Information Nondiscrimination Act of 2008 (GINA). Pub.L. 110–223, 122 Stat. 881 (2008).

Gold, L. H., & Shuman, D. W. (2009). *Evaluating mental health disability in the workplace*. New York: Springer Science & Business Media.

Greenberg, S. A., & Shuman, D. W. (1997). Irreconcilable conflict between therapeutic and forensic roles. *Professional Psychology: Research and Practice, 28*, 50–57.

Greenberg, S. A., & Shuman, D. W. (2007).When worlds collide: Therapeutic and forensic roles. *Professional Psychology: Research and Practice, 38*(2), 129–132.

Grisso, T. (1986). *Evaluating competencies: Forensic assessments and instruments*. New York: Plenum.

Grisso, T. (2003). *Evaluating competencies: Forensic assessments and instruments* (2nd ed.). New York: Kluwer Academic/Plenum Press.

Health Insurance Portability and Accountability Act (HIPAA). Title 45, Subtitle A, Subchapter C, Part 160, General Administrative Requirements (2000a).

Health Insurance Portability and Accountability Act (HIPAA) Privacy Rule. Title 45, Subtitle A, Subchapter C, Part 164, Subpart E, Privacy of Individually Identifiable Health Information (2000b).

Heilbrun, K. (2001). *Principles of forensic mental health assessment*. New York: Kluwer Academic/Plenum.

Heilbrun, K., Grisso, T., & Goldstein, A. M. (2009). *Foundations of forensic mental health assessment*. New York: Oxford University Press.

Heilbrun, K., Warren, J., & Picarello, K. (2003). Third party information in forensic assessment. In A. M. Goldstein & I. B. Weiner (Eds.), *Forensic psychology* (Vol. 11, pp. 69–86). Hoboken, NJ: John Wiley.

International Association of Chiefs of Police. (2009). *Psychological fitness-for-duty evaluation guidelines*. Arlington, VA: International Association of Chiefs of Police. Retrieved August 25, 2010, from http://theiacp.org/psych_services_section/pdfs/Psych-FitnessforDutyEvaluation.pdf

Koocher, G. P. (2007). Twenty-first century ethical challenges for psychology. *American Psychologist, 62*, 375–384.

Mariani, R. C., & Avelenda, S. M. (2009). Mental health issues under the ADA. Retrieved December 15, 2009, http://www.cnapro.com/docs/ada_mental_health_issues.doc

McDonald, J. J., Kulick, F. B., & Creighton, M. K. (1995). Mental disabilities under the ADA: A management rights approach. *Employee Relations Law Journal, 20*(4), 541–569.

Melton, G. B., Petrila, J., Poythress, N. G., Slobogin, C., Lyons, P. M., & Otto, R. K. (2007). *Psychological evaluations for the courts*. New York: Guilford.

Morse, S. (1978). Law and mental health professionals: The limits of expertise. *Professional Psychology, 9*, 389–399.

OPM Medical Qualification Determinations. 5 C.F.R. §339 (1995).

Otto, R. K., & Krauss, D. A. (2009, August 10). Contemplating the presence of third party observers and facilitators in psychological evaluations. *Assessment Online First*. doi:10.1177/1073191109336267

Rehabilitation Act of 1973, 29 U.S.C.A. §706 (1973).

Rogers, R. (Ed.). (1997). *Clinical assessment of malingering and deception* (2nd ed.). New York: Guilford.

Rostow, C. D., & Davis, R. D. (2004). *A handbook for psychological fitness-for-duty evaluations in law enforcement*. Binghamton, NY: Haworth Press.

Shuman, D. (2005). *Psychiatric and psychological evidence*. St. Paul, MN: Thomson-West.

Stone, A.V. (2000). *Fitness for duty: Principles, methods and legal issues*. New York: CRC Press.

U.S. Department of Defense. (1997). Directive 6490.1, Mental Health Evaluations of Members of the Armed Forces, October 1, 1997.

U.S. Department of Health & Human Services. (2000, December 28). Standards for Privacy of Individually Identifiable Health Information, *Federal Register, 65*(250), 82554.

CASES CITED

AFGE Local 596 v. Department of Justice et al. (Sherman, 2007).

Albert v. Runyon, 6 F.Supp.2d 57, 1998 U.S. Dist. Lexis 7505 (D. Mass. 1998).

Anderson v. Little League Baseball, Inc., 794 F.Supp. 342, 61 USLW 2050 (D. Ariz. 1992).

Arkansas Attorney General Opinion No. 2000-338 (1-21-2001).

Barnett v. U.S. Air., Inc., 228 F.3d 1105 (9th Cir. 2000).

Bass v. City of Albany, 968 F.2d 1067 (11th Cir. 1992).

Bauschard v. Martin, 1993 WL 79259 (N.D. Ill. 1993) (not reported).

Bonsignore v. City of New York, 683 F.2d 635 (2d Cir. 1982).

Brownfield v. City of Yakima, No. 09-35628, (9th Cir. July 27, 2010).

Brumbalough v. Camelot Care Centers, Inc., 427 F.3d 996 (6th Cir. 2005).

Butler v. Thornburgh, 900 F.2d 871, 876 (5th Cir. 1990), cert. denied, 498 U.S. 998 (1990).
Cannice v. Norwest Bank Iowa N.A., 189 F.3d 723 (8th Cir. 1999).
Carrillo v. National Council of Churches of Christ in the USA, 976 F.Supp. 254 (SDNY 1997).
Cleghorn v. Hess, 853 P.2d 1260 (Nev. 1993).
Cleveland Board of Education v. Loudermill, 470 U.S. 532, 105 S.Ct. 1487, 84 L.Ed.2d 494 (1985).
Cody v. CIGNA Healthcare of St. Louis, Inc.139 F.3d 595 (8th Cir. 1998).
Colon v. City of Newark, 909 A.2d 725 (NJAD 2006), 2006 WL 1194230 (unpublished decision).
Conte v. Horcher, 365 N.E.2d 567 (Ill. App. 1977).
Crandall v. Michaud, 603 So. 2d 637, 637 (Fla. 1992).
Cripe v. City of San Jose, 261 F.3d 877 (9th Cir. 2001).
Deen v. Darosa, 414 F.3d 731 (7th Cir. 2005).
Denhof et al. v. City of Grand Rapids, 494 F.3d 534 (6th Cir. 2007).
Elkins v. Syken, 672 So.2d 517, 519 (Fla. 1996).
Galieti v. State Farm Mutual Automobile Insurance Co. et al., 154 FRD 262; 1994 U.S. Dist. LEXIS 8835; 29 Fed. R. Serv. 3d (Callaghan) 183.
Gardner v. Broderick, 392 U.S. 273 (1968).
Garrity v. New Jersey, 385 U.S. 493 (1967).
Gilbert v. Daimler Chrysler Corp., 685 N.W.2d 391 (Mich. 2004).
Guice-Mills v. Derwinski, 967 F.2d 794 (2nd Cir. 1992).
Hammon v. DHL Airways, Inc., 980 F.Supp. 919 (S.D. Ohio 1997), aff'd, 165 F.3d 441, 450 (6th Cir. 1999).
Hill v. Winona, 454 NW 2d 659 (Minn.App. 1990).
Hogarth v. Thornburgh, 833 F.Supp. 1077 (SDNY 1993).
Holst v. Veterans Affairs, 106 MSPR 499 (2007).
Jackson v. Lake County, 2003 WL 22127743 (N.D. Ill. 2003) (not reported).
Jackson v. Wilson, 262 S.E.2d 547, 152 Ga.App. 250 (Ga.App. 1979).
Knill v. Principi, EEOC DOC 01984220, 2001 WL 683335 (EEOC), citing Universal Camera Corp. v. NLRB, 340 US 474, 477 (1951).
Kraft v. Police Commissioner of Boston, 417 Mass. 235, 629 NE 2d 995, 1994 Mass. Lexis 93 (1994).
Larson v. Koch Refining Co., 920 F.Supp. 1000 (D. Minn. 1996).
Lassiter v. Department of Justice, 60 M.S.P.R. 138 (December 21, 1993).
Lassiter v. Reno, 86 F.3d 1151 (4th Cir. 1996), cert. denied, 519 U.S. 1091 (1997).
Lefkowitz v. Turley, 414 U.S. 70 (1973).
Leonel v. American Airlines, Inc., 400 F.3d 702 (9th Cir. 2005).
Marino v. U.S. Postal Service et al., 25 F.3d 1037, 3 A.D. Cases 704 (1st Cir. 1994).
Mazzarella v. U.S. Postal Service, 849 F.Supp. 89 (D.Mass. 1994).
McGreal v. Ostrov, 368 F.3d 657 (7th Cir. 2004).
McKnight v. Monroe Co. Sheriff's Dept. (S.D.Ind. 2002).
Myers v. Hose, 50 F.3d 278 (4th Cir. 1995).
National Treasury Employees Union v. Von Raab, 489 U.S. 656, 109 S.Ct. 1384, 103 L.Ed.2d 685 (1989).
NLRB v. Weingarten, Inc., 420 US 251 (1975).
Nuss v. Township of Falls, et al., 89 Pa. Commw. 97; 491 A.2d 971, 1985 Pa. Commw. LEXIS 1029.
Palmer v. Circuit Court of Cook County, 117 F.3d 351 (7th Cir. 1997).
Pettus v. Cole, 57 Cal.Rptr.2d 46, 49 Cal.App. 4th 402 (Cal.App. 1 Dist. 1996).
Policemen's Benevolent Association of New Jersey v. Township of Washington, 850 F.2d 133 (3rd Cir. 1988).
Ragge v. MCA/Universal Studios et al., 165 FRD 601 (CD Cal. 1995); 1995 U.S. Dist. LEXIS 20669.
Richardson v. City of Pasadena, 500 S.W. 2d 175 (Tex.Civ.App.—Houston [14th Dist.] 1973), rev'd on procedural ground, 513 S.W. 2d 1 (Tex. 1974).
Sager v. County of Yuba, 68 Cal.Rptr.3d 1, 156 Cal.App.4th 1049 (Cal.App. 2007).
Schloendorff v. Society of New York Hospital, 211 NY 125, 105 N.E. 92 (N.Y. 1914).
Schuman v. City of Philadelphia, 470 F.Supp. 449 (E.D. Pa. 1979).
Sehie v. City of Aurora, 432 F.3d 749 (7th Cir. 2005).
Simmons v. Rehab Xcel, Inc., 731 So.2d 529, 531–532 (La. App. 1999).
Slater v. Dept. of Homeland Security, 108 MSPR 419, 2008 MSPB 73.
Stewart v. Pearce, 484 F.2d 1031 (9th Cir. 1973).
Sullivan v. River Valley School District, 197 F3d 804, 9 AD 1711(6th Cir. 1999).
Thomas v. Corwin, 483 F.3d 516 (8th Cir. 2007), U.S. App. Lexis 7601, 100 FEP Cases (BNA) 297.
Thompson v. City of Arlington, 838 F.Supp. 1137; 1993 U.S. Dist. LEXIS 17093; 2 Am.Disabilities Cas. (BNA) 1756.

Tingler v. City of Tampa, 400 So.2d 146 (Fla. App. 1981).

Todd v. Lexington Fayette Urban County Government, 2009 U.S. Dist. LEXIS 115183 (C.D. KY 2009).

Tomlin v. Holecek et al., 150 FRD 628 (D.Minn. 1993); 1993 U.S. Dist. LEXIS 16851; 27 Fed. R. Serv. 3d (Callaghan) 977.

Universal Camera Corp. v. National Labor Relations Board, 340 U.S. 474 (1951).

Vinson v. The Superior Court of Alameda County, 43 Cal.3d 833, 239 Cal.Rptr. 292 (1987).

Watson v. City of Miami Beach, 177 F.3d 932 (11th Cir. 1999).

Yin v. California, 95 F.3d 864 (9th Cir. 1996).

14 Methods for Real-Time Assessment of Operational Stress During Realistic Police Tactical Training

Riccardo Fenici

Donatella Brisinda

Anna Rita Sorbo

INTRODUCTION

Numerous studies have shown that factors related to organizational structure, inappropriate authoritarian management, poor interpersonal relationships with supervisors, lack of adequate participation in planning and of autonomy in performing duties, and lack of recognition for work accomplishments are usually reported as the major source of stress for police officers. On the other hand, there are other risk factors such as alteration of normal sleep patterns because of shift schedules, daily exposure to interpersonal violence, personal endangerment with fear of revenge from criminals, and interactions with an ambivalent public, which induce chronic emotional effects that jeopardize the physical and psychological balance of police officers with their families. A chronic burden of negative emotions such as anger, anxiety, or depression can lead to psychological burnout, whereas continuous activation of the stress response systems (i.e., the hypothalamus-pituitary-adrenal axis and the autonomic nervous system [ANS]) can induce alterations of the neuroautonomic and endocrine balance, leading to higher incidence of hypertension, cardiovascular disease, metabolic syndrome, and even cancer.

Under such unfavorable basal conditions, law enforcement officers may be suddenly called to respond to critical situations implying an appropriate use of tactics and force to protect their lives and the lives of others. In front of a potentially lethal threat, although in the grip of *fight or flight*–induced psychophysiological alterations, the police officer is required to maintain vigilance, dynamic threat assessment, sound judgment, and appropriate tactical decision making. Instead, uncontrolled stress-induced emotions (i.e., fear and anger), perceptual anomalies (tunnel vision, auditory exclusion, and altered sense of space and time), memory loss, and intrusive distractive thoughts may induce behavioral alterations (automatic pilot, dissociation, and freezing) with tragic consequences. In spite of the high risk of stress-induced errors, accidents, or overreaction that can compromise performance, jeopardize public safety, and determine liability, the training of police officers on tactical stress management is still more empirical than based on scientific knowledge. From real-life experience, we have to acknowledge that empirical police training is often insufficient to guarantee operational success and officers' survival. Thus, an unquestionable mandatory commitment of any modern police institution should be to favor research in the psychophysiology of officers' behavior under critical tactical stress and to develop more efficient scientifically based training to improve officers' survival on the street.

During the last decade, only a few attempts have been reported in such direction; however, there could be others that have not been disclosed to the public (as in our case) for institutional classification of the information. Available data are still limited and in most cases rather empirical. The purpose of this chapter is to summarize present experience and to provide suggestions about how to design more comprehensive investigational protocols to evaluate police tactical stress, using scientific methods and available technologies gathered from experimental and clinical psychophysiology.

TACTICAL STRESS

It is well known by police officers that *when something is going to be wrong* for an unexpected sudden threat occurring during a boring night shift or the best-planned SWAT operation, there are immediate, uncontrollable physical reactions (one for all, a marked increase of the heart rate), which alarm the mind about the impending danger and trigger the *Oh shit!* statement (Solomon, 1991). At that point, the officer may do the right thing, react and survive, or lose control and be defeated.

The empirical experience of survivors is an inestimable wealth that must be transferred to other officers, to prepare them for the danger before they run into troubles themselves (Solomon, 1991; Solomon & Horn, 1986). However, besides *fate*, common sense suggests that there have to be critical differences in the *functioning* of officers who performed well and those who failed. In order to inoculate this precious experience into operational efficiency with more efficient training, it is necessary to study and understand such psychophysiological differences. The problem is that acute psychophysiological stress occurring during high-risk police operations is difficult to study and may elude an accurate quantification because it consists of several (interrelated) mechanisms, including psychological, endocrine, immunologic, and physical involvement, which reciprocal interaction is characterized by a pronounced interindividual and situational variability. To achieve a comprehensive understanding, high competence in very different fields and an appropriate interdisciplinary approach are required. Scientists and police officers have to work together to understand the weak points of present knowledge and to design a better training, based on scientific evidence of efficacy. On the contrary, at the moment, the majority of police instructors are highly experienced street veterans, but usually have not had much knowledge about how to use scientific methods in training. On the other hand, scientists skilled in research useful to studying police tactical stress are usually closed in psychophysiology laboratories and very far away from the street and from the real-life stress occurring in highly demanding police tactical tasks. Thus, a first mandatory step is to create an appropriate communication between such different professionals, by overcoming the diffidence of police officers who usually don't like to deal with doctors (especially "shrinks") and to have such people telling them theories about what works (or not) on the street and by pulling the "scientist" out of the laboratory and into the police reality, at least in the training arena where such a realm can be realistically reconstructed and studied. An excellent example of such fruitful interaction and integration can be found in Matthew J. Sharp's recent book *Processing Under Pressure* (2010), where a lot of scientific knowledge has been provided in an understandable style and has been used to interpret real operational situations.

EMOTIONS AND COGNITIVE FUNCTION UNDER TACTICAL STRESS

Indeed, the relationship between emotion and cognition has been a matter of scientific debate for decades, and a systematic treatment of such a complex matter is obviously beyond the scope of this chapter. Here, we will briefly summarize only basic information useful to understand what happens to police officers when a tactical scenario turns into violence and needs force-on-force action. In such a situation, major emotional reactions to perceived danger trigger the officer's defensive response, mobilizing strength for survival through ANS adaptations, but inducing significant *body dysfunction* (e.g., perceptual distortion and modification of cardiorespiratory function) (Grossman & Siddle,

1998; Honig & Roland, 1998; Solomon & Horn, 1986) with possible derangement of cognitive function and rational control. Initially, cognitive and emotional functions were viewed as largely separated, with belief that emotion was primary to and independent of cognition (Kunst-Wilson & Zajonc, 1980). Modern research in neuroscience and psychophysiology has significantly modified this interpretation. An important progress in understanding the relationship between cognition and emotion in humans has become possible after the advent of modern neuroimaging, especially the functional MRI, which confirmed that cognitive processes occur in cortical regions of the brain (Gazzaniga, Ivry, & Mangun, 2008) and that brain structures linked to emotion are mostly subcortical. However, there is a more complex network, including the anterior cingulate and prefrontal cortex, which provides the mechanism for self-regulation of cognition and emotion (Allman, Hakeem, Erwin, Nimchinsky, & Hof, 2001; Bush, Luu, & Posner, 2000; Posner & Rothbart, 2007; Posner, Rothbart, Rueda, & Tang, 2009). The anterior cingulate cortex also (1) regulates the processing of information from other brain areas, (2) is sensitive to reward and pain (Eisenberger, Lieberman, & Williams, 2003; Hampton & O'Doherty, 2007), and (3) serves as part of a controlling network in coupling cognitive and emotional areas during task performance (Crottaz-Herbette & Menon, 2006; Etkin, Egner, Peraza, Kandel, & Hirsch, 2006; Posner, Rothbart, Sheese, & Tang, 2007). In addition, subcortical structures (e.g., the amygdala, the ventral striatum, and the hypothalamus), which are considered part of the primitive brain and capable of operating fast and in automatic fashion to evoke survival responses (Whalen et al., 2004), are widely networked to integrate emotion and cognition. In this way, typical cognitive functions, such as perception, attention, and memory, are largely dependent on emotional stimuli. In summary, it is now evident that in the real world, there are situations in which cognition and emotion are acting simultaneously, and it is difficult to separate their reciprocal interaction; therefore, they are now considered as interdependent and integrated functions in controlling human thought and behavior (Duncan & Barrett, 2007; Gray, Braver, & Raichle, 2002; Pessoa, 2008; Sergerie, Lepage, & Armony, 2006), especially under high-stress situations.

THE AMYGDALA AND THE RESPONSE TO THREAT AND FEAR

The key brain structure that coordinates behavioral, immunological, and neuroendocrine responses to environmental threats and fear reaction is the amygdala, a multinuclear structure located deep within the temporal lobes, medial to the hypothalamus, and adjacent to the hippocampus, well situated to integrate and distribute information through widespread projections with the rest of the brain. The amygdala serves in assessing the environment, stores emotional memories within the brain, and compares incoming emotional signals with previous emotional memories in order to make instantaneous decisions about the threat level of new incoming sensory information. The emotional content can change the formation and recollection of a memory event. In animals, the enhancement of memory owing to an emotion is due more to the induced arousal level than to the positive or negative valence of the emotion per se (McGaugh, 2004; Phelps, Ling, & Carrasco, 2006). In humans, the amygdala is known to be a critical structure for the enhancement of emotional memory (Adolphs, Cahill, Schul, & Babinsky, 1997; Phelps, 2004) and to identify new items as opposed to old (Sergerie et al., 2007). The right amygdala is more involved in the formation of emotional memory, whereas the left amygdala is activated by the retrieval of those memories (Sergerie et al., 2006). The amygdala and the associated basal forebrain system play a major role in emotional memory storage (McGaugh, 2004) by modulating activation in a network of brain regions, including the hippocampus, which is centrally involved in memory formation, and in other brain structures (e.g., the nucleus accumbens, caudate nucleus, entorhinal cortex) and cortical regions (McGaugh, 2002). Experiments on fear conditioning have shown that the amygdala participates in the acquisition, storage, and expression of the conditioned fear response (i.e., when an animal learns that a neutral stimulus predicts an aversive event). In humans, integrity of the left amygdala is necessary for physiological reaction to the threat stimulus (Olsson & Phelps, 2007) also in the case of instructed fear (Funayama, Grillon, Davis, & Phelps, 2001; Hugdahl & Ohman, 1977; Phelps et al., 2001) and observational fear (Ohman & Mineka, 2001).

Moreover, the link between perception, attention, and emotion is mediated by the amygdala. In fact, visual responses are stronger when subjects view emotional scenes. It appears that the amygdala may provide a form of emotional attention that enhances visual information under emotional stress (Pessoa, Kastner, & Ungerleider, 2002; Vuilleumier, 2005) and responds to emotional faces of which subjects are not conscious (Whalen et al., 2004). Through its extensive connections to the hypothalamus and other autonomic nervous system centers, the amygdala is able to shortcut neural signals activating the ANS and emotional response before the higher brain centers receive sensory information. In this way, it provides fast and automatic—fight or flight—behavioral responses important for survival, following the "low route" suggested by LeDoux (1996).

To date, little knowledge exists on the molecular basis of stress-induced defense (fight or flight) response underlying the simultaneous coordinated changes in the cardiovascular, respiratory, sensory, and behavioral parameters. To explore neural mechanisms of stress-related adjustments of central autonomic regulation, research has recently focused on several neurotransmitters possibly involved in modulation of the efferent pathways during defense responses. Among them, the orexin system can possibly serve as one essential modulator among many for coordinating circuits controlling autonomic function and behavior. Orexin-containing cells are widely distributed in the hypothalamus, thalamus, cerebral cortex, brain stem, and spinal cord, with widespread connections with other brain regions to control multiple physiological functions, including motivation and regulation of autonomic and neuroendocrine systems (Kuwaki, Zhang, Nakamura, & Deng, 2008). At the perception of a life-threatening attack, the effects of fear, anxiety, and anger are so automatic and rapid to preclude analytical thinking of what objectively occurs. In front of a real-life operational danger, the information-processing situation, the officer might unconsciously switch to the *experiential thinking mode* that occurs when a perceived emergency requires a quick response (Artwohl, 2008; Epstein, 1994). As opposed to the deliberative, analytical *rational thinking mode*, experiential thinking is seized by emotions and oriented toward immediate action. This is confirmed by the fact that 74% of the police officers studied by Artwohl (2002, 2008), under a sudden, life-threatening attack, responded "automatically to the perceived threat, giving little or no conscious thought to their actions," in a way very consistent with the experiential thinking mode. The same author reports also that about 20% of the officers involved in a shooting incident "feel" that the information provided by "self-evidently valid experiential thinking" was more real than what actually happened during the incident, even when confronted with a videotape proving that they saw things that didn't happen.

Another cognitive process relevant to police work is the so-called *behavioral (or response) inhibition*—the process required to cancel an intended action. Behavioral inhibition involves several areas of the prefrontal cortex (e.g., dorsolateral prefrontal cortex, anterior cingulate cortex, and inferior frontal cortex) (Aron, Robbins, & Poldrack, 2004; Rubia, Smith, Brammer, & Taylor, 2003) and is usually studied in the laboratory by using the so-called GO/NO-GO tasks in which subjects are asked to execute a motor response when shown the GO stimulus (e.g., press a key as fast as possible when you see a GO stimulus), but to withhold the response to the NO-GO stimulus. An equivalent situation in police work typically occurs in a SHOOT/NO-SHOOT scenario. A recent study investigated the interaction between the processing of emotional words and response inhibition. Response inhibition following negative words engaged in the dorsolateral prefrontal cortex. However, this region was not recruited by negative valence or inhibitory task demands per se while it was sensitive to the explicit interaction between behavioral inhibition and the processing of words with a negative valence (Goldstein et al., 2007). This might suggest a possible mechanism for emotional interference on the officer's decision-making capability when he is in the empirical thinking mode piloted by the fear and/or anger emotional state. Thus, the experiential thinking mode has obvious advantages in life-threatening situations demanding an immediate response because it rapidly processes information to pilot almost automatically a survival response; however, it doesn't guarantee that such automatic responses will always be the appropriate ones, from both tactical and legal points of view. This fact, in association with stress-induced memory distortion and fragmentation (Grossman & Siddle, 1998), might have serious implications in the postshooting aftermath, especially if officers have to provide justification for the use of deadly force. On the other hand, when officers have to make split-second decisions about the use of force, the automatic processing of the experiential system is dominant over the rational system and becomes the default option. As experiential thinking mode is based on "past experiences" (Epstein, 1994), it seems evident that in order to improve officers' survival in a force-on-force confrontation, appropriate training should provide "past experiences" of proven efficacy. This cannot be achieved by theoretical teaching of police tactics and skills only, but also requires providing coached repetition under realistic stress, to verify the achievement of emotional control by the trainees and that their "automatic behaviors" under stress will be adaptive and efficient to solve tactical problems, within the law (Artwohl, 2002, 2008; Artwohl & Christensen, 1997; Humes, 1992). Moreover, police training must be redesigned, taking into account modern knowledge in psychophysiology to provide officers with the capability to keep the highest possible degree of emotional and situational control. This is obviously a challenging task because it implies filling the gap between scientific knowledge on psychophysiology gathered in the laboratory and the lack of methods to quantify what extent emotions affect individual tactical behavior in operational scenarios, in order to apply this knowledge in the demanding practice of police work.

AUTONOMIC REACTION TO THREAT, FEAR, AND ANGER

In a life-threatening situation, emotional responses in the brain orchestrate bodily resources in an integrated fashion to secure specific functional adaptations to different and complex demands, finalizing them to survival; however, the debate of whether fear and anger drive specific physiological responses, useful to differentiate them, is still controversial. A first meta-analysis of 22 studies on somatovisceral responses sampled during a variety of emotional states indicated that discrete emotions couldn't be fully differentiated by visceral activity alone (Cacioppo, Berntson, Larsen, Poehlmann, & Ito, 2000). Instead, a meta-analysis of previous research, focusing on the possibility to separate the effects of anger from those of fear, has demonstrated that the simultaneous effects of such emotions and of different behavioral responses (e.g., approach and withdrawal) (Christie & Friedman, 2004) can be at least in part be differentiated by measuring several physiological parameters related to bodily adaptation (Stemmler, 2004). A recent work of the same author has confirmed that anger could be somehow differentiated from fear by measuring bodily reactions (Stemmler, Aue, & Wacker, 2007). In extreme synthesis, the results confirmed that somatovisceral response to anger is characterized by a mixture of adrenaline and noradrenaline effects (Breggin, 1964; Funkenstein, 1955, 1956; Funkenstein, King, & Drolette, 1954; Wagner, 1989) with a relatively larger noradrenergic influence, some vagal withdrawal, and a slight α-adrenergic activation (Weiss, del-Bo, Reichek, & Engelman, 1980), with resultant bradycardia and periferal vasoconstriction, without blood pressure increase. Instead, somatovisceral response to fear is characterized by a relatively larger adrenergic influence and comprises vagal withdrawal, slight α-adrenergic activation, and diverse signs for β1-adrenergic activation, which are consistent with the action of adrenaline (Fahrenberg & Foerster, 1989; Funkenstein, 1955) (see Figure 14.1).

The dominant autonomic response to threat is characterized by the prevalence of the sympathetic nervous activity over the parasympathetic tone. The enhancement of sympathetic activity generates energy, diverts blood flow away from the gastrointestinal tract and skin via vasoconstriction, enhances blood flow to skeletal muscles (by as much as 1200%) and to the lungs, dilates bronchioles for greater alveolar oxygen exchange, increases heart rate (HR) and contractility, dilates pupils, and relaxes the lens, allowing more light to enter the eye. The prevalence of sympathetic effects and concomitant adrenergic neuroendocrine response are finalized to increase strength, resistance, and attention for survival; however, they induce functional alterations (visual, auditory,

Anger	Fear
• Dominant noradrenaline effects mixed with adrenergic effects • Bradycardia • Stroke volume increase • Vagal withdrawal	• Dominant adrenaline-like pattern • Increased LV contractility • Smaller T-wave, larger P-wave amplitudes • Stronger vagal withdrawal

ADRENALINE

    Stimulates alpha-, beta1, and beta2- adrenergic receptors.
      ⇓ Finger temperature, diastolic blood pressure, <u>total peripheral resistance</u>
      ⇑ <u>Heart rate,</u> systolic blood pressure, stroke volume, left-ventricular contractility, cardiac output, number of skin conductance responses, and respiration rate

NORADRENALINE

    stimulates alpha- and beta1 adrenergic receptors
      ⇓ Heart rate and finger temperature
      ⇑ Systolic and diastolic blood pressure, total peripheral resistance

FIGURE 14.1 Autonomic response to anger and fear, according to the meta-analysis of Stemmler (2004). Relatively stronger noradrenergic effects characterize anger, whereas fear is characterized by relatively dominant adrenergic response. Major physiological effects of adrenaline and noradrenaline are also summarized.

cardiac, and so on), which largely affect the officer's capability to move and act with the same flexibility available during training, in the absence of life-threatening stress (Siddle, 1999).

Now, the question is whether it is possible to objectively quantify the kind and the amount of individual emotional reaction of a police officer involved in a critical operation, by measuring physiological parameters affected by dominant autonomic reactions, and how to do that. Thus, the challenge is to develop reliable, scientifically validated methods to evaluate such psychophysiological response during tactical tasks.

METHODS TO MEASURE STRESS REACTIONS IN THE LABORATORY

In the psychophysiology laboratory, somatovisceral responses to emotions can be investigated under controlled conditions by monitoring a variety of physiologic signals such as electroencephalogram, electrocardiogram (ECG), electromyogram, impedance cardiogram, blood pressure, skin conductance, skin temperature, pulse volume, and respiration (Kreibig, Wilhelm, Roth, & Gross, 2007; Stemmler et al., 2007). Interestingly, it has also been recently suggested that the amplitude of resting ECG waveform contains information related to emotional personality and brain activity in the amygdala and hippocampus (Koelsch et al., 2007). Most of such recordings are feasible and reliable only when the investigated subject is sitting quietly to prevent movement artifacts, although even in the laboratory the quality of the recordings can be altered by several factors, which might jeopardize the reliability of the result. Such technical difficulty is obviously higher when attempting physiological recordings in the realm of police operational scenarios. For this reason, most parameters usually monitored to measure stress reactions in experimental psychology are not reliably obtainable on the field. Therefore, it is difficult to transfer scientific investigations from the laboratory in the training range and even less in the operational realm. In fact, although the wide experience developed in sports medicine and experimental psychology might help to find some technical solutions, the complexity of the dynamic variables that have to be monitored during realistic police scenarios implying the use of force is too wide to be covered with presently available technology. It turns out that there is a very limited experience on direct measurement of human physiology during force-on-force encounters by law enforcement and that the only parameter that has been studied so far is the HR obtained with ECG recording or with HR monitoring devices used for sports activity, both methods having pros and cons. In addition to physiological signals, several humoral stress markers can be also measured. Salivary Dehydroepiandrosterone (DHEA), Cortisol, and Secretory Immunoglobulin A (S-IgA) are the most frequently used, because they can be easily sampled without any subject discomfort, even in an outdoor situation. DHEA and its sulfated metabolite DHEA-S are hormones secreted by the adrenal cortex in response to pituitary adrenocorticotropic hormone (ACTH) production. DHEA-S is the most abundant circulating steroid hormone in humans and its measurement has been of interest, especially because reduced levels of both DHEA and DHEA-S are associated with aging. DHEA is also the precursor to the human sex hormones (estrogen and testosterone) and has been found to be deficient in people suffering from many diseases including obesity, diabetes, hypertension, cancer, Alzheimer's, immune deficiency, coronary artery disease, and various autoimmune disorders. Cortisol, a glucocorticoid hormone, is involved in protein, carbohydrate, and fat metabolism, and it is widely known as the stress hormone because it is secreted in excessive amounts when people are under stress. Cortisol is tightly regulated by feedback mechanisms in both the hypothalamus and the pituitary glands, where the original hormonal signals trigger its production. As in other systems, the hypothalamus begins the process by secreting corticotropin-releasing factor (CRF) in response to a variety of stressors. Then, CRF triggers the anterior pituitary to release ACTH that increases the adrenal cortex secretion of cortisol. Salivary cortisol levels have been compared to serum cortisol levels in a variety of patients, founding a very reliable measurement (Aardal-Eriksson, Karlberg, & Holm, 1998). The advantages of using salivary measurements include noninvasive sample collecting anytime and anywhere without inducing cortisol/stress due to venipuncture for blood sampling. Salivary cortisol levels have been used to measure acute stress induced by consecutive parachute jumps (Deinzer, Kirschbaum, Gresele, & Hellhammer, 1996) or by a psychosocial stress test involving free speech and mental arithmetic in front of an audience for 15 minutes (Kirschbaum, Wust, & Hellhammer, 1992). DHEA/cortisol ratio has been proposed as an important marker of stress and aging. When individuals are under prolonged stress, a divergence in this ratio results, because cortisol levels continue to rise while DHEA levels decrease significantly. The effects of DHEA/cortisol imbalance can be severe and may include elevated blood sugar levels, increased bone loss, compromised immune function, decreased skin repair and regeneration, increased fat accumulation, and brain cell destruction. A significant increase in DHEA/cortisol ratio was found in volunteers who showed a significant reduction in stress, burnout, and negative emotion as a result of stress management intervention. Reduced stress diminishes the system's cortisol demand and can result in the diversion of pregnenolone, a common precursor of DHEA and cortisol, from cortisol production into DHEA synthesis (McCraty, Barrios-Choplin, Rozman, Atkinson, & Watkins, 1998). S-IgA is produced by B-lymphocytes, a major component of the immune system, and it is viewed as the first defending line against pathogens in the upper respiratory tract, the gastrointestinal system, and the urinary tract. Salivary S-IgA levels were inversely correlated to perceived stress in emergency department nurses (Yang et al., 2002). In healthy volunteers, salivary S-IgA levels were measured before and after experiencing the emotional states of either positive feeling of care and compassion or negative feeling of anger. Self-induced positive feeling states produced a significant increase in S-IgA levels, while 5 minutes of self-induced anger feeling produced a significant inhibition of S-IgA lasting from 1 to 5 hours after the emotional experience (Rein, Atkinson, & McCraty, 1995). Thus, salivary S-IgA level can provide information about stress-induced depression of immune defense. Stress-induced activation of mononuclear interleukin 1β (IL-1β) is a mechanism potentially linking stress with immune and endocrine status and with heart disease. Regardless of the nature of the stress, the effects of IL-1β include the stimulation of ACTH secretion, with a consequent increase in glucocorticoid levels and activation of the sympathetic nervous system, followed by a release of catecholamines. Salivary IL-1β concentration is another easily measurable marker of psychological stress (Brydon et al.,

2005; Ilardo et al., 2001). However, costs and organization might be the only limitations in testing the above biomarkers of stress on a large scale. Finally, the degree of individual emotional involvement is usually rated on the basis of self-reports of emotions and motivational approach (Kreibig et al., 2007; Stemmler et al., 2007).

HISTORY OF TACTICAL STRESS AND HEART RATE

In 1984, Massad F. Ayoob, in his book *Stress Fire*, described how survival stress reactions, induced by a deadly force confrontation, could affect defensive efficacy and provided fundamental suggestions for coping with stress, to control physiological symptoms, and to be efficient in an armed confrontation. Since that reading, we started to figure out how to find a way to objectively quantify individual stress in police officers exposed to acute operational pressure implying the use of force and shootings. As cardiologists, we thought the easiest way was to monitor the HR continuously; however, wearable Holter recorders were bulky at that time and much vulnerable to mechanical shock. Thus, we had to wait for the first solid-state recorders to initiate in 1990, the first pilot study evaluating the feasibility to capture the heart rates of law enforcement officers during actual force-on-force scenarios. Bruce Siddle, in *Sharpening the Warrior's Edge: The Psychology & Science of Training* and in a subsequent publication (Siddle, 1995, 1999), reviewed previous research and discussed how survival stress reactions might affect the law enforcement officer when placed in a life or death situation, taking into account the neural basis of survival motor programs, motor skills classification, reaction time, and the psychology of survival training. Most important, he attempted an integration of available information about HR levels, motor skills, and associated cognitive performance, in a model correlating different levels of survival stress reaction, based on the elevation of the HR. In his model, fine motor skills (such has finger dexterity and eye–hand coordination) deteriorate above 115 beats per minute (bpm), whereas complex motor skills (i.e., ability to track and shoot a moving target, which involves eye–hand coordination, timing, and balance) begin to deteriorate when the HR reaches 145 bpm. With HR above 145 bpm, perception begins to be altered, leading to auditory exclusion and narrowing of the visual system (tunnel vision). With further increase of the HR, a progressive deterioration of cognitive control of action can occur, with a sort of functional shut-off of prefrontal cortical areas, and irrational behavior prevails when HR exceeds 175 bpm. The gross motor skill controlling the actions of the large muscle group such as the thighs, chest, back, and arms is enhanced and maximized with increasing level of stress, although excessive blood reduces flexibility and capability to run well. Siddle as well as other authors (Grossman & Christensen, 2004) suggest that, as in athletic competitions, the optimal tactical HR "zone" should be between 115 and 145 bpm. Instead, when HR raises above 175 bpm, tactical efficiency may be lost because of a progressive trend toward irrationality, favored by perceptual and memory distortion (Klinger, 2001), reduced functioning of the prefrontal cortex, and prevalence of amygdala activation under uncontrolled fight-or-flight response (Sharps, 2010). Bruce Siddle's research about the effects of stress on HR and their physiological consequences on the human body were paramount for police instructors who started to figure out that officers have to receive and practice realistic force-on-force training, because only in that way they can be prepared to deal with the real-life operational stress (Olson, 1998). However, in spite of the unquestionable merit of Siddle's intuition and attempt to correlate the intensity of operational stress with the HR response, the significance of HR increase is still questionable. In particular, experimental evidence that the absolute value of HR achieved can be an index of individual stress and predictive of operational behavior is lacking at the moment. In 1999, Fenici et al. reported about ECG and blood pressure monitoring in six healthy adult athletes (five were police officers) to evaluate if there was indeed an elevation in the HR and blood pressure of law enforcement officers under the stress of a competitive pistol shooting. Four shooters' heartbeats reached above 180 bpm and in two cases the HR exceeded 200 bpm, for the occurrence of paroxysmal arrhythmias. The study demonstrated that under competition stress, healthy athletes had elevated heart rates but reported different subjective stress perception. The highest level of stress was achieved during "man-versus-man" shoot-offs, which better mimic a defensive situation, affecting shooting precision and the outcome of the competition. The authors recommended that further studies were needed to evaluate cardiovascular stress and the coping capabilities of the law enforcement officer in operational scenarios. However, it was also evident that the pure measure of HR increase could be misleading, if not interpreted in the context of the event dynamics. In fact, in action shooting, as in the realm of a police tactical scenario, an overlap can occur of physical effort and psychological strain, both contributing to increase HR. It is possible that the same 175 bpm might have a very different effect on behavioral appropriateness if predominantly generated by physical effort and not by psychological stress. Moreover, the results of few studies, carried out by monitoring the HR during realistic tactical training, seem partially in disagreement with Siddle's model and suggest the need for more sophisticated methods to quantify the individual psychological stress during police tactical tasks. At the Federal Law Enforcement Training Centers, Meyerhoff et al. (2004) found a significant elevation in HR and blood pressure during very stressful realistic scenarios simulating highly dangerous situations, created to evaluate the performance of law enforcement personnel with a protocol measuring indices of stress and impact on performance. Differences in HR responsivity were observed between officers who achieved passing scores and those who failed. However, successful officers displayed additional HR acceleration while in the passenger role during a stressful driving episode as well as during the gunfight, whereas officers who received failing scores on those elements had lower HR than the successful ones. Unfortunately, absolute HR values were not reported in this study. Another study, conducted at the Texas State University at San Marcos in connection with the Advanced Law Enforcement Rapid Response Training (ALERRT), was recently presented at the Annual Conference of the Society of Police and Criminal Psychology (SPCP) in 2008. The authors concluded that in the 42 investigated officers, (1) there was no significant correlation between the amount of experience and training of the officers and average or maximum HR achieved during force-on-force scenarios, (2) training doesn't affect management aspect, and (3) there is no relationship between HR and Body Mass Index. However, they also correctly suggested that, as the HR was not measured with continuous ECG recording, some measurements could have been affected by technical limitation of the HR monitor used (Kemp & Diez, 2008). A larger prospective research project, carried out in Italy since 1992 by monitoring ECG and blood pressure of police officers undergoing realistic training in medium- to high-stress tactical scenarios, including force-on-force and gunfight with Simunitions®, has provided evidence that the resting HR and blood pressure values of the police officers tended to be significantly enhanced already before action. Their HR suddenly increased (even above 150% of the basal state) during life-threatening confrontations. However, the absolute value of HR and the percent of HR increase did not predict the tactical behavior of individual officers or the outcome of their action. In fact, about half of the officers acted properly in spite of very high HRs, whereas half of those who failed had a lower HR increase and their HR was sometime still within the "ideal combat range" (Fenici, 2008; Fenici & Brisinda, 2008b). In summary, the results of previous research could raise doubts about the information that can be gathered with measurements of the HR when the intention is to evaluate the amount of individual stress induced by police tactical operation and/or to predict appropriate tactical behavior as a function of individual HR reaction. Moreover, when tactical tasks implied an amount of physical effort, it was difficult to distinguish to what extent the HR acceleration was due to emotional involvement or to physical activity.

In order to separate these two effects, knowledge of mechanisms underlying HR regulation in different physiological and emotional conditions is required.

HEART RATE REGULATION

Daily life is characterized by alternation of rest and activity, requiring adjustments of the ANS to adapt cardiorespiratory function for bodily demands. The ANS controls body's visceral functions,

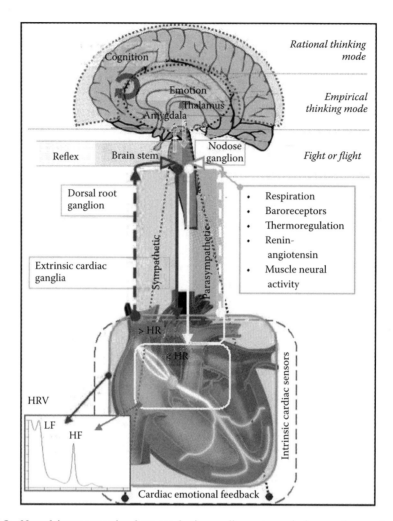

FIGURE 14.2 Neural interconnection between brain, cardiac autonomic innervation, and other visceral inputs to the brain stem modulating heart rate (HR) and its variability (HRV). Sympathetic (max effect in 4 s) and parasympathetic (max effect in 0.6 s) "efferent" (solid arrows) and "afferent" (dashed arrows) limbs are shown. The afferent signals from the heart reach the medulla, then travel to the subcortical and cortical areas of the brain, affecting feeling states, mental processes and emotional balance.

including heart activity, gastrointestinal tract movement, and endocrine secretion. The normal sinus rhythm is generated by the intrinsic automaticity of the physiological pacemaker of the heart, which is largely modulated by the ANS through the interplay of sympathetic and vagal outflows (see Figure 14.2). In most physiological conditions, the efferent sympathetic and parasympathetic branches regulate HR, influencing the activity of ion channels involved in the regulation of depolarization of the cardiac pacemaker cells (Piot, Copie, Guize, Lavergne, & Le Heuzey, 1997). The sympathetic system enhances automaticity by increasing the rate of pacemaker depolarization, whereas vagal stimulation causes hyperpolarization and reduces the rate of autodepolarization, with consequent reduction of HR.

HEART RATE VARIABILITY

Although the heart beating at rest was once believed to be regular, it is actually known that the sinus rhythm of a healthy heart is slightly irregular because of three major physiological originating factors: (1) a quasi-oscillatory fluctuations in blood-pressure control, (2) respiration, and (3) oscillations due to thermal regulation. This phenomenon is named *HR variability* (HRV). The dynamic modulation of HR is provided by the interaction of the sympathetic system (which has a response time in the order of a few seconds) and of parasympathetic activity (which works much faster: response time 0.2–0.6 seconds) (Berntson et al., 1997). Such continuous modulation by ANS results into HR fluctuation or variability. Whereas the measure of HR is a static index of autonomic input to the sinus node, which doesn't provide direct information on sympathetic or parasympathetic function in a given state, HRV analysis provides a quantitative assessment of cardiac autonomic regulation (ESC and NASPE Task Force on Heart Rate Variability, 1996; Lahiri, Kannankeril, & Goldberger, 2008; Perini & Veicsteinas, 2003). Thus, HRV analysis may be a useful clinical tool to assess the dynamics of sympathovagal balance in a given situation.

Even though HRV has been extensively studied during the last decades, its clinical application has reached general consensus (ESC and NASPE Task Force on Heart Rate Variability, 1996) only as a predictor of risk after myocardial infarction (Fox et al., 2007, 2008) and as an early warning sign of diabetic neuropathy (Braune & Geisenörfer, 1995; Pagani, 2000). However, HRV analysis is nowadays also increasingly used as a research tool to quantify emotional response in social and psychopathological processes, since theoretical and empirical rationale for its use as an index of individual differences in emotional response has been given recently by Appelhans and Luecken (2006).

QUANTITATIVE ASSESSMENT OF HRV

HRV is usually measured from changes in heartbeat interval, which is the reciprocal of HR. The starting point for HRV analysis is the ECG recording from which the HRV time series are extracted. The sinus interval is generally defined as the time difference between two successive P-waves. However, as the P-wave is usually a low-amplitude signal, in order to improve the accuracy of detection of the heart rate, the heartbeat period is usually evaluated as the time difference between two consecutive QRS complexes, which are signals 10 times larger in amplitude. After QRS peaks have been properly detected (with a time accuracy of 1–2 ms), the HRV time series (or tachogram) can be derived. Any technical (e.g., errors in QRS detection) or physiological (e.g., arrhythmic events) artifacts in the RR interval (i.e., the interval between two consecutive R waves) time series, which may affect HRV analysis, must be manually removed and only artifact-free sections should be included in the analysis (ESC and NASPE Task Force on Heart Rate Variability, 1996). An example of an HRV tachogram in different physiological conditions is shown in Figure 14.3a.

Quantitative assessment of HRV is performed with time-domain, frequency-domain, and nonlinear methods. For a comprehensive description of HRV analysis, the interested reader is addressed to more specific literature (ESC and NASPE Task Force on Heart Rate Variability, 1996; Lahiri et al., 2008; Sztajzel, 2004; Tarvainen, Georgiadis, Ranta-aho, & Karjalainen, 2006). This chapter will mainly describe the fundamentals of frequency domain analysis, because it is the most suitable for short-time analysis and useful to study stress-induced transient fluctuations of autonomic balance potentially affecting tactical behavior of police officers. The time-domain parameters (see Table 14.1) are statistical calculations directly applied to the series of successive RR interval values. Nonlinear methods are increasingly used in clinical studies, but the physiological interpretation of their results is still difficult (Carrasco, Caitan, Gonzàlez, & Yànez, 2001; Zbilut, Thomasson, & Webber, 2002). Frequency domain analysis describes the periodic oscillations of the HR signal decomposed into different frequencies and amplitudes. It can be performed with nonparametric methods, such as the Fast Fourier Transform (FFT), which is characterized by discrete peaks for the several frequency components, or with parametric methods, such as the autoregressive model estimation (ARMA), resulting in a continuous and smoother spectrum of activity, more suitable for very short-term HRV changes evaluation. The spectral components (see Table 14.2) are evaluated in frequency (Hertz: Hz) and amplitude, the latter assessed by the area

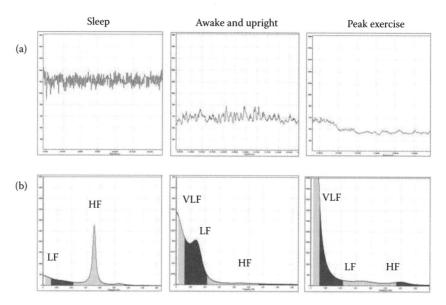

FIGURE 14.3 HRV analysis in different physiological conditions. (a) Tachograms (time variation of RR interval). (b) Power spectral analysis (5' intervals - ARMA model) shows a prevalence of vagal tone (HF) during sleep; and a clear-cut increase in LF power (and LF/HF ratio) occurs when awake and upright, predominantly due to an increase in direct neural stimulation of sympathetic tone. At the peak of exercise, the HRV total power decreases, with dominance of the VLF component.

below each component (power spectral density). Short-term (5 minutes) spectral recordings are mainly characterized by two components: the low frequency (LF: 0.04–0.15 Hz) and the high frequency (HF: 0.15–0.4 Hz). The most relevant periodic determinant of HRV is the respiratory sinus arrhythmia due to the physiological influence of breathing, which is measured by the HF component and generally believed to be of parasympathetic origin. The frequency components within the LF band are considered of both sympathetic and parasympathetic origin (Berntson et al., 1997) even though some researchers have suggested them to be mainly of sympathetic genesis (Malliani, Pagani, Lombardi, & Cerutti, 1991). Furthermore, there are also feedback mechanisms providing quick reflexes. The most relevant is the arterial baroreflex, based on specialized stretching sensors (baroreceptors) located on the walls of some large vessels and activated by blood pressure increase. Baroreceptors activation is known to inhibit sympathetic outflow from the brain to periferal vascular bed, whereas psychological stress enhances sympathetic outflow by inhibition baroreflex activity (Eckberg et al., 1988). Within the LF band, the frequency range around 0.1 Hz (named also middle frequency or MF band) is considered as due to baroreceptor activity and reflecting the blood

TABLE 14.1
Time Domain HRV Parameters

Variable	Units	Description
SDNN	msec	Standard deviation of all NN intervals
SDANN	msec	Standard deviation of average of NN intervals in all 5-minute segments of entire recording
rMSSD	msec	Square root of the mean of the sum of the squares of differences between adjacent NN intervals
SDNN index	msec	Mean of the standard deviations of all NN intervals for all 5-minute segments of the entire recording
NN50		Numbers of pairs of adjacent NN intervals differing by more than 50 msec in the entire recording
pNN50	%	NN50 count divided by the total number of all NN intervals

---

TABLE 14.2
Frequency Domain HR Parameters

Absolute values (expressed in ms^2)

• Total power	= variance of all NN intervals	<0.4 Hz
• ULF (24h)	ultra-low frequency	<0.003 Hz
• VLF	very low frequency	<0.003–0.04 Hz
• LF	low frequency power	0.04–0.15 Hz
• MF	middle frequency power	0.08–0.1 Hz
• HF	high frequency power	0.15–0.4 Hz
• LF/HF	ratio of low-high frequency power	

Normalization of LF and HF (in n.u.) by subtracting VLF component:

$$\text{LF or HF norm (nu)} = \frac{\text{LF or HF (ms}^2)}{\text{total power (ms}^2) - \text{VLF(ms}^2)} \times 100$$

Relative values (in %) of each component (LF and HF) in proportion to total power

---

pressure feedback signals sent from the heart back to the brain (Aguirre, Wodicka, Maayan, & Shannon, 1990; Pitzalis et al., 1997; Robbe et al., 1987; Tiller, McCraty, & Atkinson, 1996). On the other hand, HR fluctuations below 0.04 Hz have not been studied as much as higher frequencies. They are usually divided into very low frequency (VLF: 0.003–0.04 Hz) and ultra-low frequency (ULF: 0–0.003 Hz) bands, the latter generally omitted in case of short-term recordings (ESC and NASPE Task Force on Heart Rate Variability, 1996). These lowest frequency components of HRV have been related to humoral factors such as thermoregulatory processes and renin-angiotensin system (Berntson et al., 1997). The power of spectral densities can be expressed in absolute values (ms^2/Hz) and in normalized units (n.u.). The normalization is performed by subtracting the VLF component from the total power, to minimize the effects of the changes in total power on the LF and HF components (Sztajzel, 2008). The total power of HRV is the total variance RR intervals and corresponds to the sum of the four spectral bands, ULF, VLF, LF, and HF. The power of the single spectral peaks is not a direct measure of the autonomic activities (Kamath & Fallen, 1993), but can be accepted as a quantifier of autonomic responsiveness (Saul, Rea, Eckberg, Berger, & Cohen, 1990). In particular, the LF/HF ratio is generally accepted as an index of instantaneous sympatho-vagal balance (ESC and NASPE Task Force on Heart Rate Variability, 1996; Lahiri et al., 2008; Perini & Veicsteinas, 2003; Sztajzel, 2004). Therefore, relative (%) changes in LF and HF powers and variations of LF/HF ratio indicate a shift from the vagal to sympathetic dominance and vice versa, induced by situational changes or stimuli (e.g., awakeness, sleep, and moving from supine to upright position) (see Figure 14.3b). Besides HRV, other markers of autonomic activity are HR recovery after exercise (Lahiri et al., 2008), HR turbulence, QT interval, and baroreflex sensitivity (Sztajzel, 2004).

HRV AND PHYSICAL EFFORT

Power spectral analysis of HRV has been also used to evaluate the respective sympathetic and vagal roles in controlling HR during and after muscular work (Buchheit, Laursen, & Ahmaidii, 2007, Perini & Veicsteinas, 2003; Pichon, de Bisschop, Roulaud, & Papelier, 2004). Interestingly, although HRV analysis is reliable to highlight modifications in autonomic activities induced by different physiological conditions at rest (e.g., hypoxia exposure, training, water immersion), changes in HF and LF powers and in LF/HF ratio during exercise don't reflect the withdrawal of vagal activity and the sympathetic activation occurring at increasing loads. In fact, Perini and Veicsteinas (2003) have shown that LF power doesn't change during low-intensity exercise and decreases to negligible values at medium-high intensity, albeit an enhancement of sympathetic activity. The same authors suggest that changes in LF power observed at medium-high intensity might be the expression of the modifications in arterial pressure control mechanisms occurring with exercise and that LF changes are affected also by body position. In fact, the LF component increases at medium-high intensities when exercise is performed in the supine position but has an opposite trend in the sitting position, maybe in relation to different muscular inputs in the two conditions. In the same study, the HF component was appreciable in the entire range of relatively intensive exercise, and it was accounting for the most part of the total power, which usually decreases at maximal load. This peculiar finding was interpreted by Perini and Veicsteinas (2003) as possibly due to a modulation of the HF component by a direct mechanical effect of the increased respiratory activity induced by exercise.

HRV AND EMOTIONAL STRESS

As noted earlier in the chapter, normal HR variability is due to the synergic action of the two branches of the ANS with other neural, humoral, and physiological reflexes finalized to keep cardio-vascular adaptation in the optimal range for appropriate reaction to changes of external or internal conditions. These changes are also influenced by emotional reactions (Berntson et al., 1997). In fact, several studies carried out in the controlled laboratory environment have shown the relationship between exposure to acute psychological stress and alteration of cardiovascular ANS response (Delaney & Brodie, 2000; Orsila et al., 2008; Pagani et al., 1991; Salahuddin, Cho, GiJeong, & Kim, 2007; Shapiro et al., 2000). The acute effects of short-term psychological stress on time and frequency domains of HRV has been mainly investigated in the laboratory using different kinds of mental stress (e.g., stroop conflict color test, arithmetic calculation, computer controlled mental tasks, or stressful interview).

Three main stress-induced adaptations have been described: (1) a significant enhancement of HR indicating a shift toward sympathetic predominance, which is also evidenced by increase of skin conductance and decrease of skin temperature; (2) enhancement of the LF component with consequent increase of the LF/HF ratio (Orsila et al., 2008; Salahuddin et al., 2007); and (3) vagal withdrawal demonstrated by the reduction of total power (RR variance). It was also shown that additional stress (e.g., that induced by painful stimulation during mental stress) increases HR without significant changes of HRV parameters, probably because of a compensatory sympathoadrenal activation releasing catecholamine into the circulation (Terkelsen, Mølgaard, Hansen, Andersen, & Jensen, 2005).

The effects of specific emotions have been also investigated in the psychology laboratory, monitorizing multiple physiological and behavioral parameters during exposure to standardized video clips inducing discrete emotions, with evidence that the simultaneous effects of different emotions and motivational direction (approach and withdrawal) can be separated with HRV analysis (Kreibig et al, 2007; Stemmler et al., 2007) (no data on spectral parameters are available from those studies). Relatively few studies have addressed the association between real-life stress and cardiac autonomic response in humans (Lucini, Di Fede, Parati, & Pagani, 2005; Lucini, Norbiato, Clerici, & Pagani, 2002). Even less is known about acute autonomic adaptations in police officers exposed to threat-induced stress, because a systematic investigation of autonomic reactions induced by dangerous tactical tasks is still lacking. We believe research should be carried out to fill this lack of knowledge and that HRV evaluation might be a powerful, objective, and noninvasive tool to explore dynamic interactions between physiological, mental, emotional, and behavioral processes. In fact, previous work showed that changes in heart rhythms affect not only heart function but also brain ability to process information, including decision making, problem solving, and creativity (McCraty, 2002), and that real-time assessment of HRV fluctuation is a reliable method to differentiate positive and negative emotional changes (McCraty, Atkinson, Tiller, Rein, & Watkins, 1995). For almost a decade, Fenici and colleagues have shown that simple

HR analysis was not sufficient to validate Siddle's model, because the level of stress-induced HR increase, although statistically significant (Fenici, 1999; Fenici, Brisinda, & Fenici, 2002), has a wide interindividual variability, and a lower level of tachycardia is not univocally a predictor of individual tactical efficiency (Fenici & Brisinda, 2004). More recently, the same authors have applied spectral analysis of HR variability from the same dataset to attempt a dynamic imaging of the interplay between sympathetic and parasympathetic control on the HR, timed and correlated with situational monitoring of individual tactical behavior during threat-induced stress reactions (Fenici & Brisinda, 2008a, 2008b). One hundred and ten police officers volunteered for that study, all of whom were previously evaluated to exclude any cardiac and/or psychological abnormalities. 12-lead ECG was continuously recorded (Mortara-Rangoni H-Scribe Holter System), along a realistic training session. At the beginning, after a preliminary 10-minute rest period in supine position, allowed for stabilization, ECG was recorded over a 10-minute supine baseline, over a 5-minute of controlled breathing, and over a subsequent 10-minute period of active standing. Blood pressure was measured in both postures. After about 2 hours of normal low-stress daily activity, each subject participated in a briefing, describing the high-stress police tactical tasks to be performed during realistic training. At the end of the scenario, all subjects underwent a debriefing session where their performance was discussed and confronted with instructors, using video recordings as objective reference. ECG Holter recording was continued until at least 1 hour after the end of the training session. The high-stress realistic training session consisted of active participation in scenarios simulating risky police tactical operations including a building search, intervention for domestic violence, and force-on-force confrontations with professional role players. The officers' behavior during the scenarios was continuously monitored with multiple video cameras synchronized with the Holter recorder's timer, for off-line evaluation by police instructors. Power spectral analysis of HRV was performed with a parametric autoregressive model (ARMA model) estimation, which provides a continuous, smooth spectrum of different components and quantification of their relative intensity (Tarvainen, Georgiadis, Ranta-aho, & Karjalainen, 2006), from standard time intervals of 5 minutes (ESC and NASPE Task Force on Heart Rate Variability, 1996) and from ultra-short time intervals (30–50 seconds) during the phases of highest stress (Salahuddin et al., 2007). One relevant finding of the study is the observation that ultra-short term analysis of HRV is necessary to quantify acute perturbations of cardiovascular autonomic balance induced by acute stress response. In fact, standard HRV power spectral analysis, calculated from 5-minute intervals (see Figure 14.4), was inadequate to evidence sudden, short-lasting changes of the HRV pattern correlated with the phases of maximum tactical stress. In fact, the 5-minutes analysis at peak stress showed a sudden decrease of total power characterized by prevalence of the VLF component, with a time-averaging effect of rapidly changing events impairing the evaluation accuracy of peak HR and the LF/HF ratio (see values in Figure 14.4 and Figure 14.5).

Instead, in the 50-second analysis, the VLF component was absent, whereas the LF components were well evident before (Figure 14.5a) and after (Figure 14.5c) peaks of danger, but disappeared at the nadir of HR, when one or more HF components became appreciable, usually with inversion of the LF/HF ratio (Figure 14.5b). Such a kind of transient fluctuation of LF and HF relative power was highly reproducible in the same subject, as a function of the onset/offset of subsequent bursts of threat. Each time the level of threat decreased, HRV was reproducibly characterized by the reappearance and progressive increase of the LF component (Figure 14.5c). The same pattern was observed in the majority of the investigated subjects during similar events, thus only ultra-short term analysis identifies fluctuations of HRV spectral components, at the onset/offset of sudden threat. This study represents a first attempt to image the dynamicity of cardiovascular autonomic fluctuation in a model of human acute psychophysiological reaction induced by real-life police tactical stress. The main new finding is that, under the fight-or-flight response grip, fast dynamic changes in cardiovascular autonomic regulation occur, inducing rapid changes of HRV parameters within seconds. To attempt an interpretation of such peculiar transient fluctuations in HRV power

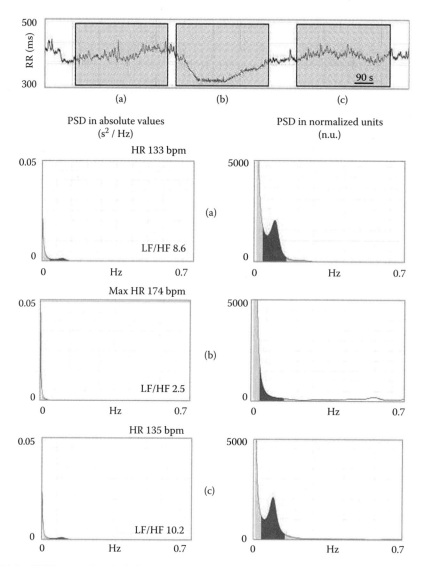

FIGURE 14.4 HRV spectral analysis from 5'intervals (shaded rectangles on the tachogram) (a) before, (b) during, and (c) after an episode of transient increase of HR caused by a sudden threat. Power spectral densities (PSD) are expressed in s²/Hz (left panels) and in normalized units (right panels). LF/HF ratio is also shown. The averaging effect of 5'analysis determines underestimation of the peak HR (174 bpm whereas the real was 190 bpm). At peak stress, PSD shows dominance of the VLF, and reduced LF power and LF/HF ratio (2.5).

spectral components during defense-arousal, it must be realized that spectral analysis of HRV can only give a partial estimate of autonomic function (because this method does not measure nervous activity directly) and that other mechanisms, such as circulating epinephrine or saturation kinetics of the sympathetic and vagal efferent nerve activity on the sinus node, might contribute to induce extreme tachycardia during acute stress (Ahmed, Kadish, Parker, & Goldberger, 1994; Malik & Camm, 1993; Tulen et al., 1994).

The reproducible pattern characterized by a marked decrease of HRV total power, LF component disappearance, and VLF dominance suggests an "adrenaline-like pattern of fear" (Stemmler et al., 2007) rather than enhanced neurosympathetic drive as the most relevant mechanism of threat-induced sudden burst of tachycardia. The relative dominance and fluctuations of HF component evidenced by ultra-short term analysis at peak-stress (Figure 14.5b) could be due

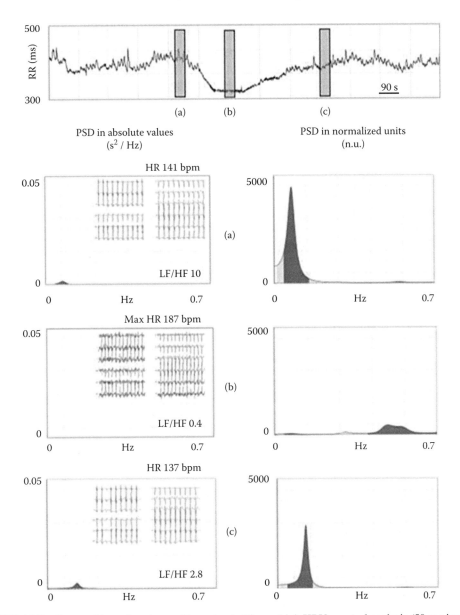

FIGURE 14.5   Same subject, situation and layout as in Figure 14.4. HRV spectral analysis (50 sec intervals) shows: dominance of the LF component in (a) and marked drop of the TP with a delayed HF component in (b - sudden threat). In (c), recovery of HRV is sustained by reappearance of a delayed LF peak. No VLF in all phases. Compared to 5'intervals, ultra-short term analysis estimates more appropriately peak HR (187 bpm) and evidences an inversion of LF/HF ratio, not appreciable in Figure 14.4. 12-lead ECG is also shown.

to stress-induced alteration of the respiratory rate and rhythm (Perini & Veicsteinas, 2003). The above provides evidence that, as happens during high-intensity physical exercise (Perini & Veicsteinas, 2003; Casadei, Cochrane, Johnston, Conway, & Sleight, 1995), HRV analysis might suggest mechanisms different from simple sympathovagal interaction as the cause of HR increase (Perini & Veicsteinas, 2003). As blood pressure cannot be continuously monitored during realistic scenarios, we cannot exclude that the modification of LF components could be also related to arterial pressure fluctuations, via baroreceptorial mechanisms (Perini & Veicsteinas, 2003; Saul et al., 1990).

METHODOLOGICAL PROBLEMS WITH HRV MEASUREMENTS

The Italian study has demonstrated that spectral analysis of HRV from ECG data is feasible and reliable to discover transient changes of cardiac sympathovagal modulation induced by acute real-life police stress, and provided that ultra-short term analysis is used. In fact, we found that transient and fast changes of autonomic balance were evidenced only using intervals of 30 to 50 seconds, which, according to Salahuddin et al. (2007), are the minimum required for an adequate estimation of HF and LF components and LF/HF ratio and represent a validated method for assessing acute stress-induced HRV variations. However, a better way to image acute changes of HRV spectral density during nonstationary events could be the use of time-frequency and time-variant methods (Mainardi, Bianchi, & Cerutti, 2002; Martinmäki & Rusko, 2008), which provide quantitative beat-to-beat evaluation of HRV parameters fluctuation (Petrucci et al., 1996) (see Figure 14.6).

Furthermore, more advanced mathematical algorythms seem promising to achieve a more selective quantification and separation of cardiac sympathetic and parasympathetic activities useful to improve the assessment of acute stress by HRV measuring of the autonomic response (Zhong, Jan, Hwan Ju, & Chon, 2006; Chen & Mukkamala, 2008). Another relevant point is that presently available hardware for digital Holter ECG recording, although reliable for clinical purposes, is too bulky, expensive, and fragile to be extensively used in tactical situations. For that purpose,

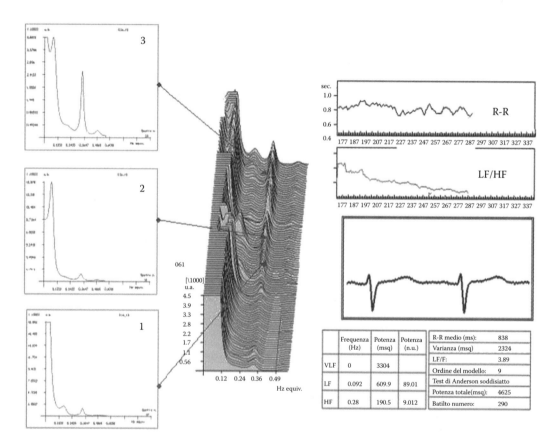

FIGURE 14.6 Example of dynamic beat-to-beat imaging of acute changes of HRV spectral density, in a healthy 18-year-old subject during postural change, from upright (1) to supine (3) position. In the middle: sequence of beat-to beat spectral densities. On the left: selected instantaneous spectral images are shown, with prevalence of LF in the upright (1 and 2) and of HF in the supine (3). On the right: windows monitoring the dynamics of RR interval, of LF/HF ratio, and of the ECG waveform.

commercial HR/RR interval recorders developed for sports activity may offer a simple, inexpensive alternative to standard ECG recording (Kemp & Diets, 2008). However, the reliability of such devices for short-term HRV measurements under heavy-duty dynamic conditions has not been validated so far. In fact, only a few studies assessing the agreement with standard ECG recordings are available at the moment (Nunan et al., 2008, 2009; Salahuddin et al., 2007) but performed in quiet resting laboratory conditions. In the latter two studies, carried out to assess the reliability of short-term resting HRV measured from Polar S810 heart-rate data, it was shown that the number of RR intervals obtained with the S810 showed excellent and interchangeable agreement with ECG recordings, but that some of the HRV parameters derived from the RR interval recorder did not agree with those derived from standard ECG, when the two data sets were processed in the same way. Thus, the authors concluded that users should be aware that HRV measures, derived from factory default settings of different systems, might yield widely varying outcomes (Nunan et al., 2008). In the most recent study, only marginal differences between the mean measures of HRV with the Polar S810 and with reference ECG recording were found, except for the LF and HF normalized units (Nunan et al., 2009). However, in both studies, prior to HRV analysis, raw RR intervals derived from both equipments had to be edited and compared to discriminate error caused by S810 acquisition or by artifacts. Manual editing before HRV analysis is at the moment unavoidable, especially when dealing with data acquired during heavy and uncontrollable tactical dynamicity. Thus, to optimize monitoring of personnel exposed to high-stress activity and to evaluate their performance under heavy-duty conditions, such as during police tactical training or even real operational deployment, a robust miniaturized personal monitoring device (i.e., a digital ECG recorder with a sampling frequency of 1 KHz), compatible with tactical equipment and with wireless connection to wearable low-noise ECG electrode systems (such as Quasar, Smartshirt, Sensotex, and so on), should be manufactured. The next step of technological development should be the inclusion of on-board capability for real-time HRV evaluation and wireless data transmission for Web remote monitoring (Salahuddin et al., 2007; Salahuddin & Kim, 2006). Obviously, for a more accurate dynamic evaluation of police stress-related ANS adaptation, other physiological parameters such as blood pressure, posture, respiration rate, skin conductance, and temperature also should be monitored simultaneously with ECG, but again such recordings are difficult and poorly reliable under dynamic action. Especially a continuous noninvasive blood pressure monitoring is impossible at the moment because of the high sensitivity to movement artifacts, even with the most recent technology (Nair et al., 2008).

HRV MONITORING TO FAVOR HEART–BRAIN COHERENCE

Research suggests that HRV monitoring during tactical training can be useful to improve the operational efficiency and success of police officers. In fact, it might help to increase insight into the complexity of human cognition/emotion interaction under threat-induced fear and to study how heart–brain interaction might affect officers' behavior when they automatically switch to the empirical thinking mode. Furthermore, HRV can be used as a sort of biofeedback tool to train people to improve emotional control.

It has been shown that cardiac oscillators involved in HRV modulation, besides regulating cardiac function, also send messages to the brain that affect perceptions, mental processes, feeling states and human performance (see Figure 14.2). Other biological oscillators—located in the brain, intestinal walls, lungs, and smooth muscles of the vascular system—are strictly involved in psychophysiological modulation. It is well known that, by intentionally focusing on one or more of these systems, it is possible to alter their rhythm and indirectly affect the cardiac activity and the cognitive and emotional functions of brain. This has been empirically achieved for hundreds of years, with meditation (affecting directly the brain), yoga (working on lungs), chi-kung (affecting the gut), and in several martial arts. Recently, research has investigated mechanisms underlying the positive effects of such traditional methods by spectral analysis of HRV. Experiments combining HRV indexes and observation of animals' behavior in a rat model of severe cardiac failure has demonstrated that abnormal sensory messages from the periphery (the failing heart) to the central nervous structures produces an abnormal cardiovascular autonomic regulation and favor an abnormally anxious response and behavior (Henze et al., 2008). Conversely, if the heart sends positive messages to the brain, as in a deliberate feeling of positive affection, the modification of cardiac sympatovagal balance might induce better heart–brain coherence in humans (Tiller et al., 1996), with resultant enhancement of mental clarity, emotional balance, and personal efficiency (McCraty et al., 1995). Thus, HRV is a simple noninvasive method to measure in humans the reflex feedback of the primitive brain stem to the afferent information sent by the heart to the brain and the complex psychophysiological reactions to activation of the upper-emotional and cognitive brain centers critical for decision making and integration of reason and feelings under stress (see Figure 14.2). From a clinical point of view, all of the above can be used to cure patients affected by cardiac disease, improving their rehabilitation in order to reduce future adverse cardiac events (Pagani & Lucini, 2008). Similarly, the same knowledge and methods might be utilized to design more appropriate training programs and preventive interventions for police officers exposed to demanding tactical stress. In fact, it is well known that relaxation training programs may significantly improve cardiac autonomic nervous tone. For example, relaxation by yoga training is associated with a significant increase of cardiac vagal modulation (Khattab et al., 2007). More interestingly, 5 days of integrative body–mind training (IBMT) improve attention and self-regulation in comparison with the same amount of relaxation training, with significantly better physiological reactions evidenced by HRV, EEG, and brain imaging data (Tang, 2008; Tang et al., 2007, 2009). An additional confirmation suggesting the need of a more holistic approach to police training can be found in the positive results obtained by teaching methods for self-induction of better heart–brain coherence in police officers (McCraty, Tomasino, Atkinson, & Sundram, 1999) and in correctional officers (McCraty, Atkinson, & Tomasino, 2003).

REFERENCES

Aardal-Eriksson, E., Karlberg, B. E., & Holm, A. C. (1998). Salivary cortisol: An alternative to serum cortisol determinations in dynamic function tests. *Clinical Chemistry and Laboratory Medicine*, *36*(4), 215–222.

Adolphs, R., Cahill, L., Schul, R., & Babinsky, R. (1997). Impaired declarative memory for emotional material following bilateral amygdala damage in humans. *Learning and Memory*, *4*, 291–300.

Aguirre, A., Wodicka, G. R., Maayan, C., & Shannon, D. C. (1990). Interaction between respiratory and RR interval oscillations at low frequencies. *Journal of the Autonomic Nervous System*, *29*, 241–246.

Ahmed, M. W., Kadish, A. H., Parker, M. A., & Goldberger, J. J. (1994). Effect of physiologic and pharmacologic adrenergic stimulation on heart rate variability. *Journal of American College of Cardiology*, *24*(4), 1082–1090.

Allman, J. M., Hakeem, A., Erwin, J. M., Nimchinsky, E., & Hof, P. (2001). The anterior cingulate cortex: The evolution of an interface between emotion and cognition. *Annals of New York Academy of Sciences*, *935*, 107–117.

Appelhans, B. M., & Luecken, L. J. (2006). Heart rate variability as an index of regulated emotional responding. *Review of General Psychology*, *10*(3), 229–240.

Aron, A. R., Robbins, T. W., & Poldrack, R. A. (2004). Inhibition and the right inferior frontal cortex. *Trends in Cognitive Sciences*, *8*, 170–177.

Artwohl, A. (2002, October). Perceptual and memory distortions during officer involved shootings. *FBI Law Enforcement Bulletin.*

Artwohl, A. (2008). *Perceptual and memory distortions during officer involved shootings.* AELE Lethal & Less Lethal Force Workshop.

Artwohl, A., & Christensen, L. (1997). *Deadly force encounters: What cops need to know to mentally and physically prepare for and win a gunfight.* Boulder, CO: Paladin.

Ayoob, M. F. (1986). *Stress fire*. (Vol. 1 of *Gunfighting for police: Advanced tactics and techniques*. Concord, NH: Police Bookshelf.

Berntson, G. G., Bigger, J. T., Jr., Eckberg, D. L., Grossman, P., Kaufmann, P. G., Malik, M., et al. (1997). Heart rate variability: Origins, methods, and interpretive caveats. *Psychophysiology, 34*, 623–648.

Braune, H. J., & Geisenörfer, U. (1995). Measurement of heart rate variations: influencing factors, normal values and diagnostic impact on diabetic autonomic neuropathy. *Diabetes Research and Clinical Practice, 29*, 179–187.

Breggin, P. R. (1964). The psychophysiology of anxiety. *Journal of Nervous and Mental Disease, 139*, 558–568.

Brydon, L., Edwards, S., Jia, H., Mohamed-Ali, V., Zachary, I., Martin, J. F., & Steptoe, A. (2005). Psychological stress activates interleukin-1β gene expression in human mononuclear cells. *Brain, Behavior, and Immunity, 19*, 540–554.

Buchheit, M., Laursen, P. B., & Ahmaidii, S. (2007). Parasympathetic reactivation after repeated sprint exercise. *American Journal of Physiology Heart and Circulation Physiology, 293*, 133–141.

Bush, G., Luu, P., & Posner, M. I. (2000). Cognitive and emotional influences in anterior cingulate cortex. *Trends in Cognitive Sciences, 4*, 215–222.

Cacioppo, J. T., Berntson, G. G., Larsen, J. T., Poehlmann, K. M., & Ito, T. A., (2000). The psychophysiology of emotion. In M. Lewis & J. M. Haviland-Jones (Eds.), *Handbook of emotions* (2nd ed., pp. 173–191). New York: Guilford.

Carrasco, S., Caitan, M. J., Gonzàlez, R., & Yànez, O. (2001). Correlation among Poincarè plot indexes and time and frequency domain measures of heart rate variability. *Journal of Medical Engineering and Technology, 25*(6), 240–248.

Casadei, B., Cochrane, S., Johnston, J., Conway, J., & Sleight, P. (1995). Pitfalls in the interpretation of spectral analysis of the heart rate variability during exercise in humans. *Acta Physiological Scandinavian, 153*(2), 125–131.

Chen, X., & Mukkamala, R. (2008). Selective quantification of the cardiac sympathetic and parasympathetic nervous systems by multisignal analysis of cardiorespiratory variability. *American Journal of Physiology Heart and Circulation Physiology, 294*(1), 362–371.

Christie, I. C., & Friedman, B. H. (2004). Autonomic specificity of discrete emotion and dimensions of affective space: a multivariate approach. *International Journal of Psycophysiology, 51*(2), 143–153.

Crottaz-Herbette, S., & Menon, V. (2006). Where and when the anterior cingulate cortex modulates attentional response: Combined fMRI and ERP evidence. *Journal of Cognitive Neuroscience, 18*, 766–780.

Deinzer, R., Kirschbaum, C., Gresele, C., & Hellhammer, D. H. (1996). Adrenocortical responses to repeated parachute jumping and subsequent h-CRH challenge in inexperienced healthy subjects. *Physiology and Behavior, 61*(4), 507–511.

Delaney, J. P., & Brodie, D. A. (2000). Effects of short-term psychological stress on the time and frequency domains of heart-rate variability. *Perceptual and Motor Skills, 91*(2), 515–524.

Duncan, S., & Barrett, L. F. (2007). Affect is a form of cognition: A neurobiological analysis. *Cognition and Emotion, 21*, 1184–1211.

Eckberg, D. L., Rea, R. F., Andersson, O. K., Hedner, T., Pernow, J., Lundberg, J. M., et al. (1988). Baroreflex modulation of sympathetic activity and sympathetic neurotransmitters in humans. *Acta Physiological Scandinavian, 133*(2), 221–231.

Eisenberger, N. I., Lieberman, M. D., & Williams, K. D. (2003). Does rejection hurt? An fMRI study of social exclusion. *Science, 302*, 290–292.

Epstein, S. (1994). The integration of the cognitive and psychodynamic unconscious. *American Psychologist, 49*, 709–723.

Etkin, A., Egner, T., Peraza, D. M., Kandel, E. R., & Hirsch, J. (2006). Resolving emotional conflict: A role for the rostral anterior cingulate cortex in modulating activity in the amygdala. *Neuron, 51*, 871–882.

Fahrenberg, J., & Foerster, F. (1989). *Nicht-invasive Methodik für die kardiovasculäre Psychophysiologie* [Non-invasive methods for cardiovascular psychophysiology]. Frankfurt: Lang.

Fenici, R. (1999). Cardiac factors in critical incidents. 27th Annual Conference of the SPCP, Port Jefferson, NY.

Fenici, R., & Brisinda, D. (2004). Cardiac and psycho-physiological reactions induced by police tactical tasks and combat shooting. Presented at the 32nd Annual Conference of the Society for Police and Criminal Psychology, Rome, October 11–15.

Fenici, R., & Brisinda, D. (2008a). Evaluation of stress-related heart-rate variability in police officers during operational training for high-risk tactical tasks. Edward Shaeffer Award at the 34th Annual Conference of the Society for Police and Criminal Psychology, Walnut Creek, CA, October 16–18.

Fenici, R., & Brisinda D. (2008b). Stress-induced changes of heart rate variability in police officers during operational training for demanding tactical tasks. *European Heart Journal*, Suppl. 29, Abs 4424, 750.

Fenici, R., Brisinda, D., & Fenici, P. (2002). Cardiovascular and psycho-physiological reaction during police action and combat shooting. Proceedings of XIV World Congress of Cardiology.

Fenici, R., Ruggieri, M. P., Brisinda, D., & Fenici, P. (1999). Cardiovascular adaptation during action pistol shooting. *Journal of Sports Medicine and Physical Fitness*, *39*(3), 259–266.

Fox, K., Borer, J. S., Camm, A. J., Danchin, N., Ferrari, R., Lopez Sendon, J. L., et al. (2007). Heart rate working group: Resting heart rate in cardiovascular disease. *Journal of American College of Cardiology*, *50*(9), 823–830.

Fox, K., Ford, I., Steg, P. G., Tendera, M., Robertson, M., & Ferrari, R. (2008). Heart rate as a prognostic risk factor in patients with coronary artery disease and left-ventricular systolic dysfunction (BEAUTIFUL): A subgroup analysis of a randomized controlled trial. *Lancet*, *372*(9641), 817–821.

Funayama, E. S., Grillon, C., Davis, M., & Phelps, E. A. (2001). A double dissociation in the affective modulation of startle in humans: effects of unilateral temporal lobectomy. *Journal of Cognitive Neuroscience*, *13*, 721–729.

Funkenstein, D. H. (1955). The physiology of fear and anger. *Scientific American*, *192*, 74–80.

Funkenstein, D. H. (1956). Nor-epinephrine-like and epinephrine-like substances in relation to human behavior. *Journal of Nervous and Mental Disease*, *124*, 58–68.

Funkenstein, D. H., King, S. H., & Drolette, M. (1954). The direction of anger during a laboratory stress-inducing situation. *Psychosomatic Medicine*, *16*, 404–413.

Gazzaniga, M. S., Ivry, R. B., & Mangun, G. R. (2008). *Cognitive neuroscience* (3rd ed.). New York. W. W. Norton.

Goldstein, M., Brendel, G., Tuescher, O., Pan, H., Epstein, J., Beutel, M., & Silbersweig, D. (2007). Neural substrates of the interaction of emotional stimulus processing and motor inhibitory control: An emotional linguistic go/no-go fMRI study. *Neuroimage*, *36*, 1026–1040.

Gray, J. R., Braver, T. S., & Raichle, M. E. (2002). Integration of emotion and cognition in the lateral prefrontal cortex. *Proceedings of the National Academy of Sciences*, *99*, 4115–4120.

Grossman, D., & Siddle, B. K. (1998). *The physiological basis and implications of memory loss during extreme survival stress situations. Critical Incident Amnesia.* Millstadt, IL: PPCT Management Systems.

Grossman, D., & Christensen, L. W. (2004). *On combat: The psychology and physiology of deadly conflict in war and peace.* Millstadt, IL: WSG Research Publications.

Hampton, A. N., & O'Doherty, J. P. (2007). Decoding the neural substrates of reward-related decision making with functional MRI. *Proceedings of the National Academy of Sciences*, *104*, 1377–1382.

Henze, M., Hart, D., Samarel, A., Barakat, J., Eckert, L., & Scrogin, K. (2008). Persistent alterations in heart rate variability, baroreflex sensitivity, and anxiety-like behaviors during development of heart failure in the rat. *American Journal of Physiology Heart and Circulation Physiology*, *295*, 29–38.

Honig, A. L., & Roland, J. E. (1998, October). Shots fired: Officer involved. *The Police Chief.*

Hugdahl, K., & Ohman, A. (1977). Effects of instruction on acquisition and extinction of electrodermal responses to fear-relevant stimuli. *Journal of Experimental Psychology [Human Learning]*, *3*, 608–618.

Humes, C. (1992). *The flashlight dilemma.* Doylestown, PA: Tactical Edge.

Ilardo, C., Toniolo, A. M., Aimone-Gastin, I., Abdelmouttaleb, I., Guéant, J. L., & Desor, D. (2001). Effects of psycho-physical stress (competitive rafting) on saliva interleukin-1 beta. *Stress and Health*, *17*, 9–15.

Kamath, M. V., & Fallen, E. L. (1993). Power spectral analysis of heart rate variability: Non invasive signature of cardiac autonomic function. *Critical Reviews in Biomedical Engineering*, *21*, 245–311.

Kemp, M., & Diez, A. S. (2008, October 16–18). "And the beat goes on": Heart rates of law enforcement officers during deadly force scenarios). Presented at the 34th Annual Conference of the Society for Police and Criminal Psychology, Walnut Creek, CA.

Khattab, K., Khattab, A. A., Ortak, J., Richardt, G., & Bonnemeier, H. (2007). Iyengar yoga increases cardiac parasympathetic nervous modulation among healthy yoga practitioners. *Evidence Based Complement Alternative Medicine, 4,* 511–517.

Kirschbaum, C., Wust, S., & Hellhammer, D. H. (1992). Consistent sex differences in cortisol responses to psychological stress. *Psychosomatic Medicine*, *54*(6), 648–657.

Klinger, D. (2001). *Police responses to officer-involved shootings.* Washington, DC: U.S. Government Printing Office.

Koelsch, S., Remppis, A., Sammler, D., Jentschke, S., Mietchen, D., Fritz, T., & Siebel, W. A. (2007). A cardiac signature of emotionality. *European Journal of Neuroscience*, *26*(11), 3328–3338.

Kreibig, S. D., Wilhelm, F. H., Roth, W. T., & Gross, J. J. (2007). Cardiovascular, electrodermal, and respiratory response patterns to fear- and sadness-inducing films. *Psychophysiology*, *44*(5), 787–806.

Kunst-Wilson, W. R., & Zajonc, R. B. (1980). Affective discrimination of stimuli that cannot be recognized. *Science, 207*, 557–558.

Kuwaki, T., Zhang, W., Nakamura, A., & Deng, B. S. (2008). Emotional and state-dependent modification of cardiorespiratory function: Role of orexinergic neurons. *Autonomic Neuroscience, 142*(1–2), 11–16.

Lahiri, M. K., Kannankeril, P. J., & Goldberger, J. J. (2008). Assessment of autonomic function in cardiovascular disease physiological basis and prognostic implications. *Journal of the American College of Cardiology, 51*, 1725–1733.

LeDoux, J. E. (1996). *The emotional brain*. New York: Simon & Schuster.

Lucini, D., Di Fede, G., Parati, G., & Pagani, M. (2005). Impact of chronic psychosocial stress on autonomic cardiovascular regulation in otherwise healthy subjects. *Hypertension, 46*(5), 1201–1206.

Lucini, D., Norbiato, G., Clerici, M., & Pagani, M. (2002). Hemodynamic and autonomic adjustments to real life stress conditions in humans. *Hypertension, 39*(1), 184–188.

Mainardi, L. T., Bianchi, A. M., & Cerutti, S. (2002). Time-frequency and time varying analysis for assessing the dynamic responses of cardiovascular control. *Critical Review in Biomedical Engineering, 30*(1–3), 175–217.

Malik, M., & Camm, A. J. (1993). Components of heart rate variability: What they really mean and what we really measure. *American Journal of Cardiology, 72*(11), 821–822.

Malliani, A., Pagani, M., Lombardi, F., & Cerutti, S. (1991). Cardiovascular neural regulation explored in the frequency domain. *Circulation, 84*(2), 482–492.

Martinmäki, K., & Rusko, H. (2008). Time-frequency analysis of heart rate variability during immediate recovery from low and high intensity exercise. *European Journal of Applied Physiology, 102*(3), 353–360.

McCraty, R. (2002). Influence of cardiac afferent input on heart–brain synchronization and cognitive performance. *International Journal of Psychophysiology, 45*(1–2), 72–73.

McCraty, R., Atkinson, M., Tiller, W. A., Rein, G., & Watkins, A. D. (1995). The effects of emotions on short-term power spectrum analysis of heart rate variability. *American Journal of Cardiology, 76*(14), 1089–1093.

McCraty, R., Barrios-Choplin, B., Rozman, D., Atkinson, M., & Watkins, A. D. (1998). The impact of a new emotional self-management program on stress, emotions, heart-rate variability, DHEA and cortisol. *Integrative Physiological and Behavioral Science, 33*(2), 151–170.

McCraty, R., Tomasino, D., Atkinson, M., & Sundram, J. (1999). *Impact of the HeartMath Self-Management Skills Program on physiological and psychological stress in police officers* (Publication no. 99–075). Boulder Creek, CA: HeartMath Research Center, Institute of HeartMath.

McCraty, R., Atkinson, M., & Tomasino, D. (2003). Impact of a workplace stress reduction program on blood pressure and emotional health in hypertensive employees. *Journal of Alternative and Complementary Medicine, 9*(3), 355–369.

McGaugh, J. L. (2002). Memory consolidation and the amygdala: A systems perspective. *Trends in Neurosciences, 25*, 456.

McGaugh, J. L. (2004) The amygdala modulates the consolidation of memories of emotionally arousing experiences. *Annual Review of Neuroscience, 27*, 1–28.

Meyerhoff, J. L., Norris, W., Saviolakis, G. A., Wollert, T., Burge, B., Atkins, V., & Spielberger, C. (2004). Evaluating performance of law enforcement personnel during a stressful training scenario. *Annals of the New York Academy of Sciences, 1032*, 250–253.

Nair, D., Tan, S. Y., Gan, H. W., Lim, S. F., Tan, J., Zhu, M., et al. (2008). The use of ambulatory tonometric radial arterial wave capture to measure ambulatory blood pressure: The validation of a novel wrist-bound device in adults. *Journal of Human Hypertension, 22*, 220–222.

Nunan, D., Donovan, G., Jakovljevic, D. G., Hodges, L. D., Sandercock, G. R., & Brodie, D. A. (2009). Validity and reliability of short-term heart-rate variability from the Polar S810. *Medicine and Science in Sports and Exercise, 41*(1), 243–250.

Nunan, D., Jakovljevic, D. G., Donovan, G., Hodges, L. D., Sandercock, G. R., & Brodie, D. A. (2008). Levels of agreement for RR intervals and short-term heart rate variability obtained from the Polar S810 and an alternative system. *European Journal of Applied Physiology, 103*(5), 529–537.

Ohman, A., & Mineka, S. (2001). Fears, phobias, and preparedness: Toward an evolved module of fear and fear learning. *Psychology Review, 108*, 483–522.

Olson, D. T. (1998). Improving deadly force decision-making. *FBI Law Enforcement Bulletin, 67*, 1–9.

Olsson, A., & Phelps, E. A. (2007). Social learning of fear. *Nature Neuroscience, 10*, 1095–1102.

Orsila, R., Virtanen, M., Luukkala, T., Tarvainen, M., Karjalainen, P., Viik, J., & Nygård, C. H. (2008). Perceived mental stress and reactions in heart rate variability: A pilot study among employees of an electronics company. *International Journal of Occupational Safety and Ergonomics, 14*(3), 275–283.

Pagani, M. (2000). Heart rate variability and autonomic diabetic neuropathy. *Diabetes Nutrition & Metabolism*, *13*(6), 341–346.

Pagani, M., & Lucini, D. (2008). Cardiovascular physiology, emotions, and clinical applications: Are we ready for prime time? *American Journal of Physiology Heart and Circulatory Physiology*, *295*(1), H1–3.

Pagani, M., Mazzuero, G., Ferrari, A., Liberati, D., Cerutti, S., Vaitl, D., et al. (1991). Sympathovagal interaction during mental stress: A study using spectral analysis of heart rate variability in healthy control subjects and patients with a prior myocardial infarction. *Circulation*, *83*(2), 43–51.

Perini, R., & Veicsteinas, A. (2003). Heart rate variability and autonomic activity at rest and during exercise in various physiological conditions. *European Journal of Applied Physiology*, *90*(3–4), 317–325.

Pessoa, L. (2008). On the relationship between emotion and cognition. *Nature Reviews Neuroscience*, *9*, 148–158.

Pessoa, L., Kastner, S., & Ungerleider, L. G. (2002). Attentional control of the processing of neutral and emotional stimuli. *Cognitive Brain Research*, *15*, 31–45.

Petrucci, E., Mainardi, L. T., Balian, V., Ghiringhelli S., Bianchi A. M., Bertinelli M., et al. (1996). Assessment of heart rate variability changes during dipyridamole infusion and dipyridamole-induced myocardial ischemia: A time variant spectral approach. *Journal of the American College of Cardiology, 28*(4), 924–934.

Phelps, E. A. (2004). Human emotion and memory: Interactions of the amygdala and hippocampal complex. *Current Opinion in Neurobiology, 14*, 198–202.

Phelps, E. A., Ling, S., & Carrasco, M. (2006). Emotion facilitates perception and potentiates the perceptual benefits of attention. *Psychological Science, 17*, 292–299.

Phelps, E. A., O'Connor, K. J., Gatenby, J. C., Gore, J. C., Grillon, C., & Davis, M. (2001). Activation of the left amygdala to a cognitive representation of fear. *Nature Neuroscience, 4*, 437–441.

Pichon, A. P., de Bisschop, C., Roulaud, A., & Papelier, Y. (2004). Spectral analysis of heart rate variability during exercise in trained subjects. *Medicine and Science in Sports and Exercise, 36*, 1702–1708.

Piot, O., Copie, X., Guize, L., Lavergne, T., & Le Heuzey, J. Y. (1997). Variabilité de la fréquence cardiaque: physiologie et méthodologie. *Réalités cardiologiques, 120*, 8–14.

Pitzalis, M. V., Mastropasqua, F., Massari, F., Passantino, A., Colombo, R., Mannarini, A., et al. (1998). Effect of respiratory rate on the relationships between RR interval and systolic blood pressure fluctuations: A frequency-dependent phenomenon. *Cardiovascular Research, 38*, 332–339.

Posner, M. I., & Rothbart, M. K. (2007). *Educating the human brain*. Washington, DC: American Psychological Association.

Posner, M. I., Rothbart, M. K., Rueda, M. R., & Tang, Y. Y. (2009). Training effortless attention. In B. Bruya (Ed.), *Effortless attention: A new perspective in the cognitive science of attention and action*. Cambridge, MA: MIT Press.

Posner, M. I., Rothbart, M. K., Sheese, B. E., & Tang, Y. (2007). The anterior cingulate gyrus and the mechanism of self-regulation. *Cognitive, Affective, & Behavioral Neuroscience, 7*, 391–395.

Rein, G., Atkinson, M., & McCraty, R. (1995). Physiological and psychological effects of compassion and anger. *Journal of Advancement in Medicine, 8*(2), 87–105.

Robbe, H. W. J., Mulder, L. J. M., Ruddel, H., Langewitz, W. A., Veldman, J. B. P., & Mulder, G. (1987). Assessment of baroreceptor reflex sensitivity by means of spectral analysis. *Hypertension, 10*, 538–543.

Rubia, K., Smith, A. B., Brammer, M. J., & Taylor, E. (2003). Right inferior prefrontal cortex mediates response inhibition while mesial prefrontal cortex is responsible for error detection. *Neuroimage, 20*, 351–358.

Salahuddin, L., Cho, J., GiJeong, M., & Kim, D. (2007). Ultra short term analysis of heart rate variability for monitoring mental stress in mobile settings. *Conference Proceedings: IEEE Engineering in Medicine and Biology Society, 1*, 4656–4659.

Salahuddin, L., & Kim, D. (2006). Detection of acute stress by heart rate variability using a prototype of a mobile ECG Sensor. International Conference on Hybrid Information Technology (ICHIT06, IEEE CS), vol. 2, 453–459.

Saul, J. P., Rea, R. F., Eckberg, D. L., Berger, R. D., & Cohen, R. J. (1990). Heart rate and muscle sympathetic nerve variability during reflex changes of autonomic activity. *American Journal of Physiology, 258*(3), H713–721.

Sergerie, K., Lepage, M., & Armony, J. L. (2006). A process-specific functional dissociation of the amygdala in emotional memory. *Journal of Cognitive Neuroscience, 18*, 1359–1367.

Sergerie, K., Lepage, M., & Armony, J. L. (2007). Influence of emotional expression on memory recognition bias: A functional magnetic resonance imaging study. *Biological Psychiatry, 62*, 1126–1133.

Shapiro, P. A., Sloan, R. P., Bagiella, E., Kuhl, J. P., Anjilvel, S., & Mann, J. J. (2000). Cerebral activation, hostility and cardiovascular control during mental stress. *Journal of Psychosomatic Research, 48*, 485–491.

Sharps, M. J. (2010). *Processing under pressure: Stress, memory and decision-making in law enforcement.* New York: Looselaf Law Publications.

Siddle, B. K. (1995). *Sharpening the warrior's edge: The psychology & science of training.* Millstadt, IL: PPCT Research Publications.

Siddle, B. K. (1999). *The impact of the sympathetic nervous system on use of force investigation.* Millstadt, IL: PPCT Research Publications.

Solomon, R. (1991). The dynamics of fear in critical incidents: Implications for training and treatment. In J. T. Reese, J. M. Horn, & C. Dunning (Eds.), *Critical incidents in policing* (pp. 347–358). Washington, DC: U.S. Department of Justice.

Solomon, R. M., & Horn, J. M. (1986). Post-shooting traumatic reactions: A pilot study. In J. T. Reese & A. H. Goldstein (Eds), *Psychological services for law enforcement.* Washington, DC: U.S. Government Printing Office.

Stemmler, G. (2004). Physiological processes during emotion. In P. Philippot & R. S. Feldman (Eds.), *The regulation of emotion* (pp. 33–70). Mahwah, NJ: Lawrence Erlbaum.

Stemmler, G., Aue, T., & Wacker, J. (2007). Anger and fear: Separable effects of emotion and motivational direction on somatovisceral responses. *International Journal of Psychophysiology, 66*(2),141–153.

Sztajzel, J. (2004). Heart rate variability: A non-invasive method to measure the autonomic nervous system. *Swiss Medical Weekly, 134*, 514–522.

Tang, Y. Y. (2008). *Exploring the brain, optimizing the life.* Beijing: Science Press.

Tang, Y. Y., Ma, Y., Wang, J., Fan, Y., Feng, S., Lu, Q., et al. (2007). Short-term meditation training improves attention and self-regulation. *Proceedings of the National Academy of Sciences, 104*, 17152–17156.

Tang, Y. Y., Ma, Y., Fan, Y., Feng, H., Wang, J., Feng, S., et al. (2009). Central and autonomic nervous system interaction is altered by short-term meditation. *Proceedings of the National Academy of Sciences, 106*(22), 8865–8870.

Tarvainen, M. P., Georgiadis, S. D., Ranta-aho, P. O., & Karjalainen, P. A. (2006). Time-varying analysis of heart rate variability signals with Kalman smoother algorithm. *Physiological Measurement, 27*(3), 225–239.

Task Force of the European Society of Cardiology and the North American Society of Pacing and Heart Rate Variability. (1996). Standards of measurement, physiological interpretation, and clinical use. *European Heart Journal, 17*, 354–381.

Terkelsen, A. J., Mølgaard, H., Hansen, J., Andersen, O. K., & Jensen, T. S. (2005). Acute pain increases heart rate: Differential mechanisms during rest and mental stress. *Autonomic Neuroscience, 121*(1–2), 101–109.

Tiller, W. A., McCraty, R., & Atkinson, M. (1996). Cardiac coherence: a new non invasive measure of autonomic nervous system order. *Alternative Therapies, 2*(1), 52–65.

Tulen, J. H., Man int 'Veld, A. J., VanRoon, A. M., Moleman, P., Van Steenis, H. G., Blankestijn, P. J., et al. (1994). Spectral analysis of hemodynamics during infusions of epinephrine and norepinephrine in men. *Journal of Applied Physiology, 76*(5), 1914–1921.

Vuilleumier, P. (2005). How brains beware: neural mechanisms of emotional attention. *Trends in Cognitive Sciences, 9*, 585–594.

Wagner, H. (1989). The peripheral physiological differentiation of emotions. In H. Wagner & A. Manstead (Eds.), *Handbook of social psychophysiology* (pp. 77–98). Chichester, UK: Wiley.

Weiss, T., del-Bo, A., Reichek, N., & Engelman, K. (1980). Pulse transit time in the analysis of autonomic nervous system effects on the cardiovascular system. *Psychophysiology, 17*, 202–207.

Whalen, P. J., Kagan, J., Cook, R. G., Davis, F. C., Kim, H., Polis, S., et al. (2004). Human amygdala responsivity to masked fearful eye whites. *Science, 306*, 2061.

Yang, Y., Koh, D., Ng, V., Lee, C. Y., Chan, G., Dong, F., & Chia, S. E. (2002). Self-perceived work related stress and the relation with salivary IgA and lysozyme among emergency department nurses. *Occupational and Environmental Medicine, 59*, 836–841.

Zbilut, J. P., Thomasson, N., & Webber, C. L. (2002). Recurrence quantification analysis as a tool for the nonlinear exploration of nonstationary cardiac signals. *Medical Engineering & Physics, 24*, 53–60.

Zhong, Y., Jan, K. M., Hwan Ju, K., & Chon, K. H. (2006). Quantifying cardiac sympathetic and parasympathetic nervous activities using principal dynamic modes analysis of heart rate variability. *American Journal of Physiology Heart and Circulatory Physiology, 291*, 1475–1483.

Part IV

Police Procedure

15 Police Use of Force

Frank J. Gallo

Under statute, police have the lawful authority to use force for self-defense, defense of others, crime prevention, and law enforcement tasks (Gallo, Collyer, & Gallagher, 2008). Conceptually speaking, force is a coercive action to make somebody do something. Police may use different degrees of force against citizens who violate the law. Forceful responses can range from mere police presence to the use of weaponry. The use of force is a central part of the police profession. The authority to use it makes policing one of the most powerful professions in society. If left unchecked, such power may lead to excessive force problems.

Some of what police stakeholders know about police use of force comes from the police psychology profession. Three professional delivery-related services to the police that psychologists have traditionally participated in are assessment related activities, intervention services, and operational support (Aumiller & Corey, 2007). The purpose of this chapter is to discuss some of the salient core proficiencies that comprise these psychological services and to review how psychologists who establish a practice in the delivery of these services generate and apply psychological knowledge to issues surrounding police use of force.

The chapter begins with a discussion of four core assessment-related proficiencies: (1) a job task analysis to identify essential job functions that involve police use of force, (2) the pre-employment post-offer psychological evaluation of police candidates, (3) the pre-offer suitability screening of job applicants for potential job-related performance problems with the use of force, and (4) the fitness for duty evaluation of incumbent officers who develop on-the-job excessive force problems. Next, we discuss the ways in which a psychologist may approach the delivery of psychological intervention services to treat police officers who have excessive problems. Finally, we review psychological and social science data from empirical research on police use of force and other psychological topics central to police operations in this area.

ASSESSMENT-RELATED ACTIVITIES

Psychologists may establish a practice in any of the police psychology proficiencies that comprise assessment-related activities. These include the job task analysis, pre-employment post-offer psychological evaluations of police candidates, pre-offer suitability screenings of job applicants, and fitness-for-duty evaluations of incumbent officers, which are core proficiencies that have long been a part of the selection and evaluation of police officers' ability to effectively perform essential job-related functions that involve the use of force.

JOB TASK ANALYSIS

Industrial-organizational psychologists have contributed much to what psychologists, police agencies, and its employees know about what police do at work. The job task analysis is the primary method for determining police responsibilities, tasks, knowledge and skills, and results achieved (Cascio & Aguinis, 2006; Gallo, 2008b; Seberhagen, 1995). The methodology primarily involves reviewing the literature on policing; reviewing police department operational manuals, rules and procedures, policies, and general orders; observing police at work by participating in ride-alongs and attending trainings; conducting interviews with police personnel; and administering survey questionnaires to police agency employees. This battery of techniques produces an exhaustive list of job duties, such as crime prevention and law enforcement, and job tasks such as making arrests and writing reports. Police agencies use this information to make informed human resource decisions about such things as employee selection, position classification, major duties, and hiring and promotional procedures, training, job evaluation and professional standards and policies (Seberhagen, 1995).

A job task analysis is a timely and expensive activity for psychologists and police agencies to ensure the reliable performance of police officers. It requires organizational cooperation and commitment at all levels. It helps to validate employment standards of the police profession. The American Psychological Association's (APA) Division of Industrial-Organizational Psychology specifies procedures for conducting job and task analyses and validating personnel selection methods (Society for Industrial & Organizational Psychology, 2003). The U.S. Equal Employment Opportunity Commission (1978) also provides guidelines for employee selection procedures. In addition, the Americans with Disabilities Act (ADA; 1990) and the APA (2002) have standards for psychological practice in this specialty area.

There are job task analyses for police position classifications such as an entry level officer (e.g., patrol officer), a first-line supervisor (e.g., sergeant), and mid-level (e.g., lieutenant) and executive (e.g., chief) police positions. For example, the California Peace Officers Standards and Training Commission (2006) identified 10 essential job performance areas for the patrol officer: social competence, teamwork, adaptability/flexibility, conscientiousness/dependability, impulse control/attention to safety, integrity/ethics, emotional regulation and stress tolerance, decision making and judgment, assertiveness/persuasiveness, and avoiding substance abuse and other risk-taking behavior. Emotional regulation and stress tolerance-related job behaviors included ones tied to police use of force. Some examples were the officer stays calm in the face of verbal abuse, uses proper escalation and de-escalation of force, uses force only when necessary, and adjusts the amount of force needed to enforce laws. A counterproductive behavior was excessive, unrestrained use of force.

In Michigan, the Commission on Law Enforcement Standards (2006) also reported on a statewide job task analysis of the patrol officer position. The core use-of-force tasks officers must perform ranged from speaking and building rapport with a person to discharging a firearm at the person. Another report on the job tasks of entry-level law enforcement officers in the State of Rhode Island (Rhode Island Peace Officers Standards and Training Commission, 2009) identified 16 essential job functions of the municipal police officer, of which 8 involved uses of force such as controlling human conflict, using physical force and exertion to perform duties, and arresting and detaining people.

Despite agency type or geographic area, the use of force is a central part of policing to maintain order, to safeguard the well-being of citizens, to prevent criminal activity, and to enforce laws. The job and task analysis for police positions define the essential components of the job that police hiring authorities should carefully consider in establishing hiring and training standards for its employees. In fact, the central question for determinations of the psychological fitness of employees is: Does the person present psychological characteristics that would probably and substantially impair him or her from performing essential job-related tasks with or without reasonable accommodations? Licensed psychologists (or psychiatrists) perform these employment evaluations.

PRE-EMPLOYMENT POST-OFFER PSYCHOLOGICAL EVALUATIONS

The pre-employment post-offer psychological evaluation (PEPOPE) of police candidates' suitability for police work is a usual part of the selection process (Gallo, 2008b). The goal of the PEPOPE is not psychiatric diagnosis, but instead a determination of whether candidates have psychological characteristics that would probably and substantially impair them from performing essential job-related functions with or without reasonable accommodations. Pre-employment psychological screenings help police hiring authorities make informed employment decisions.

Most police departments today employ psychologists to perform PEPOPEs of its candidates (Craig, 2005; Detrick, Chibnall, & Rosso, 2001). Police departments recognize that a failure to screen the psychological suitability of police candidates could amount to a negligent hiring practice (*Bonsignore v. City of New York*, 1981/1982). In fact, police departments are aware of their duty to protect the public from the hiring of psychologically unqualified candidates with mental disabilities that would impair their ability to perform police work (*McKenna v. Fargo*, 1978/1979).

For psychologists who perform PEPOPEs, standards and guidelines exist in several professional organizations, in government legislation, and in law enforcement protocols (e.g., ADA, 1990; American Psychological Association [APA], 2002; Dantzker & McCoy, 2006; International Association of Chiefs of Police [IACP] Psychological Services Section, 2004; Inwald, 1987). The PEPOPE is medical, of course, because psychologists use tests such as the Minnesota Multiphasic Personality Inventory (MMPI; Hathaway & Mckinley, 1943) that may lead to confirmation of a candidate' diagnosable psychiatric condition as specified by *DSM-IV-TR*. Therefore, psychologists conduct PEPOPEs only after the police hiring authority makes a conditional offer of employment to the candidate (ADA, 1990; Gallo & Halgin, 2010).

Psychological tests validated for use in pre-employment screenings of police candidates include those that assess psychopathology such as the MMPI (Hathaway & Mckinley, 1943) or its restandardized form, the MMPI-2 (Butcher, Dahlstrom, Graham, Tellegen, & Kaemmer, 1989), in which its standard scales are essentially identical, ensuring the continuity of previous research (Nichols, 2001); those that assess normal psychological functioning such as the California Psychological Inventory (CPI; Gough, 1975); and those that assess traits relevant to law enforcement such as the Inwald Personality Inventory (IPI; Inwald, Knatz, & Shusman, 1983). Cochrane, Tett, and Vandecreek (2003) published the results of a national survey of psychological testing practices in police settings, and Varela, Boccaccini, Scogin, Stump, and Caputo (2004) published a meta-analytic review of psychological tests used to predict the job performance of police officers.

The MMPI and CPI are the more widely used PEPOPE tests for which there are data linking police candidates' test responses to eventual job-related problems with uses of force. The most frequently used test is the MMPI (Cochrane et al., 2003; Kornfeld, 1995; Varela et al., 2004; Wrightsman & Fulero, 2005). It is a self-report objective test that assesses adult personality characteristics and provides information relevant for screening candidates for maladaptive personality functioning on the job. The test's current version has 567 items or personal statements, which candidates respond to by indicating true or false. Test data provide a summary of each candidate's personality characteristics, and behavioral proclivities such as aggressiveness, anger proneness, psychoticism, interpersonal passivity, and other clinical conditions that would put him or her at significant risk for future performance difficulty in a police employment position. MMPI comparison group test data for police employment positions are available.

Published studies that have linked police candidates' test responses on the MMPI to job difficulties with uses of force include Hargrave, Hiatt, and Gaffney (1988), who found that elevated MMPI scale scores on *Infrequency* (*F*), *Psychopathic Deviate* (*Pd*), *Hypomania* (*Ma*), and *Control* (*Cn*) correctly classified incumbent officers who received disciplinary actions for aggressive misconduct against offenders, inmates, coworkers, or family members. Costello, Schneider, and Schoenfeld (1996) also observed that police responses to MMPI scales *F*, *Pd*, and *Ha* predicted suspensions of officers with 3 years of service.

The CPI, similar to the MMPI, is a self-report objective test of adult personality, but one that involves a nonmedical assessment of normal traits. The inventory's current version has 434 items or personal statements, which candidates respond to by indicating true or false. Test data provide a summary of each candidate's personality structure and orientations. For example, there would be data on the extent to which a candidate's orientation to other people, societal values, and law enforcement may impact his or her future performance in a police employment position. CPI comparison group test data for police employment positions are also available.

In addition, published studies in the literature have established the CPI's success at predicting police abuses of force. For example, Hargrave and Hiatt (1989) reported a correlation between incumbent police officers' low CPI scale scores on *Socialization* (*So*), *Self-Control* (*Sc*), and *Well-being* (*Wb*), and disciplinary actions against them for unnecessary uses of force. Fitzgerald (1987) found that incumbent officers with low scale scores on *Responsibility* (*Re*) had more citizen complaints filed against them such as uses of unnecessary force than their normative counterparts. Sarchione, Cutler, Muchinsky, and Nelson-Gray (1998) reported that low scale scores on *Re*, *So*, and *Sc* discriminated officers who received disciplinary action from officers who did not. Job-related problems that led to disciplinary actions included uses of excessive force and inappropriate language. These validity studies make the CPI an appealing test not only to use in PEPOPEs of police candidates, but also to use in pre-offer suitability screenings of police job applicants.

Pre-Offer Suitability Screenings

Psychologists may conduct pre-offer suitability screenings of job applicants whom the police hiring authority have not given a conditional offer of employment. This type of pre-employment screening is a nonmedical assessment of normal psychological functioning. In a pre-offer suitability screening, psychologists may include psychological tests, personal history questionnaires, and other assessment instruments that would not lead to confirmation that an applicant has a diagnosable psychiatric condition as specified by the *DSM-IV-TR* (ADA, 1990; Aumiller & Corey, 2007; IACP, 2004). Similar to the PEPOPE is that the goal of the pre-offer suitability screening is not psychiatric diagnosis. It is to help police hiring authorities make informed employment decisions about whether applicants demonstrate traits, behaviors, and competencies to complete police recruit training and then perform essential job-related functions.

There are published psychological tests available that researchers have validated for use with police populations and have linked test responses to police uses of force and that psychologists may use for pre-offer suitability screenings of job applicants. For example, the *Buss-Perry Aggression Questionnaire* (AQ; Buss & Perry, 1992) is a widely used and established self-report nonmedical test for evaluating aggression (Suris et al., 2004). Five subscales comprise the AQ: physical aggression, verbal aggression, indirect aggression, hostility, and anger (Buss & Warren, 2000). Respondents who complete the questionnaire describe the extent to which statements are characteristic or uncharacteristic of them using a Likert-type response scale. Greenberg, Riggs, Bryant, and Smith (2003) found that incumbent police officers' responses to the physical aggression subscale of a 12-question modified version of the AQ correlated with complaints filed by police departments for excessive force and the number of officer-involved shootings; responses to the verbal aggression subscale correlated with complaints filed by citizens for verbal discourtesy or abuse; and responses to the anger and hostility subscales correlated with the number of officer-involved shootings.

Psychologists may also use the NEO Personality Inventory-Revised (NEO PI-R; Costa & McCrae, 1992) to screen job applicants. Test administrators use it to measure five major personality dimensions or factors (i.e., neuroticism, extraversion, openness to experience, agreeableness, and conscientiousness) that have shown to be a replicable and robust taxonomy for classifying normal adult personality traits (Barrick & Mount, 1994; Costa & McCrae, 1990; Costa & Widiger, 2002). The test consists of 240 items that define these five higher-order personality factors from which there are 30 narrower middle-order traits derived (e.g., Hostility and Impulsiveness derived from Neuroticism). Respondents rate each test item using a five-point Likert-type response scale, which ranges from *strongly disagree* to *strongly agree*. Black (2000) investigated whether the NEO PI-RI had utility in evaluating the job performance of police recruits during basic training. He found significant correlations between recruits' higher-order (extraversion) and middle-order (warmth, positive emotions, actions, assertiveness, activity, and excitement-seeking) personality traits and job performance scores on firearm and self-defense skills. Generally, police recruits who were reliable, determined, self-confident, and goal oriented were likely forceful and assertive when required and higher performers during training.

Besides the administration of paper-and-pencil tests, psychologists may administer computerized situational tests designed to measure what applicants might say or what they might do in response to interactive videos that depict police work-related events (Gallo, 2008b). For example, a psychologist can present an applicant a video that shows a potential interaction with someone. The applicant must quickly make an appraisal (judgment) as to how dangerous the person's behavior is (e.g., using a scale ranging from *not at all* dangerous to *very* dangerous), then make a decision as to how forcefully he or she would respond (e.g., using a scale ranging from an *escapable action* to a *lethal action*). The psychologist can evaluate the applicant's judgments and decisions, which may expose aggressive tendencies. For example, the applicant on average sees most interpersonal contacts as very dangerous and on average uses less lethal to lethal actions to control them. The police applicant may deliberately hide this tendency from pencil-and-paper tests and interviews, but demonstrate it under conditions that require quick judgments and decisions.

Results from situational tests can round out the applicant's pre-employment evaluation. However, when performing such evaluations, psychologists generally should not expect police applicants to have the same fund of knowledge as would incumbent officers have to make danger appraisals and use of force decisions about potential job-related events. Psychologists should look for applicants' personal experiences they bring to the job and how they use those experiences in reaction to potential real-life events.

Given the lifelike quality of computerized situational tests today, many law enforcement agencies use computer technology to deliver use of force and firearms training and to evaluate officers' performance at the recruit and in-service training levels. The *Milo Range Pro* (available from IE Interactive Training at http://www.ies-usa.com) and the *XVT Law Enforcement Trainer* (available from Meggitt Training Systems at http://www.meggitttrainingsystems.com) are popular computer software packages that provide virtual training solutions for law enforcement agencies.

Despite the practical appeal of computer situational tests as a tool for both selection and training, a search of the databases PsycINFO and Criminal Justice Abstracts using the terms *police use of force*, *police psychological testing*, and *police situational tests* yielded no published studies in the psychological literature on the use of computerized situational tests for police pre-employment screenings, pre-offer or post-offer ones. Some reasons may be that situational tests require purchasing expensive computer equipment to administer them, are time-consuming for evaluators, are costly for a police agency to have psychologists include them in a pre-employment test battery, or require a lengthy validation process for use with police populations. Nevertheless, psychologists should consider including computerized situational tests (1) to account for the influence of moderating situational variables that attitudes and personality traits may not account for in street-level judgments and decisions, and (2) to complete comprehensive psychological evaluations that help police managers make better-informed employment decisions to hire psychologically healthy police officers.

PSYCHOLOGICAL FITNESS-FOR-DUTY EVALUATIONS

Not all psychologically healthy police officers whom police agencies hire, though, may be free from abuses of force (Toch, 1995). The Independent Commission on the Los Angeles Police Department (ICLAPD; 1991) found that police supervisors gave superior performance ratings to officers who had high rates of excessive force complaints and whom psychologists rated as suitable for police work. If pre-employment psychological tests were contributing some knowledge about aggressive tendencies, then being prone to abuses of force may be more than a matter of measuring personality traits (Grant & Grant, 1995). Situational factors may contribute to aggressive overreactions (Benner, 1986; Megargee, 1970; Mills & Stratton, 1982). Abuses of force may be consequences of attitudes, beliefs, and changing personality traits that develop after selection (Beutler, Nussbaum, & Meredith, 1988; Broderick, 1977; Brown, 1988; Gallo, 2008a, 2008b; ICLAPD, 1991; Manning, 1997; Muir, 1977; Toch, 1995; White, 1972; Wilson, 1973; Worden, 1995b) and not predicted by applicants' or candidates' psychological test data. These possible determinants of excessive force may trigger a fitness-for-duty evaluation.

Police departments have a responsibility to monitor the psychological fitness of its officers to perform job tasks and to retain officers who are psychological healthy (*Bonsignore v. City of New York*, 1981/1982). In fact, police departments have the right to order an officer to participate in a psychological fitness-for-duty evaluation (FFDE; *Conte v. Harcher*, 1977) for which there are guidelines available (IACP Police Psychological Services, 2009). The objective of a psychological FFDE is to determine whether the officer's psychological characteristics may be substantially impairing him or her from performing essential job-related functions with or without reasonable accommodations. Psychologists perform FFDEs only after referring police agencies provide valid evidence (e.g., direct observations or credible third-party observations) that shows the officer may not be able to perform essential job-related functions because of psychological factors.

Psychological Hypotheses About Excessive Force Problems

In the published literature, one can find psychological hypotheses about typologies of officers with excessive force problems that police agencies may refer to psychologists for FFDEs. For example, Scrivner (1994) classifies officers with excessive force problems according to officers with personality disorders, which psychologists rarely evaluate; officers with previous job-related trauma experiences, which psychologists evaluate some of the time; officers with early career problems, which psychologists evaluate a good bit of the time; officers with inappropriate patrol styles, which psychologists evaluate much of the time; and officers with personal problems, which psychologists evaluate mostly.

Officers with personality disorders have a chronic risk of abusing force because of their enduring personality traits. Their personality characteristics manifest in antisocial, narcissistic, paranoid, and abusive tendencies that interfere with judgments and decisions that affect how they interact with citizens—especially when they perceive citizens as challenging or threatening their authority during police–citizen contacts. They also show a lack of empathy for others, have difficulties learning from their work experiences, and have problems with taking responsibility for their behaviors, all which put them at a greater risk for citizen complaints.

Officers with previous job-related trauma experiences such as officer-involved shootings are at risk for uses of excessive force. They have job stress that causes them to isolate themselves from their peers to shield posttraumatic stress reactions that manifest later in uses of excessive force.

Officers with early career problems have little police experience, are impressionable, are impulsive, and have low frustration tolerance that leads to problems with uses of force. They are young and inexperienced officers who engage in an aggressive, macho style of policing. Other early career problems involve officers who develop a heavy-handed patrol style of policing that causes them problems with the use of force. They perceive a demand to always highlight their authority. They become more rigid and sensitive to challenges by citizens, which can lead to responses against citizens that are more forceful when less forceful ones would be reasonable.

Officers with personal problems such as marital separation, divorce, or a perceived loss of status is the most frequent group of officers whom police agencies refer for FFDEs because of excessive force problems. They have a fragile sense of self-worth and higher levels of anxiety compared to their normative peer counterparts. Dangerous police–citizen contacts may threaten their self-confidence and unmask fear-based responses that involve excessive force. An erratic pattern of patrol behavior is a signpost of a loss of self-control and eventual use of excessive force.

Besides Scrivner's (1994) profiles of excessive force–prone officers, there are studies that have constructed attitudinal typologies of officers' policing styles that differ in their propensities to have excessive force problems (Broderick, 1977; Brown, 1988; Muir, 1977; White, 1972).

Tough cops (White, 1972), *enforcers* (Broderick, 1977; Muir, 1977), and *clean beat crime fight-ers* (Brown, 1988) are probably the most likely to have such problems. These officers generally perceive the primary role of the police as controlling crime. They engage an aggressive style of patrol work in which they are rigid rule appliers who enforce all laws from minor types of viola-tions to felonies. They prefer to make arrests than to handle order-maintenance calls for service. They believe the citizenry hold hostile attitudes toward the police, and are generally suspicious of them. They perceive police department rules and procedures and court decisions as tying their hands and protecting the citizenry, who hate the police, from good street policing. This causes frustration and job dissatisfaction, and stirs emotions. To do their job, they are willing to bend the rules or violate department procedures. The consequences usually involve inappropriate uses of force as street justice or just deserts. Often, when they enforce laws they have difficulty balancing the force they use with the force they need to use in particular situations, and thus they tend to use disproportionate amounts of force and to have excessive force problems. Yet, they continue to act as tough cops, which they believe cops are supposed to be, and continue to engage a macho posturing policing style.

Another psychological hypothesis apparent in studying police use of force is the police personal-ity. The debate over a police personality, as it appears in the literature, suggests there is a lack of evidence to support a specific cluster of characteristics, which tend to remain stable over the course of officers' careers, and which, relate to excessive force problems on the job (e.g., Balch, 1972; Beutler et al., 1988; Carpenter & Raza, 1987; Gould, 2000; Laguna, Linn, Ward, & Rupslaukyte, 2009; Langworthy, 1987; Lefkowitz, 1975; Skolnick, 1977; Turner, 2004). Supposedly psychologi-cally healthy police candidates who enter police work show changing personality patterns because of what happens to them on the job. Changes continue to happen and shape their work styles over the course of their careers. Some officers may become cynical, suspicious, secretive, pessimistic, authoritarian, reclusive, or prejudicial. Unwanted or negative police qualities such as these may contribute individually to excessive force problems but do not collectively as a specific entity as research on the police personality shows.

With regard to the evidence that supports psychological hypotheses about attitudinal typologies, much of it is impressionistic and grounded in unsystematic observations of few officers. Empirical tests generally show little support, variation in police behavior within and across typologies, incon-sistency in police behavior from one police–citizen encounter to the other, a weak association between police attitudes and behavior, and, again, an occupational context that largely affects police behavior (e.g., Balch, 1972; Brown, 1988; Snipes & Mastrofski, 1990; Worden, 1995a, 1995b).

Occupational Socialization and Excessive Force Problems

Excessive force problems that trigger FFDEs are probably the consequences of the confluence of officers' traits and the occupational context in which they work. Police occupational socialization (on-the-job experiences) shapes the character of police (Gallo, 2008a). Officers learn the police occupation through formal and informal lessons given during recruit training (Chappell, Lanza-Kaduce, & Johnston, 2010; Kappeler, Sluder, & Alpert, 2010). Formal lessons involve instruction on topics such as the administration of justice, fitness, law, police procedures, use of force, police professionalism, and community relations.

Informal lessons about the job usually take the form of war stories told by police academy instructors. Instructors also teach recruits about unwritten rules, values, and beliefs police gener-ally hold of the job. These lessons continue to happen on the job where officers learn what their peers consider to be normative and expected street behavior. Two salient occupational socialization effects that may lead to excessive force problems are the guiding beliefs of thinking and doing as others (conformity) and seeing the world as a dangerous place (police worldview).

Police are conformists. They learn to follow shared rules of conduct, which help to shape the quality of interactions with their peers. If they are to act comfortably with their peers on the job, they follow the rules. Officers learn quickly that there is a price to pay for violating the rules. For example, a rookie officer responds with incumbent officers to a dispatched call for disorderly conduct. The incumbent officers endorse exaggerated values of toughness, aggressiveness, and respect. These officers *don't take shit from anyone*. When the officers arrive, a male suspect insults and swears at the rookie. Although the rookie has a range of verbal skills available to manage the suspect's behaviors, the rookie fears "losing face" and the consequences of outside-the-box behaviors such as the incumbent officers labeling him or her a *wimp* or *not a real cop*. The rookie mixes his or her response choices with ideals of either managing the conflict or preserving group norms. The rookie decides to be tough and aggressive, discounts low-level intrusive responses, and uses a physical tactic where none is necessary. In this way, the rookie earns respect, meets the expectations of the incumbent officers, and avoids peer labeling, but at the cost of using excessive force against the suspect.

A police worldview of danger stems from recruit and inservice trainings and on-the-job experiences (Kappeler et al., 2010). Officers learn to see the world as a dangerous place and to see citizens as potential assailants who want to harm the police and who may have weapons with them (Broderick, 1977; Brown, 1988; Muir, 1977; Skolnick, 1994; Walker, 1983; White, 1972). Bayley (1976) concluded that danger "dominates perceptions of what a policeman must be prepared to do. The possibility of armed confrontation shapes training, patrol preoccupations, and operating procedures" (p. 171). Although officers learn to work in condition yellow, their preoccupations with the notion of danger are greater than are the real dangers associated with police work (Cullen, Link, Travis, & Lemming, 1983). In fact, most citizens are cooperative with the police even in arrest situations that have the greatest potential for violence (Gallo et al., 2008; Garner, Maxwell, & Heraux, 2002; Garner, Schade, Hepburn, & Buchanan, 1995). So an exaggerated preoccupation with the idea of danger may become an occupational hazard.

According to emotional processing theory, maybe officers' exaggerated preoccupations with danger evolve into a distorted fear structure in their memory to deal with pseudogenetic threats to survival (Foa, Hembree, & Olasov Rothbaum, 2007; Foa & Kozak, 1985, 1986; Öhman & Mineka, 2001). A normal fear structure would include representations of feared stimuli (e.g., a person is holding a weapon), the fear responses (e.g., my heart beats fast), and the meaning associated with the stimuli (e.g., this person is dangerous) and the fear responses (e.g., my heart is beating fast so I'm afraid). In this example, the fear structure represents a realistic threat to which the officer responds. An officer's fear structure becomes distorted when the officer associates ordinarily harmless stimuli with threat and danger, which easily, excessively, and automatically activate fear responses without conscious awareness of the triggering stimuli. Exaggerated threat and danger appraisals may lead to disproportionate force responses to harmless situations.

In contrast, cognitive processing models may explain how officers' exaggerated preoccupations with danger develop into excessive force problems (e.g., Beck, 1985; Beck & Clark, 1997; Beck & Greenberg, 1988; Clark & Beck, 2010; Ehlers & Clark, 2000). For example, there is an experience or situation, and maybe a pre-existing personality or schema (mental plan) vulnerability. This activates pre-attentive, automatic, and strategic processing of all incoming information through an enhanced encoding lens, which is bias for threatening and dangerous aspects of the situation, with an inability to process harmless features. This triggers the activation of three core maladaptive memory structures (schemata): (1) negative beliefs about the world and other people (e.g., the world is a dangerous place and people want to harm me), (2) negative beliefs about the situation (e.g., ordinarily harmless stimuli are dangerous or there are no harmless stimuli), and (3) negative beliefs about the self (e.g., I am vulnerable to harm). Hyperarousal symptoms and excessive force problems are probable consequences of this occupational mental playbook that involves distorted and influencing cognitive processes of attention, encoding, retrieval, and inference.

Other effects of the police occupational socialization process that may breed excessive force problems that trigger FFDEs are bravery (Pogrebin & Poole, 1991), secrecy (Fyfe, 2010; Westley, 2006), autonomy (Skolnick & Fyfe, 1993), social isolation (Manning, 2006; Skolnick, 1994;

Westley, 1970, 2006), and solidarity (Harris, 1973; Skolnick, 1994; Stoddard, 2006; Westley, 1970, 2006).

In summary, at the heart of any pre- or post-employment psychological evaluation for excessive force problems is the determination of whether applicants, candidates, or incumbent officers demonstrate characteristics that make them substantially vulnerable to uses of excessive force or excessive uses of force; and whether they demonstrate characteristics not only that show a willingness to use force but also that show an ability to use restraint. Psychologists may use nonmedical tests for pre-offer suitability screenings and medical ones for PEPOPEs and FFDEs. There is a rich discussion in the literature on using psychological tests to predict police officer performance on the job. However, much of the empirical evidence available usually ties test scores mostly to job performance measures such as disciplinary actions, absenteeism, citizen complaints, or supervisory performance ratings (Varela et al., 2004). Some disciplinary actions and citizen complaints may actually be composite measures that include excessive force problems but that researchers fail to report.

Generally though, there appears limited literature available that connects specific psychological constructs to excessive force problems (Grant & Grant, 1995). There are psychological consequences of being a police officer besides what predispositions, traits, and experiences officers bring with them to the job. Police officers do experience work-related cognitive, affective, and behavioral changes. These changes may be necessary and useful at times and may be maladaptive at other times, which triggers a FFDE. Constant negative job effects may change the psychological makeup of police officers, harden them, and make them more vulnerable to excessive force problems for which there are psychological interventions available besides the FFDE.

INTERVENTION SERVICES

The case of Mr. Patient, whom I constructed from my experience as a police officer and from my work as a clinician, provides an opportunity to explain the ways in which a psychologist may work with a police officer who presents with excessive force problems. The case of Mr. P is a compilation of my clinical work with clients, and in no way does he represent a single case. Mr. P, a 30-year-old male, sought treatment for problems with speaking aggressively to citizens, pushing and grabbing them when such behaviors were unnecessary.

PRECIPITANTS

When Mr. P's brother was hospitalized for a mental illness 4 months ago, he began to develop symptoms of anxiety. Mr. P feared he would follow in the psychological footsteps of his brother. For example, one day when Mr. P found himself crying with joy about his wife's graduation from college, he began to ruminate about his brother's hospitalization. He was becoming increasingly anxious and demonstrating a heavy-handed style of policing.

CROSS-SECTIONAL VIEW

A typical current problem situation is as follows: Mr. P is watching a television movie with his wife. He sees a man crying on the television, which triggers the automatic thoughts, "That's what my brother did in the hospital. He's weak. I'm like my brother." These thoughts evoke heightened anxiety, and fear that he would be like his brother. So Mr. P says to his wife, "This guy needs to toughen up and act like a man." In a second typical situation, Mr. P responds to a police call for service that involves a neighbor dispute. The event triggers the automatic thoughts, "What will these people think of me? They'll think I'm weak. I'm not in control." These thoughts evoke heightened anxiety and anger, which cause Mr. P to yell at the neighbors, "This is what you're gonna do," and then, "I grabbed one of the neighbors and told him to come here."

Longitudinal View

Mr. P's childhood data show that his father often said, "Can't you get it right?" when Mr. P did things. After a fight in school, his father would only ask, "Did you win?" When Mr. P cried, his father would say, "Boys don't cry. You need to toughen up. Act like a man." These data precipitated early on in Mr. P the core belief that he was helpless. He has developed the automatic thoughts, "I'm weak. I'm ineffective. I can't get it right." He has developed the following key conditional assumptions: "If I'm not in control, I'll get hurt. If I'm perfect, in control, and don't get it wrong, I'll be okay." His compensatory behavioral strategies have included striving to get whatever he is doing always right, being tough and in control all the time, and never showing weakness.

Working Hypothesis

Mr. P came to view himself as helpless because of the circumstances surrounding his childhood. His brother's hospitalization exacerbated this belief. Thinking about these thoughts and experiences has reinforced Mr. P's negative view of himself. He typically activates this perspective in interpersonal and work situations in which he perceives that he may be imperfect, powerless, not in control, or weak. To disengage his negative views of himself and function in the world, he has established rigid assumptions/rules for himself: "I must be perfect, or people will perceive me as ineffective. I must be tough and in control, or people will perceive me as weak." To operationalize his assumptions, he has developed certain behavioral compensatory strategies: perfectionism, toughness, control, and alertness. Mr. P's professional life requires him to be in a position of authority, which reinforces his coping strategies that may lead to unnecessary and excessive uses of force such as grabbing citizens and using verbal commands where none are necessary.

Treatment

Mr. P's treatment involved cognitive-behavioral therapy (CBT; Beck, 1995, 2005). He learned standard cognitive-behavioral tools (e.g., evidence for/against, advantages disadvantages, rational-emotional role-playing, imagery, decision making, problem solving, coping cards, behavioral experiments, and exposure techniques) to evaluate, modify, and respond to his negative automatic thoughts, dysfunctional self-schemas, and maladaptive assumptions. For example, Mr. P conducted behavioral experiments (e.g., kept a messy desk at work) to test his negative assumptions, for instance, "I must be perfect or people will perceive me as ineffective." Mr. P provided ongoing evidence that he is effective (e.g., listed work-related tasks he performed successfully) and different from his brother (e.g., wrote down his personal narrative). Mr. P confronted feared situations (e.g., admitted to making mistakes). In summary, he can now evaluate his distorted logic, which has reduced anxiety symptoms and danger misappraisals that most often lead to inappropriate uses of force at work. Mr. P has developed relapse prevention skills, has transitioned to self-help, and has been discharged from active treatment after 12 sessions.

The above case vignette highlights the facts that Mr. P carried with him to the job, cognitive, affective, and behavioral baggage. Mr. P's excessive force problems stem from personal ones, which the PEPOPE maybe missed. In addition, this case highlights the use of an evidence-based treatment, CBT, that would also help officers with distorted worldviews of danger and with other reasons for excessive force problems. Although one may consider other psychotherapies (e.g., Barlow, 2008; Gurman & Messer, 2005), such therapies should be clinically efficacious (as determined through clinical trials) and effective (in field studies).

Another mechanism of change to consider when working with police officers is the importance of the therapist's qualities such as attunement to police work (Wampold, 2001; Wampold et al., 1997). Psychologists, who know the job and the specific ingredients of an evidence-based psychotherapy, may provide a convincing explanation to an officer for a particular treatment plan that fits the officer's problems. These psychologists should remember though to start therapy from a position of ignorance because even if they know the job well they may not know what the job is like for that officer. In contrast, psychologists who are naïve to police work, not so uncommon among clinical psychologists, must first evaluate themselves before they opt to evaluate and treat police officers with excessive force problems. Psychologists must honestly ask about the extent of their knowledge of policing, about the extent of their training and experience in working with the police population, and about their understanding of the ethical standards of practice in being competent and sensitive to diverse populations (APA, 2002), which in many ways police officers are.

Psychologists should remember that the different reasons for officers' excessive force problems may involve the confluence of pre-employment baseline predispositions and personality traits and occupational hazards (organizational, physical, and mental). It is for this confluence that police departments bear some responsibility for calling on psychologists to conduct research on the use of force and to deliver education and trainings on psychological topics that are important to the police use of force.

OPERATIONAL SUPPORT

Police use of force is a critical operation issue. Psychologists and other social scientists have engaged research, education, and training activities to enhance the performance of police departments and its officers.

RESEARCH

Studies of the prevalence of police force have measured a variety of sorts of force, from the use of mere police presence to the use of police weaponry. What researchers know today about police use of force, which has implications for police policies, procedures, education and trainings, has come from some recurring sampling strategies (Gallo et al. 2008): making independent field observations of police–citizen interactions (e.g., Bayley & Garofalo, 1989; Klinger, 1995; Terrill & Mastrofski, 2002), surveying the public about their contacts with the police (e.g., Durose, Schmitt, & Langan, 2005; Langan, Greenfeld, Smith, Durose, & Levin, 2001), administering multi-agency surveys about the incidence and prevalence of force (e.g., IACP, 2001; Pate & Fridell, 1993), using use-of-force report forms (e.g., Croft, 1985; McLaughlin, 1992), and sampling police arrests (e.g., Gallo et al., 2008; Garner et al., 1995; Garner et al., 2002; Garner & Maxwell, 2002; Garner, Schade, Hepburn, Fagan, & Mulcahy, 1996).

Individually and collectively, these sampling strategies and the studies that use them have particular strengths for certain purposes but also have potential limitations (Gallo et al., 2008). For instance, field observations provide independent observations of trained observers who directly record the dynamics of police–citizen encounters. However, the presence of observers might temper some officers' uses of force against citizens, and thus results would reflect a restricted range of behaviors used and would generally underestimate the use of force. Public contact surveys impart information on citizens' experiences with the police. However, some citizens could exaggerate police behaviors, which would inflate the extent to which police use force against them. Performing multi-agency surveys provides many interactions between police and citizens across jurisdictions. Yet police concerns about the anonymity or the confidentiality of the results might lead to lower participation, which would attenuate estimates of the extent to which police use force. Use-of-force report forms and arrest reports are more structured data sources of incidents where police use force, except these sources of data echo police self-reports, in which some officers might report their behavior in the best possible light to avoid civil or criminal litigation.

In the final analysis, results from studies that use these sampling strategies generally reflect the facts that a small percentage of police–suspect contacts involve police using physical force, that police mostly employ bodily force tactics such as grabbing, that police rarely use weaponry, and that the best predictor of police use of force is suspect resistance.

Existing studies also reflect the fact that much of what researchers know about the variation in police use of force comes from sociological studies of police–citizen encounters. The social dynamics of police–citizen encounters are easily accessible observations available to researchers compared to what happens in the minds of officers before and when they use force. In addition, entering the field of policing and conducting research are sometimes fraught with police and union apprehension, suspiciousness, and the perceived threat of punitive sanctions (civil, criminal, and departmental), all which may lead to social desirable, deviant, or acquiescent participation, or nonparticipation. Psychological inquiries intrude on the privacy of officers for which there are legal protections in place (ADA, 1990). So gaining rapport and support and investigating psychological hypotheses about the variation in police use of force because of officers' mental processes or psychological attributes can be a challenge.

Despite the problems and limitations in this arena of research, there is some recent psychological inquiry into making improvements at the measurement stage. For example, Garner et al. (2002) constructed a maximum force measure in which they weighted the different types of force used by and against police during arrests with the perceived average rankings of force severity (1 to 100) derived from a sample of police raters who completed a survey questionnaire. The average rankings ranged from an officer's use of a conversational voice ($M = 15.6$) to an officer's use of a handgun ($M = 81.7$). They did not report the average rankings of suspect behaviors. This measurement strategy explained more variance (26.2%) in police use of force than did using the traditional physical force dichotomy (22.0%), and more variance than did earlier measurement models that used it (3.8%, Bayley & Garofalo, 1989; 12.8%, Friedrich, 1980).

Gallo and Collyer (2010) extended the work of Garner et al. (2002). They recruited a panel of police raters not only to construct a maximum force measure but also to construct a maximum danger measure. Raters completed a questionnaire that asked them to use their personal experience to rate the severity of different forceful behaviors (1 = *minimum force*, 9 = *maximum force*) used by and against police during arrests and to rate the dangerousness (1 = *minimum danger*, 9 = *maximum danger*) of different event variables available at arrests such as time of day, location of arrest, and type of call for police service. The authors weighted these variables with the raters' average ratings. Ratings of forceful behaviors used by police ranged from a conversational voice ($M = 1.69$) to the use of a handgun ($M = 8.94$). In contrast, ratings of forceful behaviors used by suspects against the police ranged from a conversational voice ($M = 1.50$) to the use of a knife ($M = 8.93$). Raters thought, on average, that a male ($M = 4.75$) who was 25 to 29 years old ($M = 4.49$), taller than 6′ 5″ ($M = 5.82$), weighed 250 lbs. or greater ($M = 5.59$), and who reached under a car seat ($M = 7.70$), was under the influence of drugs ($M = 6.75$), and was known to carry a weapon ($M = 7.90$) was the most dangerous suspect to arrest. This scaling and weighting strategy explained roughly 61% of the variability in police use of force. In fact, the best predictor of police use of force was suspect use of force, which was similar to Garner et al.'s (2002) findings.

What's also different in Gallo and Collyer (2010) is that the theoretical underpinning of their measurement approach involves the application of a schema-based processing model that considers the police worldview of danger. Simply, officers have a pre-existing mental playbook for use-of-force encounters. Their schemata involve influencing cognitive processes of attention, encoding, retrieval, and inference that trigger acts of force to stay safe and make arrests. Other studies also show officers use schemata as a basis for law enforcement decisions (e.g., Robinson, 2000; Stalans, 2008; Stalans & Finn, 1995).

EDUCATION AND TRAINING

Although officers may rely on schemata to make appraisals of threat and danger and subsequent decisions to use force, other factors contribute to the cognitive operation of officers in use-of-force encounters. Some of the salient ones are the stress response, heuristics and biases, and associated decision errors for which there are psychological data that psychologists can translate into police education and trainings.

The Stress Response

Stress is a state of psychological tension, a reaction or effect caused by perceived threat and danger stimuli (e.g., a person holding a handgun). Stress is a normal reaction to nonnormal threat and danger conditions. It is an evolutionary response that prepares officers to defend against assailants and other threats to survival. Perceived threat and danger stimuli (alarm signal) activate the stress response.

The strength of an alarm signal depends on the magnitude of the threat, the probability of the threat occurring if the officer takes no protective action, and the probability of the officer's protective action being effective. A strong alarm signal mobilizes brain regions, hormones, and neurotransmitter systems that start to facilitate peak performance (Southwick et al., 2007). The sympathetic nervous system becomes overactive. A chain of hormonal discharges energizes the officer's body. The alarm signal excites the hypothalamus, which causes the synthesis and secretion of corticotropin-releasing factor (CRF), which excites the pituitary gland to synthesize and secrete adrenocorticotropic hormone (ACTH), which excites the adrenal gland to synthesize and secrete adrenocortical glucocorticoids, epinephrine (adrenaline), norepinephrine (noradrenaline), and other adrenally derived neuroactive steroids such as cortisol (corticosteroid hormone or glucocorticoid). All of this prepares the officer to do his or her best in defense against the alarm signal.

Although stress can facilitate peak performance, too much stress can cause sensory, cognitive, and affective distortions that have behavioral consequences. The pupils, for example, dilate in states of peak stress to gather extra information, but the perceptual system narrows its field of focus (Easterbrook, 1959). There is a loss of peripheral vision and officers may retreat to widen their peripheral field. They may also overlook important visual cues and develop a less than optimal plan of action that involves inappropriate uses of force. Peak stress affects the memory system. Elevated levels of cortisol can impair memory functions (Newcomer et al., 1999). So officers may find it difficult to access their long-term memory and match sensory input with force responses that best fit the demands of situations. Memory impairment, though, is temporary, and normal memory functions return as cortisol levels deplete. In addition, peak stress can affect task performance, selection of responses to threat, and response time to threat: performance is usually best with moderate arousal (Hick, 1952; Levitt & Gutin, 1971; Martens & Landers, 1970; Wood & Hokanson, 1965; Yerkes & Dodson, 1908). Hypervigilance, the dominant response to peak stress, is a state of panic or near panic in which an individual becomes hypersensitive to threat and danger stimuli (Selye, 1956). The individual cannot discriminate threatening from nonthreatening cues. A lack of attention to important situational variables may lead to incorrect responses to threat.

Officers may experience other distortions in response to threat (Klinger, 2002). Sensory distortions may include auditory blunting, auditory exclusion, or altered perceptions of time such as things slow down or speed up (Tachypsychia). Cognitive distortions may involve dissociation, and thoughts of disbelief that may cause startle. Officers may experience episodic or delayed affective distortions, which involve fear, anxiety, sadness, numbness, guilt, or nightmares. Negative sequelae such as these are common in states of peak stress, when traumatic stressors are recurrent, and when officers perceive situations as uncontrollable and overwhelming (Southwick et al., 2007). Stress affects the cognitive processes that span encoding information, making a decision to act, developing a plan of action, initiating action, and observing the present status of threat and danger (Gallo, 2008c). Stress is a highly subjective experience in which officers' skills, fund of knowledge, coping abilities, physical and psychological fitness levels can offset its negative effects on performance.

Heuristics and Biases

Given the physiological reactions to threat and danger coupled with the need for officers to respond quickly and defend against, officers may rely on mental short cuts such as heuristics to solve problems that require force. How should an officer respond to a suspect wielding a knife? This problem, for example, requires the officer to think about how best to handle successfully what may be a novel situation. The officer may try a trial-and-error strategy before stumbling on a force response that works. Alternatively, the officer may apply a step-by-step procedure that he or she learned in training to deal with the problem. However, these techniques are time-consuming. When officers need to make quick decisions to use force under stressful conditions of uncertainty, mental short cuts such as heuristics, which are rules of thumb, or past experience strategies can serve to help officers disambiguate uncertain situations and simplify novel decision tasks. Two heuristics well recognized in the literature are the representative and availability heuristics (Kahneman, Slovic, & Tversky, 1982; Kahneman & Tversky, 1982).

"If something looks like a duck, walks like a duck, and talks like a duck, it's probably a duck." This is an example of the representative heuristic, which is a tendency for people to assume that if a person resembles members of a particular group, that person is probably a member. The assumption may be correct in some situations, but it may lead people astray in others. Consider this example: suppose a detective observes a female dressed provocatively, pacing a street corner at 2:00 a.m., and waving down motor vehicles in an area known for prostitution. The female's behavior coupled with the detective's prior knowledge of the area raise the detective's suspicion of prostitution. The detective's observations collectively reveal a mental pattern that matches characteristics of prostitution. Sometimes recognizing a pattern is rather simple and other times difficult. Recognizing a prostitute or other offender is a matter of predicting group membership from the variables (e.g., sex, clothing, time of day, location, and behavior) that provide the best information. However, even the best information can be imperfect. So if the female were actually a broken-down motorist looking for help, the detective's suspicion of prostitution and subsequent decision to conduct an investigatory stop would be incorrect.

In contrast, the availability heuristic is a tendency for people to assume that how easily they remember an event implies how usual that event happens. When people try to guess how often something happens, they usually start by trying to think of examples. For instance, an officer thinks, "Am I more likely to use force against whites than I am against nonwhites?" If all the officer can recall are examples of shootings and knife assaults involving nonwhite offenders, the officer intuitively thinks nonwhites. Because it is easier for the officer to think of these extreme examples of force that stick out in the officer's memory, the officer assumes that more force situations involve offenders of this type. The officer remembers more extreme events and ignores less severe ones that are available but less memorable. Although this tendency may prime the officer to defend against an actual nonwhite offender, the consequence of an uncertain situation may be excessive force such as physically acting on mistaken fears.

Whether officers rely on a representative or availability heuristic, the implications for using them may be decision errors. Ignoring base rates, expressing in-group favoritism and intergroup discrimination, being overconfident, forming quick impressions, holding onto beliefs even when confronted with contrary evidence, responding intuitively, using common sense instead of formal inquiry, and looking only for observations that support hypotheses of threat and danger are other cognitive operations that also raise issues of bias-based processing and associated decision errors, especially under conditions of uncertainty.

Decision Errors and Consequences

Recall the prostitute example. The detective suspects the female is a prostitute because she matches the detective's mental prototype. There is some uncertainty though in a decision to conduct an investigatory stop, so the detective may be wrong and there are associated costs. The detective would be incorrect (False Alarm error) if the decision were suspicious when the female's actual status is innocent (broken-down motorist). The detective would also be incorrect (Miss error) if the decision were not suspicious when the female's actual status is an offender (prostitute). On the other hand, the detective would be correct (Hit) if the decision were suspicious when the female's actual status is an offender. The detective would also be correct (Correct No) if the decision were not suspicious when the female's actual status is innocent.

The payoffs and costs for decisions to use force under conditions of uncertainty are not the same, though, in all use-of-force encounters. Consider the gun or wallet dilemma in which an officer must decide whether a person is holding a gun or a wallet, and then decide what to do. If the officer were to think gun when there is a gun (Hit), then the payoff would be the officer shoots an armed suspect and saves his or her life. If the officer were to think no gun when there is a wallet (Correct No), then the payoff would be the officer does nothing or the status quo. Obviously, the officer wants to be correct, but the situation is uncertain, so the officer must also consider the costs of making certain decision errors. For example, if the officer were to think gun when there is no gun (False Alarm error), then the cost would be the officer shoots an unarmed suspect. However, if the officer were to think no gun when there is a gun (Miss error), then the cost would be the suspect shoots the officer.

Which error is worse? Officers would probably think the suspect has a gun because people naturally assign a self-biased value to the False Alarm and Miss error possibilities, especially in survival situations. Such a tendency raises the issue of response bias. If officers were suspicious of everyone, then all their outcomes in any situation would be either Hits or False Alarms. They would be extreme in a way that eliminated Misses but at the cost of an unreasonable number of False Alarms. Conversely, if officers were never suspicious of anyone, then all their outcomes in any situation would be either Misses or Correct No's. They would be extreme in a way that eliminated False Alarms but at the cost of an unreasonable number of Misses. Obviously, officers want to avoid extreme suspicion and extreme nonsuspicion for a balance. What police stakeholders want are high correlations between officers' decisions and the actual status of people in any given situation.

Unfortunately, there are no precise formulas for choosing a single or best force option to handle force events. What is reasonable is a matter in which courts consider whether the totality of circumstances of any given situation justifies a particular use of force (Gallo, 2008c; *Graham v. Connor*, 1989). Police stakeholders cannot expect or insist on perfect decisions by imperfect people. What they can hold the police to is a professional standard of making reasonable decisions. What would it take to maximize Hits and minimize the total number of False Alarm and Miss errors? A good start would be for police to recognize their human vulnerabilities and become critical thinkers about everyday information: evaluate assumptions, recognize personal hidden values, consider the evidence, calculate probabilities, and evaluate conclusions. If police were more aware of the possible errors in their thinking, then they may be more alert to avoid them.

CONCLUSION

The purpose of this chapter has been to discuss some of the salient core proficiencies that comprise the police psychology profession in which psychologists have established practices and have generated and applied psychological knowledge to issues surrounding police use of force: job task analysis, pre-employment post-offer psychological evaluations of police candidates, pre-offer suitability screenings of job applicants, fitness-for-duty evaluations of incumbent officers, psychological intervention services, research, education, and trainings.

The use of force is a central part of policing. In no way does this chapter provide an exhaustive review of its many manifestations in the delivery of psychological services to the police involving assessment-related activities (e.g., evaluations for high-risk assignments), intervention services (e.g., critical incident therapy), operational support activities (e.g., crisis and hostage negotiation), and organizational development (e.g., developing performance appraisal systems). Psychologists may establish a practice in any of these areas and may conduct research that generates psychological data that have implications for assessment (e.g., screening criteria), intervention services (e.g., excessive force problems), operational support (e.g., police policies), and organizational development (e.g., performance criteria).

Some suggestions for looking at the future of research in the delivery of psychological services pertaining to police use of force, especially where what psychologists know is insufficient would include as follows: (1) examine the predictive validity of psychological tests (measures of psychopathology and measures of normative personality traits) in predicting the performance of officers on essential job-related functions that involve force, (2) use cognitive modeling methodologies to examine officers' judgment and decision approaches to the use of force, and (3) develop and validate computerized situational tests for different police classification positions. The research should involve scientific rigor. Researchers should carefully formulate their designs using a sound body of knowledge, and appropriate measures and multivariate statistical procedures while considering real-world constraints. Researchers should translate their data into evidence-based programs, policies, and professional practices that are responsive to the needs of the police profession. They should convey the data through the delivery of high-quality psychological services to police agencies, their administrators, and their employees that support the development of police officers.

In closing, this chapter benefits college students and experienced clinical practitioners who are looking at a career in police psychology and want to establish a practice in delivering psychological services related to issues surrounding police use of force. It also benefits college students and experienced police practitioners who want to establish a career in law enforcement in which they can apply psychological principles to this important topic area.

REFERENCES

American Psychological Association. (2002). Ethical principles of psychologists and code of conduct. *American Psychologist, 57*, 1060–1073.

Americans with Disabilities Act of 1990, 42 U.S.C.A. § 12101 *et seq.* (West 1993).

Aumiller, G. S., & Corey, D. (2007). Defining the field of police psychology: Core domains & proficiencies. *Journal of Police and Criminal Psychology, 22*, 65–76.

Balch, R. W. (1972). The police personality: Fact or fiction? *The Journal of Criminal Law, Criminology and Police Science, 63*, 106–119.

Barlow, D. H. (Ed.). (2008). *Clinical handbook of psychological disorders: A step-by-step treatment manual* (4th ed.). New York: Guilford.

Barrick, M. R., & Mount, M. K. (1994). The big five personality dimensions and job performance: A meta-analysis. *Personnel Psychology, 44*, 1–26.

Bayley, D. H. (1976). *Forces of order: Police behavior in Japan and the United States.* Berkeley: University of California Press.

Bayley, D. H., & Garofalo, J. (1989). The management of violence by police patrol officers. *Criminology, 27*(1), 1–25.

Beck, A. T. (1985). Theoretical perspectives on clinical anxiety. In A. H. Tuna & J. Maser (Eds.), *Anxiety and the anxiety disorders* (pp. 183–196). Hillsdale, NJ: Erlbaum.

Beck, A. T., & Clark, D. A. (1997). An information processing model of anxiety: Automatic and strategic processes. *Behaviour Research and Therapy, 35*, 49–58.

Beck, A. T., & Greenberg, R. L. (1988). Cognitive therapy of panic disorder. In R. E. Hales & A. J. Frances (Eds.), *Review of psychiatry* (Vol. 7, pp. 571–583). Washington, DC: American Psychiatric Press.

Beck, J. S. (1995). *Cognitive therapy: Basics and beyond.* New York: Guilford Press.

Beck, J. S. (2005). *Cognitive therapy for challenging problems: What to do when the basics don't work.* New York: Guilford Press.

Benner, A. W. (1986). Psychological screening of police applicants. In J. T. Reese & H. A. Goldstein (Eds.), *Psychological services for law enforcement* (pp. 11–18). Washington, DC: U.S. Government Printing Office.

Beutler, L. E., Nussbaum, P. D., & Meredith, K. E. (1988). Changing personality patterns of police officers. *Professional Psychology: Research and Practice, 19*, 503–507.

Black, J. (2000). Personality testing and police selection. *New Zealand Journal of Psychology, 29*, 2–9.

Broderick, J. J. (1977). *Police in a time of change*. Morristown, NJ: General Learning Press.

Brown, M. K. (1988). *Working the street: Police discretion and the dilemmas of reform*. New York: Russell Sage Foundation.

Buss, A. H., & Perry, M. (1992). The aggression questionnaire. *Journal of Personality and Social Psychology, 63*, 452–459.

Buss, A. H., & Warren, W. L. (2000). *Aggression Questionnaire manual*. Los Angeles: Western Psychological Services.

Butcher, J. N., Dahlstrom, W. G., Graham, J. R., Tellegen, A., & Kaemmer, B. (1989). *Minnesota multiphasic personality inventory-2: Manual for administration and scoring*. Minneapolis: University of Minnesota Press.

California Peace Officers Standards and Training Commission. (2006). *Patrol officer psychological screening dimensions*. Retrieved June 10, 2009, from http://www.post.ca.gov/selection/psychological-traits.pdf

Carpenter, B. N., & Raza, S. M. (1987). Personality characteristics of police applicants: Comparisons across subgroups and with other populations. *Journal of Police Science and Administration, 15*, 10–17.

Cascio, W. F., & Aguinis, H. (2006). *Applied psychology in human resource management* (6th ed.). Upper Saddle River, NJ: Pearson Prentice Hall.

Chappell, A. T., Lanza-Kaduce, L., & Johnston, D. H. (2010). Law enforcement training: Changes and challenges. In R. G. Dunham & G. P. Alpert (Eds.), *Critical issues in policing*: Contemporary readings (6th ed., pp. 53–70). Long Grove, IL: Waveland Press.

Clark, D. A., & Beck, A. T. (2010). *Cognitive therapy of anxiety disorders: Science and practice*. New York: Guilford.

Cochrane, R. E., Tett, R. P., & Vandecreek, L. (2003). Psychological testing and the selection of police officers. *Criminal Justice and Behavior, 30*, 511–537.

Costa, P. T., Jr., & McCrae, R. R. (1990). Personality disorders and the five-factor model of personality. *Journal of Personality Disorders, 4*, 362–371.

Costa, P. T., Jr., & McCrae, R. R. (1992). *NEO PI-R professional manual*. Odessa, FL: Psychological Assessment Resources.

Costa, P. T., Jr., & Widiger, T. A. (Eds.). (2002). *Personality disorders and the five-factor model of personality*. Washington, DC: American Psychological Association.

Costello, R. M., Schneider, S. L., & Schoenfeld, L. S. (1996). Validation of a preemployment MMPI index correlated with disciplinary suspension days of police officers. *Psychology, Crime and Law, 2*, 299–306.

Craig, R. J. (2005). *Personality-guided forensic psychology*. Washington, DC: American Psychological Association.

Croft, E. B. (1985). *Police use of force: An empirical analysis*. (Doctoral dissertation, State University of New York at Albany, 1985). Dissertation Abstracts International, *46*(8–A), 2449.

Cullen, F. T., Link, B. G., Travis, L. F., & Lemming, T. (1983). Paradox in policing: A note on perceptions of danger. *Journal of Police Science and Administration, 2*, 457–462.

Dantzker, M. L., & McCoy, J. H. (2006). Psychological screening of police recruits: A Texas perspective. *Journal of Police and Criminal Psychology, 21*, 23–32.

Detrick, P., Chibnall, J. T., & Rosso, M. (2001). Minnesota Multiphasic Inventory-2 in police officer selection: Normative data and relation to the Inwald Personality Inventory. *Professional Psychology*: Research and Practice, *32*, 484–490.

Durose, M. R., Schmitt, E. L., & Langan, P. A. (2005). *Contacts between police and the public: Findings from the 2002 national survey*. Washington, DC: Bureau of Justice Statistics.

Easterbrook, J. A. (1959). The effect of emotion on cue utilization and the organization of behavior. *Psychological Review, 66*, 183–201.

Ehlers, A., & Clark, D. M. (2000). A cognitive model of posttraumatic stress disorder. *Behaviour Research and Therapy, 38*, 319–345.

Fitzgerald, P. R. (1987). The prediction of police performance using the MMPI and CPI. (Doctoral dissertation, St. Louis University, 1987). *Dissertation Abstracts International, 47*, 3519.

Foa, E. B., Hembree, E. A., & Olasov Rothbaum, B. (2007). *Prolonged exposure therapy for PTSD: Emotional processing of traumatic experiences*. New York: Oxford University Press.

Foa, E. B., & Kozak, M. J. (1985). Treatment of anxiety disorder: Implications for psychopathology. In A. H. Tuma & D. Maser (Eds.), *Anxiety and the anxiety disorders* (pp. 421–452). Hillsdale, NJ: Erlbaum.

Foa, E. B., & Kozak, M. J. (1986). Emotional processing of fear: Exposure to corrective information. *Psychological Bulletin, 99*, 20–35.

Friedrich, R. J. (1980). Police use of force: Individuals, situations, and organizations. *Annals of the American Academy of Political and Social Science, 452*, 82–97.

Fyfe, J. J. (2010). The split-second syndrome and other determinants of police violence. In R. G. Dunham & G. P. Alpert (Eds.), *Critical issues in policing: Contemporary readings* (6th ed., pp. 466–480). Long Grove, IL: Waveland Press.

Gallo, F. J. (2008a). Police occupational socialization. In B. Cutler (Ed.), *Encyclopedia of psychology and law* (Vol. 2, pp. 572–575). Newbury Park, CA: Sage.

Gallo, F. J. (2008b). Police selection. In B. Cutler (Ed.), *Encyclopedia of psychology and law* (Vol. 2, pp. 584–587). Newbury Park, CA: Sage.

Gallo, F. J. (2008c). Police use of force. In B. Cutler (Ed.), *Encyclopedia of psychology and law* (Vol. 2, pp. 593–596). Newbury Park, CA: Sage.

Gallo, F. J. & Collyer, C. E. (2010). *Police use of force measurement: The importance of danger and officers' schemata.* Manuscript submitted for publication.

Gallo, F. J., Collyer, C. E., & Gallagher, P. L. (2008). Prevalence of force by and against police in Rhode Island jurisdictions: Implications for use-of-force training and reporting. *Criminal Justice Review, 33*, 480–501.

Gallo, F. J., & Halgin, R. P. (2010). *A guide for establishing a practice in conducting preemployment post-offer psychological evaluations of police candidates.* Manuscript submitted for publication.

Garner, J. H., & Maxwell, C. D. (2002). *Understanding the use of force by and against the police in six jurisdictions* (Final report to National Institute of Justice, 95-IJ-CX-0066). Williamston, MI: Joint Centers for Justice Studies.

Garner, J. H., Maxwell, C. D., & Heraux, C. G. (2002). Characteristics associated with the prevalence and severity of force used by the police. *Justice Quarterly, 19*(4), 705–746.

Garner, J., Schade, T., Hepburn J., & Buchanan, J. (1995). Measuring the continuum of force used by and against the police. *Criminal Justice Review, 20*, 146–168.

Garner, J., Schade, T., Hepburn, J., Fagan. J., & Mulcahy, A. (1996). *Understanding the use of force by and against police.* Washington, DC: National Institute of Justice.

Gough, H. G. (1975). *Manual for the California Psychological Inventory.* Palo Alto, CA: Consulting Psychological Press.

Gould, L. A. (2000). A longitudinal approach to the study of the police personality: Race/gender differences. *Journal of Police and Criminal Psychology, 15*, 41–51.

Grant, J. D., & Grant, J. (1995). Officer selection and the prevention of abuse of force. In W. A. Geller & H. Toch (Eds.), *And justice for all: Understanding and controlling police abuse of force* (pp. 151–162). Washington, DC: Police Executive Research Forum.

Greenberg, B. E., Riggs, M., & Bryant, F. B. (2003). Validation of a short aggression inventory for law enforcement. *Journal of Police and Criminal Psychology, 18*, 12–19.

Gurman, A. S., & Messer, S. B. (Eds.). (2005). *Essential psychotherapies: Theory and practice* (2nd ed.). New York: Guilford.

Hargrave, G. E., & Hiatt, D. (1989). Use of the California psychological inventory in law enforcement officer selection. *Journal of Personality Assessment, 53*, 267–277.

Hargrave, G. E., Hiatt, D., & Gaffney, T. W. (1988). F+4+9+Cn: An MMPI measure of aggression in law enforcement officers and applicants. *Journal of Police Science and Administration, 16*, 268–273.

Harris, R. (1973). *The police academy: An insider's view.* New York. John Wiley.

Hathaway, S. R., & Mckinley, J. C. (1943). *The Minnesota Multiphasic Personality Inventory* (Rev. ed.). Minneapolis: University of Minnesota Press.

Hibler, N. S., & Kurke, M. I. (1995). Ensuring personal reliability through selection and training. In M. I. Kurke & E. M. Scrivner (Eds.), *Police psychology into the 21st century* (pp. 57–91). Hillsdale, NJ: Erlbaum.

Hick, W. E. (1952). On the rate of gain of information. *Quarterly Journal of Experimental Psychology, 4*, 11–26.

Independent Commission on the Los Angeles Police Department. (1991). *Report of the independent commission on the Los Angeles police department.* Los Angeles, CA: Independent Commission on the Los Angeles Police Department.

International Association of Chiefs of Police. (2001). *Police use of force in America.* Alexandria, VA: International Association of Chiefs of Police.

International Association of Chiefs of Police Psychological Services Section. (2004). *Pre-employment psychological services guidelines.* Retrieved June 10, 2009, from http://theiacp.org/psych_services_section/pdfs/Psych-PreemploymentPsychEval.pdf

International Association of Chiefs of Police Psychological Services Section. (2009). *Psychological fitness-for-duty evaluation guidelines*. Retrieved August 27, 2010, from http://theiacp.org/psych_services_section/pdfs/Psych-FitnessforDutyEvaluation.pdf

Inwald, R. E. (1987). Use of psychologists for selecting and training police. In H. W. More & P. C. Unsinger (Eds.), *Police managerial use of psychology and psychologists* (pp. 107–139). Springfield, IL: Charles C Thomas.

Inwald, R. E., Knatz, H., & Shusman, L. (1983). *Inwald personality inventory manual*. New York: Hilson Research.

Kahneman, D., Slovic, P., & Tversky, A. (Eds.). (1982). *Judgment under uncertainty: Heuristics and biases*. New York: Cambridge University Press.

Kahneman, D., & Tversky, A. (1982). Judgment under uncertainty: Heuristics and biases. In D. Kahneman, P. Slovic, & A. Tversky (Eds.), *Judgment under uncertainty: Heuristics and biases* (pp. 3–20). New York: Cambridge University Press.

Kappeler, V. E., Sluder, R. D., & Alpert, G. P. (2010). Breeding deviant conformity: The ideology and culture of police. In R. G. Dunham & G. P. Alpert (Eds.), *Critical issues in policing*: *Contemporary readings* (6th ed., pp. 265–291). Long Grove, IL: Waveland Press.

Klinger, D. A. (1995). The micro-structure of nonlethal force: Baseline data from an observational study. *Criminal Justice Review*, *20*, 169–186.

Klinger, D. A. (2002). *Police responses to officer-involved shootings* (192286). Washington, DC: U.S. Department of Justice. Retrieved August 27, 2010, from the National Criminal Justice Reference Service from http://www.ncjrs.gov/pdffiles1/nij/grants/192286.pdf

Kornfeld, A. D. (1995). Police officer candidate MMPI-2 performance: Gender, ethnic, and normative factors. *Journal of Clinical Psychology*, *51*, 536–540.

Laguna, L., Linn, A., Ward, K., & Rupslaukyte, R. (2009). An examination of authoritarian personality traits among police officers: The role of experience. *Journal of Police and Criminal Psychology, 25*, 99–104.

Langan, P. A., Greenfeld, L. A., Smith, S. K., Durose, M. R., & Levin, D. J. (2001). *Contacts between police and the public: Findings from the 1999 national survey*. Washington, DC: Bureau of Justice Statistics.

Langworthy, R. H. (1987). Police cynicism: What we know from the Niederhoffer Scale. *Journal of Criminal Justice*, *15*, 17–35.

Lefkowitz, J. (1975). Psychological attributes of policemen: A review of research and opinion. *Journal of Social Issues*, *31*, 3–26.

Levitt, S., & Gutin, B. (1971). Multiple choice reaction time and movement time during physical exertion. *Research Quarterly*, *42*, 405–410.

Manning, P. K. (1997). *Police work: The social organization of policing* (2nd ed.). Prospect Heights, IL: Waveland Press.

Manning, P. K. (2006). The police: Mandate, strategies and appearances. In V. E. Kappeler (Ed.), *The police & society: Touchstone readings* (3rd ed., pp. 94–122). Long Grove, IL: Waveland Press.

Martens, R., & Landers, D. M. (1970). Motor performance under stress: A test of the inverted-U hypothesis. *Journal of Personality and Social Psychology*, *16*, 29–37.

McLaughlin, V. (1992). *Police and the use of force*: *The savannah study*. Westport, CT: Praeger.

Megargee, E. I. (1970). The prediction of violence with psychological tests. In C. D. Spielberger (Ed.), *Current topics in clinical and community psychology* (Vol. 2, pp. 97–156). New York: Academic Press.

Michigan Commission on Law Enforcement Standards. (2006, October). *Statewide job analysis of the patrol position*. Retrieved June 10, 2009, from http://www.michigan.gov/documents/mcoles/Full_Report_2006_185893_7.pdf

Mills, M. C., & Stratton, J. G. (1982). The MMPI and the prediction of police job performance. *FBI Law Enforcement Bulletin*, *51*(2), 10–15.

Muir, W. K. (1977). *Police: Streetcorner politicians*. Chicago: University of Chicago Press.

Newcomer, J. W., Selke, G., Melson, A. K., Hershey, T., Craft, S., Richards, K., & Alderson, A. L. (1999). Decreased memory performance in healthy humans induced by stress-level cortisol treatment. *Archives of General Psychiatry*, *56*, 527–533.

Nichols, D. S. (2001). Essentials of the MMPI-2 assessment. In A. S. Kaufman & N. L. Kaufman (Series Eds.), *Essentials of psychological assessment series*. New York: John Wiley.

Öhman, A., & Mineka, S. (2001). Fears, phobias, and preparedness: Toward an evolved module of fear and fear learning. *Psychological Review*, *108*, 483–522.

Pate, A. M., & Fridell, L. A. (1993). *Police use of force: Official reports, citizen complaints, and legal consequences*. Washington, DC: Police Foundation.

Pogrebin, M. R., & Poole, E. D. (1991). Police and tragic events: The management of emotions. *Journal of Criminal Justice, 19*, 395–403.

Rhode Island Peace Officers Standards and Training Commission. (2009, May). *Final report on the job task analysis study of entry level law enforcement officers in the State of Rhode Island.* Lincoln, RI: Rhode Island Municipal Police Academy.

Robinson, A. L. (2000). The effect of a domestic violence policy change on police officers' schemata. *Criminal Justice and Behavior, 27*, 600–624.

Sarchione, C. D., Cutler, M. J., Muchinsky, P. M., & Nelson-Gray, R. O. (1998). Prediction of dysfunctional job behaviors among law enforcement officers. *Journal of Applied Psychology, 83*, 904–912.

Scrivner, E. M. (1994). *Controlling police use of excessive force: The role of the police psychologist* (NIJ 150063). Washington, DC: National Institute of Justice. Retrieved July 29, 2010, from the National Criminal Justice Reference Service, http://www.ncjrs.gov/txtfiles/ppsyc.txt

Seberhagen, L. W. (1995). Human resources management. In M. I. Kurke & E. M. Scrivner (Eds.), *Police psychology into the 21st century* (pp. 435–466). Hillsdale, NJ: Erlbaum.

Selye, H. (1956). *Stress of life*. New York: McGraw-Hill.

Skolnick, J. H. (1994). *Justice without trial: Law enforcement in a democratic society* (3rd ed.). New York: Macmillan.

Skolnick, J. H. (1977). A sketch of the policeman's working personality. In D. B. Kennedy (Ed.), *The dysfunctional alliance: Emotion and reason in justice administration* (pp. 10–25). Cincinnati, OH: Anderson.

Skolnick, J. H., & Fyfe, J. J. (1993). *Above the law: Police and the excessive use of force.* New York: The Free Press.

Snipes, J. B., & Mastrofski, S. D. (1990). An empirical test of Muir's typology of police officers. *American Journal of Criminal Justice, 14*, 268–296.

Society for Industrial & Organizational Psychology. (2003, August). *Principles for the validation and use of personnel selection procedures.* Retrieved June 10, 2009, from http://www.siop.org/_Principles/principles.pdf

Southwick, S. M., Davis, L. L., Aikins, D. E., Rasmusson, A., Barron, J., & Morgan III, C. A. (2007). Neurobiological alterations associated with PTSD. In M. J. Friedman, T. M. Terence, & P. A. Resick (Eds.), *Handbook of PTSD: Science and practice* (pp. 166–189). New York: Guilford.

Stalans, L. J. (2008). Police decision making and domestic violence. In B. Cutler (Ed.), *Encyclopedia of psychology and law* (Vol. 2, pp. 567–569). Newbury Park, CA: Sage.

Stalans, L. J., & Finn, M. A. (1995). How novice and experienced officers interpret wife assaults: Normative and efficiency frames. *Law & Society Review, 29*, 287–320.

Stoddard, E. R. (2006). The informal code of police deviancy: A group approach to blue-coat crime. In V. E. Kappeler (Ed.), *The police & society: Touchstone readings* (3rd ed., pp. 201–222). Long Grove, IL: Waveland Press.

Suris, A., Lind, L., Emmett, G., Borman, P. D., Kashner, M., & Barratt, E. S. (2004). Measures of aggressive behavior: Overview of clinical and research instruments. *Aggression and Violent Behavior, 9*, 165–227.

Terrill, W., & Mastrofski, S. D. (2002). Situational and officer-based determinants of police coercion. *Justice Quarterly, 19*, 215–248.

Toch, H. (1995). The violence-prone police officer. In W. A. Geller & H. Toch (Eds.), *And justice for all: Understanding and controlling police abuse of force* (pp. 99–112). Washington, DC: Police Executive Research Forum.

Turner, L. J. (2004). Police personality: A comparative analysis of authoritarianism, aggression, and cynicism. *Dissertation Abstracts International: Section B: Sciences and Engineering, 64*(10), 5239.

U.S. Equal Employment Opportunity Commission. (1978). Employee selection procedures: Adoption by four agencies of uniform guidelines. *Federal Register, 43*, 38290–38315.

Varela, J. G., Boccaccini, M. T., Scogin, F., Stump, J., & Caputo, A. (2004). Personality testing in law enforcement employment settings. *Criminal Justice and Behavior, 3*, 649–675.

Varela, J. G., Scogin, F. R., & Vipperman, R. K. (1999). Development and preliminary validation of a semi-structured interview for the screening of law enforcement candidates. *Behavioral Sciences and the Law, 17*, 467–481.

Walker, S. (1983). *The police in America: An introduction.* New York: McGraw-Hill.

Wampold, B. E. (2001). *The great psychotherapy debate: Models, methods and findings.* Mahwah, NJ. Erlbaum.

Wampold, B. E., Mondin, G. W., Moody, M., Stich, E., Benson, K., & Ahn, H. (1997). A meta-analysis of outcome studies comparing bona fide psychotherapies: Empirically "all must have prizes." *Psychological Bulletin, 122*, 203–215.

Westley, W. A. (1970). *Violence and the police: A sociological study of law, custom and morality.* Cambridge, MA: MIT Press.

Westley, W. A. (2006). Violence and the police. In V. E. Kappeler (Ed.), *The police & society: Touchstone readings* (3rd ed., pp. 326–338). Long Grove, IL: Waveland Press.

White, S. O. (1972). A perspective on police professionalization. *Law & Society Review, 7,* 61–85.

Wilson, J. Q. (1973). *Varieties of police behavior.* New York: Atheneum.

Wood, C. G., & Hokanson, J. E. (1965). Effects of induced muscle tension on performance and the inverted-U. *Journal of Personality and Social Psychology, 1,* 506–510.

Worden, R. E. (1995a). Police officers' belief systems: A framework for analysis. *American Journal of Police, 14,* 49–81.

Worden, R. E. (1995b). The "causes" of police brutality: Theory and evidence on police use of force. In W. A. Geller & H. Toch (Eds.), *And justice for all: Understanding and controlling police abuse of force* (pp. 99–112). Washington, DC: Police Executive Research Forum.

Wrightsman, L. S., & Fulero, S. M. (2005). *Forensic psychology* (2nd ed.). Belmont, CA: Wadsworth.

Yerkes, R. M., & Dodson, J. D. (1908). The relation of strength of stimulus to rapidity of habit formation. *Journal of Comparative Neurology of Psychology, 18,* 459–482.

CASES CITED

Bonsignore v. City of New York, 521 F. Supp. 394 (S.O.N.Y. 1981), *aff'd,* 683 F.2d 635 (2nd Cir. 1982).

Conte v. Harcher, 365 N.E. 2d 567 (Ill. App. 1977).

Graham v. Connor, 490 U.S. 386 (1989).

McKenna v. Fargo, 451 F. Supp. 1355 (D. N.J. 1978), *aff'd,* 601 F.2d 573 (3rd Cir. 10 1979).

16 The Role of Psychologist as a Member of a Crisis Negotiation Team

Wayman C. Mullins

Michael J. McMains

The vast majority of police departments, other law enforcement agencies (i.e., FBI, NCIS, ATF, etc.), and most correctional facilities have crisis response teams (CRT). These teams are composed of several elements, including Incident Command staff, the Tactical Response Unit, and the Crisis Negotiation Team (CNT). Whether employed full-time, part-time, or on a consulting/as needed basis, psychologists can perform a valuable function as the mental health consultant to both the CRT and CNT. This chapter will explore these functions.

THE CRISIS RESPONSE PROCESS

The authors were recently given a letter mailed to, we presume, numerous police departments. The writer of the letter was a civilian who appeared from the writing to have had no law enforcement experience. He/she was offering his/her services as a hostage negotiator to these departments. He/she was a civilian not employed by any law enforcement or criminal justice agency, but was in the mental health field and was offering his/her services on a consultant if the need arose. No resume was included with the letter, and it was clear that he/she understood nothing about the crisis response process, the required response elements of a high-risk incident, or anything about accepted practices *vis a vis* negotiations. From more than 20 years of working in the field of law enforcement and hostage negotiations, it is our experience that, while not common, this is not an isolated and one-time event. Psychologists (and other professionals), because of their educational training, sometimes assume they have the skills necessary to serve law enforcement as negotiators. This is not the case.

A trained psychologist can provide valuable services and support to a crisis negotiation team and to the crisis response process. By *trained*, we are referring to general education received as part of a doctoral program and internship as well as specific training through continuing education seminars and specific training in hostage/crisis negotiations (same as law enforcement receives). To understand how a psychologist can serve on a CNT, it is important to understand the crisis response process itself as well as the responsibilities of each component of the CRT, and the overall structure and functioning of the CNT.

To many people (including some police agencies), *crisis incidents* is synonymous with *hostage-taking incidents*. In the more stereotypical hostage incident, a person or persons enters a facility to commit a crime of some type, the most common being robbery. But the person'a plan is somehow interrupted (e.g., a silent alarm is pressed), and the police show up. The criminal then takes both employees and customers hostage to be used as bargaining chips for demands (which generally focus on his or her escape). This scenario illustrates the basic elements of a hostage event. *Hostage* can be defined as a "person held as security for the fulfillment of certain terms" (*American Heritage*

Dictionary, 1980; McMains & Mullins, 2010). While simplistic, this definition contains several important points. Most important, hostages have to be persons. They cannot be pets, livestock, vehicles, or any inanimate objects. Implied in the definition is that hostages are held by force and cannot leave of their own volition. Hostages are bargaining chips. They are being held against their will as security for something the actor wants from the responding authorities. The actor may be willing to make a *quid pro quo* trade for hostages. While hostage callouts are one type of crisis incident to which the CRT may respond, there are many others.

A negotiated response is the first and best option in the above example, because it is the safest for all involved and least likely to result in injury or death. The other response options the police could employ include assaulting the location with sniper fire or chemical agents (Schlossberg, 1979b). Each of these other options, however, is highly likely to result in injury or death to one or more of the participants. In addition to actors taking hostages during the commission of a crime, hostage takers may also be emotionally disturbed. They may also be terrorists using hostages to secure political or criminal goals, or prisoners who riot and take hostages in the process (Goldaber, 1983; Hassel, 1975; Miron & Goldstein, 1979; Soskis & VanZandt, 1986). All of these hostage situations are ones in which a MHC (mental health consultant, a common term used in the field of negotiations) can play an important and active role in helping resolve as a team member.

The most familiar, or "classic," hostage-taking incident is actually a small portion of a CRT's work (nationally, less than 5% of all CRT/CNT responses involve hostage incidents; McMains & Mullins, 2006). By far the most common incident CRTs respond to are barricade subjects, of which there are several kinds. Barricade subjects account for over 70% of CRT callouts (FBI HOBAS data, in McMains & Mullins, 2006, 2010). HOBAS is the Hostage Barricade Database System maintained by the FBI. It is a national compilation of hostage/barricade incidents in the United States. The data in HOBAS is provided on a volunteer basis by local agencies. Use of the full data is restricted to law enforcement personnel and is available by registering on the FBI LEO (Law Enforcement Online). Attempted suicides and high-risk suicides account for almost all the rest. Barricade subjects are persons threatening to harm themselves (and sometimes others by their actions), but have no hostages. High-risk suicides are barricade subjects. Something happens to interrupt the actor's plan and the police intervene and are tasked with trying to defuse the actor's immediate crisis. In some cases, the actor's actions are less a serious suicide attempt and more a plea for help. Both of the authors of this chapter are active members of CNTs and have been for years. In one of the earliest incidents worked by one author's team, the negotiators negotiated with an actor threatening to commit suicide. His wife had left, taken the daughter, and hired a prominent divorce attorney. The actor had no money and was afraid the lawyer would really "do a number on me." The CNT explained he could get a pro bono attorney and fight back, and if he surrendered, CNT team members would put him in contact with an attorney. Upon hearing that, the actor surrendered.

Another type of barricade subject is one who barricades with victims. This type of incident is typically seen in domestic situations where one parent threatens family members. For example, John and Mary are divorced and John has no visitation rights. One day while Mary is at work, John goes over to Mary's, runs the babysitter off at gunpoint, and tries to flee with the children. A neighbor hears the commotion and calls the police. John locks himself in the house with the children. While there is risk to the children, they are not hostages in the normal sense of the word. They are victims of John's actions. This does not mean to imply that the children are in no danger. One of the common threats in these situations is "If I can't have them, no one will." And there are plenty of examples of the barricade subject killing the family members and then committing suicide.

Barricade incidents are often resolved using a heavy dose of crisis intervention, a skill which is a forte of MHCs psychologists, psychiatrists, or social workers specially trained in working with police crisis teams. While hostage incidents rely primarily on bargaining and mediation skills, barricade situations (with or without victims), high-risk suicides, and attempted suicides, rely on crisis intervention skills (Hatcher, Mohandie, Turner, & Gelles, 1998). In all these incidents, the role of the MHC may be greatly expanded by the team leader by virtue of the training and expertise of the MHC.

One central difference between hostage events and barricade subjects is the issuance of demands by the actor. In a hostage incident, the actor needs the police to secure freedom, money, rights, and privileges, for example, in a prison incident inmates may want more recreation, better food, or safety. In a barricade incident, the actor typically wants nothing from the police and may question why the police even responded (McMains & Mullins, 2006, 2010). Part of the goal of the CNT in these incidents is to develop a reason for the actor to talk to the police, and to surrender. As an example, in a recent incident involving one author's team, the negotiator convinced the actor to come out of his residence for a medical check by paramedics.

Regardless of whether it is a hostage or barricade situation, the general police response is the same. All elements of the CRT respond. It takes a full team effort to resolve these types of incidents. Incident Command staff are responsible for coordinating all responders, ensuring necessary resources are immediately available, establishing and maintaining communications (intra- and interteam), and making decisions. All decisions are made by Incident Command from giving the actor something as basic as water to possibly ordering a tactical resolution. The most critical decision an IC (Incident Commander) can make is whether to continue negotiations or go to a tactical response. Noesner (1999) has suggested a three-part test for IC regarding a tactical resolution: (1) is the action necessary? (2) is the action risk-effective? and (3) is the action acceptable? The answer to these questions should guide the IC rather than other considerations (such as the investment of time or money, and so on). The responsibility of the tactical unit is to provide the threat of force or the use of actual force to the incident. The goal of the tactical unit, just as with IC and CNT, is to save lives (Stites, 2005). In order of priority, CRT efforts are directed at saving the lives of hostages and innocents, saving the lives of responding law enforcement officers, and, finally, saving the life of the actor. Without the threat of force, there is no reason for the actor to speak with negotiators. The tactical unit provides containment of the actor and establishes an inner perimeter to isolate the actor and hostages. This perimeter is not only physical, but also may be electronic (such as cutting off phone lines or systems, disabling power to turn off computers, etc.). The tactical unit also provides intelligence regarding the actor, where the actor is, and hostages. For example, the tactical unit may provide information on the structure of the dwelling where the hostages are being held as well as on environmental or any other aspects of the situation relevant to resolving the incident. The tactical unit may employ an assault team or sniper team to provide force to save innocent lives. If the actor is actively threatening to harm a hostage, Incident Command may then order the tactical unit to employ appropriate force against the actor.

NEGOTIATION AND CNT DYNAMICS

Negotiators are highly successful at resolving crisis incidents without the loss of life or the use of tactical force. In fact, negotiators can peacefully resolve over 90% of the incidents they negotiate (McMains & Mullins, 2006). Negotiating is a team process that relies on the skillful use of communication and active listening strategies, using time as a tool in the negotiation dynamic, and properly addressing demand issues.

First, it is important to stress that crisis negotiations are a team effort. Crisis incidents are not resolved by any one person. Most teams have changed their name from *hostage negotiators* to *crisis negotiators* to more accurately reflect the work they do. Most incidents involve barricade subjects (with or without victims) and are actors in some major (perceived) life crisis. The goal of negotiations is to resolve the actor's immediate crisis, bring some level of immediate stability to their life, and then make a long-term referral (which could be criminal charges, inpatient admittance to a mental health facility, or even a trip to the hospital). The definition of a crisis, in fact, is an event where the person's ability to cope has been exceeded (Hoff, 1989). The goal of negotiations is to help develop some immediate coping skills. Negotiators rely on five principles to help resolve the actor's immediate crisis: (1) empathy, (2) active listening skills, (3) setting boundaries for conduct, (4) reframing the crisis into understandable terms and doable behaviors, and (5) problem solving (Regini, 2004). Even in the more classical type of hostage-taking incidents, negotiators can view the event as a crisis that has exceeded the subject's ability to cope; thus the name *crisis negotiator* more clearly identifies the CNT.

There are clearly defined roles on the CNT, and each member has to fulfill his or her mission for negotiations to be successful. At the minimum, a CNT should have five members. The primary negotiator talks to the actor. The primary is responsible for direct communications, gathering intelligence, and developing strategies and tactics for resolving the incident. The secondary negotiator is one of the most crucial roles on the CNT. The secondary is responsible for listening to communications with the actor (both sides) and helping plan what to say and the direction to take negotiations. The secondary is responsible for planning future conversations and helping establish a direction for negotiations. The MHC is part of the communication triad (team speaking with the actor) and is responsible for making assessments of the actor's mental state, emotional state, and potential for violence. The MHC also monitors stress levels among team members (all the CRT, not just negotiators) and helps develop negotiation strategies. The Intelligence Officer is responsible for gathering intelligence regarding the incident. Intelligence information about the actor, hostages, and victims is crucial to a successful resolution. In addition, the intelligence officer collects, analyzes, and disseminates intelligence regarding the physical layout of the scene, information related to the incident onset or dynamics, and any other information that may be needed and useful for incident command and tactical personnel. The team leader commands the CNT and provides a liaison with incident command and the tactical team. The team leader also assigns team roles (most CNTs are generic in that team members can fill most roles on the team), makes sure negotiations are progressing, ensures that team members are following accepted practices, and makes the initial decision on any demand issues, trades, or items to provide the actor (such as a cigarette, water, or other consumables).

Crisis incidents, whether hostage or barricade, go through clearly identifiable stages (McMains & Mullins, 2006, 2010). At the onset of the incident, the actor is in the crisis stage. The incident has just begun and emotions are high. When emotions are high, the ability to think and make rational decisions is low. The actor is operating on emotions (most generally anger, rage, and so forth). During this stage, the role of negotiations is to simply try and reduce emotions through the use of active listening skills. Rational decisions cannot be made during the crisis stage. Once emotions have calmed somewhat, the incident enters the accommodation/negotiation stage. Emotions are lowered, and decision making can occur. This is the stage where negotiations occur and the incident gets resolved. The final stage is the resolution stage, where the actor gives up and surrenders. This stage is almost as dangerous as the crisis stage, as the actor's emotions again rise (because they are surrendering to the police and coming out into the unknown). To help control these emotions, negotiators give very clear instructions and take great care to explain what will occur when the actor surrenders to the police.

The proper use of time as a negotiating tool is critical to the success of negotiations. Time can be used by the negotiators to reduce emotions, wear down the actor, and give the actor the opportunity to realize his best course of action is to cooperate with the police (actors will be referred to as *he* as almost all in the United States are male). For the CRT, time allows a tactical plan to be developed and put in place, and IC time to establish a command post, establish communications, and start making decisions. Negotiators usually make the use of time part of the negotiating strategy, often slowing an incident down (much to the frustration of other response elements), what Schlossberg (1979a) referred to as *dynamic inactivity*. What is crucial is not slowing and expanding the time factor, but properly managing time during the incident.

At the heart of the process is the handling of demand issues. Demands may be either instrumental or expressive (Bazan, 2009; Miron & Goldstein, 1979; Noesner & Webster, 1998).

Instrumental demands are tangible items like money, freedom, a car or plane to another country, visitation rights, and so on. Expressive demands are the unstated demands that negotiators sometimes have to intuit and are used by the actor to ventilate, reduce emotions, or try to establish power in the actor–negotiator relationship, or as a plea for recognition and attention (e.g., with borderline personalities). An instrumental demand may be appearing to win or save face. In some instances, the actor may be embarrassed or ashamed to state the demand. In a prison incident, for example, an inmate may demand to be transferred to another institution. He may claim he wants to be closer to family members. In truth, he may want to be moved to another cell or wing of the prison because he is tired of being sexually abused by a roommate. Without ultimately addressing and dealing with the expressive demands, an incident will not be successfully resolved (Borum & Strentz, 1992). The borderline personality may take hostages at the workplace and demand a promotion, more pay, better work hours, and so forth. The important issues, however, are likely what is not stated; the actor wants to be recognized for the work he is doing and receive attention by the bosses.

Negotiators will spend time discussing almost any demand issue. To the actor, when demands are given to negotiators, there are several conditions on those demands. First, the demands are not open to negotiations. To the actor, the demand(s) are the solution to his crisis. All the police are needed for is to provide the demand and end the crisis. Second, there is no room for compromise on demands. If the actor asks for an airplane, a helicopter is not an acceptable alternative. Third, demands have definitive time limits attached. The time limit itself is a demand. Fourth, there are consequences attached to each demand. If the actor does not get what he wants, he will harm hostages, victims, destroy property, or even harm himself. Negotiators generally ignore these conditions. The purpose of negotiating is to reduce demand issues to ones that are acceptable to both the actor and negotiators. Discussing a demand does not mean the actor will get the demand. An actor asking for a plane to another country does not mean the police are going to provide that transportation. But, by discussing the demand, negotiators can open the door to the discussion of many other and more relevant issues that will get the incident concluded. There are, however, some demands that are not going to be discussed (and the actor will usually be told those are not on the table) and time is not wasted talking about them. Weapons, illicit drugs, release of prisoners, and the exchange of hostages are demand issues that negotiators will not waste time on.

THE ROLE OF THE PSYCHOLOGIST ON THE CNT

The above discussion is a brief overview of the crisis incident response paradigm and negotiation process. It is not intended to be inclusive, but merely to provide a frame of reference for this chapter. Any psychologist (for the rest of the chapter, the psychologist will be referred to as the MHC) who joins a negotiating team should attend a basic negotiator school as well as ongoing training and advanced negotiation schools when possible. He or she should be familiar with the literature in the field of hostage/crisis negotiations, critical incident response, SWAT operations, and high-risk operations. Additionally, the MHC should be selected by the team and go through the same selection process as any team member. The MHC should also take part in team activities; training, exercises, and qualifications. One of the worst things the MHC can do is show up just for callouts. Crisis negotiations is a team effort. If the MHC is going to be a team member, it is critical they be a *team* member.

The MHC is an integral part of a CNT and can bring a variety of knowledge, skills, and abilities to the team; assist the team in many areas; and be a valuable resource for not only the negotiating team but also the CRT as a whole (FBI, 1993; Fuselier, 1986, 1988; McMains & Mullins, 2006, 2010). It is important to stress that the MHC is only one piece of a much larger component. The MHC can bring a wide variety of benefits to the CNT, not only during a crisis incident but at other times as well.

The MHC at a Crisis Incident

On negotiating teams, the MHC is the only specialized function. Because of the MHC's training, education, and background, they serve a specialized role. The MHC should not be the primary or secondary negotiator, nor the intelligence officer, equipment manager, team leader, or any other role on the CNT. The MHC's most valuable role is to utilize expertise in making mental health and risk assessments of the actor, hostages, victims, and any others involved in an incident (Hatcher et al., 1998).

In regard to the actor, the primary role of the MHC is to make personality and mental illness assessments. In the past, it was common to type actors according to personality style. Hostage takers were generally considered paranoid schizophrenics, manic-depressed psychotics, inadequate (dependent) personality types, and antisocial personalities. Recently, the field has moved away from making those types of absolute assessments. Most personality and behavioral disorders are on a continuum and usually involve more than one specific type of disorder. For example, an antisocial personality may also exhibit paranoid or narcissistic characteristics. Rather than make a personality assessment by category, the MHC today makes a more dynamic personality assessment and makes communication and behavioral recommendations to the primary and secondary negotiator based on that assessment. That is, instead of labeling an actor as antisocial, the MHC may recommend that the negotiators avoid talking about the actor's ex-spouse because it will likely elevate anger and rage, but instead to focus on the actor's children. The end result is the same; the path to that result is different.

Making assessments of emotionally disturbed individuals is a critical function for the MHC. Most incidents negotiators respond to involve emotionally disturbed actors (Butler, Leitenberg, & Fuselier, 1993; Head, 1990; Strentz, 1985). Some research has found that 52–85% of hostage incidents can involve emotionally disturbed actors (Austin Police Department, 1991; Fuselier, 1981). In 2005, HOBAS data (reported in McMains & Mullins, 2006) found that nationally, almost 20% of all hostage incidents involved actors who had been in treatment, were in therapy, or had been committed in the past to a psychiatric treatment facility. In 2001, Feldman reported that 94% of the 120 incidents reviewed involved emotionally disturbed actors.

The MHC should also assist in ongoing risk assessments. During any incident, risk varies with time (McMains & Mullins, 2010). Risk can increase just as it decreases. Previously, the stages of an incident were described. Incidents do not always move linearly through those stages. During the course of an incident, stages will vacillate as does the risk of violence. For example, a negotiator could convince an actor to surrender. When the actor exits the location, he sees something he was not expecting, rushes back into the location, and re-enters the crisis stage. Some actors (maybe because of drug or alcohol consumption) will vacillate between emotion and reason for long periods of time. One of the authors was involved in an incident where the actor talked calmly for long stretches of time and then, without warning, went off on an emotional tangent. This roller-coaster lasted for several hours, until finally the actor tired and walked out (also entirely unexpected).

In addition to the overall risk assessment, the MHC should conduct ongoing emotional, behavioral, and cognitive assessments of the participants (McMains & Mullins, 2010). These should be included as part of the global risk assessment, but may require independent assessments and recommendations by the MHC. For example, the MHC may do a risk assessment and conclude the actor is acting rationally and negotiations should proceed in the direction they are going, but miss in the cognitive assessment that the negotiator is using language the actor cannot understand, and frustration is building beneath the surface. Further, negotiations may proceed for several hours, and the CNT thinks they are making progress until the actor unexpectedly fires a shot at the police. In a later debriefing of the actor, the actor reveals that he spent several hours listening to the negotiator and, not understanding most of what was said, he "exploded." In other instances, an actor's affect may be extremely influenced by drug or alcohol usage, and there is a seeming disconnect between affect and behavior. So, while the risk assessment is the overall assessment of potential for violence, separate assessments of emotions, behavior, and cognition can add to the overall evaluation of the actor (and/or hostages, victims, and so on).

Because of personality disorders, mental illness, brain injury, developmental disorders, drug/alcohol abuse, poor learning history, and so on, actors in crisis (and in a crisis incident) are somewhat unpredictable and prone to violent emotional outbursts. The actor has created a crisis incident because he does not know how to cope and adapt to events in his life. The MHC can provide an invaluable service in giving the negotiator strategies for coping and adapting to the current crisis. And this is the primary reason the MHC should not be the primary negotiator. The objective is to resolve the immediate crisis, not provide counseling for the actor's long-term issues. A crisis incident is neither therapy nor the forum to get into discussions regarding the actor's long-term problems. The CNT is present to resolve the immediate crisis and get the actor removed to some other environment.

The MHC has a critical role when the CNT is negotiating with high-risk suicides and/or suicide-by-cop actors. The expertise of the MHC is vital to helping the CNT resolve suicide situations. Generally, the MHC has much more training and expertise in dealing with suicidal actors than do other members of the CNT. The MHC should take an active role in working directly with the primary negotiator to mitigate the suicide risk. Negotiating with a potential suicide requires active negotiations with little "off-phone" time. Lanceley (1999) has suggested that with suicide actors, negotiators should use active listening to explore emotions, allow the actor to vent, focus on the cause of the actor's problem, discuss the reality of death with the actor, disrupt the actor's plan as they describe the plan to the negotiator, explore with the actor meaningful things in the actor's life, use time to stall the actor's plan, and select an alternative that meets the actor's immediate goals.

A much more dangerous type of incident for negotiators is the suicide-by-cop actor. This is the person who is afraid (for whatever reason) to commit suicide and is going to provoke the police to kill him. In addition to being suicidal, these actors can be violent and aggressive (VanZandt, 1993). In fact, in officer shooting incidents, the rate of suicide-by-cop cases may be much higher that anyone would have thought (Mohandie & Meloy, 2000). Pre-incident, the MHC can assist the CNT in developing a suicide assessment checklist for evaluating and assessing risk and suicide-by-cop potential. One example of such a checklist can be found in McMains and Mullins (2006). During the incident, the MHC can keep the team focused on the risk factors for suicide-by-cop and help develop strategies and tactics to reduce those risk factors.

The MHC should also provide ongoing evaluations of hostages and victims. Most people do not receive training in how to act as a hostage, and being taken hostage may overwhelm them (McMains & Mullins, 2006). Hostages have been injured or killed because they act in inappropriate ways. A hostage may argue with their captor; may engage in philosophical/religious/political debates with the actor; may refuse to believe the incident is occurring and try to leave (and get injured or killed); or may become overly complaint and bring attention to themselves in the eyes of the hostage taker because of their tendency to "suck up" to the hostage taker. The MHC should be making ongoing assessments of hostage behavior, and if necessary, give suggestions to the primary negotiator for speaking with hostages. If, for example, a hostage is overly compliant (i.e., using "yes sir/no sir" every time the hostage taker says something, or obeying orders from the hostage taker in a rapid manner, faster and more docile than any other hostage) and being noticed by the actor, the negotiator could ask to speak to the hostage and tell the hostage to sit in the corner and be absolutely still and quiet. Part of the responsibility of the MHC is to bring hostage behavior to the attention of the negotiator and then offer suggestions on how that behavior can be altered to be more conducive to survival. Most people rely on past behavior in an attempt to adapt and cope to the hostage situation. The MHC must be part of the intelligence-gathering process and use intelligence to understand how hostages/victims responded to stress and uncertainty in the past, and use that information to predict how the hostage/victim may act in the current incident, and then give suggestions to the

ator for helping control hostage/victim behavior so they do not do something inap-
injured or killed.

≥ empirical data regarding hostage behavior. Though widely known, the Stockholm
not occur frequently, and little systematic research exists on the phenomenon. Most
on hostage behavior comes from ex-POW research. Tom Strentz (retired FBI crisis negotiator) did some excellent work on hostage behavior and was able to classify hostages as either
survivors or succumbers (Strentz, 1982, 1984; Strentz & Auerback, 1988). While there is not room
in this chapter to more completely identify differences between survivors and succumbers, Table
16.1 provides a general breakdown of the known differences. The MHC should be familiar with
these differences and then assist the primary or secondary in using communication skills to adjust
hostage behavior as needed.

There is also not much known about victim behavior, such as might occur in barricade situations involving family members. In such cases, the MHC has to understand the dynamics of prior
relationships. Crisis incidents do not occur in a vacuum. The MHC has to work with the intelligence
officer in learning as much as possible about the relationships and interactions of all involved. In
domestically motivated situations involving custody issues, the MHC could, for example, suggest
to a negotiator that he or she recommend to the actor that the children could live with the maternal
grandmother while a custody agreement is being redrafted. Without proper intelligence, the MHC
could unwittingly be elevating the risk to the children and actor. In this instance, for example, what
if the maternal grandmother is the reason the other spouse left with the children?

The MHC should make recommendations concerning communications between the primary
negotiator and the actor. The MHC, like the secondary negotiator, is part of the team effort in communicating with the actor. Questions to ask, statements that can calm emotions, the direction for
future communications, and phrasing and specific words to use or avoid are all part of the MHC's
responsibility. Reminding of and giving suggestions for using active listening skills are also part of
the communication process and one the MHC should be involved with. Often, during the heat of

---

TABLE 16.1

Difference Between Hostage Survivors and Succumbers as Identified by Dr. Thomas Strentz

Survivors	Succumbers
Fit/blend in with other hostages	Do things to stand apart from others
Avoid being a leader	Want/try to lead
Contain and hide negative feelings toward captors	Show negative feelings toward captors
Avoid political, religious, hostile language	Debate and use hostile language
Concentrate on survival	Concentrate on retaliation
Control emotions and behaviors	Do not control emotions/behavior and raise everyone's attention toward them
Confident and have good self-esteem	Afraid and anxious
Keep positive mental attitude and faith in rescuers	Feel forgotten by outside world
Use positive defense mechanisms	Use negative defense mechanisms
Establish and keep routines	Do not have any routines
Affiliate with other hostages	Loners that keep to themselves
Accept and adjust to fate	Engage in constant second-guessing
Use humor and imagery	Focus on seriousness/morbidity

Source: Based on Strentz, T., The Stockholm syndrome: Law enforcement policy and hostage behavior, in F. M.
Ochberg & D. A. Soskis (Eds.), *Victims of terrorism* (pp. 149–164), Westview Press, Boulder, CO, 1982; Strentz, T.,
Preparing the person with high potential for victimization as a hostage, in J. T. Turner (Ed.), *Violence in the medical
care setting: A survival guide* (pp. 183–208), Aspen Press, Rockville, MD, 1984.

negotiations, communicators can forget to use active listening skills (Ware, 2009). The MHC should pay attention to the communicators and be alert to active listening skills not being used. By knowing and understanding what active listening skills are, the MHC can assess if they are being correctly used. Active listening skills typically used by negotiators, include effective/extended pauses, I-messages, minimal encouragers, paraphrasing, reflected feelings (or mirroring), reflecting meaning (or emotional labeling), and summative reflection (Bolton, 1984).

The MHC can also be part of the intelligence-gathering, collation, and dissemination process. Crisis negotiations are, at heart, about changing behavior. Gathering appropriate intelligence can help accomplish behavioral change. Intelligence also allows the CNT to understand the actor's motivation, predict the risk posed to others, and predict the risk the actor poses to himself (McMains & Mullins, 2006). Understanding the total context of the incident is critical for accomplishing this task. In addition to gathering, collating, and disseminating information, intelligence officers have to assess the credibility of the source of the information they gather. An assessment has to be made regarding the relevance of that intelligence and deductions made from available intelligence that are helpful in planning the management of the incident. The MHC can assist in all of these processes, but especially in evaluating credibility of the source. Their training and experience in interviewing people should translate to the crisis incident. By virtue of such training, the MHC can obtain intelligence information that others may not ask for. For example, the intelligence officer may ask about drug abuse, multiple drug use, when and how often the actor uses drugs, and so on. The MHC may also ask about behavioral changes as a function of dose level. The intelligence officer may ask an available family member about relationship dynamics while the MHC asks about initiator behaviors or emotions. If the incident is protracted (or in the case of a prison incident, becomes a siege, a long-term protracted incident that can last several days or weeks), the MHC can help in the development of negotiator position papers. These position papers are summaries of events to date in the incident. They summarize gathered intelligence, situation boards, and communications with the actor. Dalfonzo (2003) recommends one be completed after each conversation with the actor.

Part of the responsibility of the MHC is to make stress assessments of all participants, actors, hostages, negotiators, and all members of the CRT. The MHC should be an expert in stress and stress-related issues. The MHC is responsible for monitoring stress in the participants and helping provide strategies to manage stress. For the actor and hostages, this can be accomplished through communication patterns or direct statements (e.g., "Tell him to take two deep breaths!"). For members of the CNT or CRT, it may be through performing short exercises or reminders of what they learned in training (a later section talks about training responsibilities of the MHC). Earlier in this chapter, time as a tool was discussed, and the benefits of using time were identified. Time also has some negative effects. For the actor, with the passage of time, there is a "creeping-up" effect, where the walls (i.e., the tactical team) appear to be closing in. This creeping-up effect may elevate emotions and make the actor more prone to use violence. As the actor gets fatigued, he may also become more emotional. The passage of time makes the response team fatigued as well. Decision making and performance suffer. A tired incident commander may make decisions based more on his or her fatigue than on situational dynamics. As is the case with fatigue, a tactical sniper lying in a Ghilli Suit (a type of full-body camouflage clothing) for several hours in a south Texas summer (100+ degrees) will experience decreased performance.

A crisis incident is a high-stress event by definition. Situational factors may worsen the stress for the CRT. What if the actor or hostage is a fellow police officer, or a family member of a police officer or someone on the CRT? What if children are involved? What if it is a high-profile event with a lot of media present? Or in a public venue such as an apartment complex with a lot of bystanders that cannot be evacuated? It is the responsibility of the MHC to monitor these situational factors and recommend strategies and tactics for mitigating their stress effects.

The MHC may be asked for input into decisions being considered by the team leader or incident commander. And it must be remembered it is just that: *input*. The authors have known MHCs who took it personally when their input was not acted on. The input of the MHC in not necessarily more or less valuable than the input of any other member of the CRT or CNT. A skilled team leader and incident commander will maximize input before making a decision. The input of the MHC is one piece of a much larger puzzle, not more or less valuable than anyone else's. If the MHC disagrees with a decision, that disagreement must be ignored until after the incident is resolved. There will be a time and place to discuss disagreements—during an incident is neither the time nor the place. At times, the decision may involve a tactical resolution (either assault or sniper). At that point, the MHC should work with the primary and secondary negotiator and engage in tactical negotiations, doing everything possible to assist the tactical team in accomplishing its mission.

When a crisis incident is resolved, the work of the MHC is not finished. Most CRTs and CNTs will hold a series of operational and emotional debriefings. The operational debriefings are designed to review the facts of what members of the CRT did or did not do, evaluate their performance and discuss decision making. These are part of the best practices developed in the field (Kidd, 2005). The emotional debriefing is designed to evaluate and begin resolving any emotional reactions team members had to what may or may not have occurred during the incident. If hostages were killed, children injured or sexually assaulted, a police officer killed or injured, or other participants or citizens injured or killed, an emotional debriefing can begin the healing process and reduce stress/PTSD.

Most teams hold a series of debriefings. After every incident, the CRT should conduct an operational debriefing with all response personnel. A critical component of this general debriefing is to not only assess actions and decision making, but also to discuss intrateam communication issues. For example, did intelligence information gathered by negotiators make it to the tactical team? Did the tactical team have time to prepare and implement a plan to give the actor food? All facets of the response effort have to be critically analyzed with all brass taken off (all members must have equal rank and be able to freely speak). One of the things the authors have observed over the years is a tendency of CRTs to pat themselves on the back for a job well done when an incident is successfully resolved, without critically evaluating their performance. Over time, little mistakes become big mistakes, or even critical errors that lead to someone getting killed. Then everyone tends to wonder what went wrong.

Following this briefing (and sometimes a few days later), each response component will brief their team performance. Incident command, tactical unit, and CNT will conduct independent briefings to evaluate their own team performance. The objective of this debriefing is the same as the more general debriefing. In both debriefings, the primary role of the MHC, in addition to evaluating their own performance, is to make sure an accurate assessment of performance is presented and not a glad handing. Granted, the MHC is a participant, not a leader, but he or she must still keep an objective ear tuned to the debriefings being an accurate and objective evaluation.

If an emotional debriefing is necessary, the MHC should take a lead role. This is, in fact, a point of expertise for the MHC. There may be occasions when the MHC is "too close to the action," and it may be necessary to bring in an outside psychologist to conduct the emotional debriefing. The primary purpose of this debriefing is to begin normalizing the team's emotional reaction and stop any second-guessing that may occur. The emotional debriefing is not therapy, but the MHC may see if there is a need for actual longer-term therapeutic interventions. In this case, the MHC should arrange to provide counseling services or arrange counseling with an outside counselor. The authors recommend an outside counselor or psychologist for such services.

As part of after-incident activities, the MHC may also arrange to interview the actor, hostages, victims, and other participants in order to improve future callouts. Using their background in mental health, the MHC can do a lot to prevent the negative after-effects of captivity on ex-hostages and ex-victims and even possibly prevent the onset of PTSD in some (McMains & Mullins, 2006).

One tremendous hole in our understanding regarding the long-term effects of having been taken hostage in a criminal incident is the lack of follow-up to crisis incidents using structured interviews with actors and ex-hostages. There is virtually no literature dealing with ex-hostage takers. And what little that has been done is not generalizable enough to be of practical value to police CNTs. Follow-up interviews and research with hostage takers, barricade subjects, and other actors would be valuable for CNTs and help increase success rates. The MHC is the ideal person to conduct this research because of their background in social science research methodology and statistics.

TEAM MEMBER SELECTION

Most psychologists working for or with police agencies have done preselection evaluations and may even have done evaluations for officers selected for special operation units, using standardized, clinically based, psychological testing instruments. It is common practice to do psychological evaluations for tactical team members. Many departments do them for negotiators as well. Fewer still do evaluations for incident commanders. That is one selection role for the MHC, although the authors do not believe psychological evaluations using testing instruments are necessary for negotiators or incident command staff. We do agree with the practice of evaluating potential tactical team members, however, because they provide important information on issues like self-control, impulse control, and anger management

Without using clinical testing the MHC can assume a critical role in helping develop a standardized selection sequence for team members. Using technology from organizational psychology, the MHC can do a mini-job analysis and identify the relevant knowledge, skills, and abilities (KSAs) for each role on the CRT and CNT. They can then develop standardized testing and scoring procedures for the selection process can help validate those procedures, train existing team members in their use, and then guide the team through the selection cycle.

For negotiators, some of the critical KSAs include communication ability, ability to listen, ability to manage stress, ability to work in a team, knowledge of police procedures and penal code (including any relevant Codes of Criminal Procedure or Family Codes), temperament, ability to adapt to a variety of situations, ability to control emotions, and ability to think and make decisions (Mullins, 2000, 2001, 2003). Additionally, the ability to empathize and gather intelligence is important attributes for negotiators. Some teams may have to assess an applicant's physical skills (Hogewood, 2005) because of the area they operate in or type of agency they are with. Logan (2004) found also that dealing with the public, good self-image, sensitivity to others, level of arousal, sense of morality, emphasis on cooperation versus manipulation, resourcefulness, maturity, mental agility, and intelligence were important KSAs for negotiators.

A generic negotiator selection sequence may be as follows:

1. Post an announcement asking for volunteers (and all members of the CRT should be volunteers) and outlining the job responsibilities. It should be clear that callouts can come at any time and team members will be on 24-hour call cycles. The authors have seen excellent candidates drop out of the pool because of the callout requirements.
2. Obtain a letter of recommendation from the applicant's supervisor. Less a letter of recommendation, this is more of a method of gaining a supervisor's approval for the candidate's membership on the team. Later when the team member is called out and taken away from his or regular duties, the supervisor cannot prohibit the person from the callout (which has been known to happen). Some teams even require a letter of support from the chief, director, or warden.
3. Interview with the team leader. This should be a structured interview that is scored by the team leader. Part of the purpose of this interview is to more fully explain the requirements of being on the negotiating team, callout schedule, and training requirements, and to assess the applicant's attitude toward being in the background and out of the spotlight. The authors have known of applicants that withdrew after this interview because they did not want to be away from home for a week or two at a time for training.

4. Team interview. This is a second structured interview conducted by team members (partial or full team) and the questions should be more job specific. For example, one question may be "Identify (without using names) a coworker you do not like or get along with and describe what you do to work effectively with that person?" The team should also evaluate how well the applicant fits in with the team (subjective, but can be scored). The team will operate in confined spaces under highly charged and stressful situations, so they must be able to get along with each other.

5. Scenario. The applicants should be put through a basic telephone scenario and evaluated on the relevant KSAs. They should not be evaluated on what they will be taught in training, but rather a basic level of proficiency or general ability. That is, applicants should not be scored on specific active listening skills, but their general ability to listen to and pay attention to what an actor is telling them.

The MHC can perform the same function for Incident Command staff and the tactical team. For the tactical team, the MHC may also perform fitness for duty evaluations on a periodic basis.

Team Training

It has already been stated that the MHC should go through the same training regimen as any team member (basic, advanced, ongoing). But the MHC can also be a valuable resource in conducting training. After going through advanced training and being on the team for a period of time, the MHC can conduct or lead basic training negotiation schools. The standard basic training is 40 hours (although some agencies conduct 80-hour schools). The MHC can take a lead role in training, facilitating other instructors, and writing curricula.

The MHC can conduct advanced and ongoing negotiator training in a variety of topics. Much of the training and education the MHC received is relevant and can easily be translated into training for negotiators. The authors have conducted negotiator training in courses as varied as psychopathology, social psychology, depression and suicide, domestic violence, organizational behavior modification, classic Skinnerian behavior modification, communication skills, team building, and developmental psychology, along with the more standard negotiator topics. In addition to conducting this training, the MHC can be a facilitator, finding other subject matter experts to come in and teach courses. Training courses can range from a couple of hours to a week, and utilize persons who work in women's centers, on suicide hotlines, at financial institutions, and at drug/alcohol counseling centers. Some of these trainers can be medical personnel and others relevant to the negotiation environment. There are, in fact, very few topics that cannot be translated into relevancy for negotiators.

The MHC can conduct or facilitate monthly, quarterly, semiannual, or annual team training days. There are many group exercises that can be done to facilitate communication skills, active listening skills, team building, and group dynamics. Two specific exercises the MHC could lead are the Fish Bowl and Round Table exercises. Both are designed to improve communication skills. The Fish Bowl is used to help improve active listening skills. Two team members sit back-to-back. One is the negotiator, the other the actor. The rest of the team sits in a circle around the two players. The actor is assigned a role to play, and when some signal is given the negotiator and actor to begin negotiating. The negotiator cannot problem-solve, and must only use active listening skills. Team members stop the negotiator if he or she engages in problem solving, while writing down all the active listening techniques utilized. After 15–20 minutes, the exercise is halted and the active listening skills discussed. In the Round Table exercise, negotiators are given paper and write a response to a variety of statements an actor may make during negotiations. For example, the exercise leader may say, "If my boss doesn't quit hounding me, I'm going to kill him!" Each team member writes down the first response that comes to mind. After a series of statements are read (usually about ten), the team discusses their responses to each statement. What this exercise accomplishes is to build a response repertoire to a wide variety of statements an actor could make during an actual incident.

The MHC can build and facilitate team-building exercises that can be anything from classroom projects to field exercises. The MHC can develop a series of group projects or exercises designed to increase group cohesion, reduce group tension, and improve intergroup communications. One author was instrumental in helping his team acquire a negotiation vehicle. The vehicle was a very used school bus, and one of the conditions for getting it was that the team would do the majority of the work in bringing it up to speed as a negotiator vehicle. Over a year later, after the team had gutted and rebuilt the interior, updated the electronics, and installed new electronic and lighting systems, sanded and painted the exterior, and completed thousands of other little tasks, the school bus had been transformed into a negotiation vehicle. The team did almost 100% of all work. An unexpected side benefit that no one anticipated was how building the bus became a tremendous team-building exercise.

Finally, the MHC can build, script, and manage role-playing exercises. Some of these exercises should be negotiator specific; others should involve the entire CRT. It is recommended that at least once every 2 years, a major exercise be performed that involves the CRT, department as a whole, other response elements such as utility companies, neighboring agencies, the Red Cross, EMTs, and others relevant (such as school administrators and teachers for a school situation). Role-play exercises serve several benefits for the CNT. These exercises help develop team functioning, improve individual skills, identify areas of weakness for future training, help reduce stress in real incidents, and allow for the correction of critical mistakes with no fear of injury or death.

Exercises can replicate a variety of situations and environments. They can be face-to-face, voice-to-voice, or utilize a team's equipment. Virtually any eventuality can be trained for. The level of detail can be tailored to the specific exercise. For example, a prison scenario would require a much higher level of detail than would a domestic disturbance. The MHC should be able to not only script an exercise but also develop the necessary dossiers on actors and hostages, including psychological and personality profiles to fit the scenario. One of the problems with scenario training the authors have observed over the years is a disconnect between the actor's role and their personality. For example, a retired police chief who was going to assist his terminal spouse in suicide was acted as an antisocial personality, screaming and shouting at the negotiators—totally out of character for the scripted role. The MHC can also develop a full motivation and adjust the emotions and behavioral risk based upon those motivations.

The MHC should clearly establish the goals of the exercise; identify the negotiation and crisis intervention skills needed to resolve the scenario; complete all personality profiles of the actors, hostages, victims, and so on; develop characters that will provide realistic intelligence; and include information for risk, behavioral, personality, and cognitive profiling. Role-play training without clearly defined roles, characters, actions, and so forth is worse than no training at all (Burrows, 2004; Maher, 2004; Mullins, 2001, 2003). In addition to character development, the environment for the exercise should be included. The exercise should realistically follow the progression of stages present in a real incident (crisis, accommodation/negotiation, and resolution).

The MHC should be responsible for training the actors and then being present to control the actor's during the exercise. Actors left alone will seldom follow the script, but will instead go where they want. For the past 20 years, the authors have hosted an annual hostage negotiation competition at Texas State University in San Marcos. Lasting a total of 3 days, up to 20 negotiating teams at a time are negotiating a standardized problem. All of the actors are located in a single room. The actors spend at least 1 day in training, are heavily scripted, and practice their role. In addition, during the competition, three to five *controllers* (at least one experienced negotiator, a psychologist, and one person who is not a negotiator) are present with the actors to assist them and keep them on script. Even with that level of oversight, every year at least one actor goes off script and does things completely contrary to their role.

It is a good idea in the middle of the exercise to stop and evaluate/critique performance. At the conclusion of the exercise, full debriefings should be conducted. All personnel should take part in an operational debriefing, each team should conduct an operational debriefing, and then (for practice) the MHC should facilitate an emotional debriefing.

The MHC can facilitate and conduct training that focuses on case studies. Case studies can be used to teach or reinforce specific points, be used to teach critical evaluation skills to assess CNT actions, and reverse unfavorable trends (Howard, 2003). Selecting to review incidents that were successfully resolved is just as important as studying incidents that were not successfully resolved or where lives were lost.

The MHC can facilitate regional training for CNTs. In many localities, CNTs will support and back up each other. If called, a county sheriff team will back up the city police team, and vice versa. Neighboring agencies will likely have MOUs (Memorandums of Understanding) in place that outline the specific support roles, command issues, finances, and so on they will provide one another, if needed. These teams need to train and work together prior to an actual incident. The MHC can use their skills and training to facilitate team building and group processes.

Other CNT and MHC Activities

Resolving crisis incidents are what negotiators are trained for. There are a variety of other activities suited to negotiator involvement, and the MHC can take a lead role in guiding the negotiating team in these arenas. One valuable service negotiators can provide is conducting debriefings for persons involved in other crisis/disaster incidents. One author took his team to the scene of a mass drowning and conducted emotional debriefings for the rescue workers. Hurricanes, tornadoes, and other natural disasters are situations in which negotiators can provide a valuable service in debriefing victims. Negotiators can also debrief rescue workers, good Samaritans, and others who assist survivors at the scene of manmade disasters such as plane crashes caused by human error, terrorist incidents, fires, and so on. The MHC can take a lead in training negotiators for conducting debriefings, facilitating debriefings, providing assistance to negotiators conducting debriefings, and coordinating the conduct of emotional debriefings.

The MHC can take the lead in preparing training and seminars on workplace and school violence issues. The MHC can develop curricula for such courses, train negotiators to conduct seminars, schedule training, and conduct training evaluations. The MHC can develop risk assessment instruments for schools and workplaces and then help train those personnel to accurately use the instruments. In a similar vein, the MHC can take the lead in stalking situations. The MHC can develop a protocol which negotiators can use when talking to and counseling stalking victims. They can also interview stalkers and prepare to negotiate with stalkers.

The MHC can assist the CNT in developing intelligence files on potential actors the team may have to deal with in the future. There are identifiable individuals in the community who can be predicted to engage in a negotiated incident. Intelligence files can be developed and prepared, and the CNT can be briefed and strategies developed for negotiating with such individuals. Risk, behavioral, emotional, and cognitive assessments can be completed and stored; intelligence sources identified; and potential locations identified (such as the actor's house or workplace) and plans developed for a CRT and CNT response. When doing pre-incident workups on individuals, check first with your investigative and legal sections to make sure you follow local laws governing such activities. In some jurisdictions, it is illegal for the police to keep intelligence files on persons who have not committed a crime.

The MHC can also arrange for the team to tour facilities that may have a hostage/barricade incident. For example, the local jurisdiction may have a state or federal penitentiary/prison and that facility does not have a negotiating team. It may be the case that the facility has an MOU with the local police agency to provide CRT or CNT services. In January 2004, Lewis Prison in Arizona was the site of a hostage taking where two inmates took two correctional officers hostage in a control tower. It was physically impossible for a tactical team to assault the tower fast enough to prevent the hostage takers from killing the correctional officers. The prison was forced to negotiate with the inmates. The only problem was the prison did not have a negotiating team. Instead, police negotiators from local jurisdictions were tasked with negotiating the incident. Lasting 15 days, over 10 agencies, 30 primary negotiators, and more than 60 other police negotiators were involved in the process. A vast amount of time was spent by the police negotiators becoming familiar with the prison environment, prison/inmate issues, differences (police vs. prison) in responding to demands, chain of command issues, and other aspects of the prison environment that was unique. It was time that could have been better spent by the CNT in trying to free the hostages and resolve the incident (as a side note, the incident was successfully resolved: both hostages were released, and the inmates surrendered). Having familiarity with the facility prior to an incident will help increase the odds of success, be it a prison, factory, school, government building, and so on.

SUMMARY

As has been shown, there are a wide variety and diversity of tasks the MHC can perform as an active member of the CNT. Responsibilities are not just limited to assistance during an incident. There are plenty of tasks and roles for the MHC prior to an incident including selecting team members, training, pre-incident assessments, and intelligence preparation. During an incident, the role of the MHC is as important as that of any other team member. Depending on the dynamics of the situation, the MHC has very specific tasks to perform and roles to fill. Unlike other team members, the MHC is a specialized role. While other team members can be assigned to virtually any team role, the MHC is always an MHC, regardless of the type of incident. After the crisis has been resolved and the actor is in custody or in the hospital, the MHC has additional duties. After an incident that has been successfully resolved, the MHC should take part in any operational debriefings as does any other team member. If there were injuries or deaths, the MHC should facilitate the emotional debriefings. This may also mean that the MHC finds another psychologist to conduct those debriefings. The MHC may also have to arrange for long-term treatment.

MHCs need to take a more active role in researching hostage and barricade incidents. Much of what we know about the process of negotiations is best practices by virtue of many teams engaging in the same or similar processes. But are these processes really best practices? We do not know the answer because the research has not been done. The MHC is the proper team member to conduct this research. The MHC should also be involved in research involving actor, hostage and victim issues. As pointed out, much of what we know about the behavioral dynamics in critical incidents comes from the POW literature. While there is some transfer of knowledge, there is much still to be done before we can truly understand actor, hostage, and victim behavior and improve the success rate to even greater rates.

REFERENCES

American Heritage Dictionary. (1980). New York: Houghton Mifflin.

Austin Police Department. (1991, September). *Communication skills*. Presented at SAPD Basic Hostage Negotiation School, San Antonio, TX.

Bazan, V. (2009, January). *Negotiating issues*. Seminar at the 19th Annual Hostage Negotiation Seminar, Texas State University, San Marcos, TX.

Bolton, R. (1984). *People skills*. Englewood Cliffs, NJ: Prentice-Hall.

Borum, R., & Strentz, T. (1992). The borderline personality: Negotiating strategies. *FBI Law Enforcement Bulletin, 61*, 6–10.

Burrows, S. (2004, November). *Negotiator team training*. Presentation at the Annual Convention of the Texas Association of Hostage Negotiators, Austin, TX.

Butler, W. M., Leitenberg, J. H., & Fuselier, G. D. (1993). The use of mental health professional consultants to police hostage negotiation teams. *Behavioral Science and the Law, 11*, 212–221.

Dalfonzo, V. A. (2003). Negotiation position papers: A tool for negotiators. *FBI Law Enforcement Bulletin*, *72*(10), 18–24.

Dubina, J. (2005, June). *Lewis prison hostage-taking incident*. Presentation at the Arkansas Association of Hostage Negotiators Annual Conference. Little Rock, AR.

Dubina, J., & Ragsdale, R. (2005, April). *Lewis prison incident debriefing*. Presentation at the Annual Crisis Negotiation Conference of the National Tactical Officers Association, Nashville, TN.

Federal Bureau of Investigation. (1993, Spring). Advanced Hostage Negotiation Seminar, San Antonio, TX.

Feldman, T. B. (2001). Characteristics of hostage and barricaded incidents: Implications for negotiation strategies and training. *International Journal of Police Negotiations and Crisis Management*, *1*(1), 1–15.

Fuselier, D. (1981). A practical overview of hostage negotiations. *FBI Law Enforcement Bulletin*, *50*(6), 1–11.

Fuselier, D. (1986). What every negotiator would like his chief to know. *FBI Law Enforcement Bulletin*, *55*, 12–15.

Fuselier, D. (1988). Hostage negotiation MHC: Emerging role for the clinical psychologist. *Professional Psychology: Research and Practice*, *19*, 175–179.

Goldaber, I. (1983, September). *Hostage rescue operations*. Presentation at the International Chiefs of Police Seminar, San Antonio, TX.

Hassel, C. V. (1975). The hostage situation: Exploring the motivation and cause. *The Police Chief*, *42*, 55–58.

Hatcher, C., Mohandie, K., Turner, J., & Gelles, M. (1998). The role of the psychologist in crisis/hostage negotiations. *Behavioral Science and the Law*, *16*(4), 455–472.

Head, W. B. (1990). The history response: An examination of U.S. law enforcement practices concerning hostage incidents. (Doctoral dissertation, State University of New York at Albany). *Dissertation Abstracts International*: *50*:4111A.

Hoff, L. E. (1989). *People in crisis: Understanding and helping*. Menlo Park, CA: Addison-Wesley.

Hogewood, W. (2005). AFT's SRT negotiation team. *NTOA Crisis Negotiator Journal*, *5*, 1–3.

Howard, L. M. (2003, November). *Effective techniques for teaching crisis negotiations*. Presentation at the Annual Convention of the Texas Association of Hostage Negotiators, Addison, TX.

Kidd, W. (2005, August). *Peak performance: "Best standards" for negotiators/CNT*. Presentation at the Kansas Association of Hostage Negotiators, Olathe, KS.

Lanceley, F. (1999). *On-scene guide for crisis negotiators*. Boca Raton, FL: CRC Press.

Logan, M. (2004). Selection and training of crisis negotiators in policing. *Crisis Negotiator Journal*, *3*(2), 5–7.

Maher, J. R. (2004). Role-play training for negotiators in diverse environments. *FBI Law Enforcement Bulletin*, *73*(6), 10–12.

McMains, M. J., & Mullins, W. C. (2006). *Crisis negotiations: Managing critical incidents and hostage situations in law enforcement and corrections* (3rd ed). Albany, NY: Anderson/LexisNexis.

McMains M. J., & Mullins, W. C. (2010). *Crisis negotiations: Managing critical incidents and hostage situations in law enforcement and corrections* (4th ed.). Albany, NY: Anderson/LexisNexis.

Miron, M. S., & Goldstein, A. P. (1979). *Hostage*. New York: Pergamon.

Mohandie, K., & Meloy, J. R. (2000). Clinical and forensic indicators of "suicide-by-cop." *Journal of Forensic Sciences*, *45*, 384–389.

Mullins, W. C. (2000, November). *Hostage negotiator team formation and selection*. Presentation at the Annual Convention of the Texas Association of Hostage Negotiators, San Antonio, TX.

Mullins, W. C. (2001, January). *Negotiator team selection*. Seminar at the 9th Annual Hostage Negotiation Competition, Texas State University, San Marcos, TX.

Mullins, W. C. (2003, January). *Negotiator practices: Results of a survey assessing selection practices*. Seminar at the 13th Annual Hostage Negotiation Competition, Texas State University, San Marcos, TX.

Noesner, G. (1999). Negotiation concepts for commanders. *FBI Law Enforcement Bulletin*, *68*, 6–14.

Noesner, G., & Webster, M. (1998). Crisis negotiations as crisis intervention. In Crisis Negotiation Unit (Ed.), *Crisis negotiations: A compendium* (pp. 3–19). Quantico, VA: Critical Incident Response Group, FBI Academy.

Null, S. (2001, January). *Team training issues*. Seminar at the 11th Annual Hostage Negotiation Competition, Texas State University, San Marcos, TX.

Regini, C. (2004). Crisis intervention for law enforcement negotiators. *FBI Law Enforcement Bulletin*, *73*(10), 1–4.

Schlossberg, H. (1979a). *Hostage negotiations school*. Austin: Texas Department of Public Safety.

Schlossberg, H. (1979b). Police response to hostage situations. In J. T. O'Brien & M. Marcus (Eds.), *Crime and justice in America* (pp. 209–220). New York: Pergamon.

Soskis, D. A., & VanZandt, C. R. (1986). Hostage negotiations: Law enforcement's most effective non-lethal weapon. *FBI Management Quarterly, 6*, 1–8.

Stites, R. (2005, August). *Tactical techniques for negotiators.* Presentation at the Hostage/Crisis Negotiator Conference, Olathe, KS.

Strentz, T. (1982). The Stockholm syndrome: Law enforcement policy and hostage behavior. In F. M. Ochberg & D. A. Soskis, (Eds.), *Victims of terrorism* (pp. 149–164). Boulder, CO: Westview Press.

Strentz, T. (1984). Preparing the person with high potential for victimization as a hostage. In J. T. Turner, (Ed.), *Violence in the medical care setting: A survival guide* (pp. 183–208). Rockville, MD: Aspen Press.

Strentz, T. (1985). *A statistical analysis of American hostage situations.* Unpublished manuscript, FBI Academy, Quantico, VA.

Strentz, T., & Auerbach, S. M. (1988). Adjustment to the stress of simulated captivity: Effects of emotion-focused versus problem-focused preparation on hostages differing in locus of control. *Journal of Personality and Social Psychology, 55*, 652–660.

Ware, B. (2009, November). *Active listening skills.* Seminar at the Annual Meeting of the Texas Association of Hostage Negotiators, Lewisville, TX.

17 Domestic Violence
An Analysis of the Crime and Punishment of Intimate Partner Abuse

Trisha K. Straus

Stephanie L. Brooke

INTRODUCTION: THE CASE OF MELANIE

It was a storybook meeting. In her last year of college, Melanie found herself at a party staring across a room full of people at him, Joe. As he crossed the room, she felt her heart race so fast that she could barely hear the music. They talked all night long, Joe telling her how beautiful she was and how she made him laugh. Melanie was overcome with happiness in the days and weeks to come as Joe continued to make her feel like a princess. Despite arguments against it from her parents, after a few short months of dating, the two were married. At the time they met, Melanie was in school following her lifelong dream to be an architect. Her dream was cut short, however, when she discovered after just a few months of marriage that she was pregnant. Joe explained that the children would have to come first and that Melanie's goal of a career in architecture would have to wait. It would take too much time and money away from the children, he reasoned, to go beyond her degree for the necessary architecture licensing. Melanie acquiesced, disappointed but happy about her newfound role as a mother.

Just after graduation, Melanie and Joe became the proud parents of twin girls. It is here that the storybook life for Melanie turns into a downward spiral of self-hate, resentment, fear, and anger. Joe began calling her names and belittling her for not working harder to resume her once slimmer figure. He moved the family to a small farmhouse away from her relatives and friends, essentially limiting her sphere of daily interaction to just him. Likewise, he limited her financial independence by refusing to allow her to work or maintain her own bank accounts. Her very existence was ruled and dictated by him. When she would take the girls to visit a family member, she knew upon return that she would endure an interrogation similar to that experienced by a war prisoner. Many nights, she sat home alone while he gallivanted about the town seeking the company and often pleasure of other women. When he did return home, it was a requirement that his sexual needs were met until he was satisfied. She often woke in the mornings aching and sore from having to pleasure him numerous times the night before.

Through the ensuing years, his demands escalated, requiring her to re-create pornographic instances. While he never raised a hand to her, the threats were persistent. Without actual physical contact, however, Melanie was told by her local law enforcement no crime was occurring and nothing would happen to Joe. Finally, after 13 years of imprisonment, one day Joe came home and told her he had found someone better, someone thinner and prettier, and he wanted a divorce. After so many years being put down, instead of being elated for her freedom, Melanie sunk into a deep depression lasting more than a year, where she blamed herself for the failed marriage. Without any work experience, Melanie took an hourly job as a school secretary so she could still be around her children. With such limited income, however, paying the bills was near impossible. In her deep depression, Melanie sought out therapy. It was finally there that she discovered the true nature of her trauma, that she was in fact a domestic violence victim. Armed with this knowledge, Melanie vowed to turn her tragedy into success. Today, she lives in a home owned by a family friend who allows her to pay whatever she can in rent. She has sought a government grant and is currently going back to school to become a nurse. Melanie is a domestic violence survivor. She walks around with scars that are hidden behind a warm smile and infectious laugh. Behind the smiles, however, are real fears that will never relinquish. Fear that he will return and want her back, fear that she will not be able to refuse him, fear that suddenly she will be forced back into her life of isolation and torture, and fear that someday this too will be a fate her daughters will suffer.

Melanie is just one face showing the scars received from the destructive and devastating impacts of domestic violence. While her story is beyond comprehension and words, its progress, patterns, and composition are all quite typical. The intimate details of every domestic violence story will vary based on the particular psychological nature and background of the people that are involved. Likewise, each relationship that suffers from domestic violence will weave its own course through the criminal justice system. Some cases will resolve on their own, such as Melanie's, and the violence will stop without intervention. Others, however, will progress through each phase of intervention the system has to offer. Some will find success and will escape the daily terror, while others will search unendingly without relief and will meet an untimely and unnecessary fate. In the voices of past victims that have been silenced, their pain and loss can still be heard. In the past, their voices were only whispers of their struggles and anguish. Today, their voices are spoken out, trying to reach others before it is too late. The hope for tomorrow is that their voices will be shouted by way of legislative reform and earlier intervention by police and social services. Ultimately, however, they challenge each and every one of us to see that "every life lost is a call for change" (Starr, 2006, p. 2a-4).

In this chapter, we will provide an outline of what domestic violence entails. Next, we will discuss different types of domestic violence. Additionally, we will outline a psychological profile of the perpetrator as well at the victim. This chapter also discusses the cycle of breaking domestic violence, looking at the reasons people stay in abusive relationships, developing a safety plan, looking at shelters, and more. Next, the chapter will focus on legal issues like orders of protection, law enforcement intervention, prosecution, and sentencing procedures. Last, the chapter will discuss possible reforms in law enforcement, prosecution, judicial procedures, and legislation. The chapter concludes with a forward focus on awareness of social welfare reform.

WHAT IS DOMESTIC VIOLENCE?

DEFINING DOMESTIC VIOLENCE

While every state statute will vary in terminology, there are several consistent understandings on what the crime of domestic violence entails. Domestic violence is an abusive confrontation that occurs between two people who maintain or who have maintained an intimate relationship together (McCue, 1995). Additionally, domestic violence has often been called interchangeably spousal abuse, intimate partner violence, domestic abuse, domestic battery, and, more recently, "terrorism in the home" (McCue, 1995, p. 2). While in the past, domestic violence was thought to be simply limited to those who are married, as the face of the average American relationship has changed, so too has the understanding of what relationships can suffer from domestic violence. Today, not only does domestic violence include the traditional married couple of man and woman, but it also includes couples who have a nonmarital relationship together such as those who live together or even just date and maintain separate residences. As our society has evolved to accept homosexual relationships, our eyes have been opened to see that the evils of domestic violence exist in homosexual relationships as well (Haugen, 2005). Sadly, no relationship seems safe from the dangers of abuse and victimization. Similarly, there is no race, ethnicity, religious practice, social status, or age that is exempt from domestic violence (Haugen, 2005). Domestic violence occurs "in our neighborhoods, community centers and parking lots, and on our streets, sidewalks and doorsteps" (Starr, 2006, p. 2a-9). Domestic violence, for those who have not lived it, is often an unthinkable, unimaginable act. Even many trained criminal justice experts such as law enforcement officers, prosecutors or defense attorneys, and counselors, struggle with the psychological dynamics that allow one person to impose such an indestructible hold on another (Zerwick, 2009). The simplest way for one to begin to understand the crime of domestic violence is to consider separately the three components present in every act of domestic violence: the violent confrontation, the abuser, and the victim.

The ultimate goal of domestic violence for the abuser is to gain and maintain complete and utter control over the victim in how she thinks, acts, and speaks. To gain such control, an abuser will employ any tactic to overcome his victim. Typically, domestic violence comes in the form of physical assaults, sexual abuse, financial abuse, and emotional battering. Regardless of the form of violence used, because the purpose behind the abuse is domination, "any act that causes the victim to do something she does not want to do, prevents her from doing something she wants to do, or causes her to be afraid" qualifies as domestic violence (McCue, 1995, p. 2). While in some instances, domestic violence will be one single act, more often it is a "systemic pattern of [control and] abuse that escalates overt time, in frequency and severity" (McCue, 1995, p. 3). This pattern of escalation is perhaps the most frightening component of domestic violence. There is no rationale to the escalation; it can occur slowly over time or instantaneously. While not every instance of domestic violence will involve every form of violence, due to the devastating nature of partner battery, however, emotional abuse is present in nearly every act of domestic violence.

Forms of Domestic Violence

Each victim of domestic violence will suffer some form of psychological or emotional battering. Emotional battering is "psychological or mental violence" imposed by the batterer "to rob the victim of self-esteem and a sense of personal security" (Jenesse Center, 2009a, para. 1). Because the victim's psyche is so beaten down and damaged, it is common that "[v]ictims of domestic violence often lose confidence in themselves" (Edwards, 2003, p. 5). Emotional abuse starts by demeaning jokes, insults, name-calling, or ignoring the victim's feelings (Jenesse Center, 2009a). As the batterer begins to wield more power, the abuse elevates to acts of damage and destruction to the victim's property, humiliation, and stalking the victim at work or in social settings (Jenesse Center, 2009a). Among the most severe sufferings of emotional abuse occurs through the use of threats. The batterer can verbally threaten the victim or threaten to harm those close to the victim such as children, family members, or family pets. Threats can come nonverbally as well where a batterer exposes firearms or weapons during an argument or takes weapons to bed at night (Jenesse Center, 2009a). Emotional abuse is rarely used in isolation from other forms of violence and is most commonly seen employed in tandem with either physical battering, sexual violence, or financial abuse

The physical assaults suffered at the hands of domestic violence come in many forms and in many varying levels of severity. Physical abuse occurs when a "batterer uses a show of physical strength to cower and intimidate" a victim (Jenesse Center, 2009b, para. 1). Physical attacks can include grabbing, shoving, hitting with a fist or an object, kicking, or slapping (Haugen, 2005). In more severe instances, an abuser will use a knife or gun to cause bodily harm. Physical abuse usually begins with the batterer striking his victim in places hidden from visibility, such as the stomach or torso. As the abuse escalates and the abuser feels his control grow greater, he flaunts the victim by physical assaults that are visible to others. This requires the victim to formulate some cover story for her injuries, thereby protecting him and further alienating herself into his power. The greatest escalation of physical abuse occurs when the victim is disabled, disfigured, or at the worst murdered at the hands of the abuser. While physical abuse can be quite visible to others, victims of sexual assault will often suffer greatly in isolation because it occurs within the privacy of the mutual residence.

Plaguing victims of sexual abuse is the inherent yet misplaced belief that the sexual acts conducted by two people involved in an intimate relationship are always consensual. In relationships infected by domestic violence, sexual intercourse and other sexual acts are anything but consensual; to the contrary, they often occur under stressful conditions and are a means of compliance in lieu of other more torturous threats being actualized. A person is a victim of sexual abuse when he or she is forced to take part in unwanted sexual activity (Jenesse Center, 2009c). Sexual abuse can begin with sexual jokes made at the victim's expense, criticizing or demeaning comments regarding the victim's sexuality, or making sexual innuendos toward others in front of the victim (Jenesse Center, 2009c). Quite often, the batterer will insist the victim is monogamous while he is able to go seek pleasure from others. As the pattern of violence escalates, the abuser will become jealous and oppressive over the victim's other relationships, often accusing her of affairs. This may be a form of projection as the abuser is the one typically having affairs outside of the relationship. The victim's sexual needs are always secondary to the batterer's and are usually ignored completely. At its worst, sexual abuse victims find themselves forced to perform unwanted sexual acts that are often humiliating, under duress, and even physically painful. Regardless of marital status, the crime of rape occurs when anyone is forced to have sexual intercourse against their own will. Sadly, all too many crimes of sexual abuse go unreported and unpunished when they are cloaked in the vows of marriage or intimate relationships. Similar to sexual abuse, often a victim suffers silently from financial violence.

While less discussed when compared to physical or sexual assaults, often domestic violence victims find themselves suffering from financial abuse. Economic or financial abuse occurs when an abuser attempts to control and dominate his victim through deprivation of financial resources (Jenesse Center, 2009d). An abuser might employ tactics such as maintaining physical control over all family finances, by holding all checkbooks, financial accounts, and bank cards (Jenesse Center, 2009d). Often, a victim of economic abuse finds herself without sufficient money to buy daily necessities such as food, gas, or personal items. She is required to ask for money to acquire things for her needs, usually requiring exact itemization of the expenditure, and even then it can be denied (Jenesse Center, 2009d). A victim of economic abuse has little say in what her personal needs are and how they will be financially supported. In early phases of economic abuse, a victim may be required to hand over any pay she has earned independently (Jenesse Center, 2009d). In more advanced stages, and as the abuse escalates, the batterer will harass the victim at her work, causing her trouble. The batterer wins total financial control over the victim when the victim becomes totally reliant on her abuser for economic security. As each instance of domestic violence abuse is different—whether emotional, physical, sexual, or economical in nature—so too is the face of each batterer.

The Face of the Abuser

The face of a domestic violence abuser is not exceptional. There are no distinguishing features or characteristic exteriors that can predict who will evolve into a domestic violence abuser. One cannot survey a room full of couples and conclude with any certainty the existence of domestic violence in any relationship. A batterer often is the last person anyone would think could be capable of such a horrific crime. Abusers "appear to be law-abiding citizens outside of their own homes and do not come across as abusive individuals in public, but maintain an image as friendly and devoted to their families" (McCue, 1995, p. 108). Because their violence is primarily limited to their intimate partners, many batterers have no other criminal record. A batterer becomes good at hiding the monster that lurks beneath; they are noted for being "extremely manipulative and charming"

(McCue, 1995, p. 108). Despite these outward appearances of self-confidence and control, many abusers lack self-esteem (McCue, 1995). Typically, an abuser maintains very "rigid, stereotypical thinking about men's and women's roles" in the household and in society in general (McCue, 1995, p. 108). The most common traits noted as typical of an abusive person are (1) tendency to blame others for their actions, (2) pathological jealousy, (3) dual personality, (4) severe stress reactions, (5) frequent use of sex as an act of aggression, and (6) refusal to believe their actions should have negative consequences (McCue, 1995). In carrying out abusive acts, an abuser will "commonly blame their violence on the victims" and will deny and minimize the effect of the abuse on the victim (McCue, 1995, p. 108). While many agree on the traits common to an abuser, the debate is not as clear when it comes to determining whether men or women are more frequently responsible for the violence.

While it has been historically thought that men were the primary if not sole perpetrators of domestic violence, current views are changing to see that men and women equally are capable of abusive acts. The earliest responses by the criminal justice system perpetuated the belief that men commit acts of violence and women are victims (Edwards, 2003). As far back a biblical times, in 200 B.C.E., men were prohibited from beating their wives, "unless he ha[d] suffered a grievance sufficient for divorce" (McCue, 1995, p. 26). During colonial days, the primary governing body of law was the "Body of Liberties" drafted in 1641 (McCue, 1995, p. 27). This law included a provision that married women should be free from bodily correction by her husband (McCue, 1995). As the laws of domestic violence both in America and in other countries evolved through time, they have always been drafted with the purpose of protection for the wife from a husband's abusive hands. Likewise, when considering the statistics obtained through criminal justice records, studies, and surveys, it appears as though men are the primary batterers (U.S. Department of Justice, 1998). The U.S. Department of Justice reports that in "92% of all domestic violence incidents, crimes are committed by men against women" (U.S. Department of Justice, 1998). Further, it has been reported that "[h]usbands and boyfriends commit 13,000 acts of violence against women in the workplace every year" (U.S. Department of Justice, 1994, para. 20). As times are changing, however, so too do the statistics. In 1977, the National Institute of Mental Health conducted a survey of more than 2,000 couples in the United States. Research results indicated that "men and women were equally apt to resort to minor incidents of violence (shoving, slapping, throwing objects) in domestic disputes" (Haugen, 2005, p. 13). More recently, in 1999, several studies were released with the conclusion that "men and women commit intimate violence at similar rates" (Cotton, 2006, p. 1c-3). Over the past 25 to 30 years, studies have repeatedly supported the conclusion that men and women equally abuse their partners (Cotton, 2006). Interestingly, in "more severe incidents of violence (kicking, hitting with a fist, threatening with or using a knife or gun), [surveys have] revealed that women were more likely to be the perpetrators and not the victims" (Haugen, 2005, p. 14). While both men and women alike are guilty of battering and abusing an intimate partner, when it comes to considering the victim, women are given greater attention and resources than male victims. Next, we will provide a brief profile of an abuser. Please bear in mind that much research focuses on the male abuser, but new research is now focusing on the female abuser.

Discussing a profile of an abuser can be difficult as they tend to come from all walks of life—professionals, blue-collar workers, and people from different ethnicities and religions. Specifically, research suggests that batterers are a heterogeneous group with diverse behavioral, cognitive, and emotional characteristics (Holtzworth-Munroe & Stuart, 1994). The myth that abusers are angry and hostile is not always the case; some can be very charming and kind. "Perpetrators do share a behavioral profile that is described as an ongoing pattern of coercive control involving various forms of intimidation, and psychological and physical abuse" (Child Welfare Information Gateway, 2009, para. 1). Behaviorally, batters distinguish themselves by using tactics such as abusing power and control, having different public and private behavior, projecting blame, claiming loss of control or anger problems, and minimizing or denying the abuse.

In 2009, Mauricio and Lopez did a latent classification of male batterers. In trying to identify batterer subgroups, they examined distinct violence patterns as well as associations between class membership, adult attachment associations, and antisocial and borderline personality characteristics. They used attachment theory as a basis for developing a profile of batterers (Dutton, Saunders, Starzomski, & Bartholomew, 1994). People with anxious attachment who experience their intimate partner as unavailable and suffer from abandonment anxiety may respond to their fear of abandonment with hostile or angry feelings toward their partner. With a negative model of others and strong avoidant tendencies, dismissive adults are likely to be self-centered and lacking the capacity for empathy, possibly making them more prone to violence in intimate relationships.

In addition, Mauricio and Lopez (2009) looked at personality theory to help develop a profile of batterers. For instance, Holtzworth-Munroe and Stuart (1994) asserted that an antisocial, generally violent batterer can be distinguished from a borderline batterer subtype. On the one hand, the borderline batterer was hypothesized to exhibit partner-specific violence that is less severe than that of the antisocial batterer. On the other hand, the antisocial batterer was hypothesized the most violent batterer subgroup and have greater levels of psychopathology.

They found three batterer subgroups. The first group was the high-level violence class, consisting of 40% of the batterers, who were both anxious and avoidant adult attachment orientations as well as borderline. Second, 35% of the sample, the moderate-level violence class demonstrated adult anxious attachment orientation. Representing 25% of the sample, the third group was the low-level violence class. Mauricio and Lopez stated that neither attachment orientation nor personality characteristics predicted membership in this class.

WHO ARE THE VICTIMS?

A victim of domestic violence, like a batterer, presents nothing exceptional outwardly that speaks to the vicious cycle of violence that he or she survives daily. Surveying any number of victims, there are no distinguishing features present prior to or during the abuse, other than those physically imposed by the batterer. Some victims may have been raised in an abusive home, thus conditioned that a life of violence is normal and acceptable (McCue, 1995). Lack of self-confidence is commonly seen in a domestic violence victim, attributable in great part to the repetitious and dominating impact that domestic violence inherently has on the victim (Edwards, 2003). Victims are very adept at concealing both the physical and emotional trauma going on in their lives. Depending on what statistics one considers, it is generally believed that women are more often than not the victims of domestic violence. For instance, the Centers for Disease Control estimates that roughly 25% of all women will be victimized by acts of domestic violence (Friedman, 2009). "Domestic violence is the leading cause of injury and death to American women, causing more harm than vehicular accidents, rapes, and muggings combined" (Haugen, 2005, p. 21). In 1998, the National Crime Victimization Survey (NCVS) concluded:

> [Eighty-five] percent of victims were women. The NCVS also reported that half of those female victims had sustained injuries, whereas only 32 percent of male victims of domestic violence had acknowledged any injuries. Of those people killed by violent partners, 72 percent were women. (Haugen, 2005, p. 15)

Because the victimization of women receives so much mainstream attention, the abused male victim is at times completely ignored by society.

Male victims of domestic violence are pleading for society to embrace their pain with the same compassion and empathy as that given to female victims. Where female victims of domestic violence are often called "battered women," men who are victims of domestic violence are said to suffer from the "battered husband syndrome" (Haugen, 2005, p. 23; McCue, 1995, pp. 93, 97). As the statistics today "show the numbers being roughly equal between men and women aggressors in the home" there is clearly a need for assistance for the male victim (Haugen, 2005, p. 36). For many male victims, however, assistance does not come. One primary reason males lack adequate victim resources when finding themselves as victims is because of the stereotypical perceptions society has on male strength; as a result, many "men are reluctant to acknowledge that they have been beaten up" by their female partner (Haugen, 2005, p. 36). "The humiliation and embarrassment that accompanies all [domestic violence victims] may be even greater for male[s]" (Haugen, 2005, p. 37). Additionally, when a male victim does choose to speak out, he finds few if any advocacy programs available to assist him (Cotton, 2006). It is clear that our society needs to adopt gender blindness for all instances of domestic abuse, so that each individual victim has the opportunity to escape the violence. Next, we will provide a brief profile of a victim of domestic violence.

Boyd and Klingbeil (n.d.) state that domestic violence victims come from all socioeconomic, racial, ethnic, educational, and age groups. They tend to show excessive minimalization and denial of the abuse. Additionally, they show passive acceptance and often internalize their anger. Domestic violence victims suffer from stress disorders and psychosomatic complaints. Due to economic and psychological dependency, they are prone to depression, substance abuse, and eating disorders (Brooke, 2009). Boyd and Klingbeil (n.d.) state that victims are often unaware of their ego needs; thus, they tend to define themselves in terms of partner, children, family, and/or job. Domestic violence victims are marked by low self-esteem. Also, victims are marked by the inability to convince partners of loyalty; futilely guarding against accusations of seductive behavior toward others; compliant; helpless; and powerless (Boyd & Klingbeil, n.d.). Living in constant fear of violence, helplessness, losing sight of personal boundaries, accepting blame, emotional acceptance and/or guilt for batter's behavior, suicidal ideation or attempt, and poor sexual self-image characterize the domestic violence victim. They often struggle to maintain the rights of children and often have a history of being a victim of violence as a child or witnessing violence as a child.

Caetano, Vaeth, and Ramisetty-Mikler (2008) did find that age was a variable that distinguished between domestic violence victims in that older individuals were less likely to be a victim of intimate partner violence. They conducted a longitudinal study and interviewed cohabitating and married couples in 48 states. "Other variables such as ethnicity, marital status, drinking, impulsivity, depression and powerlessness are either gender or status-specific in their ability to predict victimization, perpetration or victimization/perpetration" (p. 517). Women with high levels of powerlessness were more likely to be involved in violent relationships. It should be noted that the sample was heavily weighted with African Americans and Hispanics, which made any references to relationships to race questionable in this study.

ESCAPING THE CYCLE OF VIOLENCE

WHY DOES THE VICTIM STAY?

All too often, the question will arise in domestic violence cases: Why does the victim stay? While many victims scream out silently wanting to leave, a number of factors limit a victim's ability to escape the violence. For those cut off or geographically dislocated from family and friends, there may be limited access to find safe, affordable housing that is separate from the abuser. For those forced to rely on their batterers for economic support, there is little to no means of independent financial support if they leave. Additionally, many times a victim has been forced to leave the workforce to attend to the batterer's needs; in such instances, an abused partner is without the employment and life skills to live independent of the abuser. For those who have mutual children with the abuser, the choice to leave is almost nonexistent. A parent risks criminal and civil implications when he or she chooses to flee with the children (Starr, 2006). A parent who turns underground, choosing to run away with children parented mutually by the abuser, will soon have local and federal enforcement agencies searching for his or her whereabouts. A warrant for kidnapping can be obtained, and when the fleeing parent is located, he or she will be charged with crimes such as kidnapping, parental abduction, child concealment, or criminal custodial interference (McCue, 1995). In such instances, the abuser usually obtains full custody of the children, thereby achieving complete control of the children while the victim is routed through the criminal justice system. Ultimately, the choice of whether to leave is really a choice of survival. In many instances, "the rates of lethality for victims increase substantially when attempting to leave violent relationships" (Ainsworth, 2006, pp. 5b-5). Because leaving an abusive relationship can often be a long, arduous process, victims might seek out resources aimed at stopping partner abuse.

For a victim who remains in a relationship tarnished by domestic violence, he or she can seek out several avenues for relief. Where the perpetrator of abuse is amicable to the concept, couples counseling can be one means of stopping the violence while keeping in tact a family unit (Haugen, 2005). In sessions with trained marriage and family therapists, victims and their abusers are able to discuss what causes the instances of violence and victims are able to confront their abusers thereby finding a voice again in the relationship. One significant limitation to using this method, however, is being able to identify relationships stable enough to ensure the victim's safety during and after treatment (Haugen, 2005). Additionally, opponents of counseling argue that a batterer acts deliberately and in control, such that customary counseling sessions will provide no resolution (Haugen, 2005). When a victim cannot discuss the problems face to face with a counselor, crisis hotlines are a means of reaching out for support. Hotline staff are able to listen to the victim's situation, offer advice, and can provide referrals to local resources for help. By far, the most accessible phone resources for domestic violence victims is the National Domestic Violence Hotline, which is staffed around the clock 365 days per year, and is accessible in every state (National Domestic Violence Hotline, n.d.). When it becomes evident that the abuse will not stop, a victim's first step toward escaping the violence is to create a plan of personal protection and safety.

Why do victims stay? This is the predominant question when people try to understand the nature of domestic violence. Domestic abuse survivors often show ambivalence. For instance, the victim is often isolated by the abuse and begins to accept the abuser's depiction of being worthless, stupid, ugly, or undesirable. A distorted, negative self-image develops and, as self-esteem is undermined, the ability to make autonomous decisions declines (Brooke, 2009). In addition, there is a dearth of socioeconomic resources available to female survivors let alone male victims of domestic violence, which further complicates the difficulty of leaving.

The Family Violence Law Center (FVLC, 2009) provides some insight on why people, women in particular, stay in abusive relationships. Three major reasons are cited as why women stay in abusive relationships: lack of resources, institutional responses, and traditional philosophies. Clergy often do not know how to respond to reports of domestic violence. One of the authors served on the Catholic Diocese Committee to Stop Violence Against Women (Brooke, 1999). During the 6 months on this committee, we developed a letter to send to the Bishop outlining issues related to domestic violence and suggesting ways that clergy could respond to help them. The lack of understanding sometimes generalizes to other groups like police and law officials, as this chapter outlines in more detail. The FVLC also added that women sometimes hold the following traditional beliefs that may prevent them from leaving a domestic violence situation:

- Many women do not believe divorce is a viable alternative.
- Many women believe that a single-parent family is unacceptable, and that even a violent father is better than no father at all.
- Many women are socialized to believe they are responsible for making their marriage work. Failure to maintain the marriage equals failure as a woman.
- Many women become isolated from friends and families, either by the jealous and possessive abuser, or to hide signs of the abuse from the outside world. The isolation contributes to a sense that there is nowhere to turn.

- Many women rationalize their abuser's behavior by blaming stress, alcohol, problems at work, unemployment, or other factors.
- Many women are taught that their identity and worth are contingent on getting and keeping a man. (para. 5)

Research by Fanti, Vanman, Henrich, and Avaraamides (2009) suggests that as people watch more media violence, they become desensitized, making them less empathetic toward victims of violence. Participants watched nine violent movie scenes and nine comedy scenes. They were asked to report what scenes they enjoyed and were rated on how empathetic they were toward the victims. The researchers found:

> Desensitization to media violence was better represented by a curvilinear pattern, whereas desensitization to comedy scenes was better represented by a linear pattern. Finally, trait aggression was not related to the pattern of change over time, although significant effects were found for initial reports of enjoyment and sympathy. (p. 179)

Personal Safety Plan

Every victim of domestic violence must create a personal safety plan. The single objective of this goal is self-preservation from the abuser. A personal safety plan is a very practical and often sobering consideration of just how dire one's situation is. Among the first considerations of a safety plan is to establish and forge connections with people and agencies outside the situation for help. Creating a list of emergency numbers for the police, domestic violence shelters, and trusted people gives the victim quick access to external means of assistance (Jenesse Center, 2009e). Whether it be a neighbor, relative, physician, or minister, it is imperative to establish a relationship with someone who is aware of the direness of the situation. Once these initial steps toward protection are taken, the victim must then begin preparation for escape. Because victims often have to leave in a hurry, "[t]hey might only be able to take a few things with them" (Edwards, 2003, p. 22). Accordingly, a victim should create a "crisis stash" that includes money, car keys, clothes, and copies of important papers such as identification cards, birth certificates, or driver's licenses (Jenesse Center, 2009e, para. 5). A victim considering escape should open separate banking, insurance, and financial accounts, located at facilities disconnected with the abuser (Jenesse Center, 2009e). Victims of domestic violence may be able to change their Social Security numbers so that upon escape, it is easier "to elude their abusers" (Jenesse Center, 2009e, para. 18). A victim who chooses to remain in the mutual home must change the locks and install additional security and lighting devices (Jenesse Center, 2009e). The victim who chooses to flee, however, must seek out a location of refuge; while this can be with a close friend or family member, more often than not to completely break the cycle of violence a victim will have to escape to a shelter.

Shelters

When fleeing from an abusive home, victims often turn to community locations designed to support the specific needs of domestic violence victims. Since 1974, domestic violence victims in the United States can escape the horror of their existence in shelters (McCue, 1995). A shelter is an "environment where [domestic violence victims] can obtain, food, shelter, and emotional support, as well as helpful information, advocacy, and services" (McCue, 1995, p. 117). Offering similar resources, refuges provide all the same protection as shelters while offering an additional cloak of protection as they are secret, nondescript homes, without identity, and are only disclosed through a private network (Edward, 2003). A shelter is often the first stop a victim of domestic violence makes along his journey toward rebuilding his life. Due to the demand as well as reality that many of these locations are maintained on limited budgets and resources, shelters generally limit residence to 30 days for emergent cases and up to 2 years for families residing in transitional centers (Jenesse Center, 2009f). Upon entering a facility, a person is evaluated, an individual plan is created, and case managers are assigned to monitor progress (McCue, 1995). Because many victims also flee with young children, many shelters offer children's programs to assist with medical, psychological, and daily needs. For many domestic violence victims, however, the protection offered by these shelters is out of reach.

Despite growth in the number of shelters, many domestic violence victims are unable to avail themselves of the vast resources they offer. "In the United States, there are nearly three times as many shelters available for homeless animals as there are for homeless women" (McCue, 1995, p. 119). In many instances, the need is greater than a shelter can handle, and many victims who muster up the strength and courage to leave are often turned away (McCue, 1995). In 1990, the New York Department of Social Services reported denying 71% of the requests made for emergency shelter care due to lack of space (McCue, 1995). In that same year, Washington, D.C., victims were turned away eight times out of ten, and 90% of battered victims of Los Angeles County were denied access to shelters (McCue, 1995). When there is space, depending on location, many shelters are just out of reach. In some states, victims "must travel over 100 miles to reach the shelter" (McCue, 1995, p. 119). Despite the many shortcomings inherent in shelters, they offer among the most effective means of protection against future abuse. Additionally, research has shown that only "about one-third of the residents return to their batterer upon leaving the shelter" (McCue, 1995, p. 122). Quite possibly, the low return rate is attributable to the life skills training residents are able to avail themselves of while residing in shelters.

RECOVERY PROGRAMS AND SERVICES FOR THE VICTIM

Besides providing physical protection for domestic violence victims, shelters work to assist a victim in changing his or her life through a variety of resources. The programs and services for shelters will vary based on staffing as well as budgets. Vocational education is a critical resource for a victim of domestic violence. Victims are given instruction on topics such as independent living skills or basic computer training, taught subjects such as "resume writing, career choices, and budgeting," and provided with job search assistance (Jenesse Center, 2009f, para. 3). Because victims are so broken down by the psychological impacts of domestic violence, mental health treatment is an essential service offered in shelters. Likewise, often victims come to shelters with many medical needs, worsened by their abuser. Medical referrals and services are offered by shelters. The provision of legal services can be a critical program in a shelter. By informing victims of their legal rights and options, essential assistance is provided to prevent future acts of violence. Lastly, children's programs are an invaluable component for many shelters. Children who have witnessed acts of domestic violence require their own unique attention and counseling to rebuild themselves and their relationship with their abused parent. Likewise, parents who have been abused are offered parenting classes to rebuild their skills and confidence to raise their children. While physical protection is essential to break the pattern of domestic violence, the aforementioned services are crucial to achieve change; unfortunately, the range and access for such resources are not equal at all shelters.

The success of shelters is often limited by its operating budget and staff. "Shelters are costly to operate, due partly to the number of staff required to operate a 24-hour program and the extensive amount of time required per [victim] for advocacy" (McCue, 1995, p. 120). Despite the great financial need of shelters, funding at both the state and federal levels is often limited. For example, from 1989 to 1990, "total federal assistance for each domestic violence victim was [only] $27" (McCue, 1995, p. 121). In comparison, for that same fiscal year, $166.65 was given in federal support for homeless shelters and $8,000.00 was given in federal support for residents in mental institutions (McCue, 1995). Inevitably, when budget restraints are imposed, the first things cut from a shelter are its programs and services. In the summer of 2009, California Governor Arnold Schwarzenegger eliminated funding from the state's budget for all 94 of its shelters (Blake, 2009).

One shelter, The Women's Resource Center of Oceanside, refused to cut even one of its services or programs, acknowledging each one as vital to helping the victims of domestic violence recover and rebuild their lives (Blake, 2009). To be able to retain all of its services, however, the staff took an extensive pay cut and the facility is currently operating with ten less staff members necessary to meet the needs of the residents. The commitment and dedication demonstrated in Oceanside, California, are echoed around the country as many shelters are only able to operate with staff working exhausting shifts or many services are performed by volunteers. With community outreach so limited for many domestic violence victims, often abused partners turn toward the criminal justice system for relief.

LEGAL RESPONSES TO DOMESTIC VIOLENCE

ORDERS OF PROTECTION

The criminal justice system of each state offers a variety of tools for the domestic violence victim. Among the most commonly used method of keeping a violent person away from another is through the use of court orders. Depending on the laws of the jurisdiction, up to five court order options are available to any victim of domestic violence. The most widely used order is a restraining order, which can be obtained by those who are married or have a child in common. A restraining order prevents contact of any kind between the two parties; removes the assaulting party from the shared home; can order counseling or treatment; can include provisions for child support, child custody, and the division of joint property; and can order spousal maintenance income to the victim (Collings, Jahns, & Riehl, 2006). This order can be obtained in superior court as part of a family law action for divorce, separation, or child custody disputes (Collings et al., 2006). A violator of a restraining order may be arrested, but arrest is not mandatory in all jurisdictions (Collings et al., 2006). Similar to a restraining order, an order of protection can be sought by a victim who fears or has been subject to acts of domestic violence to prohibit contact from the abuser, remove the battering partner from the family home, establish a temporary child custody plan where applicable, and may order counseling services (Collings et al., 2006). To qualify for a protection order, the victim and the abuser must either be married, have a child in common, be related, be living together, or be over the age of 16 and are dating (Collings et al., 2006). A protection order may be obtained in any local courthouse and can be effective for up to 1 year (Collings et al., 2006). If a protection order is violated in many jurisdictions, it is mandatory that the violator is arrested (Collings et al., 2006). A sexual harassment order is similar to a protection order in the safety it offers for a victim, how it is obtained, and the repercussions for violation; the key difference, however, is that it can only be obtained by someone who has been a "victim of nonconsensual sexual conduct" (Collings et al., 2006, pp. 3–5). An antiharassment order is available to any victim who has been continuously victimized by conduct that annoys or harasses without any legitimate or lawful purpose (Collings et al., 2006). The court order prevents harassment and contact by restraining the abusive person from "coming within a specific distance from [the victim's] workplace, school, [or] residence" (Collings et al., 2006, pp. 3–4). It can be obtained through a local courthouse and can be imposed for up to 1 year; additionally, if an antiharassment order is violated, arrest may occur (Collings et al., 2006). Lastly, a victim can obtain a no-contact order to prevent contact of any form during the proceedings a criminal case. A no-contact order applies to persons who are victims of a crime where the alleged defendant is a family member or resides in the same household as the victim (Collings et al., 2006). If the no-contact order is violated, arrest is mandatory (Collings et al., 2006). Regardless of the type of order available to a victim based on his or her particular needs, many times a court order is not sufficient protection for a victim.

Despite the severe legal ramifications offered, court orders provide a limited veil of protection at best for many victims. Timing is key in enforcing court orders. When a judge enters a court order into the system, depending on the jurisdiction, it can take hours to days for the police to have notification. Without the order entered into the system, police cannot enforce any violations and the victim is essentially left without protection. Additionally, there are many offenders who taunt the court system. These offenders will adhere to the terms of the court orders, but will still find ways to harass their victim. In one instance, a woman obtained an emergency protective order against her husband. While she was at work one day, her abuser came onto the property of their joint home and dug holes in the yard (Zerwick, 2009). He then called and left repeated messages on the answering machine that told her the holes he had dug were going to be the graves for her and their children (Zerwick, 2009). Despite the valid court order, police refused to arrest her abuser because there were no witnesses to validate who did the digging, despite the answering machine message (Zerwick, 2009). Other offenders will taunt the law enforcement by driving by the victim's home or places of employment, limiting police response without adequate proof or positive identification. For some victims, facing their abusers in court to obtain an order of protection is not possible. Many fear the extreme retribution that will most assuredly await them after the court proceedings are over. For those without physical scars, they may feel embarrassment or question whether anyone will actually believe their claims. Sadly, many victims never attempt to avail themselves of the help offered by the system. Those who do choose to seek protection from the criminal justice system usually begin with help at the law enforcement level.

Law Enforcement Intervention

Often, the first call for assistance beyond a friend or family member a victim makes is to local law enforcement. Calls for assistance in family or domestic violence "constitute the largest single category of calls received by police departments each year" (McCue, 1995, p. 124). In fact, "police respond to up to 8 million times per year to violence that involves a spouse or lover" (Haugen, 2005, p. 21). When police are called to the scene, a variety of tools are at their disposal in choosing how to resolve the situation and response is based on experience, training, and intuition to determine fault. Upon arrival, law enforcement will generally use one of the four crisis management intervention styles: therapeutic, compensatory, conciliatory, and penal (Buzawa & Buzawa, 1990). Therapeutic police response "attempts to identify and solve the underlying problems leading to the act of domestic violence, while the compensatory response attempts to the injuries suffered by a victim" (Buzawa & Buzawa, 1990, pp. 39–40). Unfortunately, however, many officers use the less effective conciliatory response where the violence is viewed as a single-sided conflict without regard to who is right or wrong (Buzawa & Buzawa, 1990). Once a determination of fault is made, an officer can use the penal response by imposing punishment on one party (Buzawa & Buzawa, 1990). Legislative changes have taken much choice away from officers, however, as today many states operate under the mandatory arrest rule. Mandatory arrest laws dictate that when a domestic disturbance call is placed and police are dispatched to respond, police are required to arrest one of the two parties to the dispute. In instances where mandatory arrest laws are still not in place, law enforcement officers will still revert to the crisis management responses along with considering other factors such as the relationship of the party, police response, and perception of the victim's lifestyle and conduct as well as a consideration of the abuser's demeanor and conduct (Buzawa & Buzawa, 1990). Officers will also consider the degree of violence and victim injuries, at times going as far as applying the informal *stitch rule,* where no charges are filed if the victim's injuries do not qualify for medical attention (McCue, 1995). Regardless of the means of intervention used by the responding officer, the primary goal of the victim in calling for help is to prevent further injury. Based on the misconceptions maintained by many law enforcement agents about domestic violence cases, however, victims do not always achieve impartial protection or treatment when calling for help.

Within law enforcement, many inherent biases exist when handling cases of domestic violence. "At one time [domestic violence] was considered the most dangerous police call; now it is generally accepted as the most frequent form of violence in the United States." (Haugen, 2005, p. 20).

Like all cases of violent crimes, law enforcement agents do admittedly risk personal injury when responding to a domestic violence call. Accordingly, many officers come to domestic calls with a "defensive/reactive strategy to protect their own safety" rather than giving sole focus to the victim's safety (Buzawa & Buzawa, 1990, p. 31). Additionally, many officers do not see domestic disturbance calls as worthy of their time (Buzawa & Buzawa, 1990). Arresting a battering spouse as compared to a high-profile felon is viewed as unproductive and unbeneficial for career progress. Many officers do not believe police response is even appropriate for domestic calls and instead would view social worker intervention as more suitable to handling such matters (Buzawa & Buzawa, 1990). Lastly, victims, fearing retaliation for assisting with the arrest process and knowing their abuser will be released within days and will quickly return to settle the score, will insist against pressing charges, thereby making the police efforts worthless. Victim interference, regardless of basis, inhibits the criminal justice system not just during the arrest process but also in the prosecution of a domestic violence charge.

PROSECUTION

Following the arrest for a charge of domestic violence, the long road begins for the victim to actually receive justice. Where a police officer determines whether a domestic dispute will enter the criminal justice system through a formal arrest, a government attorney determines whether the allegations are sufficient to support prosecution. Prosecution is the formal action taken by a state, county, city, or state "in response to an alleged criminal violation in order to move the case toward adjudication" (McCue, 1995, p. 132). A case comes into the criminal justice system for prosecution either by arrest or a victim complaint where the victim files a probable cause affidavit swearing under oath that based on the reported facts and circumstances, a crime has occurred (McCue, 1995). To initiate court proceedings, a summons is issued, which requires the accused to report to a court on a given day to hear the specifics of the charges he or she is accused of. At this point, often a court may issue *sua sponte*, on its own merit, orders of protection for the victim if they are not already in place. As in all court cases, there are two sides arguing in a domestic violence case. When the case is put forward by the prosecutor, the government—and, to a greater extent, society—is responsible for insisting on justice. In criminal cases, "victims do not have the right to insist upon prosecution," and the ultimate resolution to the case does not ask for or require the victim's consent (Buzawa & Buzawa, 1990, p. 55). Because the victim's voice is not an integral part of the decision-making process toward achieving justice, often victims feeling discounted and discontented with the system serves as a deterrent to justice rather than as a positive resource toward achieving it.

Despite the many complaints initiated in the criminal justice system for crimes of domestic violence, few actually achieve the justice so desperately sought by the victims. As an example, from 1989 to 1990, the Philadelphia Municipal Court heard almost 800 cases involving domestic violence; however, only 67 cases achieved conviction (McCue, 1995). As recently as 2008, the U.S. Department of Justice reported only 37% of all domestic violence cases result in arrest; of those, only half conclude with a conviction (U.S. Department of Justice, 2008). When trying to determine what component of the criminal justice is at fault, there seems to be no single answer. Many could cite law enforcement to blame for lack of making arrests and getting domestic abusers into the system; on the other hand, others argue that the prosecution refuses to push cases forward regardless of the sufficiency of the evidence consistent with the statutory violations argued (Buzawa & Buzawa, 1990). Sadly, a good amount of case attrition is attributed to the victim. Victim noncompliance has been found to cause between 60% and 80% of all cases being dropped (Buzawa & Buzawa, 1990). For fear of retaliation or overall lack of confidence in the system, many victims refuse to appear or testify as a witness or will drop any charges initiated. Attitudes from within the criminal justice system have discouraged victim participation where victims are made to feel responsible for their plight by untrained and insensitive court personnel (Buzawa & Buzawa, 1990). Additionally, due to the complex and highly psychological hold that batterers have on their victims, often the victim's own attitude toward the crime and offender will decline during the prolonged journey toward justice (Buzawa & Buzawa, 1990). Regardless of why many cases fail to come full circle to achieving a conviction, for those cases that actualize punishment against a domestic violence offender, a variety of tools are at the court's discretion to rehabilitate an abuser and protect a victim against future violence.

SENTENCING

Achieving justice in domestic violence cases is often a long road for the victim, law enforcement, prosecutors, and the court systems. Once conviction is achieved, however, there are a variety of court-mandated treatment options available to hold an abuser accountable for his or her actions. The primary purpose behind treatment is to prevent future injury to a victim when the abuser reinitiates contact upon release. One commonly invoked form of punishment is pretrial diversion or referred prosecution, which allows a convicted offender to have a charge reduced or an arrest and conviction expunged, or removed, from his or record by successful completion of counseling and therapy (McCue, 1995). The other primary sentencing tool used by the judicial community is the imposition of court-ordered treatment to be carried out during or following serving time in a correction institution. Most treatment programs have a mental health component to them, attempting to teach the offender how to manage anger and stress and to recognize issues with imposing control over another, and providing education on interpersonal skills (McCue, 1995). Treatment can be conducted in both peer and individual settings with the overall goal to have the abuser recognize, become accountable for, and work toward changing abusive patterns. While the various treatment and counseling options are beneficial for an offender, such tools are only successful where a batterer is required to attend such training as a result of a court-imposed sentence. Due to the lenient sentences imposed and loose legislative terming of domestic violence crimes, however, many offenders are getting off quite easy when convicted of a crime of domestic violence.

Until recent years, the sentences imposed on many convicted domestic violence offenders were considered disproportionate when compared to other violent crimes. "Research indicates that the injuries battered [victims] receive are at least as serious as injuries suffered in many violent felony crimes, yet under state laws they are many times classified as misdemeanors" (McCue, 1995, p. 133). A misdemeanor is generally a crime punishable by serving less than 1 year incarcerated, usually in a local jail; a felony, on the other hand, is any crime punished by serving a sentence greater than a year with incarceration in a state level facility. When discussing crimes of rape, physical assault, or murder, in nearly every state such crimes would be prosecuted as felonies. When those same criminal acts are prosecuted under the classification of domestic violence, however, they are prosecuted as misdemeanors. In one study conducted by the National Crime Survey, it was reported that nearly one-third of all domestic violence cases charged as misdemeanors would have been charged as felonies if they had been committed between strangers (Buzawa & Buzawa, 1990). Additionally, because cases of spousal assault are generally treated as independent acts, the pattern of abusive behavior is not usually admissible when entering sentences. In contrast, previous criminal behaviors "for serial drug offenders, car thieves and other chronic criminals" are admissible to allow the full impact of sentencing guidelines to be imposed (Durbin, 2009, para. 17). Despite the many shortcomings inherent in the criminal justice system, change strives toward freedom, safety, and justice for domestic violence victims.

THE FUTURE OF DOMESTIC VIOLENCE

LAW ENFORCEMENT AND PROSECUTION REFORM

Reform is underway to overhaul how domestic violence cases are handled by the criminal justice system. The primary method of reform focuses on coordinating efforts between the police departments and the court systems. At the law enforcement level, new approaches are being adopted by police departments which change how a domestic violence call is handled. Police are given specialized training on domestic disputes, with the focus of seeing the act as the crime that it is, and not to view the matter as a private dispute. Computerized systems have been created that track requests for police response for domestic disputes, record any reports that are filed, and alert to any charges or orders of protection that have been issued (Buzawa & Buzawa, 1990). Many departments have adopted pro-arrest policies that require or prefer its officers make an arrest when dispatched to the scene where an officer has probable cause based on the facts to reasonably believe an incident of domestic violence occurred (*Domestic Violence: Arrest Policies*, n.d.). Police departments are introducing specialized crisis response teams for domestic cases as well (Buzawa & Buzawa, 1990). These response teams are comprised of a cadre of officers, specially trained in mediation and crisis intervention techniques by mental health experts and other local resources specializing in the crime of domestic violence (Buzawa & Buzawa, 1990). Due to budgetary constraints, in lieu of a specialized team of officers for domestic disputes, some departments utilize law enforcement and social worker teams to respond to homes that regularly report incidents of intimate partner violence (Buzawa & Buzawa, 1990). While reform at the law enforcement level is essential to moving domestic violence cases forward in the criminal justice system, reform at each superseding level is just as important for justice to ultimately be served.

Prosecution offices are undergoing reform as well to ensure their efforts are coordinated with and complemented by law enforcement. Many prosecution offices have created a streamlined approach for domestic cases by implementing a policy of vertical prosecution. Vertical prosecution occurs where the same prosecutor handles all aspects of a domestic violence case from court hearings to victim communication (Domestic Violence Prosecution Committee, 2004). Many offices are also taking on a more aggressive policy for violation of court protection and restraining orders as well as an overall no-drop policy whereby all appropriate cases of domestic violence will be prosecuted regardless of victim cooperation and impose restrictions on victims to prevent them from dropping charges (Buzawa & Buzawa, 1990; Domestic Violence Prosecution Committee, 2004). Recognizing that the judicial system can often be harsh on victims, many prosecutor offices have established or work in conjunction with victim-witness advocates. Victim-witness programs offer specialized support to the victim of a domestic violence, communicating progress of the case as well as informing the victim of upcoming court hearings, explaining the availability of local and community resources, and serving as a means for the victim's voice to be heard. Where a victim feels more involved with the case, he or she is likely to continue to support the prosecution rather than to impede it. Reform does not just stop, however, with law enforcement and prosecution offices; rather, it continues upward, demanding change at the judicial and legislative levels as well.

JUDICIAL AND LEGISLATIVE REFORM

As the ultimate decision makers in domestic violence cases, the judiciary must undergo reform to adequately address the needs of today's domestic violence victim. Similar to law enforcement and prosecutors, judges are receiving training on domestic violence cases, learning how to assess the danger and lethality of an abuser (Starr, 2006). With the continued growth of technology in the courtroom, a judge can make an order of protection effective immediately, thereby giving law enforcement the tools it needs to protect victims in a more timely manner (Buckley, 2009). Additionally, judges in many jurisdictions are fully exploring their discretionary powers when granting orders of protection. Where victims were once simply using protective orders to relieve themselves from the physical presence of their abuser, judges are now ordering offenders to pay financial restitution, giving a victim exclusive access to personal property of the batterer, and even ordering the abusive spouse to pay any attorney fees incurred by the victim (Buzawa & Buzawa, 1990; Collings et al., 2006). Several judicial districts are exploring the use of pretrial safety programs. Such programs operate with the goal of ensuring the victim's safety during the period of time before a case is brought to trial. Pretrial safety programs work to achieve their goal by requiring, when possible, the retention of one judge from start to completion of a case, establishing protected times on court dockets when solely domestic cases are heard, enhancing services offered to victims while expanding monitoring services over the accused, and seeking expanded support of cases from both the prosecutorial office as well as law enforcement (National Institute of Justice, 2009). In jurisdictions that are unable to retain one judge with a case, it is argued that at a minimum, judges should be required to examine the entire case history through computerized databases tracking criminal history, discussions with the victim, and overall court docket summaries to see the progress of the case in the court system (Starr, 2006). Even where the police, prosecution, and judiciary act in concert with one another, without changes in domestic violence laws, victims are still without justice.

Legislation is among the most crucial areas of need for domestic violence reform. Because a systemic limitation is imposed on the classification of crimes for domestic violence, legislatures must change the language of current statutes for crimes of partner abuse to receive the same treatment as stranger crimes. The primary federal law governing crimes of domestic violence is the Violence Against Women Act (VAWA), enacted in 1994 (Groban, n.d.). Each state has subsequently enacted its own laws as well to complement or complete the VAWA. Despite the vast legislation, a gap still exists today when crimes of assault or rape occurring under the umbrella of domestic violence are given lesser punishment than those same crimes occurring between strangers (McCue, 1995). Laws must be revised and amended to equalize the crime regardless of the relationship between the victim and offender, which will additionally serve as a catalyst to encourage police, prosecutors, and judges alike to likewise treat domestic violence cases equal to all other crimes. Further, legislative reform must include provisions to allow prosecutors to present evidence for judicial consideration of prior convictions for domestic violence crimes. Where history of prior domestic violence can be presented in trial, it is more likely that the full range of a sentence will be imposed (Durbin, 2009). Even to a lesser extent, legislative reform for treatment of domestic victims can work to reshape the overall societal stigma attributed to those who suffer from acts of domestic violence. Currently, "domestic violence is a pre-existing condition that can be used to deny coverage to battered [victims]" (Silverleib, 2009, para. 1). Legislators are vowing to remove this provision through federal health care reform, and independently 42 states have already banned such practices (Silverleib, 2009). Beyond the criminal justice system and the legislative drafters of domestic violence, society itself can reform to better support and protect domestic violence victims.

Avenues for Social Welfare Reforms

Where a victim lacks a voice for reporting domestic violence abuse, often key members of society provide that voice. When a victim is physically injured from domestic battery, he or she may seek medical attention. It is roughly estimated that between 22% and 35% of all women seen in emergency rooms are treated for domestic violence–related injuries (McCue, 1995). Similar to the specialized training for law enforcement or prosecutors, health care professionals should receive instruction on how to question battered victims, recognizing injury patterns consistent with partner abuse, and be knowledgeable about the services available to such victims (McCue, 1995). Additionally, hospitals should establish protocols for handling cases to ensure the abuser is not notified of the victim's disclosure and for contacting the authorities when necessary to prevent further harm to the victim (McCue, 1995). While many states today require medical professionals to contact authorities when any injuries are known or believed to be caused from domestic assault, legislative reform should occur to mandate reform throughout the country. Currently, nearly every state has in place mandatory reporting laws for suspected cases of child abuse. By enacting analogous mandatory reporting laws for domestic violence cases, victims would receive additional protection from society at large through social workers, teachers or school staff, child care providers, and all medical and mental health professionals. For the face of domestic violence to realize reform, it is ultimately society that must serve as the catalyst for change.

Historically, domestic violence has been viewed by society as a private matter, between a married or intimate couple. Unlike abuse on an innocent, defenseless child or animal, many people have operated under the misguided notion that adults can take care of themselves, that they can flee situations dangerous to themselves, and that anyone not party to the relationship should employ a hands-off approach to the situation. In 1993, however, sentiments began to change when Nicole Brown Simpson was killed. Although acquitted of all charges, her former husband, O.J. Simpson, stood trial for the crimes. Their relationship was presented to the public eye, where a detailed history of domestic violence was revealed (McCue, 1995). As a result of the public response from Nicole Brown's death, legislators began passing mandates and bills strengthening existing domestic violence laws. Despite intermediate cases of spousal abuse reported locally or even nationally, media coverage and societal response went largely silent until early 2009, when photographs of pop singer Rihanna were released, showing domestic abuse by her then-boyfriend, rapper Chris Brown (Friedman, 2009, para. 5). When there is little media fodder to fuel the topic, progress and societal awareness of domestic violence come from committed groups. Feminist organizations responsible for instituting shelters remain at the forefront in advocating for more protective laws for victims (McCue, 1995). The psychological community has advanced domestic violence awareness through innumerable studies that have helped to profile the abuser, as well as have created the backbones for many treatment and prevention programs (McCue, 1995). Studies presented by sociologists have provided quantitative data that serve as the basis for institutional and systemic changes (McCue, 1995). The media, however, by far seems to reach the greatest number of society. Between television, film, radio, and print forums, the media reaches nearly every citizen, multiple times a day, imparting a profound impact on public attitude. Those who argue for media reform would be the first to point to the degrading lyrics of songs, violent video games, or the film glamorization of violence against a spouse or lover as depicted in Jean Kilbourne's films about gender advertising in *Killing Us Softly* (1979) and *Still Killing Us Softly* (1987) (as cited in Kilbourne, n.d.). Media reform should work to address the proven connection between the "steady diet of violent entertainment and aggressive and antisocial behavior" seen in the millions of domestic violence cases adjudicated by the criminal justice system (McCue, 1995, p. 23). Ultimately, there is no single entity responsible for domestic violence, but rather it is the individual offender who is solely at fault. Likewise, there is no one means of reform that will work to protect the individual victim. However, where there is a concerted and united effort of reform by all the components of the criminal justice system as well as society at large, the victim of domestic violence will no longer stand alone in the fight for protection, self-preservation, or justice.

REFERENCES

Ainsworth, S. L. (2006, October 13). How to structure a parenting plan: Creative language. In *The nexus of domestic violence and family law: Meeting the challenges* (pp. 5b-1–5b-20). SeaTac: Washington State Bar Association.

Blake, K. (2009). *Local domestic violence shelters seek assistance amid tough times*. San Diego News Network. Retrieved November 28, 2009, from http://www.sdnn.com/sandiego/2009-11-25/politics-city-county-government/local-domestic-violence-shelters-seek-assistance-amid-tough-times#ixzz0YBtvOzf8

Boyd, V. D., & Klingbeil, K. S. (n.d.). *Behavioral characteristics of domestic violence*. Retrieved December 19, 2009, from http://crisis-support.org/behav.htm#table

Brooke, S. L. (1999). Catholic Diocese Committee to stop violence against women. Rochester, New York.

Brooke, S. L. (2008). *The use of the creative therapies with eating disorder*. Springfield, IL: Charles C Thomas.

Brooke, S. L. (Ed.). (2009). *The use of the creative therapies with survivors of domestic violence*. Springfield, IL: Charles C Thomas.

Buckley, M. (2009, July 14). Courtrooms to get computers. *South Bend Tribune*, pp. B1, B2.

Buzawa, C. G., & Buzawa, E. S. (1990). *Domestic violence: The criminal justice response.* Newbury Park, CA: Sage.

Ceatano, R., Vaeth, P. A., & Ramisetty-Mikler, S. (2008). Intimate partner violence victim and perpetrator characteristics among couples in the United States. *Journal of Family Violence, 23*(6), 507–518.

Child Welfare Information Gateway. (2009). *Perpetrators of domestic violence.* Retrieved December 19, 2009, from http://www.enotalone.com/article/10004.html

Collings, K., Jahns, J., & Riehl, J. (2006, October 13). The nexus of domestic violence and family law: Avoiding conflicting court orders. In *The nexus of domestic violence and family law: Meeting the challenges* (pp. 3-1–3-8). SeaTac: Washington State Bar Association.

Cotton, J. (2006). Ethical representation of (alleged) batterers. In *The nexus of domestic violence and family law: Meeting the challenges.* SeaTac: Washington State Bar Association.

Domestic violence: Arrest policies. (n.d.). Law Library: American Law and Legal Information. Retrieved November 29, 2009, from http://law.jrank.org/pages/1004/Domestic-Violence-Arrest-policies.html#ixzz0YIcPsPSI

Domestic Violence Prosecution Committee. (2004). *Guidelines for prosecution of domestic violence cases.* Alabama Coalition Against Domestic Violence. Retrieved November 29, 2009, from http://www.acadv.org/Prosecutionguidelines.pdf

Durbin, K. (2009, November 26). Domestic violence sentencing criticized: McKenna proposal would hold repeat offenders longer. *The Spokesman-Review.* Retrieved November 29, 2009, from http://www.spokesman.com/stories/2009/nov/26/domestic-violence-sentencing-criticized

Dutton, D. G., Saunders, K., Starzomski, A., & Bartholomew, K. (1994). Intimacy-anger and insecure attachment as precursors of abuse in intimate relationships. *Journal of Applied Social Psychology, 24,* 1367–1386.

Edwards, N. (2003). *Talking about domestic violence.* North Mankato, MN: Chrysalis Education.

The Family Violence Law Center. (2009). *Why do women stay?* Retrieved December 19, 2009, from http://www.fvlc.org/gethelp_whywomenstay.html

Fanti, K. A., Vanman, E., Henrich, C. C., & Avaraamides, M. N. (2009). Desensitization to media violence over a short period of time. *Aggressive Behavior, 35*(2), 179–187.

Friedman, E. (2009, February 20). *Leaked Rihanna photo could harm domestic abuse victims: Advocates debate whether Rihanna photo changes landscape for abuse victims.* ABC News. Retrieved October 20, 2009, from http://abcnews.go.com/print?id=6922697

Groban, M. (n.d.) *The federal domestic violence laws and the enforcement of these laws.* Minnesota Center Against Violence and Abuse. Retrieved November 29, 2009, from http://www.mincava.umn.edu/documents/ffc/chapter5/chapter5.html

Haugen, D. (Ed.). (2005). *Domestic violence: Opposing viewpoints.* Farmington Hills, MI: Greenhaven Press.

Holtzworth-Munroe, A., & Stuart, G. L. (1994). Typology of male batterers: Three subtypes and the differences among them. *Psychological Bulletin, 116,* 476–497.

Jenesse Center. (2009a). *Psychological/emotional battering.* Retrieved November 2, 2009, from http://www.jenesse.org/psy_abuse.html

Jenesse Center. (2009b). *Physical abuse.* Retrieved November 2, 2009, from http://www.jenesse.org/phy_abuse.html

Jenesse Center. (2009c). *Sexual abuse.* Retrieved November 2, 2009, from http://www.jenesse.org/sex_abuse.html

Jenesse Center. (2009d). *Economic abuse.* Retrieved November 2, 2009, from http://www.jenesse.org/economic_abuse.html

Jenesse Center. (2009e). *Personal safety plan.* Retrieved November 2, 2009, from http://www.jenesse.org/safety_plan.html

Jenesse Center. (2009f). *Jenesse center services.* Retrieved November 2, 2009, from http://www.jenesse.org/services.html

Kilbourne, J. (n.d.). *Jean Kilbourne.* Retrieved on December 10, 2009, from http://www.jeankilbourne.com/video.html

Lemon, N. K. (2005). *Domestic violence law* (2nd ed.). Eagan, MN: Thomson/West.

Mauricio, A. M., & Lopez, F. G. (2009). A latent classification of male batterers. *Violence and Victims, 24*(4), 419–438.

McCue, M. L. (1995). *Domestic violence: A reference handbook.* Santa Barbara, CA: ABC-CLIO.

National Domestic Violence Hotline. (n.d.). Home page. Retrieved on November 28, 2009, from http://www.ndvh.org

National Institute of Justice. (2009, August 3). *Domestic violence courts: Implementing a pretrial safety program for victims of domestic violence.* Retrieved November 29, 2009, from http://www.ojp.usdoj.gov/nij/topics/courts/domestic-violence-courts/judicial-oversight-implementing.htm

Silverleib, A. (2009, October 6). Democrats vow to ban domestic violence as 'pre-existing condition'. *CNNPolitics.com*. Retrieved October 6, 2009, from http://www.cnn.com/2009/POLITICS/10/06/domestic. violence.insurance

Starr, K. (2006, October 13). Findings and recommendations from the Washington state domestic violence fatality review. In *The nexus of domestic violence and family law: Meeting the challenges* (pp. 2a-1–2a-34). SeaTac: Washington State Bar Association.

U.S. Department of Justice. (1994). *Violence and theft in the workplace*. AARDVARG: An Abuse, Rape and Domestic Violence Aid and Resource Collection. Retrieved November 11, 2009, from http://www. aardvarc.org/dv/statistics.shtml

U.S. Department of Justice. (1998). *Violence by intimates: Analysis of data on crimes by current or former spouses, boyfriends, and girlfriends*. Retrieved October 15, 2009, from http://www.rensco.com/social_ dviolence.asp

U.S. Department of Justice. (2008). *Domestic violence arrests increase, but conviction rates are low*. Retrieved November 29, 2009, from http://www.ojp.usdoj.gov/nij/Features/dv-dual-arrest-10-22-2008.htm

Zerwick, P. (2009). Why didn't they stop him? *O: The Oprah Magazine, 10*(8), 154–158, 171–173.

18 Police Interviews With Suspects
International Perspectives

Karl A. Roberts

Victoria Herrington

INTRODUCTION

The purpose of this chapter is to review theory, research, and practice concerning police interviews with the suspects of crime. The aim of the chapter is to illustrate how a knowledge of psychology and suspect behavior can contribute to the planning and execution of suspect interviews in order to maximize the quantity, quality, and reliability of the information obtained.

In any police investigation, the interview is one of the primary methods used to obtain information from suspects. The interview process however, is not without risks, and high among these is the risk of collecting unreliable and/or misleading information. Such information has frequently—and regrettably—led to miscarriages of justice across the world, with attendant damage to the public's perception of the integrity and reputation of the police and the broader criminal justice system (e.g., Gudjonsson, 2003). Indeed, research from a procedural justice perspective reveals that bad experiences with the police—for example, mistreatment during an interview—has a negative impact on public perceptions of police legitimacy, trust in the police, and the likelihood of future cooperation with the police (e.g., Tyler, 1989; Tyler & Blader, 2003). The personal harm to the individual at the center of a miscarriage of justice is axiomatic.

There has been much research interest internationally on the conditions giving rise to miscarriages of justice, and the behavior of police interviewers has been found to be a significant contributing factor. Such behavior need not include overtly nefarious tactics. Subtle characteristics of the police–suspect interaction, including signs of disbelief, poor listening skills, poor questioning skills, and the use of tacit threats and aggression, all serve to produce unreliable accounts from suspects (Gudjonsson, 2003; Savage & Milne, 2007). In this chapter, we will explore police interview methods, identify the strengths and weaknesses of approaches used across the world, and identify international examples of best practice to help inform practitioners who seek to record accurate and reliable accounts in interviews with suspects.

THE SUSPECT INTERVIEW

In Western criminal justice systems, a *suspect* is an individual the police think may have committed a crime. When a suspect is apprehended, the person generally is arrested and subject to an interview with police officers. In most jurisdictions, criminal and case law govern the ways in which police officers make decisions about grounds for arrest. In the United Kingdom, this is the Police and Criminal Evidence Act in 1984 (PACE). In the United States, this is the Fourth and Fifth Amendments to the U.S. Constitution as well as the U.S. Supreme Court case of *Miranda v. Arizona* (1966) and subsequent related cases.

The Police and Criminal Evidence Act requires police to have some evidence constituting reasonable grounds or suspicion to justify an arrest before it takes place. It is important to note that being a suspect is not equivalent to being the offender, so one important purpose of the suspect interview is to explore the likelihood of whether or not the suspect was even involved in the offense in question (Ord, Shaw, & Green, 2008). Thus, a good suspect interview must not only explore the likelihood that the individual was involved in the offense, but accept that he or she may be able to provide a convincing alibi if given an opportunity to present it. As such, the purpose of a suspect interview should be to increase or decrease the belief by the police that a suspect is an offender, rather than only setting out to prove that this is the case. This is an important distinction, given the popularity of some approaches toward suspect interviewing that stress the importance of obtaining a confession from the suspect during the encounter (Inbau, Reid, Buckley, & Jayne, 2004).

The basic structure of the police interview across Western jurisdictions in the world is broadly similar, consisting of at least one (sometimes two) interviewer(s) present with the suspect, with the suspect asked a series of questions and invited to offer a reply. The *right to silence*—the right of the suspect to decline to offer any answer to a question posed—differs across the world. In most instances across Australian and U.S. jurisdictions, suspects have a right to silence (see *Miranda,* mentioned above), and a court can draw no inferences about the silence. In other countries, most notably England and Wales, if the case goes to court, inferences about the suspect's refusal to answer questions in a police interview may be drawn, and the suspect's innocence may therefore be questioned. In all jurisdictions, suspects must be notified of their rights (to silence or otherwise) before the interview commences, although the extent to which some suspects, particularly vulnerable ones, understand these rights, and the extent to which police officers undertaking the interview recognize this lack of comprehension and take steps to address it, as well as the implications that this may have for the interview and the veracity of the information collected are debatable (Savage & Milne, 2007). These issues will be explored further below.

QUESTION AND ANSWER

The psychological literature tells us that the manner and order in which questions are asked, their tone and wording, the characteristics of the interviewer and interviewee, and the nature of the crime and evidence will all impact an interview with a suspect and the reliability of the information obtained from the interaction (Ord et al., 2008; Savage & Milne, 2007). Many of the earliest approaches to police suspect interviews used a simple question–answer format, whereby the interviewer asked a series of questions designed to elicit the required information. Little attempt was made to build rapport or otherwise engage the suspect; *control*—in terms of questions, topics, and progression of the encounter—was in the hands of the interviewer entirely. This method appealed to a notion that interviewers should direct the suspect exclusively toward areas of interest to the police and that other information was spurious and/or represented attempts by the suspect to deflect the interviewer from the information required.

A considerable limitation with this question-and-answer approach is that it fails to appreciate that the suspect may have an *answering agenda* of his or her own, and that this may contain useful information above and beyond the narrow focus of the known investigation (Shepherd, 1991). In other words, this approach assumes that the police are in possession of all the facts about the case, although experience tells us that this is rarely true. It does not account for the possibility that the suspect may be in possession of other relevant information and that this may rule them out as a suspect and implicate other individuals.

Interrogation can be considered an extreme form of question-answer interviewing. An interrogation is characterized as an asymmetrical *conversation* between an interviewer and suspect and a questioning style in which the interviewer dominates the encounter. Interrogations may also include implied or explicit threats and coercion (Gudjonsson, 2003). Although such approaches undoubtedly serve to retain *control* in the hands of the interviewer, they also suffer from the same difficulties as traditional question–answer approaches with little opportunity for the suspect to discuss their agenda and provide information outside the narrow focus of the questioning. Moreover, this style of encounter—particularly if threats and coercion are implied and/or used—can increase an individual's anxiety, which the psychological literature tells us in turn serves to increase an individual's uncertainty and doubt about events they have experienced (Gudjonsson, 2003). In this psychological state, individuals are much more sensitive to the reactions of the interviewer—and are often looking for signals from the interviewer that their responses are acceptable and that their discomfort is coming to an end—and so are prone to tailor their answers in order to elicit a favorable reaction from the interviewer. Accuracy and detail, we argue, is therefore secondary to an individual's desire to minimize their experience of anxiety and fear, all of which serve to increase suggestibility and the likelihood that interviewees will accept the information provided to them by the interviewer and/or confabulate accounts (Gudjonsson, 2003).

THE CONFESSION OBSESSION

Traditionally, police interviews with suspects are regarded as an opportunity for the suspect to tell the truth, admit their offending, and confess their sins to the police (Ord et al., 2008). As this is the aim of the interview, it therefore follows that the interaction will be characterized by accusations and statements such as "I put it to you that you were involved..." or speculative remarks that assume the guilt of the suspect such as "Why did you do...?" Returning to our introductory remarks and the notion that being a suspect does not always equate with being an offender, such interview aims are at best problematic, and at worst ethically and procedurally dangerous. If the aim of the suspect interview is to obtain a confession, then when does the interview stop? When an interviewer is faced with a suspect reluctant to admit guilt, what tactics might he or she use to achieve his or her stated aim? The psychological literature and international police experience tell us the troubling answer to this question, and the tactics employed almost always involve some element of persuasion—to speak and ultimately confess—and if this fails in extremis perhaps even to threaten (Gudjonsson, 2003; Savage & Milne, 2007). Although one's moral reasoning may defend this as acceptable in cases where the suspect is indeed a dangerous offender (Levin, 1982), this is (arguably increasingly) not always the case. For example, in the United Kingdom in 2007–2008, an estimated 1,475,266 persons were arrested for recorded crimes, of which 4,244 were detained by the police for more than 24 hours and then released without charge.* This is an increase of 111% from the 2006–2007 figures of 2,013, and says nothing of the numbers released without charge after being held for less than 24 hours (Povey, Smith, Hand, & Dodd, 2009). Although there are a number of reasons why police may choose not to charge a suspect with an offense (including lack of evidence and the charge not in the public interest), these data clearly suggest that not all suspects are guilty of the offense for which they have been detained. Any investigation and interview approach designed to obtain a confession does not account for this eventuality.

Moreover, for confession-focused interviews, success is naturally measured by obtaining a confession, and interviewer behavior is likely to be geared to this end (Ord et al., 2008). This has a number of less obvious implications for the interaction and the veracity of the information elicited. Interviews tend to be longer (Savage & Milne, 2007) as the interviewer continues until a confession is elicited. This is likely to increase the risk of repetition of questions and statements to the suspect, especially if—due to the one-sided and narrow focus of the interaction—the interviewer completes all of the questions early in the interview. Repetition of questions raises uncertainty within a suspect and can lead to changing their account and/or agreeing to information presented to them (Gudjonsson, 2003; Ord et al., 2008), which ironically increases the suspicion among police officers as to the likelihood that the suspect is lying to hide guilt (Gudjonsson,

---

* In the United Kingdom, under section 42 of PACE, an individual can be detained on the authority of the police for a maximum of 24 hours, and up to 36 hours on the authority of a superintendent (Povey et al., 2009).

2003). When interviews are long, fatigue becomes an issue, and coupled with suspects' anxiety may lead to unreliable information and acceding to interviewers' demands. False confessions may even result through suspects' desire to simply end the—by now—uncomfortable interview (Gudjonsson, 2003).

Confession-focused interviews stress the importance of persuasion, and a key tool in the interviewer's arsenal is trying to persuade a suspect that it is in their best interests to confess to the crime. In some instances, this even goes a step further and involves interviewers persuading a suspect that they have committed a crime (Ord et al., 2008). These so-called *persuasive interview approaches* are highly likely to produce poor and unreliable accounts. Suspects may begin to doubt their own account or recollection of events, leading to actual increased unreliability of their accounts (Gudjonsson, 2003). This is strongly related to increased suggestibility and confabulation, that is, incorporating information provided by the interviewer either intentionally or unintentionally into their own account (Gudjonsson, 2003). Persuasive interview approaches are particularly problematic where the cognitive reserves of the suspect are compromised through lack of sleep, heightened anxiety, or congenital disorders and pose a particular problem for officers interviewing vulnerable suspects (we explore more later in this chapter). It bears repeating that although this arguably works in favor of natural justice and the criminal justice system when the suspect is indeed the offender, the risks of these techniques leading to a miscarriage of justice—with all the attendant risks to public confidence and perceived legitimacy of the police and criminal justice system as well as to the individual involved—outweigh any possible benefits. As such, more ethical approaches to interviewing, built on the evidenced-based literature from the psychological, sociological, and criminological fields, are needed.

ETHICAL INTERVIEWING

In a number of countries across the world, interview methods have developed that are nested within an understanding of the psychological aspects inherent in police suspect interviews, and the impact that the stressors peculiar to this interaction can have on this encounter and on the information elicited from such interviews (Shepherd, 1991). These methods are variously termed *investigative interviewing* and/or *ethical interviewing*, but share the same key aim—that the interview will provide an opportunity to obtain reliable information that rules a suspect in or out of involvement in an offense, rather than eliciting a confession per se. Central to these models is the open-mindedness of the interviewer about the suspects' guilt or innocence, at least in terms of the procedures he or she undertakes, including giving the suspect every opportunity to provide an account of his or her movements, for example. Once a full account is given, and where discrepancies are found between the account given by the suspect and evidence gathered from other witnesses, victims, and investigative methods, the police can be sure that the unreliability of the account has little to do with inadvertent pressures placed on the suspect by the police. All of this serves to increase the reliability of the information extracted and a firmer foundation on which to challenge a willfully inaccurate suspect account.

One widely adopted structure for suspect interviewing under this ethical interviewing approach is the PEACE interview model. During the 1990s in the United Kingdom, a series of miscarriages of justice cited police interviewing methods as causal factors (Savage & Milne, 2007), which led to a number of reviews of police interviewing tactics. These reviews revealed, in particular, an overreliance on the use of threats, persuasion, and coercion and a near ubiquitous use of the question-and-answer format as outlined above (Baldwin, 1993). In order to identify best practices for police interviews, psychological research and theory concerning human memory and human interaction, as well as questioning style and the impact of interviewer behavior on interviewees was reviewed, and police interview practitioners and police trainers were consulted (Bull & Milne, 2004). From this, an approach to police interviewing was devised to minimize the risks to the integrity of police investigations, and balancing this with the human rights of the interviewee and the legitimate needs of the police to obtain information from a suspect. This approach is known by the acronym PEACE, which stands for Planning, Engage and Explain, Account, Closure, and Evaluate and describes five stages that an interview should go through to meet these aims (Milne & Bull, 2003).

The PEACE interview model stresses the development of rapport with the suspect, on the understanding that rapport engenders trust between the suspect and interviewer, which minimizes the possibility of anxiety and distress on the part of the suspect and maximizes the likelihood that he or she will answer the interviewer's questions and feel able to disclose other relevant information. Practitioners may criticize this approach by pointing to their experiences with many suspects who are unreceptive in interview situations at best, with truculence, belligerence, and even aggressiveness. In such situations, one might suggest that the interviewer has little to lose by attempting to build rapport and potentially much to gain.

The *planning* phase stresses the planning of an interview ahead of time. In this phase, the interviewer should be active in considering both the aims and desired outcomes of the interview (and accepting that the aim is not simply to elicit a confession), how best to order and phrase the key questions that need to be put to the suspect, and how to consider the personality characteristics of the suspect and the reactions these are likely to produce. Special considerations may need to be given to vulnerable suspects, whose characteristics (as will be discussed later in this chapter) and other personal attributes may influence the pace and flow of the interview encounter. Further, without clear aims and outcomes of an interview, it is impossible to adequately evaluate it; one needs clear aims to be able to identify if and when they have been met. Clear aims for an interview also have an impact on the length and duration of interviews; more specifically, when the aims of the interview are met, the interview can end.

In the *engage and explain* phase, the interviewer should (attempt to) build rapport with the suspect, to put the suspect at ease and explain how the interview will operate in order to reduce anxiety and uncertainty, and to create a climate of cooperation. Interviewees come to the interview situation with a host of expectations about the encounter. For some, this will be based on previous experience; for others, it will have been gained vicariously through the experiences of friends and acquaintances; and for still others, particularly first-time suspects, it will be the result of popular media depictions of interview situations such as those found in mainstream cop dramas like *Criminal Minds* in the United States, *City Homicide* in Australia, and *The Bill* in the United Kingdom. By building rapport and explaining how the interview will progress, the suspect is put at ease. By putting the suspect at ease, anxiety will be reduced; by reducing anxiety, the suspect will be better able to give as full and accurate an account as he or she is willing, which gives the police a version of events against which to hold the suspect to account, should other evidence identify flaws in this.

In the *account* phase of the interview, the suspect is invited to provide a full account of his or her behavior relevant to the investigation based on topics of interest identified by the interviewer during the planning phase. For example, this may involve a suspect being asked to give an account of his or her movements from a given time on the day in question, details of their friends and contacts, and relevant background. The PEACE approach advises that the suspect should not be overtly challenged while he or she is providing an initial account. Although interviewers might ask for clarification of points raised, overt challenge is discouraged on the grounds that they are very likely to create doubt and uncertainty in the suspect (Gudjonsson, 2003) or may alert the suspect to evidence that contradicts their account early enough for a suspect to change their version of events to accommodate the interviewer's expressed doubts.

When the suspect has given as full an account as can be reasonably expected and has accepted that this is their account, interviewers can move on to challenge the account. Here, the interviewers may explicitly challenge inconsistencies and inaccuracies and invite the suspect to account for them within the bounds of their previously given account. This is not an aggressive or threatening phase of the interview, and some of the very best practitioners in the field adopt what might be termed a

"Colombo-esque" approach to this phase (couching the challenges in apologetic and self-effacing language), although many suspects frequently find this uncomfortable.

The PEACE model advises interviewers how to end the interview. In the *closure* phase, the interviewer brings the interaction to a comfortable conclusion, maintaining rapport with the suspect and avoiding negative emotional reactions such as anger or anxiety on both sides. Suspects should be thanked, and interviewers should ensure that suspects understand what has happened during the interview and what will happen in the future. Suspects should also be given the opportunity to ask any questions and add any further comments to their accounts that they had not had a chance to present during the interview. Why is this important? Well, pragmatically, the suspect may need to be reinterviewed at a later date, and building rapport a second time may be difficult if the interviewer ended the first interview badly. Moreover, as we noted above, many of these suspects will be released without charge, and a good proportion of them may well be innocent. There are additional benefits that go beyond the immediate interview situation. Individuals generally have a need to be treated in an unbiased, fair, and supportive manner in which they perceive that their needs are considered and that they are listened to when dealing with the police. This has been termed *procedural fairness* (Tyler, 1989). Where individuals perceive they have received treatment of this sort, there are positive impacts for the police, including enhanced perceptions of police legitimacy, trust in the police, and greater likelihood of future cooperation (Tyler & Blader, 2003).

Finally, each interview should be subject to *evaluation*. Here, the interview is evaluated against the aims and objectives set out in the planning phase as well as other evidence and intelligence the police may have. The behavior of the suspect is also considered here, both in and out of the interview situation. This can identify inconsistencies and inaccuracies which can be used to challenge the suspect's account at a later date as well as areas requiring further clarification and investigation.

Ultimately, within the PEACE approach, interviewers explicitly give suspects every opportunity to account for themselves in as supportive an environment as possible. Rapport is built and maintained throughout the interview, reducing the potential for feelings of threat and uncertainty and improving the reliability of accounts, which exonerate the innocent and give the willfully deceitful the opportunity to present their case, provide testable statements, and effectively paint themselves into a corner. Evaluation of the use of the PEACE model by United Kingdom Police has indicated an improvement in the reliability of suspect accounts and a reduction of miscarriages of justice where interviewing practices were cited by the appellant (Bull & Milne, 2004).

CONVERSATION MANAGEMENT

Whereas PEACE provides a general structure for how investigative interviews should be planned and evaluated and the order in which investigators should carry out certain tasks, *conversation management* (Shepherd, 1991) is the method through which the structure of an interview is managed, and the notion of ethical interviewing is translated from theory into practice. It fits within the PEACE framework, within the *account* phase, and stresses the order in which investigators should approach the interview.

The conversation management approach is based on psychological principles of how individuals recall and manage information and the impact of questioning on recall (Shepherd, 1991). This approach has three phases: the suspect agenda, the police agenda, and the challenge phase.* Within the suspect agenda, the suspect is permitted to say whatever they wish concerning their involvement in and recollections about the offense. The interviewer allows the suspect to speak in

---

* At the end of the interview, following the completion of the challenge phase, suspects are invited to add anything else they consider relevant, giving further opportunity to add to or modify their account and/or to provide new information in areas not covered by the interviewers, as is the case under the *closure* phase of PEACE.

his or her own words and does not interrupt (with the rationale that interruption increases the risk of suggestibility because it raises doubt on the part of the suspect about their account; see, e.g., Gudjonsson, 2003). Only when the suspect's initial account has been given can the interviewer ask questions to further clarify the events. This moves the conversation from suspect to police agenda.

During the police agenda, the interviewer's aim is to clarify the suspect's account, not challenge it. For example, if a suspect suggests he or she was driving a red car, the interviewer would ask for more details of the car; its registration, the interior color, and so on. Within the police agenda, the interviewer obtains *fine-grained detail* about the actions and events described in a suspect's account. The clear advantage of this is that the more detail police have, the more information there is to test the suspect's account with reference to witness and other evidence. Two terms highlight the useful information that can be obtained during this investigative phase: *checkable lies* and *provable facts*. Essentially, interviewers are tasked with finding as much information as possible that can be verified from other sources.

Should a suspect decline to provide an account during the suspect agenda phase (as is their right in most jurisdictions), the interview moves into the police agenda phase directly. However, the interviewer should move into the challenge phase only when this police agenda phase is complete.

In the challenge phase, investigators challenge the suspect's account using inconsistencies and inaccuracies identified from the information provided by witnesses and other sources (including forensic evidence). By coming to this stage at the end of the interview process rather than earlier, there is less likelihood that the interview process will create suspect uncertainty about their account and with it an increased risk of suggestibility and/or confabulation—the spontaneous recall by an interviewee of events that did not occur. Moreover, it also limits the "wriggle room" available for a willfully deceitful suspect to change their account and accommodate the information provided by police in their challenges. Challenges should be delivered in a calm and controlled manner without anger or threat. Again, anger, threats, and coercion raise the risk of suggestibility, and this model recommends that challenges are presented in a matter-of-fact way that merely asks the suspect to account for the evident disparity in their account against the information from another source (Ord et al., 2008). This also limits the possibility that interview evidence will be dismissed from court on the grounds of oppressive interview tactics.

Between each of the three phases, the conversation management structure suggests taking a break in order to allow time for police to evaluate the process and products of the phase. This evaluation can shape the development of further questions and ensure that all areas have been covered before moving on to the next stage; for example, a break after the police agenda allows interviewers to reflect on the extent to which they have covered all areas they wished to cover.

INTERVIEW PLANNING

Information is the lifeblood of any police investigation. As we have noted above, given the risks of entering an interview with the aim of securing a confession, maximizing the quality and quantity of information obtained should be the overall aim of the interview (Ord et al., 2008). Within the PEACE model, the *planning* and *evaluation* phases are most critical to interview planning. They identify, and make explicit, the aims of the interview and develop a strategy to achieve these. Those involved in this process need to answer several important questions, including:

- *What are the legal points to prove?* What information is required under the law to charge a suspect?
- *What are the relevant topic areas?* Some of the topics are highly relevant to an investigation (including perhaps the suspect's movements at key times, and the attitudes and interests of the suspect), while others are of more peripheral relevance (perhaps their living arrangements and social history). This is dependent on the context of the offense, of course.

- *Are there any topic areas that could and should be avoided?* Certain topics are less relevant to an investigation than others (such as a suspect's sexual interests in a fraud investigation), while others may be threatening to the suspect and may act as barriers to communication (including, for example, childhood trauma and sexual abuse), and investigators need to consider whether exploring these areas is necessary in the suspect interview by weighing their relevance against the risks to rapport.

- *In what order should topics be introduced during the interview?* In principle, interviewers can ask questions about any topic in any order, although beginning an interview with highly emotive topics (such as an individual's experiences of abuse) may serve as a barrier to communication (Ord et al., 2008) and interviewers may be better off *progressing slowly* to such discussions.

- *What is the most effective way of asking key questions?* Open questions allow for greater exposition and do not constrain the interviewee to a particular response, whereas leading questions assume a response and can impact negatively on the reliability of an account (Ord et al., 2007). Wording also plays a role, and certain phrases or types of language may increase feelings of anger or distress in an individual (Ord et al., 2007).

- *What should be the first question asked?* Often it is useful to ask directly if the suspect has any knowledge of or involvement in the offense for which they are being questioned. One of the authors of this chapter has experienced the utility of this technique in practice and has been involved in several cases where suspects confessed to an offense when asked, or explained at the conclusion of an interview period that they "would have told [the police] this 3 days ago if only [the police] had bothered to ask." This underscores our previous point regarding expectations, that many suspects have little understanding of how the interview will progress (unless this is explained to them at the outset) and may blithely follow police questioning, even if they are keen to impart useful information, unless given the opportunity to provide an account of their own as suggested under the suspect agenda aspect of conversation management (see previous discussion of conversation management).

- *What characteristics of the interviewer—skills, experience, background, appearance, and so on—would maximize the information obtained?* The best person to build rapport with a suspect may not always be the person most willing to carry out the interview, or even the lead investigator on the case. On occasion, the best interviewer may be someone with similar characteristics or experiences as the suspect such as someone of with similar physical characteristics or from a similar ethnic, religious, or socioeconomic group, who is skilled and experienced in interviewing individuals with similar characteristics to the suspect or who is able to behave in a manner that develops rapport with the suspect. The interviewer's understanding of the offense under investigation, physical characteristics, age, and gender will impact the judgments that suspects make about them and their willingness to disclose information during the interview (Ord et al., 2007).

- *How can rapport be most effectively built?* Building rapport is not a swift or brief process, and PEACE suggests that it should be engaged prior to the first interview through to charging or releasing the suspect. Skills such as active listening refers to the interviewer illustrating interest in what the suspect has said by using strategies to indicate that they are listening and engaging. Examples include use of verbal sounds in response to suspect comments (e.g., "mmm," "uh huh," thanking the suspect for a response, and paraphrasing responses), attentiveness, and paying attention to the comfort needs of the suspect. The careful ordering of topics covered in the interview (as noted above) also serves to build and maintain rapport.

- *What are the behavioral characteristics of the suspect?* It is useful during the planning and evaluation of any interview to give consideration to the behavioral characteristics of the suspect. This allows investigators to predict likely interview behavior, judge the best way to build rapport with the suspect, and decide how best to present challenging material.

Such behavioral characteristics include suspects' attitudes, beliefs, cultural background, lifestyle characteristics, fears, and perceived threats, as well as any psychological and social problems. In the next section, we will further explore the relevance of these and consider how an awareness of these issues can have an impact on police behavior in a suspect interview setting.

SUSPECT CHARACTERISTICS AND INTERVIEW CONSIDERATIONS

In very simplistic terms, human behavior is a result of complex interactions between the characteristics of an individual and the situation in which an individual finds him- or herself (Pervin & John, 1999). In other words, behavior = individual disposition × environment. If it is possible to identify something about an individual's particular characteristics, then it is possible to make some prediction about that individual's behavior in a given situation (e.g., an interview).

During a suspect interview, interviewers can control many of the characteristics of the situation (within certain legally defined constraints, of course). Such characteristics include the physical characteristics of the interview room, the physical characteristics of the interviewers, and their behavior toward the suspect (including, as previously noted, their attitude; the type, order, and style of questions asked; the duration of interviews; and so forth). These situational characteristics interact with the characteristics of the suspect to produce behavior. Clearly, then, knowledge of the suspect is useful in identifying the interview strategy most likely to elicit desired behaviors (such as answering questions and giving a full account) and reduce undesirable behavior (such as noncompliance or aggression). What is and is not desired behavior will have been identified in the planning phase and relates to the specific aims of the interview. Within the conversation management model, for example, the aim of early interviews—the suspect agenda—is to obtain a first account concerning the suspect's behavior relevant to the offense in question. This requires use of an interview strategy that makes it likely that the suspect will talk; this can be challenging because some suspects may be initially unwilling to engage with interviewers, hostile to police, traumatized, and suspicious or even fearful of police. Knowledge of the suspect's behavioral characteristics will allow interviewers to maximize the development of rapport and can assist in providing an environment idiosyncratic to the suspect's needs (i.e., an environment in which the suspect is most likely to feel most comfortable and unthreatened and to perceive that the interviewers are taking them seriously and are interested in what they have to say). This may be as simple as understanding a suspect's interests—his or her favorite football team, for example—allowing for an opportunity to engage in a safe conversational theme and reduce initial barriers to communication.* It is important to get such information right, however. As an example, the views of one of the authors of this chapter on the greatness of a particular football team do not coincide with the views of the other and have on occasion led to a breakdown in communication, albeit briefly.

Considerations of suspect behavioral characteristics are important at the evaluation stage of the process, and behavior during the interview should be considered alongside the nature of the information obtained. Evaluation within and across interviews will help identify signs of vulnerability and distress; the degree to which rapport has been achieved; the extent to which the suspect is engaging with the interviewers; and interaction strategies specific to the suspect such as interruption, silence, or disruption. All of these can shape the interview strategy and lead to modification if necessary (Gelles, McFadden, Borum, & Vossekuil, 2006).

---

* It must be noted here that investigators must be careful that their interview questions are relevant to the inquiry. Questions about interests, although unthreatening and likely to engender rapport with some individuals, are unlikely to be regarded as relevant by legal authorities; their inclusion within an interview may invite challenge of their relevance and attendant disruption to the interview should the suspect have a legal representative present. This type of question may be better placed outside of an interview should the investigator have an opportunity to engage the suspect prior to interview.

Assessing Suspect Behavioral Characteristics

Having explored the relevance of suspect behavioral characteristics, it is important to consider how investigators can identify these and the useful sources of information available to those making these assessments. In psychological practice, a behavioral assessment of an individual involves making judgments about data from a range of sources, including observation of behavior, interviews with the individual and others who know them, a consideration of an individual's background, an examination of their social circumstances, and even formalized psychometric assessment (Groth-Marnat, 2003). In an investigative context, this is clearly not always possible because of legal constraints on police interactions with suspects and, more pressingly, because police simply do not have the time to do this. This means that accessing analogous sources of information is important.

Police inquiries generate substantial information about individual suspects, and this information can be useful for its behavioral as well as its evidential content. To be sure, the amount of this information available about different suspects will vary from situation to situation. In some cases, police can draw from large reservoirs of lifestyle information from intelligence work and other investigations. Others, particularly those with no prior dealings with police investigators, may have to rely on their observations of the suspects' demeanor during the current investigation, including reactions and behavior following arrest and while awaiting interview. Even in the face of limited information about an individual, time spent considering their behavioral characteristics is likely to pay dividends (Ord et al., 2008).

Statements from people who know a suspect—such as friends, family, and professionals (doctors, psychiatrists, social workers)—are routinely collected during a police investigation. These statements offer insight into how that person behaves in their day-to-day life, their interests, hobbies, attitudes, and beliefs. They give a sense of the situations that anger and frustrate the suspect, how they deal with stress, and what they need for their own well-being. These should not be used blindly, though, and some can be self-serving or may be unfairly critical of the individual, particularly if the statements are obtained from adversaries or former partners. Thus, triangulating information from a range of different sources is important. For example, statements gained from a jilted lover may help contextualize an individual's negative characteristics against the backdrop of positive information provided by close friends. Information from sources such as other police, prison officers, and health professionals is also worth obtaining. A suspect's attitude to previous offending can be useful in predicting how they might view their current situation and how they might present for interview. Some individuals experience high levels of guilt, others try hard to conceal their offending, and still others might feel entirely justified in their actions and may be proud of their acts.

Assessing Offense Characteristics

The characteristics of the offense and of any previous offenses are useful to consider. Of particular interest here is the way in which the offender carried out the offense. During the commission of an offense, offenders can behave in ways that are important to them and may show something of their particular abilities, needs, and interests. In considering the characteristics of an offense, three key and interrelated questions should be asked:

- *What does the offender do that they have to do to commit the offense?* This invites the investigator to consider the basic offense and the minimum behavior the offender needs to do to succeed. For example, robbery requires an item to be stolen using threats of violence or actual violence; rape requires sexual penetration without the consent of the victim.
- *What does the offender do that they do not need to do?* This asks the investigator to consider how the offense differs from the basic offense and what behaviors the offender brings to the offense that take it beyond what is needed to succeed. This can uncover

the particular interests and motives of the offender. For example, one rapist may engage the victim in conversation and may be complimentary to her during and after the sexual assault. Another might say nothing to the victim, and yet another might gratuitously beat the victim during the rape. These different behaviors allow us to hypothesize about the offender's attitude to the victim and the offense.

- *What does the offender not do that they could have done?* In any offense, the offender could have carried out any number of possible acts. Returning to our rape example, an offender might gain control over a victim, but may choose not to rape him or her; another may attempt to kiss the victim and, having met with resistance, not pursue this. One offender may take steps to hide his identity, while another may take no such precautions and may leave considerable forensic evidence.

By way of an example, consider the following case. One of the authors consulted on a case where the offender spent over an hour talking to a woman he had raped at knifepoint. He told her how sorry he was and how attractive she looked; he even arranged a date with her for the next evening. All this time, the victim was able to get a good look at the offender and to produce a good description of him. In answering the three questions above, what do we see? *What does the offender do that he has to do?* To commit the rape, he must gain control over the victim to extinguish her resistance; he does this by brandishing the knife and by brute force. Having gained control over her, he completes the rape. *What does the offender do that he doesn't have to do?* Here, the offender spends time talking with the victim; he arranged a date with her and allowed her to get a good description of him. *What does the offender not do that he could have done?* Here, the offender fails to attempt to hide his identity, he was not profane, and he used minimal force—indeed, only as much force as was required to obtain control over her. He did not use the knife on the victim.

What does this behavior suggest about our offender, and about how he might react in a suspect interview situation? One hypothesis is that the offender was motivated by the need for a relationship with the victim, and that this need was so important that it overrode concerns for his personal safety (i.e., not getting caught). We might also suggest that the offender may not have regarded the encounter as a rape and may be able to justify and minimize his actions to himself. This is potentially useful information for investigators in designing an interview strategy and can inform our understanding of how the individual regards himself, the victim, and his behavior, and therefore how investigators might best approach the offense during the interview.[*]

Broaching the subject of the offense can be an important consideration in a suspect interview. Readers are invited to consider the impact the terms *rape* and *rapist* might have on a suspect who does not consider himself a rapist, such as the offender in the case referred to above, and whether this might provoke anger and act as a barrier to communication.

CHARACTERISTICS OF SUSPECTS RELEVANT TO INTERVIEWS

An individual's behavior will be governed by the interaction of a range of interrelated individual characteristics, and there are several of these that are particularly important within an interview setting because they impact on a suspect's ability to understand and engage in the process. Such characteristics are rarely completely independent, and we frequently find an interplay of these, which will impact behavior. To preempt what is to follow, an individual with high intelligence, highly developed social skills, or a high degree of empathy is likely to interact in an interview situation very differently from someone who is low on these three counts. Thus, identifying low intelligence, for example, may not be enough.

---

[*] In this particular case, the investigators employed the PEACE model and the conversation management framework, and the offender was successfully prosecuted for rape, largely on the strength of information obtained from the interviews.

INTELLIGENCE

Broadly, *intelligence* can be defined as the ability to reason, imagine, and process information (Salter, 1982). Highly intelligent individuals can be creative and imaginative and may often plan their actions in advance of the interview. In assessing an individual's intelligence, lifestyle and behavioral characteristics are important as is their previous offending behavior. Intelligent individuals may be academically successful and/or may hold demanding skilled occupations that make use of their abilities. This does not characterize all intelligent individuals, of course, although most will demonstrate their skills through their behavior and lifestyle choices, through their hobbies or interests, the books they read, the television programs they watch, and Internet sites they visit. Issues to be considered here are the complexity of the material, the need for planning, and continuity of thought—with the rule of thumb as the greater the demands on the individual, the greater the intelligence level. The way an individual communicates, that is, their vocabulary and/or the logic of their arguments and written material, can give insights into their levels of intelligence. Offending behavior too may also give an indication of intelligence; with the greater the complexity of the offense and the greater the degree of planning and imagination involved indicating higher intelligence. Within an interview context, investigators may also need to be alert to the possibility of these suspects engaging in counterstrategies to disrupt the interviews or to mislead the investigation.

In contrast, individuals at the opposite end of the intelligence spectrum (those with low intelligence) are most likely to struggle to understand complex questions and police lines of questioning. Individuals with very low intelligence (i.e., IQs less than 70) may be defined as intellectually disabled (if they have concomitant deficits in adaptive behavior such as looking after oneself in the social world). This group presents particular problems in terms of whether they should be interviewed at all, as they often fail to understand the reasons for their detention, the police cautions, and the questions posed. Suggestibility increases with low intelligence as does the likelihood of false confessions (Gudjonsson, 2003) and the prevalence of low IQ among the offending population (certainly among those who have been caught and detained by police) is high (Irving, 1980; Irving & McKenzie, 1989; Lyall, Holland, Collins, & Styles, 1995; Medford, Gudjonsson, & Pearse, 2000; Winter, Holland, & Collins, 1997). For example, Gudjonsson et al. (1993) found almost 9% of suspects with IQ scores below 70 and 42% with IQ scores in the borderline range of cognitive impairment (between 70 and 79). Herrington (2009) found that 93% of her sample of remand prisoners had an IQ less than 100, 10% had IQs less than 70, and 24% had IQs in the borderline range of functioning (between 70 and 79). There are significant risks in interviewing individuals with very low intelligence in terms of the reliability of the information provided. Moreover, identification of these individuals and catering to their special needs is not always done. Even where systems are in place to provide additional support services for this group, these services are not always activated. Gudjonsson et al. (1993) found that 20% of interviewed suspects fulfilled the criteria for needing additional support during interviews (e.g., needing an appropriate adult with them), but only 4% were correctly identified as such by the police.

SOCIAL SKILLS

We define *social skills* as an ability to relate to and communicate with others in social situations. Individuals with good social skills are comfortable communicating with a range of different individuals and frequently have a wide circle of friends and acquaintances. Such individuals may communicate readily in police interview situations and may even put the interviewers at ease through their social skills. They are often easy to interview and are capable of answering questions clearly and giving detailed accounts. The flip side of this, of course, is that willfully deceitful suspects with good social skills may manipulate the interviewer; creating conditions where the interviewer is placed at ease and considers the flow of information as being good, when in reality information may be limited in relevant detail. This illustrates the need for the content of interviews to be subjected to continuous evaluation to identify such situations. In contrast, individuals with social deficits—particularly those who also have low IQ—may find the interview situation particularly uncomfortable, may not respond to an investigator's attempt to build rapport, and may be uncommunicative.

EMPATHY

Empathy or *empathic concern* is the extent an individual is able to take account of the feelings or perspectives and needs of others. There are two important aspects to empathy relevant to behavior in an interview situation: *perspective taking*, the extent to which an individual is able to consider another's perspective, to acknowledge that others have different attitudes and opinions, and to place themselves in another's shoes and consider things from their point of view; and *emotional empathy*, the extent to which an individual is able to identify with and feel the emotions of others. Individuals vary on the degree of empathy they have. Individuals with high levels of empathy are regarded as sympathetic and are often individuals who others will turn to for advice. Those with low empathy are regarded as unsympathetic, tough-minded, and even selfish. Such individuals struggle to consider the feelings and views of others. Suspects with high levels of empathy are often most able to identify with the impact of their actions, and may experience guilt and even remorse about their actions (particularly if their offense was a sudden, uncontrolled, and unplanned act). They can relate to the victim and will be likely to struggle to rationalize their behavior, especially if the victim has suffered. By contrast, those with low empathy are unlikely to experience such guilt and may be most interested in how the situation impacts them. Having a sense of the likely level of a suspect's empathy may suggest strategies, for example, those with high empathy may be responsive to approaches that invite them to consider the victim and his or her family.

It is axiomatic that high empathy is also useful among interviewers, with good perspective-taking abilities allowing them to consider the likely impact of their own behavior on the interviewee.

SELF-ESTEEM

Self-esteem can be simplistically defined as the sense of self-worth of an individual (Branden, 1969). Individuals with high self-esteem are confident and not easily intimidated by others. Individuals with low self-esteem generally regard themselves as having lesser value and may be easily intimidated. In an interview context, interviewees with low self-esteem find it difficult to relate to interviewers and may benefit from attempts to raise their self-esteem levels through rapport building and compliments, and by interviewers showing interest in them. This may be important in getting them to speak to interviewers at all.

PSYCHOLOGICAL VULNERABILITY

Psychological vulnerability refers to the effects of individuals who have cognitive problems resulting from their age, intellectual disabilities, learning difficulties, and/or mental health problems that can impact their interactions with police in an interview situation (Milne, Shaw, & Smith, 2009). It is associated with an individual's reduced ability to deal with the stress and anxiety provoked by the interview situation as well as their ability to cope with and adapt to the demands placed on them by the interview (Gudjonsson, 2003). Vulnerable individuals, for the purpose of police interviews, include those with a history of mental illness such as schizophrenia, major depression, anxiety-related disorders, drug and alcohol problems, and learning difficulties, as well as the elderly and young children. This incorporates those with low IQ (discussed above), but vulnerability is not bounded by intelligence. Much like low IQ, however, psychological vulnerability is relatively common within criminal justice contexts. For example, Pearce (1995) estimated that 33% of suspect interviews involved a suspect with some form of psychological vulnerability. Failure to take account of these vulnerabilities may lead to unreliable accounts and even false confessions. These individuals may fail to cope adequately with the stress of the interview situation, and they may experience excessive anxiety. This anxiety is likely to exacerbate existing mental health, memory, or social problems, which in turn contribute to their inability to cope effectively with the interview. Individuals may struggle to maintain a coherent account and can be highly susceptible to poor questioning styles such as overly complex questions and leading questions. They are likely to struggle if faced with anger or threats on the part of the interviewer, which are more likely in these interviews as the police involved are frustrated by the inabilities of the suspect to communicate (Gudjonsson, 2003).

Intellectual disabilities (ID) are characterized by a significant impairment of intelligence concurrent with a significant impairment in adaptive behavior (i.e., a diminished ability to adapt to the daily demands of the normal social environment) that manifests before the age of 18. Research on ID has found that interview performance among this group is at particular risk. These individuals often suffer low self-efficacy and rely on cues from other people to help them make sense of their environment (Bybee & Zigler, 1992; Fulero & Everington, 2004). Overreliance on others in the interview context presents particular problems, and intellectually disabled individuals may struggle to adequately differentiate between different cues to identify those that are useful and those that are unhelpful (Bybee & Zigler, 1992). Again due to low self-efficacy, intellectually disabled individuals are also prone to make socially desirable responses when questioned by individuals in positions of authority, such as police officers, and this may well serve to mask their cognitive deficits (Shaw & Budd, 1982). They may acquiesce or "yes-say" to any questions asked, regardless of the appropriateness of the answer (Fulero & Everington, 2004, p. 169; Kebbell & Hatton, 1999; Sigelman, Winer, & Schoenrock, 1982) and may have difficulties processing socially significant information and understanding the reasons for other people's behavior (Fulero & Everington, 2004). Research has found that individuals with intellectual disabilities are overrepresented in the criminal justice system, particularly those who might be regarded as falling into the borderline group. Crocker et al. (2006) found that individuals with mild or borderline ID were more likely to have had the police called in response to an aggressive incident than those with more severe ID; and were ten times more likely to have been arrested at some point in their lifetime. Young males living independently with mild or borderline ID were more likely to misuse substances (typically the overuse of alcohol) leading to problematic behaviors such as aggression and erratic mood changes than those with more profound disabilities (Taggart, McLaughlin, Quinn, & Milligan, 2006). This borderline group—rather than those fulfilling the diagnostic criteria for ID—is most vulnerable in the criminal justice system and in the context of the police interview, as they are less likely to be identified by officers and more likely to mask their deficits and/or for their noncompliance to be regarded as deliberately troublesome, rather than the result of a lack of understanding.

Vulnerable interviewees are more likely to have difficulty providing clear, coherent accounts about their actions than other suspects. The uncertainty they experience with their recall serves to increase a sense of doubt about the veracity of their account for themselves as well as for the police interviewer. Accounts may change over time and with greater questioning, and increased uncertainty may lead to contradiction and confabulation, suggestibility, and—potentially—false confession (Savage & Milne, 2007).

For vulnerable individuals, an interview strategy should (attempt to) minimize stress and anxiety and be aware of any signs of distress, suggestibility, and confabulation such as agreeing with police or incorporating details of police questions into an account. Rapport-based strategies minimize these risks; however, investigators need to remain vigilant for signs of excessive distress. Repetition of questions should also be kept to a minimum as this gives a powerful implicit signal that the answers provided are unsatisfactory and can increase uncertainty on the part of the suspect. Nonverbal cues can also be influential in the context of anxiety and uncertainty, and the vulnerable suspect—sensitive to the interviewers' responses and wishing to please by giving the desired response—may be attuned to the nonverbal communication by the interviewer (Milne et al., 2009).

The problem for interviewers is a need to identify a suspect's vulnerability and to design an interview approach that seeks to minimize distress. Identifying vulnerability is problematic. A few individuals have obvious vulnerabilities; they may be actively psychotic or have limited functioning and may be unable to understand their situation. Many of these individuals may be judged unfit for interview. However, some individuals mask their vulnerabilities, either intentionally to hide their problems or because they can function well enough, although when placed in difficult situations (such as a suspect interview) their vulnerabilities impact negatively on performance. It is important that interviewers are sensitive to changes in behavior and demeanor and identify changes in mental state and functioning. If a vulnerable suspect becomes distressed and/or distracted during an interview, it may be appropriate to end the interview and give the suspect a break, perhaps require medical assessment of the suspect before continuing, or end the interviews altogether. This again illustrates the importance of an ongoing evaluation of the interview.

ATTITUDES

Attitudes are feelings and thoughts toward some object (Fazio, 1986); these can be associated with varying degrees of emotion. Attitudes can relate to any topic or issue, for example, race, sexuality, or gender. Friends, relations, and work colleagues may comment on a suspect's attitudes, and if they are strongly held, perhaps even witnesses noticed the suspect's passing comment. Attitudes can be related to an individual's motivation for offending. Some terrorists for example, justify their behavior on the basis of their political attitudes. Often, the attitudes give individuals permission to act by suggesting that a particular individual deserves to be attacked or abused. Attitudes may also impact strongly on how an individual responds to an interviewer. For example, a highly sexist individual may refuse to speak to a female interviewer. A radical Islamist may refuse to speak to someone who is a nonbeliever. Knowledge about an individual's attitude may therefore be useful in determining the characteristics of the interview team as well as in deciding how to approach the suspect. During the interview, where a suspect has strongly held attitudes, individuals may be willing to discuss their views. It is a decision for the interviewers, given the aims of the interview, whether or not they choose to follow this avenue. If unchallenged, an individual may make useful disclosures; however, it may be important for an interviewer to closely control when and if an individual discusses their views.

NEEDS

Individuals have various needs. At a basic level, everyone has a need for food, water, shelter, and so on (Maslow, 1954). At a more esoteric level, needs can be highly specific. These needs have a large impact on an individuals' behavior. If personal needs can be identified, they are useful in predicting how the individual will behave when needs are met. Achieving a need means an individual is likely to experience positive emotions (such as happiness). When needs are thwarted, a range of negative emotions may be prompted, including anger and sadness. When given an opportunity, individuals will behave in a manner designed to satisfy their personal needs whenever possible. Needs may also form part of the motivation for the offense, for example, many rapists will describe feeling an immense sense of excitement and happiness when achieving power and control over a victim, and for some individuals the pursuit of such power and control can become one of the main reasons for repeating an offense. In interviews, it is important, when possible, to try to identify a suspect's personal needs as their behavior will be influenced to some extent by the needs in question. It is for interviewers to decide whether or not to allow a suspect to realize these needs during the interview.

PUTTING IT ALL TOGETHER: DOING THE INTERVIEW

Each interview is unique and is dependent on the nature of the offense, the aims of the interview, and the characteristics of the interviewee. The planning of the interview should be influenced by all three of these factors, which lead to decisions on the particular strategy taken, the nature and order of topics, the style of questioning, and who should carry out the interview. Depending on the interview's aims, the strategy may allow a suspect to take control of the interview and present their views unchallenged in the first instance. At a stage when interviewers feel they need to challenge this first account, however, it is perhaps of greater value to keep the individual focused on the questions presented and minimize the opportunity for the suspect to lead the interview. All police behavior directed toward the suspect before, during, or after an interview can affect the likelihood that they will provide a reliable (insofar as the suspect is willing for it to be) account. Thus, the entire experience, from first to last contact, can be influential and should be subject to the strategy. This may mean that the arrest characteristics are planned, and it may suit the purposes of the strategy that the interviewers themselves carry out the arrest and transport the suspect to the police station to enable them to begin building rapport, although in some situations separating the two encounters in the mind of the suspect may be preferable. While a suspect is in custody, the impact of the behavior of other police personnel should be considered, and a misplaced comment may undermine the rapport that interviewers have worked to build. The layout of an interview room can have a strong impact on a suspect as well. Consider the position of the lead interviewer relative to the suspect, being too close may impact negatively on individuals with low self-esteem and may provoke anger or discomfort in others. Choice of interviewer is closely linked to the characteristics of the interviewee. An individual whose only experience of men is of abuse and violence may struggle to trust or build rapport with a male interviewer; an individual who has a distrust and hatred of women may not communicate with a female interviewer. Of course, if the aim of the interview is to demonstrate the hostility of an individual to a particular race or gender, then an interviewer with these characteristics could be used; however, this will be a strong barrier to communication and may simply serve to limit disclosure.

Once in the interview room, terms of address may be important. If an individual has a strong need for respect, for example, they may be angered if referred to by their first name. Likewise, a medical professional might expect to be called "Doctor" and not doing this may challenge expectations and limit rapport. Use of a first name suggests familiarity, and this may serve to put a suspect at ease. Here, we are suggesting that interviewers close the emotional distance between them and the suspect and create an unchallenging atmosphere—at least at the outset.

Sometimes, props can be useful. Photographs of a victim, a location, clothing worn by significant individuals, maps of areas can all serve as a reminder to help re-create persons, situations, and events for interviewees when these objects are viewed. This can be particularly useful when investigating cold cases in which events may have happened many years previously. These should be used judiciously, of course, so as not to stray into the techniques labeled oppressive. As noted above, the delivery and wording of questions should be considered, and use of pejorative or threatening terms may provoke anger from a suspect and limit communication. Exploring the characteristics of the suspect and knowing one's audience may minimize this risk.

Ultimately, the way an interview is carried out and its relative successes are measured against the aims and objectives of the interview. We advocate an ethical approach to suspect interviews that aims to elicit information which can be tested against evidence gleaned elsewhere to increase or decrease police suspicion that an individual was responsible for an offense.

These ethical approaches are suspect rather than police centered and actively seek to minimize stress and anxiety and maximize the quality and quantity of the information obtained. Internationally, PEACE has been adopted as a best practice interview model, and conversation management is a technique that works within this framework to provide the nuts-and-bolts of the approach for officers in the field. The success of these tools is in the hands of the investigation team who must effectively plan and prepare for their encounter with a suspect. Suspect behavioral characteristics are crucial, and interviewers must know their audience well. We conclude by reiterating that suspect interviews are a high-stakes game, and the risks associated with miscarriages of justice are considerable not only for the individuals involved but also for wider confidence and trust in the police and criminal justice system. It therefore pays to minimize the possibilities of this by engaging in an ethical interview approach.

REFERENCES

Baldwin, J. (1993). Police interview techniques—Establishing truth or proof? *Criminology, 36,* 109–134.

The Bill [Television series]. London: Talkback Thames.

Branden, N. (1969). *The psychology of self-esteem.* New York: Bantam.

Bull, R., & Milne, R. (2004). Attempts to improve police interviewing of suspects. In G. D. Lassiter (Ed.), *Interrogation, confessions and entrapment* (pp. 33–67). New York: Kluwer Plenum.

Bybee, J., & Zigler, E. (1992). Outdirectedness in individuals with and without intellectual disability. In J. A. Burack, R. M. Hodapp, & E. Zigler (Eds.), *Handbook of mental retardation* (pp. 434–462). Cambridge, UK. Cambridge University Press.

City Homicide [Television series]. Sydney, Australia: Channel 7.

Criminal Minds [Television series]. Hollywood, CA: CBS.

Crocker, A. G., Mercier, C., Lachapelle, Y., Brunet, A., Morin, D., & Roy, M. E. (2006). Prevalence and types of aggressive behaviour among adults with intellectual disabilities. *Journal of Intellectual Disability Research, 50*(9), 652–661.

Fazio, R. H. (1986). How do attitudes guide behavior? In R. M. Sorrentino & E. T. Higgins (Eds.), *The handbook of motivation and cognition: Foundations of social behavior* (pp. 204–243). New York: Guilford.

Fulero, S. M., & Everington, C. (2004). Assessing the capacity of persons with mental retardation to waive Miranda rights: A jurisprudent psychology perspective. *Law and Contemporary Problems, 28,* 53–69.

Gelles, M., McFadden, R., Borum, R., & Vossekuil, B. (2006). Interviewing Al-Qaeda-related subjects: A law enforcement perspective. In T. Williamson (Ed.), *Investigative interviewing: Developments in research, rights and regulation* (pp. 23–41). Devon, UK: Willan.

Groth-Marnat, G. (2003). *Handbook of psychological assessment* (4th ed.). Hoboken, NJ: John Wiley.

Gudjonsson, G. (2003). *The psychology of interrogations and confessions: A handbook.* Chichester, UK: Wiley.

Gudjonsson, G., Clare, I., Rutter, S., & Pearse, J. (1993). *Persons at risk during interviews in police custody: The identification of vulnerabilities.* The Royal Commission on Criminal Justice. Research Study 12. London: HMSO.

Herrington, V. (2009). Assessing the prevalence of intellectual disability among young male prisoners. *Journal of Intellectual Disability Research, 53*(5), 397–410.

Inbau, F. E., Reid, J. E., Buckley, J. P., & Jayne, B. C. (2004). *Criminal interrogations and confessions* (4th ed.). Hoboken, NJ: John Wiley.

Irving, B. (1980). *Police interrogation: A case study of current practice.* The Royal Commission on Criminal Procedure Research Study 2. London: HMSO.

Irving, B., & McKenzie, I. (1989). *Police interrogation: The effects of the Police and Criminal Evidence Act 1984.* London: The Police Foundation.

Kebbell, M. R., & Hatton, C. (1999). People with mental retardation as witnesses in court. *Mental Retardation, 3,* 179–187.

Levin, M. (1982, June). The case for torture. *Newsweek, 13,* 1–2

Lyall, I., Holland, A., Collins, S., & Styles, P. (1995). Incidence of persons with a learning disability detained in police custody: A needs assessment for service development. *Medicine, Science and the Law, 35*(1), 61–71.

Maslow, A. (1954). *Motivation and personality.* New York: HarperCollins.

Medford, S., Gudjonsson, G., & Pearse, J. (2000). *The identification of persons at risk in police custody.* London: Metropolitan Police.

Milne, R., & Bull, R. (2003). Interviewing by the police. In D. Carson & R. Bull (Eds.), *Handbook of psychology in legal contexts* (pp. 21–38). Chichester, UK: Wiley.

Milne, R., Shaw, G., & Smith, K. (2009). *Achieving best evidence in criminal proceedings: Guidance on interviewing victims and witnesses, and using special measures.* London: Crown Prosecution Service.

Ord, B., Shaw, G., & Green, T. (2008). *Investigative interviewing explained* (2nd ed.). Chatswood, Australia: Lexis Nexis.

Pearce, J. P. (1995). Police interviewing: The identification of vulnerabilities. *Journal of Community & Applied Social Psychology, 5,* 147–159.

Pervin, L. A., & John, O. P. (1999). *Handbook of personality: Theory and research.* New York: Guilford.

Police and Criminal Evidence Act, 1984. (1984). London: HMSO.

Povey, D., Smith, K., Hand, T., & Dodd, L. (2009). *Home office statistical bulletin: Police powers and procedures, England and Wales 2007/08.* London: HMSO.

Salter, W. (1982). *Handbook of human intelligence.* Cambridge, UK: Cambridge University Press.

Savage, S., & Milne, R. (2007). Miscarriages of justice: The role of the investigative process. In T. Newburn, T. Williamson, & A. Wright (Eds.), *Handbook of criminal investigation* (pp. 195–216). Cullompton, Devon, UK: Willan.

Shaw, J. A., & Budd, E. D. (1982). Determinants of acquiescence and naysaying of mentally retarded persons. *American Journal of Mental Deficiency, 87,* 108–110.

Shepherd, E. (1991). Ethical interviewing. *Policing, 7,* 42–60.

Sigelman, C., Winer, J., & Schoenrock, C. (1982). Response biases in interviews of individuals with limited mental ability. *Journal of Intellectual Disability, 39*(4), 331–340.

Taggart, L., McLaughlin, D., Quinn, B., & Milligan, V. (2006). An exploration of substance misuse in people with intellectual disabilities. *Journal of Intellectual Disability Research, 50*(8), 588–597.

Tyler, T. R. (1989). The psychology of procedural justice: A test of the group value model. *Journal of Personality and Social Psychology, 57,* 830–838.

Tyler, T. R., & Blader, S. L. (2003). The group engagement model: Procedural justice, social identity and cooperative behaviour. *Personality and Social Psychology Review, 7,* 349–361.

Winter, N., Holland, A. J., & Collins, S. (1997). Factors predisposing to suspected offending by adults with self-reported learning disabilities. *Psychological Medicine, 27,* 595–607.

CASE CITED

Miranda v. Arizona, 384 U.S. 436 (1966).

19 Applying Restorative Justice Principles in Law Enforcement

Roslyn Myers

RESTORATIVE JUSTICE AS AN ALTERNATIVE TO TRADITIONAL LEGAL RESPONSES TO CRIME

Restorative justice (RJ) is a voluntary victim-centered mechanism for offender accountability. RJ models provide a framework in which the stakeholders in a given case—typically victims, offenders, their respective family members and friends, and sometimes community leaders—explore the full effects of an offense in a mediated forum under the guidance of a facilitator (McCold, 1996; Moore & O'Connell, 1994). RJ principles, described in detail below, serve as channels of repair for the disrupted relationships that result from crime by holding offenders responsible for their actions and giving victims a supportive atmosphere in which to speak to their experience of the crime and its aftermath (Center for Restorative Justice and Mediation, 1996; Wilmerding, 1997). These practices create connections among the stakeholders of a criminal incident, which form the cornerstones of the repair that eventually can follow.

Satisfaction with the current justice system is abysmally low (Rosenbaum, 2004). Proponents of RJ have long been advancing RJ-based practices as one antidote to the chronic malaise of criminal justice participants (see, e.g., Braithwaite, 2002; Cragge, 1992; Strang, 2004; Zehr, 2002). At the forefront of the justice system is law enforcement, and the officers who serve as first responders in crime and the gatekeepers to the criminal justice system share this widespread discontent. And for good reason: on one hand, police officers are charged with the responsibility of maintaining order in their communities; and, on the other hand, they are often short changed when it comes to appropriate resources and decision-making authority to address low-level disputes or minor infractions that detract from the quality of life in their communities. RJ principles and practices can serve police officers effectively as part of their toolbox of responses in the face of crimes and minor infractions.

PRINCIPLES OF RESTORATIVE JUSTICE

RJ can be distinguished from retributive systems, like the U.S. criminal justice system. Retributive systems seek punishment for violations of law, and those punishments are almost always in the form of prison time or monetary fines. In contrast, RJ views crime as a breach of the community, and it is therefore designed to repair that breach by restoring the relationships among the victim, the offender, and the members of the community. Its practices help participants reassert their shared values, reestablish trust, define the harm caused, and establish restorative measures to address the harms. RJ requires the victim and the offender to play an active role in addressing the harm done. The general goals of RJ include:

- A "meeting of the minds" between those harmed and those causing harm
- Offender accountability, which it is hoped (but not required) stems from the offender's empathetic understanding of the victim or the community's point of view
- Offender apology, which might not be sincerely felt at the time it is given but must reflect a commitment to avoid future wrongdoing

- Reparation to the victim and/or community in the form of financial reimbursements, community service, or other forms of direct repair
- Reintegration of the offender into the community, with the caveat that gestures of repair might be ongoing to promote continued conformity with community expectations and values

For police officers, RJ holds new possibilities for dealing with crime and other violations that take place in their communities. It is generally experienced by victims and offenders as a more humane approach than traditional legal sanctions, in part because its core principles are aligned with notions of mutual respect and human dignity that are vital to a sense of true justice and restoration. They are also the foundation of good police–community relations.

The process of RJ, as described below, is flexible and rests on various principles. These include:

- The *focus* is repair of the harm caused by the offender, not punishment for the wrongdoing.
- The *process* is oriented around the needs of the victim(s).
- The *aim* of the process is to give victims a sense of relief (emotional, physical, and financial) from the harm, and give communities assurance that the offender will not engage in similar wrongdoing in the future.
- The offender is required to be *accountable*, including the often difficult moment of naming without euphemism the harm he or she caused (the crime perpetrated) and apologizing to the victims.
- The process is consummated by a formal *agreement of reparation* between the victim and the offender that outlines the steps the offender will take to make amends—financially, physically, and spiritually—to the people harmed by his or her actions.
- The process of RJ does not require forgiveness from the victim(s). Remorse on the part of the offender(s) is also not required; however, accountability is.

To make concrete the outcomes of the meeting, the victim and the offender (or, in some instances, the offender and the community) come to an agreement that describes in detail how the offender will make restitution for the damage caused, and complete other meaningful forms of repair to restore the victim as much as possible, in light of the facts of the crime (McCold, 2003). When the community is directly affected by a crime, stakeholders are asked to collectively seek appropriate methods of restoration so that the resolution is not imposed by any single participant or by the mediator, but instead develops organically from the interactions of the participants. From these processes, the aim is that victims will find a sense of relief or release that reduces the negative effects of the crime on their present emotional condition and their ability to function, and liberates their future from the damaging effects of the crime.

Although restorative justice approaches have been criticized as "soft," "liberal," or not amounting to justice at all (Levrant et al., 1999), these critiques reflect an old-school understanding of the purpose of the justice system as retributive and punishment driven. But in light of financial pressures and the impractical nature of warehousing offenders, this view is, at long last, being displaced by a more practical, restoration-driven approach that directs its attention to arguably the most important constituent: the victim. As the first contact point for victims and offenders in the criminal justice process, police officers are in a unique position to address the needs and disputes of the parties and the community while upholding the law and maintaining peace in their communities.

SUCCESSFUL APPLICATION OF RESTORATIVE JUSTICE PRINCIPLES

Because RJ is driven by principles, not ironclad procedures, restorative practices are not limited to the commonly known formal models (described in detail below) such as circle sentencing, family group decision making (also known as family group conferencing, or FGC), victim–offender restorative practices (VORP), or victim–offender mediation dialogue (VOMD). They can be as simple and informal as "affective statements/questions," which help victims and offenders articulate their respective feelings, motivations, and beliefs, and uncover "incorrect" or "antisocial" or "othering" dynamics (Jamieson & McEvoy, 2005), and reflect on how their behavior has affected others; they can be as impromptu as restorative "conversations," which have been used successfully for minor crimes in victims' services departments to expand the RJ options available to victims who do not have the interest or resources to engage in formal, long-term discourses inherent in RJ models. Formal models of RJ require more intensive planning and preparation, are more structured and therefore more heavily mediated, and sometimes involve a greater number of people.

All forms of RJ are expected to have positive results. Proponents of RJ believe it is more successful at achieving just resolutions than traditional forms of retributive justice (Walsh, 2003), and, because RJ is flexible enough to meet the needs of any victim of any type of crime, the appropriate model of RJ—whether formal or informal—has been shown to lead to high levels of victim and community satisfaction. A discussion on the difficulty of standardizing measures of success in RJ program implementation can be found in McCold (2003) and Friday (1999).

RJ has had consistent support from its "graduates" in a justice system that is otherwise not highly regarded. Compared to traditional legal responses, studies have found decreased levels of recidivism after RJ (see, e.g., Chan, 2003; Doolan, 1999; Hoyle, Young, & Hill, 2002; Rowe, 2002; Wilson & Prinzo, 2001). For studies finding slight reduction in recidivism rates, see Geudens (1998), Luke and Lind (2002), McGarrell et al. (2000), Trimboli (2000), and Umbreit (1994). For studies finding no variation in recidivism rates as compared with traditional legal system procedures, see Davis (1982), McCold (1998), Niemeyer and Shichor (1996), and Roy (1995). Increased levels of satisfaction among victims, greater bonding among families and friends affected by crime, and increased community empowerment have been found by Chan (2003), Davis (1982), Doolan (1999), Geudens (1998), Luke and Lind (2002), McCold (1998), McGarrell et al. (2000), Niemeyer and Shichor (1996), Rowe (2002), Roy (1995), Sherman et al. (2000), Trimboli (2000), Umbreit (1994), and Wilson and Prinzo (2001). For satisfaction rates for offenders of approximately 80% to 95%, see Coates and Gehm (1985), McCold and Stahr (1996), and Umbreit (1996). For studies concluding that the variation among outcomes in satisfaction can be correlated with the programs' fidelity to restorative justice principles, see McCold and Wachtel (2000). While the levels of these positive outcomes vary from study to study, remarkably no study has found that RJ leads to negative outcomes (e.g., increased recidivism or decreased victim satisfaction) (Braithwaite, 2002).

RESTORATIVE JUSTICE MODELS

The number and variety of RJ models are almost infinite, and the decision about which form to choose can and should be determined by the circumstances of the criminal event and the victim. In addition to the type of crime and the feelings of the victim, the decision will also depend on the offender's ability to accept responsibility for his or her wrongdoing, to commit to a plan to repair the harm, and to earn the desired reintegration into the community.

Because RJ is an extrajudiciary conflict resolution strategy, its uses are not confined to events defined as legal infractions or crimes. For example, it has been used increasingly in schools and workplace settings as a technique for dealing with citizen complaints against police officers and as part of an overall probation plan. RJ principles also work on the national level to address years or even decades of violence and oppression, most notably as seen in the Truth and Reconciliation Commissions in South Africa (Myers, 2009).

RJ has been adopted with ease in many jurisdictions, especially in the United Kingdom, as a diversionary program from the justice system for first-time juvenile offenders in cases of minor crimes or violations. RJ has also been used as a postadjudication procedure in serious criminal cases handled by an experienced mediator.

The following are the most common models of RJ:

- Victim–offender conferencing or family group conferencing/decision making
- Reparative boards or community panels
- Circle sentencing
- Victim–offender mediation dialogue

In all these RJ models, the decision about whom to include in the RJ meeting begins with the victim, who might express a preference for either a one-on-one meeting or broader inclusion (e.g., family members and loved ones of the victim). The facilitator should offer guidance about the RJ model best suited to the case. If broader inclusion is appropriate, the participants will be defined by how and to what degree they were affected by the crime or violation. Their harm does not have to be physical; it can be emotional. The harm also does not need to be direct: It can involve family members who observe the victim (their loved one) suffering from depression, physical impairments, or other alterations in the quality of their relationships. If it is decided that victim supporters should be included in the meeting, the offender's supporters also should be included.

Supporters not only provide emotional and moral support to the parties but also are important components in the communal demand for accountability. Their very presence creates a moral pressure on the offender and can moderate any extreme emotions that might turn counterproductive. Supporters can be part of the post-RJ mechanism by which the offender carries out his or her obligations under the agreement. They also provide substance to the ongoing web of relationships and community structures into which the offender is, ideally, reintegrated.

Because one primary value in RJ is the ability of the participants to speak openly and without interruption, a tool is often used to keep order as the participants share their stories. Known as a "talking piece," usually in the form of a stone or shell or other neutral item, the object is placed in the middle of the gathering until someone is ready to speak. It is held by the speaker until he or she is finished, then it is replaced in the center for the next person. Those who are not holding the object are asked to hold their thoughts until it is their turn. Because RJ is a victim-centered process, the talking piece is always offered to the victim first, unless there are specific reasons for changing the order. The offender typically speaks after the victim, and other participants, if any, are then able to contribute.

Nearly all RJ models are designed to result in a written document outlining the offender's restorative plan. The specifics of the document are among the primary subjects of discussion among participants and should provide time frames and dollar amounts. However, because the document reflects the consensus of an emotional—often grueling—discussion, it will not necessarily look like a legal settlement or other document prepared for the legal system. Instead, it will reflect the nature of the discussion; thus, the agreement of the participants might be expressed in just a few sentences or in several pages. It might include a preamble, stating the offender's regrets for the itemized acts that lead to the document, and/or it might include notations about the meeting similar to minutes. Whether or not the offender is facing jail time, many victims choose to include their views on whether the offender should be sentenced to prison and the length of the sentence that should be imposed. Once an RJ agreement is made, it can be used for many additional purposes, including supplementing a previously devised probation plan or as part of a victim impact statement in a criminal case. In the United Kingdom where RJ practices are employed with increasing frequency in juvenile cases or minor violations, the offender—in conjunction with an RJ program—might be given a formal police "caution," which would remain on the books for consideration in any future repeat offenses. An RJ approach allows the offender to take responsibility for his or her behavior and keeps the complainant involved and feeling valued.

In whatever way the agreement is employed, it usually represents "a major moral and material part of an offender's life" (Sherman & Strang, 2007, p. 39).

CONFERENCING MODELS

Conferencing models—which include victim–offender conferences (VOCs), family group conferences (FGCs), and community conferences (CCs)—are all organized around a face-to-face meeting among stakeholders, with formalized opportunities to speak and be heard on topics relevant to the crime and related events. The goal of the meeting is to negotiate an agreement by which the offender takes actions to rebuild trust and repair the damage he or she caused.

VOCs, in which the offender and victim are the primary participants, are appropriate for cases in which the harm is restricted to one or a few victims and do not involve broad harm, vandalism, quality-of-life offenses, or other violations to the community. The goal of the meeting(s) is to produce an agreement that outlines the offender's method of repair, but this process is not the same as mediation as used in alternative dispute resolution (ADR) approaches to lawsuits (see Nolan-Haley, 2008). For one thing, RJ is victim-oriented, while mediation and other forms of ADR are democratic; both parties stand on equal footing and mediation attempts to find common ground between them that can serve the ultimate resolution. RJ processes are careful to not revictimize the victim by attempting to equalize his or her position with that of the offender. Furthermore, in guiding the parties toward the ultimate agreement that signals the end of the meetings, the facilitator promotes an open dialogue to air grievances and grief and to express rage or regret. The process must include apologetic discourse by the offender for his or her violations.

If the two people refuse to meet in person, the facilitator can mediate between them separately. While the emotional transformation that is possible in a face-to-face meeting is unlikely to occur when the parties use the facilitator as a go-between, there is no impediment to reaching a satisfactory agreement. And, even after the discussions have begun, the parties can still decide to meet together.

Another form of RJ that follows a similar format is FGC. Because this model includes as primary participants the family of the offender (and can include the victim's family, if there is a victim in the case), it is typically used with juvenile offenders. While not considered victims or offenders, the family is viewed as an essential part of both the framework of accountability the juvenile offender must accept, as well as the offender's necessary ongoing behavioral modifications. This type of RJ is especially appropriate in circumstances in which greater family involvement and attention to the juvenile's development would positively affect his or her ability to avoid future reoffending. The two distinguishing features of FGC are family involvement and revised strategies for decision making, both in the individual offender and on a familial or communal level. This is not surprising, since FGC originated in New Zealand around 1989 as an alternative to the then-standard practices involved in child protection and youth justice system cases with the indigenous Maori people, which gave family members decision-making authority over their own children, subject to the review of the court.

In cases of juvenile crime, conferences can also be organized on a wider scale and include community leaders, religious elders, school officials, "Big Brothers/Sisters," or other mentors, friends, or people who—while not directly affected by the crime—have influential roles in relation to the offender.

In addition to the standard goals of all RJ models, CCs also use the meeting to explore the negative indirect effects of the offender's behavior on his or her broader relationships. In some instances, when people close to the young offender express disappointment, embarrassment, or disapproval, it creates powerful emotional pressure that encourages the minor to reengage his or her identity with a sense of purpose in productive activities.

REPARATIVE BOARDS AND COMMUNITY PANELS

Reparative boards and community panels (also called integrity boards) use a small group of trained volunteers who represent the community to meet with offenders and victims to negotiate the contact. The training of the members of the board varies, depending on site and circumstances, but all follow the foundational aspects of RJ with a focus on restoration, not punishment. As the alternative nomenclature suggests, the emphasis is on integrity—both the personal integrity of the offender, which needs to be reestablished, and the overall integrity of the community ties that were breached by the crime or violation. These models reflect the basic underpinnings of RJ, which strive to restore not only the physical damage caused by the offender's actions, but also the destruction of trust, shared values, community safety, and common goals shared by the community.

CIRCLE SENTENCING

This model, as its name implies, is aimed at designing a sentence for an offender—a legal sentence, as opposed to a reparation agreement—by inviting input from many members of the community. It is used in conjunction with a court appearance and must be approved by the court before it can be implemented. The participants sit in a circle, with the facilitator seated next to the offender; seated on the other side is the victim if he or she chooses to join the circle. The "talking piece" is used to keep order as participants share their views, all of which suggest factors that should be contemplated when determining an appropriate sentence. The commentary often reveals significant differences in opinions about the severity of the sentence. The facilitator encourages participants to explain the factors that influenced their views and to consider the factors raised by other members of the circle, particularly the comments shared by offenders and victims. Like reparative boards, the dialogue in circle sentencing is intended to help participants reestablish shared values and community goals, which go beyond the immediate crime.

VICTIM–OFFENDER MEDIATION DIALOGUE

Victim–offender mediation dialogue (VOMD) has been used in a variety of cases, but is among the few is suitable for extreme violations, such as those involving severe violent interpersonal crime. In VOMD, the victim requests an in-person meeting with the offender, which is coordinated and supervised by a trained mediator. In the most successful cases, the mediator works with each party separately for a long duration—usually from 6 months to 2 years —until the mediator is certain that both sides are sufficiently prepared for the dialogue. The preparatory work generally includes significant self-assessment activities, grief worksheets, and journaling, all of which help the participants develop both a greater awareness of the tapestry of emotion and needs related to the crime and to the upcoming dialogue and greater clarity about their expectations for the meeting. Participants also often exchange correspondence and/or photos—all of which help the parties explore the panoply of emotions they feel about each other and the event, their hopes and expectations for the meeting, and their particular needs to find release from the past event.

When both parties are prepared to meet, the mediator schedules the session. The offender must be ready to apologize for his actions, to name without evasion his or her wrongdoing, and to take whatever steps are necessary to make reparations. The victim must be ready to hear the truth of crime, often a difficult emotional experience, particularly if the case involved murder or a sexual offense; to hear the offender's apology (without pressure to forgive or even affirmatively accept the apologetic gestures); and to ultimately explore means of repair. In cases of severe crime, the ability to make repair is often impossible. This is one feature that distinguishes VOMDs from VOCs. To even suggest that a deceased is a form of "harm" that can be redressed or that a rape victim can place a value on what was taken during the crime is against the principles of RJ. Thus, in many VOMDs, "repair" arises in intangible ways from the meeting itself. Facing each other allows both parties to overcome intense fears; dialogue can supply precious information, such as the victim's last words or the offender's motivations, and explain the seemingly inexplicable; and the offender's willingness to respond to the victim's needs—her need for information, to hear words of regret, and to know that the offender has not forgotten the details of an event that was, for the victim, life-transforming.

VOMDs are typically held in private and can last as long as a day or several days. When they are used post-adjudication in criminal cases, they can be held at the prison. With the permission of the participants, they can be videotaped to extend the learning experience of each party or simply for posterity.

RESTORATIVE JUSTICE IN POLICING

The U.S. criminal justice system (USCJS) is founded on an untenable premise: that arresting and imprisoning offenders is a satisfactory method of dealing with misconduct and protecting society. As their part in the USCJS machinery, police officers are charged with "enforcing the law" (California Advisory Committee, 2000; U.S. Commission on Civil Rights, 2000; see also Napa Valley Criminal Justice Training Center, 2010). In contrast, in the United Kingdom, emphasis is placed on "keeping the Crown's peace" (UK Home Office, 2003, 2007). While this might seem like a matter of semantics, it results in a subtle but complex difference in police culture and reveals much about the organizing principles of an officer's daily routine. The charge to seek peace in the community implies a level of autonomy and discretion that is crucial to the professionalism and success of "beat" cops, many of whom have amassed considerable personal knowledge about their own beat and people who live there. Restorative justice measures require the officer's involvement in equal measure to his or her responsibilities as peacekeeper and police presence.

The implementation of RJ through policing is relatively new and not widespread. Initial experiments with RJ in policing have shown promising results—both for victims and communities as well as for police officers. (For a discussion of the first such experiment, in Wagga Wagga, New South Wales, Australia, in 1992, see Forsythe [1995], noting that the Wagga model, a modification of New Zealand's family group conferencing model, conferenced offenders, victims, and family and friends in a session mediated by a police officer, to decide how to respond to the offense; see also Moore & O'Connell, 1994.) Police-based restorative practices have been implemented by police officers and agencies to address recidivist crimes, disorderly conduct, and other suitable violations by innovative police departments across the United States (Nicholl, 1999) and abroad (Marshall & Merry, 1990). More than 368 police officers have been trained in RJ practices (McCold, 2003) in 141 U.S. police departments.

The RJ process brings together offenders, victims, and community members who have a stake in the crime or violation, either in person or by communication through a facilitator (the police officer), to discuss the events and find a suitable resolution. The procedures comprise three stages: adopting cases in which parties consent, carrying out the appropriate RJ model, and implementing RJ agreements. When RJ is employed to augment traditional USCJS procedures, a final stage requires the submission of a written agreement to the court, referee, or other entity in charge of the case.

ASSESSING THE SUITABILITY OF THE CASE

The first step in a restorative program is to screen cases for those suitable for RJ. Police officers are in an ideal position to lead this part of the process, as they often know the individuals or communities involved in the crime and they certainly are familiar with the circumstances surrounding the events. Police-based RJ allows officers to divert cases from the traditional legal venues, and in some way exert greater influence on the outcomes in their communities.

The first question is whether the case is appropriate to the officer's level of training, which might preclude cases involving severe interpersonal crimes. Some RJ experts believe that cases involving domestic violence, incest, or some types of sexual assault are not suitable for RJ because of the inherent power imbalance between the parties and the inability to reduce such cycle-driven harms to a written document that adequately deals with the dynamics.

Second, relying on his or her policing knowledge, the officer will assess whether the circumstances of the crime or violation lend themselves to a restorative agreement—that is, can the harm be addressed by financial repair, emotional repair, and/or community service activities? This assessment can be seen as an extension of the officer's expertise in policing that comports with RJ principles.

Finally, the parties must be amenable to an RJ process. It is preferable, but not essential, that the parties agree to meet in person because the potential for personal transformation generated by in-person meetings is critical to the restorative process. Face-to-face RJ entails direct deliberation among those affected by a crime. When one or all of the parties are unwilling to meet, however, indirect mediation or discussion with only the victim or the offender is often used to process the crime. Parties who do not wish to meet in person or to communicate through a mediator/facilitator will not be able to engage in an RJ model.

Obtaining Consent

Although some RJ adherents believe its victim orientation requires that the victim request the process first, this is not always practical in the context of police-based RJ. Because police-based RJ should be implemented at the community level for crime or violations that affect quality-of-life issues, property damage, or crimes to persons that do not involve severe violence or intimate relationships, victim initiation is usually less of an issue. While it is preferable that the mediator/facilitator approach the offender only after a victim expresses interest, some RJ practitioners believe that first obtaining consent from the offender protects victims from the often difficult emotional turmoil of considering whether or not to face the offender.

In all cases, the offender must be willing to be communicative about the events and to be accountable for his or her actions. The officer's concern when meeting with an offender is whether he or she is truly suitable for RJ, even if he or she has outwardly expressed an interest. Thus, offenders who deny guilt, express rage at the victim, or reveal themselves as unable to hold themselves personally accountable must be excluded from consideration for RJ. However, if the victim specifically requests an RJ meeting with the offender, the officer should reassess the offender's suitability again, in case there has been any change.

It is important to distinguish accountability from remorse. Being accountable has to do with the offender's ability to speak fully about the crime and to completely "own" his or her part in it. This process does not require the offender to feel guilt or regret, although such genuine reactions are desirable. Most offenders (and victims) cannot anticipate the transformative potential of such a meeting, and they approach the prospect of a resolution by an RJ model with an intellectual understanding of the potential for healing, but not fully comprehending its potential to create a truly satisfying resolution. Once an appropriately willing offender has given consent, RJ facilitators contact victims to seek their consent.

Who Is Invited to Attend?

Because RJ is intended to repair the breach of community caused by crime, the people who should be included in the meeting are those who have a stake in the event. Whether someone has a stake in the event is often defined not by physical damage to person or property, but by emotional damage or investment. Thus, in addition to the stakeholders enumerated above, there might be other victims who did not initially report the crime, or peers of the offender who contributed to the event, or even other officers who have previously dealt with the offender and want to be part of the meeting.

THE RESTORATIVE MEETING

The Officer's Role as Facilitator

In a face-to-face RJ conference, the police officer serves as the mediator or facilitator, whose job it is to prompt the parties through the RJ process. The facilitator strives for a complete expression of several important ideas: the victim's subjective feelings around his or her victimization and specific needs for repair and the offender's apology for causing harm and willingness to restore the physical and emotional damage (if at all possible).

The Body of the Meeting

The meeting itself can take on a variety of forms and hybridizations of traditional RJ models (described above). Depending on the parties involved and the type of offenses, the model can occur in a face-to-face meeting, a circle that includes community stakeholders, or as a negotiated process in which the parties communicate through the facilitator. Because RJ is intended to strengthen communal bonds, the moral and restorative themes that drive RJ make face-to-face meetings the preferable mode. "The criminological theory derived from the evidence on patterns of criminal offending and desistance over the life-course predicts that only face-to-face RJ could provide an experience with enough emotional power to substantially reduce repeat offending" (Sherman & Strang, 2007, p. 33).

Following is a general outline of an RJ model:

1. The facilitator introduces the parties and makes a brief statement about the reasons for the meeting and its restorative goals.
2. The victim describes the event and the aftermath, such that she is able to explain in full detail the effects of the crime on her and her family and friends, including the emotional landscape in which she now exists as a result of the trauma of the crime.
3. The offender(s) gives details about the crime, supplies any explanation (not justifications) describing how it came about, and offers statements of apology, including noneuphemistic words of what exactly he or she did that was wrong.
4. The victim and offender then exchange questions and answers about the crime and their experience of it; they may talk about their families, their backgrounds, and their futures, particularly those things that have been foreclosed or otherwise affected by the crime.
5. If members of the community are present, they share their understanding and experience of the crime and their need for reassurance by the offender that such actions will not occur again.
6. Community members and supporters of the victim and offender express support for the parties.
7. Under the focused guidance of the facilitator, the victim explains her desires for the restorative agreement and the offender expresses his desires for the agreement.
8. As the parties develop the restoration agreement, community and family members offer input.
9. An agreement is finalized and signed by the parties; it is considered a binding agreement and should encompass both physical and property repair as well as words and gestures necessary to restore the victim's emotional health.

Often, community members such as clergy, teachers, or Big Brothers/Sisters, or relatives of the offender in juvenile cases, are recruited to serve as mentors or supervisors to ensure that the offender carries out the agreement. If the RJ conference and agreement were undertaken to suspend a criminal case or a civil lawsuit, the case can be pursued if the offender does not fulfill the agreement.

Training Is Essential to RJ Success

Because the facilitator is the fulcrum by which balance and order is maintained at an RJ meeting, his or her skills are crucial to its success. Facilitators must be impartial; they must not dominate the session, yet they must maintain control and ensure that participants feel physically and psychologically safe throughout the process.

The facilitator is not expected to participate or lead the substance of the discussion. The facilitator is trained to keep parties focused on the reasons for the RJ meeting, the goal of repair, and the necessity of civility in communications.

The officer/facilitator's role is to provide a safe structure for full participation by the stakeholders. Officer training is well suited to this role because they are charged with maintaining public safety. As part of that safe structure, the meeting should have opportunities for participants to interact informally. Sometimes casual conversations among stakeholders can lead to shifts in their thinking, so that a roadblock that emerges during the conference can be alleviated almost imperceptibly.

POLICE-BASED RJ IN PRACTICE

In practice, the most common use of RJ in police work has been conferencing with victims, communities, and offenders. A police department in Bethlehem, Pennsylvania, has used a police-based RJ program that has been shown to be successful for both community members and officers. In the Bethlehem experiment, the primary method of RJ was conferencing. Using a scripted approach, which ensured quality and consistency (see Moore & O'Connell, 1994), the officers, acting as facilitators, read from a prewritten document to outline the framework and goals of the conferences. The outline included a formal statement about the meeting's restorative goals, which set the tone for the meeting and prepared the participants for the type of exchange that would follow. The officer/facilitator then asked a series of open-ended questions, cycling among the participants to establish each party's experience of the crime and its aftermath. Unlike traditional RJ methods, the Bethlehem facilitators began with the offender, allowing him or her the opportunity to speak, before turning to the victim, followed by the victim's supporters, and then the offender's supporters. To return the focus of the meeting to a concrete outcome, the victim was asked first what he or she would like to get from the RJ process, and the other participants were invited to comment, when appropriate, depending on the circumstances of the case. This ultimate agreement, which parties signed, reduced to writing the consensus on what restorative actions the offender was obligated to undertake.

DECISIONS TO BE MADE BY POLICE BEFORE THE RJ PROGRAM IS STARTED

Some of the decisions that must be made before a police-based RJ program is established include the following:

- What department or agency will be the administrative umbrella for the program?
- What types of offenses and offenders will be eligible for the program?
- At what point will RJ be used as an intervention?
- How will facilitators be trained?

An example of a police-based RJ program is the Bethlehem Police Family Group Conferencing Project, which trained officers in RJ and implemented the processes in the community, randomly assigned first-time moderately serious juvenile offenders to either formal adjudication or a diversionary police-facilitated conference (McCold & Wachtel, 1998). The Bethlehem experiment was essentially a diversion program. Police officers were trained to hold conferences as part of a larger community policing effort.

RJ AS PART OF AN OVERALL APPROACH: POLICING AT A COMMUNITY LEVEL

Police officers are one piece of the vast machinery that is the retributive U.S. criminal justice system. Their role is, in some way, ill-defined: Are they public service providers? Are they street judges who serve as gatekeepers to the rest of the system? Are they a form of militia hired to do the dangerous job of keeping order in society? The answer is complex because police officers are active in all these roles and many more, yet they are not often given the authority to make decisions about the way they carry out these roles.

Of the five basic "hats" worn by police officers—enforcing laws, preventing crime, keeping order in society, upholding civil rights, and providing services or referring citizens to services—the last category of activity is the one in which they are most heavily engaged on a day-to-day basis. Given that the typical police officer's role is approximately 90% doing social service functions (Wrobleski & Hess, 2000), it is surprising that he or she is not given the appropriate tools to accomplish this part of the job.

Yet police training focuses on the officer's role as a crime prevention specialist. Even though providing services and referring people to services is the primary police officer's function, the day-to-day work of policing in the United States is organized around street crime prevention almost exclusively. Police are trained to focus their energies on catching the offenders, processing them, and helping to send them to prison (Moriarty, 2002). The unfortunate outcome of this "law and order" approach is that many police officers feel they have no say in their own job goals, victims often feel their needs are not being addressed, and some communities resent police intervention that simply removes "bad elements" from the community. These are temporary solutions that do not solve the underlying problem (see, e.g., Beloof, 1999; Clear, 1994, 2009). RJ models can resolve many of these problems by giving officers a method for directly addressing the violations that occur in their communities.

The community policing movement has several generally accepted tenets:

1. It relies on partnerships with community institutions and leaders, in both private and public spheres.
2. As the relationships between officers and community leaders become more personalized, policing efforts become increasingly more effective.
3. The goal is problem solving, which relies on the officer's first-hand knowledge of the people in his or her community.
4. The culture of policing is a cooperative endeavor, with the officer serving as the instrument through which crimes, infractions, and community problems are resolved.

In short, the motto is, "Keep it local."

RJ promises that communities, victims, and offenders are given the opportunity to be as involved and autonomous in determining the outcome of a given infraction or crime as early and as fully as they choose. This allows officers to be instrumental in shaping the RJ model without the oppositional sensibilities that can develop when a decision is imposed from the outside. Police responsibility thus shifts from upholding law or imposing punishment to acting as a catalyst for stakeholder decision-making about their community and its members.

PSYCHOLOGICAL BENEFITS FOR OFFICERS

In the traditional criminal justice system, the needs of the victim are seldom considered; if they are, it is done in a shallow, incomplete way. Most officers are simply not trained to understand the views of the victim on a moral plane, on an emotional level, or in terms of the ongoing consequences of the trauma victimization (see Moriarty, 2002).

Similarly, seldom are police themselves viewed as having been affected by crime in a personal way. While it would be an overstatement to equalize the officer's experience with that of victims of serious crime, it is a major failing of the law enforcement field that the vicarious trauma experienced by police officers as a consequence of their ongoing exposure to serious danger and crime is not sufficiently recognized.

Officers, no less than civilians, suffer from posttraumatic stress disorder (PTSD), which includes characteristic symptoms following an extremely traumatic stressor caused by direct personal experience involving actual or threatened death or serious injury or other threat to one's physical integrity (Foa, 2004). The focus on the physical, while typical of the legal system, is not the best place to focus our attentions. Trauma can be experienced through vicarious exposure to physical injury, and the reaction is the same: fear, helplessness, and horror (Foa, 2004). PTSD results in recurrent intrusive distressing recollections of the event, reliving the experiences of the event, hypervigilance and heightened arousal for danger, and physiological aspects when the event is relived. The coping mechanisms are overwhelmed and the person is no longer able to manage the emotional overload, resulting in crisis reactions that most often involve fight or flight responses (Foa, 2004).

RJ offers some psychological relief for police officers who have experienced repeated vicarious damage in their jobs. The principles of RJ, no less than its methods, allow officers to process their own traumatic experiences from exposure to crime. First, RJ is founded on the goal of offender accountability. In traditional legal proceedings, the officer(s) who initially discovered the crime or arrested the offender is not present at the time guilt or innocence is determined or a sentence is handed down. The outcome of the case is a remote proceeding in most cases. RJ allows the officer to see a case to its end, and the results are often more satisfying—morally and professionally—than cases that are processed through plea bargains or even trials. Second, RJ gives officers some control over their cases; it allows them to resolve local problems using hands-on proceedings that are highly beneficial for all parties. Furthermore, psychology has long known that describing the event and the emotional aftermath improves recovery from the trauma (Myers, 2009). By facilitating RJ models, police officers participate—albeit from a different vantage point than a true victim—in the same processes of grieving, raging, accepting, releasing, and so forth that victims experience.

RESTORATIVE JUSTICE GIVES POLICE BOTH PROFESSIONAL AND PERSONAL BENEFITS

The emergence of restorative justice programs in a wide variety of cases reflects both dissatisfaction in all camps—from the crime victims, to the general public, to policy makers—with traditional legal responses to crime and the concomitant need for alternatives to retributive measures, which are no longer financially feasible. Its victim orientation, which places unwavering attention on victim needs and offender accountability, makes RJ a palatable alternative for the injured parties and their families, communities and the general public, offenders, as well as politicians (Clear, 1994; Levrant et al. 1999; Zehr, 1990). The appeal of restorative principles has been institutionalized in the RJ principles adopted in the United Nations Commission on Crime Prevention and Criminal Justice (2002), among other international protocols, and it has seeds domestically in the crime victims' rights provisions that have been legislated in either state constitutional provisions or statutory provisions at the state and federal levels.

There have been more than 100 published restorative justice program evaluations, all of which generally show satisfaction among victim participants (see, e.g., Chan, 2003; Davis, 1982; Doolan, 1999; Geudens, 1998; Luke & Lind, 2002; McCold, 1998; McGarrell et al. 2000; Niemeyer & Shichor, 1996; Rowe, 2002; Roy, 1994; Trimboli, 2000; Umbreit, 1994; Wilson & Prinzo, 2001). Satisfaction rates for offenders approach 80% to 95% (Coates & Gehm, 1985; Dignan, 1990; McCold & Stahr, 1996; Umbreit, 1996). Various studies have shown that the variation among outcomes in satisfaction can be correlated with the programs' fidelity to restorative justice principles (see, e.g., McCold & Wachtel, 2000). A few researchers have exclusively examined victim satisfaction with RJ, and many have included this measure as part of a larger study of RJ effectiveness. For example:

> These findings generally confirm the conclusions about restorative justice programs made two decades ago: disputing parties typically hold positive views of restorative justice programs; they feel satisfied with the process and would return under similar circumstances in the future. Assessments involving different settings and types of disputes found disputants perceived the outcomes of mediation hearings to be significantly fairer than those of court proceedings. (McCold, 2003)

Although there is wide support for RJ and satisfaction rates are vastly higher than other proceedings, very few police officers have heard of RJ. (Shapland et al., 2004, 2006a, 2006b, noted that only 3% of officers in the United Kingdom have heard of RJ.) The code of conduct for police officers is ideally suited to the principles of RJ. Most codes of conduct address such values as honesty, integrity, fairness, impartiality, courtesy, confidentiality, tolerance for difference, restrictions on use of force, prohibitions against the abuse of authority, and professionalism in the performance of duties, among other matters. These are precisely the ingredients that make an RJ process successful.

REFERENCES

Bazemore, G., & Maloney, D. (1994). Rehabilitating community service: Toward restorative service sanction in a balanced justice system. *Federal Probation, 58*(1), 24–35.

Bazemore, G., & Umbreit, M. (1995). Rethinking the sentencing function in juvenile court: Retributive or restorative responses to youth crime. *Crime & Delinquency, 41,* 296–316.

Bazemore, G., & Umbreit, M. S. (1999). *Conferences, circles, boards, and mediations: Restorative justice and citizen involvement in the response to youth crime.* St. Paul: Center for Restorative Justice and Mediation, University of Minnesota.

Beloof, D. (1999). *Victims in criminal procedure.* Durham, NC: Carolina Academic Press.

Bonta, J., Rooney, J., & Wallace-Capretta, S. (1998). *Restorative justice: An evaluation of the restorative resolutions project.* Ottawa: Solicitor General Canada.

Bonta, J. L., Boyl, J., Motiuk, L. L., & Sonnichsen, P. (1983). Restitution in correctional half-way houses: Victim satisfaction, attitudes, and recidivism. *Canadian Journal of Corrections, 20,* 140–152.

Bradshaw, W., & Umbreit, M. S. (1998). Crime victims meet juvenile offenders: Contributing factors to victim satisfaction with mediated dialogue in Minneapolis. *Juvenile & Family Court Journal, 49*(3), 17–25.

Braithwaite, J. (2002). *Restorative justice and responsive regulation.* Oxford: Oxford University Press.

Braithwaite, J., & Makkai, T. (1994). Trust and compliance. *Policing & Society, 4,*1–12.

California Advisory Committee to the U.S. Commission on Civil Rights. (2000, May). *Community concerns about law enforcement in Sonoma County.* Los Angeles: Author.

Center for Restorative Justice and Mediation. (1996). *Restorative justice: For victims, communities, and offenders.* Minneapolis: University of Minnesota, Center for Restorative Justice.

Chan, W. (2003).Victim-offender mediation, making amends, and restorative justice in Singapore. In Tatsuya Ota (Ed.), *Victims and criminal justice: Asian perspective* (pp. 227–260). Tokyo: Hogaku-Kenkyu-Kai, Keio University.

Clairmont, D. (1994). *Alternative justice issues for Aboriginal justice.* Paper prepared for the Department of Justice, Ottawa, Aboriginal Justice Directorate, Canada.

Clear, T. (2009). Presidential address. John Jay College of Criminal Justice, American Society of Criminology Annual Meeting, November 3–6, Philadelphia, PA.

Clear, T. R. (1994). *Harm in American penology: Offenders, victims, and their communities.* Albany: State University of New York Press.

Coates, R. B., & Gehm, J. (1985). *Victim meets offender: An evaluation of victim offender reconciliation programs.* Valparaiso, IN: PACT Institute of Justice.

Coates, R. B., & Gehm, J. (1989). An empirical assessment. In M. Wright & B. Galaway (Eds.), *Mediation and criminal justice* (pp. 251–263). London: Sage.

Cragg, W. (1992). *The practice of punishment: Towards a theory of restorative justice.* London: Routledge.

Daly, K. (1996). *Diversionary conferences in Australia: A reply to the optimists and skeptics.* Paper presented at the American Society of Criminology Annual Meeting, Chicago, IL.

Davis, R., Tichane, M., & Grayson, D. (1980). *Mediation and arbitration as alternative to prosecution in felony arrest cases: An evaluation of the Brooklyn Dispute Resolution Center.* New York: Vera Institute of Justice.

Davis, R. C. (1982). Mediation: The Brooklyn experiment. In R. Tomasic & M. Feeley (Eds.), *Neighborhood justice: Assessment of an emerging idea* (pp. 154–170). New York: Longman.

Dignan, J. (1990a). *An evaluation of an experimental adult reparation scheme in Kettering, Northamptonshire, United Kingdom.* Sheffield, UK: University of Sheffield, Centre for Criminological and Legal Research.

Dignan, J. (1990b). *Repairing the damage.* Sheffield, UK: University of Sheffield, Centre for Criminological and Legal Research.

Doolan, M. (1999). *The family group conference—10 years on.* Paper presented at Building Strong Partnerships for Restorative Practices Conference, August 7, Burlington, VT. Retrieved September 3, 2010, from http://www.iirp.org/article_detail.php?article_id=NDg1

Foa, E., Keane, T., & Friedman, M. (2004). *Effective treatments for PTSD*. New York: Guilford.

Forsythe, L. (1995). An analysis of juvenile apprehension characteristics and reapprehension rates. In D. Moore, with L. Forsythe & T. O'Connell (Eds.), *A new approach to juvenile justice: An evaluation of family conferencing in Wagga Wagga: A Report to the Criminology Research Council*. Wagga Wagga, Australia: Charles Sturt University.

Friday, P. C. (1999, November). *United Nations overview of restorative justice: Working group of Resource Committee No. 1, Victims, Report on restorative justice issues*, for the International Scientific and Professional Advisory Council of the United Nations Crime Prevention and Criminal Justice Programme.

Gehm, J. (1990). Mediated victim-offender restitution agreements: An exploratory analysis of factors related to victim participation. In B. Galaway & J. Hudson (Eds.), *Criminal justice, restitution, and reconciliation* (pp. 177–182). Monsey, NY: Criminal Justice Press.

Gehm, J. R. (1992). The function of forgiveness in the criminal justice system. In H. Messmer & H.-U. Otto (Eds.), *Restorative justice on trial* (pp. 541–550). Dordrecht, Netherlands: Kluwer.

Geudens, H. (1998). The recidivism of community service as a restitutive judicial sanction in comparison with the traditional juvenile justice measures. In L. Walgrave (Ed.), *Restorative justice for juveniles: Potentialities, risks, and problems for research* (pp. 335–350). Leuven, Belgium: Leuven University Press.

Harris, M. K. (1989). Alternative visions in the context of contemporary realities. In P. Arthur (Ed.), *Justice: The restorative vision: New perspective on crime and justice, #7*. Akron, PA: Mennonite Central Committee.

Hoyle, C., Young, R., & Hill, R. (2002). *Proceed with caution: An evaluation of the Thames Valley Police Initiative in restorative cautioning*. Oxford: Oxford Centre for Criminological Research.

Jamieson, R., & McEvoy, K. (2005). State crime by proxy and juridical othering. *British Journal of Criminology, 45*, 504–527.

Koski, D. D. (2003). *The jury trial in criminal justice*. Durham, NC: Carolina Academic Press.

Levrant, S., Cullen, F. T., Fulton, B., & Wozniak, J. F. (1999). Reconsidering restorative justice: The corruption of benevolence revisited? *Crime & Delinquency, 45*(1), 3–28.

Luke, G., & Lind, B. (2002).Reducing juvenile crime: Conferencing versus court. *Crime & Justice Bulletin: Contemporary Issues in Crime & Justice, 69,* 1–20.

Marshall, T. F., & Merry, S. (1990). *Crime and accountability: Victim offender mediation in practice*. London: Home Office.

Maxwell, G. A., & Morris, A. (1993). *Family, victims, and culture: Youth justice in New Zealand*. Wellington, New Zealand: University of Victoria University, Social Policy Agency and Institute of Criminology.

Maxwell, G. A., & Morris, A. (1996). Research on family group conferences with young offenders in New Zealand. In J. Hudson, A. Morris, G. Maxwell, & B. Galaway (Eds.), *Family group conferences: Perspectives on policy and practice*. Sydney, Australia: Federation Press and Criminal Justice Press.

Maxwell, G. A., & Morris, A. (2001). Family group conferences and re-offending. In A. Morris & G. Maxwell (Eds.), *Restorative justice for juveniles: Conferencing, mediation, and circles*. Portland, OR: Hart.

Maxwell, G. A., Morris, A., & Anderson, T. (1999). *Community panel adult pretrial diversion: Supplementary evaluation*. Research Report, Crime Prevention Unit, Department of Prime Minister and Cabinet and Institute of Criminology. Wellington, New Zealand: Victoria University of Wellington.

McCold, P. (1996). Restorative justice and the role of the community. In B. Galaway & J. Hudson (Eds.), *Restorative justice: International perspectives* (pp. 85–115). Monsey, NY: Criminal Justice Press.

McCold, P. (1998). *Police-facilitated restorative conferencing: What the data show*. International Institute for Restorative Practices. Paper presented to the Second Annual International Conference on Restorative Justice for Juveniles, Florida Atlantic University, and the International Network for Research on Restorative Justice for Juveniles, November 7–9, Fort Lauderdale, FL.

McCold, P. (2003). A survey of assessment research on mediation and conferencing. In L. Walgrave (Ed.), *Repositioning restorative justice* (pp. 67–120). Devon, UK: Willan.

McCold, P. (2008). Protocols for evaluating restorative justice programmes. *British Journal of Community Justice 6*(2), 9–28.

McCold, P., & Stahr, J. (1996). *Bethlehem police: Family group conferencing project*. Paper presented at the American Society of Criminology Annual Meeting, Chicago, IL.

McCold, P., & Wachtel, B. (1998). *Restorative policing experiment: The Bethlehem Pennsylvania Police Family Group Conferencing Project*. Pipersville, PA: Community Service Foundation.

McCold, P., & Wachtel, B. (2000). *Restorative justice theory validation*. Paper presented at the Fourth International Conference on Restorative Justice for Juveniles, October 1–4, Tübingen, Germany.

McElrea, F. W. M. (1995, May). *Accountability in the community: Taking responsibility for offending*. Paper presented at the Legal Research Foundation Conference, Auckland, New Zealand.

McGarrell, E. F., Olivares, K., Crawford, K., & Kroovand, N. (2000). *Returning justice to the community: The Indianapolis juvenile restorative justice experiment*. Indianapolis, IN: Hudson Institute.

Messmer, H., & Ouo, H. (1992). Restorative justice: Steps on the way toward a good idea. In H. Messmer & H.-U. Otto (Eds.), *Restorative justice on trial*. Dordrecht, Netherlands: Kluwer.

Moore, D. B., & O'Connell, T. (1994). Family conferencing in Wagga-Wagga: A communitarian model of justice. In C. Adler & J. Wundersitz (Eds.), *Family conferencing and juvenile justice: The way forward or misplaced optimism?* Canberra, Australia: Australian Institute of Criminology.

Moriarty, L. (2002). *Policing and victims*. Upper Saddle River, NJ: Prentice Hall.

Myers. R. (2009).Truth and reconciliation commissions 101: What TRCs can teach the United States justice system about justice. *RevistaJurídica Univ. P.R., 78*(1), 95–128.

Napa Valley Criminal Justice Training Center Basic Police Academy. (2010). *Cadet information handbook: A guide for student success*. Retrieved September 3, 2010, from http://www.nvccjtc.org/text/Cadet%20 Information%20Handbook.pdf

Nicholl, C. G. (1999). *Community policing, community justice, and restorative justice: Exploring the links for the delivery of a balanced approach to public safety*. Washington, DC: U.S. Department of Justice, Office of Community Oriented Policing Services.

Niemeyer, M., & Shichor, D. (1996). A preliminary study of a large victim/offender reconciliation program. *Federal Probation, 60*(3), 30–35.

Nixon, K., Canter, D., & Hiropoulos, A. (2006). *Patterns of offending behaviour in domestic violence*. Liverpool, UK: University of Liverpool, Centre for Investigative Psychology.

Nixon, P. (1999). Family group conference connections: Shared problems and joined up solutions. Bethlehem, PA: International Institute for Restorative Practices.

Nolan-Haley, J. (2008). *Alternative dispute resolution in a nutshell*. Eagan, MN: West.

Nugent, W. R., & Paddock, J. (1996). Evaluation of the effects of a victim-offender reconciliation program on reoffense. *Research on Social Work Practice, 6*(2), 155–178.

Nugent, W. R., & Paddock, J. B. (1995). The effect of victim–offender mediation on severity of reoffense. *Mediation Quarterly, 12,* 353–367.

Office for Victims of Crime. (1982). *Final report*. President's Task Force on Victims of Crime. Washington, DC: U.S. Department of Justice, Office of Justice Programs.

Office of Victims of Crime. (2000, April). *Multicultural implications of restorative justice: Potential pitfalls*. Washington, DC: U.S. Department of Justice, Office of Justice Programs.

Office for Victims of Crime. (2000, July). The restorative justice and mediation collection: Executive summary. *OVC Bulletin*. Retrieved September 3, 2010, from http://www.ojp.usdoj.gov/ovc/publications/infores/ restorative_justice/bulletin1/rjmc_3.html

O'Haley, J. O. (1992). Victim-offender mediation: Japanese and American comparisons. In H. Messmer & H.-U. Otto (Eds.), *Restorative justice on trial: Pitfalls and potentials of victim offender mediation–International research perspectives*. Dordrecht, Netherlands: Kluwer.

Pate, K. (1990). Victim-offender restitution programs in Canada. In B. Galaway & J. Hudson (Eds.), *Criminal justice, restitution, and reconciliation*. New York: Willow Tree.

Pennell, J., & Burford, G. (1996). Family group decision making in Canada. In J. Hudson, A. Morris, G. Maxwell, & B. Galaway (Eds.), *Family group conferences: Perspectives on policy and practice*. Sydney, Australia: Federation Press and Criminal Justice Press.

Perry, L., Lajeunesse, T., & Woods, A. (1987). *Mediation services: An evaluation*. Winnipeg, MB: Research, Planning, and Evaluation Office of the Attorney General.

Peters, T., & Aertsen, I. (1995). Restorative justice: In search of new avenues in the judicial dealing with crime: The presentation of a project of mediation for reparation. In C. Fijnaut et al. (Eds.), *Changes in society, crime, and criminal justice in Europe*. Antwerp: Kluwer.

Reske, H. (1995, February). Victim-offender mediation catching on. *American Bar Association Journal,* 14–15.

Roehl, J., & Cook R. (1982). Neighborhood justice centers field test. In R. Tomasic & M. M. Feeley (Eds.), *Neighborhood justice: Assessment of an emerging idea* (pp. 91–110). New York: Longman.

Roehl, J., & Cook, R. (1989). Mediation in interpersonal disputes: Effectiveness and limitations. In K. Kressel, D. Pruit, & Associates (Eds.), *Mediation research: The process and effectiveness of third-party intervention* (pp. 31–52). San Francisco: Jossey-Bass.

Rosenbaum, T. (2004).*The myth of moral justice*. New York: HarperCollins.

Rowe, W. (2002). *A meta-analysis of six Washington state restorative justice projects*. Bellingham, WA: Cambie Group International.

Roy, S. (1995). Juvenile restitution and recidivism in a midwestern county. *Federal Probation, 59*(1), 55–63.

Ruddick, R. (1989). A court-referred scheme. In M. Wright & B. Galaway (Eds.), *Mediation and criminal justice: Victims, offenders, and community* (pp. 82–98). London: Sage.

Schriff, M. F. (1998). Restorative justice interventions for juvenile offenders: A research agenda for the decade. *Western Criminology Review, 1*(1). Retrieved September 3, 2010, from http://wcr.sonoma.edu/v1n1/schiff.html

Schriff, M. F. (1999). The impact of restorative interventions on juvenile offenders. In G. Bazemore & L. Walgrave (Eds.), *Restorative juvenile justice: Repairing the harm of youth crime* (pp. 328–356). Monsey, NY: Criminal Justice Press.

Shapland, J., Atkinson, A., Atkinson, H., Chapman, B., Colledge, E., Dignan, J., et al. (2006a). Restorative justice in practice—Findings from the second phase of the evaluation of three schemes. *Home Office Research Findings 274*. London: Home Office. Retrieved September 3, 2010, from at http://www.homeoffice.gov.uk/rds/pdfs06/r274.pdf

Shapland, J., Atkinson, A., Atkinson, H., Chapman, B., Colledge, E., Dignan, J., et al. (2006b). *Restorative justice in practice: The second report from the evaluation of three schemes*. Sheffield, UK: University of Sheffield, Centre for Criminological Research.

Shapland, J., Atkinson, A., Atkinson, H., Chapman, B., Colledge, E., Dignan, J., et al. (2006c). Situating restorative justice within criminal justice. *Theoretical Criminology, 10*, 505–532.

Shapland, J., Atkinson, A., Atkinson, H., Chapman, B., Colledge, E., Dignan, J., et al. (2007). *Restorative justice: The views of victims and offenders: The third report from the evaluation of three schemes*. Sheffield, UK: Centre for Criminological Research, University of Sheffield.

Shapland, J., Atkinson, A., Colledge, E., Dignan, J., Howes, M., Johnstone, J., et al. (2004). Implementing restorative justice schemes (Crime Reduction Programme): A report on the first year. *Home Office Online Report 32/04*. London: Home Office. Retrieved September 3, 2010, from http://www.homeoffice.gov.uk/rds/pdfs04/rdsolr3204.pdf

Sharpe, S. (1998). *Restorative justice: A vision for healing and change*. Edmonton, Alberta, Canada: The Edmonton Victim Offender Mediation.

Sherman, L. W., & Strang, H. (2007). *Restorative justice: The evidence*. London: The Smith Institute.

Sherman, L. W., Strang, H., & Woods, D. (2000a). Recidivism patterns in the Canberra Reintegrative Shaming Experiments (RISE). Canberra, Australia: Australian National University, Centre for Restorative Justice.

Sherman, L. W., Strang, H., & Woods, D. (2000b). *Captains of restorative justice: Experience, legitimacy, and recidivism by type of offense*. Paper presented at the International Conference on Restorative Justice, Tübingen, Germany.

Smith, M. E. (2001). What future for "public safety" and "restorative justice" in community corrections. *Sentencing and Corrections: Issues for the 21st Century. No. 11*. Washington, DC: National Institute of Justice.

Strang, H. (2004). *Repair or revenge: Victims and restorative justice*. Oxford: Oxford University Press.

Strang, H., & Sherman, L. W. (1997). *The victim's perspective*. Paper 2, RISE Working Paper, Law Program, Australian National University, Canberra.

Trimboli, L. (2000). *An evaluation of the NSW youth justice conference scheme*. Sydney, Australia: New South Wales Bureau of Crime Statistics and Research.

Tyler, T. R. (2006). *Why people obey the law*. New Haven, CT: Yale University Press.

Tyler, T. R. (1994). Psychological models of the justice motive. *Journal of Personality & Social Psychology, 67*, 850–863.

Umbreit, M. S. (1994). Crime victims confront their offenders: The impact of a Minneapolis mediation program. *Journal of Research on Social Work Practice 4*(4), 436–447.

Umbreit, M. S. (1995). The development and impact of victim-offender mediation in the U.S. *Mediation Quarterly, 12*(3), 263–276.

Umbreit, M. (1996). Restorative justice through mediation: The impact of offenders facing their victims in Oakland. *The Journal of Law & Social Work, 5*(1), 1–13.

Umbreit, M. (1998). Restorative justice through victim-offender mediation: A multi-site assessment. *Western Criminology Review, 1*(1), 1–29.

Umbreit, M., & Bradshaw, W. (1997). Crime victim experience with mediation: A comparison of mediation with adult vs. juvenile offenders. *Federal Probation, 61*(4), 33–39.

Umbreit, M., & Coates, R. B. (1993). Cross-site analysis of victim-offender mediation in four states. *Crime & Delinquency, 39*(4), 565–585.

Umbreit, M., Coates, R., & Kalanj, B. (Eds.). (1994). *Victim meets offender: The impact of restorative justice and mediation*. Monsey, NY: Criminal Justice Press.

Umbreit, M., Coates, R. B., & Roberts, A. (1998). Impact of victim-offender mediation in Canada, England, and the United States. *Crime Victims Report, 1*(6), 83, 90–92.

Umbreit, M., & Greenwood, J. (1999). National survey of victim-offender mediation programs in the United States. *Mediation Quarterly, 16*(3), 235–251.

Umbreit, M., Greenwood, J., Fercello, C., & Umbreit, J. (2000, April). *Directory of victim offender mediation programs in the United States.* Washington, DC: U.S. Department of Justice.

Umbreit, M., & Warner-Roberts, A. (1996). *Mediation of criminal conflict in England: An assessment of services in Coventry and Leeds.* St. Paul: University of Minnesota, Center for Restorative Justice & Mediation.

UK Home Office. (2003, May). *Bind overs: A power for the 21st century.* Retrieved September 3, 2010, from http://www.homeoffice.gov.uk/documents/cons-2003-bind-over2835.pdf?view=Binary

UK Home Office. (2007). *The role of the police service.* Retrieved September 3, 2010, from http://www.asb.homeoffice.gov.uk/members/article.aspx?id=8214

United Nations Commission on Crime Prevention and Criminal Justice. (2002). *Report of the group of experts on restorative justice.* E/CN.15/2002/5/Add.1. Vienna: Center for International Crime Control.

United Nations Office for Drug Control and Crime Prevention. (1999). *Handbook on justice for victims: On the use and application of the United Nations Declaration of Basic Principles of Justice for Victims of Crime and Abuse of Power.* New York: U.N. Centre for International Crime Prevention.

U.S. Commission on Civil Rights. (2000, November). *Revisiting who is guarding the guardians? A report on police practices and civil rights in America.* Retrieved September 3, 2010, from http://www.usccr.gov/pubs/guard/main.htm

U.S. Department of Justice, Bureau of Justice Statistics. (2006a). *Criminal victimization 2006, statistical tables.* NCJ 223436. Retrieved September 3, 2010, from http://bjs.ojp.usdoj.gov/content/pub/pdf/cvus0606.pdf

U.S. Department of Justice, Bureau of Justice Statistics. (2006b). *Criminal and victim statistics 2006.* Retrieved from http://www.ojp.usdoj.gov/bjs/cvict.htm#summary

U.S. Department of Justice, Bureau of Justice Statistics. (2008). *Criminal victimization 2008, summary.* Retrieved September 3, 2010, from http://www.ojp.usdoj.gov/bjs/abstract/cv08.htm

Van Ness, D. W. (1986). *Crime and its victims.* Downers Grove, IL: InterVarsity Press.

Van Ness, D. W., & Strong, K. (1997). *Restoring justice.* Cincinnati, OH: Anderson.

Walgrave, L. (1993). *In search of limits to the restorative justice for juveniles.* Paper presented at the International Congress on Criminology, Budapest.

Walsh, A. (2003). Placebo justice: Victim recommendations and offender sentences in sexual assault cases. In D. Koski (Ed.), *The jury trial in criminal justice* (p. 161). Durham, NC: Carolina Academic Press.

Weitekamp, E. H. (2000). Research on victim-offender mediation: Findings and needs for the future. In The European Forum for Victim-Offender Mediation and Restorative Justice (Ed.), *Victim-offender mediation in Europe: Making restorative justice work* (pp. 99–121). Leuven, Belgium: Leuven University Press.

Williams, H. (2000, June 16). *Statement on national police practices and civil rights.* Statement on behalf of the Police Foundation before the United States Commission on Civil Rights, Washington, D.C.

Wilmerding, J. (1997). Healing lives, mending society. *Quaker Abolitionist, 3*(2), 4–5.

Wilson, R., & Prinzo, M. (2001). Circles of support: A restorative justice initiative. In M. H. Miner & E. Coleman (Eds.), *Sex offender treatment: Accomplishments, challenges, and future directions* (pp. 59–77). Binghamton, NY: Haworth Press.

Wright, M. (1996). *Justice for victims and offenders.* Philadelphia: Open University Press.

Wright, M., & Galaway, B. (1989). *Mediation and criminal justice.* London: Sage.

Wrobleski, H., & Hess, K. (2000). *An introduction to law enforcement and criminal justice* (6th ed.) Belmont, CA: Wadsworth.

Wynne, J. (1996). Leeds Mediation and Reparation Service: Ten years experience with victim-offender mediation. In B. Galaway & J. Hudson (Eds.), *Restorative justice: International perspectives* (pp. 445–461). Monsey, NY: Criminal Justice Press.

Zehr, H. (1990). *Changing lenses: A new focus for crime and justice.* Scottsdale, PA: Herald Press.

Zehr, H. (2002). *The little book of restorative justice.* Intercourse, PA: Good Books.

Zimring, F. (1971). *Perspectives on deterrence.* Washington, DC: National Institute of Mental Health.

CASE CITED

In the Matter of John Duffy, Appellant v. Benjamin Ward, as Police Commissioner of the City of New York, et al., Respondents, 81 N.Y.2d 127, 612 N.E.2d 1213, 596 N.Y.S.2d 746 (1993).

Part V

Clinical Practice

20 Police Personality
Theoretical Issues and Research

Gwendolyn L. Gerber

Kyle C. Ward

INTRODUCTION

People have conflicting stereotypes about police officers and their personality traits. Some are convinced that police officers are responsible, dedicated guardians of society, while others are certain that police officers are authoritarian individuals who are prone to abusing their authority (Yarmey, 1990). The assumption underlying both of these stereotypes is that police officers as a group are characterized by the same personality traits. This assumption is also reflected in the traditional approach to studying police personality, which postulates there is a "modal police personality" that characterizes police officers and distinguishes them from other members of the population (Leftowitz, 1975).

The view that all police officers have similar personality traits has been primarily explained by the *predispositional* and *socialization models* (Burbeck & Furnham, 1985). According to the predispositional model, certain types of individuals are attracted to the field of police work. By contrast, the socialization model postulates that strong pressures affect individuals after they become police officers, thereby modifying and shaping their personality attributes (McNamara, 1999; Niederhoffer, 1967; Skolnick, 1994). It is also possible that a wide range of personality types seek to become police officers, but the screening processes used by many police departments select for particular kinds of candidates (Burbeck & Furnham, 1985).

This chapter reviews theory and research related to the traditional approach to police personality. By focusing on the traits assumed to characterize all police officers, the traditional approach emphasizes the *differences* between police officers and members of other population groups. Much of this work has focused on authoritarianism, cynicism, and psychopathology, which continue to be discussed in the literature on policing (Bartol & Bartol, 2004; Graves, 1996; McNamara, 1999; Skolnick, 1994; Wilson & Braithwaite, 1995; Yarmey, 1990). In addition, the chapter describes a current approach to police personality, the status model of personality. The status model focuses on the effect of situational factors involving status on personality and emphasizes the *similarities* between police officers and members of other groups. In this view, police officers are subject to the same kinds of status processes and situational pressures that affect members of other task-oriented groups, and these processes have similar effects on their personality attributes (Gerber, 2001).

Most of the work on police personality has focused on men. Another issue involves the personality traits that characterize women police officers. There has been a paucity of research in this area, but a growing number of studies now include women. In addition to other issues, women police officers' personality traits are discussed in terms of women's lower status within policing.

DIFFERENCES BETWEEN POLICE OFFICERS' PERSONALITY TRAITS AND MEMBERS OF OTHER POPULATION GROUPS

The traditional view of personality is that "individuals are characterized by *stable* and *broadly generalized* dispositions that endure over long periods of time and that generate consistencies in their ... behavior across a wide range of situations" (Mischel, 1990, p. 112). Regardless of whether personality traits stem from predispositional factors or socialization practices, the traditional view holds that these are long-standing characteristics that underlie the way people think, behave, and relate to others in different situations (Pervin, 1990). From this point of view, knowledge of the personality traits that characterize police personnel and differentiate them from members of other population groups would help explain why they think and act as they do.

Although some investigators have described the police as having positive personality attributes, most of the research has been concerned with negative aspects of personality such as authoritarianism, cynicism, and psychopathology (Biggam & Power, 1996; Fenster, Wiedemann, & Locke, 1977). In addition, most of the research has been conducted with men. Methodological problems, particularly with the earlier studies, have included the absence of appropriate control groups and a lack of uniformity in measures (Balch, 1972; Biggam & Power, 1996). Studies have been conducted in different urban and rural locales in different parts of the United States, as well as in other countries, without taking into account the variations in policies and procedures characterizing different police departments.

Authoritarianism

The concept of *authoritarianism*, researched by Adorno and his colleagues (Adorno, Frenkel-Brunswik, Levinson, & Sanford, 1950), was an attempt to link deep-seated personality dispositions with social behavior that adhered to an ideology that was rigid, dogmatic, authority-dependent, and intolerant (Shaver, 1973). The book *The Authoritarian Personality* (Adorno et al., 1950) presented a theoretical framework for understanding authoritarianism, in addition to a measurement scale. The F (*fascism*) scale was designed primarily to tap fascistic proclivities–personality characteristics that make a person susceptible to an extremely rightist or conservative political agenda. This scale has been widely used in laboratory settings and nationwide surveys (Christie, 1991).

Niederhoffer (1967) applied the concept of authoritarianism to the police and postulated that the socialization that takes place within the police system was the source of this authoritarianism: "The police system transforms a man into the special type of authoritarian personality required by the police role" (p. 125). Because the patrolman *on the beat* was involved in most incidents that required a display of authority, Niederhoffer postulated that the patrolman was the most authoritarian member of the force.

Studies investigating authoritarianism in police reached their peak in the 1970s and 1980s and, with less frequency, have continued to the present time. Based on several published reviews, the consensus has been that the evidence regarding authoritarianism in police is inconclusive. In his 1972 review, Balch summarized the findings by stating there was not enough good evidence to support or refute either side of the controversy, and it was possible that police were not any more authoritarian than people from similar backgrounds. In 1975, Lefkowitz reviewed research on the police personality and concluded that police officers scored, almost without exception, as not particularly authoritarian or dogmatic on the F scale or other modifications of this scale. Further, no evidence supported the existence of pathological personality traits in police. On the contrary, some studies had found that police scored *lower* on authoritarianism than various civilian groups, including college students and teachers. Almost all the studies reviewed were methodologically inadequate, and no evidence supported the primacy of either organizational or predispositional influences in creating authoritarian personalities.

A more recent review by Burbeck and Furnham (1985) concurred that the work on authoritarianism and conservatism in police was inconclusive. One reason was that studies frequently suffered from methodological inadequacies, and these problems could account for some of the contradictory findings among the studies. Questions had been raised by various critics about the reliability and "fakeability" of some of the instruments that had been used. Most important, the matching of police with control samples was a problem for much of the research. In comparing police with civilians, some studies used control samples from other studies and others used normative data. As a result, significant differences between police and controls could be accounted for by sample differences and could have been unrelated to whether or not someone was a police officer. Part of the difficulty has involved the determination of an appropriate comparison group. Should it be the public at large or men and women of similar age, education, and social background?

Scales for Measuring Authoritarianism

The most widely used measure of authoritarianism is the California F Scale (Adorno et al., 1950). The scale was criticized as a measure of right-wing political conservatism that neglected authoritarianism of the political left (Christie, 1991). In response, Rokeach (1960) designed a scale to tap an individual's antidemocratic tendencies without being restricted to a rightist political ideology. The Rokeach Dogmatism Scale was designed to measure *closed mindedness* independent of a particular ideology, in addition to *opinionation*, another characteristic of closed-minded individuals who accept or reject other people on the basis of whether they hold similar opinions (Shaver, 1973). A further criticism of both the F Scale and the Dogmatism Scale was that items were all worded in such a way that an endorsement of an item yielded a higher score (Christie, 1991). This made it impossible to distinguish between respondents who agreed with the ideological content of the statements and respondents who would agree with almost any item. This led to the development of other scales in which some items were reversed.

Questions have been raised about the sensitivity and reliability of the various instruments that have been used in research with the police (Burbeck & Furnham, 1985). In addition, results from different scales for measuring authoritarianism and conservatism, including the F Scale and the Dogmatism Scale, are not always consistent within the same study (Colman & Gorman, 1982). Another approach to measuring authoritarianism involves the use of the MMPI-2 supplemental content scales for cynicism, anger, and antisocial practices (Laguna, Linn, Ward, & Rupslaukyte, 2010). These content scales were intercorrelated and, according to the investigators, provided a measure of the personality traits of police officers who fit the stereotypic police authoritarian personality.

Difference Between Authoritarianism and "Authority Orientation"

An *authority orientation* refers to the desire to have authorities make decisions because of their superior experience, prestige, and accumulated knowledge (Cochran, 1975). Individuals can be characterized as having an authority orientation without having the more pathological characteristics, such as dogmatism, repressive denial, ethnocentrism, and anti-Semitism, that make up the authoritarian syndrome. Police departments are characterized by strong hierarchical structures and clear-cut chains of command. In addition, police hold a special position of authority in relation to others in the community. According to Cochran (1975), it would be expected that individuals with a strong authority orientation would choose policing as an occupation without necessarily being authoritarian. The Hierarchical Control Scale is a bipolar scale in which one pole indicates a preference for decisions to be made by persons in a position of power and authority, and the other pole indicates a preference for decisions to be made by the person most affected, regardless of that individual's status. Research found that male police officers scored significantly higher than a group of male controls on hierarchical control, but did not differ on authoritarianism, as measured by the Dogmatism scale. Therefore, police supported a rigid, authoritative type of social control without showing any of the other characteristics associated with authoritarianism as it is traditionally defined. These results emphasize the importance of distinguishing between the constructs of authority orientation and authoritarianism: an individual can prefer a hierarchical control structure without possessing the other characteristics associated with authoritarianism.

POLICE CYNICISM

Cynicism is defined as a lack of belief in the sincerity or goodness of human motives and actions and is manifested in feelings ranging from "distrustfulness [and] doubt to contemptuous and mocking disbelief" (Regoli, 1976, p. 341). In Arthur Niederhoffer's (1967) classic book *Behind the Shield: The Police in Modern Society*, he described *police cynicism*, a type of cynicism that characterizes police officers. Because of the nature of their work, police officers constantly are faced with keeping people in line. To do so, they need to anticipate that most people intend to break the law. As a result, police officers become cynical and develop the idea that all people are motivated by evil and self-ishness. They come to mistrust the people they are charged to protect and, as a result, "lose faith in people, society, and eventually in themselves. In their Hobbesian view, the world becomes a jungle in which crime, corruption, and brutality are normal features of the terrain" (Niederhoffer, 1967, p. 9). In addition to a loss of faith in other people, there is a loss of enthusiasm for the high ideals of police work and a loss of personal pride and integrity.

According to Niederhoffer (1967), there are two kinds of cynicism: one is directed at life, the world, and people in general, and the other is directed at the police system. The first type of cynicism derives from exposure to the worst life has to offer and is found in police at all levels, from those who work on patrol to the police chief. The second type of cynicism is directed at the police system, and comes from the push toward professionalism in police work, which started during the 1960s. The change in the nature of policing from a *tough cop* style of policing to the *social science police officer* primarily affected lower ranking patrol officers. The changes in the system of values that accompanied these changes led to confusion, a sense of *anomie* or absence of standards, and the development of increased cynicism among police, particularly in the lower ranks. Because they want to transform and eventually control the system, professional police personnel, such as those with higher ranks and better education, are protected from this type of cynicism.

Niederhoffer believed that cynicism is learned as part of the socialization process that takes place in the police occupation. He divided cynicism into four stages related to a police officer's age and experience. The preliminary stage, *pseudo-cynicism*, arises in police recruits at the police academy, who still are idealistic beneath the surface. The second stage, *romantic cynicism*, surfaces during the first 5 years of police work, and it is the most idealistic stage where young members of the force are most vulnerable. *Aggressive cynicism*, the third stage, gradually builds and is most prevalent 10 years into police service. It corresponds with the resentment and hostility which, Niederhoffer claimed, are prevalent during this time period. The final stage, *resigned cynicism*, appears in the last few years of police work. It is at this stage that the individual may experience detachment that may be "passive and apathetic or may express itself as a form of mellow if mild good will" (Niederhoffer, 1967, p. 104). There is an acceptance of the job situation and a coming to terms with the flaws of the criminal justice system.

Research on Cynicism

Niederhoffer's theory and the questionnaire he developed have generated more research than any other issue involving the police (Langworthy, 1987). The cynicism scale has been applied to numerous populations, including rural and urban U.S. police departments, small and large departments, and even internationally. Most studies of police cynicism were conducted during the 1970s through the 1980s, and research has slowed in recent years.

Niederhoffer formulated a number of research hypothesis based on his theory and tested these hypotheses with personnel in the New York City Police Department (NYPD). The hypothesis that has received the most attention from other researchers deals with the relationship between cynicism and length of service. This hypothesis predicted a curvilinear relationship between length of service and the average level of cynicism. Specifically, the hypothesis predicted an increase in cynicism during the first few years of a police career, which would tend to level off between the fifth and tenth years of service and then decrease toward the end of a career as members of the force approached retirement (Niederhoffer, 1967). In his analysis of the NYPD data, Niederhoffer found that on the first day of training, the mean cynicism score of new recruits was significantly lower than the mean scores of any of the other groups. However, his claim of support for the curvilinear hypothesis was based primarily on a graph that compared the mean cynicism scores of patrolmen with varying lengths of service—from recruits with 2 to 3 months of experience to patrolmen with 15 to 19 years of service (Niederhoffer, 1967, p. 239).

A review of research that followed the publication of Niederhoffer's book (Langworthy, 1987) found that most of the early studies rarely examined whether the observed differences in cynicism scores were statistically significant. These studies based their conclusions of support for the curvilinear hypothesis on an examination of graphs portraying the mean cynicism scores of groups with varying lengths of service. The few studies that did provide statistics reported no significant differences in cynicism scores as a function of length of service. Langworthy (1987) reanalyzed Niederhoffer's data using a more sophisticated statistical technique and found that only those new recruits tested on their first day of training differed significantly from any of the other groups. These results correspond with Niederhoffer's (1967) analysis and other studies in which statistically significant differences in cynicism between those just beginning police training and those who had even very little police experience were found (Langworthy, 1987).

Niederhoffer postulated that professional police personnel, such as higher ranking personnel, would experience less cynicism than those in the lower ranks. Although Niederhoffer's results did not reach significance, he suggested that the results were in the predicted direction. However, subsequent research has failed provide support for this contention (Regoli, 1977). Wilt and Bannon (1976) concluded that their results hinted toward a relationship, but no statistical tests were run to support their claim. With respect to the hypothesis that more educated patrolmen would experience less cynicism, Niederhoffer found a statistically significant difference. However, these findings have not been replicated in subsequent research (Langworthy, 1987).

Regoli and his colleagues tested an additional hypothesis in their studies—that there would be an inverse relation between police professionalism and cynicism (Lotz & Regoli, 1977; Poole, Regoli, & Lotz, 1978; Regoli, 1977). This hypothesis was supported—a consistent finding was that police professionalism and cynicism, as measured by Niederhoffer's scale, are inversely related.

Cynicism Scales

Niederhoffer's (1967) scale primarily deals with the cynicism that is directed toward the police system. Although he postulated that there were four different stages of cynicism, each emerging at different points during a police career, the 20-item scale he developed deals with a unitary concept of cynicism. Subsequent research with the scale in a variety of studies found that police cynicism appeared to have several different dimensions and that the factor structure failed to replicate across studies (Langworthy, 1987). Because of this, Langworthy concluded that the scale is not reliable, which makes it difficult to interpret the results of studies utilizing the scale.

A new measure of police cynicism, developed by Regoli, Crank, and Rivera (1990), has shown promise. The 16-item scale consists of four subscales: cynicism toward rules and regulations, the legal system, police superiors, and the public. These subscales were developed by means of factor analysis and were related to various aspects of job performance. The investigators found that cynical police were more likely to be involved in hostile encounters with citizens, have higher arrest rates, show greater job dissatisfaction, and have poorer overall work relations.

A further issue that has not been addressed is whether police are more or less cynical than members of other occupational groups. A national survey of 659 American workers found that 54% of blue collar workers were classified as cynics (Kanter & Mirvis, 1989). They believed that lying, putting on a false face, and doing whatever it takes to make a buck are all part of basic human nature. The cynicism scales used in police research typically have focused on the police and have made comparisons between various police personnel. The more general survey developed by Kanter and

Mirvis (1989) could be used to compare police officers with other occupational groups on the type of cynicism that is directed at life, the world, and people in general (Niederhoffer, 1967).

Assessment of Theory and Research

A considerable amount of research has examined the reliability and validity of the Niederhoffer cynicism scale and has found it to be unacceptable. Even if the scale were considered valid, however, the "overwhelming conclusion must be that police, on average, are not cynical" (Langworthy, 1987, p. 33). Only two hypotheses have obtained a significant degree of empirical support. On their first day of training, new recruits are less cynical than those with even very little police experience. Further, there appears to be an inverse relation between police professionalism and cynicism so that officers scoring high on professionalism have lower amounts of cynicism.

On a theoretical level, Niederhoffer explained the hypothesized higher amounts of cynicism among lower ranking patrol officers, as compared with higher ranking and more educated members of the force, on the basis of changes that were taking place in the style of policing. During the 1960s, when Niederhoffer was conducting his research, police departments were in a state of flux from a *tough cop* mentality to one of more professionalism. According to Niederhoffer (1967), these changing values created a sense of anomie, a "morbid condition of society characterized by the absence of standards" (p. 95), which found its expression, in part, in the development of cynicism. Major changes have taken place in policing since the 1960s, with a greater emphasis on values that are consistently centered on the professionalization of the police (Walker, 1989). So even if police were characterized by high levels of cynicism in earlier times, this would no longer be expected to be the case.

Psychopathology

Much of the early research from the 1940s through the 1970s portrayed police officers as suffering from serious psychological problems. Based on their review of the literature, Fenster and his colleagues (1977) concluded that many of the studies implying police officers were neurotic or otherwise emotionally disturbed suffered from a number of limitations. They used inadequate samples, did not present psychometric or other research evidence, used instruments of questionable reliability, and failed to make direct comparisons between police and civilians. To remedy these shortcomings, the investigators conducted a study of 722 males, which included college-educated and non-college-educated New York City police and college-educated and non-college-educated civilians. College-educated subjects who were attending introductory psychology classes each brought in a friend who had never attended college to participate in the study. Although friends of college students were perhaps more similar to their college acquaintances compared to police and civilians at large, the investigators argued that this matching procedure made comparisons between college-educated and non-college-educated groups more meaningful.

Neuroticism was measured with the Eysenck Personality Inventory, and results found that neuroticism was *not* characteristic of New York City police officers. Both groups of police scored lower on neuroticism than the two civilian groups (Fenster & Locke, 1973; Fenster et al., 1977). The possibility that the results might have been due to defensiveness on the part of the police was tested with the Eysenck Lie scale. This hypothesis was not supported: the highest scoring group on defensiveness was the college-educated civilians, with both police groups scoring significantly lower.

Research conducted during and after the 1970s addressed many of the issues raised by Fenster and his colleagues (1977): reliable measuring instruments were used, and psychometric data were presented. Although most of the studies did not make direct comparisons between police and civilians, as had been recommended, they often included comparison groups within policing and law enforcement and used established norms to evaluate scores on the clinical scales.

The most widely used psychometric test for police selection in the United States is the Minnesota Multiphasic Personality Inventory (MMPI) (Cochrane, Tett, & Landecreek, 2003). The MMPI was originally designed to diagnose psychopathology; however, it has been used over the years for personnel selection in occupations such as law enforcement, where maturity, emotional stability, and the capacity to react responsibly under stress are necessary for satisfactory job performance (Thumin, 2002). Research by numerous investigators has demonstrated the usefulness of the MMPI for job selection and performance. Within policing, the MMPI's usefulness is in providing an objective measure for *screening out* individuals who exhibit significant psychopathology (Aamodt, 2004; Burbeck & Furnham, 1985; Kenney & Watson, 1999).

When objective measures were used, research found that police, on average, did *not* suffer from serious psychological problems. A number of studies used either the MMPI or the revised MMPI-2 and found police and other law enforcement personnel to be within the normal range on the clinical scales (Hargrave, Hiatt, & Gaffney, 1986; Laguna et al., 2010; Rubin & Cruse, 1973; Saxe & Reisner, 1976; Stevens, Turcu, Iordanescu, & Pop, 2007). Because most police departments, especially those in major cities, require screening procedures for job applicants that include standardized psychological tests like the MMPI in addition to interviews and background checks, this can result in the screening out of a number of applicants (Burbeck & Furnham, 1985; Cochrane et al., 2003; Fenster et al., 1977). As a result, it would be unlikely that police as a group would exhibit significant psychopathology.

Qualities Associated With Positive Evaluations of Police

Research has shown that police score within the normal range on the MMPI clinical scales but *lower* than civilians on neuroticism. This raises the question of why the more speculative early studies, which often were not based on objective data, concluded that police suffered from a variety of psychological problems (Fenster et al., 1977). This is a question that has been addressed by other investigators (Bonifacio, 1991; Fenster et al., 1977; Yarmey, 1990) and can be explained, in part, by the power police have over individual citizens' lives and the ambivalence toward the police that ensues as a result of that power. Studies using the MMPI have explored a further issue: What personal characteristics are associated with more positive evaluations of police officers by others? Although all the scores obtained by police on the MMPI have been in the normal range, two of the scales were associated with more positive evaluations by others, the K (defensiveness) and Hy (hysteria) scales. These included evaluations of police job applicants and job performance ratings of police officers by their supervisors.

The K scale measures defensiveness but also reflects the desire and the ability of a job applicant to present him- or herself favorably (Thumin, 2002). The Hy scale contains items that suggest the individual is well socialized and well adjusted, in addition to other items. These involve the denial of the existence of problems in one's life, as would be expected among job applicants who are motivated to be hired. Consistent with research which has found that high K and Hy scores represent desirable qualities among professional job applicants (Thumin, 2002), elevations on the K and Hy scales were associated with a greater likelihood of police applicants being hired (Saxe & Reisner, 1976). Elevations on these scales also were associated with successful applicants continuing to work in the department for at least 3 years without attrition. Further, the K and Hy scales were associated with more effective job performance evaluations in policing. Police officers who obtained better supervisory ratings had higher scores on both these scales (Bartol, 1991). Additionally, experienced police officers scored higher on the Hy scale than those with less experience (results for the K scale were not reported in this study; Laguna et al., 2010). As in other occupational fields (Cochrane et al., 2003), the ability to present oneself favorably and deny emotional problems or psychological weaknesses leads to more favorable evaluations by others (Bartol, 1982).

THE NEED FOR A NEW APPROACH TO "POLICE PERSONALITY"

Empirical research has failed to support the idea that police officers are characterized by authoritarianism, cynicism, and psychopathology, as compared with other occupational or civilian groups

(Balch, 1972; Burbeck & Furnham, 1985; Fenster et al., 1977; Langworthy, 1987; Lefkowitz, 1975). On the contrary, some studies have found that male officers are lower in authoritarianism, lower in cynicism, and psychologically healthier than other population groups (Fenster et al., 1977; Lefkowitz, 1973, 1975). Despite the lack of support from empirical research, the idea that police officers are characterized by pathological attributes, including authoritarianism and cynicism, persists throughout the literature on policing (Graves, 1996; Yarmey, 1990).

In his early review of the literature on police personality, Balch (1972) described the "unproductiveness of the personality model" (p. 118) and called for an alternative approach to understanding police behavior. He questioned the existence of modal personality characteristics among police officers and called, instead, for an emphasis on the organizational factors that shape police behavior and personality traits. Gerber (2001) has proposed a further change: instead of focusing exclusively on the personality traits assumed to differentiate police from other occupational groups, the focus needs to widen to include the *similarities* between police officers and members of other task-oriented and occupational groups. This would make it possible to explore the extent to which the situational processes that take place in other task-oriented groups have similar effects on police officers' behaviors and personality traits.

EFFECT OF STATUS ON POLICE OFFICERS' PERSONALITY TRAITS: SIMILARITIES WITH MEMBERS OF OTHER TASK-ORIENTED GROUPS

In order to effectively enforce the law, police officers need to exercise authority (Skolnick, 1994). In doing so, they need to engage in behaviors that reflect the special status they hold within society. This includes the legitimate right to exercise power, including coercive power. These high-status behaviors involve both dominance and assertiveness (Gerber, 2001). In addition, police officers need to exercise behaviors, at times, that reflect a lower status position. Because they work within a hierarchical status structure with clear lines of authority, officers are required to manifest behaviors involving accommodation to those with higher ranks. These status-related behaviors are similar to those that characterize members of other occupational and task-oriented groups and would be reflected in police officers' personality traits (Gerber, 2009). This includes the dominating or authoritative traits and the instrumental or assertive traits associated with high status, in addition to the expressive or accommodating traits associated with low status. These are the same traits associated with status in other occupational groups (Anastasia & Miller, 1998; Brenner, 1982; Moskowitz, Suh, & Desaulniers, 1994; Rose, Fogg, Helmreich, & McFadden, 1994; Rose, Helmreich, Fogg, & McFadden, 1993; Rosen, Weber, & Martin, 2000).

The focus on status reflects a recent view of personality in which "[p]ersonality is not represented as a stable constant that drives behavior, but … is contingent, responsive to the social world, and calibrated to the situation and particular task at hand" (Cross & Markus, 1999, p. 392). In this view, personality traits reflect peoples' behaviors; they summarize the way people behave over time (Buss & Craik, 1983). When an individual engages in multiple interactions over a period of time which involves either a high- or low-status position, the personality traits attributed to the self would reflect this status position. These interactions could involve multiple interchanges with others within a particular relationship with another individual, such as a partner, or within a larger organizational context, such as a police department (Gerber, 2009).

STATUS AND PERSONALITY TRAITS

Studies have shown that the personality traits related to status and power are the *gender-stereotyped personality traits* that people associate with men and women (Bem, 1974; Spence, Helmreich, & Holahan, 1979; Spence, Helmreich, & Stapp, 1975). High-status individuals of both genders perceive themselves as having more of the *instrumental-dominating traits* and *instrumental-assertive traits* associated with men (Gerber, 2009). The instrumental-dominating traits refer to socially undesirable, instrumental, goal-oriented, dominating attributes such as being dictatorial and arrogant; the instrumental-assertive traits refer to socially desirable, self-assertive, agentic or goal-oriented attributes, such as being decisive and independent (Bem, 1974; Spence et al., 1975; Spence et al., 1979). In contrast, low-status individuals of both genders perceive themselves as having more of the *expressive traits* associated with women (Gerber, 2009). The expressive traits refer to socially desirable, interpersonally oriented, communal, or accommodating attributes, such as being warm and helpful to others (Bem, 1974; Spence et al., 1975).

EFFECT OF STATUS ON BEHAVIOR AND PERSONALITY TRAITS

Status characteristics theory addresses the way status affects the behaviors that take place in task-oriented interactions (Berger, Fisek, Norman, & Wagner, 1985; Berger, Fisek, Norman, & Zelditch, 1977). When people work together on a common task, they develop expectations about each other's ability. These expectations are based on information about their status characteristics: attributes, such as work experience and gender, that are assumed to be related to task performance. *Specific status characteristics* refer to attributes related to particular tasks such as those involved in police work. Consequently, when two male police officers or two female officers work together as partners, the officer with more experience would be assumed more competent and would have higher status (Gerber, 2001). *Diffuse status characteristics* refer to socially recognized distinctions, such as gender (Berger et al., 1977). Gender serves as a diffuse status characteristic because of the cultural belief that men perform most tasks more effectively than women (Dovidio, Brown, Heltman, Ellyson, & Keating, 1988). Thus, when a man and woman work together as police partners, the man would have the higher status. Differences in dyad members' status lead to differences in the way they behave. The person with higher status engages in more dominating or authoritative behaviors in addition to more instrumental or assertive behaviors (Berger, Rosenholtz, & Zelditch, 1980). By contrast, the person with lower status engages in more expressive or accommodating behaviors.

The *status model of personality* (Gerber, 2009) extends the theory, which focuses on people's behaviors, to explain the way status affects perceptions of people's personality traits. Because the high-status individual behaves in a more dominating and instrumental way, he or she is perceived, by the self and others, as having more instrumental-dominating and instrumental-assertive traits. Because the low-status person behaves in a more expressive way, he or she is perceived, by the self and others, as having more expressive traits (Gerber, 2001).

Individual Status and Group Status

The status order that evolves within an interacting dyad in which one person has high status and the other person has low status is called *individual status* (Gerber, 1996). *Group status* refers to the status ranking of the dyad as a whole within the context of a larger organization. Since policing is a highly masculine-typed occupation, gender is an extremely salient status characteristic (Martin, 1990). Because of this, the proportions of men and women in different police partnerships determines their group status. All-male police partnerships are highest, male-female partnerships are intermediate, and all-female partnerships are lowest in group status. Both types of status rankings, individual status and group status, affect the behavior and perceived personality traits of dyad members (Gerber, 1996).

STATUS IN POLICING: EFFECT ON PERSONALITY TRAITS

Police officers who work together as partners have an intensive work relationship. They often work closely together 5 days a week over long periods of time. Not only must they cooperate with one another in order to perform their job effectively, they are dependent on one another for their safety. A study of police officers who worked together as partners examined the effect of status on officers' perceptions of their personality traits (Gerber, 1996). Three types of partnerships were included: all-male, male-female, and all-female. In the all-male and all-female teams, the more experienced officer was designated high status, and in the male-female teams, the male officer was designated high status. Police officers' perceptions of their personality traits varied with their status—both their individual status and group status. In all three partnerships, the higher status officer tended to perceive him- or herself as having more instrumental-dominating traits than did the lower status officer. In addition, higher group status was associated with more self-perceived instrumental-dominating traits, with members of the highest status all-male teams perceiving themselves as most dominant, members of intermediate-status male-female teams perceiving themselves as intermediate in dominance, and members of the lowest status all-female teams perceiving themselves as least dominant.

Status also was related to police officers' self-perceived expressive traits. Lower status officers of both genders perceived themselves as having more expressive traits than higher status officers in all three partnership types (Gerber, 1996). In addition, officers' self-perceived expressive traits varied with their group status—the lowest status all-female teams were highest, intermediate status male-female teams were intermediate, and the highest status all-male teams were lowest in expressiveness. Contrary to prediction, the instrumental-assertive traits did not vary as a function of status. All officers, regardless of their status or gender, perceived themselves as high on the instrumental-assertive traits (Gerber, 1996). This suggests that high levels of assertiveness are necessary for the performance of the role of police officer (Skolnick, 1994).

Status and Personality Traits in Policing: Further Issues

According to the status model of personality (Gerber, 2009), the status processes that affect the personality attributes of members of other task-oriented interactions are similar to the processes that affect the personality attributes of police personnel. Because of this, research in other settings, such as the military, can help to further understand the situational factors that may impact on the personality traits of police personnel.

Status plays a central role in policing and includes both formal and informal status rankings. The research with police partners, described previously, demonstrates the way in which informal status orderings affect police officers' perceptions of their personality traits (Gerber, 2001). A further issue involves the effect that formal status rankings within the police department have on personality. A study of male military personnel found that the instrumental-dominating traits varied with their formal rank (Rosen et al., 2000). The instrumental-dominating traits were *negatively* correlated with rank, indicating that lower ranking military personnel manifested more of these traits than higher ranking personnel. This suggests that the greater legitimacy associated with the exercise of power by higher ranking personnel may create less of a necessity to employ the more authoritative methods of exercising power associated with the instrumental-dominating traits. *Legitimacy* refers to a process by which high-ranking individuals can mobilize the support or resources necessary to ensure that others will comply with their directives (Ridgeway, Johnson, & Diekema, 1994). The findings from the military study suggest that there may be a negative correlation between the instrumental-dominating traits and rank for members of police departments as well. This would mean that higher ranking police personnel would perceive themselves as having fewer instrumental-dominating traits than would lower ranking personnel.

Sometimes police officers work in larger units or squads, which raises the question of the effect this would have on officers' personality traits. Whereas the expressive traits are most commonly associated with lower status (Gerber, 2009), in a group situation that calls for cooperation, these traits can be associated with higher status (Ridgeway, 1988). NASA astronauts have to be prepared to live together on a space station for extended periods of time. A sample of NASA astronauts described their personality attributes on a scale similar to expressiveness, which emphasized the ability to cooperate with others (Rose et al., 1993, 1994). Astronauts' self-perceived cooperative or expressive attributes were positively correlated with ratings by peers of their leadership, interpersonal competence, and technical competence as well as with supervisor's ratings of effectiveness. These results suggest that in larger working groups of police officers, such as squads, the expressive traits may be associated with higher status and higher perceived competence.

Finally, research has suggested that crime rates in the larger social environment can impact on the personality attributes of the police (Brown & Willis, 1985). A study of New York City police officers (Gerber & Fuller, 1998) found that the level of violent crimes in police precincts throughout New York City was associated with police officers' perceptions of their personality traits. Precincts were classified into low, medium, and high violence levels, depending on the percentage of violent crimes in relation to the population in each precinct. Officers' expressive and submissive traits were negatively correlated with precinct violence, indicating that officers in precincts with greater levels of violence perceived themselves as less accommodating and less submissive than those in precincts with lower levels of violence. In addition, results found that police officers' instrumental-dominating and instrumental-assertive traits were unrelated to precinct violence, which has implications for officers' use of force. According to these results, officers were less acquiescent in precincts with high levels of violent crimes, but were not more authoritative in their use of power. Other issues for future research involve the effect of urban and rural environments on police officers' traits and the effect of the larger national context on police in different countries.

WOMEN POLICE OFFICERS' PERSONALITY TRAITS

Research on police personality generally has involved men, but as more women have entered policing, the research has been extended to include women. Some investigators have proposed that women are less authoritarian and cynical than men; however, there is no evidence to support that position (Lunneborg, 1989). Few empirical studies have examined authoritarianism and cynicism in women police, and conflicting results have been found in comparisons between women and men (Austin & O'Neill, 1985; Davis, 1984; Dorsey & Giacopassi, 1986). Methodological weaknesses have contributed to the difficulty (Lunneborg, 1989).

With respect to psychopathology, studies using the MMPI and MMPI-2 found that women police applicants, on average, scored within the normal range on all of the clinical scales (Carpenter & Raza, 1987; Kornfeld, 1995). The MMPI MF (Masculinity-Femininity) scale was within the normal range for both genders, but women applicants scored higher than men applicants, indicating that they were less likely to identify with traditional gender roles. This would be expected of women applicants in the nontraditional, masculine-typed occupation of policing. In addition, women police applicants were likely to be more assertive, nonconforming, and energetic, as compared to women in general, than were men police applicants, compared to men in general.

WOMEN'S STATUS WITHIN POLICING: EFFECT ON PERSONALITY TRAITS

A concern expressed throughout the literature on the *woman police officer personality* is whether women need to be *defeminized* and manifest masculine-typed personality traits in order to be successful in police work (Berg & Budnick, 1986; Kennedy & Homant, 1981; Lunneborg, 1989). The assumption underlying this concern is the traditional view that women and men have different personality traits. A more recent view emphasizes the proximal determinants of people's personality traits, which are highly flexible and influenced by situational factors such as status (Deaux & LaFrance, 1998; Deaux & Major, 1987). According to the more recent approach and the body of supporting research (Gerber, 2009), personality traits are neither *feminine* nor *masculine*; the traits people associate with women and men stem from the status relation between the genders. Because men typically have higher status than women (Hollander & Offerman, 1990; Steil, 1997), they appear to have different personality attributes. However, when men and women have equal status, they perceive themselves as similar in their personality attributes.

Instrumental-Dominating and Expressive Traits

Most studies that examine personality differences between women and men police simply compare groups of women and men and look for overall gender differences. When male and female police officers are compared without taking status into account, stereotypic gender differences are generally found (Gerber, 2001). Men perceive themselves as higher on the instrumental-dominating traits, and women see themselves as higher on the expressive traits. However, when status is taken into account, these apparent gender differences disappear and status accounts for all of the variability in male and female police officers' perceptions of their instrumental-dominating and expressive traits (Gerber, 2001). This indicates that the apparent personality differences between male and female police officers actually result from the difference in their status.

Instrumental-Assertive Traits

Women police have been characterized as highly assertive in a number of investigations (Carpenter & Raza, 1987; Martin, 1990; Martin & Jurik, 1996; Sterling & Owen, 1982). Women police recruits scored significantly higher on the instrumental-assertive traits compared with women college students (Lester, Gronau, & Wondrack, 1982). In the study of police partners, described previously (Gerber, 1996), all officers, women as well as men, perceived themselves as extremely high in instrumental-assertiveness—higher than the norm for college males. The instrumental-assertive traits have been found in most research to be associated with high status (Gerber, 2009). Consequently, these results suggest that the socially desirable instrumental-assertive traits that characterize all police officers reflect the special status that women and men police officers hold within society as a whole. This grants them the legitimate right to exercise authority, including, when necessary, the use of force.

Complaining Traits

Research involving police personnel has found that women are more outspoken and verbally assertive than men and experience more aversive emotions (Biggam & Power, 1996; Kennedy & Homant, 1981; Price, 1974). Female police officers were more outspoken than a comparison group of female nurses (Kennedy & Homant, 1981), and female police executives scored higher than male police executives on verbal aggression (Price, 1974). Complaining is considered an aversive characteristic (Kowalski, 1996) and is associated more with women than with men (Spence et al., 1979). The *complaining traits* reflect an indirect way of exercising influence through an outspoken verbal assertiveness (Gerber, 2009). Although complaining is usually considered socially undesirable (Kowalski, 1996; Spence et al., 1979), it can benefit low-status dyad members by enabling them to cope more effectively with their low-status position (Wagner & Berger, 1998). At the same time as low-status individuals attempt to exercise influence, they defer to the higher status partner's right to accept or reject that influence. Research with police officers who work as partners suggested that complaining can be functional for women, who generally hold lower status positions than men within policing. Policing is one of the most highly masculine-typed occupational fields, and men are assumed to be more competent than women (Martin & Jurik, 1996). As a result, when a man and woman work together as police partners, the man is expected to enact the higher status role. Even when the woman officer is more experienced than the man, she still is expected to assume a lower status role. The only way the woman police officer can gain influence is by using an indirect form of power, like complaining.

In male-female police partnerships, the low-status woman was perceived (by herself and her male partner) as having more complaining traits than her partner, particularly when she had relatively more work experience (Gerber, 2001). Her self-perceptions on the complaining traits were correlated with her influence in the partnership, as perceived by herself and her partner, suggesting that complaining enabled the low-status woman to exercise power indirectly. Further, complaining by the low-status woman was functional for both her and her male partner. The low-status woman's complaining traits were positively correlated with her and her partner's evaluations of their own job performances, indicating that the woman's complaining was associated with better assessments by both police partners of their work effectiveness.

The Status-Related Personality Traits

The traditional approach to personality conceptualizes the personality traits associated with women and with men as *feminine* and *masculine*. However, the research reviewed here has demonstrated that status, not gender, is the primary determinant of women's—and men's—perceptions of their *gender-stereotyped* personality traits. Conceptualizing these traits in terms of status can help to better understand the issues that confront women in policing. The organization of the police department and the status expectations that govern that system help perpetuate apparent gender differences in personality. These expectations often go unexamined but have important implications for policing because they can have a major impact on the functioning of women—and men—police officers.

CONCLUSION

The traditional approach to studying *police personality* has emphasized the differences between police officers and other population groups and has concentrated on negative aspects of personality, namely, authoritarianism, cynicism, and psychopathology. Although this approach has dominated the field since the 1960s, empirical research has failed to find support for the proposition that police as a group are characterized by these negative attributes.

One of the problems in developing new approaches to the study of police officers' personality attributes has been the absence of theoretical models (Balch, 1972). The status model of personality provides a theoretical framework for the study of police personality and is rooted in a substantial body of theory and research (Berger & Zelditch, 1985; Gerber, 2001, 2009; Webster & Foschi, 1988). It postulates that the same kinds of status-related factors that affect members of other task-oriented groups impact on the personality traits of police personnel. Instead of focusing on negative aspects of personality, it is concerned with the *functions* that different behaviors and the corresponding personality traits serve in interactions between people. The personality attributes affected by these status processes reflect broad aspects of instrumentality and expressiveness and include the instrumental-dominating, instrumental-assertive, expressive, and complaining traits (Gerber, 2001, 2009; Spence et al., 1979).

The status model of personality is particularly relevant to studying the personality attributes of police personnel. Not only do they work within a hierarchical setting with formal ranks, but also the informal status orderings that emerge between police personnel are similar to those that occur in other task-oriented groups. Most important, the status model recognizes that police are not a homogeneous entity. Future research needs to move beyond studying police officers as a group, or even comparing women and men police, to examine the particular situational demands that affect the personality traits of the individuals who work in policing.

Author Note

Correspondence concerning this chapter should be addressed to Gwendolyn L. Gerber, Department of Psychology, John Jay College of Criminal Justice, The City University of New York, 445 West 59th Street, New York, New York. E-mail: ggerber@jjay.cuny.edu

REFERENCES

Aamodt, M. G. (2004). Special issue on using MMPI-2 scale configurations in law enforcement selection: Introduction and meta-analysis. *Applied H.R.M. Research, 9*(2), 41–52.

Adorno, T. W., Frenkel-Brunswik, E., Levinson, D. J., & Sanford, R. N. (1950). *The authoritarian personality* (Rev. ed.). New York: Harper.

Anastasia, I., & Miller, M. D. (1998). Sex and gender: A study of university professors. *Sex Roles, 38,* 675–683.

Austin, T. L., & O'Neill, J. J. (1985). Authoritarianism and the criminal justice student: A test of the predispositional model. *Criminal Justice Review, 10,* 33–40.

Balch, R. W. (1972). The police personality: Fact or fiction. *The Journal of Criminal Law, Criminology, and Police Science, 63,* 106–119.

Bartol, C. R. (1982). Psychological characteristics of small town police officers. *Journal of Police Science and Administration, 10,* 548–563.

Bartol, C. R. (1991). Predictive validation of the MMPI for small-town police officers who fail. *Professional Psychology: Research and Practice, 22,* 127–132.

Bartol, C. R., & Bartol, A. M. (2004). *Psychology and law: Theory, research and application* (3rd ed.). Belmont, CA: Wadsworth.

Bem, S. L. (1974). The measurement of psychological androgyny. *Journal of Consulting and Clinical Psychology, 42,* 155–162.

Berg, B. L., & Budnick, K. J. (1986). Defeminization of women in law enforcement: A new twist in the traditional police personality. *Journal of Police Science and Administration, 14,* 314–319.

Berger, J., Fisek, M. H., Norman, R. Z., & Wagner, D. G. (1985). Formation of reward expectations in status situations. In J. Berger & M. Zelditch, Jr. (Eds.), *Status, rewards, and influence* (pp. 215–261). San Francisco: Jossey-Bass.

Berger, J., Fisek, M. H., Norman, R. Z., & Zelditch, M., Jr. (1977). *Status characteristics and social interaction: An expectation states approach.* New York: Elsevier.

Berger, J., Rosenholtz, S. J., & Zelditch, M., Jr. (1980). Status organizing processes. *Annual Review of Sociology, 6,* 479–508.

Berger, J., & Zelditch, M., Jr. (Eds.). (1985). *Status, rewards, and influence: How expectations organize behavior.* San Francisco: Jossey-Bass.

Biggam, F. H., & Power, K. O. (1996). The personality of the Scottish police officer: The issue of positive and negative affectivity. *Personality and Individual Differences, 20,* 661–667.

Bonifacio, P. (1991). *The psychological effects of police work: A psychodynamic approach.* New York: Plenum.

Brenner, O. C., (1982). Relationship of education to sex, managerial status, and the managerial stereotype. *Journal of Applied Psychology, 67,* 380–383.

Brown, L., & Willis, A. (1985). Authoritarianism in British police recruits: Importation, socialization or myth? *Journal of Occupational Psychology, 58,* 97–108.

Burbeck, E., & Furnham, A. (1985). Police officer selection: A critical review of the literature. *Journal of Police Science and Administration, 13,* 58–69.

Buss, D. M., & Craik, K. H. (1983). The act frequency approach to personality. *Psychological Review, 90,* 105–126.

Carpenter, B. N., & Raza, S. M. (1987). Personality characteristics of police applicants: Comparisons across subgroups and with other populations. *Journal of Police Science and Administration, 15,* 10–17.

Christie, R. (1991). Authoritarianism and related constructs. In J. P. Robinson, P. R. Shaver, & L. S. Wrightsman (Eds.), *Measures of personality and social psychological attitudes* (Vol. 1, pp. 501–571). New York: Academic Press.

Cochran, N. (1975). Authority orientations of police. *Journal of Applied Psychology, 60,* 641–643.

Cochrane, R. E., Tett, R. P., & Landecreek, L. (2003). Psychological testing and the selection of police officers: A national survey. *Criminal Justice and Behavior, 30,* 511–537.

Colman, A. M., & Gorman, L. P. (1982). Conservatism, dogmatism and authoritarianism in British police officers. *Sociology, 16,* 1–11.

Cross, S. E., & Markus, H. R. (1999). The cultural constitution of personality. In L. A. Pervin & O. P. Johns (Eds.), *Handbook of personality: Theory and research* (2nd ed., pp. 378–396). New York: Guilford.

Davis, J. A. (1984). Perspectives of policewomen in Texas and Oklahoma. *Journal of Police Science and Administration, 12,* 395–403.

Deaux, K., & LaFrance, M. (1998). Gender. In D. T. Gilbert, S. T. Fiske, & G. Lindzey (Eds.), *The handbook of social psychology* (4th ed., Vol. 1, pp. 788–827). New York: McGraw-Hill.

Deaux, K., & Major, B. (1987). Putting gender into context: An interactive model of gender-related behavior. *Psychological Review, 94,* 369–389.

Dorsey, R. R., & Giacopassi, D. J. (1986). Assessing gender differences in the levels of cynicism among police officers. *American Journal of Police, 5,* 91–112.

Dovidio, J. F., Brown, C. E., Heltman, K., Ellyson, S. L., & Keating, C. F. (1988). Power displays between women and men in discussions of gender-linked tasks: A multichannel study. *Journal of Personality and Social Psychology*, *55*, 580–587.

Fenster, C. A., & Locke, B. (1973). Neuroticism among policemen: An examination of police personality. *Journal of Applied Psychology*, *57*, 358–359.

Fenster, C. A., Wiedemann, C. F., & Locke, B. (1977). Police personality: Social science folklore and psychological measurement. In B. D. Sales (Ed.), *Psychology in the legal process* (pp. 89–109). New York: Spectrum.

Gerber, G. L. (1996). Status in same-gender and mixed-gender police dyads: Effects on personality attributions. *Social Psychology Quarterly*, *59*, 350–363.

Gerber, G. L. (2001). *Women and men police officers: Status, gender, and personality*. Westport, CT: Praeger.

Gerber, G. L. (2009). Status and the gender stereotyped personality traits: Toward an integration. *Sex Roles*, *61*, 297–316.

Gerber, G. L., & Fuller, S. (1998). *Violent crime rates in New York City police precincts: Effect on male and female police officers' personality traits*. Unpublished manuscript, John Jay College of Criminal Justice, New York.

Graves, W. (1996). Police cynicism: Causes and cures. *The FBI Law Enforcement Bulletin*, *65*(6), 16–21.

Hargrave, G. E., Hiatt, D., & Gaffney, T. W. (1986). A comparison of MMPI and CPI test profiles for traffic officers and deputy sheriffs. *Journal of Police Science and Administration*, *14*, 250–258.

Hollander, E. P., & Offermann, L. R. (1990). Power and leadership in organizations: Relationships in transition. *American Psychologist*, *45*, 179–189.

Kanter, D. L., & Mirvis, P. H. (1989). *The cynical Americans: Living and working in an age of discontent and disillusion*. San Francisco: Jossey-Bass.

Kennedy, D. B., & Homant, R. J. (1981). Nontraditional role assumption and the personality of the policewoman. *Journal of Police Science and Administration*, *9*, 346–355.

Kenney, D. J., & Watson, T. S. (1999). Intelligence and the selection of police recruits. In D. J. Kenney & R. P. McNamara (Eds.), *Police and policing: Contemporary issues* (2nd ed., pp. 15–36). Westport, CT: Praeger.

Kornfeld, A. D. (1995). Police officer candidate MMPI-2 performance: Gender, ethnic, and normative factors. *Journal of Clinical Psychology*, *51*, 536–540.

Kowalski, R. M. (1996). Complaints and complaining: Functions, antecedents, and consequences. *Psychological Bulletin*, *119*, 179–196.

Laguna, L., Linn, A., Ward, K., & Rupslaukyte, R. (2010). An examination of authoritarian personality traits among police officers: The role of experience. *Journal of Police and Criminal Psychology*, *25*, 99–104.

Langworthy, R. H. (1987). Police cynicism: What we know from the Niederhoffer scale. *Journal of Criminal Justice*, *15*, 17–35.

Lefkowitz, J. (1973). Attitudes of police toward their job. In J. R. Snibbe & H. M. Snibbe (Eds.), *The urban policeman in transition* (pp. 203–232). Springfield, IL: Charles C Thomas.

Lefkowitz, J. (1975). Psychological attributes of policemen: A review of research and opinion. *Journal of Social Issues*, *31*, 3–26.

Lester, D., Gronau, F., & Wondrack, K. (1982). The personality and attitudes of female police officers: Needs, androgyny, and attitudes toward rape. *Journal of Police Science & Administration*, *10*, 357–360.

Lotz, R., & Regoli, R. (1977). Police cynicism and professionalism. *Human Relations*, *30*, 175–186.

Lunneborg, P. W. (1989). *Women police officers: Current career profile*. Springfield, IL: Charles C Thomas.

Martin, S. E. (1990). *On the move: The status of women in policing*. Washington, DC: Police Foundation.

Martin, S. E., & Jurik, N. C. (1996). *Doing justice, doing gender: Women in law and criminal justice occupations*. Thousand Oaks, CA: Sage.

McNamara, R. P. (1999). The socialization of the police. In D. J. Kenney & R. P. McNamara (Eds.), *Police and policing: Contemporary issues* (2nd ed., pp. 1–12). Westport, CT: Praeger.

Mischel, W. (1990). Personality dispositions revisited and revised: A view after three decades. In L. A. Pervin (Ed.), *Handbook of personality: Theory and research* (pp. 111–134). New York: Guilford.

Moskowitz, D. S., Suh, E. J., & Desaulniers, J. (1994). Situational influences on gender differences in agency and communion. *Journal of Personality and Social Psychology*, *66*, 753–761.

Niederhoffer, A. (1967). *Behind the shield: The police in urban society*. Garden City, NY: Doubleday.

Pervin, L. A. (1990). A brief history of modern personality theory. In L. A. Pervin (Ed.), *Handbook of personality: Theory and research*. New York: Guilford.

Poole, E., Regoli, R., & Lotz, R. (1978). Linkages between professionalism, work alienation and cynicism in large and small police departments. *Social Science*, *59*, 525–534.

Price, B. R. (1974). A study of leadership strength of female police executives. *Journal of Police Science and Administration, 2*, 219–226.

Regoli, R. M. (1976). The effects of college education on the maintenance of police cynicism. *Journal of Police Science and Administration, 4*, 340–345.

Regoli, R. M. (1977). *Police in America.* Washington, DC: University Press of America

Regoli, R. M., Crank, J., & Rivera, G. (1990). The construction and implementation of an alternative measure of police cynicism. *Criminal Justice and Behavior, 17*, 395–409.

Ridgeway, C. (1988). Gender differences in task groups: A status and legitimacy account. In M. Webster, Jr., & M. Foschi (Eds.), *Status generalization: New theory and research* (pp. 108–206). Stanford, CA: Stanford University Press.

Ridgeway, C. L., Johnson, C., & Diekema, D. (1994). External status, legitimacy, and compliance in male and female groups. *Social Forces, 72*, 1051–1077.

Rokeach, M. (1960). *The open and closed mind.* New York: Basic Books.

Rose, R. M., Fogg, L. F., Helmreich, R. L., & McFadden, T. J. (1994). Psychological predictors of astronaut effectiveness. *Aviation, Space, and Environmental Medicine, 65*, 910–915.

Rose, R. M., Helmreich, R. L., Fogg, L., & McFadden, T. J. (1993). Assessments of astronaut effectiveness. *Aviation, Space, and Environmental Medicine, 64*, 789–794.

Rosen, L. N., Weber, J. P., & Martin, L. (2000). Gender-related personal attributes and psychological adjustment among U.S. Army soldiers. *Military Medicine, 165*, 54–59.

Rubin, J., & Cruse, D. (1973). Police behavior: II. *Journal of Psychiatry & Law, 1*, 353–375.

Saxe, S. J., & Reiser, M. (1976). Comparison of three police applicant groups using the MMPI. *Journal of Police Science and Administration, 4*, 419–425.

Shaver, P. (1973). Authoritarianism, dogmatism and related measures. In J. P. Robinson & P. R. Shaver (Eds.), *Measures of social psychological attitudes* (pp. 295–451). Ann Arbor: Institute for Social Research, University of Michigan.

Skolnick, J. H. (1994). A sketch of the police officer's "working personality." In J. H. Skolnick (Ed.), *Justice without trial: Law enforcement in democratic society* (pp. 41–68). New York: Macmillan.

Spence, J. T., Helmreich, R. L., & Holahan, C. K. (1979). Negative and positive components of psychological masculinity and femininity and their relationships to self-reports of neurotic and acting out behaviors. *Journal of Personality and Social Psychology, 37*, 1673–1682.

Spence, J. T., Helmreich, R. L., & Stapp, J. (1975). Ratings of self and peers on sex-role attributes and their relation to self-esteem and conceptions of masculinity and femininity. *Journal of Personality and Social Psychology, 32*, 29–39.

Steil, J. M. (1997). *Marital equality: Its relationship to the well-being of husbands and wives.* Thousand Oaks, CA: Sage.

Sterling, B., & Owen, J. (1982). Perceptions of demanding versus reasoning male and female police officers. *Personality and Social Psychology Bulletin, 8*, 336–340.

Stevens, M. J., Turcu, M., Iordanescu, E., & Pop, S. (2007). MMPI-2 indicators of the psychological adjustment of Romanian verses U.S. police officers. *International Psychology Bulletin, 11*(4), 12–14.

Thumin, F. J. (2002). Comparison of the MMPI and MMPI-2 among job applicants. *Journal of Business and Psychology, 17*, 73–86.

Wagner, D. G., & Berger, J. (1998). Gender and interpersonal task behaviors: Status expectation accounts. In J. Berger & M. Zelditch, Jr. (Eds.), *Status, power, and legitimacy* (pp. 229–261). London: Transaction.

Walker, S. (1989). Conclusion: Paths to police reform—reflections on 25 years of change. In D. J. Kenney (Ed.), *Police & policing: Contemporary issues* (pp. 271–284). Westport, CT: Praeger.

Webster, M., Jr., & Foschi, M. (Eds.). (1988). *Status generalization: New theory and research.* Stanford, CA: Stanford University Press.

Wilson, C., & Braithwaite, H. (1995). Police patrolling, resistance, and conflict resolution. In N. Brewer & C. Wilson (Eds.), *Psychology and policing* (pp. 5–29). Hillsdale, NJ: Erlbaum.

Wilt, G. M., & Bannon, J. D. (1976). Cynicism or realism: A critique of Niederhoffer's research into police attitudes. *Journal of Police Science and Administration, 4*, 38–45.

Yarmey, A. D. (1990). *Understanding police and police work.* New York: New York University Press.

21 Police and Public Safety Complex Trauma and Grief

An Eco-Ethological Existential Analysis

Daniel Rudofossi

INTRODUCTION

A theory must stand up to scrutiny, testifiability, and falsifiability to be scientific (Popper, 1963). It must also pass the litmus test of colleagues who are leaders in that specific field endorsing the work, and most importantly by proxy, where scientific practitioners use the method presented in a clinical context. Publications in the field are one component of gathering evidence that one's theory and treatment are accepted, endorsements by leaders in the field are another means of gathering evidence by contemporaries indicating that one's theory is accepted as being novel (Cohen, 1985; Kuhn, 1962).

This is especially true when one presents a new synergy of theory building interlinking efficacy as a lattice that drapes the exterior method, reflecting the interior quality of impact as treatment. Biography cannot be unwed from the theory supporting any treatment; the origin of any approach is sown from the experiences and motivation of the scientist. All medicine, including the branch of science born from that hub and broadly called psychology, is no different. The craft and science of therapy are facilitating healing in a patient within that larger hub of medicine, or in the branch of psychology as a clinical application of that science. Healing is coalesced on the three dimensions of applied psychology as clinical intervention: the dimension of the patient, the dimension of the participant-observer as therapist, and the third dimension of the fluid nature of each session that melds into the next in the surround of resistance and growth.

These three dimensions create an individual motif along the palette of the ecological impact of trauma and loss as color, the style and approach of the therapist as active artist, their work of art as the therapy goals, and progress as the collaborative impact on the meaning of the art that progressively emerges. Artists work within the shadow of their expression regardless of medium, and science is a medium that can be expanded to include an artistic expression, as I am suggesting by analogy and metaphor, and not a literal construction. It is within this frame that my theory and technique may be used as a fulcrum toward defining and treating complex trauma syndromes (such as posttraumatic stress disorder [PTSD]) in public safety-military populations.

To present a technique without theory is heuristically blind; it is like tactics without strategy. I have been invited to write a chapter as an expert in my field of trauma and grief therapy. In this context, my biography is worth a brief introduction to you as a reader, as a theory is never divorced from the biography of the author and in fact makes the treatment more meaningful and credible in its benefit.

The author of this chapter has been a street cop, a psychologist, a poet, and a writer who is skilled and trained in four therapies of value: psychoanalytic, rational emotive behavior/cognitive behavioral therapy, logotherapy, and Rogerian therapy. It is not adequate to not highlight the grace of God to have had the mentoring of the finest psychologists and psychiatrists in learning the craft of applying psychotherapy through my clinical supervisors in cognitive behavioral (REBT) therapy: Albert Ellis, Ph.D. and Janet Wolfe, Ph.D.; psychoanalytic therapy supervision by Charles Brenner, MD, and Bob Scharf, MD; in logotherapy, Bob Barnes, Ph.D., and Ann Graber, Ph.D.; and Rogerian and grief therapy exemplar Richard R. Ellis, Ph.D.

By invitation, the responsibility for writing a chapter on my own original theory of complex trauma and grief for this encyclopedic work as author necessitated a careful choice of a case example to highlight the foundation of my theory and therapy approach. In doing so, I will focus on the salient points of theory and technique by using a composite case example from my decade and a half as a "cop doc" with city, state, and federal law enforcement officers and support staff.

My case presentation will illustrate why and how to effect understanding and healing via my eco-ethological existential analysis with an active law enforcement officer/military seasoned soldier overseas from the battlefield in Iraq to the battlefield on the streets, from a foreign warzone to a domestic war zone. This case example is presented in my two books working with traumatized police officer patients: *A Clinician's Guide to Complex PTSD Syndromes in Public Safety Professionals* (2007) and *A Cop Doc's Guide to Public Safety Complex Trauma Syndrome: Using Five Police Personality Styles* (2009). I have selected additional clinical components to illustrate the dialogue between cop and cop doc.

In my theory, I use the terms *ecological* and *ethological* to highlight the operational definitions that in practice are learned with one officer-patient and cop therapist at a time. It is critical to qualify what is presented in this chapter: a basic outline of one intervention with one police personality style of five that are operationally defined. It is in reading my original guide to Police and Public Safety Complex PTSD [PPS-CPTSD] and understanding the basics of operational definitions in the original texts that a deeper cultural competence and outline of how to use my approach may be learned by a mental health professional (Rudofossi, 2007).

However, any student of medicine, psychology, psychiatry, social work, nursing, biology, ethology, counseling, sociology, anthropology, criminology, or criminal justice will be able to understand the fundamental operational definitions that follow: I have minimized the definitions to what is necessary to follow the case that illustrates my theory and treatment of complex PTSD and grief syndromes. I posit that the core component of ecology and ethology informs the perceptual process of traumatic memory in the niches developed and nesting components of police trauma and grief. The active safety officer seeks meaningful information that affords a primal level of security. That primal security is inextricably linked with the infusion of survival value (ethological motivation) and shaped in the context of what each officer's ecological niche affords. The survival value is defined by what I have defined as threefold needs (on three levels as primary, secondary, and tertiary). Primary survival value is represented in terms of the officer's explicit status in rank and the explicit rules of force within his or her ecological niche; a secondary level of valued defenses and rewards is related to the assignment the officer has achieved in practice within the microcultural eco-ethological niche and what that implicitly affords and empowers each member(s) of his or her unit; and a tertiary level of symbolic significance specialized within his or her unit and offers a selective advantage to the officer within that unit. That selective advantage is doubled on an emotional and existential dimension one may even call wisdom within that unit. The complementarity of the officer and other members of this eco-ethological niche we are used to calling a unit, platoon, or squad is symbiotically worked on in the economics of survival as an ethological motivation. It is within this specialized identity mode(s) surrounded by ethological motivation to survive that the officer patient's success or failure impacts on the depth of the quantum psychic moment of trauma. His or her ecological niche may in part afford the unique expression of survival value in achieving status, protection, nurturance, succorance, social support, security, and levels of comfort through adaptation.

That adaptation, whether through cooperation or intense competition, is guided by the personality, style, and accepted norms of the unit. On a microcultural dimension, adaptation within a military, police, or public safety unit is highly idiosyncratic and not to be confused with my personality style by that same name (Rudofossi, 1999, 2009). Aggression, dominance, alexithymia, and action empathy are all expressed and in part motivated by ethological feedback loops forged within one's niche. It is important to understand that such ecology is impacted by massive loss due to trauma. That trauma is on some level conscious and on some deeper level unconscious. The consequent defenses that shape mal(adaptation) ward off expression of the multiple manifestations of loss.

I suggest the defenses of warding off of loss serve an evolutionary mechanism of defense and are motivated by selective and natural selection. Defenses need not be taken as only eco-ethological, nor does my assertion in any way eclipse the concept of ego mechanisms of defense (Freud, 1937); nor the existential defenses against transcendence (Rudofossi, 1997). My concept of eco-ethological defenses underscores aggression and necessary ethological defenses against assailants within that officer-patient's eco-ethologic niche. The existential defenses I am currently working out and refining are always an amalgam of eco-ethological both/and existential dimensions of wisdom and are at a deeper dimension amenable to my treatment. When following my method, which is the only one I know that makes the target of assessing the specific ecologic and ethologic vectors of complex trauma as the elixir to our work as clinicians, I strongly suggest that elixir is unraveling those very losses in the eco-ethological existential analytic approach. By clarifying the ecological niche and ethological vectors of complex losses in trauma, the existential analyst redirects the energy lost in fractured human time when the officer's invariant space was violated with violence with unique meaning jointly derived. While my method and treatment is labor intensive, it is rewarding to the therapist who chooses it. It does not seek a physical method, although any and all methods may compliment my approach, including EMDR and hypnotherapy as much as psychopharmacologic therapy. It is the relationship and understanding that emerges in the therapy between clinician and officer-patient in which durable achievement is garnered. In other words, my treatment approach demands an idiosyncratic sacred exploration of the black hole that trauma rips open, and hence freezing time at the rupture point, making the profane inexplicably relevant and the specific skeletons of the work of substantive pain and suffering crucial to allow the meaningful to emerge: In order to work through the losses, the gain must overwhelm the losses and be defined by it. The therapeutic alliance forged must tolerate the raw material and be refined collaboratively in the process of creative discovery that fill and effectively lay out the treatment of that officer-patient's loss.

Loss experienced by officer-patients when innocent peers are violently injured creates an increased likelihood of aggressive behavior in counterresponse. To deny this forced response from an ethological level is like denying death and human nature. The spontaneous release of aggression as an eco-ethologic defense behavior categorized as *force used over the top* when directed at homegrown terrorists or foreign murderers as brutality is anathema to a scientific and even a human approach. Clinicians as well as administrators need to understand this context of police trauma and loss in order to be able to permeate their own biases and subjective values when assessing and intervening with officers suffering from complex trauma after harm reduction exercises that follow tactical strikes on terrorists, hostage takers, and violent felons.

Aggression is shaped and selected within certain aspects of ethological motivation for the officer to act decisively to optimize a *command presence* for duty—that is, a readiness in the officer to confront a perpetrator/terrorist (foreign/domestic). Loss expressed and fostered in such an ecological niche serves to diminish the enforcement purpose and the survival value. It is to the anti-terrorist/criminal attitude for clinicians who intend to dismantle trauma and loss in a public safety population would be best advised to direct therapy endeavors. Denial, suppression, and eventually repression to an unconscious level are possible in terms of evolutionary mechanisms that defend against loss. In an ecology of violence, an internalized social distance makes superb evolutionary sense and is an equally deleterious psychological maladaptation in reintegration to post police complex ex-trauma adjustment and redeployment (Rudofossi, 1997, 2007). When a moment in experience rips through the dimension of space, that moment freezes time in an ever-contracting space. When the force of losses strikes with quantum moment the surrounding breach cauterizes the movement of space from fluid to frozen. Losses such as sudden failure in proven ecologically sophisticated functions motivated by ethological survival contracts psychological motivation in frozen craters. That crater limits and constricts fluid conscious awareness for that officer into concrete impasses of complex trauma.

The officer-patient's existential and ethological trajectory is frozen in the impact of an original quantum psychic moment as a breach in the layout of what have been affordances in the anticipatory scanning of the officer-patient. It is processed as a trauma in psychophysiological memories of the trauma event and the ecological niche it occurs in. The occlusion of the surface of the anticipated eco-ethological existential mapping of the officer is breached violently with novel and complex aspects anchored in loss in the eco-ethological existential analytic paradigm. It is described as *surreal* because one's perspective of reality is suddenly shattered and unalterably lost to any attempt to repair that loss. The trauma is at once a unique cognitive-behavioral event; it is complex in its multiple situational demands of disrupted trajectories, ethological motivation, and ecological sensibility, and in the interpretation of each participant in terms of his or her identity mode and existential meaning lost in chaos without a map. No map exists at the time of impact, and it is the therapeutic task to make sense together with the officer-patient exactly what that loss is, why that unique fracture occurred on an eco-ethological dimension, and ultimately the existential experience of loss on a macro and individual level of meaning—left ruptured. This is necessary in heuristically reconstructing the impact of trauma to forge the new layout of redirected meaning layered in loss that is seeking meaning to fill the rupture of mapped schemas.

Nonvariable aspects selected may be looked at as invariants (ethological invariants) that are layered from what is afforded and selected as meaningful in one's ecological niche. Consistency in the active participant experiences affords predictability in self-efficacy in human space—a psychological surface. These invariants are anchors helping the individual achieve competence to move with confidence in a constantly fluid and changing world. Examples of ethological invariants I have observed in officer accounts are designated routine's, objects that are symbolically meaningful in policing, interactional patterns between certain officers and ecological niches or beats, customary unit and culturally sanctioned larger police rituals, and patterns of self-efficacy that repeatedly yield successful mastery in training and actual events such as arrests, containment, perimeter setting, negotiated spaces, and community interactions. These invariants are psychological meaningful existential coordinates—animate to physical anchors—in the ecological niche establishing perceived security as survival value for each officer within a unit, platoon, or battalion. These anchors are consistent qualities in experiencing one's personal and shared world as safe.

The destruction of these perceived ethological invariants in an ecological niche through trauma creates an eco-ethological perception and more complex layered existential experiences of loss and trauma. That loss elicits a range of disturbing emotions, cognitions, and behaviors. Included is de-realization. This may be expressed as a perceptual experience when patients call the event *surreal*. Surreal meaning in this perspective makes superb evolutionary sense; it is the loss of the ethological invariants that give meaning to what was real in human time and space and is now experienced as loss. Being aware—this surreal experience may be grounded in the loss of *ethological invariants* disrupted and initially undefined—is important to clarify and support in facilitating the loss expressed. The parallels in ecological and ethological affordances and disenfranchised losses to redeeming the existential meaning and faith are laid out without losing the humanity and prized unique humane-being of this officer-patient.

I will present through a case example what I mean by the ecological and ethological motivational influence and the clarification of these drive derivatives and how, why, and when to intervene within this individualized approach to complex trauma with the impact of a collaborative eco-ethological existential analysis. I will use the following composite example of one officer-patient who serves as a ranking police officer who uses his skill he learned as a special-forces soldier and emergency service police officer in an event one ought to never experience—yet for this officer it is a staple of his ecological-ethological niche—and the constructs of his world of experience.

I will work through the ecological affordances and the ethological motivation that in part shape the special affordances that impact on how and why he is experiencing the specific aspect of losses in trauma that have left him with the five spires of loss inherent in trauma (Rudofossi, 2009). Ecology is not only the physical sense of the environment and human relationship that is bidirectional but also the added dimensions of two cultures within the larger public safety ethnological dimension of phenomenology. One is the police culture on a macrocosmic level, known as *the job* or *the corps*, in distinction to the culture of the command and the unit one has initiated into as a police officer/special agent or military officer, known as being *in the bag* or *in the saddle* as a baseline level for adaptation and speciation for officers. The powerful impact of loss in trauma shapes the formation of police identity and the interplay with what I would eventually discover as the five styles of police personality. In police identity, traumatic loss contributes to an expansive sense of lost-being in the survivor of trauma, which includes almost all officers. That existential state of a sense of loss that permeates aspects of identity modes or the forging of personality as a police officer is not so easily disentangled from the reality of one's peacetime identity or off-duty personality (Rudofossi, 1997, 2007, 2009).

The command and unit one is a member of are as critical as the incident of trauma one experiences in the field of police war zones. The macrocultural experience is distinct from the internal journey of how one internally witnesses one's own actions, thoughts, and emotions in the field of one's own eco-ethological niche. It is in a union of the ecological niche where an officer acculturates and envelops his or her personality identity modes, and this includes the selective speciation in an evolutionary sense as key information for therapy: That is why a certain behavior, idea, or tendency is piqued in one officer in distinction to another. Personality is layered in adaptation and maladaptive strategies of survival; survival is not only on a ethological dimension of sexual/aggressive drive derivatives, but also nested in an existential dimension related to the macrocultural level of learned behaviors, acceptable semantic expressions, and their analogs in acceptable cognitive and emotional schemas. Integral in the eco-ethological existential analysis of PPS-Complex PTSD is the dual goal of uncovering the hidden unconscious sexual/aggressive drive derivatives within a parallel existential/transcendental unconscious dimension. This means that the therapist facilitates his intervention as an active participant observer using an existential-analytic attitude to reflect a gradual understanding of the ethological motivation at the core of the significance of the individual officer-patient's experience of the quantum psychic moment of complex trauma.

It is within this larger framework that complex PTSD cannot be divorced from the individual officer's selection of what affordances are selected in the ecology of evolutionary motivation for survival. This complexity underscores the confusion and challenge to the therapist who can yield to the complexity and raise the proverbial surrender to general tactics to feel better, or ferret out the "A-ha" with the officer-patient who beckons an answer in part that is eco-ethological, dynamic, cognitive, behavioral, and existential. We make take the types of traumatic events police, public safety and military officer-patients experience to frame what I call *internal-witnessing* of the selection of what component of complex trauma is selected as the most impactful crater in the wound of losses trauma has spread to (Rudofossi, 2007). Internal-witnessing is the ability of the officer to learn (scaffold) his or her *owned* courage and resilience to other experiences of trauma and self, that is, to soothe oneself in the knowledge he or she has acted as best and courageous in the moment of challenge. It is the specific impact of trauma and what aspect is selected as so damaging in the officer-patient narrative that emerges that offers the material to jointly create the antidote. The clinician as participant observer navigates by clarification and repeated interpretation reflected back and forth with the officer-patient in the trauma therapy work, session by session. The complexity of the event itself leads to exploration as to the *why* it has such force and what aspect is selectively remembered in seeking understanding. Using that understanding to reestablish power after the force of the traumatic event invigorates reworking meaning in a manner that enhances the resilience and courage to existential adaptation.

OVERVIEW

Our initial goal is to help the officer-patient unravel his or her losses within the eco-ethological dimensions of PPS-CPTSD, as both adaptation and maladaptation. In doing this, we will help keep our activity focused on eliciting the officer-patient's ability to recognize where choice in his or her interpretation of the trauma lies: attributions of resilience, meaningful suffering where unavoidable, self-change in place of guilt, and losses to be mourned. Our Socratic task is to facilitate the officer-patient's ability to mourn the *tragic past of disenfranchised losses* while helping to identify resilience and meaningful choices for inner strength, including the promise of the future. The language of experiences an officer-patient uses in a meaningful way to express loss may open doors to the often neglected ecological and ethological context. Meaning may be given context through the officer-patient's verbal and nonverbal expressions: from concrete to abstract, formal to slang, and symbolic to ritualistic. Unless we can communicate in the language and dialectic the native speaker uses, we may not be able to speak the language of interest with any acumen. Communication is tri-directional with each individual officer-patient, nested in the therapist's participant observer attitude with the individual officer-patient and their unique experiences of loss in trauma made existentially sensible, together.

THERAPISTS' ATTITUDE

How can we as therapists persuade an officer to choose to help him- or herself if he or she is bound by the trappings of a present and future surrounded by trauma and loss? I suggest that many otherwise effective techniques fail to reach most officers because the officers require motivation in the face of human cruelty and evil. Terrorism (domestic or international) is not diplomacy by other means—it is an act of evil—and suffering whitewashed away in platitudes degrades the officer's experience. An officer-patient no less than a people defending their right to survive terrorism is not violent; rather, he or she is using power to stop terror's force while being human and living humanly at the highest existential dimension. That highest existential dimension is the courage to serve. My theory and therapy of complex trauma as a cop doc boldly assert that blaming the victim makes one a coconspirator with the perpetrators: when police, public safety, and military forces (domestic or foreign) fight terrorists—whether homegrown serial killers, violent gangs, Hamas, or the Taliban—where calling them evil is not anti-psychological, it is an operational definition. Speaking honestly, evil is actions of what is beyond doubt a unique and tragic choice of some human beings to devolve to a primal level of violence, rage, and murder without cause except that their victim somehow deserves to be destroyed. As George Orwell said, "Political language is designed to make lies sound truthful and murder respectable and to give an appearance of solidity to pure wind" (Orwell, 2005, p. 62). What implication for meaning do trauma, death, and brutality hold in this general context if it is not to be interpreted by the seasoned officer and returning veteran as pure wind in their courageous fight to uphold the very society they are protecting and serving? It has to do with speaking honestly and starts with calling evil, frankly, *evil*!

The first meaning for the officer-patient may occur when she or he learns you are a competent professional with the ability to listen to the violence of trauma directed at him or her. You understand and relate to the officer-patient that you know it is not he or she who causes death, brutality, and trauma. You also know that he or she has genuinely witnessed and experienced each event on multiple levels. This seems common-sense, but sensibility may not be all that common. For example, as one seasoned detective informed me, a therapist asked her, "Why don't you choose another line of work?" Another asked within the first 15 minutes of the first meeting, "Do you get the connection between your aggression and people responding with rage?" Another therapist suggested after two sessions that the detective's problems were caused by "her underlying authoritarian and aggressive impulses." Another officer-patient informed me that within three sessions, her therapist opined that "my trauma was an exaggeration to divert attention from other deeper issues." These explicit and premature confrontations are likely to turn off the patient. They are examples you and I are not likely to practice. However, effectively responding to the officer-patient's overwhelming loss with a compassionate understanding of the eco-ethological influences in the context of PPS-CPTSD may act as a catalyst for the long process of working through trauma.

THE ECO-ETHOLOGICAL STANCE TOWARD PPS-CPTSD

Ecological and ethological insight offers awareness of the dynamics of why and how trauma has influenced the shaping of the officer-patient's cognitions, behaviors, feelings, and meaningfulness for life and living. This is achieved by initially putting secondary aspects of trauma and loss into a context that is comprehensible from the officer-patient's frame of reference. I suggest that may give the officer-patient a partial freedom from self-denigration, phrenophobia (the fear of being crazy), being ostracized for weakness, and overwhelming guilt and anxiety. Your task here is to achieve a joint understanding with the officer-patient of the evolutionary significance of the ecological and ethological demands that trauma afforded him or her in surviving. That understanding is where you make explicit that the officer-patient's original adaptation to trauma in different contexts made superb evolutionary sense.

You may guide the officer-patient toward reconstructing how the initial context of an original psychic quantum moment (see Rudofossi, 2007) has such strong survival value. Using the Socratic method, you can then coax the answer to the how it made superb sense to adaptively respond to trauma as he or she did, and likely still does! You may then prepare the officer-patient for the difficult work ahead in working through what has become maladaptive into more adaptive behaviors, cognitions, and emotional expressiveness.

That task in trauma therapy is helpful in a twofold way: The officer-patient may be given a freedom of energy via an explanation he or she can use, in believing that what has become maladaptive not only is sensible but also indicates that he or she is far from crazy. Energy concentrated into a hostile self, and other evaluation, is now energy apt to be available for personal change.

How is that challenge successfully achieved? Subtly, as you guide the officer-patient's insight with your useful and compassionate reflections largely through Socratic clarification. This allows such an officer-patient to relate to his or her own meaningful experience as insight. The promise of change now becomes tangible. That explicit realization that you feel as the officer-patient's pulse of grief in his or her good time, not your own, is part of our professional stance and facilitates healing.

That stance is engaging, respectful, and likely to help bring out resilience in the difficult relationship that all trauma and loss therapy entails in real human space and time. I suggest this aspect of relating is fundamental. That brings us to the eco-ethological approach as a fundamental therapy. By that affirmation, I mean it stands as a foundation in itself. But, it also may anchor other established approaches by increasing efficacy through meaningful insight and intervention. You may then be able to implement my primary therapy method while implementing your own style and tradition of therapy. Your therapy style may include logotherapy, REBT-CBT, psychodynamic, EMDR, and configurational-analysis, among others. I will present you with an unadulterated but intensified approach that accounts for environment (ecological) and endogenous (ethological) vulnerability.

GENERAL FRAMEWORK FOR USING THE ECO-ETHOLOGICAL APPROACH TO PPS-CPTSD

One of our therapeutic tasks is to normalize the experience of stress related to objective trauma, and to assist the officer-patient to work through to insight. That insight follows a flexible path;

hence, I will offer a general approach. My approach is achieved in part by moving through five phases that enable the officer-patient to begin working through the loss in trauma. I do not believe this process can be hastened; it can only be pursued within the context of each and every officer-patient as an individual. I defer from offering a delimited—and what I consider a belied—time frame.

With that said, I suggest the eco-ethological approach offers a rediscovery of meaningfulness in each officer-patient's life. It is therefore an optimistic as well as existential approach. Many officers are challenged by sustaining meaning in their lives via the realms of spiritual, religious, existential, and philosophical beliefs. The ecological and ethological influences are cumulative and do represent a very real counterchallenge. More often than not, substitutes that may be unusually toxic and destructive in the officer's life are chosen, including alcohol, gambling, volatile risk-taking, and impulsive short-term hedonism. In many cases, losses that are disenfranchised may lead to a self-induced numbness and dissociation (Rudofossi, 2007, 2009; Rudofossi & Ellis, 1999). Overwhelming feelings of guilt and despair over what is viewed often enough as brutal and violent events become tolerable, but only at a high personal cost. Much of public service professionals' extraordinary courage goes unnoticed as the traumatic losses endured pile up into disenfranchised heaps, left unmourned.

That is one part of the picture. Your counterposition is another. You bring into the sphere of the officer-patient's experience your passion, creative influence, and commitment. Being confident in your goal of healing helps initiate a valuing of his or her own disenfranchised reservoirs of unrealized resilience, courage, and commitment. Meaning may be rediscovered through joint exploration to identify novel means of mourning losses, while accepting the reality of trauma and harvesting the hidden resilience.

Your attention toward how and when the officer-patient may denigrate his or her action as meaningless is an inroad toward healing as much as psychopathology. That is achieved via your persistence in Socratic elicitation of painful moments. By eliciting what is very painful, the officer-patient may get to review the possibility of redeeming what was valuable in his or her actions and perhaps as never before consider it as empowering. Reservoirs of optimism are framed in one's unheard courage, commitment, and resilience only if they are brought to awareness to counter the despair of the existential vacuum (Frankl, 1978, 2000; Graber 2004), angst of psyche ache (Schneidman, 1996), disenfranchised loss (Doka, 2002), and complicated grief (Worden, 2001) and complicated mourning (Rando, 1993).

Meaningful growth may be concomitant with the unraveling of loss. How you achieve that goal is part of my approach. In part, insight-oriented therapy suggests the officer-patient's transference to you, if not neglected, is an opportunity to frame optimism where the officer's unique contributions are defined and supportively enhanced. Insight may be used to appreciate the rich motifs of the unconscious myths and symbols that emerge. By understanding one's own countertransference, an equally valuable, positive insight into the patient's unconscious motivations may be achieved as well (Brenner, 1974, 1976, 1982, 2003; Freud, Ferenczi, Abraham, Simmel, & Jones, 1921). For example, you may become aware on some level that an officer-patient is censoring his or her expression of some frightening event. Your hypothesis is he or she may be too scared to express that fear. You may then relate your picking up of that fear by articulating your heuristic experience as a hypothesis. You may then gently present your hunch and then feel, observe and listen to the officer-patient's response. If you are feeling a strong visceral response, be reasonably assured your patient is too. Making that strong visceral experience explicit is helpful within the context of your countertransference experience as it is developing.

Keeping these few suggestions and qualifications in mind, let's move on to the five tasks of my eco-ethological method. On the surface, it will appear that the five tasks have some parallels to other trauma reduction interventions: it will become obvious in its applications as presented in my case examples that my approach varies in its complexity and focus.

THE FIVE TASKS OF THE ECO-ETHOLOGICAL METHOD

1. **Facilitate the patient's style of expressing the most distressing traumatic event.** The officer may present his or her material in a number of ways to you. For example, he or she may begin with a narration, a sketch, a file of papers, or pictures. To iterate, I suggest that while some articulate patients do well expressing themselves verbally, other patients may best express their material via written form or other nonverbal means. I suggest supporting whatever medium the officer-patient chooses to present the trauma event. That medium may indicate a preference the officer-patient is initially most comfortable with in communicating the trauma to you.

   You note details at this time. For example, you may observe what selected affordances (Rudofossi, 2007, 2009) the patients laid out prior to the traumatic event, and the selection of what cues support the quality and intensity of these prior selected affordances. Note the prior adaptation levels within the unit at the time of the event in comparison to the present level of maladaptation/adaptation. The quantum psychic moment may be formulated as an hypothesis at this point; it is important to listen on all levels of sensory-output the officer-patient presents with. The task is to formulate an initial hypothesis of the officer's complex trauma. This task also includes discussing that hypothesis with the officer-patient, while clarifying the eco-ethological approach to loss in trauma.

2. **Have the patient narrate his or her thoughts about each aspect of the traumatic event.** Encourage his or her ideas about the event, geographical aspects, and sensory experiences. Ask yourself the following questions: Does the memory have an eidetic quality to it? Does the choice of words of the officer-patient match the intensity as the officer-patient recalls his or her experience of the traumatic event? Do you hear certain words repeated? If so, are those repeated words used in the specific context of loss, trauma, confusion, agitation, excitement, and aversion? Is there a link to what may be a quantum psychic moment?

   If so, explore how the officer-patient felt about what he or she selected as aspects or items included in recounting the trauma, that is, items (physical or geographically located items) that may symbolize important aspects of what he or she has experienced as loss. What meaning do these selected items have within her ecological niche and status? Cue in on items referred to often. Are they emotionally evocative? Items can be highly significant to loss, and they may be interjected in a repetitive manner without any apparent context offered at first. Items can also be representative of affordances. Are you actively listening for pauses, followed by sighs or a segue to another charged but distracting topic?

   To illustrate, let's review the case of officer-patient Q. Officer Q's husband was a public safety officer who died on duty of a medical condition. Officer Q expressed consternation over her emotional distress. She felt weak and like she was really losing it over what she considered an exaggerated response to his death more than 2 years ago. While initially complicated, grief (Rando, 1993; Worden, 2001) was the diagnostic likelihood, the eco-ethological approach facilitated the grieving process. Officer Q became concerned over her symptoms of grieving. One of those symptoms she was distressed about was considering herself as possibly going crazy after experiencing spontaneous crying bouts. At times, she expressed that "without a clue, and for no apparent reason—I just don't know why—I break down and cry." We observed with more attention the situations when this would happen. We established a connection. That connection was her observation, "When I saw loose rounds [bullets] I had placed on the night table, I would just erupt in tears."

   Typically, a therapist may trivialize such reported behavior or discount it as inconsequential. However, in the eco-ethological framework, we are aware of the invariant (see Rudofossi, 2007, 2009) nature of affordances related to the bond between the deceased and the survivor. After the death of her loved one, loose rounds have become a link to what is now missing day in and day out. The loose rounds may now represent a shared ritual through the latent and symbolic meaning. Both husband and wife would play with this ritual, where separate loose rounds, left in one way or another, symbolized different meanings. Using the associations that came to mind, Officer Q was able to associate the loose rounds as invariant affordances that were disrupted by the death of her husband. That led to the dream they shared of her becoming an assistant district attorney and he a squad supervisor. That would lead to retirement and a change in her career. The roles both she and he lived, shared, and labored for, and the shared meaning of these rituals, were now gone.

That loss on multiple levels remained elusive save the affordance that led to it and made it more palatable for Officer Q to express. It put into focus a process of acceptable emotional grieving within a context that made sense to Officer Q. Prior to the eco-ethological approach, she had been unable to express the pain and anguish over his on-duty death due to a medical condition, including her anger at his death as a betrayal by abandonment. Officer Q believed—as would many therapists—that she was genuinely perseverating to meaningless aspects of inanimate objects, and if she expressed such loss, she would be labeled a *basket case* by peers and administration.

In our example, we gradually rediscovered the symbolic meaning of the loose rounds that were placed in a specific location as a latent symbol of her husband's perpetual presence. A habit of leaving these loose rounds in a certain way on the desk made sense as we explored what was significant in the niche she and her husband had forged as law enforcement officers. It was a symbol of their bond on and off duty. She broke into tears as she began to express how much she missed him. Once she realized the symbolic meaning of the loose rounds, his death was—in a special sense to her—more tangible and more acceptable within the ecological and ethological approach. While my focus on the loose rounds might seem trivial, her attention to those rounds triggered her direct emotional expression.

What seemed for no apparent reason to be eliciting so much pain was given all the reason in her voice, in her world. In the context of ecology and ethology, that symbolic significance led to other associations; it was significant in allowing her to begin to mourn other losses associated with his death. You think this step was unnecessary. You may ask, Why not just facilitate the expression of loss directly?

Remember, often the stop gap of expression of loss in police and public safety is unacceptable in this alexithymic culture (i.e, where feelings cannot be expressed with words). The ecological ethological approach helps the officer-patient to own his or her insight into behaviors, emotions, and cognitions (less self-blame and toxic misattributions). That is achieved through this phase where the maladaptation is constructed as having evolutionary sensibility and made explicit. This gives the officer-patient the opportunity for existential and psychological insight into an otherwise unapparent expression of emotion. Without ever asking why, she may suffer silently and without grasping the meaningful relation to the current ecology and ethology. Not knowing then leads into the existential issues. As Officer Q put it, "I break down and cry." But now, in our view, "It is not without any apparent reason." In this example, it was identifying Officer Q's emotional upset as having evolutionary significance. The identification of a connection between inexplicable crying and what seemed to be innocuous items helped her to accept her own insight. Overall, that insight most likely helps facilitate the alliance and trust between you and the officer-patient.

3. **You can now begin to move the officer-patient toward expressing his or her thoughts and feelings including quality and intensity of affect.** It is important to realize that identifying feelings may be requisite in an educative, supportive, and active way. The feelings of fear, disgust, happiness, and loathing may not be expressed and may even be excessively inhibited for that officer-patient. However, this inhibition is far from insurmountable.

For example, initially you may be able to gauge only the intensity of affect through a response on a scale, or subjective self-report. Underscoring a response of *slightly angry* after an officer has been personally assaulted, followed by a narrative that expresses the injustices of the system, may be an inroad to get him or her to express how angry he or she is about being assaulted.

That same approach may expand the use of identification of feelings associated with specific cognitions. While the officer-patient's affect may be elusive, you can apply all your senses. By acutely listening, you can gain a closer approximation of the state of affairs. You can utilize what you hear by gently clarifying contradictory feelings you pick up while the officer-patient is expressing trauma and loss. Contradictions can be enlightening, and may help you understand the individual context in which it emerges through the series of sessions.

4. **Separate the adaptive thoughts and behaviors from maladaptive thoughts, behaviors, and emotions.** In that separation between adaptive and maladaptive, the context of utility, survival, and motivation becomes important.

It is here that your knowledge of the officer-patient's unit and status at the time of traumatic loss helps shed light on the context of his or her personal identity and development. The validation of the officer-patient's experience in field actions is key to maintaining realistic motivation. Rank, status, and assignment are all important in your assessment, which is a key factor in our eco-ethological perspective. That is so because the status of the officer, prior expectations, and investment in his or her status provide an important link to a prior level of adaptation and affordance.

What has become maladaptation, framed by a quantum psychic moment, is made tangible by understanding where the officer-patient was psychologically at the time of the event. That consideration includes whether the officer was off-duty or on-duty; whether or not disciplinary charges were pending; whether a divorce or breakup with a significant other was imminent. While I am not talking about these considerations in detail—keep in mind these ongoing situational pressures as part of the stress and strain. The issues vary as greatly as does the affordances each rank endows within each eco-ethological niche. The weight of responsibility, the selected demands of a police event, and the consequent losses are, in part, products of that officer-patient's rank (see Rudofossi, 2007). For example, the patrol officer who is assigned as the sergeant's driver may be responsible for many operational responses, including gathering information by interviewing potential witnesses from door to door. That gathering of information can involve dealing with projections of guilt displaced onto the officer, and the impact of grief related firsthand by witnesses to a crime.

Another example is the officer on community patrol who may be responsible for an entire small community and have intimate knowledge and responsibility for ensuring the safety of seniors. In one case, a community patrol officer recounted the rape of a senior citizen at a community center. That officer-patient was particularly fond of that senior, whom he knew quite well. While anger was acceptable, a feeling of loss was not, and the feeling remained unspoken and thus more so unidentified. In yet another case, a duty captain responded to an off-duty police lieutenant who was driving while intoxicated (the first time in her life). The captain had neither choice nor discretion in processing her arrest. The police lieutenant sustained minor injuries and began to express suicidal ideations. The lieutenant now discloses that she and the captain were academy recruits together and had remained friends. To complicate matters, the lieutenant is up for promotion and is married to a detective in the captain's command. The captain had to face rancor over his command decision.

In the few examples outlined, you can see how and why rank and the eco-ethological influences are so important. Finding out the specifics makes all the difference. The meaning of the anti-affordance, including the maladaptation, helps you create strategic emphasis in forging insight with the joint work laid out before you and the officer-patient. Your understanding of the ecological and ethological dimensions of status, rank, and affordance in the context of the officer-patient may be a critical factor in the officer-patient appreciating your professionalism. Relating your understanding to the individual officer-patient may be the thread that binds. Bear in mind, that thread will become ropes over sessions where trust and commitment foster collaboration during the upheaval that grief work invariably entails.

Our task in the eco-ethological approach is to help the officer-patient to see that her or his maladaptive behaviors were and are sensible human responses in the context of her or his status as an officer and within the unit at the time of the event. This is an important task and distinction to be aware of. For instance, the lieutenant detective who is sharing a current trauma with you may be more impacted by an original trauma that occurred in her first year as a detective.

The dysfunctional is what was initially maladaptive and may be approached by empirical evaluation of what has also evolved as a healthier adaptation. Observing and accentuating strengths, resilience, and abilities—not despite trauma experienced but as adaptation to trauma—are other therapy tasks in this phase. You are neither fabricating nor creating value where it doesn't exist. Your task is identifying what has been disenfranchised and facilitating the officer-patient's reenfranchisement of that loss in trauma into a personally meaningful gain. She has gained strength from her own history—not in spite of but because of the suffering and loss she has endured.

Your task entails using your own creative intelligence in helping the officer-patient reclaim what has been largely hidden by his or her own "existential blind spot." That "spot" consists of behaviors the officer-patient never considered as his or her helpful contribution. By discovering what has eluded the officer-patient, you share in this uplifting exercise with each officer-patient encounter as it evolves. The encounter increases your experience with this population. You are not inventing what is not there but discovering what is already there. The potential for positive growth is made tangible. Mobilizing a higher frustration tolerance and active involvement includes rescripting the interpretation of the event as meaningful and fluid, not without meaning and not static.

5. **You facilitate the officer-patient retelling his or her own thoughts, behaviors, feelings, and emotions expanded within an eco-ethological existential analysis of his or her complex trauma experience(s).** The officer-patient's involvement and expanding conscious awareness of personal resilience, adaptation and courage at varying levels may overshadow the challenges of maladaptive guilt, shame, and perfectionist standards. The patient now moves beyond his or her thoughts and effective behaviors during a trauma into an existential stance he or she can use in an adaptive style with other situations. The officer-patient's choice, responsibility, and active involvement in living become core targets of this phase, a basis for empowerment and survivorship. A grounding in being able to use empirical and functional evidence for oneself is made tangible in a new mode of adaptation in her or his identity as a public service officer. One focus of this grounding in new skills is having the officer-patient identify maladaptive strategies that deter him or her from reaching new areas of social support, changing self-schemas, and finding meaning in his or her life. Trauma is no longer a series of hidden and shameful episodes. Trauma is placed in the officer-patient's life history as an experience with motive force that can shape the officer-patient's return to adaptation. For most officer-patients this achievement necessitates the retelling of the loss in their own words, and within their own sense of meaning. At this point—while shame, humiliation, and guilt may exist on some level—it is not an oppressive and stultifying shame or humiliation requiring guilt over the losses in trauma. An optimal goal is mourning of the loss which now occupies a more meaningful position

in their histories. It is at this fifth task that we may revisit our observations and review the changes in officer-patients from initial assessment to therapy at this point. This task entails an active involvement of each officer-patient in using imagery and pro-active rehearsal of effective assertiveness in response to the types of trauma encountered.

The acceptance of the loss and trauma experienced dilutes the earlier need for denial and minimization. They no longer are dominant defenses. The qualification of an officer for return to field duty (the vast majority) is best served by having the officer develop adaptive skills for dealing with the toxic impact of trauma.

This task involves the following specific objectives being achieved along a continuum:

i. Disabusing of self by not owning up to guilt, shame, and avoidance of one's role as a public safety officer.
ii. Developing a sense of meaningfulness in the choice one has made in becoming and remaining or having been a police and public safety officer. If the officer-patient has realized that the profession is not for him or her, then the objective is accepting that choice and acting on it. If one is retired or disabled, then the objective is to redeem what is of value and to use that as a point of strength and continuity in living and growing regardless of age or condition.
ii. Choosing to assert one's own ability to choose, and not dissociate from the moments so important in one's trauma history.
iv. Accessing strengths, not self-accusations, from the experiences of gains and losses the officer-patient has worked through. Realizing that choice and responsibility generate a healthy attitude that encompasses resistance in the face of conformity, nihilism, or reduced meaningfulness in one's professional achievements, actions, and interpretations of each trauma.
v. Choice and responsibility empower reaching out for social support, including nontoxic relationships, expression of one's inner and existential voice, and achieving the acceptance of limitations as strength.
vi. Resolving phrenophobia (fear of going crazy) by replacing cognitions, behaviors and feelings that were maladaptive and offering the officer-patient a sensibility by understanding the eco-ethological influences in one's unit that provoked that maladaptation in the first place. The key is mobilizing a higher frustration tolerance and active involvement through rescripting the outcome in the here and now as challenging, active, and evolving.

An achievement of this phase is evident when the officer retires, changes assignment, or stays on in his or her unit based on the meaningfulness that he or she has found through personal choice. Trauma and loss worked through is never without pain and suffering and perhaps never fully worked through. Meaningfulness may entail the choice of the officer-patient to realize his or her work as a calling absent the guilt, suffering, and pain of unmourned losses. It may be said that being able to reach out and give voice to one's pain and suffering to another significant person may be the critical factor between mental health and illness, between immunity and susceptibility, and between life and the choice to end it. You are most likely to be that significant person. However, what you initiate will hopefully be expanded in the officer-patient's ability to grow and develop meaningfulness that uses the trauma for adaptation.

For most of us, it is an awesome responsibility, choice, and ultimate reward in non-tangible and existential growth. That point of reaching out and helping the officer-patient give voice to his or her trauma is the theme throughout our five tasks of the eco-ethological method. In our approach we are aware of an aspect of positive learning, redemption, and a quality of existential meaning that can be missed. We cannot afford to be passive in our approach of PPS-CPTSD for it is anything but submissive, by operational definition trauma punctuates adaptation with violence and noise. The goal is not to avoid angst, violence, and noise, but to commit to dealing with it—committing to deal with the ongoing chaotic and at times violent and unfair aspects of the profession, without succumbing to emotional and mental burnout, behavioral helplessness, and cognitive hopelessness. In not avoiding the deleterious effect of passive withdrawal from trauma, Viktor Frankl sheds light by asserting *tragic optimism* in asserting the existential attitude (Frankl, 1978, 2000; Graber, 2004). I suggest that meaning may be rediscovered through joint exploration to identify novel means of mourning losses while accepting the reality of trauma and the tragic comedy it almost always exemplifies. Now that we have reviewed the general aspects of the eco-ethological method, we go on to look at this approach as a fundamental therapy in its own right.

THE ECO-ETHOLOGICAL APPROACH AS A FUNDAMENTAL THERAPY

The eco-ethological method is a fundamental therapy. By that affirmation, I mean it is a foundation that anchors other established approaches; it is a glue that lends itself to increased efficacy when used with other approaches. Yet, I hope it will facilitate other approaches by targeting the amelioration of symptoms and by providing an increase in insight for the real battlefield of trauma that persists in the embedded psychology of the individual officer-patient, which includes the neurobiological substrates.

Rational Emotive Behavior Therapy/Cognitive Behavior Therapy [REBT/CBT] has a significant place in the eco-ethological approach toward reassessing thoughts, behaviors, feelings, and objectives while being respectful of individual differences. Motivational interviewing techniques, paradoxical interventions, supportive empathy, and almost complete unconditional patient acceptance are effective. I chose four specific Rational Emotive Behavior Therapy styles of challenging maladaptive schemas and irrational beliefs in an acronym easily remembered, PEPE, for Philosophic, Empirical/Functional, Paradoxical and Existential challenges to maladaptive beliefs about trauma and loss. PEPE is tailored collaboratively for use with each patient. PEPE complements the heuristic-driven empirical approach with each individual officer-patient and the type of trauma and loss he or she experienced (Ellis, 1962, 1985; Frankl, 1978, 2000; Rudofossi, 1999, 2007).

The other therapy approach having a significant place in the eco-ethological approach is psychodynamic therapy. Among many useful techniques is understanding transference development in the context of trauma. Therapists from different traditional approaches understand this. In my specific approach, transference offers an economic assessment of how therapy is moving along in balancing the patient's relationship with the therapist. The psychologist cannot just leave it to chance that the officer who might have a scheduled appointment in 2 weeks will be okay. This is true of police populations, as they have many unresolved and active losses and acute trauma that the skillful assessor can elicit and cannot ignore in its ambulatory form. Dr. Benner highlighted the fact that ambulatory intervention is not a choice; it is the necessary strategy of action for all cop docs and those we educate as both officers and psychologists. Dr. Benner coined these traumatized officers the *walking wounded* who are in a state of functional motor responsiveness and on automatic run (Benner, 1999, 2004). A dissociated mind-set may underlie despair and loneliness in which a desperate pining away tears at the officer-patient's existence. One's own existential and dynamic intuition are wonderful and insightful keys to picking up on despair that is not easily expressed by the officer-patient. Awareness of countertransference is invaluable when used in this context and in a modified approach with officer-patients. Your genuine regard and respect will assist in the listening process beyond any technique.

Exploration of existential meaning and psychodynamic insight has its place in supplanting cynicism, pessimism, and burnout replete in the public service sector with healthier optimism, self- and other-appreciation, and a less gullible or invincible attitude in the officer-patient. In the eco-ethological approach, the trauma and grief therapies we reviewed as well as the aforementioned therapies are part of our armamentarium.

Consider even within the armamentarium of our eco-ethological approach to trauma: the impact of the traumatic event itself holds little valuable information without your insight into each officer-patient's perceptual, ethological, ecological, and psychic processing of that traumatic event and where that event stands in relationship to other traumatic events. Why? Because the selective perception of which event is most disturbing and why certain aspects of the traumatic event stand out and others recede are questions that remain elusive without understanding personal motivation in terms of that officer-patient's personality style. Motivation in terms of ethology includes understanding the conferring of *survival value,* that is, asking what selective advantage is offered by the persistence of certain defenses and constellations of behaviors in response to the distress of experiencing trauma. The ecological motivation looks into what specialization of the officer's repertoires is influenced by and in turn impacted by the traumatic event. Keep in mind that the ecological niche includes the ambient environment of development (Rudofossi, 1997, 2007, 2009). That ambient environment includes the unique niche that is relative to the development, vulnerability, defenses, and maturity of the individual officer. These elements generate adaptive and maladaptive responses to trauma. They are distinct from the cultural mores and taboos of the larger and more general culture and social structure.

The mechanisms of expressing drive derivatives, endogenous tendencies, and styles, while perhaps in part determined as constructs of maladaptation, are secondary to the hope we share in our therapeutic attitude for confidence that insight, choice, and responsibility can be highly developed in the officer-patient. The work of ciphering through this complexity holds the possibility of a venture in which your stance is existentially analytic, Socratic, compassionate, and cognitively aware. Motivation can change direction. You can affect the placement of the fulcrum. Hence, our eco-ethological approach offers you the benefit regardless of the initial psychological mindedness and mental health or lack thereof in the individual officer-patient. Our benefit is not without cost in terms of our own responsibility of service to the officer-patient. Frankl's existential analysis and logotherapy is the fulcrum toward effective and the core of the central intervention with Public Safety and Military CPTSD.

PRELUDE TO THE ECO-ETHOLOGICAL EXISTENTIAL ANALYSIS OF PPS-CPTSD

> The lesson I had to learn in three years spent in Auschwitz was the awareness that life has a meaning to be fulfilled … uncounted examples of heroism bear witness to the uniquely human potential to find and fulfill meaning even in extremis … we must never forget that we may also find meaning in life when confronted with a hopeless situation when facing fate that cannot be changed. For what then counts and matters is to bear witness to the unique human potential at its best which is to transform a tragedy into a personal triumph. (Frankl, 1978, p. 37)

Taking heed of Frankl's exquisite humanity is digging our heels into the depth of loss through current moments of therapy as existential opportunities to redress distortions, lessen the effective compromise formations, and correct self-destructive cognitive, emotional, and behavioral patterns. Emerging existential opportunities unfurl in the context of our focus on listening to moments that are deeply influenced by the eco-ethological niches that support the psychological context of each officer's daily life. How you go about enhancing meaning within the nondescript poverty of death, violence, deception, betrayal, and cruelty aimed at the officer-patient's experience? The drill to break the frozen tundra of traumatic loss is provoking expression of that very loss in the officer-patient by reflecting that you are actively listening and heuristically discovering the quantum psychic moment of traumas' impact. Finding motivation within the existential meaning of each officer's pain and suffering is not a byproduct of therapy—it is an explicit and potent core of the therapist's intervention. In part, achieving motivation means understanding why the officer-patient's guilt, rage, depression, and anxiety not only are overwhelming but also is a self-imposed prison of denying the trauma and the mortality we all face.

Gaining a different perspective of the same situation in which he or she has persecuted him- or herself, the same officer-patient may redeem his or her own strength, resilience, and courage through insight. Losses accumulated over time and left disenfranchised and ungrieved are toxic to healthful living: losses are poison in trauma. Left untouched, they remain preserved in timeless tumors in the walls of the officer-patient's life. Gaining insight for the officer-patient is facilitated via healing of toxic loss and human freedom to choose another path that ought not to be passed over. In my clinical judgment, putting a time frame on the process of grieving is like putting a time frame on any fluid process: it is illusory at best, and a shared delusion at worst.

By returning to the pain, suffering, and human anguish of trauma, there is much unacknowledged in the police culture, specific unit, and community that highlights what was done right with courage, responsibility, compassion, and humanity by the officer in the face of very harsh losses. That task of discovering the courage, humanity, compassion, and resilience for motivation and creativity is in the real and personal level of encounter and responsibility in both participants in the eco-ethological existential analysis. The task of therapist and officer-patient becomes visible through identifying and validating the courage, resilience, and ultimate humanity of each officer's experience with his or her own trauma. What may be most helpful in an age of terrorism is an existential attitude to grab logos that humanizes the officer-patient, the therapist, and the therapy process. It is so basic to all therapy that it may go unacknowledged as one of the most important and neglected of all tasks to achieve.

That most difficult of tasks for the therapist is helping the officer-patient confront very human disappointments, suffering, and anguish at intimate moments experienced in blinking terror, shame, and anguish. Facilitating the mourning of these losses can be fully achieved only by understanding the individual manifestation of such losses. Some are as follows: personal redemption of the officer-patient's will to live without slow self-suicide-addiction, depression, and nihilism of sorts is replaced with a desire to live a healthier lifestyle. Social contributions and the impact officer-patients have had on other lives is redeemed from the ugly trauma they have endured in silence.

Clinicians who worked with the combat veterans of both world wars shed light into the darkness with clearly calling horror what it was—horror! The treatment approach was to identify what was called the *culminating event* (Rado, 1939, 1956) in the soldier-patient's experience that is similar although expanded in what I have called an *original traumatic event* (Rudofossi, 1997, 2007) in the officer-patient's experience of trauma (Freud et al., 1921; Myers, 1940; Rado, 1939, 1956; Rudofossi, 2007; Solomon & Yakovlev, 1945). What is timeless is Rado's advice to the clinician on how to deal with combat trauma's immediate systemic effect on terrorizing and agitating the soldier-patient, which stands as informative and relevant today as it was to his contemporaries:

> The decisive factor to be introduced into the therapeutic procedure is de-sensitization of the patient to all memories of the war, whether repressed or not. In other words: his war memories must be stripped of their power to perturb him again and again and be turned into a source of repeated pride and satisfaction. (Rado, 1956, p. 162)

I suggest facilitating what I have called an internalized witnessing with each police officer by building an introspective view of his or her own hidden resilience. That hidden resilience exposed provokes redemption of courage and meaning from past trauma facilitating a self-initiated rediscovery of renewed commitment. This renewed courage enhances an ability to tolerate tragedy and maintain one's own sacred optimism, not in spite of terrorism but in the face of terrorism. My hope is that the inherent challenge in this process may be a motivation for you as it is for me when each session brings an evolving renewal of moments of opportunity for encounter as an exquisite hidden pleasure of therapy; it is unique in potential for each therapist as it is with each officer-patient. We accept a special responsibility when we choose to tend to the needs of public safety and police officers.

In light of the prolific nature of PPS-CPTSD, I suggest our special responsibility is to reconsider the level of disturbance evidenced when we first observe public safety officers in a clinical setting. Kelly suggests the impact of trauma evidenced through military veterans is infused with loss, guilt, and traumatic neurosis (Kelly, 1985). Sudden and unpredictable trauma is a dimension of experience that puts the officer-patient into a position similar to that of the military combat veteran. I suggest the officer-patient must make *quantum judgments* in response to *quantum moments* of unfolding traumatic events as his or her counterpart in military service (Rudofossi, 2007). The judgments the officer makes carry consequences that radically alter the landscape laid out through prior affordances: expectations, anticipations of how things will unfold, predictability, security, and survival value. The boundaries of each dimension of trauma are not cut with a razor's exactitude. In fact, the first is the most likely to be unheard, disenfranchised loss, that is, until you listen well and clarify with poignant empathy.

TRAUMATIC LOSS AT THE HUB OF PPS-COMPLEX PTSD

Digging our heels into the ground of loss in trauma includes dealing with sensitive and particularly difficult problems the officer-patient presents to the therapist. Achieving a successful intervention leads to a more effective navigational chart for the therapist treating PPS-CPTSD in officer-patients. Tapping out a heuristic cadence orchestrates the impact of loss each trauma makes, regardless of therapy.

Presented in the current moments of therapy are existential opportunities to redress distortions, lesser then effective compromise formations, and to correct self-destructive cognitive, emotional, and behavioral patterns. Emerging existential opportunities unfurl in the context of all therapy hours. However hearing them and acting in the moment on these opportunities requires a therapist who has gained the skill to listen to what is said on a number of levels. What I offer here is a focus on listening to the moments that are deeply influenced by the eco-ethological niches that support the psychological context of each officer's daily life. Enhancing meaning as it emerges in shattered lives within the nondescript poverty of death, violence, and cruelty of the officer-patient's experience is the core of my suggested approach to PPS-CPTSD. Finding motivation within the existential meaning of each officer's pain and suffering is not a byproduct of therapy—it is an explicit and potent core of the therapist's intervention. My supervisor in the NYPD, Chief Surgeon Dr. Martin Symonds (1997), left a strong prescription for me. He said, "If you can figure out how to motivate an officer-patient to keep up his or her resilience in the face of trauma then you have the key to healing" (M. Symonds, personal communication, 1997). While I suspect that key may have rough edges and be fragile, in part I suggest his wish and dream is closer to fulfillment: Frankl was a master teacher who suggested how important redemption is for human beings; the motivation of redemption is sweetest in the bitter desert of losses unrequited. He quotes Einstein, who summed it up well: "The man who regards his life as meaningless is not merely unhappy but hardly fit for life" (1954). Professor Dr. Frankl elaborates on Einstein's point:

> This is not only a matter of success and happiness but also of survival in the terminology of modern psychology. The will to meaning has survival value. This was the lesson I had to learn in three years spent in Auschwitz and Dachau…it is true that if there was anything to uphold man in such an extreme situation as Auschwitz it was the awareness that life has a meaning to be fulfilled…uncounted examples of such heroism and martyrdom bear witness to the uniquely human potential to find and fulfill meaning even in extremis…we must never forget that we may also find meaning in life when confronted with a hopeless situation as its helpless victim when facing fate that cannot be changed. For what then counts and matters is to bear witness to the unique human potential at its best which is to transform a tragedy into a personal triumph, to turn one's predicament into a human achievement. (Frankl, 1978, p. 37)

Nothing is static and complete in any psychological manifestation whether it be trauma, loss, mental health, psychological growth, or resilience. I suggest rather than this being a dreaded problem for the therapist and for the officer-patient, this is an opportunity where the process of genuine growth in therapy is forged. Extending Frankl's suggestions into a core approach to dealing with loss in trauma, I use the term *redemption*, as in correction of misconceptions—conscious and unconscious—in the officer-patient's maladaptation to the events in the past. The event of the past, whether the recent past or the distant echoes of the past, is what needs to be worked through to get to the opportunity awaiting the officer-patient in the here and now of human time stuck in the fractured human space of trauma. Hence, listening and achieving insight into the context of loss in trauma the officer-patient presents is key to intervention. That loss in trauma always is an issue of individual responses and different manifestations on an unconscious and conscious level. Encounter is the ongoing process that is ever changing in the dialogue of loss and redemption. Encounter is fostered in the major core of the eco-ethological approach to trauma and loss by using your insightful understanding for provoking existential insight and change.

Establishing your encounter with the officer-patient means that you understand his or her impulses; satisfaction of those impulses as wishes may be at the level of an unconscious wish influenced by tendencies of an aggressive and at times sexual nature (drive derivatives). Yet, conflicts emerge over the fulfillment of that officer-patient's wishes, and the defenses against fulfillment of those wishes. The result of these wishes and the defenses is what Brenner has originally supported and established as compromise formations (Brenner, 1974, 1976, 1982). Compromise formations are fluid and dynamic and open to change. They are ubiquitous. What Brenner suggests is original and relevant to my approach where the therapist is seeking to effect change with an officer patient who is traumatized. This is evidenced when the officer-patient presents his or her own unique compromise formations that are ever changing in the face of conflict. Brenner's science of conflict suggests the therapist's attitude and stance toward conflict is critical in effecting change in the patient. Brenner' suggests an effective therapist's attitude includes consistency in terms of his or her stance by empathically listening, clarifying, elaborating and confronting the officer-patients conflicts of which his or her defenses are an important component. Looking at the defense against losses in trauma in the same light underscored in the eco-ethological perspective where the therapist identifies, clarifies, elaborates and interprets losses through many iterations existentially is a center that militates a variation in focus as to the meaning lost and the opportunity to be regained. The impact of Brenner's science of conflict (Brenner, 1974, 1976, 1982, 2003) complements my suggested approach to therapists intervening with officer patients suffering from PPS-CPTSD (Rudofossi, 2007, 2009).

The immediate benefit is the therapist's illusions for a quick cure for the officer-patient is less likely: the consequence of this is that the patient is gradually familiarized with the toxic and cumulative layers of loss in trauma—premature termination is countered by a more effective integration which now becomes possible. The alliance as enduring and evolving complements the approach suggested in a consistent and reliable means through the therapist's stance toward PPS-CPTSD.

For our purpose, in terms of ethology and ecology, compromise formations make superb and parsimonious sense in approaching loss in trauma. A point that may be missed as long as rigidity in any therapist's approach does not blind him or her is that the insight gained may be used from approaches that differ from a psychoanalytic perspective with benefit for the officer-patient. This point becomes evident as we realize compromise formations are not only fluid in the patient's development but may be changed in response to and effected by insight and associational growth through the process of therapy (Brenner, 1974, 1976, 1982, 2003; Scharf, 2004).

To effect such a stance, the therapist would be well informed to learn about each officer-patient's unique and evolving constellation of compromise formations within his or her ecological niche. Therapist's understanding includes specifically learning 'what' meaning a traumatic event has in that officer's life. That understanding is still insufficient until the therapist learns *how* the officer-patient unconsciously and consciously uses his or her own ethological strategies for preserving motivation in defending against cumulative losses he or she experiences. The therapist's understanding of the specific strategy and motivation underlying each officer-patient's defenses, includes the specific understanding of *what* challenges, impulses, and defenses will emerge in each officer-patient's uniquely individual response to intrapsychic conflict. Ethological influence and drive derivatives in my approach are given substance and undeniably assist in working through the uncomfortable gruesome experiences without a likelihood of acting out.

The compromise formations of conflict that the officer-patient presents initially hold promise in durable change effected over time and with a consistent approach; they also infuse preventive insight. In other words, by the therapist's intervention, the individual officer-patient may achieve compromise formations that are healthier as a result of achieved insight. When insight is reached it is almost never complete—yet the severity of symptomatic presentation is likely to be reduced. Helping the officer-patient reach a level of insight takes time, effort, and an attitude that demands repeated attention to what is ethological, ecological, and largely unconscious and conscious, real and fantasized in each officer-patient's individual response to trauma. That insight in the eco-ethological approach includes the third core for building a psychological context—identity modes and multiple losses in the officer patient's handling of past cumulative and daily trauma (see Rudofossi, 2007). Rather than engaging in a passive, descriptive accounting of trauma and loss, the eco-ethological therapist actively seeks to understand the unconscious and conscious impact of loss in all trauma as a means to build a strategy one officer-patient at a time. The direction of evolution is hardly conscious in any of the world's species including human beings. Yet the unconscious pursuit of sexualized aggressive satisfaction, however hidden, can hardly be denied. Psychoanalytic insight in a classical sense may shed light on this process regardless of treatment modality. Classical analysis does not deny sexualized aggression which is active in all trauma syndromes.

However, as Frankl put it, "Destiny is not fate" (2000, p. 70). Drive derivatives may be the rake of destiny until the field is exposed and tilled a different way. The harvest from exposed loss in trauma takes time to ripen from the initial sprout of its promise in change and development along new furrows for each officer patient in his or her unique compromise formations and existentially meaningful path. This harvest cannot be achieved with a cookie cutter approach according to this author and others who include private and police practitioners (Barnes, 2005; Benner, 1999, 2004; Brenner, 1974, 1976, 1982, 2003; Mansfield, 2004; Myers, 1940; Reese, 1991, 1996; Rudofossi & Ellis, 1999; Scharf, 2004; Thorp, 2005). Gain may be achieved by taking the humble goal of improvement, rather than attempting to extinguish trauma and loss by instituting treatment plans forced upon all officer-patients. What is economical is based on sound theory—economical in terms of psychological, mental, and existentially sound cost-effective efforts. Simplicity is slicing away with an Ockham's razor the idealism in mass-producing a linear all-encompassing treatment plan. Improvement is a substantive gain. Improvement demands an approach that deals with realistic differences, one case at a time. When disenfranchised losses are made tangible and concrete, the grief may be then expressed.

I suggest that the witnessing of one's own trauma may eventually be shifted from an external source (namely, the therapist) to an internalized witnessing in each officer-patient's own conscience. This internalization is not a simple externalized witnessing by others via the therapist as yet another cliché and proscribed strategy. In a sense, I suggest we can anticipate with confidence that internalized witnessing occurs as the officer-patient achieves a worthwhile and meaningful change in other people's lives through his or her own police actions.

How important internalized witnessing may be, in a case by case approach with police and public safety patients, is suggested by the accumulated wisdom and the historical context of clinicians dealing with war trauma. The therapist's goal in combat trauma therapy was to help each soldier-patient reenfranchise what was horrific and traumatic by not watering down or insulting his or her sensibilities by grouping together his or her unique experiences.

No hell is as vivid as war with its dehumanization, death, and losses that heap upon a never-ending pyre—no matter how legitimate, the combatants never remain unscathed—except for war fought in one's own backyard, which is the additional shock, disgust, guilt, anxiety, and depressive affect that police officer-patients deal with. Clarifying that truth is therapeutic.

While many differences can be garnered to challenge the combat experiences of the soldier-patient during both world wars and police special agents, enough similarities exist in the disruption of intrapsychic development for the officer-patient that is relevant to the attitude gained within the eco-ethological approach to PPS-CPTSD throughout this chapter. What is timeless is military and cop docs unapologetically confirming the *terror* in the terrorists' attempt toward terrorizing and agitating the soldier-patient, which stands as relevant today as it was to our contemporaries half a century ago.

Frankly speaking, terrorism is a human evil crime that attempts to dehumanize victims, survivors, and the military and public safety officers who combat it. Affirming the officer's stance as courageous is the therapeutic and bottom line in clinical police psychology. Valuing his or her efforts is crucial in treatment of police and military trauma.

This means the officer-patient is guided through clarification and elaboration to take an active and introspective look at his or her trauma and reprocessing through his or her own initiative. That may be achieved in the transference during the therapy situation if handled with support, clarification, elaboration, and confrontation while helping the patient gain insight to his or her successes that remain hidden and disenfranchised in the losses unveiled. Facilitating an internalized witnessing of one's personal achievement as a police and public safety officer may help create a meaningful bridge on which the officer may move toward asking for social support and love of family members and friends. An internalized witnessing of one's resilience and redemption may facilitate a self-initiated renewed commitment to public service. That renewed commitment can enhance an ability to tolerate tragedy and maintain one's own sacred optimism triggering other areas of growth and healing.

Expanding your unconscious and emotional wisdom as a therapist seeking to do work or to enhance your work with police and public safety officer-patients cannot be offered in cookbook fashion. What I hope to relate are ways to facilitate initial interventions likely to work with officer-patients. I present a real composite case example of trauma and loss to guide your odyssey. The inherent challenge in this process may be a motivation for you, as it was for me—each session an evolving renewal of moments of opportunity for encounter. That sensibility is bidirectional and an exquisite hidden pleasure of therapy; it is unique in potential for each therapist.

CASE OF SGT. Z: PPS-CPTSD: EXPERIMENTAL TRAUMATIC NEUROSIS—EXCITED TYPE

BIOGRAPHY

Sgt. Z is a German American First Rescue Responder. His background includes being a veteran of the Iraqi war with two tours under his Sam Brown belt. His significant other is an emergency room physician. Although an intimation of *folie a deux* related to a craving for excitement and hyper-stimulation may exist, intimacy and love in this couple have sustained the relationship. Another dynamic here is that both are highly committed, no-nonsense professionals who share a goal of work as the *sine qua non* of meaning in their life. Both have a hyperfocus toward achieving those goals. Predictably, each also helps the other when there is a crisis.

Sgt. Z expressed one problem he had in his mid-40s. He believed that "life is too unpredictable after so much crap on the street, I cannot commit to marriage." This fear of commitment is related to intense worry about loss. That fear of loss through violence and death has kept him from expressing the love he feels. In place of this love, he will allow expression of overprotectiveness for those he considers significant in his life: his significant other, family, friends, and the officers in his elite unit of hypervigilance (Gilmartin, 2002). Hypervigilance is a cognitive schema of constant guardedness against non-police-oriented culture and perceived *outsiders.*

Sgt. Z's major complaint was sleep disturbance. He wrote down his dreams in a log as per our behavioral plan. He reported feeling "bored, unappreciated and upset about a lot of things on the job. Recently it's caught up with me."

Paradoxically, Sgt. Z focuses on doing a great job, "I will be one of the best bosses in the Department. I loved being a cop. I will be a great boss as a sergeant, too." Over 7 years Sgt. Z responded to an estimated 300 emergency situations involving officers and civilians in dire straits. This is likely an underestimation. He presented me with multiple letters indicating risk-taking and bravery. But he was not foolhardy, and did not run in without caution.

He is a highly trained and skillful police supervisor. Sgt. Z expressed "loving the mean streets and the excitement from rescue calls." Yet, Sgt. Z has expressed exasperation with these same jobs. He "demands perfection or nothing," and is hyperfocused in his approach to public service. He presented with many achievements and commendations and training certifications requiring a great deal of savvy and increasing sophistication. He is very involved with officers who work for him on- and off-duty. While I was taking his trauma history, he described one of the worst events in his career.

SGT. Z's ACCOUNT OF HIS MOST TRAUMATIC EVENT

About seven years ago, I responded to an emotionally disturbed person (EDP) job in the confines of Pct X. Upon arrival, we were informed by the sectors on the scene that there was an EDP in the house, possibly with a gun. The male involved was at the window shouting at the police. I made contact with him by telling him my name was Sgt. Z and I that was here to help him. I do not remember exactly how he responded. But I do remember it was with viciousness. For about 130 minutes, I tried to talk with this male and establish some kind of rapport and mutual trust. No matter what I said, he would not respond directly to me. He responded only with hate toward the police, including me.

Because the radio run said he was armed, I came in armed with an automatic weapon. This made him even more mad. I tried to explain why I was armed; he didn't want to hear it. No matter how I tried, and I really tried to give him a pitch, it failed.

He would not have a dialogue with me. During my attempts to talk with him, he would leave the window, come back a short time later, and then back and forth. After waiting a while, we tried to talk again, but he would get that look of hate, then pain in his face, then hate again. The last time he came back with a gun in his hand. Before I could say anything, I saw his face and eyes filled with extreme hate. He looked straight at me and said, "Let my blood be on your hands." He then put the gun into his mouth, and blew his brains out.

I remembered a short time later him lying on the floor with brain matter all over. I wondered why he did this. I did not understand. I still don't understand. I remember we were all getting our gear together. We were then called to another EDP job. I didn't have any time to talk about this. I do remember going home and wondering all night "Why did he do this?" I had a lot of dreams. Why couldn't I reach him? I didn't ever discuss this, until now with you. This was one of the worst things that happened to me in my life. I just feel this can never go away.

HEURISTIC RECONSTRUCTION OF PPS-CPTSD WITH SGT. Z

Sgt. Z's dominant sensory mode and memory appear to be primarily eidetic, in both visual and auditory modalities. It is likely that Sgt. Z has a more than average awareness of emotional expression in others (i.e., hate, viciousness, and fear). The keen perceptual skill is likely endogenous and, in strong measure, exogenous. My use of the term *exogenous* is nested in the ecological with ethological shaping of behavioral and cognitive patterns. In Sgt. Z's case, his behavioral and cognitive appraisals are influenced by evolutionary demands. After all, Sgt. Z's survival value depends on being correctly attuned to severely disturbed and violent offenders.

Sgt. Z's experience with situational demands remain indeterminate, volatile, and uncertain. Sgt. Z's identity modes are not sharply delineated for any long period of containment. Sgt. Z's event ends with the death of the emotionally disturbed person. Sgt. Z's experience of complex trauma are substantive and core dimensions of what I have discovered and call *police experimental traumatic neurosis.*

The substantive dimensions include a minimum of intense situational demands that rapidly change, are simultaneously experienced, or are so vague as to be indeterminate to the participant. To these extreme ecological demands, the infusion of ethological motivation of survival is framed in rapidly changing identity mode conflicts the sergeant is forced to make as commander. Let us review why this is so.

In Sgt. Z's own words, the existential conflict is intolerable and is evidenced by the symptoms replete for development of a trauma syndrome. Sgt. Z is forced to become active and hold himself back simultaneously. He is unsure of what will come next for 130 minutes. Yes, 130 minutes! The stimulation is as intense as it gets. A psychotic man is threatening to kill himself and possibly Sgt. Z and anyone who gets in his way. This person is attempting to place the full responsibility for his destined outcome on Sgt. Z through unrelenting and extremely unstable behavior.

The situation is not simple. The possibilities make it a complex situation that demands the utmost of emotional intelligence and strategic cognitive intelligence. The strain on Sgt. Z's ability to inhibit his own ethological arousal toward self-defense, and the increasing provocation toward confrontation, is exhausting. Sgt. Z's emotional and visceral memory is absorbing these toxic elements into his neurological encoding tracks, both limbic and frontal executive structure and function. This memory may become part of his *ethological memory* triggered whenever cues and stimuli are evoked during similar trauma he is likely to experience in the future. It is imperative his trauma is understood as he experiences it, and which he may not be able to be aware of until you use the eco-ethological existential analysis collaboratively.

What is evoked with certainty is a simultaneous collision between two opposing forces—inhibition and excitation. Here is a reconstruction of that collision into four parts:

1. The inhibition of the use of ultimate physical force is effected in the context of the pursuit/attack and confrontation identity mode evoked by the armed, barricaded EDP.
2. The EDP is exhibiting a *cry for help* through his erratic actions of hate and extreme aggressive gestures and behaviors. The words spoken by the barricaded EDP betray a possibility that communication may be bridged. Sgt. Z is attuned to his own voice of conscience to effect his custodial and his rescue identity mode.
3. That psychophysiological conflict is complicated by yet another conflict in the existential realm. That conflict revolves around whether or not action that affects the pursuit and confrontation which might result in potentially lethal identity modes, force, or, alternatively, great personal risk to Sgt. Z and his troops by inhibiting pursuit in an attempt to persuade the EDP to drop his firearms through hostage negotiation techniques. Taser or not is the question that may make all the difference in the world for Sgt. Z and his troops to be or not to be.
4. The existential dimension of Sgt. Z's compassion and mercy toward this disturbed person is intense. His investment in success as rescuer and investment in his idealistic goal are enhanced by the highest standards he has learned as a member and commander of his elite unit. While the result of his intention could very well end in his own loss of life, he is not naïve or ignorant of this choice. He chooses to place himself in the front line and to resolve this event.

What remains unclear is how much neurological, ethological, emotional, cognitive, and behavioral aftershocks will reverberate in the trauma syndrome that follows Sgt. Z's traumatic experience. What we are certain of at this point are Sgt. Z's supervisory responsibility and indeterminate identity modes relating to the extremely inchoate field demands of a barricaded and volatile psychotic person who is armed, suicidal, and homicidal.

To begin to appreciate Sgt. Z's experience, an individual perspective enhances our understanding. Our approach to Sgt. Z targets maximizing specificity in treatment plans, facilitating his healing process, and redeeming the positive outcomes equally disenfranchised from his own interpretation of trauma.

First, he seeks out excitement and the challenge of his detail. However, unlike the officer who has a hyperexcited style and may be addicted to trauma, he appears to get little pleasure in being the first in the line of fire. Rather, we will now touch on his style of being hyperfocused on achieving ideals of perfection in his work. Specifically in this trauma, Sgt. Z's hyperfocus includes success as he sees it unroll through his anticipatory schemas of trajectories—involving the identity-modes of pursuit, confrontation, arrest, custody, and rescue identity modes.

Elaborating on what we do know: Sgt. Z still is a sergeant and evaluates his sense of self and identity with his successes on the job. Being a boss on the job is not being a little Caesar—it is safeguarding your troop's welfare with your life. In the hyperfocused Sgt. Z, it is exponentially magnified.

We need to remember this original trauma was experienced 7 years ago. Remember that Sgt. Z called this event "one of the worst things to happen to me, and what I did not discuss, until now." The hyperfocus afforded by his elite unit's survival value compliments his perfectionism. His eco-ethological niche afforded the specific evocation of his development of PPS-CPTSD. While the psychotic man did not succeed in getting Sgt. Z to shoot him, he did not even get a chance to Taser him. The EDP unconsciously used a form of projective identification to hook Sgt. Z into absorbing the hate, torment, and anguish from the initiation of the first event until his suicide. The suicide triggered the emotions of guilt, uncertainty, and doubt. The personality style of Sgt. Z suggests his vulnerability to absorb these toxic projections anteing up the pain in his heart and soul as a sergeant for believing he failed the ill man and his troops.

Thus, the various identity modes anticipated in the ecology of conditional situational demands could have unfolded at any time in many different ways. Sgt. Z was keenly aware and hyperfocused for 130 minutes. The investment he chose was preventing death to himself, other sacred victims, and the person barricading himself. We know Sgt. Z had no chance to debrief, moving on to the next job. A critical factor of the shock and loss after intense investment is that his experience was disenfranchised. Seven years later, his impressions have gone through many permutations through a series of subsequent traumas. Strong evidence suggests an Experimental Police Traumatic Neurosis—Excited Type for Sgt. Z.

His extraordinary courage was not acknowledged in the least. The reality was his bravery was considered a failure by performance standards. He did not prevent the suicide. While no one berated him, no one acknowledged the magnitude of this trauma either, thereby adding another to the many losses for Sgt. Z.

Finally, in our initial heuristic construction, the stimulation that comes with highly exciting and dangerous events for ego enhancement or for thrills is not congruent with Sgt. Z's style. That raises a question about why motivation and desire to continue in his special line of work continues. It is here that ethological motivation can explain this desire to reenact the original trauma successfully. This type of trauma may offer an ecological reexperiencing of the psychophysical threshold of the original experimental traumatic neurosis. It makes exceptional sense that the repetition compulsion to search for this type of situation is, in part, a result of conditioning and reinforcement; in part, the dynamics of heightened arousal in a sexualized aggression outlet; and, finally, the need to master a trauma that Superman could not solve with a better outcome. In his own existential angst, this is irrelevant until it is unraveled in our work together and it is intense and takes passion, reason, and compassion from both parties to achieve.

As a sergeant, his existential angst motivates schemas for anger, hopelessness, guilt, and self-recriminations in what he appraises as an unsuccessful conclusion—suicide. Every time he is successful in a barricaded situation, proof is garnered by gathering what he considers self-deficiencies.

Behaviorally, this self-reinforcement becomes psychologically toxic. The invariable success and failure stimulate variable self-conditioning schedules in the ecology of his world of trauma, which paradoxically reinforce the persistence of his search for an ever elusive solution of freedom from self-censure and unwarranted guilt.

The personal toll emotionally, cognitively, behaviorally, and existentially is excessive. This type of trauma is what officers deal with repetitively as chronic, overwhelming, and extreme strain. It is overly complex and intense emotional shock that is inescapable. Pavlov relied on his theory using animals and predicted that "the excitatory type loses almost completely, (his/her) ability for inhibition, and seeks unusual arousal to repeat the excessive stimulation" (Pavlov, 1941, p. 112). Our work suggests clinically in the eco-ethological approach that we are ethologically as humans even more apt to suffer this traumatic neurosis; however, we can reverse and redeem the trauma with tragic optimism through our persistent interventions.

Eco-Ethological—Existential Analytic Intervention With Sgt. Z

Let's review the anticipatory and trajectory schema in Sgt. Z's executive strategy. His goal is establishing a relationship and reaching this psychotic fellow emotionally. His attitude is to stave off a confrontation. Sgt. Z established a high level of expectation, and anticipation of disarming, taking custody, and rescuing. At the same time, his role as a supervisor demands personal safety that weighs heavily on his tactical approach. His ethological motivation is to defend himself and others with the full weight of personal survival.

Existentially, an intense desire for rescue and connecting through his exquisite empathy is countered by the situational demands of confrontation with an armed and seriously disturbed man. This is a severe conflict including unconscious and conscious conflicts (too elaborate to present, here). Tactically, Sgt. Z has assessed three possible and radically different outcomes as follows:

1. Arrest and custodial identity-mode with all the tactics in anticipation of a nonarmed struggle ensuing, including Tasering the psychotic fellow
2. Custodial and rescue identity-mode if the person surrenders to assistance (this man's injuries are undetermined)
3. The ultimate confrontation identity-mode if the EDP moves into an assault mode, entailing a full-blown firearm life/death struggle

These outcomes are dependent on the situational demands that unfold in relation to the EDP behavior, the ecology, and Sgt. Z's response. Each outcome demands radically different approaches in terms of safety, action, or inhibition of action. To iterate, the investment and response to any outcome involves risk to life for all involved. Sgt. Z has not dehumanized the EDP, and chooses, as far as he can, to desperate attempt at extreme risk, to establish an encounter. He has the following identity modes actively and simultaneously stimulated.

Sgt. Z has activated the identity mode of strategic pursuit: following every move, tactic, point by point intention that the aggressor makes (there is an attunement and identification with the aggressor). This carries unconscious and conscious awareness of hate, rage, despair, excessive anxiety, sadism, masochism, and chaotic impressions as well as existential synchronized attunement.

Sgt. Z has activated the identity mode of arrest and custody: following every opportunity to capture this highly volatile emotionally disturbed person without effecting harm and using the necessary force to accomplish this goal, including using the Taser gun. What this entails is uncertain throughout.

Sgt. Z has activated the identity mode of confrontation the moment he tried to encounter the emotionally disturbed man with a possible deadly weapon. He has anticipated whether or how he will use deadly physical force if necessary to stop him. He has also no doubt anticipated his own death if he is shot point blank. Sgt. Z reported he went over multiple times the alternative tactics to stop this person. This has been ethologically motivated and practiced many times. It is likely that vicarious trauma and anticipatory schemas complicate the experience. Sgt. Z is constantly monitoring the ecological opportunity to end the barricaded situation with the least harm to all participants. He no doubt has fully activated his unconscious existential voice and his conflicting ethological demand for his troops and his own survival.

Sgt. Z has activated his rescue identity mode as the most desirable. It is the most difficult in the face of all the other contradictory and oppositional roles. He anticipates gaining an inroad to lessen the strain and stress of the emotionally distraught and psychotic person. This person thwarts each attempt with extreme rejection. Sgt. Z is painfully aware of the desire of the psychotic man to either commit suicide, or attempt to kill Sgt. Z.

Factually, these identity modes are all activated, and the potential outcomes are all lived through as trajectories with different intensities. Our specific understanding is clarified through the following facts as we reconstruct the trauma with Sgt. Z.

Sgt. Z led the work of his unit with this EDP barricaded person who threatened suicide in an escalating ultimate confrontation through potential suicide and/or homicide.

Hateful emotions and vicious expressions were picked up as invariants that Sgt. Z learned to pick up accurately as affordances in his ecological niche as an emergency first responder.

There is communication for 130 minutes. High-ranking officers are controlling the outer scene, yet another factor of escalation and performance anxiety. Perimeters of safety are set, and established preparation is forged for contingencies where he is at the heart of the negotiations. If you have flown on a plane that has turbulence, magnify that by 100 times and think of being on board for 130 minutes.

The ambient internal perimeter is highly charged. At extreme levels of sustained attention for Sgt. Z, the emotional intensity and mental exhaustion are neurologically overwhelming. Sgt. Z's communication with his unit, his bosses (superior officers), the sounds and cues of his ambient environment, and general communications, are all in addition to his communication with the EDP. Keep in mind, action and outcome is indeterminate. Indeterminate stress has been conclusively associated with high levels of cortisol, strain, and stress. The extreme affordances for all-out combat is established tactically. Sgt. Z adapts by what I have already proposed as adaptive-functional dissociation, and adaptive-depersonalization due to the sustained attention the situation affords. The splits sustained by Sgt. Z may support crystallized splits of consciousness. He is running the equivalent of an emotional marathon.

The EDP's pattern of leaving the window and coming back and forth heightens intermittent stimulation and inhibition, episodic moments of uncertainty with peaks of aggressive readiness, and anxious inhibition. Escalating rage by the EDP is in striking opposition to Officer B's strategic counterinvestment in establishing nonviolent rescue. Keep in mind that this suggests his adaptation level is one of confidence in the success of his approach. Sgt. Z is left with imprinting of traumatic shock and loss when the involved victim commits suicide, setting the fertile ground for delayed PPS Experimental Traumatic Neurosis—Excitatory Type, and Disenfranchised Complicated Grief within Complex PTSD.

With the clear understanding of how significant this trauma is, our approach to the PPS-CPTSD is not to force change for Sgt. Z. That choice is ultimately Sgt. Z's. Our choice is first to understand the toxicity. I structure understanding within the patient's style and the specific event in mind.

Eight Steps to Effectively, Existentially, and Heuristically Intervene With Complex Trauma and Grief: The Case Example of Sgt. Z

1. I support and validate the patient's free association to the trauma in his good time with my tool of active listening.
2. I heuristically clarify all points of trauma and losses embedded in anticipatory schemas, trajectories of those schemas, the roles conflicts and situational demands and investments

as delineated in my heuristic reconstruction. We will go back in Sgt. Z's good time. I will elicit the unspeakable disenfranchised losses visible and heard so he need not harm himself in an overactive identification with the aggressor.

3. I will explicitly validate the impact of the multiple events separately. We clarify how these events can yield a quantum psychic moment with many anti-affordances for a sergeant assigned to an elite unit responsible for rescue work: Sgt. Z's experience and the meaning this layered event(s) holds for him will be allowed support and a voice bolted with validation and compassion for him to counter the extreme trauma he has tragically absorbed. This counts and must never be minimized. This is not advocacy; it is the power that confronts the extreme violent force used against this officer. It is life saving for the officer-patient who may never come again if you fail to let him know his work is vital and he or she is valued unequivocally by you.

4. I clarify how stressful the simultaneous potential and actual unidentified expectations of model performance clash with reality including behaviors, and emotional responses in terms of stimulation and inhibition. This of course is done in language that the sergeant can understand and relate to.

5. Our attempt is to bring Sgt. Z to verbally express his identity modes, behavioral repertoire, and emotional distress. He now begins to express the unacceptable and understand how complex his situation was and how incredible the fact is that he did stood his ground and attempted to achieve the best he could. I never fail to let an officer-patient know "God gave free will and we can only achieve what we can as mere mortals, even if we are on the side of angels and do our darnedest to win the devil!"

6. Sgt. Z's narration of each potential outcome is highlighted with his enhanced understanding of why each of his identity modes emerged. I lay out the frame for further and more in depth clarification and confrontation by beginning to de-stigmatize aggressive, depressive, and guilty self-recriminations in thoughts, behavior, and emotion as affordances shaped by field trauma from the onset.

7. Shifts in his awareness call for cognitive, behavioral, affective, and emotional states where altered consciousness may be allowed expression under the safe haven of the therapeutic encounter. The defined highly chaotic situation as a whole event produces extreme emotional arousal and inhibition and a maladaptive pattern takes shape. This perspective helps bring the motivational change necessary by my facilitating Sgt. Z's emotional drainage of what had been compartmentalized through counterphobic defenses. Those defenses are given substance and understanding as evolutionary mechanisms. This understanding, while fundamental, begins to allow expression, and reenfranchising what has been disenfranchised for so long.

8. Sgt. Z's courage, compassion, and wisdom that have gone unheard are given expression each step of the way in our joint exploration. That positive aspect of his existential sensibility had been disenfranchised up to this point in our work.

While as a reader, many case examples are offered in my published guides to complex PTSD, I would be remiss if I did not end this chapter with a snippet of how to facilitate an alliance as happened between myself and Sgt. Z, whom I was privileged to have worked with in the moment of time that was ripe for intervention.

In the following case example (a snippet of our work), I will skip ahead to Sgt. Z, with whom I have established an initial alliance. I have begun working with Sgt. Z's hyperfocus on how he perceives his failure as a sergeant when the emotionally disturbed person as described in this chapter commits suicide.

Sgt. Z's self-blame is very harsh, and his guilt is overwhelming—he expresses feeling he messed up and how he will have to pay for what in his mind is moral turpitude. At this juncture in which you are invited to view what is an initial clarification of his nightmare which is a gift he presents begrudgingly to me to help open up our working through his experience of complex loss in his traumatic experiences as an important aspect of the eco-ethological existential analysis. Our task is to facilitate a lucid and direct expression of loss in the trauma while valuing the highly courageous, intelligent, humane Sgt. Z.

Sgt. Z: Doc Dan, I am not having any real nightmares, you know what I mean? [Sweaty and wipes brow off forehead.] I mean I am just going through some weird type of stuff at night but I am fine. Really, I am not really seeing anything weird like images of dead people or anything weird like that. I mean it is really nothing anyhow. You know what I mean it is just one of those things I mean stuff like seeing DOA's.

Hey, how are you feeling Doc? [This is a way of diversion I will answer and immediately redirect our attention.]

Dr. Dan: I am fine, thanks Z. I may be wrong but it seems like you are having a hell of a rough time around some very intense dreams at night. Talk to me Z; why do you think you needed to look away and give me a whole pitch as to why you are okay and not seeing anything weird? [Sgt. Z has an eye aversion from my eyes and looking downward and wiping mouth.]

Sgt. Z: [Pausing and looking at me with his head tilted and with a slant of his eyebrow.] Maybe I could have gotten the guy to drop the firearm and connect with him. It was a while ago. I never failed like that. I was worried the job would get my own throat cut, maybe even demote me, I know I let my guys down, they could have been killed but I could have tried harder to get him to look at me. I could have gotten him to drop the piece and let me take him into custody like XX, remember that one I told you about, Doc? [I nod a yes, staying silent, allowing Sgt. Z time to express his thoughts as they emerge.] What is happening is I guess I am paying for kind of like penance for my allowing a guy who couldn't help himself to kill himself on my tour as the boss. It is okay doc as I tell you I am really not upset at all. I mean he told me I have his blood on my hands. [Silence for a few moments.] I am not sleeping so well I need to hit the gym again—been getting a real belly [pointing to his stomach]. Hey anyhow what are you doing for New Year?

Dr. Dan: It is hard real hard to tell me I imagine you are feeling guilty as if you caused this guy Henry's death, his name is Henry right? [Sgt. Z nods and turns away.] You are blaming yourself. [Stopping and looking Sgt. Z in the eyes.] Sgt. Z did you see Henry in your dreams. Is he ghosting you? [Sgt. Z teary eyed, face becomes flush and looking away, I gently and in a very subdued voice turn again to engage Sgt. Z.] Talk to me, I am listening with my big ears…. [Silent and intuitively feeling and sensing extreme discomfort, I respond by heuristically moving with my own intuitive sense as a cop doc.]

Sgt. Z: I am not seeing him exactly you know Doc; I am kind of visualizing him in the moments and feeling very weird. Look it is really nothing and you got other patients this is not that important. Is it really that important?

Dr. Dan: [without missing a beat] I think it is, and I think you really want to let me know what you are going through at night but may be worried I may think you are ready to be put in the Psych Unit. What do you say if I tell you it is not abnormal to see an image or flash back even when you are alone in the room at night. [Although I have iterated this before, I never tire of letting Sgt. Z, as is true of other public safety officers, know it is safe to share their fears and traumas with me.] I am all ears; take a look at my big ones, I am listening Z.

Sgt. Z: [Looking away but moving toward eye contact and moving forward to gain security and connection with another human being, expressing a willingness to trust and be vulnerable.] I had a really freaky dream like he was going to take me with him. I felt I could not wake up from my nightmare and when I did I could not breathe. I awoke screaming in the night. I was awoken finally by my wife asking me if I was okay. It was humiliating. It was that I could not rid myself of his presence.

Doc Dan: [I chose to reflect and chain Sgt. Z's references.] So Henry is present in more than your dreams. Does he sometimes appear in your waking vision or just in your sleep? Do you ever speak with him?

Sgt. Z: I am not crazy doc; I am no shrink like you but I do know I do not speak with him. I kind of see him at least sometimes at night right before I sleep.

Dr. Dan: I wonder if there are certain times you tend to see him and do you remember him ever telling you anything?

Sgt. Z: Do we have to do this, Doc?

Doc Dan: We are here and I am interested in knowing what is going on so we can approach this together. Yes, if it is too painful we can stop, but I would really like you to help me understand what is going on in your mind because that can help us figure out how to lesson some of the pain you are in.

Sgt. Z: The dream is very vivid like when I told you but in my dream he is in my room and cuts into his arms in front of me and I tell him stop, please it is okay, I am here to help. He says you cannot help me no one can. I look on in terror as he just [pausing while his breathing is labored but hardly heard and his eyes averting me], he does not care at all that I am there as if I am not real he just starts to cut into his flesh and I see blood it is very painful and he looks at me and lets me know he is dead and says why did you kill me? I know I am dreaming but I am not able to wake up. Doc I wake up and will not allow myself to go to back to sleep. It is hell for me and I do not know what to do? I can't take a pill for it, I know you think it will help but no I can't anyhow it is just a dream but...

Doc Dan: Do you think you killed Henry still or has our review of the incredible catch 22 and the tension between your own survival and your need to act as a boss by backing up your guys, maintaining a perimeter, needing to be armed yourself and ready to shot to stop him, gain custody, deal with his being extremely dangerous, mentally ill and psychotic, and at the same time you were trying to let him know in real time and real space you cared and tried your very best to save this man's life and protect your troops as well? Let me ask you: who cared and protected Sgt. Z and allowed him some slack? It is amazing that you hold a standard for yourself that is superhuman, and who willed himself to die Sgt. Z?

Sgt. Z: I don't know! You know Doc, please help me get rid of this nightmare and stop seeing this guy.

Dr. Dan: Tell me Sgt. Z; please help me out here, will you?

Sgt. Z: How Doc?

Dr. Dan: By answering my question, which is very hard to imagine that unless you were the Angel Gabriel how could you have possibly saved Henry when he had planned to do himself in and commit suicide by cop. Yet before you do, do you remember the breakdown of what we both learned together as to your courage and will to believe in being compassionate to a person who could not even be compassionate to himself, what does that really mean to who you really are at your core, Sgt. Z? Tell me can you answer that question?

Sgt. Z: [Silence and sadness in tone of voice, teary-eyed no expression for a few minutes, a deep sigh.] It is very disturbing like the feeling I told you about I remember now, I did not cause his death I could not prevent him from doing it. I tried hard real hard and I did care enough I guess like you said I put myself in the front line like any boss would including you Doc.

Dr. Dan: I do not know if I would have the superb courage you did when called on to be as courageous as you were in the moment you were called to act as you did. Is it possible you could allow yourself to revisit your incredible ability to stay with it when most people would run the other way. Can you accept your only being human even if at times you take on superman human tasks that only by the grace of God can they turn out as we may wish? It appears you did the best you could and in this case it is tragic Henry died but you did not cause it and in fact you gave him every opportunity to retreat and surrender. Z, he already wrote his own script to die and attempt to put his own tragic choice and his own responsibility on your hands. Is it possible to pray for him in your own way and forgive yourself for an act you had tried to help avert and had no responsibility for?!?

Sgt. Z: I know you are right Doc. It is hard to believe after this I truly could not have done better for him. I mean I know what you are saying is true that Henry wanted to kill himself. But why out of the blue?

Dr. Dan: [I will explore that question with Sgt. Z including his own self destructive impulses to punish himself later in the session. In the here and now, I will not miss my opportunity to further solidify the gain he has made in realizing, even if only in part and for now, he is not a failure and he in fact has the power of compassion and courage.] It is clearly because Henry had not sought help, it is easier in the short term to avoid the painful work of being vulnerable to therapy, and I do not have the wisdom as to why he needed to kill himself then. I do know he was very ill and as we discussed he tried to drag you into his hell by lying to you and blaming you for his own death. It is very clear to me and I wonder if you ever pause as we discussed and reflect real deeply as to how you care so much that even after 7 years your compassion is so intense you are worried you may not have superseded the angels for even God himself gave free will and it appears you did everything humanly possible to save this tragic man's self-destructive choice. What do you think Sgt. Z?

[This is a paradoxical intervention to help Sgt. Z realize through an existential level of experience I witness and value the pain and loss underlying his experience as I support a powerful reflection for him to use for internal witnessing of his existential nightmare he did not cause, and the residual and cumulative losses through modeling and positive reinforcement we are committed to work through step by step in taking away his nightmares and self-abuse, which he never caused. My intervention tends to be helpful to Sgt. Z; he will incorporate our work in his own internal witnessing when he is long done with our work in therapy.]

Sgt. Z: [A slight expression of relief that is genuine] I mean, I am sorry he died but I did not cause his death; it is this crazy job which is what it is! Imagine, a young guy killing himself? Over what, Doc? Blaming me when I put myself out for him, that's crazy. Why would he hurt me—it is crazy, isn't it? It's not me, it's the shitty situation and I did do the best I can, right?

Dr. Dan: No, it's not you! Yes, it's been hard to allow yourself permission to express your compassion, which cuts like pain as you're doing right now and to realize Henry was a very sick man who tragically lost his life in the face of the remarkable efforts and decency you did when you were placed in a crazy situation you never created. [Our work continues; the paradoxical intervention worked well in this session, and many more revisits will create the web of strands that cohere as a bridge to healthier wellness for Sgt. Z in his own unique ecological and ethological niches with soulful motivation. There is a lot left to do but this example hopefully suffices to give a taste to you of how complex trauma is and how durable it is unless the commitment and the wisdom is generated one officer-patient and one police and public safety therapist at a time.]

FINAL COMMENTS AND CONCLUSION: PPS-CPTSD

Taken as a whole, this one composite case may serve as a tentative outline toward understanding complex PTSD in police and public safety populations. In presenting this example, personality dynamics have not been included as one can find in my recent publication (Rudofossi, 2009). In looking at my approach to complex trauma, a parable toward why we need to look at the whole picture within context is worth illustrating, that context may be taken from economics. You may say to yourself, look, a general eco-ethological understanding is a good way to go, but finding out the specifics of each officer-patient is daunting and time consuming. That point is true! Yet, without understanding the context of the individual officer-patient, your technique and method that may be right on the money is likely to be squandered. Why? Because demand can only command a response of supply once that need is established on a fundamental level.

Put another way, the economic laws of supply and demand hold in trauma: what is demanded to be effective is an understanding that reaches the reality of what is experienced in the field of meaning for your officer-patient. Until you can relate that field of meaning in the individual officer-patient's way of looking at his or her construction of loss in trauma, you are making a pitch in a sea of unanchored chance.

Ethology and ecology are disciplines with great potential for our population of police and public safety. It speaks to the experience of officers' traumas and losses in the field of their historical evolution. That evolution is relevant to cultural competence and individual development. Doing our work requires challenges to our own intellect, and more so to our passion and the existential meaningfulness we invest in our own work and those with whom we work. Yet, that is not an impossible task, but one where patience and curiosity engenders an attitude is likely to facilitate a probable humane and scientific understanding that is effective. To achieve your task, learning the language goes beyond the macro-culture and the official line of the public safety department. It entails your understanding and knowledge of the experience of demands in the officer-patient's ecological niche. That understanding is the currency we need to invest and trade in the market economy of trauma and loss with the officer-patient.

A demoralized participant may opt out of the journey of life. Their investments may be largely in destructive stock. Our challenge to that option is possible if we are clear on what currency the participant is using, what options for reinvestment may be considered, and we have a meaningful investment available to redirect the officer-patient investor. Once that is known, then all your training and experience is put to the best selective advantage in a competitive market economy. While you and I may not prefer to speak of trauma and loss in terms of trade and market economies, it may be the most economical metaphor available. That is markedly salient in a market economy anchored in limiting therapy to *briefer as better*. However, when you meet the needs of a goldfish, you can use a bowl; when you need to meet the needs of a blue whale, you had better be thinking expansion—that blue whale is trauma being hidden in our bathtub. Something's gotta give. Understanding the economy and the specific investments the officer-patient has made may help us suggest a reinvestment of static, into dynamic redirection and growth. I suggest that grasping this reality deepens insight, boosts realistic assessment and sharpens strategic treatment in working through complex PTSD we are likely to encounter in our expanded domain of trauma work.

The vast majority of public safety officers will be referred by agencies, some through peer-support and trauma team members, and some will be walk-ins without any prodding and seek out a mental health practitioner for the first time. Many will come forward with the dysfunctional myths we discussed. Some will be green with idealism, some tarnished with the gray of pessimism, and many soaked in the red shock of war wounds—so many tattered rags on the warfronts—in the intrapsychic conflicts of their psyches. Existential meaning is invariably personal and relates back to being invested in the patient's way of looking at the universe without losing yours. If you conceptualize this approach as a multicultural venture with a specific goal of understanding culture in terms of the ecological and ethological influences, you can connect with an increased chance of encounter. A potential caveat is a misinterpretation of the stance I advocate. That is working on an anti-reductionistic approach to eco-ethological etiology with the gestalt in mind. If as clinicians we reduce our approach to a formula, we endanger prepackaging the human being invariably winding up caught in the lining from which we construct our weblike designs. That snare has always been alluring to me. I suggest sharing the real person behind the therapist's approach is the way to bring out the real patient one is evolving with. Each real interaction is a step in one's own choice to grow, regress, or stagnate. That intangible encounter is irreducible and is the apogee of the intervention's crest to take away as a crosswind from this book on your own rewarding voyage with public servants of red, white, or blue hues. To infuse the wisdom of Talmudic sages, "To save one life is to save a world," if you prevent an officer's suicide, you have saved a world, not only his or her own but also the world at large! Please do so!

REFERENCES

Barnes, R. (2005). Personal correspondence on trauma and police issues from a logotherapy and forensic perspective. Retired Veteran and Psychologist President, Viktor Frankl Institute, Harding Simmons Professor, and Chair of Psychology and Counseling.

Benner, A. (1999). Personal correspondence on cop doc and the forging of a new role for the uniformed psychologist by founder of Cop Doc's National Association and cofounder of West Coast Post Trauma Retreat. United States Marine Corp Pilot and Captain San Francisco Police Department.

Benner, A. (2004). Personal correspondence on cop doc guide and emotional exhaustion fatigue in peer support officers and uniformed psychologist cop docs.

Brenner, C. (1974). *An elementary textbook of psychoanalysis.* New York: Anchor Books.

Brenner, C. (1976*). Psychoanalytic technique and intra-psychic conflict.* New Haven, CT: International University Press.

Brenner, C. (1982). *The mind in conflict.* New Haven, CT: International University Press.

Brenner, C. (2003). Personal correspondence on the iatrogenic casting of trauma without accounting for the deeper layers of personality and why an individualized approach is optimal.

Cohen, B. I. (1985). *Revolution in science.* Boston: Harvard University Belknap Press.

Doka, K. J. (Ed.). (1989). *Disenfranchised grief: Recognizing hidden sorrow.* Lexington, KY: Research Press.

Doka, K. J. (2002). *Disenfranchised grief: New directions, challenges, and strategies for practice.* Champaign, IL: Research Press

Einstein, A. (1954). *Ideas and opinions.* New York: Crown.

Ellis, A. (1962). *Reason and emotion in psychotherapy.* Secaucus, NJ: Lyle Stuart.

Ellis, A. (1985). *Overcoming resistance: Rational-emotive therapy with difficult patients.* New York: Springer.

Frankl, V. (1978). *The unheard cry for meaning.* New York: Simon & Schuster.

Frankl, V. (2000). *Man's search for ultimate meaning.* Cambridge, MA: Perseus.

Freud, A. (1937). *Ego and the mechanisms of defense.* New York: International University Press.

Freud, S. (1924). Recollection, repetition and working through. In J. Strachey & A. Freud (Eds.), *The complete psychological works of Sigmund Freud* (Vol. 12, pp. 366–376). London: The Hogarth Press.

Freud, S., Ferenczi, S., Abraham, K., Simmel, E., & Jones, E. (1921). *Psychoanalysis and the war neuroses.* London: International Psycho-Analytic Press.

Gilmartin, K. M. (2002). *Emotional survival for law enforcement.* Tucson, AZ: E-S Press.

Graber, A. V. (2004). *Viktor Frankl's logotherapy.* Lima, OH: Wyndham Hall Press.

Kelly, W. (1985). *Post traumatic stress disorder and the war veteran patient.* New York: Brunner/Mazel.

Kuhn, T. (1962). *The structure of scientific revolutions.* Chicago: University of Chicago Press.

Mansfield, V. (2004). Personal correspondence on a chief's viewpoint of three decades of executive police leadership and Rudofossi's construct of PPS-CPTSD.

Myers, C. (1940). *Shell shock in France 1914–1918.* Cambridge: Cambridge University Press.

Orwell, G. (2005). *Why I write.* New York: Penguin Books.

Pavlov, I. (1941). *Conditioned reflexes and psychiatry.* New York: International Publishers.

Popper, K. (1963). *Conjectures and refutations: The growth of scientific knowledge.* New York: Harper & Row.

Rado, S. (1939). Developments in the psychoanalytic conception and treatment of the neuroses. *Psychoanalytic Quarterly, 8,* 427.

Rado, S. (1956). *Psychoanalysis of behavior.* New York: Grune and Stratton.

Rando, T. (1993). *Treatment of complicated mourning: Clinicians guide.* Champaign, IL: Research Press.

Reese, J. (1991). *Critical incidents in policing.* Washington, DC: Department of Justice, Federal Bureau of Investigation.

Reese, J. (1996). Personal correspondence regarding *Federal Bureau of Investigation Agent Cop Doc advice in setting up a program for trauma and support in conducting research on PTSD and services.*

Rudofossi, D. (1997). *The impact of trauma and loss on affective differential profiles of police officers.* Ann Arbor: University of Michigan.

Rudofossi, D., & Ellis, R. R. (1999, August). *Differential police personality styles use of coping strategies, ego mechanism of defenses in adaptation to trauma and loss.* Symposium conducted at the annual meeting of the American Psychological Association, Boston, MA.

Rudofossi, D. M. (2007). *Working with traumatized police officer patients: A clinician's guide to complex PTSD.* Amityville, NY: Baywood.

Rudofossi, D. M. (2009). *A cop doc's guide to public safety complex trauma syndrome: Using five police personality styles:* Amityville, NY. Baywood.

Rudofossi, D. M., & Ellis, R. R. (1999, August). *Differential police personality styles use of coping strategies, ego mechanisms of defense in adaptation to trauma and loss.* Symposium conducted at the meeting of the American Psychological Association, Boston, Massachusetts.

Scharf, R. (2004). Personal correspondence regarding *Trauma and organizational character traits and issues from a psychoanalytic perspective.* New York Psychoanalytic Institute and Society.

Schneidman, E. (1996). *The suicidal mind.* Oxford: Oxford University Press.

Solomon, H., & Yakovlev, P. (1945) *Manual of military neuropsychiatry.* Philadelphia: W. B. Saunders.

Symonds, M. (1997). Personal correspondence regarding Chief Surgeon supervision of clinical cases and resistance to intervention of disabled officer.

Thorp, J. A. (2005). Personal correspondence on the need to expand ones approach to work with the traumatized patient.

Worden, J. (2001). *Grief counseling & grief therapy.* New York: Springer.

22 Suicide and Law Enforcement
What Do We Know?

Alan A. Abrams

Alice Liang

Kyleeann Stevens

Brenda Frechette

More police in the United States die from self-inflicted injuries than are killed in the line of duty (Mohandie & Hatcher, 1999). Many aware of this see this fact as proof that law enforcement is an exceptionally stressful occupation and that police work takes enormous emotional tolls on those who enter the field (Volanti, 2004). No definitive study on police suicide exists to answer the many questions that exist about the mental health stresses of police work. This chapter will review what is known about suicide in relation to law enforcement, and what inferences and extrapolations are warranted.

Discussions about the relationship of suicide and occupation confront problems of defining who is included and what the appropriate comparison population should be. Not all states or jurisdictions report occupation at the time of death—how should data from recording jurisdictions be applied to other geographical areas? What occupations should be counted as law enforcement? What time periods for measuring suicides are reasonable (Loo, 2003)? Are only completed suicides certified by the medical examiner the correct measure? Should suspicious deaths be included? Should nonfatal, self-inflicted injuries or thoughts of self-harm be included? Should suicides by retired former law enforcement agents be included? Should the comparison group be the general population, corrected for age and sex distributions, or should it be further narrowed and matched for say marital status, income, length of employment in the occupation at death, specific medical or psychiatric conditions, access to guns, exposure to sunlight, having been medically psychologically screened prior to hiring (healthy worker effect), or comorbid substance abuse? Different studies have produced widely differing conclusions based on these definitional decisions. One review reported that 11 of 18 studies of police suicide report a high rate, 3 report an average rate, and 4 conclude that police have a low rate (Stack & Kelley, 1994).

The purposes for which the outcomes of the studies are cited may not even require a showing that police in fact have an elevated incidence of self-injury and suicide. Identifying those stresses that can be reduced or better managed, and diverting those on a trajectory toward self-destruction remain important objectives. Regardless of the specific statistics, all professionals who work with lethal means such as guns or poisons need to be educated about suicide prevention, recognizing depression or suicidality in oneself, coworkers, or family; have emotional assistance programs available; have mental health issues destigmatized; and have access to effective education and treatment of substance abuse. Regardless of the risk of suicide, law enforcement officers are exposed to particular occupational traumas such as duty deaths and injury, use of deadly force, intervening in mass shootings, mass fatalities, witnessing suicides, intervening in domestic violence, handling dead bodies, and so forth (Dowling, Moynihan, & Genet, 2006). Regardless of the study findings on suicide, law enforcement workers need to have evidence-based programs for dealing with occupational trauma, stress, and posttraumatic responses (Becker et al., 2009; O'Hara & Violanti, 2009; Violanti et al., 2006).

It is not established that there is an elevated suicide rate in police. At present, the best answer to the question of whether completed suicide is an occupational hazard for law enforcement is: probably not (Agerbo, Gunnell, Bonde, Mortensen, & Nordentoft, 2007). The more complex question of whether police work causes an occupation specific mental illness or a generalized alteration (positive or negative) in mental health is not answered by the findings on suicide rates.

RISK FACTORS IN SUICIDE

The epidemiology of suicide is constantly changing, both regarding rates, methods, risk factors and characteristics of those who die by suicide. In 2005, the rate of suicide in the United States was 11 per 100,000, and there were 32,637 total deaths by suicide in the United States (Kung, Hoyert, Xu, & Murphy, 2008). Suicide is best defined as fatal, intentional, self-inflicted injury with the intent to end life (O'Carroll et al., 1996). However, any study showing an occupation with a suicide rate greater than the baseline rate does not establish that the occupation has any correlation or relationship with the number of suicides. A number of historical, demographic, and clinical factors have been associated with increased risk of suicide, and others with decreased risk (protective factors). Any study of suicide rates among law enforcement officers has to account for both risk and protective factors contributing to an accurate comparison control group. Identified risk factors for suicide include advanced age, male gender, non-Hispanic Caucasians, Native American ethnicity, psychosis, personality disorder, a prior history of a suicide attempt, a prior history of violence to others, impulse control disorder, traumatic brain injury, chronic or terminal physical illness, affective disorders, anxiety disorders, substance abuse disorders, a history of sexual assault or abuse, a family history of suicide or mental illness, access to lethal methods, hopelessness, intoxication, economic stress, and comorbid substance abuse. Protective factors include personal resilience; cultural and religious beliefs that discourage suicide; good physical and mental health; access to effective treatments for mental, physical, and substance use disorders; restricted access to highly lethal means of suicide; and strong connections to family and community support. An ideal study that accounts for all the demographic, clinical, and historical factors regarding occupation and suicide has yet to be conceived.

OCCUPATION AND SUICIDE

The risk of suicide varies across occupational groups (Agerbo et al., 2007; Boxer, Burnett, & Swanson, 1995; Kposowa, 1999; Meltzer, Griffiths, Brock, Rooney, & Jenkins, 2008; Stack, 2001). Is there something inherently protective about certain occupations with low risks of death by suicide or inherently toxic about those occupations with elevated risk? Do occupations with higher risk of suicide attract those with a greater burden of mental illness or greater resistance to treatment of mental illness (Agerbo et al., 2007)? A model for a causal relationship between suicide and occupation would need to separate out whether the field selected out or attracted applicants with preexisting physical or psychiatric morbidity, whether the field merely provided more lethal means but the rate of serious suicide attempts were not elevated, and whether persons with increased demographic risk remained in the field longer, and look for occupation related hazards and stresses. Posttraumatic stress, shift work, police culture, job dissatisfaction, burnout, gender tensions for female officers in a traditionally male occupation, alcohol abuse, marital instability, and managerial stress have been postulated as occupational hazards in law enforcement (Decker, 2006; Stuart, 2008).

A number of studies have consistently shown a highly significant relationship, that is, elevated relative risk odds ratio (RR) or proportional mortality ratios (PMRs), between the medical fields—physicians, nurses, veterinarians, dentists, social workers—and suicide (Agerbo et al., 2007; Center et al., 2003; Hawton, Malmberg, & Simkin, 2004; Hawton & Vislisel, 1999; Mellanby, 2005; Meltzer et al., 2008; Schernhammer, 2005; Schernhammer & Colditz, 2004; Stack, 2004). This elevated risk may be even greater for women (Lindeman, Laara, Hakko, & Lonnqvist, 1996). While most occupations do not increase risk of suicide among the mentally ill, the health fields apparently do (Agerbo et al., 2007). Many studies have also shown a relationship between unemployment or menial employment and suicide (Agerbo, 2003; Agerbo et al., 2007; Blakely, Collings, & Atkinson, 2003). In both groups, the risk is two to three times that of the adjusted general population. Inferences from these relatively consistent findings have included that larger numbers of severely mental ill persons are chronically unemployed or underemployed (Agerbo, Byrne Eaton, & Mortensen, 2004; Tohen, Bromet, Murphy, & Tsuang, 2000), that the health fields attract people with affective disorders (Wieclaw, Agerbo, Mortensen, & Bonde, 2006), or that access to lethal poison is so easy in the health fields that suicide attempts are likely to become fatal.

LAW ENFORCEMENT AND COMPLETED SUICIDE

In fact, police suicide is generally a low-probability event, with most years marked by zero or one suicide and the unusual year marked by several suicides. Reviews of early studies of completed police suicide have commented on methodological problems in reaching conclusions (Violanti, 2008). Predominantly, concerns have been raised about data collection methods and the appropriate control groups for comparison. General population comparisons do not control for differences in age, marital status, race, or gender, or provide comparison rates appropriate to the subpopulation of those involved in the work force (Stuart, 2008). Loo (2003) argued that the tendency to publish studies because they reported police suicides creates a bias against the unpublished studies that examined police forces with no suicides. A similar sentiment regarding publication bias was later expressed by Hem et al., (2004). Loo (1986, 2003) further stated shorter time frames can distort suicide rates, while studying small police forces can give the impression of an alarming picture even if only one suicide occurred in a given year. Likewise, Marzuk, Leon, Tardiff, and Nock (2004) highlighted the importance of examining longer time periods given the instability of suicide rates. Following a meta-analysis involving 101 samples of police suicide statistics (Loo, 2003), results confirmed that time periods of less than 10 years reflected high, atypical suicide rates in comparison to evaluation periods which spanned at least 10 years. Furthermore, findings indicated that suicide rates for the United States police were not significantly different from those for the comparable male population.

Another significant matter has to do with whether the deaths of police officers were reported or classified correctly. It has been repeatedly mentioned that administrators are reluctant to keep records of police suicides and if records are kept, the information is either incomplete or not made easily accessible (Heiman, 1975; Heiman, 1977; Loo, 1999). There is also the tendency of administration to believe the causes of suicides are outside the realm of the work environment and that to admit to such a problem would reveal weaknesses (Warne, 2008). Moreover, there is a strong sense of denial that suicide is a problem (Violanti, 1996). Rates reported may reflect an underestimation as many questionable deaths classified due to other causes are actually disguised or undetermined suicides (Mohandie & Hatcher, 1999). Hence, suicides may be underreported due to stigma or from being misclassified as an accident (Loo, 1986). According to Warne (2007), it is believed that there is an error of at least 30% over a 40-year period in the misclassification of some police suicides because of what is believed to be an effort to protect the department, the officer's family, and the officer's death itself.

Loo (2003) suggested that differences in societal values and legislation toward discriminatory employment practices can impact suicide rates. Stuart (2008) has asserted that the lack of standardized comparisons and conflicting results regarding the magnitude of suicide risk present methodological challenges that render the epidemiology of police suicide inconclusive.

An early study in the United States revealed that the average police officer who inflicted fatal self-harm was in his late 40s, was divorced or seeking divorce, was at or near retirement after at least 15 years of service, and suffered problems with alcohol (Heiman, 1977).

Stack and Kelley (1994) reported a suicide rate of 25.6 per 100,000 for police, which was only slightly greater than men of the same age. The difference was not statistically significant (Stack & Kelley, 1994). Boxer, Burnett, and Swanson (1995), using data from 26 states, also reported only a slightly elevated suicide rate for police.

Marzuk, Nock, Leon, Portera, and Tardiff (2002) conducted a study of New York City police officers that covered the years from 1977 to 1996. In this sample of 668 officer deaths, 80 were classified as suicides, which resulted primarily from the use of firearms (93.8%), followed by hanging, carbon monoxide poisoning, and falling from height. Of particular importance was that the suicide rate of male officers was lower or equal to the suicide rate of a comparable New York City population. Though the number of female police suicides was small, women posed a higher risk of suicide in comparison to the city's residents. Loo (1986) similarly found a high rate of suicide by firearm in a sample of the Canadian Federal Police force. Of the 34 suicides that occurred in a 23-year period, 29 of the officers had chosen a firearm as the method of suicide. Among the 29 deaths, 27 of the guns used were service revolvers.

Recent large studies with better attempts to find comparable control groups for comparison with completed suicides among law enforcement personnel have not found significant elevations.

Stack analyzed the U.S. national mortality file tapes, which covered 21 states that reported cause of death and decedent's occupation. In 1990, there were 9,499 suicides and 134,386 deaths from all other causes reported (Stack, 2001). He employed a multivariate model to remove the demographic covariates of occupation such as age, race, marital status, and gender. After bivariate logistic regression analyses controlling for the demographic factors, the risk of suicide in an occupation field was assessed against that in all other occupations in the labor force. After controlling for gender, age, race, and marital status, the odds ratio for police death by suicide was 0.92 and thus not significantly elevated or reduced (Stack, 2001).

Agerbo et al. (2007) did a nested case control study with 3,195 suicides in Denmark compared with 63,900 demographically matched controls. The studied suicides were all suicides completed between 1991 and 1997 by persons 25–60 years old. There were only 10 completed suicides by police during that time period. The risk of suicide was estimated as a RR 0.85, which was not significantly elevated or reduced (Agerbo et al., 2007).

Meltzer et al. (2008) studied mortality data collated by the Office for National Statistics (ONS) in England and Wales from 2001 to 2005. They calculated the proportional mortality ratios (PMRs) for both men and women according to their occupation. They defined the PMR as the ratio of how more or less likely a death in a given occupation is to be from suicide as opposed to other causes, than a death of someone of the same age and gender in England and Wales as a whole. Police did not show excess mortality from suicide, though the exact rate was not reported (Meltzer et al. 2008).

LAW ENFORCEMENT, STRESS, SUICIDAL IDEATION, OR ATTEMPTED SUICIDE

All the methodological problems of addressing completed suicides among law enforcement personnel are greatly multiplied in the attempt to study attempted or considered suicide, or other self-injurious behaviors. Berg et al. reported that among Norwegian police, there was a lifetime prevalence of reporting on a questionnaire of 24% for ever having the feeling that life was not worth living, 6.4% for ever having seriously considered suicide, and 0.7% for ever attempting suicide (Berg, Hem, Lau, Loeb, & Ekeberg, 2003). Violanti reported a lifetime prevalence of suicidal ideation in female police of 25% and in male police of 23.1% (Violanti et al., 2008). Violanti concluded that exposure to stress, PTSD, and alcohol use increase suicidal ideation among the police he examined by tenfold (Violanti, 2004). According to Violanti (2004), officers identified eight work events perceived as traumatic or disturbing: homicide of another officer, involvement in a shooting, abused children, serious traffic accidents, witnessing death, seeing deceased bodies, seeing serious assault victims, and homicide victims. Further analyses indicated persons dying had the greatest impact on PTSD symptoms, followed by miscellaneous disturbing incidents and homicide of a fellow officer, which subsequently increased the risk of alcohol use and suicide ideation. Shooting incidents have consistently been reported as the most stressful experience, not only due to the trauma associated with the actual shooting but also because officers may have to relive the incident via investigations into the legality of the shooting (Violanti, 1996). Violanti has also reported that shift work interacting with other factors affects suicidal ideation among police (Violanti et al., 2008).

A study in Brazil also showed a relationship between PTSD in police and suicidal ideation (Maia et al., 2007). In a study of police in South Africa, 7% reported current suicide ideation (Pienaar, Rothmann, & van de Vijver. 2007).

In one review of fitness-for-duty examinations, 55% of those referred admitted to previous suicide attempts (Janik & Kravitz, 2001). K. P. Decker, in her thoughtful 2006 book *Fit, Unfit or Misfit? How to Perform Fitness for Duty Evaluations in Law Enforcement Professionals,* provides interview data collected during her performance of fitness-for-duty evaluations after referral for behavioral or psychiatric problems. She reported that 31% had recent suicidal ideation and that 11% had made a recent suicide attempt (Decker, 2006). Interestingly, in her group, suicide attempts were most likely by overdose.

Because of the significant methodological problems, it is not possible to determine whether there is a higher lifetime prevalence of suicide attempts or suicidal ideation among law enforcement personnel. What the studies do suggest is that police personnel with identified behavior or psychiatric problems, substance misuse problems, marital problems, recent suspensions from duty, and exposure to stress or trauma may develop suicidal ideation or make a suicide attempt. This is not particularly different from those at risk in the general adult population. Predictions of who is likely to attempt suicide are plagued by large numbers of false positives.

CONCLUSIONS

Numerous studies have consistently demonstrated an elevated risk of completed suicide for persons working in the health-care fields. It is reasonable to assume that if an elevated risk of suicide is connected with a particular occupation, it will be regularly demonstrated in a variety of studies and in studies from different countries. A consistent relationship between completed suicides and work in law enforcement has not been found.

Law enforcement personnel are exposed to a variety of stressors, both on the job and in their personal life. The lack of an elevated suicide rate does not reduce the importance of the toll that such stressors take on law enforcement personnel. Regardless of the relative risk of suicide among law enforcement compared to other occupations, active efforts to reduce deaths by suicide are essential (Moscicki, 2001). Suicide prevention is still in the early phases of efficacy assessment (Mann et al. 2005). In their recent review, Mann et al. (2005) identified general suicide-prevention interventions as (1) awareness and education, (2) primary care physicians, (3) gatekeepers, (4) screening, (5) treatment interventions (pharmacotherapy, psychotherapy, chain of care after attempt), (6) means restriction, and (7) the media. The most promising interventions for decreasing suicide rates are educating primary care physicians in depression recognition and treatment, and restricting access to lethal methods.

REFERENCES

Agerbo, E. (2003). Unemployment and suicide. *Journal of Epidemiology & Community Health*, *57*, 560–561.

Agerbo, E., Byrne Eaton, W. W., & Mortensen, P. B. (2004). Marital and labor market status in the long run in schizophrenia. *Archives of General Psychiatry*, *61*, 28–33.

Agerbo, E., Gunnell, D., Bonde, J. P., Mortensen, P. B., & Nordentoft, M. (2007). Suicide and occupation: the impact of socio-economic, demographic and psychiatric differences. *Psychological Medicine, 37*, 1131–1140.

Becker, C. B., Meyer, G., Price, J. S., Graham, M. M., Arsena, A., Armstrong, D. A., & Ramon E. (2009). Law enforcement preferences for PTSD treatment and crisis management alternatives. *Behaviour Research and Therapy, 47*, 245–253.

Berg, A. M., Hem, E., Lau, B., Loeb, M., & Ekeberg, O. (2003). Suicidal ideation and attempts in Norwegian police. *Suicide and Life-Threatening Behavior, 33*(3), 302–312.

Blakely, T. A., Collings, S. C., & Atkinson J. (2003). Unemployment and suicide. Evidence for a causal association? *Journal of Epidemiology & Community Health, 57*, 594–600.

Boxer, P. A., Burnett, C., & Swanson, N. (1995). Suicide and occupation: A review of the literature. *Journal of Occupational and Environmental Medicine, 37*, 442–452.

Center, C., Davis, M., Detre, T., Ford, D. E., Hansbrough, W., Hendin, H., et al. (2003). Confronting depression and suicide in physicians: A consensus statement. *Journal of the American Medical Association, 289*, 3161–3166.

Decker, K. P. (2006). *Fit, unfit or misfit? How to perform fitness for duty evaluations in law enforcement professionals.* Springfield, IL: Charles C Thomas.

Dowling, F. G., Moynihan, G., & Genet, B. (2006). A peer-based assistance program for officers with the New York City Police Department: Report of the effects of Sept. 11, 2001. *American Journal of Psychiatry, 63*, 151–153.

Hawton, K., Malmberg, A., & Simkin, S. (2004). Suicide in doctors: A psychological autopsy study. *Journal of Psychosomatic Research, 57*, 1–4.

Hawton, K., & Vislisel, L. (1999). Suicide in nurses. *Suicide and Life-Threatening Behavior, 29*, 86–95.

Heiman, M. F. (1975). Police suicides revisited. *Suicide, 5*, 5–20.

Heiman, M. F. (1977). Suicide among police. *American Journal of Psychiatry, 134*, 1286–1290.

Hem, E., Berg, A. M., & Ekeberg, O. (2001). Suicide in police: A critical review. *Suicide and Life-Threatening Behavior, 31*, 224–233.

Hem, E., Berg, A. M., & Ekeberg, O. (2004). Suicide among police officers. Letter to the editor. *American Journal of Psychiatry, 161*, 767–768.

Janik, J., & Kravitz, H. M. (2001). Linking work and domestic problems with police suicide. *Suicide and Life-Threatening Behavior, 31*(2), 224–233.

Kposowa, A. J. (1999). Suicide mortality in the United States: Differentials by industrial and occupational groups. *American Journal of Industrial Medicine, 36*, 645–652.

Kung, H. C., Hoyert, D. L., Xu, J. Q., & Murphy, S. L. (2008). Deaths: Final data for 2005. *National Vital Statistics Reports, 56*(10), 1–124.

Lindeman, S., Laara, E., Hakko, H., & Lonnqvist, J. (1996). A systematic review on gender-specific suicide mortality in medical doctors. *The British Journal of Psychiatry, 168*, 274–279.

Loo, R. (1986). Suicide among police in a federal force. *Suicide and Life-Threatening Behavior, 16*, 379–388.

Loo, R. (2003). A meta-analysis of police suicide rates: Findings and issues. *Suicide and Life-Threatening Behavior, 33*, 313–325.

Maia, D. B., Marmar, C. R., Metzler, T., Nóbrega, A., Berger, W., Mendlowicz, V., et al. (2007). Posttraumatic stress symptoms in an elite unit of Brazilian police officers: Prevalence and impact on psychosocial functioning and on physical and mental health. *Journal of Affective Disorders, 97*, 241–245.

Mann, J. J., Apter, A., Bertolote, J., Beautrais, A., Currier, D., Haas, A., et al. (2005). Suicide prevention strategies: A systematic review. *Journal of the American Medical Association, 294*, 2064–2074.

Marzuk, P. M., Leon, A. C., Tardiff, K., & Nock, M. K. (2004). Suicide among police officers. Reply to letters to the editor. *American Journal of Psychiatry, 161*, 768.

Marzuk, P. M., Nock, M. K., Leon, A. C., Portera, L., & Tardiff, K. (2002). Suicide among New York City police officers, 1977–1996. *American Journal of Psychiatry, 159*, 2069–2071.

Mellanby, R. J. (2005). Incidence of suicide in the veterinary profession in England and Wales. *The Veterinary Record, 157*, 415–417.

Meltzer, H., Griffiths C., Brock A., Rooney, C., & Jenkins, R. (2008). Patterns of suicide by occupation in England and Wales: 2001–2005. *The British Journal of Psychiatry, 193*, 73–76.

Mohandie, K., & Hatcher, C. (1999). Suicide and violence risk in law enforcement: Practical guidelines for risk assessment, prevention, and intervention. *Behavioral Sciences & the Law, 17*, 357–376.

Moscicki, E. K. (2001). Epidemiology of completed and attempted suicide: Toward a framework for prevention. *Clinical Neuroscience Research, 1*, 310–323.

O'Carroll, P. W., Berman, A. L., Maris, R. W., Moscicki, E. K, Tanney, B. L., & Silverman, M. M. (1996). Beyond the Tower of Babel: A nomenclature for suicidology. *Suicide and Life-Threatening Behavior, 26*, 237–252.

O'Hara A. F., & Violanti, J. M. (2009). Police suicide: A Web surveillance of national data. *International Journal of Emergency Mental Health, 11*(1), 17–23.

Pienaar J., Rothmann S., & van de Vijver, F. J. R. (2007). Occupational stress, personality traits, coping strategies, and suicide ideation in the South African Police Service. *Criminal Justice and Behavior, 34*, 246–258.

Schernhammer, E. S. (2005). Taking their own lives: The high rate of physician suicide. *New England Journal of Medicine, 352*, 2473–2476.

Schernhammer, E. S., & Colditz, G. A. (2004). Suicide rates among physicians: A quantitative and gender assessment (meta-analysis). *American Journal of Psychiatry, 161*, 2295–2302.

Stack, S. (2001). Occupation and suicide. *Social Science Quarterly, 82*, 384–396.

Stack, S. (2004). Suicide among social workers: A research note. *Archives of Suicide Research, 8*, 379–388.

Stack, S., & Kelley, T. (1994). Police suicide: An analysis. *American Journal of Police, 13*(4), 73–90.

Stuart, H. (2008). Suicidality among police. *Current Opinion in Psychiatry, 21*(5), 505–509.

Tohen, M., Bromet, E., Murphy, J. M., & Tsuang, M. T. (2000). Psychiatric epidemiology. *Harvard Review of Psychiatry, 8*, 111–125.

Violanti, J. M. (2004). Predictors of police suicide ideation. *Suicide and Life-Threatening Behavior, 34*(3), 277–283.

Violanti, J. M. (2008). Police suicide research: Conflict and consensus. *International Journal of Emergency Mental Health, 10*(4), 299–307.

Violanti, J. M., Andrew, M. E., Burchfiel, C. M., Dorn, J., Hartley, T., & Miller, D. B. (2006). Posttraumatic stress symptoms and subclinical cardiovascular disease in police officers. *International Journal of Stress Management, 13*(4), 541–554.

Violanti, J. M., Charles, L. E., Hartley, T. A., Mnatsakanova, A., Andrew, M. E., Fekedulegn, D., et al. (2008). Shift-work and suicide ideation among police officers. *American Journal of Industrial Medicine, 51*(10), 758–768.

Violanti, J. M., Vena, J. E., Marshall, J. R., & Petralia, S. (1996). A comparative evaluation of police suicide rate validity. *Suicide and Life-Threatening Behavior, 26*, 79–85.

Warne, R. (2008). Police suicides: The unidentified assailant. In G. W. Doherty (Ed.), *Proceedings of the 6th Rocky Mountain Region Disaster Mental Health Conference* (pp. 1–13). Ann Arbor, MI: Rocky Mountain DMH Institute Press/Loving Healing Press.

Wieclaw, J., Agerbo, E., Mortensen, P. B., & Bonde, J. P. (2006). Risk of affective and stress related disorders among employees in human service professions. *Occupational and Environmental Medicine, 63*, 314–319.

Part VI

Treatment and Dysfunction

23 Cops in Trouble

Psychological Strategies for Helping Officers Under Investigation, Criminal Prosecution, or Civil Litigation

Laurence Miller

You receive a referral to see an officer who is the subject of an Internal Affairs investigation, disciplinary proceeding, administrative action, or legal charge. The referral may come from the officer's law enforcement agency or from the officer himself. Or the officer may be dragged in by a family member, sent to you following a suicidal gesture, or referred by his lawyer. Finally, you may have been treating this officer in the past or currently, and this new charge is a sudden, unexpected stressor.

Helping officers in distress, let alone those whose troubles may at least be partially self-induced, takes all the skills of a crisis counselor, psychotherapist, and patient advocate (Blau, 1994; Miller, 1995, 1999, 2000, 2006c, 2007c, 2007d; Russell & Beigel, 1990). The purpose of this chapter is not to provide legal advice, nor to encourage you to second-guess the decisions of your officer's administrators or command staff, the overwhelming majority of whom are honorable public servants, dedicated to the welfare of their personnel and their communities. This chapter will provide the police psychologist and other mental health practitioners who work with law enforcement and public safety personnel with practical information on the main reasons why law enforcement officers find themselves in internal investigatory and/or legal trouble; the types of consequences for such actions; the range of psychological reactions to an internal investigation; the main coping strategies that police psychologists can help these officers utilize to psychologically survive the ordeals of investigation, prosecution, possible incarceration, and civil litigation; specific psychotherapy techniques for special cases of officers in trouble; and suggestions for ethical collaboration between the police psychologist and the officer's legal counsel. The emphasis throughout this chapter is on the police psychologist's role as a treating clinician and advocate for the officer's psychological well-being, and is not intended to provide legal advice. [Note: For linguistic ease, the male pronoun will be used to denote both male and female officers.]

REASONS FOR AN INVESTIGATION OR LEGAL ACTION

Police officers are hardly the only professionals who are investigated, disciplined, prosecuted, and/or sued for unprofessional and/or illegal conduct (Miller, 2004, 2006c, 2008a). A comprehensive but nonexhaustive list includes federal agents, local police officers, firefighters, paramedics, medical and mental health clinicians, attorneys and judges, protective services and court personnel, clergy, airline and other transportation workers, corporate or government managers or executives, political figures, and military personnel.

What all these professionals have in common is that they all occupy positions of *high public authority and trust*. Society places great power and responsibility in their hands and so we hold them to a higher standard of personal and professional conduct than other types of workers. Supervisors in these fields generally take the position that tolerating even a few bad apples can have devastating repercussions—practical, professional, political, and financial—on their respective fields as a whole. Hence, to preserve the honor and integrity of these professions and the public trust on which they rely, investigators may be especially zealous in pursuing those who are suspected of breaking the rules.

For most police officers, the range of infractions includes, but is not limited to, the following (Hughes, 2001; Kaeppler, 1997; Kaeppler, Kaeppler, & del Carmen, 1993; Shev & Howard, 1977; Vaughn, Cooper, & del Carmen, 2001; Walker, 1997).

Excessive force. This is typically the largest category of police violation to come to the attention of investigators and other third parties. Despite training and official guidelines, in most real-life situations encountered by police officers, the line between proper and improper force is hardly clear cut. The amount of force necessary to a secure the situation is often a judgment call, and that means some misjudgments are inevitable. *Excessive force* has been defined as the use of more force than is reasonably necessary in a given situation, whereas *unnecessary force* involves the use of force where none at all is necessary (Scrivner, 1999).

Because the definition depends on the situation, confusions and disagreements are predictable. Generally, what citizens commonly understand by *excessive* is any behavior that ignores or tramples on what they feel are their full rights and dignity in a free society (Klockars, 1996). This can involve the officer's use of abusive language or curt commands to "move along." It can include stopping, questioning, and searching citizens on the street or in their cars; implicit or explicit threats to use physical force if not obeyed; direct physical threats with a baton or firearm; the actual use of violent physical force; or the unjustified killing of a suspect (Fyfe, 1988; Geller & Toch, 1996; Miller, 2004, 2006a; Walker, 1997).

Police corruption and misconduct. This is when a police officer uses his or her status or power to wrongfully achieve some personal benefit or gain (McCafferty & McCafferty, 1998), and is the other main cause of action for an internal investigation or legal charge. Some authorities (Beigel & Beigel, 1977; McCafferty & McCafferty, 1998; McCafferty, Souryal, & McCafferty, 1998) have subcategorized police corruption to include the following:

1. *Mooching*: receiving gratuities (such as free meals), sometimes in return for favoritism
2. *Chiseling*: demanding free or discounted admission to sports or other events not connected with police duties
3. *Favoritism*: granting immunity from police action to certain citizens or peers, such as "fixing" parking or traffic violations
4. *Prejudice*: treating certain groups differently, particularly minority groups who are less likely to cause trouble for the officer
5. *Shopping:* stealing small items from an unsecured place of business on one's beat
6. *Extortion:* explicitly demanding a cash payment in return for protection against police action
7. *Bribes:* accepting an unsolicited cash payment in order to avoid arrest
8. *Shakedown:* stealing expensive items from a crime scene and attributing their loss to criminal activity
9. *Perjury:* lying to protect a fellow officer or oneself when under oath in a court of law or during an Internal Affairs Division investigation
10. *Premeditated theft:* carrying out a planned burglary
11. *Carrying unauthorized weapons*
12. *Taking property* from recovered stolen cars
13. *Keeping weapons or drugs* that are confiscated from suspects
14. *Having sex with informants* in vice and narcotics investigations

15. *Selling confidential information* to lawyers and insurance companies
16. *Loafing or attending to personal business* while on duty
17. *Using deceptive or aggressive means in interrogation* of subjects
18. *Collecting kickbacks* from lawyers for driving arrests or auto accident investigations
19. *Direct assaults and violence*

Anyone who has worked for any length of time with a major police agency can no doubt add his or her own items to this list.

CONSEQUENCES OF AN INTERNAL INVESTIGATION

Although there can be several kinds of administrative and legal repercussions from a particular action, probably the one that is feared and loathed the most is the departmental Internal Affairs investigation, because this comes from inside "the tribe," from one's professional peers, the people who should understand. While the details vary from agency to agency, there are several possible outcomes of a departmental internal investigation.

Exoneration. The charges are found to have an insufficient basis to be sustained. The officer is thanked for his cooperation and is returned to duty.

Discipline. The investigating panel concludes that the officer did do something wrong, but not severe enough to be terminated, so he or she may be subject to a range of sanctions, from suspension without pay to demotion in rank, reassignment to other duties, removal from a special unit, verbal or written reprimand, or other measures.

Termination. The charges are either serious enough in themselves, or the infractions show a recurring pattern, to warrant the officer being fired from the agency.

Criminal prosecution. The case is serious enough to be turned over to local or federal prosecutors for further investigation that may lead to criminal charges being brought against the officer. This is seen most commonly in excessive force cases or where the officer was involved in outright criminal activity.

Civil lawsuit. This is an action that may be taken by a third party who sues the officer—and typically the department and the municipality as well—for physical, emotional, financial, or other damages. Most commonly, the plaintiff is either the complainant in an action for alleged police misbehavior (such as a police beating, Tasing, shooting, or sexual assault) or the surviving family member of a decedent who was the victim of deadly force by police). The plaintiff may also allege insufficient action by the police (officer incompetence or neglect of procedure in protecting a victim), negligence, or improper behavior (a pedestrian is severely injured in a crash involving an unsafe police vehicle chase, or is hit by a stray round during a gun battle). Even if the department or agency is not directly involved in this lawsuit, the officer's personnel file and other records may be subpoenaed by plaintiff or defense counsel for use in the case.

Personal damage. Ruined reputation, family crisis, financial disruption, reduced employment prospects, media intrusion, and mental health and substance abuse problems are all possible consequences of the stress of being investigated and possibly charged.

PSYCHOLOGICAL REACTIONS TO AN INTERNAL INVESTIGATION OR OTHER DISCIPLINARY OR LEGAL ACTION

While each officer will respond individually based on his unique personality, temperament, and personal history (Miller, 2003, 2005, 2006c, 2008a), certain reaction patterns occur fairly commonly following an internal investigation, disciplinary action, or legal charge.

Fear. Suddenly, the officer's career is on the line, and with it his whole sense of personal and professional identity. Often, the greatest anxiety comes from not knowing what will happen next. As the crisis unfolds, there are good moments, when the officer is able to put it out of his mind and hope for the best, and bad moments when he or she is close to panic.

Anger. "I can't believe this is how I get treated for doing my job!" is a typical reaction. If the officer feels that his actions were justified or that the department is making too big a deal of this case because of political pressure, a personal vendetta, or just because the powers-that-be can't or won't understand the full story behind the officer's conduct, then he or she may be fuming. Even worse is when the officer believes that the discipline was meted out unfairly: "I know a dozen guys/gals who've done the same thing as me—or far worse—and nothing happened to them!" Fear and anger typically alternate in a swirling spiral of emotions that may make it difficult for the officer to think clearly at just the time that clear-headedness is vital.

Hopelessness/helplessness. Many investigated or charged officers go through periods during which they just crash and feel demoralized and defeated: "If something like this can happen, then what the hell's the point of anything?" Motivation is sapped, energy is drained, and the officer may shuffle around like the living dead. Then, boom—something happens and the anger and panic come flooding in again. These kinds of roller-coaster emotional cycles can prove debilitating over time and may start to convince the officer that he or she is going insane.

Recklessness/revenge. Sometimes, as a reaction against feeling like an impotent victim, the officer will get the urge to act out is some way: "Okay, they think I'm a friggin' criminal—I'll show them how bad I can really be!" This is probably a subset of the angry response discussed above. In these instances, it may be very difficult for the officer to fight his temptation to figuratively stick a thumb in the eye of the officer's perceived tormentors, but, as further discussed below, it is vitally important to encourage the officer to consider the big picture and to keep such impulses in check.

Guilt. In many cases, as much as the officer hates to admit it, there may have been some way he contributed to his own plight. Sometimes it may have been outright illicit or criminal behavior, but more often it represents one of those "tipping point" moments when the officer made a choice to behave one way and not another. Perhaps a suspect jabbed him with a hidden syringe while he was trying to cuff him, and he gave him an extra thump as a thank you. Or he did get overly flirty with the cute college student at the crash scene and spent far too much time attending to her minor wounds, to the neglect of the trucker with the compound fracture. Or some cash was found at a crime scene and nobody was around (they thought), so the investigating officers picked it up and pocketed it. And, besides, even if the officers knew they were doing something wrong, they never thought they'd get nailed, because everybody does it and gets away with it but—just our damn luck—we got pinched. In such cases, fear, guilt, anger, and paranoia may all percolate and magnify the officer's distress: "What was I thinking?" "How could I have been so stupid?" "Everybody does it and I get screwed!" "I'll bet this was a set-up—they've had it in for me for a long time!"

Clinical syndromes. These may be physical, such as headaches, stomach problems, or sleep disruption; or psychological, including panic disorder, depression, or sometimes full-blown posttraumatic stress disorder (PTSD). Alcohol or substance abuse is a distinct risk, further compounding the problem and further elevating the risk of suicidal behavior (Miller, 2005). It is usually at the point where the officer begins to get so overwhelmed by the stress of the investigation that he is not able to function, and will admit that it's time to get help.

PSYCHOLOGICAL STRATEGIES FOR HELPING OFFICERS DEAL WITH AN INTERNAL INVESTIGATION OR LEGAL ACTION

The following are some psychological coping strategies you can utilize and adapt to the unique circumstances and personality of your officer and his particular administrative and/or legal situation. As a mental health clinician working with officers in trouble, your roles may well span those of coach, therapist, parent, anger-projection target, toxic pain absorber, crisis manager, and hand holder. Officers may skip several sessions, and then abruptly demand immediate unscheduled time. They may appear calm, even cheerful one session, and then call you a day later in near-mental meltdown. This section will focus on practical advice you can give your officer that can aid in his self-help efforts to deescalate from further trouble and productively work with his attorney (Miller, 2006b, 2006c, 2008a). The following section will discuss some more intensive and extensive psychotherapeutic strategies for officers in distress.

Don't panic. There's no way your officer will avoid experiencing a certain degree of anxiety from now until the case is resolved one way or another, but the goal is to help him deal with it without becoming too overwhelmed to function. Teach the officer a number of basic stress-management techniques and cognitive-behavioral coping strategies to encourage the sense that he can at least control something. Utilize whatever works: tapes and manuals or in-office relaxation or biofeedback exercises. Encourage the officer to practice these techniques so that he can use them whenever necessary.

Strategize. Another good reason to control anxiety is to keep it from overwhelming productive thinking and problem-solving skills. At some point the officer has to sit down and figure out what he is going to do. While you are not the officer's attorney, one important therapeutic task is to lease out your frontal lobes to the officer who is having difficulty thinking clearly about his case. Help the officer review the actions that led to the investigation. Help him be clear about what's being charged and what the realistic options are. The game plan you and the officer develop may be modified multiple times as new information comes in and contingencies change, but at least he will have a game plan, which will give the officer a greater feeling of control.

Get legal help. Encourage the officer to retain competent, qualified legal representation. Usually, officers under investigation or charged with a violation are assigned a union legal representative, but complex or difficult cases may require the officer to retain specialized independent counsel. The rule of thumb before an officer takes any action on his own behalf is "Ask your lawyer first," and that may include what is said in the clinical session. The officer can disagree with his attorney, argue with the attorney and, ultimately, choose to reject the attorney's advice, but the officer should use the attorney's knowledge and experience to guide his efforts so that they'll be maximally productive. With the officer's permission, offer to make yourself available to speak with the attorney: the more everybody involved in the case is on the same page, the smoother things will go. At times, the attorney may contact you for advice on how to deal with certain psycho-legal issues; in such cases, don't be shy about giving your frank opinions about the case and offering your best clinical recommendations in the service of the officer's psychological health and well-being.

Keep a low profile. Especially when the case appears to drag on and anxiety and paranoia continue to fester, the officer may begin to feel a great temptation to "take it to the streets" to publicize his trials and tribulations so that the whole world will rise up and denounce the cosmic injustice he has been dealt. Discuss this with the officer and in most cases discourage it. Remind the officer that, except for a few close family members and allies, most people's reaction will be somewhere between a yawn and "better you than me." Aside from this apathetic response, turning the case into a crusade and acting like the poster-boy/gal for wrongful discipline will, in most cases, only backfire and damage the officer's chances of being exonerated or reinstated by backing the decision makers into an us-versus-them contest of wills. In the same way, encourage the officer to be very wary of those who may want to make his case their *cause célèbre,* because these third parties usually have their own political or social agendas that have little to do with the officer's welfare.

Keeping a low profile also means staying out of further trouble. During a suspension, with too much free time on the officer's hands and too much dysphoric rumination percolating in his head, the officer may be tempted to go out, have some fun, and raise a little hell while he still can. Your response: *Don't.* From now until this case is resolved, the officer should behave as if there is a surveillance camera trained on him 24/7. It may not be fair to be trapped in virtual house arrest, not working or going out, but encourage the officer to look at the big picture. Would he want his review or appeals board to be on the verge of cutting him a break, only to learn at the last minute that he was involved in further illegal, obnoxious, or just embarrassingly stupid behavior? Sometimes your therapeutic coaching role may include telling your officer, "Don't be a schmuck." Encourage him to tough it out and work toward a favorable resolution. (Note: This includes mouthing off on Facebook, blogs, or other Internet outlets.)

Work the case. The opposite extreme from the "crusader for justice" syndrome is often demoralized apathy; often these moods will alternate in a bipolar manner. Sometimes, productive action is the best medicine. After getting approval from the attorney, remind the officer that even the best lawyer can't do everything by herself. Consequently, one way for a downtrodden officer to jump-start his mojo—or, alternatively, to burn up some of that surplus of nervous energy that might otherwise lead to trouble—is to "obsess constructively" and serve as the pointperson on the case. This means doing research, creating a card or computer file on the case and relevant resources, keeping the information organized and up to date, and passing it on to the officer's attorney. Just remind the officer to check everything with his lawyer first to be a helper, not a pest, so the activity is empowering and not further demoralizing.

Don't lie. This is crucial. Experienced clinicians know that our patients don't always tell us the truth—and we're trying to help them! Under the intense adversarial circumstances of an investigation or legal charge, the temptation to bend the story will be extreme for the officer, but if the powers-that-be suspect he is lying, and certainly if the officer is caught in a direct fabrication, it could blow the whole case and even lead to additional criminal charges. More commonly, officers may not flat-out make things up out of thin air, but, like most people, they will self-defensively spin the events to accord with their interpretation of their actions. Again, with attorney approval, encourage your officer to relate and process the events until a consistent and comprehensible narrative emerges. Remember that your job is not to tell the officer *what* to say, but to help him express thoughts as clearly as possible.

Have a plan B. And, preferably, a C and a D, too. An important component of productive problem solving is contingency planning. If, despite his best efforts, worse comes to worst and it looks like the officer's law enforcement career is over, it is vital to have some plans made ahead of time for what the former officer going to do in his new life. Understandably, this kind of advance planning is harder than it seems because the mere acknowledgment of any alternate plans will seem like a pessimistic capitulation to the possibility of failure. Nevertheless, encourage the officer to make these contingency plans for the same reason people buy insurance: you hope the big one doesn't hit, but if it does, you want to be prepared.

PSYCHOTHERAPY FOR LAW ENFORCEMENT INVESTIGATORY, DISCIPLINARY, OR LEGAL STRESS

Not everyone, even those under severe stress, needs to be in psychotherapy on general principles. If an officer feels he can deal with this on his own, all power to him. But the right counselor can make a tremendous difference at those times when it looks like it's all going to hell and there's no one else the officer can vent to, either because the usual sounding boards are getting tired of hearing it or the officer doesn't want to further burden them. Many officers who have faced disciplinary or legal action have noted that having a mental health clinician in their corner was not only a source of emotional support but also an invaluable resource for providing frequent, needed reality checks that kept the officer from acting like a royal jerk and screwing up his own case.

ADMINISTRATIVE AND LEGAL ISSUES

Again, whether self- or department referred, if your services are sought by an officer under investigation or legal action, give his attorney a courtesy call unless the officer specifically forbids it (very rare, in my experience). Of course, utilize the appropriate written release and permission forms.

A special application of the earlier issue of what and how much to say to whom sometimes arises in the psychotherapy context: "Look, doc, I don't know if I told this part of the story yet, but I'm afraid if I tell you something, you'll report it—we're protected by confidentiality, right?" Answer: doctor–patient confidentiality says you as the clinician can't violate confidentiality unless the officer presents a clear and imminent danger to self or others, or if you become aware that the officer is physically or sexually abusing a child or other dependent person. I can't think of a single case in my own or my colleagues' practices where this has actually happened. And even then, as a mandated reporter, the clinician would be duty-bound to disclose only the danger or offense in question, but still not be allowed to reveal unrelated confidential material. However, in most jurisdictions, doctor–patient confidentiality is still not as inviolate as attorney–client privilege (or, for that matter, clergy–parishioner privilege) so, theoretically at least, a judge could issue a court order for your records and even jail you for contempt if you refused to produce them. Again, in all my years of practice, this has never happened to me or to any psychologist I know, and it would probably have to be a matter of national security for something like this to occur—but, theoretically, it could happen.

Even then, by the time the officer gets to your office, he has probably told his story so many times to so many people, that it's unlikely you're going to learn anything startlingly new at that point. Nevertheless, for the officer's own peace of mind, if there's something he doesn't feel 100% safe telling you at the moment, validate his decision to protect himself. Encourage the officer to talk it over with his attorney, and if the lawyer says it's okay, then offer to listen to whatever the officer has to say. However, if the officer's legal counsel tells him to clam up about a particular detail, then respect that. As a competent mental health clinician, you can still productively steer the officer's therapy around those little holes in the road.

Speaking of attorneys, you may be asked to give your opinion about an officer's condition. Bear in mind that your clinical treatment of an officer, even when mandated by that officer's department, does not comprise a psychological fitness-for-duty (FFD) evaluation (Decker, 2006; IACP, 2005; Miller, 2004, 2007a; Rostow & Davis, 2002, 2004; Stone, 1995, 2000), which is an objective, specialized assessment used to determine whether an officer's actions are primarily related to a mental disorder. If such an examination is ordered, it will be conducted by another psychologist not connected to the clinical treatment of your officer. However, as a treating clinician, you may be asked for your input in the form of your notes or verbal consultation with the examiner. Consult with the officer and with his attorney before complying with this request, and make sure all appropriate informed consent paperwork is completed.

Whether self-referred, mandated by the department, or a little of both, psychotherapy with law enforcement officers requires some special considerations (Miller, 1995, 1999, 2005, 2006a, 2006c, 2007c, 2007d, 2008c, 2009).

TRUST AND THE THERAPEUTIC RELATIONSHIP

Difficulty with trust appears to be an occupational hazard for law enforcement officers, who typically maintain a strong sense of self-sufficiency and insistence on solving their own problems. The development of trust during the establishment of the therapeutic alliance depends on the therapist's skill in interpreting the officer's statements, thoughts, feelings, reactions, and nonverbal behavior. In the best case, the officer begins to feel at ease with the therapist and finds comfort and a sense of predictability from the psychotherapy process. This requires *accurate empathy* without premature emotional "crowding"; *genuineness* in communication and interaction style; *respect* for the officer by treating him as an adult and as a professional; *concreteness,* at least initially, in providing down-to-earth interpretations and solutions; and *availability* in being flexible with scheduling appointments and responding to between-session contacts (Silva, 1991).

THERAPEUTIC STRATEGIES AND TECHNIQUES

Many law enforcement and emergency services personnel come under psychotherapeutic care in the context of some form of critical incident posttraumatic stress reaction or other crisis context (Blau, 1994; Fullerton et al., 1992; Kirschman, 1997; Miller, 2007c, 2007d), and this will probably be the case with the officer who suddenly finds himself under investigation or facing criminal charges. In general, the effectiveness of any therapeutic technique will be determined by the timeliness, tone, style, and intent of the intervention. Effective psychological interventions with law enforcement officers share in common the elements of briefness, focus on specific symptomatology or conflict issues, and direct operational efforts to resolve the conflict or problem and to reach a satisfactory short-term conclusion, while planning for the future if necessary. A straightforward, goal-directed, problem-solving therapeutic intervention approach includes the following components: creating a sanctuary; focusing on critical areas of concern; specifying desired outcomes; reviewing assets; developing a general plan; identifying practical initial implementations; encouraging self-efficacy; and setting appointments for review, reassurance, and further implementation (Blau, 1994; Miller, 1999, 2006c).

Blau (1994) delineates a number of effective individual intervention strategies for police officers, which are directly applicable to officers under investigatory or legal stress.

Attentive listening. This includes good eye contact, appropriate body language, genuine interest, and interpersonal engagement, without inappropriate comment or interruption. Clinicians will recognize this type of intervention as a form of "active listening."

Being there with empathy. This therapeutic attitude conveys availability, concern, and awareness of the disruptive emotions being experienced by the traumatized or distressed officer. It is also helpful to let the officer know, in a nonalarming manner, what he is likely to experience in the days and weeks ahead, consistent with the "reality check" function of counseling noted in the first section of this chapter.

Reassurance. In acute stress situations such as facing the possible loss of one's career or jail time, this should take the form of realistically reassuring the officer that routine matters will be taken care of, deferred responsibilities will be handled by others, and the officer has administrative and command support. This, of course, must be realistically based.

Supportive counseling. This includes active listening, restatement of content, clarification of feelings, and validation. In cases of investigatory or legal stress, this also may include such concrete services as liaising with attorneys and other third parties, as appropriate. Third parties, incidentally, may well include the officer's family, as bolstering this support system in times of crisis can be a powerful therapeutic adjunct (Kirschman, 1997; Miller, 2006c, 2007b).

Interpretive counseling. This type of intervention should be used when the officer's emotional reaction is significantly greater than the circumstances of the critical incident seem to warrant. In appropriate cases, this therapeutic strategy can stimulate the officer to explore underlying emotional or psychodynamic issues that intensify a naturally stressful traumatic event, such as an internal investigation or legal charge. In a few cases, this may lead to continuing, ongoing psychotherapy (Blau, 1994; Miller 1999, 2006c).

UTILIZING COGNITIVE DEFENSES

In psychology, *defense mechanisms* are mental stratagems that the mind uses to protect itself from unpleasant thoughts, feelings, impulses, and memories. While the normal use of such defenses enables the average, nonpathologically affected person to avoid conflict and ambiguity and maintain some consistency to his personality and belief system, most psychologists would agree that an overuse of defenses to wall off too much painful thought and feeling leads to an overly rigid and dysfunctional coping style. Accordingly, much of the ordinary psychotherapeutic process involves carefully helping patients to relinquish pathological defenses so that they can learn to deal with internal conflicts constructively. However, in the face of immediate and ongoing severe stress, the last thing a traumatized officer needs is to have his defenses stripped away. If anything, the proper utilization of psychological defenses can serve as an important "psychological splint" that enables the officer to function during the prolonged crisis of an investigation or legal action (Janik, 1991; Miller, 2008c, 2008d).

Indeed, law enforcement and other emergency services personnel usually need little help in applying defense mechanisms on their own. Examples (Durham, McCammon, & Allison, 1985; Fullerton et al., 1992; Henry, 2004; Taylor, Wood, & Lechtman, 1983) include the following:

- *Denial.* "I'll just put it out of my mind; focus on other things; avoid situations or people who remind me of it."
- *Rationalization.* "I had no choice; things happen for a reason; it could have been worse; other people have it worse; most people would react this way."
- *Displacement/projection.* "It was Command's fault for issuing such a stupid order; I didn't have the right backup; they're all trying to blame me for everything."
- *Refocus on positive attributes.* "Hey, this was a one-shot deal—I'm usually a great cop. I'm not gonna let this get me down."
- *Refocus on positive behaviors.* "Okay, I'm gonna get through this investigation, get more training, increase my knowledge and skill, and stay out of trouble, so I never get into this kind of jam again."

Janik (1991) proposes that, in the short term, therapists actively support and bolster psychological defenses that temporarily enable the officer to continue functioning. Just as a physical crutch is an essential part of orthopedic rehabilitation when an injured patient is learning to walk again, a psychological crutch is perfectly adaptive and productive if it enables the officer to stay on his psychological two feet during a prolonged professional and personal crisis like an investigation or legal action. Only later, when he is making the bumpy transition back to normal routine functioning, are the defenses revisited as possible bars to progress. Indeed, rare among us is the person who is completely defense free. It is only when defenses are used inappropriately and for too long that they constitute a "crutch" in the pejorative sense. In fact, many of the adaptive defenses noted above will seem familiar to psychologists as *cognitive-restructuring* techniques from the cognitive therapy toolkit.

SURVIVAL RESOURCE TRAINING

A recent trend in clinical services for law enforcement has been a deemphasis on remediating pathological reactions to stressful events, and focusing more on marshalling the officer's innate capacities of strength and resilience (Miller, 2008b, 2008c, 2008d). One of the early developers of this approach was Solomon (1988, 1991), who pointed out that officers often dwell on their mistakes and misdeeds following actions that led to a deleterious outcome, and thereby overlook anything they might have done right in mitigating the crisis. Thus, being realistically reminded by the therapist of their own adaptive coping efforts may prove especially empowering because it draws upon strengths that came from the officer himself. Termed *survival resource training,* this intervention, as originally conceived, allows officers to utilize their original fear response to gain access to a psychological state characterized by controlled strength, increased awareness, confidence, and clarity of mind.

In this technique, the therapist encourages the officer to view the critical incident he or she was involved in from a detached, objective point of view, "like you were watching a movie of yourself," and to go through the incident "frame by frame." At the point where he visualizes himself fully engaging in his activity (negotiating, arresting, securing a crime scene, firing his weapon, and so on), the officer is instructed to "focus on the part of you enabling you to respond." In most cases, this leads to a mental reframe characterized by controlled strength, heightened awareness, confidence, and mental clarity, as the officer mentally zooms in on his capability to respond, instead of fixating on the immobilizing fear, perceptions of weakness, loss of control, or perceptual distortions.

In applying this to officers whose alleged misdeeds led to their investigation or legal charges, I have found the frame-by-frame approach to have a powerful clarifying and empowering effect, while at the same time allowing officers to break through maladaptive denial and blame-shifting and take ownership of what they're truly responsible for. This occurs when officers are able to analyze and separate what they did and what others did, what was a legitimate response to the situation and what was bending or breaking the rules, how they handled or mishandled the situation and how others handled or mishandled it, what their thinking and motivation were at the time of an alleged misdeed and why they went through with it ("What stopped you from stopping yourself?"), and, finally, identifying the "tipping points" at which they made the ill-fated decision to proceed with the bad behavior. This latter insight often enables the officer to get a feeling of control over the incident by assuring himself that he will never do it again and, at the same time, functions as form of internal atonement by allowing the officer, by virtue of that confidence, to say to himself, "I'm not that person anymore."

CONCLUSIONS

Remember, the therapist is not a moralist, and the purpose of psychotherapy for an investigative or disciplinary crisis is to help the officer maintain psychological stability, not effect a radical personality overhaul. But if, in the process, the officer can learn something about himself that leads to a sincere adjustment in attitude and behavior, then you will quite possibly have made a positive and wide-ranging impact on the future trajectory of that officer's life and career.

REFERENCES

Beigel, H., & Beigel, A. (1977). *Beneath the badge: A study of police corruption.* New York: Harper & Row.

Blau, T. H. (1994). *Psychological services for law enforcement.* New York: Wiley.

Decker, K. P. (2006), *Fit, unfit, or misfit? How to perform fitness for duty evaluations in law enforcement professional.* Springfield, IL: Charles C Thomas.

Durham, T. W., McCammon, S. L., & Allison, E. J. (1985). The psychological impact of disaster on rescue personnel. *Annals of Emergency Medicine, 14,* 664–668.

Fullerton, C. S., McCarroll, J. E., Ursano, R. J., & Wright, K. M. (1992). Psychological responses of rescue workers: Firefighters and trauma. *American Journal of Orthopsychiatry, 62,* 371–378.

Fyfe, J. J. (1988). Police use of deadly force: Research and reform. *Justice Quarterly, 5,* 165–205.

Geller, W. A., & Toch, H. (1996). Understanding and controlling police abuse of force. In W. A. Geller & H. Toch (Eds.), *Police violence: Understanding and controlling police abuse of force* (pp. 292–328). New Haven, CT: Yale University Press.

Henry, V. E. (2004). *Death work: Police, trauma, and the psychology of survival.* New York: Oxford University Press.

Hughes, T. (2001). Police officers and civil liability: "The ties that bind"? *Policing, 24,* 240–262.

International Association of Chiefs of Police. (2005). Psychological fitness for duty evaluation guidelines. *The Police Chief,* September, pp. 70–74.

Janik, J. (1991). What value are cognitive defenses in critical incident stress? In J. Reese, J. Horn, & C. Dunning (Eds.), *Critical incidents in policing* (pp. 149–158). Washington, DC: U.S. Government Printing Office.

Kaeppler, V. E. (1997). *Critical issues in police civil liability* (2nd ed.). Prospect Heights, IL: Waveland.

Kaeppler, V. E., Kappeler, S. F., & del Carmen, R. V. (1993). A content analysis of police civil liability cases: Decisions of the federal district courts, 1978–1990. *Journal of Criminal Justice, 21,* 325–337.

Kirschman, E. F. (1997). *I love a cop: What police families need to know.* New York: Guilford.

Klockars, C. B. (1996). A theory of excessive force and its control. In W. A. Geller & H. Toch (Eds.), *Police violence: Understanding and controlling police abuse of force* (pp. 1–22). New Haven, CT: Yale University Press.

McCafferty, F. L., & McCafferty, M. A. (1998). Corruption in law enforcement: A paradigm of occupational stress and deviancy. *Journal of the American Academy of Psychiatry and Law, 26,* 57–65.

McCafferty, F. L., Souryal, S., & McCafferty, M. A. (1998). The corruption of a law enforcement officer: A paradigm of occupational stress and deviancy. *Journal of the American Academy of Psychiatry and Law, 26,* 433–458.

Miller, L. (1995). Tough guys: Psychotherapeutic strategies with law enforcement and emergency services personnel. *Psychotherapy, 32,* 592–600.

Miller, L. (1999). Psychotherapy with law enforcement and emergency services personnel: Principles and practical strategies. In L. Territo & J. D. Sewell (Eds.), *Stress management in law enforcement* (pp. 317–332). Durham, NC: Carolina Academic Press.

Miller, L. (2000). Traumatized psychotherapists. In F. M. Dattilio & A. Freeman (Eds.), *Cognitive-behavioral strategies in crisis intervention* (2nd ed., pp. 429–445). New York: Guilford.

Miller, L. (2003, May). Police personalities: Understanding and managing the problem officer. *The Police Chief,* pp. 53–60.

Miller, L. (2004). Good cop—bad cop: Problem officers, law enforcement culture, and strategies for success. *Journal of Police and Criminal Psychology, 19,* 30–48.

Miller, L. (2005). Police officer suicide: Causes, prevention, and practical intervention strategies. *International Journal of Emergency Mental Health, 7,* 101–114.

Miller, L. (2006a). Officer-involved shooting: Reaction patterns, response protocols, and psychological intervention strategies. *International Journal of Emergency Mental Health, 8,* 239–254.

Miller, L. (2006b, October). On the spot: Testifying in court for law enforcement officers. *FBI Law Enforcement Bulletin,* pp. 1–6.

Miller, L. (2006c). *Practical police psychology: Stress management and crisis intervention for law enforcement.* Springfield, IL: Charles C Thomas.

Miller, L. (2007a, August). The psychological fitness-for-duty evaluation. *FBI Law Enforcement Bulletin,* pp. 10–16.

Miller, L. (2007b). Police families: Stresses, syndromes, and solutions. *American Journal of Family Therapy, 35,* 21–40.

Miller, L. (2007c). Crisis intervention strategies for treating law enforcement and mental health professionals. In F. M. Dattilio & A. Freeman (Eds.), *Cognitive-behavioral strategies in crisis intervention* (3rd ed., pp. 93–121). New York: Guilford.

Miller, L. (2007d). Law enforcement traumatic stress: Clinical syndromes and intervention strategies. In L. Territo & J. D. Sewell (Eds.), *Stress management in law enforcement* (2nd ed., pp. 381–397). Durham, NC: Carolina Academic Press.

Miller, L. (2008a). You're it! Psychological survival tips for dealing with an excessive force investigation. *ILEETA Use of Force Journal, 8*(4), 18–22.

Miller, L. (2008b). Military psychology and police psychology: Mutual contributions to crisis intervention and stress management. *International Journal of Emergency Mental Health, 10,* 9–26.

Miller, L. (2008c). Stress and resilience in law enforcement training and practice. *International Journal of Emergency Mental Health, 10,* 109–124.

Miller, L. (2008d). *METTLE: Mental toughness training for law enforcement.* Flushing, NY: Looseleaf Law Publications.

Miller, L. (2009). Criminal investigator stress: Symptoms, syndromes, and practical coping strategies. *International Journal of Emergency Mental Health, 11,* 87–92.

Rostow, C. D., & Davis, R. D. (2002, September). Psychological fitness for duty evaluations in law enforcement. *The Police Chief,* pp. 58–66.

Rostow, C. D., & Davis, R. D. (2004). *A handbook for psychological fitness-for-duty evaluations in law enforcement.* New York: Haworth.

Russell, H. E., & Beigel, A. (1990). *Understanding human behavior for effective police work* (3rd ed.). New York: Basic Books.

Scrivner, E. M. (1999). Controlling police use of excessive force: The role of the police psychologist. In L. Territo & J. D. Sewell (Eds.), *Stress management in law enforcement* (pp. 383–391). Durham, NC: Carolina Academic Press.

Shev, E. E., & Howard, J. J. (1977). *Good cops, bad cops.* San Francisco: San Francisco Book Co.

Silva, M. N. (1991). The delivery of mental health services to law enforcement officers. In J. T. Reese, J. M. Horn, & C. Dunning (Eds.), *Critical incidents in policing* (pp. 335–341). Washington, DC: Federal Bureau of Investigation.

Solomon, R. M. (1988). Mental conditioning: The utilization of fear. In J. T. Reese & J. M. Horn (Eds.), *Police psychology: Operational assistance* (pp. 391-407). Washington, DC: Federal Bureau of Investigation.

Solomon, R. M. (1991). The dynamics of fear in critical incidents. In J. T. Reese, J. M. Horn, & C. Dunning (Eds.), *Critical incidents in policing* (pp. 347–358). Washington, DC: Federal Bureau of Investigation.

Stone, A. V. (1995). Law enforcement psychological fitness for duty: Clinical issues. In M. I. Kurke & E. M. Scrivner (Eds.), *Police psychology into the 21st century* (pp. 109–131). Hillsdale, NJ: Lawrence Erlbaum.

Stone, A. V. (2000). *Fitness for duty: Principles, methods, and legal issues.* Boca Raton, FL: CRC Press.

Taylor, S. E., Wood, J. V., & Lechtman, R. R. (1983). It could be worse: Selective evaluation as a response to victimization. *Journal of Social Issues, 39,* 19–40.

Vaughn, M. S., Cooper, T. W., & del Carmen, R. V. (2001) Assessing legal liabilities in law enforcement: Police chiefs' views. *Crime and Delinquency, 47,* 3–27.

Walker, S. (1997). Complaints against the police: A focus group study of citizen perceptions, goals, and expectations. *Criminal Justice Review, 22,* 207–226.

24 Critical Incidents

Suzanne Best

Alexis Artwohl

Ellen Kirschman

The term *critical incident* used in the context of emergency services has been defined in a number of ways since it first came into vogue in the early 1990s. Rather than insisting on a universally agreed upon meaning, law enforcement experts have actually stressed the importance of maintaining a flexible definition because of the wide variation in officer responses to duty-related events (Bohl, 1995; Federal Bureau of Investigation [FBI], 1996). Thus, while definitions vary, it is generally understood that line-of-duty events, which for officers are "outside the range of normal activity" (Paton & Violanti, 1996, p. 183) or involve serious threat or loss (Gentz, 1990), are considered critical incidents. For some experts, it is the officer's reaction rather than event characteristics themselves that makes an incident *critical* (Fay, 2000; Mitchell & Everly, 2001). This mirrors the American Psychiatric Association's criteria of an event eliciting an intense emotional reaction in the exposed individual in order for it to be considered "traumatic" in the *Diagnostic and Statistical Manual* (DSM-IV-TR, 2000). However, unlike the now controversial restrictions imposed by the DSM-IV's PTSD Criterion A2 (Kilpatrick, Resnick, & Acierno, 2009; Weathers & Keane, 2007), *critical* reactions to police incidents have been characterized in such vague, broad terms as "strong emotional reactions" (Mitchell, 1983), an overwhelming of coping mechanisms (Mitchell & Everly, 2001), or a "psychological crisis" (Faye, 2000). Regardless, certain police encounters are routinely categorized as critical incidents, or as incidents more likely to cause a critical response. These include such potentially traumatic events as line-of-duty deaths or serious injuries, shooting incidents, and child deaths or significant injuries (DSM-IV PTSD, Criterion A; Mitchell & Everly, 2001; Paton & Violanti, 1996). In addition, some psychologists identify stressful situations such as facing legal charges or the threat of dismissal, or experiencing intense media or public scrutiny as potential critical incidents (Faye, 2000; Gentz, 1990; Mitchell & Bray, 1990). This inclusion of both stressful and traumatic events under the heading of *critical incidents* has been criticized as an "overstatement" that leads to the excessive use and support of certain debriefing interventions (Stuhlmiller & Dunning, 2000).

CRITICAL INCIDENT ASSESSMENT

The National Center for Post-Traumatic-Stress Disorder (PTSD) lists 12 separate measures of trauma exposure, including one well-known instrument designed to assess exposure to traumatic events specific to combat (Combat Exposure Scale; Keane et al., 1989). While the type of traumatic exposure has been identified as a crucial aspect of PTSD diagnosis and symptom development (Kessler, 1995; Peterson, Prout, & Schwarz, 1991), not one of these instruments adequately measures the array of events encountered in the line of police duty. Even with the ever-burgeoning interest in the impact of traumatic events on law enforcement personnel, the most widely used measure of critical incident exposure remains the Police Stress Survey (PSS) published in 1981 (PSS; Spielberger, Westberry, & Greenfield, 1981). The PSS includes both organizational and "intrinsic" stressors. While many of these intrinsic stressors are PTSD Criterion A1 level events (e.g., "physical attack on one's person"), others are clearly not (e.g., "making critical decisions"). This necessitates a continued need for a clear measure of traumatic exposure relevant to policing. One such measure, in press at the time of this writing, is the Critical Incident History Questionnaire (CIHQ; Weiss et al., in press). This 34-item self-report measure was validated in a sample of 719 urban officers and includes severity ratings for each incident that were negatively correlated with exposure frequency, internally consistent, and stable.

FREQUENCY OF CRITICAL INCIDENT EXPOSURE

Given the lack of agreement on what constitutes a critical incident and the corresponding need for a clearly focused published measure, there are little data on the overall incidence of critical incident exposure in law enforcement professionals. In the study of the CIHQ's properties (Weiss et al., 2010), the rates of occurrence of each of the measure's 34 measures indicate that in terms of life-threatening incidents, being shot at occurred at least once for 38% and 10–20 times for nearly 2% of the officers surveyed, while over 20% reported having been present when a fellow officer was killed. Nearly two-thirds had encountered a badly beaten child at least once in their careers, and nearly 90% had encountered a sexually assaulted adult.

SEVERITY OF CRITICAL INCIDENT EXPOSURE

When examining officers' self-identified worst police experiences, two broad categories of critical incident types emerge: (1) active participation in a very violent incident that carried a high level of personal threat, and (2) confrontation with a very depressing or otherwise disturbing incident that did not involve a direct threat of personal death or injury. Interestingly, the retrospectively reported perceived severity of a critical incident was found to be more powerful than event type in predicting subsequent psychological disturbance (Carlier, Lamberts, & Gersons, 1997). Research using the PSS (Paton & Violanti, 1996; Spielberger et al., 1981), and the CIHQ indicate that the death of a fellow officer and killing someone in the line of duty are rated as the most stressful incidents encountered in police work (Spielberger et al., 1981; Weiss et al., 2010). In a study utilizing the same sample as the CIHQ research, officers were asked to select a single critical incident that they identified as "the most troublesome, disturbing or distressing." Of these, 1.2% were vehicular accidents; .6% were natural disasters; 23% were physical assaults; 2% were sexual assaults; 64% involved illness, injury or death; and 6% involved harassment or threats (Brunet et al., 2001).

IMMEDIATE CRITICAL INCIDENT REACTIONS

While the importance of event type has been highlighted in studies involving civilian populations (Breslau et al., 1998; Kessler et al., 1995), *peritraumatic dissociation* (dissociative reactions at the time of a traumatic event and immediately following) has been shown to be the most powerful predictor of subsequent PTSD development (Ozer et al., 2003). More extreme dissociative symptoms such as depersonalization, derealization, and disorientation seem to interfere with the processing of traumatic memories (Zoellner, Alvarez-Conrad, & Foa, 2002) and to disrupt physiological arousal functioning (Pole et al., 2005). In the field of police psychology, less intense dissociative symptoms such as altered sense of time, tunnel vision, and memory loss, generally referred to in terms of perceptual distortion or disturbance, are not necessarily considered to be maladaptive (Artwohl, 2002; Honig & Sultan, 2004).

ATTENTION, PERCEPTION, AND MEMORY

When human beings are forced to make quick decisions in response to sudden threats, their attention tends to become very narrowly and externally focused on the perceived threat. Because humans can only attend to a small portion of their environment at any given time, this is an adaptive mechanism that allows people to pay intense attention to cues that are relevant for survival while ignoring other cues. This alteration in attention and perception in sudden, dynamic situations is a normal and adaptive survival response causing memory gaps as nonrelevant information fails to be encoded. Such alterations in visual perception are commonly referred to as *tunnel vision*, but are more accurately a reflection of the well-studied phenomenon of selective attention (Lewinski, 2008). This selective attention process transforms broadly focused ambient (peripheral) vision to focal vision that narrowly focuses on threat cues, creating the tunnel-vision phenomenon.

Selective attention can take many other forms. For instance, in officer-involved shootings the most common form of selective attention is "inattentional deafness" by which officers commonly do not hear very loud sounds such as gunfire (Artwohl, 2002, Honig & Sultan, 2004; Klinger, 2001). Auditory exclusion likely occurs during this time because processing visual threat cues such as a suspect's hand motions is the attentional process most essential for survival, causing the brain to ignore or suppress any conscious attention to auditory cues (Shomstein & Yantis, 2004). Visual and auditory selective attention explains why officers involved in shootings often do not know how many rounds they fired or what other officers were doing at the scene.

Differences in decision-making strategies have also been identified as relevant to attention and memory during critical incidents (Epstein, 1994; Klein, 1998 Sharps, 2010). *Rational* decision making is often characterized as slow, logical, sequential, conscious, analytical, effortful, fact based, reflective, oriented toward delayed action, and based on rules. This powerful analytical tool enables humans to build skyscrapers, send people to the moon, and be less likely to jump to conclusions, and helps detectives solve complex investigative cases. However, rational decision making has a potentially fatal flaw in the context of critical incidents in that officers may be killed or injured if they face a situation that requires a rapid response. Therefore, humans have another method of decision making, known as *intuitive,* that can take place much faster than rational thought. When faced with a sudden, potentially threatening event, the brain switches to this intuitive mode of processing, which is characterized by very fast, emotionally based, effortless, automatic, subconscious thought, which is associative rather than sequential, less open to change, less reflective and introspective, more action oriented, and more influenced by immediate contextual cues. The strategy involved in the intuitive mode of processing is often referred to as *gut instinct, sixth sense,* and other terms that highlight the fact that the decision making is experienced at a subconscious level (i.e., below the level of conscious awareness). Klein (1998) found that first responders such as firefighters used this type of decision making, which he termed *recognition primed decision making* and that due to its rapid, subconscious nature they had difficulty articulating exactly why they chose a certain response. Artwohl (2002) found the same phenomenon with 157 police officers involved in shootings: 74% reported that they gave little or no conscious thought to what they did. This subconscious decision making can further impair memory for details of the event.

Research has established that memory is highly prone toward a variety of errors even under the relatively low stress of daily life (Schacter, 2001). Higher stress levels can have an effect on memory but the interaction of stress and memory is complex (Sapolsky, 2004). According to Sapolsky, "Recent research shows just how short-term stressors of mild to moderate severity enhance cognition and memory, whereas major or prolonged stressors disrupt them" (p. 28). Therefore, while mild to moderate stressors may temporarily enhance memory, humans in extreme stress situations will normally experience an increase memory gaps, time distortion, false memories, and memories that are out of order and change over time (British Psychological Society Research Board, 2008; Fisher & Geiselman, 1992). This can even include situations where officers discharge their weapons at the scene of a critical incident yet have no memory of doing so (Artwohl, 2003). For police psychologists, administrators, and investigators, it is important to understand that these memory errors are normal and are not necessarily an indication of incompetence, lying, or the inability to cope with extreme stressors.

IMMEDIATE EMOTIONAL REACTIONS

While dissociative reactions have been positively related to the degree of threat posed to an officer, emotional reactions have not (McCaslin et al., 2006). Perceptual and memory distortions at the time of a critical incident may, however, be evoked or enhanced by emotional reactions (Honig & Sultan, 2004; Koopman, Classen, & Spiegel, 1994). Emotional reactions at the time of a critical incident are particularly salient in a culture that values and fosters a sense of invulnerability (Paton & Violanti, 1996) and stigmatizes the experience and particularly the expression of intense emotions. In fact, the ability to emotionally distance oneself from the experiences of death and danger is considered to be an essential skill of policing (Henry, 1995). However, when asked to select the most distressing incident of their careers, police officers have reported experiencing fear, helplessness, and/or horror at rates similar to their traumatized civilian counterparts, though the most frequently endorsed items in both groups were anger/frustration, sadness/grief, and helplessness. Possibly the most startling finding is that female officers but not males experienced significantly less distress at the time of a traumatic incident than their same-sex civilian comparison group (Brunet et al., 2001).

The importance of emotional control is arguably most salient in situations of personal life threat and use of lethal force. In spite of the time and resources invested in firearms training, shooting incidents are generally experienced as sudden and unexpected events (Paton & Violanti, 1996). Consequently, a sense of helplessness is not uncommon (Brunet et al., 2001; Honig & Sultan, 2004), though complete helplessness, that is, the perception that "the suspect definitely had the upper hand," is rare (Honig & Sultan, 2004, p. 5). It should be noted that not all emotional reactions for officers involved in shootings are negative. In fact, according to our collective clinical observations, many if not the majority of officers react to their first shooting incident with a profound sense of relief and bolstered confidence that their substantial training "kicked in" when put to the test. Klinger (2001) found that in 33 out of 113 shootings, officers reported the feeling of elation. This positive emotional response was related to joy over having survived a life-threatening event and having passed the ultimate test that demonstrated their competence to themselves and others.

SHORT-TERM POSTINCIDENT REACTIONS

In the general population, trauma victims are typically shown to experience a postevent surge of psychological reactions followed by a gradual reduction of symptoms over time (Galea et al., 2002). In the majority of cases, this reduction occurs within the first month. In a smaller portion of cases however, symptomatic reactions may initially fluctuate, be delayed, or develop into a chronic course of posttraumatic stress disorder (PTSD) (Bonano, 2004). In regard to post-incident reactions, the primary focus in police psychology has been on officer-involved shootings. Within this context, three reaction "typologies" have been proposed (Miller, 2006b). The first, defined as a *transitory period of post-incident psychological distress,* mirrors the more typical reaction noted above and is characterized by a rather rapid amelioration of symptoms that do not at any time interfere with the officer's daily functioning. The second, *intermediate response*, involves fluctuating symptoms that persist over the initial weeks and potential months, while a *severe psychological disability* significantly impairs an officer's functioning.

That many if not most officers will experience some acute symptoms in the first few days postincident has been well documented (Artwohl & Christensen, 1997; Klinger, 2001; Solomon & Horn, 1986). Klinger (2001) asked officers to list the symptoms they experienced in the first 24 hours after being in an officer-involved shooting and found physical reactions such as fatigue (39%), headache (6%), and loss of appetite (16%); emotional responses such as elation (26%), sadness (18%), anxiety (37%), and numbness (18%); and cognitive symptoms such as recurrent thoughts (82%), guilt (10%), and fear of legal and administrative problems (31%). When officers were asked about their experience of specific acute stress symptoms within the first 3–5 days post-incident, nearly half reported reexperiencing symptoms including intrusive images and nightmares. While the majority of these were mild in nature, 15–21% reported severe levels of intrusions (Honig & Sultan, 2004). Other commonly noted acute responses include sleep disturbance, anger, increased startle response, and hypervigilence (Honig & Sultan, 2004; Miller, 2006; Solomon & Horn, 1986).

Again in the police population, perceptions of control and vulnerability are paramount and considered key predictors of symptom development and persistence (Honig & Sultan, 2004; McCaslin et al., 2006; Miller, 2006). In addition, in shooting incidents in which a suspect or bystander is killed, the degree of conflict experienced by the officer over having taken a life has been shown to be associated with the severity of the reaction (Miller, 1998, 2006b). It is thus interesting to note that Honig and Sultan (2004) reported "second guessing" as the most common reaction 3–5 days post-incident as well as the second most utilized coping mechanism.

FAMILY REACTIONS

Behind every law enforcement officer who experiences a shooting or other critical incident is a nearly invisible family whose lives can be deeply affected by the trauma but for whom few services exist. This is a remarkable oversight considering ample evidence that work-related stress, acute and chronic, affects the family at the same time, and that family support plays a crucial role in mitigating the effects of such stress on the officer. How family members, parents, siblings, spouses, children, and significant others react to a critical incident depends on a wide variety of factors: the nature of the incident, whether the officer was injured, community reaction, organizational response, and media reaction as well as the strength of preincident family relationships and individual coping skills. The range of family reactions can vary from mild to a more disruptive condition known as *vicarious or secondary trauma* that mimics acute stress or PTSD (Artwohl & Christensen, 1997; Batten et al., 2009; Kirschman, 2004, 2007; Regehr, 2005).

PHYSICAL SAFETY

The family's first concern is for the physical safety of the officer. Their primary need is to communicate with their officer face to face or, when that is not possible, by telephone. When accurate information is not available, as often happens in a prolonged event or a major catastrophe, this leads to increased fear, frustration, anger, and, in some cases, panic. Depending on the circumstances, families may even have reason to fear for their own safety, as defendants and their cohorts have been known to make threats against an arresting officer's family. In rural communities, the officer's family and the defendant's family may know each other and their children may even attend the same school.

PSYCHOLOGICAL SAFETY

Once concern for the officer and family's physical well-being is alleviated, the family may then have concerns about how the incident will affect the officer emotionally. Their concerns may be influenced by intimate and unique knowledge of the officer's pre-incident stability and postincident behavior. In common parlance, the family worries about changes in the officer's personality, attitude, and ability to work and interact with his or her loved ones.

The two predominant emotions experienced by family members are anger and fear—anger that family life has been disrupted by this event and fear that things will never return to normal. When the officer's physical safety is not an issue, anxiety and fear can quickly build around legal consequences of the incident including the possibility of an internal affairs investigation, criminal charges, a civil suit, job loss, and other employment actions affecting the officer's job and the family's financial security. In instances of actual or perceived administrative betrayal, family members can react with rage and/or anxiety. The type of reactions experienced by the family is as much determined by preincident coping skills as it is by circumstances in the environment, most prominently the manner in which the employing agency responds to the officer and his or her family.

Public Scrutiny

One of the givens of being a law enforcement family is public scrutiny. If the incident receives widespread media attention, particularly negative attention, the entire family loses its privacy. This can be especially damaging to children (see "Children's Reactions," below). Seeing your loved one vilified in the news or having the facts of the incident inaccurately reported creates pain and anger for the family. Intrusive questions or comments from friends, neighbors, and even strangers can provoke anger and isolation as the family retreats from ordinary social activities. Oftentimes, the family, not the officer, bears the burden of fielding these questions, and family members may themselves become the source of the negative comments.

Impact on Family Relationships

An officer who has experienced a significant critical incident is often very self-involved or symptomatic, even in the absence of a diagnosable condition. As a result, the spouse/significant other may bear more than his or her usual share of household and child-rearing tasks. Family members might feel shut out, ignored, and devalued because their loved one won't talk about the event or only wants to talk about it with other officers (Artwohl & Christensen, 1997). This can lead to depression, isolation, and exhaustion. In some circumstances, family members feel angry and neglected when all the attention—positive and negative—is focused on the law enforcement professional, and the family's concerns or contributions are not acknowledged.

A significant critical incident calls attention to the dangers of the job. Because some officers choose not to share these dangers with their families, the incident may come as a surprise to some and a validation of their unspoken fears to others. Difficulty arises when there is conflict among family members, such as when frightened parents or spouses demand that the officer find a less dangerous job. In some cases, especially if the incident involved children, family members may become overprotective or restrictive, placing overly rigid limits on the family's normal social activities. This can be quite difficult for children.

Partner Competence

Family members are not trained mental health professionals, nor are they generally properly prepared for dealing with someone who may be showing symptoms of acute stress or PTSD. If they are also isolated and without significant support systems, they are further at risk for having unrealistic expectations of themselves and their officer–family member. They can feel confused, overwhelmed, and helpless. They may feel responsible for their loved one's situation. Such reactions may range from irrational guilt over having harsh words prior to the incident to a loss of self-worth because whatever they do or say has no effect on their loved one's emotional condition. Without information about critical incident stress, family members may personalize the officer's behavior. For example, spouses may feel rejected because their mate is withdrawn, is depressed, and has no interest in sex (Armstrong, Best, & Domenici, 2006; Cukor et al., 2009; Kirschman, 2007).

Children's Reactions

Children are like litmus paper: they soak up tensions in their environment and are prone to be emotionally upset in proportion to their parents' level of upset. Young children may be especially reactive because they don't have the language needed to put their feelings into words. Older children and teens are vulnerable to the social whims of their peers. Following a critical incident, they may resent the unwanted attention they get because of something their parent did.

Younger children are mostly concerned with separation and safety. They need reassurance that they will be looked after. Reassurance comes with a return to normal routines and familiar surroundings. They may demonstrate their concerns by separation anxiety, school phobias, whining or clinging behavior, and bedtime problems such as refusing to go to sleep or to sleep in their own beds, or nightmares. They may regress to an earlier level of behavior, demanding to be fed or dressed when they were previously able to do that for themselves. Regressive reactions may also include thumb sucking, bedwetting, and temper tantrums. Because small children have no concrete understanding of death and insufficient language to express their emotions, they may engage in repetitive play in an attempt to master their fears or they may repeatedly ask the same questions (Armstrong et al., 2006).

Older children are prone to act out their fears and anxieties. They may become socially withdrawn and silent, concerned that the fears they have following the incident are childish. They may be moody and get in fights at school. Their concentration may suffer along with their grades. Like younger children, teens can develop school phobias based on separation anxiety. Some teens may be inclined to numb their feelings with alcohol or marijuana. Others may assume an overly adult role and try to fix things for their parents.

Children of all ages may experience mood swings in the wake of a critical incident or manifest physical ailments that have no apparent medical cause. Some can assume irrational guilt for their parents' troubles. If only they had behaved better, Mother or Father would not have been in a shooting. Following such incidents, all children need to have their TV viewing, news programs in particular, monitored by an adult. The reactions most in need of attention are aggressive behavior, hypervigilance, serious acting out, radical mood changes, listlessness, and major social withdrawal.

ADDRESSING OFFICER-INVOLVED SHOOTINGS

The Police Psychological Services Section of the International Association of Chiefs of Police (PSS/IACP) has published guidelines on a variety of topics to assist law enforcement agencies and mental health professionals in achieving best practices. These guidelines are periodically updated to reflect current research and can be viewed on the IACP website. The *Officer-Involved Shooting Guidelines*, which are highlighted below, include recommendations targeted toward providing individual officers with optimum aid and support. Although some of these recommendations may be specific to shootings, many will apply to any significant critical incident an officer may encounter.

AGENCY RESPONSE

It is widely accepted that officers involved in shootings (OIS) or other significant critical incidents require immediate support. From an administrative perspective, this includes assisting the officer in stepping away from the scene to a private location insulated from the media and the public, assistance in contacting family members, access to peer support and other supportive individuals, personal statements of concern and support from command staff, and guidance about what to expect during the investigative process.

ON-SCENE RESPONSE

As discussed earlier, an officer's peritraumatic or immediate reactions to a critical incident are powerful predictors of the officer's long-term psychological response. The first step toward lowering arousal is to ensure the officer's safety and provide reassurance that the incident is over. Because an officer's weapon is immediately taken into evidence when it is discharged, it is essential that it be replaced without delay. This not only helps the officer to feel less vulnerable, but also conveys "support, confidence, and trust" (Guideline 3.3; IACP PSS OIS Guidelines, 2010) at a time when it is most needed. While it may be essential for investigatory personnel to remain at the scene for hours, involved officers should ideally be transported away from the scene as soon as is practically possible. During the time that an officer remains on scene, he or she should be gently guided away from any suspects or potentially disturbing images and be shielded from distraught victims, curious onlookers, and media.

As is recommended in the OIS Guidelines, officers should be assisted as soon as possible in contacting their families. Not only will this ensure that family members do not first hear of the incident through media or neighbors, but also speaking with a loved one may provide the officer with added support and reassurance. If the officer is injured or unable to make a call, a previously designated coworker should do so and family members should be offered transportation to the hospital where the officer may be receiving care.

Legal Concerns

Police officers involved in on-duty shootings face an unusual situation; they are a rare group of employees who, simply by virtue of performing their job function, will now become de facto suspects in a felony crime. *De facto suspect* means they are not criminal suspects in that they have not been arrested on probable cause of having committed any crimes. However, in most jurisdictions, officers are automatically subjected to a criminal investigation that could result in conviction and perhaps imprisonment as well as an administrative investigation that could result in discipline and/or termination. While these investigations are done to enhance the accountability and transparency of police use of force, it puts officers in a unique situation that few other employees or citizens will face. Other use-of-force incidents might also trigger the investigative process. Officers and agencies also face the prospect of civil litigation based on claims that officers used unjustified or excessive force. Thus, officers are simultaneously de facto suspects, victims of a violent crime, and witnesses during an investigation. This unique circumstance places these officers in legal jeopardy and contributes to the stress of the aftermath (Americans for Effective Law Enforcement, 2008).

Because of this, care must be taken to avoid needlessly jeopardizing the officers' legal situation. During of the potentially confusing aftermath of officer-involved shootings, officers may wish to consult legal advisors of their choice, such as union representatives and attorneys, for education. The officers and all on-scene responders need to be aware of who has legally privileged status with regard to communication from involved officers so that statements made in the context of garnering emotional support or legal counsel are afforded legally privileged confidentiality. This education can be done within the context of training prior to incidents and by consulting legal advisors during the aftermath. Trainings should also include basic information regarding post-incident administrative and investigative procedures, and this information should be reviewed by a legal representative, supervisor, or peer support member within the initial hours after a shooting.

Investigations should be conducted in a manner that does not exacerbate stress during the post-incident aftermath. Although the officers involved in shootings are de facto suspects, they are not *criminal* suspects and should not be treated as such. Investigators should be trained in the latest research on the complex physics and biomechanics of officer-involved shootings, such as eyewitness perception and memory, and use interview methods specifically designed to facilitate fuller and more accurate accountings from cooperative witnesses (Artwohl, 2002; Fisher & Geiselman, 1992; Honig & Lewinski, 2008; Pinizotto et al., 2007). These practices will help ensure the accuracy and thoroughness of the investigation and mitigate further needless stress for officers and their families during the investigative process.

Peer Support

Peer support in the aftermath of critical incidents is helpful to involved personnel, especially when it is provided by those who have been through a similar experience (Artwohl & Christensen, 1997; Clark & Haley, 2007; IACP PSS Peer Support Guidelines; Miller, 2006a, c). The formation, training, and sponsorship of peer support teams by agencies are a wise investment. Like all interventions, peer support is most effective when provided by experienced and well- trained individuals. It is advisable that peer support teams have close working relationships with mental health professionals who are experienced with critical incident stress interventions and law enforcement culture and who can provide supervision, consultation, and work with peer supporters as a team to facilitate post-shooting interventions. The *Peer Support Guidelines* published by the IACP Psychological Services Section were written to assist agencies, officers, and mental health professionals in developing, training, and mobilizing peer support teams.

In addition to peer support teams, agency personnel should receive regular training and written information on common physical and psychological reactions to critical incidents. Training should include the appropriate ways to respond to and support peers who have been exposed to a critical incident as well as local resources for psychological services.

ADMINISTRATIVE LEAVE

In the wake of officer-involved shootings and other use-of-force situations, it has become standard practice in most agencies for involved personnel to be provided with administrative leave so they can have time to decompress and marshal their coping skills before returning to work. The IACP/PSS OIS Guidelines recommend a minimum of 3 days leave, although more may be advisable depending on the circumstances and the status of the officer. If officers are on extended administrative leave due to physical and/or psychological injury or other circumstances, they should be assisted during the return-to-work process with training and psychological counseling as needed.

PUBLIC EDUCATION

Critical incidents in law enforcement, especially officer-involved shootings, may attract negative media and community reactions that can cause distress to involved personnel and their families. Agencies are well advised to develop ongoing community education and outreach programs that foster understanding and support for police operations as well as timely debriefings to the media and the community to allay concerns regarding specific incidents (Pinizotto et al., 2007). Officers and their families should be prepared to cope with negative publicity that could include television, newspapers, and the Internet.

AGENCY DEBRIEFINGS

In addition to educating the public, it is advisable for agencies to educate personnel within their agency when a stressful, high-profile event has occurred involving its officers. Lack of knowledge about the details of the event can fuel rumors and does nothing to allay the anxiety of the personnel who were not directly impacted but may still have concerns. Rumors that begin to circulate may also be harmful to the involved personnel when inaccuracies and speculations about their performance come to their attention (Artwohl & Christensen, 1997). It is important to note that neither agency nor tactical/operational debriefings in first responder settings should take the form of a psychological intervention. Rather, such debriefings are forums in which information is shared in order to assist agency personnel in developing a more coherent narrative of the incident from which they can learn and better support affected officers.

ON-SCENE PSYCHOLOGICAL INTERVENTIONS

While some agencies support a contracted or in-house psychologist or clergy member to provide on-scene services, others may rely on trained peer support teams or simply well-educated fellow officers and supervisors to address an involved officer's immediate needs. A variety of models and strategies can be used to provide mental health support and services to officers (Finn & Tomz,

1997). Substantial research supports the indication of two primary targets for on-scene interventions: physiological arousal (Ozer et al., 2003; Pitman et al., 2004) and emotional distress (Brunet et al., 2001).

A quick visual assessment of the involved officer may provide needed information concerning their level of physiological arousal. While states of complete panic are rare (Miller, 2006c), rapid breathing, trembling, and pronounced sweating may be observed. Leading the officer through a slow breathing exercise can help reduce these immediate symptoms. In addition, because police officers are highly sensitive to the sense or appearance of being "out of control," it is important to normalize these reactions in a calm and reassuring tone. If an officer appears confused, dazed, or disoriented, grounding techniques should be employed. These may include saying the officer's name, requesting eye contact, and providing repeated reassurance that the incident is indeed over and the officer is safe. Physical grounding techniques may also be helpful such as having the officer plant his or her feet firmly on the ground or providing something of substance to hold. In some cases, physical contact such as a hand on the shoulder can be used to ground a disoriented officer, but this should only be done with extreme caution as any contact may be perceived as threatening rather than comforting.

Expressions of emotional distress at the scene of a shooting or other significant critical incident can be quite varied. While anger is an understandable reaction in life-threatening situations, extreme rage not only serves to increase autonomic arousal but also may be misinterpreted by supervisors and any members of the public or the media who are at the scene. Again, normalization and slow breathing can assist the officer in managing his or her reaction. Crying is also not uncommon, but may cause the officer to feel shame or to perceive themselves as "weak," and so this too should be normalized and reassurances provided. Negative self-statements, particularly those that include irrational generalizations (e.g., "I can't do this job," or "I'm such an idiot") or begin with "I should have..." are to be gently challenged and discouraged. Second guessing of self and others is a common emotional response after critical incidents and has been observed in officers involved in shootings (Artwohl & Christensen, 1997; Honig & Sultan, 2004; Miller, 2006a, b). This form of hindsight bias reflects a highly personal emotional reaction, not objective facts about the event, and should not be interpreted as an indication that any of the incident participants have done something wrong. It is helpful in these situations to know as much as possible about the details of the incident prior to arriving on scene so that inaccurate or unfounded statements can be challenged. Above all, on-scene emotional retellings of the incident should not be encouraged as this may exacerbate peritraumatic reactions with potentially harmful effects (Brymer et al., 2006; Gist et al., 1997).

POSTINCIDENT INTERVENTIONS

Much has been written about postincident interventions. We will focus here on early interventions provided to police officers during the first few weeks of experiencing a critical incident. For purposes of the general discussion in this chapter, the use of terms such as *Critical Incident Stress Management* (CISM) or *Critical Incident Stress Debriefing* (CISD) will be avoided as they represent specific models of postincident intervention.

Researchers in this area agree that continued scientific investigation is necessary to determine the most effective approaches to postincident interventions (Creamer, 2006; Dunning, 2004; Mitchell & Everly, 1993; Parker et al., 2006; Pender & Prichard, 2008; Raphael & Wilson, 2000; Robinson, 2008; Sanders, 2008). While some controversy remains, there is wide agreement that psychological assistance provided during the acute phase of a potentially distressing critical incident can be valuable. As with any medical or psychological intervention, quality is the key. Poorly administered or inappropriate treatment may be not only ineffective but also iatrogenic. This potential for harm does not mean that postincident interventions are to be avoided, but that techniques and intervention models should be approached with an eye toward proven efficacy in the specific population to whom they will be applied.

Although there are many useful components within a variety of postintervention models, rigid adherence to any protocol is ill advised. Interventions should be tailored to the particular incident, available personnel and resources, and the specific needs of involved individuals or groups. Certain critical incidents such as line-of-duty deaths may require special considerations and procedures. Individuals may also have special concerns (e.g., religious concerns) that are best addressed through pastoral counseling or unusually distressed family members who may benefit from individual and/or family interventions. It is also important to recognize that critical incidents may trigger underlying clinical pathology in vulnerable individuals for whom clinical treatment, including psychotherapy and medication, may be part of the postintervention process.

One of the unresolved controversies surrounding early postincident interventions is whether they are effective in preventing the development of PTSD in vulnerable individuals. Even if postincident interventions do not prevent posttraumatic stress in vulnerable individuals, these interventions for law enforcement can be helpful for the following reasons (Artwohl & Christensen, 1997; Bohl, 1995; Clark & Haley, 2007; Miller, 2006a, b, c):

- Because of the attentional and perceptual demands of performing under sudden, dynamic, life-threatening circumstances, it is normal for individuals involved in critical incidents to have memory gaps, false memories, memories that are out of order, and memories that change over time (Artwohl, 2002; Artwohl & Christensen, 1997; Honig & Sultan, 2004. Klinger, 2001). Officers may be unaware that these reactions are normal and may therefore be troubled by them. It is often helpful for officers to be educated about the normalcy of these occurrences so they can cope better with concerns about their own performance and/ or the performance of other officers who may have been at the same event. In the case of events that trigger the investigatory process, this education can help them cope better with the investigation process, where they will be subjected to detailed questioning about the incident. Education concerning normal memory functioning should therefore be an essential component of any individual or group debriefing.
- Group debriefings can provide involved personnel with additional details that provide a more complete and accurate picture of the incident. This will facilitate understanding of the event and closure about memory gaps and distortions.
- Group debriefings mobilize peer support, enhancing a supportive social milieu that has been shown to help individuals in stressful situations.
- Postincident interventions are a demonstration by the agency and peers that they have concern for the officers and want to help them.
- Although most officers are emotionally resilient and can expect normal recovery, a few susceptible individuals will go on to develop PTSD and/or other related mental health problems with or without postincident interventions. It's important that these officers be educated about what to expect, be able to recognize when longer term problems are developing, and know where and how they can seek further help if needed.
- Debriefings provide an opportunity to discuss the impact of the event on significant others. Helping officers understand how loved ones are affected and how they can be supported after an incident can help to mitigate any potentially negative effects on these relationships.
- Even for the majority of officers who will progress resiliently with postincident recovery, there are other normal but negative acute emotional reactions that can result from critical incidents such as confusion, situational anxiety, and feelings of isolation and being misunderstood. For officers involved in use-of-force incidents, the aftermath can be particularly stressful as they are subjected to investigations and potentially negative reactions from the media and community. Again, postincident education in a group or individual setting can assist officers in the acute phase of adjustment.

ASSUMPTION OF RESILIENCE AND NORMAL RECOVERY

As noted earlier, the vast majority of trauma survivors do not go on to develop PTSD. Police officers have been shown to be particularly resilient with reported PTSD rates of only 7–10% (Clark & Haley, 2007; Marmar et al., 1999), although many may have acute reactions in the mild to moderate range (Honig & Sultan, 2004). As Creamer (2006) points out, "A fundamental starting point in the immediate aftermath of trauma is to expect normal recovery" (p. 135). Any postincident interventions that lead participants to expect overwhelmingly negative short-term or long-term responses are not appropriate and may in fact be deleterious.

PROVIDERS AND CONFIDENTIALITY

There may be a wide range of providers involved in the postincident intervention process, including licensed mental health providers, peer supporters, and members of the clergy. Each type of provider should be well trained in evidence-based postincident interventions appropriate to their discipline. Another area of agreement among experts is that providers of postincident interventions should be culturally competent. All individuals providing services to law enforcement should familiarize themselves with the language, job demands, and subculture of police service.

Many groups have their own cultural identity, and those who are members of that group will usually perceive each other as "insiders." They may view those who are not members of the group as "outsiders" and view them with some degree of suspicion. This is often the case with police officers. While police officers who are peer supporters will already be perceived as insiders and thus more readily accepted by the officers, clinicians attempting to provide services may be viewed as outsiders and viewed with suspicion. Until they have demonstrated cultural competence and gained the trust and acceptance of the officers, their ability to be effective may be compromised.

Because critical incidents in law enforcement may involve events such as officer-involved shootings that place the officers in legal jeopardy, special care should be taken to scrupulously define contexts and relationships that provide legally privileged confidentiality, and the exact extent and limits of confidentiality of any postincident intervention should be explicitly explained to the officers (Artwohl & Christensen, 1997; Miller, 2006c). This should be done verbally and in writing. For instance, officers, like most consumers of psychological services, may be unaware that by filing a disability claim, they are granting access to their medical records, including postincident interventions conducted by mental health professionals (Kirschman, 2007). Providers of mental health services to officers under these circumstances should always be mindful of the legal risks their clients face and how these risks interface with the limits of confidentiality.

INTERVENTION TYPES AND PURPOSES

Besides onscene psychological first aid, the two major types of postincident psychological intervention typically offered are individual debriefings with a mental health professional and group debriefings. The purpose of each of these interventions includes education about common trauma reactions including memory errors and gaps, review of internal and external coping mechanisms, mobilizing social support for the officers and their families, stigma reduction, reviewing facts about the particular incident, processing feelings about the particular incident, and providing information regarding where and how to seek out further assistance if needed. There is no conclusive evidence that either individual or group debriefing is superior for all individuals. Each has its advantages, and it is advisable to offer both when time and resources permit.

Individual Debriefings

Individual debriefings should be conducted by licensed mental health professionals with expertise in trauma, postincident interventions, and knowledge of law enforcement culture. These debriefings should be confidential (with the usual exceptions that would apply to any consumer of mental health services) and no report should be provided to the officer's agency or supervisors. In order to avoid confusion, it should be clearly stressed to agency commanders and involved human resources personnel that postincident interventions are not evaluative in nature and should not be utilized to determine an officer's fitness for duty. It is the position of the IACP/PSS that merely being involved in a shooting does not render an officer unfit for duty and therefore does not necessitate a fitness-for-duty exam prior to returning to work. However, if a fitness-for-duty exam should be required, it should be conducted by a different mental health professional than the one who provided the debriefing or any other counseling services to the officer.

There is some controversy over whether or not officers involved in shootings or other major critical incidents should be mandated to attend a postshooting debriefing. It is the position of the IACP/PSS that because many officers would choose not to attend if given a choice, they should be required to attend at least one session so they may receive basic education about trauma reactions, coping resources, and where to get further help if needed. Although officers can be ordered to attend they should never be ordered by their department or anyone providing the debriefings to discuss any details of the event or their own reactions. Such discussion should be strictly voluntary on the part of the officers. In a study conducted by Honig and Sultan (2004) with the Los Angeles County Sheriff's Department, 60% of almost 1,000 officers involved in critical incidents (90% were officer-involved shootings) said they would not have attended an individual debriefing had they not been ordered, yet 100% found it helpful. This finding may not, however, generalize to all jurisdictions. In other situations where officers were referred to mental health professionals with whom they did not feel comfortable and whom they did not trust, negative outcomes resulted (Klinger, 2001).

Individual sessions with trusted mental health professionals offer the advantage of a private, legally privileged setting where officers can safely discuss concerns that they may not feel comfortable discussing in front of other individuals, including other officers who were at the same incident. For the small number of significantly traumatized individuals, individual sessions also offer a safe venue where they can confront the event at their own pace without being exposed to the stories and reactions of others.

Family members also can benefit from debriefings. This may include totally separate individual debriefings, joint sessions, or both, according to the discretion of the officer and the mental health provider. Regardless of the format, some attempt should be made to see that family members receive basic education and access to resources as needed.

Group Debriefings

Group debriefings are typically conducted by a team composed of mental health professionals and peers trained in postintervention strategies. It is the position of the IACP/PSS that attendance at group debriefings be voluntary rather than mandatory. Group experiences of any sort are not for everyone, and there may be particular group compositions with which individuals may not feel comfortable. If officers are ordered to attend such a session, it should be made clear that active participation is voluntary. These sessions should also be confidential and no report should be provided to the agency. Confidentiality may not be legally privileged; this varies from state to state. Some states such as Oregon and Washington have passed laws providing some degree of legal privilege to sanctioned peer support groups, so knowledge of state laws and local policies is important. Regardless of whatever legal privilege is afforded to group sessions, it is likely that discussions in any group setting have a greater risk of breach of confidentiality than an individual setting with a professional who is legally and ethically bound by confidentiality mandates. This is especially a concern when officers have been involved in an event that may put them in legal jeopardy such as an officer-involved shooting (Artwohl & Christensen, 1997; Miller, 2006a, c). Each officer will have to decide based on his or her individual circumstances and level of comfort with group attendance and/or participation.

Group debriefings have the advantage of mobilizing peer support and providing the opportunity to discuss the event with others who have been through similar experiences. It can enhance unit cohesion and morale through discussion and resolution of a shared experience and clarification of the roles that each individual played in the event. It is also an opportunity to hear what the other participants in the event experienced, thus providing all involved officers with richer and more accurate details about the event.

Participants in the group are usually limited to personnel directly involved in the incident. While this obviously includes the involved officers, the group may choose to invite other emergency services personnel (such as dispatchers) who played a role in the event. This should be at the discretion of each group and can be influenced by a variety of factors.

TIMING OF DEBRIEFINGS

While on-scene first aid is obviously offered immediately after the event, debriefings are more typically done sometime during the first week, after the officers have had an opportunity to decompress and have one or more sleep cycles. The exact timing of both individual and group debriefings should be up to the officers and the providers of the debriefings based on event, individual, and group circumstances (Artwohl & Christensen, 1997; Bohl, 1995, Miller, 2006a, c).

FOLLOW-UP INTERVENTIONS

Because of the variable course of postincident reactions, it is important that follow-up services be available. For officers exhibiting more significant acute reactions, these services may include a more immediate follow-up session and provision of or referral to ongoing treatment. As delayed reactions are not uncommon, the IACP/PSS OIS Guidelines recommend that a follow-up contact, whether in person or by phone or e-mail, be made within the first 4 months post-incident. The needs of family members should be considered as well when making follow-up interventions. Finally, the potential for anniversary reactions (a resurgence in traumatic stress symptoms that occurs around the anniversary of a traumatic incident; American Psychiatric Association, 2000) deems it important to contact officers just prior to the first-year anniversary of a significant critical incident.

REFERENCES

Americans for Effective Law Enforcement. (2008). Administrative investigations of police shootings and other critical incidents: Officer statements and use of force reports part one: The prologue. *AELE Monthly Law Journal, 201*(6), 201–211.

Americans for Effective Law Enforcement. (2008). Administrative investigations of police shootings and other critical incidents: Officer statements and use of force reports part two: The basics. *AELE Monthly Law Journal, 201*(8), 201–216.

American Psychiatric Association. (2000). *Diagnostic and statistical manual of mental disorders* (4th ed., text revision). Washington, DC: Author.

Armstrong, K., Best, S., & Domenici, P. (2006). *Courage after fire: Coping strategies for troops returning from Iraq and Afghanistan and their families.* Berkeley, CA: Ulysses Press.

Artwohl, A. (2002). Perceptual and memory distortions in officer-involved shootings. *FBI Law Enforcement Bulletin, 71*(10), 18–24.

Artwohl, A. (2003). No recall of weapons discharge. *Law Enforcement Executive Forum, 3*(2), 41–49.

Artwohl, A., & Christensen, L. (1997). *Deadly force encounters: What cops need to know to mentally and physically prepare for and survive a gunfight.* Boulder, CO: Paladin Press.

Batten, S., Drapalski, A., Decker, M., DeViva, J., Morris, L., Mann, M., et al. (2009). Veteran interest in family involvement in PTSD treatment. *Psychological Services, 6*(3), 184.

Bohl, N. (1995). Professionally administered critical incident debriefings for police officers. In M. Kurke (Ed.), *Police psychology into the 21st century* (pp. 169–188). Washington, DC: American Psychological Association.

Bonano, G. A. (2004). Loss, trauma, and human resilience: Have we underestimated the human capacity to thrive after extremely adverse events? *American Psychologist, 59*, 20–28.

Breslau, N., Kessler, R. C., Chilcoat, H. D., Schultz, L. R., Davis, G. C., & Andreski, P. (1998). Trauma and posttraumatic stress disorder in the community: The Detroit area survey of trauma. *Archives of General Psychiatry, 55*, 626–632.

Brewin, C. R., Andrews, B., Rose, S., & Kirk, M. (1999). Acute stress disorder and posttraumatic stress disorder in victims of violent crime. *The American Journal of Psychiatry, 156*(3), 360–366.

British Psychological Society Research Board. (2008). *Guidelines on memory and the law: Recommendations from the scientific study of human memory.* Retrieved August 10, 2010, from http://www.psychiatry.ox.ac.uk/epct/emily_holmes/articles/bpsmemorylaw

Brunet, A., Weiss, D. S., Metzler, T. J., Best, S. R., Neylan, T. C., Rogers, C., et al. (2001). The Peritraumatic Distress Inventory: A proposed measure of PTSD Criterion A2. *American Journal of Psychiatry, 158*(9), 1480–1485.

Brymer M., Jacobs C., Layne C., Pynoos, R., Ruzek, J., Steinberg A., et al. (2006). *Psychological first aid: Field operations guide* (2nd ed.). Retrieved August 10, 2010, from http://ncptsd.va.gov/ncmain/ncdocs/manuals/PFA_2ndEditionwithappendices.pdf

Carlier, I., Lamberts, R. D., & Gersons, B. P. (1997). Risk factors for posttraumatic stress symptomatology in police officers: A prospective analysis. *Journal of Nervous and Mental Disease, 185*(8), 498–506.

Clark, D. W., & Haley, M. (2007). Crisis response tools for law enforcement. *The Police Chief, 24*(8), 94–101.

Creamer, M. (2006). Acute psychological intervention for law enforcement following trauma exposure: What is current best practice? *Law Enforcement Executive Forum, 6*(3), 135–150.

Cukor, J., Spitalnick, J., Difede, J., Rizzo, A., & Rothbaum, B. (2009). Emerging treatments for PTSD. *Clinical Psychology Review, 29*(8), 715–726.

Dunning, C. (2004). Maintaining police officers at peak mental functioning: Risk management of on-the-job mental injuries sustained in response to violent, catastrophic, and disastrous events. *Law Enforcement Executive Forum, 4*(2), 129–146.

Epstein, S. (1994). Integration of the cognitive and psychodynamic unconscious. *American Psychologist, 49*(8), 709–721.

Finn, P., & Tomz, J. E. (1997). *Developing a law enforcement stress program for officers and their families.* Washington, DC: National Institute of Justice.

Fisher, R. P., & Geiselman, R. E. (1992). *Memory-enhancing techniques for investigative interviewing.* Springfield, IL: Charles C Thomas.

Fay, J. (2000). *A narrative approach to critical and sub-critical incident debriefings.* Unpublished doctoral dissertation, American School of Professional Psychology, San Francisco.

Federal Bureau of Investigation. (1996). Critical incident stress in law enforcement. *Law Enforcement Bulletin,* February.

Galea, S., Ahern, J., Resnick, H., Kilpatrick, D., Bucuvalas M., Gold, J., et al. (2002). Psychological sequelae of the September 11th attacks in Manhattan, New York City. *New England Journal of Medicine, 346*, 982–987.

Gentz, D. (1990). The psychological impact of critical incidents on police officers. In J. T. Reese, J. M. Horne, & C. Dunning (Eds.), *Critical incidents in policing* (pp. 175–181). Washington, DC: Federal Bureau of Investigations.

Gist, R., Lohr, J. M., Kenardy, J., Bergmann, L., Meldrum, L., Redburn, B. G., et al. (1997). Researchers speak on CISM. *Journal of Emergency Medical Services, 22*(5), 27–28.

Henry, V. E. (1995). The police officer as survivor: Death confrontations and the police subculture. *Behavioral Sciences and the Law, 13*, 93–112.

Honig, A., & Sultan, S. (2004). Reactions and resilience under fire: What an officer can expect. *The Police Chief, 71*(12), 54–60.

Honig, A. L., & Lewinski, W. J. (2008). A survey of the research on human factors related to lethal force encounters: Implications for law enforcement training, tactics, and testimony. *Law Enforcement Executive Research Forum, 8*(4), 129–152.

International Association of Chiefs of Police /Psychological Services Section. (2000). *Peer support guidelines.* Alexandria, VA: IACP.

International Association of Chiefs of Police/Psychological Services Section. (2010). *Officer-involved shooting guidelines.* Alexandria, VA: IACP.

Kahneman, D. (2003). A perspective on judgment and choice: Mapping bounded rationality. *American Psychologist, 58*(9), 697–720.

Keane, T., Fairbank, J., Caddell, J., Zimering, R., Taylor, K., & Mora, C. (1989). *Clinical evaluation of a measure to assess combat exposure. Psychological Assessment, 1*, 53–55.

Kessler R. C., Sonnega, A., Bromet, E., Hughes, M., & Nelson, C. B. (1995). Posttraumatic stress disorder in the national comorbidity survey. *Archives of General Psychiatry, 52*, 1048–1060.

Koopman C., Classen, C., & Spiegel, D. (1994). Predictors of posttraumatic stress symptoms among survivors of the Oakland/Berkeley, CA firestorm. *American Journal of Psychiatry, 151*, 888–894.

Kilpatrick, Resnick, & Acierno. (2009). Should PTSD Criterion A be retained? *Journal of Traumatic Stress, 22*(5), 374–383.

Kirschman, E (2004). *I love a firefighter: What the family needs to know.* New York: Guilford.

Kirschman, E. (2007). *I love a cop* (Rev. ed.). New York: Guilford.

Klein, G. (1998). *Sources of power: How people make decisions.* Cambridge, MA: MIT Press.

Klinger, D. (2001). *Police responses to officer involved shootings.* Washington, DC: U.S. Government Printing Office.

Lewinski, W. (2008). The attention study: A study on the presence of selective attention in firearms officers. *Law Enforcement Executive Forum, 8*(6), 107–138.

Liberman, A., Best, S. R., Metzler, T. J., Fagan, J. A., Weiss, D. S., & Marmar, C. R. (2002). Routine occupational work stress as a risk factor for stress reactions among police officers. *Policing: An International Journal of Police Strategies and Management, 25*, 421–439.

Marmar, C. R., Weiss, D. S., Metzler, T. J., Delucchi, K. L., Best, S. R., & Wentworth, K. A. (1999). Longitudinal course and predictors of continuing distress following critical incident exposure in emergency services personnel. *Journal of Nervous and Mental Disease, 187*(1), 15–22.

McCaslin, S. E., Rogers, C. E., Metzler, T. J., Best, S. R., Weiss, D. S., Fagan, J. A., et al. (2006). The impact of personal threat on police officers' responses to critical incident stressors. *Journal of Nervous and Mental Diseases, 194*, 591–597.

Miller, L. (1998). *Shocks to the system: Psychotherapy of traumatic disability syndromes.* New York: Norton.

Miller, L. (2006a). Critical incident stress debriefing for law enforcement: Practical models and special applications. *International Journal of Emergency Mental Health, 8*(3), 189–201.

Miller, L. (2006b). Officer-involved shooting: Reaction patterns, response protocols, and psychological intervention strategies. *International Journal of Emergency Mental Health, 8*(4), 239–254.

Miller, L. (2006c). *Practical police psychology: Stress management and crisis intervention for law enforcement.* Springfield, IL: Charles C Thomas.

Mitchell, J. T. (1983). When disaster strikes: The critical incident stress debriefing process. *Journal of Emergency Medical Services, 8*, 35–39.

Mitchell, J., & Bray, G. (1990). *Emergency services stress: Guidelines for preserving the health and careers of emergency services personnel.* Englewood Cliffs, NJ: Prentice Hall.

Mitchell, J. T., & Everly, G. S. (1993). *Critical incident stress debriefing: An operations manual for CISD, defusing, and other group crisis intervention services.* Ellicott City, MD: Chevron.

Mitchell, J. T., & Everly, G. S. (2001). *Critical incident stress debriefing: An operations manual for CISD, defusing and other group crisis intervention services* (3rd ed.). Ellicott City, MD: Chevron.

Ozer, E. J., Best, S. R., Lipsey, T. L., & Weiss D. S. (2003). Predictors of posttraumatic stress disorder and symptoms in adults: A meta-analysis. *Psychological Bulletin, 129*(1), 52–73.

Parker, C. L., Every, G. S., Barnett, D. J., & Links, J. M. (2006). Establishing evidence-informed core intervention competencies in psychological first aid for public health personnel. *International Journal of Emergency Mental Health, 8*(2), 83–92.

Paton, D., & Violanti, J. (1996). *Traumatic stress in critical occupations: Recognition, consequences and treatment.* Springfield, IL: Charles C Thomas.

Pender D. A., & Prichard, K. K. (2008). Group process research and emergence of therapeutic factors in critical incident stress debriefing. *International Journal of Emergency Mental Health, 10*(1), 39–48.

Peterson, K. C., Prout, M. F., & Schwarz, R. A. (1991). *Post-traumatic stress disorder: A clinician's guide.* New York: Plenum.

Pinizotto, A. J., David, E. F., & Miller, C. E. (2007). The deadly mix. *FBI Law Enforcement Bulletin, 76*(3), 1–9.

Pitman, R. K., Sanders, K. M., Zusman, R. M., Healy, A. R., Cheema, F., Lasko, N. B., et al. (2004). A pilot study of secondary prevention of posttraumatic stress disorder with propranolol. *Biological Psychiatry, 51*(2), 189–192.

Pole, N., Cumberbatch, E., Taylor, W. M., Metzler, T., Marmar, C. R., & Neylan, T. (2005). Comparisons between high and low peritraumatic dissociators in cardiovascular and emotional activity while remembering trauma. *Journal of Trauma and Dissociation, 6*, 51–67.

Raphael, B., & Wilson, J. P. (Eds.). (2000). *Psychological debriefing: Theory, practice, and evidence*. Cambridge, UK: Cambridge University Press.

Regehr, C., & Bober, T. (2005). *In the line of fire: Trauma in the emergency services*. Oxford, UK: Oxford University Press.

Robinson, R. (2008). Reflections on the debriefing debate. *International Journal of Emergency Mental Health, 10*(4), 253–259.

Sanders, S. (2008). Certification and the pledge of excellence in traumatic stress interventions. *International Journal of Emergency Mental Health, 10*(1), 61–66.

Sapolsky, R. M. (2004). Stressed out memories. *Scientific American Mind, 14*(5), 28–34.

Schacter, D. (2001). *The seven sins of memory*. New York: Houghton Mifflin.

Sharps, M. J. (2010). *Processing under pressure: Stress, memory and decision making in law enforcement*. Flushing, NY: Looseleaf Law Publications.

Shomstein, S., & Yantis, S. (2004). Control of attention shifts between vision and audition in human cortex. *The Journal of Neuroscience, 24*(47), 10702–10706.

Solomon, R. M., & Horn, J. M. (1986). Post-shooting traumatic reactions: A pilot study. In J. T. Reese & H. A. Goldstein (Eds.), *Psychological services for law enforcement* (pp. 383–394). Washington, DC: U.S. Government Printing Office.

Spielberger, C. D., Westberry, L. G., Grier, K. S., & Greenfield, G. (1981). *The police stress survey: Sources of stress in law enforcement*. Tampa, FL: Human Resources Institute.

Stuhlmiller, C., & Dunning, C. (2000). Concerns about debriefing: Challenging the mainstream. In B. Raphael & J. Wilson (Eds.), *Psychological debriefing: Theory, practice and evidence* (pp. 305–320). Cambridge, UK: Cambridge University Press.

Weathers, F., & Keane, T. (2007). The Criterion A problem revisited: Controversies and challenges in defining and measuring psychological trauma. *Journal of Traumatic Stress, 20*(2), 107–121.

Weiss, D. S., Brunet, A., Best, S. R., Metzler, T. J., Liberman, A., Pole, N., et al. (in press). The Critical Incident History Questionnaire: A method for measuring total cumulative exposure to critical incidents in police officers. *Journal of Traumatic Stress, 23*.

Zoellner, L. A., Alvarez-Conrad, J., & Foa, E. B. (2002). Peritraumatic dissociative experiences, trauma narratives, and trauma pathology. *Journal of Traumatic Stress, 15*, 49–57.

25 Developing and Maintaining Successful Peer Support Programs in Law Enforcement Organizations

Jocelyn E. Roland

Human beings have a natural inclination to rely on one another, be it in the personal or professional spheres of their lives. When one considers the amount of time most people spend in the workplace, it is easy to see why professional relationships are influential, significant, and inescapable. Smart employers have been aware of these natural relationships and have used them to develop programs to improve, enhance, and maintain employee well-being, knowing full well that mental health is crucial to productivity in the workplace.

A HISTORICAL PERSPECTIVE OF PEER SUPPORT PROGRAMS

Both government and private industry have been aware of the fact that the health of an organization is dependent on the health of the people who make up the organization (Reese, 1995). In the 1940s, employee well-being came to light as an important part of organizational functioning. This led to the development of Employee Assistance Programs (EAPs) that help employees resolve both personal and professional problems with the knowledge that job performance and productivity are impacted by impaired employees (Gund & Elliott, 1995). The first EAPs primarily focused on alcohol addiction and frequently employed the assistance of Alcoholics Anonymous and/or its model of self-help (Reese, 1995). Therefore, peer counseling is hardly a new concept and has been applied in a variety of professional forums for more than 60 years (Linden & Klein, 1988). Starting in the 1950s, police departments began implementing similar programs, again primarily addressing alcohol abuse (Mullins, 1994; Reese, 1995). Police departments in cities such as Boston, Chicago, and New York considered the benefits of such programs and first began to use them. Starting in the 1970s, the Los Angeles Sheriff's Department followed suit with an alcohol program, and in 1983 the San Francisco Police Department developed a stress program (Reese, 1995). In 1981, a Peer Counseling Program was initiated by the Los Angeles Police Department, and was reported to have had more than 230 members in 2001 (Los Angeles Police Beat, 2001; Reiser, 1995). According to Reese (1995), "In 1986, the major police departments in the United States had some form of a stress unit" (p. 35). Therefore, for nearly 30 years the concept of peers helping peers within law enforcement organizations has been formalized into programmatic systems to provide basic support to coworkers across ranks, addressing a wide variety of topics.

Aside from alcohol-related problems, law enforcement agencies have also focused on decreasing stress, particularly critical incidents, as an area of concern. While historically "worst case scenarios" have been in the limelight (e.g., officer-involved shootings, injured officers, and line-of-duty deaths), more recently there has been a shift to recognize that events that impact officers go beyond the discharging of a firearm and that, for example, performing CPR on a nonresponsive baby can be traumatic and upsetting as well. Other considerations have come to include some of the work tasks that are basic requirements of the job such as responding to gruesome murder scenes, traffic collisions with multiple casualties, investigating child pornography cases, and responding to and handling sexual assault cases. Combating and decreasing the possibility of posttraumatic stress disorder and other acute stress reactions have therefore become focuses of peer support as well (Gund & Elliott, 1995).

The success of mental health service delivery to law enforcement has been mixed (Mullins, 1994). The police organizational culture has historically been skeptical of the value and merit of psychological services. Mental health professionals are often viewed as unfamiliar with the rigors of the job, seen as tools of management or the brass, and are associated with the stigma of mental illness, not mental health. These fears and perpetual false beliefs lead to distrust and suspicion of the mental health professional (Mullins, 1994). Carlan and Nored (2008) note that even with an increase in staff psychologists in larger departments and contracted providers for smaller agencies, the negative connotation of seeking psychological assistance remains.

In contrast to these perceived "outsiders," peers trained to offer basic counseling and support provide a bridge between servicing the psychological and emotional needs of police and their suspicions. Peer support persons and groups challenge mental health professionals because of their familiarity with the work and culture, the level of trust that already exists, and the sense of mutual support and connection from having worked together, sometimes for many years. In these days of managed care and reduced mental health benefits through insurance plans, trained peers are comparatively inexpensive and easily accessible. Their onsite, round-the-clock availability makes them handy. Peers offer instant credibility and the perception (both real and fantasized) of a higher level of empathy than professionals (Finn & Tomz, 1997; Linden & Klein, 1988; Mullins, 1994). Through regular contact and positive working experiences, peers are obviously, and not surprisingly, able to be accepted in a way that is rare and uncommon for the "outsider."

Because of peer support teams' acceptance, they are uniquely positioned to provide early intervention and a proactive—rather than a reactive—approach to service delivery (Mullins, 1994). When a crisis occurs on duty, peer support members and supervisors can be advised of the event and quickly mobilize. Assistance may come as an informal intervention such as a casual hallway contact between peers after briefing, or a formalized interaction such as a critical incident stress debriefing. While frequently the "rumor mill" of law enforcement organizations is not used effectively, crisis and critical incident response is one of the clear exceptions to this rule. Usually when there is a lightning-fast spread of information, it relates to a bit of juicy gossip: affairs, discipline, or other negative types of fodder. This type of information spread can, however, also be used for beneficial purposes. Now more than ever, with the advances in technology (e.g., e-mail, cell phone calls, or text messages), the opportunities to "spread the word" in order to aid and assist impacted officers can be implemented as quickly as the data can be sent. This rapid information dissemination allows for quicker responses by peers with needed service being offered in a timelier manner. An example of this was noted recently by this author when during a counseling session I was asked by staff to step outside for an emergency. When I returned to the session no more than 3 minutes later, the officer said, "I know you have to go, there's been a shooting."

Carlan and Nored (2008) have addressed the fact that both personal and organizational stressors in policing are well documented. Personal stressors include such factors as having a hard-charging personality style and rigidity in cognitive style. Even introversion contributes to the stress that the individual brings to the table. Organizationally, challenges range from internal factors such as shift work, management complaints and frustrations, internal affairs, and investigations; to external concerns such as one's exposure to death and violence, regular interactions with criminals, and shortcomings of the judicial system. The negative consequences for police officers are myriad including hypertension, coronary heart disease, stroke, sexual dysfunction, anxiety, depression, and substance abuse (Carlan & Nored, 2008). These are problems not just for the officer and his or her family, but for the agency as well. Workers' Compensation, absenteeism, increased supervision, and overtime costs are all associated with the losses when officers are not functioning at optimal levels. These problems are not micro, but macro. Peer support provides a potentially cost effective means of intervention, positively exploiting the benefits of preexisting relationships between employees.

A secondary benefit to peer support programs is that they offer another bridge: to the mental health professional. While some peer support programs have started more by grassroots means, such as the impetus for Alcoholics Anonymous, most programs have been developed and supported by professionals, particularly the police psychologist (Scrivner & Kurke, 1995). The natural connection between the paraprofessional and the licensed mental health professional is obvious to anyone who has worked in or with agencies who have peer support personnel. The contacts with officers made by peer counselors provides a natural referral source for the mental health professional when a conflict or matter is beyond the peer support person's skill level or expertise (Carlan & Nored, 2008; Linden & Klein, 1988). This is similar to many police psychologists' experiences of meeting an officer in one context (e.g., as a member of a crisis negotiation team) and having a successful relationship, and as a result of the level of comfort and connectedness attained, that officer refers his friend to the psychologist for marital counseling. The positive experience of the individual in one environment naturally leads to expectations of success in another.

DEVELOPING PEER SUPPORT PROGRAMS

The success of peer support teams relies on good people and good training. As noted previously, humans have a natural tendency to rely on one another for support and comfort. Informal support groups are well known in police history and in many ways make sense, and can be beneficial. However, there are times when such support groups can be detrimental (Klein, 1994; Mullins, 1994). Informal group leaders have no training, and the information they provide may be untrue, based on myth, or counterproductive. "Choir practice"—that is, drinking after a shift no matter what time of day or night—is probably the most well-known example of a problematic law enforcement support group because it focuses on using alcohol as a stress reliever. The behavior also offers tacit acceptance of alcohol as a means to deal with uncomfortable feelings and experiences (Klein, 1994; Mullins, 1994). Often, telling "war stories" is part of this ritual. Many officers relish the opportunity to get together and discuss gruesome, harrowing, and often titillating stories for a variety of reasons. Sometimes it is the one-upmanship of who has seen the bloodiest homicide. Sometimes it is to share the details of a call that was funny and entertaining. However, there are times when the intent of the discussion is a compulsion to retell in an effort to process and make sense cognitively of an event or critical incident that is beyond comprehension. In these cases, the repetition of the story becomes an opportunity to further burn into memory the unexplainable event, increasing its memory recall strength and exacerbating the problem by making the event prominent in their cognition. This is the exact opposite of what the officer expects to occur through the repetitive dialogue. Instead of processing the distressing event in a way that decreases the affective and cognitive upset, they practice the event in their head, increasing the likelihood of reexperiencing it. Without knowing it, the officer has effectively ensured upset through behavior that was expected to decrease it (Breslau & Davis, 1992; Van der Kolk, 1991).

It is critical to set up a peer support program in a manner that ensures its success organizationally because it is embraced by the agency's stakeholders as well as found to be effective by the clients who use it. Like any effort, it takes time to figure out what makes something successful, the normal course of experimentation. At this point in time, there have been numerous successful peer support programs, and as a result of these accomplishments there now exist guidelines that can help give direction to the development of a successful program. The International Association of Chiefs of Police (IACP) Police Psychological Services Section is one of the major groups of police psychologists from around the United States and internationally that have pooled their collective experiences to develop guiding principles that provide a useful framework for making intelligent, experience-based decisions regarding peer support programs. The most recent version of the Peer Support Guidelines was ratified at the annual conference in Boston, Massachusetts, in 2006. The document states, "The goal of peer support is to provide all public safety employees in an agency the opportunity to receive emotional and tangible peer support through times of personal or professional crisis and to help anticipate and address potential difficulties" (IACP, 2006, p. 1).

The Guidelines emphasize the importance of programs being "developed and implemented under the organizational structure of the parent agency" (IACP, 2006, p. 1). One set of authors, Gund and Elliott (1995), addressed the challenges the Fairfax County Police Department (Virginia) had in setting up a peer support team. After several unsuccessful attempts, it finally became fully operational, but only when the department decided it wanted a team and took responsibility for it.

Another critical component of success is a formal policy statement that grants peer support teams departmental confidentiality to maximize success while recognizing the legal limitations of privilege. It is suggested that any agency taking on the task of developing a peer support program investigate the state and federal statutes regarding privacy of communications. Most departments that have implemented teams acknowledge that peers may not have legal confidentiality but respect the privacy of the communications and do not mix such relationships with Internal Affairs investigations or other types of supervisory or disciplinary actions (Finn & Tomz, 1997; Fuller, 1991; Gund & Elliott, 1995).

The Guidelines also suggest oversight of the program by a steering committee from inception through implementation and that the members of this committee represent the agency in terms of employees who work for it: sworn, nonsworn, line personnel, and supervisors. One of the most important components of the program for various reasons (e.g., clinical oversight, clinical supervision, liability management, or referral resource) is the inclusion of a licensed mental health professional, a position that has increasingly become an experienced police psychologist. Each peer support program should have a written procedural manual or governing departmental order that is available to all personnel so that it is clear how the program functions and what one might expect to get through a peer support contact.

SUPPORT AND ACCEPTANCE OF PROGRAMS

One of the other matters to consider in a peer support team's success is the relationship between the parent department and the other major player involved in public safety employment: unions. Frequently, there are contentious relationships between these two parties, and without union support there is little that management can implement successfully, particularly an endeavor like peer support where cynicism around mental health services already exists. When it comes to policies and procedures, a rule can be a rule. With psychological service delivery, a fragile relationship exists at the start when you have a group of skeptical consumers. Add to this mix a union that tells its members to not trust the peer support program, and failure is inevitable. It is therefore wise and prudent to work closely with these organizations to ensure the message the union puts forth is one of support and backing. Eliminating this tension by building a good working relationship with this stakeholder paves the way for success.

Top-down support is therefore critical in ensuring the peer support program both gets off the ground and has the internal structure to thrive and prosper. Similarly though, bottom-up support is critical as well. As discussed earlier, "Peer counseling programs are based on the premise that with proper guidance, police officers are in many cases more appropriate helpers for the majority of the problems faced by police officers, at least for initial contact" (Jones, 1995, p. 223). Jones (1995) also wisely notes that peer support may be particularly effective with minority groups. The peer counselor offers a number of advantages compared with traditional mental health providers. These include the innate familiarity with the police work, their availability on-site (which includes a broad range of coverage as a result of how most agencies deploy personnel with overlapping shifts), and the perception that another officer is their equal (Carlan & Nored, 2008). In a nutshell, nobody understands a police officer like another police officer (Klein, 1994).

Consumer acceptance is therefore a crucial component to the success of any peer support program. If the persons within the organization are not using the services, the program will be perceived as having no merit by management, the team members will feel bored and unappreciated, and eventually the effort will die. It is therefore critical that recruiting members of a peer support team be done in a thoughtful manner. Team members should be volunteers who are in good standing with their departments and are respected within the organization (IACP, 2006; Mullins, 1994). They should be individuals who have an excellent work record and hold the esteem of their comrades. Consideration for team member traits include (but are not limited to) reputation, approval by peers and supervisors, time on the department, personal experiences with situations that give them unique or valued experiences (e.g., shootings, cancer survival, or divorce), and innate personal qualities and characteristics consistent with success as a confidant such as empathy, compassion, concern, judgment, maturity, and both political and social tact (Finn & Tomz, 1997; IACP, 2006). One other consideration is not a requirement but makes good common sense: the individual's willingness to use professional or paraprofessional counseling services themselves (Finn & Tomz, 1997).

INDENTIFYING, RECRUITING, AND SELECTING PEERS

Smart recruiting and solicitation of volunteers are critical components of team development. One element to consider is whether or not the position truly is volunteer or if there will be some form of compensation as a result of appointment to the team (e.g., a salary percentage increase because it is characterized as a special assignment). In the latter case, there may be departmental rules or a Memorandum of Understanding (MOU) regarding the selection process because it is associated with financial benefits. Most agencies have volunteers for the position, but remunerated for their time assisting a contact or responding to a critical incident should it occur off-duty. Developing these standards as part of the program's operational guidelines is crucial in ensuring there are no abuses of compensation or concerns by management as to what will and will not be remunerated. Sad but true: there are people who will not join a program because of the time they may have to give up outside of paid employment.

With consideration given to employee's personality styles, experiences, and level of commitment, the next consideration is "shoulder tapping." This is where for a new team, the steering committee, or an existing team, team members consider who in their organization they would like to see on the team should those individuals have the desire to join. In every organization, law enforcement, public safety, or otherwise, there are invariably people who are seen as natural leaders, confidants, good listeners, are objective in their problem assessment. Ask any supervisor, and they will easily be able to tell you who they would go to for assistance and who their subordinates seek out. As noted earlier, beyond the desired innate personality traits, there are also coworkers who have "been there, done that." These are the kind of people others turn to when they feel that their experience is similar, recognizing the success their shift partner had in dealing with a parallel situation. People gain reputations, for good or for bad, for a reason. In developing or enhancing a peer support team, assessing who the respected department members are is one relatively easy and thoughtful way to augment the cadre of peer support persons.

An important consideration in regard to team selection is the peer's willingness to tolerate psychological and emotional discomfort. It is not unusual to hear of important people in police officers' lives—such as spouses, significant others, parents, and nonpolice friends—who are not willing to listen to the particulars of horrific events (Klein, 1994). When it comes to the particularly ugly stuff—rapes, sexual assault and abuse, child pornography, and homicides—understandably, many civilians do not want to know the details. The details should be processed and addressed appropriately as a step toward maintaining or regaining mental health. This is particularly relevant for investigators and crime scene personnel who collect evidence and witness autopsies. The required extended exposure to these horrors is exactly the kind of experience that can lead to stress-related illnesses and conditions if not addressed appropriately. Tolerating the retelling of such critical incidents is an absolute necessity and obviously requires a certain type of peer. According to Carlan and Nored (2008), departments with counseling options report a decrease in stress levels, while personal demographics counted for very little. This provides support for such programs. Knowing that police personnel in every agency will be exposed to some form of trauma, direct or vicariously, peer support programs offer another option to ensuring the mental health of employees.

As far as logistics go, it is suggested that recruiting efforts be seen as fair and based on a clearly defined process. Again, this process may be dictated by department policy or an MOU. When advertising for the team, this announcement should be distributed to all agency employees who are eligible to join. Frequently a letter of interest is requested, and some agencies provide a specific form for the candidate to fill out inquiring about their interests and experiences (Finn & Tomz, 1997). Practical application or participating in role play or scenarios is another option for assessing the innate personality traits a team may be interested in seeing in their new members. Interviewing potential members is one way to discuss relevant matters, assess level of commitment, and get an overall feel for the applicant. Most notably, however, is the direct recommendation of an individual by supervisors and peers. This is also one of the suggestions made in the IACP Guidelines (2006).

In order to maximize success, the IACP Guidelines suggest that an agency endeavor to train as many peers as possible, taking into account the demographics of the department and considering the client base in this manner. This includes considering position within the agency, rank, shifts, and divisions or departments. It is also suggested that interagency relationships be built, recognizing the fact that critical incidents as well as the "everyday emergency" frequently involve multiagency responses (e.g., police, fire, paramedics, dispatch, and other law enforcement agencies) (IACP, 2006). Steering committees or existing teams must at all times be seen by their potential consumers as fair and objective, and that includes when they are starting from scratch or considering new members for an established team.

Another critical component of program success is deselection. There are times when it becomes clear that for any one of numerous reasons a team member should not be actively functioning on the team. Bad things sometimes happen to good people. People make poor choices. In these situations, deselection may be warranted for not adhering to program rules such as maintaining confidentiality or losing one's standing within the organization (IACP, 2006). In other cases, the reason for deselection may be the team member's failure to abide by training requirements or submitt required paperwork such as confidential contact hours. Sometimes peers themselves recognize that they may need to remove themselves from the team, and on other occasions a steering committee or other oversight delegate may have to step in. Regardless of the cause for deselection, the ability to maintain the integrity and quality of the team is critical.

Short-term breaks are also occasionally warranted, and one option is to allow team members to take a leave of absence when they are faced with professional and/or personal challenges that might impair their ability to provide quality contacts. Certain work-related dilemmas pose complications that, in the interest of maintaining team perception, require members to take a leave. Examples include being under investigation oneself or being assigned to the Internal Affairs unit. While neither of these examples should connote guilt or prejudice respectively, the reality is that potential contacts may believe there has been a compromise in the peer's ability to be of service. For the officer who is the subject of an investigation and cleared, he should be able to reinstate with a "cleared name." For the sergeant who was assigned to Internal Affairs for her required tour of duty, rescind the leave of absence when she is moved back to a noninvestigative position. In both cases, it is time to welcome back a valued member of the team.

TRAINING

Once a cadre of peer support persons has been selected through a careful and thoughtful process, the next step is to train them, usually over a number of days starting with the rules and guidelines of the program. This would include reviewing a written procedures manual that is suggested by the IACP (2006). Providing a clear outline of expectations—both the do's and the don'ts—is vital. The following is a list of possible topics to be covered:

1. Manual guidelines
2. Confidentiality
3. Role conflicts
4. Referrals
5. Deselection and leave of absence
6. Continuing training requirements
7. Performance expectations
8. Administrative responsibilities

Similar to any successful program, implementation is critical to let individuals know upfront exactly what may be expected of them. To some degree, this should have occurred at the time the peer was selected, however, reiterating the expectations in a group setting may be useful in exerting additional emphasis on the importance of these issues to the team's success. Law enforcement personnel are already aware of the skepticism and cynicism that may surround psychological intervention, and it will be no surprise to them that the success of their program is determined by their behavior and the choices they make in regard to interventions and contacts.

In reviewing the above list, confidentiality is probably one of the most important and continually addressed topics when it comes to peer support (Finn & Tomz, 1997; Fuller, 1991; Mullins, 1994). Again, this grows partly from the police culture of distrust and partly from the fears (both real and imagined) that anyone may have when confiding in someone other than a friend. Each program should have a very clear policy "that clarifies confidentiality guidelines and reporting requirements and avoids role conflicts and dual relationships" (IACP, 2006, p. 4). It is this author's experience in working with peer support personnel that the matter of confidentiality comes up frequently as an area of concern. Part of this comes from the normal anxiety associated with following any important rule, feelings most mental health professionals feel when starting in the field and continue to experience when faced with challenging clinical cases. This is probably one of the most important reasons for having a licensed mental health professional, someone with experience working with public safety personnel, involved with the running of the peer support team. In this situation, not only does the licensed professional serve as a consultant to the team but also is at times a resource for members who themselves need counsel on how to clearly assess the potential ethical legal ramifications of a quandary. The relationship also allows a peer to "hand off" a contact if the matter requires legal privilege. Any missteps in this area can potentially damage a peer support program as quickly as it was established.

Peer support persons should be aware of the state and federal laws surrounding confidentiality, which includes danger to self and others, child or elder abuse, and other serious violations of the law (IACP, 2006). Departments must abide by the guidelines they provide in this area so that there is no attempt to gather information for investigative purposes when an appropriate peer-contact relationship exists.

Dovetailing the topic of confidentiality is role conflict, which includes dual relationships and potential conflicts that arise out of natural work relationships. Law enforcement careers by nature have the built-in potential for role conflict. Examples include extended tenures that cross multiple units, divisions, and ranks; peer and supervisory duties that may have inquisitive and/or investigative tasks; as well as personal comingling of coworkers that includes romantic relationships and legally binding contracts such as marriage or the dissolution of those relationships. While one may endeavor to steer clear of such complications, particularly in smaller agencies, these lines will get crossed. It is imperative that peer support persons be prepared to deal with these possible concerns and navigate them as smoothly as possible whether the decision is to maintain the contact, refer to another peer, or refer to a licensed therapist.

Knowing one's limitations as a peer support person is another important issue to be addressed, and leads to the discussion regarding referrals. A referral may be made because the intensity of the problem exceeds what the peer is capable of handling. This is particularly important regarding issues such as suicide, alcohol or substance abuse, or other medical/life-threatening issues. Of note for law enforcement is what seems to this author to be a more frequently emerging issue: addiction to prescribed medications resulting from bona fide on-the-job injuries handled through Workers' Compensation. Police recognize the problems with addiction quite readily. However, they seem to struggle with identifying a coworker as an addict when the medications are legally prescribed and taken for a justified injury.

Referrals may also be made because the situation presented by the contact would be best served by someone with expertise on a specific topic. On occasion, transfer to another peer may be an option, such as referring a contact that has specific questions about the perceptual disturbances they experienced during a critical incident to another peer support person who was involved in two officer-involved shootings. A grieving parent may feel that a peer who has not experienced the loss of someone close to him or her can understand their pain as well as someone with a similar sorrow. Whether or not the contact's belief is valid, it remains incumbent upon the peer to accept the referral request. These examples provide the support for ensuring that programs are developed with sufficient numbers of personnel who have a variety of experiences relevant to the potential needs of the program's consumers. It also supports "shoulder tapping," when a member of a department is identified as having the unique experiences that make him or her a valued addition to a team. Referrals outside the program should be discussed as well, understanding that clergy, legal counsel, financial consultants, addiction specialists, and physicians may all have relevance when it comes to issues that require a higher level of care and attention.

Deselection and leave of absences should be discussed, although the former matter is likely more of an administrative decision. Peer support persons by nature, with their high levels of empathy and concern, can run the risk of not recognizing when they need to say no, or when they need to take a break. Clear-cut situations such as grief, injury, or movement into a position of investigative responsibility can signal an obvious time for a break. However, there are more subtle circumstances that may not be clear and require the intervention of the program coordinator, frequently the police psychologist or other mental health provider. Things like multiple stressors, job promotion, and relationship problems may provide enough noise in the peer's head, making it hard for the person to provide solid, objective, and useful support. These complications may also make peer support itself feel like one more burden the peer has to contend with. By character, people who select into this position are likely to be givers, and it is important that they recognize when they have given too much and need to step back, regroup, and engage in self-care in order to be effective for someone else.

Continuing training requirements, performance expectations, and administrative responsibilities should be clearly delineated. One of the challenges of any volunteer program is maintaining enthusiasm and connectivity. Offering interesting, relevant, and informational training is one way to keep programs up and running. It also provides benefits to the program that are not so obvious such as allowing team leaders to monitor performance and to identify deficits in members. It is suggested that a minimum of four trainings per year be conducted to keep programs running and members connected. Topics can range from a basic review of skills to a specialized area of interest (e.g., cancer treatment and recovery, dealing with adolescents, financial hardship, and so on). It is also suggested that there be time to debrief contacts who were difficult, challenging, or unique. Group learning is a benefit to be taken advantage of. Furthermore, this type of sharing provides an opportunity for members to learn more about others' strengths and weaknesses, area(s) of specialty, and general personality style or approach—all critical when it comes to referral.

Performance expectations should be consistent with those laid out in the agency's guidelines regarding the peer support program. This would include the minimum number of trainings to be attended yearly, duties of report, and any administrative duties required. Smart peer support programs should require anonymous and confidential statistics gathered solely for the purpose of supporting the work efforts of the team members and documenting the overall success of the program in terms of number of contacts, time spent at each encounter, topics addressed, and so forth. In larger agencies, the option to obtain more data such as rank, unit, and/or division may exist as long as such data are not identifying. Having the program coordinator gather and summarize the data, someone who can maintain the confidentiality of even this general information, is suggested in an effort to maintain privacy of the contacts while being able to show the agency that the investment in the program is worthwhile.

The length of the initial training program should be determined by the steering committee and/ or trainers. In a review of the literature, programs range from 24 to 64 hours of initial training, with varying rates of follow-up training thereafter (Finn & Tomz 1997; Linden & Klein, 1988; Mullins, 1994). One obvious issue is that extended training has a variety of costs associated with it, from real monies laid out for peers to attend the training to the costs associated with the absence of the employees from their regularly assigned duties. This is another critical juncture wherein the department's support needs to be fully behind the team's efforts, considering peer support team training as valuable as a narcotics school, crisis negotiations training, or time spent on the range. Again, when an agency recognizes that peer contacts are cost effective for a variety of reasons, they are more likely to stand behind the costs associated with the team. Securing a budget or identified funding source for a team ensures there will be sufficient monetary support to maintain and enhance skill sets as well as being able to provide interesting and innovative training. This improves the chances of keeping team members challenged and interested in the valuable services they provide.

Once the "housekeeping" is taken care of, training should focus on the task at hand: fundamental communication and problem resolution skills. A solid foundation in one-on-one interventions is the origin for good interventions. It is likely that the majority of, if not all, volunteers will already inherently have many of the skills that will be presented. However, it remains crucial to go through the training naming, identifying and organizing the natural process of support so that peers can better understand the development of interpersonal connection that is believed to be the heart of effective interactions. It is also critical for peer support persons to recognize that even while they may be naturally inclined in one area, for example problem solving, they may be deficient in another area such as listening. Suggested topics in the arena of basic counseling skills include but are not limited to the following:

1. Extending the invitation
2. Active listening skills
3. Paraphrasing
4. Eliciting feelings and emotions
5. Discerning the difference between content and process
6. Problem solving

Law enforcement personnel are, like military personnel, used to repetition training and practical application. However, when it comes to role-playing and scenario-based training in peer support, many team members become shy and reticent to perform in front of others. There is no better way to practice the above listed skills than in real time. Part of the reason why training programs should be extended over a number of days is that it allows the team member sufficient practical experience along with the opportunity to get feedback (from both trainers and peers) as well as to observe others. There is no definitive score to achieve, but a baseline to surpass. Police personnel like to function with clear markers indicating success or failure, but with this type of work those markers are not readily identified, and as a result it becomes very important to allow sufficient time for confidence in skills to be obtained so that when they are sent off to do this important work they feel capable, informed, and supported with a back-up system that is there to help when needed.

One of the most frequent applications of peer support is in managing critical incident stress. Bohl (1995) notes that while originally within the law enforcement milieu, officer-involved shootings were first the focus of critical incident response, somewhere in the 1980s it was recognized that there exists a whole constellation of other events police personnel encounter that can be equally—if not more—distressing than a shooting. Historically the perception was that the discharging of one's firearm was the cause of distress, ignoring the fact that *not* discharging it for any number of reasons (e.g., sniper fire, civilians in the backdrop, or malfunction) could be even more distressing than being able to respond to the threat. In studies addressing feelings of control and security for officers involved in critical incidents (over 90% were shootings), numbers stayed relatively stable over the years indicating that on average, about 50% of officers involved experienced a sense of vulnerability (Honig & Roland, 1998; Honig & Sultan, 2004). This feeling is enhanced by the inability to react. The previously limited definition of critical incidents in policing does a grave disservice in understanding what makes an impact on the individual in a time of crisis.

With the broader view of critical incidents in policing reaching beyond the previous boundaries of shootings also came the recognition that a critical incident could be the catalyst to a host of problematic outcomes for employees. These include decreased work performance, alcohol and substance abuse, suicide, and posttraumatic stress disorder (Bohl, 1995). Combine this acknowledgment with the fact that police personnel are not readily willing to admit stress or distress from such events because they are trained to handle such events, and that such extreme incidents happen relatively rarely (Bohl, 1995). From the supervisor's perspective, there is no need to intervene. The supervisor sees no reaction because line personnel keep their feelings under wraps, and exposure to the distressing event is an assumed part of the job. These types of assumptions are exactly the impetus for peer support: departments need people who are trained to be attuned to the process, not just the content. They need people who see beyond what is overtly expressed because by the time that point is reached, the damage is done and manifest. Peer support persons are a first-line defense to avoid and defuse potential damage that costs the organization significantly more in the long run.

Successful Critical Incident Stress Management (CISM) is facilitated by teams of trained peers to help avoid the damage just discussed. Sheehan, Everly, and Langlieb (2004) report in a survey examining 11 emergency service related organizations' responses to critical incidents that there were five best practices that emerged. The first is early intervention. Second, offering complete care that includes multicomponent short- and long-term services, which indicates that strategic planning to deliver such services needs to be in place before the crisis. Next is peer support, which was understood as just that and not as a substitute for professional intervention or service delivery. Fourth is specialized training in CISM, for both peers and professionals. Last, appropriate assistance delivery based on the situation, logistics, and personnel involved (e.g., one-on-one vs. group interventions, spiritual assistance, family support, and so on). While peers may make up the majority of a CISM team, it is recommended that these responses occur under the guidance of a mental health professional (Bohl, 1995, Mitchell, 1994) and can include clergy as well.

As noted earlier, one of the keys to successful CISM interventions is rapid response. Prior to a formal debriefing, peer support persons can play a critical role in offering a wide range of aid. These include one-to-one interactions such as normalizing the event, discussing common reactions, providing factual information regarding departmental policy and procedure (particularly in the case of a shooting), as well as validating emotional responses (Gund & Elliott, 1995). In cases where an employee must not discuss the event because of procedural and investigative policy, the peer support person should be well versed and know what can and cannot be discussed. Ultimately, the goal in this situation is for the impacted employee to feel supported and cared for, and that affective experience comes from the connection as much as, if not more so, from the peer's empathy and presence.

SPECIALIZED PEER SKILLS

Besides responding to a critical incident, peers can provide a variety of contacts with the benefit of personal experience and training in specialized areas. The literature addresses two primary areas particularly relevant to police personnel: officer-involved shootings and substance abuse recovery (Finn & Tomz, 1997; Gund & Elliott, 1995). In regard to alcoholism, officers sometimes feel constrained by the very nature of their jobs as law enforcers to seek treatment and support for addiction in the community. This is particularly common in smaller constituencies where services are limited and some of those being provided services are the same people the officer has arrested. The recovering peer support person who has struggled with these same issues may be a critical link in getting a coworker into treatment and encouraging long-term sobriety.

Officers involved in shootings share a common bond that is unique in law enforcement. Peer support persons with these experiences provide an option for the police officer to discuss the event (aside from a recommended formalized debriefing with a properly trained mental health professional [IACP, 2004]]) with a comrade who has undergone a similar experience but with the added training that makes the peer distinctly able to offer understanding and explanation (Trompetter, 1994). The Los Angeles Sheriff's Department has gone so far as developing a subset of peer support persons who have been in shootings that function as the "buddy" for an officer after a shooting. Members of this team keep the deputy company and attend to the person's basic needs such as calling loved ones or securing food, and in their discussions following the shooting the peer knows full well the rules regarding not discussing the event details until investigations are complete. One of the outcomes of this intervention is a reduced level of management concern regarding policy violation, because the department is confident in the peer's knowledge of rules and their adherence to them.

Other types of specialized persons to consider are those with military experience, especially those who have been deployed, served in combat zones, and successfully reintegrated into civilian life. Another suggested constituent of a peer support team is someone who has dealt with serious injury, whether it was on or off the job. It is not uncommon for employees to feel invisible after an injury and time away from the department. Serving as a liaison, the peer support person can help to maintain a level of connection during recuperation and rehabilitation. There is a strong parallel for employees on administrative leave. While there may be some limitations for contact or discussion per department policy and procedure, abandoning an employee because of allegations should not be seen as acceptable behavior. Again, the peer support person is in the unique position to be trained, including instruction by the investigative arm of the agency, to follow rules while providing relief from feelings of rejection, embarrassment, shame, and disgrace. Peer support teams have the possibility to intervene in the potentially destructive process of isolation.

The benefit of having chaplains or clergy on a team is apparent. Many agencies have clergy that assist in death notifications and public relations. Some agencies have developed relationships with spiritual leaders who provide counsel to personnel for both personal and professional issues. While functioning as a member of a peer support team, it is essential that the person approaches interventions in a nondenominational manner. This is imperative for group interventions where religious preference is not known. In one-on-one interventions a contact may request support that is consistent with the chaplain's area of practice, but overall, maintaining a position as a leader of faith and spirituality without designating a particular set of beliefs or values is likely to best serve everyone with whom they come in contact. Being sensitive to cultural and religious issues reflects the fact that the clergy member is there to assist one and all, equally. It is crucial that the allegiance of the chaplain be known as a supporter of the law enforcement mission. If there is any sense that the chaplain has not been supportive, that person's role on the team will be questioned and could have negative consequences for the team as a whole.

One of the hidden benefits to specialized team member's skills and encompassing employees in need who may not recognize they need assistance is the good will engendered both for the team and the agency. By maintaining contact with the officer who is off for the long term due to a back injury sustained in an on-duty traffic collision, the officer feels connected and does not return to work disgruntled and angry with his department for feeling abandoned. The dispatcher who returns from administrative leave after an allegation of misconduct, with her name cleared, feels that even while the Internal Affairs investigation had to be completed, there was someone in the unit who cared enough to check in with her. Peers who make contacts as early interventions, whether they provide the service or refer on to an expert, may have just prevented long-term psychological trauma from setting in, leading to Workers' Compensation claims and costs that are expensive in terms of both time lost and money expended. In these instances, peer support is a valuable tool for departments maintaining employee well-being and productivity.

LONG-TERM SUCCESS OF PEER SUPPORT PROGRAMS

Initial training of peer support personnel is an obvious component of any successful program; however, ongoing training is just as important. As discussed earlier, a successful program is one that lasts, and longevity requires continued efforts and energies be put into the program not only by its members but also by its leaders. One of the best ways to keep teams invigorated is through training that they perceive as relevant and useful. An instructor may feel that certain topics must be addressed or revisited, but encouraging team members to suggest topics of interest is just as valuable. This has been noted when certain issues are pressing from either the micro- or macro-environment they are functioning in. At press time, the United States will have been in a notable recession and time of financial crisis for nearly 2 years. There is no doubt this is a matter peers would need to address and comprehend better. In this case, training could include bringing in financial experts. Other specialized topics could be germane to the agency itself, such as the arrest of one of their own for alleged misdoing. It is also crucial for team leaders to be aware that sometimes training takes place in a one-on-one capacity, and that mentoring peer support persons is a critical role for such individuals.

The following is a suggested list of training topics by the IACP (2006):

1. Confidentiality
2. Role conflict
3. Limits and liability
4. Ethical issues
5. Communication facilitation and listening skills
6. Nonverbal communication
7. Problem assessment
8. Problem-solving skills
9. Cross-cultural issues
10. Psychological diagnoses
11. Medical conditions often confused with psychiatric disorders
12. Stress management
13. Burnout
14. Grief management
15. Domestic violence
16. AIDS
17. Suicide assessment
18. Crisis management

19. Trauma intervention
20. Alcohol and substance abuse
21. When to seek mental health consultation and referral information

Long-term success for the team will be based on a number of achieved goals: acceptance of the program by department administrators, an agency's acceptance of the rules of confidentiality and maintaining the privacy of peer contacts, program use that comes from both the requesting individual as well as referrals by peers and supervisors, and word of mouth success from accomplishments the team makes, most notably in high-profile situations. Engendering the good will, acceptance, and referrals of unions will ensure that the value of the team is seen from an agent whose primary goal is to support the interests of department employees. Top-down and bottom-up support helps to create and maintain the framework for a successful team that only needs to be fleshed out by solid team members. Program marketing is essential to the team's staying power (Finn & Tomz, 1997).

Maintaining a visible profile within the department is another tool for survival. Staying connected to supervisors helps to keep the services of the peer support team on their minds when a critical incident occurs, or they notice changes in an employee's behavior. Providing in-service training on the role of the team and the benefits it can offer help to make it one of the many items on their list to attend to when a crisis occurs. It seems apparent from this author's experience that certain employees consider peer support a valuable tool, and others hardly give it a second thought. It is frequently their direct experience with a crisis and the team's response or witnessing a friend/coworker benefit from the interaction that makes a sale. Because nobody is hoping for a crisis, it is the team members themselves who need to sell the program. The perfect example is the respected officer who struggled with his own shooting, connected with a member of peer support, and was able to successfully process the event. He continued to be a valued, respected member of the department, and as a result of his experience, he joined the peer support team to help others as he was helped.

Another component of long-term success is for team leaders and peers themselves to be aware of potential conflicts of interest and how to avoid them. This includes avoiding situations where investigations and disciplinary issues might present potential conflicts for team members who may be compelled to report behavior that is against policy. Another area of relevance is substance use and/or abuse. It is in these situations where the benefit of a licensed mental health professional is most clearly recognized. It is at times like these where the peer support member can halt a conversation, acknowledge his or her requirements in regard to departmental misconduct, and refer to the professional who has legal standing in regard to confidentiality. Without this relationship, peer support persons are left with a contact in need and no clear place to hand over the person with the assurance that his or her needs will be met. Besides taking care of the employee whose crisis extends beyond the skills and abilities of the peer, the relationship with a licensed mental health professional helps to reduce some of the anxiety peer support persons can feel should they be faced with this exact scenario.

Breaches of confidentiality, both real and imagined, are another important area to attend to in ensuring the longevity of the peer support program. Human beings are fallible. It seems safe to assume that someone who would choose to volunteer for such a program, put forth the effort to train, and give of themselves in what can be a demanding exercise would not intentionally share a secret or violate a confidentiality. When such a breach occurs, it is best to deal with it head-on and attempt damage control. It should be noted that many organizations, law enforcement among them, have reputations for passing around information lightning fast. With mobile access to information through e-mail, instant messaging, and text messaging, the speed of data transmission is almost immediate. It is important to also remember that many people will share their secrets with more than one person, even if they don't remember having done so or admitting it. Given these potential scenarios, it is wise to act quickly, try to squash the misconceptions, and work closely with the individual who believes he or she has been wronged.

CARING FOR PEER SUPPORT PERSONS

Keeping teams innervated and excited can present challenges over the long haul. Besides providing ongoing training that is interesting and valuable, ensuring that members are utilized is another key component to team success. While individual contacts most frequently seem to be prompted by those seeking help, team members who are aware of crises or intervention opportunities can self-initiate contacts and should be encouraged to do so. Team members should also consider the importance of referring to others when a specialty topic makes their compatriot uniquely poised to offer their experience and wisdom. In regard to CISM and debriefings, the team leader should be aware of the need to take turns among the members to ensure that everyone gets a chance to participate and contribute. One should strive to have team members feel as though there are no favorites, and that there is a balanced approach to using the team roster when a call-out occurs.

"Debriefing the debriefers" is another important concept, both for sustaining the team over time as well as in terms of the peers' mental health. Regular team meetings facilitate the discussion of contacts that have proved taxing for a variety of reasons (e.g., the intensity of the event, the length or number of contacts, or the issue hitting "close to home" for the team member). A positive working relationship with the team leader, preferably a mental health professional capable of facilitating the debriefing process, allows for the dissipation of affect associated with contacts, feedback on interventions, and encouragement in their skills, contributions and value to the organization and the team. Validation by the rest of the team is critical in terms of feeling supported by one's comrades as well as normalizing the challenges anybody, professional or otherwise, can feel when dealing with highly emotionally charged situations. Consultation and mentoring should be an integral part of the process, and the team leader needs to be readily accessible for team members who need feedback, support, and direction sooner than when the teams itself may be scheduled to meet.

INNOVATIVE USES FOR PEER SUPPORT TEAMS

With the increased approval of peer support teams, there is greater opportunity to grow and stretch beyond the limits of the parent agency. For smaller departments that have close working relationships with other agencies in their immediate geographic area, developing multiagency teams is a step toward expanding police mental health assistance. Interagency assists are common between departments whose boundaries touch, particularly in high-risk or "Code 3" situations. There is no reason then for neighboring departments to not connect when it comes to psychological or emotional aid. Of particular importance is when a smaller agency suffers a critical incident that impacts the entire department, peer support members included. Who are they going to call on in their time of need? Strategic planning should therefore consider the value of multiagency teams, noting that they can still maintain their autonomy in appropriate situations. By occasionally training together team members get to know each other and can sell to their agency the merit of the team that comes to assist them when necessary. It will be much easier to sell the value of an assisting team when familiarity, credibility, and prior experience can be proved.

Another option provided by multiagency familiarity is referring a contact to a peer outside one's agency in a situation where disclosure is not comfortable for a contact. Particularly in small agencies where everybody knows everybody else, it may be difficult for the contact to discuss the matter without sufficient feelings of safety. For example, the contact may feel comfortable talking to a peer about many matters, but not the conflict she is having with her supervisor, who is the peer support person's brother-in-law. Whether or not the contact's fears and concerns are valid in regard to the team member remaining objective, the validity of the feelings are meritorious. Having a solid relationship with neighboring teams may allow for a referral that yields another example of successful peer support while respecting and valuing the contact's concerns.

An additional value to multiagency teams is when CISM debriefings are multiagency. When police, dispatch, fire, ambulance, and other public safety personnel respond to a single event, there exists the opportunity to provide intervention to a larger group, which may be necessary to understand "the whole picture." Conducting a multiagency debriefing with members of two or more of these teams presents the opportunity to benefit from the various members' experiences, training, and unique perspective on the critical incident based on the differences in the various jobs they do. The fire service in particular has rapidly embraced the value of peer support and CISM. Perhaps part of this grows from one of the inherent differences in how police and fire personnel work: fire personnel almost always work in teams versus police who mostly work independently, particularly in tight budgetary times where one-man units are the norm, rather than the exception.

Other benefits to a multiagency approach is the opportunity for combined training, increasing the breadth of experiences peers can share and learn from as well as pooling funds for educational opportunities. Sharing resources is a win–win situation for everyone.

Lastly, depth and breadth allow for innovative training. Practicing how to respond to larger scale crises is feasible for small departments when they share in the exercise. When conducting role-playing exercises, the chance to have another team observe adds another level of distance that can make the scenario seem more realistic and less contrived, a problem experienced when the same people practice with each other over and over. Also, a little personal distance might allow for more honest, and therefore instructive, feedback. This same distance can also provide a forum for objective criticism which can facilitate growth for the individual as well as the team as a whole.

CONCLUSION

The future of peer support groups in law enforcement is bright. As teams are more readily accepted, increasingly formed and encouraged, and utilized with increased frequency, the benefits that can be reaped from them will continue to be mined. As noted earlier, effective peer support teams offer organizations more than simply responding to critical incidents a few times a year. They bridge the gap between personnel in need and the department psychologist or other licensed mental health professional. They reduce costs for agencies by improving employee well-being through early intervention, modeling effective and healthy psychological stress management, and can assist in returning injured, investigated, or military personnel to work. The peer support person in recovery from alcohol abuse can help his shift partner find an Alcoholics Anonymous meeting geared toward public safety personnel so that he may disclose his addiction in a room with people he feels will safeguard his admission in a way the general public may not. And, perhaps most important, police work is a 24/7 job, and when peer support persons work the same or similar schedules, the likelihood of contacts increases because of the easy access to trained coworkers. The value that these teams provide is vast, and for those delivering support, personal growth and satisfaction make it all worthwhile.

REFERENCES

Aumiller, G. S., Corey, D., Allen, S., Brewster, J. Cuttler, M., Gupton, H., et al. (2007). Defining the field of police psychology: Core domains and proficiencies. *Journal of Police & Criminal Psychology, 22*(2), 65–76.

Bohl, N. (1995). Professionally administered critical incident debriefing for police officers. In M. I. Kurke & E. M. Scrivner (Eds.), *Police psychology into the 21st century* (pp. 169–188). Hillsdale, NJ: Lawrence Erlbaum.

Breslau, N., & Davis, G. C. (1992). Posttraumatic stress disorder in an urban population of young adults: Risk factors for chronicity. *American Journal of Psychiatry, 149*(5), 671–675.

Carlan, P. E., & Nored, L. S. (2008). An examination of officer stress: Should police departments implement mandatory counseling? *Journal of Police & Criminal Psychology, 23*(1), 8–15.

Clark, D. W., & Haley, M. (2007). Crisis response tools for law enforcement. *The Police Chief, 74*(8), 94–101.

Davis, C. D., & Breslau, N. (1994). Post-traumatic stress disorder in victims of civilian trauma and criminal violence. *Psychiatric Clinics of North America, 17*(2), 289–298.

Finn, P., & Tomz, J. E. (1997). *Developing a law enforcement stress program for officers and their families.* Washington, DC: U.S Department of Justice, Office of Justice Programs, National Institute of Justice.

Fishkin, G. L. (1987). *Police burnout: Signs, symptoms and solutions for all law enforcement and public safety personnel.* Gardena, CA: Harcourt, Brace, Jovanovich.

Fuller, R. A. (1991). An overview of the process of peer support team development. In J. T. Reese, J. M. Horn, & C. Dunning (Eds.), *Critical incidents in policing, revised* (pp. 99–105). Washington, DC: U.S. Department of Justice, Federal Bureau of Investigation.

Gund, N., & Elliott, B. (1995). Employee assistance programs in police organizations. In M. I. Kurke & E. M. Scrivner (Eds.), *Police psychology into the 21st century* (pp. 149–167). Hillsdale, NJ: Lawrence Erlbaum.

Honig, A. L., & Roland, J. E. (1998). Shots fired: Officer involved. *The Police Chief, 65*(10), 116–120.

Honig, A. L., & Sultan, S. E. (2004). Reactions and resilience under fire: What an officer can expect. *The Police Chief, 71*(12), 54–60.

International Association of Chiefs of Police, Police Psychological Services Section.(2004). *Officer-involved shooting guidelines.* Retrieved January 28, 2010, from http://www.theiacp.org/psych_services_section/

International Association of Chiefs of Police. (2006). Peer support guidelines. Arlington, VA: Author. Retrieved July 13, 2009, from http://www.theiacp.org/psych_services_section/

Jones, J. W. (1995). Counseling issues and police diversity. In M. I. Kurke & E. M. Scrivner (Eds.), *Police psychology into the 21st century* (pp. 207–254). Hillsdale, NJ: Lawrence Erlbaum.

Klein, R. (1991). The utilization of police peer counselors in critical incidents. In J. T. Reese, J. M. Horn, & C. Dunning (Eds.), *Critical incidents in policing, revised* (pp. 159–168). Washington, DC: U.S. Department of Justice, Federal Bureau of Investigation.

Klein, R. (1994). Training peer counselors to provide the initial intervention in law enforcement relationship problems. In J. T. Reese & E. Scrivner (Eds.), *Law enforcement families: Issues and answers* (pp. 345–351). Washington, DC: U.S. Department of Justice, Federal Bureau of Investigation.

Linden, J., & Klein, R. (1988). Police peer counseling: An expanded perspective. In J. T. Reese & J. M. Horn (Eds.), *Police psychology: Operational assistance* (pp. 241–244). Washington, DC: U.S. Department of Justice, Federal Bureau of Investigation.

Mashburn, M. D. (1993). Critical incident counseling: Importance of counseling for police officers. *FBI Law Enforcement Bulletin, 62.* Retrieved January 17, 2010, from http://findarticles.com/p/articles/mi_m2194/?tag=content;col1

McCammon, S., Durham, T. W., Allison, E. J., Jr., & Williamson, J. E. (1988). Emergency workers' cognitive appraisal and coping with traumatic events. *Journal of Traumatic Stress, 1*(3), 353–372.

Mitchell, J. T. (1994). Critical incident stress interventions with families and significant others. In J. T. Reese & E. Scrivner (Eds.), *Law enforcement families: Issues and answers* (pp. 195–215). Washington, DC: U.S. Department of Justice, Federal Bureau of Investigation.

Mullins, W. C. (1994). Peer support team training and intervention for the police family. In J. T. Reese & E. Scrivner (Eds.), *Law enforcement families: Issues and answers* (pp. 205–215). Washington, DC: U.S. Department of Justice, Federal Bureau of Investigation.

Peer counseling program turns 20 years old. (2001). *Los Angeles Police Beat, 47*(8), p. 6.

Reese, J. T. (1995). A history of police psychological services. In M. I. Kurke & E. M. Scrivner (Eds.), *Police psychology into the 21st century* (pp. 31–44). Hillsdale, NJ: Lawrence Erlbaum.

Reiser, M. (1995). Foreward. In M. I. Kurke & E. M. Scrivner (Eds.), *Police psychology into the 21st century* (pp. xi–xiv). Hillsdale, NJ: Lawrence Erlbaum.

Scrivner, E. M., & Kurke, M. I. (1995). Police psychology at the dawn of the 21st century. In M. I. Kurke & E. M. Scrivner (Eds.), *Police psychology into the 21st century* (pp. 3–29). Hillsdale, NJ: Lawrence Erlbaum.

Sheehan, D. C., Everly, G. S., Jr., & Langlieb, A. (2004). Current best practices: Coping with major critical incidents. *FBI Law Enforcement Bulletin, 73,* 1–13.

Slate, R. N., Johnson, W. W., & Colbert, S. S. (2007). Police stress: A structural model. *Journal of Police & Criminal Psychology, 22*(2), 102–112.

Trompetter, P. S. (1994). Conjoint critical incident debriefings. In J. T. Reese & E. Scrivner (Eds.), *Law enforcement families: Issues and answers* (pp. 233–238). Washington, DC: U.S. Department of Justice, Federal Bureau of Investigation.

Van der Kolk, B. (1991). The psychological processing of traumatic events: The personal experience of post-traumatic stress disorder. In J. T. Reese, J. M. Horn, & C. Dunning (Eds.), *Critical incidents in policing, revised* (pp. 359–364). Washington, DC: U.S. Department of Justice, Federal Bureau of Investigation.

26 The Disconnected Values Model

A Brief Intervention for Improving Healthy Habits and Coping With Stress in Law Enforcement

Mark H. Anshel

Maintaining healthy habits that provide the proper energy and quality of life is a primary goal for any individual, but particularly for law enforcement personnel. Law enforcement is a profession that requires extensive physical stamina as well as successful adaptation to an array of stressful events. Possible "storms" intrinsic to job demands include addiction to alcohol and tobacco, poor work–life balance, the need to maintain positive relationships among work colleagues, lack of supervisory support, racism, relatively high rates of divorce and suicide, sexual harassment, violence, dealing with the court system, and maintaining a passion for a career that experiences only a 30% retention rate after 3 years on the job (Anshel, 2000; Aumiller & Corey, 2007; Rybicki & Nutter, 2002). Unhealthy habits exacerbate the deleterious effects of these storms on job satisfaction and performance. Thus, it is apparent that detecting and attempting to change unhealthy behavior patterns are especially important in law enforcement.

ANTECEDENTS OF POOR HEALTH IN LAW ENFORCEMENT

OBESITY, LOW FITNESS, AND POOR NUTRITION

Not unlike most professions, law enforcement has more than its share of obese members (Hoffman & Collingwood, 2005). Obesity often leads to low energy on the job and for family, poor health, and increased incidences of type 2 diabetes, a medical condition that is often an outcome of obesity and that reduces life span by about 10 years (Dunn, Andersen, & Jakicic, 1998). The obesity epidemic among law enforcement personnel is a function of overeating in both frequency and amount per sitting, eating diets relatively high in fat and low in fiber, and leading a sedentary existence, characterized in part by a lack of regular exercise (Hoffman & Collingwood, 2005).

In their study on the effects of a 10-week fitness program intervention among 67 police officers (54 men and 13 women) from the southeastern United States, Anshel and Kang (2008) found that 86% of participants were diagnosed as obese immediately prior to the study. The intervention, based on the Disconnected Values Model (described later), resulted in significantly improved cardiovascular and strength fitness, a relatively high exercise adherence rate of 80%, increased cardiovascular activity, and a 75% increase for strength training.

HIGH STRESS

The literature is replete with evidence of excessive stress in law enforcement, as described fully in other chapters of this book (also see Anshel, 2000). In their study of police stress and well-being, Hart, Wearing, and Headey (1995) found that "police organizations are the main source of psychological distress among police officers" (p. 150). Thus, due to the intrinsic nature of stress in law enforcement, Hart et al. contend that the goal of programs intended to improve coping skills cannot be to eliminate stress, but rather to help the individual better manage it, thereby reducing its unpleasant effect on job performance and mental, emotional, and physical well-being.

In their description of core domains in police psychology, Aumiller and Corey (2007) recommend the need for interventions related to improved wellness. These include disability and substance abuse recovery, and programs that "assist law enforcement officers with psychological preparation that helps them gain self-confidence and an ability to coordinate cognitions, emotions, and behavior in an optimally adaptive manner" (p. 72). The authors further describe the importance of mental preparation to combat the potential sources of high stress and to make cognitive appraisals of stressful events as "challenges or opportunities rather than risks or potential failures" (p. 72). Perhaps at the heart of effective stress management is the ability to apply proper coping skills.

Poor Coping Skills

Coping is a term—and a process—that has been misunderstood and misused over the years (Anshel, 2000). Coping is typically and traditionally defined as constantly changing conscious cognitive and behavioral attempts to manage the specific external and internal demands of a situation that is perceived as stressful (Lazarus & Folkman, 1984). This definition does not, in itself, presume that coping is always effective (i.e., often referred to as *adaptive*), nor that it is performed automatically. *Adaptive coping*, according to Zeidner and Saklofske (1996), should lead to a safe, legal, and permanent resolution of the problem, with no additional conflict, while maintaining a positive emotional state. *Maladaptive coping*, on the other hand, may consist of strategies, either planned or unplanned, that are illegal, contribute to the person's additional stress level or stress intensity, lead to undesirable performance outcome, or result in negative emotion.

Snyder and Dinoff (1999) correctly contend that "the effectiveness of the coping strategy rests on its ability to reduce immediate distress, as well as to contribute to more long-term outcomes such as psychological well-being" (p. 5). Coping is a skill and, like any skills, must be learned and practiced in order to properly reduce external demands (e.g., removal of the stressor, altering the situation) and/or build internal resources (e.g., confidence, hardiness). The use of coping strategies, therefore, is a learned and conscious process.

Evidence abounds that attempts at coping in law enforcement are too often maladaptive (Hart et al., 1995). Sample maladaptive coping strategies reported in the law enforcement literature (e.g., Anshel, 2000) include excessive alcohol intake, tobacco use, sudden and explosive anger, impatience, and physical confrontation. Adaptive coping includes dealing directly and professionally with the problem through discussion, avoiding the stressor, exercise, prayer, meditation, psychological distancing, and various forms of distraction. Poor coping skills, addressed in the Disconnected Values Model, carry costs to the officer's mental and physical well-being. These include, according to Loehr and Schwartz (2003), reduced fitness, weight gain, low energy, persistent higher stress and anxiety, hypertension, heart disease, low attention span, distraction from the task at hand, job burnout, and leaving the law enforcement profession.

There are long-term consequences of unhealthy habits. The human body will respond unfavorably to leading a sedentary lifestyle, not engaging in regular exercise, poor diet, high stress, and poor sleep. From the perspective of job effectiveness in law enforcement, maintaining an unhealthy lifestyle eventually leads to highly undesirable outcomes—physically, mentally, emotionally, and spiritually (Loehr & Schwartz, 2003). Police personnel, for instance, report markedly reduced passion for their job, leading to chronic stress, burnout (defined as a state of emotional, physical, and mental exhaustion that occurs in persons who encounter long-term stress from engaging in particular activities), and quitting the force as a result of the effects of prolonged negative behavioral patterns (Baumeister, Faber, & Wallace, 1999; Slate, Johnson, & Colbert, 2007).

WELLNESS PROGRAMS AND INTERVENTIONS IN LAW ENFORCEMENT

Aumiller and Corey (2007) recommend that wellness programs in law enforcement focus on reducing stress and promoting good physical and mental health for police officers. McCarty, Zhao, and Garland (2007) also found that wellness programs in law enforcement, for both male and female police officers, target similar health-related issues.

In a more recent study, Tanigoshi, Kontos, and Remley (2008) attempted to determine the effectiveness of wellness counseling on improving health outcomes among 51 volunteer law enforcement officers. The experimental group met with a counselor to determine personal wellness needs and program goals based on the results of a wellness inventory that reflected both physical and mental well-being (e.g., improved motivation, managing anxiety, overcoming low self-esteem, planning a fitness program, starting proper dietary habits). The control group participants, on the other hand, did not meet with a counselor. Instead, they were offered counseling services free of charge at the end of the study. Members of both groups completed a 107-item inventory called the 5F-Wel, which provides "a comprehensive and systematic measure for assessing total wellness" (p. 67), prior to and immediately following the 15-week intervention period. It was hypothesized that individuals in the counseling (intervention) group would more likely engage in health-related programs and improve their fitness and diet as a result. All data were based on self-report. The results indicated a significant groups × time (pretest–posttest) interaction, in which the wellness counseling group significantly improved wellness scores between pretest and posttest, whereas the control group's wellness levels remained unchanged from pretest to posttest. Limitations of his study included the exclusive use of self-report, and the failure to include fitness or nutrition coaching and testing, which did not allow for detecting changes in fitness or any other objective measures that would have reflected health behavior change.

Clearly, law enforcement members both need and will benefit from developing habits that improve fitness and nutrition to reduce the onset of obesity and obesity-related diseases, and increase energy and job performance. The existing health behavior change literature, however, is replete with interventions that have yielded only equivocal results. The amount of outcome variance explained in studies testing the efficacy of exercise interventions has rarely been above 30% (Baranowski, Anderson, & Carmack, 1998).

According to Dishman and Buckworth (1997), who conducted a meta-analysis of 127 studies and 14 dissertations to determine the effectiveness of interventions to enhance exercise adherence in a healthy population, physical activity or fitness associated with the interventions diminished with time; in other words, there was *poor adherence*. The equivocal findings of studies on the effectiveness of these interventions may be due, at least in part, to limitations in the use of these interventions. These limitations include the absence of a theoretical framework, poor inclusion and exclusion criteria of research participants, and the use of strategies and programs that have been imposed on the individual, such as program goals, and allowing participants choices, a strategy called *perceived choice* (Markland, 1999) in which participants select the time, location, and type of exercises to perform (Buckworth & Dishman, 2002). Oldridge (2001) suggests that exercise strategies should be implemented as an integral part of one's daily routines, a strategy rarely addressed in the health behavior change literature.

As Glasgow et al. (2004) have concluded from their review of related literature, "it is well documented that the results of most behavioral and health promotion studies have not been translated into practice" (p. 3). As indicated earlier, unknown to researchers and practitioners are the *mechanisms* that lead to health and exercise behavior change. Ockene (2001) correctly concludes that "change is a process, not a one-time event, and we can't expect people to make changes at a level for which they're not ready. Our interventions need to be directed to where the individual is" (p. 45).

These limitations are addressed in a health behavior change intervention called the Disconnected Values Model (DVM).

ANTECEDENTS OF THE DISCONNECTED VALUES MODEL: STARTING POINTS FOR BUILDING HEALTHY HABITS

Few would argue that changing one's health behavior habits is very challenging (Loehr, 2007; Ockene, 2001). This is partly because our habits have been formed over many years, have become automatic behavior patterns, and consequently are firmly entrenched in our lifestyle, represented by routines. To paraphrase Loehr (2007), we are who we train to be. If we fail to challenge our cardiovascular system through vigorous physical activity, we literally train our body to be unfit through a sedentary lifestyle. Not surprisingly, attempting to increase fitness through exercise becomes difficult and unpleasant due to making sudden, highly intense demands on our physiological systems. Resuming a sedentary lifestyle, therefore, becomes increasingly attractive.

Other challenges to health behavior changes, especially related to increasing physical activity, is partially due to an array of long-held feelings and attitudes that may reflect negative previous experiences in exercise settings. Examples include the physical education teacher who used exercise as a form of discipline, or exercise burnout resulting from too much physical training as a former athlete, or experiencing an injury from previous exercise attempts. Along these lines, an improper diet (e.g., high fat, low fiber) and poor eating patterns (e.g., excessive portions in one sitting, late-night eating), and several eating disorders (e.g., anorexia, emotional eating) reflect habits that are formed early in life and usually result in long-term unpleasant consequences.

Five components are needed to change health behavior. These components are based on reviewing the existing clinical and empirical literature (e.g., Loehr, 2007; Loehr & Schwartz, 2003; Rollnick, Mason, & Butler, 1999; Shumaker, Ockene, & Riekert, 2009), my own published research (Anshel, 2008; Anshel & Kang, 2007a, 2007b, 2008), and my experience as practitioner in wellness settings, including a 2-year grant as the director of the Middle Tennessee State University Employee Health and Wellness Program. These components are (1) having a mission and developing a mission statement; (2) obtaining social support such as coaching, verbal support from family and friends, and exercising with others; (3) using quantitative data, such as fitness test scores or a lipids profile; (4) developing routines—habits of desirable behaviors—based on proper time management strategies; and (5) acknowledging one's values. Although these components will be discussed later when reviewing the model's action plan, a brief review of each is important to lend further credence of the current model.

DEVELOPING A MISSION STATEMENT

A mission statement is usually defined as a declaration of specific goals and the intent about how the person intends to reach these goals (Loehr & Schwartz, 2003). The statement reflects the person's most important values and serves as a blueprint for how the person will invest his or her energy. Here are two sample mission statements obtained from two law enforcement officers who experienced a program in which the DVM was administered to a police detective and a police officer, respectively (Anshel & Kang, 2008).

Detective-personal. I plan to maintain a weight of 115 by exercise and changing a few eating habits. This is the healthiest for me physically and mentally. I am going to increase my overall health for my immediate family as well as my mother who has supranuclear palsy. I will work on bettering my attitude toward my family and life in general. I will keep in close contact with a few friends who I have put on the back burner lately.

Detective-professional. I want to be able to perform well at work and not feel tired by lunchtime. I will eat every 2–3 hours to maintain my energy and keep me more alert. I will try to have a good attitude toward work and the people I work with.

Officer-personal. I plan to spend more time doing things I like to do. Since recently ending a marriage, I want to rebuild my life and find out who I really am. With the work of my psychologist, I plan to work out some previous issues that I have with life. I want to become more physically active and try new hobbies. I adopted a new pet and plan on incorporating him into my schema. I plan on reconnecting with old friends from the past.

Officer-professional. I am going to be more assertive and stand up for myself at work. I am going to work on being on time daily and not let my personal life affect my professional career. I am going to try to be more compassionate and receptive to others and their feelings.

Obtaining Social Support

A person's social environment is a very important factor for promoting exercise habits. The extent to which an individual receives various forms of support from others, either directly as a co-exerciser or indirectly through verbal messages of approval and motivation, is referred to as social support (Anshel, 2006; Berger, Pargman, & Weinberg, 2007). In their extensive review of the literature, Berger et al. concluded that "social support from family friends, and significant others has been consistently related to adult physical activity and adherence to structured exercise programs" (p. 237). Hoffman and Collingwood (2005) found similar patterns among law enforcement supervisors who offered positive messages for improved fitness to subordinates. Anshel and Kang (2007a, 2007b) found that wellness programs resulted in significantly improved fitness, changes in dietary habits, and high exercise adherence rates if participants in their 10-week wellness program interacted intermittently with fitness and nutrition coaches during the program. Developing desirable, permanent changes in health behavior, therefore, is more likely if individuals in law enforcement receive coaching and/or exercise with others.

Receiving Numerical (Quantitative) Data

Loehr and Schwartz (2003), based on extensive empirical evidence, contend that most individuals are motivated by numbers. That is, the use of quantitative data powerfully influence health behavior change because the person being evaluated has an objective health measure that provides a value that is perceived by the individual as desirable or undesirable. Thus, testing serves two purposes: (1) to indicate a starting point or baseline measure (i.e., a "pretest") that allows individuals to compare their progress on the same measure(s) after a period of time (i.e., a "posttest"), or (2) as an objective measure or some deficiency or need for improvement. The undesirable number provides a strong incentive to change the behavior pattern perceived as responsible for this outcome (Anshel, 2006, 2008).

Developing Routines

Of central importance to replacing unhealthy habits is for the individual to develop new routines—habits of desirable behaviors—that are scheduled and based on proper time management strategies in which the ritual will be carried out as planned.

Why are new rituals so important to developing new habits? As Loehr and Schwartz (2003) explain, "rituals serve as anchors, insuring that even in the most difficult circumstances, we will continue to use our energy in service of the values that we hold most dear" (p. 167). It is common for us, especially in the face of challenges, to revert to what we know and what feels comfortable. This is where our routines become central to our comfort zone and maintaining a high quality of life; we "do" what we "know." Loehr and Schwartz contend that "rituals are a powerful means by which to translate our values and priorities into action—to embody what matters most to us in our everyday behaviors" (p. 166).

Acknowledging Values

The fifth and last component of health behavior change is a person's values. According to Rokeach (1973), values are core beliefs that guide and provide the impetus for motivating behavior, and provide standards against which we assess behavior. Values differ from interests and attitudes, the latter of which are more situational and transitory, and derived from a core set of values (Super, 1995). In addition, interests, attitudes, and needs are transitory, and once satiated, attitudes and needs may not influence behavior to a similar extent as do values. Hogan and Mookherjee (1981) contend that values guide behavior, and that sharing values with others strongly affects a person's commitment to benefit others.

Members of law enforcement, for instance, whose values include family, faith, health, or high-quality job performance will more likely perceive healthy habits, such as engaging in regular exercise, proper sleep, or proper eating habits, as consistent with their values and to the benefit of others who are considered important. Habits that benefit our quality of life and our physical and mental well-being fulfill our sense of purpose (Loehr & Schwartz, 2003). Our sense of purpose results in becoming more concerned with serving and meeting the needs of others, and are less concerned with self-focusing on our own needs (Loehr, 2007). For instance, police officers who consider *performance competence* as an important value will want to develop habits that promote good health and energy in order to meet job demands. Failing to maintain habits that are consistent with one's values form "disconnects" that have short-term costs (e.g., weight gain) and long-term consequences (e.g., type 2 diabetes, heart disease). Whether these costs and consequences are acceptable to the officer forms the basis for making a conscious decision to retain the negative habit or to replace it with positive, healthier alternative behaviors. This decision is at the heart of the Disconnected Values Model, a brief intervention for use by law enforcement that does not require licensure in psychology or counseling.

THE DISCONNECTED VALUES MODEL (DVM): A BRIEF INTERVENTION FOR LAW ENFORCEMENT

The DVM is predicated on two postulates, often missing from existing health behavior change intervention research. The first postulate is that a person's decision to initiate a behavior pattern reflects his or her deepest values and beliefs, also called the *power of purpose* (Loehr & Schwartz, 2003). An individual's sense of purpose fosters the desire to become fully engaged in activities that the person feels is of genuine importance in meeting personal goals.

The second DVM postulate is that individuals prefer behavioral patterns consistent with those values and that acknowledged inconsistencies between the person's values and behaviors is uncomfortable. The challenge for most individuals is to consistently hold ourselves accountable to them. Thus, an individual whose values include health, family, faith, and performance excellence should be self-motivated to regularly engage in at least some behavior patterns that reflect these values. As Loehr and Schwartz (2003) conclude, "deeply held values fuel the energy on which purpose is built" (p. 140).

The DVM, illustrated in Figure 26.1, requires that individuals exhibit high self-awareness that their unhealthy habits form the underlying causes of their poor health, unhappiness, or lack of energy. Additional self-awareness is important in acknowledging the undesirability of maintaining these self-destructive behavioral patterns; if individuals fail to change these habits, there will be long-term consequences to health and quality of life.

Because the DVM consists of a set of cognitive and behavioral strategies, conducted in a structured sequence, and does not warrant psychotherapy, it can be administered by individuals who are not licensed, registered, or certified mental health professionals. In fact, the use of professional counseling techniques and other clinical interventions is contrary to the model's strengths. Application of the DVM has similarities to the conceptual framework of motivational interviewing.

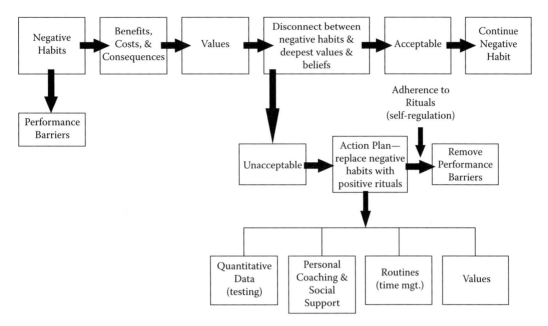

FIGURE 26.1   The Disconnected Values Model.

As described by Hecht et al. (2005) and Miller and Rollnick (2002), motivational interviewing (MI) is a client-centered method to enhance intrinsic motivation for health behavior change by performing three essential functions: (1) collaborating with the client to create a safe, supportive, and nonjudgmental environment within which to initiate the client's behavior change; (2) exploring with the client reasons for and against behavior change, the goal of which is to resolve ambivalence; and (3) developing the client's sense of autonomy (responsibility) for making behavior change. Hecht et al. contend that "it is the client, not the counselor, who must decide if, how, and when change will occur" (p. 30). To Miller and Rollnick, MI is "a client-centered directive method for enhancing intrinsic motivation to change by exploring and resolving ambivalence" (p. 25).

Unlike MI, the DVM is a values-based approach to assist clients in detecting at least one misalignment between their unhealthy habits and their deepest values about what they are most passionate about, and to help them determine if the disconnect is acceptable, given the disconnect's short-term costs and long-term consequences. The DVM also provides guidelines for a self-regulation action plan, unlike MI. In summary, then, the DVM posits that changing unhealthy behavior patterns is a function of three processes: (1) that individuals agree that these undesirable behavior patterns—bad habits—are inconsistent with their values; (2) that this inconsistency between values and bad habits is unacceptable because of the costs and consequences of persisting in these actions; and (3) that these individuals are willing to follow an action plan that replaces negative habits with positive routines. The model begins with acknowledging negative habits.

Negative Habits

Negative habits, in this model, consist of an individual's thoughts, emotions, or actions that are acknowledged by the person as unhealthy (e.g., overweight, physical fatigue) or undesirable (e.g., feelings of discomfort or unhappiness), and yet, the individual persists in voluntarily maintaining them. Quality of life often suffers.

The two primary reasons individuals engage in negative habits is because (1) the perceived benefits of maintaining the habit outweigh its costs and long-term consequences, and (2) the benefits are short term, whereas the consequences (e.g., heart disease) take years to manifest (Anshel, 2006;

Loehr, 2007). A habit does not exist without benefits. For example, the negative habit of impatience in response to frustration has the perceived benefits of prompting action by others, and perhaps releasing unpleasant feelings. The costs, however, include alienating others, being avoided by others, and increased stress. Long-term consequences might include hypertension and a lack of respect and trust by others. The individual makes a judgment call whether the benefits outweigh the costs and consequences of their habitual impatience.

Performance Barriers

Performance barriers are operationally defined as a persistent thought, emotion, or action that compromises and creates obstacles to high-quality performance (Dunn et al., 1998). The barriers are almost always controllable—with the exception of many addicted behaviors, which are not always controllable—and, thus, changeable because they are manifestations of the individual's negative habits. Thus, the negative habit of not exercising often leads to performance barriers such as physical or mental fatigue, lack of concentration, poor sleep, low self-confidence, or poor communication skills. The model requires individuals to identify their negative habits and the consequent barriers to high performance that often result.

In examples related to law enforcement, the emotional negative habit of persistent anxiety will lead to the performance barrier of slow, often inaccurate decision-making. The negative physical habit of poor work–life balance results in the performance barrier of poor relationships with family. One function of the model, then, is to help the client detect their negative habits and how they lead to undesirable job performance and in other areas of life. The next stage is to self-examine the reasons, or benefits, of maintaining these negative habits.

Perceived "Benefits" of Negative Habits

Without benefits, we would not persist in having unhealthy habits. The so-called benefits of not exercising, for example, include more time to do other things, not experiencing the discomfort of physical exertion, and avoiding the expense of purchasing fitness club memberships and exercise clothing. Of course, there are also "costs" and "long-term consequences" of not exercising.

Costs and Long-Term Consequences of Negative Habits

Before individuals are prepared to make changes in any unhealthy habit, they must be able to identify the short-term costs and long-term consequences of this habit. The short-term costs of not engaging in regular exercise, for instance, includes reduced fitness, weight gain, less energy, and higher stress and anxiety. The long-term consequences of not exercising include poorer physical and mental health, reduced quality of life, greater likelihood of contracting certain diseases, and, in some cases, shorter life span. If the person considers these costs acceptable, then the negative habit of not exercising and maintaining a sedentary lifestyle will likely continue. However, if the costs and long-term consequences are viewed as far greater than the benefits, *and* the person concludes that these costs and consequences are unacceptable, than a change in behavior is far more likely.

While the cost–benefit paradigm seems like a powerful tool to instigate behavior change, there is a missing "ignition point." The DVM is values based; therefore, the individual is asked to identify the misalignment between the designated negative habit and the person's deepest values and beliefs.

Determining Our Deepest Values and Beliefs

The DVM includes an intervention component that reflects the person's sense of purpose, that is, "the energy derived from connecting to deeply held values and a purpose beyond one's self-interest"

(Loehr & Schwartz, 2003, p. 131). Loehr and Schwartz explain self-destructive behaviors and negative habits (e.g., poor nutrition, lack of exercise, lack of recovery from chronic stress) as reflecting a "lack of…firm beliefs and compelling values [that are] easily buffeted by the prevailing winds. If we lack a strong sense of purpose [i.e., what really matters to us; our passion] we cannot hold our ground when we are challenged by life's inevitable storms" (p. 133).

It is suggested that individuals be presented with a list of values—what they consider to be their beliefs about what is really important to them—rather than to ask them to generate their own list. The latter invites underreporting. Approximately 40 values have been identified by Loehr and Schwartz (2003) and Anshel and Kang (2007a, 2007b; 2008). Next, they are asked to select and then rank their five most important values. The values most likely to be ranked as highly important include health, faith, family, integrity, happiness, honesty, character, performance excellence, commitment, and concern for others.

In summary, the decision to replace an unhealthy habit with desirable routines is more likely if (1) a person acknowledges that the costs and long-term consequences of a negative habit are greater than the benefits, (2) these costs run counter to the person's deepest values and beliefs about what is important, and (3) this discrepancy between their negative habits and their values is unacceptable. Thus, behavior change is more likely to be permanent when the patient, client, or law enforcement officer concludes that health, quality of life, and high job performance and job satisfaction are linked to behaving in a way that is consistent with one's deepest values.

Establishing a Disconnect

To help law enforcement officers detect an inconsistency between their values and their negative (self-destructive) habits, the consultant or police supervisor might ask, "To what extent are your values consistent with your actions? If you value your health, for instance, do you have habits that are not good for you, and therefore, inconsistent with your values? What about your family? Do you value your family? If you lead a sedentary lifestyle and are not involved in a program of exercise and proper nutrition, yet one of your deepest values is to maintain good health, to what extent is your health value consistent with your behavior? Do you detect a 'disconnect,' or inconsistency, between your beliefs about good health and your unhealthy behavioral patterns?"

Acceptability of the Disconnect

If a person acknowledges that his or her negative habits (e.g., not engaging in regular exercise; not getting sufficient sleep; having a poor work–life balance; following a nonnutritious diet, eating large portions of food, especially close to bedtime, and/or allowing excessive weight gain; impatience; anger) are inconsistent with the person's deepest values and beliefs about what is really important to him or her, the follow-up question must be asked: "Given the short-term costs and long-term consequences of your negative habit(s), is the disconnect between your lack of exercise and your values of health, family, faith, and job performance acceptable to you?" If the disconnect *is* acceptable—and for many individuals who feel that changing the negative habit is either undesirable or beyond their control—then no change will likely occur. It is necessary, therefore, to identify another disconnect between the person's negative habit and his or her values. Only when an acknowledged disconnect is *unacceptable* to the individual will there be a commitment to change behavior and replace the negative habit with a new, more desirable routine. If a disconnect is viewed as unacceptable, the individual should be ready to develop and carry out an action plan.

Developing an Action Plan

The decision to initiate an exercise program, ostensibly because there is a disconnect between the individual's negative habit and his or her deepest values and beliefs, is followed by developing a self-regulation detailed action plan. The plan consists of using time management skills in creating a schedule for initiating and maintaining the new, desirable ritual. For starting an exercise program, for example, this might include determining the location of the exercise venue, scheduling one or more sessions with an exercise (fitness) coach, determining the exercise type and schedule (i.e., days of the week, time of day for exercise), and planning exercise tests to establish a baseline of fitness and other health indicators. In addition, the action plan should examine availing oneself of social support (e.g., exercising with a friend, exercising as a group or class), and perhaps obtaining nutritional coaching to establish proper eating patterns. Only qualified individuals, such as a registered dietician, should be consulted for this information. Studies have indicated that specificity of timing and precision of behavior dramatically increase the probability of successfully carrying out a self-controlled action plan (Loehr, 2007; Loehr & Schwartz, 2003).

The action plan consists primarily of three factors that will markedly enhance the individual's *permanent* commitment to health behavior change. For developing a habit of regular exercise, for example, the plan consists of (1) a specific time of day for exercising; (2) a set of routines that support the exercise habit (e.g., selected thoughts and behaviors prior to, during, and following the exercise session; exercising with a friend and promoting other forms of social support; minimizing distractions that will interfere with exercise plans; and choosing the proper clothing and venue); and (3) linking these specific times and routines to the individual's deepest values and beliefs about the benefits of this new habit, and removing the existing disconnect.

Finally, someone called an orientation coach, who introduces the model's procedures and establishes at least one disconnect, or a fitness coach and the client will work together to develop a 24-hour self-regulation action plan consisting of new routines that are built into one's workday. The scheduled activities will include presleep rituals (e.g., no excessive food or alcohol intake within 2 hours before bedtime); activity that induces positive emotion and positive communication with family members); sleep (e.g., times for lights out and waking); specified times for exercise, water intake (i.e., hydration), meals, snacks, and recovery breaks; connecting with family members and significant others; and other rituals linked to each dimension and the client's values.

The DVM meets six criteria of a practical intervention, as suggested by Brawley (1993): (1) that processes being studied are changeable, (2) that the links between key factors are described so that they are targeted for change, (3) that assessment measures of these factors and the relationships between them are accurate, (4) that the theory or model shows external validity, (5) that the model's concepts lead to a direct or indirect change in cognition and behavior, and (6) that a framework can explain the reasons an intervention failed to produce change.

EMPIRICAL RESEARCH SUPPORT FOR THE DVM

Three outcome-based studies, including one involving police officers, have provided support for the DVM. In one study, Anshel and Kang (2007a) tested the DVM on replacing negative habits with positive routines for improving full engagement at work among 41 university faculty. Results indicated statistically significant improvements in fitness and dietary habits, time management and organizational skills, positive mood state, adaptation to work-related stressors, improved work–life balance, and self-reported reduced disconnects between undesirable habits and the person's values.

In two additional tests of the DVM, Anshel and Kang (2007b, 2008) examined the effect of a 10-week intervention on selected measures of fitness and nutrition among university faculty and staff, and 67 male and female members of a city police department, respectively, both located in the southeastern United States. Both studies, using an action research methodology, consisted of teaching components of the DVM to all participants in a 90-minute orientation. Individuals were then assigned a fitness coach who tested and then trained their clients over the 10-week program. Participants in both studies were given a series of fitness tests prior to (pretest) and immediately following (posttest) the program. The tests measured changes in aerobic fitness, strength, and percentage of body fat. In addition, pre- and postprogram blood tests measured changes in their lipids profile (e.g., high- and low-density lipoproteins, or "good" and "bad" cholesterol, and triglycerides). Weekly seminars on proper dietary habits were also offered by a registered dietician.

Results of the multivariate analyses in both studies indicated significantly improved fitness scores (e.g., increased cardiovascular ability, improved strength, lower percentage of body fat), and significantly reduced low-density (not high-density) lipoproteins, an indication of favorable changes in dietary habits. That is, "bad" cholesterol was markedly reduced. Exercise adherence for cardiovascular activity averaged 22 of 30 sessions (73%), and strength-training adherence averaged 13 of 20 sessions (65%) for the faculty study and 80% and 75% in the police study, respectively. These are relatively high adherence rates, as indicated by existing research literature. The results of these outcome-based studies suggest that the DVM provides an effective cognitive-behavioral approach to promoting changes in selected health behaviors, in particular, exercise and nutritional habits. The DVM has been validated in these studies.

According to Mills (2003), action research, employed in the two Anshel and Kang studies described previously, includes five forms of validation that were confirmed in the two Anshel and Kang studies: theoretical, evaluative, outcome, process, and catalytic. *Theoretical validity* is the ability of the study to explain the DVM. The Anshel and Kang studies of university employees (2007a, 2007b) and of police officers (2008) included an initial 3-hour seminar and subsequent action plan. The participants exhibited increased insight into the negative habits that compromised their health, happiness, and quality of life, while acknowledging their values and the disconnect between their values and their negative habits. They also replaced these negative habits with positive routines, particularly related to changes in exercise and nutritional habits, that ostensibly would improve selected measures of health and psychological well-being, and they willingly worked with a performance coach in carrying out the action plan, followed by adherence to these new rituals.

Evaluative validity (i.e., the results were obtained and reported in an unbiased manner) was evident by significant improvements in selected fitness and blood lipid measures.

Outcome validity (i.e., the action plan leads to resolving selected problems successfully) was obtained by significant improvements from pretest to posttest indicating strong adherence to program concepts.

Process validity (i.e., the study was conducted in a dependable and competent manner) was achieved in these studies by including trained, professional coaches, including the seminar leader who provided initial information and nurtured participant motivation to engage in the program.

Catalytic validity, according to Mills (2003), indicates that participants take action on the basis of their heightened understanding of the study's subject. This was apparent in the Anshel and Kang (2008) study partially based on the officers' high exercise adherence rates and statistically significant improvements on all fitness and lipids scores. The results of quantitative analyses provided further evidence of self-reported outcomes. While the DVM has been empirically shown in these studies to change health behavior, further research is needed to determine the effects of the model on long-term adherence to the newly acquired habits. A particularly relevant form of research in health behavior change that is common in the clinical literature is the case study.

BRIEF CASE STUDY OF JAMES, A LAW ENFORCEMENT OFFICER

James is a 42-year-old married male with two children. James is 6 feet, 2 inches tall and weighs 265 pounds. He has 38% body fat (i.e., the degree to which his weight consists of fat, as opposed to lean body tissue; the average for males is 20–25%), and a waist circumference of 51 inches. James listed five "negative habits" that he acknowledged compromises his health: the absence of regular (daily) exercise, a diet high in fat and low in fiber, poor sleep, high daily stress accompanied by poor coping habits, and smoking one pack of cigarettes a day. Two years earlier, he had engaged in a strength-training program and enjoyed it but does not enjoy aerobic exercise, particularly at his excessive weight. He has no apparent symptoms of heart disease, although his physician has strongly recommended changes in lifestyle. His goals were to lose weight, exercise regularly to enhance both muscular strength and aerobic fitness, sleep better, reduce his daily stress level, and have more energy.

Three individuals, called *coaches*, who were experts in their respective areas of specialization, assisted James through the 10-week program. The orientation coach served the mutual roles of program organizer and researcher who organized data collection, and worked privately with the client during an initial 90-minute session; the session consisted of presenting the client with completing segments of a workbook and reviewing each component of the model (e.g., reviewing the costs and benefits of their self-described negative habits, identifying their values and the disconnects between those values and their negative habits, and so on), and developing the client's action plan. The nutrition coach, who was a registered dietician, interpreted the blood lipids profile scores, provided education about proper nutrition and eating habits, and counseled the client on overcoming current undesirable eating habits. The fitness coach (personal trainer) who administered pre- and postintervention fitness tests, provided a fitness prescription and met with the client once per week to teach weight-training skills.

The registered dietician recorded James' current diet and helped him make proper food choices that were sensitive to his highly restricted dietary preferences. The exercise coach, who was a university student in the exercise science program, administered five fitness tests: cardiovascular fitness, upper-body strength, lower-body strength, percent body fat, and waist circumference prior to the program, soon followed by an exercise prescription. Although James was asked to commit to three 1-hour sessions of exercise per week, coaching was provided only 1 hour per week. The coaching consisted of exercise instruction using weights and monitoring cardiovascular exercise so that James's heart rate could approach "training level." James was retested following the 10-week program for fitness and blood lipids.

Applying the DVM in the orientation segment prior to the formal coaching program included five steps. The first step consisted of James developing a mission statement about his intended outcomes of this 10-week program and the need to maintain a lifestyle that was consistent with his values. He needed to identify the reasons he wished to improve his health and energy. The second segment consisted of the model's cost–benefit tradeoff. James identified the negative habits he felt most impaired his quality of life, energy, and career in law enforcement. He also listed the benefits, costs, and consequences of maintaining those unhealthy habits. For example, the benefits of eating a fast-food, high-calorie lunch (and often dinner, too) included good taste, low cost, fast and convenient restaurant service, and feeling satiated until the next meal; the issue of nutritional value was not a perceived benefit. Then he listed the "costs" of these habits, including high fat content, high number of ingested calories, feeling uncomfortably full, and high fat content. Long-term consequences included increased "bad" cholesterol, weight gain, and the possibility of heart disease, type 2 diabetes (associated with severe obesity), and some forms of cancers associated with a high-fat diet.

In the third segment, James was asked to identify five of his most important values. He listed family, faith, health, job performance, and integrity. James was then asked to make two lists, his unhealthy habits (e.g., eating three donuts for breakfast daily, eating large portions of food at lunch and dinner, minimizing fresh vegetables, not exercising, and feeling excessive stress at work). The fourth step consisted of comparing the contents of each list and identifying and articulating any "disconnects," that is, areas in which a negative habit was inconsistent with a particular value. James acknowledged three disconnects between his negative (unhealthy) habits and his most important values. The orientation coach then asked James to think about and react to the following statement: "Given the costs and long-term consequences of any negative habit that is inconsistent with any of your values, is this disconnect acceptable?" James was reminded that if he concluded that the disconnect was acceptable, then the negative habit would continue; he would not be open to replacing it with a healthier ritual. However, if he concluded that any particular disconnect was unacceptable, again, due to its costs and consequences, this would indicate that James is ready for behavior change by planning and carrying out an action plan that replaced the unhealthy habit with a more desirable routine.

For example, family was one of James' primary values. He has two sons, which contributed to his conclusion that his current lifestyle was inconsistent with his belief in being a good father and having sufficient energy to play with and mentor his sons. Having the energy to enjoy his relationship with family members was an important outcome of this program. He agreed, for example, that his wife would help him eat meals with smaller portions, which were low in fat and consistent with the registered dietician's recommendations. He and his wife also agreed to exercise together at least twice per week.

The fifth and final segment consisted of developing and agreeing to carry out a time-management action plan based on inserting specific behaviors into James' revised 24-hour schedule. Sample tasks included planned times to awake in the morning (law enforcement personnel also work a night shift, requiring a different schedule, but behavioral patterns would be similar), preferred bedtime, times for eating several small meals each day, snacking, exercise, recovery periods (e.g., including times to connect with family and friends), and a 2-hour segment before bedtime called *presleep rituals*. The coaches served as strong sources of support for developing these new routines.

Fitness and blood tests were conducted immediately before and after the intervention to determine the extent to which the intervention resulted in desirable changes in the dependent measures, called *change scores*. Results of the blood test indicated improved lipids profile scores, with all scores categorized as "normal." Postintervention fitness tests indicated improved upper- and lower-body strength—as determined by one maximal lift using arms and legs, respectively—and superior cardiovascular fitness. Cardiovascular fitness is determined by a submaximal VO^2 test, which consists of walking on a treadmill for 8 minutes at a predetermined speed. Individuals with higher cardiovascular fitness will have lower increased heart rate on the treadmill, and their heart rate will return to "normal" (i.e., recover) after the walking task more quickly. The data also revealed a three-inch reduction in James' waistline and a reduction in percent body fat (from 38% to 32%).

On qualitative measures, James reported a high rate of adherence to his exercise regimen. Full adherence was defined as attending exercise sessions a minimum of three times per week over the 10-week program, or a total of 30 sessions. James attended 26 of the 30 sessions, for a compliance rate of 87%. Prior to the intervention, James revealed that he was failing to show his love of his family, his highest ranked value, and allowed job-related stress to dominate his thoughts and emotions almost every waking hour.

In a postintervention interview, James was adamant about his commitment to overcome his disconnected values (e.g., family, health, faith) in contrast to maintaining unhealthy habits and maintaining his new set of routines, particularly related to eating behavior and exercise. James reported improved energy at work and when he was with his family.

James commented about the 10-week program that lent insights into its influence on his behavior. His positive feelings toward the three coaches enhanced his motivation, commitment, and satisfaction in establishing new routines, especially those related to exercise and diet. Establishing good rapport with coaches is central to intervention effectiveness because changing behavior begins with establishing trust and credibility with a client (Rollnick et al., 1999).

A second factor that influenced James's behavior changes were test scores he received prior to the program. Although his lack of fitness was assumed, his poor lipids profile scores were "eye-opening," to use his terms. Without making a diagnosis, the dietician informed him that certain scores were often predictive of advance heart disease and type 2 diabetes. As indicated earlier, quantitative data are important motivators of behavior change because they are objective and promote a sense of authenticity and validity to the person's health assessment (Anshel, 2006). As Loehr and Schwartz (2003) assert, people are motivated by numbers, usually in the form of test data.

A final factor that promoted adherence to James' action plan was establishing routines that were consistent with his values and his passion about what is really important in his personal life and career. More specifically, his routines were consistent with the program's goals of improved fitness, blood lipids, and energy. His action plan provided specific tasks that were to be performed at specific times, another component of the model. Scheduled tasks such as times for exercise, meals, snacks, recovery breaks, contact with loved ones and colleagues, presleep rituals, scheduled times for sleep and waking, and other activities that were consistent with his most important values resulted in strong plan adherence, an outcome consistent with past related group studies with university employees (Anshel & Kang, 2007a, 2007b) and police officers (Anshel & Kang, 2008).

CONCLUSIONS AND FUTURE DIRECTIONS

Values are core beliefs that guide behavior, provide impetus for motivating behavior, and provide standards against which we assess behavior (Rokeach, 1973). Values are highly relevant to establishing a person's individuality and help our understanding of one's behavior. And yet, interventions intended to change health behaviors have heretofore ignored adding a person's values as an intrinsic component of these programs. As Rokeach contends, a person who values health will tend to develop daily rituals and long-term habits that enhance health and general well-being. Hogan and Mookherjee (1981) describe values as "one of the most distinguishing characteristics motivating human beings; the likely effects of values on human behavior, beliefs, and attitudes are indisputable" (p. 29). One strength of the DVM is the recognition that identifying one's values guide the person's behavior and that sharing values with others strongly influences the person's willingness to sacrifice personal, self-serving needs for the benefit of others.

Values, according to Super (1995), are more central determinants of behavior than interests and attitudes, the latter of which are more situational and derived from a core set of values. Thus, a plethora of interests and attitudes are derived from a relatively reduced number of values. Unlike interests and attitudes, which are transitory, and once satiated, may not influence behavior, values are almost always firmly entrenched and stable, and, therefore, transcend situations and guide behavior over a long period of time. It is likely, therefore, that values predict behavior (Brown & Crace, 1996; Hogan & Mookherjee, 1981). Ostensibly, if health forms part of a person's value system, more time and effort will go toward engaging in regular exercise and other behavioral patterns endorsed by a person's personal care provider or personal trainer.

While the DVM is intended as a form of brief therapy that can be administered by individuals without a credential as a mental health professional, client issues may surface prior to or during the program that may require the services of a licensed psychologist or therapist. For example, wellness programs for law enforcement participants often require counseling skills on issues that are central to mental well-being, such as depression, low self-esteem, posttraumatic stress disorder, various addictions, work-related stress, irrational thinking, and burnout (Tanigoshi et al., 2008). Concomitant with these conditions are psychological tests that measure evidence of psychopathology. The administration and interpretation of such tests require licensure as a mental health professional that serves diagnostic purposes (Quick et al., 1997).

As Quick et al. and Tanigoshi et al. contend, mental health issues often accompany dropout from most health-related programs for an array of reasons. The need to address mental health issues also exists to a similar extent for both male and female law enforcement officers (McCarty et al., 2007). Thus, a wellness program in law enforcement based on the DVM should either include a licensed psychologist whose role it is to test and, if needed, to meet with any individual whose test scores suggest psychopathology, or includes an option for any participant to receive counseling.

Nevertheless, the DVM has been shown to address issues of immense importance to most individuals, and has particular relevance to law enforcement: the inconsistency between people are passionate about—their values—and their lifestyle in numerous studies, as reviewed earlier.

Using the model's sequential steps, a person's willingness to gain insights into his or her self-destructive nature, and to conclude that the inconsistency between their habits and values carries consequences that are simply unacceptable, is a powerful tool in the fight against unhealthy habits considered the antecedents of low job satisfaction, poor job performance, burnout, and leaving the profession of law enforcement. Efficacy of the DVM among various positions and roles of law enforcement and follow-up programs that detect adherence to initiating new health-related routines await further experimental and case study research.

REFERENCES

Anshel, M. H. (2000). A conceptual model and implications for coping with stressful events in police work. *Criminal Justice and Behavior: An International Journal, 27*, 375–400.

Anshel, M. H. (2006). *Applied exercise psychology: A practitioner's guide to improving client health and fitness.* New York: Springer.

Anshel, M. H. (2008). The Disconnected Values Model: Intervention strategies for health behavior change. *Journal of Clinical Sport Psychology, 2,* 357–380.

Anshel, M. H., & Kang, M. (2007a). Effect of an intervention on replacing negative habits with positive routines for improving full engagement at work: A test of the Disconnected Values Model. *Journal of Consulting Psychology: Practice and Research, 59,* 110–125.

Anshel, M. H., & Kang, M. (2007b). An outcome-based action study on changes in fitness, blood lipids, and exercise adherence based on the Disconnected Values Model. *Behavioral Medicine, 33,* 85–98.

Anshel, M. H., & Kang, M. (2008). Effectiveness of motivational interviewing on changes in fitness, blood lipids, and exercise adherence among police officers. *Journal of Correctional Health Care, 14,* 48–62.

Aumiller, G. S., & Corey, D. (2007). Defining the field of police psychology: Core domains & proficiencies. *Journal of Police and Criminal Psychology, 22,* 65–76.

Baranowski, T., Anderson, C., & Carmack, C. (1998). Mediating variable framework in physical activity interventions. How are we doing? How might we do better? *American Journal of Preventive Medicine, 15,* 266–297.

Baumeister, R. F., Faber, J. E., & Wallace, H. M. (1999). Coping and ego depletion: Recovery after the coping process. In C. R. Snyder (Ed.), *Coping: The psychology of what works* (pp. 50–69). New York: Oxford University Press.

Berger, B., Pargman, D., & Weinberg, R. (2007). *Foundations of exercise psychology* (2nd ed). Morgantown, WV: Fitness Information Technology.

Brawley, L. R. (1993). The practicality of using social psychological theories for exercise and health research and intervention. *Journal of Applied Sport Psychology, 5,* 99–115.

Brown, D., & Crace, R. K. (1996). Values in life role choices and outcomes: A conceptual model. *Career Development Quarterly, 44,* 221–223.

Buckworth, J., & Dishman, R. K. (2002). *Exercise psychology.* Champaign, IL: Human Kinetics.

Dishman, R. K., & Buckworth, J. (1997). Adherence to physical activity. In W. P. Morgan (Ed.), *Physical activity & mental health* (pp. 63–80). Washington, DC: Taylor & Francis.

Dunn, A. L., Andersen, R. E., & Jakicic, J. M. (1998). Lifestyle physical activity interventions: History, short- and long-term effects, and recommendations. *American Journal of Preventive Medicine, 15,* 398–412.

Glasgow, R. E., Klesges, L. M., Dzewaltowski, D. A., Bull, S. S., & Estabrooks, P. (2004). The future of health behavior change research: What is needed to improve translation of research into health promotion practice. *Annals of Behavioral Medicine, 27,* 3–12.

Hart, P. M., Wearing, A. J., & Headey, B. (1995). Police stress and well-being: Integrating personality, coping and daily work experiences. *Journal of Occupational and Organizational Psychology, 68,* 133–156.

Hecht, J., Borrelli, B., Breger, R. K., DeFrancesco, C., Ernst, D., & Resnicow, K. (2005). Motivational interviewing in community-based research: Experience from the field. *Annals of Behavioral Medicine, 29,* 29–34.

Hoffman, R., & Collingwood, T. R. (2005). *Fit for duty: The police officer's guide to total fitness* (2nd ed.). Champaign, IL: Human Kinetics.

Hogan, H. W., & Mookherjee, H. N. (1981). Values and selected antecedents. *Journal of Social Psychology, 113,* 29–35.

Lazarus, R. S., & Folkman, S. (1984). *Stress, appraisal, and coping.* New York: Springer.

Loehr, J. (2007). *The power of story: Rewrite your destiny in business and in life.* New York: Free Press.

Loehr, J., & Schwartz, T. (2003).*The power of full engagement: Managing energy, not time, is the key to high performance and personal renewal.* New York: Free Press.

Markland, D. (1999). Self-determination moderates the effects of perceived competence on intrinsic motivation in an exercise setting. *Journal of Sport and Exercise Psychology, 21*, 351–361.

McCarty, W. P., Zhao, J., & Garland, B. E. (2007). Occupational stress and burnout between male and female police officers: Are there any gender differences? *Policing: An International Journal of Police Strategies & Management, 30*, 672–691.

Miller, W. R., & Rollnick, S. (2002). *Motivational interviewing: Preparing people for change.* New York: Guilford.

Mills, G. E. (2003). *Action research: A guide for the teacher researcher* (2nd ed.). Upper Saddle River, NJ: Merrill Prentice-Hall.

Ockene, J. K. (2001). Strategies to increase adherence to treatment.In L. E. Burke & I. S. Ockene (Eds.), *Compliance in healthcare and research* (pp. 43–56). Armonk, NY: Futura.

Oldridge, N. B. (2001). Future directions: What paths do researchers need to take? What needs to be done to improve multi-level compliance? In L. E. Burke & I. S. Ockene (Eds.), *Compliance in healthcare and research* (pp. 331–347). Armonk, NY: Futura.

Quick, J. C., Quick, J. D., Nelson, D. L., & Hurrell, J. J. (1997). *Preventive stress management in organizations.* Washington, DC: American Psychological Association.

Rokeach, M. (1973). *The nature of human values.* New York: Free Press.

Rollnick, S., Mason, P., & Butler, C. (1999). *Health behavior change: A guide for practitioners.* New York: Churchill Livingstone.

Rybicki, D., & Nutter, R. (2002). Employment-related psychological evaluations: Risk management concerns and current practices. *Journal of Police Criminal Psychology, 17*, 8–31.

Shumaker, S. A., Ockene, J. K., & Riekert, K. A. (Eds.). (2009). *The handbook of health behavior change* (3rd ed.). New York: Springer.

Slate, R. N., Johnson, W. W., & Colbert, S. S. (2007). Police stress: A structural model. *Journal of Police and Criminal Psychology, 22*, 102–112.

Snyder, C. R., & Dinoff, B. L. (1999). Coping: Where have you been? In C. R. Snyder (Ed.), *Coping: The psychology of what words* (pp. 3–19). New York: Oxford University Press.

Super, D. E. (1995). Values: Their nature, assessment, and practical use. In D. E. Super & B. Sverko (Eds.), *Life roles, values, and careers: International findings of the work importance study* (pp. 54–61). San Francisco: Jossey-Bass.

Tanigoshi, H., Kontos, A. P., & Remley, T. P. (2008). The effectiveness of individual wellness counseling on the wellness of law enforcement officers. *Journal of Counseling and Development, 86*, 64–74.

Zeidner, M., & Saklofske, D. (1996). Adaptive and maladaptive coping. In M. Zeidner & N. S. Endler (Eds.), *Handbook of coping: Theory, research, applications* (pp. 505–531). New York: Wiley.

Author Index

Subject Index